# The Cricketers' Who's Who 2012

*Foreword by*
**ANDREW STRAUSS**

*Editor*
**JO HARMAN**

*Compiled by*
**ED DAVIS, ED KEMP, SAM STOW, MATT THACKER & PHIL WALKER**

*Design*
**JOE PROVIS & ROB WHITEHOUSE**

*The* **Cricketers'** Who's Who *2012*

This edition first published in the UK by All Out Cricket Ltd

© All Out Cricket Ltd 2012
www.alloutcricket.com

ISBN: 978-1908051875

This book is copyright under the Berne Convention. No reproduction without permission
All rights reserved. The Publisher makes no representations, express or implied, with
regard to the accuracy of the information contained in this book and cannot accept any
legal responsibility for any errors or ommission that may be made. A CIP Catalogue record
for this book is available from the British Library.

Published under the imprint Pitch Publishing Ltd, A2 Yeoman Gate, Yeoman Way,
Worthing, BN13 3QZ.
www.pitchpublishing.co.uk

Editor: *Jo Harman;* Research and editorial: *Ed Davis, Ed Kemp, Sam Stow, Matt Thacker,
Phil Walker;* Design: *Joe Provis, Rob Whitehouse;* Images: *Getty Images unless stated;*
Print: *Jellyfish Print Solutions*

Acknowledgements
The publishers would like to thank the county clubs, the Professional Cricketers' Association
and the players for their assistance in helping to put together this book. Additional
information has been gathered from espncricinfo.com and cricketarchive.com.
Thanks also to Tom Blanchard, Dan Thacker, Sunni Upal, Jon Waring and Sam Watts
Thanks to the following for providing photographs: Sarah Ansell, James Buttler, Donald
MacLeod, Ed Melia, Chris Nash

# CONTENTS

The
Cricketers'
Who's Who
2012

# REAL PEOPLE
# REAL PLACES
# REAL NEEDS

**PCA BENEVOLENT FUND**
The Heart of the Game

The Benevolent Fund is part of the PCA's ongoing commitment to help current and former players and their dependants in times of hardship, upheaval or to readjust to the world beyond the game.

Few vocations carry so much uncertainty as that of a professional cricketer. The demands of playing any sport for a living, leaves little time to consider and plan for possible disasters or upheavals in the future.

A significant amount of money is set aside from PCA fundraising for this purpose.

Benevolent issues are those that pull at everyone's heart strings and emphasise the important work the PCA does in generating vital funds.

The Fund is part of the PCA's on-going commitment to supporting players and their dependants who might be in need of a helping hand to readjust to a world beyond cricket.

It can also help current and past players who may have fallen on hard times or are in need of specialist advice or assistance.

Every donation helps. Please give today
**www.thepca.co.uk/benevolent_fund**

Acting to safeguard the rights of present, past and future first class cricketers.

PROFESSIONAL CRICKETERS' ASSOCIATION

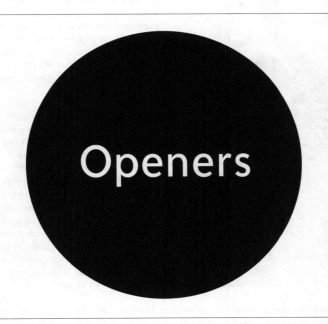

Openers

# FOREWORD

*by Andrew Strauss*

Welcome to the 2012 edition of The Cricketers' Who's Who, the book that gives you the inside track on those who are lucky enough to play this brilliant game for a living. It's a publication that has become part of the fabric of the English summer because cricket fans know that its arrival heralds the start of another fascinating season, and I expect this year to be no different.

It's a great time to be a supporter of English cricket. We're immensely proud of our achievements in both Test and Twenty20 cricket over the last few years – and know we're not far off becoming a good side in the one-day game – but we're determined not to get complacent. Every team out there will be looking to challenge us and so it's vital we maintain the passion and desire to improve that has served us so well in recent times. If we do that, I think this team has every chance of becoming something very special.

This summer sees us welcome first the West Indies and then South Africa to our shores. The men from the Caribbean are definitely a team on the rise, thanks in no small part to the leadership of their coach Ottis Gibson, a man everyone involved in the England set-up holds in the highest regard following his stint as our bowling coach. They will pose a stern challenge, while South Africa can boast some of the finest players in the game and are one of several sides vying to become the No.1 team in the world. Rest assured that we will not be taking either of these sides lightly in any way.

Looking beyond the international arena, I'm anticipating another exciting year for county cricket. While opinion varies on the structure of our domestic season, there is no denying that the LV= County Championship has thrown up plenty of white-knuckle finishes in recent years and is producing some phenomenal young players, while the showpiece finals for the Friends Life t20 and the Clydesdale Bank 40 provide all the drama and excitement a player or fan could possibly wish for.

Our domestic game has to strike a delicate balance between serving as a breeding ground for the next generation of English cricketers and providing its loyal supporters with all the thrills and spills that they deserve. I think the balance at the moment is about right. Turning back to the international game, it's fair to say that Test cricket should be given the attention and respect it deserves. I'm buoyed by what great support there is for the game in this country, but I'm aware that in other parts of the world this isn't always the case. We are in a fortunate position in the UK, but administrators all around the world need to keep working on the product to make it as desirable and attractive as possible, whether that's through giving the format context via a Test Championship or simply doing their level best to get people attending matches. Hopefully something can be agreed, because for me it remains the pinnacle of the game and the truest test of a cricketer's character and ability.

Happy reading and enjoy the summer,

Andrew Strauss
England Test Captain

**MAKE**
**THE RIGHT NOISE**

**NOT**
**WHITE NOISE**

Making sure your business is heard above the crowd is about more than increasing the volume of your communications.

For 10 years, TriNorth has been helping businesses in the sports, leisure and entertainment industries find their voice.

**Now that's something to shout about.**

**www.trinorth.co.uk**

TriNorth. Perfectly Pitched. Expertly Delivered.
EDITORIAL / DESIGN / PRINT / DIGITAL / EVENTS / COMMERCIAL

## EDITOR'S NOTES

When All Out Cricket took over compiling and producing the Cricketers' Who's Who last year, we had ideas about refreshing the format while retaining its core values, which we saw as providing interesting and unique information, both personal and statistical, about the men who spend their summers playing county cricket for a living in England.

We certainly shook things up a bit – moving away from alphabetical listings to a county-by-county format, and opting to include the Netherlands, Scotland, the Unicorns and the touring sides. Finally, we codified certain entries (such as 1,000 runs or 50 wickets in a first-class season) to allow more space for those words.

Force of circumstance – we purchased the title very late in the day when its very existence was by no means assured – meant we moved away from players completing surveys about themselves. Instead we provided a more objective view of their skills and characters, based around conversations with journalists, coaches and fellow players.

Inevitably, as with any well-loved publication, feedback followed hot on the heels of change. There was outrage in a few cases, consternation in many, congratulations in others. We invited comment, we listened to it, we weighed it up, and we have reacted.

The biggest gripe people had was that they wanted to see more of the players' characters and we had always intended to reintroduce this unique aspect of the book. Indeed, in the editor's notes last year we said: "We have changed the format in 2011 before we take stock, and decide how to approach the publication in 2012, finding a way of reintroducing player comment next year." Having had time to survey county cricketers over the course of the winter, we now have what we feel is a compelling set of pen portraits. The surveys have largely been completed online and we would like to extend our thanks to all of the players (and those county officials who have helped with the chivvying along) who have taken the time to give us a bit of themselves.

When we talked to players a year ago, many of them told us they were upset when false information was put in the Who's Who, with paper forms floating around dressing rooms and not always being completed by the intended recipient! This year we are confident the right men have completed the right forms. Now that doesn't mean all the information is 100 per cent trustworthy – you can't stop people embellishing the truth or inventing amazing but true 'facts' about themselves. But that's all part of the fun, and part of the players' characters. As with Wikipedia, approach with care and make sure you don't base any hard-hitting articles on some of the claims within these pages. Additionally, to get you closer to the players, we've included as many of their Twitter accounts as we could get hold of.

So we've returned to an alphabetical format, probably a wise decision in an era when players flit between counties far more easily than in days of yore, with the loan system adding yet more 'ownership' changes. There will doubtless be people who play this year who do not feature in the book but we've gone with the squads the counties kindly supplied to us in mid-March. Dreaming up which other overseas stars may swell the county ranks this season is beyond our skills and our remit!

We've retained the listings for Scotland, the Netherlands and the Unicorns – they are an integral and fascinating part of the summer schedule – but we have dispensed with the tourists section. We would again be relying too much on guesswork and with an increasing separation of squads for the different formats of the game, you can find anything up to 30 players from the major tourists reaching these shores. The job of giving information on these men we leave to The Wisden Guide to International Cricket 2012.

In this digital age, we are well aware that cricket lovers can access up-to-the-minute stats at the click of a mouse and that paper-based stats are now of limited value. We have stuck to the basics – last season's county-by-county numbers and each player's overall figures. You may notice that we have organised the one-day bowling stats by economy rate rather than average, an indication that the forms of the game are becoming ever more divergent.

Two little notes to end on. Firstly, we have omitted in many cases the players' answers to the question: "Who is the best player in county cricket?" There are only so many times you can type Marcus Trescothick – he is truly an institution. And finally, a word about our officials. Traditionally the umpires have been given limited space in the Who's Who but this year we surveyed them as well and came up with some interesting titbits.

As last year, we do not pretend to have all the answers and would appreciate any feedback you may have. Please drop me a line at cwweditor@alloutcricket.co.uk with any comments.

Jo Harman
March 26, 2012

# Wisden 2012

**HALF PRICE SUBSCRIBER OFFER** + free Wisden Guide book

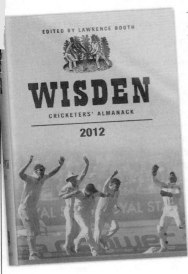

*EDITED BY LAWRENCE BOOTH*

**WISDEN**
CRICKETERS' ALMANACK
2012

The 149th edition of *Wisden Cricketers' Almanack* celebrates the rise of England's Test team to the top of the world rankings – an unprecedented feat following a triumphant 4–0 whitewash of India.

*Wisden 2012* also includes the tale of the Indians' emotional path to World Cup glory, Lancashire's nail-biting first outright County Championship success in 77 years, and the spot-fixing trial that threatened cricket's credibility.

Among the feature articles:

- **W** **Mike Brearley** and **Mike Yardy** examine the complex issue of depression in cricket

- **W** **Simon Hughes** outlines the reasons behind England's rise to the top of the Test world

- **W** **Gideon Haigh** steps into the ICC's political furnace

- **W** **Colin Shindler** looks back on the demise, 50 years ago, of the divide between amateurs and professionals

- **W** **Andy Bull** discovers why we overuse the phrase "it's not cricket"

- **W** **Peter Gibbs** remembers the day he spent with the legendary – and the legendarily grumpy – England fast bowler SF Barnes

- **W** **Andrew Renshaw** uncovers the mystery of *Wisden's* unknown soldier – a century on

**PLUS** Your chance to be published in *Wisden 2013*.

*The pleasure generated by the annual appearance of a new Wisden is reassuringly undiminished* The Guardian

## SUBSCRIBE TO WISDEN CRICKETERS' ALMANACK AND GET A FREE COPY OF THE WISDEN GUIDE 2012

You can now subscribe to *Wisden* by direct debit. The standard hardback *Wisden 2012* has a cover price of £50, but direct debit subscribers can get it at half price – £25 (plus £3.50 postage to a UK address). And if you start your subscription with *Wisden 2012*, we will guarantee that you will get the 2013 edition at the same price – *and* we will send you a free copy of *The Wisden Guide to International Cricket 2012*.

To subscribe, either download the form from **www.wisden.com**, or request it by email to **subscribe@wisden.com** or by writing to: **Wisden Subscriptions, Marketing Dept, Bloomsbury Publishing, 50 Bedford Square, London WC1B 3DP**

## SAME GAME, DIFFERENT LANDSCAPE

*With the new season upon us, All Out Cricket editor Phil Walker writes about the familiar joys of an evolving game.*

Fresh spins on old rituals herald the new season. A hoary game that once feared change can now barely get enough of it.

The various newfangled Twenty20 tournaments springing up (anyone for the Bangladesh Premier League?) aptly catch the pace of change. With the IPL and the Champions League Twenty20 – those immovable totems bookending our summer season – casually reshaping cricket's landscape, the biggest question in cricket today is simply this: where will all this lead? For the jumpy lover-guardians of international cricket, the big fear is that the players will desert their countries to chase the swag bags offered up to private guns for hire. Others are more relaxed about it all: Test cricket endures, end of story.

As for our counties, merely striving to get from here to there, there's nothing like the promise of a lucrative Champions League tilt to focus minds and treasurers. With the money on offer for qualification to the autumn tournament dwarfing all other potential payouts on county cricket's table, counties have been rushing to strengthen their Twenty20 squads with overseas stars. And why not? For many counties, a run to the Champions League can shape and solidify their financial futures. We've all got bills to pay.

Priorities shift in tune with the times. Highlights of the time-honoured 'curtain-raiser' between the MCC and the champion county – no longer beamed from Lord's but the Sheikh Zayed Stadium in Abu Dhabi – can now be watched online, as debate rages on the web about the workability of pink balls under lights in relation to day/night Test matches.

Back in the shires, the sports editor who used to send his photographer to snap the solitary spectator in the empty stand on the first day of the County Championship has been usurped by the blogger, producing over-by-over info and posting Twitter pics from Edgbaston, Taunton and Wantage Road, as all the while the Cardus disciples in the press box wrestle to condense a session into 140 characters. After-play interviews are filmed and posted within minutes, along with highlights packages. The BBC radio commentators wrap up the day's play for the last time, having provided (heroic) ball-by-ball coverage all day, as the press office prepares to go viral with their ad campaign for the next big event. Analysts for Opta, the sports data specialists, collate their accumulated stats from the day, as part of a new deal with the ECB to cover every ball of every match from this season. It's a far cry from the days of Teletext (page 340!) and the odd leaflet through the door from your local club. Today, information about who's bowled whom, how it happened and what it means, is available at the click of a button. The story of the season, presented for our pleasure like never before.

As the action takes place out in the middle, an agent sits opposite the chief executive amongst the oil paintings of pre-war amateurs in the committee room to debate contract terms for his latest starlet. Both parties know that with counties reaping decent (and excellently intentioned) bonuses from the ECB for bringing on fresh English talent, the unproven youngster holds all the cards. Meanwhile, on the pitch, the humble stalwart creaks back to the top of his mark and looks anxiously behind him.

All the while, on the online forums (the pubs of the day), county cricket's future is being picked apart following the publication of the Morgan Report. Compiled by the ex-ECB chairman and former ICC president David Morgan on behalf of the ECB, the English game's latest audit recommends cutting the number of County Championship games from 16 to 14 per side, replacing the 40-over format with a 50-over equivalent, and altering again the number of Twenty20 group matches – suggesting 14 per side this time, down from 16 in 2011, and up from the 10 fixtures slated for this season. To judge from the blogosphere, the biggest gripe concerns the proposed Championship shake-up. His proposals for reducing the fixture pile-up of an admittedly congested calendar would entail certain teams playing each other twice, and other teams just once, making it tough to refute the charge that this would corrugate the playing field. Having garnered various opinions (not least from the PCA, which broadly supports the existing system), the ECB's line is to wait and see how 2012 plays out.

Which, of course, is what we'll all be doing. The new season is here. Even as cricket leaps from the platform to catch the next hurtling train, the essential hallmarks still remain. The same smells, the same ball, the same old 22 yards. Cloud cover, threats of rain, the sunlit run-chase. The glorious uncertainty of the English cricket season. It's still the same; just different. Let's go again.

# KEY

RHB LB R1 W1 MVP2

R – 1,000 or more first-class runs in an English season (the number next to 'R' denotes how many times the player has achieved this feat)

W – 50 or more first-class wickets in an English season (the number next to 'W' denotes how many times the player has achieved this feat)

MVP – Denotes a player's presence in the top 100 places of the 2011 Overall FTI MVP Points (the number next to 'MVP' denotes the player's specific placing)

---

\* – Not out innings (e.g. 137\*)

(s) – A competition has been shared between two or more winners

CB40 – Clydesdale Bank 40 (English domestic 40-over competition)

CC1/CC2 – County Championship Division One/County Championship Division Two

FL t20 – Friends Life t20 (English domestic 20-over competition)

ICC – International Cricket Council

LB – Legbreak bowler

LF – Left-arm fast bowler

LFM – Left-arm fast-medium bowler

LHB – Left-hand batsman

LM – Left-arm medium

LMF – Left-arm medium-fast bowler

MCCU – Marylebone Cricket Club University

OB – Offbreak bowler

ODI – One-Day International

RF – Right-arm fast bowler

RFM – Right-arm fast-medium bowler

RHB – Right-hand batsman

RM – Right-arm medium bowler

RMF – Right-arm medium-fast bowler

SLA – Slow left-arm orthodox

SLC – Slow left-arm Chinaman

T20/T20I – Twenty20/Twenty20 International

UCCE – University Centre of Cricketing Excellence

WK – Wicketkeeper

---

NOTES: The stats given for a player's best batting and best bowling performance are limited to first-class cricket. If a field within a player's career statistics is left blank then the record for that particular statistic is incomplete, e.g. there is no record for how many balls a player has faced in first-class cricket. An '-' indicates that a particular statistic is inapplicable, e.g. a player has never bowled a ball in first-class cricket. All stats correct as of March 13, 2012

# SIGN UP TO GET WISDEN EXTRA – IT'S FREE!

*Wisden EXTRA* is our new online magazine, published at key points in the cricket year. A natural complement to the Almanack, it provides an authoritative and high-class take on the major cricket issues from around the world, with writing from internationally renowned names, photos from Patrick Eagar, humour from Tyers and Beach, and memorable extracts from *Wisden's* extensive archive.

*Wisden EXTRA* is free. To make sure you receive future issues, all you have to do is sign up at www.wisden.com/signup (where you can also find previous issues).

If you register by October 31, 2012 you will be entered into a prize draw to win a Gullivers Sports Travel holiday for two in New Zealand.

For our full range of
ECB Cricket Factory visit
www.cricketfactory.co.uk

"The England Cricket Team use elements of the ECB Cricket Factory Skill sets because they allow us to conduct fun and flexible fielding exercises. The skill sets can be used not only in a structured environment to suit the needs of an individual, but also in a manner that promotes creativity amongst participants"
**Richard Halsall, England Fielding Coach**

**Fielding**

**Batting**

**Throwing**

**Catching**

**Co-ordination**

**Movement**

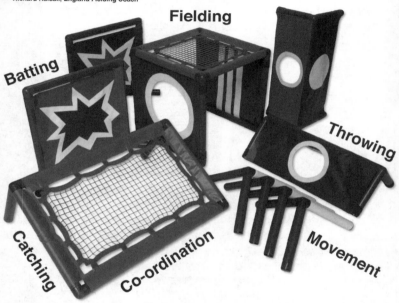

ECB Cricket Factory Core Skills Set

| Mini Slip Net | Drill Points | Action Targets | Drill Cube | Target Tunnels |

For further information email: or phone:
enquiries@cricketfactory.co.uk 01423 780373

© All content (design,and images) copyright Peter Brian Gray trading as Factory Eleven®. All rights reserved 2012

*The*
Teams

FORMED: 1870
HOME GROUND: County Ground, Derby
ONE-DAY NAME: Falcons
CAPTAIN: Wayne Madsen
2011 RESULTS: CC2: 5/9; CB40: 3/7 in Group A; FL t20: 7/9 in North Group
HONOURS: Championship: 1936; Gillette/NatWest/C&G/FP Trophy: 1981; Benson and Hedges Cup: 1993; Sunday League: 1990

### THE LOWDOWN

2011 was a season of upheaval for Derbyshire, with head of cricket John Morris leaving the club midway through the summer amidst rumours of a player revolt. Despite this turmoil, the club can look back with justifiable pride on a season of quiet progress, thanks in no small part to the efforts of Tony Palladino, Jonathan Clare and Tim Groenewald, who picked up a combined total of 143 Championship wickets. Following the retirement of skipper Luke Sutton and seamer Steffan Jones – as well as the loss of allrounder Greg Smith to Essex – the 2012 squad perhaps looks a little light on experience, but there is no doubt there is plenty of young talent within the Falcons' ranks. Throw in the services of quality overseas internationals in the form of Martin Guptill, Usman Khawaja and Rana Naved-ul-Hasan and the recruitment of canny left-arm spinner David Wainwright from Yorkshire, and it's little surprise that the Falcons are widely tipped to ruffle a few feathers in 2012.

### HEAD COACH: KARL KRIKKEN

A wicketkeeper-batsman, Krikken made his Derbyshire debut in 1987 and went on to enjoy a 16-year first-class career with the county and Griqualand West. Following his retirement, he was appointed Derbyshire's academy director, a role in which he oversaw the emergence of a number of the current first-team squad. Following the departure of John Morris, Krikken took the reins as part of a four-man collective before being confirmed as the club's new head coach in June last year. With an outstanding reputation for identifying and developing young talent, Krikken will be doing his utmost to bring out the best in the likes of Dan Redfern and Chesney Hughes.

| | Mat | Inns | NO | Runs | HS | Ave | SR | 100 | 50 | 4s | 6s |
|---|---|---|---|---|---|---|---|---|---|---|---|
| WJ Durston | 16 | 31 | 3 | 1138 | 151 | 40.64 | 65.74 | 3 | 6 | 171 | 7 |
| RA Whiteley | 11 | 20 | 4 | 644 | 130* | 40.25 | 50.58 | 2 | 2 | 82 | 14 |
| UT Khawaja | 4 | 8 | 0 | 319 | 135 | 39.87 | 53.16 | 1 | 0 | 42 | 0 |
| MJ Guptill | 8 | 16 | 2 | 537 | 143 | 38.35 | 74.79 | 1 | 4 | 95 | 3 |
| ML Turner | 7 | 11 | 8 | 113 | 27* | 37.66 | 65.31 | 0 | 0 | 13 | 0 |
| GM Smith | 13 | 24 | 3 | 726 | 130 | 34.57 | 79.17 | 1 | 5 | 104 | 0 |
| JL Clare | 14 | 23 | 2 | 688 | 130 | 32.76 | 75.77 | 1 | 3 | 99 | 4 |
| DJ Redfern | 13 | 25 | 0 | 775 | 99 | 31.00 | 51.25 | 0 | 7 | 102 | 0 |
| PM Borrington | 2 | 4 | 0 | 114 | 87 | 28.50 | 36.89 | 0 | 1 | 15 | 0 |
| CF Hughes | 14 | 27 | 0 | 741 | 167 | 27.44 | 53.85 | 2 | 2 | 104 | 5 |
| WL Madsen | 14 | 27 | 0 | 727 | 140 | 26.92 | 44.82 | 2 | 4 | 83 | 1 |
| LD Sutton | 16 | 26 | 1 | 573 | 56 | 22.92 | 39.95 | 0 | 1 | 64 | 0 |
| TD Groenewald | 14 | 21 | 8 | 281 | 60* | 21.61 | 39.30 | 0 | 1 | 31 | 6 |
| PS Jones | 2 | 4 | 1 | 54 | 27 | 18.00 | 77.14 | 0 | 0 | 8 | 0 |
| MS Lineker | 3 | 6 | 0 | 107 | 71 | 17.83 | 44.58 | 0 | 1 | 20 | 0 |
| Azeem Rafiq | 3 | 4 | 1 | 52 | 25* | 17.33 | 25.74 | 0 | 0 | 3 | 0 |
| AP Palladino | 14 | 22 | 5 | 241 | 60 | 14.17 | 52.05 | 0 | 1 | 30 | 1 |
| TC Knight | 2 | 3 | 1 | 15 | 14 | 7.50 | 39.47 | 0 | 0 | 2 | 0 |
| GT Park | 2 | 3 | 0 | 19 | 14 | 6.33 | 27.94 | 0 | 0 | 0 | 0 |
| MHA Footitt | 4 | 7 | 1 | 36 | 17 | 6.00 | 61.01 | 0 | 0 | 5 | 1 |

Batting

| | Overs | Mdns | Runs | Wkts | BBI | BBM | Ave | Econ | SR | 5w | 10w |
|---|---|---|---|---|---|---|---|---|---|---|---|
| MHA Footitt | 95.5 | 18 | 387 | 15 | 5/53 | 7/145 | 25.80 | 4.03 | 38.3 | 1 | 0 |
| AP Palladino | 435.1 | 94 | 1379 | 52 | 5/39 | 9/124 | 26.51 | 3.16 | 50.2 | 3 | 0 |
| JL Clare | 321.4 | 64 | 1165 | 43 | 5/50 | 6/100 | 27.09 | 3.62 | 44.8 | 1 | 0 |
| TD Groenewald | 469.0 | 107 | 1422 | 48 | 5/59 | 8/97 | 29.62 | 3.03 | 58.6 | 1 | 0 |
| ML Turner | 152.0 | 23 | 647 | 21 | 5/32 | 7/80 | 30.80 | 4.25 | 43.4 | 1 | 0 |
| Azeem Rafiq | 99.0 | 25 | 293 | 8 | 3/24 | 6/91 | 36.62 | 2.95 | 74.2 | 0 | 0 |
| GM Smith | 323.5 | 71 | 991 | 26 | 4/63 | 6/88 | 38.11 | 3.06 | 74.7 | 0 | 0 |
| CF Hughes | 108.0 | 16 | 370 | 9 | 2/9 | 2/17 | 41.11 | 3.42 | 72.0 | 0 | 0 |
| WJ Durston | 97.2 | 12 | 345 | 8 | 4/45 | 4/117 | 43.12 | 3.54 | 73.0 | 0 | 0 |
| PS Jones | 42.3 | 8 | 148 | 3 | 3/56 | 3/77 | 49.33 | 3.48 | 85.0 | 0 | 0 |
| RA Whiteley | 92.0 | 5 | 385 | 6 | 1/21 | 2/82 | 64.16 | 4.18 | 92.0 | 0 | 0 |
| TC Knight | 48.0 | 7 | 143 | 2 | 2/32 | 2/59 | 71.50 | 2.97 | 144.0 | 0 | 0 |
| UT Khawaja | 1.0 | 0 | 2 | 0 | - | - | - | 2.00 | - | 0 | 0 |
| GT Park | 4.0 | 0 | 16 | 0 | - | - | - | 4.00 | - | 0 | 0 |
| DJ Redfern | 3.0 | 0 | 14 | 0 | - | - | - | 4.66 | - | 0 | 0 |

Bowling

**Catches/Stumpings:**
59 Sutton (+2st), 13 Hughes, 9 Guptill, Madsen, Whiteley, 7 Clare, Durston, 6 Redfern, 5 Khawaja, Smith, 3 Borrington, Footitt, Groenewald, 2 Park, 1 Knight, Jones, Lineker, Palladino

**Batting**

|  | Mat | Inns | NO | Runs | HS | Ave | SR | 100 | 50 | 4s | 6s |
|---|---|---|---|---|---|---|---|---|---|---|---|
| MJ Guptill | 5 | 5 | 1 | 278 | 103* | 69.50 | 97.88 | 2 | 1 | 27 | 6 |
| WL Madsen | 12 | 12 | 1 | 478 | 75 | 43.45 | 90.35 | 0 | 4 | 33 | 5 |
| WJ Durston | 12 | 12 | 0 | 491 | 95 | 40.91 | 78.68 | 0 | 4 | 40 | 7 |
| UT Khawaja | 5 | 5 | 1 | 155 | 89* | 38.75 | 73.11 | 0 | 1 | 19 | 1 |
| Azeem Rafiq | 5 | 3 | 2 | 30 | 18 | 30.00 | 85.71 | 0 | 0 | 1 | 0 |
| T Poynton | 4 | 3 | 1 | 44 | 40 | 22.00 | 107.31 | 0 | 0 | 2 | 2 |
| CF Hughes | 12 | 12 | 0 | 243 | 66 | 20.25 | 87.41 | 0 | 1 | 28 | 4 |
| GM Smith | 12 | 12 | 0 | 215 | 68 | 17.91 | 75.97 | 0 | 1 | 15 | 2 |
| RA Whiteley | 7 | 7 | 1 | 106 | 40 | 17.66 | 89.07 | 0 | 0 | 13 | 1 |
| GT Park | 9 | 8 | 3 | 82 | 38 | 16.40 | 53.59 | 0 | 0 | 5 | 0 |
| TD Groenewald | 9 | 3 | 2 | 15 | 9 | 15.00 | 83.33 | 0 | 0 | 1 | 0 |
| AP Palladino | 5 | 3 | 1 | 28 | 18 | 14.00 | 164.70 | 0 | 0 | 3 | 0 |
| MS Lineker | 1 | 1 | 0 | 13 | 13 | 13.00 | 56.52 | 0 | 0 | 1 | 0 |
| PS Jones | 7 | 6 | 2 | 49 | 23 | 12.25 | 106.52 | 0 | 0 | 2 | 2 |
| LD Sutton | 8 | 6 | 2 | 25 | 16* | 6.25 | 62.50 | 0 | 0 | 0 | 0 |
| P Burgoyne | 2 | 2 | 1 | 6 | 6* | 6.00 | 85.71 | 0 | 0 | 1 | 0 |
| JL Clare | 8 | 6 | 0 | 32 | 19 | 5.33 | 72.72 | 0 | 0 | 3 | 0 |
| MHA Footitt | 2 | 1 | 0 | 4 | 4 | 4.00 | 200.00 | 0 | 0 | 1 | 0 |
| ML Turner | 2 | 2 | 1 | 2 | 1* | 2.00 | 66.66 | 0 | 0 | 0 | 0 |
| DJ Redfern | 1 | 1 | 0 | 0 | 0 | 0.00 | 0.00 | 0 | 0 | 0 | 0 |
| TC Knight | 3 | 1 | 1 | 1 | 1* | - | 100.00 | 0 | 0 | 0 | 0 |
| J Needham | 1 | 1 | 1 | 1 | 1* | - | 100.00 | 0 | 0 | 0 | 0 |

**Bowling**

|  | Overs | Mdns | Runs | Wkts | BBI | Ave | Econ | SR | 4w | 5w |
|---|---|---|---|---|---|---|---|---|---|---|
| WJ Durston | 37.0 | 1 | 165 | 8 | 3/7 | 20.62 | 4.45 | 27.7 | 0 | 0 |
| Azeem Rafiq | 25.1 | 0 | 115 | 2 | 1/29 | 57.50 | 4.56 | 75.5 | 0 | 0 |
| TC Knight | 24.0 | 0 | 113 | 5 | 2/27 | 22.60 | 4.70 | 28.8 | 0 | 0 |
| GT Park | 15.0 | 0 | 71 | 3 | 2/21 | 23.66 | 4.73 | 30.0 | 0 | 0 |
| CF Hughes | 64.0 | 2 | 310 | 14 | 3/19 | 22.14 | 4.84 | 27.4 | 0 | 0 |
| PS Jones | 47.0 | 2 | 233 | 11 | 3/38 | 21.18 | 4.95 | 25.6 | 0 | 0 |
| AP Palladino | 30.0 | 3 | 155 | 6 | 4/32 | 25.83 | 5.16 | 30.0 | 1 | 0 |
| RA Whiteley | 8.0 | 0 | 42 | 1 | 1/26 | 42.00 | 5.25 | 48.0 | 0 | 0 |
| TD Groenewald | 55.1 | 2 | 299 | 9 | 4/22 | 33.22 | 5.41 | 36.7 | 1 | 0 |
| GM Smith | 63.0 | 1 | 344 | 10 | 3/39 | 34.40 | 5.46 | 37.8 | 0 | 0 |
| JL Clare | 46.1 | 2 | 261 | 10 | 3/61 | 26.10 | 5.65 | 27.7 | 0 | 0 |
| P Burgoyne | 10.0 | 0 | 62 | 2 | 2/36 | 31.00 | 6.20 | 30.0 | 0 | 0 |
| J Needham | 5.0 | 0 | 32 | 0 | - | - | 6.40 | - | 0 | 0 |
| ML Turner | 11.0 | 0 | 72 | 2 | 2/42 | 36.00 | 6.54 | 33.0 | 0 | 0 |
| MHA Footitt | 6.0 | 0 | 72 | 0 | - | - | 12.00 | - | 0 | 0 |

**Catches/Stumpings:**
9 Sutton (+3st), 8 Park, 7 Madsen, 4 Clare, 3 Durston, Groenewald, Rafiq, Smith, 2 Guptill, Hughes, Khawaja, Poynton (+1st), Whiteley, 1 Burgoyne, Footitt, Redfern, Turner

www.derbyshireccc.com / tel: 01332 388 101

**Derbyshire FALCONS**

Batting

| | Mat | Inns | NO | Runs | HS | Ave | SR | 100 | 50 | 4s | 6s |
|---|---|---|---|---|---|---|---|---|---|---|---|
| RA Whiteley | 12 | 11 | 7 | 215 | 40* | 53.75 | 141.44 | 0 | 0 | 15 | 8 |
| MJ Guptill | 14 | 14 | 0 | 476 | 79 | 34.00 | 122.36 | 0 | 3 | 51 | 13 |
| GT Park | 13 | 13 | 6 | 222 | 50* | 31.71 | 124.71 | 0 | 1 | 18 | 4 |
| WL Madsen | 14 | 14 | 2 | 316 | 61* | 26.33 | 121.07 | 0 | 3 | 23 | 6 |
| CF Hughes | 13 | 13 | 0 | 272 | 65 | 20.92 | 105.01 | 0 | 1 | 18 | 9 |
| WJ Durston | 14 | 14 | 0 | 282 | 86 | 20.14 | 114.17 | 0 | 2 | 27 | 4 |
| TD Groenewald | 11 | 3 | 2 | 17 | 8 | 17.00 | 130.76 | 0 | 0 | 1 | 1 |
| PS Jones | 14 | 5 | 2 | 39 | 24 | 13.00 | 82.97 | 0 | 0 | 3 | 0 |
| JL Clare | 14 | 8 | 3 | 48 | 15 | 9.60 | 88.88 | 0 | 0 | 2 | 1 |
| GM Smith | 6 | 6 | 0 | 47 | 36 | 7.83 | 100.00 | 0 | 0 | 3 | 1 |
| LD Sutton | 14 | 4 | 0 | 3 | 2 | 0.75 | 23.07 | 0 | 0 | 0 | 0 |
| AL Hughes | 1 | 1 | 1 | 11 | 11* | - | 91.66 | 0 | 0 | 1 | 0 |
| TC Knight | 10 | 1 | 1 | 2 | 2* | - | 100.00 | 0 | 0 | 0 | 0 |
| ML Turner | 3 | 1 | 1 | 1 | 1* | - | 50.00 | 0 | 0 | 0 | 0 |
| MHA Footitt | 1 | - | - | - | - | - | - | - | - | - | - |

Bowling

| | Overs | Mdns | Runs | Wkts | BBI | Ave | Econ | SR | 4w | 5w |
|---|---|---|---|---|---|---|---|---|---|---|
| GM Smith | 18.0 | 0 | 119 | 4 | 2/36 | 29.75 | 6.61 | 27.0 | 0 | 0 |
| TC Knight | 30.0 | 0 | 201 | 9 | 3/16 | 22.33 | 6.70 | 20.0 | 0 | 0 |
| CF Hughes | 43.0 | 0 | 296 | 12 | 4/23 | 24.66 | 6.88 | 21.5 | 1 | 0 |
| RA Whiteley | 6.0 | 0 | 46 | 2 | 1/12 | 23.00 | 7.66 | 18.0 | 0 | 0 |
| WJ Durston | 25.2 | 0 | 201 | 9 | 2/22 | 22.33 | 7.93 | 16.8 | 0 | 0 |
| AL Hughes | 3.0 | 0 | 24 | 0 | - | - | 8.00 | - | 0 | 0 |
| TD Groenewald | 34.2 | 1 | 280 | 8 | 2/18 | 35.00 | 8.15 | 25.7 | 0 | 0 |
| PS Jones | 40.3 | 0 | 340 | 10 | 2/20 | 34.00 | 8.39 | 24.3 | 0 | 0 |
| JL Clare | 30.5 | 0 | 261 | 4 | 1/5 | 65.25 | 8.46 | 46.2 | 0 | 0 |
| ML Turner | 8.1 | 0 | 78 | 3 | 3/22 | 26.00 | 9.55 | 16.3 | 0 | 0 |
| MHA Footitt | 2.0 | 0 | 22 | 0 | - | - | 11.00 | - | 0 | 0 |

**Catches/Stumpings:**
9 Guptill, 6 Durston, 4 Clare, Madsen, Park, 3 Knight, Sutton (+5st), 2 Groenewald, Whiteley, 1 Jones, Smith

**FORMED:** 1882
**HOME GROUND:** Emirates Durham International Cricket Ground
**ONE-DAY NAME:** Dynamos
**CAPTAIN:** Phil Mustard (Championship), Dale Benkenstein (CB40 and FL t20)
**2011 RESULTS:** CC1: 3/9; CB40: Semi-finalists; FL t20: Quarter-finalists
**HONOURS:** Championship: (2) 2008, 2009; Gillette/NatWest/C&G/FP Trophy: 2007

### THE LOWDOWN

Last season promised much but delivered relatively little for Durham. Looking to recover from a disappointing 2010 where injuries took their toll, the club managed eight Division One victories, but four draws and four defeats saw them eventually finish third. A strong CB40 campaign resulted in a semi-final spot and they also reached the knockout stages of the FL t20, losing in the quarter-finals to Hampshire. If 2011 was a nearly season, 2012 could well be the year they get back to winning silverware. With a blend of talented youngsters like Scott Borthwick and Mark Wood alongside seasoned veterans like Steve Harmison and Dale Benkenstein, the squad looks well balanced, while the addition of Herschelle Gibbs to the FL t20 squad will further bolster a powerful batting line-up featuring Ian Blackwell and Phil Mustard. The potential resurrection of Graham Onions' England career may inconvenience their push for Championship wickets, but the squad looks equipped to cope.

### DIRECTOR OF CRICKET: GEOFF COOK

A very able opening batsman for Northamptonshire, Durham, Eastern Province and England, Cook took charge of Durham's youth academy following his retirement in 1992, before being promoted to director of cricket in 2007. He subsequently guided the club to their first silverware, the 2007 Friends Provident Trophy, before delivering back-to-back County Championship crowns in 2008 and 2009.

|  | Mat | Inns | NO | Runs | HS | Ave | SR | 100 | 50 | 4s | 6s |
|---|---|---|---|---|---|---|---|---|---|---|---|
| LE Plunkett | 4 | 5 | 3 | 248 | 107* | 124.00 | 60.19 | 1 | 2 | 25 | 1 |
| DM Benkenstein | 17 | 27 | 4 | 1366 | 150 | 59.39 | 55.59 | 4 | 9 | 162 | 5 |
| P Mustard | 13 | 18 | 4 | 716 | 101 | 51.14 | 71.52 | 1 | 6 | 98 | 5 |
| MD Stoneman | 7 | 11 | 0 | 556 | 128 | 50.54 | 57.43 | 1 | 5 | 87 | 1 |
| BA Stokes | 11 | 18 | 2 | 734 | 185 | 45.87 | 70.98 | 3 | 2 | 84 | 15 |
| ID Blackwell | 17 | 26 | 2 | 1063 | 158 | 44.29 | 79.38 | 3 | 6 | 121 | 18 |
| WR Smith | 15 | 25 | 0 | 978 | 179 | 39.12 | 42.01 | 3 | 4 | 139 | 4 |
| MJ Di Venuto | 16 | 25 | 1 | 935 | 132 | 38.95 | 61.31 | 3 | 4 | 130 | 0 |
| PD Collingwood | 7 | 13 | 1 | 439 | 108 | 36.58 | 56.57 | 1 | 2 | 50 | 4 |
| GJ Muchall | 15 | 24 | 1 | 836 | 175 | 36.34 | 59.97 | 1 | 7 | 124 | 2 |
| SG Borthwick | 14 | 20 | 5 | 477 | 101 | 31.80 | 57.40 | 1 | 2 | 67 | 1 |
| MA Wood | 3 | 5 | 1 | 118 | 48 | 29.50 | 73.75 | 0 | 0 | 14 | 1 |
| MJ Richardson | 5 | 8 | 1 | 167 | 73* | 23.85 | 53.35 | 0 | 2 | 20 | 1 |
| GR Breese | 1 | 2 | 0 | 42 | 38 | 21.00 | 61.76 | 0 | 0 | 5 | 1 |
| CD Thorp | 16 | 20 | 3 | 310 | 43 | 18.23 | 64.85 | 0 | 0 | 44 | 6 |
| ME Claydon | 9 | 14 | 4 | 150 | 38 | 15.00 | 54.54 | 0 | 0 | 22 | 2 |
| C Rushworth | 3 | 3 | 1 | 28 | 21 | 14.00 | 60.86 | 0 | 0 | 4 | 0 |
| SJ Harmison | 6 | 4 | 0 | 45 | 27 | 11.25 | 60.00 | 0 | 0 | 7 | 0 |
| G Onions | 11 | 14 | 5 | 100 | 28* | 11.11 | 49.50 | 0 | 0 | 13 | 1 |
| RMR Brathwaite | 7 | 7 | 4 | 27 | 13 | 9.00 | 52.94 | 0 | 0 | 2 | 1 |
| BA Raine | 1 | 2 | 0 | 11 | 7 | 5.50 | 36.66 | 0 | 0 | 1 | 0 |

*Batting*

|  | Overs | Mdns | Runs | Wkts | BBI | BBM | Ave | Econ | SR | 5w | 10w |
|---|---|---|---|---|---|---|---|---|---|---|---|
| GR Breese | 12.0 | 1 | 21 | 1 | 1/19 | 1/21 | 21.00 | 1.75 | 72.0 | 0 | 0 |
| RMR Brathwaite | 177.4 | 27 | 656 | 26 | 5/56 | 7/98 | 25.23 | 3.69 | 41.0 | 2 | 0 |
| MA Wood | 57.0 | 8 | 264 | 10 | 3/72 | 5/129 | 26.40 | 4.63 | 34.2 | 0 | 0 |
| SJ Harmison | 117.4 | 24 | 454 | 17 | 4/67 | 7/151 | 26.70 | 3.85 | 41.5 | 0 | 0 |
| G Onions | 365.3 | 72 | 1341 | 50 | 6/95 | 8/153 | 26.82 | 3.66 | 43.8 | 2 | 0 |
| SG Borthwick | 273.0 | 66 | 958 | 35 | 5/80 | 5/71 | 27.37 | 3.50 | 46.8 | 1 | 0 |
| PD Collingwood | 37.0 | 9 | 117 | 4 | 2/22 | 2/22 | 29.25 | 3.16 | 55.5 | 0 | 0 |
| ME Claydon | 226.5 | 50 | 824 | 28 | 6/104 | 8/138 | 29.42 | 3.63 | 48.6 | 2 | 0 |
| BA Stokes | 146.3 | 20 | 621 | 21 | 6/68 | 7/145 | 29.57 | 4.23 | 41.8 | 1 | 0 |
| CD Thorp | 476.4 | 124 | 1412 | 46 | 6/20 | 8/73 | 30.69 | 2.96 | 62.1 | 1 | 0 |
| ID Blackwell | 482.5 | 167 | 1172 | 38 | 5/102 | 7/91 | 30.84 | 2.42 | 76.2 | 1 | 0 |
| C Rushworth | 55.0 | 16 | 169 | 5 | 2/15 | 3/54 | 33.80 | 3.07 | 66.0 | 0 | 0 |
| LE Plunkett | 113.4 | 20 | 428 | 11 | 3/70 | 4/128 | 38.90 | 3.76 | 62.0 | 0 | 0 |
| DM Benkenstein | 80.0 | 25 | 193 | 3 | 1/6 | 1/9 | 64.33 | 2.41 | 160.0 | 0 | 0 |
| WR Smith | 5.0 | 2 | 5 | 0 | - | - | - | 1.00 | - | 0 | 0 |
| BA Raine | 3.0 | 1 | 7 | 0 | - | - | - | 2.33 | - | 0 | 0 |

*Bowling*

**Catches/Stumpings:**
48 Mustard (+2st), 27 Di Venuto, Richardson (+1st), 14 Borthwick, 11 Muchall, Smith, 9 Thorp, 7 Benkenstein, Stokes, 6 Stoneman, 4 Collingwood, 3 Breese, Onions, 2 Blackwell, Wood, 1 Brathwaite, Claydon, Plunkett, Raine, Rushworth

**Batting**

| | Mat | Inns | NO | Runs | HS | Ave | SR | 100 | 50 | 4s | 6s |
|---|---|---|---|---|---|---|---|---|---|---|---|
| GJ Muchall | 9 | 9 | 3 | 405 | 95* | 67.50 | 85.44 | 0 | 5 | 36 | 2 |
| BA Stokes | 8 | 8 | 1 | 357 | 150* | 51.00 | 106.56 | 1 | 2 | 38 | 9 |
| PD Collingwood | 6 | 6 | 1 | 243 | 96 | 48.60 | 96.04 | 0 | 2 | 16 | 6 |
| MJ Di Venuto | 3 | 3 | 0 | 135 | 70 | 45.00 | 105.46 | 0 | 2 | 15 | 0 |
| P Mustard | 12 | 12 | 2 | 417 | 139* | 41.70 | 116.80 | 2 | 1 | 46 | 9 |
| DM Benkenstein | 11 | 10 | 2 | 308 | 82 | 38.50 | 96.25 | 0 | 2 | 21 | 4 |
| KJ Coetzer | 6 | 6 | 1 | 166 | 110* | 33.20 | 86.91 | 1 | 0 | 19 | 1 |
| MD Stoneman | 4 | 4 | 0 | 130 | 73 | 32.50 | 81.76 | 0 | 1 | 15 | 0 |
| ID Blackwell | 9 | 8 | 1 | 227 | 98 | 32.42 | 122.04 | 0 | 1 | 19 | 10 |
| GR Breese | 12 | 8 | 3 | 159 | 47* | 31.80 | 98.14 | 0 | 0 | 10 | 6 |
| CD Thorp | 4 | 3 | 1 | 37 | 17 | 18.50 | 119.35 | 0 | 0 | 2 | 2 |
| SG Borthwick | 8 | 3 | 0 | 43 | 32 | 14.33 | 84.31 | 0 | 0 | 1 | 1 |
| C Rushworth | 4 | 2 | 1 | 12 | 12* | 12.00 | 100.00 | 0 | 0 | 1 | 0 |
| WR Smith | 4 | 2 | 0 | 11 | 7 | 5.50 | 84.61 | 0 | 0 | 0 | 0 |
| G Onions | 9 | 3 | 2 | 5 | 4 | 5.00 | 62.50 | 0 | 0 | 1 | 0 |
| ME Claydon | 12 | 5 | 1 | 14 | 9 | 3.50 | 45.16 | 0 | 0 | 0 | 0 |
| MA Wood | 3 | 2 | 0 | 6 | 5 | 3.00 | 50.00 | 0 | 0 | 0 | 0 |
| BW Harmison | 4 | 1 | 1 | 3 | 3* | - | 75.00 | 0 | 0 | 0 | 0 |
| RMR Brathwaite | 1 | - | - | - | - | - | - | - | - | - | - |
| LE Plunkett | 2 | - | - | - | - | - | - | - | - | - | - |
| BA Raine | 1 | - | - | - | - | - | - | - | - | - | - |

**Bowling**

| | Overs | Mdns | Runs | Wkts | BBI | Ave | Econ | SR | 4w | 5w |
|---|---|---|---|---|---|---|---|---|---|---|
| MA Wood | 14.0 | 0 | 62 | 1 | 1/28 | 62.00 | 4.42 | 84.0 | 0 | 0 |
| G Onions | 62.0 | 3 | 307 | 8 | 3/46 | 38.37 | 4.95 | 46.5 | 0 | 0 |
| BA Stokes | 25.2 | 0 | 128 | 9 | 4/29 | 14.22 | 5.05 | 16.8 | 1 | 0 |
| ID Blackwell | 53.0 | 3 | 271 | 9 | 3/49 | 30.11 | 5.11 | 35.3 | 0 | 0 |
| DM Benkenstein | 21.0 | 0 | 109 | 1 | 1/24 | 109.00 | 5.19 | 126.0 | 0 | 0 |
| C Rushworth | 26.3 | 2 | 140 | 7 | 2/15 | 20.00 | 5.28 | 22.7 | 0 | 0 |
| KJ Coetzer | 2.0 | 0 | 11 | 0 | - | - | 5.50 | - | 0 | 0 |
| GR Breese | 59.5 | 2 | 336 | 13 | 4/21 | 25.84 | 5.61 | 27.6 | 1 | 0 |
| ME Claydon | 78.3 | 4 | 447 | 21 | 3/16 | 21.28 | 5.69 | 22.4 | 0 | 0 |
| SG Borthwick | 44.3 | 0 | 256 | 6 | 2/31 | 42.66 | 5.75 | 44.5 | 0 | 0 |
| PD Collingwood | 13.0 | 0 | 76 | 3 | 2/19 | 25.33 | 5.84 | 26.0 | 0 | 0 |
| CD Thorp | 22.0 | 1 | 152 | 6 | 3/56 | 25.33 | 6.90 | 22.0 | 0 | 0 |
| LE Plunkett | 4.0 | 0 | 29 | 0 | - | - | 7.25 | - | 0 | 0 |
| WR Smith | 3.0 | 0 | 23 | 0 | - | - | 7.66 | - | 0 | 0 |
| RMR Brathwaite | 6.0 | 0 | 49 | 0 | - | - | 8.16 | - | 0 | 0 |
| BW Harmison | 1.0 | 0 | 15 | 0 | - | - | 15.00 | - | 0 | 0 |

**Catches/Stumpings:**
13 Mustard (+2st), 7 Collingwood, 4 Coetzer, Smith, 3 Benkenstein, Blackwell, Borthwick, Breese, 2 Stokes, Stoneman, 1 Claydon, B.Harmison, Muchall, Onions, Raine, Thorp, Wood

www.durhamccc.co.uk / tel: 0844 499 4466

# DURHAM DYNAMOS

| | Mat | Inns | NO | Runs | HS | Ave | SR | 100 | 50 | 4s | 6s |
|---|---|---|---|---|---|---|---|---|---|---|---|
| P Mustard | 16 | 13 | 1 | 366 | 75 | 30.50 | 122.00 | 0 | 2 | 46 | 7 |
| WR Smith | 4 | 3 | 2 | 29 | 11* | 29.00 | 138.09 | 0 | 0 | 3 | 0 |
| DM Benkenstein | 16 | 11 | 2 | 254 | 60 | 28.22 | 150.29 | 0 | 2 | 27 | 7 |
| BA Stokes | 1 | 1 | 0 | 28 | 28 | 28.00 | 121.73 | 0 | 0 | 2 | 1 |
| ID Blackwell | 16 | 13 | 2 | 293 | 77 | 26.63 | 127.94 | 0 | 1 | 25 | 11 |
| DA Miller | 13 | 10 | 2 | 212 | 54 | 26.50 | 119.10 | 0 | 1 | 19 | 4 |
| SG Borthwick | 10 | 4 | 2 | 51 | 30 | 25.50 | 98.07 | 0 | 0 | 3 | 1 |
| GR Breese | 16 | 11 | 4 | 148 | 34 | 21.14 | 130.97 | 0 | 0 | 16 | 5 |
| GJ Muchall | 16 | 13 | 0 | 254 | 64 | 19.53 | 113.39 | 0 | 2 | 28 | 2 |
| LE Plunkett | 16 | 9 | 2 | 127 | 41 | 18.14 | 135.10 | 0 | 0 | 7 | 6 |
| ME Claydon | 16 | 4 | 2 | 26 | 19 | 13.00 | 89.65 | 0 | 0 | 2 | 1 |
| PD Collingwood | 13 | 9 | 0 | 96 | 29 | 10.66 | 96.96 | 0 | 0 | 5 | 2 |
| C Rushworth | 14 | 3 | 2 | 2 | 2 | 2.00 | 66.66 | 0 | 0 | 0 | 0 |
| G Onions | 9 | 2 | 2 | 0 | 0* | - | - | 0 | 0 | 0 | 0 |

| | Overs | Mdns | Runs | Wkts | BBI | Ave | Econ | SR | 4w | 5w |
|---|---|---|---|---|---|---|---|---|---|---|
| PD Collingwood | 27.0 | 0 | 157 | 16 | 5/6 | 9.81 | 5.81 | 10.1 | 1 | 1 |
| DM Benkenstein | 16.0 | 0 | 111 | 5 | 2/14 | 22.20 | 6.93 | 19.2 | 0 | 0 |
| GR Breese | 38.0 | 0 | 283 | 13 | 3/23 | 21.76 | 7.44 | 17.5 | 0 | 0 |
| G Onions | 26.0 | 0 | 194 | 6 | 2/18 | 32.33 | 7.46 | 26.0 | 0 | 0 |
| ID Blackwell | 27.0 | 0 | 215 | 4 | 2/30 | 53.75 | 7.96 | 40.5 | 0 | 0 |
| ME Claydon | 45.4 | 2 | 369 | 15 | 3/6 | 24.60 | 8.08 | 18.2 | 0 | 0 |
| LE Plunkett | 41.0 | 0 | 332 | 13 | 5/31 | 25.53 | 8.09 | 18.9 | 0 | 1 |
| SG Borthwick | 12.0 | 0 | 100 | 4 | 3/19 | 25.00 | 8.33 | 18.0 | 0 | 0 |
| C Rushworth | 39.0 | 0 | 342 | 11 | 3/20 | 31.09 | 8.76 | 21.2 | 0 | 0 |

**Catches/Stumpings:**
10 Mustard (+2st), 9 Breese, Miller, 6 Benkenstein, Claydon, 5 Muchall, 3 Blackwell, Collingwood, Smith, 2 Borthwick, Onions, Plunkett, Rushworth

**FORMED:** 1876
**HOME GROUND:** The Ford County Ground, Chelmsford
**ONE-DAY NAME:** Eagles
**CAPTAIN:** James Foster
**2011 RESULTS:** CC2: 7/9; CB40: 3/7 in Group C; FL t20: 6/9 in South Group
**HONOURS:** Championship: (6) 1979, 1983, 1984, 1986, 1991, 1992; Gillette/NatWest/ C&G/FP Trophy: (3) 1985, 1997, 2008; Benson and Hedges Cup: (2) 1979, 1998; Pro40/ National League/CB40: (2) 2005, 2006; Sunday League: (3) 1981, 1984, 1985

## THE LOWDOWN

Last season was another ultimately frustrating one for Essex. With Championship promotion high on the priority list, the team were unable to close out games, drawing half of their four-day matches en route to finishing seventh. Although they performed well in the CB40, their T20 form was poor, all the more surprising considering their pedigree in the short form. The captures of allrounder Greg Smith and left-arm seamer Charl Willoughby will add depth and experience to the squad, while overseas players Alviro Petersen and Peter Siddle will bring international class and expertise. They will complement the array of talented youngsters the Eagles have on their books, with fans hoping Tymal Mills, Reece Topley and Tom Craddock can build on impressive breakthrough performances last term. Guided by a respected coach and a popular captain who was in fine form throughout last season, the ingredients are there for a successful campaign this time round.

### HEAD COACH: PAUL GRAYSON

Born and bred in Yorkshire, Essex's coach enjoyed a decent career with his home county before moving to Chelmsford, where he played for eight years. After retiring from the first-class game in 2005 with two ODI appearances to his name, he turned his hand briefly to minor counties cricket with Suffolk before returning to Essex as coach. Approachable, flinty and quietly authoritative, his character and coaching methods are universally respected in the Essex dressing room.

| | Mat | Inns | NO | Runs | HS | Ave | SR | 100 | 50 | 4s | 6s |
|---|---|---|---|---|---|---|---|---|---|---|---|
| JS Foster | 16 | 28 | 7 | 964 | 117* | 45.90 | 50.05 | 2 | 4 | 111 | 3 |
| AN Cook | 7 | 14 | 0 | 634 | 155 | 45.28 | 61.31 | 2 | 3 | 90 | 1 |
| AJ Wheater | 11 | 20 | 1 | 804 | 164 | 42.31 | 82.80 | 2 | 4 | 109 | 17 |
| RS Bopara | 11 | 20 | 1 | 776 | 178 | 40.84 | 48.92 | 3 | 3 | 86 | 2 |
| RN ten Doeschate | 9 | 14 | 1 | 501 | 164 | 38.53 | 81.33 | 2 | 2 | 62 | 5 |
| GR Napier | 7 | 12 | 1 | 383 | 196 | 34.81 | 80.63 | 1 | 1 | 42 | 22 |
| OA Shah | 10 | 18 | 1 | 574 | 118 | 33.76 | 52.85 | 2 | 2 | 63 | 5 |
| MJ Walker | 11 | 21 | 2 | 587 | 97 | 30.89 | 43.09 | 0 | 4 | 73 | 1 |
| T Westley | 11 | 20 | 0 | 549 | 99 | 27.45 | 54.79 | 0 | 5 | 88 | 0 |
| JC Mickleburgh | 16 | 30 | 0 | 793 | 112 | 26.43 | 45.86 | 1 | 4 | 105 | 2 |
| BA Godleman | 13 | 24 | 0 | 634 | 130 | 26.41 | 44.30 | 1 | 3 | 74 | 3 |
| CJC Wright | 5 | 9 | 0 | 217 | 77 | 24.11 | 54.25 | 0 | 1 | 31 | 1 |
| ML Pettini | 8 | 14 | 2 | 285 | 67* | 23.75 | 39.52 | 0 | 2 | 32 | 2 |
| TJ Phillips | 10 | 16 | 4 | 273 | 58 | 22.75 | 36.89 | 0 | 2 | 41 | 1 |
| DD Masters | 16 | 24 | 2 | 234 | 48 | 10.63 | 48.34 | 0 | 0 | 33 | 1 |
| TR Craddock | 8 | 11 | 4 | 65 | 21 | 9.28 | 31.86 | 0 | 0 | 9 | 1 |
| MA Chambers | 12 | 17 | 4 | 108 | 30 | 8.30 | 32.53 | 0 | 0 | 20 | 0 |
| LL Tsotsobe | 3 | 4 | 3 | 6 | 6 | 6.00 | 15.78 | 0 | 0 | 1 | 0 |
| BT Foakes | 1 | 1 | 0 | 5 | 5 | 5.00 | 27.77 | 0 | 0 | 1 | 0 |
| TS Mills | 4 | 6 | 2 | 19 | 8 | 4.75 | 46.34 | 0 | 0 | 4 | 0 |
| RJW Topley | 9 | 11 | 5 | 21 | 9 | 3.50 | 29.16 | 0 | 0 | 1 | 0 |

| | Overs | Mdns | Runs | Wkts | BBI | BBM | Ave | Econ | SR | 5w | 10w |
|---|---|---|---|---|---|---|---|---|---|---|---|
| DD Masters | 637.1 | 169 | 1687 | 93 | 8/10 | 9/55 | 18.13 | 2.64 | 41.1 | 8 | 0 |
| MJ Walker | 25.0 | 5 | 60 | 3 | 2/15 | 2/15 | 20.00 | 2.40 | 50.0 | 0 | 0 |
| RJW Topley | 222.5 | 44 | 801 | 34 | 5/46 | 7/114 | 23.55 | 3.59 | 39.3 | 2 | 0 |
| GR Napier | 192.4 | 37 | 690 | 28 | 6/53 | 8/116 | 24.64 | 3.58 | 41.2 | 2 | 0 |
| TR Craddock | 204.2 | 35 | 628 | 22 | 4/59 | 6/71 | 28.54 | 3.07 | 55.7 | 0 | 0 |
| RN ten Doeschate | 69.3 | 3 | 270 | 9 | 2/33 | 2/33 | 30.00 | 3.88 | 46.3 | 0 | 0 |
| RS Bopara | 239.0 | 37 | 803 | 24 | 3/45 | 4/139 | 33.45 | 3.35 | 59.7 | 0 | 0 |
| TS Mills | 65.0 | 11 | 241 | 7 | 3/48 | 3/99 | 34.42 | 3.70 | 55.7 | 0 | 0 |
| MA Chambers | 293.1 | 45 | 1063 | 26 | 3/34 | 5/120 | 40.88 | 3.62 | 67.6 | 0 | 0 |
| CJC Wright | 147.0 | 19 | 521 | 12 | 3/109 | 4/127 | 43.41 | 3.54 | 73.5 | 0 | 0 |
| TJ Phillips | 181.3 | 29 | 657 | 11 | 4/97 | 5/110 | 59.72 | 3.61 | 99.0 | 0 | 0 |
| LL Tsotsobe | 84.0 | 8 | 388 | 5 | 2/71 | 2/128 | 77.60 | 4.61 | 100.8 | 0 | 0 |
| T Westley | 61.5 | 10 | 184 | 2 | 2/45 | 2/45 | 92.00 | 2.97 | 185.5 | 0 | 0 |
| OA Shah | 2.5 | 0 | 4 | 0 | - | - | - | 1.41 | - | 0 | 0 |

**Catches/Stumpings:**
48 Foster (+4st), 15 Shah, 13 Walker, 11 Mickleburgh, Westley, 10 ten Doeschate, 7 Phillips, 5 Cook, Godleman, Wheater (inc 1 outfield, +0st), 4 Masters, Pettini, 3 Foakes (+0st), Napier, 2 Mills, 1 Bopara, Chambers, Craddock, Topley, Tsotsobe

# LIST A AVERAGES 2011

## Batting

| | Mat | Inns | NO | Runs | HS | Ave | SR | 100 | 50 | 4s | 6s |
|---|---|---|---|---|---|---|---|---|---|---|---|
| JS Foster | 9 | 4 | 1 | 211 | 77 | 70.33 | 122.67 | 0 | 3 | 23 | 3 |
| RS Bopara | 9 | 6 | 2 | 233 | 75* | 58.25 | 81.46 | 0 | 2 | 14 | 3 |
| AN Cook | 4 | 3 | 0 | 151 | 96 | 50.33 | 91.51 | 0 | 1 | 22 | 0 |
| OA Shah | 7 | 6 | 1 | 242 | 104 | 48.40 | 102.54 | 1 | 1 | 23 | 6 |
| ML Pettini | 12 | 10 | 3 | 297 | 104 | 42.42 | 80.05 | 1 | 1 | 25 | 3 |
| TJ Phillips | 12 | 4 | 2 | 80 | 58* | 40.00 | 86.02 | 0 | 1 | 5 | 2 |
| CJC Wright | 7 | 2 | 0 | 60 | 42 | 30.00 | 84.50 | 0 | 0 | 7 | 0 |
| JC Mickleburgh | 3 | 2 | 0 | 57 | 56 | 28.50 | 90.47 | 0 | 1 | 7 | 0 |
| GR Napier | 12 | 7 | 1 | 153 | 41 | 25.50 | 96.83 | 0 | 0 | 14 | 5 |
| DD Masters | 8 | 3 | 2 | 20 | 19* | 20.00 | 50.00 | 0 | 0 | 2 | 0 |
| RJW Topley | 3 | 1 | 0 | 19 | 19 | 19.00 | 95.00 | 0 | 0 | 1 | 0 |
| AJ Wheater | 12 | 8 | 1 | 122 | 40 | 17.42 | 99.18 | 0 | 0 | 14 | 4 |
| T Westley | 5 | 4 | 0 | 65 | 50 | 16.25 | 71.42 | 0 | 1 | 6 | 1 |
| RN ten Doeschate | 7 | 5 | 1 | 32 | 30 | 8.00 | 65.30 | 0 | 0 | 3 | 0 |
| TS Mills | 1 | 1 | 0 | 0 | 0 | 0.00 | 0.00 | 0 | 0 | 0 | 0 |
| MJ Walker | 5 | 2 | 2 | 116 | 71* | - | 96.66 | 0 | 1 | 15 | 0 |
| TR Craddock | 4 | 2 | 2 | 5 | 5* | - | 38.46 | 0 | 0 | 0 | 0 |
| MA Comber | 5 | - | - | - | - | - | - | - | - | - | - |
| SB Styris | 2 | - | - | - | - | - | - | - | - | - | - |
| LL Tsotsobe | 5 | - | - | - | - | - | - | - | - | - | - |

## Bowling

| | Overs | Mdns | Runs | Wkts | BBI | Ave | Econ | SR | 4w | 5w |
|---|---|---|---|---|---|---|---|---|---|---|
| T Westley | 6.0 | 0 | 18 | 1 | 1/18 | 18.00 | 3.00 | 36.0 | 0 | 0 |
| TR Craddock | 25.0 | 1 | 117 | 3 | 2/38 | 39.00 | 4.68 | 50.0 | 0 | 0 |
| DD Masters | 53.0 | 1 | 252 | 8 | 4/32 | 31.50 | 4.75 | 39.7 | 1 | 0 |
| RS Bopara | 61.0 | 0 | 303 | 17 | 3/27 | 17.82 | 4.96 | 21.5 | 0 | 0 |
| TJ Phillips | 75.0 | 0 | 380 | 17 | 5/28 | 22.35 | 5.06 | 26.4 | 0 | 1 |
| MA Comber | 12.0 | 0 | 65 | 0 | - | - | 5.41 | - | 0 | 0 |
| RJW Topley | 20.0 | 0 | 109 | 3 | 2/45 | 36.33 | 5.45 | 40.0 | 0 | 0 |
| CJC Wright | 36.0 | 3 | 202 | 8 | 4/20 | 25.25 | 5.61 | 27.0 | 1 | 0 |
| LL Tsotsobe | 38.3 | 0 | 242 | 8 | 4/43 | 30.25 | 6.28 | 28.8 | 1 | 0 |
| GR Napier | 77.0 | 1 | 493 | 12 | 4/38 | 41.08 | 6.40 | 38.5 | 1 | 0 |
| TS Mills | 8.0 | 0 | 52 | 1 | 1/52 | 52.00 | 6.50 | 48.0 | 0 | 0 |
| RN ten Doeschate | 17.5 | 0 | 124 | 1 | 1/28 | 124.0 | 6.95 | 107.0 | 0 | 0 |
| OA Shah | 2.0 | 0 | 14 | 0 | - | - | 7.00 | - | 0 | 0 |

**Catches/Stumpings:**
6 Napier, Wheater (inc 4 outfield, +0st), 5 Pettini, Foster (+0st), 4 Bopara, Phillips, Wright, 3 Mickleburgh, 2 Craddock, Masters, Shah, ten Doeschate, 1 Tsotsobe, Walker, Westley

| | Mat | Inns | NO | Runs | HS | Ave | SR | 100 | 50 | 4s | 6s |
|---|---|---|---|---|---|---|---|---|---|---|---|
| SB Styris | 9 | 8 | 2 | 220 | 47 | 36.66 | 160.58 | 0 | 0 | 14 | 13 |
| JS Foster | 13 | 11 | 5 | 174 | 31 | 29.00 | 111.53 | 0 | 0 | 14 | 0 |
| OA Shah | 15 | 14 | 1 | 363 | 78* | 27.92 | 126.04 | 0 | 2 | 31 | 13 |
| TJ Phillips | 15 | 8 | 5 | 76 | 33 | 25.33 | 146.15 | 0 | 0 | 9 | 2 |
| ML Pettini | 13 | 12 | 0 | 271 | 81 | 22.58 | 118.34 | 0 | 1 | 29 | 5 |
| RS Bopara | 12 | 12 | 0 | 237 | 72 | 19.75 | 113.39 | 0 | 1 | 19 | 5 |
| RN ten Doeschate | 15 | 14 | 3 | 181 | 32* | 16.45 | 113.12 | 0 | 0 | 12 | 3 |
| TG Southee | 15 | 12 | 3 | 135 | 74 | 15.00 | 170.88 | 0 | 1 | 12 | 7 |
| GR Napier | 8 | 7 | 0 | 86 | 26 | 12.28 | 145.76 | 0 | 0 | 7 | 5 |
| AJ Wheater | 11 | 10 | 0 | 121 | 29 | 12.10 | 122.22 | 0 | 0 | 15 | 2 |
| MJ Walker | 13 | 10 | 1 | 95 | 28 | 10.55 | 97.93 | 0 | 0 | 10 | 0 |
| CJC Wright | 7 | 2 | 0 | 1 | 1 | 0.50 | 25.00 | 0 | 0 | 0 | 0 |
| DD Masters | 13 | 4 | 4 | 3 | 2* | - | 100.00 | 0 | 0 | 0 | 0 |
| T Westley | 3 | 1 | 1 | 2 | 2* | - | 100.00 | 0 | 0 | 0 | 0 |
| AN Cook | 1 | - | - | - | - | - | - | - | - | - | - |
| TR Craddock | 2 | - | - | - | - | - | - | - | - | - | - |

| | Overs | Mdns | Runs | Wkts | BBI | Ave | Econ | SR | 4w | 5w |
|---|---|---|---|---|---|---|---|---|---|---|
| OA Shah | 1.0 | 0 | 5 | 1 | 1/5 | 5.00 | 5.00 | 6.0 | 0 | 0 |
| T Westley | 2.0 | 0 | 13 | 1 | 1/7 | 13.00 | 6.50 | 12.0 | 0 | 0 |
| DD Masters | 40.5 | 1 | 279 | 5 | 2/25 | 55.80 | 6.83 | 49.0 | 0 | 0 |
| TJ Phillips | 49.0 | 0 | 344 | 26 | 4/22 | 13.23 | 7.02 | 11.3 | 3 | 0 |
| SB Styris | 22.0 | 0 | 159 | 7 | 3/12 | 22.71 | 7.22 | 18.8 | 0 | 0 |
| GR Napier | 29.0 | 1 | 220 | 5 | 2/9 | 44.00 | 7.58 | 34.8 | 0 | 0 |
| RS Bopara | 25.3 | 0 | 195 | 6 | 2/28 | 32.50 | 7.64 | 25.5 | 0 | 0 |
| TG Southee | 52.0 | 2 | 417 | 22 | 6/16 | 18.95 | 8.01 | 14.1 | 0 | 1 |
| RN ten Doeschate | 29.0 | 0 | 254 | 8 | 3/18 | 31.75 | 8.75 | 21.7 | 0 | 0 |
| CJC Wright | 17.0 | 0 | 167 | 4 | 2/20 | 41.75 | 9.82 | 25.5 | 0 | 0 |
| TR Craddock | 2.0 | 0 | 23 | 0 | - | - | 11.50 | - | 0 | 0 |

**Catches/Stumpings:**
8 ten Doeschate, 7 Phillips, 6 Foster (+4st), Pettini, Southee, 5 Bopara, 4 Walker, 3 Craddock, Styris, 1 Masters, Napier, Shah, Wright, Westley

TEAM PROFILE

FORMED: 1888
HOME GROUND: SWALEC Stadium, Cardiff
ONE-DAY NAME: Welsh Dragons
CAPTAIN: Mark Wallace (Championship and CB40), Jim Allenby (FL t20)
2011 RESULTS: CC2: 6/9; CB40: 5/7 in Group C; FL t20: 7/9 in South Group
HONOURS: Championship: (3) 1948, 1969, 1997; Pro40/National League/CB40: (2) 2002, 2004; Sunday League: 1993

## THE LOWDOWN

After another disappointing season in 2011 and the acrimonious departure of the Maynards from the club in 2010 still leaving a bitter taste in the mouth, the last thing Glamorgan needed was more controversy. Unfortunately for their loyal and enduring fans, that's what they got with Alviro Petersen turning down a contract before signing for Essex. The return of Simon Jones to his home county offers some hope if he can remain injury free, while the overseas additions of Marcus North and Moises Henriques look to be shrewd acquisitions. Head coach Matthew Mott and newly installed skipper Mark Wallace will need to establish unity if the club is to enjoy a successful season, but with experienced players like Jim Allenby and talented youngsters such as James Harris at their disposal, the raw materials are there.

### HEAD COACH: MATTHEW MOTT

Mott has endured a turbulent start to his Glamorgan career, but the Queenslander is a proven winner who possesses the experience and expertise to succeed. A left-handed batsman who played for Victoria and Queensland, he became New South Wales coach in 2007 and guided them to the Champions League Twenty20 tournament in 2009. Prior to signing a three-year deal with Glamorgan in 2011, Mott joined John Buchanan as assistant coach with IPL side Kolkata Knight Riders.

| | Mat | Inns | NO | Runs | HS | Ave | SR | 100 | 50 | 4s | 6s |
|---|---|---|---|---|---|---|---|---|---|---|---|
| SJ Walters | 7 | 14 | 4 | 508 | 147 | 50.80 | 55.15 | 2 | 1 | 61 | 6 |
| AN Petersen | 15 | 27 | 2 | 1069 | 210 | 42.76 | 59.92 | 2 | 5 | 141 | 4 |
| MA Wallace | 16 | 29 | 4 | 1020 | 107 | 40.80 | 61.96 | 2 | 7 | 122 | 9 |
| WD Bragg | 16 | 30 | 0 | 1033 | 110 | 34.43 | 56.17 | 1 | 8 | 139 | 1 |
| AJ Norman | 1 | 1 | 0 | 34 | 34 | 34.00 | 41.97 | 0 | 0 | 4 | 0 |
| J Allenby | 9 | 17 | 1 | 517 | 113 | 32.31 | 57.57 | 1 | 4 | 68 | 5 |
| MJ Powell | 12 | 23 | 2 | 675 | 99 | 32.14 | 49.63 | 0 | 5 | 91 | 2 |
| HT Waters | 3 | 5 | 2 | 93 | 54 | 31.00 | 27.19 | 0 | 1 | 11 | 0 |
| GP Rees | 16 | 31 | 0 | 954 | 126 | 30.77 | 49.58 | 1 | 8 | 132 | 8 |
| BJ Wright | 9 | 16 | 1 | 460 | 101 | 30.66 | 64.06 | 1 | 3 | 66 | 1 |
| JAR Harris | 10 | 17 | 3 | 403 | 60* | 28.78 | 47.80 | 0 | 3 | 53 | 1 |
| NA James | 4 | 7 | 0 | 186 | 49 | 26.57 | 38.11 | 0 | 0 | 21 | 0 |
| WT Owen | 9 | 11 | 4 | 167 | 69 | 23.85 | 70.46 | 0 | 1 | 24 | 4 |
| GG Wagg | 14 | 23 | 1 | 446 | 70* | 20.27 | 73.47 | 0 | 3 | 67 | 6 |
| JC Glover | 3 | 4 | 2 | 35 | 16* | 17.50 | 42.68 | 0 | 0 | 5 | 0 |
| DA Cosker | 16 | 24 | 4 | 314 | 39 | 15.70 | 41.26 | 0 | 0 | 37 | 4 |
| RDB Croft | 9 | 14 | 2 | 182 | 33 | 15.16 | 42.22 | 0 | 0 | 22 | 0 |
| AJ Shantry | 3 | 6 | 4 | 25 | 14 | 12.50 | 18.51 | 0 | 0 | 2 | 0 |
| Alex J Jones | 2 | 3 | 0 | 34 | 26 | 11.33 | 48.57 | 0 | 0 | 4 | 1 |
| CP Ashling | 2 | 3 | 2 | 9 | 7 | 9.00 | 33.33 | 0 | 0 | 1 | 0 |

*Batting*

| | Overs | Mdns | Runs | Wkts | BBI | BBM | Ave | Econ | SR | 5w | 10w |
|---|---|---|---|---|---|---|---|---|---|---|---|
| NA James | 24.0 | 2 | 79 | 5 | 2/28 | 4/79 | 15.80 | 3.29 | 28.8 | 0 | 0 |
| J Allenby | 228.3 | 51 | 654 | 25 | 5/44 | 6/86 | 26.16 | 2.86 | 54.8 | 1 | 0 |
| JAR Harris | 340.2 | 63 | 1186 | 44 | 5/39 | 8/101 | 26.95 | 3.48 | 46.4 | 3 | 0 |
| WD Bragg | 10.0 | 1 | 27 | 1 | 1/4 | 1/5 | 27.00 | 2.70 | 60.0 | 0 | 0 |
| CP Ashling | 44.0 | 2 | 183 | 6 | 4/47 | 4/77 | 30.50 | 4.15 | 44.0 | 0 | 0 |
| AJ Shantry | 93.5 | 20 | 291 | 9 | 3/42 | 6/107 | 32.33 | 3.10 | 62.5 | 0 | 0 |
| DA Cosker | 613.1 | 162 | 1650 | 49 | 5/48 | 8/91 | 33.67 | 2.69 | 75.0 | 1 | 0 |
| WT Owen | 229.2 | 26 | 1041 | 30 | 5/124 | 6/61 | 34.70 | 4.53 | 45.8 | 1 | 0 |
| JC Glover | 52.0 | 4 | 201 | 5 | 4/49 | 5/99 | 40.20 | 3.86 | 62.4 | 0 | 0 |
| GG Wagg | 401.2 | 64 | 1380 | 33 | 3/52 | 6/138 | 41.81 | 3.43 | 72.9 | 0 | 0 |
| RDB Croft | 295.1 | 49 | 831 | 19 | 3/80 | 4/116 | 43.73 | 2.81 | 93.2 | 0 | 0 |
| HT Waters | 59.0 | 14 | 161 | 3 | 2/16 | 2/16 | 53.66 | 2.72 | 118.0 | 0 | 0 |
| Alex J Jones | 36.0 | 4 | 158 | 2 | 1/50 | 1/79 | 79.00 | 4.38 | 108.0 | 0 | 0 |
| AN Petersen | 55.0 | 11 | 160 | 1 | 1/37 | 1/44 | 160.00 | 2.90 | 330.0 | 0 | 0 |
| AJ Norman | 17.0 | 4 | 49 | 0 | - | - | - | 2.88 | - | 0 | 0 |

*Bowling*

**Catches/Stumpings:**
39 Wallace (+5st), 13 Rees, 8 Powell, 6 Allenby, Bragg, Cosker, Harris, Petersen, 5 Wagg, Walters, 3 Wright, 2 Glover, Shantry, 1 A.Jones, Owen

**Batting**

| | Mat | Inns | NO | Runs | HS | Ave | SR | 100 | 50 | 4s | 6s |
|---|---|---|---|---|---|---|---|---|---|---|---|
| GP Rees | 12 | 12 | 2 | 567 | 110* | 56.70 | 93.10 | 2 | 4 | 49 | 13 |
| AN Petersen | 12 | 12 | 2 | 547 | 144 | 54.70 | 98.20 | 1 | 2 | 47 | 16 |
| DA Cosker | 11 | 5 | 4 | 51 | 39* | 51.00 | 127.50 | 0 | 0 | 2 | 1 |
| SJ Walters | 11 | 11 | 2 | 302 | 79 | 33.55 | 85.79 | 0 | 3 | 26 | 7 |
| CB Cooke | 7 | 6 | 1 | 126 | 75 | 25.20 | 111.50 | 0 | 1 | 10 | 6 |
| NA James | 3 | 2 | 0 | 47 | 43 | 23.50 | 81.03 | 0 | 0 | 2 | 0 |
| GG Wagg | 11 | 11 | 1 | 195 | 34 | 19.50 | 116.07 | 0 | 0 | 18 | 6 |
| J Allenby | 9 | 9 | 0 | 169 | 41 | 18.77 | 84.50 | 0 | 0 | 12 | 3 |
| BJ Wright | 5 | 5 | 1 | 71 | 28* | 17.75 | 70.29 | 0 | 0 | 2 | 1 |
| RDB Croft | 5 | 1 | 0 | 16 | 16 | 16.00 | 84.21 | 0 | 0 | 0 | 0 |
| AJ Norman | 1 | 1 | 0 | 15 | 15 | 15.00 | 107.14 | 0 | 0 | 0 | 1 |
| MA Wallace | 12 | 11 | 1 | 111 | 29 | 11.10 | 84.73 | 0 | 0 | 9 | 1 |
| MP O'Shea | 9 | 7 | 1 | 53 | 25 | 8.83 | 73.61 | 0 | 0 | 6 | 0 |
| Alex J Jones | 3 | 2 | 1 | 3 | 3* | 3.00 | 50.00 | 0 | 0 | 0 | 0 |
| WD Bragg | 1 | 1 | 0 | 0 | 0 | 0.00 | 0.00 | 0 | 0 | 0 | 0 |
| JAR Harris | 7 | 4 | 4 | 42 | 19* | - | 123.52 | 0 | 0 | 3 | 0 |
| WT Owen | 9 | 2 | 2 | 3 | 3* | - | 37.50 | 0 | 0 | 0 | 0 |
| SP Jones | 3 | - | - | - | - | - | - | - | - | - | - |
| HT Waters | 1 | - | - | - | - | - | - | - | - | - | - |

**Bowling**

| | Overs | Mdns | Runs | Wkts | BBI | Ave | Econ | SR | 4w | 5w |
|---|---|---|---|---|---|---|---|---|---|---|
| WD Bragg | 1.0 | 0 | 2 | 0 | - | - | 2.00 | - | 0 | 0 |
| GP Rees | 0.3 | 0 | 2 | 0 | - | - | 4.00 | - | 0 | 0 |
| AJ Norman | 7.0 | 0 | 31 | 0 | - | - | 4.42 | - | 0 | 0 |
| DA Cosker | 56.0 | 0 | 276 | 11 | 4/30 | 25.09 | 4.92 | 30.5 | 2 | 0 |
| RDB Croft | 23.0 | 3 | 122 | 1 | 1/43 | 122.00 | 5.30 | 138.0 | 0 | 0 |
| MP O'Shea | 29.0 | 0 | 157 | 5 | 2/32 | 31.40 | 5.41 | 34.8 | 0 | 0 |
| J Allenby | 32.3 | 0 | 179 | 5 | 2/26 | 35.80 | 5.50 | 39.0 | 0 | 0 |
| JAR Harris | 27.5 | 2 | 156 | 9 | 3/39 | 17.33 | 5.60 | 18.5 | 0 | 0 |
| WT Owen | 40.0 | 3 | 233 | 15 | 4/31 | 15.53 | 5.82 | 16.0 | 2 | 0 |
| NA James | 15.0 | 1 | 88 | 5 | 3/36 | 17.60 | 5.86 | 18.0 | 0 | 0 |
| SP Jones | 8.0 | 1 | 52 | 2 | 2/9 | 26.00 | 6.50 | 24.0 | 0 | 0 |
| GG Wagg | 60.1 | 0 | 416 | 7 | 3/35 | 59.42 | 6.91 | 51.5 | 0 | 0 |
| AN Petersen | 1.0 | 0 | 7 | 0 | - | - | 7.00 | - | 0 | 0 |
| Alex J Jones | 18.0 | 0 | 128 | 3 | 1/38 | 42.66 | 7.11 | 36.0 | 0 | 0 |
| HT Waters | 3.0 | 0 | 27 | 0 | - | - | 9.00 | - | 0 | 0 |

**Catches/Stumpings:**
8 Wallace (+3st), 6 Rees, 4 Petersen, 3 Cosker, 3 Wagg, 2 A.Jones, O'Shea, Walters, 1 Allenby, Cooke, Owen, Wright

www.glamorgancricket.com / tel: 029 2040 9380

WELSH
DRAGONS

| | Mat | Inns | NO | Runs | HS | Ave | SR | 100 | 50 | 4s | 6s |
|---|---|---|---|---|---|---|---|---|---|---|---|
| DA Cosker | 12 | 4 | 3 | 38 | 21* | 38.00 | 111.76 | 0 | 0 | 4 | 0 |
| SJ Walters | 4 | 2 | 0 | 74 | 37 | 37.00 | 102.77 | 0 | 0 | 6 | 1 |
| AN Petersen | 16 | 15 | 2 | 423 | 72 | 32.53 | 117.82 | 0 | 2 | 43 | 7 |
| J Allenby | 12 | 11 | 1 | 264 | 63 | 26.40 | 110.46 | 0 | 1 | 20 | 7 |
| GG Wagg | 11 | 9 | 2 | 151 | 46 | 21.57 | 123.77 | 0 | 0 | 8 | 5 |
| JAR Harris | 4 | 4 | 3 | 21 | 17* | 21.00 | 131.25 | 0 | 0 | 3 | 0 |
| MJ Cosgrove | 16 | 15 | 1 | 293 | 47 | 20.92 | 114.00 | 0 | 0 | 38 | 7 |
| GP Rees | 9 | 8 | 0 | 152 | 38 | 19.00 | 112.59 | 0 | 0 | 11 | 5 |
| DO Brown | 5 | 3 | 1 | 38 | 31* | 19.00 | 131.03 | 0 | 0 | 4 | 1 |
| CB Cooke | 16 | 14 | 2 | 224 | 47 | 18.66 | 140.00 | 0 | 0 | 8 | 14 |
| MA Wallace | 15 | 11 | 4 | 109 | 40* | 15.57 | 100.00 | 0 | 0 | 8 | 0 |
| NA James | 4 | 2 | 0 | 20 | 13 | 10.00 | 133.33 | 0 | 0 | 0 | 1 |
| BJ Wright | 6 | 5 | 1 | 39 | 23 | 9.75 | 69.64 | 0 | 0 | 2 | 0 |
| MP O'Shea | 2 | 2 | 0 | 18 | 11 | 9.00 | 163.63 | 0 | 0 | 1 | 1 |
| RDB Croft | 14 | 5 | 2 | 23 | 5* | 7.66 | 92.00 | 0 | 0 | 3 | 0 |
| Alex J Jones | 14 | 5 | 3 | 9 | 4* | 4.50 | 50.00 | 0 | 0 | 1 | 0 |
| SP Jones | 10 | 2 | 1 | 1 | 1* | 1.00 | 33.33 | 0 | 0 | 0 | 0 |
| WT Owen | 6 | - | - | - | - | - | - | - | - | - | - |

**Batting**

| | Overs | Mdns | Runs | Wkts | BBI | Ave | Econ | SR | 4w | 5w |
|---|---|---|---|---|---|---|---|---|---|---|
| RDB Croft | 42.0 | 2 | 237 | 15 | 3/9 | 15.80 | 5.64 | 16.8 | 0 | 0 |
| AN Petersen | 13.1 | 0 | 80 | 5 | 1/5 | 16.00 | 6.07 | 15.8 | 0 | 0 |
| NA James | 15.0 | 1 | 92 | 4 | 2/22 | 23.00 | 6.13 | 22.5 | 0 | 0 |
| MP O'Shea | 8.0 | 0 | 50 | 1 | 1/25 | 50.00 | 6.25 | 48.0 | 0 | 0 |
| GG Wagg | 30.3 | 1 | 201 | 10 | 3/30 | 20.10 | 6.59 | 18.3 | 0 | 0 |
| DA Cosker | 36.4 | 1 | 253 | 9 | 3/11 | 28.11 | 6.90 | 24.4 | 0 | 0 |
| WT Owen | 16.3 | 0 | 114 | 7 | 3/21 | 16.28 | 6.90 | 14.1 | 0 | 0 |
| SP Jones | 35.5 | 1 | 250 | 11 | 2/18 | 22.72 | 6.97 | 19.5 | 0 | 0 |
| MJ Cosgrove | 4.2 | 0 | 31 | 2 | 1/12 | 15.50 | 7.15 | 13.0 | 0 | 0 |
| Alex J Jones | 32.0 | 0 | 256 | 15 | 3/16 | 17.06 | 8.00 | 12.8 | 0 | 0 |
| J Allenby | 12.0 | 0 | 97 | 3 | 1/16 | 32.33 | 8.08 | 24.0 | 0 | 0 |
| JAR Harris | 11.2 | 0 | 98 | 3 | 2/38 | 32.66 | 8.64 | 22.6 | 0 | 0 |
| DO Brown | 4.0 | 0 | 45 | 0 | - | - | 11.25 | - | 0 | 0 |
| GP Rees | 2.0 | 0 | 25 | 0 | - | - | 12.50 | - | 0 | 0 |

**Bowling**

**Catches/Stumpings:**
9 Petersen, 8 Cooke, 6 Wallace (+2st), 4 Cosgrove, Croft, 3 Cosker, James, Wagg, Walters, Wright, 2 Allenby, 1 A.Jones, S.Jones

TEAM PROFILE

FORMED: 1871
HOME GROUND: County Ground, Bristol
ONE-DAY NAME: Gladiators
CAPTAIN: Alex Gidman
2011 RESULTS: CC2: 4/9; CB40: 6/7 in Group C; FL t20: 8/9 in South Group
HONOURS: Gillette/NatWest/C&G/FP Trophy: (5) 1973, 1999, 2000, 2003, 2004; Benson and Hedges Cup: (3) 1977, 1999, 2000; Pro40/National League/CB40: 2000

## THE LOWDOWN

Gloucestershire's glory days in one-day cricket felt like a fading memory last season. The Gladiators finished second-bottom in their respective CB40 and FL t20 groups, with the batsmen consistently failing to post competitive scores. But the County Championship was a different story, with six victories sealing fourth place and offering the fans hope of a promotion push in 2012. Will Gidman in particular enjoyed an outstanding season playing under his older brother Alex and will be looking to build on his 2011 'double' of 1,000 first-class runs and 50 wickets. The loss of stalwarts Jon Lewis and Chris Taylor leaves the squad light on experience, but the capture of talented young batsman Dan Housego and the retention of Muttiah Muralitharan for the FL t20 are a boost to the club. Off the field, ground development disputes continue but supporters will be buoyed by the news that coach John Bracewell has agreed a new contract to oversee the progression of his young squad.

### HEAD COACH: JOHN BRACEWELL

The New Zealander has become synonymous with Gloucestershire, his presence defined by the successes he enjoyed with them as both player and coach. Returning to his native country as national coach in 2003, Bracewell led the Black Caps to their first Chappell-Hadlee Trophy victory and the semi-finals of the 2007 World Cup. Bracewell left the post in 2008, returning to his beloved Bristol base in 2009.

## Batting

| | Mat | Inns | NO | Runs | HS | Ave | SR | 100 | 50 | 4s | 6s |
|---|---|---|---|---|---|---|---|---|---|---|---|
| WRS Gidman | 16 | 28 | 6 | 1006 | 116* | 45.72 | 51.24 | 1 | 8 | 134 | 3 |
| EGC Young | 3 | 5 | 2 | 129 | 51* | 43.00 | 41.88 | 0 | 1 | 12 | 0 |
| CG Taylor | 16 | 29 | 1 | 1139 | 196 | 40.67 | 62.41 | 3 | 6 | 160 | 2 |
| APR Gidman | 15 | 27 | 3 | 903 | 168 | 37.62 | 62.27 | 1 | 6 | 117 | 7 |
| KS Williamson | 13 | 23 | 0 | 831 | 149 | 36.13 | 57.38 | 1 | 5 | 119 | 0 |
| CDJ Dent | 12 | 21 | 2 | 649 | 100 | 34.15 | 52.63 | 1 | 3 | 90 | 1 |
| IA Cockbain | 12 | 21 | 1 | 542 | 127 | 27.10 | 45.54 | 1 | 3 | 71 | 2 |
| RG Coughtrie | 16 | 30 | 5 | 632 | 54* | 25.28 | 36.32 | 0 | 2 | 69 | 1 |
| J Lewis | 16 | 25 | 2 | 525 | 71 | 22.82 | 77.43 | 0 | 4 | 58 | 8 |
| HJH Marshall | 11 | 19 | 1 | 401 | 72 | 22.27 | 47.62 | 0 | 2 | 61 | 0 |
| JMR Taylor | 3 | 5 | 0 | 111 | 39 | 22.20 | 58.11 | 0 | 0 | 17 | 1 |
| LC Norwell | 3 | 5 | 2 | 59 | 26 | 19.66 | 30.89 | 0 | 0 | 5 | 0 |
| JN Batty | 6 | 10 | 0 | 179 | 70 | 17.90 | 32.31 | 0 | 1 | 21 | 0 |
| V Banerjee | 3 | 5 | 2 | 52 | 25 | 17.33 | 24.29 | 0 | 0 | 6 | 0 |
| DA Payne | 14 | 21 | 6 | 255 | 62 | 17.00 | 41.12 | 0 | 1 | 34 | 0 |
| ID Saxelby | 15 | 23 | 6 | 238 | 34* | 14.00 | 40.47 | 0 | 0 | 21 | 1 |
| CN Miles | 1 | 2 | 0 | 24 | 19 | 12.00 | 25.80 | 0 | 0 | 3 | 0 |
| JK Fuller | 1 | 1 | 0 | 4 | 4 | 4.00 | 80.00 | 0 | 0 | 0 | 0 |

## Bowling

| | Overs | Mdns | Runs | Wkts | BBI | BBM | Ave | Econ | SR | 5w | 10w |
|---|---|---|---|---|---|---|---|---|---|---|---|
| CG Taylor | 5.0 | 1 | 11 | 1 | 1/7 | 1/7 | 11.00 | 2.20 | 30.0 | 0 | 0 |
| WRS Gidman | 375.2 | 84 | 1088 | 51 | 6/92 | 6/114 | 21.33 | 2.89 | 44.1 | 3 | 0 |
| J Lewis | 513.3 | 109 | 1521 | 65 | 5/65 | 8/100 | 23.40 | 2.96 | 47.4 | 1 | 0 |
| LC Norwell | 86.5 | 16 | 341 | 12 | 6/46 | 7/112 | 28.41 | 3.92 | 43.4 | 1 | 0 |
| DA Payne | 345.2 | 61 | 1298 | 42 | 6/26 | 9/96 | 30.90 | 3.75 | 49.3 | 2 | 0 |
| ID Saxelby | 393.2 | 53 | 1529 | 49 | 6/69 | 10/142 | 31.20 | 3.88 | 48.1 | 2 | 1 |
| CN Miles | 19.0 | 1 | 80 | 2 | 2/80 | 2/80 | 40.00 | 4.21 | 57.0 | 0 | 0 |
| HJH Marshall | 94.1 | 20 | 274 | 6 | 2/18 | 2/19 | 45.66 | 2.90 | 94.1 | 0 | 0 |
| JMR Taylor | 78.0 | 4 | 355 | 6 | 2/81 | 2/81 | 59.16 | 4.55 | 78.0 | 0 | 0 |
| JK Fuller | 19.0 | 3 | 62 | 1 | 1/49 | 1/62 | 62.00 | 3.26 | 114.0 | 0 | 0 |
| APR Gidman | 32.0 | 4 | 127 | 2 | 2/33 | 2/33 | 63.50 | 3.96 | 96.0 | 0 | 0 |
| KS Williamson | 94.0 | 10 | 332 | 5 | 2/39 | 3/100 | 66.40 | 3.53 | 112.8 | 0 | 0 |
| V Banerjee | 100.0 | 17 | 307 | 4 | 3/134 | 3/135 | 76.75 | 3.07 | 150.0 | 0 | 0 |
| CDJ Dent | 2.0 | 0 | 8 | 0 | - | - | - | 4.00 | - | 0 | 0 |
| EGC Young | 6.0 | 1 | 23 | 0 | - | - | - | 3.83 | - | 0 | 0 |

**Catches/Stumpings:**
36 Coughtrie (inc 1 outfield +0st), 28 Batty (+0st), 17 Dent, 12 Williamson, A.Gidman, 10 Cockbain, 9 Marshall, 5 Lewis, Payne, C.Taylor, 4 W.Gidman, 2 Saxelby, 1 Fuller, J.Taylor

**GLADIATORS**

## Batting

| | Mat | Inns | NO | Runs | HS | Ave | SR | 100 | 50 | 4s | 6s |
|---|---|---|---|---|---|---|---|---|---|---|---|
| APR Gidman | 12 | 12 | 1 | 463 | 106* | 42.09 | 88.86 | 1 | 3 | 46 | 5 |
| CG Taylor | 12 | 11 | 2 | 333 | 100* | 37.00 | 85.38 | 1 | 1 | 32 | 2 |
| IA Cockbain | 12 | 11 | 2 | 309 | 79 | 34.33 | 89.30 | 0 | 3 | 32 | 0 |
| KJ O'Brien | 8 | 8 | 2 | 170 | 46 | 28.33 | 129.77 | 0 | 0 | 16 | 7 |
| WRS Gidman | 8 | 6 | 2 | 108 | 40* | 27.00 | 76.05 | 0 | 0 | 6 | 0 |
| KS Williamson | 11 | 11 | 0 | 288 | 64 | 26.18 | 74.61 | 0 | 1 | 20 | 1 |
| CDJ Dent | 1 | 1 | 0 | 25 | 25 | 25.00 | 83.33 | 0 | 0 | 5 | 0 |
| HJH Marshall | 7 | 7 | 0 | 161 | 60 | 23.00 | 94.70 | 0 | 2 | 15 | 2 |
| JK Fuller | 8 | 7 | 3 | 86 | 33 | 21.50 | 97.72 | 0 | 0 | 9 | 0 |
| JN Batty | 12 | 9 | 1 | 162 | 32 | 20.25 | 92.04 | 0 | 0 | 12 | 2 |
| RKJ Dawson | 3 | 3 | 1 | 37 | 23 | 18.50 | 123.33 | 0 | 0 | 5 | 0 |
| EGC Young | 11 | 9 | 3 | 108 | 50 | 18.00 | 81.20 | 0 | 1 | 8 | 1 |
| JMR Taylor | 5 | 3 | 1 | 18 | 9* | 9.00 | 180.00 | 0 | 0 | 0 | 2 |
| J Lewis | 4 | 1 | 0 | 6 | 6 | 6.00 | 60.00 | 0 | 0 | 0 | 0 |
| DA Payne | 9 | 3 | 2 | 3 | 2* | 3.00 | 50.00 | 0 | 0 | 0 | 0 |
| ID Saxelby | 4 | 2 | 0 | 2 | 2 | 1.00 | 33.33 | 0 | 0 | 0 | 0 |
| MD Taylor | 2 | 1 | 1 | 7 | 7* | - | 140.00 | 0 | 0 | 1 | 0 |
| V Banerjee | 1 | - | - | - | - | - | - | - | - | - | - |
| CN Miles | 2 | - | - | - | - | - | - | - | - | - | - |

## Bowling

| | Overs | Mdns | Runs | Wkts | BBI | Ave | Econ | SR | 4w | 5w |
|---|---|---|---|---|---|---|---|---|---|---|
| EGC Young | 86.0 | 2 | 397 | 9 | 2/32 | 44.11 | 4.61 | 57.3 | 0 | 0 |
| APR Gidman | 9.0 | 0 | 43 | 4 | 3/24 | 10.75 | 4.77 | 13.5 | 0 | 0 |
| RKJ Dawson | 18.0 | 0 | 93 | 2 | 1/21 | 46.50 | 5.16 | 54.0 | 0 | 0 |
| WRS Gidman | 42.2 | 0 | 230 | 4 | 2/29 | 57.50 | 5.43 | 63.5 | 0 | 0 |
| CN Miles | 11.0 | 1 | 63 | 2 | 2/32 | 31.50 | 5.72 | 33.0 | 0 | 0 |
| V Banerjee | 8.0 | 0 | 46 | 1 | 1/46 | 46.00 | 5.75 | 48.0 | 0 | 0 |
| JK Fuller | 56.0 | 3 | 326 | 16 | 4/33 | 20.37 | 5.82 | 21.0 | 1 | 0 |
| JMR Taylor | 25.4 | 0 | 151 | 7 | 3/37 | 21.57 | 5.88 | 22.0 | 0 | 0 |
| KS Williamson | 35.0 | 0 | 213 | 4 | 1/26 | 53.25 | 6.08 | 52.5 | 0 | 0 |
| DA Payne | 65.1 | 4 | 415 | 12 | 4/23 | 34.58 | 6.36 | 32.5 | 1 | 0 |
| MD Taylor | 13.5 | 2 | 89 | 4 | 2/43 | 22.25 | 6.43 | 20.7 | 0 | 0 |
| J Lewis | 27.0 | 2 | 183 | 8 | 4/41 | 22.87 | 6.77 | 20.2 | 1 | 0 |
| KJ O'Brien | 27.0 | 0 | 183 | 3 | 1/31 | 61.00 | 6.77 | 54.0 | 0 | 0 |
| ID Saxelby | 30.5 | 1 | 246 | 7 | 3/63 | 35.14 | 7.97 | 26.4 | 0 | 0 |
| HJH Marshall | 2.0 | 0 | 17 | 0 | - | - | 8.50 | - | 0 | 0 |

**Catches/Stumpings:**
9 Batty (+2st), 8 Cockbain, 6 C.Taylor, 5 A.Gidman, Williamson, Young, 4 Marshall, 3 O'Brien, 2 Fuller, W.Gidman, Payne, 1 Dawson, J.Taylor, M.Taylor

www.gloscricket.co.uk / tel: 0117 910 8000

## GLADIATORS

Batting

| | Mat | Inns | NO | Runs | HS | Ave | SR | 100 | 50 | 4s | 6s |
|---|---|---|---|---|---|---|---|---|---|---|---|
| KJ O'Brien | 14 | 14 | 2 | 365 | 119 | 30.41 | 161.50 | 1 | 1 | 36 | 21 |
| IA Cockbain | 12 | 12 | 1 | 281 | 78 | 25.54 | 116.59 | 0 | 1 | 26 | 6 |
| HJH Marshall | 15 | 15 | 0 | 367 | 102 | 24.46 | 129.22 | 1 | 1 | 44 | 6 |
| APR Gidman | 6 | 6 | 1 | 107 | 43* | 21.40 | 128.91 | 0 | 0 | 7 | 4 |
| CG Taylor | 14 | 14 | 2 | 236 | 51 | 19.66 | 110.28 | 0 | 1 | 27 | 2 |
| KS Williamson | 15 | 15 | 1 | 248 | 50 | 17.71 | 103.76 | 0 | 1 | 21 | 5 |
| WRS Gidman | 8 | 7 | 1 | 78 | 40* | 13.00 | 86.66 | 0 | 0 | 5 | 0 |
| JMR Taylor | 7 | 7 | 1 | 51 | 38 | 8.50 | 89.47 | 0 | 0 | 8 | 0 |
| EGC Young | 15 | 12 | 2 | 78 | 28 | 7.80 | 100.00 | 0 | 0 | 6 | 1 |
| J Lewis | 8 | 6 | 2 | 28 | 11 | 7.00 | 107.69 | 0 | 0 | 2 | 1 |
| CDJ Dent | 1 | 1 | 0 | 7 | 7 | 7.00 | 63.63 | 0 | 0 | 1 | 0 |
| RG Coughtrie | 13 | 10 | 2 | 54 | 18 | 6.75 | 83.07 | 0 | 0 | 3 | 2 |
| DA Payne | 10 | 5 | 1 | 13 | 10 | 3.25 | 86.66 | 0 | 0 | 0 | 1 |
| M Muralitharan | 15 | 9 | 4 | 14 | 8* | 2.80 | 73.68 | 0 | 0 | 1 | 0 |
| ID Saxelby | 9 | 5 | 1 | 11 | 5 | 2.75 | 45.83 | 0 | 0 | 0 | 0 |
| JN Batty | 2 | 1 | 1 | 19 | 19* | - | 158.33 | 0 | 0 | 2 | 0 |
| JK Fuller | 1 | - | - | - | - | - | - | - | - | - | - |

Bowling

| | Overs | Mdns | Runs | Wkts | BBI | Ave | Econ | SR | 4w | 5w |
|---|---|---|---|---|---|---|---|---|---|---|
| EGC Young | 50.0 | 0 | 325 | 11 | 2/14 | 29.54 | 6.50 | 27.2 | 0 | 0 |
| KS Williamson | 34.4 | 0 | 226 | 9 | 2/18 | 25.11 | 6.51 | 23.1 | 0 | 0 |
| M Muralitharan | 54.0 | 0 | 372 | 12 | 2/15 | 31.00 | 6.88 | 27.0 | 0 | 0 |
| JMR Taylor | 16.1 | 0 | 118 | 8 | 4/16 | 14.75 | 7.29 | 12.1 | 1 | 0 |
| ID Saxelby | 28.0 | 1 | 219 | 7 | 2/23 | 31.28 | 7.82 | 24.0 | 0 | 0 |
| DA Payne | 26.0 | 0 | 221 | 12 | 3/20 | 18.41 | 8.50 | 13.0 | 0 | 0 |
| J Lewis | 22.0 | 0 | 199 | 5 | 3/31 | 39.80 | 9.04 | 26.4 | 0 | 0 |
| WRS Gidman | 8.0 | 0 | 76 | 1 | 1/18 | 76.00 | 9.50 | 48.0 | 0 | 0 |
| KJ O'Brien | 15.5 | 0 | 156 | 2 | 1/21 | 78.00 | 9.85 | 47.5 | 0 | 0 |
| JK Fuller | 2.0 | 0 | 23 | 0 | - | - | 11.50 | - | 0 | 0 |
| APR Gidman | 1.0 | 0 | 13 | 0 | - | - | 13.00 | - | 0 | 0 |

**Catches/Stumpings:**
8 Marshall, 6 Cockbain, Coughtrie (+5st), O'Brien, 5 C.Taylor, 4 Williamson, 2 W.Gidman, Lewis, Saxelby, 1 Batty (+0st), J.Taylor

# HAMPSHIRE

**HAMPSHIRE**
CRICKET

FORMED: 1863
HOME GROUND: The Ageas Bowl
ONE-DAY NAME: Royals
CAPTAIN: Jimmy Adams (Championship and CB40), Dimitri Mascarenhas (FL t20)
2011 RESULTS: CC1: 9/9; CB40: 4/7 in Group B; FL t20: Semi-finalists
HONOURS: Championship: (2) 1961, 1973; Gillette/NatWest/C&G/FP Trophy: (2) 1991, 2005; Benson and Hedges Cup: (2) 1988, 1992; Sunday League: (3) 1975, 1978, 1986; Twenty20 Cup: 2010

## THE LOWDOWN

A poor County Championship season saw Hampshire relegated from Division One for the first time since 2002. A lack of threatening bowling options and the loss of key players like Michael Carberry for a large part of the season saw them achieve just three wins in the competition. They fared better in one-day cricket, however, reaching the semi-finals of the FL t20 competition, but were unable to retain the trophy after a one-over eliminator defeat to Somerset. Captain Dominic Cork and veteran keeper Nic Pothas have both departed, but while domestic signings have been scarce, the signing of Simon Katich as their overseas player will add steel and undoubted class to the squad. Keeping players fit will be key to any success, but if they can do that they will be a force to be reckoned with on all fronts.

### TEAM MANAGER: GILES WHITE

A talented top-order batsman and part-time legbreak bowler, White began his career in the minor counties with Devon before graduating from Loughborough University. After spending time on the staff at Somerset, he joined Hampshire in 1994, scoring over 6,000 first-class runs across an 11-year career. Upon retirement, he joined the Royals' coaching staff and was promoted to the role of team manager in 2008 after Paul Terry stepped down from the position.

| | Mat | Inns | NO | Runs | HS | Ave | SR | 100 | 50 | 4s | 6s |
|---|---|---|---|---|---|---|---|---|---|---|---|
| MA Carberry | 9 | 15 | 1 | 793 | 300* | 56.64 | 57.54 | 3 | 1 | 116 | 4 |
| ND McKenzie | 16 | 28 | 2 | 1120 | 237 | 43.07 | 46.24 | 3 | 3 | 145 | 2 |
| LA Dawson | 15 | 26 | 1 | 908 | 169 | 36.32 | 49.86 | 2 | 5 | 103 | 2 |
| JHK Adams | 15 | 26 | 0 | 935 | 207 | 35.96 | 42.83 | 2 | 4 | 129 | 1 |
| BAC Howell | 1 | 2 | 0 | 71 | 71 | 35.50 | 39.44 | 0 | 1 | 7 | 1 |
| SM Ervine | 14 | 24 | 2 | 663 | 128 | 30.13 | 54.79 | 1 | 3 | 78 | 2 |
| JM Vince | 16 | 27 | 2 | 723 | 157 | 28.92 | 56.57 | 2 | 2 | 111 | 2 |
| JG Myburgh | 6 | 11 | 0 | 287 | 80 | 26.09 | 49.31 | 0 | 2 | 41 | 2 |
| CP Wood | 8 | 11 | 1 | 259 | 56* | 25.90 | 73.37 | 0 | 1 | 33 | 4 |
| DG Cork | 10 | 15 | 1 | 317 | 50 | 22.64 | 58.81 | 0 | 1 | 39 | 6 |
| N Pothas | 8 | 15 | 1 | 303 | 72 | 21.64 | 50.58 | 0 | 3 | 34 | 3 |
| Kabir Ali | 5 | 9 | 4 | 98 | 32 | 19.60 | 38.58 | 0 | 0 | 11 | 0 |
| MD Bates | 8 | 12 | 1 | 204 | 58* | 18.54 | 37.02 | 0 | 1 | 27 | 0 |
| F de Wet | 4 | 6 | 3 | 49 | 16* | 16.33 | 44.14 | 0 | 0 | 6 | 0 |
| AD Mascarenhas | 8 | 14 | 2 | 190 | 50 | 15.83 | 49.47 | 0 | 1 | 26 | 1 |
| Imran Tahir | 8 | 10 | 3 | 74 | 22* | 10.57 | 66.66 | 0 | 0 | 7 | 2 |
| JA Tomlinson | 6 | 10 | 6 | 36 | 12* | 9.00 | 17.06 | 0 | 0 | 2 | 0 |
| MJ Lumb | 1 | 2 | 0 | 17 | 11 | 8.50 | 29.31 | 0 | 0 | 1 | 0 |
| DR Briggs | 11 | 17 | 2 | 103 | 29 | 6.86 | 33.33 | 0 | 0 | 14 | 1 |
| DA Griffiths | 6 | 10 | 4 | 19 | 6* | 3.16 | 21.11 | 0 | 0 | 2 | 0 |
| SP Jones | 1 | 1 | 0 | 0 | 0 | 0.00 | 0.00 | 0 | 0 | 0 | 0 |

Batting

| | Overs | Mdns | Runs | Wkts | BBI | BBM | Ave | Econ | SR | 5w | 10w |
|---|---|---|---|---|---|---|---|---|---|---|---|
| Imran Tahir | 235.2 | 40 | 685 | 28 | 6/132 | 6/146 | 24.46 | 2.91 | 50.4 | 2 | 0 |
| AD Mascarenhas | 229.2 | 61 | 581 | 21 | 6/62 | 6/62 | 27.66 | 2.53 | 65.5 | 1 | 0 |
| CP Wood | 192.4 | 39 | 671 | 24 | 4/35 | 5/65 | 27.95 | 3.48 | 48.1 | 0 | 0 |
| Kabir Ali | 129.0 | 21 | 437 | 13 | 4/43 | 6/116 | 33.61 | 3.38 | 59.5 | 0 | 0 |
| DA Griffiths | 172.5 | 41 | 607 | 18 | 6/85 | 7/102 | 33.72 | 3.51 | 57.6 | 1 | 0 |
| DG Cork | 278.3 | 60 | 802 | 22 | 5/75 | 8/126 | 36.45 | 2.87 | 75.9 | 1 | 0 |
| DR Briggs | 449.5 | 89 | 1393 | 38 | 6/65 | 7/156 | 36.65 | 3.09 | 71.0 | 3 | 0 |
| JA Tomlinson | 173.1 | 39 | 573 | 15 | 4/13 | 7/84 | 38.20 | 3.30 | 69.2 | 0 | 0 |
| F de Wet | 124.0 | 15 | 470 | 9 | 2/78 | 3/96 | 52.22 | 3.79 | 82.6 | 0 | 0 |
| SM Ervine | 220.2 | 33 | 896 | 15 | 3/66 | 3/53 | 59.73 | 4.06 | 88.1 | 0 | 0 |
| SP Jones | 18.3 | 1 | 65 | 1 | 1/59 | 1/65 | 65.00 | 3.51 | 111.0 | 0 | 0 |
| JG Myburgh | 15.0 | 1 | 66 | 1 | 1/30 | 1/50 | 66.00 | 4.40 | 90.0 | 0 | 0 |
| LA Dawson | 61.0 | 9 | 231 | 3 | 1/5 | 1/5 | 77.00 | 3.78 | 122.0 | 0 | 0 |
| MA Carberry | 8.3 | 3 | 18 | 0 | - | - | - | 2.11 | - | 0 | 0 |
| ND McKenzie | 2.0 | 0 | 23 | 0 | - | - | - | 11.50 | - | 0 | 0 |

Bowling

**Catches/Stumpings:**
20 Pothas (+0st), 18 Bates (+4st), 17 Dawson, 13 Adams, 12 McKenzie, 9 Vince, 6 Carberry, Cork, Ervine, 5 de Wet, 4 Tahir, Wood, 2 Briggs, Mascarenhas, Myburgh, 1 Ali, Tomlinson

HAMPSHIRE
ROYALS

## Batting

| | Mat | Inns | NO | Runs | HS | Ave | SR | 100 | 50 | 4s | 6s |
|---|---|---|---|---|---|---|---|---|---|---|---|
| ND McKenzie | 6 | 6 | 2 | 244 | 87* | 61.00 | 88.08 | 0 | 2 | 24 | 1 |
| BAC Howell | 11 | 8 | 2 | 340 | 122 | 56.66 | 96.31 | 1 | 2 | 25 | 9 |
| JM Vince | 12 | 12 | 0 | 473 | 131 | 39.41 | 99.16 | 1 | 2 | 52 | 4 |
| JHK Adams | 10 | 10 | 2 | 314 | 113 | 39.25 | 93.17 | 1 | 1 | 35 | 2 |
| LA Dawson | 12 | 10 | 2 | 282 | 70 | 35.25 | 104.44 | 0 | 1 | 23 | 7 |
| SM Ervine | 10 | 10 | 2 | 273 | 136 | 34.12 | 100.36 | 1 | 0 | 26 | 5 |
| JG Myburgh | 3 | 3 | 0 | 81 | 64 | 27.00 | 102.53 | 0 | 1 | 11 | 1 |
| H Riazuddin | 4 | 1 | 0 | 22 | 22 | 22.00 | 81.48 | 0 | 0 | 1 | 0 |
| N Pothas | 1 | 1 | 0 | 15 | 15 | 15.00 | 48.38 | 0 | 0 | 0 | 0 |
| AD Mascarenhas | 7 | 5 | 0 | 64 | 26 | 12.80 | 80.00 | 0 | 0 | 7 | 1 |
| CP Wood | 10 | 5 | 1 | 44 | 14* | 11.00 | 83.01 | 0 | 0 | 2 | 0 |
| MD Bates | 11 | 5 | 2 | 33 | 24* | 11.00 | 82.50 | 0 | 0 | 2 | 0 |
| DR Briggs | 8 | 5 | 1 | 30 | 16 | 7.50 | 100.00 | 0 | 0 | 4 | 0 |
| MA Carberry | 6 | 4 | 0 | 29 | 22 | 7.25 | 50.87 | 0 | 0 | 1 | 0 |
| DA Griffiths | 3 | 1 | 0 | 7 | 7 | 7.00 | 63.63 | 0 | 0 | 1 | 0 |
| DG Cork | 7 | 6 | 1 | 27 | 10 | 5.40 | 77.14 | 0 | 0 | 2 | 0 |
| TJ Ravenscroft | 1 | 1 | 0 | 5 | 5 | 5.00 | 50.00 | 0 | 0 | 0 | 0 |
| Imran Tahir | 5 | 1 | 0 | 3 | 3 | 3.00 | 100.00 | 0 | 0 | 0 | 0 |
| SP Jones | 5 | 3 | 3 | 1 | 1* | - | 25.00 | 0 | 0 | 0 | 0 |

## Bowling

| | Overs | Mdns | Runs | Wkts | BBI | Ave | Econ | SR | 4w | 5w |
|---|---|---|---|---|---|---|---|---|---|---|
| Imran Tahir | 27.0 | 0 | 131 | 5 | 2/45 | 26.20 | 4.85 | 32.4 | 0 | 0 |
| MA Carberry | 7.0 | 0 | 36 | 0 | - | - | 5.14 | - | 0 | 0 |
| AD Mascarenhas | 53.0 | 3 | 275 | 9 | 3/24 | 30.55 | 5.18 | 35.3 | 0 | 0 |
| DA Griffiths | 16.0 | 1 | 86 | 4 | 3/36 | 21.50 | 5.37 | 24.0 | 0 | 0 |
| DG Cork | 35.0 | 0 | 195 | 2 | 1/49 | 97.50 | 5.57 | 105.0 | 0 | 0 |
| SM Ervine | 49.0 | 0 | 277 | 6 | 2/23 | 46.16 | 5.65 | 49.0 | 0 | 0 |
| SP Jones | 36.1 | 3 | 205 | 8 | 4/52 | 25.62 | 5.66 | 27.1 | 1 | 0 |
| DR Briggs | 55.4 | 0 | 323 | 9 | 3/30 | 35.88 | 5.80 | 37.1 | 0 | 0 |
| CP Wood | 59.3 | 1 | 359 | 18 | 4/34 | 19.94 | 6.03 | 19.8 | 1 | 0 |
| LA Dawson | 24.0 | 0 | 149 | 1 | 1/32 | 149.00 | 6.20 | 144.0 | 0 | 0 |
| H Riazuddin | 14.0 | 0 | 92 | 5 | 3/37 | 18.40 | 6.57 | 16.8 | 0 | 0 |
| BAC Howell | 6.0 | 0 | 40 | 0 | - | - | 6.66 | - | 0 | 0 |
| JG Myburgh | 2.4 | 0 | 19 | 0 | - | - | 7.12 | - | 0 | 0 |

**Catches/Stumpings:**
6 Vince, 5 Bates (+2st), Dawson, 4 Carberry, Wood, 3 Briggs, Howell, 2 Adams, Ervine, McKenzie, Riazuddin, 1 Cork, Mascarenhas, Ravenscroft

HAMPSHIRE
ROYALS

Batting

| | Mat | Inns | NO | Runs | HS | Ave | SR | 100 | 50 | 4s | 6s |
|---|---|---|---|---|---|---|---|---|---|---|---|
| LA Dawson | 5 | 3 | 2 | 49 | 26 | 49.00 | 100.00 | 0 | 0 | 4 | 0 |
| ND McKenzie | 17 | 15 | 4 | 408 | 89* | 37.09 | 114.60 | 0 | 2 | 38 | 7 |
| JM Vince | 17 | 16 | 3 | 445 | 85* | 34.23 | 125.00 | 0 | 4 | 44 | 11 |
| SM Ervine | 13 | 11 | 4 | 219 | 45 | 31.28 | 115.87 | 0 | 0 | 18 | 4 |
| MJ Lumb | 9 | 9 | 1 | 197 | 53 | 24.62 | 150.38 | 0 | 1 | 25 | 8 |
| JHK Adams | 17 | 17 | 3 | 319 | 47 | 22.78 | 110.76 | 0 | 0 | 32 | 9 |
| Shahid Afridi | 10 | 9 | 0 | 180 | 80 | 20.00 | 145.16 | 0 | 1 | 15 | 8 |
| N Pothas | 11 | 5 | 3 | 34 | 15* | 17.00 | 82.92 | 0 | 0 | 1 | 0 |
| DG Cork | 17 | 7 | 4 | 44 | 21 | 14.66 | 122.22 | 0 | 0 | 3 | 2 |
| BAC Howell | 7 | 6 | 2 | 43 | 16 | 10.75 | 79.62 | 0 | 0 | 3 | 0 |
| AD Mascarenhas | 17 | 9 | 1 | 85 | 25 | 10.62 | 141.66 | 0 | 0 | 7 | 3 |
| MD Bates | 6 | 1 | 0 | 10 | 10 | 10.00 | 76.92 | 0 | 0 | 1 | 0 |
| DR Briggs | 16 | 4 | 2 | 8 | 4* | 4.00 | 100.00 | 0 | 0 | 0 | 0 |
| CP Wood | 7 | 1 | 0 | 3 | 3 | 3.00 | 100.00 | 0 | 0 | 0 | 0 |
| Imran Tahir | 16 | 2 | 2 | 18 | 17* | - | 138.46 | 0 | 0 | 2 | 0 |
| SP Jones | 2 | - | - | - | - | - | - | - | - | - | - |

Bowling

| | Overs | Mdns | Runs | Wkts | BBI | Ave | Econ | SR | 4w | 5w |
|---|---|---|---|---|---|---|---|---|---|---|
| Shahid Afridi | 34.3 | 0 | 190 | 17 | 5/20 | 11.17 | 5.50 | 12.1 | 0 | 1 |
| Imran Tahir | 48.0 | 1 | 287 | 17 | 3/13 | 16.88 | 5.97 | 16.9 | 0 | 0 |
| SM Ervine | 2.0 | 0 | 12 | 1 | 1/9 | 12.00 | 6.00 | 12.0 | 0 | 0 |
| AD Mascarenhas | 53.0 | 1 | 341 | 21 | 3/19 | 16.23 | 6.43 | 15.1 | 0 | 0 |
| SP Jones | 5.0 | 0 | 33 | 3 | 2/2 | 11.00 | 6.60 | 10.0 | 0 | 0 |
| DR Briggs | 50.1 | 0 | 343 | 23 | 5/19 | 14.91 | 6.83 | 13.0 | 2 | 1 |
| DG Cork | 46.3 | 0 | 343 | 17 | 2/23 | 20.17 | 7.37 | 16.4 | 0 | 0 |
| CP Wood | 17.0 | 0 | 135 | 6 | 2/17 | 22.50 | 7.94 | 17.0 | 0 | 0 |

**Catches/Stumpings:**
11 Vince, 7 Pothas (+3st), Tahir, 6 Ervine, 5 McKenzie, 4 Adams, 4 Bates (+3st), 3 Cork, 2 Afridi, Briggs, Dawson, Mascarenhas, 1 Lumb.

# KENT

**FORMED:** 1870
**HOME GROUND:** St Lawrence Ground, Canterbury
**ONE-DAY NAME:** Spitfires
**CAPTAIN:** Rob Key
**2011 RESULTS:** CC2: 8/9; CB40: 4/7 in Group A; FL t20: Quarter-finalists
**HONOURS:** Championship: (7) 1906, 1909, 1910, 1913, 1970, 1977(s), 1978; Gillette/NatWest/C&G/FP Trophy: (2) 1967, 1974; Pro40/National League/CB40: 2001; Sunday League: (4) 1972, 1973, 1976, 1995; Twenty20 Cup: 2007

## THE LOWDOWN

With former West Indies batsman Jimmy Adams freshly installed as director of cricket and their collection of youngsters a season older and wiser, Kent will be hoping for big things in 2012, despite losing the services of aggressive opening batsman Joe Denly to Middlesex, injury-plagued seamer Robbie Joseph to Leicestershire and middle-order run-machine Martin van Jaarsveld to retirement. They've done their best to add experience to their squad during the winter, bringing in seasoned campaigners in batsman Michael Powell, seamer Charlie Shreck and allrounder Ben Harmison, while Middlesex opener Scott Newman will spend the start of the season with them on loan. If their 1st XI is fit and firing they look a match for anyone – especially in the shorter forms of the game – but there will be a few nervous supporters should any of their key bowlers – England spinner James Tredwell foremost among them – break down.

### DIRECTOR OF CRICKET: JIMMY ADAMS

A left-handed middle-order batsman who racked up more than 3,000 runs across his 54-Test career, Adams was a lynchpin of the West Indies' batting line-up for nine years. Since retiring in 2004, Adams has coached the West Indies U19 team and served as technical director of Jamaica Cricket. Renowned as an intelligent and affable figure, as well as a devoted student of the game, he succeeds former coach Paul Farbrace, who stood down at the end of 2011 season. Reportedly hugely excited at the level of young talent the club having coming through their ranks, Adams will be doing his utmost to help the likes of Daniel Bell-Drummond, Adam Ball and Sam Northeast kick on.

**Batting**

| | Mat | Inns | NO | Runs | HS | Ave | SR | 100 | 50 | 4s | 6s |
|---|---|---|---|---|---|---|---|---|---|---|---|
| Azhar Mahmood | 7 | 13 | 3 | 521 | 97 | 52.10 | 63.22 | 0 | 5 | 63 | 4 |
| RWT Key | 12 | 24 | 2 | 895 | 162 | 40.68 | 53.43 | 2 | 5 | 104 | 3 |
| JL Denly | 14 | 28 | 1 | 1024 | 199 | 37.92 | 61.87 | 2 | 5 | 148 | 3 |
| M van Jaarsveld | 14 | 28 | 3 | 755 | 95 | 30.20 | 51.46 | 0 | 6 | 97 | 4 |
| SA Northeast | 17 | 33 | 0 | 880 | 176 | 26.66 | 55.45 | 2 | 4 | 113 | 7 |
| DI Stevens | 16 | 31 | 0 | 819 | 143 | 26.41 | 70.66 | 1 | 4 | 122 | 6 |
| SA Shaw | 4 | 5 | 3 | 50 | 22* | 25.00 | 71.42 | 0 | 0 | 11 | 0 |
| GO Jones | 16 | 31 | 1 | 699 | 79 | 23.30 | 49.57 | 0 | 4 | 91 | 2 |
| DJ Bell-Drummond | 4 | 7 | 0 | 147 | 80 | 21.00 | 60.99 | 0 | 1 | 21 | 2 |
| AJ Blake | 9 | 17 | 0 | 345 | 96 | 20.29 | 60.52 | 0 | 3 | 54 | 2 |
| MT Coles | 10 | 16 | 4 | 242 | 50* | 20.16 | 66.85 | 0 | 1 | 36 | 3 |
| SJ Cook | 7 | 14 | 2 | 237 | 51 | 19.75 | 52.66 | 0 | 1 | 27 | 3 |
| SW Billings | 1 | 1 | 0 | 19 | 19 | 19.00 | 51.35 | 0 | 0 | 3 | 0 |
| JC Tredwell | 12 | 22 | 2 | 362 | 47 | 18.10 | 47.82 | 0 | 0 | 46 | 1 |
| JE Goodman | 4 | 7 | 0 | 121 | 56 | 17.28 | 41.86 | 0 | 1 | 16 | 0 |
| AJ Ball | 9 | 15 | 1 | 184 | 46 | 13.14 | 35.24 | 0 | 0 | 23 | 2 |
| Wahab Riaz | 5 | 9 | 1 | 85 | 34 | 10.62 | 56.66 | 0 | 0 | 11 | 1 |
| CD Piesley | 2 | 3 | 0 | 26 | 22 | 8.66 | 41.93 | 0 | 0 | 2 | 0 |
| RH Joseph | 7 | 12 | 6 | 42 | 19* | 7.00 | 21.98 | 0 | 0 | 6 | 0 |
| DJ Balcombe | 5 | 8 | 2 | 40 | 12 | 6.66 | 45.97 | 0 | 0 | 7 | 0 |
| NC Saker | 4 | 5 | 0 | 29 | 18 | 5.80 | 23.01 | 0 | 0 | 4 | 0 |
| AEN Riley | 6 | 8 | 4 | 17 | 5 | 4.25 | 37.77 | 0 | 0 | 2 | 0 |
| CE Shreck | 1 | 2 | 1 | 4 | 4 | 4.00 | 23.52 | 0 | 0 | 1 | 0 |
| JD Nel | 1 | 2 | 1 | 2 | 2* | 2.00 | 22.22 | 0 | 0 | 0 | 0 |

**Bowling**

| | Overs | Mdns | Runs | Wkts | BBI | BBM | Ave | Econ | SR | 5w | 10w |
|---|---|---|---|---|---|---|---|---|---|---|---|
| DJ Balcombe | 174.5 | 40 | 588 | 33 | 6/51 | 10/102 | 17.81 | 3.36 | 31.7 | 4 | 1 |
| DI Stevens | 288.2 | 74 | 862 | 41 | 7/21 | 11/70 | 21.02 | 2.98 | 42.1 | 2 | 1 |
| Azhar Mahmood | 210.1 | 63 | 546 | 23 | 6/36 | 7/108 | 23.73 | 2.59 | 54.8 | 1 | 0 |
| RH Joseph | 145.1 | 30 | 552 | 20 | 4/25 | 6/52 | 27.60 | 3.80 | 43.5 | 0 | 0 |
| JC Tredwell | 394.5 | 78 | 1175 | 42 | 5/35 | 6/141 | 27.97 | 2.97 | 56.4 | 2 | 0 |
| M van Jaarsveld | 14.0 | 0 | 60 | 2 | 2/33 | 2/41 | 30.00 | 4.28 | 42.0 | 0 | 0 |
| NC Saker | 111.0 | 18 | 392 | 13 | 5/112 | 5/112 | 30.15 | 3.53 | 51.2 | 1 | 0 |
| MT Coles | 284.3 | 51 | 1020 | 32 | 5/29 | 7/149 | 31.87 | 3.58 | 53.3 | 2 | 0 |
| Wahab Riaz | 121.4 | 24 | 436 | 13 | 4/94 | 4/58 | 33.53 | 3.58 | 56.1 | 0 | 0 |
| SA Shaw | 81.1 | 5 | 400 | 11 | 5/118 | 6/175 | 36.36 | 4.92 | 44.2 | 1 | 0 |
| AJ Ball | 143.0 | 25 | 560 | 15 | 3/36 | 3/45 | 37.33 | 3.91 | 57.2 | 0 | 0 |
| AEN Riley | 131.2 | 14 | 547 | 14 | 5/76 | 5/76 | 39.07 | 4.16 | 56.2 | 1 | 0 |
| SJ Cook | 144.1 | 28 | 448 | 11 | 3/40 | 5/83 | 40.72 | 3.10 | 78.6 | 0 | 0 |
| JL Denly | 92.0 | 10 | 305 | 7 | 3/43 | 6/114 | 43.57 | 3.31 | 78.8 | 0 | 0 |
| JD Nel | 15.0 | 1 | 60 | 1 | 1/60 | 1/60 | 60.00 | 4.00 | 90.0 | 0 | 0 |
| AJ Blake | 6.0 | 0 | 27 | 0 | - | - | - | 4.50 | - | 0 | 0 |
| JE Goodman | 7.5 | 0 | 21 | 0 | - | - | - | 2.68 | - | 0 | 0 |
| RWT Key | 0.4 | 0 | 8 | 0 | - | - | - | 12.00 | - | 0 | 0 |
| CE Shreck | 25.0 | 8 | 69 | 0 | - | - | - | 2.76 | - | 0 | 0 |

**Catches/Stumpings:**
57 Jones (+4st), 24 van Jaarsveld, 14 Tredwell, 13 Stevens, 11 Key, 9 Mahmood, Northeast, 6 Blake, 5 Ball, Goodman, 4 Denly, 3 Bell-Drummond, Coles, Shaw, 2 Billings (+0st), Riley, Saker, 1 Balcombe, Cook, Joseph, Riaz

# LIST A AVERAGES 2011

## Batting

| | Mat | Inns | NO | Runs | HS | Ave | SR | 100 | 50 | 4s | 6s |
|---|---|---|---|---|---|---|---|---|---|---|---|
| M van Jaarsveld | 12 | 12 | 0 | 538 | 124 | 44.83 | 105.07 | 1 | 4 | 53 | 8 |
| DI Stevens | 12 | 12 | 1 | 386 | 70 | 35.09 | 103.48 | 0 | 3 | 34 | 10 |
| AJ Ball | 9 | 8 | 6 | 62 | 19 | 31.00 | 93.93 | 0 | 0 | 6 | 0 |
| SA Northeast | 12 | 12 | 2 | 308 | 63* | 30.80 | 74.75 | 0 | 3 | 18 | 1 |
| Azhar Mahmood | 10 | 9 | 0 | 246 | 68 | 27.33 | 91.44 | 0 | 2 | 26 | 2 |
| RWT Key | 5 | 5 | 0 | 126 | 59 | 25.20 | 69.23 | 0 | 1 | 12 | 1 |
| DJ Bell-Drummond | 5 | 5 | 0 | 111 | 42 | 22.20 | 98.23 | 0 | 0 | 15 | 2 |
| Wahab Riaz | 3 | 2 | 1 | 22 | 12* | 22.00 | 110.00 | 0 | 0 | 2 | 0 |
| JL Denly | 6 | 6 | 0 | 123 | 46 | 20.50 | 75.46 | 0 | 0 | 9 | 3 |
| SW Billings | 3 | 3 | 0 | 54 | 26 | 18.00 | 100.00 | 0 | 0 | 8 | 1 |
| GO Jones | 10 | 9 | 0 | 159 | 39 | 17.66 | 82.38 | 0 | 0 | 11 | 0 |
| JC Tredwell | 12 | 10 | 2 | 121 | 37 | 15.12 | 98.37 | 0 | 0 | 11 | 3 |
| MT Coles | 5 | 5 | 0 | 70 | 47 | 14.00 | 109.37 | 0 | 0 | 7 | 1 |
| AJ Blake | 7 | 6 | 0 | 72 | 19 | 12.00 | 80.00 | 0 | 0 | 8 | 0 |
| SA Shaw | 6 | 5 | 3 | 8 | 4* | 4.00 | 88.88 | 0 | 0 | 1 | 0 |
| CD Piesley | 1 | 1 | 0 | 4 | 4 | 4.00 | 40.00 | 0 | 0 | 0 | 0 |
| DJ Balcombe | 3 | 2 | 0 | 6 | 6 | 3.00 | 35.29 | 0 | 0 | 0 | 0 |
| SJ Cook | 4 | 2 | 2 | 9 | 7* | - | 90.00 | 0 | 0 | 1 | 0 |
| AEN Riley | 6 | 1 | 1 | 3 | 3* | - | 42.85 | 0 | 0 | 0 | 0 |
| CK Langeveldt | 1 | 1 | 1 | 0 | 0* | - | 0.00 | 0 | 0 | 0 | 0 |

## Bowling

| | Overs | Mdns | Runs | Wkts | BBI | Ave | Econ | SR | 4w | 5w |
|---|---|---|---|---|---|---|---|---|---|---|
| CK Langeveldt | 8.0 | 0 | 33 | 0 | - | - | 4.12 | - | 0 | 0 |
| JC Tredwell | 88.0 | 1 | 383 | 11 | 2/27 | 34.81 | 4.35 | 48.0 | 0 | 0 |
| DJ Balcombe | 16.3 | 1 | 86 | 6 | 4/38 | 14.33 | 5.21 | 16.5 | 1 | 0 |
| Wahab Riaz | 22.3 | 0 | 120 | 9 | 5/46 | 13.33 | 5.33 | 15.0 | 0 | 1 |
| AJ Ball | 52.3 | 2 | 283 | 12 | 2/31 | 23.58 | 5.39 | 26.2 | 0 | 0 |
| AEN Riley | 36.0 | 0 | 197 | 5 | 2/32 | 39.40 | 5.47 | 43.2 | 0 | 0 |
| DI Stevens | 61.0 | 2 | 336 | 8 | 2/27 | 42.00 | 5.50 | 45.7 | 0 | 0 |
| JL Denly | 15.0 | 3 | 87 | 3 | 3/42 | 29.00 | 5.80 | 30.0 | 0 | 0 |
| M van Jaarsveld | 13.0 | 0 | 77 | 0 | - | - | 5.92 | - | 0 | 0 |
| Azhar Mahmood | 73.3 | 2 | 437 | 18 | 4/52 | 24.27 | 5.94 | 24.5 | 2 | 0 |
| SJ Cook | 25.0 | 1 | 155 | 5 | 3/40 | 31.00 | 6.20 | 30.0 | 0 | 0 |
| AJ Blake | 2.0 | 1 | 13 | 2 | 2/13 | 6.50 | 6.50 | 6.0 | 0 | 0 |
| SA Shaw | 27.0 | 1 | 184 | 5 | 3/26 | 36.80 | 6.81 | 32.4 | 0 | 0 |
| MT Coles | 29.0 | 0 | 218 | 5 | 2/37 | 43.60 | 7.51 | 34.8 | 0 | 0 |

**Catches/Stumpings:**
9 Jones (inc 2 outfield +4st), 7 van Jaarsveld, 6 Tredwell, 5 Stevens, 3 Billings (+2st), Blake, Coles, Mahmood, 1 Balcombe, Cook, Denly, Key, Northeast, Riaz

| | Mat | Inns | NO | Runs | HS | Ave | SR | 100 | 50 | 4s | 6s |
|---|---|---|---|---|---|---|---|---|---|---|---|
| JC Tredwell | 15 | 5 | 4 | 61 | 34* | 61.00 | 112.96 | 0 | 0 | 3 | 2 |
| M van Jaarsveld | 9 | 8 | 4 | 215 | 63* | 53.75 | 148.27 | 0 | 2 | 26 | 3 |
| DI Stevens | 16 | 16 | 8 | 375 | 68 | 46.87 | 143.12 | 0 | 2 | 25 | 22 |
| Azhar Mahmood | 15 | 14 | 2 | 485 | 106* | 40.41 | 143.91 | 1 | 3 | 50 | 12 |
| JL Denly | 16 | 16 | 1 | 420 | 100 | 28.00 | 113.82 | 1 | 3 | 38 | 9 |
| Wahab Riaz | 13 | 5 | 2 | 78 | 32* | 26.00 | 173.33 | 0 | 0 | 6 | 5 |
| SA Northeast | 15 | 9 | 4 | 115 | 39* | 23.00 | 121.05 | 0 | 0 | 11 | 1 |
| CK Langeveldt | 15 | 2 | 1 | 20 | 13* | 20.00 | 105.26 | 0 | 0 | 3 | 0 |
| RWT Key | 15 | 15 | 0 | 269 | 75 | 17.93 | 114.46 | 0 | 1 | 30 | 2 |
| GO Jones | 16 | 7 | 2 | 79 | 30* | 15.80 | 92.94 | 0 | 0 | 6 | 2 |
| DJ Bell-Drummond | 1 | 1 | 0 | 11 | 11 | 11.00 | 183.33 | 0 | 0 | 1 | 1 |
| AJ Ball | 13 | 3 | 0 | 22 | 15 | 7.33 | 95.65 | 0 | 0 | 1 | 1 |
| MT Coles | 3 | 1 | 0 | 5 | 5 | 5.00 | 166.66 | 0 | 0 | 1 | 0 |
| AJ Blake | 6 | 3 | 0 | 5 | 5 | 1.66 | 45.45 | 0 | 0 | 0 | 0 |
| SW Billings | 4 | 2 | 0 | 3 | 2 | 1.50 | 60.00 | 0 | 0 | 0 | 0 |
| SJ Cook | 2 | 1 | 1 | 4 | 4* | - | 80.00 | 0 | 0 | 0 | 0 |

Batting

| | Overs | Mdns | Runs | Wkts | BBI | Ave | Econ | SR | 4w | 5w |
|---|---|---|---|---|---|---|---|---|---|---|
| M van Jaarsveld | 4.0 | 0 | 20 | 3 | 3/20 | 6.66 | 5.00 | 8.0 | 0 | 0 |
| JC Tredwell | 53.0 | 0 | 352 | 10 | 2/14 | 35.20 | 6.64 | 31.8 | 0 | 0 |
| DI Stevens | 19.0 | 0 | 131 | 8 | 4/21 | 16.37 | 6.89 | 14.2 | 1 | 0 |
| AJ Ball | 38.0 | 0 | 280 | 10 | 2/28 | 28.00 | 7.36 | 22.8 | 0 | 0 |
| MT Coles | 8.0 | 0 | 60 | 0 | - | - | 7.50 | - | 0 | 0 |
| DJ Balcombe | 3.0 | 0 | 23 | 1 | 1/23 | 23.00 | 7.66 | 18.0 | 0 | 0 |
| Azhar Mahmood | 52.2 | 0 | 414 | 14 | 3/14 | 29.57 | 7.91 | 22.4 | 0 | 0 |
| Wahab Riaz | 46.2 | 1 | 397 | 20 | 5/17 | 19.85 | 8.56 | 13.9 | 0 | 1 |
| JL Denly | 5.0 | 0 | 44 | 0 | - | - | 8.80 | - | 0 | 0 |
| CK Langeveldt | 50.0 | 0 | 463 | 15 | 3/37 | 30.86 | 9.26 | 20.0 | 0 | 0 |
| AEN Riley | 3.0 | 0 | 34 | 1 | 1/34 | 34.00 | 11.33 | 18.0 | 0 | 0 |
| SJ Cook | 3.0 | 0 | 55 | 0 | - | - | 18.33 | - | 0 | 0 |

Bowling

**Catches/Stumpings:**
9 Ball, 8 Jones (+1st), 6 Denly, 5 Northeast, Stevens, 4 Blake, Tredwell, 3 Key, Langeveldt, 2 Mahmood, 1 Billings, van Jaarsveld

TEAM PROFILE

**Lancashire County Cricket Club**

™

**FORMED:** 1864
**HOME GROUND:** Old Trafford
**ONE-DAY NAME:** Lightning
**CAPTAIN:** Glen Chapple
**2011 RESULTS:** CC1: Champions; CB40: 4/7 in Group C; FL t20: Semi-finalists
**HONOURS:** Championship: (9) 1897, 1904, 1926, 1927, 1928, 1930, 1950(s) (Div 2: 2005), 2011; Gillette/NatWest/C&G/FP Trophy: (7) 1970, 1971, 1972, 1985, 1990, 1996, 1998; Benson and Hedges Cup: (4) 1984, 1990, 1995, 1996; Pro40/National League/CB40: 1999; Sunday League: (4) 1969, 1970, 1989, 1998

### THE LOWDOWN

For the first time in recent memory, Lancashire entered last season with almost no one in the media talking up their chances of taking the title. A small squad, no big name overseas player and a worrying bank balance were all cited as reasons why they'd be amongst the also-rans, but Glen Chapple's side – a team of hungry and largely homegrown cricketers – confounded everyone by storming to their first outright Championship victory in 77 years. And having added the vastly experienced South African international batsman Ashwell Prince to their ranks in 2012 – not to mention the fact that the likes of talented left-arm spinners Simon Kerrigan and Steve Parry are a year further on in their development – there's every chance that they could defend their four-day title and improve on their impressive showing in the FL t20, which saw them narrowly miss out to eventual winners Leicestershire following a semi-final one-over eliminator defeat.

### HEAD COACH: PETER MOORES

Hugely respected throughout the game, Moores made his name as a coach by leading Sussex to their first-ever Championship title in 2003 before succeeding Rod Marsh as director of the ECB academy in 2005. Appointed as England coach following the resignation of Duncan Fletcher in 2007, he struggled to see eye-to-eye with then skipper Kevin Pietersen, a situation that ultimately forced the ECB to dismiss both men back in 2009. Lancashire promptly came calling, and it proved an ideal match as Moores helped turn a county that had fallen at the final hurdle on countless occasions into four-day champions.

| | Mat | Inns | NO | Runs | HS | Ave | SR | 100 | 50 | 4s | 6s |
|---|---|---|---|---|---|---|---|---|---|---|---|
| LA Procter | 7 | 10 | 1 | 366 | 89 | 40.66 | 42.70 | 0 | 2 | 43 | 5 |
| SC Moore | 16 | 28 | 3 | 1013 | 169* | 40.52 | 56.43 | 2 | 5 | 135 | 5 |
| MF Maharoof | 5 | 7 | 1 | 241 | 102 | 40.16 | 65.31 | 1 | 0 | 24 | 3 |
| PJ Horton | 17 | 30 | 1 | 1099 | 99 | 37.89 | 50.04 | 0 | 9 | 145 | 2 |
| OJ Newby | 4 | 5 | 3 | 75 | 29* | 37.50 | 51.72 | 0 | 0 | 12 | 0 |
| KR Brown | 17 | 30 | 2 | 997 | 114 | 35.60 | 50.17 | 1 | 7 | 146 | 0 |
| SJ Croft | 17 | 29 | 1 | 842 | 122 | 30.07 | 53.32 | 2 | 5 | 98 | 9 |
| MJ Chilton | 14 | 23 | 1 | 647 | 117 | 29.40 | 43.74 | 1 | 3 | 84 | 0 |
| JM Anderson | 2 | 3 | 2 | 28 | 18* | 28.00 | 50.90 | 0 | 0 | 2 | 0 |
| TC Smith | 12 | 19 | 1 | 459 | 89 | 25.50 | 43.50 | 0 | 4 | 69 | 0 |
| GD Cross | 17 | 27 | 0 | 611 | 125 | 22.62 | 58.35 | 1 | 2 | 77 | 6 |
| KW Hogg | 12 | 19 | 1 | 370 | 52 | 20.55 | 70.20 | 0 | 2 | 51 | 3 |
| SC Kerrigan | 5 | 7 | 3 | 80 | 40 | 20.00 | 44.94 | 0 | 0 | 11 | 1 |
| G Chapple | 13 | 22 | 1 | 380 | 97 | 18.09 | 70.76 | 0 | 1 | 44 | 7 |
| SI Mahmood | 11 | 17 | 0 | 287 | 50 | 16.88 | 77.98 | 0 | 1 | 39 | 3 |
| G Keedy | 16 | 24 | 15 | 111 | 20 | 12.33 | 34.47 | 0 | 0 | 12 | 0 |
| AP Agathangelou | 1 | 2 | 0 | 18 | 18 | 9.00 | 31.03 | 0 | 0 | 0 | 0 |
| Junaid Khan | 1 | 2 | 0 | 16 | 16 | 8.00 | 106.66 | 0 | 0 | 1 | 2 |

Batting

| | Overs | Mdns | Runs | Wkts | BBI | BBM | Ave | Econ | SR | 5w | 10w |
|---|---|---|---|---|---|---|---|---|---|---|---|
| SC Kerrigan | 213.0 | 49 | 494 | 26 | 9/51 | 12/192 | 19.00 | 2.31 | 49.1 | 2 | 1 |
| KW Hogg | 311.0 | 68 | 953 | 50 | 7/28 | 11/59 | 19.06 | 3.06 | 37.3 | 3 | 1 |
| G Chapple | 434.3 | 104 | 1126 | 57 | 6/70 | 9/117 | 19.75 | 2.59 | 45.7 | 3 | 0 |
| G Keedy | 562.4 | 110 | 1442 | 61 | 6/133 | 10/177 | 23.63 | 2.56 | 55.3 | 3 | 1 |
| OJ Newby | 78.0 | 17 | 323 | 12 | 4/63 | 4/63 | 26.91 | 4.14 | 39.0 | 0 | 0 |
| SI Mahmood | 270.4 | 36 | 1093 | 39 | 5/74 | 10/186 | 28.02 | 4.03 | 41.6 | 2 | 1 |
| TC Smith | 226.3 | 44 | 747 | 25 | 4/32 | 4/50 | 29.88 | 3.29 | 54.3 | 0 | 0 |
| JM Anderson | 71.3 | 20 | 165 | 5 | 3/57 | 3/88 | 33.00 | 2.30 | 85.8 | 0 | 0 |
| LA Procter | 83.0 | 8 | 332 | 9 | 3/33 | 4/50 | 36.88 | 4.00 | 55.3 | 0 | 0 |
| SJ Croft | 83.0 | 17 | 242 | 6 | 2/10 | 2/10 | 40.33 | 2.91 | 83.0 | 0 | 0 |
| MF Maharoof | 112.5 | 18 | 397 | 9 | 4/35 | 5/74 | 44.11 | 3.51 | 75.2 | 0 | 0 |
| Junaid Khan | 27.0 | 4 | 90 | 1 | 1/44 | 1/90 | 90.00 | 3.33 | 162.0 | 0 | 0 |
| AP Agathangelou | 4.0 | 0 | 12 | 0 | - | - | - | 3.00 | - | 0 | 0 |

Bowling

**Catches/Stumpings:**
48 Cross (+10st), 32 Horton, 22 Smith, 21 Croft, 8 Brown, Chilton, Moore, 5 Keedy, 4 Agathangelou, Maharoof, 3 Anderson, Mahmood, 2 Chapple, Hogg, Procter, 1 Kerrigan

## Batting

| | Mat | Inns | NO | Runs | HS | Ave | SR | 100 | 50 | 4s | 6s |
|---|---|---|---|---|---|---|---|---|---|---|---|
| PJ Horton | 12 | 11 | 4 | 403 | 97* | 57.57 | 92.64 | 0 | 3 | 32 | 3 |
| SJ Croft | 12 | 12 | 1 | 494 | 107 | 44.90 | 97.62 | 1 | 3 | 36 | 11 |
| TC Smith | 7 | 7 | 0 | 282 | 117 | 40.28 | 104.05 | 1 | 1 | 38 | 3 |
| OJ Newby | 6 | 2 | 1 | 37 | 35* | 37.00 | 194.73 | 0 | 0 | 4 | 2 |
| KR Brown | 11 | 11 | 2 | 329 | 101* | 36.55 | 90.63 | 1 | 0 | 36 | 3 |
| GD Cross | 11 | 9 | 2 | 235 | 66* | 33.57 | 106.81 | 0 | 2 | 16 | 5 |
| SC Moore | 12 | 11 | 0 | 300 | 69 | 27.27 | 101.69 | 0 | 3 | 37 | 5 |
| MJ Chilton | 1 | 1 | 0 | 25 | 25 | 25.00 | 104.16 | 0 | 0 | 3 | 0 |
| LA Procter | 9 | 8 | 4 | 77 | 24 | 19.25 | 80.20 | 0 | 0 | 3 | 0 |
| SD Parry | 12 | 4 | 3 | 15 | 9* | 15.00 | 83.33 | 0 | 0 | 1 | 0 |
| SI Mahmood | 5 | 3 | 0 | 42 | 26 | 14.00 | 110.52 | 0 | 0 | 2 | 2 |
| MF Maharoof | 5 | 4 | 1 | 41 | 38* | 13.66 | 110.81 | 0 | 0 | 4 | 1 |
| J Clark | 3 | 1 | 0 | 8 | 8 | 8.00 | 61.53 | 0 | 0 | 0 | 0 |
| SC Kerrigan | 10 | 2 | 0 | 8 | 5 | 4.00 | 88.88 | 0 | 0 | 1 | 0 |
| G Chapple | 2 | 1 | 0 | 4 | 4 | 4.00 | 100.00 | 0 | 0 | 0 | 0 |
| G Keedy | 4 | 1 | 0 | 2 | 2 | 2.00 | 50.00 | 0 | 0 | 0 | 0 |
| KW Hogg | 3 | 2 | 2 | 15 | 10* | - | 100.00 | 0 | 0 | 2 | 0 |
| AL Davies | 1 | 1 | 1 | 6 | 6* | - | 85.71 | 0 | 0 | 0 | 0 |

## Bowling

| | Overs | Mdns | Runs | Wkts | BBI | Ave | Econ | SR | 4w | 5w |
|---|---|---|---|---|---|---|---|---|---|---|
| G Chapple | 13.0 | 0 | 54 | 3 | 3/25 | 18.00 | 4.15 | 26.0 | 0 | 0 |
| MF Maharoof | 36.0 | 0 | 184 | 4 | 3/33 | 46.00 | 5.11 | 54.0 | 0 | 0 |
| SC Kerrigan | 62.0 | 2 | 317 | 6 | 2/21 | 52.83 | 5.11 | 62.0 | 0 | 0 |
| SD Parry | 75.5 | 0 | 420 | 13 | 3/40 | 32.30 | 5.53 | 35.0 | 0 | 0 |
| G Keedy | 26.0 | 0 | 151 | 4 | 2/45 | 37.75 | 5.80 | 39.0 | 0 | 0 |
| JM Anderson | 15.0 | 2 | 89 | 2 | 1/42 | 44.50 | 5.93 | 45.0 | 0 | 0 |
| SJ Croft | 18.1 | 0 | 112 | 1 | 1/19 | 112.00 | 6.16 | 109.0 | 0 | 0 |
| SI Mahmood | 37.0 | 2 | 233 | 7 | 4/24 | 33.28 | 6.29 | 31.7 | 1 | 0 |
| Junaid Khan | 23.3 | 0 | 148 | 5 | 4/29 | 29.60 | 6.29 | 28.2 | 1 | 0 |
| TC Smith | 34.0 | 0 | 239 | 7 | 4/48 | 34.14 | 7.02 | 29.1 | 1 | 0 |
| LA Procter | 20.0 | 0 | 143 | 2 | 1/19 | 71.50 | 7.15 | 60.0 | 0 | 0 |
| KW Hogg | 19.0 | 1 | 151 | 6 | 3/63 | 25.16 | 7.94 | 19.0 | 0 | 0 |
| OJ Newby | 25.4 | 0 | 228 | 5 | 2/43 | 45.60 | 8.88 | 30.8 | 0 | 0 |

**Catches/Stumpings:**
8 Cross (+4st), 7 Croft, 5 Parry, 3 Kerrigan, Horton, 2 Keedy, Procter, Smith, 1 Brown, Mahmood, Moore

| | Mat | Inns | NO | Runs | HS | Ave | SR | 100 | 50 | 4s | 6s |
|---|---|---|---|---|---|---|---|---|---|---|---|
| SC Moore | 17 | 17 | 2 | 522 | 76 | 34.80 | 133.16 | 0 | 4 | 53 | 13 |
| TC Smith | 16 | 16 | 3 | 413 | 75 | 31.76 | 132.37 | 0 | 2 | 35 | 12 |
| KR Brown | 11 | 9 | 1 | 240 | 51 | 30.00 | 129.03 | 0 | 2 | 18 | 8 |
| SJ Croft | 17 | 15 | 2 | 380 | 55 | 29.23 | 133.33 | 0 | 4 | 32 | 12 |
| J Clark | 9 | 8 | 2 | 127 | 38 | 21.16 | 138.04 | 0 | 0 | 9 | 5 |
| LA Procter | 15 | 10 | 5 | 85 | 25* | 17.00 | 91.39 | 0 | 0 | 3 | 2 |
| PJ Horton | 8 | 8 | 1 | 117 | 49* | 16.71 | 102.63 | 0 | 0 | 8 | 0 |
| KW Hogg | 6 | 2 | 1 | 15 | 14* | 15.00 | 107.14 | 0 | 0 | 1 | 0 |
| GD Cross | 17 | 14 | 1 | 156 | 30 | 12.00 | 113.86 | 0 | 0 | 9 | 4 |
| MF Maharoof | 10 | 7 | 2 | 59 | 27 | 11.80 | 85.50 | 0 | 0 | 2 | 1 |
| SD Parry | 17 | 7 | 3 | 35 | 11 | 8.75 | 109.37 | 0 | 0 | 3 | 0 |
| SI Mahmood | 11 | 8 | 1 | 42 | 20 | 6.00 | 144.82 | 0 | 0 | 2 | 3 |
| G Keedy | 15 | 3 | 2 | 6 | 3 | 6.00 | 50.00 | 0 | 0 | 0 | 0 |
| Junaid Khan | 8 | 3 | 1 | 11 | 8 | 5.50 | 64.70 | 0 | 0 | 0 | 0 |
| JM Anderson | 1 | 1 | 0 | 1 | 1 | 1.00 | 50.00 | 0 | 0 | 0 | 0 |
| G Chapple | 3 | 2 | 2 | 7 | 5* | - | 233.33 | 0 | 0 | 1 | 0 |
| SC Kerrigan | 6 | 1 | 1 | 0 | 0* | - | - | 0 | 0 | 0 | 0 |

Batting

| | Overs | Mdns | Runs | Wkts | BBI | Ave | Econ | SR | 4w | 5w |
|---|---|---|---|---|---|---|---|---|---|---|
| G Keedy | 58.0 | 0 | 342 | 20 | 3/14 | 17.10 | 5.89 | 17.4 | 0 | 0 |
| MF Maharoof | 38.0 | 0 | 228 | 10 | 2/13 | 22.80 | 6.00 | 22.8 | 0 | 0 |
| Junaid Khan | 31.0 | 0 | 186 | 12 | 3/12 | 15.50 | 6.00 | 15.5 | 0 | 0 |
| SD Parry | 67.0 | 1 | 424 | 17 | 4/23 | 24.94 | 6.32 | 23.6 | 1 | 0 |
| SI Mahmood | 41.2 | 0 | 299 | 12 | 3/13 | 24.91 | 7.23 | 20.6 | 0 | 0 |
| G Chapple | 11.0 | 0 | 80 | 3 | 1/17 | 26.66 | 7.27 | 22.0 | 0 | 0 |
| SC Kerrigan | 24.0 | 0 | 175 | 4 | 2/32 | 43.75 | 7.29 | 36.0 | 0 | 0 |
| LA Procter | 11.0 | 0 | 94 | 4 | 3/22 | 23.50 | 8.54 | 16.5 | 0 | 0 |
| KW Hogg | 15.5 | 0 | 159 | 4 | 2/22 | 39.75 | 10.04 | 23.7 | 0 | 0 |
| TC Smith | 21.4 | 0 | 226 | 6 | 2/34 | 37.66 | 10.43 | 21.6 | 0 | 0 |
| SJ Croft | 8.0 | 0 | 87 | 1 | 1/23 | 87.00 | 10.87 | 48.0 | 0 | 0 |
| JM Anderson | 4.0 | 0 | 54 | 2 | 2/54 | 27.00 | 13.50 | 12.0 | 0 | 0 |

Bowling

**Catches/Stumpings:**
10 Croft, Cross (+8st), 5 Proctor, 4 Clark, Maharoof, Parry, Smith, 3 Brown, Horton, Keedy, Mahmood, Moore, 2 Hogg, 1 Khan

# LEICESTERSHIRE

**LEICESTERSHIRE**
COUNTY CRICKET CLUB

FORMED: 1879
HOME GROUND: County Ground, Grace Road
ONE-DAY NAME: Foxes
CAPTAIN: Matthew Hoggard
2011 RESULTS: CC2: 9/9; CB40: 6/7 in Group B; FL t20: Champions
HONOURS: Championship: (3) 1975, 1996, 1998; Benson and Hedges Cup: (3) 1972, 1975, 1985; Sunday League: (2) 1974, 1977; Twenty20 Cup: (3) 2004, 2006, 2011

## THE LOWDOWN

In 2011 a disappointing County Championship season – in which Leicestershire managed a solitary win – and a poor CB40 campaign were eclipsed by a stunning triumph in the FL t20. Andrew McDonald starred at the top of the order throughout the campaign, with veteran Paul Nixon inspiring his side to victory to seal a fairytale ending to his 22-year career, and their exits – as well as the loss of James Taylor and Harry Gurney to Nottinghamshire – are a significant blow to the Foxes. But with a host of talented youngsters such as England Lions paceman Nathan Buck and stylish strokemaker Josh Cobb at their disposal, led by an inspirational leader in the form of Matthew Hoggard, there is room for cautious optimism. Overseas signings Ramnaresh Sarwan and Abdul Razzaq – who will be available for the FL t20 – will bring some much-needed experience to the squad and the bowling department looks nicely balanced.

### HEAD COACH: PHIL WHITTICASE

After leading Leicestershire to the T20 title in his first year in charge, Whitticase looks to be an inspired appointment by the club. As a player the wicketkeeper spent all of his 11-year career at Grace Road, scoring 3,113 first-class runs. He took the reins in November 2010 after Tim Boon left the Foxes to take up a role with England's Development Programme.

| | Mat | Inns | NO | Runs | HS | Ave | SR | 100 | 50 | 4s | 6s |
|---|---|---|---|---|---|---|---|---|---|---|---|
| JWA Taylor | 15 | 28 | 3 | 1335 | 237 | 53.40 | 52.53 | 3 | 7 | 130 | 12 |
| EJ Eckersley | 4 | 8 | 0 | 321 | 106 | 40.12 | 46.25 | 1 | 2 | 38 | 2 |
| AB McDonald | 5 | 10 | 2 | 312 | 164 | 39.00 | 71.39 | 1 | 1 | 44 | 2 |
| SJ Thakor | 3 | 5 | 0 | 190 | 134 | 38.00 | 54.13 | 1 | 0 | 20 | 2 |
| WI Jefferson | 15 | 29 | 1 | 1007 | 133 | 35.96 | 53.16 | 3 | 3 | 145 | 4 |
| WA White | 14 | 26 | 1 | 789 | 83* | 31.56 | 58.40 | 0 | 6 | 109 | 9 |
| MAG Boyce | 15 | 30 | 0 | 815 | 119 | 27.16 | 41.09 | 2 | 0 | 121 | 6 |
| GP Smith | 12 | 24 | 0 | 620 | 108 | 25.83 | 49.63 | 1 | 3 | 81 | 2 |
| PG Dixey | 6 | 10 | 1 | 228 | 72* | 25.33 | 46.62 | 0 | 2 | 34 | 1 |
| CW Henderson | 13 | 22 | 3 | 435 | 80* | 22.89 | 60.00 | 0 | 3 | 61 | 3 |
| JKH Naik | 17 | 32 | 7 | 545 | 77* | 21.80 | 39.04 | 0 | 2 | 58 | 3 |
| TJ New | 10 | 19 | 0 | 412 | 76 | 21.68 | 47.35 | 0 | 4 | 48 | 0 |
| RML Taylor | 4 | 8 | 0 | 160 | 70 | 20.00 | 47.47 | 0 | 1 | 19 | 2 |
| J du Toit | 6 | 11 | 0 | 217 | 97 | 19.72 | 54.93 | 0 | 1 | 25 | 4 |
| Kadeer Ali | 1 | 2 | 0 | 34 | 33 | 17.00 | 45.33 | 0 | 0 | 5 | 0 |
| PA Nixon | 4 | 7 | 0 | 97 | 46 | 13.85 | 32.88 | 0 | 0 | 10 | 0 |
| JJ Cobb | 9 | 18 | 0 | 215 | 44 | 11.94 | 50.35 | 0 | 0 | 31 | 4 |
| MN Malik | 11 | 17 | 8 | 71 | 12 | 7.88 | 21.84 | 0 | 0 | 7 | 1 |
| NL Buck | 13 | 22 | 5 | 124 | 26 | 7.29 | 30.61 | 0 | 0 | 11 | 0 |
| MJ Hoggard | 12 | 19 | 7 | 68 | 19* | 5.66 | 22.22 | 0 | 0 | 6 | 0 |
| ACF Wyatt | 4 | 4 | 2 | 10 | 4* | 5.00 | 50.00 | 0 | 0 | 2 | 0 |
| WS Jones | 2 | 4 | 0 | 12 | 10 | 3.00 | 31.57 | 0 | 0 | 1 | 0 |
| HF Gurney | 1 | 1 | 0 | 2 | 2 | 2.00 | 100.00 | 0 | 0 | 0 | 0 |
| SJ Cliff | 1 | - | - | - | - | - | - | - | - | - | - |
| LA Radford | 1 | - | - | - | - | - | - | - | - | - | - |

*Batting*

| | Overs | Mdns | Runs | Wkts | BBI | BBM | Ave | Econ | SR | 5w | 10w |
|---|---|---|---|---|---|---|---|---|---|---|---|
| SJ Thakor | 17.0 | 2 | 74 | 3 | 3/57 | 3/57 | 24.66 | 4.35 | 34.0 | 0 | 0 |
| J du Toit | 7.0 | 2 | 27 | 1 | 1/17 | 1/17 | 27.00 | 3.85 | 42.0 | 0 | 0 |
| SJ Cliff | 17.0 | 3 | 56 | 2 | 2/56 | 2/56 | 28.00 | 3.29 | 51.0 | 0 | 0 |
| WA White | 295.0 | 45 | 1134 | 38 | 4/37 | 6/61 | 29.84 | 3.84 | 46.5 | 0 | 0 |
| ACF Wyatt | 111.0 | 29 | 395 | 13 | 2/28 | 4/65 | 30.38 | 3.55 | 51.2 | 0 | 0 |
| JKH Naik | 462.4 | 73 | 1528 | 49 | 5/34 | 7/109 | 31.18 | 3.30 | 56.6 | 2 | 0 |
| CW Henderson | 495.1 | 127 | 1269 | 40 | 4/43 | 7/128 | 31.72 | 2.56 | 74.2 | 0 | 0 |
| LA Radford | 15.0 | 3 | 64 | 2 | 2/47 | 2/64 | 32.00 | 4.26 | 45.0 | 0 | 0 |
| MN Malik | 314.4 | 78 | 1006 | 29 | 4/62 | 5/92 | 34.68 | 3.19 | 65.1 | 0 | 0 |
| MJ Hoggard | 323.0 | 70 | 993 | 28 | 4/66 | 6/100 | 35.46 | 3.07 | 69.2 | 0 | 0 |
| HF Gurney | 35.3 | 6 | 113 | 3 | 2/64 | 3/113 | 37.66 | 3.18 | 71.0 | 0 | 0 |
| AB McDonald | 87.0 | 11 | 303 | 8 | 3/51 | 3/51 | 37.87 | 3.48 | 65.2 | 0 | 0 |
| NL Buck | 345.4 | 83 | 1197 | 25 | 5/99 | 5/124 | 47.88 | 3.46 | 82.9 | 1 | 0 |
| RML Taylor | 67.1 | 5 | 300 | 5 | 3/53 | 3/88 | 60.00 | 4.46 | 80.6 | 0 | 0 |
| JJ Cobb | 24.0 | 3 | 79 | 1 | 1/41 | 1/41 | 79.00 | 3.29 | 144.0 | 0 | 0 |
| Kadeer Ali | 1.0 | 1 | 0 | 0 | - | - | - | 0.00 | - | 0 | 0 |
| WS Jones | 3.0 | 1 | 6 | 0 | - | - | - | 2.00 | - | 0 | 0 |

*Bowling*

**Catches/Stumpings:**
24 Jefferson, 20 New (+1st), 15 Dixey (+1st), 13 Boyce, Eckersley (inc 1 outfield +0st), 12 Taylor, 8 Smith, 6 Cobb, Naik, 5 Henderson, White, 4 du Toit, 2 Hoggard, McDonald, Taylor, 1 Malik

**Batting**

|  | Mat | Inns | NO | Runs | HS | Ave | SR | 100 | 50 | 4s | 6s |
|---|---|---|---|---|---|---|---|---|---|---|---|
| Kadeer Ali | 1 | 1 | 0 | 60 | 60 | 60.00 | 101.69 | 0 | 1 | 3 | 0 |
| JWA Taylor | 9 | 8 | 1 | 408 | 101 | 58.28 | 96.68 | 1 | 3 | 30 | 0 |
| JJ Cobb | 11 | 10 | 1 | 485 | 91* | 53.88 | 106.35 | 0 | 5 | 58 | 9 |
| AB McDonald | 3 | 1 | 0 | 35 | 35 | 35.00 | 184.21 | 0 | 0 | 6 | 1 |
| J du Toit | 11 | 10 | 0 | 259 | 56 | 25.90 | 84.64 | 0 | 1 | 31 | 2 |
| PA Nixon | 5 | 5 | 0 | 118 | 54 | 23.60 | 83.09 | 0 | 1 | 9 | 0 |
| TJ New | 4 | 1 | 0 | 20 | 20 | 20.00 | 62.50 | 0 | 0 | 1 | 0 |
| MAG Boyce | 9 | 8 | 0 | 144 | 48 | 18.00 | 80.00 | 0 | 0 | 10 | 2 |
| WA White | 11 | 10 | 2 | 123 | 29* | 15.37 | 72.78 | 0 | 0 | 5 | 2 |
| WI Jefferson | 5 | 4 | 0 | 52 | 26 | 13.00 | 88.13 | 0 | 0 | 5 | 2 |
| SJ Thakor | 2 | 2 | 0 | 26 | 13 | 13.00 | 65.00 | 0 | 0 | 1 | 1 |
| PG Dixey | 6 | 6 | 0 | 63 | 42 | 10.50 | 78.75 | 0 | 0 | 8 | 0 |
| MJ Hoggard | 7 | 5 | 1 | 42 | 23 | 10.50 | 95.45 | 0 | 0 | 4 | 1 |
| CW Henderson | 8 | 7 | 2 | 50 | 18* | 10.00 | 64.10 | 0 | 0 | 2 | 1 |
| JKH Naik | 6 | 4 | 2 | 15 | 9* | 7.50 | 53.57 | 0 | 0 | 0 | 0 |
| NL Buck | 5 | 3 | 0 | 14 | 7 | 4.66 | 48.27 | 0 | 0 | 0 | 0 |
| WS Jones | 1 | 1 | 0 | 3 | 3 | 3.00 | 25.00 | 0 | 0 | 0 | 0 |
| GP Smith | 2 | 2 | 1 | 2 | 2 | 2.00 | 13.33 | 0 | 0 | 0 | 0 |
| HF Gurney | 3 | 2 | 0 | 2 | 1 | 1.00 | 50.00 | 0 | 0 | 0 | 0 |
| MN Malik | 7 | 3 | 1 | 2 | 2 | 1.00 | 20.00 | 0 | 0 | 0 | 0 |
| ACF Wyatt | 5 | 2 | 2 | 3 | 2* | - | 60.00 | 0 | 0 | 0 | 0 |

**Bowling**

|  | Overs | Mdns | Runs | Wkts | BBI | Ave | Econ | SR | 4w | 5w |
|---|---|---|---|---|---|---|---|---|---|---|
| AB McDonald | 11.0 | 0 | 54 | 0 | - | - | 4.90 | - | 0 | 0 |
| CW Henderson | 63.1 | 3 | 324 | 9 | 2/34 | 36.00 | 5.12 | 42.1 | 0 | 0 |
| MJ Hoggard | 51.0 | 2 | 265 | 11 | 2/26 | 24.09 | 5.19 | 27.8 | 0 | 0 |
| MN Malik | 48.0 | 2 | 267 | 10 | 3/37 | 26.70 | 5.56 | 28.8 | 0 | 0 |
| JKH Naik | 38.0 | 0 | 224 | 3 | 2/38 | 74.66 | 5.89 | 76.0 | 0 | 0 |
| ACF Wyatt | 26.0 | 2 | 161 | 4 | 2/36 | 40.25 | 6.19 | 39.0 | 0 | 0 |
| JJ Cobb | 42.0 | 0 | 273 | 5 | 2/35 | 54.60 | 6.50 | 50.4 | 0 | 0 |
| NL Buck | 36.0 | 0 | 235 | 5 | 3/54 | 47.00 | 6.52 | 43.2 | 0 | 0 |
| WA White | 63.0 | 1 | 422 | 9 | 2/37 | 46.88 | 6.69 | 42.0 | 0 | 0 |
| HF Gurney | 19.4 | 0 | 135 | 3 | 2/40 | 45.00 | 6.86 | 39.3 | 0 | 0 |

**Catches/Stumpings:**
6 Cobb, 5 Boyce, 4 du Toit, New (+1st), 3 McDonald, White, 2 Buck, Dixey (+0st), Henderson, Hoggard, Nixon (outfield), 1 Gurney, Naik, Smith, Taylor, Wyatt

www.leicestershireccc.co.uk / tel: 0871 282 1879

| | Mat | Inns | NO | Runs | HS | Ave | SR | 100 | 50 | 4s | 6s |
|---|---|---|---|---|---|---|---|---|---|---|---|
| WA White | 19 | 11 | 9 | 111 | 21* | 55.50 | 152.05 | 0 | 0 | 8 | 4 |
| AB McDonald | 19 | 19 | 7 | 628 | 96* | 52.33 | 128.42* | 0 | 7 | 58 | 10 |
| JWA Taylor | 18 | 15 | 6 | 342 | 53 | 38.00 | 112.13 | 0 | 1 | 25 | 8 |
| Abdul Razzaq | 17 | 13 | 3 | 300 | 62* | 30.00 | 140.18 | 0 | 1 | 26 | 14 |
| JJ Cobb | 19 | 19 | 2 | 378 | 60 | 22.23 | 155.55* | 0 | 2 | 40 | 18 |
| WI Jefferson | 19 | 17 | 2 | 323 | 63 | 21.53 | 144.84 | 0 | 1 | 41 | 12 |
| PA Nixon | 19 | 9 | 0 | 174 | 44 | 19.33 | 101.75 | 0 | 0 | 11 | 3 |
| J du Toit | 19 | 14 | 3 | 136 | 33 | 12.36 | 114.28 | 0 | 0 | 15 | 1 |
| CW Henderson | 18 | 3 | 2 | 0 | 0* | 0.00 | 0.00 | 0 | 0 | 0 | 0 |
| MJ Hoggard | 14 | 1 | 1 | 10 | 10* | - | 500.00 | 0 | 0 | 1 | 1 |
| MAG Boyce | 9 | 2 | 2 | 8 | 4* | - | 266.66 | 0 | 0 | 2 | 0 |
| JKH Naik | 5 | 1 | 1 | 0 | 0* | - | - | 0 | 0 | 0 | 0 |
| HF Gurney | 14 | - | - | - | - | - | - | - | - | - | - |

Batting

| | Overs | Mdns | Runs | Wkts | BBI | Ave | Econ | SR | 4w | 5w |
|---|---|---|---|---|---|---|---|---|---|---|
| CW Henderson | 65.0 | 0 | 447 | 17 | 3/25 | 26.29 | 6.87 | 22.9 | 0 | 0 |
| HF Gurney | 49.5 | 2 | 354 | 23 | 3/25 | 15.39 | 7.10 | 13.0 | 0 | 0 |
| JKH Naik | 13.0 | 0 | 96 | 7 | 3/3 | 13.71 | 7.38 | 11.1 | 0 | 0 |
| AB McDonald | 56.4 | 0 | 439 | 15 | 3/18 | 29.26 | 7.74 | 22.6 | 0 | 0 |
| Abdul Razzaq | 59.2 | 1 | 461 | 19 | 3/12 | 24.26 | 7.76 | 18.7 | 0 | 0 |
| MJ Hoggard | 39.0 | 1 | 310 | 14 | 3/21 | 22.14 | 7.94 | 16.7 | 0 | 0 |
| JJ Cobb | 29.0 | 0 | 231 | 13 | 4/22 | 17.76 | 7.96 | 13.3 | 1 | 0 |
| WA White | 35.0 | 0 | 343 | 5 | 1/8 | 68.60 | 9.80 | 42.0 | 0 | 0 |

Bowling

**Catches/Stumpings:**
13 McDonald, 10 Cobb, 9 Jefferson, Nixon (+4st), 8 White, 7 Taylor, 6 Henderson, 5 Razzaq, 2 du Toit, Hoggard, 1 Gurney, Naik

# MIDDLESEX

**FORMED:** 1864
**HOME GROUND:** Lord's
**ONE-DAY NAME:** Panthers
**CAPTAIN:** Neil Dexter
**2011 RESULTS:** CC2: Champions; CB40: 2/7 in Group A; FL t20: 9/9 in South Group
**HONOURS:** Championship: (12) 1903, 1920, 1921, 1947, 1949(s), 1976, 1977(s), 1980, 1982, 1985, 1990, 1993; Gillette/NatWest/C&G/FP Trophy: (4) 1977, 1980, 1984, 1988; Benson and Hedges Cup: (2) 1983, 1986; Sunday League: 1992; Twenty20 Cup: 2008

## THE LOWDOWN

A successful County Championship campaign saw Middlesex claim the Division Two title last year and return to the-top flight for the first time since 2006. Australian opener Chris Rogers starred with the bat, notching four centuries and amassing 1,303 first-class runs, while promising young batsman Sam Robson enhanced his reputation with some assured performances. While their CB40 efforts were also impressive, the club's poor form in the FL t20 led to a bottom-place finish in the South Group. The signing of Joe Denly could be the answer to their T20 shortcomings, while the acquisition of offspinner Ollie Rayner – who is familiar with the Home of Cricket having spent some time on loan at Middlesex last season – looks to be a shrewd piece of business. After achieving their primary aim of County Championship promotion last season, Middlesex will be now be looking to establish themselves as a force to be reckoned with in Division One.

## MANAGING DIRECTOR OF CRICKET: ANGUS FRASER

Fraser delivered his first trophy last season after being appointed managing director of cricket in 2009. He brings a winning mentality to the club, forged throughout his successful 18-year career with Middlesex and the England national side, whom he represented in 46 Test matches and 42 ODIs. Upon retiring from first-class cricket in 2002, he worked as a journalist for The Independent before returning to his spiritual home.

| | Mat | Inns | NO | Runs | HS | Ave | SR | 100 | 50 | 4s | 6s |
|---|---|---|---|---|---|---|---|---|---|---|---|
| AJ Strauss | 6 | 10 | 2 | 614 | 241* | 76.75 | 66.95 | 3 | 0 | 84 | 2 |
| CJL Rogers | 16 | 27 | 3 | 1303 | 148 | 54.29 | 61.03 | 4 | 6 | 183 | 6 |
| SD Robson | 12 | 20 | 3 | 903 | 146 | 53.11 | 54.00 | 2 | 4 | 131 | 2 |
| GK Berg | 8 | 11 | 2 | 406 | 130* | 45.11 | 71.98 | 1 | 2 | 46 | 8 |
| OP Rayner | 9 | 9 | 3 | 269 | 58* | 44.83 | 77.74 | 0 | 3 | 40 | 2 |
| JA Simpson | 18 | 26 | 6 | 869 | 143 | 43.45 | 50.43 | 1 | 7 | 111 | 5 |
| DJ Malan | 17 | 28 | 2 | 947 | 143 | 36.42 | 57.84 | 3 | 2 | 126 | 6 |
| JWM Dalrymple | 12 | 19 | 3 | 531 | 122* | 33.18 | 53.63 | 2 | 1 | 64 | 6 |
| SA Newman | 13 | 22 | 1 | 694 | 95 | 33.04 | 62.57 | 0 | 4 | 116 | 1 |
| DM Housego | 8 | 15 | 2 | 407 | 104 | 31.30 | 44.57 | 1 | 0 | 45 | 0 |
| NJ Dexter | 13 | 22 | 3 | 561 | 145 | 29.52 | 58.62 | 1 | 3 | 72 | 4 |
| TJ Murtagh | 16 | 19 | 5 | 269 | 55 | 19.21 | 48.46 | 0 | 1 | 39 | 1 |
| TS Roland-Jones | 7 | 8 | 2 | 109 | 28 | 18.16 | 42.24 | 0 | 0 | 13 | 0 |
| AJ Ireland | 3 | 5 | 0 | 75 | 29 | 15.00 | 48.70 | 0 | 0 | 10 | 2 |
| GS Sandhu | 1 | 2 | 1 | 15 | 8 | 15.00 | 51.72 | 0 | 0 | 2 | 0 |
| ST Finn | 8 | 9 | 1 | 108 | 32 | 13.50 | 51.92 | 0 | 0 | 17 | 0 |
| SP Crook | 11 | 9 | 1 | 64 | 13 | 8.00 | 47.05 | 0 | 0 | 8 | 0 |
| TMJ Smith | 4 | 6 | 0 | 42 | 16 | 7.00 | 27.27 | 0 | 0 | 6 | 0 |
| CD Collymore | 16 | 15 | 7 | 43 | 8* | 5.37 | 35.83 | 0 | 0 | 7 | 0 |
| AM Rossington | 1 | 2 | 0 | 4 | 4 | 2.00 | 26.66 | 0 | 0 | 1 | 0 |
| TW Parsons | 1 | 1 | 1 | 7 | 7* | - | 77.77 | 0 | 0 | 1 | 0 |

Batting

| | Overs | Mdns | Runs | Wkts | BBI | BBM | Ave | Econ | SR | 5w | 10w |
|---|---|---|---|---|---|---|---|---|---|---|---|
| GK Berg | 175.5 | 30 | 564 | 28 | 6/58 | 7/90 | 20.14 | 3.20 | 37.6 | 1 | 0 |
| ST Finn | 241.2 | 55 | 705 | 34 | 5/113 | 6/110 | 20.73 | 2.92 | 42.5 | 1 | 0 |
| TJ Murtagh | 514.5 | 103 | 1774 | 85 | 5/27 | 10/128 | 20.87 | 3.44 | 36.3 | 4 | 1 |
| CD Collymore | 456.2 | 100 | 1289 | 49 | 4/28 | 6/100 | 26.30 | 2.82 | 55.8 | 0 | 0 |
| TS Roland-Jones | 188.5 | 25 | 684 | 26 | 5/91 | 7/185 | 26.30 | 3.62 | 43.5 | 1 | 0 |
| DJ Malan | 62.5 | 11 | 212 | 7 | 4/80 | 4/80 | 30.28 | 3.37 | 53.8 | 0 | 0 |
| SP Crook | 172.5 | 18 | 812 | 26 | 5/94 | 5/94 | 31.23 | 4.69 | 39.8 | 1 | 0 |
| OP Rayner | 184.5 | 36 | 523 | 13 | 4/43 | 4/85 | 40.23 | 2.82 | 85.3 | 0 | 0 |
| NJ Dexter | 118.1 | 25 | 411 | 9 | 3/46 | 3/60 | 45.66 | 3.47 | 78.7 | 0 | 0 |
| JWM Dalrymple | 174.4 | 18 | 553 | 12 | 3/21 | 3/64 | 46.08 | 3.16 | 87.3 | 0 | 0 |
| TMJ Smith | 103.0 | 13 | 369 | 8 | 3/38 | 4/107 | 46.12 | 3.58 | 77.2 | 0 | 0 |
| AJ Ireland | 80.3 | 14 | 285 | 5 | 2/51 | 3/108 | 57.00 | 3.54 | 96.6 | 0 | 0 |
| SA Newman | 1.0 | 0 | 2 | 0 | - | - | - | 2.00 | - | 0 | 0 |
| TW Parsons | 21.0 | 1 | 83 | 0 | - | - | - | 3.95 | - | 0 | 0 |
| SD Robson | 1.0 | 0 | 8 | 0 | - | - | - | 8.00 | - | 0 | 0 |
| GS Sandhu | 13.0 | 0 | 69 | 0 | - | - | - | 5.30 | - | 0 | 0 |
| AJ Strauss | 1.0 | 0 | 2 | 0 | - | - | - | 2.00 | - | 0 | 0 |

Bowling

**Catches/Stumpings:**
67 Simpson (+1st), 25 Malan, 15 Rayner, 12 Robson, 11 Dexter, Newman, 9 Dalrymple, 7 Berg, Rogers, 6 Strauss, 4 Crook, Murtagh, 3 Roland-Jones, 2 Housego, 1 Collymore, Finn, Rossington

## Batting

| | Mat | Inns | NO | Runs | HS | Ave | SR | 100 | 50 | 4s | 6s |
|---|---|---|---|---|---|---|---|---|---|---|---|
| PR Stirling | 12 | 12 | 2 | 535 | 109 | 53.50 | 128.60 | 1 | 2 | 63 | 13 |
| SD Robson | 2 | 2 | 0 | 96 | 65 | 48.00 | 82.05 | 0 | 1 | 7 | 0 |
| DJ Malan | 12 | 12 | 0 | 510 | 107 | 42.50 | 90.74 | 1 | 3 | 62 | 3 |
| OP Rayner | 5 | 4 | 2 | 80 | 34* | 40.00 | 103.89 | 0 | 0 | 11 | 1 |
| NJ Dexter | 10 | 10 | 4 | 214 | 58 | 35.66 | 85.94 | 0 | 1 | 23 | 1 |
| CJL Rogers | 9 | 9 | 2 | 237 | 51* | 33.85 | 92.94 | 0 | 2 | 18 | 2 |
| GK Berg | 6 | 5 | 1 | 129 | 52 | 32.25 | 77.24 | 0 | 1 | 11 | 1 |
| AJ Ireland | 5 | 2 | 1 | 26 | 22* | 26.00 | 70.27 | 0 | 0 | 3 | 0 |
| SA Newman | 12 | 12 | 1 | 275 | 73 | 25.00 | 75.96 | 0 | 1 | 39 | 2 |
| SP Crook | 6 | 4 | 0 | 71 | 61 | 17.75 | 122.41 | 0 | 1 | 6 | 2 |
| BJM Scott | 4 | 3 | 0 | 45 | 19 | 15.00 | 56.96 | 0 | 0 | 1 | 0 |
| TE Scollay | 3 | 3 | 0 | 37 | 17 | 12.33 | 78.72 | 0 | 0 | 4 | 0 |
| JWM Dalrymple | 5 | 3 | 1 | 24 | 14 | 12.00 | 64.86 | 0 | 0 | 0 | 0 |
| TJ Murtagh | 10 | 5 | 3 | 19 | 7 | 9.50 | 45.23 | 0 | 0 | 0 | 0 |
| TMJ Smith | 7 | 4 | 0 | 35 | 27 | 8.75 | 79.54 | 0 | 0 | 1 | 0 |
| JA Simpson | 8 | 3 | 0 | 18 | 12 | 6.00 | 78.26 | 0 | 0 | 2 | 0 |
| ST Finn | 5 | 1 | 0 | 0 | 0 | 0.00 | 0.00 | 0 | 0 | 0 | 0 |
| TS Roland-Jones | 5 | 3 | 1 | 0 | 0* | 0.00 | 0.00 | 0 | 0 | 0 | 0 |
| CD Collymore | 5 | 2 | 2 | 3 | 2* | - | 60.00 | 0 | 0 | 0 | 0 |
| REM Williams | 1 | - | - | - | - | - | - | - | - | - | - |

## Bowling

| | Overs | Mdns | Runs | Wkts | BBI | Ave | Econ | SR | 4w | 5w |
|---|---|---|---|---|---|---|---|---|---|---|
| OP Rayner | 31.0 | 0 | 151 | 6 | 2/20 | 25.16 | 4.87 | 31.0 | 0 | 0 |
| ST Finn | 32.0 | 2 | 158 | 12 | 5/33 | 13.16 | 4.93 | 16.0 | 0 | 1 |
| CD Collymore | 34.5 | 4 | 175 | 8 | 3/17 | 21.87 | 5.02 | 26.1 | 0 | 0 |
| TMJ Smith | 45.0 | 1 | 229 | 5 | 2/37 | 45.80 | 5.08 | 54.0 | 0 | 0 |
| TS Roland-Jones | 34.4 | 0 | 194 | 8 | 3/51 | 24.25 | 5.59 | 26.0 | 0 | 0 |
| SP Crook | 39.3 | 2 | 222 | 6 | 2/38 | 37.00 | 5.62 | 39.5 | 0 | 0 |
| TJ Murtagh | 67.2 | 4 | 381 | 7 | 2/29 | 54.42 | 5.65 | 57.7 | 0 | 0 |
| GK Berg | 30.0 | 1 | 172 | 7 | 4/24 | 24.57 | 5.73 | 25.7 | 1 | 0 |
| NJ Dexter | 38.1 | 1 | 219 | 5 | 2/26 | 43.80 | 5.73 | 45.8 | 0 | 0 |
| JWM Dalrymple | 13.0 | 0 | 76 | 2 | 1/41 | 38.00 | 5.84 | 39.0 | 0 | 0 |
| AJ Ireland | 21.4 | 1 | 131 | 1 | 1/31 | 131.00 | 6.04 | 130.0 | 0 | 0 |
| PR Stirling | 22.0 | 0 | 138 | 2 | 2/38 | 69.00 | 6.27 | 66.0 | 0 | 0 |
| DJ Malan | 15.0 | 0 | 100 | 4 | 1/18 | 25.00 | 6.66 | 22.5 | 0 | 0 |
| REM Williams | 7.0 | 0 | 57 | 0 | - | - | 8.14 | - | 0 | 0 |

**Catches/Stumpings:**
6 Simpson (+0st), 5 Crook, Stirling, 4 Malan, 3 Dexter, Murtagh, Newman, Robson, 2 Berg, Dalrymple, Rogers, Scott (+0st), 1 Collymore, Scollay, Smith, Williams

PANTHERS

Batting

| | Mat | Inns | NO | Runs | HS | Ave | SR | 100 | 50 | 4s | 6s |
|---|---|---|---|---|---|---|---|---|---|---|---|
| JH Davey | 4 | 3 | 2 | 31 | 18* | 31.00 | 114.81 | 0 | 0 | 3 | 0 |
| DJ Malan | 6 | 5 | 1 | 113 | 32 | 28.25 | 110.78 | 0 | 0 | 13 | 0 |
| TMJ Smith | 16 | 11 | 7 | 110 | 36* | 27.50 | 118.27 | 0 | 0 | 10 | 0 |
| SD Robson | 4 | 4 | 2 | 53 | 28* | 26.50 | 103.92 | 0 | 0 | 5 | 0 |
| SA Newman | 16 | 15 | 2 | 314 | 61 | 24.15 | 100.64 | 0 | 1 | 35 | 4 |
| CJL Rogers | 9 | 7 | 0 | 154 | 46 | 22.00 | 120.31 | 0 | 0 | 15 | 3 |
| NJ Dexter | 14 | 12 | 0 | 236 | 49 | 19.66 | 108.25 | 0 | 0 | 16 | 8 |
| JWM Dalrymple | 12 | 10 | 2 | 148 | 48 | 18.50 | 98.01 | 0 | 0 | 12 | 3 |
| JA Simpson | 16 | 13 | 1 | 214 | 60* | 17.83 | 132.09 | 0 | 1 | 20 | 6 |
| PR Stirling | 13 | 13 | 1 | 213 | 51* | 17.75 | 150.00 | 0 | 1 | 29 | 9 |
| R McLaren | 15 | 13 | 4 | 136 | 35* | 15.11 | 97.84 | 0 | 0 | 6 | 3 |
| TS Roland-Jones | 2 | 1 | 0 | 12 | 12 | 12.00 | 200.00 | 0 | 0 | 1 | 1 |
| SP Crook | 14 | 10 | 2 | 94 | 29 | 11.75 | 113.25 | 0 | 0 | 7 | 4 |
| TE Scollay | 5 | 4 | 0 | 36 | 15 | 9.00 | 90.00 | 0 | 0 | 3 | 1 |
| AJ Ireland | 9 | 4 | 3 | 8 | 6* | 8.00 | 88.88 | 0 | 0 | 1 | 0 |
| AM Rossington | 4 | 4 | 0 | 27 | 25 | 6.75 | 112.50 | 0 | 0 | 3 | 1 |
| TJ Murtagh | 9 | 3 | 0 | 17 | 9 | 5.66 | 85.00 | 0 | 0 | 2 | 0 |
| ST Finn | 8 | 2 | 1 | 4 | 4* | 4.00 | 80.00 | 0 | 0 | 1 | 0 |

Bowling

| | Overs | Mdns | Runs | Wkts | BBI | Ave | Econ | SR | 4w | 5w |
|---|---|---|---|---|---|---|---|---|---|---|
| ST Finn | 28.0 | 1 | 175 | 7 | 2/19 | 25.00 | 6.25 | 24.0 | 0 | 0 |
| NJ Dexter | 41.0 | 0 | 281 | 12 | 4/21 | 23.41 | 6.85 | 20.5 | 1 | 0 |
| TMJ Smith | 52.0 | 0 | 400 | 12 | 2/25 | 33.33 | 7.69 | 26.0 | 0 | 0 |
| SP Crook | 43.1 | 3 | 365 | 17 | 3/21 | 21.47 | 8.45 | 15.2 | 0 | 0 |
| TS Roland-Jones | 8.0 | 0 | 70 | 2 | 2/42 | 35.00 | 8.75 | 24.0 | 0 | 0 |
| R McLaren | 52.5 | 0 | 464 | 14 | 3/7 | 33.14 | 8.78 | 22.6 | 0 | 0 |
| JWM Dalrymple | 20.0 | 0 | 176 | 3 | 2/23 | 58.66 | 8.80 | 40.0 | 0 | 0 |
| AJ Ireland | 25.0 | 1 | 230 | 7 | 3/7 | 32.85 | 9.20 | 21.4 | 0 | 0 |
| PR Stirling | 9.0 | 0 | 84 | 2 | 2/25 | 42.00 | 9.33 | 27.0 | 0 | 0 |
| TJ Murtagh | 26.1 | 0 | 267 | 2 | 1/24 | 133.50 | 10.20 | 78.5 | 0 | 0 |

**Catches/Stumpings:**
10 Smith, 9 Simpson (+5st), 6 McLaren, 4 Rogers, Dexter, 3 Dalrymple, 2 Robson, Rossington, Malan, Murtagh, Stirling, Crook, Newman, 1 Scollay, Ireland

TEAM PROFILE

FORMED: 1878
HOME GROUND: County Ground, Wantage Road
ONE-DAY NAME: Steelbacks
CAPTAIN: Andrew Hall
2011 RESULTS: CC2: 3/9; CB40: 3/7 in Group B; FL t20: 9/9 in North Group
HONOURS: Gillette/NatWest/C&G/FP Trophy: (2) 1976, 1992; Benson and Hedges Cup: 1980

### THE LOWDOWN

Last season was ultimately a frustrating one for Northants, as they missed out on County Championship promotion by a single point, as Surrey pipped them to second place. But they can take encouragement from a positive season in four-day cricket, underpinned by the stand-out performances of captain Andrew Hall with the bat and Chaminda Vaas with the ball. Unsurprisingly, the Steelbacks have retained Vaas as their overseas player for 2011, and the Sri Lankan veteran forms a dangerous seam attack with England Lion Jack Brooks and Lee Daggett. The loss of veterans Mal Loye and David Lucas will be felt, but the capture of Scotland international Kyle Coetzer will bolster the middle-order. County Championship promotion will be the ultimate goal after coming so close last year, but they will also be targeting an improved performance in the FL t20 after finishing bottom of the North Group in 2011.

### HEAD COACH: DAVID CAPEL

Capel has been a loyal servant of Northamptonshire both as a player and a coach throughout his cricketing career. He represented his hometown club as a player for 17 years, scoring more than 12,000 first-class runs and taking 546 wickets. After retiring he became the Steelbacks' academy director before taking charge of first-team affairs in 2006. Capel also represented his country, playing 15 Tests and 23 ODIs for England between 1987 and 1990.

| | Mat | Inns | NO | Runs | HS | Ave | SR | 100 | 50 | 4s | 6s |
|---|---|---|---|---|---|---|---|---|---|---|---|
| DJ Willey | 2 | 2 | 1 | 118 | 64 | 118.00 | 68.60 | 0 | 2 | 17 | 3 |
| D Murphy | 4 | 4 | 1 | 164 | 79 | 54.66 | 55.97 | 0 | 1 | 18 | 2 |
| AJ Hall | 16 | 23 | 4 | 960 | 146 | 50.52 | 47.88 | 2 | 5 | 116 | 9 |
| SD Peters | 15 | 21 | 1 | 864 | 222 | 43.20 | 54.13 | 3 | 2 | 120 | 0 |
| JD Middlebrook | 16 | 20 | 5 | 644 | 109 | 42.93 | 54.66 | 3 | 1 | 75 | 8 |
| AG Wakely | 16 | 22 | 0 | 869 | 98 | 39.50 | 54.04 | 0 | 5 | 109 | 8 |
| NJ O'Brien | 14 | 22 | 4 | 676 | 166 | 37.55 | 60.03 | 1 | 4 | 86 | 2 |
| RI Newton | 8 | 14 | 1 | 478 | 113 | 36.76 | 64.76 | 1 | 2 | 74 | 0 |
| KJ Coetzer | 4 | 7 | 1 | 214 | 84 | 35.66 | 50.47 | 0 | 2 | 34 | 0 |
| RA White | 13 | 18 | 0 | 599 | 140 | 33.27 | 60.14 | 1 | 2 | 85 | 4 |
| MB Loye | 8 | 12 | 0 | 393 | 87 | 32.75 | 40.85 | 0 | 4 | 55 | 2 |
| WPUJC Vaas | 14 | 16 | 1 | 403 | 96 | 26.86 | 39.01 | 0 | 2 | 48 | 1 |
| LM Daggett | 15 | 17 | 9 | 189 | 50* | 23.62 | 36.98 | 0 | 1 | 28 | 0 |
| DS Lucas | 10 | 12 | 2 | 199 | 60 | 19.90 | 51.28 | 0 | 1 | 27 | 1 |
| JA Brooks | 9 | 8 | 5 | 58 | 15* | 19.33 | 42.02 | 0 | 0 | 10 | 0 |
| DJG Sales | 12 | 16 | 1 | 267 | 65 | 17.80 | 50.66 | 0 | 1 | 40 | 2 |
| BHN Howgego | 6 | 8 | 0 | 142 | 41 | 17.75 | 38.06 | 0 | 0 | 18 | 0 |
| L Evans | 2 | 1 | 0 | 5 | 5 | 5.00 | 55.55 | 0 | 0 | 1 | 0 |
| DA Burton | 1 | 2 | 0 | 8 | 6 | 4.00 | 29.62 | 0 | 0 | 1 | 0 |
| T Brett | 1 | 1 | 0 | 2 | 2 | 2.00 | 15.38 | 0 | 0 | 0 | 0 |
| PM Best | 1 | 1 | 1 | 31 | 31* | - | 70.45 | 0 | 0 | 3 | 1 |

Batting

| | Overs | Mdns | Runs | Wkts | BBI | BBM | Ave | Econ | SR | 5w | 10w |
|---|---|---|---|---|---|---|---|---|---|---|---|
| DJ Willey | 59.2 | 12 | 168 | 13 | 5/29 | 10/75 | 12.92 | 2.83 | 27.3 | 2 | 1 |
| AG Wakely | 8.2 | 0 | 32 | 2 | 1/0 | 1/0 | 16.00 | 3.84 | 25.0 | 0 | 0 |
| WPUJC Vaas | 499.0 | 119 | 1501 | 70 | 6/46 | 10/82 | 21.44 | 3.00 | 42.7 | 6 | 1 |
| JA Brooks | 289.0 | 68 | 942 | 43 | 5/23 | 7/97 | 21.90 | 3.25 | 40.3 | 2 | 0 |
| L Evans | 35.0 | 8 | 125 | 5 | 3/21 | 3/21 | 25.00 | 3.57 | 42.0 | 0 | 0 |
| DS Lucas | 242.4 | 48 | 915 | 32 | 5/20 | 9/75 | 28.59 | 3.77 | 45.5 | 1 | 0 |
| JD Middlebrook | 426.4 | 86 | 1307 | 43 | 5/123 | 9/190 | 30.39 | 3.06 | 59.5 | 2 | 0 |
| LM Daggett | 451.5 | 91 | 1551 | 46 | 4/35 | 6/132 | 33.71 | 3.43 | 58.9 | 0 | 0 |
| AJ Hall | 351.1 | 66 | 1267 | 28 | 3/8 | 4/81 | 45.25 | 3.60 | 75.2 | 0 | 0 |
| T Brett | 30.4 | 8 | 94 | 2 | 1/29 | 2/94 | 47.00 | 3.06 | 92.0 | 0 | 0 |
| RA White | 65.0 | 4 | 264 | 2 | 2/51 | 2/51 | 66.00 | 4.06 | 97.5 | 0 | 0 |
| DA Burton | 30.0 | 9 | 142 | 2 | 2/55 | 2/142 | 71.00 | 4.73 | 90.0 | 0 | 0 |
| PM Best | 47.0 | 12 | 153 | 2 | 1/47 | 2/153 | 76.50 | 3.25 | 141.0 | 0 | 0 |
| D Murphy | 1.0 | 0 | 3 | 0 | - | - | - | 3.00 | - | 0 | 0 |

Bowling

**Catches/Stumpings:**
49 O'Brien (+4st), 31 Hall, 16 Murphy (+0st), 15 Peters, 13 Sales, 9 White, 8 Middlebrook, Wakely, 5 Howgego, 3 Newton, 2 Brooks, Daggett, 1 Best, Coetzer, Lucas

**Batting**

| | Mat | Inns | NO | Runs | HS | Ave | SR | 100 | 50 | 4s | 6s |
|---|---|---|---|---|---|---|---|---|---|---|---|
| NJ O'Brien | 9 | 9 | 1 | 393 | 121 | 49.12 | 118.01 | 1 | 3 | 45 | 7 |
| AJ Hall | 11 | 9 | 4 | 242 | 67 | 48.40 | 88.97 | 0 | 2 | 18 | 2 |
| AG Wakely | 10 | 10 | 2 | 376 | 94 | 47.00 | 96.16 | 0 | 3 | 31 | 6 |
| WPUJC Vaas | 6 | 5 | 2 | 109 | 68 | 36.33 | 76.22 | 0 | 1 | 10 | 1 |
| DJG Sales | 8 | 8 | 3 | 176 | 60* | 35.20 | 79.27 | 0 | 1 | 18 | 0 |
| JD Middlebrook | 11 | 7 | 4 | 101 | 31* | 33.66 | 121.68 | 0 | 0 | 4 | 4 |
| DJ Willey | 12 | 7 | 1 | 199 | 74 | 33.16 | 103.10 | 0 | 2 | 16 | 7 |
| SD Peters | 8 | 8 | 0 | 221 | 63 | 27.62 | 62.96 | 0 | 2 | 19 | 0 |
| RA White | 9 | 8 | 0 | 210 | 47 | 26.25 | 83.66 | 0 | 0 | 16 | 2 |
| RI Newton | 6 | 5 | 0 | 121 | 49 | 24.20 | 121.00 | 0 | 0 | 11 | 4 |
| L Evans | 2 | 1 | 0 | 18 | 18 | 18.00 | 40.00 | 0 | 0 | 3 | 0 |
| MB Loye | 5 | 5 | 0 | 89 | 63 | 17.80 | 76.72 | 0 | 1 | 9 | 2 |
| BHN Howgego | 2 | 1 | 0 | 12 | 12 | 12.00 | 85.71 | 0 | 0 | 1 | 0 |
| D Murphy | 4 | 3 | 2 | 12 | 10* | 12.00 | 36.36 | 0 | 0 | 0 | 0 |
| BM Shafayat | 1 | 1 | 0 | 11 | 11 | 11.00 | 183.33 | 0 | 0 | 1 | 1 |
| DS Lucas | 8 | 2 | 0 | 7 | 4 | 3.50 | 77.77 | 0 | 0 | 1 | 0 |
| PM Best | 3 | 3 | 2 | 3 | 2* | 3.00 | 50.00 | 0 | 0 | 0 | 0 |
| KJ Coetzer | 1 | 1 | 1 | 54 | 54* | - | 84.37 | 0 | 1 | 6 | 1 |
| JA Brooks | 4 | 1 | 1 | 2 | 2* | - | 100.00 | 0 | 0 | 0 | 0 |
| LM Daggett | 7 | - | - | - | - | - | - | - | - | - | - |
| SA Sweeney | 1 | - | - | - | - | - | - | - | - | - | - |

**Bowling**

| | Overs | Mdns | Runs | Wkts | BBI | Ave | Econ | SR | 4w | 5w |
|---|---|---|---|---|---|---|---|---|---|---|
| T Brett | 8.0 | 0 | 29 | 2 | 2/29 | 14.50 | 3.62 | 24.0 | 0 | 0 |
| AG Wakely | 16.0 | 0 | 70 | 2 | 1/7 | 35.00 | 4.37 | 48.0 | 0 | 0 |
| JD Middlebrook | 84.0 | 0 | 423 | 9 | 3/37 | 47.00 | 5.03 | 56.0 | 0 | 0 |
| WPUJC Vaas | 33.0 | 3 | 168 | 8 | 3/37 | 21.00 | 5.09 | 24.7 | 0 | 0 |
| JA Brooks | 29.0 | 1 | 148 | 5 | 2/35 | 29.60 | 5.10 | 34.8 | 0 | 0 |
| DA Burton | 9.0 | 1 | 47 | 3 | 3/25 | 15.66 | 5.22 | 18.0 | 0 | 0 |
| LM Daggett | 50.0 | 1 | 271 | 6 | 2/30 | 45.16 | 5.42 | 50.0 | 0 | 0 |
| DJ Willey | 68.0 | 0 | 397 | 14 | 3/49 | 28.35 | 5.83 | 29.1 | 0 | 0 |
| AJ Hall | 68.2 | 2 | 432 | 19 | 5/22 | 22.73 | 6.32 | 21.5 | 1 | 1 |
| DS Lucas | 46.0 | 0 | 314 | 10 | 5/48 | 31.40 | 6.82 | 27.6 | 0 | 1 |
| PM Best | 24.0 | 0 | 179 | 4 | 3/53 | 44.75 | 7.45 | 36.0 | 0 | 0 |
| L Evans | 8.0 | 0 | 71 | 0 | - | - | 8.87 | - | 0 | 0 |
| SA Sweeney | 3.0 | 0 | 31 | 0 | - | - | 10.33 | - | 0 | 0 |
| RA White | 1.2 | 0 | 24 | 0 | - | - | 18.00 | - | 0 | 0 |

**Catches/Stumpings:**
13 (O'Brien (inc 1 outfield +1st), 8 Wakely, 6 Willey, 5 Sales, 3 Hall, Loye, 2 Burton, Daggett, Lucas, Middlebrook, 1 Coetzer, Evans, Sweeney, White

www.northantscricket.com / tel: 01604 514455

| | Mat | Inns | NO | Runs | HS | Ave | SR | 100 | 50 | 4s | 6s |
|---|---|---|---|---|---|---|---|---|---|---|---|
| AG Wakely | 13 | 13 | 1 | 360 | 62 | 30.00 | 127.20 | 0 | 3 | 34 | 4 |
| J Botha | 13 | 13 | 1 | 245 | 54* | 20.41 | 99.59 | 0 | 1 | 19 | 3 |
| NJ O'Brien | 7 | 7 | 1 | 118 | 33 | 19.66 | 94.40 | 0 | 0 | 8 | 2 |
| RA White | 11 | 11 | 0 | 204 | 51 | 18.54 | 83.95 | 0 | 1 | 22 | 2 |
| BM Shafayat | 6 | 6 | 0 | 81 | 37 | 13.50 | 91.01 | 0 | 0 | 8 | 0 |
| D Murphy | 7 | 6 | 2 | 54 | 20 | 13.50 | 114.89 | 0 | 0 | 6 | 0 |
| SD Peters | 7 | 6 | 0 | 78 | 22 | 13.00 | 79.59 | 0 | 0 | 6 | 1 |
| RI Newton | 6 | 6 | 1 | 64 | 37 | 12.80 | 91.42 | 0 | 0 | 4 | 1 |
| AJ Hall | 11 | 10 | 2 | 93 | 28 | 11.62 | 108.13 | 0 | 0 | 8 | 1 |
| JA Brooks | 11 | 7 | 3 | 46 | 33* | 11.50 | 124.32 | 0 | 0 | 6 | 1 |
| DJ Willey | 10 | 8 | 4 | 43 | 22* | 10.75 | 107.50 | 0 | 0 | 3 | 1 |
| JD Middlebrook | 10 | 10 | 2 | 74 | 20 | 9.25 | 104.22 | 0 | 0 | 5 | 1 |
| DJG Sales | 2 | 2 | 1 | 7 | 7* | 7.00 | 77.77 | 0 | 0 | 1 | 0 |
| WPUJC Vaas | 4 | 4 | 0 | 21 | 19 | 5.25 | 52.50 | 0 | 0 | 2 | 0 |
| BHN Howgego | 1 | 1 | 0 | 3 | 3 | 3.00 | 37.50 | 0 | 0 | 0 | 0 |
| LM Daggett | 12 | 4 | 3 | 1 | 1* | 1.00 | 20.00 | 0 | 0 | 0 | 0 |
| RI Keogh | 3 | 1 | 0 | 1 | 1 | 1.00 | 14.28 | 0 | 0 | 0 | 0 |
| DS Lucas | 5 | 2 | 0 | 1 | 1 | 0.50 | 11.11 | 0 | 0 | 0 | 0 |
| OP Stone | 1 | 1 | 0 | 0 | 0 | 0.00 | 0.00 | 0 | 0 | 0 | 0 |
| L Evans | 3 | - | - | - | - | - | - | - | - | - | - |

Batting

| | Overs | Mdns | Runs | Wkts | BBI | Ave | Econ | SR | 4w | 5w |
|---|---|---|---|---|---|---|---|---|---|---|
| J Botha | 50.0 | 0 | 282 | 12 | 4/16 | 23.50 | 5.64 | 25.0 | 1 | 0 |
| DS Lucas | 16.0 | 0 | 101 | 7 | 3/19 | 14.42 | 6.31 | 13.7 | 0 | 0 |
| WPUJC Vaas | 13.0 | 1 | 88 | 2 | 1/17 | 44.00 | 6.76 | 39.0 | 0 | 0 |
| LM Daggett | 34.5 | 0 | 238 | 9 | 2/17 | 26.44 | 6.83 | 23.2 | 0 | 0 |
| JA Brooks | 33.0 | 1 | 235 | 6 | 2/23 | 39.16 | 7.12 | 33.0 | 0 | 0 |
| JD Middlebrook | 35.0 | 0 | 255 | 3 | 1/24 | 85.00 | 7.28 | 70.0 | 0 | 0 |
| DJ Willey | 17.0 | 0 | 130 | 9 | 3/31 | 14.44 | 7.64 | 11.3 | 0 | 0 |
| AJ Hall | 34.3 | 0 | 267 | 14 | 4/23 | 19.07 | 7.73 | 14.7 | 1 | 0 |
| L Evans | 9.0 | 0 | 70 | 3 | 1/15 | 23.33 | 7.77 | 18.0 | 0 | 0 |
| BM Shafayat | 1.0 | 0 | 8 | 0 | - | - | 8.00 | - | 0 | 0 |
| RI Keogh | 2.0 | 0 | 18 | 0 | - | - | 9.00 | - | 0 | 0 |
| AG Wakely | 1.0 | 0 | 18 | 0 | - | - | 18.00 | - | 0 | 0 |

Bowling

**Catches/Stumpings:**
5 O'Brien (+1st), 4 Daggett, Murphy (+2st), Wakely, Willey, 2 Keogh, Hall, Middlebrook, Shafayat, 1 Botha, Brooks, Lucas, Peters, Stone, Vaas, White

TEAM PROFILE

**NOTTINGHAMSHIRE**
COUNTY CRICKET CLUB ®

FORMED: 1841
HOME GROUND: Trent Bridge, Nottingham
ONE-DAY NAME: Outlaws
CAPTAIN: Chris Read
2011 RESULTS: CC1: 6/9; CB40: 2/7 in Group C; FL t20: Quarter-finalists
HONOURS: Championship: (6) 1907, 1929, 1981, 1987, 2005, 2010; Gillette/NatWest/C&G/FP Trophy: 1987; Benson and Hedges Cup: 1989; Sunday League: 1991

## THE LOWDOWN

Nottinghamshire were aiming to secure back-to-back County Championship titles last season, but could only register a disappointing sixth-place finish as they struggled to score runs at the top of the order. Although Alex Hales enjoyed an impressive season, scoring 1,035 runs, he could not rely on his opening partners for support. The signings of Michael Lumb and James Taylor should ensure plenty of middle-order runs though. The bowling department is less of an issue, with Andre Adams performing brilliantly last season and combining well with Luke Fletcher and Darren Pattinson. A clear priority for the Outlaws this season will be to better their second-place group-stage finish in the CB40 and improve on their FL t20 quarter-final place, with a first one-day trophy for 21 years being a priority.

### DIRECTOR OF CRICKET: MICK NEWELL

Newell spent eight years with Nottinghamshire, opening the batting for the county between 1984 and 1992. Ten years later he took control of team affairs on a temporary basis, guiding the Outlaws to the top tier of county cricket in 2007. As a result he was rewarded with a permanent role, and delivered the Division One title three years later. Newell has also played a role in the England Lions and U19 set-ups.

| | Mat | Inns | NO | Runs | HS | Ave | SR | 100 | 50 | 4s | 6s |
|---|---|---|---|---|---|---|---|---|---|---|---|
| AC Voges | 12 | 20 | 1 | 845 | 165 | 44.47 | 54.09 | 1 | 7 | 121 | 0 |
| AD Hales | 14 | 26 | 2 | 1043 | 184 | 43.45 | 65.26 | 3 | 7 | 152 | 7 |
| SR Patel | 13 | 23 | 1 | 887 | 128 | 40.31 | 59.21 | 2 | 6 | 135 | 3 |
| CMW Read | 18 | 32 | 4 | 993 | 133* | 35.46 | 58.27 | 2 | 5 | 136 | 7 |
| DM Bravo | 4 | 7 | 0 | 248 | 70 | 35.42 | 43.50 | 0 | 2 | 32 | 3 |
| AD Brown | 5 | 9 | 2 | 229 | 128* | 32.71 | 67.35 | 1 | 1 | 34 | 0 |
| PJ Franks | 15 | 27 | 3 | 695 | 96 | 28.95 | 47.83 | 0 | 5 | 105 | 1 |
| K Turner | 5 | 9 | 0 | 227 | 64 | 25.22 | 49.45 | 0 | 1 | 32 | 0 |
| AR Adams | 16 | 27 | 4 | 551 | 64 | 23.95 | 100.73 | 0 | 5 | 60 | 31 |
| DJ Pattinson | 7 | 10 | 4 | 136 | 35* | 22.66 | 51.71 | 0 | 0 | 16 | 5 |
| SJ Mullaney | 18 | 32 | 0 | 649 | 83 | 20.28 | 54.72 | 0 | 3 | 95 | 2 |
| MH Wessels | 10 | 19 | 0 | 384 | 84 | 20.21 | 56.97 | 0 | 3 | 53 | 4 |
| SCJ Broad | 3 | 5 | 0 | 97 | 26 | 19.40 | 91.50 | 0 | 0 | 10 | 3 |
| A Carter | 1 | 1 | 0 | 17 | 17 | 17.00 | 89.47 | 0 | 0 | 2 | 0 |
| MA Wagh | 9 | 18 | 2 | 268 | 48 | 16.75 | 46.68 | 0 | 0 | 41 | 2 |
| GG White | 6 | 10 | 1 | 140 | 54* | 15.55 | 48.78 | 0 | 1 | 17 | 4 |
| NJ Edwards | 8 | 16 | 3 | 184 | 64 | 14.15 | 51.25 | 0 | 1 | 30 | 0 |
| A Patel | 3 | 6 | 0 | 74 | 24 | 12.33 | 38.34 | 0 | 0 | 12 | 0 |
| LJ Fletcher | 14 | 23 | 5 | 189 | 39 | 10.50 | 54.15 | 0 | 0 | 23 | 5 |
| GP Swann | 2 | 4 | 0 | 42 | 25 | 10.50 | 56.75 | 0 | 0 | 6 | 0 |
| DJ Hussey | 1 | 2 | 0 | 18 | 13 | 9.00 | 58.06 | 0 | 0 | 2 | 0 |
| CE Shreck | 10 | 13 | 10 | 25 | 7* | 8.33 | 24.75 | 0 | 0 | 4 | 0 |
| S Kelsall | 1 | 2 | 0 | 15 | 11 | 7.50 | 41.66 | 0 | 0 | 2 | 0 |
| BA Hutton | 1 | 2 | 0 | 9 | 9 | 4.50 | 50.00 | 0 | 0 | 2 | 0 |
| JT Ball | 1 | 2 | 1 | 4 | 4 | 4.00 | 57.14 | 0 | 0 | 1 | 0 |
| BJ Phillips | 1 | 1 | 1 | 71 | 71* | - | 68.26 | 0 | 1 | 8 | 3 |

Batting

| | Overs | Mdns | Runs | Wkts | BBI | BBM | Ave | Econ | SR | 5w | 10w |
|---|---|---|---|---|---|---|---|---|---|---|---|
| A Carter | 25.0 | 9 | 63 | 3 | 2/37 | 3/63 | 21.00 | 2.52 | 50.0 | 0 | 0 |
| AR Adams | 479.3 | 93 | 1515 | 67 | 6/31 | 11/85 | 22.61 | 3.15 | 42.9 | 7 | 2 |
| DJ Pattinson | 167.1 | 36 | 529 | 20 | 5/44 | 8/90 | 26.45 | 3.16 | 50.1 | 1 | 0 |
| CE Shreck | 281.5 | 62 | 945 | 34 | 5/52 | 6/77 | 27.79 | 3.35 | 49.7 | 1 | 0 |
| SR Patel | 346.0 | 68 | 1042 | 37 | 7/68 | 11/111 | 28.16 | 3.01 | 56.1 | 1 | 1 |
| LJ Fletcher | 456.0 | 104 | 1378 | 48 | 5/82 | 8/131 | 28.70 | 3.02 | 57.0 | 1 | 0 |
| SCJ Broad | 111.3 | 24 | 384 | 11 | 5/95 | 6/162 | 34.90 | 3.44 | 60.8 | 1 | 0 |
| JT Ball | 21.0 | 1 | 106 | 3 | 3/72 | 3/106 | 35.33 | 5.04 | 42.0 | 0 | 0 |
| GG White | 119.0 | 19 | 463 | 13 | 4/72 | 7/89 | 35.61 | 3.89 | 54.9 | 0 | 0 |
| GP Swann | 42.0 | 5 | 144 | 3 | 2/69 | 2/116 | 48.00 | 3.42 | 84.0 | 0 | 0 |
| PJ Franks | 360.0 | 66 | 1215 | 25 | 4/50 | 4/83 | 48.60 | 3.37 | 86.4 | 0 | 0 |
| SJ Mullaney | 142.3 | 31 | 436 | 6 | 1/13 | 2/71 | 72.66 | 3.05 | 142.5 | 0 | 0 |
| AD Hales | 1.0 | 0 | 1 | 0 | - | - | - | 1.00 | - | 0 | 0 |
| BA Hutton | 18.0 | 3 | 69 | 0 | - | - | - | 3.83 | - | 0 | 0 |
| A Patel | 1.5 | 0 | 10 | 0 | - | - | - | 5.45 | - | 0 | 0 |
| BJ Phillips | 37.2 | 5 | 139 | 0 | - | - | - | 3.72 | - | 0 | 0 |
| SKW Wood | 4.0 | 1 | 8 | 0 | - | - | - | 2.00 | - | 0 | 0 |

Bowling

**Catches/Stumpings:**
52 Read (+4st), 20 Voges, 16 Mullaney, 14 Hales, 9 Edwards, 8 Patel, 6 Wessels, 5 Adams, Franks, Hussey, 4 White, 3 Fletcher, Wagh, 2 Brown, Shreck, 1 Bravo, Hutton, Kelsall, Pattinson, Phillips, Swann, Turner

# LIST A AVERAGES 2011

**OUTLAWS**

## Batting

| | Mat | Inns | NO | Runs | HS | Ave | SR | 100 | 50 | 4s | 6s |
|---|---|---|---|---|---|---|---|---|---|---|---|
| AC Voges | 8 | 8 | 3 | 336 | 103* | 67.20 | 107.34 | 1 | 3 | 33 | 4 |
| AD Hales | 6 | 6 | 0 | 266 | 116 | 44.33 | 120.90 | 1 | 2 | 35 | 7 |
| S Kelsall | 1 | 1 | 0 | 40 | 40 | 40.00 | 64.51 | 0 | 0 | 1 | 0 |
| CMW Read | 12 | 11 | 2 | 340 | 68* | 37.77 | 109.32 | 0 | 3 | 26 | 5 |
| SR Patel | 10 | 10 | 0 | 318 | 69 | 31.80 | 81.95 | 0 | 2 | 36 | 1 |
| DM Bravo | 3 | 3 | 0 | 94 | 62 | 31.33 | 95.91 | 0 | 1 | 11 | 1 |
| MA Wagh | 1 | 1 | 0 | 31 | 31 | 31.00 | 86.11 | 0 | 0 | 2 | 0 |
| NJ Edwards | 2 | 2 | 0 | 54 | 33 | 27.00 | 101.88 | 0 | 0 | 10 | 0 |
| MH Wessels | 10 | 10 | 0 | 239 | 57 | 23.90 | 105.75 | 0 | 2 | 27 | 9 |
| SL Elstone | 9 | 9 | 1 | 185 | 40 | 23.12 | 102.77 | 0 | 0 | 12 | 6 |
| SJ Mullaney | 12 | 11 | 0 | 232 | 61 | 21.09 | 87.54 | 0 | 2 | 19 | 4 |
| BA Hutton | 2 | 2 | 1 | 20 | 17* | 20.00 | 117.64 | 0 | 0 | 0 | 1 |
| A Patel | 4 | 4 | 0 | 79 | 35 | 19.75 | 77.45 | 0 | 0 | 11 | 2 |
| BJ Phillips | 12 | 9 | 4 | 96 | 16* | 19.20 | 100.00 | 0 | 0 | 7 | 3 |
| AD Brown | 6 | 6 | 1 | 94 | 27 | 18.80 | 96.90 | 0 | 0 | 14 | 0 |
| GG White | 7 | 4 | 1 | 52 | 25 | 17.33 | 96.29 | 0 | 0 | 4 | 1 |
| PJ Franks | 10 | 8 | 4 | 67 | 28* | 16.75 | 89.33 | 0 | 0 | 8 | 0 |
| K Turner | 2 | 2 | 0 | 22 | 18 | 11.00 | 100.00 | 0 | 0 | 4 | 0 |
| LJ Fletcher | 6 | 2 | 0 | 18 | 16 | 9.00 | 138.46 | 0 | 0 | 0 | 2 |
| DJ Pattinson | 9 | 3 | 2 | 9 | 7 | 9.00 | 112.50 | 0 | 0 | 1 | 0 |
| AR Adams | 2 | 2 | 0 | 7 | 7 | 3.50 | 140.00 | 0 | 0 | 0 | 1 |
| SKW Wood | 4 | 3 | 0 | 8 | 8 | 2.66 | 47.05 | 0 | 0 | 0 | 0 |
| JT Ball | 5 | 3 | 3 | 35 | 19* | - | 152.17 | 0 | 0 | 5 | 0 |

## Bowling

| | Overs | Mdns | Runs | Wkts | BBI | Ave | Econ | SR | 4w | 5w |
|---|---|---|---|---|---|---|---|---|---|---|
| AR Adams | 13.0 | 0 | 58 | 3 | 2/23 | 19.33 | 4.46 | 26.0 | 0 | 0 |
| PJ Franks | 56.5 | 2 | 300 | 17 | 5/43 | 17.64 | 5.27 | 20.0 | 0 | 1 |
| SJ Mullaney | 61.0 | 0 | 325 | 8 | 2/42 | 40.62 | 5.32 | 45.7 | 0 | 0 |
| SR Patel | 64.0 | 3 | 357 | 10 | 4/37 | 35.70 | 5.57 | 38.4 | 1 | 0 |
| DJ Pattinson | 53.0 | 4 | 302 | 12 | 3/45 | 25.16 | 5.69 | 26.5 | 0 | 0 |
| GG White | 26.4 | 0 | 168 | 3 | 1/19 | 56.00 | 6.30 | 53.3 | 0 | 0 |
| SKW Wood | 11.0 | 0 | 72 | 3 | 2/24 | 24.00 | 6.54 | 22.0 | 0 | 0 |
| BJ Phillips | 69.0 | 3 | 457 | 6 | 1/17 | 76.16 | 6.62 | 69.0 | 0 | 0 |
| LJ Fletcher | 42.2 | 0 | 286 | 8 | 3/27 | 35.75 | 6.75 | 31.7 | 0 | 0 |
| JT Ball | 27.0 | 1 | 189 | 2 | 1/35 | 94.50 | 7.00 | 81.0 | 0 | 0 |
| BA Hutton | 14.0 | 0 | 101 | 1 | 1/60 | 101.00 | 7.21 | 84.0 | 0 | 0 |

**Catches/Stumpings:**
6 Read (+1st), 5 Mullaney, Patel, 3 Hales, Phillips, Wessels, 2 Bravo, Elstone, Franks, Pattinson, Voges, Wood, 1 Adams, Brown, Edwards, Fletcher, Hutton

## OUTLAWS

| | Mat | Inns | NO | Runs | HS | Ave | SR | 100 | 50 | 4s | 6s |
|---|---|---|---|---|---|---|---|---|---|---|---|
| DJ Hussey | 10 | 10 | 1 | 357 | 73 | 39.66 | 168.39 | 0 | 4 | 26 | 15 |
| AD Hales | 16 | 16 | 0 | 544 | 78 | 34.00 | 146.63 | 0 | 5 | 65 | 14 |
| AC Voges | 16 | 16 | 0 | 484 | 74 | 30.25 | 135.19 | 0 | 2 | 52 | 2 |
| CMW Read | 15 | 15 | 8 | 199 | 34* | 28.42 | 136.30 | 0 | 0 | 11 | 6 |
| SR Patel | 13 | 13 | 2 | 287 | 70* | 26.09 | 141.37 | 0 | 2 | 25 | 10 |
| MH Wessels | 16 | 16 | 0 | 392 | 76 | 24.50 | 136.11 | 0 | 2 | 43 | 12 |
| Tamim Iqbal | 5 | 5 | 0 | 104 | 47 | 20.80 | 110.63 | 0 | 0 | 11 | 3 |
| SL Elstone | 15 | 13 | 8 | 91 | 21* | 18.20 | 135.82 | 0 | 0 | 8 | 1 |
| SJ Mullaney | 16 | 12 | 3 | 162 | 35* | 18.00 | 140.86 | 0 | 0 | 16 | 2 |
| AR Adams | 6 | 3 | 2 | 18 | 8* | 18.00 | 200.00 | 0 | 0 | 2 | 1 |
| LJ Fletcher | 13 | 3 | 2 | 5 | 5 | 5.00 | 62.50 | 0 | 0 | 1 | 0 |
| DJ Pattinson | 16 | 4 | 4 | 13 | 12* | - | 185.71 | 0 | 0 | 2 | 0 |
| BJ Phillips | 4 | 1 | 1 | 2 | 2* | - | 100.00 | 0 | 0 | 0 | 0 |
| JT Ball | 1 | - | - | - | - | - | - | - | - | - | - |
| A Carter | 8 | - | - | - | - | - | - | - | - | - | - |
| GG White | 6 | - | - | - | - | - | - | - | - | - | - |

*Batting*

| | Overs | Mdns | Runs | Wkts | BBI | Ave | Econ | SR | 4w | 5w |
|---|---|---|---|---|---|---|---|---|---|---|
| AC Voges | 5.0 | 0 | 34 | 0 | - | - | 6.80 | - | 0 | 0 |
| SR Patel | 47.0 | 0 | 340 | 10 | 2/27 | 34.00 | 7.23 | 28.2 | 0 | 0 |
| GG White | 14.0 | 0 | 103 | 5 | 2/26 | 20.60 | 7.35 | 16.8 | 0 | 0 |
| AR Adams | 21.4 | 0 | 160 | 7 | 2/19 | 22.85 | 7.38 | 18.5 | 0 | 0 |
| BJ Phillips | 10.3 | 0 | 78 | 3 | 2/31 | 26.00 | 7.42 | 21.0 | 0 | 0 |
| LJ Fletcher | 43.0 | 1 | 327 | 17 | 4/30 | 19.23 | 7.60 | 15.1 | 1 | 0 |
| SJ Mullaney | 47.0 | 0 | 368 | 10 | 3/26 | 36.80 | 7.82 | 28.2 | 0 | 0 |
| DJ Pattinson | 49.1 | 0 | 400 | 23 | 5/25 | 17.39 | 8.13 | 12.8 | 0 | 1 |
| A Carter | 26.5 | 0 | 229 | 9 | 4/20 | 25.44 | 8.53 | 17.8 | 1 | 0 |
| DJ Hussey | 7.0 | 0 | 72 | 3 | 1/9 | 24.00 | 10.28 | 14.0 | 0 | 0 |
| JT Ball | 1.0 | 0 | 11 | 0 | - | - | 11.00 | - | 0 | 0 |
| AD Hales | 0.1 | 0 | 2 | 0 | - | - | 12.00 | - | 0 | 0 |

*Bowling*

**Catches/Stumpings:**
5 Read (+5st), 8 Mullaney, 7 Elstone, Voges, 6 Hussey, 5 Fletcher, 3 Carter, Hales, Pattinson, Wessels, 2 Tamim Iqbal, 1 Adams, Patel

TEAM PROFILE

SOMERSET
CRICKET CLUB

FORMED: 1875
HOME GROUND: County Ground, Taunton
CAPTAIN: Marcus Trescothick
2011 RESULTS: CC1: 4/9; CB40: Finalists; FL t20: Finalists
HONOURS: Gillette/NatWest/C&G/FP Trophy: (3) 1979, 1983, 2001; Benson and Hedges Cup: (2) 1981, 1982; Sunday League: 1979; Twenty20 Cup: 2005

### THE LOWDOWN

Runners-up for successive seasons in the CB40 and FL t20 competitions, Somerset struggled to shed their bridesmaid tag. Favoured for both limited-overs competitions in 2011, they were unable to deliver at the last. The signings of Chris Gayle and Albie Morkel for the FL t20 competition signals their intent, with Gayle joining captain Marcus Trescothick to form an opening partnership which will have bowlers up and down the country quaking in their boots. While Craig Kieswetter and Jos Buttler may be away with England for some of the season, a batting line-up containing James Hildreth, Nick Compton and Peter Trego looks well equipped to cope, and having secured the services of the highly impressive Vernon Philander for April and May, they have more than enough ammunition to be in the running for all three competitions once again.

### HEAD COACH: ANDY HURRY

The former Royal Marines fitness instructor joined Somerset in 2001 as fitness coach, introducing a modern regime including yoga to improve player fitness. Four years later he was appointed 2nd XI coach, before leaving to take on a coaching role with the UAE. Hurry spent only a year on foreign soil though, returning to Somerset in 2006 to assume control of the first team after Mark Garraway left to join England's coaching staff.

|  | Mat | Inns | NO | Runs | HS | Ave | SR | 100 | 50 | 4s | 6s |
|---|---|---|---|---|---|---|---|---|---|---|---|
| AJ Strauss | 1 | 2 | 1 | 187 | 109* | 187.00 | 80.25 | 1 | 1 | 34 | 1 |
| ME Trescothick | 13 | 23 | 2 | 1673 | 227 | 79.66 | 69.94 | 6 | 6 | 242 | 18 |
| NRD Compton | 14 | 23 | 4 | 1098 | 254* | 57.78 | 47.51 | 2 | 6 | 124 | 1 |
| C Kieswetter | 9 | 14 | 0 | 572 | 164 | 40.85 | 64.48 | 2 | 3 | 68 | 6 |
| JC Hildreth | 16 | 25 | 1 | 923 | 186 | 38.45 | 63.26 | 2 | 4 | 129 | 6 |
| AV Suppiah | 17 | 31 | 3 | 961 | 156 | 34.32 | 52.91 | 1 | 6 | 133 | 4 |
| AC Thomas | 8 | 10 | 0 | 333 | 94 | 33.30 | 46.90 | 0 | 1 | 44 | 2 |
| PD Trego | 17 | 26 | 5 | 676 | 120 | 32.19 | 71.91 | 1 | 4 | 80 | 15 |
| JC Buttler | 13 | 18 | 1 | 524 | 100 | 30.82 | 58.94 | 1 | 3 | 83 | 5 |
| M Kartik | 8 | 13 | 3 | 285 | 65* | 28.50 | 60.25 | 0 | 2 | 33 | 6 |
| CAJ Meschede | 5 | 8 | 1 | 149 | 53 | 21.28 | 46.13 | 0 | 1 | 16 | 3 |
| AJ Dibble | 2 | 4 | 2 | 40 | 39* | 20.00 | 59.70 | 0 | 0 | 5 | 2 |
| AWR Barrow | 7 | 11 | 0 | 218 | 69 | 19.81 | 47.70 | 0 | 1 | 32 | 0 |
| CR Jones | 8 | 12 | 1 | 169 | 55 | 15.36 | 37.72 | 0 | 2 | 28 | 0 |
| L Gregory | 5 | 8 | 1 | 98 | 48 | 14.00 | 45.58 | 0 | 0 | 16 | 0 |
| GH Dockrell | 1 | 1 | 0 | 14 | 14 | 14.00 | 43.75 | 0 | 0 | 2 | 0 |
| BAW Mendis | 2 | 4 | 0 | 52 | 28 | 13.00 | 100.00 | 0 | 0 | 8 | 1 |
| SP Kirby | 16 | 24 | 3 | 143 | 19 | 6.80 | 30.62 | 0 | 0 | 21 | 1 |
| GM Hussain | 9 | 14 | 2 | 75 | 42 | 6.25 | 26.40 | 0 | 0 | 10 | 0 |
| CM Willoughby | 15 | 19 | 8 | 50 | 23* | 4.54 | 56.81 | 0 | 0 | 8 | 1 |
| SD Snell | 1 | 1 | 0 | 4 | 4 | 4.00 | 44.44 | 0 | 0 | 0 | 0 |
| MTC Waller | 1 | - | - | - | - | - | - | - | - | - | - |

*Batting*

|  | Overs | Mdns | Runs | Wkts | BBI | BBM | Ave | Econ | SR | 5w | 10w |
|---|---|---|---|---|---|---|---|---|---|---|---|
| AC Thomas | 236.5 | 44 | 840 | 33 | 6/60 | 10/88 | 25.45 | 3.54 | 43.0 | 2 | 1 |
| MTC Waller | 5.2 | 0 | 28 | 1 | 1/7 | 1/28 | 28.00 | 5.25 | 32.0 | 0 | 0 |
| SP Kirby | 490.5 | 89 | 1672 | 53 | 6/115 | 6/115 | 31.54 | 3.40 | 55.5 | 1 | 0 |
| CM Willoughby | 507.3 | 106 | 1721 | 53 | 6/76 | 6/92 | 32.47 | 3.39 | 57.4 | 1 | 0 |
| M Kartik | 322.2 | 75 | 893 | 26 | 5/137 | 6/109 | 34.34 | 2.77 | 74.3 | 1 | 0 |
| AWR Barrow | 7.0 | 0 | 36 | 1 | 1/4 | 1/4 | 36.00 | 5.14 | 42.0 | 0 | 0 |
| GH Dockrell | 18.0 | 1 | 76 | 2 | 2/76 | 2/76 | 38.00 | 4.22 | 54.0 | 0 | 0 |
| PD Trego | 293.4 | 43 | 1078 | 28 | 4/22 | 7/93 | 38.50 | 3.67 | 62.9 | 0 | 0 |
| AV Suppiah | 149.1 | 29 | 447 | 10 | 2/16 | 2/16 | 44.70 | 2.99 | 89.5 | 0 | 0 |
| GM Hussain | 247.1 | 41 | 987 | 22 | 6/33 | 6/70 | 44.86 | 3.99 | 67.4 | 1 | 0 |
| L Gregory | 48.0 | 2 | 222 | 4 | 1/15 | 1/38 | 55.50 | 4.62 | 72.0 | 0 | 0 |
| CAJ Meschede | 34.1 | 5 | 141 | 2 | 1/14 | 1/37 | 70.50 | 4.12 | 102.5 | 0 | 0 |
| AJ Dibble | 36.0 | 4 | 142 | 2 | 1/26 | 1/57 | 71.00 | 3.94 | 108.0 | 0 | 0 |
| BAW Mendis | 66.1 | 3 | 285 | 4 | 4/183 | 4/183 | 71.25 | 4.30 | 99.2 | 0 | 0 |

*Bowling*

**Catches/Stumpings:**
31 Buttler (inc 3 outfield +1st), 29 Trescothick, 27 Kieswetter (+1st), 22 Hildreth, 11 Suppiah, 10 Trego, 5 Compton, Jones, Kirby, 4 Barrow, Kartik, 2 Hussain, Willoughby

**SOMERSET**
CRICKET CLUB

### Batting

| | Mat | Inns | NO | Runs | HS | Ave | SR | 100 | 50 | 4s | 6s |
|---|---|---|---|---|---|---|---|---|---|---|---|
| JC Buttler | 13 | 10 | 7 | 411 | 94* | 137.00 | 133.44 | 0 | 4 | 45 | 10 |
| CR Jones | 2 | 2 | 1 | 78 | 45* | 78.00 | 89.65 | 0 | 0 | 10 | 0 |
| C Kieswetter | 10 | 9 | 2 | 399 | 108* | 57.00 | 96.84 | 2 | 1 | 35 | 10 |
| NRD Compton | 12 | 10 | 3 | 280 | 104 | 40.00 | 78.21 | 1 | 0 | 19 | 3 |
| ME Trescothick | 12 | 11 | 2 | 338 | 111* | 37.55 | 113.04 | 1 | 2 | 44 | 4 |
| PD Trego | 14 | 13 | 1 | 444 | 100 | 37.00 | 105.96 | 1 | 2 | 45 | 13 |
| JC Hildreth | 14 | 11 | 2 | 268 | 50* | 29.77 | 87.01 | 0 | 1 | 32 | 0 |
| AV Suppiah | 14 | 7 | 2 | 131 | 57 | 26.20 | 110.08 | 0 | 1 | 14 | 1 |
| M Kartik | 5 | 3 | 0 | 74 | 40 | 24.66 | 96.10 | 0 | 0 | 9 | 2 |
| AC Thomas | 9 | 3 | 0 | 46 | 22 | 15.33 | 67.64 | 0 | 0 | 4 | 0 |
| CAJ Meschede | 9 | 5 | 0 | 66 | 19 | 13.20 | 80.48 | 0 | 0 | 5 | 0 |
| L Gregory | 7 | 2 | 0 | 12 | 11 | 6.00 | 50.00 | 0 | 0 | 1 | 0 |
| SD Snell | 1 | 1 | 1 | 18 | 18* | - | 128.57 | 0 | 0 | 2 | 0 |
| GM Hussain | 4 | 1 | 1 | 16 | 16* | - | 114.28 | 0 | 0 | 0 | 1 |
| MTC Waller | 6 | 2 | 2 | 1 | 1* | - | 33.33 | 0 | 0 | 0 | 0 |
| SP Kirby | 9 | 1 | 1 | 0 | 0* | - | 0.00 | 0 | 0 | 0 | 0 |
| AJ Dibble | 4 | - | - | - | - | - | - | - | - | - | - |
| GH Dockrell | 5 | - | - | - | - | - | - | - | - | - | - |
| BAW Mendis | 4 | - | - | - | - | - | - | - | - | - | - |

### Bowling

| | Overs | Mdns | Runs | Wkts | BBI | Ave | Econ | SR | 4w | 5w |
|---|---|---|---|---|---|---|---|---|---|---|
| GH Dockrell | 30.0 | 0 | 133 | 5 | 3/27 | 26.60 | 4.43 | 36.0 | 0 | 0 |
| AV Suppiah | 45.3 | 0 | 207 | 9 | 2/2 | 23.00 | 4.54 | 30.3 | 0 | 0 |
| BAW Mendis | 27.0 | 1 | 135 | 8 | 4/35 | 16.87 | 5.00 | 20.2 | 1 | 0 |
| AC Thomas | 48.2 | 0 | 252 | 7 | 2/36 | 36.00 | 5.21 | 41.4 | 0 | 0 |
| MTC Waller | 28.4 | 0 | 156 | 5 | 1/14 | 31.20 | 5.44 | 34.4 | 0 | 0 |
| CAJ Meschede | 28.0 | 0 | 160 | 5 | 2/16 | 32.00 | 5.71 | 33.6 | 0 | 0 |
| L Gregory | 32.0 | 0 | 189 | 13 | 4/27 | 14.53 | 5.90 | 14.7 | 2 | 0 |
| PD Trego | 60.0 | 1 | 355 | 10 | 3/33 | 35.50 | 5.91 | 36.0 | 0 | 0 |
| M Kartik | 32.0 | 2 | 191 | 5 | 2/24 | 38.20 | 5.96 | 38.4 | 0 | 0 |
| AJ Dibble | 26.0 | 1 | 170 | 5 | 3/52 | 34.00 | 6.53 | 31.2 | 0 | 0 |
| SP Kirby | 47.2 | 1 | 321 | 20 | 3/24 | 16.05 | 6.78 | 14.2 | 0 | 0 |
| GM Hussain | 25.0 | 0 | 182 | 3 | 2/40 | 60.66 | 7.28 | 50.0 | 0 | 0 |

**Catches/Stumpings:**
10 Kieswetter (+0st), 7 Buttler (inc 3 outfield + 0st), Hildreth, 5 Suppiah, Trego Trescothick, 4 Kartik, Meschede, 3 Compton, Dockrell, 2 Hussain, Snell (+0st), 1 Gregory, Kirby, Mendis, Waller

www.somersetcountycc.co.uk / tel: 0845 337 1875

## SOMERSET
### CRICKET CLUB

| | Mat | Inns | NO | Runs | HS | Ave | SR | 100 | 50 | 4s | 6s |
|---|---|---|---|---|---|---|---|---|---|---|---|
| RE van der Merwe | 5 | 4 | 1 | 169 | 89* | 56.33 | 169.00 | 0 | 2 | 12 | 12 |
| ME Trescothick | 16 | 16 | 3 | 507 | 108* | 39.00 | 162.50 | 1 | 3 | 65 | 19 |
| KA Pollard | 11 | 10 | 4 | 234 | 47* | 39.00 | 162.50 | 0 | 0 | 17 | 11 |
| NRD Compton | 2 | 1 | 0 | 37 | 37 | 37.00 | 94.87 | 0 | 0 | 2 | 1 |
| JC Hildreth | 16 | 15 | 3 | 346 | 64* | 28.83 | 120.13 | 0 | 2 | 28 | 5 |
| C Kieswetter | 7 | 7 | 0 | 166 | 59 | 23.71 | 137.19 | 0 | 1 | 23 | 4 |
| JC Buttler | 16 | 14 | 3 | 259 | 72* | 23.54 | 148.00 | 0 | 1 | 21 | 12 |
| M Kartik | 16 | 6 | 3 | 63 | 25* | 21.00 | 112.50 | 0 | 0 | 5 | 1 |
| PD Trego | 16 | 16 | 1 | 304 | 55 | 20.26 | 122.08 | 0 | 1 | 28 | 10 |
| CAJ Meschede | 12 | 9 | 1 | 125 | 53 | 15.62 | 119.04 | 0 | 1 | 10 | 6 |
| AV Suppiah | 16 | 9 | 4 | 75 | 23* | 15.00 | 102.73 | 0 | 0 | 3 | 1 |
| SP Kirby | 14 | 4 | 3 | 8 | 7 | 8.00 | 100.00 | 0 | 0 | 1 | 0 |
| AC Thomas | 5 | 1 | 0 | 7 | 7 | 7.00 | 87.50 | 0 | 0 | 0 | 0 |
| L Gregory | 12 | 5 | 1 | 27 | 15 | 6.75 | 69.23 | 0 | 0 | 0 | 0 |
| MTC Waller | 8 | 2 | 1 | 5 | 3 | 5.00 | 62.50 | 0 | 0 | 0 | 0 |
| GM Hussain | 3 | 1 | 0 | 4 | 4 | 4.00 | 28.57 | 0 | 0 | 0 | 0 |
| GH Dockrell | 1 | - | - | - | - | - | - | - | - | - | - |

Batting

| | Overs | Mdns | Runs | Wkts | BBI | Ave | Econ | SR | 4w | 5w |
|---|---|---|---|---|---|---|---|---|---|---|
| AV Suppiah | 26.4 | 0 | 150 | 14 | 6/5 | 10.71 | 5.62 | 11.4 | 0 | 1 |
| M Kartik | 56.0 | 0 | 353 | 17 | 2/7 | 20.76 | 6.30 | 19.7 | 0 | 0 |
| MTC Waller | 22.0 | 0 | 140 | 9 | 2/20 | 15.55 | 6.36 | 14.6 | 0 | 0 |
| RE van der Merwe | 16.0 | 0 | 124 | 4 | 2/15 | 31.00 | 7.75 | 24.0 | 0 | 0 |
| CAJ Meschede | 10.3 | 0 | 82 | 6 | 3/9 | 13.66 | 7.80 | 10.5 | 0 | 0 |
| SP Kirby | 33.1 | 1 | 273 | 8 | 2/17 | 34.12 | 8.23 | 24.8 | 0 | 0 |
| L Gregory | 37.0 | 1 | 306 | 18 | 4/15 | 17.00 | 8.27 | 12.3 | 1 | 0 |
| PD Trego | 14.3 | 0 | 121 | 4 | 2/24 | 30.25 | 8.34 | 21.7 | 0 | 0 |
| AC Thomas | 18.5 | 0 | 160 | 5 | 2/25 | 32.00 | 8.49 | 22.6 | 0 | 0 |
| KA Pollard | 37.3 | 0 | 323 | 12 | 3/25 | 26.91 | 8.61 | 18.7 | 0 | 0 |
| GM Hussain | 9.0 | 0 | 78 | 5 | 3/40 | 15.60 | 8.66 | 10.8 | 0 | 0 |
| GH Dockrell | 2.0 | 0 | 19 | 1 | 1/19 | 19.00 | 9.50 | 12.0 | 0 | 0 |

Bowling

**Catches/Stumpings:**
9 Pollard, 8 Buttler (inc 6 outfield +5st), Hildreth, 7 Kieswetter (+1st), 6 Gregory, 5 Trego, 4 Kartik, Kirby, Suppiah, Trescothick, van der Merwe, Waller, 2 Meschede, 1 Thomas

TEAM PROFILE

**FORMED:** 1845
**GROUND:** The Kia Oval
**ONE-DAY NAME:** Lions
**CAPTAIN:** Rory Hamilton-Brown
**2011 RESULTS:** CC2: 2/9; CB40: Champions; FL t20: 5/9 in South Group
**HONOURS:** Championship: (19) 1890, 1891, 1892, 1894, 1895, 1899, 1914, 1950, 1952, 1953, 1954, 1955, 1956, 1957, 1958, 1971, 1999, 2000, 2002; Gillette/NatWest/C&G/FP Trophy: 1982; Benson and Hedges Cup: (3) 1974, 1997, 2001; Pro40/National League/CB40: (2) 2003, 2011; Sunday League: 1996; Twenty20 Cup: 2003

### THE LOWDOWN

After promising to rebuild the Surrey squad at the start of his tenure, Chris Adams led his side to a promotion and a CB40 title last season. With the likes of Jason Roy, Tom Maynard, Steve Davies and Rory Hamilton-Brown in their ranks, Surrey aren't short of exciting young batting talent, whilst the addition of Jacques Rudolph for the start of the season will add both experience and quality. With the ball, Jade Dernbach and Stuart Meaker appear ready for the challenge of Division One cricket, while Murali Kartik will add real value towards the back end of the season. The Lions look a good bet to make the knockout stages of the FL t20 this year, and their chances will only be improved by the re-signing of short-form specialist and former Aussie international Dirk Nannes.

### PROFESSIONAL CRICKET MANAGER: CHRIS ADAMS

Renowned for his achievements in the domestic game as a player, Adams also represented his country, playing five Tests and five ODIs for England. A dependable runscorer for Derbyshire in his earlier career, he moved to Sussex where he masterminded their maiden County Championship success in 2003. He retired at the end of the 2008 season as Sussex's longest-serving captain, immediately moving into coaching at Surrey, where he has recruited a number of former Surrey stars to his staff.

| | Mat | Inns | NO | Runs | HS | Ave | SR | 100 | 50 | 4s | 6s |
|---|---|---|---|---|---|---|---|---|---|---|---|
| CP Schofield | 3 | 4 | 1 | 179 | 99 | 59.66 | 84.83 | 0 | 1 | 22 | 4 |
| Z de Bruyn | 16 | 27 | 2 | 1383 | 179 | 55.32 | 59.76 | 4 | 9 | 194 | 9 |
| KP Pietersen | 2 | 3 | 0 | 136 | 58 | 45.33 | 77.27 | 0 | 1 | 16 | 4 |
| TL Maynard | 16 | 28 | 3 | 1022 | 141 | 40.88 | 68.82 | 3 | 3 | 123 | 13 |
| SM Davies | 16 | 27 | 1 | 1035 | 156 | 39.80 | 58.84 | 2 | 5 | 143 | 3 |
| RJ Hamilton-Brown | 16 | 30 | 2 | 1039 | 159 | 37.10 | 78.29 | 1 | 5 | 163 | 9 |
| MR Ramprakash | 13 | 23 | 2 | 700 | 141 | 33.33 | 51.35 | 1 | 3 | 92 | 0 |
| A Harinath | 2 | 4 | 0 | 128 | 80 | 32.00 | 46.37 | 0 | 1 | 16 | 1 |
| TM Jewell | 2 | 3 | 0 | 92 | 61 | 30.66 | 53.17 | 0 | 1 | 12 | 0 |
| JJ Roy | 12 | 22 | 1 | 623 | 106* | 29.66 | 83.96 | 1 | 1 | 83 | 9 |
| CJ Jordan | 7 | 9 | 1 | 228 | 79* | 28.50 | 48.61 | 0 | 2 | 22 | 1 |
| Yasir Arafat | 8 | 11 | 2 | 255 | 65 | 28.33 | 60.00 | 0 | 1 | 33 | 1 |
| GJ Batty | 16 | 24 | 4 | 532 | 79 | 26.60 | 55.70 | 0 | 4 | 73 | 3 |
| RJ Burns | 1 | 2 | 0 | 35 | 26 | 17.50 | 45.45 | 0 | 0 | 4 | 0 |
| TJ Lancefield | 1 | 2 | 0 | 35 | 35 | 17.50 | 28.68 | 0 | 0 | 4 | 0 |
| MNW Spriegel | 1 | 2 | 0 | 34 | 30 | 17.00 | 79.06 | 0 | 0 | 5 | 0 |
| GC Wilson | 4 | 7 | 0 | 110 | 42 | 15.71 | 37.67 | 0 | 0 | 16 | 0 |
| CT Tremlett | 3 | 4 | 1 | 47 | 17 | 15.66 | 51.08 | 0 | 0 | 6 | 2 |
| MJ Brown | 3 | 5 | 0 | 78 | 46 | 15.60 | 40.20 | 0 | 0 | 11 | 0 |
| GA Edwards | 1 | 2 | 0 | 29 | 19 | 14.50 | 34.11 | 0 | 0 | 5 | 0 |
| SC Meaker | 10 | 12 | 1 | 143 | 55* | 13.00 | 34.62 | 0 | 1 | 20 | 1 |
| JW Dernbach | 9 | 11 | 4 | 51 | 19 | 7.28 | 61.44 | 0 | 0 | 8 | 2 |
| ZS Ansari | 3 | 6 | 0 | 43 | 21 | 7.16 | 38.39 | 0 | 0 | 4 | 0 |
| SJ King | 1 | 2 | 0 | 13 | 13 | 6.50 | 39.39 | 0 | 0 | 2 | 0 |
| TE Linley | 14 | 24 | 5 | 122 | 21 | 6.42 | 30.88 | 0 | 0 | 13 | 2 |
| PP Ojha | 4 | 5 | 3 | 12 | 5* | 6.00 | 37.50 | 0 | 0 | 0 | 0 |
| FOE van den Bergh | 1 | 1 | 0 | 0 | 0 | 0.00 | 0.00 | 0 | 0 | 0 | 0 |
| MP Dunn | 3 | 5 | 5 | 3 | 2* | - | 11.53 | 0 | 0 | 0 | 0 |

*Batting*

| | Overs | Mdns | Runs | Wkts | BBI | BBM | Ave | Econ | SR | 5w | 10w |
|---|---|---|---|---|---|---|---|---|---|---|---|
| PP Ojha | 150.4 | 52 | 311 | 24 | 6/8 | 10/90 | 12.95 | 2.06 | 37.6 | 2 | 1 |
| TE Linley | 482.3 | 102 | 1339 | 73 | 6/57 | 10/107 | 18.34 | 2.77 | 39.6 | 2 | 1 |
| TM Jewell | 30.4 | 5 | 117 | 6 | 5/49 | 5/49 | 19.50 | 3.81 | 30.6 | 1 | 0 |
| JJ Roy | 6.2 | 0 | 43 | 2 | 2/29 | 2/43 | 21.50 | 6.78 | 19.0 | 0 | 0 |
| SC Meaker | 279.1 | 48 | 993 | 44 | 5/37 | 8/81 | 22.56 | 3.55 | 38.0 | 3 | 0 |
| ZS Ansari | 50.0 | 6 | 158 | 6 | 2/39 | 2/39 | 26.33 | 3.16 | 50.0 | 0 | 0 |
| FOE van den | 24.0 | 5 | 79 | 3 | 3/79 | 3/79 | 26.33 | 3.29 | 48.0 | 0 | 0 |
| KP Pietersen | 14.0 | 3 | 27 | 1 | 1/24 | 1/24 | 27.00 | 1.92 | 84.0 | 0 | 0 |
| MNW Spriegel | 17.0 | 1 | 56 | 2 | 2/56 | 2/56 | 28.00 | 3.29 | 51.0 | 0 | 0 |
| MP Dunn | 39.1 | 4 | 193 | 6 | 5/56 | 5/68 | 32.16 | 4.92 | 39.1 | 1 | 0 |
| GJ Batty | 390.5 | 69 | 1200 | 36 | 5/76 | 6/124 | 33.33 | 3.07 | 65.1 | 1 | 0 |
| Z de Bruyn | 189.0 | 38 | 589 | 15 | 3/39 | 4/90 | 39.26 | 3.11 | 75.6 | 0 | 0 |
| JW Dernbach | 307.1 | 71 | 872 | 22 | 5/41 | 7/92 | 39.63 | 2.83 | 83.7 | 1 | 0 |
| CP Schofield | 72.0 | 13 | 230 | 5 | 2/57 | 2/73 | 46.00 | 3.19 | 86.4 | 0 | 0 |
| Yasir Arafat | 276.0 | 56 | 948 | 20 | 5/86 | 7/162 | 47.40 | 3.43 | 82.8 | 1 | 0 |
| CJ Jordan | 144.0 | 26 | 528 | 11 | 4/57 | 4/71 | 48.00 | 3.66 | 78.5 | 0 | 0 |
| CT Tremlett | 96.0 | 20 | 306 | 6 | 2/19 | 3/152 | 51.00 | 3.18 | 96.0 | 0 | 0 |
| RJ Hamilton-Brown | 25.5 | 2 | 107 | 1 | 1/19 | 1/19 | 107.00 | 4.14 | 155.0 | 0 | 0 |
| TL Maynard | 2.0 | 0 | 7 | 0 | - | - | - | 3.50 | - | 0 | 0 |
| SJ King | 18.0 | 2 | 81 | 0 | - | - | - | 4.50 | - | 0 | 0 |
| GA Edwards | 18.3 | 3 | 82 | 0 | - | - | - | 4.43 | - | 0 | 0 |

*Bowling*

**Catches/Stumpings:**
53 Davies (+2st), 20 Batty, 14 Maynard, 12 Hamilton-Brown, 11 Roy, 10 Ramprakash, 7 de Bruyn, 4 Linley, 3 Dernbach, Jordan, Wilson, 2 Burns (+0st), Meaker, Yasir Arafat, 1 Ansari, Edwards, Lancefield, Pietersen, Spriegel

### Batting

|  | Mat | Inns | NO | Runs | HS | Ave | SR | 100 | 50 | 4s | 6s |
|---|---|---|---|---|---|---|---|---|---|---|---|
| MNW Spriegel | 13 | 12 | 4 | 424 | 86 | 53.00 | 106.53 | 0 | 3 | 35 | 10 |
| JJ Roy | 13 | 13 | 0 | 585 | 131 | 45.00 | 111.00 | 2 | 4 | 59 | 12 |
| TL Maynard | 13 | 13 | 1 | 481 | 79 | 40.08 | 106.88 | 0 | 5 | 35 | 10 |
| CP Schofield | 13 | 12 | 5 | 246 | 72 | 35.14 | 105.57 | 0 | 1 | 20 | 6 |
| Z de Bruyn | 13 | 13 | 3 | 328 | 84* | 32.80 | 83.88 | 0 | 1 | 26 | 2 |
| SM Davies | 13 | 13 | 0 | 395 | 96 | 30.38 | 110.64 | 0 | 2 | 57 | 4 |
| RJ Hamilton-Brown | 13 | 13 | 0 | 372 | 78 | 28.61 | 120.77 | 0 | 3 | 54 | 4 |
| ZS Ansari | 7 | 5 | 3 | 47 | 22 | 23.50 | 114.63 | 0 | 0 | 1 | 2 |
| Yasir Arafat | 12 | 9 | 5 | 85 | 30* | 21.25 | 106.25 | 0 | 0 | 6 | 1 |
| GJ Batty | 10 | 5 | 1 | 29 | 14 | 7.25 | 70.73 | 0 | 0 | 3 | 0 |
| SC Meaker | 3 | 2 | 1 | 6 | 5 | 6.00 | 46.15 | 0 | 0 | 0 | 0 |
| CJ Jordan | 2 | 1 | 0 | 0 | 0 | 0.00 | 0.00 | 0 | 0 | 0 | 0 |
| GC Wilson | 2 | 1 | 0 | 0 | 0 | 0.00 | 0.00 | 0 | 0 | 0 | 0 |
| PP Ojha | 1 | 1 | 1 | 1 | 1* | - | 50.00 | 0 | 0 | 0 | 0 |
| TE Linley | 6 | 1 | 1 | 0 | 0* | - | - | 0 | 0 | 0 | 0 |
| JW Dernbach | 8 | - | - | - | - | - | - | - | - | - | - |

### Bowling

|  | Overs | Mdns | Runs | Wkts | BBI | Ave | Econ | SR | 4w | 5w |
|---|---|---|---|---|---|---|---|---|---|---|
| GJ Batty | 63.0 | 1 | 301 | 13 | 3/31 | 23.15 | 4.77 | 29.0 | 0 | 0 |
| JW Dernbach | 65.1 | 2 | 324 | 23 | 4/7 | 14.08 | 4.97 | 17.0 | 3 | 0 |
| TE Linley | 28.4 | 1 | 150 | 7 | 3/50 | 21.42 | 5.23 | 24.5 | 0 | 0 |
| MNW Spriegel | 52.0 | 0 | 299 | 11 | 3/39 | 27.18 | 5.75 | 28.3 | 0 | 0 |
| RJ Hamilton-Brown | 30.0 | 0 | 174 | 3 | 3/38 | 58.00 | 5.80 | 60.0 | 0 | 0 |
| CP Schofield | 66.2 | 3 | 393 | 17 | 4/22 | 23.11 | 5.92 | 23.4 | 2 | 0 |
| Yasir Arafat | 74.4 | 2 | 460 | 19 | 5/45 | 24.21 | 6.16 | 23.5 | 0 | 1 |
| Z de Bruyn | 28.0 | 0 | 187 | 7 | 3/47 | 26.71 | 6.67 | 24.0 | 0 | 0 |
| SC Meaker | 16.3 | 0 | 111 | 4 | 3/22 | 27.75 | 6.72 | 24.7 | 0 | 0 |
| ZS Ansari | 24.0 | 0 | 169 | 4 | 1/22 | 42.25 | 7.04 | 36.0 | 0 | 0 |
| PP Ojha | 5.0 | 0 | 37 | 0 | - | - | 7.40 | - | 0 | 0 |
| CJ Jordan | 10.0 | 0 | 92 | 1 | 1/39 | 92.00 | 9.20 | 60.0 | 0 | 0 |

**Catches/Stumpings:**
13 Davies (+4st), 10 Maynard, 7 Hamilton-Brown, Spriegel, 6 Roy, 5 Batty, 4 Ansari, de Bruyn, Schofield, 1 Dernbach, Linley, Meaker

| | Mat | Inns | NO | Runs | HS | Ave | SR | 100 | 50 | 4s | 6s |
|---|---|---|---|---|---|---|---|---|---|---|---|
| TL Maynard | 15 | 13 | 4 | 392 | 76 | 43.55 | 133.33 | 0 | 2 | 25 | 13 |
| ZS Ansari | 10 | 6 | 3 | 108 | 34* | 36.00 | 145.94 | 0 | 0 | 12 | 2 |
| Z de Bruyn | 15 | 11 | 3 | 275 | 70* | 34.37 | 103.38 | 0 | 2 | 18 | 5 |
| SM Davies | 15 | 13 | 2 | 365 | 99* | 33.18 | 154.66 | 0 | 3 | 56 | 8 |
| KP Pietersen | 2 | 1 | 0 | 30 | 30 | 30.00 | 107.14 | 0 | 0 | 2 | 0 |
| JJ Roy | 15 | 13 | 0 | 363 | 53 | 27.92 | 135.44 | 0 | 4 | 41 | 10 |
| Yasir Arafat | 11 | 7 | 4 | 71 | 28* | 23.66 | 129.09 | 0 | 0 | 5 | 2 |
| CP Schofield | 9 | 3 | 1 | 37 | 30* | 18.50 | 115.62 | 0 | 0 | 1 | 2 |
| RJ Hamilton-Brown | 15 | 13 | 0 | 232 | 51 | 17.84 | 128.88 | 0 | 1 | 33 | 4 |
| SC Meaker | 10 | 3 | 2 | 17 | 17 | 17.00 | 154.54 | 0 | 0 | 2 | 1 |
| GJ Batty | 14 | 5 | 2 | 24 | 12* | 8.00 | 80.00 | 0 | 0 | 3 | 0 |
| GC Wilson | 4 | 2 | 0 | 11 | 11 | 5.50 | 68.75 | 0 | 0 | 0 | 0 |
| MNW Spriegel | 4 | 3 | 0 | 16 | 8 | 5.33 | 47.05 | 0 | 0 | 0 | 0 |
| JW Dernbach | 6 | 3 | 1 | 4 | 4 | 2.00 | 33.33 | 0 | 0 | 0 | 0 |
| DP Nannes | 15 | 2 | 2 | 0 | 0* | - | 0.00 | 0 | 0 | 0 | 0 |
| TE Linley | 2 | - | - | - | - | - | - | - | - | - | - |
| CT Tremlett | 3 | - | - | - | - | - | - | - | - | - | - |

*Batting*

| | Overs | Mdns | Runs | Wkts | BBI | Ave | Econ | SR | 4w | 5w |
|---|---|---|---|---|---|---|---|---|---|---|
| JW Dernbach | 22.3 | 0 | 153 | 13 | 3/27 | 11.76 | 6.80 | 10.3 | 0 | 0 |
| ZS Ansari | 31.0 | 0 | 221 | 4 | 1/19 | 55.25 | 7.12 | 46.5 | 0 | 0 |
| GJ Batty | 37.0 | 0 | 265 | 8 | 2/23 | 33.12 | 7.16 | 27.7 | 0 | 0 |
| RJ Hamilton-Brown | 9.0 | 0 | 65 | 2 | 1/10 | 32.50 | 7.22 | 27.0 | 0 | 0 |
| DP Nannes | 52.4 | 0 | 381 | 19 | 5/40 | 20.05 | 7.23 | 16.6 | 0 | 1 |
| TE Linley | 6.0 | 0 | 44 | 3 | 2/28 | 14.66 | 7.33 | 12.0 | 0 | 0 |
| CT Tremlett | 12.0 | 0 | 94 | 6 | 4/16 | 15.66 | 7.83 | 12.0 | 1 | 0 |
| Z de Bruyn | 18.1 | 0 | 148 | 6 | 2/18 | 24.66 | 8.14 | 18.1 | 0 | 0 |
| Yasir Arafat | 34.0 | 0 | 284 | 10 | 3/15 | 28.40 | 8.35 | 20.4 | 0 | 0 |
| MNW Spriegel | 5.0 | 0 | 44 | 0 | - | - | 8.80 | - | 0 | 0 |
| CP Schofield | 20.0 | 0 | 183 | 3 | 2/28 | 61.00 | 9.15 | 40.0 | 0 | 0 |
| SC Meaker | 26.0 | 0 | 254 | 6 | 2/16 | 42.33 | 9.76 | 26.0 | 0 | 0 |

*Bowling*

**Catches/Stumpings:**
10 Davies (+3st), 9 Roy, 5 Meaker, 4 Maynard, 3 Nannes, 2 Ansari, Batty, de Bruyn, Hamilton-Brown, Pietersen, Yasir Arafat, 1 Linley, Schofield, Spriegel, Wilson

**TEAM PROFILE**

FORMED: 1839
HOME GROUND: County Ground, Hove
ONE-DAY NAME: Sharks
CAPTAIN: Michael Yardy
2011 RESULTS: CC1: 5/9; CB40: Semi-finalists; FL t20: Quarter-finalists
HONOURS: Championship: (3) 2003, 2006, 2007; Gillette/NatWest/C&G/FP Trophy: (5) 1963, 1964, 1978, 1986, 2006; Pro40/National League/CB40: (2) 2008, 2009; Sunday League: 1982; Twenty20 Cup: 2009

## THE LOWDOWN

Always a force in one-day cricket, Sussex reached the knockout stages of both the CB40 and the FL t20 last season, but fell at the semi-finals and quarter-finals respectively. With batsmen like Murray Goodwin, Chris Nash and Ed Joyce in their ranks, and Luke Wright appearing to be overlooked by England, runscoring should not be an issue for the Sharks, but Monty Panesar's recent successes with England mean that the bowling ranks may be more stretched. With Matt Prior out of favour in England's one-day side, Michael Yardy will be hoping to get a bit more playing time out of the world's best stumper, while many good judges are tipping young gloveman Ben Brown to impress this year. Having gone a couple of years without a trophy, the Hove faithful will be hungry for success in 2012.

## CRICKET MANAGER: MARK ROBINSON

An honest seamer, Robinson enjoyed a 15-year first-class career, plying his trade with Yorkshire, Northamptonshire and finally Sussex before retiring in 2002. He became club coach in 2005 when Peter Moores vacated the role to become ECB academy director, leading the Sharks to a superb double in his second season in charge. Known for possessing an excellent track record in nurturing young talent, Robinson will be excited by the players at his disposal this season.

| | Mat | Inns | NO | Runs | HS | Ave | SR | 100 | 50 | 4s | 6s |
|---|---|---|---|---|---|---|---|---|---|---|---|
| MW Machan | 2 | 2 | 0 | 170 | 99 | 85.00 | 80.56 | 0 | 2 | 28 | 0 |
| MW Goodwin | 16 | 29 | 3 | 1372 | 274* | 52.76 | 51.09 | 4 | 4 | 166 | 1 |
| JS Gatting | 7 | 11 | 1 | 513 | 116* | 51.30 | 66.19 | 2 | 3 | 78 | 1 |
| EC Joyce | 16 | 29 | 1 | 1269 | 140 | 45.32 | 53.79 | 2 | 9 | 181 | 3 |
| MH Yardy | 10 | 16 | 2 | 617 | 130 | 44.07 | 51.84 | 2 | 3 | 68 | 4 |
| MJ Prior | 5 | 8 | 1 | 284 | 97* | 40.57 | 79.10 | 0 | 2 | 44 | 1 |
| KO Wernars | 3 | 4 | 1 | 104 | 53 | 34.66 | 40.31 | 0 | 1 | 12 | 0 |
| OP Rayner | 5 | 10 | 3 | 240 | 62* | 34.28 | 51.50 | 0 | 2 | 34 | 1 |
| LJ Wright | 4 | 7 | 0 | 237 | 116 | 33.85 | 63.03 | 1 | 0 | 33 | 1 |
| CD Nash | 15 | 28 | 0 | 928 | 120 | 33.14 | 57.81 | 1 | 7 | 133 | 3 |
| Naveed Arif | 4 | 7 | 2 | 165 | 100* | 33.00 | 49.54 | 1 | 0 | 17 | 4 |
| WAT Beer | 1 | 1 | 0 | 33 | 33 | 33.00 | 57.89 | 0 | 0 | 3 | 0 |
| LWP Wells | 14 | 27 | 2 | 824 | 174 | 32.96 | 44.92 | 3 | 0 | 123 | 3 |
| BC Brown | 11 | 19 | 2 | 504 | 112 | 29.64 | 61.23 | 2 | 2 | 74 | 0 |
| AJ Hodd | 9 | 16 | 4 | 320 | 67 | 26.66 | 43.89 | 0 | 1 | 36 | 0 |
| L Vincent | 1 | 2 | 0 | 49 | 36 | 24.50 | 125.64 | 0 | 0 | 8 | 1 |
| WD Parnell | 5 | 7 | 1 | 143 | 44 | 23.83 | 49.82 | 0 | 0 | 16 | 3 |
| WA Adkin | 4 | 6 | 2 | 74 | 29* | 18.50 | 32.17 | 0 | 0 | 9 | 0 |
| Naveed-ul-Hasan | 9 | 13 | 1 | 186 | 43* | 15.50 | 77.82 | 0 | 0 | 19 | 8 |
| A Khan | 13 | 18 | 5 | 186 | 65 | 14.30 | 39.82 | 0 | 1 | 18 | 1 |
| JE Anyon | 15 | 22 | 3 | 269 | 53 | 14.15 | 36.64 | 0 | 2 | 29 | 1 |
| MS Panesar | 16 | 22 | 8 | 120 | 20 | 8.57 | 26.43 | 0 | 0 | 9 | 3 |
| JA Glover | 1 | - | - | - | - | - | - | - | - | - | - |
| LJ Hatchett | 1 | - | - | - | - | - | - | - | - | - | - |
| CJ Liddle | 1 | - | - | - | - | - | - | - | - | - | - |

*Batting*

| | Overs | Mdns | Runs | Wkts | BBI | BBM | Ave | Econ | SR | 5w | 10w |
|---|---|---|---|---|---|---|---|---|---|---|---|
| WAT Beer | 16.0 | 8 | 36 | 3 | 3/36 | 3/36 | 12.00 | 2.25 | 32.0 | 0 | 0 |
| CJ Liddle | 15.0 | 7 | 14 | 1 | 1/14 | 1/14 | 14.00 | 0.93 | 90.0 | 0 | 0 |
| LJ Hatchett | 20.0 | 6 | 45 | 2 | 2/45 | 2/45 | 22.50 | 2.25 | 60.0 | 0 | 0 |
| Naveed Arif | 98.4 | 12 | 388 | 15 | 4/41 | 7/127 | 25.86 | 3.93 | 39.4 | 0 | 0 |
| CD Nash | 92.0 | 18 | 291 | 11 | 4/103 | 5/113 | 26.45 | 3.16 | 50.1 | 0 | 0 |
| MS Panesar | 750.3 | 223 | 1880 | 69 | 5/58 | 7/134 | 27.24 | 2.50 | 65.2 | 3 | 0 |
| KO Wernars | 29.5 | 7 | 109 | 4 | 2/13 | 2/13 | 27.25 | 3.65 | 44.7 | 0 | 0 |
| LJ Wright | 49.0 | 8 | 146 | 5 | 3/54 | 3/54 | 29.20 | 2.97 | 58.8 | 0 | 0 |
| A Khan | 381.5 | 72 | 1259 | 39 | 4/70 | 6/85 | 32.28 | 3.29 | 58.7 | 0 | 0 |
| JE Anyon | 450.1 | 50 | 1785 | 55 | 5/136 | 8/156 | 32.45 | 3.96 | 49.1 | 1 | 0 |
| Naveed-ul-Hasan | 279.4 | 58 | 921 | 27 | 5/79 | 10/161 | 34.11 | 3.29 | 62.1 | 2 | 1 |
| JS Gatting | 12.0 | 3 | 36 | 1 | 1/8 | 1/8 | 36.00 | 3.00 | 72.0 | 0 | 0 |
| WD Parnell | 154.0 | 20 | 611 | 15 | 3/60 | 5/153 | 40.73 | 3.96 | 61.6 | 0 | 0 |
| OP Rayner | 99.1 | 26 | 284 | 6 | 2/38 | 3/73 | 47.33 | 2.86 | 99.1 | 0 | 0 |
| JA Glover | 14.0 | 4 | 52 | 1 | 1/52 | 1/52 | 52.00 | 3.71 | 84.0 | 0 | 0 |
| LWP Wells | 44.0 | 7 | 170 | 2 | 2/28 | 2/33 | 85.00 | 3.86 | 132.0 | 0 | 0 |
| WA Adkin | 63.0 | 17 | 174 | 1 | 1/28 | 1/45 | 174.00 | 2.76 | 378.0 | 0 | 0 |
| MW Machan | 1.0 | 0 | 4 | 0 | - | - | - | 4.00 | - | 0 | 0 |
| MH Yardy | 3.0 | 0 | 7 | 0 | - | - | - | 2.33 | - | 0 | 0 |

*Bowling*

**Catches/Stumpings:**
22 Joyce, 20 Hodd (inc 2 outfield +1st), 17 Yardy, 14 Brown (inc 3 outfield +2st), 16 Prior (inc 10 outfield + 2st), 9 Khan, Nash, 6 Goodwin, Wells, 5 Anyon, 4 Adkin, 3 Gatting, Parnell, Rayner, Wernars, 2 Panesar, Vincent, 1 Naveed-ul-Hasan

**SUSSEX SHARKS**

### Batting

| | Mat | Inns | NO | Runs | HS | Ave | SR | 100 | 50 | 4s | 6s |
|---|---|---|---|---|---|---|---|---|---|---|---|
| LJ Wright | 3 | 3 | 1 | 135 | 71* | 67.50 | 100.00 | 0 | 1 | 22 | 1 |
| EC Joyce | 12 | 12 | 2 | 562 | 120 | 56.20 | 104.85 | 2 | 2 | 59 | 8 |
| MW Machan | 1 | 1 | 0 | 56 | 56 | 56.00 | 90.32 | 0 | 1 | 5 | 0 |
| CD Nash | 12 | 11 | 1 | 557 | 124* | 55.70 | 107.11 | 1 | 5 | 64 | 5 |
| WD Parnell | 5 | 3 | 1 | 107 | 47 | 53.50 | 112.63 | 0 | 0 | 9 | 2 |
| BC Brown | 8 | 7 | 3 | 187 | 60 | 46.75 | 111.97 | 0 | 2 | 18 | 1 |
| JS Gatting | 8 | 8 | 0 | 277 | 122 | 34.62 | 102.97 | 1 | 0 | 29 | 7 |
| MW Goodwin | 12 | 10 | 2 | 270 | 109* | 33.75 | 115.87 | 1 | 0 | 34 | 2 |
| MH Yardy | 11 | 7 | 1 | 184 | 53 | 30.66 | 91.54 | 0 | 1 | 12 | 2 |
| WAT Beer | 2 | 2 | 1 | 29 | 27* | 29.00 | 93.54 | 0 | 0 | 2 | 0 |
| L Vincent | 9 | 9 | 1 | 216 | 71 | 27.00 | 102.85 | 0 | 1 | 26 | 6 |
| KO Wernars | 1 | 1 | 0 | 21 | 21 | 21.00 | 84.00 | 0 | 0 | 0 | 1 |
| Naved-ul-Hasan | 7 | 5 | 2 | 53 | 25* | 17.66 | 80.30 | 0 | 0 | 4 | 1 |
| Naveed Arif | 11 | 7 | 3 | 64 | 22 | 16.00 | 65.30 | 0 | 0 | 3 | 1 |
| WA Adkin | 2 | 1 | 0 | 10 | 10 | 10.00 | 33.33 | 0 | 0 | 0 | 0 |
| LWP Wells | 4 | 2 | 0 | 19 | 17 | 9.50 | 82.60 | 0 | 0 | 1 | 1 |
| AJ Hodd | 5 | 3 | 1 | 14 | 6* | 7.00 | 66.66 | 0 | 0 | 1 | 0 |
| A Khan | 4 | 2 | 0 | 14 | 8 | 7.00 | 82.35 | 0 | 0 | 2 | 0 |
| MJ Prior | 2 | 2 | 0 | 11 | 7 | 5.50 | 78.57 | 0 | 0 | 2 | 0 |
| CJ Liddle | 11 | 5 | 0 | 20 | 8 | 4.00 | 100.00 | 0 | 0 | 2 | 0 |
| MS Panesar | 12 | 4 | 2 | 1 | 1* | 0.50 | 20.00 | 0 | 0 | 0 | 0 |
| OP Rayner | 1 | - | - | - | - | - | - | - | - | - | - |

### Bowling

| | Overs | Mdns | Runs | Wkts | BBI | Ave | Econ | 5R | 4w | 5w |
|---|---|---|---|---|---|---|---|---|---|---|
| OP Rayner | 6.0 | 0 | 25 | 0 | - | - | 4.16 | - | 0 | 0 |
| LJ Wright | 12.0 | 0 | 53 | 2 | 2/26 | 26.50 | 4.41 | 36.0 | 0 | 0 |
| MS Panesar | 83.0 | 2 | 440 | 12 | 2/28 | 36.66 | 5.30 | 41.5 | 0 | 0 |
| Naved-ul-Hasan | 52.0 | 0 | 277 | 13 | 3/21 | 21.30 | 5.32 | 24.0 | 0 | 0 |
| CD Nash | 43.1 | 0 | 233 | 7 | 3/30 | 33.28 | 5.39 | 37.0 | 0 | 0 |
| Naveed Arif | 69.1 | 0 | 390 | 9 | 3/54 | 43.33 | 5.63 | 46.1 | 0 | 0 |
| WAT Beer | 17.0 | 0 | 96 | 0 | - | - | 5.64 | - | 0 | 0 |
| A Khan | 24.3 | 1 | 142 | 1 | 1/33 | 142.0 | 5.79 | 147.0 | 0 | 0 |
| CJ Liddle | 61.0 | 3 | 362 | 16 | 4/38 | 22.62 | 5.93 | 22.8 | 1 | 0 |
| MH Yardy | 68.2 | 0 | 432 | 18 | 4/10 | 24.00 | 6.32 | 22.7 | 1 | 0 |
| WA Adkin | 10.0 | 0 | 64 | 1 | 1/39 | 64.00 | 6.40 | 60.0 | 0 | 0 |
| WD Parnell | 32.0 | 0 | 237 | 8 | 3/31 | 29.62 | 7.40 | 24.0 | 0 | 0 |
| JS Gatting | 2.0 | 0 | 17 | 0 | - | - | 8.50 | - | 0 | 0 |
| LWP Wells | 4.5 | 0 | 42 | 0 | - | - | 8.68 | - | 0 | 0 |
| KO Wernars | 2.0 | 0 | 18 | 0 | - | - | 9.00 | - | 0 | 0 |

**Catches/Stumpings:**
8 Brown (+2st), Vincent, 6 Joyce, 5 Goodwin, Hodd (+0st), Naveed Arif, 3 Nash, Panesar, 2 Gatting, 1 Adkin, Liddle, Machan, Naved-ul-Hasan, Parnell, Rayner, Wright, Yardy

www.sussexcricket.co.uk / tel: 0844 264 0202

**SUSSEX**
**SHARKS**

|  | Mat | Inns | NO | Runs | HS | Ave | SR | 100 | 50 | 4s | 6s |
|---|---|---|---|---|---|---|---|---|---|---|---|
| LJ Wright | 10 | 10 | 1 | 332 | 81* | 36.88 | 155.14 | 0 | 3 | 33 | 14 |
| MW Goodwin | 15 | 14 | 3 | 332 | 100* | 30.18 | 127.20 | 1 | 1 | 33 | 5 |
| MJ Prior | 6 | 6 | 0 | 167 | 89 | 27.83 | 135.77 | 0 | 1 | 16 | 4 |
| CD Nash | 16 | 16 | 3 | 335 | 64* | 25.76 | 109.12 | 0 | 1 | 39 | 4 |
| Naved-ul-Hasan | 11 | 8 | 3 | 118 | 34 | 23.60 | 137.20 | 0 | 0 | 7 | 5 |
| AJ Hodd | 9 | 4 | 2 | 43 | 18* | 21.50 | 81.13 | 0 | 0 | 1 | 1 |
| L Vincent | 16 | 16 | 3 | 262 | 44* | 20.15 | 107.37 | 0 | 0 | 23 | 5 |
| MH Yardy | 9 | 8 | 3 | 97 | 24 | 19.40 | 85.84 | 0 | 0 | 3 | 0 |
| BC Brown | 9 | 9 | 0 | 155 | 68 | 17.22 | 111.51 | 0 | 1 | 13 | 4 |
| CJ Liddle | 16 | 4 | 3 | 14 | 9 | 14.00 | 66.66 | 0 | 0 | 1 | 0 |
| EC Joyce | 2 | 2 | 0 | 22 | 15 | 11.00 | 95.65 | 0 | 0 | 2 | 0 |
| WD Parnell | 7 | 4 | 2 | 20 | 12* | 10.00 | 105.26 | 0 | 0 | 0 | 0 |
| KO Wernars | 2 | 1 | 0 | 9 | 9 | 9.00 | 90.00 | 0 | 0 | 0 | 0 |
| OP Rayner | 12 | 8 | 3 | 37 | 15 | 7.40 | 84.09 | 0 | 0 | 2 | 1 |
| JS Gatting | 10 | 9 | 1 | 46 | 20 | 5.75 | 75.40 | 0 | 0 | 2 | 0 |
| LWP Wells | 1 | 1 | 0 | 3 | 3 | 3.00 | 50.00 | 0 | 0 | 0 | 0 |
| Naveed Arif | 5 | 2 | 0 | 4 | 2 | 2.00 | 66.66 | 0 | 0 | 0 | 0 |
| Umar Gul | 8 | 2 | 0 | 1 | 1 | 0.50 | 20.00 | 0 | 0 | 0 | 0 |
| MS Panesar | 12 | 1 | 0 | 0 | 0 | 0.00 | 0.00 | 0 | 0 | 0 | 0 |

|  | Overs | Mdns | Runs | Wkts | BBI | Ave | Econ | SR | 4w | 5w |
|---|---|---|---|---|---|---|---|---|---|---|
| CD Nash | 18.0 | 0 | 112 | 9 | 4/7 | 12.44 | 6.22 | 12.0 | 1 | 0 |
| Naved-ul-Hasan | 36.2 | 0 | 248 | 16 | 5/17 | 15.50 | 6.82 | 13.6 | 0 | 1 |
| OP Rayner | 43.0 | 1 | 297 | 12 | 5/18 | 24.75 | 6.90 | 21.5 | 0 | 1 |
| MS Panesar | 42.0 | 0 | 297 | 15 | 3/14 | 19.80 | 7.07 | 16.8 | 0 | 0 |
| CJ Liddle | 49.5 | 1 | 361 | 21 | 4/20 | 17.19 | 7.24 | 14.2 | 1 | 0 |
| LJ Wright | 17.0 | 0 | 127 | 6 | 2/24 | 21.16 | 7.47 | 17.0 | 0 | 0 |
| MH Yardy | 36.0 | 0 | 271 | 7 | 2/22 | 38.71 | 7.52 | 30.8 | 0 | 0 |
| Naveed Arif | 11.0 | 0 | 83 | 1 | 1/26 | 83.00 | 7.54 | 66.0 | 0 | 0 |
| WD Parnell | 23.0 | 0 | 197 | 6 | 2/26 | 32.83 | 8.56 | 23.0 | 0 | 0 |
| Umar Gul | 28.2 | 1 | 251 | 12 | 3/24 | 20.91 | 8.85 | 14.1 | 0 | 0 |
| KO Wernars | 1.0 | 0 | 20 | 0 | - | - | 20.00 | - | 0 | 0 |

**Catches/Stumpings:**
9 Nash, 8 Hodd (+1st), Vincent, 7 Rayner, 5 Gatting, Naved-ul-Hasan, 4 Brown (+0st), Wright, 3 Liddle, Yardy, 1 Goodwin, Naveed Arif, Panesar, Parnell, Prior (+1st), Wernars

**TEAM PROFILE**

FORMED: 1882
HOME GROUND: Edgbaston
ONE-DAY NAME: Bears
CAPTAIN: Jim Troughton
2011 RESULTS: CC1: 2/9; CB40: 5/7 in Group B; FL t20: 8/9 in North Group
HONOURS: Championship: (6) 1911, 1951, 1972, 1994, 1995, 2004; Gillette/NatWest/C&G/FP Trophy: (5) 1966, 1968, 1989, 1993, 1995; Benson and Hedges Cup: (2) 1994, 2002; CB40: 2010; Sunday League: (3) 1980, 1994, 1997

### THE LOWDOWN

Last season Warwickshire were able to address their County Championship woes of previous seasons, but at the same time their one-day form dipped. Consistent performances in the four-day format saw the Bears enter the final game of the season as title favourites, but they were unable to secure the victory they needed against Hampshire to take the title. They failed to defend their CB40 crown, finishing fifth in Group B, while their T20 form was similarly disappointing. Talented allrounder Chris Woakes starred with bat and ball, confirming his England credentials, while Varun Chopra began the season in scintillating fashion with back-to-back double hundreds. This season's permanent signing of another ex-Essex cricketer in Chris Wright brings depth to an already potent bowling line-up that contains Boyd Rankin, Rikki Clarke and overseas spinner Jeetan Patel. If they can start firing on all fronts this season then big things are expected from the Bears.

### DIRECTOR OF CRICKET: ASHLEY GILES

Warwickshire favourite Giles arrived at Edgbaston in 1993 and spent 14 years as a player for the club, before making a seamless transition into coaching and becoming director of cricket in 2007. The Ashes-winner played in 54 Tests and 62 ODIs for England, calling time on his international career in Australia in 2006. He is also an England selector and is tipped to coach the national side at some point in the future.

| | Mat | Inns | NO | Runs | HS | Ave | SR | 100 | 50 | 4s | 6s |
|---|---|---|---|---|---|---|---|---|---|---|---|
| S Chanderpaul | 5 | 7 | 1 | 539 | 193 | 89.83 | 58.84 | 3 | 1 | 63 | 7 |
| IR Bell | 3 | 6 | 1 | 256 | 139 | 51.20 | 57.91 | 1 | 0 | 36 | 1 |
| CR Woakes | 11 | 16 | 4 | 579 | 129 | 48.25 | 63.55 | 1 | 5 | 77 | 1 |
| AG Botha | 2 | 3 | 1 | 92 | 64 | 46.00 | 63.88 | 0 | 1 | 15 | 1 |
| V Chopra | 17 | 28 | 1 | 1203 | 228 | 44.55 | 57.64 | 3 | 4 | 158 | 8 |
| KHD Barker | 10 | 12 | 1 | 473 | 118 | 43.00 | 59.19 | 2 | 2 | 70 | 1 |
| TR Ambrose | 16 | 22 | 3 | 744 | 95* | 39.15 | 52.54 | 0 | 8 | 93 | 0 |
| IJ Westwood | 13 | 19 | 1 | 693 | 171 | 38.50 | 50.07 | 3 | 2 | 87 | 2 |
| DL Maddy | 8 | 11 | 1 | 354 | 76 | 35.40 | 61.56 | 0 | 2 | 54 | 1 |
| JO Troughton | 14 | 21 | 2 | 634 | 151 | 33.36 | 42.83 | 1 | 3 | 80 | 2 |
| M Yousuf | 6 | 11 | 0 | 353 | 109 | 32.09 | 63.26 | 1 | 2 | 49 | 2 |
| LJ Evans | 3 | 4 | 0 | 124 | 52 | 31.00 | 40.00 | 0 | 1 | 14 | 0 |
| JS Patel | 3 | 4 | 0 | 114 | 65 | 28.50 | 82.01 | 0 | 1 | 12 | 3 |
| R Clarke | 15 | 22 | 1 | 558 | 126 | 26.57 | 60.85 | 1 | 2 | 75 | 12 |
| WTS Porterfield | 16 | 25 | 1 | 583 | 87 | 24.29 | 45.83 | 0 | 5 | 78 | 2 |
| CL Metters | 10 | 12 | 5 | 167 | 30 | 23.85 | 39.66 | 0 | 0 | 17 | 0 |
| TP Milnes | 1 | 1 | 0 | 23 | 23 | 23.00 | 38.33 | 0 | 0 | 1 | 0 |
| NM Carter | 2 | 3 | 0 | 66 | 40 | 22.00 | 68.75 | 0 | 0 | 10 | 0 |
| CJC Wright | 4 | 3 | 2 | 19 | 13* | 19.00 | 61.29 | 0 | 0 | 2 | 0 |
| IJL Trott | 3 | 5 | 0 | 93 | 39 | 18.60 | 53.75 | 0 | 0 | 15 | 0 |
| NS Tahir | 4 | 6 | 0 | 93 | 53 | 15.50 | 31.63 | 0 | 1 | 13 | 0 |
| WB Rankin | 13 | 16 | 7 | 133 | 28 | 14.77 | 52.77 | 0 | 0 | 15 | 0 |
| SA Piolet | 1 | 1 | 0 | 6 | 6 | 6.00 | 35.29 | 0 | 0 | 1 | 0 |
| RM Johnson | 1 | 2 | 0 | 10 | 5 | 5.00 | 21.27 | 0 | 0 | 1 | 0 |
| AS Miller | 6 | 9 | 4 | 15 | 8 | 3.00 | 22.05 | 0 | 0 | 0 | 0 |
| PM Best | 1 | 2 | 0 | 3 | 2 | 1.50 | 5.45 | 0 | 0 | 0 | 0 |
| MG Holmes | 2 | 3 | 1 | 1 | 1* | 0.50 | 4.16 | 0 | 0 | 0 | 0 |

Batting

| | Overs | Mdns | Runs | Wkts | BBI | BBM | Ave | Econ | SR | 5w | 10w |
|---|---|---|---|---|---|---|---|---|---|---|---|
| TP Milnes | 12.0 | 3 | 39 | 4 | 4/15 | 4/39 | 9.75 | 3.25 | 18.0 | 0 | 0 |
| AG Botha | 32.0 | 8 | 80 | 5 | 3/39 | 5/80 | 16.00 | 2.50 | 38.4 | 0 | 0 |
| NM Carter | 60.4 | 11 | 197 | 10 | 6/30 | 8/103 | 19.70 | 3.24 | 36.4 | 1 | 0 |
| JS Patel | 117.1 | 20 | 344 | 17 | 6/111 | 10/163 | 20.23 | 2.93 | 41.3 | 2 | 1 |
| CR Woakes | 406.4 | 90 | 1220 | 56 | 7/20 | 10/123 | 21.78 | 3.00 | 43.5 | 3 | 1 |
| CL Metters | 221.4 | 32 | 695 | 29 | 6/65 | 8/186 | 23.96 | 3.13 | 45.8 | 2 | 0 |
| CJC Wright | 167.1 | 35 | 535 | 22 | 5/31 | 7/96 | 24.31 | 3.20 | 45.5 | 2 | 0 |
| WB Rankin | 387.5 | 42 | 1419 | 55 | 5/57 | 8/115 | 25.80 | 3.65 | 42.3 | 2 | 0 |
| R Clarke | 410.5 | 70 | 1225 | 46 | 5/10 | 7/32 | 26.63 | 2.98 | 53.5 | 1 | 0 |
| PM Best | 15.0 | 1 | 82 | 3 | 2/69 | 3/82 | 27.33 | 5.46 | 30.0 | 0 | 0 |
| MG Holmes | 33.3 | 8 | 118 | 4 | 2/54 | 3/86 | 29.50 | 3.52 | 50.2 | 0 | 0 |
| SA Piolet | 13.0 | 0 | 59 | 2 | 2/26 | 2/59 | 29.50 | 4.53 | 39.0 | 0 | 0 |
| DL Maddy | 116.0 | 29 | 336 | 11 | 3/29 | 6/103 | 30.54 | 2.89 | 63.2 | 0 | 0 |
| NS Tahir | 119.0 | 33 | 348 | 11 | 4/36 | 4/70 | 31.63 | 2.92 | 64.9 | 0 | 0 |
| KHD Barker | 250.0 | 46 | 803 | 25 | 5/31 | 8/129 | 32.12 | 3.21 | 60.0 | 1 | 0 |
| AS Miller | 124.0 | 25 | 434 | 7 | 2/15 | 4/65 | 62.00 | 3.50 | 106.2 | 0 | 0 |
| IJL Trott | 6.0 | 0 | 18 | 0 | - | - | - | 3.00 | - | 0 | 0 |
| IJ Westwood | 3.0 | 0 | 16 | 0 | - | - | - | 5.33 | - | 0 | 0 |

Bowling

**Catches/Stumpings:**
39 Ambrose (+2st), Clarke, 18 Porterfield, 16 Chopra, 15 Metters, Westwood, 13 Troughton, 8 Maddy, 6 Johnson (+0st), Woakes, 5 Barker, Botha, 4 Trott, 3 Rankin, 2 Chanderpaul, Patel, 1 Bell, Best, Carter, Evans, Holmes, Piolet

**Batting**

| | Mat | Inns | NO | Runs | HS | Ave | SR | 100 | 50 | 4s | 6s |
|---|---|---|---|---|---|---|---|---|---|---|---|
| IR Bell | 2 | 2 | 0 | 114 | 88 | 57.00 | 92.68 | 0 | 1 | 11 | 1 |
| Mohammad Yousuf | 6 | 6 | 2 | 213 | 74* | 53.25 | 110.93 | 0 | 3 | 14 | 4 |
| DL Maddy | 6 | 5 | 2 | 135 | 49 | 45.00 | 119.46 | 0 | 0 | 13 | 2 |
| V Chopra | 11 | 11 | 0 | 448 | 115 | 40.72 | 87.15 | 1 | 3 | 37 | 9 |
| WTS Porterfield | 12 | 12 | 0 | 444 | 95 | 37.00 | 94.26 | 0 | 4 | 49 | 6 |
| A Javid | 1 | 1 | 0 | 34 | 34 | 34.00 | 66.66 | 0 | 0 | 0 | 1 |
| R Clarke | 12 | 10 | 1 | 288 | 76 | 32.00 | 126.87 | 0 | 3 | 31 | 7 |
| CR Woakes | 8 | 7 | 3 | 106 | 34* | 26.50 | 108.16 | 0 | 0 | 4 | 4 |
| JO Troughton | 11 | 11 | 2 | 235 | 61 | 26.11 | 86.71 | 0 | 2 | 18 | 4 |
| SA Piolet | 7 | 4 | 2 | 50 | 39 | 25.00 | 116.27 | 0 | 0 | 7 | 1 |
| NM Carter | 6 | 6 | 0 | 112 | 53 | 18.66 | 97.39 | 0 | 1 | 16 | 1 |
| TR Ambrose | 9 | 5 | 0 | 93 | 39 | 18.60 | 56.70 | 0 | 0 | 3 | 0 |
| AG Botha | 4 | 4 | 1 | 55 | 45 | 18.33 | 152.77 | 0 | 0 | 3 | 3 |
| S Chanderpaul | 1 | 1 | 0 | 17 | 17 | 17.00 | 141.66 | 0 | 0 | 2 | 1 |
| KHD Barker | 11 | 9 | 1 | 135 | 56 | 16.87 | 97.82 | 0 | 1 | 8 | 5 |
| PM Best | 3 | 1 | 0 | 12 | 12 | 12.00 | 38.70 | 0 | 0 | 0 | 0 |
| RM Johnson | 3 | 3 | 1 | 16 | 15 | 8.00 | 106.66 | 0 | 0 | 1 | 0 |
| AS Miller | 4 | 2 | 1 | 4 | 2* | 4.00 | 57.14 | 0 | 0 | 0 | 0 |
| MG Holmes | 3 | 2 | 0 | 5 | 5 | 2.50 | 100.00 | 0 | 0 | 1 | 0 |
| CL Metters | 3 | 2 | 0 | 3 | 2 | 1.50 | 30.00 | 0 | 0 | 0 | 0 |
| IJL Trott | 1 | 1 | 0 | 0 | 0 | 0.00 | 0.00 | 0 | 0 | 0 | 0 |
| TW Allin | 1 | 1 | 1 | 2 | 2* | - | 16.66 | 0 | 0 | 0 | 0 |
| CJC Wright | 1 | 1 | 1 | 2 | 2* | - | 66.66 | 0 | 0 | 0 | 0 |
| WB Rankin | 2 | 1 | 1 | 1 | 1* | - | 50.00 | 0 | 0 | 0 | 0 |
| JS Patel | 3 | - | - | - | - | - | - | - | - | - | - |

**Bowling**

| | Overs | Mdns | Runs | Wkts | BBI | Ave | Econ | SR | 4w | 5w |
|---|---|---|---|---|---|---|---|---|---|---|
| CJC Wright | 7.0 | 0 | 30 | 1 | 1/30 | 30.00 | 4.28 | 42.0 | 0 | 0 |
| IJL Trott | 2.0 | 0 | 9 | 0 | - | - | 4.50 | - | 0 | 0 |
| AS Miller | 31.0 | 2 | 145 | 6 | 2/31 | 24.16 | 4.67 | 31.0 | 0 | 0 |
| AG Botha | 22.0 | 1 | 104 | 3 | 1/17 | 34.66 | 4.72 | 44.0 | 0 | 0 |
| R Clarke | 63.0 | 0 | 329 | 12 | 4/28 | 27.41 | 5.22 | 31.5 | 1 | 0 |
| CL Metters | 18.0 | 0 | 94 | 2 | 2/41 | 47.00 | 5.22 | 54.0 | 0 | 0 |
| JS Patel | 27.0 | 0 | 144 | 7 | 3/41 | 20.57 | 5.33 | 23.1 | 0 | 0 |
| MG Holmes | 22.0 | 0 | 119 | 2 | 2/47 | 59.50 | 5.40 | 66.0 | 0 | 0 |
| PM Best | 18.0 | 0 | 101 | 1 | 1/34 | 101.00 | 5.61 | 108.0 | 0 | 0 |
| SA Piolet | 36.0 | 0 | 224 | 5 | 2/52 | 44.80 | 6.22 | 43.2 | 0 | 0 |
| DL Maddy | 40.0 | 1 | 254 | 11 | 4/29 | 23.09 | 6.35 | 21.8 | 1 | 0 |
| CR Woakes | 50.0 | 0 | 319 | 10 | 2/30 | 31.90 | 6.38 | 30.0 | 0 | 0 |
| NM Carter | 28.5 | 1 | 186 | 3 | 1/23 | 62.00 | 6.45 | 57.6 | 0 | 0 |
| A Javid | 4.0 | 0 | 27 | 0 | - | - | 6.75 | - | 0 | 0 |
| KHD Barker | 67.1 | 0 | 485 | 10 | 3/36 | 48.50 | 7.22 | 40.3 | 0 | 0 |
| WB Rankin | 11.0 | 0 | 96 | 0 | - | - | 8.72 | - | 0 | 0 |
| TW Allin | 2.0 | 0 | 29 | 0 | - | - | 14.50 | - | 0 | 0 |

**Catches/Stumpings:**
5 Ambrose (+2st), 4 Chopra, Clarke, Porterfield, Troughton, 3 Barker, Maddy, Woakes, 2 Best, Holmes, Johnson (+0st), Patel, Piolet, 1 Bell, Metters, Miller, Mohammad Yousuf

www.edgbaston.com / tel: 0844 635 1902

| | Mat | Inns | NO | Runs | HS | Ave | SR | 100 | 50 | 4s | 6s |
|---|---|---|---|---|---|---|---|---|---|---|---|
| TR Ambrose | 13 | 10 | 5 | 170 | 44* | 34.00 | 112.58 | 0 | 0 | 9 | 2 |
| WTS Porterfield | 14 | 14 | 0 | 437 | 83 | 31.21 | 125.93 | 0 | 4 | 56 | 4 |
| JO Troughton | 15 | 15 | 4 | 326 | 55* | 29.63 | 113.58 | 0 | 1 | 26 | 6 |
| CR Woakes | 9 | 8 | 4 | 101 | 44* | 25.25 | 124.69 | 0 | 0 | 8 | 3 |
| DL Maddy | 14 | 13 | 0 | 239 | 61 | 18.38 | 121.31 | 0 | 1 | 17 | 10 |
| NM Carter | 12 | 12 | 0 | 181 | 38 | 15.08 | 119.07 | 0 | 0 | 26 | 5 |
| V Chopra | 14 | 14 | 0 | 203 | 40 | 14.50 | 105.72 | 0 | 0 | 23 | 4 |
| R Clarke | 15 | 15 | 4 | 157 | 25* | 14.27 | 113.76 | 0 | 0 | 11 | 4 |
| SA Piolet | 15 | 6 | 2 | 53 | 21 | 13.25 | 103.92 | 0 | 0 | 3 | 1 |
| AG Botha | 8 | 5 | 2 | 37 | 14* | 12.33 | 132.14 | 0 | 0 | 3 | 2 |
| KHD Barker | 15 | 9 | 1 | 77 | 23 | 9.62 | 90.58 | 0 | 0 | 5 | 1 |
| JS Patel | 15 | 4 | 2 | 9 | 6* | 4.50 | 69.23 | 0 | 0 | 0 | 0 |
| IJL Trott | 1 | 1 | 0 | 1 | 1 | 1.00 | 100.00 | 0 | 0 | 0 | 0 |
| RM Johnson | 2 | 1 | 1 | 0 | 0* | - | - | 0 | 0 | 0 | 0 |
| AS Miller | 3 | 1 | 1 | 0 | 0* | - | - | 0 | 0 | 0 | 0 |

Batting

| | Overs | Mdns | Runs | Wkts | BBI | Ave | Econ | SR | 4w | 5w |
|---|---|---|---|---|---|---|---|---|---|---|
| AG Botha | 25.0 | 0 | 162 | 6 | 2/19 | 27.00 | 6.48 | 25.0 | 0 | 0 |
| SA Piolet | 52.0 | 0 | 357 | 18 | 3/25 | 19.83 | 6.86 | 17.3 | 0 | 0 |
| JS Patel | 48.3 | 0 | 333 | 11 | 3/19 | 30.27 | 6.86 | 26.4 | 0 | 0 |
| DL Maddy | 20.0 | 0 | 150 | 12 | 3/10 | 12.50 | 7.50 | 10.0 | 0 | 0 |
| CR Woakes | 29.5 | 0 | 227 | 10 | 2/15 | 22.70 | 7.60 | 17.9 | 0 | 0 |
| KHD Barker | 40.4 | 0 | 328 | 14 | 3/18 | 23.42 | 8.06 | 17.4 | 0 | 0 |
| AS Miller | 8.0 | 0 | 69 | 3 | 2/16 | 23.00 | 8.62 | 16.0 | 0 | 0 |
| NM Carter | 34.1 | 0 | 302 | 6 | 2/34 | 50.33 | 8.83 | 34.1 | 0 | 0 |
| R Clarke | 7.0 | 0 | 80 | 0 | - | - | 11.42 | - | 0 | 0 |

Bowling

**Catches/Stumpings:**
10 Clarke, 8 Barker, 7 Porterfield, Woakes, 4 Ambrose (+3st), Carter, Troughton, 3 Patel, 2 Maddy, Miller, Piolet, 1 Botha, Chopra, Johnson (+1st)

TEAM PROFILE

FORMED: 1865
HOME GROUND: New Road, Worcester
ONE-DAY NAME: Royals
CAPTAIN: Daryl Mitchell
2011 RESULTS: CC1: 7/9; CB40: 7/7 in
Group A; FL t20: 5/9 in North Group
HONOURS: Championship: (5) 1964, 1965,
1974, 1988, 1989; Gillette/Natwest/C&G/
FP Trophy: 1994; Benson and Hedges Cup:
1991; Pro40/National League/CB40: 2007;
Sunday League: (3) 1971, 1987, 1988.

## THE LOWDOWN

Worcestershire defied the odds last year to preserve their Division One status in the County Championship and will be looking to improve upon their seventh-place finish in 2012. The evergreen Vikram Solanki registered yet another 1,000 run first-class season and Moeen Ali enjoyed his most prolific campaign in a Royals shirt to date across all competitions, but their fellow batsmen failed to turn in such consistent performances. In the bowling department, veteran seamer Alan Richardson led the line brilliantly in four-day cricket with 73 wickets, and while Gareth Andrew provided some excellent support, they lacked depth in the seam department. The signing of experienced left-armer David Lucas from Northamptonshire should help to address this issue, while promising paceman Richard Jones will be hoping for more four-day cricket in this campaign. Mystery spinner Saeed Ajmal has been retained for the FL t20 to complement a squad containing the exciting, hard-hitting Alexei Kervezee and promising bowler Jack Shantry for a competition which may well turn out to be the county's best hope for silverware.

### DIRECTOR OF CRICKET: STEVE RHODES

Rhodes began his career with home side Yorkshire before making the move to New Road in 1985 where he became a Worcestershire institution. A talented wicketkeeper and pugnacious batsman, Rhodes was named as one of Wisden's Five Cricketers of the Year in 1994, making his Test debut in the same year against New Zealand at Trent Bridge. He went on to represent England a further 10 times in Test matches and played in nine one-day internationals.

| | Mat | Inns | NO | Runs | HS | Ave | SR | 100 | 50 | 4s | 6s |
|---|---|---|---|---|---|---|---|---|---|---|---|
| Shakib Al Hasan | 1 | 1 | 0 | 54 | 54 | 54.00 | 85.71 | 0 | 1 | 9 | 0 |
| VS Solanki | 16 | 30 | 3 | 1148 | 173 | 42.51 | 58.78 | 3 | 6 | 162 | 10 |
| MM Ali | 16 | 29 | 1 | 930 | 158 | 33.21 | 49.75 | 1 | 5 | 131 | 11 |
| DKH Mitchell | 13 | 25 | 2 | 751 | 66 | 32.65 | 45.98 | 0 | 5 | 111 | 0 |
| BJM Scott | 12 | 20 | 5 | 463 | 73 | 30.86 | 58.68 | 0 | 2 | 59 | 2 |
| AN Kervezee | 16 | 29 | 1 | 800 | 128 | 28.57 | 65.35 | 1 | 6 | 126 | 4 |
| JG Cameron | 12 | 23 | 1 | 578 | 98 | 26.27 | 48.90 | 0 | 3 | 80 | 2 |
| GM Andrew | 16 | 29 | 2 | 666 | 67 | 24.66 | 58.99 | 0 | 4 | 90 | 6 |
| JD Shantry | 7 | 11 | 4 | 148 | 47* | 21.14 | 63.24 | 0 | 0 | 26 | 0 |
| MG Pardoe | 13 | 26 | 0 | 507 | 74 | 19.50 | 37.41 | 0 | 4 | 77 | 2 |
| A Kapil | 5 | 8 | 0 | 139 | 54 | 17.37 | 48.26 | 0 | 1 | 18 | 2 |
| Saeed Ajmal | 3 | 6 | 1 | 86 | 47 | 17.20 | 61.42 | 0 | 0 | 10 | 0 |
| DG Wright | 7 | 13 | 0 | 212 | 65 | 16.30 | 71.62 | 0 | 1 | 34 | 2 |
| OB Cox | 4 | 8 | 1 | 86 | 23 | 12.28 | 34.12 | 0 | 0 | 11 | 1 |
| MS Mason | 3 | 6 | 0 | 67 | 63 | 11.16 | 89.33 | 0 | 1 | 9 | 1 |
| A Richardson | 16 | 26 | 11 | 151 | 41 | 10.06 | 53.73 | 0 | 0 | 23 | 3 |
| RA Jones | 6 | 10 | 2 | 51 | 23* | 6.37 | 42.14 | 0 | 0 | 4 | 2 |
| SH Choudhry | 2 | 4 | 0 | 23 | 9 | 5.75 | 17.29 | 0 | 0 | 2 | 0 |
| KAJ Roach | 4 | 6 | 1 | 17 | 6 | 3.40 | 23.94 | 0 | 0 | 2 | 0 |
| JK Manuel | 1 | 2 | 0 | 5 | 5 | 2.50 | 45.45 | 0 | 0 | 1 | 0 |
| ND Pinner | 1 | 1 | 0 | 0 | 0 | 0.00 | 0.00 | 0 | 0 | 0 | 0 |
| A Shankar | 1 | 1 | 1 | 10 | 10* | - | 16.66 | 0 | 0 | 0 | 0 |
| CD Whelan | 1 | 1 | 1 | 11 | 11* | - | 40.74 | 0 | 0 | 0 | 0 |

*Batting*

| | Overs | Mdns | Runs | Wkts | BBI | BBM | Ave | Econ | SR | 5w | 10w |
|---|---|---|---|---|---|---|---|---|---|---|---|
| Shakib Al Hasan | 38.2 | 5 | 127 | 7 | 4/42 | 7/127 | 18.14 | 3.31 | 32.8 | 0 | 0 |
| A Richardson | 663.1 | 179 | 1783 | 73 | 6/22 | 9/114 | 24.42 | 2.68 | 54.5 | 3 | 0 |
| DG Wright | 272.4 | 55 | 827 | 31 | 6/56 | 8/96 | 26.67 | 3.03 | 52.7 | 3 | 0 |
| Saeed Ajmal | 164.1 | 31 | 471 | 17 | 6/124 | 8/168 | 27.70 | 2.86 | 57.9 | 2 | 0 |
| GM Andrew | 384.1 | 63 | 1545 | 52 | 5/59 | 8/106 | 29.71 | 4.02 | 44.3 | 1 | 0 |
| RA Jones | 109.4 | 14 | 500 | 16 | 3/38 | 6/132 | 31.25 | 4.55 | 41.1 | 0 | 0 |
| A Kapil | 30.2 | 1 | 138 | 4 | 2/38 | 3/64 | 34.50 | 4.54 | 45.5 | 0 | 0 |
| KAJ Roach | 133.0 | 25 | 550 | 14 | 3/44 | 6/113 | 39.28 | 4.13 | 57.0 | 0 | 0 |
| MS Mason | 95.3 | 19 | 290 | 7 | 3/72 | 3/86 | 41.42 | 3.03 | 81.8 | 0 | 0 |
| JD Shantry | 204.1 | 42 | 634 | 14 | 3/65 | 3/85 | 45.28 | 3.10 | 87.5 | 0 | 0 |
| MM Ali | 267.2 | 21 | 925 | 18 | 4/53 | 4/105 | 51.38 | 3.46 | 89.1 | 0 | 0 |
| SH Choudhry | 11.0 | 2 | 70 | 1 | 1/14 | 1/39 | 70.00 | 6.36 | 66.0 | 0 | 0 |
| DKH Mitchell | 28.0 | 6 | 82 | 1 | 1/11 | 1/11 | 82.00 | 2.92 | 168.0 | 0 | 0 |
| JG Cameron | 7.0 | 0 | 42 | 0 | - | - | - | 6.00 | - | 0 | 0 |
| CD Whelan | 8.0 | 0 | 35 | 0 | - | - | - | 4.37 | - | 0 | 0 |

*Bowling*

**Catches/Stumpings:**
33 Mitchell, 31 Scott (+4st), 23 Solanki, 15 Cox (+0st), 12 Ali, 8 Andrew, 7 Cameron, 5 Richardson, 4 Kervezee, 3 Pardoe, Wright, 2 Kapil, 1 Choudhry, Pinner, Shakib Al Hasan, Shantry

### Batting

|  | Mat | Inns | NO | Runs | HS | Ave | SR | 100 | 50 | 4s | 6s |
|---|---|---|---|---|---|---|---|---|---|---|---|
| MM Ali | 12 | 12 | 0 | 612 | 158 | 51.00 | 122.64 | 3 | 1 | 87 | 12 |
| JG Cameron | 12 | 12 | 2 | 453 | 69 | 45.30 | 79.33 | 0 | 4 | 32 | 7 |
| VS Solanki | 8 | 8 | 0 | 289 | 84 | 36.12 | 94.13 | 0 | 4 | 36 | 2 |
| DKH Mitchell | 10 | 10 | 2 | 250 | 81* | 31.25 | 88.33 | 0 | 1 | 21 | 0 |
| AN Kervezee | 9 | 9 | 0 | 238 | 69 | 26.44 | 81.22 | 0 | 1 | 20 | 1 |
| JK Manuel | 5 | 5 | 0 | 116 | 48 | 23.20 | 95.86 | 0 | 0 | 15 | 2 |
| A Kapil | 6 | 6 | 1 | 105 | 44 | 21.00 | 74.46 | 0 | 0 | 6 | 2 |
| GM Andrew | 10 | 9 | 0 | 176 | 48 | 19.55 | 90.25 | 0 | 0 | 12 | 7 |
| ND Pinner | 9 | 9 | 0 | 122 | 37 | 13.55 | 72.61 | 0 | 0 | 8 | 0 |
| BJM Scott | 7 | 7 | 2 | 60 | 22* | 12.00 | 89.55 | 0 | 0 | 6 | 0 |
| MG Pardoe | 1 | 1 | 0 | 11 | 11 | 11.00 | 55.00 | 0 | 0 | 0 | 0 |
| JD Shantry | 11 | 7 | 5 | 20 | 14 | 10.00 | 100.00 | 0 | 0 | 3 | 0 |
| OB Cox | 5 | 3 | 1 | 16 | 8* | 8.00 | 59.25 | 0 | 0 | 0 | 0 |
| SH Choudhry | 9 | 8 | 3 | 31 | 10 | 6.20 | 67.39 | 0 | 0 | 2 | 0 |
| Saeed Ajmal | 4 | 4 | 2 | 10 | 5* | 5.00 | 55.55 | 0 | 0 | 0 | 0 |
| RA Jones | 2 | 1 | 0 | 4 | 4 | 4.00 | 50.00 | 0 | 0 | 0 | 0 |
| CD Whelan | 3 | 2 | 0 | 7 | 6 | 3.50 | 58.33 | 0 | 0 | 0 | 0 |
| DG Wright | 2 | 1 | 0 | 1 | 1 | 1.00 | 33.33 | 0 | 0 | 0 | 0 |
| MS Mason | 1 | 1 | 0 | 0 | 0 | 0.00 | 0.00 | 0 | 0 | 0 | 0 |
| A Shankar | 1 | 1 | 0 | 0 | 0 | 0.00 | 0.00 | 0 | 0 | 0 | 0 |
| NL Harrison | 4 | 1 | 1 | 2 | 2* | - | 50.00 | 0 | 0 | 0 | 0 |
| BL D'Oliveira | 1 | - | - | - | - | - | - | - | - | - | - |

### Bowling

|  | Overs | Mdns | Runs | Wkts | BBI | Ave | Econ | SR | 4w | 5w |
|---|---|---|---|---|---|---|---|---|---|---|
| JG Cameron | 2.0 | 0 | 9 | 1 | 1/9 | 9.00 | 4.50 | 12.0 | 0 | 0 |
| Saeed Ajmal | 33.0 | 1 | 158 | 11 | 4/24 | 14.36 | 4.78 | 18.0 | 1 | 0 |
| DG Wright | 15.4 | 0 | 79 | 2 | 1/36 | 39.50 | 5.04 | 47.0 | 0 | 0 |
| DKH Mitchell | 46.5 | 0 | 266 | 6 | 1/6 | 44.33 | 5.67 | 46.8 | 0 | 0 |
| JD Shantry | 77.2 | 2 | 442 | 14 | 3/39 | 31.57 | 5.71 | 33.1 | 0 | 0 |
| MM Ali | 81.0 | 1 | 483 | 5 | 2/25 | 96.60 | 5.96 | 97.2 | 0 | 0 |
| NL Harrison | 29.0 | 1 | 180 | 3 | 2/43 | 60.00 | 6.20 | 58.0 | 0 | 0 |
| MS Mason | 5.0 | 1 | 32 | 0 | - | - | 6.40 | - | 0 | 0 |
| GM Andrew | 62.5 | 1 | 410 | 11 | 3/41 | 37.27 | 6.52 | 34.2 | 0 | 0 |
| SH Choudhry | 47.0 | 1 | 311 | 5 | 2/46 | 62.20 | 6.61 | 56.4 | 0 | 0 |
| BL D'Oliveira | 6.0 | 0 | 40 | 1 | 1/40 | 40.00 | 6.66 | 36.0 | 0 | 0 |
| ND Pinner | 3.0 | 0 | 20 | 0 | - | - | 6.66 | - | 0 | 0 |
| CD Whelan | 21.0 | 1 | 146 | 1 | 1/82 | 146.00 | 6.95 | 126.0 | 0 | 0 |
| A Kapil | 22.0 | 1 | 159 | 3 | 1/18 | 53.00 | 7.22 | 44.0 | 0 | 0 |
| RA Jones | 9.3 | 0 | 86 | 1 | 1/33 | 86.00 | 9.05 | 57.0 | 0 | 0 |
| VS Solanki | 1.1 | 0 | 14 | 0 | - | - | 12.00 | - | 0 | 0 |

**Catches/Stumpings:**
9 Cameron, 6 Mitchell, 5 Andrew, Ali, 4 Solanki, 3 Choudhry, Scott (+2st), Shantry, 2 Ajmal, Cox (+0st) Kapil, Pinner, 1 D'Oliveira, Kervezee, Manuel, Pardoe

WORCESTERSHIRE ROYALS

Batting

| | Mat | Inns | NO | Runs | HS | Ave | SR | 100 | 50 | 4s | 6s |
|---|---|---|---|---|---|---|---|---|---|---|---|
| GM Andrew | 13 | 12 | 4 | 257 | 65* | 32.12 | 138.17 | 0 | 3 | 16 | 11 |
| DKH Mitchell | 13 | 12 | 4 | 224 | 45 | 28.00 | 117.27 | 0 | 0 | 17 | 2 |
| SH Choudhry | 8 | 7 | 5 | 46 | 26* | 23.00 | 127.77 | 0 | 0 | 3 | 0 |
| MM Ali | 13 | 13 | 0 | 297 | 53 | 22.84 | 118.32 | 0 | 2 | 41 | 2 |
| JG Cameron | 13 | 12 | 1 | 223 | 55 | 20.27 | 112.06 | 0 | 1 | 9 | 8 |
| VS Solanki | 11 | 11 | 1 | 194 | 62* | 19.40 | 101.57 | 0 | 1 | 25 | 1 |
| AN Kervezee | 13 | 13 | 1 | 220 | 56 | 18.33 | 121.54 | 0 | 1 | 22 | 4 |
| A Kapil | 6 | 4 | 2 | 26 | 13 | 13.00 | 104.00 | 0 | 0 | 2 | 1 |
| BJM Scott | 13 | 10 | 2 | 102 | 22 | 12.75 | 100.99 | 0 | 0 | 10 | 0 |
| JK Manuel | 2 | 2 | 0 | 25 | 21 | 12.50 | 108.69 | 0 | 0 | 4 | 0 |
| Shakib Al Hasan | 12 | 12 | 0 | 110 | 21 | 9.16 | 85.93 | 0 | 0 | 5 | 2 |
| Saeed Ajmal | 8 | 2 | 1 | 7 | 5 | 7.00 | 77.77 | 0 | 0 | 0 | 0 |
| JD Shantry | 13 | 4 | 3 | 3 | 3* | 3.00 | 60.00 | 0 | 0 | 0 | 0 |
| CD Whelan | 4 | 2 | 0 | 3 | 2 | 1.50 | 42.85 | 0 | 0 | 0 | 0 |
| DG Wright | 1 | - | - | - | - | - | - | - | - | - | - |

Bowling

| | Overs | Mdns | Runs | Wkts | BBI | Ave | Econ | SR | 4w | 5w |
|---|---|---|---|---|---|---|---|---|---|---|
| A Kapil | 9.0 | 0 | 53 | 3 | 3/9 | 17.66 | 5.88 | 18.0 | 0 | 0 |
| Saeed Ajmal | 30.3 | 1 | 182 | 16 | 4/14 | 11.37 | 5.96 | 11.4 | 1 | 0 |
| Shakib Al Hasan | 46.0 | 0 | 315 | 19 | 4/31 | 16.57 | 6.84 | 14.5 | 1 | 0 |
| SH Choudhry | 19.0 | 0 | 131 | 4 | 2/24 | 32.75 | 6.89 | 28.5 | 0 | 0 |
| VS Solanki | 2.0 | 0 | 14 | 1 | 1/14 | 14.00 | 7.00 | 12.0 | 0 | 0 |
| MM Ali | 36.0 | 0 | 261 | 9 | 2/14 | 29.00 | 7.25 | 24.0 | 0 | 0 |
| JD Shantry | 46.4 | 1 | 339 | 16 | 3/31 | 21.18 | 7.26 | 17.5 | 0 | 0 |
| CD Whelan | 14.0 | 0 | 108 | 6 | 4/21 | 18.00 | 7.71 | 14.0 | 1 | 0 |
| GM Andrew | 43.5 | 0 | 343 | 19 | 3/17 | 18.05 | 7.82 | 13.8 | 0 | 0 |
| DKH Mitchell | 7.0 | 0 | 55 | 2 | 1/7 | 27.50 | 7.85 | 21.0 | 0 | 0 |
| DG Wright | 2.0 | 0 | 17 | 0 | - | - | 8.50 | - | 0 | 0 |

**Catches/Stumpings:**
11 Cameron, 7 Mitchell, Scott (+7st), Solanki, 6 Shakib Al Hasan, 5 Ali, Andrew, Kervezee, 3 Ajmal, Shantry, 2 Cox (2st), Kapil, 1 Whelan

TEAM PROFILE

**THE YORKSHIRE COUNTY CRICKET CLUB**

FORMED: 1863
HOME GROUND: Headingley Carnegie
ONE-DAY NAME: Carnegie
CAPTAIN: Andrew Gale
2011 RESULTS: CC1: 8/9; CB40: 6/7 in Group A; FL t20: 6/9 in North Group
HONOURS: Championship (31): 1893, 1896, 1898, 1900, 1901, 1902, 1905, 1908, 1912, 1919, 1922, 1923, 1924, 1925, 1931, 1932, 1933, 1935, 1937, 1938, 1939, 1946, 1949, 1959, 1960, 1962, 1963, 1966, 1967, 1968, 2001; Gillette/NatWest/C&G/FP Trophy: (3) 1965, 1969, 2002; Benson and Hedges Cup: 1987; Sunday League: 1983

### THE LOWDOWN

The disappointment of relegation to the bottom tier of the County Championship marked the lowest point in an indifferent season for the Tykes. A lack of runs and experience at the top of the order led to an emergency recall of Jacques Rudolph for a limited stint, who quickly showed the county what they were missing. The capture of Australian opener Phil Jaques should address the issue this season, bringing some nous to a batting order packed with exceptionally talented youngsters like Jonny Bairstow, Joe Root and Gary Ballance. The bowling department remains well-stocked, spearheaded by crowd-favourite Ryan Sidebottom, Ajmal Shahzad and young legspinner Adil Rashid, who will hope to improve on the performances he turned in last season. Returning to the top tier of the County Championship at the first attempt is the firm priority this season for Jason Gillespie and his side.

### HEAD COACH: JASON GILLESPIE

The legendary Australian fast-bowler replaces Martyn Moxon for the upcoming season as the county look to undertake a major restructuring following a poor 2011 season. As a player, Gillespie took 259 wickets in 71 Tests for his national side, also playing in 97 ODIs. He represented Yorkshire in the 2006 and 2007 seasons, and has maintained a close relationship with the county ever since.

| | Mat | Inns | NO | Runs | HS | Ave | SR | 100 | 50 | 4s | 6s |
|---|---|---|---|---|---|---|---|---|---|---|---|
| GS Ballance | 12 | 23 | 5 | 862 | 111 | 47.88 | 51.34 | 1 | 10 | 108 | 5 |
| JM Bairstow | 13 | 24 | 2 | 1015 | 205 | 46.13 | 69.14 | 2 | 6 | 158 | 9 |
| JA Rudolph | 4 | 8 | 1 | 318 | 120 | 45.42 | 61.74 | 1 | 1 | 39 | 6 |
| GL Brophy | 7 | 11 | 3 | 355 | 177* | 44.37 | 50.07 | 1 | 1 | 45 | 1 |
| TT Bresnan | 3 | 5 | 1 | 175 | 87 | 43.75 | 44.87 | 0 | 1 | 22 | 1 |
| AW Gale | 12 | 22 | 3 | 769 | 145* | 40.47 | 52.52 | 2 | 4 | 92 | 3 |
| JJ Sayers | 11 | 22 | 2 | 773 | 139 | 38.65 | 40.79 | 1 | 6 | 75 | 4 |
| JE Root | 15 | 30 | 4 | 937 | 160 | 36.03 | 43.66 | 1 | 4 | 119 | 1 |
| CJ Geldart | 1 | 1 | 0 | 34 | 34 | 34.00 | 60.71 | 0 | 0 | 4 | 0 |
| DJ Wainwright | 4 | 6 | 1 | 146 | 62 | 29.20 | 55.30 | 0 | 1 | 14 | 0 |
| A Lyth | 11 | 22 | 1 | 553 | 74 | 26.33 | 52.21 | 0 | 6 | 82 | 1 |
| RM Pyrah | 11 | 16 | 1 | 376 | 117 | 25.06 | 59.77 | 1 | 1 | 51 | 3 |
| AU Rashid | 16 | 26 | 3 | 556 | 82 | 24.17 | 47.35 | 0 | 3 | 76 | 0 |
| A Shahzad | 11 | 16 | 2 | 320 | 70 | 22.85 | 44.50 | 0 | 1 | 35 | 6 |
| A McGrath | 12 | 23 | 0 | 485 | 115 | 21.08 | 45.84 | 1 | 1 | 67 | 2 |
| RJ Sidebottom | 16 | 25 | 6 | 389 | 61 | 20.47 | 38.70 | 0 | 2 | 58 | 1 |
| SA Patterson | 11 | 16 | 6 | 130 | 53 | 13.00 | 29.81 | 0 | 1 | 18 | 0 |
| SM Guy | 1 | 2 | 0 | 15 | 8 | 7.50 | 35.71 | 0 | 0 | 1 | 0 |
| GS Randhawa | 1 | 1 | 0 | 5 | 5 | 5.00 | 23.80 | 0 | 0 | 1 | 0 |
| MA Ashraf | 7 | 9 | 1 | 27 | 8* | 3.37 | 16.77 | 0 | 0 | 4 | 0 |
| OJ Hannon-Dalby | 5 | 8 | 2 | 10 | 6* | 1.66 | 7.63 | 0 | 0 | 1 | 0 |
| AZ Lees | 1 | 1 | 0 | 0 | 0 | 0.00 | 0.00 | 0 | 0 | 0 | 0 |
| AE Lilley | 1 | 1 | 0 | 0 | 0 | 0.00 | 0.00 | 0 | 0 | 0 | 0 |
| BP Gibson | 1 | 1 | 1 | 1 | 1* | - | 100.00 | 0 | 0 | 0 | 0 |
| I Wardlaw | 1 | - | - | - | - | - | - | - | - | - | - |

| | Overs | Mdns | Runs | Wkts | BBI | BBM | Ave | Econ | SR | 5w | 10w |
|---|---|---|---|---|---|---|---|---|---|---|---|
| JJ Sayers | 13.2 | 3 | 31 | 3 | 3/15 | 3/15 | 10.33 | 2.32 | 26.6 | 0 | 0 |
| TT Bresnan | 97.0 | 27 | 252 | 13 | 4/50 | 5/59 | 19.38 | 2.59 | 44.7 | 0 | 0 |
| RJ Sidebottom | 467.4 | 107 | 1364 | 62 | 7/37 | 11/98 | 22.00 | 2.91 | 45.2 | 3 | 1 |
| GS Randhawa | 21.0 | 4 | 62 | 2 | 2/54 | 2/62 | 31.00 | 2.95 | 63.0 | 0 | 0 |
| RM Pyrah | 266.4 | 54 | 956 | 29 | 5/58 | 8/131 | 32.96 | 3.58 | 55.1 | 1 | 0 |
| A Shahzad | 301.3 | 46 | 1116 | 30 | 5/61 | 5/91 | 37.20 | 3.70 | 60.3 | 2 | 0 |
| DJ Wainwright | 143.5 | 31 | 451 | 12 | 6/40 | 7/115 | 37.58 | 3.13 | 71.9 | 1 | 0 |
| AU Rashid | 448.3 | 56 | 1692 | 39 | 6/77 | 11/114 | 43.38 | 3.77 | 69.0 | 2 | 1 |
| JE Root | 84.3 | 13 | 319 | 7 | 3/33 | 3/33 | 45.57 | 3.77 | 72.4 | 0 | 0 |
| SA Patterson | 294.5 | 55 | 973 | 21 | 4/51 | 4/79 | 46.33 | 3.30 | 84.2 | 0 | 0 |
| MA Ashraf | 158.0 | 28 | 561 | 11 | 3/71 | 3/77 | 51.00 | 3.55 | 86.1 | 0 | 0 |
| A McGrath | 21.0 | 2 | 56 | 1 | 1/14 | 1/14 | 56.00 | 2.66 | 126.0 | 0 | 0 |
| I Wardlaw | 13.0 | 0 | 68 | 1 | 1/68 | 1/68 | 68.00 | 5.23 | 78.0 | 0 | 0 |
| OJ Hannon-Dalby | 121.0 | 10 | 398 | 4 | 1/28 | 2/73 | 99.50 | 3.28 | 181.5 | 0 | 0 |
| GS Ballance | 2.0 | 0 | 11 | 0 | - | - | - | 5.50 | - | 0 | 0 |
| GL Brophy | 2.0 | 0 | 6 | 0 | - | - | - | 3.00 | - | 0 | 0 |
| AE Lilley | 13.0 | 4 | 34 | 0 | - | - | - | 2.61 | - | 0 | 0 |
| A Lyth | 2.0 | 1 | 10 | 0 | - | - | - | 5.00 | - | 0 | 0 |
| JA Rudolph | 6.0 | 0 | 28 | 0 | - | - | - | 4.66 | - | 0 | 0 |

**Catches/Stumpings:**
43 Bairstow (+0st), 20 Lyth, 12 McGrath, 9 Rashid, 7 Ballance, Brophy (inc 2 outfield, +1st), 6 Gibson (+0st), 5 Sayers, Root, 4 Patterson, 3 Gale, 2 Pyrah, Rudolph, Sidebottom, 1 Bresnan, Geldart, Guy (+0st)

## LIST A AVERAGES 2011

### Batting

| | Mat | Inns | NO | Runs | HS | Ave | SR | 100 | 50 | 4s | 6s |
|---|---|---|---|---|---|---|---|---|---|---|---|
| JA Rudolph | 4 | 4 | 1 | 282 | 132* | 94.00 | 95.91 | 1 | 1 | 25 | 4 |
| GS Ballance | 9 | 9 | 3 | 331 | 81* | 55.16 | 97.35 | 0 | 2 | 28 | 8 |
| JM Bairstow | 10 | 10 | 0 | 385 | 114 | 38.50 | 115.96 | 1 | 2 | 27 | 15 |
| AW Gale | 9 | 9 | 0 | 316 | 112 | 35.11 | 75.05 | 1 | 2 | 26 | 5 |
| JE Root | 6 | 6 | 1 | 172 | 62 | 34.40 | 67.18 | 0 | 1 | 12 | 0 |
| AU Rashid | 11 | 8 | 4 | 124 | 43 | 31.00 | 88.57 | 0 | 0 | 7 | 1 |
| A Lyth | 11 | 11 | 0 | 314 | 73 | 28.54 | 80.51 | 0 | 2 | 29 | 5 |
| RM Pyrah | 7 | 6 | 2 | 93 | 69 | 23.25 | 83.03 | 0 | 1 | 8 | 0 |
| A McGrath | 5 | 5 | 1 | 76 | 63 | 19.00 | 87.35 | 0 | 1 | 6 | 1 |
| A Shahzad | 9 | 8 | 2 | 105 | 59* | 17.50 | 94.59 | 0 | 1 | 10 | 5 |
| RJ Sidebottom | 7 | 4 | 1 | 40 | 29 | 13.33 | 117.64 | 0 | 0 | 2 | 2 |
| JJ Sayers | 6 | 6 | 0 | 71 | 25 | 11.83 | 62.83 | 0 | 0 | 8 | 0 |
| GL Brophy | 6 | 6 | 1 | 53 | 28 | 10.60 | 72.60 | 0 | 0 | 4 | 0 |
| TT Bresnan | 1 | 1 | 0 | 9 | 9 | 9.00 | 128.57 | 0 | 0 | 1 | 0 |
| DJ Wainwright | 10 | 5 | 3 | 17 | 8* | 8.50 | 68.00 | 0 | 0 | 2 | 0 |
| BW Sanderson | 3 | 1 | 0 | 2 | 2 | 2.00 | 100.00 | 0 | 0 | 0 | 0 |
| I Wardlaw | 1 | 1 | 0 | 1 | 1 | 1.00 | 25.00 | 0 | 0 | 0 | 0 |
| LJ Hodgson | 2 | 1 | 0 | 0 | 0 | 0.00 | 0.00 | 0 | 0 | 0 | 0 |
| AZ Lees | 1 | 1 | 1 | 12 | 12* | - | 85.71 | 0 | 0 | 2 | 0 |
| SA Patterson | 6 | 1 | 1 | 0 | 0* | - | - | 0 | 0 | 0 | 0 |
| OJ Hannon-Dalby | 4 | - | - | - | - | - | - | - | - | - | - |

### Bowling

| | Overs | Mdns | Runs | Wkts | BBI | Ave | Econ | SR | 4w | 5w |
|---|---|---|---|---|---|---|---|---|---|---|
| I Wardlaw | 4.0 | 0 | 15 | 0 | - | - | 3.75 | - | 0 | 0 |
| LJ Hodgson | 12.0 | 1 | 53 | 2 | 1/14 | 26.50 | 4.41 | 36.0 | 0 | 0 |
| JE Root | 18.4 | 1 | 89 | 2 | 1/1 | 44.50 | 4.76 | 56.0 | 0 | 0 |
| TT Bresnan | 7.0 | 0 | 34 | 2 | 2/34 | 17.00 | 4.85 | 21.0 | 0 | 0 |
| AU Rashid | 80.0 | 1 | 427 | 21 | 3/30 | 20.33 | 5.33 | 22.8 | 0 | 0 |
| DJ Wainwright | 65.3 | 2 | 350 | 10 | 2/27 | 35.00 | 5.34 | 39.3 | 0 | 0 |
| RJ Sidebottom | 50.0 | 0 | 273 | 11 | 2/19 | 24.81 | 5.46 | 27.2 | 0 | 0 |
| SA Patterson | 40.0 | 2 | 224 | 12 | 4/28 | 18.66 | 5.60 | 20.0 | 1 | 0 |
| A McGrath | 7.0 | 0 | 40 | 0 | - | - | 5.71 | - | 0 | 0 |
| A Shahzad | 63.4 | 2 | 387 | 10 | 2/22 | 38.70 | 6.07 | 38.2 | 0 | 0 |
| BW Sanderson | 13.0 | 1 | 80 | 1 | 1/36 | 80.00 | 6.15 | 78.0 | 0 | 0 |
| RM Pyrah | 34.0 | 1 | 213 | 7 | 3/41 | 30.42 | 6.26 | 29.1 | 0 | 0 |
| OJ Hannon-Dalby | 21.4 | 1 | 144 | 5 | 2/22 | 28.80 | 6.64 | 26.0 | 0 | 0 |
| JA Rudolph | 2.0 | 0 | 14 | 0 | - | - | 7.00 | - | 0 | 0 |
| MA Ashraf | 17.5 | 0 | 129 | 2 | 1/29 | 64.50 | 7.23 | 53.5 | 0 | 0 |
| JJ Sayers | 1.0 | 0 | 8 | 0 | - | - | 8.00 | - | 0 | 0 |

**Catches/Stumpings:**
7 Wainwright, 6 Bairstow (inc 1 outfield, +1st), 5 Brophy (+2st), 4 Ballance, Gale, Lyth, Rashid, Shahzad, 3 Hannon-Dalby, Sidebottom, 2 Guy (+1st), Pyrah, Root, 1 Ashraf, Sanderson

www.yorkshireccc.com / tel: 0871 971 1222

| | Mat | Inns | NO | Runs | HS | Ave | SR | 100 | 50 | 4s | 6s |
|---|---|---|---|---|---|---|---|---|---|---|---|
| AW Gale | 15 | 13 | 0 | 418 | 67 | 32.15 | 135.27 | 0 | 4 | 53 | 4 |
| JJ Sayers | 7 | 6 | 0 | 154 | 44 | 25.66 | 127.27 | 0 | 0 | 17 | 3 |
| A Lyth | 15 | 13 | 1 | 306 | 45 | 25.50 | 114.60 | 0 | 0 | 31 | 4 |
| GS Ballance | 13 | 10 | 1 | 215 | 48 | 23.88 | 125.73 | 0 | 0 | 15 | 7 |
| Azeem Rafiq | 8 | 4 | 3 | 22 | 11* | 22.00 | 122.22 | 0 | 0 | 3 | 0 |
| JE Root | 9 | 7 | 2 | 106 | 46* | 21.20 | 100.00 | 0 | 0 | 8 | 0 |
| JM Bairstow | 15 | 12 | 1 | 203 | 41* | 18.45 | 118.02 | 0 | 0 | 15 | 7 |
| RJ Sidebottom | 8 | 7 | 4 | 53 | 16* | 17.66 | 129.26 | 0 | 0 | 4 | 0 |
| A Shahzad | 9 | 7 | 2 | 82 | 20 | 16.40 | 170.83 | 0 | 0 | 8 | 3 |
| A McGrath | 9 | 7 | 0 | 92 | 28 | 13.14 | 103.37 | 0 | 0 | 5 | 1 |
| RM Pyrah | 15 | 10 | 3 | 62 | 17* | 8.85 | 126.53 | 0 | 0 | 5 | 2 |
| GL Brophy | 7 | 6 | 0 | 45 | 22 | 7.50 | 107.14 | 0 | 0 | 4 | 0 |
| AU Rashid | 14 | 9 | 1 | 50 | 13* | 6.25 | 74.62 | 0 | 0 | 2 | 0 |
| TT Bresnan | 3 | 1 | 1 | 25 | 25* | - | 147.05 | 0 | 0 | 2 | 1 |
| DJ Wainwright | 8 | 3 | 3 | 14 | 6* | - | 77.77 | 0 | 0 | 0 | 0 |
| SA Patterson | 4 | - | - | - | - | - | - | - | - | - | - |
| BW Sanderson | 2 | - | - | - | - | - | - | - | - | - | - |
| I Wardlaw | 4 | - | - | - | - | - | - | - | - | - | - |

Batting

| | Overs | Mdns | Runs | Wkts | BBI | Ave | Econ | SR | 4w | 5w |
|---|---|---|---|---|---|---|---|---|---|---|
| I Wardlaw | 11.1 | 0 | 65 | 2 | 2/17 | 32.50 | 5.82 | 33.5 | 0 | 0 |
| BW Sanderson | 8.0 | 0 | 48 | 5 | 4/21 | 9.60 | 6.00 | 9.6 | 1 | 0 |
| Azeem Rafiq | 31.0 | 0 | 227 | 8 | 3/15 | 28.37 | 7.32 | 23.2 | 0 | 0 |
| RJ Sidebottom | 28.3 | 1 | 218 | 5 | 2/18 | 43.60 | 7.64 | 34.2 | 0 | 0 |
| DJ Wainwright | 24.0 | 0 | 185 | 3 | 1/22 | 61.66 | 7.70 | 48.0 | 0 | 0 |
| RM Pyrah | 53.0 | 0 | 417 | 21 | 5/16 | 19.85 | 7.86 | 15.1 | 1 | 1 |
| AU Rashid | 51.0 | 0 | 417 | 15 | 4/26 | 27.80 | 8.17 | 20.4 | 1 | 0 |
| A Shahzad | 29.0 | 0 | 242 | 9 | 3/30 | 26.88 | 8.34 | 19.3 | 0 | 0 |
| TT Bresnan | 11.0 | 0 | 106 | 2 | 1/32 | 53.00 | 9.63 | 33.0 | 0 | 0 |
| SA Patterson | 14.5 | 0 | 146 | 1 | 1/34 | 146.0 | 9.84 | 89.0 | 0 | 0 |
| A McGrath | 4.0 | 0 | 42 | 3 | 3/17 | 14.00 | 10.50 | 8.0 | 0 | 0 |
| JE Root | 3.0 | 0 | 34 | 1 | 1/12 | 34.00 | 11.33 | 18.0 | 0 | 0 |

Bowling

**Catches/Stumpings:**
6 Lyth, 5 Pyrah, Rafiq, Rashid, Sidebottom, 3 Ballance, Brophy (+0st), Wainwright, 2 Bairstow (inc 1 outfield, +1st), McGrath, Patterson, Root, 1 Gale

ENJOY

# MICHAEL VAUGHAN'S

## VALUABLE BETTING INSIGHTS
## EXCLUSIVELY ON BETFAIR

Sign up at
betfair.com
Enter promo code
AOC123 for a

# £20

risk free bet, plus

# £1000

Cash Back!

18+ Please gamble responsibly
www.gambleaware.co.uk

Follow us on Twitter @Betfairsports.
Visit the Michael Vaughan Zone www.betting.betfair.com/cricket/michaelvaughan

▲▼ betfair
The World's Biggest Betting Community

ALLOUTCRICKET

*The*
Players

**NOTTINGHAMSHIRE**

FULL NAME: Andre Ryan Adams
BORN: July 17, 1975, Auckland, New Zealand
SQUAD NO: 41
HEIGHT: 5ft 11in
NICKNAME: Dre, Doctor, Dizzy
EDUCATION: West Lake Boys, Auckland
TEAMS: New Zealand, Auckland, Essex, Herefordshire, Kolkata Tigers, Nottinghamshire
CAREER: Test: 2002; ODI: 2001; T20I: 2005; First-class: 1998; List A: 1997; T20: 2004

BEST BATTING: 124 Essex vs Leicestershire, Leicester, 2004
BEST BOWLING: 6-25 Auckland vs Wellington, Auckland, 2005
COUNTY CAPS: 2004 (Essex); 2007 (Nottinghamshire)

WHY CRICKET? Parents are West Indian. I had no choice!
CAREER HIGHLIGHTS? Winning the Championship, playing in a World Cup, playing a Test
CRICKETING HEROES? Michael Holding, Viv Richards
BEST PLAYER IN COUNTY CRICKET? Alex Hales
TIPS FOR THE TOP? Alex Hales, Jos Buttler
IF YOU WEREN'T A CRICKETER? Running a hunting lodge
FAVOURITE FILM? The Usual Suspects
DREAM HOLIDAY? Rarotonga
AMAZE ME! My grandfather is Corsican and my grandmother is Scottish. I actually really like classical music
TWITTER FEED: @andreadams

| Batting | Mat | Inns | NO | Runs | HS | Ave | SR | 100 | 50 | Ct | St |
|---|---|---|---|---|---|---|---|---|---|---|---|
| Tests | 1 | 2 | 0 | 18 | 11 | 9.00 | 90.00 | 0 | 0 | 1 | 0 |
| ODIs | 42 | 34 | 10 | 419 | 45 | 17.45 | 100.47 | 0 | 0 | 8 | 0 |
| T20Is | 4 | 2 | 1 | 13 | 7 | 13.00 | 108.33 | 0 | 0 | 1 | 0 |
| First-class | 137 | 191 | 21 | 3916 | 124 | 23.03 | | 3 | 18 | 91 | 0 |
| List A | 165 | 119 | 29 | 1504 | 90* | 16.71 | | 0 | 1 | 40 | 0 |
| Twenty20 | 60 | 37 | 12 | 352 | 54* | 14.08 | 132.83 | 0 | 1 | 18 | 0 |

| Bowling | Mat | Balls | Runs | Wkts | BBI | BBM | Ave | Econ | SR | 5w | 10 |
|---|---|---|---|---|---|---|---|---|---|---|---|
| Tests | 1 | 190 | 105 | 6 | 3/44 | 6/105 | 17.50 | 3.31 | 31.6 | 0 | 0 |
| ODIs | 42 | 1885 | 1643 | 53 | 5/22 | 5/22 | 31.00 | 5.22 | 35.5 | 1 | 0 |
| T20Is | 4 | 77 | 105 | 3 | 2/20 | 2/20 | 35.00 | 8.18 | 25.6 | 0 | 0 |
| First-class | 137 | 26858 | 13180 | 560 | 6/25 | | 23.53 | 2.94 | 47.9 | 27 | 5 |
| List A | 165 | 7561 | 5957 | 209 | 5/7 | 5/7 | 28.50 | 4.72 | 36.1 | 4 | 0 |
| Twenty20 | 60 | 1240 | 1580 | 71 | 5/20 | 5/20 | 22.25 | 7.64 | 17.4 | 1 | 0 |

FULL NAME: James Henry Kenneth Adams
BORN: September 23, 1980, Winchester, Hampshire
SQUAD NO: 4
HEIGHT: 6ft 1in
NICKNAME: Bison
EDUCATION: Sherborne School; Loughborough University
TEAMS: Auckland, British Universities, England Lions, Hampshire, Hampshire 2nd XI, Loughborough MCCU
CAREER: First-class: 2002; List A: 2002; T20: 2005

HAMPSHIRE

BEST BATTING: 262* Hampshire vs Nottingham, Nottingham, 2006
BEST BOWLING: 2-16 Hampshire vs Durham, Chester-le-Street, 2004
COUNTY CAP: 2006

CAREER HIGHLIGHTS? Playing and winning the 50-over comp in 2009 at Lord's and the T20 win at The Rose Bowl in 2010
SUPERSTITIONS? Routines…
CRICKETING HEROES? Robin Smith – everything was put on hold when he was batting on the TV. For obvious reasons I used to hope [the West Indian] Jimmy Adams did well
NON-CRICKETING HEROES? I watch in awe whenever I see a musician play (I have a signed Jimmy Page book which is probably my most prized possession). Currently I'm belatedly paying homage to Rory Gallagher, Muhammad Ali (though I've only really seen footage from When We Were Kings), Wolverine and Calvin And Hobbes
AMAZE ME! The first album I ever bought was by New Kids On The Block, I don't see the fun of rollercoasters and I have the largest big toe in the world
FANTASY SLIP CORDON? Keeper: Wolverine (he must have good hands), 1st: Noddy Holder (not the dude from Slade but the batting guru from Perth), 2nd: Jimmy Page (legend), 3rd: Bill Bailey (funny), Gully: My youngest brother and his Southern BBQ van (he employs my other siblings too and would provide a constant source of grub). If I have to be in it, I'd jump in at 1st – the armchair

| Batting | Mat | Inns | NO | Runs | HS | Ave | SR | 100 | 50 | Ct | St |
|---|---|---|---|---|---|---|---|---|---|---|---|
| First-class | 126 | 224 | 16 | 7773 | 262* | 37.37 | | 13 | 42 | 112 | 0 |
| List A | 57 | 54 | 5 | 1868 | 131 | 38.12 | 84.60 | 2 | 13 | 21 | 0 |
| Twenty20 | 78 | 70 | 11 | 1578 | 101* | 26.74 | 120.55 | 2 | 4 | 19 | 0 |

| Bowling | Mat | Balls | Runs | Wkts | BBI | BBM | Ave | Econ | SR | 5w | 10 |
|---|---|---|---|---|---|---|---|---|---|---|---|
| First-class | 126 | 961 | 662 | 11 | 2/16 | | 60.18 | 4.13 | 87.3 | 0 | 0 |
| List A | 57 | 79 | 105 | 1 | 1/34 | 1/34 | 105.00 | 7.97 | 79.0 | 0 | 0 |
| Twenty20 | 78 | 36 | 60 | 0 | - | - | - | 10.00 | - | 0 | 0 |

# WILLIAM ADKIN LHB RM

**SUSSEX**

FULL NAME: William Anthony Adkin
BORN: April 9, 1990, Redhill, Surrey
SQUAD NO: 21
HEIGHT: 6ft 9in
NICKNAME: Avatar, Adders
EDUCATION: Sackalle School
TEAMS: Sussex, Sussex 2nd XI
CAREER: First-class: 2010; List A: 2010; T20: 2012

BEST BATTING: 45 Sussex vs Surrey, Guildford, 2010
BEST BOWLING: 1-28 Sussex vs Worcestershire, Worcester, 2011

WHY CRICKET? Father made me play in the back garden at the age of four
CAREER HIGHLIGHTS? Gaining professional contract. 1st XI debut
SUPERSTITIONS? None
CRICKETING HEROES? Glenn McGrath, Graham Thorpe
BEST PLAYER IN COUNTY CRICKET? Marcus Trescothick
TIP FOR THE TOP? Chris Woakes
IF YOU WEREN'T A CRICKETER? Chef or actor
WHEN RAIN STOPS PLAY? I tell jokes
FAVOURITE FILM? Wedding Crashers
FAVOURITE TV? Celebrity Juice
DREAM HOLIDAY? Barbados
ACCOMPLISHMENTS? Graduating from university
SURPRISING SKILL? I'm good at card tricks
FANTASY SLIP CORDON? Keeper: Michael Jordan, 1st: David Beckham, 2nd: Me, 3rd: Ricky Gervais, Gully: Alan Shearer
TWITTER FEED: @WillAdkin

| Batting | Mat | Inns | NO | Runs | HS | Ave | SR | 100 | 50 | Ct | St |
|---|---|---|---|---|---|---|---|---|---|---|---|
| First-class | 5 | 7 | 2 | 119 | 45 | 23.80 | 32.24 | 0 | 0 | 4 | 0 |
| List A | 3 | 2 | 0 | 40 | 30 | 20.00 | 58.82 | 0 | 0 | 1 | 0 |
| Twenty20 | 2 | 2 | 1 | 9 | 8* | 9.00 | 52.94 | 0 | 0 | 1 | 0 |

| Bowling | Mat | Balls | Runs | Wkts | BBI | BBM | Ave | Econ | SR | 5w | 10 |
|---|---|---|---|---|---|---|---|---|---|---|---|
| First-class | 5 | 444 | 212 | 2 | 1/28 | 1/38 | 106.00 | 2.86 | 222.0 | 0 | 0 |
| List A | 3 | 96 | 80 | 2 | 1/16 | 1/16 | 40.00 | 5.00 | 48.0 | 0 | 0 |
| Twenty20 | 2 | 30 | 37 | 1 | 1/28 | 1/28 | 37.00 | 7.40 | 30.0 | 0 | 0 |

# SHAHID AFRIDI

## RHB LB

FULL NAME: Sahibzada Mohammad Shahid Khan Afridi
BORN: March 1, 1980, Khyber Agency, Pakistan
SQUAD NO: 00
HEIGHT: 5ft 11in
NICKNAME: Boom Boom
TEAMS: Pakistan, Deccan Chargers, Dhaka Gladiators, Griqualand West, Habib Bank Limited, Hampshire, ICC World XI, Karachi, Leicestershire, Melbourne Renegades, South Australia
CAREER: Test: 1998; ODI: 1996; T20I: 2006; First-class: 1995; List A: 1995; T20: 2004

HAMPSHIRE

BEST BATTING: 164 Leicestershire vs Northamptonshire, Northampton, 2001
BEST BOWLING: 6-101 Habib Bank Limited vs Khan Research Laboratories, Rawalpindi, 1997
COUNTY CAP: 2001 (Leicestershire)

NOTES: Hit the fastest ever ODI hundred at the age of 16 in only his second match, bringing up his century in just 37 balls; hitting 11 sixes and six fours. Player of the Tournament World T20 2007. Captained Pakistan in 34 ODIs, 19 T20Is and one Test

| Batting | Mat | Inns | NO | Runs | HS | Ave | SR | 100 | 50 | Ct | St |
|---|---|---|---|---|---|---|---|---|---|---|---|
| Tests | 27 | 48 | 1 | 1716 | 156 | 36.51 | 86.97 | 5 | 8 | 10 | 0 |
| ODIs | 339 | 315 | 19 | 6999 | 124 | 23.64 | 113.89 | 6 | 33 | 110 | 0 |
| T20Is | 48 | 46 | 3 | 748 | 54* | 17.39 | 141.93 | 0 | 3 | 13 | 0 |
| First-class | 111 | 183 | 4 | 5631 | 164 | 31.45 | | 12 | 30 | 75 | 0 |
| List A | 430 | 403 | 22 | 9649 | 124 | 25.32 | | 8 | 52 | 133 | 0 |
| Twenty20 | 108 | 96 | 7 | 1704 | 80 | 19.14 | 157.19 | 0 | 5 | 29 | 0 |

| Bowling | Mat | Balls | Runs | Wkts | BBI | BBM | Ave | Econ | SR | 5w | 10 |
|---|---|---|---|---|---|---|---|---|---|---|---|
| Tests | 27 | 3194 | 1709 | 48 | 5/52 | 5/43 | 35.60 | 3.21 | 66.5 | 1 | 0 |
| ODIs | 339 | 14802 | 11364 | 343 | 6/38 | 6/38 | 33.13 | 4.60 | 43.1 | 8 | 0 |
| T20Is | 48 | 1085 | 1115 | 56 | 4/11 | 4/11 | 19.91 | 6.16 | 19.3 | 0 | 0 |
| First-class | 111 | 13493 | 7023 | 258 | 6/101 | | 27.22 | 3.12 | 52.2 | 8 | 0 |
| List A | 430 | 18897 | 14522 | 447 | 6/38 | 6/38 | 32.48 | 4.61 | 42.2 | 10 | 0 |
| Twenty20 | 108 | 2362 | 2513 | 137 | 5/20 | 5/20 | 18.34 | 6.38 | 17.2 | 1 | 0 |

## ANDREA AGATHANGELOU · RHB LB

FULL NAME: Andrea Peter Agathangelou
BORN: November 16, 1989, Rustenberg, South Africa
SQUAD NO: 11
HEIGHT: 6ft 3in
NICKNAME: Aggers
EDUCATION: UNISA
TEAMS: Lancashire, Lancashire 2nd XI, North West, North West Under-19s, South Africa Under-19s
CAREER: First-class: 2008; List A: 2008

BEST BATTING: 158 North West vs KwaZulu-Natal, Potchefstroom, 2010
BEST BOWLING: 2-62 North West vs KwaZulu-Natal Inland, Potchefstroom, 2009

CAREER HIGHLIGHTS? Representing my province in all age groups and South Africa at U19. Playing first-class cricket at 17. Representing Highveld Lions. Representing SA Amateurs. Signing a contract with Lancashire and being part of the Championship-winning squad
CRICKETING HEROES? Sachin Tendulkar, Rahul Dravid, Jacques Kallis, Matthew Hayden
NON-CRICKETING HEROES? My mother and father, my grandparents, John Openshaw (mentor)
BEST PLAYER IN COUNTY CRICKET? Marcus Trescothick
TIP FOR THE TOP? Simon Kerrigan
IF YOU WEREN'T A CRICKETER? I would be taking over the world!
WHEN RAIN STOPS PLAY? Relaxing and being part of the banter in the changing room
FAVOURITE TV? Friends, Two And A Half Men
FAVOURITE FILM? The Replacements, The Warrior
FAVOURITE BOOK? Eagle In The Sky – Wilbur Smith
DREAM HOLIDAY? Cyprus, the Maldives
GUILTY PLEASURES? I have a massive sweet tooth! And often need to hide my stash away from the fitness staff
SURPRISING FACTS? I speak three languages – English, Afrikaans and bettering my hand at Greek. Was a provincial squash player
TWITTER FEED: @Agathangelou11

| Batting | Mat | Inns | NO | Runs | HS | Ave | SR | 100 | 50 | Ct | St |
|---|---|---|---|---|---|---|---|---|---|---|---|
| First-class | 27 | 53 | 2 | 1831 | 158 | 35.90 | 53.60 | 4 | 11 | 41 | 0 |
| List A | 23 | 22 | 2 | 654 | 94 | 32.70 | 78.13 | 0 | 5 | 9 | 1 |

| Bowling | Mat | Balls | Runs | Wkts | BBI | BBM | Ave | Econ | SR | 5w | 10 |
|---|---|---|---|---|---|---|---|---|---|---|---|
| First-class | 27 | 465 | 311 | 6 | 2/62 | 3/66 | 51.83 | 4.01 | 77.5 | 0 | 0 |
| List A | 23 | 30 | 35 | 0 | - | - | - | 7.00 | - | 0 | 0 |

# SAEED AJMAL

## RHB OB

FULL NAME: Saeed Ajmal
BORN: October 14, 1977, Faisalabad, Punjab
SQUAD NO: 50
HEIGHT: 5ft 4in
TEAMS: Pakistan, Dhaka Gladiators, Faisalabad, Islamabad Cricket Association, Khan Research Labs, Water and Power Development Authority, Worcestershire
CAREER: Test: 2009; ODI: 2008; T20I: 2009; First-class: 1996; List A: 1995; T20: 2005

BEST BATTING: 53 Faisalabad vs Quetta, Sargodha, 2004
BEST BOWLING: 7-55 Pakistan vs England, Dubai, 2012

NOTES: Man of the Series in this winter's 3-0 drubbing of England by Pakistan, Ajmal is widely recognised as one of the best spinners in world cricket. He was ranked second in both Test and one-day formats at the end of March. At 30, Ajmal came late to international cricket – he was 32 before he played a Test – but he has made up for lost time. He was the leading wicket-taker in Tests in 2011 with 50 in eight games, then took a further 24 in the three-match series at 14.70 against the world's No.1 Test side. He is also a key one-day bowler, regularly choking the opposition's scoring in the middle overs

| Batting | Mat | Inns | NO | Runs | HS | Ave | SR | 100 | 50 | Ct | St |
|---|---|---|---|---|---|---|---|---|---|---|---|
| Tests | 20 | 28 | 9 | 227 | 50 | 11.94 | 39.75 | 0 | 1 | 6 | 0 |
| ODIs | 62 | 38 | 18 | 183 | 33 | 9.15 | 57.18 | 0 | 0 | 11 | 0 |
| T20Is | 37 | 13 | 9 | 52 | 21* | 13.00 | 118.18 | 0 | 0 | 5 | 0 |
| First-class | 107 | 142 | 45 | 1199 | 53 | 12.36 | | 0 | 3 | 34 | 0 |
| List A | 164 | 90 | 43 | 380 | 33 | 8.08 | | 0 | 0 | 37 | 0 |
| Twenty20 | 83 | 24 | 15 | 94 | 21* | 10.44 | 109.30 | 0 | 0 | 14 | 0 |

| Bowling | Mat | Balls | Runs | Wkts | BBI | BBM | Ave | Econ | SR | 5w | 10 |
|---|---|---|---|---|---|---|---|---|---|---|---|
| Tests | 20 | 6551 | 2857 | 107 | 7/55 | 11/111 | 26.70 | 2.61 | 61.2 | 5 | 2 |
| ODIs | 62 | 3230 | 2227 | 93 | 5/43 | 5/43 | 23.94 | 4.13 | 34.7 | 1 | 0 |
| T20Is | 37 | 804 | 837 | 51 | 4/19 | 4/19 | 16.41 | 6.24 | 15.7 | 0 | 0 |
| First-class | 107 | 23498 | 10675 | 395 | 7/55 | | 27.02 | 2.72 | 59.4 | 24 | 3 |
| List A | 164 | 8501 | 6228 | 246 | 5/18 | 5/18 | 25.31 | 4.39 | 34.5 | 2 | 0 |
| Twenty20 | 83 | 1799 | 1905 | 121 | 4/14 | 4/14 | 15.74 | 6.35 | 14.8 | 0 | 0 |

## KABIR ALI                                    RHB RMF W5

HAMPSHIRE

FULL NAME: Kabir Ali
BORN: November 24, 1980, Moseley, Birmingham, Warwickshire
SQUAD NO: 33
HEIGHT: 6ft
NICKNAME: Kabby, Taxi
EDUCATION: Moseley School; Wolverhampton University
TEAMS: England, Barisal Burners, England A, Hampshire, Marylebone Cricket Club, Rajasthan, Worcestershire
CAREER: Test: 2003; ODI: 2003; First-class: 1999; List A: 2000; T20: 2004

BEST BATTING: 84* Worcestershire vs Durham, Stockton, 2003
BEST BOWLING: 8-50 Worcestershire vs Lancashire, Manchester, 2007

FAMILY TIES? Father played club cricket. Cousin Moeen plays for Worcerstershire and cousin Kadeer played for Gloucestershire
CAREER HIGHLIGHTS? Playing for England
OTHER SPORTS PLAYED? Football, snooker
RELAXATIONS? Playing snooker and spending time with family and friends
NOTES: Took five wickets in the match in his first and only Test appearance for England, against South Africa at Headingley in 2003

| Batting | Mat | Inns | NO | Runs | HS | Ave | SR | 100 | 50 | Ct | St |
|---|---|---|---|---|---|---|---|---|---|---|---|
| Tests | 1 | 2 | 0 | 10 | 9 | 5.00 | 35.71 | 0 | 0 | 0 | 0 |
| ODIs | 14 | 9 | 3 | 93 | 39* | 15.50 | 86.11 | 0 | 0 | 1 | 0 |
| First-class | 122 | 173 | 27 | 2481 | 84* | 16.99 | | 0 | 7 | 33 | 0 |
| List A | 157 | 98 | 26 | 1092 | 92 | 15.16 | | 0 | 3 | 27 | 0 |
| Twenty20 | 34 | 25 | 7 | 309 | 49 | 17.16 | 134.93 | 0 | 0 | 8 | 0 |
| Bowling | Mat | Balls | Runs | Wkts | BBI | BBM | Ave | Econ | SR | 5w | 10 |
| Tests | 1 | 216 | 136 | 5 | 3/80 | 5/136 | 27.20 | 3.77 | 43.2 | 0 | 0 |
| ODIs | 14 | 673 | 682 | 20 | 4/45 | 4/45 | 34.10 | 6.08 | 33.6 | 0 | 0 |
| First-class | 122 | 20826 | 12445 | 461 | 8/50 | | 26.99 | 3.58 | 45.1 | 23 | 4 |
| List A | 157 | 6683 | 5752 | 227 | 5/36 | 5/36 | 25.33 | 5.16 | 29.4 | 2 | 0 |
| Twenty20 | 34 | 695 | 956 | 40 | 4/44 | 4/44 | 23.90 | 8.25 | 17.3 | 0 | 0 |

# MOEEN ALI

## LHB OB R1 MVP13

FULL NAME: Moeen Munir Ali
BORN: June 18, 1987, Birmingham
SQUAD NO: 8
HEIGHT: 6ft
NICKNAME: Moe, Brother Mo
EDUCATION: Moseley School
TEAMS: England Lions, England Under-19s, Moors Sports Club, Warwickshire, Worcestershire
CAREER: First-class: 2005; List A: 2006; T20: 2007

BEST BATTING: 158 Worcestershire vs Somerset, Worcester, 2011
BEST BOWLING: 5-36 Worcestershire vs Middlesex, Lord's, 2010
COUNTY CAP: 2007 (Worcestershire)

FAMILY TIES? Dad is a cricket coach. Kadeer Ali (former Leicestershire, Worcestershire, Gloucestershire) is my brother, Kabir Ali (Hampshire) is my cousin
CAREER HIGHLIGHTS? Playing for England and captaining Worcestershire. Being promoted twice with Worcestershire. Winning the CB40. Scoring 136 against Sri Lanka
CRICKETING HEROES? Brian Lara, Saeed Anwar, Marcus Trescothick, Saeed Ajmal
NON-CRICKETING HEROES? Prophet Muhammad (peace be upon him), Abu Bakr, Umar, Uthman, Ali (may Allah be pleased with them all)
TIPS FOR THE TOP? Aneesh Kapil, Ben Stokes
IF YOU WEREN'T A CRICKETER? Own and run a chippy called Big Mo's
FAVOURITE BOOK? Al-Quran (the recitation) Aurther-Allah (One true God)
DREAM HOLIDAY? Saudi Arabia or Palestine
ACCOMPLISHMENTS? Hajj, performing the fifth pillar of Islam
SURPRISING FACT? Big Liverpool fan. I wear my trousers above my ankles. My grandmother is a white English woman
FANTASY SLIP CORDON? Keeper: Superman, 1st: Spiderman, 2nd: Batman, 3rd: Me, Gully: Ironman

| Batting | Mat | Inns | NO | Runs | HS | Ave | SR | 100 | 50 | Ct | St |
|---|---|---|---|---|---|---|---|---|---|---|---|
| First-class | 68 | 118 | 8 | 3962 | 158 | 36.01 | 53.65 | 7 | 25 | 36 | 0 |
| List A | 75 | 71 | 2 | 2119 | 158 | 30.71 | 99.48 | 6 | 9 | 22 | 0 |
| Twenty20 | 50 | 48 | 3 | 1024 | 72 | 22.75 | 118.51 | 0 | 5 | 14 | 0 |

| Bowling | Mat | Balls | Runs | Wkts | BBI | BBM | Ave | Econ | SR | 5w | 10 |
|---|---|---|---|---|---|---|---|---|---|---|---|
| First-class | 68 | 4293 | 2753 | 48 | 5/36 | 6/39 | 57.35 | 3.84 | 89.4 | 1 | 0 |
| List A | 75 | 1344 | 1288 | 24 | 3/32 | 3/32 | 53.66 | 5.75 | 56.0 | 0 | 0 |
| Twenty20 | 50 | 499 | 611 | 24 | 3/19 | 3/19 | 25.45 | 7.34 | 20.7 | 0 | 0 |

## JIM ALLENBY RHB RM

GLAMORGAN

FULL NAME: James Allenby
BORN: September 12, 1982, Western Australia, Australia
SQUAD NO: 5
HEIGHT: 6ft
NICKNAME: Hank
EDUCATION: Christ Church Grammar School, Perth
TEAMS: Durham Cricket Board, Glamorgan, Leicestershire, Western Australia, Western Australia Under-19s
CAREER: First-class: 2006; List A: 2003; T20: 2005

BEST BATTING: 138* Leicestershire vs Bangladesh A, Leicester, 2008
BEST BOWLING: 5-44 Glamorgan vs Derbyshire, Cardiff, 2011
COUNTY CAP: 2010 (Glamorgan)

CAREER HIGHLIGHTS? Signing first pro contract in 2005 after three years trialling all over the country. Winning the T20 with Leicestershire in 2006 and playing Finals Day in 2005. Century on County Championship debut. T20 century for Leicestershire
SUPERSTITIONS? Prepare for each ball in same way and walk out on left hand side
CRICKETING HEROES? Steve Waugh, Dean Jones, Paul Nixon, Matt Maynard
NON-CRICKETING HEROES? Family
BEST PLAYER IN COUNTY CRICKET? Dale Benkenstein
TIPS FOR THE TOP? James Harris, Tom Maynard
IF YOU WEREN'T A CRICKETER? Probably still doing landscaping or coaching cricket. Alternatively I would have set up a business to encourage school age kids to be active and play all sports to avoid becoming unhealthy
WHEN RAIN STOPS PLAY? Pool table in dressing room gets a workout!
DREAM HOLIDAY? Yallingup, Western Australia
AMAZE ME! 1. I support Wales in the rugby 2. Cousin Robert is a top 50 world golfer 3. It is all my own hair, no Tweed!

| Batting | Mat | Inns | NO | Runs | HS | Ave | SR | 100 | 50 | Ct | St |
|---|---|---|---|---|---|---|---|---|---|---|---|
| First-class | 72 | 113 | 16 | 3692 | 138* | 38.06 | 56.83 | 5 | 29 | 66 | 0 |
| List A | 68 | 63 | 7 | 1358 | 91* | 24.25 | 82.95 | 0 | 6 | 19 | 0 |
| Twenty20 | 67 | 62 | 10 | 1410 | 110 | 27.11 | 117.89 | 1 | 9 | 22 | 0 |

| Bowling | Mat | Balls | Runs | Wkts | BBI | BBM | Ave | Econ | SR | 5w | 10 |
|---|---|---|---|---|---|---|---|---|---|---|---|
| First-class | 72 | 7430 | 3431 | 124 | 5/44 | 6/86 | 27.66 | 2.77 | 59.9 | 3 | 0 |
| List A | 68 | 1963 | 1703 | 54 | 5/43 | 5/43 | 31.53 | 5.20 | 36.3 | 1 | 0 |
| Twenty20 | 67 | 820 | 1083 | 40 | 5/21 | 5/21 | 27.07 | 7.92 | 20.5 | 2 | 0 |

FULL NAME: Thomas William Allin
BORN: November 27, 1987, Devon
SQUAD NO: 87
HEIGHT: 5ft 11in
NICKNAME: Muscles, Guetta, TA
EDUCATION: Bideford College; UWIC University
TEAMS: Cardiff MCCU, Devon, Warwickshire
CAREER: List A: 2011

**WARWICKSHIRE**

FAMILY TIES? Dad [Tony] used to play professionally
CAREER HIGHLIGHTS? Signing for Warwickshire and subsequently making my debut
SUPERSTITIONS? Three practice balls to mid on, left pad on first, lucky socks
CRICKETING HEROES? Sachin Tendulkar
NON-CRICKETING HEROES? Kauto Star
BEST PLAYER IN COUNTY CRICKET? Chris Woakes
TIP FOR THE TOP? Tom Milnes
IF YOU WEREN'T A CRICKETER? Involved in horse racing or a teacher
WHEN RAIN STOPS PLAY? iPhone
FAVOURITE TV? Channel 4 Racing or Hustle
FAVOURITE FILM? The Next Three Days
FAVOURITE BOOK? Paul Nicholls – Lucky Break
DREAM HOLIDAY? Sydney
ACCOMPLISHMENTS? Degree
SURPRISING SKILL? I'm class at Mario Kart on N64, lost once in 10 years!
GUILTY PLEASURES? Gambling
AMAZE ME! I want to be a jockey, I love rain, I only hit my first six when I was 16
TWITTER FEED: @tommya87

| Batting | Mat | Inns | NO | Runs | HS | Ave | SR | 100 | 50 | Ct | St |
|---------|-----|------|-----|------|-----|------|-------|-----|-----|-----|-----|
| List A | 1 | 1 | 1 | 2 | 2* | - | 16.66 | 0 | 0 | 0 | 0 |

| Bowling | Mat | Balls | Runs | Wkts | BBI | BBM | Ave | Econ | SR | 5w | 10 |
|---------|-----|-------|------|------|-----|-----|-----|-------|-----|-----|-----|
| List A | 1 | 12 | 29 | 0 | - | - | - | 14.50 | - | 0 | 0 |

## TIM AMBROSE                                    RHB WK

**FULL NAME:** Timothy Raymond Ambrose
**BORN:** December 1, 1982, Newcastle, New South Wales, Australia
**SQUAD NO:** 12
**HEIGHT:** 5ft 7in
**NICKNAME:** Freak
**EDUCATION:** Merewether Selective High, NSW
**TEAMS:** England, Sussex, Warwickshire
**CAREER:** Test: 2008; ODI: 2008; T20I: 2008; First-class: 2001; List A: 2001; T20: 2003

**BEST BATTING:** 251* Warwickshire vs Worcestershire, Worcester, 2007
**COUNTY CAPS:** 2003 (Sussex); 2007 (Warwickshire)

**FAMILY TIES?** Father played for Nelson Bay
**CAREER HIGHLIGHTS?** Winning the Championship with Sussex in 2003, any time I've played for England
**CRICKETING HEROES?** Steve Waugh, Adam Gilchrist, Mushtaq Ahmed
**NON-CRICKETING HEROES?** Peter Griffin, Eric Cantona
**BEST PLAYER IN COUNTY CRICKET?** Marcus Trescothick
**TIP FOR THE TOP?** Laurie Evans
**WHEN RAIN STOPS PLAY?** Debating random topics – North vs South is always fun!
**FAVOURITE TV?** Dexter, Family Guy
**FAVOURITE FILM?** Cool Hand Luke
**FAVOURITE BOOK?** Bravo Two Zero
**DREAM HOLIDAY?** Nelson Bay

| Batting | Mat | Inns | NO | Runs | HS | Ave | SR | 100 | 50 | Ct | St |
|---|---|---|---|---|---|---|---|---|---|---|---|
| Tests | 11 | 16 | 1 | 447 | 102 | 29.80 | 46.41 | 1 | 3 | 31 | 0 |
| ODIs | 5 | 5 | 1 | 10 | 6 | 2.50 | 29.41 | 0 | 0 | 3 | 0 |
| T20Is | 1 | - | - | - | - | - | - | - | - | 1 | 1 |
| First-class | 136 | 207 | 18 | 6277 | 251* | 33.21 | 51.56 | 9 | 39 | 318 | 21 |
| List A | 120 | 99 | 14 | 2351 | 135 | 27.65 | 72.89 | 3 | 8 | 120 | 22 |
| Twenty20 | 55 | 43 | 13 | 800 | 77 | 26.66 | 114.77 | 0 | 2 | 32 | 17 |

| Bowling | Mat | Balls | Runs | Wkts | BBI | BBM | Ave | Econ | SR | 5w | 10 |
|---|---|---|---|---|---|---|---|---|---|---|---|
| Tests | 11 | - | - | - | - | - | - | - | - | - | - |
| ODIs | 5 | - | - | - | - | - | - | - | - | - | - |
| T20Is | 1 | - | - | - | - | - | - | - | - | - | - |
| First-class | 136 | 6 | 1 | 0 | - | - | - | 1.00 | - | 0 | 0 |
| List A | 120 | - | - | - | - | - | - | - | - | - | - |
| Twenty20 | 55 | - | - | - | - | - | - | - | - | - | - |

# JAMES ANDERSON                              LHB RFM W2

FULL NAME: James Michael Anderson
BORN: July 30, 1982, Burnley, Lancashire
SQUAD NO: 9
HEIGHT: 6ft 2in
NICKNAME: Jimmy, Jimbo, Jimbob
EDUCATION: St Theodore's RC High School;
St Theodore's RC Sixth Form Centre, Burnley
TEAMS: England, Auckland, England Under-
19s, Lancashire, Lancashire Cricket Board
CAREER: Test: 2003; ODI: 2002; T20I: 2007;
First-class: 2002; List A: 2000; T20: 2004

BEST BATTING: 37* Lancashire vs Durham, Manchester, 2005
BEST BOWLING: 7-43 England vs New Zealand, Nottingham, 2008
COUNTY CAP: 2003; BENEFIT YEAR: 2012

CAREER HIGHLIGHTS? Two Ashes wins
CRICKETING HEROES? Allan Donald, Peter Martin
TIP FOR THE TOP? Simon Kerrigan
IF YOU WEREN'T A CRICKETER? Busking with my recorder
WHEN RAIN STOPS PLAY? Cards, sleeping, singing a cappella with Swann, Cook and Bresnan
FAVOURITE TV? Peppa Pig
FAVOURITE FILM? Les Enfants Terribles (1950)
SURPRISING SKILL? I can peel a potato in 2.4 seconds
AMAZE ME! I have a personality. I'm allergic to mushrooms
FANTASY SLIP CORDON? Keeper: Inspector Gadget, Gully: Me
TWITTER FEED: @JimmyAnderson9

| Batting | Mat | Inns | NO | Runs | HS | Ave | SR | 100 | 50 | Ct | St |
|---|---|---|---|---|---|---|---|---|---|---|---|
| Tests | 66 | 87 | 34 | 626 | 34 | 11.81 | 36.93 | 0 | 0 | 34 | 0 |
| ODIs | 154 | 63 | 34 | 199 | 20* | 6.86 | 42.16 | 0 | 0 | 42 | 0 |
| T20Is | 19 | 4 | 3 | 1 | 1* | 1.00 | 50.00 | 0 | 0 | 3 | 0 |
| First-class | 130 | 153 | 60 | 960 | 37* | 10.32 | | 0 | 0 | 63 | 0 |
| List A | 207 | 84 | 51 | 292 | 20* | 8.84 | | 0 | 0 | 51 | 0 |
| Twenty20 | 40 | 9 | 6 | 23 | 16 | 7.66 | 92.00 | 0 | 0 | 8 | 0 |

| Bowling | Mat | Balls | Runs | Wkts | BBI | BBM | Ave | Econ | SR | 5w | 10 |
|---|---|---|---|---|---|---|---|---|---|---|---|
| Tests | 66 | 14192 | 7587 | 249 | 7/43 | 11/71 | 30.46 | 3.20 | 56.9 | 11 | 1 |
| ODIs | 154 | 7652 | 6414 | 208 | 5/23 | 5/23 | 30.83 | 5.02 | 36.7 | 1 | 0 |
| T20Is | 19 | 422 | 552 | 18 | 3/23 | 3/23 | 30.66 | 7.84 | 23.4 | 0 | 0 |
| First-class | 130 | 25150 | 13402 | 485 | 7/43 | | 27.63 | 3.19 | 51.8 | 23 | 3 |
| List A | 207 | 10062 | 8210 | 282 | 5/23 | 5/23 | 29.11 | 4.89 | 35.6 | 1 | 0 |
| Twenty20 | 40 | 855 | 1190 | 37 | 3/23 | 3/23 | 32.16 | 8.35 | 23.1 | 0 | 0 |

## GARETH ANDREW — LHB RMF W1 MVP2

**WORCESTERSHIRE**

FULL NAME: Gareth Mark Andrew
BORN: December 27, 1983, Yeovil, Somerset
SQUAD NO: 14
HEIGHT: 6ft
NICKNAME: Gaz, Brad, Alfie, Sobers
EDUCATION: Ansford Communtity School;
Richard Huish College, Taunton
TEAMS: Somerset, Somerset Cricket Board,
Worcestershire, Worcestershire 2nd XI
CAREER: First-class: 2003; List A: 2000; T20:
2003

BEST BATTING: 92* Worcestershire vs Nottinghamshire, Worcester, 2009
BEST BOWLING: 5-58 Worcestershire vs Middlesex, Kidderminster, 2008

WHY CRICKET? Wasn't good enough to be a footballer!
CAREER HIGHLIGHTS? Winning 2005 T20 with Somerset. Division Two promotions with Worcestershire in 2008 and 2010
NON-CRICKETING HEROES? Jeremy Clarkson, Steve McQueen
BEST PLAYER IN COUNTY CRICKET? Marcus Trescothick
TIPS FOR THE TOP? Jos Buttler, Aneesh Kapil
IF YOU WEREN'T A CRICKETER? Racing something with an engine
WHEN RAIN STOPS PLAY? You'll find me annoying the physio!
FAVOURITE TV? Top Gear
FAVOURITE FILM? Man On Fire
FAVOURITE BOOK? The Alchemist by Paulo Coelho
ACCOMPLISHMENTS? GCSEs, A-Levels, passing my driving test!
GUILTY PLEASURES? Coffee
FANTASY SLIP CORDON? Keeper: Chris Evans, 1st: Steve McQueen, 2nd: Jenson Button, 3rd: Penelope Cruz, 4th: Me, Gully: Fearne Cotton
TWITTER FEED: @GAndrew14

| Batting | Mat | Inns | NO | Runs | HS | Ave | SR | 100 | 50 | Ct | St |
|---|---|---|---|---|---|---|---|---|---|---|---|
| First-class | 58 | 88 | 12 | 1844 | 92* | 24.26 | 53.37 | 0 | 11 | 20 | 0 |
| List A | 93 | 62 | 14 | 816 | 104 | 17.00 | | 1 | 1 | 30 | 0 |
| Twenty20 | 76 | 45 | 16 | 456 | 65* | 15.72 | 131.79 | 0 | 3 | 20 | 0 |

| Bowling | Mat | Balls | Runs | Wkts | BBI | BBM | Ave | Econ | SR | 5w | 10 |
|---|---|---|---|---|---|---|---|---|---|---|---|
| First-class | 58 | 7800 | 5199 | 153 | 5/58 | | 33.98 | 3.99 | 50.9 | 3 | 0 |
| List A | 93 | 3077 | 3235 | 94 | 5/31 | 5/31 | 34.41 | 6.30 | 32.7 | 1 | 0 |
| Twenty20 | 76 | 1341 | 1915 | 71 | 4/22 | 4/22 | 26.97 | 8.56 | 18.8 | 0 | 0 |

# ZAFAR ANSARI                                   LHB SLA

FULL NAME: Zafar Shahaan Ansari
BORN: December 10, 1991, Ascot, Berkshire
SQUAD NO: 22
HEIGHT: 5ft 11in
NICKNAME: Zaf, PM
EDUCATION: Hampton School; University of Cambridge
TEAMS: Cambridge MCCU, England Under-19s, Surrey, Surrey 2nd XI, Surrey Under-13s, Surrey Under-15s, Surrey Under-17s, Surrey Under-19s
CAREER: First-class: 2011; List A: 2010; T20: 2011

SURREY

BEST BATTING: 41 CMCCU vs Surrey, Fenner's, 2011
BEST BOWLING: 5-33 CMCCU vs Surrey, Fenner's, 2011

FAMILY TIES? My dad played three first-class matches in Pakistan. My brother [Akbar] has played a lot of county 2nd XI cricket (Surrey, Worcestershire, Nottinghamshire, Hampshire) and captained Cambridge Blues for two years
CAREER HIGHLIGHTS? T20 debut, winning the CB40 at Lord's
CRICKETING HEROES? Garry Sobers, Graham Thorpe, Wasim Akram, Chris Scott
NON-CRICKETING HEROES? Akbar Ansari, Costas Douzinas
BEST PLAYER IN COUNTY CRICKET? Steve Davies
TIPS FOR THE TOP? Jason Roy, Tom Maynard, Chris Jones, Aneesh Kapil
IF YOU WEREN'T A CRICKETER? Law or American footballer
WHEN RAIN STOPS PLAY? Reading, drinking tea
FAVOURITE TV? The West Wing
FAVOURITE FILM? Biutiful
FAVOURITE BOOK? Half Of A Yellow Sun by Chimamanda Adichie
DREAM HOLIDAY? Barcelona
ACCOMPLISHMENTS? Starred 1st in first-year Cambridge exams
FANTASY SLIP CORDON? Keeper: Malcolm X, 1st: Michael Vick, 2nd: Leon Trotsky, 3rd: Me, Gully: Mike Hussey

| Batting | Mat | Inns | NO | Runs | HS | Ave | SR | 100 | 50 | Ct | St |
|---|---|---|---|---|---|---|---|---|---|---|---|
| First-class | 6 | 10 | 0 | 90 | 41 | 9.00 | 45.68 | 0 | 0 | 4 | 0 |
| List A | 9 | 7 | 4 | 76 | 23* | 25.33 | 105.55 | 0 | 0 | 5 | 0 |
| Twenty20 | 10 | 6 | 3 | 108 | 34* | 36.00 | 145.94 | 0 | 0 | 2 | 0 |

| Bowling | Mat | Balls | Runs | Wkts | BBI | BBM | Ave | Econ | SR | 5w | 10 |
|---|---|---|---|---|---|---|---|---|---|---|---|
| First-class | 6 | 765 | 402 | 12 | 5/33 | 5/39 | 33.50 | 3.15 | 63.7 | 1 | 0 |
| List A | 9 | 210 | 225 | 6 | 1/22 | 1/22 | 37.50 | 6.42 | 35.0 | 0 | 0 |
| Twenty20 | 10 | 186 | 221 | 4 | 1/19 | 1/19 | 55.25 | 7.12 | 46.5 | 0 | 0 |

# JAMES ANYON LHB RFM W1

**SUSSEX**

FULL NAME: James Edward Anyon
BORN: May 5, 1983, Lancaster
SQUAD NO: 30
HEIGHT: 6ft 2in
NICKNAME: Jimmy
EDUCATION: Gorsbory High School; Preston College; Loughborough University
TEAMS: Cumberland, Loughborough MCCU, Surrey, Sussex, Warwickshire
CAREER: First-class: 2003; List A: 2003; T20: 2005

---

BEST BATTING: 53 Sussex vs Yorkshire, Scarborough, 2011
BEST BOWLING: 6-82 Warwickshire vs Glamorgan, Cardiff, 2008
COUNTY CAP: 2011 (Sussex)

---

FAMILY TIES? Dad and uncle were good village players. They started me off, playing when they were short of players when I was only nine or 10
CAREER HIGHLIGHTS? My T20 hat-trick vs Somerset in 2005. My Man of the Match performance against Nottinghamshire in 2011
CRICKETING HEROES? Curtly Ambrose, Glenn McGrath, Darren Gough, Michael Atherton
NON-CRICKETING HEROES? Paul Scholes, Sir Alex Ferguson, Winston Churchill
TIP FOR THE TOP? Ben Brown
IF YOU WEREN'T A CRICKETER? A fitness instructor
WHEN RAIN STOPS PLAY? Reading
FAVOURITE TV? Anything on the History or Discovery channels
FAVOURITE FILM? The Godfather
GUILTY PLEASURES? Basshunter – shocking!
FANTASY SLIP CORDON? Keeper: Andy Hodd (he cracks me up all game and can keep pretty well, to be fair), 1st: Brian Cox (when it gets boring, at least I could learn something), 2nd: Me, 3rd: Eva Mendes (so she would be stood in front of me), Gully: Winston Churchill (for some useful inspiration)

| Batting | Mat | Inns | NO | Runs | HS | Ave | SR | 100 | 50 | Ct | St |
|---|---|---|---|---|---|---|---|---|---|---|---|
| First-class | 73 | 96 | 28 | 807 | 53 | 11.86 | 33.69 | 0 | 2 | 23 | 0 |
| List A | 38 | 11 | 5 | 34 | 12 | 5.66 | 80.95 | 0 | 0 | 8 | 0 |
| Twenty20 | 22 | 4 | 3 | 16 | 8* | 16.00 | 69.56 | 0 | 0 | 3 | 0 |
| Bowling | Mat | Balls | Runs | Wkts | BBI | BBM | Ave | Econ | SR | 5w | 10 |
| First-class | 73 | 11428 | 7061 | 196 | 6/82 | | 36.02 | 3.70 | 58.3 | 3 | 0 |
| List A | 38 | 1375 | 1254 | 41 | 3/6 | 3/6 | 30.58 | 5.47 | 33.5 | 0 | 0 |
| Twenty20 | 22 | 351 | 498 | 25 | 3/6 | 3/6 | 19.92 | 8.51 | 14.0 | 0 | 0 |

FULL NAME: Naveed Arif Gondal
BORN: November 2, 1981, Mandi Bahauddin, Punjab, Pakistan
SQUAD NO: 8
HEIGHT: 5ft 11in
NICKNAME: Nav
EDUCATION: F.A College
TEAMS: Gujranwala Cricket Association, Sialkot, Sialkot Stallions, Sussex
CAREER: First-class: 2001; List A: 2003; T20: 2009

SUSSEX

BEST BATTING: 100* Sussex vs Lancashire, Hove, 2011
BEST BOWLING: 7-66 Sialkot vs Abbottabad, Abbottabad, 2009

WHY CRICKET? Attracted watching the 1992 World Cup
CAREER HIGHLIGHTS? Pakistan Best Bowler of 2008/09. Selection for Pakistan A. Selection for Sussex CCC
CRICKETING HEROES? Wasim Akram
NON-CRICKETING HEROES? My father
BEST PLAYER IN COUNTY CRICKET? Luke Wright
TIP FOR THE TOP? Raza Hassan (Pakistan A)
IF YOU WEREN'T A CRICKETER? Business
WHEN RAIN STOPS PLAY? Chatting with players
FAVOURITE TV? Sky Sports
FAVOURITE FILM? Gladiator
DREAM HOLIDAY? Australia, Dubai
NOTES: Arif's first name is commonly misspelt as 'Naved'. His maiden first-class century enabled Sussex to pull off an unlikely draw against Lancashire last year

| Batting | Mat | Inns | NO | Runs | HS | Ave | SR | 100 | 50 | Ct | St |
|---|---|---|---|---|---|---|---|---|---|---|---|
| First-class | 35 | 46 | 14 | 575 | 100* | 17.96 | | 1 | 0 | 11 | 0 |
| List A | 22 | 11 | 3 | 141 | 49 | 17.62 | 88.12 | 0 | 0 | 8 | 0 |
| Twenty20 | 16 | 6 | 2 | 20 | 12 | 5.00 | 66.66 | 0 | 0 | 3 | 0 |

| Bowling | Mat | Balls | Runs | Wkts | BBI | BBM | Ave | Econ | SR | 5w | 10 |
|---|---|---|---|---|---|---|---|---|---|---|---|
| First-class | 35 | 6981 | 3885 | 163 | 7/66 | | 23.83 | 3.33 | 42.8 | 10 | 1 |
| List A | 22 | 787 | 773 | 18 | 3/19 | 3/19 | 42.94 | 5.89 | 43.7 | 0 | 0 |
| Twenty20 | 16 | 285 | 317 | 12 | 3/12 | 3/12 | 26.41 | 6.67 | 23.7 | 0 | 0 |

GLAMORGAN

FULL NAME: Chris Paul Ashling
BORN: November 26, 1988, Manchester, Lancashire
SQUAD NO: 32
HEIGHT: 5ft 9in
NICKNAME: Tevez
EDUCATION: Sale Grammar; Millfield; UWIC; Staffs Uni
TEAMS: Glamorgan, Lancashire 2nd XI, Wales Minor Counties
CAREER: First-class: 2009; List A: 2009; T20: 2010

BEST BATTING: 20 Glamorgan vs Derbyshire, Derby, 2010
BEST BOWLING: 4-47 Glamorgan vs Surrey, The Oval, 2011

FAMILY TIES? My dad Paul played league cricket for many years in Cheshire, as do my brothers Patrick and Dominic
CAREER HIGHLIGHTS? Taking 4-47 against Surrey at The Oval in 2011. 2-37 against Lancashire in a Pro40 in 2009
CRICKETING HEROES? Darren Gough
NON-CRICKETING HEROES? Zinedine Zidane
BEST PLAYER IN COUNTY CRICKET? Marcus Trescothick
TIP FOR THE TOP? Tom Maynard
IF YOU WEREN'T A CRICKETER? Hopefully a journalist
WHEN RAIN STOPS PLAY? Mucking about in the changing room
FAVOURITE TV? Only Fools And Horses
ACCOMPLISHMENTS? Scoring two goals for Man City U13 against Man Utd U13 in a hard-fought 2-1 victory
SURPRISING SKILL? Played for Man City youth teams. Doing a Sports Journalism degree at Staffordshire University
TWITTER FEED: @ChrisAshling32

| Batting | Mat | Inns | NO | Runs | HS | Ave | SR | 100 | 50 | Ct | St |
|---|---|---|---|---|---|---|---|---|---|---|---|
| First-class | 6 | 9 | 4 | 58 | 20 | 11.60 | 37.66 | 0 | 0 | 0 | 0 |
| List A | 8 | 6 | 4 | 11 | 6* | 5.50 | 33.33 | 0 | 0 | 0 | 0 |
| Twenty20 | 4 | 2 | 0 | 6 | 6 | 3.00 | 66.66 | 0 | 0 | 0 | 0 |

| Bowling | Mat | Balls | Runs | Wkts | BBI | BBM | Ave | Econ | SR | 5w | 10 |
|---|---|---|---|---|---|---|---|---|---|---|---|
| First-class | 6 | 763 | 499 | 15 | 4/47 | 4/77 | 33.26 | 3.92 | 50.8 | 0 | 0 |
| List A | 8 | 274 | 304 | 5 | 2/33 | 2/33 | 60.80 | 6.65 | 54.8 | 0 | 0 |
| Twenty20 | 4 | 66 | 118 | 3 | 2/39 | 2/39 | 39.33 | 10.72 | 22.0 | 0 | 0 |

## MOIN ASHRAF RHB RFM

FULL NAME: Moin Aqeeb Ashraf
BORN: January 5, 1992, Bradford, Yorkshire
SQUAD NO: 23
HEIGHT: 6ft 3in
NICKNAME: Mo, Prince
EDUCATION: Dixons City Academy, Leeds
Metropolitan University
TEAMS: Yorkshire, Yorkshire 2nd XI,
Yorkshire Academy, Yorkshire Under-17s
CAREER: First-class: 2010; List A: 2011

YORKSHIRE

BEST BATTING: 10 Yorkshire vs Kent, Leeds, 2010
BEST BOWLING: 5-32 Yorkshire vs Kent, Leeds, 2010

FAMILY TIES? All my brothers play and my uncles played
CAREER HIGHLIGHTS? 5-32 vs Kent at Headingley on my home Championship debut
CRICKETING HEROES? Imran Khan, Darren Gough, Shoaib Akhtar, Darren Gough
NON-CRICKETING HEROES? Malcolm X, Muhammad Ali
BEST PLAYER IN COUNTY CRICKET? Jonny Bairstow
TIPS FOR THE TOP? James Taylor, Alex Hales, Matthew Dunn
IF YOU WEREN'T A CRICKETER? Studying or journalism
WHEN RAIN STOPS PLAY? Catching up with scores elsewhere or university work
FAVOURITE TV? Celebrity Juice
FAVOURITE FILM? Four Lions
FAVOURITE BOOK? Imran Khan: The Celebrity, The Politician, The Cricketer
DREAM HOLIDAY? Dubai
ACCOMPLISHMENTS? Being an honest person and charity work
GUILTY PLEASURES? Maryland Cookies
AMAZE ME! Enjoy rapping for my charity work
FANTASY SLIP CORDON? Keeper: Cristiano Ronaldo, 1st: Neymar, 2nd: Malcolm X, 3rd: Lionel
Messi
TWITTER FEED: @MoinA23

| Batting | Mat | Inns | NO | Runs | HS | Ave | SR | 100 | 50 | Ct | St |
|---|---|---|---|---|---|---|---|---|---|---|---|
| First-class | 11 | 13 | 1 | 42 | 10 | 3.50 | 18.26 | 0 | 0 | 1 | 0 |
| List A | 4 | - | - | - | - | - | - | - | - | 1 | 0 |

| Bowling | Mat | Balls | Runs | Wkts | BBI | BBM | Ave | Econ | SR | 5w | 10 |
|---|---|---|---|---|---|---|---|---|---|---|---|
| First-class | 11 | 1398 | 773 | 22 | 5/32 | 6/45 | 35.13 | 3.31 | 63.5 | 1 | 0 |
| List A | 4 | 143 | 154 | 4 | 2/25 | 2/25 | 38.50 | 6.46 | 35.7 | 0 | 0 |

**YORKSHIRE**

FULL NAME: Jonathan Marc Bairstow
BORN: September 26, 1989, Bradford, Yorkshire
SQUAD NO: 21
HEIGHT: 6ft
NICKNAME: Bluey, Ronald
EDUCATION: St Peter's, York; Leeds Metropolitan University
TEAMS: England, England Lions, Yorkshire, Yorkshire 2nd XI
CAREER: ODI: 2011; T20I: 2011; First-class: 2009; List A: 2009; T20: 2010

BEST BATTING: 205 Yorkshire vs Nottinghamshire, Nottingham, 2011

FAMILY TIES? My father [David] played for Yorkshire and England
CAREER HIGHLIGHTS? My Yorkshire debut and scoring 41* on debut for England
CRICKETING HEROES? Anthony McGrath
NON-CRICKETING HEROES? Jonny Wilkinson
BEST PLAYER IN COUNTY CRICKET? Marcus Trescothick
TIP FOR THE TOP? James Wainman
IF YOU WEREN'T A CRICKETER? I'd play rugby
WHEN RAIN STOPS PLAY? Play on my iPhone or catch up on sleep
FAVOURITE TV? The Inbetweeners
FAVOURITE FILM? The Hangover
GUILTY PLEASURES? Large cod and chips
AMAZE ME! I'm ginger
FANTASY SLIP CORDON? Keeper: Mila Kunis, 1st: Jonny Wilkinson, 2nd: Daniela Hantuchova, 3rd: James Corden
TWITTER FEED: @jbairstow21

| Batting | Mat | Inns | NO | Runs | HS | Ave | SR | 100 | 50 | Ct | St |
|---|---|---|---|---|---|---|---|---|---|---|---|
| ODIs | 6 | 5 | 1 | 90 | 41* | 22.50 | 87.37 | 0 | 0 | 3 | 0 |
| T20Is | 6 | 5 | 3 | 91 | 60* | 45.50 | 109.63 | 0 | 1 | 6 | 0 |
| First-class | 46 | 81 | 17 | 2889 | 205 | 45.14 | | 3 | 22 | 98 | 5 |
| List A | 46 | 41 | 5 | 989 | 114 | 27.47 | 99.69 | 1 | 4 | 30 | 3 |
| Twenty20 | 38 | 32 | 7 | 518 | 60* | 20.72 | 117.99 | 0 | 1 | 14 | 4 |

| Bowling | Mat | Balls | Runs | Wkts | BBI | BBM | Ave | Econ | SR | 5w | 10 |
|---|---|---|---|---|---|---|---|---|---|---|---|
| ODIs | 6 | - | - | - | - | - | - | - | - | - | - |
| T20Is | 6 | - | - | - | - | - | - | - | - | - | - |
| First-class | 46 | - | - | - | - | - | - | - | - | - | - |
| List A | 46 | - | - | - | - | - | - | - | - | - | - |
| Twenty20 | 38 | - | - | - | - | - | - | - | - | - | - |

# DAVID BALCOMBE

## RHB RMF

FULL NAME: David John Balcombe
BORN: December 24, 1984, City of London
SQUAD NO: 84
HEIGHT: 6ft 4in
NICKNAME: Balcs, Spalko
EDUCATION: St John's School Leatherhead;
Durham University
TEAMS: Durham MCCU, Hampshire, Surrey
2nd XI
CAREER: First-class: 2005; List A: 2007; T20:
2006

BEST BATTING: 73 DUCCE vs Leicestershire, Leicester, 2005
BEST BOWLING: 6-51 Kent vs Essex, Canterbury, 2011

CAREER HIGHLIGHTS? Taking maiden first-class five-wicket haul against Durham. Making my Championship and Pro40 debuts for Hampshire
CRICKET MOMENTS TO FORGET? Bowling two overs for 35 in a one-day game
CRICKETERS PARTICULARLY ADMIRED? Shane Warne
FAVOURITE BAND? Five For Fighting, Kings Of Leon
RELAXATIONS? Sleeping, films
SUPERSTITIONS? Left equipment on first, i.e. left shoe, left pad

| Batting | Mat | Inns | NO | Runs | HS | Ave | SR | 100 | 50 | Ct | St |
|---|---|---|---|---|---|---|---|---|---|---|---|
| First-class | 34 | 44 | 9 | 462 | 73 | 13.20 | 46.38 | 0 | 1 | 9 | 0 |
| List A | 12 | 5 | 0 | 10 | 6 | 2.00 | 32.25 | 0 | 0 | 4 | 0 |
| Twenty20 | 2 | 1 | 0 | 3 | 3 | 3.00 | 60.00 | 0 | 0 | 0 | 0 |

| Bowling | Mat | Balls | Runs | Wkts | BBI | BBM | Ave | Econ | SR | 5w | 10 |
|---|---|---|---|---|---|---|---|---|---|---|---|
| First-class | 34 | 5607 | 3420 | 105 | 6/51 | | 32.57 | 3.65 | 53.4 | 5 | 1 |
| List A | 12 | 483 | 464 | 16 | 4/38 | 4/38 | 29.00 | 5.76 | 30.1 | 0 | 0 |
| Twenty20 | 2 | 30 | 38 | 1 | 1/23 | 1/23 | 38.00 | 7.60 | 30.0 | 0 | 0 |

## ADAM BALL RHB LFM

**KENT**

FULL NAME: Adam James Ball
BORN: March 1, 1993, Greenwich, London
SQUAD NO: 24
HEIGHT: 6ft 2in
NICKNAME: Bally
EDUCATION: Beths Grammar School, Bexley
TEAMS: England Under-19s, Kent, Kent 2nd XI, Kent Academy XI, Kent Under-13s, Kent Under-15s, Kent Under-17s
CAREER: First-class: 2011; List A: 2010; T20: 2011

BEST BATTING: 46 Kent vs Gloucestershire, Canterbury, 2011
BEST BOWLING: 3-36 Kent vs Leicestershire, Leicester, 2011

CRICKETING HEROES? Andrew Flintoff
FAVOURITE MUSICIAN? Taio Cruz
FAVOURITE FOOD? Nando's
FAVOURITE FILM? Ali G Indahouse
BEST CRICKETING MOMENT? Playing in the T20 quarter-finals
CAREER HIGHLIGHTS? Signing my first professional contract with Kent and being named as England U19 captain
NOTES: Will captain the England U19 tour of Australia in April and, consequently, will miss the start of the domestic season

| Batting | Mat | Inns | NO | Runs | HS | Ave | SR | 100 | 50 | Ct | St |
|---|---|---|---|---|---|---|---|---|---|---|---|
| First-class | 9 | 15 | 1 | 184 | 46 | 13.14 | 35.24 | 0 | 0 | 5 | 0 |
| List A | 10 | 9 | 6 | 67 | 19 | 22.33 | 91.78 | 0 | 0 | 0 | 0 |
| Twenty20 | 13 | 3 | 0 | 22 | 15 | 7.33 | 95.65 | 0 | 0 | 9 | 0 |

| Bowling | Mat | Balls | Runs | Wkts | BBI | BBM | Ave | Econ | SR | 5w | 10 |
|---|---|---|---|---|---|---|---|---|---|---|---|
| First-class | 9 | 858 | 560 | 15 | 3/36 | 3/45 | 37.33 | 3.91 | 57.2 | 0 | 0 |
| List A | 10 | 345 | 299 | 13 | 2/31 | 2/31 | 23.00 | 5.20 | 26.5 | 0 | 0 |
| Twenty20 | 13 | 228 | 280 | 10 | 2/28 | 2/28 | 28.00 | 7.36 | 22.8 | 0 | 0 |

# JAKE BALL

**RHB RFM**

FULL NAME: Jacob Timothy Ball
BORN: March 14, 1991, Mansfield, Nottinghamshire
SQUAD NO: 28
EDUCATION: Meden School, Mansfield
TEAMS: England Under-19s, Nottinghamshire, Nottinghamshire 2nd XI
CAREER: First-class: 2011; List A: 2009; T20: 2011

---

BEST BATTING: 4 Nottinghamshire vs MCC, Abu Dhabi, 2011
BEST BOWLING: 3-72 Nottinghamshire vs MCC, Abu Dhabi, 2011

---

FAMILY TIES? Brother played for Lincolnshire and Nottinghamshire U15, U17 and 2nd XI
NOTES: Played for England U19 before signing a professional contract with Nottinghamshire in October 2010. Took 3-32 on his home debut against Leicestershire in the CB40 in 2010. Nephew of former Nottinghamshire and England wicketkeeper, and current England wicketkeeping coach, Bruce French

| Batting | Mat | Inns | NO | Runs | HS | Ave | SR | 100 | 50 | Ct | St |
|---|---|---|---|---|---|---|---|---|---|---|---|
| First-class | 1 | 2 | 1 | 4 | 4 | 4.00 | 57.14 | 0 | 0 | 0 | 0 |
| List A | 7 | 5 | 3 | 41 | 19* | 20.50 | 132.25 | 0 | 0 | 0 | 0 |
| Twenty20 | 1 | - | - | - | - | - | - | - | - | 0 | 0 |

| Bowling | Mat | Balls | Runs | Wkts | BBI | BBM | Ave | Econ | SR | 5w | 10 |
|---|---|---|---|---|---|---|---|---|---|---|---|
| First-class | 1 | 126 | 106 | 3 | 3/72 | 3/106 | 35.33 | 5.04 | 42.0 | 0 | 0 |
| List A | 7 | 246 | 254 | 6 | 3/32 | 3/32 | 42.33 | 6.19 | 41.0 | 0 | 0 |
| Twenty20 | 1 | 6 | 11 | 0 | - | - | - | 11.00 | - | 0 | 0 |

FULL NAME: Gary Simon Ballance
BORN: November 22, 1989, Harare, Zimbabwe
SQUAD NO: 19
HEIGHT: 6ft
NICKNAME: Gazza
EDUCATION: Peterhouse, Zimbabwe; Harrow School
TEAMS: Derbyshire, Derbyshire 2nd XI, Mid West Rhinos, Yorkshire, Zimbabwe Under-19s
CAREER: First-class: 2008; List A: 2006; T20: 2010

BEST BATTING: 210 Midwest Rhinos vs Southern Rocks, Masvingo, 2011

FAMILY TIES? Nephew of former Zimbabwe captain Dave Houghton
CRICKETING HEROES? Andy Flower, Shane Warne
NOTES: On the books at Derbyshire as a 16-year-old where he made a handful of appearances for them in 2006 and 2007 before joining the Yorkshire academy. Forced his way into the Yorkshire 1st XI last season and scored 717 runs at 42.17 in the Championship even as the club suffered relegation. Also impressed in the CB40 competition with 331 runs at 55.16

| Batting | Mat | Inns | NO | Runs | HS | Ave | SR | 100 | 50 | Ct | St |
|---|---|---|---|---|---|---|---|---|---|---|---|
| First-class | 33 | 59 | 9 | 2763 | 210 | 55.26 | 52.39 | 11 | 14 | 39 | 0 |
| List A | 28 | 27 | 6 | 1101 | 135* | 52.42 | 90.17 | 3 | 4 | 12 | 0 |
| Twenty20 | 28 | 25 | 3 | 533 | 67 | 24.22 | 116.37 | 0 | 2 | 7 | 0 |
| Bowling | Mat | Balls | Runs | Wkts | BBI | BBM | Ave | Econ | SR | 5w | 10 |
| First-class | 33 | 24 | 17 | 0 | - | - | - | 4.25 | - | 0 | 0 |
| List A | 28 | - | - | - | - | - | - | - | - | - | - |
| Twenty20 | 28 | - | - | - | - | - | - | - | - | - | - |

FULL NAME: Keith Hubert Douglas Barker
BORN: October 21, 1986, Manchester, Lancashire
SQUAD NO: 13
HEIGHT: 6ft 2in
NICKNAME: Barksy
EDUCATION: Moorhead High School
TEAMS: Warwickshire, Warwickshire 2nd XI
CAREER: First-class: 2009; List A: 2009; T20: 2009

**WARWICKSHIRE**

BEST BATTING: 118 Warwickshire vs Sussex, Birmingham, 2011
BEST BOWLING: 5-31 Warwickshire vs DMCCU, Durham University, 2011

FAMILY TIES? My father Keith Barker played for British Guinea, and my godfather Clive Lloyd was a West Indies legend
WHY CRICKET? Always enjoyed playing with friends and family
CAREER HIGHLIGHTS? Winning the CB40 competition
NON-CRICKETING HEROES? Lewis Hamilton
BEST PLAYER IN COUNTY CRICKET? Marcus Trescothick
TIP FOR THE TOP? Chris Woakes
IF YOU WEREN'T A CRICKETER? Cricket coach
WHEN RAIN STOPS PLAY? Resting or playing cricket inside with a tennis ball
FAVOURITE TV? Family Guy, Man Versus Food
ACCOMPLISHMENTS? Playing international football at age-group level
GUILTY PLEASURES? Everything that tastes good
AMAZE ME! My heart stopped beating during an operation when I was 15 and I was brought back to life. Played football in the UEFA Cup for Blackburn Rovers
FANTASY SLIP CORDON? Keeper: James Corden, 1st: Karl Pilkington, 2nd: Keith Barker Jnr, 3rd: Keith Barker Snr, Gully: Chris Tucker

| Batting | Mat | Inns | NO | Runs | HS | Ave | SR | 100 | 50 | Ct | St |
|---|---|---|---|---|---|---|---|---|---|---|---|
| First-class | 17 | 21 | 2 | 558 | 118 | 29.36 | 58.06 | 2 | 2 | 6 | 0 |
| List A | 34 | 24 | 6 | 356 | 56 | 19.77 | 89.67 | 0 | 1 | 8 | 0 |
| Twenty20 | 40 | 21 | 3 | 274 | 46 | 15.22 | 111.38 | 0 | 0 | 11 | 0 |
| Bowling | Mat | Balls | Runs | Wkts | BBI | BBM | Ave | Econ | SR | 5w | 10 |
| First-class | 17 | 2035 | 1113 | 28 | 5/31 | 8/129 | 39.75 | 3.28 | 72.6 | 1 | 0 |
| List A | 34 | 1169 | 1210 | 36 | 4/33 | 4/33 | 33.61 | 6.21 | 32.4 | 0 | 0 |
| Twenty20 | 40 | 745 | 961 | 51 | 4/19 | 4/19 | 18.84 | 7.73 | 14.6 | 0 | 0 |

## ALEX BARROW                                          RHB OB

SOMERSET

**FULL NAME:** Alexander William Rodgerson Barrow
**BORN:** May 6, 1992, Bath, Somerset
**SQUAD NO:** 18
**HEIGHT:** 5ft 7in
**NICKNAME:** Baz, Wheels, Pocket Rocket
**EDUCATION:** King's College Taunton
**TEAMS:** England Under-19s, Somerset, Somerset 2nd XI, Somerset Under-17s
**CAREER:** First-class: 2011

BEST BATTING: 69 Somerset vs Yorkshire, Leeds, 2011
BEST BOWLING: 1-4 Somerset vs Hampshire, Southampton, 2011

CAREER HIGHLIGHTS? My highlights so far would be representing England U19, my first-class debut and my maiden first-class 50 against Yorkshire
SUPERSTITIONS? I have a few routines but they are not superstitions as such
CRICKETING HEROES? When I was young my heroes were Darren Gough and Jonty Rhodes. Ian Bell and Sachin Tendulkar are two batters I really like watching and Paul Collingwood is my inspiration in the field
NON-CRICKETING HEROES? Jonny Wilkinson is someone I always admire – he puts his all into everything he does
BEST PLAYER IN COUNTY CRICKET? Marcus Trescothick. It may sound biased but you just have to look at his record
TIPS FOR THE TOP? Jos Buttler and Matthew Dunn (Surrey)
IF YOU WEREN'T A CRICKETER? I think I would go into coaching rugby and cricket. I quite like the sound of being a batmaker too
SURPRISING SKILL? I love drawing – my sister and I are both artistic. Although I must admit she's better than me
GUILTY PLEASURES? Making 'rocky road' cake with George Dockrell!
AMAZE ME! I'd never scored a county hundred at any level when I was signed
TWITTER FEED: @Alex_Barrow5

| Batting | Mat | Inns | NO | Runs | HS | Ave | SR | 100 | 50 | Ct | St |
|---------|-----|------|-----|------|-----|-------|-------|-----|-----|-----|-----|
| First-class | 7 | 11 | 0 | 218 | 69 | 19.81 | 47.70 | 0 | 1 | 4 | 0 |

| Bowling | Mat | Balls | Runs | Wkts | BBI | BBM | Ave | Econ | SR | 5w | 10 |
|---------|-----|-------|------|------|-----|-----|-------|------|-----|-----|-----|
| First-class | 7 | 42 | 36 | 1 | 1/4 | 1/4 | 36.00 | 5.14 | 42.0 | 0 | 0 |

# MICHAEL BATES

## RHB WK

FULL NAME: Michael David Bates
BORN: October 10, 1990, Frimley
SQUAD NO: 16
HEIGHT: 5ft 8in
NICKNAME: Batesy
EDUCATION: Yateley Manor; Lord Wandsworth College
TEAMS: England Under-19s, Hampshire, Hampshire 2nd XI
CAREER: First-class: 2010; List A: 2010; T20: 2010

---

BEST BATTING: 58* Hampshire vs Durham, Chester-le-Street, 2011

---

CAREER HIGHLIGHTS? Winning at T20 Finals Day in 2010
CRICKETING HEROES? Alec Stewart
TIPS FOR THE TOP? Jos Buttler, James Vince, Danny Briggs, Ben Stokes
IF YOU WEREN'T A CRICKETER? Don't know!
FAVOURITE TV? Scrubs
FAVOURITE FILM? Blood Diamond
FAVOURITE BOOK? Lance Armstrong's autobiography
DREAM HOLIDAY? Greece
NOTES: Represented England at U15, U17, U18 and U19 level. Played in the 2010 U19 World Cup in New Zealand

| Batting | Mat | Inns | NO | Runs | HS | Ave | SR | 100 | 50 | Ct | St |
|---|---|---|---|---|---|---|---|---|---|---|---|
| First-class | 16 | 23 | 4 | 296 | 58* | 15.57 | 37.99 | 0 | 1 | 46 | 4 |
| List A | 17 | 8 | 3 | 36 | 24* | 7.20 | 66.66 | 0 | 0 | 10 | 4 |
| Twenty20 | 16 | 3 | 1 | 25 | 10 | 12.50 | 89.28 | 0 | 0 | 10 | 4 |

| Bowling | Mat | Balls | Runs | Wkts | BBI | BBM | Ave | Econ | SR | 5w | 10 |
|---|---|---|---|---|---|---|---|---|---|---|---|
| First-class | 16 | - | - | - | - | - | - | - | - | - | - |
| List A | 17 | - | - | - | - | - | - | - | - | - | - |
| Twenty20 | 16 | - | - | - | - | - | - | - | - | - | - |

**SURREY**

FULL NAME: Gareth Jon Batty
BORN: October 13, 1977, Bradford, Yorkshire
SQUAD NO: 13
HEIGHT: 5ft 11in
NICKNAME: Bats, Keith, Boris, Boom Boom, Mick Hucknall, Jack Bauer, Red
EDUCATION: Bingley Grammar
TEAMS: England, Surrey, Surrey Cricket Board, Worcestershire, Yorkshire
CAREER: Test: 2003; ODI: 2002; T20I: 2009; First-class: 1997; List A: 1998; T20: 2003

BEST BATTING: 133 Worcestershire vs Surrey, The Oval, 2004
BEST BOWLING: 7-52 Worcestershire vs Northamptonshire, Northampton, 2004

FAMILY TIES? My dad was academy coach at Yorkshire and brother played for Yorkshire and Somerset
CAREER HIGHLIGHTS? Playing for England
CRICKETING HEROES? Alec Stewart, Adam Hollioake, Graeme Hick
NON-CRICKETING HEROES? Jack Bauer
BEST PLAYER IN COUNTY CRICKET? Mark Ramprakash and Marcus Trescothick
TIPS FOR THE TOP? Jason Roy, Tom Maynard, Stuart Meaker
WHEN RAIN STOPS PLAY? Babysitting Jason Roy
FAVOURITE TV? Only Fools And Horses, 24, Celebrity Juice
DREAM HOLIDAY? Scarborough
ACCOMPLISHMENTS? Building my house
SURPRISING SKILL? I play the drums and I do the caterpillar very well

| Batting | Mat | Inns | NO | Runs | HS | Ave | SR | 100 | 50 | Ct | St |
|---|---|---|---|---|---|---|---|---|---|---|---|
| Tests | 7 | 8 | 1 | 144 | 38 | 20.57 | 27.01 | 0 | 0 | 3 | 0 |
| ODIs | 10 | 8 | 2 | 30 | 17 | 5.00 | 41.09 | 0 | 0 | 4 | 0 |
| T20Is | 1 | 1 | 0 | 4 | 4 | 4.00 | 57.14 | 0 | 0 | 0 | 0 |
| First-class | 166 | 252 | 42 | 5384 | 133 | 25.63 | | 2 | 28 | 123 | 0 |
| List A | 204 | 158 | 32 | 2079 | 83* | 16.50 | | 0 | 5 | 71 | 0 |
| Twenty20 | 72 | 54 | 14 | 481 | 87 | 12.02 | 110.06 | 0 | 1 | 25 | 0 |

| Bowling | Mat | Balls | Runs | Wkts | BBI | BBM | Ave | Econ | SR | 5w | 10 |
|---|---|---|---|---|---|---|---|---|---|---|---|
| Tests | 7 | 1394 | 733 | 11 | 3/55 | 5/153 | 66.63 | 3.15 | 126.7 | 0 | 0 |
| ODIs | 10 | 440 | 366 | 5 | 2/40 | 2/40 | 73.20 | 4.99 | 88.0 | 0 | 0 |
| T20Is | 1 | 18 | 17 | 0 | - | - | - | 5.66 | - | 0 | 0 |
| First-class | 166 | 30779 | 15276 | 446 | 7/52 | | 34.25 | 2.97 | 69.0 | 17 | 1 |
| List A | 204 | 7985 | 6092 | 185 | 5/35 | 5/35 | 32.92 | 4.57 | 43.1 | 1 | 0 |
| Twenty20 | 72 | 1254 | 1596 | 56 | 4/23 | 4/23 | 28.50 | 7.63 | 22.3 | 0 | 0 |

FULL NAME: Jonathan Neil Batty
BORN: April 18, 1974, Chesterfield, Derbyshire
SQUAD NO: 1
HEIGHT: 5ft 10in
NICKNAME: JB
EDUCATION: Wheatley Park School; Repton School; Durham University; Oxford University
TEAMS: Oxford University, Oxfordshire, Surrey
CAREER: First-class: 1994; List A: 1994; T20: 2003

**GLOUCESTERSHIRE**

BEST BATTING: 168* Surrey vs Essex, Chelmsford, 2003
BEST BOWLING: 1-21 Surrey vs Lancashire, Manchester, 2001
COUNTY CAPS: 2001 (Surrey); 2010 (Gloucestershire); BENEFIT YEAR: 2009 (Surrey)

FAMILY TIES? My father played for Nottinghamshire Schools and a good standard of league cricket
CAREER HIGHLIGHTS? Winning three County Championships in 1999, 2000 and 2002, winning the T20 Cup in 2003 and being appointed Surrey captain for 2004
CRICKETING HEROES? David Gower, Bruce French, Deryck Murray, Alec Stewart and Jack Russell
NON-CRICKETING HEROES? Ayrton Senna, Jonny Wilkinson
BEST PLAYER IN COUNTY CRICKET? Mark Ramprakash
TIP FOR THE TOP? Cameron Herring
IF YOU WEREN'T A CRICKETER? Prime minister
DREAM HOLIDAY? Diva Maldives
ACCOMPLISHMENTS? Gaining my degree and postgraduate diploma
SURPRISING SKILL? Latin American dancing. I've got the best teacher in the world!
GUILTY PLEASURES? Fish and chips
AMAZE ME! Won Mr and Mr on Cricket AM with Ian Salisbury
TWITTER FEED: @jonathanbatty

| Batting | Mat | Inns | NO | Runs | HS | Ave | SR | 100 | 50 | Ct | St |
|---|---|---|---|---|---|---|---|---|---|---|---|
| First-class | 212 | 334 | 36 | 9417 | 168* | 31.60 | | 20 | 40 | 581 | 67 |
| List A | 197 | 161 | 27 | 2970 | 158* | 22.16 | | 1 | 14 | 204 | 36 |
| Twenty20 | 57 | 48 | 19 | 631 | 59 | 21.75 | 112.88 | 0 | 2 | 33 | 20 |

| Bowling | Mat | Balls | Runs | Wkts | BBI | BBM | Ave | Econ | SR | 5w | 10 |
|---|---|---|---|---|---|---|---|---|---|---|---|
| First-class | 212 | 78 | 61 | 1 | 1/21 | | 61.00 | 4.69 | 78.0 | 0 | 0 |
| List A | 197 | - | - | - | - | - | - | - | - | - | - |
| Twenty20 | 57 | - | - | - | - | - | - | - | - | - | - |

# WILL BEER                                                    RHB LB

**SUSSEX**

FULL NAME: William Andrew Thomas Beer
BORN: October 8, 1988, Crawley, Sussex
SQUAD NO: 18
HEIGHT: 5ft 10in
NICKNAME: Beery
EDUCATION: Reigate Grammar
TEAMS: Sussex, Sussex 2nd XI
CAREER: First-class: 2008; List A: 2009; T20: 2008

BEST BATTING: 37* Sussex vs Worcestershire, Worcester, 2010
BEST BOWLING: 3-31 Sussex vs Worcestershire, Worcester, 2010

FAMILY TIES? Dad played for Sussex 2nd XI
CAREER HIGHLIGHTS? Winning the T20 domestic tournament in 2009 and going to the Champions League
CRICKETING HEROES? Shane Warne, Michael Yardy
NON-CRICKETING HEROES? David Beckham, Joey Essex
BEST PLAYER IN COUNTY CRICKET? Marcus Trescothick
TIPS FOR THE TOP? Matt Machan, Luke Wells
IF YOU WEREN'T A CRICKETER? Professional golfer
WHEN RAIN STOPS PLAY? Play Monopoly with teammates on my iPad – it can get very competitive! Dressing room golf
FAVOURITE FILM? Snakes On A Plane
FAVOURITE TV? The Only Way Is Essex
FAVOURITE BOOK? Harry Potter series
DREAM HOLIDAY? New York
GUILTY PLEASURES? Dairy Milk Buttons
TWITTER FEED: @Willbeer18

| Batting | Mat | Inns | NO | Runs | HS | Ave | SR | 100 | 50 | Ct | St |
|---|---|---|---|---|---|---|---|---|---|---|---|
| First-class | 5 | 4 | 2 | 76 | 37* | 38.00 | 38.97 | 0 | 0 | 1 | 0 |
| List A | 16 | 6 | 1 | 63 | 27* | 12.60 | 80.76 | 0 | 0 | 4 | 0 |
| Twenty20 | 31 | 16 | 5 | 86 | 22 | 7.81 | 108.86 | 0 | 0 | 5 | 0 |

| Bowling | Mat | Balls | Runs | Wkts | BBI | BBM | Ave | Econ | SR | 5w | 10 |
|---|---|---|---|---|---|---|---|---|---|---|---|
| First-class | 5 | 388 | 228 | 9 | 3/31 | 3/36 | 25.33 | 3.52 | 43.1 | 0 | 0 |
| List A | 16 | 642 | 516 | 8 | 2/17 | 2/17 | 64.50 | 4.82 | 80.2 | 0 | 0 |
| Twenty20 | 31 | 588 | 675 | 23 | 3/19 | 3/19 | 29.34 | 6.88 | 25.5 | 0 | 0 |

WARWICKSHIRE

FULL NAME: Ian Ronald Bell
BORN: April 11, 1982, Walsgrave, Coventry, Warwickshire
SQUAD NO: 4
HEIGHT: 5ft 10in
NICKNAME: Belly
EDUCATION: Princethorpe College, Rugby
TEAMS: England, England Lions, England Under-19s, Marylebone Cricket Club, Warwickshire, Warwickshire Cricket Board
CAREER: Test: 2004; ODI: 2004; T20I: 2006; First-class: 1999; List A: 1999; T20: 2003

BEST BATTING: 262* Warwickshire vs Sussex, Horsham, 2004
BEST BOWLING: 4-4 Warwickshire vs Middlesex, Lord's, 2004
COUNTY CAP: 2001; BENEFIT YEAR: 2011

CAREER HIGHLIGHTS? Winning County Championship with Warwickshire, Ashes victories
SUPERSTITIONS? None
CRICKETING HEROES? Ricky Ponting, Dominic Ostler, Jeetan Patel
NON-CRICKETING HEROES? Gary Shaw, Gordon Cowans
BEST PLAYER IN COUNTY CRICKET? Marcus Trescothick
TIP FOR THE TOP? Chris Woakes
IF YOU WEREN'T A CRICKETER? I'd be sitting at the Holte End watching the Villa
DREAM HOLIDAY? Maldives
ACCOMPLISHMENTS? Honorary doctorate at Coventry University

| Batting | Mat | Inns | NO | Runs | HS | Ave | SR | 100 | 50 | Ct | St |
|---|---|---|---|---|---|---|---|---|---|---|---|
| Tests | 72 | 122 | 14 | 5078 | 235 | 47.01 | 52.36 | 16 | 28 | 57 | 0 |
| ODIs | 108 | 104 | 9 | 3234 | 126* | 34.04 | 73.31 | 1 | 19 | 35 | 0 |
| T20Is | 7 | 7 | 1 | 175 | 60* | 29.16 | 119.86 | 0 | 1 | 4 | 0 |
| First-class | 195 | 328 | 35 | 13473 | 262* | 45.98 | | 38 | 67 | 136 | 0 |
| List A | 232 | 221 | 21 | 7537 | 158 | 37.68 | | 7 | 53 | 82 | 0 |
| Twenty20 | 44 | 43 | 6 | 926 | 85 | 25.02 | 114.60 | 0 | 4 | 16 | 0 |

| Bowling | Mat | Balls | Runs | Wkts | BBI | BBM | Ave | Econ | SR | 5w | 10 |
|---|---|---|---|---|---|---|---|---|---|---|---|
| Tests | 72 | 108 | 76 | 1 | 1/33 | 1/33 | 76.00 | 4.22 | 108.0 | 0 | 0 |
| ODIs | 108 | 88 | 88 | 6 | 3/9 | 3/9 | 14.66 | 6.00 | 14.6 | 0 | 0 |
| T20Is | 7 | - | - | - | - | - | - | - | - | - | - |
| First-class | 195 | 2809 | 1564 | 47 | 4/4 | | 33.27 | 3.34 | 59.7 | 0 | 0 |
| List A | 232 | 1290 | 1138 | 33 | 5/41 | 5/41 | 34.48 | 5.29 | 39.0 | 1 | 0 |
| Twenty20 | 44 | 132 | 186 | 3 | 1/12 | 1/12 | 62.00 | 8.45 | 44.0 | 0 | 0 |

## DANIEL BELL-DRUMMOND  RHB RM

**KENT**

FULL NAME: Daniel James Bell-Drummond
BORN: August 4, 1993, Lewisham, London
SQUAD NO: 23
HEIGHT: 5ft 11in
NICKNAME: DBD, Deebs
EDUCATION: Millfield School
TEAMS: England Under-19s, Kent, Kent 2nd XI
CAREER: First-class: 2011; List A: 2011; T20: 2011

---

BEST BATTING: 80 Kent vs Loughborough MCCU, Canterbury, 2011

FAMILY TIES? My father is really passionate about the sport
WHY CRICKET? My father got me into it and I've always really enjoyed spending time at Catford Wanderers CC, my local club
CAREER HIGHLIGHTS? Making my first-class debut
SUPERSTITIONS? None
CRICKETING HEROES? Brian Lara, Kevin Pietersen, Chris Gayle
NON-CRICKETING HEROES? Nelson Mandela, Muhammad Ali
BEST PLAYER IN COUNTY CRICKET? Marcus Trescothick
TIPS FOR THE TOP? Adam Ball, Ben Foakes, Sam Northeast
IF YOU WEREN'T A CRICKETER? I'd be a musician
WHEN RAIN STOPS PLAY? I listen to my iPod, read magazines or watch TV
FAVOURITE TV? Eastenders
FAVOURITE FILM? Coach Carter
FAVOURITE BOOK? Animal Farm
DREAM HOLIDAY? The Caribbean
FANTASY SLIP CORDON? Keeper: Floyd Mayweather Jr, 1st: Me, 2nd: Robin van Persie, 3rd: Lee Evans, Gully: Brian Lara
TWITTER FEED: @deebzz23

| Batting | Mat | Inns | NO | Runs | HS | Ave | SR | 100 | 50 | Ct | St |
|---|---|---|---|---|---|---|---|---|---|---|---|
| First-class | 4 | 7 | 0 | 147 | 80 | 21.00 | 60.99 | 0 | 1 | 3 | 0 |
| List A | 5 | 5 | 0 | 111 | 42 | 22.20 | 98.23 | 0 | 0 | 0 | 0 |
| Twenty20 | 1 | 1 | 0 | 11 | 11 | 11.00 | 183.33 | 0 | 0 | 0 | 0 |

| Bowling | Mat | Balls | Runs | Wkts | BBI | BBM | Ave | Econ | SR | 5w | 10 |
|---|---|---|---|---|---|---|---|---|---|---|---|
| First-class | 4 | - | - | - | - | - | - | - | - | - | - |
| List A | 5 | - | - | - | - | - | - | - | - | - | - |
| Twenty20 | 1 | - | - | - | - | - | - | - | - | - | - |

# DALE BENKENSTEIN

## RHB RM R5 MVP16

FULL NAME: Dale Martin Benkenstein
BORN: June 9, 1974, Harare, Zimbabwe
SQUAD NO: 44
HEIGHT: 5ft 7in
NICKNAME: Benki
EDUCATION: Michaelhouse School
TEAMS: South Africa, Delhi Giants, Dolphins, Durham, KwaZulu-Natal, Natal
CAREER: ODI: 1998; First-class: 1993; List A: 1992; T20: 2004

DURHAM

BEST BATTING: 259 KwaZulu-Natal vs Northerns, Durban, 2002
BEST BOWLING: 4-16 Dolphins vs Warriors, Durban, 2005
COUNTY CAP: 2005

FAMILY TIES? My father Martin, uncle Des and twin brothers, Boyd and Brett, all played first-class cricket
CAREER HIGHLIGHTS? Playing for South Africa, winning the double with the Dolphins in 1997, winning the FP Trophy final at Lord's with Durham in 2007 and our first Championship in 2008
CRICKETING HEROES? Viv Richards
NON-CRICKETING HEROES? Seb Coe, Bjorn Borg, Christian Cullen
BEST PLAYER IN COUNTY CRICKET? Marcus Trescothick
TIPS FOR THE TOP? Ben Stokes, Scott Borthwick
IF YOU WEREN'T A CRICKETER? Rugby player
FAVOURITE TV? Hawaii Five-O
FAVOURITE FILM? Hall Pass
DREAM HOLIDAY? Maldives
ACCOMPLISHMENTS? My family, and beating Jansher Khan at squash

| Batting | Mat | Inns | NO | Runs | HS | Ave | SR | 100 | 50 | Ct | St |
|---|---|---|---|---|---|---|---|---|---|---|---|
| ODIs | 23 | 20 | 3 | 305 | 69 | 17.94 | 65.87 | 0 | 1 | 3 | 0 |
| First-class | 243 | 370 | 42 | 15107 | 259 | 46.05 | | 38 | 81 | 160 | 0 |
| List A | 290 | 262 | 60 | 7134 | 107* | 35.31 | | 1 | 44 | 107 | 0 |
| Twenty20 | 90 | 81 | 16 | 1682 | 60 | 25.87 | 129.38 | 0 | 6 | 31 | 0 |

| Bowling | Mat | Balls | Runs | Wkts | BBI | BBM | Ave | Econ | SR | 5w | 10 |
|---|---|---|---|---|---|---|---|---|---|---|---|
| ODIs | 23 | 65 | 44 | 4 | 3/5 | 3/5 | 11.00 | 4.06 | 16.2 | 0 | 0 |
| First-class | 243 | 7517 | 3568 | 100 | 4/16 | | 35.68 | 2.84 | 75.1 | 0 | 0 |
| List A | 290 | 3197 | 2681 | 87 | 4/16 | 4/16 | 30.81 | 5.03 | 36.7 | 0 | 0 |
| Twenty20 | 90 | 462 | 566 | 21 | 3/10 | 3/10 | 26.95 | 7.35 | 22.0 | 0 | 0 |

**MIDDLESEX**

FULL NAME: Gareth Kyle Berg
BORN: January 18, 1981, Cape Town, South Africa
SQUAD NO: 8
HEIGHT: 6ft
NICKNAME: Ice, Bergy, Ford
EDUCATION: South African College School
TEAMS: Italy, Middlesex, Western Province
CAREER: First-class: 2008; List A: 2008; T20: 2009

BEST BATTING: 130* Middlesex vs Leicestershire, Leicester, 2011
BEST BOWLING: 6-58 Middlesex vs Glamorgan, Cardiff, 2011
COUNTY CAP: 2010

CAREER HIGHLIGHTS? Playing alongside Hansie Cronje and Shaun Pollock in a friend's benefit game. Scoring 65 in my first game at Lord's
CAREER OUTSIDE CRICKET? Professional sports coach in schools
CRICKET MOMENTS TO FORGET? Being left out of South Africa U15 World Cup squad one week before the tournament in England
SUPERSTITIONS? Always put my right boot and pad on first. Always look at the sun when stepping on to the field
CRICKETERS PARTICULARLY ADMIRED? Steve Waugh, Herschelle Gibbs, Brian McMillan
TIPS FOR THE TOP? Adam London, Sam Robson
FAVOURITE BAND? Red Hot Chili Peppers, Oasis, The Beatles, Dean Martin
NOTES: Made his Middlesex debut as a 27-year-old after a spell playing for Northamptonshire 2nd XI. Scored his maiden first-class ton against Derbyshire in 2010 and made his second ton last season after recovering from a back injury that ruled him out for much of the campaign. Took 26 wickets at 19.96 in seven County Championship matches last season. Represented Italy in the ICC World T20 qualifiers in March

| Batting | Mat | Inns | NO | Runs | HS | Ave | SR | 100 | 50 | Ct | St |
|---|---|---|---|---|---|---|---|---|---|---|---|
| First-class | 39 | 65 | 9 | 1953 | 130* | 34.87 | 68.64 | 2 | 12 | 24 | 0 |
| List A | 39 | 33 | 6 | 679 | 65 | 25.14 | 85.94 | 0 | 3 | 11 | 0 |
| Twenty20 | 24 | 19 | 7 | 333 | 41 | 27.75 | 139.91 | 0 | 0 | 8 | 0 |

| Bowling | Mat | Balls | Runs | Wkts | BBI | BBM | Ave | Econ | SR | 5w | 10 |
|---|---|---|---|---|---|---|---|---|---|---|---|
| First-class | 39 | 4272 | 2498 | 80 | 6/58 | 7/90 | 31.22 | 3.50 | 53.4 | 3 | 0 |
| List A | 39 | 954 | 876 | 31 | 4/24 | 4/24 | 28.25 | 5.50 | 30.7 | 0 | 0 |
| Twenty20 | 24 | 399 | 506 | 13 | 2/22 | 2/22 | 38.92 | 7.60 | 30.6 | 0 | 0 |

# PAUL BEST LHB SLA

FULL NAME: Paul Merwood Best
BORN: March 8, 1991, Nuneaton, Warwickshire
SQUAD NO: 15
HEIGHT: 5ft 10in
NICKNAME: Besty
EDUCATION: Bablake School, Coventry; Cambridge University
TEAMS: Cambridge MCCU, Cambridge University, England Under-19s, Northamptonshire, Warwickshire, Warwickshire 2nd XI
CAREER: First-class: 2011; List A: 2011

BEST BATTING: 150 CMCCU vs Warwickshire, Fenner's, 2011
BEST BOWLING: 6-86 Cambridge University vs Oxford University, Fenner's, 2011

FAMILY TIES? Dad played club cricket. Younger brother Mark is in the Warwickshire Academy
WHY CRICKET? Dad had a big influence – we played the game for hour after hour in the back garden, plus going to watch Warwickshire play at Edgbaston
CAREER HIGHLIGHTS? Captaining England U19 in 2009 and 2010. 150* for Cambridge MCCU vs Surrey in 2011 and winning the game. Getting a six-fer vs Middlesex for Cambridge MCCU in 2011. Making Warwickshire Championship debut. Being in the Cambridge team that won the treble vs Oxford in 2011
CRICKETING HEROES? Daniel Vettori
NON-CRICKETING HEROES? Hugh Laurie
BEST PLAYER IN COUNTY CRICKET? Marcus Trescothick
TIPS FOR THE TOP? Mark Best, Zafar Ansari, Charlie Taylor
IF YOU WEREN'T A CRICKETER? Either in the City or owning my own set of delicatessens
WHEN RAIN STOPS PLAY? Read or play cards
FAVOURITE TV? The Wire
FAVOURITE FILM? The Shawshank Redemption
AMAZE ME! The subjects I am studying at university are Anglo Saxon, Norse and Celtic
FANTASY SLIP CORDON? Keeper: Frankie Boyle, 1st: Shakespeare, 2nd: King Aethelred the Unready, 3rd: Me, Gully: Jamie Oliver

| Batting | Mat | Inns | NO | Runs | HS | Ave | SR | 100 | 50 | Ct | St |
|---------|-----|------|----|------|----|------|-------|-----|----|----|----|
| First-class | 6 | 9 | 2 | 305 | 150 | 43.57 | 50.66 | 1 | 1 | 4 | 0 |
| List A | 6 | 4 | 2 | 15 | 12 | 7.50 | 40.54 | 0 | 0 | 2 | 0 |

| Bowling | Mat | Balls | Runs | Wkts | BBI | BBM | Ave | Econ | SR | 5w | 10 |
|---------|-----|-------|------|------|------|-------|-------|------|------|----|----|
| First-class | 6 | 1615 | 901 | 26 | 6/86 | 9/131 | 34.65 | 3.34 | 62.1 | 2 | 0 |
| List A | 6 | 252 | 280 | 5 | 3/53 | 3/53 | 56.00 | 6.66 | 50.4 | 0 | 0 |

# SAM BILLINGS

## RHB WK

FULL NAME: Samuel William Billings
BORN: June 15, 1991, Pembury, Kent
SQUAD NO: 20
HEIGHT: 5ft 11in
NICKNAME: Bilbo, Doug
EDUCATION: Haileybury College
TEAMS: England Under-19s, Kent, Kent 2nd XI, Loughborough MCCU
CAREER: First-class: 2011; List A: 2011; T20: 2011

BEST BATTING: 131 Loughborough MCCU vs Northamptonshire, Loughborough, 2011

CRICKETING HEROES? Sachin Tendulkar
FAVOURITE MUSICIAN? Tinie Tempah
FAVOURITE FOOD? Roast lamb or steak and chips
QUOTE TO LIVE BY? "What you do in life echoes in eternity"
CAREER HIGHLIGHTS? My debuts for Kent and England U19

| Batting | Mat | Inns | NO | Runs | HS | Ave | SR | 100 | 50 | Ct | St |
|---|---|---|---|---|---|---|---|---|---|---|---|
| First-class | 3 | 5 | 0 | 222 | 131 | 44.40 | 49.22 | 1 | 0 | 2 | 0 |
| List A | 3 | 3 | 0 | 54 | 26 | 18.00 | 100.00 | 0 | 0 | 3 | 2 |
| Twenty20 | 4 | 2 | 0 | 3 | 2 | 1.50 | 60.00 | 0 | 0 | 1 | 0 |

| Bowling | Mat | Balls | Runs | Wkts | BBI | BBM | Ave | Econ | SR | 5w | 10 |
|---|---|---|---|---|---|---|---|---|---|---|---|
| First-class | 3 | - | - | - | - | - | - | - | - | - | - |
| List A | 3 | - | - | - | - | - | - | - | - | - | - |
| Twenty20 | 4 | - | - | - | - | - | - | - | - | - | - |

DURHAM

**FULL NAME:** Ian David Blackwell
**BORN:** June 10, 1978, Chesterfield, Derbyshire
**SQUAD NO:** 37
**HEIGHT:** 6ft 2in
**NICKNAME:** Blackdog, Donkey, Le Donk, Blackgoose
**EDUCATION:** Manor Secondary School; Brookfield Community School
**TEAMS:** England, Central Districts, Derbyshire, Durham, Somerset
**CAREER:** Test: 2006; ODI: 2002; First-class: 1997; List A: 1997; T20: 2003

**BEST BATTING:** 247* Somerset vs Derbyshire, Taunton, 2003
**BEST BOWLING:** 7-85 Durham vs Lancashire, Manchester, 2009
**COUNTY CAP:** 2001 (Somerset)

**CAREER HIGHLIGHTS?** My England ODI and Test debuts, winning the County Championship with Durham in 2009, winning Division Two, the T20 Cup and the C&G Trophy with Somerset. Winning the Walter Lawrence Trophy for the fastest hundred and also scoring the third-fastest double century (132 balls) by an Englishman during my 247* against Derbyshire. Scoring 102* vs MCC at Lord's on my Durham debut was very special too
**SUPERSTITIONS?** I always chew gum when I play and I always have a set way to get padded up
**BEST PLAYER IN COUNTY CRICKET?** Batting: Marcus Trescothick. Keeper: Chris Read. Bowler: Glen Chapple
**TIPS FOR THE TOP?** Ben Stokes, Scott Borthwick, Jack James Blackwell, Joe Root
**IF YOU WEREN'T A CRICKETER?** After my cricket career I want to become an umpire
**WHEN RAIN STOPS PLAY?** My iPad, playing 500 with the lads and of course going to the gym!
**FAVOURITE TV?** Kitchen Nightmares, Hell's Kitchen

| Batting | Mat | Inns | NO | Runs | HS | Ave | SR | 100 | 50 | Ct | St |
|---|---|---|---|---|---|---|---|---|---|---|---|
| Tests | 1 | 1 | 0 | 4 | 4 | 4.00 | 25.00 | 0 | 0 | 0 | 0 |
| ODIs | 34 | 29 | 2 | 403 | 82 | 14.92 | 86.66 | 0 | 1 | 8 | 0 |
| First-class | 198 | 297 | 23 | 10999 | 247* | 40.14 | | 26 | 61 | 63 | 0 |
| List A | 250 | 230 | 19 | 5760 | 134* | 27.29 | | 3 | 34 | 63 | 0 |
| Twenty20 | 77 | 69 | 9 | 1281 | 82 | 21.35 | 131.79 | 0 | 5 | 17 | 0 |

| Bowling | Mat | Balls | Runs | Wkts | BBI | BBM | Ave | Econ | SR | 5w | 10 |
|---|---|---|---|---|---|---|---|---|---|---|---|
| Tests | 1 | 114 | 71 | 0 | - | - | - | 3.73 | - | 0 | 0 |
| ODIs | 34 | 1230 | 877 | 24 | 3/26 | 3/26 | 36.54 | 4.27 | 51.2 | 0 | 0 |
| First-class | 198 | 30251 | 13603 | 371 | 7/85 | | 36.66 | 2.69 | 81.5 | 13 | 0 |
| List A | 250 | 8711 | 6968 | 203 | 5/26 | 5/26 | 34.32 | 4.79 | 42.9 | 1 | 0 |
| Twenty20 | 77 | 1273 | 1508 | 50 | 4/26 | 4/26 | 30.16 | 7.10 | 25.4 | 0 | 0 |

## ALEX BLAKE                                    LHB RMF

KENT

FULL NAME: Alexander James Blake
BORN: January 25, 1989, Farnborough, Kent
SQUAD NO: 18
HEIGHT: 6ft 2in
NICKNAME: Blakey, Butler, TS
EDUCATION: Hayes Secondary School;
Leeds Metropolitan University
TEAMS: Kent, Kent 2nd XI, Leeds/Bradford
MCCU
CAREER: First-class: 2008; List A: 2007; T20:
2010

BEST BATTING: 105* Kent vs Yorkshire, Leeds, 2010
BEST BOWLING: 2-9 Kent vs Pakistanis, Canterbury, 2010

CAREER HIGHLIGHTS? Maiden first-class century at Headingley. Representing England U19
CRICKETING HEROES? Graham Thorpe, Freddie Flintoff
NON-CRICKETING HEROES? David Beckham, Lance Armstrong
BEST PLAYER IN COUNTY CRICKET? Marcus Trescothick
TIPS FOR THE TOP? Ben Stokes, Matt Coles, Jonny Bairstow
IF YOU WEREN'T A CRICKETER? Busking
WHEN RAIN STOPS PLAY? Winding up Matt Coles or Fabian Cowdrey
FAVOURITE FILM? Moulin Rouge
FAVOURITE BOOK? The Game
SURPRISING SKILL? Gourmet chef
GUILTY PLEASURES? Dominos Pizza
AMAZE ME! Lived with Jonny Bairstow at university, can name all the countries of the world,
have a pet budgie
FANTASY SLIP CORDON? Keeper: Calvin Harris (to bust out some beats), 1st: Karl Pilkington
(to entertain us all day by not having a clue), 2nd: Me, 3rd: Joey Barton (chief sledger), Gully:
Joey Essex
TWITTER FEED: @aj_blake10

| Batting | Mat | Inns | NO | Runs | HS | Ave | SR | 100 | 50 | Ct | St |
|---|---|---|---|---|---|---|---|---|---|---|---|
| First-class | 23 | 39 | 1 | 829 | 105* | 21.81 | 60.07 | 1 | 3 | 12 | 0 |
| List A | 25 | 18 | 5 | 357 | 81* | 27.46 | 99.16 | 0 | 2 | 10 | 0 |
| Twenty20 | 21 | 15 | 2 | 127 | 33 | 9.76 | 118.69 | 0 | 0 | 13 | 0 |

| Bowling | Mat | Balls | Runs | Wkts | BBI | BBM | Ave | Econ | SR | 5w | 10 |
|---|---|---|---|---|---|---|---|---|---|---|---|
| First-class | 23 | 198 | 128 | 3 | 2/9 | 2/9 | 42.66 | 3.87 | 66.00 | 0 | 0 |
| List A | 25 | 84 | 74 | 3 | 2/13 | 2/13 | 24.66 | 5.28 | 28.0 | 0 | 0 |
| Twenty20 | 21 | - | - | - | - | - | - | - | - | - | - |

FULL NAME: Ravinder Singh Bopara
BORN: May 4, 1985, Forest Gate, London
SQUAD NO: 25
HEIGHT: 5ft 10in
NICKNAME: Puppy, Bops
EDUCATION: Brampton Manor School
TEAMS: England, Dolphins, England Lions, England Under-19s, Essex, Essex Cricket Board, Kings XI Punjab, Marylebone Cricket Club
CAREER: Test: 2007; ODI: 2007; T20I: 2008; First-class: 2002; List A: 2002; T20: 2003

ESSEX

BEST BATTING: 229 Essex vs Northamptonshire, Chelmsford, 2007
BEST BOWLING: 5-75 Essex vs Surrey, Colchester, 2006
COUNTY CAPS: 2005

CRICKETERS PARTICULARLY ADMIRED? Sachin Tendulkar, Jacques Kallis, Viv Richards
FAVOURITE BAND? Usher, Ne-Yo
NOTES: Made his name with 135 for Essex against the Australian tourists in 2005. Made his ODI debut in February 2007 against Australia and appeared in his first World Cup that April, when he came within one shot of beating Sri Lanka before being bowled off the final delivery. Made his Test debut in December 2007 against Sri Lanka, but after three matches he was dropped. Returned in 2009, and three hundreds in consecutive innings against the West Indies secured a place in the 2009 Ashes, but he was dropped after four Tests. Played the last two Tests against India in August 2011. In 2008 he became just the eighth man in history to make a double hundred in a one-day match when he hit 201* from 138 balls against Leicestershire

| Batting | Mat | Inns | NO | Runs | HS | Ave | SR | 100 | 50 | Ct | St |
|---|---|---|---|---|---|---|---|---|---|---|---|
| Tests | 12 | 17 | 1 | 553 | 143 | 34.56 | 53.89 | 3 | 0 | 6 | 0 |
| ODIs | 72 | 67 | 12 | 1668 | 96 | 30.32 | 75.00 | 0 | 8 | 23 | 0 |
| T20Is | 19 | 17 | 2 | 299 | 55 | 19.93 | 96.14 | 0 | 1 | 4 | 0 |
| First-class | 121 | 203 | 24 | 7452 | 229 | 41.63 | 53.45 | 20 | 29 | 72 | 0 |
| List A | 200 | 187 | 37 | 5704 | 201* | 38.02 | | 6 | 34 | 60 | 0 |
| Twenty20 | 111 | 100 | 11 | 2152 | 105* | 24.17 | 115.38 | 1 | 11 | 34 | 0 |

| Bowling | Mat | Balls | Runs | Wkts | BBI | BBM | Ave | Econ | SR | 5w | 10 |
|---|---|---|---|---|---|---|---|---|---|---|---|
| Tests | 12 | 326 | 212 | 1 | 1/39 | 1/39 | 212.00 | 3.90 | 326.0 | 0 | 0 |
| ODIs | 72 | 689 | 596 | 13 | 4/38 | 4/38 | 45.84 | 5.19 | 53.0 | 0 | 0 |
| T20Is | 19 | 106 | 109 | 9 | 4/10 | 4/10 | 12.11 | 6.16 | 11.7 | 0 | 0 |
| First-class | 121 | 8908 | 5715 | 134 | 5/75 | | 42.64 | 3.84 | 66.4 | 1 | 0 |
| List A | 200 | 4259 | 3824 | 144 | 5/63 | 5/63 | 26.55 | 5.38 | 29.5 | 1 | 0 |
| Twenty20 | 111 | 1367 | 1735 | 75 | 4/10 | 4/10 | 23.13 | 7.61 | 18.2 | 0 | 0 |

**DERBYSHIRE**

FULL NAME: Paul Michael Borrington
BORN: May 24, 1988, Nottingham
SQUAD NO: 17
HEIGHT: 5ft 10in
NICKNAME: Bozza, Boz
EDUCATION: Chellaston School; Repton School; Loughborough University
TEAMS: Derbyshire, Loughborough UCCE
CAREER: First-class: 2005; List A: 2009

BEST BATTING: 105 vs Loughborough UCCE vs Hampshire, Southampton, 2005

FAMILY TIES? Father [Tony] played for Derbyshire between 1970 and 1982
WHY CRICKET? Introduced to the game by my dad at a very young age – as soon as I could walk, basically!
CAREER HIGHLIGHTS? Maiden first-class century. Derbyshire debut vs Leicestershire at Grace Road in 2005. Winning at Lord's in the Universities Final with Loughborough. Captaining the Midlands to victory at the Bunbury Festival
CRICKETING HEROES? Michael Vaughan
WHEN RAIN STOPS PLAY? Reading a newspaper or magazine, sleeping, watching the clock!
FAVOURITE TV? An Idiot Abroad, Home And Away, Soccer Saturday
FAVOURITE FILM? Man On Fire, Pulp Fiction, The Matrix, Aladdin
GUILTY PLEASURES? The X Factor, Strictly Come Dancing
FANTASY SLIP CORDON? Keeper: Karl Pilkington, 1st: Me, 2nd: David Beckham, 3rd: Dario Gradi
TWITTER FEED: @pborrington

| Batting | Mat | Inns | NO | Runs | HS | Ave | SR | 100 | 50 | Ct | St |
|---|---|---|---|---|---|---|---|---|---|---|---|
| First-class | 28 | 46 | 5 | 1223 | 105 | 29.82 | 36.85 | 2 | 6 | 19 | 0 |
| List A | 1 | 1 | 0 | 25 | 25 | 25.00 | 67.56 | 0 | 0 | 0 | 0 |

| Bowling | Mat | Balls | Runs | Wkts | BBI | BBM | Ave | Econ | SR | 5w | 10 |
|---|---|---|---|---|---|---|---|---|---|---|---|
| First-class | 28 | 6 | 5 | 0 | - | - | - | 5.00 | - | 0 | 0 |
| List A | 1 | - | - | - | - | - | - | - | - | - | - |

FULL NAME: Scott George Borthwick
BORN: April 19, 1990, Sunderland, County Durham
SQUAD NO: 16
TEAMS: England, Durham, Durham 2nd XI, England Lions, England Under-19s
CAREER: ODI: 2011; T20I: 2011; First-class 2009; List A: 2009; T20: 2008

DURHAM

BEST BATTING: 101 Durham vs Sri Lanka A, Chester-le-Street, 2011
BEST BOWLING: 5-80 Durham vs Sussex, Hove, 2011

FAMILY TIES? Uncle [David] played for Northumberland
NOTES: Toured South Africa with England U19 in 2009, following selection for the Elite England Player Development XI in 2008. He was awarded the NBC Denis Compton Award for Durham's most promising young player in 2009. Took 35 first-class wickets, made his ODI debut for England against Ireland (August), his T20I bow (September) at The Oval vs the West Indies, and his overseas senior debut in India (October) in 2011. He spent the 2011/12 winter with the England Lions in Bangladesh

| Batting | Mat | Inns | NO | Runs | HS | Ave | SR | 100 | 50 | Ct | St |
|---|---|---|---|---|---|---|---|---|---|---|---|
| ODIs | 2 | 2 | 0 | 18 | 15 | 9.00 | 112.50 | 0 | 0 | 0 | 0 |
| T20Is | 1 | 1 | 0 | 14 | 14 | 14.00 | 87.50 | 0 | 0 | 1 | 0 |
| First-class | 28 | 39 | 9 | 821 | 101 | 27.36 | 54.04 | 1 | 4 | 23 | 0 |
| List A | 28 | 17 | 6 | 169 | 44 | 15.36 | 68.97 | 0 | 0 | 9 | 0 |
| Twenty20 | 18 | 7 | 4 | 79 | 30 | 26.33 | 91.86 | 0 | 0 | 5 | 0 |

| Bowling | Mat | Balls | Runs | Wkts | BBI | BBM | Ave | Econ | SR | 5w | 10 |
|---|---|---|---|---|---|---|---|---|---|---|---|
| ODIs | 2 | 54 | 72 | 0 | - | - | - | 8.00 | - | 0 | 0 |
| T20Is | 1 | 24 | 15 | 1 | 1/15 | 1/15 | 15.00 | 3.75 | 24.0 | 0 | 0 |
| First-class | 28 | 3010 | 1856 | 61 | 5/80 | 8/84 | 30.42 | 3.69 | 49.3 | 1 | 0 |
| List A | 28 | 910 | 846 | 18 | 2/11 | 2/11 | 47.00 | 5.57 | 50.5 | 0 | 0 |
| Twenty20 | 18 | 182 | 242 | 10 | 3/19 | 3/19 | 24.20 | 7.97 | 18.2 | 0 | 0 |

# MATT BOYCE LHB RM

**LEICESTERSHIRE**

FULL NAME: Matthew Andrew Golding Boyce
BORN: August 13, 1985, Cheltenham
SQUAD NO: 11
HEIGHT: 5ft 10in
NICKNAME: Boycey, Weasel
EDUCATION: Oakham School; Nottingham University
TEAMS: Leicestershire, Leicestershire 2nd XI
CAREER: First-class: 2006; List A: 2007; T20: 2008

---

BEST BATTING: 119 Leicestershire vs Gloucestershire, Leicester, 2011

WHY CRICKET? Enjoyed playing Kwik Cricket at school and then local club
CAREER HIGHLIGHTS? Maiden first-class hundred, winning the T20 Cup with Leicestershire
CRICKETING HEROES? Graham Thorpe, Brian Lara, Paul Nixon
NON-CRICKETING HEROES? Jonny Wilkinson, Winston Churchill
BEST PLAYER IN COUNTY CRICKET? Dave Masters and Marcus Trescothick
TIPS FOR THE TOP? Shiv Thakor, James Taylor, Josh Cobb, Nathan Buck
IF YOU WEREN'T A CRICKETER? Would be selling my soul in the City!
WHEN RAIN STOPS PLAY? Reading, playing poker, sleeping
FAVOURITE TV? Scrubs
FAVOURITE FILM? Forrest Gump
FAVOURITE BOOK? Love an autobiography, sports or otherwise
DREAM HOLIDAY? The Seychelles to relax and South America for adventure
ACCOMPLISHMENTS? Playing rugby at Twickenham twice, university degree
SURPRISING SKILL? World class singer… in the shower
GUILTY PLEASURES? Xbox
AMAZE ME! Planning on walking John O'Groats to Land's End in the autumn
TWITTER FEED: @boycey85

| Batting | Mat | Inns | NO | Runs | HS | Ave | SR | 100 | 50 | Ct | St |
|---|---|---|---|---|---|---|---|---|---|---|---|
| First-class | 64 | 115 | 6 | 3003 | 119 | 27.55 | 40.73 | 3 | 15 | 39 | 0 |
| List A | 41 | 36 | 3 | 864 | 80 | 26.18 | 79.48 | 0 | 4 | 12 | 0 |
| Twenty20 | 26 | 15 | 4 | 251 | 34 | 22.81 | 109.13 | 0 | 0 | 3 | 0 |

| Bowling | Mat | Balls | Runs | Wkts | BBI | BBM | Ave | Econ | SR | 5w | 10 |
|---|---|---|---|---|---|---|---|---|---|---|---|
| First-class | 64 | 42 | 63 | 0 | - | - | - | 9.00 | - | 0 | 0 |
| List A | 41 | - | - | - | - | - | - | - | - | - | - |
| Twenty20 | 26 | - | - | - | - | - | - | - | - | - | - |

FULL NAME: William David Bragg
BORN: October 24, 1986, Newport
SQUAD NO: 22
HEIGHT: 5ft 10in
NICKNAME: BPOT, Shelf
EDUCATION: Rougemont School, Newport;
University of Wales Institute, Cardiff
TEAMS: Glamorgan 2nd XI, Wales Minor
Counties
CAREER: First-class 2007; List A: 2005; T20:
2010

**GLAMORGAN**

---

BEST BATTING: 110 Glamorgan vs Leicestershire, Colwyn Bay, 2011
BEST BOWLING: 1-4 Glamorgan vs Kent, Canterbury, 2010

---

CAREER HIGHLIGHTS? Scoring 1,000 runs in my first full season, last season
SUPERSTITIONS? Always go to the toilet before batting!
CRICKETING HEROES? Herschelle Gibbs, Brian Lara, Daryl Cullinan
NON-CRICKETING HEROES? Kenny Powers, Ricky Gervais
BEST PLAYER IN COUNTY CRICKET? Marcus Trescothick
TIPS FOR THE TOP? Tom Maynard, James Harris, Scott Murphy
IF YOU WEREN'T A CRICKETER? Working abroad in some kind of financial environment
FAVOURITE TV? The Office
FAVOURITE FILM? Hear No Evil, See No Evil
FAVOURITE BOOK? Financial Times
DREAM HOLIDAY? Thailand
ACCOMPLISHMENTS? Getting a BSc degree in Civil Engineering
SURPRISING SKILL? I play acoustic guitar
GUILTY PLEASURES? Feeding the ducks whilst eating chocolate
FANTASY SLIP CORDON? Keeper: Ricky Gervais, 1st: Karl Pilkington, 2nd: Piers Morgan, 3rd:
Britney Spears, Gully: Peggy Mitchell
TWITTER FEED: @wdbragg22

| Batting | Mat | Inns | NO | Runs | HS | Ave | SR | 100 | 50 | Ct | St |
|---|---|---|---|---|---|---|---|---|---|---|---|
| First-class | 30 | 52 | 0 | 1507 | 110 | 28.98 | 52.93 | 1 | 10 | 13 | 1 |
| List A | 14 | 13 | 1 | 283 | 78 | 23.58 | 70.57 | 0 | 1 | 2 | 0 |
| Twenty20 | 1 | 1 | 0 | 15 | 15 | 15.00 | 68.18 | 0 | 0 | 0 | 0 |

| Bowling | Mat | Balls | Runs | Wkts | BBI | BBM | Ave | Econ | SR | 5w | 10 |
|---|---|---|---|---|---|---|---|---|---|---|---|
| First-class | 30 | 90 | 50 | 1 | 1/4 | 1/5 | 50.00 | 3.33 | 90.0 | 0 | 0 |
| List A | 14 | 12 | 17 | 0 | - | - | - | 8.50 | - | 0 | 0 |
| Twenty20 | 1 | - | - | - | - | - | - | - | - | - | - |

**B**

## RUEL BRATHWAITE                                    RHB RFM

**DURHAM**

FULL NAME: Ruel Marlon Ricardo Brathwaite
BORN: September 6, 1985, Barbados
SQUAD NO: 8
HEIGHT: 6ft 3in
NICKNAME: Brath
EDUCATION: Queen's College, Barbados;
Dulwich College; Loughborough University
TEAMS: West Indians, Cambridge MCCU,
Combined Campuses and Colleges, Durham,
Loughborough MCCU, Marylebone Cricket
Club, Surrey 2nd XI
CAREER: First-class: 2006; List A: 2007; T20:
2010

BEST BATTING: 76* LUCCE vs Worcestershire, County Ground, 2007
BEST BOWLING: 5-54 Cambridge University vs Oxford University, Fenner's, 2009

WHY CRICKET? The passion and skill levels of two great West Indian fast bowlers, Courtney
Walsh and Curtly Ambrose, first attracted me to the game
CAREER HIGHLIGHTS? Taking five wickets in an innings in the first two Championship
matches I played as a professional cricketer. Playing for a West Indies A team, captained
by Chris Gayle, in a warm-up match against the England Lions. Scoring 75* to see an MCC
Universities team to victory over Ireland A in Ireland
CRICKETING HEROES? Malcolm Marshall, Michael Holding, Courtney Walsh, Curtly Ambrose,
Brian Lara, Sir Vivian Richards, George Headley, Andrew Flintoff
NON-CRICKETING HEROES? The late Stephen Alleyne
BEST PLAYER IN COUNTY CRICKET? It's between Marcus Trescothick and Mark Ramprakash
TIP FOR THE TOP? Ben Stokes
IF YOU WEREN'T A CRICKETER? I have two degrees in Engineering and I am interested in
investment management so I would pursue a career in one of those fields
DREAM HOLIDAY? I was born in Barbados so I think I'm a little bit biased
ACCOMPLISHMENTS? Outside of cricket my greatest achievement was graduating from
Cambridge University with a Masters
AMAZE ME! I love beaches but I can't swim

| Batting | Mat | Inns | NO | Runs | HS | Ave | SR | 100 | 50 | Ct | St |
|---|---|---|---|---|---|---|---|---|---|---|---|
| First-class | 20 | 21 | 8 | 171 | 76* | 13.15 | 56.43 | 0 | 1 | 1 | 0 |
| List A | 2 | - | - | - | - | - | - | - | - | 0 | 0 |
| Twenty20 | 1 | 1 | 0 | 0 | 0 | 0.00 | 0.00 | 0 | 0 | 0 | 0 |

| Bowling | Mat | Balls | Runs | Wkts | BBI | BBM | Ave | Econ | SR | 5w | 10 |
|---|---|---|---|---|---|---|---|---|---|---|---|
| First-class | 20 | 3229 | 1950 | 56 | 5/54 | 8/130 | 34.82 | 3.62 | 57.6 | 3 | 0 |
| List A | 2 | 54 | 68 | 1 | 1/19 | 1/19 | 68.00 | 7.55 | 54.0 | 0 | 0 |
| Twenty20 | 1 | 18 | 33 | 1 | 1/33 | 1/33 | 33.00 | 11.00 | 18.0 | 0 | 0 |

**FULL NAME:** Gareth Rohan Breese
**BORN:** January 9, 1976, Montego Bay, Jamaica
**SQUAD NO:** 70
**HEIGHT:** 5ft 7in
**NICKNAME:** Briggy
**EDUCATION:** Wolmer's Boys School, Kingston
**TEAMS:** West Indies, Durham, Jamaica
**CAREER:** Test: 2002; First-class: 1995; List A: 1996; T20: 2004

**DURHAM**

**BEST BATTING:** 165* Durham vs Somerset, Taunton, 2004
**BEST BOWLING:** 7-60 Jamaica vs Barbados, Bridgetown, 2004

**FAMILY TIES?** My father is in cricket administration and used to play club cricket
**CAREER HIGHLIGHTS?** Playing Test cricket, winning trophies with Durham and Jamaica
**CRICKETING HEROES?** Jimmy Adams
**NON-CRICKETING HEROES?** My parents
**BEST PLAYER IN COUNTY CRICKET?** Marcus Trescothick
**TIPS FOR THE TOP?** Ben Stokes and Scott Borthwick
**IF YOU WEREN'T A CRICKETER?** Possibly working in a hotel as I did Hotel Management at university
**WHEN RAIN STOPS PLAY?** Messing around with my gear
**FAVOURITE TV?** Live cricket
**FAVOURITE FILM?** Man On Fire, The Patriot and The Lincoln Lawyer
**DREAM HOLIDAY?** Jamaican north coast
**ACCOMPLISHMENTS?** My family
**GUILTY PLEASURES?** Just look at me! It's sweets, of course!
**AMAZE ME!** I enjoy DIY, love playing Words With Friends, and I love spear fishing

| Batting | Mat | Inns | NO | Runs | HS | Ave | SR | 100 | 50 | Ct | St |
|---|---|---|---|---|---|---|---|---|---|---|---|
| Tests | 1 | 2 | 0 | 5 | 5 | 2.50 | 19.23 | 0 | 0 | 1 | 0 |
| First-class | 117 | 187 | 20 | 4401 | 165* | 26.35 | | 4 | 27 | 99 | 0 |
| List A | 161 | 122 | 31 | 1899 | 68* | 20.86 | | 0 | 3 | 64 | 0 |
| Twenty20 | 77 | 51 | 13 | 506 | 37 | 13.31 | 116.05 | 0 | 0 | 35 | 0 |

| Bowling | Mat | Balls | Runs | Wkts | BBI | BBM | Ave | Econ | SR | 5w | 10 |
|---|---|---|---|---|---|---|---|---|---|---|---|
| Tests | 1 | 188 | 135 | 2 | 2/108 | 2/135 | 67.50 | 4.30 | 94.0 | 0 | 0 |
| First-class | 117 | 18165 | 8390 | 281 | 7/60 | | 29.85 | 2.77 | 64.6 | 12 | 3 |
| List A | 161 | 6063 | 4750 | 168 | 5/41 | 5/41 | 28.27 | 4.70 | 36.0 | 2 | 0 |
| Twenty20 | 77 | 1260 | 1439 | 67 | 4/14 | 4/14 | 21.47 | 6.85 | 18.8 | 0 | 0 |

YORKSHIRE

**FULL NAME:** Timothy Thomas Bresnan
**BORN:** February 28, 1985, Pontefract, Yorkshire
**SQUAD NO:** 16
**HEIGHT:** 6ft
**NICKNAME:** Brezy Lad, Brez, Tikka, Brezzie
**EDUCATION:** Castleford High School; Pontefract New College
**TEAMS:** England, England Lions, England Under-19s, Marylebone Cricket Club, Yorkshire
**CAREER:** Test: 2009; ODI: 2006; T20I: 2006; First-class: 2003; List A: 2001; T20: 2003

**BEST BATTING:** 126* England Lions vs Indians, Chelmsford, 2007
**BEST BOWLING:** 5-42 Yorkshire vs Worcestershire, Worcester, 2005
**COUNTY CAP:** 2006

**FAMILY TIES?** Dad played local league cricket
**FAVOURITE BAND?** Razorlight, Snow Patrol
**RELAXATIONS?** PlayStation, cinema
**CRICKETING HEROES?** Ian Botham

| Batting | Mat | Inns | NO | Runs | HS | Ave | SR | 100 | 50 | Ct | St |
|---|---|---|---|---|---|---|---|---|---|---|---|
| Tests | 10 | 8 | 1 | 318 | 91 | 45.42 | 46.90 | 0 | 3 | 3 | 0 |
| ODIs | 58 | 45 | 13 | 673 | 80 | 21.03 | 92.44 | 0 | 1 | 15 | 0 |
| T20Is | 20 | 11 | 5 | 78 | 23* | 13.00 | 111.42 | 0 | 0 | 5 | 0 |
| First-class | 106 | 139 | 24 | 3305 | 126* | 28.73 | 48.07 | 3 | 17 | 42 | 0 |
| List A | 195 | 138 | 40 | 1857 | 80 | 18.94 | 91.07 | 0 | 4 | 51 | 0 |
| Twenty20 | 70 | 46 | 18 | 484 | 42 | 17.28 | 115.23 | 0 | 0 | 20 | 0 |

| Bowling | Mat | Balls | Runs | Wkts | BBI | BBM | Ave | Econ | SR | 5w | 10 |
|---|---|---|---|---|---|---|---|---|---|---|---|
| Tests | 10 | 2031 | 968 | 41 | 5/48 | 7/96 | 23.60 | 2.85 | 49.5 | 1 | 0 |
| ODIs | 58 | 2915 | 2598 | 69 | 5/48 | 5/48 | 37.65 | 5.34 | 42.2 | 1 | 0 |
| T20Is | 20 | 388 | 479 | 14 | 3/10 | 3/10 | 34.21 | 7.40 | 27.7 | 0 | 0 |
| First-class | 106 | 17764 | 9072 | 297 | 5/42 | | 30.54 | 3.06 | 59.8 | 5 | 0 |
| List A | 195 | 8593 | 7307 | 213 | 5/48 | 5/48 | 34.30 | 5.10 | 40.3 | 1 | 0 |
| Twenty20 | 70 | 1389 | 1712 | 63 | 3/10 | 3/10 | 27.17 | 7.39 | 22.0 | 0 | 0 |

FULL NAME: Danny Richard Briggs
BORN: April 30, 1991, Newport, Isle of Wight
SQUAD NO: 19
HEIGHT: 6ft 2in
NICKNAME: Briggsy
EDUCATION: Carisbrooke High School
TEAMS: England, Berkshire, England Lions, England Under-19s, Hampshire, Hampshire 2nd XI
CAREER: ODI: 2012; First-class: 2009; List A: 2009; T20: 2010

---

BEST BATTING: 38* England Lions vs Barbados, Bridgetown, 2011
BEST BOWLING: 6-45 England Lions vs Windward Islands, Roseau, 2011

---

WHY CRICKET? Family members played, along with friends of a similar age
CAREER HIGHLIGHTS? Winning the T20 Cup in 2010
CRICKETING HEROES? Daniel Vettori
BEST PLAYER IN COUNTY CRICKET? James Tomlinson
TIP FOR THE TOP? Jos Buttler
IF YOU WEREN'T A CRICKETER? Anything to do with sport
WHEN RAIN STOPS PLAY? Very bored, sleeping or listening to music
FAVOURITE TV? Any comedy
FAVOURITE FILM? The Shawshank Redemption
DREAM HOLIDAY? Caribbean
GUILTY PLEASURES? 80s music
FANTASY SLIP CORDON? Keeper: Happy Gilmore, 1st: Viv Richards, 2nd: James Tomlinson, 3rd: Pele
TWITTER FEED: @dannybriggs19

| Batting | Mat | Inns | NO | Runs | HS | Ave | SR | 100 | 50 | Ct | St |
|---|---|---|---|---|---|---|---|---|---|---|---|
| ODIs | 1 | - | - | - | - | - | - | - | - | 0 | 0 |
| First-class | 33 | 40 | 7 | 322 | 38* | 9.75 | | 0 | 0 | 9 | 0 |
| List A | 29 | 15 | 4 | 96 | 16 | 8.72 | 79.33 | 0 | 0 | 11 | 0 |
| Twenty20 | 43 | 10 | 5 | 27 | 10 | 5.40 | 103.84 | 0 | 0 | 6 | 0 |

| Bowling | Mat | Balls | Runs | Wkts | BBI | BBM | Ave | Econ | SR | 5w | 10 |
|---|---|---|---|---|---|---|---|---|---|---|---|
| ODIs | 1 | 60 | 39 | 2 | 2/39 | 2/39 | 19.50 | 3.90 | 30.0 | 0 | 0 |
| First-class | 33 | 6835 | 3605 | 113 | 6/45 | 9/96 | 31.90 | 3.16 | 60.4 | 5 | 0 |
| List A | 29 | 1422 | 1124 | 33 | 3/27 | 3/27 | 34.06 | 4.74 | 43.0 | 0 | 0 |
| Twenty20 | 43 | 877 | 962 | 61 | 5/19 | 5/19 | 15.77 | 6.58 | 14.3 | 1 | 0 |

**NOTTINGHAMSHIRE**

FULL NAME: Stuart Christopher John Broad
BORN: June 24, 1986, Nottingham
SQUAD NO: 16
HEIGHT: 6ft 5in
NICKNAME: Broady
EDUCATION: Oakham School
TEAMS: England, Leicestershire, Nottinghamshire
CAREER: Test: 2007; ODI: 2006; T20I: 2006; First-class: 2005; List A: 2005; T20: 2006

BEST BATTING: 169 England vs Pakistan, Lord's, 2010
BEST BOWLING: 8-52 Nottinghamshire vs Warwickshire, Birmingham, 2010
COUNTY CAP: 2007 (Leicestershire)

FAMILY TIES? Dad Chris played for Gloucestershire, Nottinghamshire and England
SUPERSTITIONS? Three warm up balls before I bowl a new spell
CRICKETERS PARTICULARLY ADMIRED? Glenn McGrath, Shaun Pollock
OTHER SPORTS PLAYED? Hockey (Midlands age group), golf
OTHER SPORTS FOLLOWED? Football (Nottingham Forest), rugby (Leicester Tigers)
RELAXATIONS? PSP, playing golf, films
NOTES: England T20 captain

| Batting | Mat | Inns | NO | Runs | HS | Ave | SR | 100 | 50 | Ct | St |
|---|---|---|---|---|---|---|---|---|---|---|---|
| Tests | 44 | 59 | 8 | 1440 | 169 | 28.23 | 64.02 | 1 | 9 | 13 | 0 |
| ODIs | 87 | 49 | 16 | 393 | 45* | 11.90 | 71.58 | 0 | 0 | 18 | 0 |
| T20Is | 34 | 14 | 6 | 44 | 10* | 5.50 | 107.31 | 0 | 0 | 16 | 0 |
| First-class | 91 | 117 | 21 | 2450 | 169 | 25.52 | 58.48 | 1 | 16 | 28 | 0 |
| List A | 104 | 55 | 17 | 439 | 45* | 11.55 | 70.46 | 0 | 0 | 20 | 0 |
| Twenty20 | 49 | 16 | 7 | 53 | 10* | 5.88 | 98.14 | 0 | 0 | 17 | 0 |

| Bowling | Mat | Balls | Runs | Wkts | BBI | BBM | Ave | Econ | SR | 5w | 10 |
|---|---|---|---|---|---|---|---|---|---|---|---|
| Tests | 44 | 9015 | 4491 | 145 | 6/46 | 8/76 | 30.97 | 2.98 | 62.1 | 4 | 0 |
| ODIs | 87 | 4412 | 3828 | 142 | 5/23 | 5/23 | 26.95 | 5.20 | 31.0 | 1 | 0 |
| T20Is | 34 | 723 | 876 | 40 | 3/17 | 3/17 | 21.90 | 7.26 | 18.0 | 0 | 0 |
| First-class | 91 | 16904 | 9084 | 325 | 8/52 | | 27.95 | 3.22 | 52.0 | 14 | 1 |
| List A | 104 | 5194 | 4516 | 167 | 5/23 | 5/23 | 27.04 | 5.21 | 31.1 | 1 | 0 |
| Twenty20 | 49 | 1070 | 1193 | 60 | 3/13 | 3/13 | 19.88 | 6.68 | 17.8 | 0 | 0 |

FULL NAME: Jack Alexander Brooks
BORN: June 4, 1984, Oxford
SQUAD NO: 9
HEIGHT: 6ft 2in
NICKNAME: Brooksy, Ferret, Animal,
Gianluigi Von Burgernips, Scrumpy, Subo,
Headband Warrior
EDUCATION: Wheatley Park School, Oxford
TEAMS: England Lions, Northamptonshire,
Northamptonshire 2nd XI, Oxfordshire
CAREER: First-class: 2009; List A: 2009; T20:
2010

**NORTHAMPTONSHIRE**

BEST BATTING: 53 Northamptonshire vs Gloucestershire, Bristol, 2010
BEST BOWLING: 5-23 Northamptonshire vs Leicestershire, Grace Road, 2011
COUNTY CAP: 2011

FAMILY TIES? Father Don played and captained local village side Tiddington for 100 years,
brother Nathan also plays for Tiddington and has represented Oxfordshire Development XI
SUPERSTITIONS? Always scratch my bowling marker with a J and change the headband now
and then
CRICKETING HEROES? Dennis Lillee, Curtly Ambrose, Colin Milburn
NON-CRICKETING HEROES? Vincent Chase, John Malkovich and Rambo
BEST PLAYER IN COUNTY CRICKET? Batsman: Marcus Trescothick. Bowler: David Masters is
an annoyingly good English seamer who is never injured!
TIPS FOR THE TOP? Rob Newton, Alex Wakely, Ben Howgego, David Murphy
WHEN RAIN STOPS PLAY? Talking about girls with Ben Howgego or annoying my teammates
FAVOURITE FILM? Rambo or The Goonies
FAVOURITE BOOK? 4,000 Days
DREAM HOLIDAY? Oxfordshire
SURPRISING SKILL? Damn good salesman and can drive a tractor
AMAZE ME! Large nipples (apparently) and I chose my middle name
TWITTER FEED: @BrooksyFerret

| Batting | Mat | Inns | NO | Runs | HS | Ave | SR | 100 | 50 | Ct | St |
|---|---|---|---|---|---|---|---|---|---|---|---|
| First-class | 26 | 31 | 11 | 255 | 53 | 12.75 | 47.30 | 0 | 1 | 5 | 0 |
| List A | 20 | 9 | 4 | 29 | 10 | 5.80 | 64.44 | 0 | 0 | 0 | 0 |
| Twenty20 | 28 | 10 | 6 | 59 | 33* | 14.75 | 134.09 | 0 | 0 | 5 | 0 |

| Bowling | Mat | Balls | Runs | Wkts | BBI | BBM | Ave | Econ | SR | 5w | 10 |
|---|---|---|---|---|---|---|---|---|---|---|---|
| First-class | 26 | 4461 | 2527 | 89 | 5/23 | 7/97 | 28.39 | 3.39 | 50.1 | 2 | 0 |
| List A | 20 | 846 | 687 | 19 | 3/35 | 3/35 | 36.15 | 4.87 | 44.5 | 0 | 0 |
| Twenty20 | 28 | 522 | 603 | 20 | 3/24 | 3/24 | 30.15 | 6.93 | 26.1 | 0 | 0 |

## GERARD BROPHY — RHB WK

FULL NAME: Gerard Louis Brophy
BORN: November 26, 1975, Welkom, Orange Free State, South Africa
SQUAD NO: 20
HEIGHT: 5ft 10in
NICKNAME: Scuba
EDUCATION: Christian Brothers College, Boksburg
TEAMS: Ireland, Free State, Gauteng, Northamptonshire, Transvaal, Yorkshire
CAREER: First-class: 1996; List A: 1997; T20: 2003

BEST BATTING: 185 South Africa Academy vs Zimbabwe Union President's XI, Harare, 1998
COUNTY CAP: 2008; BENEFIT YEAR: 2011

WHY CRICKET? Because of the pre-season tours to Barbados!
CAREER HIGHLIGHTS? Captaining Orange Free State; scoring a 13-ball 50
SUPERSTITIONS? Always put my left pad on first
CRICKETING HEROES? Ian Healy
NON-CRICKETING HEROES? Chuck Norris
BEST PLAYER IN COUNTY CRICKET? Marcus Trescothick
TIP FOR THE TOP? Jonny Bairstow
IF YOU WEREN'T A CRICKETER? I'd be a pilot
FAVOURITE TV? Two And A Half Men
FAVOURITE FILM? Heat
DREAM HOLIDAY? The Maldives
ACCOMPLISHMENTS? My daughter, Georgia
GUILTY PLEASURES? Chocolate, sweets
TWITTER FEED: @Brophy20

| Batting | Mat | Inns | NO | Runs | HS | Ave | SR | 100 | 50 | Ct | St |
|---|---|---|---|---|---|---|---|---|---|---|---|
| First-class | 122 | 195 | 25 | 5473 | 185 | 32.19 | | 8 | 27 | 293 | 22 |
| List A | 118 | 98 | 20 | 2045 | 93* | 26.21 | | 0 | 13 | 115 | 24 |
| Twenty20 | 55 | 47 | 9 | 723 | 57* | 19.02 | 120.50 | 0 | 2 | 24 | 7 |

| Bowling | Mat | Balls | Runs | Wkts | BBI | BBM | Ave | Econ | SR | 5w | 10 |
|---|---|---|---|---|---|---|---|---|---|---|---|
| First-class | 122 | 24 | 7 | 0 | - | - | - | 1.75 | - | 0 | 0 |
| List A | 118 | - | - | - | - | - | - | - | - | - | - |
| Twenty20 | 55 | - | - | - | - | - | - | - | - | - | - |

# BEN BROWN

## RHB WK

**FULL NAME:** Ben Christopher Brown
**BORN:** November 23, 1988, Crawley, Sussex
**SQUAD NO:** 26
**HEIGHT:** 5ft 8in
**NICKNAME:** Brownie
**EDUCATION:** Balcombe Primary; Ardingly College
**TEAMS:** England Under-19s, Sussex, Sussex 2nd XI
**CAREER:** First-class: 2007; List A: 2007; T20: 2008

**BEST BATTING:** 112 Sussex vs Derbyshire, Horsham, 2010

**CAREER HIGHLIGHTS?** Scoring my maiden Championship century, Sussex winning T20 in 2009
**CRICKETING HEROES?** Alec Stewart and Adam Gilchrist
**BEST PLAYER IN COUNTY CRICKET?** Chris Nash
**TIPS FOR THE TOP?** Luke Wells, Will Beer and Matt Machan
**IF YOU WEREN'T A CRICKETER?** Probably have to be a footballer
**WHEN RAIN STOPS PLAY?** Talking rubbish in the dressing room and trying to irritate anybody attempting to do a crossword or Suduko!
**FAVOURITE TV?** Match Of The Day
**FAVOURITE FILM?** Gladiator
**FAVOURITE BOOK?** One Day by David Nicolls
**DREAM HOLIDAY?** Rome
**ACCOMPLISHMENTS?** School exam results
**GUILTY PLEASURES?** Ben and Jerry's Chocolate Fudge Brownie (preferably the whole tub)
**FANTASY SLIP CORDON?** Keeper: Me, 1st: Julius Cesar (commanding leader), 2nd: Jesus (must be a good fielder), 3rd: Russell Brand, Gully: David Beckham
**TWITTER FEED:** @Ben_Brown26

| Batting | Mat | Inns | NO | Runs | HS | Ave | SR | 100 | 50 | Ct | St |
|---|---|---|---|---|---|---|---|---|---|---|---|
| First-class | 21 | 34 | 4 | 1065 | 112 | 35.50 | 65.01 | 4 | 4 | 23 | 4 |
| List A | 20 | 14 | 6 | 299 | 60 | 37.37 | 112.83 | 0 | 3 | 16 | 3 |
| Twenty20 | 22 | 18 | 1 | 264 | 68 | 15.52 | 103.93 | 0 | 1 | 9 | 1 |

| Bowling | Mat | Balls | Runs | Wkts | BBI | BBM | Ave | Econ | SR | 5w | 10 |
|---|---|---|---|---|---|---|---|---|---|---|---|
| First-class | 21 | - | - | - | - | - | - | - | - | - | - |
| List A | 20 | - | - | - | - | - | - | - | - | - | - |
| Twenty20 | 22 | - | - | - | - | - | - | - | - | - | - |

LANCASHIRE

**FULL NAME:** Karl Robert Brown
**BORN:** May 17, 1988, Bolton, Lancashire
**SQUAD NO:** 14
**HEIGHT:** 5ft 10in
**NICKNAME:** Browny, Charlie
**EDUCATION:** Hesketh Fletcher CE, Atherton, Lancashire
**TEAMS:** Lancashire, Lancashire 2nd XI, Moors Sports Club
**CAREER:** First-class: 2006; List A: 2007; T20: 2011

**BEST BATTING:** 114 Lancashire vs Sussex, Liverpool, 2011
**BEST BOWLING:** 2-30 Lancashire vs Nottinghamshire, Nottingham, 2009

**FAMILY TIES?** Dad played league cricket for Atherton CC and was professional for Clifton CC
**CAREER HIGHLIGHTS?** Scoring maiden first-class and one-day hundreds, playing for England U19
**SUPERSTITIONS?** No interesting ones
**CRICKETING HEROES?** Andrew Flintoff, Stuart Law
**NON-CRICKETING HEROES?** Kevin Davies, Lionel Messi, Ronnie O'Sullivan, Phil Taylor, Sergio Garcia
**BEST PLAYER IN COUNTY CRICKET?** Marcus Trescothick
**TIP FOR THE TOP?** Simon Kerrigan
**IF YOU WEREN'T A CRICKETER?** Not sure
**WHEN RAIN STOPS PLAY?** Playing cards or watching TV
**FAVOURITE TV?** Celebrity Juice
**FAVOURITE FILM?** Snatch, Layer Cake
**DREAM HOLIDAY?** Anywhere with a golf course
**ACCOMPLISHMENTS?** Playing football for Wigan Athletic
**GUILTY PLEASURES?** Sweets
**TWITTER FEED?** @karlos173

| Batting | Mat | Inns | NO | Runs | HS | Ave | SR | 100 | 50 | Ct | St |
|---|---|---|---|---|---|---|---|---|---|---|---|
| First-class | 27 | 47 | 3 | 1187 | 114 | 26.97 | 48.48 | 1 | 7 | 15 | 0 |
| List A | 23 | 23 | 3 | 687 | 101* | 34.35 | 84.08 | 1 | 3 | 4 | 0 |
| Twenty20 | 11 | 9 | 1 | 240 | 51 | 30.00 | 129.03 | 0 | 2 | 3 | 0 |

| Bowling | Mat | Balls | Runs | Wkts | BBI | BBM | Ave | Econ | SR | 5w | 10 |
|---|---|---|---|---|---|---|---|---|---|---|---|
| First-class | 27 | 66 | 44 | 2 | 2/30 | 2/37 | 22.00 | 4.00 | 33.0 | 0 | 0 |
| List A | 23 | - | - | - | - | - | - | - | - | - | - |
| Twenty20 | 11 | - | - | - | - | - | - | - | - | - | - |

FULL NAME: Nathan Liam Buck
BORN: April 26, 1991, Leicester
SQUAD NO: 17
HEIGHT: 6ft 3in
NICKNAME: Bucky
EDUCATION: Ashby School
TEAMS: England Lions, England Under-17s, England Under-19s, Leicestershire, Leicestershire 2nd XI
CAREER: First-class: 2009; List A: 2009; T20: 2010

LEICESTERSHIRE

BEST BATTING: 26 Leicestershire vs Middlesex, Leicester, 2011
BEST BOWLING: 5-99 Leicestershire vs Gloucestershire, Bristol, 2011
COUNTY CAP: 2011

FAMILY TIES? My older brother Mitchell played at Grace Dieu Park CC where I decided to follow in his footsteps and join in at Kwik Cricket
CAREER HIGHLIGHTS? England Lions tour to West Indies
CRICKETING HEROES? Dale Steyn, Andrew Flintoff
IF YOU WEREN'T A CRICKETER? I'd probably be studying Sport and Exercise Science at Loughborough University
FAVOURITE TV? The Inbetweeners
FAVOURITE FILM? The Hangover
DREAM HOLIDAY? Barbados
TWITTER FEED: @NathanBuck17
RELAXATIONS? Socialising and eating out
FAVOURITE BAND? Dizzee Rascal, Calvin Harris
NOTES: Trained with Stuart Broad, Simon Jones and Graham Onions at the National Performance Centre in 2006, aged 15. Took 49 first-class wickets at 27.34 in his first full season in county cricket in 2010. Toured Bangladesh and Sri Lanka with England Lions in 2011/12

| Batting | Mat | Inns | NO | Runs | HS | Ave | SR | 100 | 50 | Ct | St |
|---|---|---|---|---|---|---|---|---|---|---|---|
| First-class | 36 | 49 | 14 | 265 | 26 | 7.57 | | 0 | 0 | 6 | 0 |
| List A | 21 | 9 | 2 | 57 | 21 | 8.14 | 65.51 | 0 | 0 | 3 | 0 |
| Twenty20 | 11 | 1 | 1 | 3 | 3* | - | 100.00 | 0 | 0 | 2 | 0 |

| Bowling | Mat | Balls | Runs | Wkts | BBI | BBM | Ave | Econ | SR | 5w | 10 |
|---|---|---|---|---|---|---|---|---|---|---|---|
| First-class | 36 | 5377 | 3057 | 82 | 5/99 | 7/79 | 37.28 | 3.41 | 65.5 | 1 | 0 |
| List A | 21 | 856 | 767 | 26 | 4/39 | 4/39 | 29.50 | 5.37 | 32.9 | 0 | 0 |
| Twenty20 | 11 | 228 | 289 | 16 | 3/16 | 3/16 | 18.06 | 7.60 | 14.2 | 0 | 0 |

## PETER BURGOYNE

RHB OB

**DERBYSHIRE**

FULL NAME: Peter Burgoyne
BORN: November 11, 1993, Nottingham
SQUAD NO: 11
HEIGHT: 6ft 2in
NICKNAME: Pie Man, Burgy
EDUCATION: St John Houghton School;
Derby College
TEAMS: Derbyshire, Derbyshire 2nd XI,
Derbyshire Under-14s, Derbyshire Under-
15s, Derbyshire Under-17s, Derbyshire
Under-19s, England Under-19s
CAREER: List A: 2011

**CAREER HIGHLIGHTS?** Making my first-team debut against Middlesex. Playing for England U19 against South Africa in 2011

**SUPERSTITIONS?** Some say that when I'm about to pick the ball up in the field I keep saying 'hop, hop, hop', but other than that absolutely nothing

**CRICKETING HEROES?** Graeme Swann

**NON-CRICKETING HEROES?** Raymond van Barneveld

**TIP FOR THE TOP?** James Taylor

**WHEN RAIN STOPS PLAY?** If there is a dartboard knocking about then I'd tend to have a few throws but if not I'd most probably just go and have a cuppa

**FAVOURITE TV?** Premier League Darts, Coronation Street

**DREAM HOLIDAY?** Barbados – enough said

| Batting | Mat | Inns | NO | Runs | HS | Ave | SR | 100 | 50 | Ct | St |
|---------|-----|------|-----|------|-----|------|-------|-----|-----|-----|-----|
| List A | 2 | 2 | 1 | 6 | 6* | 6.00 | 85.71 | 0 | 0 | 1 | 0 |

| Bowling | Mat | Balls | Runs | Wkts | BBI | BBM | Ave | Econ | SR | 5w | 10 |
|---------|-----|-------|------|------|------|------|-------|------|------|-----|-----|
| List A | 2 | 60 | 62 | 2 | 2/36 | 2/36 | 31.00 | 6.20 | 30.0 | 0 | 0 |

## RORY BURNS                                          LHB WK

FULL NAME: Rory Joseph Burns
BORN: August 26, 1990, Epsom, Surrey
SQUAD NO: 17
HEIGHT: 5ft 8in
NICKNAME: Bieber, Biebs
EDUCATION: City of London Freemen's
School; UWIC
TEAMS: Cardiff MCCU, Hampshire 2nd XI,
Surrey, Surrey 2nd XI, Surrey Under-19s
CAREER: First-class: 2011

BEST BATTING: 26 CMCCU vs Surrey, Fenner's, 2011

CAREER HIGHLIGHTS? Signing professionally, any hundred scored, winning the Walter Lawrence trophy [given to the MCCU player who makes the highest score for any of the six University teams during the season – Burns made 230 against Oxford in 2010], winning BUCS one-day comp with Cardiff UCCE
SUPERSTITIONS? Not really, I just always put my kit on in the same order
CRICKETING HEROES? Kumar Sangakkara, Alec Stewart, Graham Thorpe
NON-CRICKETING HEROES? Jonny Wilkinson, Will Ferrell
BEST PLAYER IN COUNTY CRICKET? Marcus Trescothick
TIPS FOR THE TOP? Jason Roy, Jos Buttler, Paul Stirling
IF YOU WEREN'T A CRICKETER? Student
WHEN RAIN STOPS PLAY? Procrastinating, inventing any sort of game to pass time
FAVOURITE TV? Watching a lot of Modern Family at the moment, plus The OC and One Tree Hill
FAVOURITE FILM? If it's got Will Ferrell in it, it's top drawer
DREAM HOLIDAY? Somewhere sunny and where I have to do very little
SURPRISING SKILL? Used to play the saxophone
GUILTY PLEASURES? Chocolate and any food in the carbohydrate category. I'm not shy of a potato in any form
AMAZE ME! I only started wicketkeeping at 15. Justin Bieber's hair was inspired by mine. I can play golf left or right-handed
TWITTER FEED: @roryburns17

| Batting | Mat | Inns | NO | Runs | HS | Ave | SR | 100 | 50 | Ct | St |
|---------|-----|------|-----|------|-----|-------|-------|-----|-----|-----|-----|
| First-class | 1 | 2 | 0 | 35 | 26 | 17.50 | 45.45 | 0 | 0 | 2 | 0 |

| Bowling | Mat | Balls | Runs | Wkts | BBI | BBM | Ave | Econ | SR | 5w | 10 |
|---------|-----|-------|------|------|-----|-----|-----|------|-----|-----|-----|
| First-class | 1 | - | - | - | - | - | - | - | - | - | - |

## DAVE BURTON

### RHB RMF

NORTHAMPTONSHIRE

FULL NAME: David Alexander Burton
BORN: August 23, 1985, Stockwell, London
SQUAD NO: 23
HEIGHT: 5ft 11in
NICKNAME: Burts, DB, Burtna, Dizzy
EDUCATION: Allen Edwards Primary School;
Sacred Heart RC Secondary School; Lambeth
College
TEAMS: Essex 2nd XI, Gloucestershire, Kent,
Middlesex, Northamptonshire, Surrey 2nd
XI, Sussex 2nd XI
CAREER: First-class: 2006; List A: 2009; T20:
2008

BEST BATTING: 52* Gloucestershire vs Glamorgan, Cardiff, 2006
BEST BOWLING: 5-68 Middlesex vs Gloucestershire, Bristol, 2009

WHY CRICKET? The passion of the Caribbean environment I grew up in. Everyone loved cricket then I got introduced to it at primary school at the age of eight and I never looked back
CAREER HIGHLIGHTS? 52* for Gloucestershire vs Glamorgan (2006), 5-68 for Middlesex vs Gloucestershire (2009), 5-75 for Northamptonshire vs Leicestershire (2010)
BEST PLAYER IN COUNTY CRICKET? Darren Stevens
TIPS FOR THE TOP? Dom Sibley (Surrey), Luke Remice (Kent), Daniel Bell-Drummond (Kent), Rajan Soni (Surrey)
ACCOMPLISHMENTS? Forming my own car detailing business and modelling
SURPRISING SKILL? I race mountain bikes downhill and can do endless tricks at a skatepark
AMAZE ME! Was the face of Pepsi for T20 World Cup 2007. Have always been the last man standing on every bleep/yoyo fitness test taken. Have only travelled once outside the UK which was South Africa in 2007
FANTASY SLIP CORDON? Keeper: Bernie Mac (for constant comedy), 1st: Princess Diana (for the heart of gold and passion for people), 2nd: Nelson Mandela (for 100 per cent inspiration), 3rd: Ayrton Senna (for nothing but petrolhead banter), Gully: Shanaze Reade (BMX beauty is a hot dinner date)

| Batting | Mat | Inns | NO | Runs | HS | Ave | SR | 100 | 50 | Ct | St |
|---|---|---|---|---|---|---|---|---|---|---|---|
| First-class | 6 | 10 | 4 | 66 | 52* | 11.00 | 32.51 | 0 | 1 | 1 | 0 |
| List A | 5 | 1 | 0 | 2 | 2 | 2.00 | 66.66 | 0 | 0 | 3 | 0 |
| Twenty20 | 3 | - | - | - | - | - | - | - | - | 1 | 0 |

| Bowling | Mat | Balls | Runs | Wkts | BBI | BBM | Ave | Econ | SR | 5w | 10 |
|---|---|---|---|---|---|---|---|---|---|---|---|
| First-class | 6 | 878 | 692 | 16 | 5/68 | 5/68 | 43.25 | 4.72 | 54.8 | 2 | 0 |
| List A | 5 | 144 | 141 | 5 | 3/25 | 3/25 | 28.20 | 5.87 | 28.8 | 0 | 0 |
| Twenty20 | 3 | 54 | 51 | 4 | 2/13 | 2/13 | 12.75 | 5.66 | 13.5 | 0 | 0 |

# JOS BUTTLER                                          RHB WK MVP45

FULL NAME: Joseph Charles Buttler
BORN: September 8, 1990, Taunton, Somerset
SQUAD NO: 15
HEIGHT: 6ft
EDUCATION: King's College, Taunton
TEAMS: England, England Lions, England Under-19s, Somerset, Somerset 2nd XI
CAREER: ODI: 2012; T20I: 2011; First-class: 2009; List A: 2009; T20: 2009

SOMERSET

---

BEST BATTING: 144 Somerset vs Hampshire, Southampton, 2010

---

NOTES: Shares keeping duties at Somerset with fellow international Craig Kieswetter, but is yet to keep wicket for England. Came to prominence after scoring 55 from just 25 balls in the 2010 Friends Provident t20 semi-final between Somerset and Notts, and 440 runs at 55 in the 2010 CB40. Averaged 137 in last year's CB40, scoring 411 runs in 10 innings (seven not outs, four fifties) and top-scored in the final, with 86 from 72 balls. A successful tour with England Lions to Sri Lanka in early 2012 (262 runs at 87.33) led to a call-up for England's limited-overs squads for the series against Pakistan in UAE

| Batting | Mat | Inns | NO | Runs | HS | Ave | SR | 100 | 50 | Ct | St |
|---------|-----|------|----|----|----|----|----|----|----|----|----|
| ODIs | 1 | 1 | 0 | 0 | 0 | 0.00 | 0.00 | 0 | 0 | 0 | 0 |
| T20Is | 7 | 4 | 0 | 30 | 13 | 7.50 | 83.33 | 0 | 0 | 1 | 0 |
| First-class | 27 | 39 | 4 | 1123 | 144 | 32.08 | 59.57 | 2 | 5 | 54 | 1 |
| List A | 40 | 35 | 15 | 1341 | 119 | 67.05 | 127.95 | 2 | 9 | 25 | 4 |
| Twenty20 | 53 | 42 | 10 | 688 | 72* | 21.50 | 135.96 | 0 | 2 | 33 | 9 |
| Bowling | Mat | Balls | Runs | Wkts | BBI | BBM | Ave | Econ | SR | 5w | 10 |
| ODIs | 1 | - | - | - | - | - | - | - | - | - | - |
| T20Is | 7 | - | - | - | - | - | - | - | - | - | - |
| First-class | 27 | - | - | - | - | - | - | - | - | - | - |
| List A | 40 | - | - | - | - | - | - | - | - | - | - |
| Twenty20 | 53 | - | - | - | - | - | - | - | - | - | - |

# JAMES CAMERON
## LHB RM

FULL NAME: James Gair Cameron
BORN: January 31, 1986, Harare, Zimbabwe
SQUAD NO: 16
HEIGHT: 5ft 10in
NICKNAME: Jimbo
EDUCATION: St George's College, Harare; University of Western Australia
TEAMS: Worcestershire, Zimbabwe Under-19s
CAREER: First-class: 2010; List A: 2010; T20: 2010

BEST BATTING: 105 Worcestershire vs Sussex, Worcester, 2010
BEST BOWLING: 2-18 Worcestershire vs Northamptonshire, Worcester, 2010

FAMILY TIES? All my family played cricket. My brother represented Zimbabwe at age group levels, as did my uncles and grandfather
CAREER HIGHLIGHTS? My first hundred for Worcestershire to help get us promoted in 2010. It was a brilliant afternoon
TIPS FOR THE TOP? Mitchell Marsh from Western Australia is a very good young player. Alexei Kervezee and Aneesh Kapil from Worcester
WHEN RAIN STOPS PLAY? Relax! Grab a cup of tea and a paper and maybe have a lie-down
FAVOURITE TV? Any documentaries on wildlife, especially in Africa. I also enjoy the fishing programmes, like River Monsters
DREAM HOLIDAY? Any good fishing trip. The Zambezi Valley is a special place
ACCOMPLISHMENTS? Getting my B Comm degree from UWA. I played some representative rugby when I was younger, a sport which I always enjoyed
AMAZE ME! Scared of English winters. I'm from Zimbabwe and I support Crystal Palace!
FANTASY SLIP CORDON? Keeper: Warren Buffett (wouldn't mind picking his brain and possibly getting some share tips!), 1st: Tiger Woods, 2nd: Eddie Murphy (for the humour), 3rd: Me, Gully: Superman (he is responsible for catching everything while the rest of us can relax and chat)

| Batting | Mat | Inns | NO | Runs | HS | Ave | SR | 100 | 50 | Ct | St |
|---|---|---|---|---|---|---|---|---|---|---|---|
| First-class | 22 | 40 | 2 | 1154 | 105 | 30.36 | 53.17 | 1 | 6 | 14 | 0 |
| List A | 24 | 23 | 5 | 689 | 69 | 38.27 | 82.41 | 0 | 5 | 10 | 0 |
| Twenty20 | 28 | 23 | 2 | 381 | 55 | 18.14 | 110.11 | 0 | 2 | 13 | 0 |

| Bowling | Mat | Balls | Runs | Wkts | BBI | BBM | Ave | Econ | SR | 5w | 10 |
|---|---|---|---|---|---|---|---|---|---|---|---|
| First-class | 22 | 605 | 374 | 8 | 2/18 | 3/43 | 46.75 | 3.70 | 75.6 | 0 | 0 |
| List A | 24 | 277 | 301 | 8 | 4/44 | 4/44 | 37.62 | 6.51 | 34.6 | 0 | 0 |
| Twenty20 | 28 | 179 | 239 | 8 | 3/22 | 3/22 | 29.87 | 8.01 | 22.3 | 0 | 0 |

## MICHAEL CARBERRY — LHB OB R3

**FULL NAME:** Michael Alexander Carberry
**BORN:** September 29, 1980, Croydon, Surrey
**SQUAD NO:** 15
**HEIGHT:** 5ft 11in
**NICKNAME:** Carbs
**EDUCATION:** St John Rigby College
**TEAMS:** England, England Lions, Hampshire, Kent, Marylebone Cricket Club, Surrey, Surrey Cricket Board
**CAREER:** Test: 2010; First-class: 2001; List A: 1999; T20: 2003

**BEST BATTING:** 300* Hampshire vs Yorkshire, Southampton, 2011
**BEST BOWLING:** 2-85 Hampshire vs Durham, Chester-le-Street, 2006
**COUNTY CAP:** 2006 (Hampshire)

**FAMILY TIES?** My dad played club cricket
**CAREER HIGHLIGHTS?** Every day is a highlight
**CRICKETERS PARTICULARLY ADMIRED?** Ricky Ponting, Brian Lara
**RELAXATIONS?** Sleeping
**NOTES:** Toured India with England Lions in 2008. Member of the England Performance Programme squad 2009/10. Opened the batting on Test debut for England against Bangladesh in 2010, scored 30 and 34, and has not played since. In 2011, hit a career-best 300 not out against Yorkshire at The Rose Bowl

| Batting | Mat | Inns | NO | Runs | HS | Ave | SR | 100 | 50 | Ct | St |
|---|---|---|---|---|---|---|---|---|---|---|---|
| Tests | 1 | 2 | 0 | 64 | 34 | 32.00 | 45.71 | 0 | 0 | 1 | 0 |
| First-class | 121 | 213 | 19 | 8625 | 300* | 44.45 | 52.56 | 26 | 37 | 56 | 0 |
| List A | 124 | 115 | 11 | 2930 | 121* | 28.17 | | 2 | 21 | 50 | 0 |
| Twenty20 | 66 | 61 | 9 | 1441 | 90 | 27.71 | 114.54 | 0 | 10 | 30 | 0 |

| Bowling | Mat | Balls | Runs | Wkts | BBI | BBM | Ave | Econ | SR | 5w | 10 |
|---|---|---|---|---|---|---|---|---|---|---|---|
| Tests | 1 | - | - | - | - | - | - | - | - | - | - |
| First-class | 121 | 1252 | 891 | 13 | 2/85 | | 68.53 | 4.26 | 96.3 | 0 | 0 |
| List A | 124 | 216 | 206 | 4 | 2/11 | 2/11 | 51.50 | 5.72 | 54.0 | 0 | 0 |
| Twenty20 | 66 | 18 | 19 | 1 | 1/16 | 1/16 | 19.00 | 6.33 | 18.0 | 0 | 0 |

# ANDY CARTER

**RHB RFM**

NOTTINGHAMSHIRE

FULL NAME: Andrew Carter
BORN: August 27, 1988, Lincoln
SQUAD NO: 37
EDUCATION: Lincoln College
TEAMS: Essex, Essex 2nd XI, Lincolnshire,
Nottinghamshire, Nottinghamshire 2nd XI
CAREER: First-class: 2009; List A: 2009; T20:
2010

BEST BATTING: 17 Nottinghamshire vs OMCCU, The Parks, 2011
BEST BOWLING: 5-40 Essex vs Kent, Canterbury, 2010

NOTES: Given a short-term contract in April 2008 after starring in the Lincolnshire Premier
League in 2007. Took 54 Second XI wickets in the 2009 season. Made County Championship
debut against Worcestershire at New Road in August 2009, where his first wicket was that of
Steve Davies

| Batting | Mat | Inns | NO | Runs | HS | Ave | SR | 100 | 50 | Ct | St |
|---------|-----|------|----|------|----|-----|----|-----|----|----|----|
| First-class | 7 | 8 | 1 | 71 | 17 | 10.14 | | 0 | 0 | 2 | 0 |
| List A | 10 | 6 | 1 | 25 | 12 | 5.00 | 54.34 | 0 | 0 | 3 | 0 |
| Twenty20 | 10 | - | - | - | - | - | - | - | - | 3 | 0 |

| Bowling | Mat | Balls | Runs | Wkts | BBI | BBM | Ave | Econ | SR | 5w | 10 |
|---------|-----|-------|------|------|-----|-----|-----|------|----|----|----|
| First-class | 7 | 1169 | 571 | 21 | 5/40 | 7/121 | 27.19 | 2.93 | 55.6 | 1 | 0 |
| List A | 10 | 294 | 279 | 12 | 3/32 | 3/32 | 23.25 | 5.69 | 24.5 | 0 | 0 |
| Twenty20 | 10 | 203 | 298 | 9 | 4/20 | 4/20 | 33.11 | 8.80 | 22.5 | 0 | 0 |

FULL NAME: Neil Miller Carter
BORN: January 29, 1975, Cape Town, South Africa
SQUAD NO: 7
HEIGHT: 6ft 2in
NICKNAME: Carts
EDUCATION: Hottentots Holland High School
TEAMS: Boland, Cape Cobras, Matabeleland Tuskers, Middlesex, Warwickshire
CAREER: First-class: 1999; List A: 1999; T20: 2003

BEST BATTING: 103 Warwickshire vs Sussex, Hove, 2002
BEST BOWLING: 6-30 Warwickshire vs Lancashire, Liverpool, 2011
COUNTY CAP: 2005; BENEFIT YEAR: 2012

WHY CRICKET? Went to a school where you had to play summer and winter sports. Cricket was the summer sport
CAREER HIGHLIGHTS? Every trophy that I've won. PCA Player of the Year 2010
SUPERSTITIONS? None
CRICKETING HEROES? Stephen Jefferies, Allan Donald
NON-CRICKETING HEROES? Roger Federer
BEST PLAYER IN COUNTY CRICKET? Marcus Trescothick
TIPS FOR THE TOP? Chris Woakes, Tom Milnes
IF YOU WEREN'T A CRICKETER? I'd be a computer engineer
WHEN RAIN STOPS PLAY? Checking to see how long the rain will last for!
FAVOURITE TV? Ice Road Truckers
FAVOURITE FILM? Mud, Sweat And Tears
FAVOURITE BOOK? Moneyball
DREAM HOLIDAY? Cocoa Island, Maldives

| Batting | Mat | Inns | NO | Runs | HS | Ave | SR | 100 | 50 | Ct | St |
|---|---|---|---|---|---|---|---|---|---|---|---|
| First-class | 109 | 151 | 24 | 2938 | 103 | 23.13 | | 1 | 13 | 25 | 0 |
| List A | 173 | 148 | 15 | 2965 | 135 | 22.29 | | 3 | 13 | 14 | 0 |
| Twenty20 | 97 | 94 | 2 | 1528 | 58 | 16.60 | 136.67 | 0 | 2 | 15 | 0 |

| Bowling | Mat | Balls | Runs | Wkts | BBI | BBM | Ave | Econ | SR | 5w | 10 |
|---|---|---|---|---|---|---|---|---|---|---|---|
| First-class | 109 | 18089 | 10455 | 307 | 6/30 | | 34.05 | 3.46 | 58.9 | 14 | 0 |
| List A | 173 | 7360 | 5990 | 223 | 5/31 | 5/31 | 26.86 | 4.88 | 33.0 | 2 | 0 |
| Twenty20 | 97 | 1895 | 2268 | 90 | 5/19 | 5/19 | 25.20 | 7.18 | 21.0 | 1 | 0 |

ESSEX

FULL NAME: Maurice Anthony Chambers
BORN: September 14, 1987, Port Antonio, Portland, Jamaica
SQUAD NO: 29
HEIGHT: 6ft 3in
NICKNAME: Mozza
EDUCATION: Homerton College of Technology; George Monoux College
TEAMS: England Lions, Essex, Essex 2nd XI
CAREER: First-class: 2005; List A: 2008; T20: 2008

BEST BATTING: 30 Essex vs Leicestershire, Leicester, 2011
BEST BOWLING: 6-68 Essex vs Nottinghamshire, Chelmsford, 2010

SUPERSTITIONS? No sexy time before cricket
OTHER SPORTS FOLLOWED? Football (Manchester United)
FAVOURITE BAND? 50 Cent, Vybz Kartel
RELAXATIONS? Shopping, playing Xbox, listening to music and partying real hard
OTHER SPORTS PLAYED? Basketball – I just train with my cousin for the fitness. I play badminton with a few of my friends
CRICKETERS PARTICULARLY ADMIRED? Courtney Walsh, Curtly Ambrose, Stuart Broad, Brian Lara, Kevin Pietersen, Brett Lee
CRICKET MOMENTS TO FORGET? Playing for England U19 vs India, we were eight wickets down with two balls to go and I was the last batsman. I told myself I was not going to pad up, and then my mate was out and I went in to bat with no abdo guard or gloves
NOTES: Jamaica-born, awarded British Citizenship in 2007 having gained special dispensation from the ECB to represent Essex and England U19 as a non-overseas player. Returned prematurely from the England Lions tour of the West Indies in early 2011 following an injury to his left thigh

| Batting | Mat | Inns | NO | Runs | HS | Ave | SR | 100 | 50 | Ct | St |
|---|---|---|---|---|---|---|---|---|---|---|---|
| First-class | 36 | 49 | 20 | 195 | 30 | 6.72 | | 0 | 0 | 8 | 0 |
| List A | 3 | 1 | 1 | 1 | 1* | - | 100.00 | 0 | 0 | 1 | 0 |
| Twenty20 | 18 | 8 | 5 | 28 | 10* | 9.33 | 96.55 | 0 | 0 | 6 | 0 |

| Bowling | Mat | Balls | Runs | Wkts | BBI | BBM | Ave | Econ | SR | 5w | 10 |
|---|---|---|---|---|---|---|---|---|---|---|---|
| First-class | 36 | 4988 | 3006 | 90 | 6/68 | | 33.40 | 3.61 | 55.4 | 2 | 1 |
| List A | 3 | 90 | 93 | 3 | 1/26 | 1/26 | 31.00 | 6.20 | 30.0 | 0 | 0 |
| Twenty20 | 18 | 312 | 461 | 17 | 3/31 | 3/31 | 27.11 | 8.86 | 18.3 | 0 | 0 |

## GLEN CHAPPLE      RHB RMF W6 MVP52

FULL NAME: Glen Chapple
BORN: January 23, 1974, Skipton, Yorkshire
SQUAD NO: 3
HEIGHT: 6ft 2in
NICKNAME: Chappie, Boris
EDUCATION: West Craven High School;
Nelson and Colne College
TEAMS: England, Lancashire
CAREER: ODI: 2006; First-class: 1992; List A:
1993; T20: 2003

LANCASHIRE

BEST BATTING: 155 Lancashire vs Somerset, Manchester, 2001
BEST BOWLING: 7-53 Lancashire vs Durham, Blackpool, 2007
COUNTY CAP: 1994; BENEFIT YEAR: 2004

FAMILY TIES? Father played in Lancashire League for Nelson and was a professional for Darwen and Earby
SUPERSTITIONS? None
CRICKETERS PARTICULARLY ADMIRED? Dennis Lillee, Robin Smith
FAVOURITE BAND? U2, Oasis, Stone Roses
RELAXATIONS? Golf
OTHER SPORTS FOLLOWED? Football (Liverpool)

| Batting | Mat | Inns | NO | Runs | HS | Ave | SR | 100 | 50 | Ct | St |
|---|---|---|---|---|---|---|---|---|---|---|---|
| ODIs | 1 | 1 | 0 | 14 | 14 | 14.00 | 200.00 | 0 | 0 | 0 | 0 |
| First-class | 265 | 368 | 66 | 7484 | 155 | 24.78 | | 6 | 34 | 85 | 0 |
| List A | 271 | 155 | 41 | 2004 | 81* | 17.57 | | 0 | 9 | 60 | 0 |
| Twenty20 | 53 | 30 | 11 | 287 | 55* | 15.10 | 112.10 | 0 | 1 | 14 | 0 |

| Bowling | Mat | Balls | Runs | Wkts | BBI | BBM | Ave | Econ | SR | 5w | 10 |
|---|---|---|---|---|---|---|---|---|---|---|---|
| ODIs | 1 | 24 | 14 | 0 | - | - | - | 3.50 | - | 0 | 0 |
| First-class | 265 | 45376 | 22250 | 837 | 7/53 | | 26.58 | 2.94 | 54.2 | 34 | 2 |
| List A | 271 | 11661 | 8770 | 302 | 6/18 | 6/18 | 29.03 | 4.51 | 38.6 | 4 | 0 |
| Twenty20 | 53 | 1001 | 1277 | 53 | 3/36 | 3/36 | 24.09 | 7.65 | 18.8 | 0 | 0 |

**WARWICKSHIRE**

FULL NAME: Varun Chopra
BORN: June 21, 1987, Barking, Essex
SQUAD NO: 3
HEIGHT: 6ft 1in
NICKNAME: Tidz, Chops
EDUCATION: Ilford County HS
TEAMS: England Under-19s, Essex, Essex 2nd XI, Tamil Union Cricket and Athletic Club, Warwickshire
CAREER: First-class: 2006; List A: 2006; T20: 2006

---

BEST BATTING: 233* Tamil Union vs Sinhalese Sports Club, PSS Colombo, 2012

---

CAREER HIGHLIGHTS? Back-to-back double centuries in 2011
SUPERSTITIONS? None
CRICKETING HEROES? Sachin Tendulkar, Shane Warne
NON-CRICKETING HEROES? Roger Federer
BEST PLAYER IN COUNTY CRICKET? Marcus Trescothick
TIP FOR THE TOP? Adam Wheater
IF YOU WEREN'T A CRICKETER? I'd be working for a bank
FAVOURITE TV? Entourage
FAVOURITE FILM? Law Abiding Citizen
FAVOURITE BOOK? Lord Of The Rings
DREAM HOLIDAY? Maldives
GUILTY PLEASURES? Cheesecake
AMAZE ME! Went to Loughborough University for eight weeks. I can wiggle my ears
FANTASY SLIP CORDON? Keeper: Russell Peters, 1st: Tiger Woods, 2nd: Jessica Alba, 3rd: Me, Gully: Tom Cruise

| Batting | Mat | Inns | NO | Runs | HS | Ave | SR | 100 | 50 | Ct | St |
|---|---|---|---|---|---|---|---|---|---|---|---|
| First-class | 78 | 132 | 8 | 4318 | 233* | 34.82 | 51.08 | 7 | 21 | 69 | 0 |
| List A | 49 | 47 | 1 | 1783 | 115 | 38.76 | 77.11 | 3 | 15 | 14 | 0 |
| Twenty20 | 30 | 29 | 4 | 352 | 51 | 14.08 | 101.44 | 0 | 1 | 3 | 0 |

| Bowling | Mat | Balls | Runs | Wkts | BBI | BBM | Ave | Econ | SR | 5w | 10 |
|---|---|---|---|---|---|---|---|---|---|---|---|
| First-class | 78 | 137 | 90 | 0 | - | - | - | 3.94 | - | 0 | 0 |
| List A | 49 | 18 | 18 | 0 | - | - | - | 6.00 | - | 0 | 0 |
| Twenty20 | 30 | - | - | - | - | - | - | - | - | - | - |

# SHAAIQ CHOUDHRY                                      RHB SLA

FULL NAME: Shaaiq Hussain Choudhry
BORN: November 3, 1985, Rotherham, Yorkshire
SQUAD NO: 28
HEIGHT: 5ft 11in
NICKNAME: Shak, Chouds
EDUCATION: Fir Vale School; Rotherham College of Arts and Technology; University of Bradford
TEAMS: Leeds-Bradford UCCE, Marylebone Cricket Club, Warwickshire, Worcestershire
CAREER: First-class: 2007; List A: 2010; T20: 2010

WORCESTERSHIRE

BEST BATTING: 75 Warwickshire vs DUCCE, Durham University, 2009
BEST BOWLING: 1-14 Worcestershire vs Lancashire, Blackpool, 2011

WHY CRICKET? Watching my dad play as a youngster and watching cricket on TV inspired me to get involved in the game
CAREER HIGHLIGHTS? First-class debut against West Indies and scoring 54*. Championship debut for Worcestershire against Sussex, scoring 63 and taking 1-30. Taking 4-54 in a CB40 game against Surrey
SUPERSTITIONS? I tend to blink four times before facing each ball
CRICKETING HEROES? Muttiah Muralitharan, Jacques Kallis, Sachin Tendulkar
NON-CRICKETING HEROES? My dad
BEST PLAYER IN COUNTY CRICKET? Marcus Trescothick, Alan Richardson
TIP FOR THE TOP? Aneesh Kapil
IF YOU WEREN'T A CRICKETER? I would be working in graphics and photography
WHEN RAIN STOPS PLAY? Play games on my iPhone and eat!
FAVOURITE FILM? Scarface
FANTASY SLIP CORDON? Keeper: Charlie Sheen, 1st: Mario Balotelli, 2nd: Rihanna, 3rd: Me, Gully: Muhammad Ali
TWITTER FEED: @shaaiqchoudhry

| Batting | Mat | Inns | NO | Runs | HS | Ave | SR | 100 | 50 | Ct | St |
|---|---|---|---|---|---|---|---|---|---|---|---|
| First-class | 5 | 8 | 2 | 222 | 75 | 37.00 | 37.50 | 0 | 3 | 2 | 0 |
| List A | 16 | 14 | 7 | 146 | 39 | 20.85 | 89.57 | 0 | 0 | 6 | 0 |
| Twenty20 | 11 | 10 | 8 | 61 | 26* | 30.50 | 112.96 | 0 | 0 | 0 | 0 |
| Bowling | Mat | Balls | Runs | Wkts | BBI | BBM | Ave | Econ | SR | 5w | 10 |
| First-class | 5 | 204 | 156 | 2 | 1/14 | 1/32 | 78.00 | 4.58 | 102.0 | 0 | 0 |
| List A | 16 | 480 | 524 | 11 | 4/54 | 4/54 | 47.63 | 6.55 | 43.6 | 0 | 0 |
| Twenty20 | 11 | 156 | 182 | 6 | 2/24 | 2/24 | 30.33 | 7.00 | 26.0 | 0 | 0 |

**DERBYSHIRE**

FULL NAME: Jonathan Luke Clare
BORN: June 14, 1986, Burnley, Lancashire
SQUAD NO: 13
HEIGHT: 6ft 4in
NICKNAME: JC, Sidewinder, Scream
EDUCATION: St Theodores RC High and Sixth Form
TEAMS: Derbyshire, Derbyshire 2nd XI, Lancashire 2nd XI, Surrey 2nd XI
CAREER: First-class: 2007; List A: 2007; T20: 2008

BEST BATTING: 130 Derbyshire vs Glamorgan, Derby, 2011
BEST BOWLING: 7-74 Derbyshire vs Northamptonshire, Northampton, 2008

FAMILY TIES? Grandfather and father played for Burnley Cricket Club
CAREER HIGHLIGHTS? Scoring 129* and taking 7-79 in the same game vs Northants
SUPERSTITIONS? Nope, particularly as I wear the number 13!
CRICKETING HEROES? Glenn McGrath, Andrew Flintoff, Steve Waugh, Allan Donald
NON-CRICKETING HEROES? Jimmy Mullen (Burnley FC), Ted McMinn (Burnley FC and current DCCC kitman), Tiger Woods, Lance Armstrong, Michael Jordan
TIPS FOR THE TOP? Tom Knight, Pete Burgoyne
IF YOU WEREN'T A CRICKETER? I quite like the idea of being a football referee as the current crop are a disgrace!
WHEN RAIN STOPS PLAY? Gym, FIFA and a good old game of Pig
DREAM HOLIDAY? Anywhere with snow, maybe Austria or Switzerland
SURPRISING SKILL? I can play the steel drums
AMAZE ME! I turned down a schoolboy apprenticeship at Man City to pursue cricket (well, my dad did) which was probably a decent decision as I was never good enough
FANTASY SLIP CORDON? Keeper: Ricky Gervais, 1st: David Beckham, 2nd: Myself, 3rd: Alex Turner, Gully: Winston Churchill
TWITTER FEED: @jcfalcons13

| Batting | Mat | Inns | NO | Runs | HS | Ave | SR | 100 | 50 | Ct | St |
|---|---|---|---|---|---|---|---|---|---|---|---|
| First-class | 38 | 55 | 7 | 1343 | 130 | 27.97 | 68.10 | 2 | 8 | 17 | 0 |
| List A | 32 | 25 | 2 | 225 | 34 | 9.78 | 90.72 | 0 | 0 | 11 | 0 |
| Twenty20 | 26 | 16 | 5 | 111 | 18 | 10.09 | 102.77 | 0 | 0 | 10 | 0 |

| Bowling | Mat | Balls | Runs | Wkts | BBI | BBM | Ave | Econ | SR | 5w | 10 |
|---|---|---|---|---|---|---|---|---|---|---|---|
| First-class | 38 | 4903 | 2970 | 105 | 7/74 | 7/74 | 28.28 | 3.63 | 46.6 | 3 | 0 |
| List A | 32 | 1064 | 997 | 25 | 3/39 | 3/39 | 39.88 | 5.62 | 42.5 | 0 | 0 |
| Twenty20 | 26 | 238 | 333 | 6 | 2/20 | 2/20 | 55.50 | 8.39 | 39.6 | 0 | 0 |

LANCASHIRE

FULL NAME: Jordan Clark
BORN: October 14, 1990, Whitehaven, Cumbria
SQUAD NO: 16
HEIGHT: 6ft 4in
NICKNAME: Clarky
EDUCATION: Sedbergh School
TEAMS: Cumberland, England Under-15s, Lancashire, Lancashire 2nd XI
CAREER: List A: 2010; T20: 2011

WHY CRICKET? My dad's influence
CAREER HIGHLIGHTS? Taking part in T20 Finals Day and winning the County Championship
SUPERSTITIONS? Right pad first
CRICKETING HEROES? Andrew Flintoff
NON-CRICKETING HEROES? Steven Cheetham
TIP FOR THE TOP? Ben Stokes
IF YOU WEREN'T A CRICKETER? I'd be at university
WHEN RAIN STOPS PLAY? I'm bored
FAVOURITE TV? Geordie Shore
FAVOURITE FILM? I Love You Man
DREAM HOLIDAY? Barbados
GUILTY PLEASURES? Nicki Minaj

| Batting | Mat | Inns | NO | Runs | HS | Ave | SR | 100 | 50 | Ct | St |
|---------|-----|------|----|------|----|-----|----|-----|----|----|----|
| List A | 4 | 2 | 0 | 40 | 32 | 20.00 | 75.47 | 0 | 0 | 0 | 0 |
| Twenty20 | 9 | 8 | 2 | 127 | 38 | 21.16 | 138.04 | 0 | 0 | 4 | 0 |

| Bowling | Mat | Balls | Runs | Wkts | BBI | BBM | Ave | Econ | SR | 5w | 10 |
|---------|-----|-------|------|------|-----|-----|-----|------|----|----|----|
| List A | 4 | - | - | - | - | - | - | - | - | - | - |
| Twenty20 | 9 | - | - | - | - | - | - | - | - | - | - |

# RIKKI CLARKE

## RHB RFM R1 MVP9

WARWICKSHIRE

FULL NAME: Rikki Clarke
BORN: September 29, 1981, Orsett, Essex
SQUAD NO: 81
HEIGHT: 6ft 4in
NICKNAME: Clarkey, Crouchy, Rock
EDUCATION: Godalming Middle School;
Broad Water Secondary School; Godalming
College
TEAMS: England, Derbyshire, Marylebone
Cricket Club, Surrey, Warwickshire
CAREER: Test: 2003; ODI: 2003; First-class:
2002; List A: 2001; T20: 2003

BEST BATTING: 214 Surrey vs Somerset, Guildford, 2006
BEST BOWLING: 6-63 Warwickshire vs Kent, Canterbury, 2010
COUNTY CAP: 2005 (Surrey)

CAREER HIGHLIGHTS? Playing for my country in ODI and Test cricket and becoming a joint
world record-holder for seven catches in a first-class innings
CRICKETING HEROES? Freddie Flintoff, Graeme Swann and Darren Gough. All great
characters and wonderful, hard-working cricketers. Great for the game
TIPS FOR THE TOP? Laurie Evans and Jason Roy. Both are incredibly talented batsmen
ACCOMPLISHMENTS? Like to think being a good dad is one. My daughter just said I am, so
it's in!
AMAZE ME! I was mascot for Spurs vs Coventry back in 1993, with the likes of Gary
Mabbutt and Gary Lineker playing in the match. I am named after Ricky Villa, who scored
the winning FA Cup final goal in 1981. Pretty sure I am right in saying that I am the only
English cricketer to get fined half my match fee on Test debut. Not happy about it but it's a
fact you might not know
TWITTER FEED: @Rikkiclarke81

| Batting | Mat | Inns | NO | Runs | HS | Ave | SR | 100 | 50 | Ct | St |
|---|---|---|---|---|---|---|---|---|---|---|---|
| Tests | 2 | 3 | 0 | 96 | 55 | 32.00 | 37.94 | 0 | 1 | 1 | 0 |
| ODIs | 20 | 13 | 0 | 144 | 39 | 11.07 | 62.06 | 0 | 0 | 11 | 0 |
| First-class | 133 | 210 | 20 | 6581 | 214 | 34.63 | | 13 | 30 | 200 | 0 |
| List A | 162 | 134 | 19 | 2982 | 98* | 25.93 | | 0 | 15 | 74 | 0 |
| Twenty20 | 79 | 74 | 23 | 1083 | 79* | 21.23 | 121.54 | 0 | 3 | 40 | 0 |

| Bowling | Mat | Balls | Runs | Wkts | BBI | BBM | Ave | Econ | SR | 5w | 10 |
|---|---|---|---|---|---|---|---|---|---|---|---|
| Tests | 2 | 174 | 60 | 4 | 2/7 | 3/11 | 15.00 | 2.06 | 43.5 | 0 | 0 |
| ODIs | 20 | 469 | 415 | 11 | 2/28 | 2/28 | 37.72 | 5.30 | 42.6 | 0 | 0 |
| First-class | 133 | 12317 | 7823 | 214 | 6/63 | | 36.55 | 3.81 | 57.5 | 2 | 0 |
| List A | 162 | 3839 | 3626 | 92 | 4/28 | 4/28 | 39.41 | 5.66 | 41.7 | 0 | 0 |
| Twenty20 | 79 | 822 | 1127 | 42 | 3/11 | 3/11 | 26.83 | 8.22 | 19.5 | 0 | 0 |

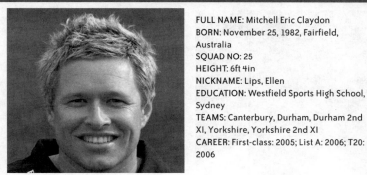

FULL NAME: Mitchell Eric Claydon
BORN: November 25, 1982, Fairfield, Australia
SQUAD NO: 25
HEIGHT: 6ft 4in
NICKNAME: Lips, Ellen
EDUCATION: Westfield Sports High School, Sydney
TEAMS: Canterbury, Durham, Durham 2nd XI, Yorkshire, Yorkshire 2nd XI
CAREER: First-class: 2005; List A: 2006; T20: 2006

BEST BATTING: 40 Durham vs Lancashire, Manchester, 2008
BEST BOWLING: 6-104 Durham vs Somerset, Taunton, 2011

CAREER HIGHLIGHTS? Being a part of two Championship winning teams. Every game I play for Durham is a highlight. Also getting the chance to play in New Zealand for Canterbury Wizards as their overseas player
NON-CRICKETING HEROES? My family
BEST PLAYER IN COUNTY CRICKET? Dale Benkenstein
TIPS FOR THE TOP? Ben Stokes and Scott Borthwick
IF YOU WEREN'T A CRICKETER? Working in a factory somewhere
WHEN RAIN STOPS PLAY? Learning new card tricks and showing them to the lads
FAVOURITE TV? Entourage
FAVOURITE FILM? Green Mile
FAVOURITE BOOK? The Blind Side
DREAM HOLIDAY? Las Vegas
ACCOMPLISHMENTS? Being a father to Lachlan Bickhoff-Claydon
SURPRISING SKILL? Card tricks and magic in general
TWITTER FEED: @mitchellclaydon

| Batting | Mat | Inns | NO | Runs | HS | Ave | SR | 100 | 50 | Ct | St |
|---|---|---|---|---|---|---|---|---|---|---|---|
| First-class | 41 | 48 | 10 | 554 | 40 | 14.57 | 56.12 | 0 | 0 | 6 | 0 |
| List A | 51 | 25 | 6 | 130 | 19 | 6.84 | 83.87 | 0 | 0 | 2 | 0 |
| Twenty20 | 54 | 15 | 10 | 85 | 19 | 17.00 | 125.00 | 0 | 0 | 14 | 0 |

| Bowling | Mat | Balls | Runs | Wkts | BBI | BBM | Ave | Econ | SR | 5w | 10 |
|---|---|---|---|---|---|---|---|---|---|---|---|
| First-class | 41 | 5629 | 3372 | 104 | 6/104 | | 32.42 | 3.59 | 54.1 | 2 | 0 |
| List A | 51 | 2210 | 1853 | 66 | 4/39 | 4/39 | 28.07 | 5.03 | 33.4 | 0 | 0 |
| Twenty20 | 54 | 1031 | 1370 | 51 | 5/26 | 5/26 | 26.86 | 7.97 | 20.2 | 1 | 0 |

# JOSH COBB        RHB LB MVP67

**LEICESTERSHIRE**

FULL NAME: Joshua James Cobb
BORN: August 17, 1990, Leicester
SQUAD NO: 5
HEIGHT: 6ft
NICKNAME: Cobby, Cobblet
EDUCATION: Bosworth College; Oakham School
TEAMS: England Under-19s, Leicestershire, Leicestershire 2nd XI
CAREER: First-class: 2007; List A: 2008; T20: 2008

BEST BATTING: 148* Leicestershire vs Middlesex, Lord's, 2008
BEST BOWLING: 2-11 Leicestershire vs Gloucestershire, Leicester, 2011

FAMILY TIES? Dad played for Leicestershire, uncle played minor counties
WHY CRICKET? Had no choice. My dad arrived at my birth during a game in his whites so I've literally been born into it
CAREER HIGHLIGHTS? Scoring 148* at Lord's to become Leicestershire's youngest Championship century maker, playing in T20 Finals Day
SUPERSTITIONS? Left shoe and pad on first, when gardening on the wicket I try and keep my taps to even numbers
BEST PLAYER IN COUNTY CRICKET? Marcus Trescothick, Darren Stevens
TIPS FOR THE TOP? Jason Roy, Shiv Thakor, Jos Buttler
WHEN RAIN STOPS PLAY? Nathan Buck and me normally go and pester the office girls downstairs. Also try to stay out of Hoggy's way if he is bored
FAVOURITE TV? Peppa Pig
FAVOURITE BOOK? Got so many favourites in my book collection it's hard to single one out
AMAZE ME! I used to be a Next model. I know, don't laugh
FANTASY SLIP CORDON? Keeper: Paul Nixon, 1st: Cheryl Cole, 2nd: Myself, 3rd: Jessica-Jane Clement, Gully: Liam Kinch
TWITTER FEED: @cobby24

| Batting | Mat | Inns | NO | Runs | HS | Ave | SR | 100 | 50 | Ct | St |
|---|---|---|---|---|---|---|---|---|---|---|---|
| First-class | 37 | 66 | 5 | 1320 | 148* | 21.63 | 43.56 | 1 | 7 | 18 | 0 |
| List A | 29 | 26 | 3 | 742 | 91* | 32.26 | 98.01 | 0 | 5 | 12 | 0 |
| Twenty20 | 30 | 27 | 4 | 435 | 60 | 18.91 | | 0 | 2 | 13 | 0 |

| Bowling | Mat | Balls | Runs | Wkts | BBI | BBM | Ave | Econ | SR | 5w | 10 |
|---|---|---|---|---|---|---|---|---|---|---|---|
| First-class | 37 | 480 | 322 | 6 | 2/11 | 2/11 | 53.66 | 4.02 | 80.0 | 0 | 0 |
| List A | 29 | 384 | 392 | 8 | 2/35 | 2/35 | 49.00 | 6.12 | 48.0 | 0 | 0 |
| Twenty20 | 30 | 228 | 332 | 15 | 4/22 | 4/22 | 22.13 | 8.73 | 15.2 | 0 | 0 |

FULL NAME: Ian Andrew Cockbain
BORN: February 17, 1987, Liverpool, Lancashire
SQUAD NO: 28
HEIGHT: 6ft
NICKNAME: Coey, Mini
EDUCATION: Maghull High School; Liverpool John Moores University
TEAMS: Gloucestershire, Gloucestershire 2nd XI, Lancashire 2nd XI, Marylebone Cricket Club Young Cricketers
CAREER: First-class: 2011; List A: 2011; T20: 2011

BEST BATTING: 127 Gloucestershire vs Middlesex, Uxbridge, 2011

FAMILY TIES? My dad played for Lancashire back in the late Seventies

CAREER HIGHLIGHTS? Making my first-class debut for Gloucestershire vs Derby and also making my first-class maiden hundred (which was all the more pleasing since my dad hasn't got one!)

BEST PLAYER IN COUNTY CRICKET? Mark Ramprakash, he just looked a different class when we played him this year

TIPS FOR THE TOP? Chris Dent who opens the batting for us and also Craig Miles, a young bowler who has come through the academy

IF YOU WEREN'T A CRICKETER? I'd hopefully be on the way to getting my qualification to work with my dad as an IFA

WHEN RAIN STOPS PLAY? Normally having a nap, doing the crossword or trying my best to wind a few of the lads up! Ian Saxelby and Richard Coughtrie are the easiest by far

DREAM HOLIDAY? I haven't had much of a chance to holiday really as my time is split between cricket here and in Australia but I would love to spend some time in the Caribbean

SURPRISING SKILL? I'm pretty boring, I'd like to say I'm a good singer but I am so bad. Just ask my housemate Richard Coughtrie

AMAZE ME! I support Everton, I'm a keen bird spotter and I love the zoo

TWITTER FEED: @IanCoey

| Batting | Mat | Inns | NO | Runs | HS | Ave | SR | 100 | 50 | Ct | St |
|---|---|---|---|---|---|---|---|---|---|---|---|
| First-class | 12 | 21 | 1 | 542 | 127 | 27.10 | 45.54 | 1 | 3 | 10 | 0 |
| List A | 12 | 11 | 2 | 309 | 79 | 34.33 | 89.30 | 0 | 3 | 8 | 0 |
| Twenty20 | 12 | 12 | 1 | 281 | 78 | 25.54 | 116.59 | 0 | 1 | 6 | 0 |

| Bowling | Mat | Balls | Runs | Wkts | BBI | BBM | Ave | Econ | SR | 5w | 10 |
|---|---|---|---|---|---|---|---|---|---|---|---|
| First-class | 12 | - | - | - | - | - | - | - | - | - | - |
| List A | 12 | - | - | - | - | - | - | - | - | - | - |
| Twenty20 | 12 | - | - | - | - | - | - | - | - | - | - |

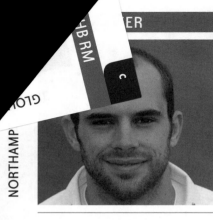

FULL NAME: Kyle James Coetzer
BORN: April 14, 1984, Aberdeen
SQUAD NO: 30
HEIGHT: 5ft 11in
NICKNAME: Costa, Meerkat
EDUCATION: Aberdeen Grammar School
TEAMS: Scotland, Durham, Scotland under 19s, Western Province, Northamptonshire
CAREER: ODI: 2008; T20I: 2008; First-class: 2004; List A: 2003; T20: 2007

BEST BATTING: 172 Durham vs MCC, Sheikh Zayed Stadium, 2010
BEST BOWLING: 2-16 Scotland vs Kenya, Gymkhana Club Ground, 2009

FAMILY TIES? Elder brothers Shaun and Stuart both played some level of cricket for Scotland. Grandfather Sid Dugmore played for Eastern Province and so did my uncle Grant Dugmore, who has coached and played for Argentina. He is now the development officer of the Americas
SUPERSTITIONS? Touch my bat in the crease after each ball
CRICKETING HEROES? Brian McMillan, Allan Donald, Jacques Kallis, Robin Smith
BEST PLAYER IN COUNTY CRICKET? Ben Stokes
TIPS FOR THE TOP? Mark Wood (Durham), Rob Newton (Northamptonshire) and also Ben Stokes (Durham)
IF YOU WEREN'T A CRICKETER? Fitness trainer
FAVOURITE TV? Outnumbered, The Inbetweeners
AMAZE ME! I have never seen a live day's play of Test cricket
FANTASY SLIP CORDON? Keeper: Will Ferrell, 1st: Lee Evans, 2nd: Phil Tufnell, 3rd: Nicky Philips, Gully: Arnold Schwarzenegger, Leg slip: Myself
TWITTER FEED: @Meergoose11

| Batting | Mat | Inns | NO | Runs | HS | Ave | SR | 100 | 50 | Ct | St |
|---|---|---|---|---|---|---|---|---|---|---|---|
| ODIs | 9 | 9 | 1 | 384 | 89* | 48.00 | 82.05 | 0 | 4 | 6 | 0 |
| T20Is | 9 | 9 | 1 | 234 | 48* | 29.25 | 104.00 | 0 | 0 | 2 | 0 |
| First-class | 50 | 88 | 10 | 2675 | 172 | 34.29 | 48.84 | 5 | 12 | 28 | 0 |
| List A | 75 | 73 | 10 | 2238 | 127 | 35.52 | 79.22 | 3 | 15 | 31 | 0 |
| Twenty20 | 24 | 22 | 2 | 469 | 64 | 23.45 | 104.92 | 0 | 1 | 5 | 0 |

| Bowling | Mat | Balls | Runs | Wkts | BBI | BBM | Ave | Econ | SR | 5w | 10 |
|---|---|---|---|---|---|---|---|---|---|---|---|
| ODIs | 9 | 114 | 125 | 1 | 1/35 | 1/35 | 125.00 | 6.57 | 114.0 | 0 | 0 |
| T20Is | 9 | 48 | 47 | 5 | 3/25 | 3/25 | 9.40 | 5.87 | 9.6 | 0 | 0 |
| First-class | 50 | 258 | 157 | 3 | 2/16 | 2/16 | 52.33 | 3.65 | 86.0 | 0 | 0 |
| List A | 75 | 258 | 253 | 1 | 1/35 | 1/35 | 253.00 | 5.88 | 258.0 | 0 | 0 |
| Twenty20 | 24 | 84 | 92 | 6 | 3/25 | 3/25 | 15.33 | 6.57 | 14.0 | 0 | 0 |

# MATT COLES LHB RMF

**FULL NAME:** Matthew Thomas Coles
**BORN:** May 26, 1990, Maidstone, Kent
**SQUAD NO:** 26
**HEIGHT:** 6ft 3in
**NICKNAME:** Colesy
**EDUCATION:** Maplesden Noakes Secondary School
**TEAMS:** Kent, Kent 2nd XI
**CAREER:** First-class: 2009; List A: 2009; T20: 2010

KENT

**BEST BATTING:** 51 Kent vs Lancashire, Canterbury, 2010
**BEST BOWLING:** 5-29 Kent vs LMCCU, Canterbury, 2011

**CRICKETING HEROES?** Andrew Flintoff
**FAVOURITE BAND?** Red Hot Chili Peppers
**FAVOURITE FOOD?** Roast lamb
**FAVOURITE FILM?** Anchorman
**QUOTE TO LIVE BY?** "Powerful dreams inspire powerful action"
**CAREER HIGHLIGHTS?** Walking out onto the pitch for the first time wearing a Kent shirt
**NOTES:** Called up for the England Lions tour of Sri Lanka in February 2012 as a replacement for the injured Stuart Meaker

| Batting | Mat | Inns | NO | Runs | HS | Ave | SR | 100 | 50 | Ct | St |
|---|---|---|---|---|---|---|---|---|---|---|---|
| First-class | 26 | 41 | 10 | 650 | 51 | 20.96 | 65.06 | 0 | 2 | 7 | 0 |
| List A | 15 | 8 | 0 | 81 | 47 | 10.12 | 97.59 | 0 | 0 | 4 | 0 |
| Twenty20 | 17 | 10 | 1 | 65 | 16* | 7.22 | 125.00 | 0 | 0 | 5 | 0 |

| Bowling | Mat | Balls | Runs | Wkts | BBI | BBM | Ave | Econ | SR | 5w | 10 |
|---|---|---|---|---|---|---|---|---|---|---|---|
| First-class | 26 | 3493 | 2190 | 61 | 5/29 | 7/149 | 35.90 | 3.76 | 57.2 | 2 | 0 |
| List A | 15 | 426 | 495 | 23 | 4/47 | 4/47 | 21.52 | 6.97 | 18.5 | 0 | 0 |
| Twenty20 | 17 | 272 | 384 | 15 | 3/30 | 3/30 | 25.60 | 8.47 | 18.1 | 0 | 0 |

# PAUL COLLINGWOOD                    RHB RM R2

FULL NAME: Paul David Collingwood
BORN: May 26, 1976, Shotley Bridge, Co Durham
SQUAD NO: 5
HEIGHT: 5ft 11in
NICKNAME: Colly
EDUCATION: Blackfyne Comprehensive School; Derwentside College
TEAMS: England, Delhi Daredevils, Durham, Impi, Perth Scorchers
CAREER: Test: 2003; ODI: 2001; T20I: 2005; First-class: 1996; List A: 1995; T20: 2005

---

BEST BATTING: 206 England vs Australia, Adelaide, 2006
BEST BOWLING: 5-52 Durham vs Somerset, Grangefield Road, 2005
BENEFIT YEAR: 2007

---

SUPERSTITIONS? Left pad on first and wearing them on the wrong legs
CRICKET MOMENTS TO FORGET? Being Matt Walker's first first-class wicket
CRICKETERS PARTICULARLY ADMIRED? Steve Waugh, Jacques Kallis, Glenn McGrath, Shane Warne
OTHER SPORTS FOLLOWED? Golf, football (Sunderland)
NOTES: He scored his maiden ODI century (100) for England against Sri Lanka at Perth in 2003. Made 112* and took 6-31 in an ODI against Bangladesh at Trent Bridge in 2005, and was Man of the Match in three consecutive matches en route to England claiming the Commonwealth Bank Series title in 2007. Made a career-best 206 at Adelaide in 2006. England's ODI captain from June 2007 until August 2008, later returning to lead England to victory in the World 20 in 2010. Quit Test cricket after winning the 2010/11 Ashes win

| Batting | Mat | Inns | NO | Runs | HS | Ave | SR | 100 | 50 | Ct | St |
|---|---|---|---|---|---|---|---|---|---|---|---|
| Tests | 68 | 115 | 10 | 4259 | 206 | 40.56 | 46.44 | 10 | 20 | 96 | 0 |
| ODIs | 197 | 181 | 37 | 5092 | 120* | 35.36 | 76.98 | 5 | 26 | 108 | 0 |
| T20Is | 35 | 33 | 2 | 583 | 79 | 18.80 | 127.01 | 0 | 3 | 14 | 0 |
| First-class | 204 | 350 | 28 | 11749 | 206 | 36.48 | | 25 | 60 | 232 | 0 |
| List A | 373 | 351 | 62 | 9826 | 120* | 34.00 | | 8 | 56 | 192 | 0 |
| Twenty20 | 85 | 73 | 5 | 1229 | 79 | 18.07 | 120.60 | 0 | 6 | 24 | 0 |

| Bowling | Mat | Balls | Runs | Wkts | BBI | BBM | Ave | Econ | SR | 5w | 10 |
|---|---|---|---|---|---|---|---|---|---|---|---|
| Tests | 68 | 1905 | 1018 | 17 | 3/23 | 3/35 | 59.88 | 3.20 | 112.0 | 0 | 0 |
| ODIs | 197 | 5186 | 4294 | 111 | 6/31 | 6/31 | 38.68 | 4.96 | 46.7 | 1 | 0 |
| T20Is | 35 | 222 | 329 | 16 | 4/22 | 4/22 | 20.56 | 8.89 | 13.8 | 0 | 0 |
| First-class | 204 | 10246 | 5184 | 132 | 5/52 | | 39.27 | 3.03 | 77.6 | 1 | 0 |
| List A | 373 | 9810 | 7926 | 229 | 6/31 | 6/31 | 34.61 | 4.84 | 42.8 | 1 | 0 |
| Twenty20 | 85 | 757 | 903 | 55 | 5/6 | 5/6 | 16.41 | 7.15 | 13.7 | 2 | 0 |

FULL NAME: Corey Dalanelo Collymore
BORN: December 21, 1977, Boscobelle, St Peter, Barbados
SQUAD NO: 32
HEIGHT: 6ft
NICKNAME: Screw, CC
EDUCATION: Alexandra Secondary School
TEAMS: West Indies, Barbados, Sussex, Warwickshire
CAREER: Test: 1999; ODI: 1999; First-class: 1999; List A: 1999; T20: 2006

MIDDLESEX

BEST BATTING: 23 Sussex vs Nottinghamshire, Horsham, 2009
BEST BOWLING: 7-57 West Indies vs Sri Lanka, Kingston, 2003
COUNTY CAP: 2011 (Middlesex)

CRICKETERS PARTICULARLY ADMIRED? Courtney Walsh, Vasbert Drakes, Steve Waugh
OTHER SPORTS FOLLOWED? Football (Arsenal and Brazil)
OPINIONS ON CRICKET? Need better wickets so as to keep fast bowlers in the game
NOTES: Represented West Indies U19 in home series vs Pakistan U19 in 1996/97. Took 4-49 in the final of the Coca Cola Cup vs India at Harare in 2001, winning the Man of the Match award. Took 5-51 vs Sri Lanka at Colombo in the LG Albans Triangular Series 2001/02, winning the Man of the Match award. Player of the [Test] Series vs Sri Lanka 2002/03, performances including 7-57 in the second Test at Kingston. Was an overseas player with Warwickshire in August and September 2003, replacing the injured Collins Obuya. Signed for Middlesex from Sussex ahead of the 2011 county season and took 49 County Championship wickets at 26.30 in the last campaign

| Batting | Mat | Inns | NO | Runs | HS | Ave | SR | 100 | 50 | Ct | St |
|---|---|---|---|---|---|---|---|---|---|---|---|
| Tests | 30 | 52 | 27 | 197 | 16* | 7.88 | 30.68 | 0 | 0 | 6 | 0 |
| ODIs | 84 | 35 | 17 | 104 | 13* | 5.77 | 39.84 | 0 | 0 | 12 | 0 |
| First-class | 150 | 202 | 92 | 862 | 23 | 7.83 | | 0 | 0 | 46 | 0 |
| List A | 136 | 52 | 27 | 154 | 13* | 6.16 | | 0 | 0 | 21 | 0 |
| Twenty20 | 6 | 2 | 1 | 5 | 4 | 5.00 | 45.45 | 0 | 0 | 4 | 0 |

| Bowling | Mat | Balls | Runs | Wkts | BBI | BBM | Ave | Econ | SR | 5w | 10 |
|---|---|---|---|---|---|---|---|---|---|---|---|
| Tests | 30 | 6337 | 3004 | 93 | 7/57 | 11/134 | 32.30 | 2.84 | 68.1 | 4 | 1 |
| ODIs | 84 | 4074 | 2924 | 83 | 5/51 | 5/51 | 35.22 | 4.30 | 49.0 | 1 | 0 |
| First-class | 150 | 25708 | 12006 | 455 | 7/57 | | 26.38 | 2.80 | 56.5 | 12 | 2 |
| List A | 136 | 6348 | 4549 | 147 | 5/27 | 5/27 | 30.94 | 4.29 | 43.1 | 2 | 0 |
| Twenty20 | 6 | 95 | 133 | 3 | 1/21 | 1/21 | 44.33 | 8.40 | 31.6 | 0 | 0 |

## MICHAEL COMBER

### RHB RFM

FULL NAME: Michael Andrew Comber
BORN: October 26, 1989, Colchester, Essex
SQUAD NO: 35
HEIGHT: 6ft 3in
TEAMS: Essex, Essex 2nd XI, Essex Under-17s
CAREER: First-class 2010; List A: 2010; T20: 2010

BEST BATTING: 19 vs Bangladeshis, Chelmsford, 2010
BEST BOWLING: 2-34 Essex vs Bangladeshis, Chelmsford, 2010

NOTES: Spent six years on Essex's academy, before signing an Academy-Professional contract in 2009. Made his senior debut in May 2010 against Bangladesh, and later that season made an unbeaten 52 against Northants to bring victory in a CB40 fixture, before making his Championship debut against Durham in the final match of the 2010 season. Brother Nicholas played in the East Anglian Premier League

| Batting | Mat | Inns | NO | Runs | HS | Ave | SR | 100 | 50 | Ct | St |
|---------|-----|------|-----|------|-----|------|--------|-----|-----|-----|-----|
| First-class | 2 | 3 | 0 | 19 | 19 | 6.33 | 27.53 | 0 | 0 | 1 | 0 |
| List A | 6 | 1 | 1 | 52 | 52* | - | 104.00 | 0 | 1 | 0 | 0 |
| Twenty20 | 1 | 1 | 0 | 5 | 5 | 5.00 | 100.00 | 0 | 0 | 0 | 0 |

| Bowling | Mat | Balls | Runs | Wkts | BBI | BBM | Ave | Econ | SR | 5w | 10 |
|---------|-----|-------|------|------|-----|-----|------|------|-----|-----|-----|
| First-class | 2 | 134 | 94 | 4 | 2/34 | 3/78 | 23.50 | 4.20 | 33.5 | 0 | 0 |
| List A | 6 | 72 | 65 | 0 | - | - | - | 5.41 | - | 0 | 0 |
| Twenty20 | 1 | - | - | - | - | - | - | - | - | - | - |

# NICK COMPTON

## RHB OB R2

FULL NAME: Nicholas Richard Denis Compton
BORN: June 26, 1983, Durban, South Africa
SQUAD NO: 3
HEIGHT: 6ft 2in
NICKNAME: Compo, Ledge, Cheser, Comp Dog
EDUCATION: Hilton College, SA; Harrow School; Durham University
TEAMS: Mashonaland Eagles, Middlesex, Somerset
CAREER: First-class: 2004; List A: 2001; T20: 2004

BEST BATTING: 254* Somerset vs Durham, Chester-le-Street, 2011
BEST BOWLING: 1-1 Somerset vs Hampshire, Southampton, 2010
COUNTY CAPS: 2006 (Middlesex); 2011 (Somerset)

FAMILY TIES? Grandfather, Denis, played cricket for Middlesex and England. Great uncle Leslie played cricket for Middlesex. Father Richard played first-class cricket in South Africa and uncle Patrick played a few games too

WHY CRICKET? Love of sport, growing up in sport-mad South Africa. Watching heroes like Jacques Kallis, Jonty Rhodes, Andrew Hudson and Gary Kirsten. My dad taking me down to the beach and playing in the garden. I just wanted to be like those guys

CAREER HIGHLIGHTS? Maiden first-class century at Lord's – getting there with a six! My Somerset county cap and being selected for the England Lions tour to Bangladesh 2007. My career best 254* vs Durham too

SUPERSTITIONS? I only walk over the white line after my batting partner – I like to feel like I've given them the respect!

CRICKETING HEROES? Jacques Kallis, Rahul Dravid and Brian Lara

IF YOU WEREN'T A CRICKETER? Trying my hand at radio, was told I had a face for it!

WHEN RAIN STOPS PLAY? Searching Facebook on my iPad, writing blogs and generally annoying teammates with my new video camera

TWITTER FEED: @nickcompton3

| Batting | Mat | Inns | NO | Runs | HS | Ave | SR | 100 | 50 | Ct | St |
|---|---|---|---|---|---|---|---|---|---|---|---|
| First-class | 82 | 143 | 17 | 4760 | 254* | 37.77 | 48.72 | 11 | 20 | 40 | 0 |
| List A | 86 | 78 | 16 | 2441 | 131 | 39.37 | 80.72 | 6 | 13 | 41 | 0 |
| Twenty20 | 56 | 48 | 4 | 846 | 74 | 19.22 | 110.87 | 0 | 5 | 21 | 0 |

| Bowling | Mat | Balls | Runs | Wkts | BBI | BBM | Ave | Econ | SR | 5w | 10 |
|---|---|---|---|---|---|---|---|---|---|---|---|
| First-class | 82 | 164 | 215 | 3 | 1/1 | 1/1 | 71.66 | 7.86 | 54.6 | 0 | 0 |
| List A | 86 | 61 | 53 | 1 | 1/0 | 1/0 | 53.00 | 5.21 | 61.0 | 0 | 0 |
| Twenty20 | 56 | - | - | - | - | - | - | - | - | - | - |

ESSEX

FULL NAME: Alastair Nathan Cook
BORN: December 25, 1984, Gloucester
SQUAD NO: 26
HEIGHT: 6ft 2in
NICKNAME: Cooky, Chef
EDUCATION: Bedford School
TEAMS: England, Bedfordshire, England
Lions, England Under-19s, Essex,
Marylebone Cricket Club
CAREER: Test: 2006; ODI: 2006; T20I: 2007;
First-class: 2003; List A: 2003; T20: 2005

BEST BATTING: 294 England vs India, Birmingham, 2011
BEST BOWLING: 3-13 Essex vs Northamptonshire, Chelmsford, 2005
COUNTY CAP: 2005

FAMILY TIES? Dad played for the local club side and was a very good opening bat, while
mum made the teas. Brothers played for Maldon Cricket Club
CAREER HIGHLIGHTS? Ashes wins home and away, becoming world No.1 Test team, Essex
winning the 50-over comp, making England debut
CRICKETING HEROES? Graham Gooch, watched him playing for Essex at the County Ground
as a kid
BEST PLAYER IN COUNTY CRICKET? Ryan ten Doeschate and James Foster
TIP FOR THE TOP? Ben Foakes
IF YOU WEREN'T A CRICKETER? Farmer
GUILTY PLEASURES? Shooting, beer and darts

| Batting | Mat | Inns | NO | Runs | HS | Ave | SR | 100 | 50 | Ct | St |
|---------|-----|------|-----|------|-----|-------|--------|-----|-----|-----|-----|
| Tests | 75 | 131 | 7 | 6027 | 294 | 48.60 | 48.32 | 19 | 27 | 66 | 0 |
| ODIs | 45 | 45 | 2 | 1781 | 137 | 41.41 | 80.62 | 4 | 11 | 17 | 0 |
| T20Is | 4 | 4 | 0 | 61 | 26 | 15.25 | 112.96 | 0 | 0 | 1 | 0 |
| First-class | 161 | 285 | 21 | 12488 | 294 | 47.30 | 53.09 | 36 | 62 | 150 | 0 |
| List A | 98 | 96 | 8 | 3560 | 137 | 40.45 | 80.83 | 8 | 21 | 40 | 0 |
| Twenty20 | 29 | 27 | 2 | 834 | 100* | 33.36 | 129.90 | 1 | 5 | 9 | 0 |

| Bowling | Mat | Balls | Runs | Wkts | BBI | BBM | Ave | Econ | SR | 5w | 10 |
|---------|-----|-------|------|------|-----|-----|-------|------|------|-----|-----|
| Tests | 75 | 6 | 1 | 0 | - | - | - | 1.00 | - | 0 | 0 |
| ODIs | 45 | - | - | - | - | - | - | - | - | - | - |
| T20Is | 4 | - | - | - | - | - | - | - | - | - | - |
| First-class | 161 | 270 | 205 | 6 | 3/13 | - | 34.16 | 4.55 | 45.0 | 0 | 0 |
| List A | 98 | 18 | 10 | 0 | - | - | - | 3.33 | - | 0 | 0 |
| Twenty20 | 29 | - | - | - | - | - | - | - | - | - | - |

FULL NAME: Simon James Cook
BORN: January 15, 1977, Oxford
SQUAD NO: 7
HEIGHT: 6ft 4in
NICKNAME: Chef
EDUCATION: Matthew Arnold School
TEAMS: Kent, Middlesex
CAREER: First-class: 1999; List A: 1997; T20: 2003

KENT

BEST BATTING: 93* Middlesex vs Nottinghamshire, Lords, 2001
BEST BOWLING: 8-63 Middlesex vs Northamptonshire, Northampton, 2002
COUNTY CAPS: 2003 (Middlesex); 2007 (Kent)

FAMILY TIES? Brothers played for Oxfordshire
CAREER OUTSIDE CRICKET? Coaching and property development
CAREER HIGHLIGHTS? Beating Australia in a one-day game at Lord's. Winning Division Two of the National League in 2004 and equalling league record for wickets in a season (39). Winning T20 Cup in 2007
CRICKET MOMENT TO FORGET? Being outside the circle in a one-day game when I was supposed to be in it. Danny Law was bowled, the ball went for four (off the stumps, making six no-balls in total) and he went on to win the game for Durham
FAVOURITE BAND? Not My Day
FAVOURITE FILM? Man On FIre
CRICKETERS PARTICULARLY ADMIRED? Angus Fraser, Glenn McGrath
OTHER SPORTS FOLLOWED? Football (Liverpool)

| Batting | Mat | Inns | NO | Runs | HS | Ave | SR | 100 | 50 | Ct | St |
|---|---|---|---|---|---|---|---|---|---|---|---|
| First-class | 139 | 184 | 31 | 2549 | 93* | 16.66 | | 0 | 7 | 34 | 0 |
| List A | 183 | 109 | 35 | 1253 | 67* | 16.93 | | 0 | 2 | 29 | 0 |
| Twenty20 | 69 | 22 | 14 | 138 | 25* | 17.25 | 117.94 | 0 | 0 | 14 | 0 |

| Bowling | Mat | Balls | Runs | Wkts | BBI | BBM | Ave | Econ | SR | 5w | 10 |
|---|---|---|---|---|---|---|---|---|---|---|---|
| First-class | 139 | 20959 | 10974 | 341 | 8/63 | | 32.18 | 3.14 | 61.4 | 12 | 0 |
| List A | 183 | 8023 | 6350 | 229 | 6/37 | 6/37 | 27.72 | 4.74 | 35.0 | 2 | 0 |
| Twenty20 | 69 | 1447 | 1816 | 81 | 3/13 | 3/13 | 22.41 | 7.53 | 17.8 | 0 | 0 |

## CHRIS COOKE  RHB WK

GLAMORGAN

FULL NAME: Christopher Barry Cooke
BORN: May 30, 1986, Johannesburg, South Africa
SQUAD NO: 24
HEIGHT: 5ft 9in
NICKNAME: Cookie, Cameron
EDUCATION: Bishops School, Cape Town; University of Cape Town
TEAMS: Glamorgan, Glamorgan 2nd XI, Hampshire 2nd XI, Western Province
CAREER: First-class: 2009; List A: 2009; T20: 2011

BEST BATTING: 44* Western Province vs Eastern Province, Newlands, 2010

FAMILY TIES? My father played for Eastern Province, whilst both my brothers played at a high standard. All three were keeper/batters
CAREER HIGHLIGHTS? My first ton as a nine-year-old. A one-day century at Newlands. Winning the Southern Electric Premier League with Bournemouth CC. Signing my first professional contract at Glamorgan. My first three scoring shots for the county 1st XI being three consecutive sixes
CRICKETING HEROES? Herschelle Gibbs, Kumar Sangakkara and Ben Wright
TIPS FOR THE TOP? Travis Townsend, Kirk Wernars, James Harris, Marty Walters, Max Waller
IF YOU WEREN'T A CRICKETER? International DJ
WHEN RAIN STOPS PLAY? Corridor cricket (you have to keep focused) or bird watching
FAVOURITE TV? 24, Modern Family, Eastbound And Down
DREAM HOLIDAY? A chartered yacht down the Croatian coastline
ACCOMPLISHMENTS? Acquiring a degree in Psychology and Media from UCT
GUILTY PLEASURES? Raw fish
AMAZE ME! I am a massive Chelsea fan, I bowl mean leggies (which no one backs) and I have to have the volume on an even number!
TWITTER FEED: @cooky_24

| Batting | Mat | Inns | NO | Runs | HS | Ave | SR | 100 | 50 | Ct | St |
|---|---|---|---|---|---|---|---|---|---|---|---|
| First-class | 6 | 11 | 1 | 186 | 44* | 18.60 | 36.97 | 0 | 0 | 12 | 1 |
| List A | 21 | 20 | 4 | 541 | 109* | 33.81 | 100.93 | 1 | 2 | 10 | 2 |
| Twenty20 | 16 | 14 | 2 | 224 | 47 | 18.66 | 140.00 | 0 | 0 | 8 | 0 |
| Bowling | Mat | Balls | Runs | Wkts | BBI | BBM | Ave | Econ | SR | 5w | 10 |
| First-class | 6 | - | - | - | - | - | - | - | - | - | - | - |
| List A | 21 | - | - | - | - | - | - | - | - | - | - | - |
| Twenty20 | 16 | - | - | - | - | - | - | - | - | - | - | - |

FULL NAME: Dean Andrew Cosker
BORN: January 7, 1978, Weymouth, Dorset
SQUAD NO: 23
HEIGHT: 5ft 11in
NICKNAME: Lurks, The Lurker, Bryn
EDUCATION: Millfield School
TEAMS: Glamorgan, England A
CAREER: First-class: 1996; List A: 1996; T20: 2003

**GLAMORGAN**

BEST BATTING: 52 Glamorgan vs Gloucestershire, Bristol, 2005
BEST BOWLING: 6-91 Glamorgan vs Essex, Cardiff, 2009
COUNTY CAP: 2000; BENEFIT YEAR: 2010

CAREER HIGHLIGHTS? Debut at Glamorgan in 1997, Championship medal in 1997, England A caps, trophies with Glamorgan, and seeing the grimace on Gareth Rees' face when he gets hit at short leg
CRICKET MOMENTS TO FORGET? Every time I bowl from the Taff End at the SWALEC Stadium in the T20 when the wind is with the batsman
OTHER SPORTS PLAYED? Golf
FAVOURITE BAND? Bananarama
OTHER SPORTS FOLLOWED? Football (Spurs and the Swans), WWF wrestling
CRICKETERS PARTICULARLY ADMIRED? Mike Kasprowicz, Matt Elliott, Matt Maynard, Robert Croft, Steve Watkin, Graham Thorpe
NOTES: Leading wicket-taker on England A tour of Zimbabwe and South Africa 1998/99. Third youngest Glamorgan player to receive his county cap

| Batting | Mat | Inns | NO | Runs | HS | Ave | SR | 100 | 50 | Ct | St |
|---|---|---|---|---|---|---|---|---|---|---|---|
| First-class | 194 | 256 | 75 | 2488 | 52 | 13.74 | | 0 | 1 | 116 | 0 |
| List A | 212 | 111 | 51 | 697 | 50* | 11.61 | | 0 | 1 | 81 | 0 |
| Twenty20 | 75 | 25 | 19 | 105 | 21* | 17.50 | 88.98 | 0 | 0 | 22 | 0 |

| Bowling | Mat | Balls | Runs | Wkts | BBI | BBM | Ave | Econ | SR | 5w | 10 |
|---|---|---|---|---|---|---|---|---|---|---|---|
| First-class | 194 | 36796 | 17540 | 494 | 6/91 | | 35.50 | 2.86 | 74.4 | 8 | 1 |
| List A | 212 | 8875 | 7098 | 216 | 5/54 | 5/54 | 32.86 | 4.79 | 41.0 | 1 | 0 |
| Twenty20 | 75 | 1306 | 1712 | 58 | 3/11 | 3/11 | 29.51 | 7.86 | 22.5 | 0 | 0 |

## RICHARD COUGHTRIE                    RHB WK

FULL NAME: Richard George Coughtrie
BORN: September 1, 1988, North Shields, Northumberland
SQUAD NO: 12
HEIGHT: 5ft 10in
NICKNAME: Coffers
EDUCATION: Royal Grammar School, Newcastle; Oxford Brookes University
TEAMS: Durham 2nd XI, Gloucestershire, Gloucestershire 2nd XI, Northumberland, Oxford MCCU
CAREER: First-class: 2009; T20: 2011

BEST BATTING: 54* Gloucestershire vs Derbyshire, Derby, 2011

WHY CRICKET? I used to watch England on the TV and then go out and play cricket with my friends in the street
CAREER HIGHLIGHTS? Making my County Championship debut and scoring the winning runs vs Somerset in the T20 at Bristol last season
SUPERSTITIONS? Not anymore, I used to have a few lucky car park spaces
CRICKETING HEROES? Jack Russell, Alec Stewart, Ian Botham and Craig White
NON-CRICKETING HEROES? Alan Shearer, Winston Churchill, Ayrton Senna and Brian Clough
BEST PLAYER IN COUNTY CRICKET? Being a keeper, I think James Foster has to be up there
TIPS FOR THE TOP? David Payne and Chris Dent
IF YOU WEREN'T A CRICKETER? I'd probably be finishing off a degree and be getting to a few more Newcastle United games
FAVOURITE TV? Porridge, Only Fools And Horses
FAVOURITE FILM? The Damned United, Mike Bassett England Manager
FAVOURITE BOOK? Colin Dexter – The Way Through The Woods
ACCOMPLISHMENTS? School exam results and building the shed in my back garden!
GUILTY PLEASURES? Wispa Golds and I drink far too much coffee
AMAZE ME! I made a couple of appearances in TV programmes when I was younger
TWITTER FEED: @rgcoughtie

| Batting | Mat | Inns | NO | Runs | HS | Ave | SR | 100 | 50 | Ct | St |
|---|---|---|---|---|---|---|---|---|---|---|---|
| First-class | 23 | 40 | 6 | 784 | 54* | 23.05 | 34.96 | 0 | 2 | 42 | 1 |
| Twenty20 | 13 | 10 | 2 | 54 | 18 | 6.75 | 83.07 | 0 | 0 | 6 | 5 |

| Bowling | Mat | Balls | Runs | Wkts | BBI | BBM | Ave | Econ | SR | 5w | 10 |
|---|---|---|---|---|---|---|---|---|---|---|---|
| First-class | 23 | - | - | - | - | - | - | - | - | - | - |
| Twenty20 | 13 | - | - | - | - | - | - | - | - | - | - |

**FULL NAME:** Fabian Kruuse Cowdrey
**BORN:** January 30, 1993, Canterbury
**SQUAD NO:** 30
**HEIGHT:** 6ft
**NICKNAME:** Cow, Fabs, Fabes
**EDUCATION:** Tonbridge School
**TEAMS:** Kent 2nd XI
**CAREER:** Yet to make first-team debut

KENT

**FAMILY TIES?** My grandfather, Colin, and father, Chris, both captained England and Kent and my uncle, Graham, played for Kent

**CAREER HIGHLIGHTS?** Breaking the all-time school record for most runs in a season at Tonbridge School and becoming the third highest-scorer ever there. Making my debut for Kent 2nd XI at 16 years old and receiving a contract in late 2011

**SUPERSTITIONS?** Thankfully none at the moment

**CRICKETING HEROES?** My dad is a hero of mine and has had a huge impact on my game. More recently, Sachin Tendulkar is one I admire and 'try' to replicate (as hard as that is!)

**NON-CRICKETING HEROES?** Jo-Wilfried Tsonga – the French tennis player

**TIP FOR THE TOP?** Jos Buttler has a unique talent that is worth looking out for

**IF YOU WEREN'T A CRICKETER?** I'd be looking for a route into the music industry or looking for a song lyricist job

**FAVOURITE TV?** Geordie Shore, Take Me Out

**FAVOURITE FILM?** The Town

**FAVOURITE BOOK?** Wisden!

**ACCOMPLISHMENTS?** Writing songs, receiving sport scholarship to school

**SURPRISING SKILL?** I can sing, but sadly gave up instruments due to my teacher in Year Four

**AMAZE ME!** Highest score of 167 on paper toss (medium level), went to the same prep school as Andrew Strauss and love writing

**FANTASY SLIP CORDON?** Keeper: Alan Knott (greatest ever), 1st: James Corden (he'd swallow it!), 2nd: Myself (amongst the banter), 3rd: Freddie Flintoff (adds a League Of Their Own vibe alongside Corden), 4th: Charlie Sheen (unique banter about beautiful individuals in crowd)

**TWITTER FEED:** @cowdreyfk

# BEN COX RHB WK

FULL NAME: Oliver Benjamin Cox
BORN: February 2, 1992, Wordsley, Stourbridge, Worcestershire
SQUAD NO: 10
TEAMS: Worcestershire, Worcestershire 2nd XI
CAREER: First-class: 2009; List A: 2010; T20: 2010

---

BEST BATTING: 61 Worcestershire vs Somerset, Taunton, 2009

---

CAREER HIGHLIGHTS? My debut vs Somerset whilst I was still at school in 2009
SUPERSTITIONS? Left pad first and not washing keeping inners!
CRICKETING HEROES? Steve Rhodes and Steve Davies
NON-CRICKETING HEROES? Jonny Wilkinson for his determination to succeed
TIPS FOR THE TOP? Christian Davies, Aneesh Kapil, Ross Whiteley
IF YOU WEREN'T A CRICKETER? Hopefully rugby for Worcester Warriors after a couple of hard years in the gym!
WHEN RAIN STOPS PLAY? Sleep, Football Manager, iPad, receiving abuse about my hairline
FAVOURITE TV? Friday Night Lights
FAVOURITE FILM? The Blind Side, Transformers
ACCOMPLISHMENTS? England U18 rugby trials and beating Millfield School 25-20
SURPRISING SKILL? Make a mean potato bake
GUILTY PLEASURES? A drink with the lads
AMAZE ME! I was close to quitting cricket to play rugby. I was once on the books at West Bromwich Albion. I trialled with Manu Tuilagi
FANTASY SLIP CORDON? Keeper: Owen Farrell, 1st: David Beckham, 2nd: Will Beer, 3rd: Lee Evans, Gully: Mila Kunis
TWITTER FEED: @BenCox10

| Batting | Mat | Inns | NO | Runs | HS | Ave | SR | 100 | 50 | Ct | St |
|---|---|---|---|---|---|---|---|---|---|---|---|
| First-class | 14 | 25 | 5 | 365 | 61 | 18.25 | 49.79 | 0 | 2 | 37 | 2 |
| List A | 12 | 6 | 3 | 25 | 9* | 8.33 | 62.50 | 0 | 0 | 9 | 2 |
| Twenty20 | 8 | 5 | 3 | 13 | 6* | 6.50 | 108.33 | 0 | 0 | 2 | 2 |

| Bowling | Mat | Balls | Runs | Wkts | BBI | BBM | Ave | Econ | SR | 5w | 10 |
|---|---|---|---|---|---|---|---|---|---|---|---|
| First-class | 14 | - | - | - | - | - | - | - | - | - | - |
| List A | 12 | - | - | - | - | - | - | - | - | - | - |
| Twenty20 | 8 | - | - | - | - | - | - | - | - | - | - |

# TOM CRADDOCK

## RHB LB

FULL NAME: Thomas Richard Craddock
BORN: July 13, 1989, Huddersfield
SQUAD NO: 20
HEIGHT: 5ft 7in
NICKNAME: Crads
EDUCATION: Holmfirth High School;
Huddersfield New College; Leeds
Metropolitan University
TEAMS: Essex, Gloucestershire 2nd XI,
Leeds/Bradford MCCU, Marylebone Cricket
Club Universities, Unicorns
CAREER: First-class: 2011; List A: 2011; T20:
2011

ESSEX

BEST BATTING: 21 Essex vs Leicestershire, Southend, 2011
BEST BOWLING: 4-59 Essex vs Leicestershire, Southend, 2011

FAMILY TIES? My grandad was a league umpire and my mother's cousins played league cricket, with one of her cousins (James Pamment) playing professionally for Yorkshire and Auckland. He is currently the U19 cricket coach for the New Zealand side
CAREER HIGHLIGHTS? Making my debut for Essex in all formats, especially my first-class debut against Sri Lanka. Taking four-fer on my County Championship debut against Northants
CRICKETING HEROES? Shane Warne
NON-CRICKETING HEROES? Lance Armstrong
TIP FOR THE TOP? Tymal Mills
FAVOURITE TV? Lost
FAVOURITE FILM? Inception
FAVOURITE BOOK? The Lord Of The Rings
DREAM HOLIDAY? Travelling across America
ACCOMPLISHMENTS? Achieving a degree
SURPRISING FACT? Broke both collar bones as a teenager, good dancer, played football for Huddersfield Town for a year aged 12
TWITTER FEED: @tcradd20

| Batting | Mat | Inns | NO | Runs | HS | Ave | SR | 100 | 50 | Ct | St |
|---|---|---|---|---|---|---|---|---|---|---|---|
| First-class | 8 | 11 | 4 | 65 | 21 | 9.28 | 31.86 | 0 | 0 | 1 | 0 |
| List A | 6 | 4 | 4 | 9 | 5* | - | 30.00 | 0 | 0 | 2 | 0 |
| Twenty20 | 2 | - | - | - | - | - | - | - | - | 3 | 0 |

| Bowling | Mat | Balls | Runs | Wkts | BBI | BBM | Ave | Econ | SR | 5w | 10 |
|---|---|---|---|---|---|---|---|---|---|---|---|
| First-class | 8 | 1226 | 628 | 22 | 4/59 | 6/71 | 28.54 | 3.07 | 55.7 | 0 | 0 |
| List A | 6 | 246 | 182 | 4 | 2/38 | 2/38 | 45.50 | 4.43 | 61.5 | 0 | 0 |
| Twenty20 | 2 | 12 | 23 | 0 | - | - | - | 11.50 | - | 0 | 0 |

# ROBERT CROFT

## RHB OB W10

FULL NAME: Robert Damien Bale Croft
BORN: May 25, 1970, Morriston, Swansea
SQUAD NO: 10
HEIGHT: 5ft 11in
NICKNAME: Crofty
EDUCATION: St John Lloyd Catholic School, Llanelli
TEAMS: England, Glamorgan
CAREER: Test: 1996; ODI: 1996; First-class: 1989; List A: 1989; T20: 2003

BEST BATTING: 143 Glamorgan vs Somerset, Taunton, 1995
BEST BOWLING: 8-66 Glamorgan vs Warwickshire, Swansea, 1992
COUNTY CAP: 1992; BENEFIT YEAR: 2000; TESTIMONIAL: 2012

CAREER HIGHLIGHTS? Playing for England and winning the Championship with Glamorgan in 1997
CRICKETERS PARTICULARLY ADMIRED? Ian Botham, Shane Warne, Viv Richards
CRICKET MOMENTS TO FORGET? None. This career is too short to forget any of it
OTHER SPORTS FOLLOWED? Football (Liverpool), rugby (Llanelli and Wales)
NOTES: Represented England in 1999 World Cup. Captained Glamorgan 2003 to 2006. Retired from international cricket in 2004. First Welshman to have scored 10,000 runs and taken 1,000 wickets in first-class cricket

| Batting | Mat | Inns | NO | Runs | HS | Ave | SR | 100 | 50 | Ct | St |
|---|---|---|---|---|---|---|---|---|---|---|---|
| Tests | 21 | 34 | 8 | 421 | 37* | 16.19 | 36.29 | 0 | 0 | 10 | 0 |
| ODIs | 50 | 36 | 12 | 345 | 32 | 14.37 | 66.47 | 0 | 0 | 11 | 0 |
| First-class | 400 | 590 | 105 | 12791 | 143 | 26.37 | | 8 | 54 | 175 | 0 |
| List A | 407 | 338 | 61 | 6490 | 143 | 23.42 | | 4 | 32 | 94 | 0 |
| Twenty20 | 82 | 49 | 13 | 693 | 62* | 19.25 | 123.97 | 0 | 4 | 25 | 0 |

| Bowling | Mat | Balls | Runs | Wkts | BBI | BBM | Ave | Econ | SR | 5w | 10 |
|---|---|---|---|---|---|---|---|---|---|---|---|
| Tests | 21 | 4619 | 1825 | 49 | 5/95 | 7/143 | 37.24 | 2.37 | 94.2 | 1 | 0 |
| ODIs | 50 | 2466 | 1743 | 45 | 3/51 | 3/51 | 38.73 | 4.24 | 54.8 | 0 | 0 |
| First-class | 400 | 88307 | 40826 | 1152 | 8/66 | | 35.43 | 2.77 | 76.6 | 49 | 9 |
| List A | 407 | 18487 | 13392 | 410 | 6/20 | 6/20 | 32.66 | 4.34 | 45.0 | 1 | 0 |
| Twenty20 | 82 | 1623 | 1884 | 83 | 3/9 | 3/9 | 22.69 | 6.96 | 19.5 | 0 | 0 |

# STEVEN CROFT          RHB RMF/OB MVP14

**FULL NAME:** Steven John Croft
**BORN:** October 11, 1984, Blackpool, Lancashire
**SQUAD NO:** 15
**HEIGHT:** 5ft 11in
**NICKNAME:** Crofty
**EDUCATION:** Highfield High, Blackpool; Myerscough College
**TEAMS:** Auckland, Lancashire, Lancashire Cricket Board
**CAREER:** First-class: 2005; List A: 2003; T20: 2006

BEST BATTING: 122 Lancashire vs Warwickshire, Liverpool, 2011
BEST BOWLING: 4-51 Lancashire vs Nottinghamshire, Nottingham, 2008
COUNTY CAP: 2010

FAMILY TIES? Father was a very poor legspinner, so I got plenty of practice hitting sixes!
CAREER HIGHLIGHTS? Winning the County Championship with Lancashire in 2011. Captaining the county
CRICKETING HEROES? Andrew Flintoff, Stuart Law, Jacques Kallis
NON-CRICKETING HEROES? Alan Shearer
BEST PLAYER IN COUNTY CRICKET? Glen Chapple
TIPS FOR THE TOP? Jos Buttler, Simon Kerrigan, Glen Chapple
WHEN RAIN STOPS PLAY? Listening to music or trying to stay awake listening to Saj Mahmood's stories
FAVOURITE TV? Modern Family
FAVOURITE FILM? Step Brothers or The Shawshank Redemption
FAVOURITE BOOK? I, Partridge: We Need To Talk About Alan
SURPRISING SKILL? Being the best PS3 player in the Lancashire team
GUILTY PLEASURES? Rioja and pizza
AMAZE ME! First person from the Fylde Coast to play for Lancashire
TWITTER FEED: @stevenjcroft

| Batting | Mat | Inns | NO | Runs | HS | Ave | SR | 100 | 50 | Ct | St |
|---|---|---|---|---|---|---|---|---|---|---|---|
| First-class | 76 | 119 | 10 | 3351 | 122 | 30.74 | 51.04 | 3 | 22 | 69 | 0 |
| List A | 88 | 79 | 16 | 2157 | 107 | 34.23 | | 1 | 14 | 34 | 0 |
| Twenty20 | 75 | 68 | 10 | 1554 | 88 | 26.79 | 122.07 | 0 | 9 | 41 | 0 |

| Bowling | Mat | Balls | Runs | Wkts | BBI | BBM | Ave | Econ | SR | 5w | 10 |
|---|---|---|---|---|---|---|---|---|---|---|---|
| First-class | 76 | 2647 | 1617 | 37 | 4/51 | 4/100 | 43.70 | 3.66 | 71.5 | 0 | 0 |
| List A | 88 | 1501 | 1353 | 40 | 4/24 | 4/24 | 33.82 | 5.40 | 37.5 | 0 | 0 |
| Twenty20 | 75 | 471 | 667 | 23 | 3/6 | 3/6 | 29.00 | 8.49 | 20.4 | 0 | 0 |

# STEVEN CROOK                                    RHB RFM

MIDDLESEX

**FULL NAME:** Steven Paul Crook
**BORN:** May 28, 1983, Adelaide, Australia
**SQUAD NO:** 25
**HEIGHT:** 5ft 11in
**NICKNAME:** Crookster, Crooky, Weirdo
**EDUCATION:** Rostrevor College, Adelaide
**TEAMS:** Lancashire, Northamptonshire,
South Australia Under-17s, South Australia
Under-19s
**CAREER:** First-class: 2003; List A: 2003; T20:
2004

**BEST BATTING:** 97 Northamptonshire vs Yorkshire, Northampton, 2005
**BEST BOWLING:** 5-71 Northamptonshire vs Essex, Northampton, 2009

**FAMILY TIES?** Brother [Andrew] played for South Australia, Lancashire and Northants
**CAREER HIGHLIGHTS?** 2011 Division Two County Championship winners
**SUPERSTITIONS?** None
**CRICKETING HEROES?** Chris Rogers
**NON-CRICKETING HEROES?** Chris Martin from Coldplay
**BEST PLAYER IN COUNTY CRICKET?** Jack Brooks
**TIP FOR THE TOP?** Adam Rossington
**IF YOU WEREN'T A CRICKETER?** Binman
**WHEN RAIN STOPS PLAY?** Sleeping
**FAVOURITE TV?** CSI
**FAVOURITE FILM?** Point Break
**FAVOURITE BOOK?** Where's Wally?
**DREAM HOLIDAY?** Phuket
**ACCOMPLISHMENTS?** Starting my own business
**SURPRISING SKILL?** I sing opera
**GUILTY PLEASURES?** Rick Astley
**AMAZE ME!** My dad had a number one hit in Australia

| Batting | Mat | Inns | NO | Runs | HS | Ave | SR | 100 | 50 | Ct | St |
|---------|-----|------|-----|------|-----|-------|--------|-----|-----|-----|-----|
| First-class | 46 | 56 | 8 | 1325 | 97 | 27.60 | 68.75 | 0 | 9 | 16 | 0 |
| List A | 36 | 24 | 2 | 352 | 72 | 16.00 | 96.96 | 0 | 2 | 11 | 0 |
| Twenty20 | 48 | 28 | 5 | 280 | 29 | 12.17 | 116.66 | 0 | 0 | 8 | 0 |

| Bowling | Mat | Balls | Runs | Wkts | BBI | BBM | Ave | Econ | SR | 5w | 10 |
|---------|-----|-------|------|------|-----|-----|-------|------|------|-----|-----|
| First-class | 46 | 5340 | 3654 | 85 | 5/71 | | 42.98 | 4.10 | 62.8 | 2 | 0 |
| List A | 36 | 1287 | 1281 | 27 | 4/20 | 4/20 | 47.44 | 5.97 | 47.6 | 0 | 0 |
| Twenty20 | 48 | 487 | 717 | 26 | 3/21 | 3/21 | 27.57 | 8.83 | 18.7 | 0 | 0 |

FULL NAME: Gareth David Cross
BORN: June 20, 1984, Bury, Lancashire
SQUAD NO: 7
HEIGHT: 5ft 9in
NICKNAME: Crossy, Manc, Gary, Monkey
EDUCATION: Moorside High School; Eccles College
TEAMS: Lancashire, Lancashire Cricket Board
CAREER: First-class: 2005; List A: 2003; T20: 2006

LANCASHIRE

BEST BATTING: 125 Lancashire vs Sussex, Hove, 2011

CAREER HIGHLIGHTS? Winning the Championship with my home club – who I have supported since I was a kid – alongside my mates is pretty difficult to beat
SUPERSTITIONS? Just the usual, right pad on before left
CRICKETING HEROES? Ian Healy's keeping, Adam Gilchrist's batting
NON-CRICKETING HEROES? George Best, Eric Cantona
BEST PLAYER IN COUNTY CRICKET? Batting: Marcus Trescothick; bowling: Glen Chapple and Jimmy Anderson
TIPS FOR THE TOP? Karl Brown, Simon Kerrigan
IF YOU WEREN'T A CRICKETER? Binman
WHEN RAIN STOPS PLAY? Joking around
FAVOURITE TV? Entourage
FAVOURITE FILM? Man On Fire
DREAM HOLIDAY? Bora Bora
ACCOMPLISHMENTS? Passing at least one GCSE
FANTASY SLIP CORDON? Keeper: Myself, 1st: Wayne Rooney, 2nd: Denzel Washington, 3rd: George Best, Gully: Eva Mendes
TWITTER FEED: @gazcross07

| Batting | Mat | Inns | NO | Runs | HS | Ave | SR | 100 | 50 | Ct | St |
|---|---|---|---|---|---|---|---|---|---|---|---|
| First-class | 32 | 51 | 2 | 1210 | 125 | 24.69 | 62.62 | 2 | 6 | 87 | 18 |
| List A | 53 | 43 | 5 | 834 | 76 | 21.94 | | 0 | 3 | 32 | 15 |
| Twenty20 | 68 | 51 | 10 | 653 | 65* | 15.92 | 128.29 | 0 | 2 | 42 | 20 |
| Bowling | Mat | Balls | Runs | Wkts | BBI | BBM | Ave | Econ | SR | 5w | 10 |
| First-class | 32 | - | - | - | - | - | - | - | - | - | - |
| List A | 53 | 36 | 26 | 2 | 2/26 | 2/26 | 13.00 | 4.33 | 18.0 | 0 | 0 |
| Twenty20 | 68 | - | - | - | - | - | - | - | - | - | - |

WORCESTERSHIRE

FULL NAME: Brett Louis D'Oliveira
BORN: February 28, 1992, Worcester
SQUAD NO: 15
HEIGHT: 5ft 11in
NICKNAME: Dolly, Bdoll
EDUCATION: Blessed Edward High School;
Worcestershire Sixth Form College
TEAMS: Worcestershire, Worcestershire
2nd XI, Worcestershire Under-13s,
Worcestershire Under-14s, Worcestershire
Under-15s, Worcestershire Under-17s
CAREER: List A: 2011

FAMILY TIES? Grandfather played for Worcestershire and England as well as coaching at Worcestershire. Father played for Worcestershire and is currently 2nd XI coach and academy director
CAREER HIGHLIGHTS? Signing my professional contract with Worcestershire. Making my debut for Worcestershire
SUPERSTITIONS? I always bat in a jumper and put my left pad on first
CRICKETING HEROES? Shane Warne, Sachin Tendulkar, Jonty Rhodes and Basil D'Oliveira
NON-CRICKETING HEROES? Nelson Mandela, Martin Luther King Jr, Rosa Parks
BEST PLAYER IN COUNTY CRICKET? There are so many but I will keep it close to home and say Alan Richardson
TIP FOR THE TOP? Alex Milton
IF YOU WEREN'T A CRICKETER? Studying Sport and Exercise Science at university
WHEN RAIN STOPS PLAY? Dressing room cricket, listening to music, doing crosswords, having banter with the lads
FAVOURITE TV? Two And A Half Men
FAVOURITE FILM? American Gangster
DREAM HOLIDAY? Cuba
GUILTY PLEASURES? Fast food
FANTASY SLIP CORDON? Keeper: Aubrey Drake Graham, 1st: John Bishop, 2nd: Michael Jordan, 3rd: Bob Marley, Gully: Cheryl Cole
TWITTER FEED: @bdolly09

| Batting | Mat | Inns | NO | Runs | HS | Ave | SR | 100 | 50 | Ct | St |
|---------|-----|------|-----|------|-----|------|------|------|------|------|------|
| List A | 1 | - | - | - | - | - | - | - | - | 1 | 0 |

| Bowling | Mat | Balls | Runs | Wkts | BBI | BBM | Ave | Econ | SR | 5w | 10 |
|---------|-----|-------|------|------|------|------|-------|------|------|------|------|
| List A | 1 | 36 | 40 | 1 | 1/40 | 1/40 | 40.00 | 6.66 | 36.0 | 0 | 0 |

## LEE DAGGETT — RHB RMF

**FULL NAME:** Lee Martin Daggett
**BORN:** October 1, 1982, Bury, Lancashire
**SQUAD NO:** 10
**HEIGHT:** 6ft
**NICKNAME:** Dags, Von Daggentooth
**EDUCATION:** Woodhey High School; Holy Cross College; Durham University; Salford University
**TEAMS:** Durham MCCU, Lancashire Cricket Board, Leicestershire, Northamptonshire, Warwickshire
**CAREER:** First-class: 2003; List A: 2006; T20: 2007

**BEST BATTING:** 50* Northamptonshire vs Leicestershire, Grace Road, 2011
**BEST BOWLING:** 8-94 DUCCE vs Durham, Riverside, 2004

**CAREER HIGHLIGHTS?** Eight wickets for Durham University whilst I didn't have a contract, six wickets against Durham for Warwickshire in 2006, T20 quarter-final win against Hampshire in 2009
**SUPERSTITIONS?** I don't like my bowling marker being moved and I never shave during a game
**CRICKETING HEROES?** Allan Donald, Brett Lee
**NON-CRICKETING HEROES?** Dave Grohl, Will Ferrell, Lance Armstrong
**TIPS FOR THE TOP?** Alex Wakely, Tom Maynard, Ollie Stone
**IF YOU WEREN'T A CRICKETER?** Physiotherapist
**DREAM HOLIDAY?** Mauritius
**AMAZE ME!** I have an Australian passport, I played at the old Wembley, and although I look 39 I'm actually only 29
**FANTASY SLIP CORDON?** Keeper: Peter Schmeichel (childhood hero), 1st: Dave Grohl (absolute legend with plenty of stories I'm sure), 2nd: Britney Spears (my number one, apart from the missus of course), 3rd: Fry and Lawrie (brilliant actors and both hilarious), Gully: Myself
**TWITTER FEED:** @LeeDaggett

| Batting | Mat | Inns | NO | Runs | HS | Ave | SR | 100 | 50 | Ct | St |
|---|---|---|---|---|---|---|---|---|---|---|---|
| First-class | 54 | 67 | 30 | 491 | 50* | 13.27 | 33.15 | 0 | 1 | 7 | 0 |
| List A | 49 | 14 | 11 | 78 | 14* | 26.00 | 70.90 | 0 | 0 | 8 | 0 |
| Twenty20 | 40 | 9 | 5 | 8 | 3* | 2.00 | 44.44 | 0 | 0 | 10 | 0 |

| Bowling | Mat | Balls | Runs | Wkts | BBI | BBM | Ave | Econ | SR | 5w | 10 |
|---|---|---|---|---|---|---|---|---|---|---|---|
| First-class | 54 | 8384 | 4879 | 137 | 8/94 | | 35.61 | 3.49 | 61.1 | 2 | 0 |
| List A | 49 | 2024 | 1690 | 60 | 4/17 | 4/17 | 28.16 | 5.00 | 33.7 | 0 | 0 |
| Twenty20 | 40 | 497 | 658 | 20 | 2/17 | 2/17 | 32.90 | 7.94 | 24.8 | 0 | 0 |

**MIDDLESEX**

FULL NAME: Joshua Henry Davey
BORN: August 3, 1990, Aberdeen
SQUAD NO: 24
EDUCATION: Culford School; Oxford Brookes University
TEAMS: Scotland, Middlesex, Middlesex 2nd XI, Suffolk
CAREER: ODI: 2010; First-class: 2010; List A: 2010; T20: 2010

BEST BATTING: 72 Middlesex vs OMCCU, The Parks, 2010
BEST BOWLING: 2-41 Middlesex vs OMCCU, The Parks, 2010

NOTES: Attended Darren Lehmann Cricket Academy in Adelaide in 2009. Holds the record for the best ever ODI bowling figures for Scotland of 5-9 against Afghanistan at Ayr in 2010. Made 72 on his first-class debut for Middlesex against Oxford University in 2010. Hit unbeaten 48 and took 3-41 against Ireland at Edinburgh in the 2011 Tri-Nation Tournament to help his side to a five-wicket win

| Batting | Mat | Inns | NO | Runs | HS | Ave | SR | 100 | 50 | Ct | St |
|---|---|---|---|---|---|---|---|---|---|---|---|
| ODIs | 8 | 8 | 1 | 147 | 48* | 21.00 | 56.75 | 0 | 0 | 4 | 0 |
| First-class | 5 | 9 | 1 | 269 | 72 | 33.62 | 41.77 | 0 | 3 | 3 | 0 |
| List A | 25 | 24 | 3 | 530 | 91 | 25.23 | 63.02 | 0 | 2 | 10 | 0 |
| Twenty20 | 6 | 5 | 3 | 38 | 18* | 19.00 | 108.57 | 0 | 0 | 2 | 0 |

| Bowling | Mat | Balls | Runs | Wkts | BBI | BBM | Ave | Econ | SR | 5w | 10 |
|---|---|---|---|---|---|---|---|---|---|---|---|
| ODIs | 8 | 284 | 220 | 13 | 5/9 | 5/9 | 16.92 | 4.64 | 21.8 | 1 | 0 |
| First-class | 5 | 198 | 133 | 3 | 2/41 | 2/65 | 44.33 | 4.03 | 66.0 | 0 | 0 |
| List A | 25 | 622 | 549 | 24 | 5/9 | 5/9 | 22.87 | 5.29 | 25.9 | 1 | 0 |
| Twenty20 | 6 | 30 | 48 | 0 | - | - | - | 9.60 | - | 0 | 0 |

## ALEX DAVIES RHB WK

FULL NAME: Alexander Luke Davies
BORN: August 23, 1994, Darwen, Lancashire
SQUAD NO: TBC
HEIGHT: 5ft 6in
NICKNAME: Big Al, AD
EDUCATION: Queen Elizabeth Grammar School
TEAMS: Lancashire, Lancashire 2nd XI, Lancashire Cricket Academy, Lancashire Under-13s, Lancashire Under-14s, Lancashire Under-15s, Lancashire Under-17s
CAREER: List A: 2011

LANCASHIRE

CAREER HIGHLIGHTS? Making Lancashire 1st XI debut and representing England at U15 and U17 level

SUPERSTITIONS? Always put my left foot on and off the field first and put my gear on in the same order

CRICKETING HEROES? Sachin Tendulkar, Mark Boucher, James Foster, AB de Villiers

NON-CRICKETING HEROES? Michael Owen, Jonny Wilkinson, Mario Balotelli

BEST PLAYER IN COUNTY CRICKET? Simon Kerrigan, Jos Buttler

TIPS FOR THE TOP? Daniel Bell-Drummond, Aneesh Kapil, Reece Topley

IF YOU WEREN'T A CRICKETER? Sports physio

WHEN RAIN STOPS PLAY? Cards, music, sleep

FAVOURITE TV? Shameless, The Only Way Is Essex

FAVOURITE FILM? Anchorman, Role Models, Billy Madison

DREAM HOLIDAY? Dubai, Ibiza

ACCOMPLISHMENTS? Playing for Blackburn Rovers FC

SURPRISING SKILL? Card tricks

GUILTY PLEASURES? Busted (the band)

AMAZE ME! Believe it or not I am the tallest member of my family

FANTASY SLIP CORDON? Keeper: Myself, 1st: Brian Potter (Peter Kay), 2nd: Mario Balotelli, 3rd: Ron Burgundy, Gully: Joey Barton

TWITTER FEED: @aldavies23

| Batting | Mat | Inns | NO | Runs | HS | Ave | SR | 100 | 50 | Ct | St |
|---------|-----|------|-----|------|-----|-----|-------|-----|-----|-----|-----|
| List A | 1 | 1 | 1 | 6 | 6* | - | 85.71 | 0 | 0 | 0 | 0 |

| Bowling | Mat | Balls | Runs | Wkts | BBI | BBM | Ave | Econ | SR | 5w | 10 |
|---------|-----|-------|------|------|-----|-----|-----|------|-----|-----|-----|
| List A | 1 | - | - | - | - | - | - | - | - | - | - |

## MARK DAVIES

### RHB RFM W1

FULL NAME: Mark Davies
BORN: October 4, 1980, Stockton-on-Tees, Co Durham
SQUAD NO: 4
HEIGHT: 6ft 2in
NICKNAME: Davo, Bob
EDUCATION: Northfield School, Billingham
TEAMS: Durham, Durham Cricket Board, Kent
CAREER: First-class: 2002; List A: 1998; T20: 2003

BEST BATTING: 62 Durham vs Somerset, Grangefield Road, 2005
BEST BOWLING: 8-24 Durham vs Hampshire, Basingstoke, 2008
COUNTY CAP: 2005 (Durham)

FAMILY TIES? My uncle Paul played for Yorkshire 2nd XI
CAREER HIGHLIGHTS? Winning back-to-back Championships with Durham. Also being picked for the England Lions tour to New Zealand was a special time for me
CRICKETING HEROES? My uncle Paul in the early years and then Glenn McGrath
NON-CRICKETING HEROES? Oasis
BEST PLAYER IN COUNTY CRICKET? Marcus Trescothick
TIP FOR THE TOP? Ben Stokes
IF YOU WEREN'T A CRICKETER? Anything to do with sport
FAVOURITE TV? This Is England
FAVOURITE FILM? Wedding Crashers
FAVOURITE BOOK? Racing Through The Dark by David Millar
ACCOMPLISHMENTS? Becoming a dad in 2008
GUILTY PLEASURES? Curries and lager
FANTASY SLIP CORDON? Keeper: Noel Gallagher, 1st: Liam Gallagher, 2nd: Gazza, 3rd: Myself, Gully: Floyd Mayweather Jr
NOTES: Will start the season on trial with Kent ahead of a possible permanent switch

| Batting | Mat | Inns | NO | Runs | HS | Ave | SR | 100 | 50 | Ct | St |
|---|---|---|---|---|---|---|---|---|---|---|---|
| First-class | 83 | 107 | 41 | 733 | 62 | 11.10 | 33.01 | 0 | 1 | 17 | 0 |
| List A | 73 | 36 | 14 | 166 | 31* | 7.54 | | 0 | 0 | 10 | 0 |
| Twenty20 | 9 | 4 | 3 | 11 | 6 | 11.00 | 78.57 | 0 | 0 | 2 | 0 |

| Bowling | Mat | Balls | Runs | Wkts | BBI | BBM | Ave | Econ | SR | 5w | 10 |
|---|---|---|---|---|---|---|---|---|---|---|---|
| First-class | 83 | 12540 | 5726 | 253 | 8/24 | | 22.63 | 2.73 | 49.5 | 12 | 2 |
| List A | 73 | 2982 | 2087 | 68 | 4/13 | 4/13 | 30.69 | 4.19 | 43.8 | 0 | 0 |
| Twenty20 | 9 | 204 | 241 | 8 | 2/14 | 2/14 | 30.12 | 7.08 | 25.5 | 0 | 0 |

## STEVE DAVIES — LHB WK R4 MVP18

FULL NAME: Steven Michael Davies
BORN: June 17, 1986, Bromsgrove, Worcestershire
SQUAD NO: 9
HEIGHT: 6ft
NICKNAME: Davo
EDUCATION: King Charles High School
TEAMS: England, England Lions, Marylebone Cricket Club, Surrey, Worcestershire, Worcestershire Cricket Board
CAREER: ODI: 2009; T20I: 2009; First-class: 2005; List A: 2003; T20: 2006

BEST BATTING: 192 Worcestershire vs Gloucestershire, Bristol, 2006

WHY CRICKET? My father introduced me to the game when I was six years old. I played most sports when I was younger but happened to be better at cricket than most of the others
CAREER HIGHLIGHTS? Worcestershire first-class debut vs Durham. Receiving my Surrey cap and representing my country in T20 and ODI cricket. Also winning the CB40 competition with Worcestershire and Surrey
CRICKETING HEROES? Adam Gilchrist, Brian Lara, Sachin Tendulkar
NON-CRICKETING HEROES? Roger Federer
BEST PLAYER IN COUNTY CRICKET? Marcus Trescothick
TIPS FOR THE TOP? Zafar Ansari, Arun Harinath
FAVOURITE FILM? Wedding Crashers
FAVOURITE BOOK? Andre Agassi – Open
DREAM HOLIDAY? New York
FANTASY SLIP CORDON? Keeper: Me, 1st: Roger Federer, 2nd: Ricky Gervais (hilarious), 3rd: Mike Tyson (fascinates me), Gully: Beyoncé (in case we need some tunes)
TWITTER FEED: @stevedavies43

| Batting | Mat | Inns | NO | Runs | HS | Ave | SR | 100 | 50 | Ct | St |
|---|---|---|---|---|---|---|---|---|---|---|---|
| ODIs | 8 | 8 | 0 | 244 | 87 | 30.50 | 105.62 | 0 | 1 | 8 | 0 |
| T20Is | 5 | 5 | 0 | 102 | 33 | 20.40 | 124.39 | 0 | 0 | 2 | 1 |
| First-class | 110 | 184 | 20 | 6567 | 192 | 40.04 | 63.04 | 10 | 34 | 336 | 16 |
| List A | 122 | 112 | 12 | 3620 | 119 | 36.20 | | 0 | 5 | 21 | 109 | 31 |
| Twenty20 | 70 | 63 | 7 | 1387 | 99* | 24.76 | 143.58 | 0 | 8 | 40 | 9 |

| Bowling | Mat | Balls | Runs | Wkts | BBI | BBM | Ave | Econ | SR | 5w | 10 |
|---|---|---|---|---|---|---|---|---|---|---|---|
| ODIs | 8 | - | - | - | - | - | - | - | - | - | - |
| T20Is | 5 | - | - | - | - | - | - | - | - | - | - |
| First-class | 110 | - | - | - | - | - | - | - | - | - | - |
| List A | 122 | - | - | - | - | - | - | - | - | - | - |
| Twenty20 | 70 | - | - | - | - | - | - | - | - | - | - |

# LIAM DAWSON

## RHB SLA

HAMPSHIRE

FULL NAME: Liam Andrew Dawson
BORN: March 1, 1990, Swindon, Wiltshire
SQUAD NO: 8
HEIGHT: 5ft 10in
NICKNAME: Daws, Chav, Leeemo, Kimya
EDUCATION: John Bentley School
TEAMS: England Lions, England Under-19s, Hampshire, Hampshire 2nd XI, Mountaineers
CAREER: First-class: 2007; List A: 2007; T20: 2008

BEST BATTING: 169 Hampshire vs Somerset, Southampton, 2011
BEST BOWLING: 7-51 Mountaineers vs Mashonaland Eagles, Mutare Sports Club, 2011

FAMILY TIES? Dad and brother played for Goatacre CC in Wiltshire
CAREER HIGHLIGHTS? Winning a Lord's final with Hampshire and winning the T20 competition at The Rose Bowl
CRICKETING HEROES? Shane Warne
BEST PLAYER IN COUNTY CRICKET? Michael Carberry
TIPS FOR THE TOP? James Vince, Jason Roy, Tom Maynard
IF YOU WEREN'T A CRICKETER? I'd be struggling
WHEN RAIN STOPS PLAY? Internet, sleeping, practising
FAVOURITE TV? TOWIE
FAVOURITE FILM? The Great Escape
DREAM HOLIDAY? Las Vegas
GUILTY PLEASURES? McDonald's, and Coco Pops at night
FANTASY SLIP CORDON? Keeper: Paul Gascogine, 1st: Derren Brown, 2nd: Cheryl Cole, 3rd: Me, Gully: Colleen Rooney
TWITTER FEED: @daws128

| Batting | Mat | Inns | NO | Runs | HS | Ave | SR | 100 | 50 | Ct | St |
|---|---|---|---|---|---|---|---|---|---|---|---|
| First-class | 45 | 72 | 8 | 2145 | 169 | 33.51 | 49.05 | 4 | 12 | 35 | 0 |
| List A | 50 | 42 | 9 | 914 | 70 | 27.69 | 96.82 | 0 | 3 | 26 | 0 |
| Twenty20 | 36 | 24 | 7 | 193 | 26 | 11.35 | 96.50 | 0 | 0 | 19 | 0 |

| Bowling | Mat | Balls | Runs | Wkts | BBI | BBM | Ave | Econ | SR | 5w | 10 |
|---|---|---|---|---|---|---|---|---|---|---|---|
| First-class | 45 | 1647 | 1056 | 27 | 7/51 | 7/84 | 39.11 | 3.84 | 61.0 | 1 | 0 |
| List A | 50 | 1185 | 1077 | 28 | 4/45 | 4/45 | 38.46 | 5.45 | 42.3 | 0 | 0 |
| Twenty20 | 36 | 262 | 355 | 8 | 3/25 | 3/25 | 44.37 | 8.12 | 32.7 | 0 | 0 |

# ZANDER DE BRUYN          RHB RMF R1 MVP25

FULL NAME: Zander de Bruyn
BORN: July 5, 1975, Johannesburg, South Africa
SQUAD NO: 58
HEIGHT: 6ft 1in
NICKNAME: Z
EDUCATION: Randburg High School; University of Johannesburg
TEAMS: South Africa, Gauteng, Lions, Marylebone Cricket Club, Somerset, Surrey, Titans, Transvaal, Warriors, Worcestershire
CAREER: Test: 2004; First-class: 1996; List A: 1996; T20: 2005

BEST BATTING: 266* Easterns vs Griqualand West, Kimberley, 2003
BEST BOWLING: 7-67 Warriors vs Titans, Port Elizabeth, 2007
COUNTY CAP: 2008 (Somerset)

CAREER HIGHLIGHTS? Playing for South Africa in India in front of 60,000 people
CRICKETING HEROES? Clive Rice, Steve Waugh
NON-CRICKETING HEROES? Superman and Gareth Batty
BEST PLAYER IN COUNTY CRICKET? Marcus Trescothick
TIPS FOR THE TOP? Jason Roy, Stuart Meaker
FAVOURITE TV? Top Gear
FAVOURITE FILM? Jerry Maguire
FAVOURITE BOOK? Steve Waugh's autobiography
DREAM HOLIDAY? Miami
ACCOMPLISHMENTS? My wife and kids
GUILTY PLEASURES? Chocolate and coffee
FANTASY SLIP CORDON? Keeper: Jeremy Clarkson, 1st: Myself, 2nd: Michael McIntyre, 3rd: Shakira, Gully: Steve Waugh

| Batting | Mat | Inns | NO | Runs | HS | Ave | SR | 100 | 50 | Ct | St |
|---|---|---|---|---|---|---|---|---|---|---|---|
| Tests | 3 | 5 | 1 | 155 | 83 | 38.75 | 37.89 | 0 | 1 | 0 | 0 |
| First-class | 198 | 332 | 34 | 12445 | 266* | 41.76 | | 27 | 69 | 119 | 0 |
| List A | 208 | 192 | 42 | 5552 | 122* | 37.01 | | 6 | 34 | 50 | 0 |
| Twenty20 | 103 | 90 | 26 | 1965 | 95* | 30.70 | 108.68 | 0 | 9 | 21 | 0 |

| Bowling | Mat | Balls | Runs | Wkts | BBI | BBM | Ave | Econ | SR | 5w | 10 |
|---|---|---|---|---|---|---|---|---|---|---|---|
| Tests | 3 | 216 | 92 | 3 | 2/32 | 2/32 | 30.66 | 2.55 | 72.0 | 0 | 0 |
| First-class | 198 | 16213 | 9195 | 236 | 7/67 | | 38.96 | 3.40 | 68.6 | 3 | 0 |
| List A | 208 | 4835 | 4473 | 143 | 5/44 | 5/44 | 31.27 | 5.55 | 33.8 | 1 | 0 |
| Twenty20 | 103 | 917 | 1346 | 47 | 4/18 | 4/18 | 28.63 | 8.80 | 19.5 | 0 | 0 |

## CON DE LANGE RHB SLA

FULL NAME: Con de Wet De Lange
BORN: February 11, 1981, Bellville, Cape Province, South Africa
SQUAD NO: 31
HEIGHT: 5ft 7in
NICKNAME: CDL, Conna, Goose
EDUCATION: Worcester Gymnasium High School; UNISA
TEAMS: Boland, Cape Cobras, Eagles, Free State, Knights, Western Province Boland
CAREER: First-class: 1998; List A: 2000; T20: 2007

BEST BATTING: 109 Boland vs Easterns, Paarl, 2003
BEST BOWLING: 7-48 Gauteng vs Boland, Randjesfontein, 2004

WHY CRICKET? As a youngster I wanted to play cricket with my dad. I quickly learned that it's a fantastic game and that it teaches you so many different and important life skills
CAREER HIGHLIGHTS? Playing for the Cape Cobras and having Newlands as my home ground. Winning the domestic one-day trophy with Boland, Cape Cobras and the Knights, and now getting the opportunity to play county cricket
BEST PLAYER IN COUNTY CRICKET? There are plenty of quality players. I will soon find out who's the best of the lot!
IF YOU WEREN'T A CRICKETER? I would love to be a pro golfer
FAVOURITE TV? Frozen Planet
FAVOURITE FILM? Gladiator, Wedding Crashers
ACCOMPLISHMENTS? Creating such a beautiful little girl called Daisy
TWITTER FEED: @cdwdelange

| Batting | Mat | Inns | NO | Runs | HS | Ave | SR | 100 | 50 | Ct | St |
|---------|-----|------|-----|------|-----|-------|-------|-----|-----|-----|-----|
| First-class | 83 | 134 | 12 | 2723 | 109 | 22.31 | | 1 | 13 | 45 | 0 |
| List A | 118 | 77 | 18 | 1373 | 66 | 23.27 | | 0 | 7 | 36 | 0 |
| Twenty20 | 16 | 7 | 2 | 23 | 8 | 4.60 | 88.46 | 0 | 0 | 10 | 0 |

| Bowling | Mat | Balls | Runs | Wkts | BBI | BBM | Ave | Econ | SR | 5w | 10 |
|---------|-----|-------|------|------|------|------|-------|------|------|-----|-----|
| First-class | 83 | 14629 | 6747 | 175 | 7/48 | | 38.55 | 2.76 | 83.5 | 5 | 1 |
| List A | 118 | 4906 | 3589 | 118 | 4/8 | 4/8 | 30.41 | 4.38 | 41.5 | 0 | 0 |
| Twenty20 | 16 | 306 | 360 | 14 | 2/14 | 2/14 | 25.71 | 7.05 | 21.8 | 0 | 0 |

FULL NAME: Joseph Liam Denly
BORN: March 16, 1986, Canterbury, Kent
SQUAD NO: 10
HEIGHT: 6ft
NICKNAME: JD, Denners, No Pants
EDUCATION: Chaucer Technology College
TEAMS: England, England Lions, England Performance Programme, England Under-19s, Kent, Kent 2nd XI
CAREER: ODI: 2009; T20I: 2009; First-class: 2004; List A: 2004; T20: 2004

MIDDLESEX

BEST BATTING: 199 Kent vs Derbyshire, Derby, 2011
BEST BOWLING: 3-43 Kent vs Surrey, The Oval, 2011
COUNTY CAP: 2008 (Kent)

FAMILY TIES? Brother Sam and dad were both Kent League players
CAREER HIGHLIGHTS? Playing for England, winning T20 Cup with Kent
SUPERSTITIONS? Left pad first
BEST PLAYER IN COUNTY CRICKET? Marcus Trescothick, Mark Ramprakash
TIPS FOR THE TOP? Sam Robson, Adam London
IF YOU WEREN'T A CRICKETER? I'd be struggling!
WHEN RAIN STOPS PLAY? TV, pranks, cards
FAVOURITE TV? Big Brother
FAVOURITE FILM? Step Brothers
DREAM HOLIDAY? Maldives
FANTASY SLIP CORDON? Keeper: Ricky Gervais, 1st: Angelina Jolie, 2nd: Jennifer Aniston, 3rd: Karl Pilkington
TWITTER FEED: @Joed1986

| Batting | Mat | Inns | NO | Runs | HS | Ave | SR | 100 | 50 | Ct | St |
|---|---|---|---|---|---|---|---|---|---|---|---|
| ODIs | 9 | 9 | 0 | 268 | 67 | 29.77 | 65.52 | 0 | 2 | 5 | 0 |
| T20Is | 5 | 5 | 0 | 20 | 14 | 4.00 | 68.96 | 0 | 0 | 1 | 0 |
| First-class | 84 | 149 | 6 | 4930 | 199 | 34.47 | 59.11 | 12 | 24 | 37 | 0 |
| List A | 83 | 81 | 7 | 2419 | 115 | 32.68 | 72.33 | 4 | 11 | 25 | 0 |
| Twenty20 | 76 | 73 | 4 | 1761 | 100 | 25.52 | 113.17 | 1 | 10 | 29 | 0 |

| Bowling | Mat | Balls | Runs | Wkts | BBI | BBM | Ave | Econ | SR | 5w | 10 |
|---|---|---|---|---|---|---|---|---|---|---|---|
| ODIs | 9 | - | - | - | - | - | - | - | - | - | - |
| T20Is | 5 | 6 | 9 | 1 | 1/9 | 1/9 | 9.00 | 9.00 | 6.0 | 0 | 0 |
| First-class | 84 | 1747 | 967 | 20 | 3/43 | 6/114 | 48.35 | 3.32 | 87.3 | 0 | 0 |
| List A | 83 | 120 | 122 | 4 | 3/42 | 3/42 | 30.50 | 6.10 | 30.0 | 0 | 0 |
| Twenty20 | 76 | 48 | 76 | 1 | 1/9 | 1/9 | 76.00 | 9.50 | 48.0 | 0 | 0 |

# CHRIS DENT LHB SLA WK

**GLOUCESTERSHIRE**

FULL NAME: Christopher David James Dent
BORN: January 20, 1991, Bristol
SQUAD NO: 15
HEIGHT: 5ft 10in
NICKNAME: Denty, Maggot, Weezle, Harry
EDUCATION: Filton College
TEAMS: England Under-19s, Gloucestershire, Gloucestershire 2nd XI
CAREER: First-class: 2010; List A: 2009; T20: 2010

BEST BATTING: 100 Gloucestershire vs Surrey, Cheltenham, 2011
COUNTY CAP: 2010

WHY CRICKET? Socialising with mates
CAREER HIGHLIGHTS? Maiden first-class hundred
CRICKETING HEROES? Brian Lara, Chris Taylor, Jack Russell
NON-CRICKETING HEROES? Tiger Woods
BEST PLAYER IN COUNTY CRICKET? Marcus Trescothick
TIP FOR THE TOP? Jos Buttler
IF YOU WEREN'T A CRICKETER? I'd be working in Mbargo in Bristol
WHEN RAIN STOPS PLAY? On my phone or sleeping
FAVOURITE TV? The Joy Of Teen Sex
FAVOURITE FILM? The Girl With The Dragon Tattoo
FAVOURITE BOOK? The Game
DREAM HOLIDAY? Las Vegas
ACCOMPLISHMENTS? Tonning up on the leaderboard and getting through college
GUILTY PLEASURES? Night out, and bubble bath in the changing rooms
FANTASY SLIP CORDON? Keeper: Rihanna, 1st: Megan Fox, 2nd: Me, 3rd: Tiger Woods, Gully: Jessica Alba
TWITTER FEED: @Cdent15

| Batting | Mat | Inns | NO | Runs | HS | Ave | SR | 100 | 50 | Ct | St |
|---|---|---|---|---|---|---|---|---|---|---|---|
| First-class | 28 | 52 | 5 | 1374 | 100 | 29.23 | 51.55 | 1 | 7 | 41 | 0 |
| List A | 8 | 5 | 0 | 49 | 25 | 9.80 | 79.03 | 0 | 0 | 2 | 0 |
| Twenty20 | 8 | 7 | 0 | 169 | 63 | 24.14 | 118.18 | 0 | 1 | 0 | 0 |

| Bowling | Mat | Balls | Runs | Wkts | BBI | BBM | Ave | Econ | SR | 5w | 10 |
|---|---|---|---|---|---|---|---|---|---|---|---|
| First-class | 28 | 78 | 51 | 0 | - | - | - | 3.92 | - | 0 | 0 |
| List A | 8 | 12 | 17 | 1 | 1/17 | 1/17 | 17.00 | 8.50 | 12.0 | 0 | 0 |
| Twenty20 | 8 | - | - | - | - | - | - | - | - | - | - |

# JADE DERNBACH

## RHB RFM W1

FULL NAME: Jade Winston Dernbach
BORN: April 3, 1986, Johannesburg, South Africa
SQUAD NO: 16
HEIGHT: 6ft 2in
NICKNAME: Dirtbag
EDUCATION: St John The Baptist, Johannesburg
TEAMS: England, England Lions, Surrey, Surrey 2nd XI
CAREER: ODI: 2011; T20I: 2011; First-class: 2003; List A: 2005; T20: 2005

SURREY

BEST BATTING: 56* Surrey vs Northamptonshire, Northampton, 2011
BEST BOWLING: 6-47 Surrey vs Leicestershire, Leicester, 2010

CRICKETING HEROES? Jacques Kallis, Jonty Rhodes, James Anderson
RELAXATIONS? Going out with friends, swimming, playing football and rugby and listening to music
NOTES: Leading wicket-taker in the 2008 NatWest Pro40, taking 24 wickets at 13.08. Took 51 first-class wickets at 27.25 in 2010. Replaced the injured Ajmal Shahzad for the knockout stages of the 2011 World Cup. Played in England's limited-overs sides against India (late 2011) and Pakistan (early 2012). Particularly impressed in the three T20Is against Pakistan, claiming four wickets at 17 with an economy of 6.18

| Batting | Mat | Inns | NO | Runs | HS | Ave | SR | 100 | 50 | Ct | St |
|---|---|---|---|---|---|---|---|---|---|---|---|
| ODIs | 14 | 4 | 1 | 13 | 5 | 4.33 | 65.00 | 0 | 0 | 3 | 0 |
| T20Is | 8 | 1 | 0 | 3 | 3 | 3.00 | 75.00 | 0 | 0 | 5 | 0 |
| First-class | 65 | 78 | 29 | 478 | 56* | 9.75 | | 0 | 1 | 8 | 0 |
| List A | 86 | 32 | 12 | 165 | 31 | 8.25 | 83.33 | 0 | 0 | 19 | 0 |
| Twenty20 | 50 | 12 | 3 | 43 | 12 | 4.77 | 79.62 | 0 | 0 | 12 | 0 |

| Bowling | Mat | Balls | Runs | Wkts | BBI | BBM | Ave | Econ | SR | 5w | 10 |
|---|---|---|---|---|---|---|---|---|---|---|---|
| ODIs | 14 | 700 | 710 | 20 | 4/45 | 4/45 | 35.50 | 6.08 | 35.0 | 0 | 0 |
| T20Is | 8 | 172 | 173 | 11 | 4/22 | 4/22 | 15.72 | 6.03 | 15.6 | 0 | 0 |
| First-class | 65 | 10326 | 5927 | 182 | 6/47 | | 32.56 | 3.44 | 56.7 | 9 | 0 |
| List A | 86 | 3676 | 3766 | 141 | 5/31 | 5/31 | 26.70 | 6.14 | 26.0 | 2 | 0 |
| Twenty20 | 50 | 944 | 1300 | 46 | 4/22 | 4/22 | 28.26 | 8.26 | 20.5 | 0 | 0 |

# NEIL DEXTER

**RHB RM**

FULL NAME: Neil John Dexter
BORN: August 21, 1984, Johannesburg, South Africa
SQUAD NO: 8
HEIGHT: 6ft
NICKNAME: Ted, Dex, Sexy Dexy
EDUCATION: Northwood School Durban; UNISA
TEAMS: Essex, Essex 2nd XI, Kent, Kent 2nd XI, Middlesex
CAREER: First-class: 2005; List A: 2005; T20: 2006

BEST BATTING: 146 Middlesex vs Kent, Uxbridge, 2009
BEST BOWLING: 3-46 Middlesex vs Surrey, Lord's, 2011
COUNTY CAP: 2010 (Middlesex)

CRICKETERS PARTICULARLY ADMIRED? Steve Waugh, Brett Lee
OTHER SPORTS PLAYED? Golf, tennis
FAVOURITE BAND? Simple Plan, Goo Goo Dolls
CRICKET MOMENTS TO FORGET? Being hit for 25 in one over against Worcestershire
RELAXATIONS? Lying around doing nothing
NOTES: Became the third youngest captain in Middlesex's history after replacing Shaun Udal midway through the 2010 county season. Signed for the club in 2008 after rejecting a three-year contract extension with Kent, who he joined as a Kolpak player in 2005. Captained Middlesex to the County Championship Division Two title in 2011. Had a loan spell with Essex in 2008. Played for Natal U13-U19, Natal Academy and Natal A in his native country of South Africa

| Batting | Mat | Inns | NO | Runs | HS | Ave | SR | 100 | 50 | Ct | St |
|---------|-----|------|-----|------|------|-------|--------|-----|----|----|----|
| First-class | 64 | 103 | 15 | 3516 | 146 | 39.95 | 55.34 | 8 | 18 | 55 | 0 |
| List A | 62 | 55 | 12 | 1464 | 135* | 34.04 | 81.55 | 2 | 6 | 15 | 0 |
| Twenty20 | 67 | 59 | 6 | 1106 | 73 | 20.86 | 110.93 | 0 | 2 | 26 | 0 |

| Bowling | Mat | Balls | Runs | Wkts | BBI | BBM | Ave | Econ | SR | 5w | 10 |
|---------|-----|-------|------|------|------|------|-------|------|------|----|----|
| First-class | 64 | 2773 | 1578 | 37 | 3/46 | | 42.64 | 3.41 | 74.9 | 0 | 0 |
| List A | 62 | 1349 | 1187 | 24 | 3/17 | 3/17 | 49.45 | 5.27 | 56.2 | 0 | 0 |
| Twenty20 | 67 | 665 | 836 | 31 | 4/21 | 4/21 | 26.96 | 7.54 | 21.4 | 0 | 0 |

# MICHAEL DI VENUTO

## LHB RM R10

FULL NAME: Michael James Di Venuto
BORN: December 12, 1973, Hobart, Australia
SQUAD NO: 23
HEIGHT: 5ft 11in
NICKNAME: Diva, Nutes
EDUCATION: St Virgil's College, Hobart
TEAMS: Australia, Italy, Australia A, Derbyshire, Derbyshire 2nd XI, Durham, Northern Territory Cricket Association Invitation XI, Sussex, Sussex 2nd XI, Tasmania
CAREER: ODI: 1997; First-class: 1991; List A: 1992; T20: 2003

DURHAM

BEST BATTING: 254* Durham vs Sussex, Chester-le-Street, 2009
BEST BOWLING: 1-0 Tasmania vs Queensland, Brisbane, 2000
COUNTY CAPS: 1999 (Sussex); 2000 (Derbyshire)

FAMILY TIES? Dad played and coached bush cricket for years. My brother Peter was also a talented cricketer
CAREER HIGHLIGHTS? Playing for Australia and winning first ever four-day titles for Tasmania and Durham
SUPERSTITIONS? I like to call them habits! Too many to list
CRICKETING HEROES? Viv Richards, Dennis Lillee
NON-CRICKETING HEROES? Gary Ablett Sr – a former Aussie rules great
BEST PLAYER IN COUNTY CRICKET? Marcus Trescothick by a distance
TIPS FOR THE TOP? Ben Stokes and Scott Borthwick are going nicely at the moment
IF YOU WEREN'T A CRICKETER? Playing Aussie rules was my dream as a kid
WHEN RAIN STOPS PLAY? Hit the papers
FAVOURITE FILM? The Hangover
FAVOURITE BOOK? In The Firing Line by Ed Cowan
SURPRISING SKILL? My dad is a concrete contractor so I'm quite handy on the trowel

| Batting | Mat | Inns | NO | Runs | HS | Ave | SR | 100 | 50 | Ct | St |
|---|---|---|---|---|---|---|---|---|---|---|---|
| ODIs | 9 | 9 | 0 | 241 | 89 | 26.77 | 85.76 | 0 | 2 | 1 | 0 |
| First-class | 331 | 581 | 42 | 24909 | 254* | 46.21 | | 60 | 145 | 406 | 0 |
| List A | 302 | 296 | 18 | 9217 | 173* | 33.15 | | 15 | 48 | 123 | 0 |
| Twenty20 | 47 | 45 | 5 | 993 | 95* | 24.82 | 125.06 | 0 | 7 | 10 | 0 |

| Bowling | Mat | Balls | Runs | Wkts | BBI | BBM | Ave | Econ | SR | 5w | 10 |
|---|---|---|---|---|---|---|---|---|---|---|---|
| ODIs | 9 | - | - | - | - | - | - | - | - | - | - |
| First-class | 331 | 807 | 484 | 5 | 1/0 | | 96.80 | 3.59 | 161.4 | 0 | 0 |
| List A | 302 | 200 | 181 | 5 | 1/10 | 1/10 | 36.20 | 5.43 | 40.0 | 0 | 0 |
| Twenty20 | 47 | 78 | 88 | 5 | 3/19 | 3/19 | 17.60 | 6.76 | 15.6 | 0 | 0 |

## ADAM DIBBLE

**RHB RMF**

**SOMERSET**

FULL NAME: Adam John Dibble
BORN: March 9, 1991, Exeter, Devon
SQUAD NO: 16
HEIGHT: 6ft 4in
NICKNAME: Dibbs, Officer
EDUCATION: St John's School, Sidmouth;
Taunton School
TEAMS: Devon, Somerset, Somerset 2nd XI
CAREER: First-class: 2011; List A: 2011; T20:
2011

---

BEST BATTING: 39* Somerset vs Nottinghamshire, Nottingham, 2011
BEST BOWLING: 1-26 Somerset vs Yorkshire, Leeds, 2011

---

FAMILY TIES? Dad plays club cricket for Sidmouth, sister for Devon and England Academy
CAREER HIGHLIGHTS? Champions League semi-final, 9-27 for Somerset 2nd XI
CRICKETING HEROES? Kumar Sangakkara, Chris Gayle
NON-CRICKETING HEROES? David Beckham, Jonny Wilkinson, Coldplay
BEST PLAYER IN COUNTY CRICKET? Marcus Trescothick
TIP FOR THE TOP? Jamie Overton
IF YOU WEREN'T A CRICKETER? Job hunting
WHEN RAIN STOPS PLAY? Music, reading
FAVOURITE TV? Sherlock
FAVOURITE FILM? Hitch
DREAM HOLIDAY? Dubai, the Maldives
ACCOMPLISHMENTS? Occasionally beating Charl Willoughby at Scrabble!
GUILTY PLEASURES? Chocolate, Westlife
FANTASY SLIP CORDON? Keeper: David Beckham, 1st: Jonny Wilkinson, 2nd: Stephen Fry,
3rd: Peter Kay, Gully: Lee Evans
TWITTER FEED: @adam_dibble

| Batting | Mat | Inns | NO | Runs | HS | Ave | SR | 100 | 50 | Ct | St |
|---------|-----|------|----|------|-----|-------|-------|-----|----|----|----|
| First-class | 2 | 4 | 2 | 40 | 39* | 20.00 | 59.70 | 0 | 0 | 0 | 0 |
| List A | 4 | - | - | - | - | - | - | - | - | 0 | 0 |
| Twenty20 | 2 | - | - | - | - | - | - | - | - | 0 | 0 |

| Bowling | Mat | Balls | Runs | Wkts | BBI | BBM | Ave | Econ | SR | 5w | 10 |
|---------|-----|-------|------|------|------|------|-------|------|-------|----|----|
| First-class | 2 | 216 | 142 | 2 | 1/26 | 1/57 | 71.00 | 3.94 | 108.0 | 0 | 0 |
| List A | 4 | 156 | 170 | 5 | 3/52 | 3/52 | 34.00 | 6.53 | 31.2 | 0 | 0 |
| Twenty20 | 2 | 48 | 44 | 2 | 1/20 | 1/20 | 22.00 | 5.50 | 24.0 | 0 | 0 |

FULL NAME: Paul Garrod Dixey
BORN: November 2, 1987, Canterbury
SQUAD NO: 10
HEIGHT: 5ft 9in
NICKNAME: Dico, Austin
EDUCATION: The King's School, Canterbury;
Durham University
TEAMS: Durham MCCU, England Under-19s,
Kent, Leicestershire, Leicestershire 2nd XI,
Marylebone Cricket Club
CAREER: First-class: 2005; List A: 2007

**LEICESTERSHIRE**

BEST BATTING: 103 DUCCE vs Lancashire, Durham University, 2009

CAREER HIGHLIGHTS? Maiden first-class hundred
SUPERSTITIONS? No, Jacques du Toit uses them all
CRICKETING HEROES? Sachin Tendulkar
NON-CRICKETING HEROES? Jonny Wilkinson
BEST PLAYER IN COUNTY CRICKET? Marcus Trescothick
TIPS FOR THE TOP? James Taylor, Josh Cobb, Sam Northeast
IF YOU WEREN'T A CRICKETER? Either looking at rocks or Excel spreadsheets
WHEN RAIN STOPS PLAY? Doing everything possible to avoid Wayne White
FAVOURITE TV? Made In Chelsea
FAVOURITE FILM? A River Runs Through It, Gladiator
DREAM HOLIDAY? A cruise around the Caribbean
ACCOMPLISHMENTS? Living with Wayne White for a season
SURPRISING SKILL? I'm a keen fly fisherman
GUILTY PLEASURES? Westlife, Made In Chelsea
FANTASY SLIP CORDON? Keeper: Myself, 1st: Karl Pilkington (entertainment value), 2nd:
Megan Fox (self-explanatory), 3rd: Andy Flower (to tell me everything I'm doing wrong),
Gully: Angelina Jolie (to up the female to male ratio a little)
TWITTER FEED: @pauldixey10

| Batting | Mat | Inns | NO | Runs | HS | Ave | SR | 100 | 50 | Ct | St |
|---|---|---|---|---|---|---|---|---|---|---|---|
| First-class | 19 | 32 | 2 | 562 | 103 | 18.73 | 44.11 | 1 | 2 | 42 | 7 |
| List A | 10 | 9 | 2 | 95 | 42 | 13.57 | 86.36 | 0 | 0 | 6 | 0 |
| Bowling | Mat | Balls | Runs | Wkts | BBI | BBM | Ave | Econ | SR | 5w | 10 |
| First-class | 19 | - | - | - | - | - | - | - | - | - | - |
| List A | 10 | - | - | - | - | - | - | - | - | - | - |

# GEORGE DOCKRELL RHB SLA

FULL NAME: George Henry Dockrell
BORN: July 22, 1992, Dublin, Ireland
SQUAD NO: 20
HEIGHT: 6ft 3in
NICKNAME: Potatoe, Doc
EDUCATION: Gonzaga College, Dublin;
Trinity College, Dublin
TEAMS: Ireland, Ireland Under-13s, Ireland
Under-15s, Ireland Under-19s, Somerset,
Somerset 2nd XI
CAREER: ODI: 2010; T20I: 2010; First-class:
2010; List A: 2010; T20: 2010

BEST BATTING: 53 Ireland vs Namibia, Belfast, 2011
BEST BOWLING: 5-37 Ireland vs Kenya, Mombasa, 2012

CAREER HIGHLIGHTS? Playing for Ireland in the World T20 in the West Indies, the World Cup in India and also playing with Somerset in the Champions League in India
CRICKETING HEROES? Daniel Vettori would be my cricketing hero. He has performed consistently for New Zealand for a long time in all forms of the game
NON-CRICKETING HEROES? Brian O'Driscoll, again for his consistent performances and his contribution to Irish rugby
TIPS FOR THE TOP? Last year was my first full season of county cricket so I haven't seen many young players, but I have seen a lot of Lewis Gregory who I think will do very well this year
ACCOMPLISHMENTS? Being selected in the Irish U16 hockey squad
GUILTY PLEASURES? Making 'rocky road' with Alex Barrow
AMAZE ME! 1. I live with Alex Barrow, Lewis Gregory, Chris Jones and Calum Haggett in Taunton 2. I cannot cook to save my life 3. I've never had a cup of tea or coffee!
TWITTER FEED: @georgedockrell

| Batting | Mat | Inns | NO | Runs | HS | Ave | SR | 100 | 50 | Ct | St |
|---|---|---|---|---|---|---|---|---|---|---|---|
| ODIs | 28 | 15 | 8 | 71 | 19 | 10.14 | 76.34 | 0 | 0 | 13 | 0 |
| T20Is | 11 | 3 | 2 | 2 | 2* | 2.00 | 25.00 | 0 | 0 | 1 | 0 |
| First-class | 8 | 9 | 1 | 117 | 53 | 14.62 | 38.23 | 0 | 1 | 4 | 0 |
| List A | 37 | 18 | 10 | 105 | 22* | 13.12 | 82.03 | 0 | 0 | 17 | 0 |
| Twenty20 | 24 | 5 | 4 | 2 | 2* | 2.00 | 22.22 | 0 | 0 | 9 | 0 |

| Bowling | Mat | Balls | Runs | Wkts | BBI | BBM | Ave | Econ | SR | 5w | 10 |
|---|---|---|---|---|---|---|---|---|---|---|---|
| ODIs | 28 | 1329 | 932 | 35 | 4/35 | 4/35 | 26.62 | 4.20 | 37.9 | 0 | 0 |
| T20Is | 11 | 243 | 197 | 20 | 4/20 | 4/20 | 9.85 | 4.86 | 12.1 | 0 | 0 |
| First-class | 8 | 1143 | 645 | 29 | 5/37 | 9/87 | 22.24 | 3.38 | 39.4 | 2 | 0 |
| List A | 37 | 1725 | 1219 | 44 | 4/35 | 4/35 | 27.70 | 4.24 | 39.2 | 0 | 0 |
| Twenty20 | 24 | 477 | 485 | 32 | 4/20 | 4/20 | 15.15 | 6.10 | 14.9 | 0 | 0 |

# JACQUES DU TOIT

## RHB RMF

FULL NAME: Jacques Du Toit
BORN: January 2, 1980, Port Elizabeth, South Africa
SQUAD NO: 8
EDUCATION: Elspark School, Germiston; Oosterlig College; University of Pretoria
TEAMS: Colombo Cricket Club, Easterns, Leicestershire
CAREER: First-class: 1999; List A: 2004; T20: 2008

**LEICESTERSHIRE**

BEST BATTING: 154 Leicestershire vs CMCCU, Fenner's, 2010
BEST BOWLING: 3-31 Leicestershire vs Gloucestershire, Leicester, 2008

NOTES: Arrived at Leicestershire via the East Anglian Leagues. Played in all competitions in 2008, scoring two centuries in the process. After his maiden first-class century (103) against Northamptonshire he went on to score 144 off 119 balls in the Pro40 game against Glamorgan at Colwyn Bay in August 2008, but couldn't prevent a four-wicket defeat. In 2010 he scored 899 first-class runs at an average of 47.31 and 485 List A runs at 44.09 and was named Leicestershire's Supporters' Player of the Year. He featured in six first-class games in 2011, with his best score for the season coming against Loughborough MCCU when he made 97

| Batting | Mat | Inns | NO | Runs | HS | Ave | SR | 100 | 50 | Ct | St |
|---|---|---|---|---|---|---|---|---|---|---|---|
| First-class | 35 | 55 | 3 | 1817 | 154 | 34.94 | | 4 | 10 | 28 | 0 |
| List A | 47 | 44 | 2 | 1147 | 144 | 27.30 | 87.69 | 2 | 4 | 19 | 0 |
| Twenty20 | 52 | 46 | 6 | 632 | 69 | 15.80 | 120.61 | 0 | 1 | 25 | 0 |

| Bowling | Mat | Balls | Runs | Wkts | BBI | BBM | Ave | Econ | SR | 5w | 10 |
|---|---|---|---|---|---|---|---|---|---|---|---|
| First-class | 35 | 516 | 382 | 6 | 3/31 | | 63.66 | 4.44 | 86.0 | 0 | 0 |
| List A | 47 | 66 | 66 | 2 | 2/30 | 2/30 | 33.00 | 6.00 | 33.0 | 0 | 0 |
| Twenty20 | 52 | 32 | 41 | 2 | 2/15 | 2/15 | 20.50 | 7.68 | 16.0 | 0 | 0 |

SURREY

FULL NAME: Matthew Peter Dunn
BORN: May 5, 1992, Egham, Surrey
SQUAD NO: 4
HEIGHT: 6ft 1in
NICKNAME: Dunny
EDUCATION: Bishopsgate School; Bearwood College
TEAMS: England Under-15s, England Under-19s, Surrey, Surrey Under-15s, Surrey Under-17s, Surrey Under-19s
CAREER: First-class: 2010; List A: 2011

BEST BATTING: 2* Surrey vs CMCCU, Fenner's, 2011
BEST BOWLING: 5-56 Surrey vs Derbyshire, Derby, 2011

CAREER HIGHLIGHTS? When I signed my first professional contract, being selected for the England U19 side and taking five wickets on debut against Derbyshire
CRICKETING HEROES? Brett Lee, Dale Steyn, Andrew Flintoff
NON-CRICKETING HEROES? James Corden, Lance Armstrong
BEST PLAYER IN COUNTY CRICKET? Marcus Trescothick
TIPS FOR THE TOP? Jason Roy, Tom Maynard, Rory Burns, Tymal Mills, Dominic Sibley
IF YOU WEREN'T A CRICKETER? Trying to become a rugby player instead or possibly working in business
WHEN RAIN STOPS PLAY? Game of eye spy, read the paper, do the crossword, have a sleep
FAVOURITE TV? An Idiot Abroad
FAVOURITE FILM? The Prestige
DREAM HOLIDAY? Grand Canyon
ACCOMPLISHMENTS? NVQ in Sporting Excellence
SURPRISING SKILL? Doing foreign accents (speciality eastern European)
GUILTY PLEASURES? Lindor chocolates
AMAZE ME! I lived in Norway for two years as a child, I was born with dark red hair, I had a panic attack the first time I ever went to a cricket club practice session because I didn't think I would be any good and went home!
TWITTER FEED: @matthewdunn05

| Batting | Mat | Inns | NO | Runs | HS | Ave | SR | 100 | 50 | Ct | St |
|---|---|---|---|---|---|---|---|---|---|---|---|
| First-class | 4 | 5 | 5 | 3 | 2* | - | 11.53 | 0 | 0 | 0 | 0 |
| List A | 1 | - | - | - | - | - | - | - | - | 1 | 0 |

| Bowling | Mat | Balls | Runs | Wkts | BBI | BBM | Ave | Econ | SR | 5w | 10 |
|---|---|---|---|---|---|---|---|---|---|---|---|
| First-class | 4 | 324 | 241 | 9 | 5/56 | 5/68 | 26.77 | 4.46 | 36.0 | 1 | 0 |
| List A | 1 | 36 | 32 | 2 | 2/32 | 2/32 | 16.00 | 5.33 | 18.0 | 0 | 0 |

# WES DURSTON

## RHB OB R1 MVP22

FULL NAME: Wesley John Durston
BORN: October 6, 1980, Taunton, Somerset
SQUAD NO: 3
HEIGHT: 5ft 9in
NICKNAME: Bestie, Durst
EDUCATION: Millfield School, Glastonbury; University College, Worcester
TEAMS: Derbyshire, Somerset, Somerset Cricket Board, Unicorns
CAREER: First-class: 2002; List A: 2000; T20: 2003

BEST BATTING: 151 Derbyshire vs Gloucestershire, Derby, 2011
BEST BOWLING: 4-45 Derbyshire vs Kent, Derby, 2011

WHY CRICKET? Watched my dad play every weekend growing up and then played at school. I've been brought up around the game and have always loved it
CAREER HIGHLIGHTS? Winning the T20 in 2005, Division Two in 2007 – both with Somerset – and also playing in the Champions League
SUPERSTITIONS? Right foot on and off the pitch first. Always place my bat over the crease in the same place as and when I return to it
CRICKETING HEROES? Ian Botham, Shane Warne, Brian Lara
NON-CRICKETING HEROES? Eric Cantona, Tiger Woods, Gary Lineker
BEST PLAYER IN COUNTY CRICKET? Marcus Trescothick
TIPS FOR THE TOP? Ross Whiteley, Jos Buttler, Joseph Durston
IF YOU WEREN'T A CRICKETER? I'd be a teacher
WHEN RAIN STOPS PLAY? Coffee and crossword
FAVOURITE TV? CSI or Criminal Minds
FAVOURITE FILM? Star Wars
FAVOURITE BOOK? Any sporting biography or Point Of Origin by Patricia Cornwell
DREAM HOLIDAY? The Caribbean
ACCOMPLISHMENTS? Being a father to Daisy and Joseph

| Batting | Mat | Inns | NO | Runs | HS | Ave | SR | 100 | 50 | Ct | St |
|---|---|---|---|---|---|---|---|---|---|---|---|
| First-class | 56 | 99 | 15 | 3104 | 151 | 36.95 | 58.55 | 4 | 20 | 50 | 0 |
| List A | 80 | 70 | 17 | 1833 | 117 | 34.58 | | | 1 | 12 | 22 | 0 |
| Twenty20 | 68 | 59 | 10 | 1113 | 111 | 22.71 | 120.32 | 1 | 5 | 26 | 0 |

| Bowling | Mat | Balls | Runs | Wkts | BBI | BBM | Ave | Econ | SR | 5w | 10 |
|---|---|---|---|---|---|---|---|---|---|---|---|
| First-class | 56 | 2837 | 1841 | 33 | 4/45 | | 55.78 | 3.89 | 85.9 | 0 | 0 |
| List A | 80 | 1245 | 1192 | 32 | 3/7 | 3/7 | 37.25 | 5.74 | 38.9 | 0 | 0 |
| Twenty20 | 68 | 474 | 678 | 32 | 3/25 | 3/25 | 21.18 | 8.58 | 14.8 | 0 | 0 |

## NED ECKERSLEY — RHB WK

**LEICESTERSHIRE**

FULL NAME: Edmund James Eckersley
BORN: August 9, 1989, Oxford
SQUAD NO: 33
HEIGHT: 6ft
EDUCATION: St Benedict's School, Ealing
TEAMS: Leicestershire, Leicestershire 2nd XI, Marylebone Cricket Club, Marylebone Cricket Club Young Cricketers, Middlesex 2nd XI, Mountaineers
CAREER: First-class: 2011; List A: 2008; T20: 2011

BEST BATTING: 106 Leicestershire vs Middlesex, Leicester, 2011

WHY CRICKET? Just loved to play all the time in the summer
CAREER HIGHLIGHTS? Scoring my maiden first-class hundred in the last game of the 2011 season
CRICKETING HEROES? Alec Stewart
BEST PLAYER IN COUNTY CRICKET? Marcus Trescothick
TIP FOR THE TOP? Alex Hales
IF YOU WEREN'T A CRICKETER? Studying at university
WHEN RAIN STOPS PLAY? Cards, listening to iPod
FAVOURITE TV? 24
FAVOURITE FILM? Blood Diamond
DREAM HOLIDAY? Cuba or Maldives
GUILTY PLEASURES? Westlife
FANTASY SLIP CORDON? Keeper: Nelson Mandela, 1st: Michael McIntyre, 2nd: Freddie Flintoff, 3rd: Myself, Gully: David Beckham
TWITTER FEED: @nedeckersley

| Batting | Mat | Inns | NO | Runs | HS | Ave | SR | 100 | 50 | Ct | St |
|---|---|---|---|---|---|---|---|---|---|---|---|
| First-class | 7 | 12 | 0 | 447 | 106 | 37.25 | 45.06 | 1 | 3 | 28 | 0 |
| List A | 4 | 3 | 1 | 28 | 27* | 14.00 | 77.77 | 0 | 0 | 6 | 0 |
| Twenty20 | 5 | 5 | 3 | 29 | 12* | 14.50 | 76.31 | 0 | 0 | 2 | 1 |

| Bowling | Mat | Balls | Runs | Wkts | BBI | BBM | Ave | Econ | SR | 5w | 10 |
|---|---|---|---|---|---|---|---|---|---|---|---|
| First-class | 7 | - | - | - | - | - | - | - | - | - | - |
| List A | 4 | - | - | - | - | - | - | - | - | - | - |
| Twenty20 | 5 | - | - | - | - | - | - | - | - | - | - |

# GEORGE EDWARDS

**RHB RFM**

FULL NAME: George Alexander Edwards
BORN: July 29, 1992, King's College Hospital, Lambeth, London
SQUAD NO: 56
HEIGHT: 6ft 5in
NICKNAME: Chicken
EDUCATION: St. Joesph's College
TEAMS: Surrey, Surrey 2nd XI
CAREER: First-class: 2011

---

BEST BATTING: 19 Surrey vs CMCCU, Fenner's, 2011

---

FAMILY TIES? Dad played a bit, as did my brother, but that's about it
CAREER HIGHLIGHTS? Making first-class debut and signing with Surrey
SUPERSTITIONS? Not really
NON-CRICKETING HEROES? My mum
IF YOU WEREN'T A CRICKETER? Who knows?
WHEN RAIN STOPS PLAY? Sleeping
GUILTY PLEASURES? Love sweets and cheese
FANTASY SLIP CORDON? Keeper: Whoopi Goldberg, 1st: Beyoncé, 2nd: Myself, 3rd: Kelly Rowland, Gully: Angelina Jolie
NOTES: Plays for Spencer CC in Battersea. Signed a professional contract with Surrey last August. Graduate of Surrey's Pemberton Greenish Academy

| Batting | Mat | Inns | NO | Runs | HS | Ave | SR | 100 | 50 | Ct | St |
|---|---|---|---|---|---|---|---|---|---|---|---|
| First-class | 1 | 2 | 0 | 29 | 19 | 14.50 | 34.11 | 0 | 0 | 1 | 0 |

| Bowling | Mat | Balls | Runs | Wkts | BBI | BBM | Ave | Econ | SR | 5w | 10 |
|---|---|---|---|---|---|---|---|---|---|---|---|
| First-class | 1 | 111 | 82 | 0 | - | - | - | 4.43 | - | 0 | 0 |

## NEIL EDWARDS                                    LHB RM R1

FULL NAME: Neil James Edwards
BORN: October 14, 1983, Treliske, Truro, Cornwall
SQUAD NO: 15
HEIGHT: 6ft 3in
NICKNAME: Toastie, Shanksy, Toast, Jedders
EDUCATION: Cape Cornwall School; Richard Huish College
TEAMS: Cornwall, England Under-19s, Somerset
CAREER: First-class: 2002; List A: 2006; T20: 2003

BEST BATTING: 212 Somerset vs LUCCE, Taunton, 2007
BEST BOWLING: 1-16 Somerset vs Derbyshire, Taunton, 2004

CAREER HIGHLIGHTS? England U19 tour of Australia, County Championship winners 2010
CRICKETING HEROES? Marcus Trescothick, Justin Langer
BEST PLAYER IN COUNTY CRICKET? Marcus Trescothick
TIP FOR THE TOP? Alex Hales
WHEN RAIN STOPS PLAY? In the gym or watching TV
FAVOURITE TV? Eastenders
FAVOURITE FILM? Anchorman
FAVOURITE BOOK? Lance Armstrong's autobiography
DREAM HOLIDAY? New York
ACCOMPLISHMENTS? Marrying my beautiful wife Kirsty
GUILTY PLEASURES? Cornish pasty
FANTASY SLIP CORDON? Keeper: Michael McIntyre, 1st: Will Ferrell, 2nd: Me, 3rd: Jennifer Aniston, Gully: Barack Obama

| Batting | Mat | Inns | NO | Runs | HS | Ave | SR | 100 | 50 | Ct | St |
|---------|-----|------|-----|------|-----|-------|-------|-----|-----|-----|-----|
| First-class | 64 | 109 | 3 | 3337 | 212 | 31.48 | 59.31 | 3 | 17 | 61 | 0 |
| List A | 10 | 9 | 0 | 195 | 65 | 21.66 | 68.90 | 0 | 1 | 3 | 0 |
| Twenty20 | 1 | 1 | 0 | 1 | 1 | 1.00 | 14.28 | 0 | 0 | 0 | 0 |

| Bowling | Mat | Balls | Runs | Wkts | BBI | BBM | Ave | Econ | SR | 5w | 10 |
|---------|-----|-------|------|------|-----|-----|-------|------|-------|-----|-----|
| First-class | 64 | 287 | 194 | 2 | 1/16 | | 97.00 | 4.05 | 143.5 | 0 | 0 |
| List A | 10 | - | - | - | - | - | - | - | - | - | - |
| Twenty20 | 1 | - | - | - | - | - | - | - | - | - | - |

# SCOTT ELSTONE — RHB OB

FULL NAME: Scott Liam Elstone
BORN: June 10, 1990, Burton-on-Trent, Staffordshire
SQUAD NO: 17
EDUCATION: Friary Grange School, Lichfield
TEAMS: Nottinghamshire, Nottinghamshire 2nd XI
CAREER: List A: 2010; T20: 2010

NOTTINGHAMSHIRE

NOTES: Joined Nottinghamshire in 2010 as a product of the academy system. Made his one-day debut in the CB40 against Scotland and scored 18 not out from 12 balls. Appeared as a substitute fielder in the Trent Bridge Test between England and India in 2011, taking two catches and in doing so becoming the youngest English substitute to take a catch on home soil since 1998

| Batting | Mat | Inns | NO | Runs | HS | Ave | SR | 100 | 50 | Ct | St |
|---|---|---|---|---|---|---|---|---|---|---|---|
| List A | 13 | 13 | 2 | 251 | 40 | 22.81 | 105.46 | 0 | 0 | 3 | 0 |
| Twenty20 | 16 | 13 | 8 | 91 | 21* | 18.20 | 135.82 | 0 | 0 | 7 | 0 |

| Bowling | Mat | Balls | Runs | Wkts | BBI | BBM | Ave | Econ | SR | 5w | 10 |
|---|---|---|---|---|---|---|---|---|---|---|---|
| List A | 13 | 22 | 22 | 1 | 1/22 | 1/22 | 22.00 | 6.00 | 22.0 | 0 | 0 |
| Twenty20 | 16 | - | - | - | - | - | - | - | - | - | - |

## SEAN ERVINE

## LHB RM MVP66

HAMPSHIRE

**FULL NAME:** Sean Michael Ervine
**BORN:** December 6, 1982, Harare, Zimbabwe
**SQUAD NO:** 7
**HEIGHT:** 6ft 2in
**NICKNAME:** Slug, Lion
**EDUCATION:** Lomagundi College
**TEAMS:** Zimbabwe, Hampshire, Midlands, Southern Rocks, Western Australia
**CAREER:** Test: 2003; ODI: 2001; First-class: 2001; List A: 2001; T20: 2005

**BEST BATTING:** 237* Hampshire vs Somerset, Southampton, 2010
**BEST BOWLING:** 6-82 Midlands vs Mashonaland, Kwekwe Sports Club, 2003
**COUNTY CAP:** 2005

**FAMILY TIES?** Father Rory played first-class cricket in Zimbabwe. Brother Craig plays for the current Zimbabwe team. Brother Ryan plays for the franchise Southern Rocks in Zimbabwe. Uncle Neil played first-class cricket in Zimbabwe
**CAREER HIGHLIGHTS?** 100 vs India at Adelaide Oval in the 2004/05 VB series. Hundreds and Man of the Match in both the semi-final and final of the C&G Trophy in 2005. Four wickets vs Australia in the first Test match in Perth in 2003 for Zimbabwe. Scoring 208 and 160 in the same game for the Southern Rocks in 2010. Playing in the 2003 World Cup in South Africa. Playing with Shane Warne at Hampshire
**TIPS FOR THE TOP?** James Vince, Chris Wood, Ben Stokes
**FAVOURITE TV?** Sky Sports News, Discovery and National Geographic
**SURPRISING SKILL?** Can open a bottle with another bottle (beer, that is)
**GUILTY PLEASURES?** Biltong, Bounty chocolate, sticky toffee pudding
**TWITTER FEED:** @Slug_7

| Batting | Mat | Inns | NO | Runs | HS | Ave | SR | 100 | 50 | Ct | St |
|---|---|---|---|---|---|---|---|---|---|---|---|
| Tests | 5 | 8 | 0 | 261 | 86 | 32.62 | 55.41 | 0 | 3 | 7 | 0 |
| ODIs | 42 | 34 | 7 | 698 | 100 | 25.85 | 85.53 | 1 | 2 | 5 | 0 |
| First-class | 132 | 211 | 22 | 6557 | 237* | 34.69 | | 12 | 33 | 103 | 0 |
| List A | 181 | 163 | 26 | 4337 | 167* | 31.65 | | 7 | 17 | 50 | 0 |
| Twenty20 | 94 | 88 | 20 | 1712 | 82 | 25.17 | 131.59 | 0 | 7 | 34 | 0 |

| Bowling | Mat | Balls | Runs | Wkts | BBI | BBM | Ave | Econ | SR | 5w | 10 |
|---|---|---|---|---|---|---|---|---|---|---|---|
| Tests | 5 | 570 | 388 | 9 | 4/146 | 4/146 | 43.11 | 4.08 | 63.3 | 0 | 0 |
| ODIs | 42 | 1649 | 1561 | 41 | 3/29 | 3/29 | 38.07 | 5.67 | 40.2 | 0 | 0 |
| First-class | 132 | 14509 | 8759 | 197 | 6/82 | | 44.46 | 3.62 | 73.6 | 5 | 0 |
| List A | 181 | 6319 | 5904 | 172 | 5/50 | 5/50 | 34.32 | 5.60 | 36.7 | 2 | 0 |
| Twenty20 | 94 | 920 | 1352 | 54 | 4/12 | 4/12 | 25.03 | 8.81 | 17.0 | 0 | 0 |

## LAURIE EVANS · RHB RMF

**FULL NAME:** Laurie John Evans
**BORN:** October 12, 1987, Lambeth, London
**SQUAD NO:** 32
**HEIGHT:** 6ft 1in
**NICKNAME:** LJ, Loz
**EDUCATION:** Whitgift School; The John Fisher School; Durham University
**TEAMS:** Durham MCCU, ECB Development of Excellence XI, Malden Wanderers, Marylebone Cricket Club, Surrey, Surrey 2nd XI, Warwickshire
**CAREER:** First-class: 2007; List A: 2009; T20: 2009

**BEST BATTING:** 133* DUCCE vs Lancashire, Durham University, 2011
**BEST BOWLING:** 1-30 Surrey vs Bangladeshis, The Oval, 2010

**CAREER HIGHLIGHTS?** Maiden first-class hundred
**SUPERSTITIONS?** None
**CRICKETING HEROES?** Viv Richards
**NON-CRICKETING HEROES?** Mick Skinner
**BEST PLAYER IN COUNTY CRICKET?** Ian Bell
**IF YOU WEREN'T A CRICKETER?** Rugby player
**WHEN RAIN STOPS PLAY?** I'm bored
**FAVOURITE FILM?** The Boat That Rocked
**DREAM HOLIDAY?** Barbados
**ACCOMPLISHMENTS?** Golf handicap of eight, going down. Won Daily Mail rugby competition. Played in Harlequins Academy
**SURPRISING SKILL?** I play piano and guitar and work as a part-time chef
**GUILTY PLEASURES?** Clothes, trainers and accessories
**AMAZE ME!** My uncle Greg Searle is an Olympic gold medallist, soon to be twice in 2012
**FANTASY SLIP CORDON?** Keeper: Justin Timberlake, 1st: Mick Jagger, 2nd: Peter Kay, 3rd: David Attenborough
**TWITTER FEED:** @lj32evans

| Batting | Mat | Inns | NO | Runs | HS | Ave | SR | 100 | 50 | Ct | St |
|---|---|---|---|---|---|---|---|---|---|---|---|
| First-class | 12 | 22 | 1 | 667 | 133* | 31.76 | 46.15 | 1 | 4 | 7 | 0 |
| List A | 2 | 2 | 1 | 39 | 36* | 39.00 | 95.12 | 0 | 0 | 2 | 0 |
| Twenty20 | 1 | 1 | 0 | 7 | 7 | 7.00 | 87.50 | 0 | 0 | 0 | 0 |

| Bowling | Mat | Balls | Runs | Wkts | BBI | BBM | Ave | Econ | SR | 5w | 10 |
|---|---|---|---|---|---|---|---|---|---|---|---|
| First-class | 12 | 36 | 30 | 1 | 1/30 | 1/30 | 30.00 | 5.00 | 36.0 | 0 | 0 |
| List A | 2 | - | - | - | - | - | - | - | - | - | - |
| Twenty20 | 1 | - | - | - | - | - | - | - | - | - | - |

# LUKE EVANS

## RHB RMF

**FULL NAME:** Luke Evans
**BORN:** April 26, 1987, Sunderland, Co Durham
**SQUAD NO:** 25
**HEIGHT:** 6ft 7in
**NICKNAME:** Daisy Duke, Longshanks, Lukey, Evo, Cool Hand
**EDUCATION:** St Aidan's RC School and Sixth Form
**TEAMS:** Durham, Durham 2nd XI, Northamptonshire
**CAREER:** First-class: 2007; List A: 2009; T20: 2011

---

**BEST BATTING:** 8* Northamptonshire vs Gloucestershire, Bristol, 2010
**BEST BOWLING:** 3-21 Northamptonshire vs LMCCU, Loughborough, 2011

---

**FAMILY TIES?** My dad played the anchor batsman role for Farringdon Comprehensive School in Sunderland
**CAREER HIGHLIGHTS?** Taking wickets against India in the 2011 tour match for Northants in front of a packed crowd at Wantage Road is something that sticks out for me. The real highlights are still to come
**CRICKETING HEROES?** Everyone associated with Chester-le-Street CC, Ian Dawson, Curtly Ambrose, Stephen Harmison, Dale Steyn
**TIP FOR THE TOP?** Ben Stokes
**WHEN RAIN STOPS PLAY?** Studying, listening to music and boring everyone with the meteorological detail of what is overhead
**FAVOURITE TV?** QI, Not Going Out, Family Guy
**FAVOURITE FILM?** The Lion King
**FAVOURITE BOOK?** The Lord Of The Rings and the works of Roald Dahl
**ACCOMPLISHMENTS?** Getting my pilot's licence
**SURPRISING SKILL?** I play guitar, bass guitar and a bit of piano, I have isolated moments of greatness on the dartboard and basketball court, I can draw quite well and can also fly aeroplanes

| Batting | Mat | Inns | NO | Runs | HS | Ave | SR | 100 | 50 | Ct | St |
|---|---|---|---|---|---|---|---|---|---|---|---|
| First-class | 6 | 7 | 4 | 26 | 8* | 8.66 | 29.21 | 0 | 0 | 1 | 0 |
| List A | 7 | 3 | 1 | 19 | 18 | 9.50 | 33.92 | 0 | 0 | 2 | 0 |
| Twenty20 | 3 | - | - | - | - | - | - | - | - | 0 | 0 |

| Bowling | Mat | Balls | Runs | Wkts | BBI | BBM | Ave | Econ | SR | 5w | 10 |
|---|---|---|---|---|---|---|---|---|---|---|---|
| First-class | 6 | 685 | 452 | 14 | 3/21 | 4/77 | 32.28 | 3.95 | 48.9 | 0 | 0 |
| List A | 7 | 192 | 227 | 5 | 2/53 | 2/53 | 45.40 | 7.09 | 38.4 | 0 | 0 |
| Twenty20 | 3 | 54 | 70 | 3 | 1/15 | 1/15 | 23.33 | 7.77 | 18.0 | 0 | 0 |

## TOM FELL                                RHB WK

FULL NAME: Thomas Charles Fell
BORN: October 17, 1993, Hillingdon, Middlesex
SQUAD NO: 29
HEIGHT: 6ft 1in
NICKNAME: Felly
EDUCATION: Oakham School
TEAMS: Staffordshire Under-13s, Staffordshire Under-14s, Staffordshire Under-15s, Staffordshire Under-17s, Worcestershire 2nd XI, Worcestershire Academy
CAREER: Yet to make first-team debut

WORCESTERSHIRE

**FAMILY TIES?** My father was a Cambridge Blue
**CAREER HIGHLIGHTS?** Playing for the MCC Schools at Lord's last year, breaking the school record for most runs scored in a season and scoring a double century for Staffs U17
**SUPERSTITIONS?** I tread on the rope as I go out to bat
**CRICKETING HEROES?** Sachin Tendulkar
**NON-CRICKETING HEROES?** Lionel Messi, Gareth Bale, Matt Hampson
**BEST PLAYER IN COUNTY CRICKET?** Marcus Trescothick
**TIPS FOR THE TOP?** Aneesh Kapil and Shiv Thakor
**IF YOU WEREN'T A CRICKETER?** I may be working harder at school!
**WHEN RAIN STOPS PLAY?** Listening to music or playing one hand-one bounce in the changing room
**FAVOURITE TV?** Sky Sports News and Top Gear
**FAVOURITE FILM?** Gladiator
**FAVOURITE BOOK?** Holes by Louis Sachar
**DREAM HOLIDAY?** Anywhere hot where they play cricket – the Caribbean probably
**SURPRISING SKILL?** I'm a mean darts player!
**GUILTY PLEASURES?** Kentucky Fried Chicken and playing FIFA on the PlayStation
**AMAZE ME!** I once sang a solo in a school musical, I can hardly swim, I am a single-figure handicapper at golf
**FANTASY SLIP CORDON?** Keeper: Me, 1st: Jeff Stelling, 2nd: Jeremy Clarkson, 3rd: Harry Redknapp, Gully: David Lloyd (Bumble)

# STEVEN FINN

## RHB RF W2

**FULL NAME:** Steven Thomas Finn
**BORN:** April 4, 1989, Watford, Hertfordshire
**SQUAD NO:** 9
**HEIGHT:** 6ft 7in
**NICKNAME:** Finny, Lurch, Neil
**EDUCATION:** Parmiter's School, Watford
**TEAMS:** England, England Lions, England Under-19s, Middlesex, Middlesex 2nd XI, Otago
**CAREER:** Test: 2010; ODI: 2011; T20I: 2011; First-class: 2005; List A: 2007; T20: 2008

BEST BATTING: 32 Middlesex vs Essex, Lord's, 2011
BEST BOWLING: 9-37 Middlesex vs Worcestershire, Worcester, 2010
COUNTY CAP: 2009

FAMILY TIES? Father played club and minor counties cricket. Grandfather played club cricket. Grew up around cricket grounds
CAREER HIGHLIGHTS? Winning the Ashes in Australia. Taking 5-87 vs Bangladesh at Lord's and being on the honours board. Test debut vs Bangladesh
CRICKETING HEROES? Glenn McGrath, Angus Fraser
BEST PLAYER IN COUNTY CRICKET? Chris Rogers, Mark Ramprakash, Glen Chapple
WHEN RAIN STOPS PLAY? iPad watching movies. Or being the butt of inappropriate jokes
FAVOURITE TV? Entourage, The Inbetweeners, The Only Way Is Essex
FAVOURITE FILM? Scarface, Carlito's Way, Gladiator
FAVOURITE BOOK? Ben Cousins – My Life Story
TWITTER FEED: @finnysteve

| Batting | Mat | Inns | NO | Runs | HS | Ave | SR | 100 | 50 | Ct | St |
|---|---|---|---|---|---|---|---|---|---|---|---|
| Tests | 12 | 13 | 9 | 35 | 19 | 8.75 | 27.34 | 0 | 0 | 3 | 0 |
| ODIs | 15 | 8 | 5 | 62 | 35 | 20.66 | 93.93 | 0 | 0 | 3 | 0 |
| T20Is | 5 | - | - | - | - | - | - | - | - | 1 | 0 |
| First-class | 66 | 80 | 24 | 402 | 32 | 7.17 | 32.36 | 0 | 0 | 17 | 0 |
| List A | 54 | 19 | 7 | 113 | 35 | 9.41 | 68.48 | 0 | 0 | 7 | 0 |
| Twenty20 | 29 | 5 | 3 | 18 | 8 | 9.00 | 90.00 | 0 | 0 | 5 | 0 |

| Bowling | Mat | Balls | Runs | Wkts | BBI | BBM | Ave | Econ | SR | 5w | 10 |
|---|---|---|---|---|---|---|---|---|---|---|---|
| Tests | 12 | 2074 | 1346 | 50 | 6/125 | 9/187 | 26.92 | 3.89 | 41.4 | 3 | 0 |
| ODIs | 15 | 856 | 670 | 28 | 4/34 | 4/34 | 23.92 | 4.69 | 30.5 | 0 | 0 |
| T20Is | 5 | 108 | 138 | 7 | 3/22 | 3/22 | 19.71 | 7.66 | 15.4 | 0 | 0 |
| First-class | 66 | 11428 | 6638 | 234 | 9/37 | | 28.36 | 3.48 | 48.8 | 7 | 1 |
| List A | 54 | 2398 | 1988 | 78 | 5/33 | 5/33 | 25.48 | 4.97 | 30.7 | 1 | 0 |
| Twenty20 | 29 | 584 | 744 | 29 | 3/22 | 3/22 | 25.65 | 7.64 | 20.1 | 0 | 0 |

FULL NAME: Luke Jack Fletcher
BORN: September 18, 1988, Nottingham
SQUAD NO: 19
HEIGHT: 6ft 6in
NICKNAME: Fletch
EDUCATION: Henry Mellish Comprehensive School
TEAMS: England Under-19s, Nottinghamshire, Nottinghamshire 2nd XI
CAREER: First-class: 2008; List A: 2008; T20: 2009

**NOTTINGHAMSHIRE**

BEST BATTING: 92 Nottinghamshire vs Hampshire, Southampton, 2009
BEST BOWLING: 5-82 Nottinghamshire vs Lancashire, Nottingham, 2011

CAREER HIGHLIGHTS? Making my debut for Notts, winning the Championship and playing in a T20 quarter-final
SUPERSTITIONS? Like to receive the ball from mid off when bowling
CRICKETING HEROES? Freddie Flintoff
BEST PLAYER IN COUNTY CRICKET? Marcus Trescothick, Andre Adams
TIPS FOR THE TOP? George Bacon, Sam Wood
IF YOU WEREN'T A CRICKETER? Still working at Hooters
WHEN RAIN STOPS PLAY? Abuse senior/veteran players
FAVOURITE TV? Take Me Out
FAVOURITE FILM? The Shawshank Redemption
DREAM HOLIDAY? Las Vegas
GUILTY PLEASURES? Chick flicks
SURPRISING FACTS? Played football at Wembley and Old Trafford as a youngster, I enjoy helping out my good friend Johnny Thrower with his groundsman duties at Papplewick and Linby CC and I'm an ex-chef at Hooters
TWITTER FEED: @fletcherluke

| Batting | Mat | Inns | NO | Runs | HS | Ave | SR | 100 | 50 | Ct | St |
|---|---|---|---|---|---|---|---|---|---|---|---|
| First-class | 29 | 40 | 11 | 406 | 92 | 14.00 | 57.67 | 0 | 1 | 5 | 0 |
| List A | 27 | 14 | 5 | 97 | 40* | 10.77 | 94.17 | 0 | 0 | 3 | 0 |
| Twenty20 | 24 | 5 | 3 | 7 | 5 | 3.50 | 46.66 | 0 | 0 | 7 | 0 |

| Bowling | Mat | Balls | Runs | Wkts | BBI | BBM | Ave | Econ | SR | 5w | 10 |
|---|---|---|---|---|---|---|---|---|---|---|---|
| First-class | 29 | 5345 | 2811 | 90 | 5/82 | 8/131 | 31.23 | 3.15 | 59.3 | 1 | 0 |
| List A | 27 | 1112 | 1029 | 28 | 3/27 | 3/27 | 36.75 | 5.55 | 39.7 | 0 | 0 |
| Twenty20 | 24 | 498 | 638 | 26 | 4/30 | 4/30 | 24.53 | 7.68 | 19.1 | 0 | 0 |

## BEN FOAKES                                          RHB WK

FULL NAME: Benjamin Thomas Foakes
BORN: February 15, 1993, Colchester, Essex
SQUAD NO: 4
TEAMS: England Under-17s, England Under-19s, Essex, Essex 2nd XI
CAREER: First-class: 2011

ESSEX

BEST BATTING: 5 Essex vs Sri Lankans, Chelmsford, 2011

NOTES: England U19 wicketkeeper-batsman who made a century batting at No.3 versus Bangladesh U19 in January 2012. Made his senior Essex debut in 2011 against the Sri Lankan tourists, catching Kumar Sangakkara as one of three dismissals. Tipped by Bruce French, the England wicketkeeping coach, as a star of the future

| Batting | Mat | Inns | NO | Runs | HS | Ave | SR | 100 | 50 | Ct | St |
|---|---|---|---|---|---|---|---|---|---|---|---|
| First-class | 1 | 1 | 0 | 5 | 5 | 5.00 | 27.77 | 0 | 0 | 3 | 0 |

| Bowling | Mat | Balls | Runs | Wkts | BBI | BBM | Ave | Econ | SR | 5w | 10 |
|---|---|---|---|---|---|---|---|---|---|---|---|
| First-class | 1 | - | - | - | - | - | - | - | - | - | - | - |

# MARK FOOTITT                                    RHB LFM

**FULL NAME:** Mark Harold Alan Footitt
**BORN:** November 25, 1985, Nottingham
**SQUAD NO:** 4
**HEIGHT:** 6ft 2in
**NICKNAME:** Footy
**EDUCATION:** Carlton Le Willows School
**TEAMS:** Derbyshire, England Under-19s, Marylebone Cricket Club, Nottinghamshire, Nottinghamshire Cricket Board
**CAREER:** First-class: 2005; List A: 2002; T20: 2005

DERBYSHIRE

**BEST BATTING:** 30 Derbyshire vs Surrey, The Oval, 2010
**BEST BOWLING:** 5-45 Nottinghamshire vs West Indies A, Nottingham, 2006

**CAREER HIGHLIGHTS?** My first game for Notts and taking five wickets for Derby
**CRICKETING HEROES?** Brett Lee
**NON-CRICKETING HEROES?** Adam Sandler
**TIP FOR THE TOP?** Ross Whiteley
**WHEN RAIN STOPS PLAY?** Reading newspapers and playing games on my phone
**FAVOURITE TV?** The Simpsons
**DREAM HOLIDAY?** The Maldives
**ACCOMPLISHMENTS?** Being a dad to Heidi Footitt
**GUILTY PLEASURES?** Cheese, garlic pizza bread, cookies
**AMAZE ME!** I started off bowling right-arm then changed to left-arm

| Batting | Mat | Inns | NO | Runs | HS | Ave | SR | 100 | 50 | Ct | St |
|---|---|---|---|---|---|---|---|---|---|---|---|
| First-class | 22 | 26 | 9 | 154 | 30 | 9.05 | 51.33 | 0 | 0 | 7 | 0 |
| List A | 11 | 3 | 1 | 5 | 4 | 2.50 | 83.33 | 0 | 0 | 1 | 0 |
| Twenty20 | 2 | - | - | - | - | - | - | - | - | 0 | 0 |

| Bowling | Mat | Balls | Runs | Wkts | BBI | BBM | Ave | Econ | SR | 5w | 10 |
|---|---|---|---|---|---|---|---|---|---|---|---|
| First-class | 22 | 2942 | 1902 | 61 | 5/45 | | 31.18 | 3.87 | 48.2 | 3 | 0 |
| List A | 11 | 348 | 363 | 10 | 3/20 | 3/20 | 36.30 | 6.25 | 34.8 | 0 | 0 |
| Twenty20 | 2 | 24 | 56 | 0 | - | - | - | 14.00 | - | 0 | 0 |

**ESSEX**

FULL NAME: James Savin Foster
BORN: April 15, 1980, Whipps Cross,
Leytonstone, Essex
SQUAD NO: 7
HEIGHT: 6ft
NICKNAME: Fozzy, Chief
EDUCATION: Forest School; Durham
University
TEAMS: England, Durham MCCU, Essex,
Marylebone Cricket Club
CAREER: Test: 2001; ODI: 2001; T20I: 2009;
First-class: 2000; List A: 2000; T20: 2003

BEST BATTING: 212 Essex vs Leicestershire, Chelmsford, 2004
BEST BOWLING: 1-122 Essex vs Northamptonshire, Northampton, 2008
COUNTY CAP: 2001; BENEFIT YEAR: 2011

FAMILY TIES? Dad played for Essex Amateurs
CAREER HIGHLIGHTS? Playing for my country
CRICKETERS PARTICULARLY ADMIRED? Nasser Hussain, Stuart Law, Robert Rollins, Ian
Healy, Jack Russell, Alec Stewart, Adam Gilchrist
OTHER SPORTS PLAYED? Hockey (Essex U21), tennis (played for GB U14 vs Sweden U14)
OTHER SPORTS FOLLOWED? Football
NOTES: Current Essex captain. Achieved the 'double' of 1,037 runs and 51 dismissals in 2004.
In Pro40 match against Durham in September 2009, he hit five sixes in consecutive balls
from Scott Borthwick

| Batting | Mat | Inns | NO | Runs | HS | Ave | SR | 100 | 50 | Ct | St |
|---|---|---|---|---|---|---|---|---|---|---|---|
| Tests | 7 | 12 | 3 | 226 | 48 | 25.11 | 34.55 | 0 | 0 | 17 | 1 |
| ODIs | 11 | 6 | 3 | 41 | 13 | 13.66 | 57.74 | 0 | 0 | 13 | 7 |
| T20Is | 5 | 5 | 2 | 37 | 14* | 12.33 | 115.62 | 0 | 0 | 3 | 3 |
| First-class | 190 | 291 | 37 | 9177 | 212 | 36.12 | | 16 | 45 | 532 | 48 |
| List A | 172 | 127 | 35 | 2622 | 83* | 28.50 | | 0 | 14 | 198 | 53 |
| Twenty20 | 90 | 75 | 22 | 1143 | 62* | 21.56 | 132.90 | 0 | 4 | 36 | 34 |

| Bowling | Mat | Balls | Runs | Wkts | BBI | BBM | Ave | Econ | SR | 5w | 10 |
|---|---|---|---|---|---|---|---|---|---|---|---|
| Tests | 7 | - | - | - | - | - | - | - | - | - | - |
| ODIs | 11 | - | - | - | - | - | - | - | - | - | - |
| T20Is | 5 | - | - | - | - | - | - | - | - | - | - |
| First-class | 190 | 84 | 128 | 1 | 1/122 | 1/122 | 128.00 | 9.14 | 84.0 | 0 | 0 |
| List A | 172 | - | - | - | - | - | - | - | - | - | - |
| Twenty20 | 90 | - | - | - | - | - | - | - | - | - | - |

## PAUL FRANKS · LHB RFM W2

**FULL NAME:** Paul John Franks
**BORN:** February 3, 1979, Mansfield, Nottinghamshire
**SQUAD NO:** 8
**HEIGHT:** 6ft 2in
**NICKNAME:** Franksie, Pike, The General
**EDUCATION:** Minster School, Southwell
**TEAMS:** England, Mid West Rhinos, Nottinghamshire
**CAREER:** ODI: 2000; First-class: 1996; List A: 1997; T20: 2003

NOTTINGHAMSHIRE

BEST BATTING: 123* Nottinghamshire vs Leicestershire, Leicester, 2003
BEST BOWLING: 7-56 Nottinghamshire vs Middlesex, Lord's, 2000
COUNTY CAP: 1999; BENEFIT YEAR: 2007

FAMILY TIES? Dad was a local league legend and general cricket tragic!
WHY CRICKET? Inspired by Ian Botham
CAREER HIGHLIGHTS? England debut , County Championship wins in 2005 and 2010, T20 Finals Day
CRICKETING HEROES? Ian Botham, Andrew Flintoff, Graeme Swann
NON-CRICKETING HEROES? Eric Cantona, Seve Ballesteros
BEST PLAYER IN COUNTY CRICKET? Marcus Trescothick, Dale Benkenstein and Michael Di Venuto
TIPS FOR THE TOP? Alex Hales, Jos Buttler
FAVOURITE FILM? Top Gun, Major League
DREAM HOLIDAY? Bali
FANTASY SLIP CORDON? Keeper: Paul Gascoigne, 1st: Me, 2nd: Elle Macpherson, 3rd: David Beckham, Gully: Luke Fletcher
TWITTER FEED: @thegeneral_8

| Batting | Mat | Inns | NO | Runs | HS | Ave | SR | 100 | 50 | Ct | St |
|---|---|---|---|---|---|---|---|---|---|---|---|
| ODIs | 1 | 1 | 0 | 4 | 4 | 4.00 | 23.52 | 0 | 0 | 1 | 0 |
| First-class | 195 | 282 | 49 | 6473 | 123* | 27.78 | | 4 | 35 | 65 | 0 |
| List A | 180 | 132 | 41 | 1899 | 84* | 20.86 | | 0 | 5 | 28 | 0 |
| Twenty20 | 50 | 30 | 13 | 287 | 29* | 16.88 | 117.62 | 0 | 0 | 8 | 0 |

| Bowling | Mat | Balls | Runs | Wkts | BBI | BBM | Ave | Econ | SR | 5w | 10 |
|---|---|---|---|---|---|---|---|---|---|---|---|
| ODIs | 1 | 54 | 48 | 0 | - | - | - | 5.33 | - | 0 | 0 |
| First-class | 195 | 29464 | 16161 | 496 | 7/56 | | 32.58 | 3.29 | 59.4 | 11 | 0 |
| List A | 180 | 6607 | 5527 | 194 | 6/27 | 6/27 | 28.48 | 5.01 | 34.0 | 3 | 0 |
| Twenty20 | 50 | 479 | 687 | 20 | 2/12 | 2/12 | 34.35 | 8.60 | 23.9 | 0 | 0 |

# TOM FRIEND                                    RHB RFM

FULL NAME: Tom Friend
BORN: May 3, 1991, Newport, Isle of Wight, Hampshire
SQUAD NO: 21
HEIGHT: 6ft 2in
NICKNAME: Friendy
EDUCATION: Carisbrooke High School; Brockenhurst College; UWIC
TEAMS: Unicorns, Worcestershire 2nd XI
CAREER: List A: 2011

**CAREER HIGHLIGHTS?** Winning the University Cup final at Lord's. Taking my first six-fer for Worcester 2nd XI

**SUPERSTITIONS?** I couldn't be less superstitious

**CRICKETING HEROES?** I always liked to watch Darren Gough bowl as a youngster. Andrew Flintoff is also someone who I was always entertained by

**NON-CRICKETING HEROES?** David Beckham has to be up there

**BEST PLAYER IN COUNTY CRICKET?** Marcus Trescothick

**TIP FOR THE TOP?** Aneesh Kapil

**IF YOU WEREN'T A CRICKETER?** I would be a footballer no doubt, similar to Gareth Bale!

**WHEN RAIN STOPS PLAY?** I work really hard on my mental game

**FAVOURITE TV?** Family Guy

**FAVOURITE FILM?** Inception

**FAVOURITE BOOK?** I Hope They Serve Beer In Hell – Tucker Max

**DREAM HOLIDAY?** Las Vegas

**SURPRISING SKILL?** I've got a great left peg

**GUILTY PLEASURES?** Football Manager

**AMAZE ME!** I'm ranked No.2 in the world on Modern Warfare 3. I own five phones

**FANTASY SLIP CORDON?** Keeper: Kevin Bridges, 1st: George Best, 2nd: Gazza, 3rd: Myself, Gully: Tucker Max

**TWITTER FEED?** @Friendy3

**NOTES:** Has also been included in the Unicorns squad for the 2012 CB40

| Batting | Mat | Inns | NO | Runs | HS | Ave | SR | 100 | 50 | Ct | St |
|---------|-----|------|-----|------|-----|------|-------|-----|-----|-----|-----|
| List A | 3 | 3 | 1 | 19 | 14 | 9.50 | 70.37 | 0 | 0 | 0 | 0 |

| Bowling | Mat | Balls | Runs | Wkts | BBI | BBM | Ave | Econ | SR | 5w | 10 |
|---------|-----|-------|------|------|------|------|--------|------|-------|-----|-----|
| List A | 3 | 114 | 122 | 1 | 1/49 | 1/49 | 122.00 | 6.42 | 114.0 | 0 | 0 |

# JAMES FULLER                                    RHB RF

**FULL NAME:** James Kerr Fuller
**BORN:** January 24, 1990, Cape Town, South Africa
**SQUAD NO:** 26
**HEIGHT:** 6ft 3in
**EDUCATION:** Westlake High School; Otago University
**TEAMS:** Gloucestershire, Gloucestershire 2nd XI, New Zealand Under-19s, Otago, Otago Under-19s
**CAREER:** First-class: 2010; List A: 2011; T20: 2011

**BEST BATTING:** 24 Otago vs Wellington, Wellington, 2010
**BEST BOWLING:** 1-33 Otago vs Northern Districts, Whangarei, 2010

**CAREER HIGHLIGHTS?** Playing first-class cricket for Otago and Gloucestershire, taking 4-33 against Essex in a CB40 match
**SUPERSTITIONS?** I put my left pad on first
**CRICKETING HEROES?** Glenn McGrath, Brett Lee and William Lillywhite
**BEST PLAYER IN COUNTY CRICKET?** Marcus Trescothick
**TIPS FOR THE TOP?** Ian Saxelby and David Payne
**IF YOU WEREN'T A CRICKETER?** I'd spend hours on the golf course and try to make it at that or go back to university
**WHEN RAIN STOPS PLAY?** On my iPhone playing games or potentially reading a book
**FAVOURITE TV?** Take Me Out and Geordie Shore
**FAVOURITE FILM?** Transformers 1, 2 and 3
**FAVOURITE BOOK?** The Harry Potters and books written by Lee Child
**DREAM HOLIDAY?** Fiji with the family
**GUILTY PLEASURES?** Fairly susceptible to the odd chocolate bar
**AMAZE ME!** I'm currently mid-way through a Neuroscience degree at Otago University. I enjoy cooking and my specialty is roasts. I'm left-footed and right-handed
**TWITTER FEED:** @James_fuller246

| Batting | Mat | Inns | NO | Runs | HS | Ave | SR | 100 | 50 | Ct | St |
|---|---|---|---|---|---|---|---|---|---|---|---|
| First-class | 3 | 4 | 0 | 35 | 24 | 8.75 | 49.29 | 0 | 0 | 2 | 0 |
| List A | 8 | 7 | 3 | 86 | 33 | 21.50 | 97.72 | 0 | 0 | 2 | 0 |
| Twenty20 | 1 | - | - | - | - | - | - | - | - | 0 | 0 |

| Bowling | Mat | Balls | Runs | Wkts | BBI | BBM | Ave | Econ | SR | 5w | 10 |
|---|---|---|---|---|---|---|---|---|---|---|---|
| First-class | 3 | 456 | 293 | 3 | 1/33 | 1/62 | 97.66 | 3.85 | 152.0 | 0 | 0 |
| List A | 8 | 336 | 326 | 16 | 4/33 | 4/33 | 20.37 | 5.82 | 21.0 | 0 | 0 |
| Twenty20 | 1 | 12 | 23 | 0 | - | - | - | 11.50 | - | 0 | 0 |

# ANDREW GALE LHB LB MVP63

**YORKSHIRE**

FULL NAME: Andrew William Gale
BORN: November 28, 1983, Dewsbury, Yorkshire
SQUAD NO: 26
HEIGHT: 6ft 2in
NICKNAME: Galey
EDUCATION: Whitcliffe Mount School; Heckmondwike Grammar School
TEAMS: England Lions, England Under-19s, Yorkshire, Yorkshire Cricket Board
CAREER: First-class: 2004; List A: 2002; T20: 2004

BEST BATTING: 151* Yorkshire vs Nottinghamshire, Nottingham, 2010
BEST BOWLING: 1-33 Yorkshire vs LUCCE, Leeds, 2007
COUNTY CAPS: 2008

FAMILY TIES? My grandad and uncles were big league cricketers
CAREER HIGHLIGHTS? Captaining England Lions and Yorkshire
SUPERSTITIONS? I don't like odd numbers
CRICKETING HEROES? Marcus Trescothick, Mark Butcher, Mike Hussey
NON-CRICKETING HEROES? Any of the Huddersfield Town players!
TIPS FOR THE TOP? Joe Root, Gary Ballance, Jonny Bairstow
IF YOU WEREN'T A CRICKETER? Running my businesses, Pro Coach Cricket Academy and All Rounder Cricket
WHEN RAIN STOPS PLAY? Bit of fitness work or catch up on the news
FAVOURITE TV? Entourage
FAVOURITE FILM? Step Brothers
DREAM HOLIDAY? Cape Town
GUILTY PLEASURES? Watching Huddersfield Town, eating Haribo!
FANTASY SLIP CORDON? Keeper: Neil Warnock, 1st: John Bishop, 2nd: Me, 3rd: David Beckham
TWITTER FEED: @galeylad

| Batting | Mat | Inns | NO | Runs | HS | Ave | SR | 100 | 50 | Ct | St |
|---|---|---|---|---|---|---|---|---|---|---|---|
| First-class | 79 | 129 | 9 | 4476 | 151* | 37.30 | | 12 | 20 | 33 | 0 |
| List A | 101 | 93 | 10 | 2601 | 125* | 31.33 | | 2 | 14 | 20 | 0 |
| Twenty20 | 71 | 64 | 9 | 1590 | 91 | 28.90 | 124.21 | 0 | 13 | 27 | 0 |
| Bowling | Mat | Balls | Runs | Wkts | BBI | BBM | Ave | Econ | SR | 5w | 10 |
| First-class | 79 | 24 | 47 | 1 | 1/33 | 1/33 | 47.00 | 11.75 | 24.0 | 0 | 0 |
| List A | 101 | - | - | - | - | - | - | - | - | - | - |
| Twenty20 | 71 | - | - | - | - | - | - | - | - | - | - |

## JOE GATTING

**RHB OB**

FULL NAME: Joe Stephen Gatting
BORN: November 25, 1987, Brighton, Sussex
SQUAD NO: 25
HEIGHT: 5ft 11in
TEAMS: Sussex, Sussex 2nd XI
CAREER: First-class: 2009; List A: 2009; T20: 2009

SUSSEX

BEST BATTING: 152 Sussex vs CUCCE, Fenner's, 2009
BEST BOWLING: 1-8 Sussex vs Nottinghamshire, Nottingham, 2011

FAMILY TIES? My uncle Mike and my dad both played
CAREER HIGHLIGHTS? Champions League in India, first centuries in first-class and List A cricket
SUPERSTITIONS? Left pad first
CRICKETING HEROES? Uncle, Brian Lara and Andrew Symonds
NON-CRICKETING HEROES? Tiger Woods
BEST PLAYER IN COUNTY CRICKET? Marcus Trescothick
TIP FOR THE TOP? Luke Wells
FAVOURITE FILM? The Next Three Days
FAVOURITE BOOK? Bounce
DREAM HOLIDAY? Barbados
ACCOMPLISHMENTS? Playing Championship football
GUILTY PLEASURES? The X Factor
AMAZE ME! Colour blind (green and red)
FANTASY SLIP CORDON? Keeper: John Bishop (good for sledging), 1st: James Corden (funny banter and would have a supply of sweets), 2nd: Me, 3rd: Eric Cantona (arrogant and skilful), Gully: Mike Tyson (to scare the batsmen)

| Batting | Mat | Inns | NO | Runs | HS | Ave | SR | 100 | 50 | Ct | St |
|---|---|---|---|---|---|---|---|---|---|---|---|
| First-class | 19 | 28 | 1 | 978 | 152 | 36.22 | 62.57 | 3 | 4 | 9 | 0 |
| List A | 31 | 30 | 3 | 832 | 122 | 30.81 | 87.21 | 1 | 4 | 9 | 0 |
| Twenty20 | 38 | 31 | 5 | 337 | 37 | 12.96 | 109.06 | 0 | 0 | 12 | 0 |

| Bowling | Mat | Balls | Runs | Wkts | BBI | BBM | Ave | Econ | SR | 5w | 10 |
|---|---|---|---|---|---|---|---|---|---|---|---|
| First-class | 19 | 102 | 55 | 2 | 1/8 | 1/8 | 27.50 | 3.23 | 51.0 | 0 | 0 |
| List A | 31 | 20 | 22 | 0 | - | - | - | 6.60 | - | 0 | 0 |
| Twenty20 | 38 | 10 | 14 | 1 | 1/12 | 1/12 | 14.00 | 8.40 | 10.0 | 0 | 0 |

# CHRIS GAYLE

**LHB OB**

**FULL NAME:** Christopher Henry Gayle
**BORN:** September 21, 1979, Kingston, Jamaica
**SQUAD NO:** 30
**HEIGHT:** 6ft 2in
**TEAMS:** West Indies, Barisal Burners, ICC World XI, Jamaica, Kolkata Knight Riders, Matabeleland Tuskers, Royal Challengers Bangalore, Somerset, Stanford Superstars, Sydney Thunder, Western Australia, Worcestershire
**CAREER:** Test: 2000; ODI: 1999; T20I: 2006; First-class: 1998; List A: 1998; T20: 2005

**BEST BATTING:** 333 West Indies vs Sri Lanka, Galle, 2010
**BEST BOWLING:** 5-34 West Indies vs England, Birmingham, 2004

**NOTES:** Eighth on the list of all-time West Indian runscorers. One of only four men to reach 300 in Tests more than once (317 against South Africa in 2005 and 333 vs Sri Lanka in 2010). Scored a 79-ball hundred against South Africa at Cape Town in 2004. Scored a 70-ball hundred against Australia at Perth in 2009. Hasn't played for West Indies since last March because of an ongoing dispute with the WICB. Leading runscorer in last season's IPL with 608 runs at 67.55 and a strike-rate of 183.33. Underwent heart surgery in 2005, having been forced to retire hurt while batting in a Test match against Australia at Adelaide

| Batting | Mat | Inns | NO | Runs | HS | Ave | SR | 100 | 50 | Ct | St |
|---|---|---|---|---|---|---|---|---|---|---|---|
| Tests | 91 | 159 | 6 | 6373 | 333 | 41.65 | 59.10 | 13 | 33 | 85 | 0 |
| ODIs | 228 | 223 | 16 | 8087 | 153* | 39.06 | 83.95 | 19 | 43 | 99 | 0 |
| T20Is | 20 | 20 | 1 | 617 | 117 | 32.47 | 144.49 | 1 | 5 | 5 | 0 |
| First-class | 166 | 294 | 21 | 12294 | 333 | 45.03 | | 30 | 59 | 144 | 0 |
| List A | 294 | 288 | 23 | 10526 | 153* | 39.72 | | 22 | 59 | 125 | 0 |
| Twenty20 | 92 | 91 | 12 | 3237 | 117 | 40.97 | 154.88 | 7 | 19 | 25 | 0 |

| Bowling | Mat | Balls | Runs | Wkts | BBI | BBM | Ave | Econ | SR | 5w | 10 |
|---|---|---|---|---|---|---|---|---|---|---|---|
| Tests | 91 | 6857 | 2995 | 72 | 5/34 | 6/81 | 41.59 | 2.62 | 95.2 | 2 | 0 |
| ODIs | 228 | 6936 | 5473 | 156 | 5/46 | 5/46 | 35.08 | 4.73 | 44.4 | 1 | 0 |
| T20Is | 20 | 209 | 254 | 12 | 2/15 | 2/15 | 21.16 | 7.29 | 17.4 | 0 | 0 |
| First-class | 166 | 12247 | 5066 | 131 | 5/34 | | 38.67 | 2.48 | 93.4 | 2 | 0 |
| List A | 294 | 9074 | 6846 | 213 | 5/46 | 5/46 | 32.14 | 4.52 | 42.6 | 1 | 0 |
| Twenty20 | 92 | 1275 | 1607 | 48 | 4/22 | 4/22 | 33.47 | 7.56 | 26.5 | 0 | 0 |

# CALLUM GELDART

**LHB RM**

**FULL NAME:** Callum John Geldart
**BORN:** December 17, 1991, Huddersfield, Yorkshire
**SQUAD NO:** 6
**HEIGHT:** 6ft
**NICKNAME:** Cal
**EDUCATION:** Shelley College; Huddersfield New College
**TEAMS:** Yorkshire, Yorkshire 2nd XI
**CAREER:** First-class: 2010

**BEST BATTING:** 34 Yorkshire vs DMCCU, Durham University, 2011

**FAMILY TIES?** Dad played in local leagues
**CAREER HIGHLIGHTS?** First first-class match
**SUPERSTITIONS?** Never tap bat any less or more than three times
**CRICKETING HEROES?** Marcus Trescothick
**TIP FOR THE TOP?** Joe Root
**IF YOU WEREN'T A CRICKETER?** Barman
**WHEN RAIN STOPS PLAY?** Fitness, watching TV
**FAVOURITE TV?** Family Guy
**FAVOURITE FILM?** Notorious
**DREAM HOLIDAY?** Rio de Janeiro
**GUILTY PLEASURES?** Ice cream

| Batting | Mat | Inns | NO | Runs | HS | Ave | SR | 100 | 50 | Ct | St |
|---|---|---|---|---|---|---|---|---|---|---|---|
| First-class | 2 | 2 | 0 | 51 | 34 | 25.50 | 42.14 | 0 | 0 | 1 | 0 |

| Bowling | Mat | Balls | Runs | Wkts | BBI | BBM | Ave | Econ | SR | 5w | 10 |
|---|---|---|---|---|---|---|---|---|---|---|---|
| First-class | 2 | - | - | - | - | - | - | - | - | - | - |

# HERSCHELLE GIBBS

**RHB LB**

DURHAM

FULL NAME: Herschelle Herman Gibbs
BORN: February 23, 1974, Green Point, Cape Town, South Africa
SQUAD NO: 7
HEIGHT: 5ft 8in
NICKNAME: Scooter
EDUCATION: Diocesan College
TEAMS: South Africa, Cape Cobras, Deccan Chargers, Glamorgan, Khulna Royal Bengals, Northern Districts, Perth Scorchers, Western Province, Yorkshire
CAREER: Test: 1996; ODI: 1996; T20I: 2005; First-class: 1990; List A: 1990; T20: 2004

BEST BATTING: 228 South Africa vs Pakistan, Cape Town, 2003
BEST BOWLING: 2-14 South Africa A vs Somerset, Taunton, 1996
COUNTY CAP: 2008 (Glamorgan)

FAMILY TIES? Father Herman is a leading sports writer
CRICKETERS PARTICULARLY ADMIRED? Peter Kirsten, Viv Richards
OTHER SPORTS PLAYED? Golf
OTHER SPORTS FOLLOWED? Football (Manchester United)
FAVOURITE MUSIC? Luther Vandross, George Benson, Frank Sinatra
RELAXATIONS? Shopping
NOTES: In a World Cup match against the Netherlands in 2007 he hit six sixes in an over off Dan van Bunge, an international ODI record. He has featured in three 300-plus opening partnerships with Graeme Smith in Test matches. He scored 175 from 111 balls to give South Africa victory against Australia at Johannesburg, 2008 in the highest ODI chase in history

| Batting | Mat | Inns | NO | Runs | HS | Ave | SR | 100 | 50 | Ct | St |
|---|---|---|---|---|---|---|---|---|---|---|---|
| Tests | 90 | 154 | 7 | 6167 | 228 | 41.95 | 50.26 | 14 | 26 | 94 | 0 |
| ODIs | 248 | 240 | 16 | 8094 | 175 | 36.13 | 83.26 | 21 | 37 | 108 | 0 |
| T20Is | 23 | 23 | 1 | 400 | 90* | 18.18 | 125.78 | 0 | 3 | 8 | 0 |
| First-class | 193 | 331 | 13 | 13425 | 228 | 42.21 | | 31 | 60 | 176 | 0 |
| List A | 389 | 370 | 32 | 11976 | 175 | 35.43 | | 27 | 62 | 171 | 0 |
| Twenty20 | 137 | 134 | 9 | 3227 | 101* | 25.81 | 125.95 | 1 | 23 | 65 | 0 |

| Bowling | Mat | Balls | Runs | Wkts | BBI | BBM | Ave | Econ | SR | 5w | 10 |
|---|---|---|---|---|---|---|---|---|---|---|---|
| Tests | 90 | 6 | 4 | 0 | - | - | - | 4.00 | - | 0 | 0 |
| ODIs | 248 | - | - | - | - | - | - | - | - | - | - |
| T20Is | 23 | - | - | - | - | - | - | - | - | - | - |
| First-class | 193 | 138 | 78 | 3 | 2/14 | | 26.00 | 3.39 | 46.0 | 0 | 0 |
| List A | 389 | 66 | 57 | 2 | 1/16 | 1/16 | 28.50 | 5.18 | 33.0 | 0 | 0 |
| Twenty20 | 137 | - | - | - | - | - | - | - | - | - | - |

**GLOUCESTERSHIRE**

**FULL NAME:** Alexander Peter Richard Gidman
**BORN:** June 22, 1981, High Wycombe, Buckinghamshire
**SQUAD NO:** 5
**HEIGHT:** 6ft 2in
**NICKNAME:** Giddo
**EDUCATION:** Wycliffe College
**TEAMS:** England A, England Lions, Gloucestershire, Gloucestershire 2nd XI, Marylebone Cricket Club, Otago
**CAREER:** First-class: 2002; List A: 2001; T20: 2003

**BEST BATTING:** 176 Gloucestershire vs Surrey, Bristol, 2009
**BEST BOWLING:** 4-47 Gloucestershire vs Glamorgan, Cardiff, 2009
**BENEFIT YEAR:** 2012

**FAMILY TIES?** Brother Will also plays for Gloucestershire
**CRICKETING HEROES?** Steve Waugh
**FAVOURITE BAND?** Oasis, Pink Floyd
**RELAXATIONS?** Just chilling out, movies, golf, playing guitar
**NOTES:** Gloucestershire Young Player of the Year 2002 and 2003. NBC Denis Compton Award for the most promising young Gloucestershire player 2002 and 2003. A member of the ECB National Academy in 2003/04 and 2004/05. Included in England's preliminary squad for the ICC Champions Trophy 2004 and represented England Lions in 2007, the same year that he made a century in each innings (130 and 105*) against Northants at Gloucester. Gloucestershire's Players' Player of the Year 2006. Vice-captain of Gloucestershire from 2006-2008 and club captain since 2009

| Batting | Mat | Inns | NO | Runs | HS | Ave | SR | 100 | 50 | Ct | St |
|---|---|---|---|---|---|---|---|---|---|---|---|
| First-class | 145 | 254 | 23 | 8251 | 176 | 35.71 | 57.14 | 16 | 46 | 92 | 0 |
| List A | 166 | 157 | 16 | 3883 | 116 | 27.53 | | 5 | 20 | 54 | 0 |
| Twenty20 | 64 | 57 | 10 | 991 | 64 | 21.08 | 116.17 | 0 | 3 | 12 | 0 |

| Bowling | Mat | Balls | Runs | Wkts | BBI | BBM | Ave | Econ | SR | 5w | 10 |
|---|---|---|---|---|---|---|---|---|---|---|---|
| First-class | 145 | 7049 | 4378 | 99 | 4/47 | | 44.22 | 3.72 | 71.2 | 0 | 0 |
| List A | 166 | 3046 | 2636 | 65 | 5/42 | 5/42 | 40.55 | 5.19 | 46.8 | 1 | 0 |
| Twenty20 | 64 | 262 | 360 | 8 | 2/24 | 2/24 | 45.00 | 8.24 | 32.7 | 0 | 0 |

# WILL GIDMAN
## LHB RM R1 W1 MVP43

GLOUCESTERSHIRE

FULL NAME: William Robert Simon Gidman
BORN: February 14, 1985, High Wycombe, Buckinghamshire
SQUAD NO: 23
HEIGHT: 6ft 2in
NICKNAME: Gidders, Giddo, Wilbur, P.T
EDUCATION: Wycliffe College, Stonehouse; Berkshire College of Agriculture
TEAMS: Durham, Durham 2nd XI, Gloucestershire, Gloucestershire 2nd XI, Marylebone Cricket Club
CAREER: First-class: 2007; List A: 2003; T20: 2011

BEST BATTING: 116* Gloucestershire vs Northamptonshire, Bristol, 2011
BEST BOWLING: 6-92 Gloucestershire vs Derbyshire, Derby, 2011

FAMILY TIES? Alex Gidman, brother and captain of Gloucestershire
CAREER HIGHLIGHTS? Maiden hundred. In fact, any time I raise my bat and any wicket I take!
CRICKETING HEROES? Quite a few, actually, but the main one is Garry Sobers
NON-CRICKETING HEROES? Muhammad Ali, Jonny Wilkinson
TIP FOR THE TOP? David Payne
IF YOU WEREN'T A CRICKETER? I'd own a coffee shop
WHEN RAIN STOPS PLAY? Reading, listening to music or playing cards
FAVOURITE TV? Friends, Scrubs
ACCOMPLISHMENTS? The birth of my baby girl and snapping up my fiancée – the phrase punching above my weight comes to mind!
GUILTY PLEASURES? Take That
AMAZE ME! I was the first ever Gloucestershire U10 player to score a century. I'm a Level 1 basketball coach. I gave away four overthrows off Freddie Flintoff's bowling whilst fielding for England!
FANTASY SLIP CORDON? Keeper: Peter Kay, 1st: Lee Evans, 2nd: Michael McIntyre, 3rd: Muhammad Ali, Gully: Jennifer Aniston

| Batting | Mat | Inns | NO | Runs | HS | Ave | SR | 100 | 50 | Ct | St |
|---|---|---|---|---|---|---|---|---|---|---|---|
| First-class | 17 | 30 | 6 | 1014 | 116* | 42.25 | 50.90 | 1 | 8 | 4 | 0 |
| List A | 26 | 16 | 4 | 213 | 40* | 17.75 | | 0 | 0 | 8 | 0 |
| Twenty20 | 8 | 7 | 1 | 78 | 40* | 13.00 | 86.66 | 0 | 0 | 2 | 0 |

| Bowling | Mat | Balls | Runs | Wkts | BBI | BBM | Ave | Econ | SR | 5w | 10 |
|---|---|---|---|---|---|---|---|---|---|---|---|
| First-class | 17 | 2390 | 1174 | 55 | 6/92 | 6/114 | 21.34 | 2.94 | 43.4 | 3 | 0 |
| List A | 26 | 816 | 653 | 23 | 4/36 | 4/36 | 28.39 | 4.80 | 35.4 | 0 | 0 |
| Twenty20 | 8 | 48 | 76 | 1 | 1/18 | 1/18 | 76.00 | 9.50 | 48.0 | 0 | 0 |

# JOHN GLOVER

## RHB RMF

FULL NAME: John Charles Glover
BORN: August 29, 1989, Cardiff
SQUAD NO: 36
HEIGHT: 6ft 4in
NICKNAME: Gloves, Glovebox, MC
EDUCATION: Llantarnam Comprehensive School; Durham University
TEAMS: Durham MCCU, Durham UCCE, Glamorgan, Wales Minor Counties
CAREER: First-class: 2008

BEST BATTING: 16* Glamorgan vs Kent, Canterbury, 2011
BEST BOWLING: 5-38 DUCCE vs Durham, Durham University, 2009

WHY CRICKET? My father played for Panteg Cricket Club so grew up watching and playing
CAREER HIGHLIGHTS? Glamorgan debut in 2011, playing in the first County Championship game under floodlights
SUPERSTITIONS? Always put left pad on first
CRICKETING HEROES? Courtney Walsh
NON-CRICKETING HEROES? Graeme McDowell, Martyn Williams, Kevin McNaughton
IF YOU WEREN'T A CRICKETER? I would be trying to find a job in sport development
WHEN RAIN STOPS PLAY? Either reading books or watching films
FAVOURITE TV? Friends
FAVOURITE FILM? Pulp Fiction, Gladiator, Inception
FAVOURITE BOOK? 1984 by George Orwell
DREAM HOLIDAY? Barry Island
ACCOMPLISHMENTS? 2:1 from Durham University
AMAZE ME! 1. Played football at Ninian Park in a schools cup final, 2. Wrestled with lion cubs in Potchefstroom, 3. Took part in salsa dancing for my dissertation
FANTASY SLIP CORDON? Keeper: Dave Grohl, 1st: Jimi Hendrix, 2nd: Flea from Red Hot Chili Peppers, 3rd: Eric Clapton, Gully: James Brown – the jam session after the game would be amazing
TWITTER FEED: @John_Gloves

| Batting | Mat | Inns | NO | Runs | HS | Ave | SR | 100 | 50 | Ct | St |
|---|---|---|---|---|---|---|---|---|---|---|---|
| First-class | 11 | 14 | 4 | 76 | 16* | 7.60 | 25.50 | 0 | 0 | 3 | 0 |

| Bowling | Mat | Balls | Runs | Wkts | BBI | BBM | Ave | Econ | SR | 5w | 10 |
|---|---|---|---|---|---|---|---|---|---|---|---|
| First-class | 11 | 1336 | 802 | 20 | 5/38 | 5/56 | 40.10 | 3.60 | 66.8 | 1 | 0 |

## BILLY GODLEMAN LHB LB

ESSEX

FULL NAME: Billy Ashley Godleman
BORN: February 11, 1989, Camden, London
SQUAD NO: 34
HEIGHT: 6ft 3in
NICKNAME: G
EDUCATION: Central Foundation School;
Islington Green School
TEAMS: England Under-19s, Essex,
Middlesex, Middlesex 2nd XI
CAREER: First-class: 2005; List A: 2007; T20:
2006

BEST BATTING: 130 Essex vs Leicestershire, Leicester, 2011

CAREER HIGHLIGHTS? Maiden first-class century – 113* vs Somerset in 2007
FAVOURITE BAND? Pink Floyd, Led Zeppelin, Fleetwood Mac
RELAXATIONS? Spending time with my little brother Johnny and family, reading, watching
Liverpool FC
OPINIONS ON CRICKET? You get out what you put in
NOTES: Made 149 for England U19 in 2007 against Pakistan – then the highest individual
innings by an English batsman at that level, having represented England at youth level from
U15 upwards. Made unbeaten 69 on his first-class debut for Middlesex in 2005; made his
maiden first-class hundred – 113* – on his Championship debut against Somerset in 2007.
He scored over 1,000 runs across all forms of cricket in 2008. Signed a three-year deal with
Essex in August 2009

| Batting | Mat | Inns | NO | Runs | HS | Ave | SR | 100 | 50 | Ct | St |
|---|---|---|---|---|---|---|---|---|---|---|---|
| First-class | 61 | 105 | 3 | 3010 | 130 | 29.50 | 41.74 | 4 | 15 | 47 | 0 |
| List A | 17 | 17 | 1 | 342 | 82 | 21.37 | 70.80 | 0 | 1 | 4 | 0 |
| Twenty20 | 24 | 23 | 0 | 419 | 69 | 18.21 | 107.43 | 0 | 3 | 11 | 0 |
| Bowling | Mat | Balls | Runs | Wkts | BBI | BBM | Ave | Econ | SR | 5w | 10 |
| First-class | 61 | 30 | 35 | 0 | - | - | - | 7.00 | - | 0 | 0 |
| List A | 17 | - | - | - | - | - | - | - | - | - | - |
| Twenty20 | 24 | - | - | - | - | - | - | - | - | - | - |

# MURRAY GOODWIN
## RHB LB R9 MVP26

FULL NAME: Murray William Goodwin
BORN: December 11, 1972, Harare
SQUAD NO: 3
HEIGHT: 5ft 9in
NICKNAME: Muzza, Fuzz, Goodie
EDUCATION: St John's, Harare;
Newtonmoore Senior High, Western
Australia
TEAMS: Netherlands, Zimbabwe,
Ahmedabad Rockets, Mashonaland, Sussex,
Warriors, Western Australia
CAREER: Test: 1998; ODI: 1998; First-class:
1994; List A: 1994; T20: 2003

SUSSEX

BEST BATTING: 344* Sussex vs Somerset, Taunton, 2009
BEST BOWLING: 2-23 Zimbabweans vs Lahore City, Lahore, 1998
COUNTY CAP: 2001; BENEFIT YEAR: 2009

FAMILY TIES? Dad is a coach. Eldest brother played for Zimbabwe
CAREER HIGHLIGHTS? Becoming the highest individual scorer in Sussex's history – 335* vs
Leicestershire, September 2003 at Hove. Broke Duleepsinhji's record of 333 from 1930
CRICKETERS PARTICULARLY ADMIRED? Allan Border, Steve Waugh, Curtly Ambrose and
Sachin Tendulkar
OTHER SPORTS PLAYED? Hockey, golf, tennis
NOTES: Scored 149 unbeaten runs (148* and 1*) in his last Test appearance, against England
at Trent Bridge in 2000. Smashed 87* from 64 balls, including a last-ball six, to snatch the
2008 Pro40 Division One title on the last day of the season. Has made 100 scores of 50 or
more (52 fifties and 48 centuries) in 302 first-class innings for Sussex

| Batting | Mat | Inns | NO | Runs | HS | Ave | SR | 100 | 50 | Ct | St |
|---|---|---|---|---|---|---|---|---|---|---|---|
| Tests | 19 | 37 | 4 | 1414 | 166* | 42.84 | 46.31 | 3 | 8 | 10 | 0 |
| ODIs | 71 | 70 | 3 | 1818 | 112* | 27.13 | 68.50 | 2 | 8 | 20 | 0 |
| First-class | 282 | 490 | 41 | 21753 | 344* | 48.44 | | 67 | 88 | 150 | 0 |
| List A | 353 | 336 | 40 | 10654 | 167 | 35.99 | | 14 | 66 | 108 | 0 |
| Twenty20 | 88 | 82 | 11 | 2003 | 102* | 28.21 | 121.54 | 2 | 10 | 16 | 0 |

| Bowling | Mat | Balls | Runs | Wkts | BBI | BBM | Ave | Econ | SR | 5w | 10 |
|---|---|---|---|---|---|---|---|---|---|---|---|
| Tests | 19 | 119 | 69 | 0 | - | | | 3.47 | - | 0 | 0 |
| ODIs | 71 | 248 | 210 | 4 | 1/12 | 1/12 | 52.50 | 5.08 | 62.0 | 0 | 0 |
| First-class | 282 | 713 | 376 | 7 | 2/23 | | 53.71 | 3.16 | 101.8 | 0 | 0 |
| List A | 353 | 351 | 306 | 7 | 1/9 | 1/9 | 43.71 | 5.23 | 50.1 | 0 | 0 |
| Twenty20 | 88 | - | - | - | - | - | - | - | - | - | - |

## RECORDO GORDON                    RHB RFM

**WARWICKSHIRE**

FULL NAME: Recordo Olton Gordon
BORN: October 12, 1991, St Elizabeth's, Jamaica
SQUAD NO: 44
NICKNAME: Ricky, Flash
EDUCATION: Aston Manor Academy; Hamstead Hall Sixth Form
TEAMS: Herefordshire, Warwickshire 2nd XI, Warwickshire Under-15s, Warwickshire Under-17s
CAREER: Yet to make first-team debut

WHY CRICKET? Watching Brian Lara bat and Walsh and Ambrose bowl
CAREER HIGHLIGHTS? Taking 4-4 in a T20 game and gaining a contract
CRICKETING HEROES? Courtney Walsh and Curtly Ambrose
NON-CRICKETING HEROES? Father
BEST PLAYER IN COUNTY CRICKET? There are a lot of good players but I really rate Alfonso Thomas as a bowler
TIPS FOR THE TOP? Jos Buttler, Ben Stokes
IF YOU WEREN'T A CRICKETER? I'd be at universiy
WHEN RAIN STOPS PLAY? Putting my feet up, getting them out of my bowling boots
FAVOURITE TV? The Big Bang Theory
FAVOURITE BOOK? The Tomb
DREAM HOLIDAY? Jamaica
ACCOMPLISHMENTS? Being head boy of my school
SURPRISING SKILL? I'm a good cook and baker
TWITTER FEED: @recordoGordon

# LEWIS GREGORY RHB RFM

FULL NAME: Lewis Gregory
BORN: May 24, 1992, Plymouth
SQUAD NO: 24
TEAMS: Devon, England Under-19s, Somerset, Somerset 2nd XI
CAREER: First-class: 2011; List A: 2010; T20: 2011

SOMERSET

BEST BATTING: 48 Somerset vs Warwickshire, Birmingham, 2011
BEST BOWLING: 1-15 Somerset vs Sussex, Hove, 2011

NOTES: Former England U19 skipper. Took a hat-trick for Somerset's 2nd XI against Essex in 2010. Played against the touring Pakistanis on List A debut, claiming 4-49 including the wickets of Shahid Afridi and Abdul Razzaq. Somerset's leading wicket-taker in last year's FL t20, claiming 18 wickets at 17 in 12 matches

| Batting | Mat | Inns | NO | Runs | HS | Ave | SR | 100 | 50 | Ct | St |
|---|---|---|---|---|---|---|---|---|---|---|---|
| First-class | 5 | 8 | 1 | 98 | 48 | 14.00 | 45.58 | 0 | 0 | 0 | 0 |
| List A | 8 | 3 | 0 | 12 | 11 | 4.00 | 46.15 | 0 | 0 | 2 | 0 |
| Twenty20 | 15 | 5 | 1 | 27 | 15 | 6.75 | 69.23 | 0 | 0 | 7 | 0 |

| Bowling | Mat | Balls | Runs | Wkts | BBI | BBM | Ave | Econ | SR | 5w | 10 |
|---|---|---|---|---|---|---|---|---|---|---|---|
| First-class | 5 | 288 | 222 | 4 | 1/15 | 1/38 | 55.50 | 4.62 | 72.0 | 0 | 0 |
| List A | 8 | 252 | 238 | 17 | 4/27 | 4/27 | 14.00 | 5.66 | 14.8 | 0 | 0 |
| Twenty20 | 15 | 240 | 324 | 20 | 4/15 | 4/15 | 16.20 | 8.10 | 12.0 | 0 | 0 |

# DAVID GRIFFITHS LHB RF

HAMPSHIRE

FULL NAME: David Andrew Griffiths
BORN: September 10, 1985, Newport, Isle of Wight
SQUAD NO: 18
HEIGHT: 6ft 1in
NICKNAME: Griff
EDUCATION: Sandown High School
TEAMS: Hampshire, Hampshire 2nd XI
CAREER: First-class: 2006; List A: 2008; T20: 2007

BEST BATTING: 31* Hampshire vs Surrey, Southampton, 2007
BEST BOWLING: 6-85 Hampshire vs Nottinghamshire, Nottingham, 2011

FAMILY TIES? Father captained Wales at minor counties level. Stepfather captained Isle of Wight. Uncles play league cricket
CAREER HIGHLIGHTS? Making Championship debut against Durham in 2007
CRICKET MOMENTS TO FORGET? My first ball in Championship cricket – Ottis Gibson hit me on the head!
SUPERSTITIONS? Always turn right at the end of run-up
CRICKETERS PARTICULARLY ADMIRED? Darren Gough, Brett Lee, Brian Lara
TIPS FOR THE TOP? Michael Bates, Danny Briggs
OTHER SPORTS FOLLOWED? Football (Manchester United), rugby league (St Helens)
FAVOURITE BAND? Any RnB music
NOTES: Played for England U19 in 2004 and 2005

| Batting | Mat | Inns | NO | Runs | HS | Ave | SR | 100 | 50 | Ct | St |
|---|---|---|---|---|---|---|---|---|---|---|---|
| First-class | 28 | 42 | 18 | 160 | 31* | 6.66 | 24.31 | 0 | 0 | 2 | 0 |
| List A | 8 | 2 | 1 | 10 | 7 | 10.00 | 40.00 | 0 | 0 | 2 | 0 |
| Twenty20 | 3 | 1 | 1 | 4 | 4* | - | 36.36 | 0 | 0 | 0 | 0 |

| Bowling | Mat | Balls | Runs | Wkts | BBI | BBM | Ave | Econ | SR | 5w | 10 |
|---|---|---|---|---|---|---|---|---|---|---|---|
| First-class | 28 | 4540 | 2910 | 83 | 6/85 | 7/102 | 35.06 | 3.84 | 54.6 | 2 | 0 |
| List A | 8 | 318 | 313 | 10 | 4/29 | 4/29 | 31.30 | 5.90 | 31.8 | 0 | 0 |
| Twenty20 | 3 | 42 | 55 | 3 | 3/13 | 3/13 | 18.33 | 7.85 | 14.0 | 0 | 0 |

G

# TIM GROENEWALD

## RHB RFM MVP89

FULL NAME: Timothy Duncan Groenewald
BORN: January 10, 1984, Pietermaritzburg, South Africa
SQUAD NO: 12
HEIGHT: 6ft 2in
NICKNAME: TG, Groeners
EDUCATION: Maritzburg College, Natal; University of South Africa
TEAMS: Derbyshire, Warwickshire, Warwickshire 2nd XI
CAREER: First-class: 2006; List A: 2006; T20: 2006

**DERBYSHIRE**

BEST BATTING: 78 Warwickshire vs Bangladesh A, Birmingham, 2008
BEST BOWLING: 6-50 Derbyshire vs Surrey, Whitgift School, 2009

WHY CRICKET? Jonty Rhodes' dad was my coach at school from age six through to 10 and this gave me a great start in the game
CAREER HIGHLIGHTS? Playing in a Friends Provident semi-final for Warwickshire against Hampshire in 2007. My two eight-wicket hauls have been special as well. Defending six runs off the last over against Lancashire in the T20 last year
CRICKETING HEROES? Hansie Cronje and Allan Donald while growing up. After playing with Dale Steyn, I now admire him massively
TIP FOR THE TOP? Jonny Bairstow
IF YOU WEREN'T A CRICKETER? I'd start my own business
WHEN RAIN STOPS PLAY? Sleeping on the physio bed, playing a few pranks on people in the changing room, watching YouTube videos
FAVOURITE TV? The Apprentice, Two And A Half Men
FAVOURITE FILM? Lincoln Lawyer, Law Abiding Citizen, Taken
FAVOURITE BOOK? The Kite Runner, The Street Lawyer
DREAM HOLIDAY? Maldives
GUILTY PLEASURES? Chocolate and afternoon sleeps!
TWITTER FEED: @timmyg12

| Batting | Mat | Inns | NO | Runs | HS | Ave | SR | 100 | 50 | Ct | St |
|---|---|---|---|---|---|---|---|---|---|---|---|
| First-class | 53 | 72 | 22 | 1059 | 78 | 21.18 | 45.74 | 0 | 4 | 19 | 0 |
| List A | 55 | 36 | 10 | 345 | 36 | 13.26 | 96.63 | 0 | 0 | 13 | 0 |
| Twenty20 | 57 | 22 | 11 | 264 | 41 | 24.00 | 127.53 | 0 | 0 | 14 | 0 |

| Bowling | Mat | Balls | Runs | Wkts | BBI | BBM | Ave | Econ | SR | 5w | 10 |
|---|---|---|---|---|---|---|---|---|---|---|---|
| First-class | 53 | 8986 | 4767 | 146 | 6/50 | 8/97 | 32.65 | 3.18 | 61.5 | 5 | 0 |
| List A | 55 | 1922 | 1782 | 50 | 4/22 | 4/22 | 35.64 | 5.56 | 38.4 | 0 | 0 |
| Twenty20 | 57 | 965 | 1300 | 47 | 3/18 | 3/18 | 27.65 | 8.08 | 20.5 | 0 | 0 |

# MARTIN GUPTILL

## RHB OB MVP97

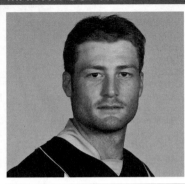

FULL NAME: Martin James Guptill
BORN: September 30, 1986, Auckland, New Zealand
SQUAD NO: 31
HEIGHT: 6ft 2in
NICKNAME: Guppy, The Fish
EDUCATION: Avondale College
TEAMS: New Zealand, Auckland, Derbyshire, New Zealand Academy, New Zealand Under-19s
CAREER: Test: 2009; ODI: 2009; T20I: 2009; First-class: 2006; List A: 2006; T20: 2006

---

BEST BATTING: 195* Auckland vs Canterbury, Rangiora, 2011
BEST BOWLING: 3-37 New Zealand vs Pakistan, Napier, 2009

---

NOTES: Made his first-team debut for Auckland in a limited-overs game against Canterbury in 2006. Is missing two toes on one of his feet following a forklift accident that occurred when he was 13. Made his maiden Test century – 189 off 310 deliveries – against Bangladesh at Hamilton in February 2010, with his second Test ton – a knock of 109 off 236 deliveries that included 11 fours and two sixes – coming against Zimbabwe at Bulawayo in November 2011. Averages 38.68 in ODI cricket when he takes the first ball in New Zealand's innings, compared to 49.17 when he bats at No.2

| Batting | Mat | Inns | NO | Runs | HS | Ave | SR | 100 | 50 | Ct | St |
|---|---|---|---|---|---|---|---|---|---|---|---|
| Tests | 20 | 37 | 1 | 1170 | 189 | 32.50 | 44.53 | 2 | 7 | 21 | 0 |
| ODIs | 60 | 58 | 6 | 2055 | 122* | 39.51 | 81.97 | 2 | 16 | 20 | 0 |
| T20Is | 29 | 27 | 5 | 788 | 91* | 35.81 | 126.48 | 0 | 4 | 14 | 0 |
| First-class | 54 | 97 | 6 | 3113 | 195* | 34.20 | 47.33 | 5 | 17 | 45 | 0 |
| List A | 99 | 95 | 9 | 3489 | 156 | 40.56 | 81.49 | 8 | 21 | 41 | 0 |
| Twenty20 | 78 | 74 | 10 | 2354 | 120* | 36.78 | 132.02 | 1 | 13 | 49 | 0 |

| Bowling | Mat | Balls | Runs | Wkts | BBI | BBM | Ave | Econ | SR | 5w | 10 |
|---|---|---|---|---|---|---|---|---|---|---|---|
| Tests | 20 | 278 | 196 | 5 | 3/37 | 3/37 | 39.20 | 4.23 | 55.6 | 0 | 0 |
| ODIs | 60 | 65 | 53 | 2 | 2/7 | 2/7 | 26.50 | 4.89 | 32.5 | 0 | 0 |
| T20Is | 29 | 6 | 11 | 0 | - | - | - | 11.00 | - | 0 | 0 |
| First-class | 54 | 446 | 297 | 6 | 3/37 | 3/37 | 49.50 | 3.99 | 74.3 | 0 | 0 |
| List A | 99 | 65 | 53 | 2 | 2/7 | 2/7 | 26.50 | 4.89 | 32.5 | 0 | 0 |
| Twenty20 | 78 | 12 | 19 | 0 | - | - | - | 9.50 | - | 0 | 0 |

# HARRY GURNEY

## RHB LFM

**FULL NAME:** Harry Frederick Gurney
**BORN:** October 25, 1986, Nottingham
**SQUAD NO:** 11
**HEIGHT:** 6ft 1in
**NICKNAME:** Sicknote, Contract, Chicken Legs, Gurns
**EDUCATION:** Garendon High School; Loughborough Grammar School; University of Leeds
**TEAMS:** Leeds/Bradford MCCU, Leicestershire, Leicestershire 2nd XI
**CAREER:** First-class: 2007; List A: 2009; T20: 2009

**BEST BATTING:** 24* Leicestershire vs Middlesex, Leicester, 2009
**BEST BOWLING:** 5-82 Leicestershire vs Surrey, Leicester, 2009

**WHY CRICKET?** I was useless at football!
**CAREER HIGHLIGHTS?** Signing first professional contract, Championship and CB40 five-wicket hauls
**CRICKETING HEROES?** Ryan Sidebottom, Dale Steyn
**NON-CRICKETING HEROES?** Peter Jones, Richard Branson, Alan Sugar
**TIP FOR THE TOP?** Joe Root
**IF YOU WEREN'T A CRICKETER?** Probably something in the financial sector in London
**WHEN RAIN STOPS PLAY?** Poker, reading, and drinking coffee
**FAVOURITE TV?** Frozen Planet
**FAVOURITE FILM?** Crash
**DREAM HOLIDAY?** St. Anton, Austria
**GUILTY PLEASURES?** Westlife, they are amazing
**SURPRISING FACTS?** I was once a sponsored poker player, I have five brothers and I support West Ham United
**FANTASY SLIP CORDON?** Keeper: Ricky Gervais, 1st: Alan Sugar, 2nd: Natalie Portman, 3rd: Me, 4th: Harry Redknapp, Gully: Tony Blair/Margaret Thatcher
**TWITTER FEED:** @gurneyhf

| Batting | Mat | Inns | NO | Runs | HS | Ave | SR | 100 | 50 | Ct | St |
|---|---|---|---|---|---|---|---|---|---|---|---|
| First-class | 17 | 18 | 8 | 63 | 24* | 6.30 | 31.65 | 0 | 0 | 2 | 0 |
| List A | 19 | 5 | 0 | 9 | 7 | 1.80 | 42.85 | 0 | 0 | 1 | 0 |
| Twenty20 | 30 | 2 | 2 | 5 | 5* | - | 100.00 | 0 | 0 | 4 | 0 |

| Bowling | Mat | Balls | Runs | Wkts | BBI | BBM | Ave | Econ | SR | 5w | 10 |
|---|---|---|---|---|---|---|---|---|---|---|---|
| First-class | 17 | 2378 | 1447 | 31 | 5/82 | 5/82 | 46.67 | 3.65 | 76.7 | 1 | 0 |
| List A | 19 | 709 | 645 | 15 | 5/24 | 5/24 | 43.00 | 5.45 | 47.2 | 1 | 0 |
| Twenty20 | 30 | 593 | 741 | 38 | 3/21 | 3/21 | 19.50 | 7.49 | 15.6 | 0 | 0 |

## ALEX HALES

### RHB RM R1 MVP23

NOTTINGHAMSHIRE

FULL NAME: Alexander Daniel Hales
BORN: January 3, 1989, Hillingdon, Middlesex
SQUAD NO: 10
HEIGHT: 6ft 5in
NICKNAME: Halsey, Trigg
EDUCATION: Chesham High School, Chesham
TEAMS: England, Buckinghamshire, England Lions, Nottinghamshire, Nottinghamshire 2nd XI
CAREER: T20I: 2011; First-class: 2008; List A: 2008; T20: 2009

BEST BATTING: 184 Nottinghamshire vs Somerset, Nottingham, 2011
BEST BOWLING: 2-63 Nottinghamshire vs Yorkshire, Nottingham, 2009

CRICKET MOMENT TO FORGET? Dropping a sitter against Kent 2nd XI for MCC Young Cricketers. If I had held the catch we would have won the game and qualified for the semi-finals!
SUPERSTITIONS? Always put my left pad on before my right one
CRICKETERS PARTICULARLY ADMIRED? Ian Bell, Nick Lines, Vinnie Fazio
OTHER SPORTS PLAYED? Play a bit of football in the winter for my local team
FAVOURITE BAND? Oasis
OTHER SPORTS FOLLOWED? Football (Arsenal)
SURPRISING FACTS? Grandfather once took Rod Laver to five sets at Wimbledon
RELAXATIONS? Enjoy playing poker

| Batting | Mat | Inns | NO | Runs | HS | Ave | SR | 100 | 50 | Ct | St |
|---|---|---|---|---|---|---|---|---|---|---|---|
| T20Is | 4 | 4 | 1 | 75 | 62* | 25.00 | 96.15 | 0 | 1 | 3 | 0 |
| First-class | 35 | 60 | 4 | 2259 | 184 | 40.33 | 58.99 | 4 | 16 | 29 | 0 |
| List A | 43 | 41 | 2 | 1397 | 150* | 35.82 | 102.41 | 3 | 7 | 18 | 0 |
| Twenty20 | 46 | 46 | 3 | 1146 | 83 | 26.65 | 134.98 | 0 | 10 | 18 | 0 |

| Bowling | Mat | Balls | Runs | Wkts | BBI | BBM | Ave | Econ | SR | 5w | 10 |
|---|---|---|---|---|---|---|---|---|---|---|---|
| T20Is | 4 | - | - | - | - | - | - | - | - | - | - |
| First-class | 35 | 281 | 167 | 3 | 2/63 | 2/63 | 55.66 | 3.56 | 93.6 | 0 | 0 |
| List A | 43 | 4 | 10 | 0 | - | - | - | 15.00 | - | 0 | 0 |
| Twenty20 | 46 | 3 | 7 | 0 | - | - | - | 14.00 | - | 0 | 0 |

# ANDREW HALL

## RHB RMF R1 MVP15

FULL NAME: Andrew James Hall
BORN: July 31, 1975, Johannesburg, South Africa
SQUAD NO: 1
HEIGHT: 6ft
NICKNAME: Hbomb, Hancock
EDUCATION: Hoerskool Alberton
TEAMS: South Africa, Africa XI, Chandigarh Lions, Dolphins, Easterns, Gauteng, Kent, Mashonaland Eagles, Northamptonshire, Transvaal, Worcestershire
CAREER: Test: 2002; ODI: 1999; T20I: 2006; First-class: 1995; List A: 1995; T20: 2003

BEST BATTING: 163 South Africa vs India, Kanpur, 2004
BEST BOWLING: 6-77 Easterns vs Western Province, Benoni, 2002
COUNTY CAPS: 2003 (Worcestershire); 2005 (Kent); 2009 (Northamptonshire)

FAMILY TIES? My brother and sister played indoor cricket for South Africa
CAREER HIGHLIGHTS? 163 opening the batting in India, 5-18 against England during the World Cup
CRICKETING HEROES? Clive Rice, Jimmy Cook and Ray Jennings
TIP FOR THE TOP? Alex Wakely
IF YOU WEREN'T A CRICKETER? Wanted to be a pilot and would have gone into the military to fly
FAVOURITE BOOK? The Gunslinger series by Stephen King
AMAZE ME! Played indoor cricket for SA when I was 17, I like classical music and was the 458th player for Northamptonshire
TWITTER FEED: @AndrewHall99

| Batting | Mat | Inns | NO | Runs | HS | Ave | SR | 100 | 50 | Ct | St |
|---|---|---|---|---|---|---|---|---|---|---|---|
| Tests | 21 | 33 | 4 | 760 | 163 | 26.20 | 46.06 | 1 | 3 | 16 | 0 |
| ODIs | 88 | 56 | 13 | 905 | 81 | 21.04 | 75.04 | 0 | 3 | 29 | 0 |
| T20Is | 2 | 1 | 0 | 11 | 11 | 11.00 | 110.00 | 0 | 0 | 0 | 0 |
| First-class | 198 | 292 | 39 | 9100 | 163 | 35.96 | | 12 | 54 | 196 | 0 |
| List A | 303 | 239 | 45 | 5731 | 129* | 29.54 | | 6 | 31 | 90 | 1 |
| Twenty20 | 97 | 85 | 20 | 1404 | 66* | 21.60 | 118.98 | 0 | 4 | 27 | 0 |

| Bowling | Mat | Balls | Runs | Wkts | BBI | BBM | Ave | Econ | SR | 5w | 10 |
|---|---|---|---|---|---|---|---|---|---|---|---|
| Tests | 21 | 3001 | 1617 | 45 | 3/1 | 5/20 | 35.93 | 3.23 | 66.6 | 0 | 0 |
| ODIs | 88 | 3341 | 2515 | 95 | 5/18 | 5/18 | 26.47 | 4.51 | 35.1 | 1 | 0 |
| T20Is | 2 | 48 | 60 | 3 | 3/22 | 3/22 | 20.00 | 7.50 | 16.0 | 0 | 0 |
| First-class | 198 | 29932 | 14588 | 533 | 6/77 | | 27.36 | 2.92 | 56.1 | 15 | 1 |
| List A | 303 | 12120 | 9616 | 352 | 5/18 | 5/18 | 27.31 | 4.76 | 34.4 | 2 | 0 |
| Twenty20 | 97 | 1894 | 2398 | 118 | 6/21 | 6/21 | 20.32 | 7.59 | 16.0 | 2 | 0 |

## RORY HAMILTON-BROWN    RHB OB R1 MVP39

**SURREY**

FULL NAME: Rory James Hamilton-Brown
BORN: September 3, 1987, Wellington Hospital, London
SQUAD NO: 27
HEIGHT: 6ft
NICKNAME: Razza, HB
EDUCATION: Dulwich Prep; Millfield School
TEAMS: England Under-19s, Mashonaland Eagles, Surrey, Surrey 2nd XI, Sussex
CAREER: First-class: 2005; List A: 2005; T20: 2008

BEST BATTING: 171* Sussex vs Yorkshire, Hove, 2009
BEST BOWLING: 2-49 Sussex vs Yorkshire, Hove, 2009

WHY CRICKET? The competitive nature and the feeling of winning
CAREER HIGHLIGHTS? Being appointed Surrey captain and winning the CB40 in 2011
CRICKETING HEROES? Jacques Kallis and Herschelle Gibbs
NON-CRICKETING HEROES? Joel Stransky and Mark Wright
BEST PLAYER IN COUNTY CRICKET? Marcus Trescothick
TIPS FOR THE TOP? Daniel Bell-Drummond, Tom Maynard and Billy Godleman
IF YOU WEREN'T A CRICKETER? I would like to be working in the City, depending on grades
WHEN RAIN STOPS PLAY? Discussing team tactics with the Sports Science Department and listening to their 80s mix CD
FAVOURITE TV? An Idiot Abroad
FAVOURITE FILM? The Other Guys
FAVOURITE BOOK? The Innocent Man by John Grisham
GUILTY PLEASURES? A love of the commentary style of Bob Willis
AMAZE ME! I like Tabasco on any food, I have a great love of street art and I never miss an episode of TOWIE
FANTASY SLIP CORDON? Keeper: Jack Whitehall, 1st: Usain Bolt, 2nd: Kate Beckinsale, 3rd: Tom Maynard, Gully: Boris Johnson

| Batting | Mat | Inns | NO | Runs | HS | Ave | SR | 100 | 50 | Ct | St |
|---|---|---|---|---|---|---|---|---|---|---|---|
| First-class | 42 | 73 | 5 | 2316 | 171* | 34.05 | 78.56 | 5 | 9 | 32 | 0 |
| List A | 62 | 55 | 2 | 1413 | 115 | 26.66 | 113.76 | 1 | 7 | 21 | 0 |
| Twenty20 | 69 | 63 | 3 | 1084 | 87* | 18.06 | 119.12 | 0 | 4 | 21 | 0 |

| Bowling | Mat | Balls | Runs | Wkts | BBI | BBM | Ave | Econ | SR | 5w | 10 |
|---|---|---|---|---|---|---|---|---|---|---|---|
| First-class | 42 | 817 | 504 | 8 | 2/49 | 3/85 | 63.00 | 3.70 | 102.1 | 0 | 0 |
| List A | 62 | 1236 | 1154 | 32 | 3/28 | 3/28 | 36.06 | 5.60 | 38.6 | 0 | 0 |
| Twenty20 | 69 | 520 | 662 | 34 | 4/15 | 4/15 | 19.47 | 7.63 | 15.2 | 0 | 0 |

# OLIVER HANNON-DALBY

## LHB RMF

FULL NAME: Oliver James Hannon-Dalby
BORN: June 20, 1989, Halifax, Yorkshire
SQUAD NO: 12
HEIGHT: 6ft 8in
NICKNAME: Bunse, Dave, OHD, Shaggy
EDUCATION: The Brooksbank School
TEAMS: Yorkshire, Yorkshire 2nd XI
CAREER: First-class: 2008; List A: 2011

BEST BATTING: 11* Yorkshire vs Lancashire, Manchester, 2010
BEST BOWLING: 5-68 Yorkshire vs Somerset, Leeds, 2010

WHY CRICKET? Went to my first match at five days old, so not much choice!
CAREER HIGHLIGHTS? Debut and first five-fer
CRICKETING HEROES? Glenn McGrath, Brett Lee
NON-CRICKETING HEROES? Lance Armstrong, my mum
BEST PLAYER IN COUNTY CRICKET? Marcus Trescothick
TIPS FOR THE TOP? Jonny Bairstow, Azeem Rafiq
IF YOU WEREN'T A CRICKETER? Teacher
WHEN RAIN STOPS PLAY? Eating or crosswords
FAVOURITE TV? Top Gear, Family Guy
FAVOURITE FILM? Blades Of Glory
FAVOURITE BOOK? Guinness World Records
DREAM HOLIDAY? Barbados
ACCOMPLISHMENTS? Buying my first house
SURPRISING SKILL? Juggle, play guitar
GUILTY PLEASURES? Guinness
AMAZE ME! Local high jump champion aged 12, Yorkshire CCC Scrabble champion 2011,
Cyril Sneer impressionist
TWITTER FEED: @OHD12

| Batting | Mat | Inns | NO | Runs | HS | Ave | SR | 100 | 50 | Ct | St |
|---|---|---|---|---|---|---|---|---|---|---|---|
| First-class | 23 | 24 | 9 | 40 | 11* | 2.66 | 10.58 | 0 | 0 | 1 | 0 |
| List A | 4 | - | - | - | - | - | - | - | - | 3 | 0 |

| Bowling | Mat | Balls | Runs | Wkts | BBI | BBM | Ave | Econ | SR | 5w | 10 |
|---|---|---|---|---|---|---|---|---|---|---|---|
| First-class | 23 | 3196 | 1884 | 39 | 5/68 | 7/122 | 48.30 | 3.53 | 81.9 | 2 | 0 |
| List A | 4 | 130 | 144 | 5 | 2/22 | 2/22 | 28.80 | 6.64 | 26.0 | 0 | 0 |

## ARUN HARINATH

### LHB OB

SURREY

**FULL NAME:** Arun Harinath
**BORN:** April 3, 1987, Sutton, Surrey
**SQUAD NO:** 10
**HEIGHT:** 5ft 11in
**NICKNAME:** Baron
**EDUCATION:** Tiffin Boys' Grammar School; Loughborough University
**TEAMS:** Loughborough MCCU, Marylebone Cricket Club, Surrey, Surrey 2nd XI
**CAREER:** First-class: 2007; List A: 2009

**BEST BATTING:** 80 Surrey vs CMCCU, Fenner's, 2011

**FAMILY TIES?** Dad played school and university cricket in Sri Lanka. My brother was also on the staff at Surrey in 2009
**CAREER HIGHLIGHTS?** Making my first team debut was pretty special
**CRICKETING HEROES?** Brian Lara, Mark Butcher, Graham Thorpe, Mark Ramprakash
**NON-CRICKETING HEROES?** Tim Tebow, Ray Lewis
**BEST PLAYER IN COUNTY CRICKET?** Marcus Trescothick
**TIPS FOR THE TOP?** Tom Maynard, Dom Sibley
**IF YOU WEREN'T A CRICKETER?** Probably still be at university attempting a Masters
**WHEN RAIN STOPS PLAY?** Watching The West Wing, reading or – if there are enough of us – playing 500
**FAVOURITE TV?** The West Wing
**FAVOURITE FILM?** Wedding Crashers
**FAVOURITE BOOK?** Catcher In The Rye
**DREAM HOLIDAY?** Hawaii
**ACCOMPLISHMENTS?** Attaining a degree
**AMAZE ME!** I'm a big NFL fan, I'm doing another degree in Politics, Philosophy and Economics and I used to play club badminton when I was younger
**FANTASY SLIP CORDON?** Keeper: Steve Carell (he would keep us all entertained), 1st: Myself, 2nd: Spiderman (someone needs to be able to catch the ball if we aren't paying attention), 3rd: Chris Martin (with guitar), Gully: Tim Tebow

| Batting | Mat | Inns | NO | Runs | HS | Ave | SR | 100 | 50 | Ct | St |
|---|---|---|---|---|---|---|---|---|---|---|---|
| First-class | 26 | 44 | 1 | 1129 | 80 | 26.25 | 41.20 | 0 | 8 | 7 | 0 |
| List A | 1 | 1 | 1 | 21 | 21* | - | 80.76 | 0 | 0 | 0 | 0 |

| Bowling | Mat | Balls | Runs | Wkts | BBI | BBM | Ave | Econ | SR | 5w | 10 |
|---|---|---|---|---|---|---|---|---|---|---|---|
| First-class | 26 | 36 | 30 | 0 | - | - | - | 5.00 | - | 0 | 0 |
| List A | 1 | - | - | - | - | - | - | - | - | - | - |

# BEN HARMISON

## LHB RMF

FULL NAME: Ben William Harmison
BORN: January 9, 1986, Ashington, Northumberland
SQUAD NO: 21
HEIGHT: 6ft 5in
NICKNAME: Harmy
EDUCATION: Ashington High School
TEAMS: Durham, Northumberland
CAREER: First-class: 2006; List A: 2005; T20: 2006

KENT

BEST BATTING: 110 Durham vs OUCCE, The Parks, 2006
BEST BOWLING: 4-27 Durham vs Surrey, Guildford, 2008

FAMILY TIES? Brother Stephen plays for Durham and England. Father Jim and brother James play league cricket for Ashington CC
CAREER HIGHLIGHTS? Signing my first professional contract at the age of 18. Consecutive hundreds in my first two first-class games for Durham
CRICKET MOMENT TO FORGET? Getting a first-baller vs Bangladesh in a one-dayer
CRICKETERS PARTICULARLY ADMIRED? Andrew Flintoff
FAVOURITE FILM? Armageddon
FAVOURITE BAND? Take That
OTHER SPORTS PLAYED? Golf, fishing, football
OTHER SPORTS FOLLOWED? Football (Newcastle United)
RELAXATIONS? Fishing, listening to music

| Batting | Mat | Inns | NO | Runs | HS | Ave | SR | 100 | 50 | Ct | St |
|---|---|---|---|---|---|---|---|---|---|---|---|
| First-class | 37 | 62 | 5 | 1488 | 110 | 26.10 | 44.44 | 3 | 7 | 23 | 0 |
| List A | 51 | 44 | 5 | 953 | 67 | 24.43 | 71.65 | 0 | 3 | 18 | 0 |
| Twenty20 | 30 | 17 | 7 | 117 | 24 | 11.70 | 107.33 | 0 | 0 | 9 | 0 |
| Bowling | Mat | Balls | Runs | Wkts | BBI | BBM | Ave | Econ | SR | 5w | 10 |
| First-class | 37 | 1557 | 1144 | 33 | 4/27 | 6/98 | 34.66 | 4.40 | 47.1 | 0 | 0 |
| List A | 51 | 865 | 855 | 24 | 3/43 | 3/43 | 35.62 | 5.93 | 36.0 | 0 | 0 |
| Twenty20 | 30 | 348 | 471 | 23 | 3/20 | 3/20 | 20.47 | 8.12 | 15.1 | 0 | 0 |

# STEVE HARMISON

### RHB RF W6

**DURHAM**

**FULL NAME:** Stephen James Harmison
**BORN:** October 23, 1978, Ashington, Northumberland
**SQUAD NO:** 10
**HEIGHT:** 6ft 4in
**NICKNAME:** Harmy
**EDUCATION:** Ashington High School
**TEAMS:** England, Durham, Durham 2nd XI, ICC World XI, Lions
**CAREER:** Test: 2002; ODI: 2002; T20I: 2005; First-class: 1996; List A: 1998; T20: 2004

**BEST BATTING:** 49* England vs South Africa, The Oval, 2008
**BEST BOWLING:** 7-12 England vs West Indies, Kingston, 2004

**FAMILY TIES?** Brother James played for Northumberland and younger brother Ben currently plays for Kent
**CRICKETERS PARTICULARLY ADMIRED?** David Boon, Courtney Walsh
**RELAXATIONS?** Spending time with the family
**OTHER SPORTS FOLLOWED?** Football (Newcastle United)
**NOTES:** He made his Test debut in 2002 against India at Trent Bridge. At The Oval in 2003 he took four second-innings wickets to help England draw the series against South Africa. In early 2004 he demolished the West Indies with 7-12 at Jamaica and 6-61 at Trinidad, taking 23 wickets in the series. After taking eight wickets in a day at The Oval against the West Indies in September 2004, he went top of the PricewaterhouseCoopers ratings for Test bowlers. He was an Ashes winner in 2005, becoming an MBE in the New Year's Honours list for 2006, and was also part of the victorious Ashes squad in 2009

| Batting | Mat | Inns | NO | Runs | HS | Ave | SR | 100 | 50 | Ct | St |
|---------|-----|------|-----|------|-----|------|-------|-----|-----|-----|-----|
| Tests | 63 | 86 | 23 | 743 | 49* | 11.79 | 57.19 | 0 | 0 | 7 | 0 |
| ODIs | 58 | 25 | 14 | 91 | 18* | 8.27 | 64.53 | 0 | 0 | 10 | 0 |
| T20Is | 2 | - | - | - | - | - | - | - | - | 1 | 0 |
| First-class | 205 | 262 | 74 | 1857 | 49* | 9.87 | | 0 | 0 | 29 | 0 |
| List A | 143 | 67 | 34 | 267 | 25* | 8.09 | | 0 | 0 | 23 | 0 |
| Twenty20 | 28 | 6 | 1 | 11 | 6 | 2.20 | 84.61 | 0 | 0 | 3 | 0 |

| Bowling | Mat | Balls | Runs | Wkts | BBI | BBM | Ave | Econ | SR | 5w | 10 |
|---------|-----|-------|------|------|-----|-----|------|------|------|-----|-----|
| Tests | 63 | 13375 | 7192 | 226 | 7/12 | 11/76 | 31.82 | 3.22 | 59.1 | 8 | 1 |
| ODIs | 58 | 2899 | 2481 | 76 | 5/33 | 5/33 | 32.64 | 5.13 | 38.1 | 1 | 0 |
| T20Is | 2 | 39 | 42 | 1 | 1/13 | 1/13 | 42.00 | 6.46 | 39.0 | 0 | 0 |
| First-class | 205 | 38784 | 20381 | 730 | 7/12 | | 27.91 | 3.15 | 53.1 | 27 | 1 |
| List A | 143 | 6838 | 5658 | 184 | 5/33 | 5/33 | 30.75 | 4.96 | 37.1 | 1 | 0 |
| Twenty20 | 28 | 505 | 668 | 29 | 5/41 | 5/41 | 23.03 | 7.93 | 17.4 | 1 | 0 |

FULL NAME: James Alexander Russell Harris
BORN: May 16, 1990, Morriston, Swansea, Glamorgan
SQUAD NO: 9
HEIGHT: 6ft 1in
NICKNAME: Lloyd Christmas, LC, Rolf, Bones
EDUCATION: Pontarddulais Comprehensive; Gorseinon College
TEAMS: England Lions, England Under-19s, Glamorgan, Glamorgan 2nd XI, Wales Minor Counties
CAREER: First-class: 2007; List A: 2007; T20: 2008

**GLAMORGAN**

BEST BATTING: 87* Glamorgan vs Nottinghamshire, Swansea, 2007
BEST BOWLING: 7-66 Glamorgan vs Gloucestershire, Bristol, 2007
COUNTY CAP: 2010

FAMILY TIES? Father played for British Universities
CAREER HIGHLIGHTS? Taking 12 wickets in my second first-class game on my 17th birthday, getting my county cap in 2010, going on the Lions tour to the West Indies in 2011
SUPERSTITIONS? Left pad before right
CRICKETING HEROES? Glenn McGrath, Jacques Kallis
NON-CRICKETING HEROES? Tiger Woods, Lance Armstrong
BEST PLAYER IN COUNTY CRICKET? Marcus Trescothick
TIPS FOR THE TOP? James Taylor, Ben Stokes, Jos Buttler
IF YOU WEREN'T A CRICKETER? Attempting to play golf, most probably
WHEN RAIN STOPS PLAY? There's now a pool table in the Glammy dressing room so playing on that. Otherwise time on the iPad
FAVOURITE TV? Entourage (highly recommended)
FAVOURITE FILM? The Shawshank Redemption, Anchorman
FAVOURITE BOOK? The Da Vinci Code, Angels And Demons
DREAM HOLIDAY? Barbados
TWITTER FEED: @James_Harris9

| Batting | Mat | Inns | NO | Runs | HS | Ave | SR | 100 | 50 | Ct | St |
|---|---|---|---|---|---|---|---|---|---|---|---|
| First-class | 59 | 84 | 16 | 1474 | 87* | 21.67 | | 0 | 7 | 16 | 0 |
| List A | 30 | 20 | 5 | 175 | 29 | 11.66 | 74.15 | 0 | 0 | 5 | 0 |
| Twenty20 | 23 | 14 | 7 | 87 | 18 | 12.42 | 120.83 | 0 | 0 | 2 | 0 |

| Bowling | Mat | Balls | Runs | Wkts | BBI | BBM | Ave | Econ | SR | 5w | 10 |
|---|---|---|---|---|---|---|---|---|---|---|---|
| First-class | 59 | 10791 | 5744 | 211 | 7/66 | 12/118 | 27.22 | 3.19 | 51.1 | 7 | 1 |
| List A | 30 | 1128 | 1005 | 40 | 4/48 | 4/48 | 25.12 | 5.34 | 28.2 | 0 | 0 |
| Twenty20 | 23 | 404 | 577 | 20 | 4/23 | 4/23 | 28.85 | 8.56 | 20.2 | 0 | 0 |

# JAMIE HARRISON

## RHB LMF

**DURHAM**

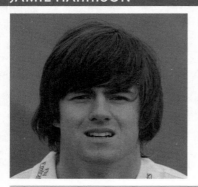

FULL NAME: Jamie Harrison
BORN: November 19, 1990, Whiston, Knowsley, Lancashire
SQUAD NO: 13
HEIGHT: 6ft 1in
NICKNAME: Justin Bieber, Jay
EDUCATION: Sedbergh School
TEAMS: Durham 2nd XI, Durham Academy, Gloucestershire 2nd XI, Sedbergh School
CAREER: Yet to make first-team debut

**WHY CRICKET?** I started playing cricket at the age of 11, at first just to try something new. I found I enjoy the one-to-one battles and the individual role you can have in contributing to your team's performance

**CAREER HIGHLIGHTS?** Joining Durham CCC after leaving school, taking 7-26 for the academy

**SUPERSTITIONS?** I like to pack my bag the night before the day's play with my warm-up kit on one side and my whites on the other. When getting to the ground I like to unpack my bag in the same order and lay it all out. I like to walk on the pitch last too

**CRICKETING HEROES?** Wasim Akram, Glenn McGrath, Dale Steyn, Simon Brown

**NON-CRICKETING HEROES?** Lance Armstrong, Sean Long, Muhammad Ali

**BEST PLAYER IN COUNTY CRICKET?** Dale Benkenstein, he is a great role model to all players

**TIPS FOR THE TOP?** Rammy Singh (Durham), Paul Coughlin (Durham)

**IF YOU WEREN'T A CRICKETER?** I'd have gone to university to study Sports Science

**FAVOURITE TV?** Geordie Shore, Shameless, Misfits, Mrs Brown's Boys

**FAVOURITE FILM?** Ali, East Is East, Four Lions, The Inbetweeners

**FAVOURITE BOOK?** Glenn McGrath – Line And Strength

**DREAM HOLIDAY?** Fiji

# NICK HARRISON RHB RMF

FULL NAME: Nicholas Luke Harrison
BORN: February 3, 1992, Bath, Somerset
SQUAD NO: 12
HEIGHT: 6ft 4in
NICKNAME: Trigger, Pablo
EDUCATION: Hardenhuish School, Chippenham
TEAMS: Wiltshire, Worcestershire, Worcestershire 2nd XI
CAREER: List A: 2011

FAMILY TIES? My dad and brothers all played, as well as my uncle and my cousins. We all played together for Chippenham 3rd XI, where eight of us out of the 11 were related!

CAREER HIGHLIGHTS? Making my debut for the first team and playing on Sky in the same game. Taking three five-wicket hauls in two weeks. Taking my first wicket for the first team

CRICKETING HEROES? Glenn McGrath and Andrew Flintoff

BEST PLAYER IN COUNTY CRICKET? Marcus Trescothick or Alan Richardson

TIPS FOR THE TOP? Aneesh Kapil

IF YOU WEREN'T A CRICKETER? I would try The X Factor! Or study to become a plumber or an electrician

WHEN RAIN STOPS PLAY? I'll be playing games on my iPod and drinking hundreds of cups of tea

FAVOURITE TV? Two And A Half Men

FAVOURITE FILM? Good Will Hunting, Rise Of The Planet Of The Apes

FAVOURITE BOOK? Ross Kemp: Pirates, The Game by Neil Strauss

DREAM HOLIDAY? Miami beach holiday

ACCOMPLISHMENTS? Played basketball for my county

GUILTY PLEASURES? Ronan Keating, McDonald's cheeseburgers

AMAZE ME! My toes are like fingers, I have produced a few music tracks that haven't quite made it into the business, I gave Katherine Jenkins a kiss on the cheek when working at the motorway services

FANTASY SLIP CORDON? Keeper: Mila Kunis, 1st: Me, 2nd: Lee Evans, 3rd: Gary Barlow, 4th: Rihanna, Gully: Peter Griffin

| Batting | Mat | Inns | NO | Runs | HS | Ave | SR | 100 | 50 | Ct | St |
|---------|-----|------|----|------|----|-----|----|-----|----|----|----|
| List A | 4 | 1 | 1 | 2 | 2* | - | 50.00 | 0 | 0 | 0 | 0 |

| Bowling | Mat | Balls | Runs | Wkts | BBI | BBM | Ave | Econ | SR | 5w | 10 |
|---------|-----|-------|------|------|-----|-----|-----|------|----|----|----|
| List A | 4 | 174 | 180 | 3 | 2/43 | 2/43 | 60.00 | 6.20 | 58.0 | 0 | 0 |

# LEWIS HATCHETT

## LHB LMF

SUSSEX

FULL NAME: Lewis James Hatchett
BORN: January 21, 1990, Shoreham-by-Sea, Sussex
SQUAD NO: 5
HEIGHT: 6ft 3in
NICKNAME: Hatch
EDUCATION: Steyning Grammar School
TEAMS: Sussex, Sussex 2nd XI
CAREER: First-class: 2010

BEST BATTING: 20 Sussex vs Middlesex, Uxbridge, 2010
BEST BOWLING: 5-47 Sussex vs Leicestershire, Leicester, 2010

CAREER HIGHLIGHTS? First-class debut, my maiden first-class five-fer, signing a contract with my home county Sussex and all of these things happening in the same year!
SUPERSTITIONS? Try not to move places when the team are doing well and sometimes shave my head before games! Always turn left at the top of my run-up
CRICKETING HEROES? Grew up watching the old West Indian bowlers such as Courtney Walsh and Curtly Ambrose. Watched a lot of Jason Lewry at Sussex, probably where I learnt my action from
NON-CRICKETING HEROES? My family. Our country's servicemen, past and present
BEST PLAYER IN COUNTY CRICKET? Batting: Marcus Trescothick; bowling: Glen Chapple
TIPS FOR THE TOP? Jos Buttler and Alex Hales look super talented, those are two who stand out for me. I'd also back my mate Luke Wells to push on to higher things
IF YOU WEREN'T A CRICKETER? Would love to have been a Marine
FAVOURITE TV? Scrubs
FAVOURITE FILM? Too many to pick just one! I'm a big fan of films though
DREAM HOLIDAY? Barbados – just to go and chill with friends out there
AMAZE ME! I suffer from Poland Syndrome, I like the countryside over the city, I have my Sussex cap number tattooed under my left arm
FANTASY SLIP CORDON? Keeper: Will Ferrell, 1st: Jim Carrey, 2nd: Me, 3rd: Jonny Wilkinson, 4th: Tiger Woods, 5th: Nicki Minaj, Gully: Rihanna
TWITTER FEED: @lewis_hatchett

| Batting | Mat | Inns | NO | Runs | HS | Ave | SR | 100 | 50 | Ct | St |
|---|---|---|---|---|---|---|---|---|---|---|---|
| First-class | 5 | 4 | 0 | 30 | 20 | 7.50 | 27.77 | 0 | 0 | 1 | 0 |

| Bowling | Mat | Balls | Runs | Wkts | BBI | BBM | Ave | Econ | SR | 5w | 10 |
|---|---|---|---|---|---|---|---|---|---|---|---|
| First-class | 5 | 520 | 301 | 14 | 5/47 | 6/92 | 21.50 | 3.47 | 37.1 | 1 | 0 |

# CLAUDE HENDERSON

## RHB SLA W1 MVP41

FULL NAME: Claude William Henderson
BORN: June 14, 1972, Worcester, Cape Province, South Africa
SQUAD NO: 15
HEIGHT: 6ft 2in
NICKNAME: Hendo
EDUCATION: Worcester High School, South Africa
TEAMS: South Africa, Boland, Cape Cobras, Leicestershire, Lions, Western Province, Worcestershire Cricket Board
CAREER: Test: 2001; ODI: 2001; First-class: 1990; List A: 1991; T20: 2004

LEICESTERSHIRE

BEST BATTING: 81 Leicestershire vs Gloucestershire, Leicester, 2001
BEST BOWLING: 7-57 Boland vs Eastern Province, Paarl, 1994
COUNTY CAP: 2004; TESTIMONIAL: 2011

FAMILY TIES? Brother James was first-class opening batter
CAREER HIGHLIGHTS? All the trophies won in SA and for Leicestershire, and playing for South Africa
CRICKETING HEROES? Graeme Pollock, Shane Warne and Jacques Kallis
NON-CRICKETING HEROES? Ernie Els and Carel du Plessis
TIP FOR THE TOP? James Taylor
IF YOU WEREN'T A CRICKETER? Spin bowling coach, commentator, restaurant owner
WHEN RAIN STOPS PLAY? Listen to banter in the changing room, reading my emails
FAVOURITE TV? National Geographic, Sky Sports
FAVOURITE FILM? Taken
GUILTY PLEASURES? I love red wine
FANTASY SLIP CORDON? Keeper: Marilyn Monroe, 1st: Lee Evans, 2nd: Elle Macpherson, 3rd: Shane Warne

| Batting | Mat | Inns | NO | Runs | HS | Ave | SR | 100 | 50 | Ct | St |
|---|---|---|---|---|---|---|---|---|---|---|---|
| Tests | 7 | 7 | 0 | 65 | 30 | 9.28 | 32.17 | 0 | 0 | 2 | 0 |
| ODIs | 4 | - | - | - | - | - | - | - | - | 0 | 0 |
| First-class | 259 | 354 | 74 | 5293 | 81 | 18.90 | | 0 | 18 | 88 | 0 |
| List A | 253 | 145 | 68 | 1160 | 45 | 15.06 | | 0 | 0 | 57 | 0 |
| Twenty20 | 97 | 36 | 14 | 179 | 32 | 8.13 | 100.00 | 0 | 0 | 26 | 0 |

| Bowling | Mat | Balls | Runs | Wkts | BBI | BBM | Ave | Econ | SR | 5w | 10 |
|---|---|---|---|---|---|---|---|---|---|---|---|
| Tests | 7 | 1962 | 928 | 22 | 4/116 | 7/176 | 42.18 | 2.83 | 89.1 | 0 | 0 |
| ODIs | 4 | 217 | 132 | 7 | 4/17 | 4/17 | 18.85 | 3.64 | 31.0 | 0 | 0 |
| First-class | 259 | 62412 | 26597 | 869 | 7/57 | | 30.60 | 2.55 | 71.8 | 33 | 2 |
| List A | 253 | 11228 | 8123 | 317 | 6/29 | 6/29 | 25.62 | 4.34 | 35.4 | 2 | 0 |
| Twenty20 | 97 | 1936 | 2232 | 89 | 3/23 | 3/23 | 25.07 | 6.91 | 21.7 | 0 | 0 |

## MOISES HENRIQUES

### RHB RFM

**FULL NAME:** Moises Constantino Henriques
**BORN:** February 1, 1987, Funchal, Portugal
**SQUAD NO:** 7
**HEIGHT:** 6ft 1in
**NICKNAME:** Moey
**TEAMS:** Australia, Australia A, Delhi Daredevils, Kolkata Knight Riders, Mumbai Indians, New South Wales, Sydney Sixers
**CAREER:** ODI: 2009; T20I: 2009; First-class: 2006; List A: 2006; T20: 2006

BEST BATTING: 82 Australia A vs Pakistan A, Townsville, 2009
BEST BOWLING: 5-17 New South Wales vs Queensland, Brisbane, 2006

NOTES: Allrounder who captained Australia U19. Made his first-class debut for New South Wales vs South Australia in 2006. Youngest player to ever take 10 wickets in a Sydney first-grade game

| Batting | Mat | Inns | NO | Runs | HS | Ave | SR | 100 | 50 | Ct | St |
|---|---|---|---|---|---|---|---|---|---|---|---|
| ODIs | 2 | 2 | 0 | 18 | 12 | 9.00 | 60.00 | 0 | 0 | 0 | 0 |
| T20Is | 1 | 1 | 0 | 1 | 1 | 1.00 | 50.00 | 0 | 0 | 0 | 0 |
| First-class | 27 | 48 | 6 | 1257 | 82 | 29.92 | 48.34 | 0 | 8 | 14 | 0 |
| List A | 50 | 44 | 7 | 885 | 65* | 23.91 | 77.29 | 0 | 2 | 23 | 0 |
| Twenty20 | 54 | 48 | 8 | 826 | 70 | 20.65 | 120.23 | 0 | 2 | 31 | 0 |

| Bowling | Mat | Balls | Runs | Wkts | BBI | BBM | Ave | Econ | SR | 5w | 10 |
|---|---|---|---|---|---|---|---|---|---|---|---|
| ODIs | 2 | 90 | 84 | 1 | 1/51 | 1/51 | 84.00 | 5.60 | 90.0 | 0 | 0 |
| T20Is | 1 | - | - | - | - | - | - | - | - | - | - |
| First-class | 27 | 2899 | 1475 | 47 | 5/17 | 5/40 | 31.38 | 3.05 | 61.6 | 2 | 0 |
| List A | 50 | 1853 | 1638 | 40 | 3/29 | 3/29 | 40.95 | 5.30 | 46.3 | 0 | 0 |
| Twenty20 | 54 | 809 | 1159 | 36 | 3/11 | 3/11 | 32.19 | 8.59 | 22.4 | 0 | 0 |

## MATT HIGGINBOTTOM                    LHB RMF

FULL NAME: Matthew Higginbottom
BORN: October 20, 1990, Stockport, Cheshire
SQUAD NO: 20
HEIGHT: 6ft 1in
NICKNAME: Higgy, Higgos, Chigs
EDUCATION: New Mills Business and
Enterprise College; Leeds Metropolitan
University
TEAMS: Leeds/Bradford MCCU, Derbyshire,
Derbyshire 2nd XI
CAREER: Yet to make first-team debut

DERBYSHIRE

FAMILY TIES? Family has always been strongly tied with the local club Hayfield, with my grandfather, father and brother all being key players at the club at various stages
CAREER HIGHLIGHTS? Playing against Australia in a tour match in 2010
CRICKETING HEROES? Glenn McGrath, Brian Lara, Brett Lee
NON-CRICKETING HEROES? Lance Armstrong
BEST PLAYER IN COUNTY CRICKET? Marcus Trescothick
TIPS FOR THE TOP? Peter Burgoyne, Tom Craddock
WHEN RAIN STOPS PLAY? Losing at poker, playing games on phone
FAVOURITE TV? One Tree Hill
FAVOURITE FILM? Step Brothers
DREAM HOLIDAY? Fiji
GUILTY PLEASURES? Crisps and sweets
FANTASY SLIP CORDON? Keeper: Me, 1st: Roger Federer (my hero), 2nd: Ricky Gervais (hilarious), 3rd: Mike Tyson (fascinates me), Gully: Beyoncé (in case we need some tunes)
TWITTER FEED: @matthigg12

## JAMES HILDRETH       RHB RM R2 MVP68

SOMERSET

FULL NAME: James Charles Hildreth
BORN: September 9, 1984, Milton Keynes
SQUAD NO: 25
HEIGHT: 5ft 10in
NICKNAME: Hildy, Hildz
EDUCATION: Millfield School, Glastonbury
TEAMS: England Lions, Somerset, Somerset Cricket Board
CAREER: First-class: 2003; List A: 2003; T20: 2004

BEST BATTING: 303* Somerset vs Warwickshire, Taunton, 2009
BEST BOWLING: 2-39 Somerset vs Hampshire, Taunton, 2009
COUNTY CAP: 2007

FAMILY TIES? Dad played league cricket in Kent and Northants
SUPERSTITIONS? Left pad before right when getting padded up
OTHER SPORTS PLAYED? Hockey (West of England), squash (South of England), football (England Independent Schools, Luton Town), rugby (Millfield)
FAVOURITE BAND? Jack Johnson
RELAXATIONS? Travelling, snowboarding, music
NOTES: Maiden first-class century in 2004 – 101 from 113 balls against Durham at Taunton. Scored 1,440 runs in 2010. Scored 210 in his final age-group match, against Bangladesh in 2004. Scored 38 off 24 balls in Somerset's famous chase against the touring Australians in 2005. Caught Ricky Ponting off the bowling of Matthew Hoggard whilst fielding in the first Ashes Test at Lord's in 2005 as a substitute. His 303* against Warwickshire in April 2009 is the earliest ever triple hundred in an English season

| Batting | Mat | Inns | NO | Runs | HS | Ave | SR | 100 | 50 | Ct | St |
|---|---|---|---|---|---|---|---|---|---|---|---|
| First-class | 134 | 216 | 16 | 8652 | 303* | 43.26 | | 23 | 41 | 111 | 0 |
| List A | 138 | 131 | 21 | 3600 | 151 | 32.72 | | 4 | 15 | 46 | 0 |
| Twenty20 | 100 | 95 | 14 | 1833 | 77* | 22.62 | 117.80 | 0 | 8 | 41 | 0 |

| Bowling | Mat | Balls | Runs | Wkts | BBI | BBM | Ave | Econ | SR | 5w | 10 |
|---|---|---|---|---|---|---|---|---|---|---|---|
| First-class | 134 | 480 | 414 | 5 | 2/39 | | 82.80 | 5.17 | 96.0 | 0 | 0 |
| List A | 138 | 150 | 185 | 6 | 2/26 | 2/26 | 30.83 | 7.40 | 25.0 | 0 | 0 |
| Twenty20 | 100 | 169 | 247 | 10 | 3/24 | 3/24 | 24.70 | 8.76 | 16.9 | 0 | 0 |

## ANDY HODD                                    RHB WK

**FULL NAME:** Andrew John Hodd
**BORN:** January 12, 1984, Chichester, West Sussex
**SQUAD NO:** 19
**HEIGHT:** 5ft 9in
**NICKNAME:** Hoddy
**EDUCATION:** Bexhill High School; Bexhill College; Loughborough University
**TEAMS:** England Under-19s, Surrey, Sussex, Sussex Cricket Board
**CAREER:** First-class: 2003; List A: 2002; T20: 2005

SUSSEX

**BEST BATTING:** 123 Sussex vs Yorkshire, Hove, 2007

**CAREER OUTSIDE CRICKET?** Coaching
**FAMILY TIES?** Long line of enthusiastic club cricketers
**SUPERSTITIONS?** Too many! Must drink coffee the morning of a game
**CRICKETERS PARTICULARLY ADMIRED?** David Hussey, Matt Prior
**OTHER SPORTS PLAYED?** Golf, football, boxing
**OTHER SPORTS FOLLOWED?** Football (Brighton and Hove Albion)
**FAVOURITE BAND?** Hard-Fi
**RELAXATIONS?** Cinema, DVDs, gym, going out
**NOTES:** England U19 wicketkeeper. Returned to Sussex in 2006 after a brief stint with Surrey. Shared keeping duties with Ben Brown and Matt Prior in 2011 – playing eight of Sussex's 16 Championship games

| Batting | Mat | Inns | NO | Runs | HS | Ave | SR | 100 | 50 | Ct | St |
|---|---|---|---|---|---|---|---|---|---|---|---|
| First-class | 57 | 84 | 15 | 2006 | 123 | 29.07 | 43.69 | 4 | 9 | 113 | 12 |
| List A | 42 | 33 | 9 | 566 | 91 | 23.58 | | 0 | 1 | 34 | 8 |
| Twenty20 | 47 | 25 | 4 | 253 | 26 | 12.04 | 103.26 | 0 | 0 | 22 | 10 |

| Bowling | Mat | Balls | Runs | Wkts | BBI | BBM | Ave | Econ | SR | 5w | 10 |
|---|---|---|---|---|---|---|---|---|---|---|---|
| First-class | 57 | 10 | 7 | 0 | - | - | - | 4.20 | - | 0 | 0 |
| List A | 42 | - | - | - | - | - | - | - | - | - | - |
| Twenty20 | 47 | - | - | - | - | - | - | - | - | - | - |

# DAN HODGSON RHB WK

**YORKSHIRE**

FULL NAME: Daniel Mark Hodgson
BORN: February 26, 1990, Northallerton, Yorkshire
SQUAD NO: 18
HEIGHT: 5ft 7in
NICKNAME: Hodgy
TEAMS: Leeds/Bradford MCCU
CAREER: Yet to make first-team debut

**FAMILY TIES?** My brothers play in the North Yorkshire South Durham league
**WHY CRICKET?** Loved playing for Aldbrough St. John village cricket club
**CAREER HIGHLIGHTS?** Signing for Yorkshire
**CRICKETING HEROES?** Shane Warne, Kumar Sangakkara
**NON-CRICKETING HEROES?** My parents, Alan Shearer, The Rock, Jay-Z
**BEST PLAYER IN COUNTY CRICKET?** Marcus Trescothick
**TIPS FOR THE TOP?** Ben Slater, Tom Craddock
**IF YOU WEREN'T A CRICKETER?** I'd be studying Sport Science and Physiology at the University of Leeds
**FAVOURITE TV?** Match Of The Day, One Tree Hill, House
**FAVOURITE FILM?** Man On Fire, Role Models, Inception
**FAVOURITE BOOK?** The Da Vinci Code
**DREAM HOLIDAY?** Anywhere with snow for skiing, or hot with a beach and windsurfing
**SURPRISING SKILL?** Fire juggling
**GUILTY PLEASURES?** Hip-Hop and RnB
**FANTASY SLIP CORDON?** Keeper: Me, 1st: Sonny Bill Williams, 2nd: P Diddy, 3rd: Peter Griffin, Gully: David Attenborough

# MICHAEL HOGAN  RHB RFM

**FULL NAME:** Michael Garry Hogan
**BORN:** May 31, 1981
**SQUAD NO:** TBC
**TEAMS:** New South Wales Country, New South Wales Second XI, Western Australia
**CAREER:** First-class: 2009; List A: 2009; T20: 2010

---

**BEST BATTING:** 41 Western Australia vs Victoria, MCG, 2011
**BEST BOWLING:** 6-70 Western Australia vs Tasmania, Hobart, 2010

---

**NOTES:** Signed for Glamorgan in March on a three-year contract and will join the county in July. "I think he'll be a great asset to our attack," Glamorgan coach Matthew Mott told the BBC after the deal was announced. "He's probably not a household name in Wales yet but he comes highly recommended, particularly from his [Western Australia] captain Marcus North. He's highly rated in Australian cricket, just recently he was polled amongst the Australian players as one of the best bowlers in the country"

| Batting | Mat | Inns | NO | Runs | HS | Ave | SR | 100 | 50 | Ct | St |
|---|---|---|---|---|---|---|---|---|---|---|---|
| First-class | 27 | 40 | 11 | 389 | 41 | 13.41 | 102.09 | 0 | 0 | 8 | 0 |
| List A | 21 | 6 | 2 | 51 | 27 | 12.75 | 94.44 | 0 | 0 | 7 | 0 |
| Twenty20 | 9 | 2 | 1 | 5 | 3* | 5.00 | 83.33 | 0 | 0 | 4 | 0 |

| Bowling | Mat | Balls | Runs | Wkts | BBI | BBM | Ave | Econ | SR | 5w | 10 |
|---|---|---|---|---|---|---|---|---|---|---|---|
| First-class | 27 | 6036 | 2846 | 100 | 6/70 | 9/86 | 28.46 | 2.82 | 60.3 | 4 | 0 |
| List A | 21 | 1186 | 946 | 26 | 5/44 | 5/44 | 36.38 | 4.78 | 45.6 | 1 | 0 |
| Twenty20 | 9 | 204 | 259 | 6 | 4/26 | 4/26 | 43.16 | 7.61 | 34.0 | 0 | 0 |

# KYLE HOGG — LHB RFM W1 MVP54

**LANCASHIRE**

FULL NAME: Kyle William Hogg
BORN: July 2, 1983, Birmingham, Warwickshire
SQUAD NO: 22
HEIGHT: 6ft 4in
NICKNAME: Hoggy, Boss
EDUCATION: Saddleworth High School
TEAMS: England Under-19s, Lancashire, Otago
CAREER: First-class: 2001; List A: 2001; T20: 2003

BEST BATTING: 88 Lancashire vs Yorkshire, Manchester, 2010
BEST BOWLING: 7-28 Lancashire vs Hampshire, Southampton, 2011
COUNTY CAPS: 2007 (Worcestershire); 2010 (Lancashire)

FAMILY TIES? Dad [William] and grandad [West Indies legend Sonny Ramadhin] both played
WHY CRICKET? Being brought up around the game
CAREER HIGHLIGHTS? Winning the Championship in 2011
CRICKETING HEROES? Ambrose, McGrath, Lara, Flintoff
NON-CRICKETING HEROES? Plenty of musicians, too many to mention
BEST PLAYER IN COUNTY CRICKET? Mark Ramprakash
TIP FOR THE TOP? Simon Kerrigan
IF YOU WEREN'T A CRICKETER? Good question!
WHEN RAIN STOPS PLAY? Cards or iPod
FAVOURITE TV? Crimewatch
FAVOURITE FILM? Control
DREAM HOLIDAY? Barbados takes some beating
SURPRISING SKILL? Can put a few chords together on the guitar
GUILTY PLEASURES? iTunes
TWITTER FEED: @kyle_hogg22

| Batting | Mat | Inns | NO | Runs | HS | Ave | SR | 100 | 50 | Ct | St |
|---|---|---|---|---|---|---|---|---|---|---|---|
| First-class | 76 | 97 | 12 | 2019 | 88 | 23.75 | 60.17 | 0 | 13 | 18 | 0 |
| List A | 129 | 80 | 23 | 950 | 66* | 16.66 | 69.44 | 0 | 1 | 22 | 0 |
| Twenty20 | 28 | 18 | 4 | 226 | 44 | 16.14 | 137.80 | 0 | 0 | 5 | 0 |

| Bowling | Mat | Balls | Runs | Wkts | BBI | BBM | Ave | Econ | SR | 5w | 10 |
|---|---|---|---|---|---|---|---|---|---|---|---|
| First-class | 76 | 10332 | 5359 | 174 | 7/28 | | 30.79 | 3.11 | 59.3 | 4 | 1 |
| List A | 129 | 4902 | 3936 | 133 | 4/20 | 4/20 | 29.59 | 4.81 | 36.8 | 0 | 0 |
| Twenty20 | 28 | 378 | 564 | 16 | 2/10 | 2/10 | 35.25 | 8.95 | 23.6 | 0 | 0 |

# MATTHEW HOGGARD

## RHB RFM W3

FULL NAME: Matthew James Hoggard
BORN: December 31, 1976, Leeds, Yorkshire
SQUAD NO: 77
HEIGHT: 6ft 2in
NICKNAME: Oggie, Hoggy
EDUCATION: Pudsey Grangefield School
TEAMS: England, Free State, Leicestershire, Yorkshire
CAREER: Test: 2000; ODI: 2001; First-class: 1996; List A: 1998; T20: 2004

**LEICESTERSHIRE**

BEST BATTING: 89* Yorkshire vs Glamorgan, Leeds, 2004
BEST BOWLING: 7-49 Yorkshire vs Somerset, Leeds, 2003
COUNTY CAPS: 2000 (Yorkshire); 2010 (Leicestershire); BENEFIT YEAR: 2008 (Yorkshire)

FAMILY TIES? Dad is a cricket badger
CRICKETING HEROES? Allan Donald, Courtney Walsh
NOTES: NBC Denis Compton Award for most promising young Yorkshire player in 1998. PCA Young Player of the Year in 2000. Took 7-63 vs New Zealand in the first Test at Christchurch 2001/02, the best innings return by an England pace bowler in Tests vs New Zealand. Took hat-trick in the third Test vs West Indies at Bridgetown 2003/04. His international awards include Man of the [Test] Series vs Bangladesh 2003/04 and Man of the Match in the fourth Test vs South Africa at Johannesburg 2004/05 (5-144/7-61) and in the first Test vs India at Nagpur 2005/06 (6-57). Appointed MBE in 2006 New Year Honours as part of 2005 Ashes-winning England team. Took 200th Test wicket in the first Test vs Sri Lanka at Lord's 2006. Took 237th Test wicket in the fourth Test vs West Indies at Riverside 2007 to move into sixth place in the England list of Test wicket-takers. Having had his Yorkshire contract terminated in October 2009, he joined Leicestershire the following month as their new captain for 2010

| Batting | Mat | Inns | NO | Runs | HS | Ave | SR | 100 | 50 | Ct | St |
|---|---|---|---|---|---|---|---|---|---|---|---|
| Tests | 67 | 92 | 27 | 473 | 38 | 7.27 | 22.63 | 0 | 0 | 24 | 0 |
| ODIs | 26 | 6 | 2 | 17 | 7 | 4.25 | 56.66 | 0 | 0 | 5 | 0 |
| First-class | 222 | 282 | 84 | 1752 | 89* | 8.84 | | 0 | 4 | 62 | 0 |
| List A | 147 | 48 | 25 | 130 | 23 | 5.65 | | 0 | 0 | 18 | 0 |
| Twenty20 | 45 | 7 | 4 | 56 | 18 | 18.66 | 175.00 | 0 | 0 | 7 | 0 |

| Bowling | Mat | Balls | Runs | Wkts | BBI | BBM | Ave | Econ | SR | 5w | 10 |
|---|---|---|---|---|---|---|---|---|---|---|---|
| Tests | 67 | 13909 | 7564 | 248 | 7/61 | 12/205 | 30.50 | 3.26 | 56.0 | 7 | 1 |
| ODIs | 26 | 1306 | 1152 | 32 | 5/49 | 5/49 | 36.00 | 5.29 | 40.8 | 1 | 0 |
| First-class | 222 | 39999 | 20503 | 746 | 7/49 | | 27.48 | 3.07 | 53.6 | 25 | 1 |
| List A | 147 | 6835 | 5164 | 201 | 5/28 | 5/28 | 25.69 | 4.53 | 34.0 | 4 | 0 |
| Twenty20 | 45 | 905 | 1267 | 45 | 3/19 | 3/19 | 28.15 | 8.40 | 20.1 | 0 | 0 |

## PAUL HORTON — RHB RM R3 MVP75

FULL NAME: Paul James Horton
BORN: September 20, 1982, Sydney, Australia
SQUAD NO: 20
HEIGHT: 5ft 10in
NICKNAME: Horts, Lefty, Aussie
EDUCATION: Colo High School, Sydney; Broadgreen Comp, Liverpool; St Margaret's High School
TEAMS: Lancashire, Lancashire 2nd XI, Matabeleland Tuskers
CAREER: First-class: 2003; List A: 2003; T20: 2005

BEST BATTING: 209 Matabeleland Tuskers vs Southern Rocks, Masvingo, 2011
COUNTY CAP: 2007

CAREER HIGHLIGHTS? Nothing can top winning the County Championship in 2011 with Lancashire, but every time I score a first-class hundred is pretty special. Back-to-back Logan Cup trophys with Matebeleland Tuskers in 2010/11 and 2011/12
CRICKETING HEROES? Mark Waugh, Dean Jones, Brian Lara
NON-CRICKETING HEROES? Roger Federer, Robbie Fowler
BEST PLAYER IN COUNTY CRICKET? Marcus Trescothick
TIPS FOR THE TOP? Simon Kerrigan, Ben Stokes
IF YOU WEREN'T A CRICKETER? Something in a suit!
WHEN RAIN STOPS PLAY? Ranges from hitting balls to talking rubbish in the dressing room
FAVOURITE TV? Location, Location, Location
FAVOURITE FILM? Notting Hill
FAVOURITE BOOK? It's Not About The Bike – Lance Armstrong
SURPRISING FACT? I once stacked shelves in Sainsbury's. Was once held as an illegal immigrant!
FANTASY SLIP CORDON? Keeper: Tiger Woods, 1st: Myself, 2nd: Robbie Fowler, 3rd: Nelson Mandela, Gully: Wonder Woman
TWITTER FEED: @Pjhorton20

| Batting | Mat | Inns | NO | Runs | HS | Ave | SR | 100 | 50 | Ct | St |
|---|---|---|---|---|---|---|---|---|---|---|---|
| First-class | 108 | 182 | 15 | 6566 | 209 | 39.31 | 49.56 | 13 | 37 | 115 | 1 |
| List A | 76 | 70 | 8 | 1898 | 111* | 30.61 | | 2 | 10 | 25 | 0 |
| Twenty20 | 52 | 50 | 9 | 972 | 71 | 23.70 | 105.42 | 0 | 2 | 18 | 0 |

| Bowling | Mat | Balls | Runs | Wkts | BBI | BBM | Ave | Econ | SR | 5w | 10 |
|---|---|---|---|---|---|---|---|---|---|---|---|
| First-class | 108 | 18 | 16 | 0 | - | - | - | 5.33 | - | 0 | 0 |
| List A | 76 | - | - | - | - | - | - | - | - | - | - |
| Twenty20 | 52 | - | - | - | - | - | - | - | - | - | - |

# DAN HOUSEGO
## RHB LB

FULL NAME: Daniel Mark Housego
BORN: October 12, 1988, Windsor, Berkshire
SQUAD NO: 3
HEIGHT: 5ft 9in
NICKNAME: The Estate Agent, Housey
EDUCATION: The Oratory School, Reading
TEAMS: Berkshire, Middlesex, Middlesex 2nd XI
CAREER: First-class: 2008; T20: 2008

BEST BATTING: 104 Middlesex vs Sri Lankans, Uxbridge, 2011

CAREER HIGHLIGHTS? Scoring a hundred against Sri Lanka
CRICKETING HEROES? Steve Waugh
BEST PLAYER IN COUNTY CRICKET? Marcus Trescothick
TIP FOR THE TOP? Alex Wakely
IF YOU WEREN'T A CRICKETER? Personal trainer
WHEN RAIN STOPS PLAY? Reading, Football Manager, anything that's not to do with cricket!
FAVOURITE TV? Only Fools And Horses
FAVOURITE FILM? Law Abiding Citizen
FAVOURITE BOOK? Any sports autobiography
DREAM HOLIDAY? Disney World, Florida
ACCOMPLISHMENTS? Oxford United footballer, 200m national prep school champion and I played for England U15, U16, U17 and U19
SURPRISING SKILL? Can sit on my own beside a fishing lake for days without getting bored!
GUILTY PLEASURES? Carp fishing, golf, movies
AMAZE ME! I am going to marry Mila Kunis one day

| Batting | Mat | Inns | NO | Runs | HS | Ave | SR | 100 | 50 | Ct | St |
|---|---|---|---|---|---|---|---|---|---|---|---|
| First-class | 15 | 29 | 3 | 703 | 104 | 27.03 | 46.92 | 2 | 0 | 5 | 0 |
| Twenty20 | 5 | 4 | 0 | 37 | 18 | 9.25 | 88.09 | 0 | 0 | 0 | 0 |

| Bowling | Mat | Balls | Runs | Wkts | BBI | BBM | Ave | Econ | SR | 5w | 10 |
|---|---|---|---|---|---|---|---|---|---|---|---|
| First-class | 15 | 7 | 17 | 0 | - | - | - | 14.57 | - | 0 | 0 |
| Twenty20 | 5 | - | - | - | - | - | - | - | - | - | - |

# BEN HOWGEGO                          LHB RM

**FULL NAME:** Benjamin Harry Nicholas Howgego
**BORN:** March 3, 1988, Kings Lynn, Norfolk
**SQUAD NO:** 27
**HEIGHT:** 5ft 11in
**NICKNAME:** Ken
**EDUCATION:** King's School, Ely; Stowe School
**TEAMS:** ECB Development of Excellence XI, Northamptonshire, Northamptonshire 2nd XI
**CAREER:** First-class: 2008; List A: 2009; T20: 2010

---

**BEST BATTING:** 80 Northamptonshire vs Derbyshire, Chesterfield, 2010

---

**FAMILY TIES?** My grandfather played cricket for Essex 2nd XI and my brother is an integral member of March Town CC
**CAREER HIGHLIGHTS?** First-class debut against Gloucestershire a few years back, scored 80 against Derbyshire in County Championship, 180 vs Yorkshire in 2nd XI Trophy
**CRICKETING HEROES?** Graham Thorpe was my cricketing hero as a young guy and Brian Lara has always been my favourite cricketer to watch
**BEST PLAYER IN COUNTY CRICKET?** Marcus Trescothick
**TIPS FOR THE TOP?** Rob Newton and Alex Wakely
**WHEN RAIN STOPS PLAY?** Talking rubbish with Rob Newton usually
**FAVOURITE TV?** Entourage
**FAVOURITE FILM?** Gladiator
**DREAM HOLIDAY?** Caribbean
**ACCOMPLISHMENTS?** University degree and three As at A-Level
**AMAZE ME!** I live in the pleasuredome, have a phobia of baked beans and love the animated series of Transformers
**FANTASY SLIP CORDON?** Keeper: Ricky Gervais (hilarious), 1st: Myself (have to be in it), 2nd: Shakira (my future wife), 3rd: David Beckham (great lid), Gullly: Borat (would definitely keep me entertained all day)

| Batting | Mat | Inns | NO | Runs | HS | Ave | SR | 100 | 50 | Ct | St |
|---|---|---|---|---|---|---|---|---|---|---|---|
| First-class | 20 | 34 | 4 | 669 | 80 | 22.30 | 39.44 | 0 | 1 | 11 | 0 |
| List A | 3 | 2 | 0 | 19 | 12 | 9.50 | 67.85 | 0 | 0 | 0 | 0 |
| Twenty20 | 2 | 2 | 0 | 4 | 3 | 2.00 | 44.44 | 0 | 0 | 0 | 0 |

| Bowling | Mat | Balls | Runs | Wkts | BBI | BBM | Ave | Econ | SR | 5w | 10 |
|---|---|---|---|---|---|---|---|---|---|---|---|
| First-class | 20 | 12 | 16 | 0 | - | - | - | 8.00 | - | 0 | 0 |
| List A | 3 | - | - | - | - | - | - | - | - | - | - |
| Twenty20 | 2 | - | - | - | - | - | - | - | - | - | - |

# ALEX HUGHES

### RHB RM

FULL NAME: Alex Lloyd Hughes
BORN: September 29, 1991, Wordsley, Staffordshire
SQUAD NO: 18
HEIGHT: 5ft 10in
TEAMS: Derbyshire, Derbyshire 2nd XI, Staffordshire
CAREER: T20: 2011

**DERBYSHIRE**

NOTES: Plays for Wombourne CC in the Birmingham and District Premier League and scored 721 runs at an average of 31.35 last season, with a top-score of 106*. His brother Liam is Wombourne's club captain, plays for Staffordshire at minor counties level and was on the Derbyshire staff between 2005 and 2007. Alex made his first-team debut against Yorkshire Carnegie at Derby in the FL t20 and made 11* batting at No.8

| Batting | Mat | Inns | NO | Runs | HS | Ave | SR | 100 | 50 | Ct | St |
|---|---|---|---|---|---|---|---|---|---|---|---|
| Twenty20 | 1 | 1 | 1 | 11 | 11* | - | 91.66 | 0 | 0 | 0 | 0 |

| Bowling | Mat | Balls | Runs | Wkts | BBI | BBM | Ave | Econ | SR | 5w | 10 |
|---|---|---|---|---|---|---|---|---|---|---|---|
| Twenty20 | 1 | 18 | 24 | 0 | - | - | - | 8.00 | - | 0 | 0 |

## CHESNEY HUGHES                    LHB SLA MVP56

DERBYSHIRE

FULL NAME: Chesney Francis Hughes
BORN: January 20, 1991, Anguilla
SQUAD NO: 20
HEIGHT: 6ft 5in
TEAMS: Anguilla, Derbyshire, Leeward Islands, West Indies Under-19s
CAREER: First-class: 2010; List A: 2007; T20: 2006

BEST BATTING: 167 Derbyshire vs Glamorgan, Derby, 2011
BEST BOWLING: 2-9 Derbyshire vs Middlesex, Derby, 2011

NOTES: Recommended to Derbyshire by former Hampshire bowler and fellow Anguillian Cardigan Connor. Represented West Indies at U19 level but does not count as an overseas player because he holds an English passport. Currently in the process of qualifying for England. Made 41 against Middlesex on Championship debut and notched his maiden first-class century – aged just 19 years and 125 days – in his third Championship match against Gloucestershire at Derby, in the process becoming the youngest player to score a first-class century for the county – a record previously held by Ian Hall who scored 113 against Hampshire at Derby, aged 19 years and 226 days

| Batting | Mat | Inns | NO | Runs | HS | Ave | SR | 100 | 50 | Ct | St |
|---|---|---|---|---|---|---|---|---|---|---|---|
| First-class | 26 | 48 | 2 | 1525 | 167 | 33.15 | 55.25 | 4 | 6 | 25 | 0 |
| List A | 40 | 39 | 1 | 881 | 81 | 23.18 | | 0 | 7 | 9 | 0 |
| Twenty20 | 34 | 31 | 0 | 572 | 65 | 18.45 | 102.69 | 0 | 3 | 6 | 0 |

| Bowling | Mat | Balls | Runs | Wkts | BBI | BBM | Ave | Econ | SR | 5w | 10 |
|---|---|---|---|---|---|---|---|---|---|---|---|
| First-class | 26 | 714 | 451 | 10 | 2/9 | 2/17 | 45.10 | 3.78 | 71.4 | 0 | 0 |
| List A | 40 | 648 | 539 | 16 | 3/19 | 3/19 | 33.68 | 4.99 | 40.5 | 0 | 0 |
| Twenty20 | 34 | 312 | 373 | 14 | 4/23 | 4/23 | 26.64 | 7.17 | 22.2 | 0 | 0 |

# PHIL HUGHES                                              LHB OB

FULL NAME: Phillip Joel Hughes
BORN: November 30, 1988, Macksville, New South Wales, Australia
SQUAD NO: 2
HEIGHT: 5ft 7in
NICKNAME: Boofa
TEAMS: Australia, Australia A, Australia Under-19s, Hampshire, Middlesex, New South Wales, New South Wales Under-19s, Western Suburbs, Worcestershire
CAREER: Test: 2009; First-class: 2007; List A: 2007; T20: 2008

---

BEST BATTING: 198 New South Wales vs South Australia, Adelaide, 2008

---

NOTES: Hughes holds an Italian passport by virtue of his Italian mother (his father was a banana farmer) and he was a talented rugby league player as a boy. He became the second youngest debutant for New South Wales and at 19, was the youngest ever player to score a century in the Pura Cup final. He also became the second youngest Australian to score a century in Tests and the youngest player in history to score centuries in both innings of the same Test. Has won the Sheffield Shield Player of the Year (2007/08) and Bradman Young Cricketer of the Year (2009) awards. In his first stint in county cricket – in 2009 – he scored 574 runs in his three first-class matches for Middlesex, including three hundreds, at an average of 143.50. In this winter's Test series between Australia and New Zealand, he was dismissed c Guptill b Martin in all four of his innings. He joins Worcestershire in late May

| Batting | Mat | Inns | NO | Runs | HS | Ave | SR | 100 | 50 | Ct | St |
|---|---|---|---|---|---|---|---|---|---|---|---|
| Tests | 17 | 32 | 1 | 1072 | 160 | 34.58 | 55.57 | 3 | 3 | 7 | 0 |
| First-class | 70 | 128 | 7 | 5648 | 198 | 46.67 | 58.28 | 17 | 29 | 45 | 0 |
| List A | 46 | 46 | 6 | 1625 | 138 | 40.62 | 72.93 | 2 | 11 | 16 | 0 |
| Twenty20 | 17 | 17 | 3 | 527 | 83 | 37.64 | 111.65 | 0 | 4 | 10 | 0 |

| Bowling | Mat | Balls | Runs | Wkts | BBI | BBM | Ave | Econ | SR | 5w | 10 |
|---|---|---|---|---|---|---|---|---|---|---|---|
| Tests | 17 | - | - | - | - | - | - | - | - | - | - |
| First-class | 70 | 18 | 9 | 0 | - | - | - | 3.00 | - | 0 | 0 |
| List A | 46 | - | - | - | - | - | - | - | - | - | - |
| Twenty20 | 17 | - | - | - | - | - | - | - | - | - | - |

## GEMAAL HUSSAIN

**RHB RMF W1**

SOMERSET

FULL NAME: Gemaal Maqsood Hussain
BORN: October 10, 1983, Waltham Forest
SQUAD NO: 27
HEIGHT: 6ft 4in
NICKNAME: G Man, Big G
EDUCATION: Top Valley Comprehensive, Nottingham; Leeds University
TEAMS: Essex 2nd XI, Gloucestershire, Leeds/Bradford MCCU, Nottinghamshire Cricket Board, Somerset, Sussex 2nd XI, Worcestershire
CAREER: First-class: 2009; List A: 2009; T20: 2009

BEST BATTING: 42 Somerset vs Lancashire, Liverpool, 2011
BEST BOWLING: 6-33 Somerset vs Worcestershire, Taunton, 2011
COUNTY CAP: 2009 (Gloucestershire)

FAMILY TIES? My cousin is coach of the Singapore cricket team. Everyone in my family loves the game and has played at least club level
CAREER HIGHLIGHTS? Finishing the 2010 season as highest wicket-taker for any English qualified player. It's a highlight because it was my first Championship season. Getting five wickets playing at Lord's for the first time
CRICKETING HEROES? Imran Khan, Wasim Akram, Shoaib Akhtar, Sachin Tendulkar, Saqlain Mushtaq, Sir Vivian Richards
BEST PLAYER IN COUNTY CRICKET? Marcus Trescothick
TIP FOR THE TOP? Jos Buttler
IF YOU WEREN'T A CRICKETER? Working in the sports industry
WHEN RAIN STOPS PLAY? Go to the gym and pretend I'm working out, watch the boys play on their iPads
FAVOURITE TV? Top Gear, Friends, The Simpsons and, of course, The Inbetweeners
FAVOURITE FILM? The Pursuit Of Happyness
DREAM HOLIDAY? Anywhere close to nature, peaceful and where I can relax
AMAZE ME! I snore like a horse and I can play the drums

| Batting | Mat | Inns | NO | Runs | HS | Ave | SR | 100 | 50 | Ct | St |
|---|---|---|---|---|---|---|---|---|---|---|---|
| First-class | 25 | 42 | 12 | 244 | 42 | 8.13 | 26.12 | 0 | 0 | 4 | 0 |
| List A | 5 | 1 | 1 | 16 | 16* | - | 114.28 | 0 | 0 | 2 | 0 |
| Twenty20 | 18 | 12 | 4 | 35 | 8 | 4.37 | 57.37 | 0 | 0 | 4 | 0 |

| Bowling | Mat | Balls | Runs | Wkts | BBI | BBM | Ave | Econ | SR | 5w | 10 |
|---|---|---|---|---|---|---|---|---|---|---|---|
| First-class | 25 | 4121 | 2591 | 91 | 6/33 | 9/98 | 28.47 | 3.77 | 45.2 | 3 | 0 |
| List A | 5 | 180 | 199 | 5 | 2/17 | 2/17 | 39.80 | 6.63 | 36.0 | 0 | 0 |
| Twenty20 | 18 | 354 | 489 | 21 | 3/22 | 3/22 | 23.28 | 8.28 | 16.8 | 0 | 0 |

# BRETT HUTTON

**RHB RM**

FULL NAME: Brett Alan Hutton
BORN: February 6, 1993, Doncaster, Yorkshire
SQUAD NO: 26
EDUCATION: Worksop College
TEAMS: England Under-19s, Nottinghamshire, Nottinghamshire 2nd XI, Nottinghamshire Under-13s, Nottinghamshire Under-14s, Nottinghamshire Under-15s, Nottinghamshire Under-17s
CAREER: First-class: 2011; List A: 2011

**NOTTINGHAMSHIRE**

BEST BATTING: 9 Nottinghamshire vs MCC, Abu Dhabi, 2011

NOTES: Made his first-class debut in Abu Dhabi against the MCC in 2011. Part of the England U19 squad that hosted South Africa in 2011. Named in the party to tour Bangladesh in 2011/12

| Batting | Mat | Inns | NO | Runs | HS | Ave | SR | 100 | 50 | Ct | St |
|---|---|---|---|---|---|---|---|---|---|---|---|
| First-class | 1 | 2 | 0 | 9 | 9 | 4.50 | 50.00 | 0 | 0 | 1 | 0 |
| List A | 2 | 2 | 1 | 20 | 17* | 20.00 | 117.64 | 0 | 0 | 1 | 0 |

| Bowling | Mat | Balls | Runs | Wkts | BBI | BBM | Ave | Econ | SR | 5w | 10 |
|---|---|---|---|---|---|---|---|---|---|---|---|
| First-class | 1 | 108 | 69 | 0 | - | - | - | 3.83 | - | 0 | 0 |
| List A | 2 | 84 | 101 | 1 | 1/60 | 1/60 | 101.00 | 7.21 | 84.0 | 0 | 0 |

## ANTHONY IRELAND

RHB RMF

MIDDLESEX

**FULL NAME:** Anthony John Ireland
**BORN:** August 30, 1984, Masvingo, Zimbabwe
**SQUAD NO:** 88
**EDUCATION:** Plumtree High School, Matabeleland
**TEAMS:** Zimbabwe, Gloucestershire, Gloucestershire 2nd XI, Midlands, Southern Rocks, Middlesex
**CAREER:** ODI: 2005; T20I: 2006; First-class: 2003; List A: 2004; T20: 2006

**BEST BATTING:** 29 Middlesex vs Essex, Chelmsford, 2011
**BEST BOWLING:** 7-36 Zimbabwe A vs Bangladesh A, Mirpur, 2006
**COUNTY CAP:** 2007 (Gloucestershire)

NOTES: Arrived in England in 2004 to play club cricket after the player rebellion in Zimbabwe but returned to represent his country in the 2007 World Cup. Retired from international cricket in April 2007 to sign for Gloucestershire as a Kolpak player. Took 36 first-class wickets in 2010 at an average of 21.77, including two five-wicket hauls. Signed for Middlesex ahead of the 2011 season, bringing an end to a four-year spell with Gloucestershire. Took four wickets in two County Championship matches in 2011

| Batting | Mat | Inns | NO | Runs | HS | Ave | SR | 100 | 50 | Ct | St |
|---|---|---|---|---|---|---|---|---|---|---|---|
| ODIs | 26 | 13 | 5 | 30 | 8* | 3.75 | 29.70 | 0 | 0 | 2 | 0 |
| T20Is | 1 | 1 | 1 | 2 | 2* | - | 66.66 | 0 | 0 | 0 | 0 |
| First-class | 39 | 58 | 16 | 210 | 29 | 5.00 | 27.88 | 0 | 0 | 10 | 0 |
| List A | 70 | 33 | 16 | 116 | 22* | 6.82 | 43.44 | 0 | 0 | 9 | 0 |
| Twenty20 | 40 | 14 | 7 | 40 | 8* | 5.71 | 65.57 | 0 | 0 | 10 | 0 |
| Bowling | Mat | Balls | Runs | Wkts | BBI | BBM | Ave | Econ | SR | 5w | 10 |
| ODIs | 26 | 1326 | 1115 | 38 | 3/41 | 3/41 | 29.34 | 5.04 | 34.8 | 0 | 0 |
| T20Is | 1 | 18 | 33 | 1 | 1/33 | 1/33 | 33.00 | 11.00 | 18.0 | 0 | 0 |
| First-class | 39 | 5796 | 3556 | 118 | 7/36 | | 30.13 | 3.68 | 49.1 | 4 | 1 |
| List A | 70 | 2935 | 2650 | 89 | 4/16 | 4/16 | 29.77 | 5.41 | 32.9 | 0 | 0 |
| Twenty20 | 40 | 719 | 1075 | 42 | 3/7 | 3/7 | 25.59 | 8.97 | 17.1 | 0 | 0 |

FULL NAME: Nicholas Alexander James
BORN: September 17, 1986, Sandwell, West Midlands
SQUAD NO: 11
HEIGHT: 5ft 10in
NICKNAME: Jaymo
EDUCATION: King Edward VI Aston
TEAMS: England Under-19s, Glamorgan, Staffordshire, Wales Minor Counties, Warwickshire, Warwickshire 2nd XI
CAREER: First-class: 2008; List A: 2006; T20: 2007

GLAMORGAN

BEST BATTING: 60* Glamorgan vs West Indies A, Cardiff, 2010
BEST BOWLING: 2-28 Glamorgan vs Kent, Canterbury, 2011

FAMILY TIES? My dad plays club cricket for Aldridge in the South Staffordshire Premier League
CAREER HIGHLIGHTS? Glamorgan 1st XI debut vs West Indies A
SUPERSTITIONS? Right pad on first, but I always forget
CRICKETING HEROES? Brian Lara, Chris Cooke, Nick Knight
NON-CRICKETING HEROES? Muhammad Ali, Remi Gaillard
BEST PLAYER IN COUNTY CRICKET? Marcus Trescothick
TIPS FOR THE TOP? Andy Miller, James Harris, Will Owen
FAVOURITE TV? I'm Alan Partridge
FAVOURITE FILM? Dumb And Dumber
FAVOURITE BOOK? The Sun
DREAM HOLIDAY? Menorca
ACCOMPLISHMENTS? Top one per cent in the world on Call Of Duty

| Batting | Mat | Inns | NO | Runs | HS | Ave | SR | 100 | 50 | Ct | St |
|---|---|---|---|---|---|---|---|---|---|---|---|
| First-class | 6 | 10 | 1 | 295 | 60* | 32.77 | 40.85 | 0 | 1 | 1 | 0 |
| List A | 16 | 11 | 2 | 174 | 43 | 19.33 | 84.87 | 0 | 0 | 3 | 0 |
| Twenty20 | 6 | 4 | 1 | 33 | 13 | 11.00 | 137.50 | 0 | 0 | 5 | 0 |

| Bowling | Mat | Balls | Runs | Wkts | BBI | BBM | Ave | Econ | SR | 5w | 10 |
|---|---|---|---|---|---|---|---|---|---|---|---|
| First-class | 6 | 168 | 86 | 6 | 2/28 | 4/79 | 14.33 | 3.07 | 28.0 | 0 | 0 |
| List A | 16 | 354 | 283 | 14 | 3/36 | 3/36 | 20.21 | 4.79 | 25.2 | 0 | 0 |
| Twenty20 | 6 | 90 | 92 | 4 | 2/22 | 2/22 | 23.00 | 6.13 | 22.5 | 0 | 0 |

YORKSHIRE

FULL NAME: Philip Anthony Jaques
BORN: May 3, 1979, Wollongong, Australia
SQUAD NO: 2
HEIGHT: 6ft 1in
NICKNAME: Pro, PJ
EDUCATION: Figtree High School; Australian College of Physical Education
TEAMS: Australia, New South Wales, Northamptonshire, Worcestershire, Yorkshire
CAREER: Test: 2005; ODI: 2006; First-class: 2001; List A: 2000; T20: 2003

BEST BATTING: 244 Worcestershire vs Essex, Chelmsford, 2006
COUNTY CAPS: 2003 (Northamptonshire); 2005 (Yorkshire)

FAMILY TIES? Dad played league cricket in Sheffield, England
CAREER HIGHLIGHTS? Playing for Australia
CRICKETING HEROES? Steve Waugh, Mark Taylor
FAVOURITE BAND? Coldplay, Bon Jovi
RELAXATIONS? Golf, beach, watching movies

| Batting | Mat | Inns | NO | Runs | HS | Ave | SR | 100 | 50 | Ct | St |
|---|---|---|---|---|---|---|---|---|---|---|---|
| Tests | 11 | 19 | 0 | 902 | 150 | 47.47 | 54.23 | 3 | 6 | 7 | 0 |
| ODIs | 6 | 6 | 0 | 125 | 94 | 20.83 | 71.02 | 0 | 1 | 3 | 0 |
| First-class | 160 | 286 | 11 | 13579 | 244 | 49.37 | | 38 | 63 | 125 | 0 |
| List A | 149 | 146 | 10 | 5670 | 171* | 41.69 | 89.82 | 14 | 30 | 40 | 0 |
| Twenty20 | 60 | 59 | 7 | 1576 | 92 | 30.30 | 127.50 | 0 | 10 | 15 | 0 |

| Bowling | Mat | Balls | Runs | Wkts | BBI | BBM | Ave | Econ | SR | 5w | 10 |
|---|---|---|---|---|---|---|---|---|---|---|---|
| Tests | 11 | - | - | - | - | - | - | - | - | - | - |
| ODIs | 6 | - | - | - | - | - | - | - | - | - | - |
| First-class | 160 | 68 | 87 | 0 | - | - | - | 7.67 | - | 0 | 0 |
| List A | 149 | 18 | 19 | 0 | - | - | - | 6.33 | - | 0 | 0 |
| Twenty20 | 60 | 6 | 15 | 0 | - | - | - | 15.00 | - | 0 | 0 |

# ATEEQ JAVID

**RHB RM**

FULL NAME: Ateeq Javid
BORN: October 15, 1991, Birmingham, Warwickshire
SQUAD NO: 17
TEAMS: England Under-19s, Warwickshire, Warwickshire 2nd XI
CAREER: First-class: 2009; List A: 2011

WARWICKSHIRE

BEST BATTING: 48 Warwickshire vs Yorkshire, Leeds, 2010

NOTES: Played four youth Tests for England U19 in 2010 against Sri Lanka, hitting 90 at Wantage Road and 89 at Scarborough. Played for England U16 Elite Player Development side in 2008, scoring 45 from 29 balls at the Bunbury Festival. Scored 21 from 119 balls on County Championship debut against Durham at Chester-le-Street in 2009

| Batting | Mat | Inns | NO | Runs | HS | Ave | SR | 100 | 50 | Ct | St |
|---|---|---|---|---|---|---|---|---|---|---|---|
| First-class | 7 | 13 | 0 | 146 | 48 | 11.23 | 29.20 | 0 | 0 | 6 | 0 |
| List A | 2 | 2 | 0 | 58 | 34 | 29.00 | 69.87 | 0 | 0 | 0 | 0 |

| Bowling | Mat | Balls | Runs | Wkts | BBI | BBM | Ave | Econ | SR | 5w | 10 |
|---|---|---|---|---|---|---|---|---|---|---|---|
| First-class | 7 | 78 | 78 | 0 | - | - | - | 6.00 | - | 0 | 0 |
| List A | 2 | 24 | 27 | 0 | - | - | - | 6.75 | - | 0 | 0 |

**LEICESTERSHIRE**

FULL NAME: William Ingleby Jefferson
BORN: October 25, 1979, Derby
SQUAD NO: 1
HEIGHT: 6ft 10in
NICKNAME: Santa, Lemar, Jeffer, Jeffo
EDUCATION: Oundle School; Durham University
TEAMS: Durham MCCU, Essex, Nottinghamshire
CAREER: First-class: 2000; List A: 2000; T20: 2003

BEST BATTING: 222 Essex vs Hampshire, Southampton, 2004
BEST BOWLING: 1-16 Essex vs Yorkshire, Leeds, 2005
COUNTY CAP: 2002 (Essex)

CAREER HIGHLIGHTS? 222 against Shane Warne's Hampshire in 2004 and one England A tour to date
CRICKETING HEROES? Mike Atherton for his stubbornness at the crease, Graeme Hick for the sheer amount of runs he scored
BEST PLAYER IN COUNTY CRICKET? It has to be Marcus Trescothick as every other batsman in the country would love to match his runscoring consistency
TIPS FOR THE TOP? Having played with him for the last two years, James Taylor will continue to score mountains of runs at county level. I like the look of Jos Buttler and Jonny Bairstow from what I have seen on TV
FAVOURITE TV? It was 24 until it got past the sixth series, and now Spooks has finished as well. The Inbetweeners is hilarious, but I would go for Downton Abbey
FAVOURITE FILM? The Shawshank Redemption
FAVOURITE BOOK? Emotional Intelligence by Daniel Goleman
ACCOMPLISHMENTS? Organising a dinner that raised £12k in one night for Bowel Cancer UK
AMAZE ME! I was a national fives champion when I was at school, I think of myself as a bit of a chef in the kitchen, all my girlfriends have been under six feet tall

| Batting | Mat | Inns | NO | Runs | HS | Ave | SR | 100 | 50 | Ct | St |
|---|---|---|---|---|---|---|---|---|---|---|---|
| First-class | 117 | 208 | 14 | 7021 | 222 | 36.19 | | 17 | 27 | 126 | 0 |
| List A | 101 | 98 | 6 | 3144 | 132 | 34.17 | | 4 | 18 | 43 | 0 |
| Twenty20 | 69 | 66 | 6 | 1254 | 83 | 20.90 | 128.48 | 0 | 6 | 25 | 0 |

| Bowling | Mat | Balls | Runs | Wkts | BBI | BBM | Ave | Econ | SR | 5w | 10 |
|---|---|---|---|---|---|---|---|---|---|---|---|
| First-class | 117 | 120 | 60 | 1 | 1/16 | | 60.00 | 3.00 | 120.0 | 0 | 0 |
| List A | 101 | 24 | 9 | 2 | 2/9 | 2/9 | 4.50 | 2.25 | 12.0 | 0 | 0 |
| Twenty20 | 69 | - | - | - | - | - | - | - | - | - | - |

# TOM JEWELL

### RHB RFM

FULL NAME: Thomas Melvin Jewell
BORN: January 13, 1991, Reading, Berkshire
SQUAD NO: 8
HEIGHT: 6ft 5in
NICKNAME: Jewellpig, TJ, Jeweller
EDUCATION: Bradfield College
TEAMS: Surrey, Surrey 2nd XI
CAREER: First-class: 2008; List A: 2009

SURREY

BEST BATTING: 61 Surrey vs CMCCU, Fenner's, 2011
BEST BOWLING: 5-49 Surrey vs CMCCU, Fenner's, 2011

CAREER HIGHLIGHTS? Making my first-class debut
SUPERSTITIONS? None
CRICKETING HEROES? Matthew Spriegel
NON-CRICKETING HEROES? Will Ferrell
BEST PLAYER IN COUNTY CRICKET? Tim Linley
TIP FOR THE TOP? Jason Roy
IF YOU WEREN'T A CRICKETER? I'd be at university
WHEN RAIN STOPS PLAY? iPad games
FAVOURITE TV? The Office or MasterChef
FAVOURITE FILM? Wedding Crashers
FAVOURITE BOOK? The Sun
DREAM HOLIDAY? Vegas
ACCOMPLISHMENTS? Completing three stars on every level of Angry Birds
GUILTY PLEASURES? Ben and Jerry's ice cream
SURPRISING FACTS? I live in Reading yet still play for Surrey, I'm the third youngest player
to ever represent Surrey, I've worked at Hollister clothing store this winter for a few shifts
and I can solve a Rubik's Cube in two minutes
TWITTER FEED: @Tomjewell8

| Batting | Mat | Inns | NO | Runs | HS | Ave | SR | 100 | 50 | Ct | St |
|---|---|---|---|---|---|---|---|---|---|---|---|
| First-class | 6 | 5 | 1 | 97 | 61 | 24.25 | 50.78 | 0 | 1 | 0 | 0 |
| List A | 2 | 2 | 1 | 1 | 1 | 1.00 | 11.11 | 0 | 0 | 0 | 0 |

| Bowling | Mat | Balls | Runs | Wkts | BBI | BBM | Ave | Econ | SR | 5w | 10 |
|---|---|---|---|---|---|---|---|---|---|---|---|
| First-class | 6 | 466 | 260 | 10 | 5/49 | 5/49 | 26.00 | 3.34 | 46.6 | 1 | 0 |
| List A | 2 | 36 | 56 | 0 | - | - | - | 9.33 | - | 0 | 0 |

# RICHARD JOHNSON

## RHB WK

**FULL NAME:** Richard Matthew Johnson
**BORN:** September 1, 1988, Solihull, West Midlands
**SQUAD NO:** 16
**HEIGHT:** 5ft 10in
**NICKNAME:** Johnno
**EDUCATION:** Solihull School
**TEAMS:** Herefordshire, Warwickshire, Warwickshire 2nd XI
**CAREER:** First-class: 2008; List A: 2008; T20: 2009

**BEST BATTING:** 72 Warwickshire vs CUCCE, Fenner's, 2008

**WHY CRICKET?** Watching it on TV and playing with friends
**CAREER HIGHLIGHTS?** Winning CB40 final vs Somerset in 2010
**SUPERSTITIONS?** Packing my bag the same way
**CRICKETING HEROES?** Keith Piper, Tony Frost, James Foster
**NON-CRICKETING HEROES?** Jamie Redknapp, Muhammad Ali
**BEST PLAYER IN COUNTY CRICKET?** Chris Woakes
**TIP FOR THE TOP?** Ateeq Javid
**IF YOU WEREN'T A CRICKETER?** Still a student
**FAVOURITE TV?** Take Me Out
**FAVOURITE FILM?** Enemy At The Gates
**FAVOURITE BOOK?** Bounce by Matthew Syed
**DREAM HOLIDAY?** Las Vegas
**GUILTY PLEASURES?** Chocolate
**AMAZE ME!** Take That are my favourite group, I played football for Wolverhampton Wanderers U10 and U13 and like to believe I was quite good, I always listen to music whilst waiting to bat
**TWITTER FEED:** @richjohnno16

| Batting | Mat | Inns | NO | Runs | HS | Ave | SR | 100 | 50 | Ct | St |
|---|---|---|---|---|---|---|---|---|---|---|---|
| First-class | 8 | 13 | 1 | 233 | 72 | 19.41 | 49.36 | 0 | 1 | 26 | 2 |
| List A | 11 | 6 | 2 | 46 | 20 | 11.50 | 80.70 | 0 | 0 | 9 | 2 |
| Twenty20 | 10 | 4 | 3 | 7 | 6* | 7.00 | 87.50 | 0 | 0 | 2 | 3 |

| Bowling | Mat | Balls | Runs | Wkts | BBI | BBM | Ave | Econ | SR | 5w | 10 |
|---|---|---|---|---|---|---|---|---|---|---|---|
| First-class | 8 | - | - | - | - | - | - | - | - | - | - |
| List A | 11 | - | - | - | - | - | - | - | - | - | - |
| Twenty20 | 10 | - | - | - | - | - | - | - | - | - | - |

## ALEX JONES                                          RHB LFM

FULL NAME: Alexander John Jones
BORN: November 10, 1988, Bridgend
SQUAD NO: 27
HEIGHT: 6ft 2in
NICKNAME: AJ, Spider, Magoo
EDUCATION: Cowbridge Comprehensive;
UWIC
TEAMS: Cardiff MCCU, Cardiff UCCE,
Glamorgan, Marylebone Cricket Club
Universities, Marylebone Cricket Club
Young Cricketers, Wales Minor Counties
CAREER: First-class: 2011; List A: 2010; T20:
2011

GLAMORGAN

BEST BATTING: 26 Glamorgan vs Northamptonshire, Northampton, 2011
BEST BOWLING: 1-50 Glamorgan vs Surrey, The Oval, 2011

WHY CRICKET? Got into cricket by watching my dad play at Ewenny and Corntown Cricket
Club as a kid and throwing a ball around with the other kids, especially Adam Weaver
CAREER HIGHLIGHTS? Playing and winning at Lord's in the MCCU final for Cardiff. Also
playing in the 2011 T20 campaign for Glamorgan
CRICKETING HEROES? Glenn McGrath, Andrew Flintoff, Kevin Pietersen
NON-CRICKETING HEROES? Muhammad Ali, Scott Gibbs
TIPS FOR THE TOP? James Harris, Aneurin Norman, Andrew Salter
IF YOU WEREN'T A CRICKETER? I'd be trying to play rugby!
WHEN RAIN STOPS PLAY? Feet up with a cup of tea enjoying some drivel from the boys
FAVOURITE TV? Dirty Sanchez, Total Wipeout
FAVOURITE FILM? Snatch
FAVOURITE BOOK? The Game
DREAM HOLIDAY? Hawaii
ACCOMPLISHMENTS? Winning the Glamorgan golf day in 2011
SURPRISING SKILL? Represented Wales in rugby sevens in South Africa, partial to a karaoke
night, used to play the trumpet
TWITTER FEED: aj_jones27

| Batting | Mat | Inns | NO | Runs | HS | Ave | SR | 100 | 50 | Ct | St |
|---|---|---|---|---|---|---|---|---|---|---|---|
| First-class | 2 | 3 | 0 | 34 | 26 | 11.33 | 48.57 | 0 | 0 | 1 | 0 |
| List A | 4 | 3 | 1 | 8 | 5 | 4.00 | 53.33 | 0 | 0 | 2 | 0 |
| Twenty20 | 14 | 5 | 3 | 9 | 4* | 4.50 | 50.00 | 0 | 0 | 1 | 0 |

| Bowling | Mat | Balls | Runs | Wkts | BBI | BBM | Ave | Econ | SR | 5w | 10 |
|---|---|---|---|---|---|---|---|---|---|---|---|
| First-class | 2 | 216 | 158 | 2 | 1/50 | 1/79 | 79.00 | 4.38 | 108.0 | 0 | 0 |
| List A | 4 | 156 | 202 | 3 | 1/38 | 1/38 | 67.33 | 7.76 | 52.0 | 0 | 0 |
| Twenty20 | 14 | 192 | 256 | 15 | 3/16 | 3/16 | 17.06 | 8.00 | 12.8 | 0 | 0 |

# CHRIS JONES

**RHB**

SOMERSET

**FULL NAME:** Christopher Robert Jones
**BORN:** November 5, 1990, Harold Wood, Essex
**SQUAD NO:** 14
**EDUCATION:** Broadstone Middle School; Poole Grammar School; Durham University
**TEAMS:** Dorset, Dorset Under-13s, Dorset Under-15s, Durham MCCU, Somerset, Somerset 2nd XI, Somerset Under-15s, Somerset Under-17s
**CAREER:** First-class: 2010; List A: 2011; T20: 2011

---

**BEST BATTING:** 69 DMCCU vs Yorkshire, Durham University, 2011

---

**NOTES:** Skippered the 2nd XI in 2010. First taste of 1st XI cricket was as a substitute for Craig Kieswetter against Lancashire in the same year. Impressed in his two CB40 appearances last year, scoring an unbeaten 45 against Essex and 33 against Durham in the semi-final. Played three matches in last year's Champions League, deputising for the absent Craig Kieswetter at the top of the order – scored 36 runs, with a top score of 16

| Batting | Mat | Inns | NO | Runs | HS | Ave | SR | 100 | 50 | Ct | St |
|---|---|---|---|---|---|---|---|---|---|---|---|
| First-class | 12 | 18 | 1 | 304 | 69 | 17.88 | 38.19 | 0 | 3 | 6 | 0 |
| List A | 2 | 2 | 1 | 78 | 45* | 78.00 | 89.65 | 0 | 0 | 0 | 0 |
| Twenty20 | 3 | 3 | 0 | 36 | 16 | 12.00 | 138.46 | 0 | 0 | 1 | 0 |

| Bowling | Mat | Balls | Runs | Wkts | BBI | BBM | Ave | Econ | SR | 5w | 10 |
|---|---|---|---|---|---|---|---|---|---|---|---|
| First-class | 12 | - | - | - | - | - | - | - | - | - | - |
| List A | 2 | - | - | - | - | - | - | - | - | - | - |
| Twenty20 | 3 | - | - | - | - | - | - | - | - | - | - |

## GERAINT JONES

### RHB WK R2

FULL NAME: Geraint Owen Jones
BORN: July 14, 1976, Kundiawa, Papua New Guinea
SQUAD NO: 9
HEIGHT: 5ft 8in
NICKNAME: Jonesy, Joner
EDUCATION: Harristown SHS, Toowoomba; MacGregor SHS, Brisbane
TEAMS: England, Papua New Guinea, Kent, Kent 2nd XI
CAREER: Test: 2004; ODI: 2004; T20I: 2005; First-class: 2001; List A: 2001; T20: 2003

KENT

BEST BATTING: 178 Kent vs Somerset, Canterbury, 2010
COUNTY CAP: 2003; BENEFIT YEAR: 2012

FAMILY TIES? James Tredwell is married to my wife's sister
CAREER HIGHLIGHTS? Debut for England vs West Indies 2004, my century vs New Zealand, the 2005 Ashes and Kent winning the T20 trophy
SUPERSTITIONS? Always left foot first. I do this away from cricket too
CRICKETING HEROES? Ian Healy, Jack Russell, Sachin Tendulkar
TIP FOR THE TOP? James Taylor
IF YOU WEREN'T A CRICKETER? Grinding doing a regular job, wishing I was a pro sportsman
WHEN RAIN STOPS PLAY? Mixture of sleeping, practising, watching TV and messing around
FAVOURITE FILM? The Hangover
FAVOURITE BOOK? Shantaram
AMAZE ME! I have a certificate in sheep shearing
TWITTER FEED: @Gojones623

| Batting | Mat | Inns | NO | Runs | HS | Ave | SR | 100 | 50 | Ct | St |
|---|---|---|---|---|---|---|---|---|---|---|---|
| Tests | 34 | 53 | 4 | 1172 | 100 | 23.91 | 54.13 | 1 | 6 | 128 | 5 |
| ODIs | 49 | 41 | 8 | 815 | 80 | 24.69 | 78.21 | 0 | 4 | 68 | 4 |
| T20Is | 2 | 2 | 1 | 33 | 19 | 33.00 | 132.00 | 0 | 0 | 2 | 0 |
| First-class | 159 | 249 | 21 | 7398 | 178 | 32.44 | | 15 | 36 | 488 | 35 |
| List A | 170 | 144 | 23 | 2861 | 86 | 23.64 | 79.76 | 0 | 11 | 183 | 39 |
| Twenty20 | 79 | 60 | 12 | 799 | 56 | 16.64 | 112.21 | 0 | 2 | 41 | 16 |

| Bowling | Mat | Balls | Runs | Wkts | BBI | BBM | Ave | Econ | SR | 5w | 10 |
|---|---|---|---|---|---|---|---|---|---|---|---|
| Tests | 34 | - | - | - | - | - | - | - | - | - | - |
| ODIs | 49 | - | - | - | - | - | - | - | - | - | - |
| T20Is | 2 | - | - | - | - | - | - | - | - | - | - |
| First-class | 159 | 24 | 26 | 0 | - | - | - | 6.50 | - | 0 | 0 |
| List A | 170 | - | - | - | - | - | - | - | - | - | - |
| Twenty20 | 79 | - | - | - | - | - | - | - | - | - | - |

# RICHARD JONES

**RHB RMF**

**FULL NAME:** Richard Alan Jones
**BORN:** November 6, 1986, Stourbridge
**SQUAD NO:** 25
**HEIGHT:** 6ft 2in
**NICKNAME:** Jonah, Dick
**EDUCATION:** Grange School, Stourbridge; Kind Edward VI College, Stourbridge
**TEAMS:** England Under-19s, Loughborough MCCU, Matabeleland Tuskers, Worcestershire, Worcestershire 2nd XI
**CAREER:** First-class: 2007; List A: 2008; T20: 2010

**BEST BATTING:** 62 Matabeleland Tuskers vs Southern Rocks, Bulawayo, 2012
**BEST BOWLING:** 7-115 Worcestershire vs Sussex, Hove, 2010
**COUNTY CAP:** 2007

**CAREER HIGHLIGHTS?** Signing my first professional contract with Worcestershire, the club I've been at since the age of nine. Getting selected in the England U19 tour of Bangladesh was also a huge honour. More recently, being part of a Worcestershire squad that so spectacularly defied the odds over the last two seasons, firstly in getting promoted to Division One and then retaining that status last season, was hugely satisfying
**SUPERSTITIONS?** Only one – sit as far away from Jack Shantry as you can, else you run the risk of losing some of your kit amongst the atrocity that is his changing area
**CRICKETING HEROES?** Graeme Hick, Darren Gough
**TIPS FOR THE TOP?** Nottinghamshire's James Taylor looks as though he has a very big future for England. As does Jonny Bairstow, Alex Hales and Ben Stokes. Closer to home, young Aneesh Kapil is a huge talent
**ACCOMPLISHMENTS?** I was a senior prefect at high school. I went for head boy but they opted for Jimmy Martin, a quieter and more obedient student. The regime couldn't handle me – I knew it and they knew it! Other than that, I had my first sports article published in All Out Cricket magazine three years ago
**TWITTER FEED:** @richardjones441

| Batting | Mat | Inns | NO | Runs | HS | Ave | SR | 100 | 50 | Ct | St |
|---|---|---|---|---|---|---|---|---|---|---|---|
| First-class | 32 | 50 | 7 | 471 | 62 | 10.95 | 39.81 | 0 | 2 | 12 | 0 |
| List A | 10 | 5 | 2 | 23 | 11* | 7.66 | 69.69 | 0 | 0 | 1 | 0 |
| Twenty20 | 6 | 2 | 1 | 14 | 9 | 14.00 | 77.77 | 0 | 0 | 7 | 0 |

| Bowling | Mat | Balls | Runs | Wkts | BBI | BBM | Ave | Econ | SR | 5w | 10 |
|---|---|---|---|---|---|---|---|---|---|---|---|
| First-class | 32 | 4579 | 3146 | 95 | 7/115 | 8/105 | 33.11 | 4.12 | 48.2 | 3 | 0 |
| List A | 10 | 333 | 380 | 3 | 1/25 | 1/25 | 126.66 | 6.84 | 111.0 | 0 | 0 |
| Twenty20 | 6 | 66 | 119 | 2 | 1/17 | 1/17 | 59.50 | 10.81 | 33.0 | 0 | 0 |

# SIMON JONES                                          LHB RFM

FULL NAME: Simon Philip Jones
BORN: December 25, 1978, Morriston, Swansea
SQUAD NO: 50
HEIGHT: 6ft 3in
NICKNAME: Horse
EDUCATION: Coedcae Comprehensive; Millfield
TEAMS: England, Glamorgan, Hampshire, Worcestershire
CAREER: Test: 2002; ODI: 2004; First-class: 1998; List A: 1999; T20: 2008

**GLAMORGAN**

BEST BATTING: 46 Glamorgan vs Yorkshire, Scarborough, 2001
BEST BOWLING: 6-45 Glamorgan vs Derbyshire, 2002
COUNTY CAP: 2002 (Glamorgan)

FAMILY TIES? My father [Jeff] played for England
CRICKET MOMENTS TO FORGET? Every injury
SUPERSTITIONS? Right boot on first
CRICKETERS PARTICULARLY ADMIRED? Allan Donald
OTHER SPORTS PLAYED? Football (trials with Leeds United)
FAVOURITE BAND? Eminem
CAREER HIGHLIGHTS? Winning the 2005 Ashes series

| Batting | Mat | Inns | NO | Runs | HS | Ave | SR | 100 | 50 | Ct | St |
|---|---|---|---|---|---|---|---|---|---|---|---|
| Tests | 18 | 18 | 5 | 205 | 44 | 15.76 | 51.89 | 0 | 0 | 4 | 0 |
| ODIs | 8 | 1 | 0 | 1 | 1 | 1.00 | 50.00 | 0 | 0 | 0 | 0 |
| First-class | 90 | 111 | 37 | 899 | 46 | 12.14 | | 0 | 0 | 17 | 0 |
| List A | 43 | 16 | 11 | 77 | 26 | 15.40 | | 0 | 0 | 2 | 0 |
| Twenty20 | 28 | 7 | 4 | 27 | 11* | 9.00 | 128.57 | 0 | 0 | 1 | 0 |

| Bowling | Mat | Balls | Runs | Wkts | BBI | BBM | Ave | Econ | SR | 5w | 10 |
|---|---|---|---|---|---|---|---|---|---|---|---|
| Tests | 18 | 2821 | 1666 | 59 | 6/53 | 7/110 | 28.23 | 3.54 | 47.8 | 3 | 0 |
| ODIs | 8 | 348 | 275 | 7 | 2/43 | 2/43 | 39.28 | 4.74 | 49.7 | 0 | 0 |
| First-class | 90 | 13242 | 8072 | 265 | 6/45 | | 30.46 | 3.65 | 49.9 | 15 | 1 |
| List A | 43 | 1767 | 1537 | 42 | 5/32 | 5/32 | 36.59 | 5.21 | 42.0 | 1 | 0 |
| Twenty20 | 28 | 607 | 751 | 36 | 4/10 | 4/10 | 20.86 | 7.42 | 16.8 | 0 | 0 |

LEICESTERSHIRE

FULL NAME: William Stephen Jones
BORN: March 29, 1990, Perth, Australia
SQUAD NO: 25
EDUCATION: Harrow School; Cardiff University
TEAMS: Hertfordshire, Leicestershire, Leicestershire 2nd XI
CAREER: First-class: 2011; List A: 2011

BEST BATTING: 10 Leicestershire vs Sri Lanka A, Leicester, 2011

CRICKETERS PARTICULARLY ADMIRED? Sachin Tendulkar, Michael Atherton, Andrew Strauss
RELAXATIONS? TV, reading, golf
NOTES: Studying at Cardiff University and in the MCCU programme. Father represented Leicestershire 2nd XI. Trialled for Leicestershire in 2010 after playing in the 2009 Minor Counties Championship for Hertfordshire. Averaged 53 in the 2nd XI Trophy in 2010 and went to the Global Cricket Academy in Pune, India with Leicestershire teammate Greg Smith in January 2011. Hit 159 for Leicestershire 2nd XI against Sussex at Stirlands CC and made his first-class debut against Sri Lanka A last season before making his County Championship debut at Grace Road in September against Middlesex. Scored 129 for MCC against Bermuda at the National Sports Centre in Hamilton later that month

| Batting | Mat | Inns | NO | Runs | HS | Ave | SR | 100 | 50 | Ct | St |
|---|---|---|---|---|---|---|---|---|---|---|---|
| First-class | 2 | 4 | 0 | 12 | 10 | 3.00 | 31.57 | 0 | 0 | 0 | 0 |
| List A | 1 | 1 | 0 | 3 | 3 | 3.00 | 25.00 | 0 | 0 | 0 | 0 |

| Bowling | Mat | Balls | Runs | Wkts | BBI | BBM | Ave | Econ | SR | 5w | 10 |
|---|---|---|---|---|---|---|---|---|---|---|---|
| First-class | 2 | 18 | 6 | 0 | - | - | - | 2.00 | - | 0 | 0 |
| List A | 1 | - | - | - | - | - | - | - | - | - | - |

# CHRIS JORDAN

## RHB RFM

FULL NAME: Christopher James Jordan
BORN: October 4, 1988, Barbados
SQUAD NO: 23
HEIGHT: 6ft 2in
NICKNAME: CJ
EDUCATION: Dulwich College
TEAMS: Barbados, Surrey, Surrey 2nd XI
CAREER: First-class: 2007; List A: 2007; T20: 2008

SURREY

BEST BATTING: 79* Surrey vs Essex, Chelmsford, 2011
BEST BOWLING: 5-77 Barbados vs Guyana, Barbados, 2012

CRICKETING HEROES? Brian Lara, Brett Lee, Dwayne Bravo
SUPERSTITIONS? Have to touch my box, my thigh pad and my pads before I settle down to bat
NOTES: Eligible to represent England through his grandmother. Took four wickets on first-class debut against Kent. Selected for the ECB Winter Performance Programme at the end of 2009. Missed the entire 2010 season due to a stress fracture. Claimed his maiden five-wicket haul in March, having registered a career-best 4-41 in Barbados' previous fixture against Guyana

| Batting | Mat | Inns | NO | Runs | HS | Ave | SR | 100 | 50 | Ct | St |
|---|---|---|---|---|---|---|---|---|---|---|---|
| First-class | 31 | 38 | 9 | 721 | 79* | 24.86 | | 0 | 3 | 16 | 0 |
| List A | 20 | 12 | 1 | 74 | 38 | 6.72 | 49.33 | 0 | 0 | 5 | 0 |
| Twenty20 | 11 | 10 | 2 | 111 | 31 | 13.87 | 104.71 | 0 | 0 | 4 | 0 |

| Bowling | Mat | Balls | Runs | Wkts | BBI | BBM | Ave | Econ | SR | 5w | 10 |
|---|---|---|---|---|---|---|---|---|---|---|---|
| First-class | 31 | 4365 | 2555 | 64 | 5/77 | 5/73 | 39.92 | 3.51 | 68.2 | 1 | 0 |
| List A | 20 | 763 | 747 | 23 | 3/28 | 3/28 | 32.47 | 5.87 | 33.1 | 0 | 0 |
| Twenty20 | 11 | 174 | 259 | 5 | 2/34 | 2/34 | 51.80 | 8.93 | 34.8 | 0 | 0 |

## ROBBIE JOSEPH

### RHB RFM W1

LEICESTERSHIRE

FULL NAME: Robert Hartman Joseph
BORN: January 20, 1982, Antigua
SQUAD NO: 4
HEIGHT: 6ft 2in
NICKNAME: RJ
EDUCATION: Sutton Valence School; St. Mary's University, Twickenham; University of Kent
TEAMS: England Lions, First-Class Counties XI, Kent, Kent 2nd XI, Leeward Islands, Leicestershire
CAREER: First-class: 2000; List A: 2004; T20: 2008

BEST BATTING: 36* Kent vs Sussex, Hove, 2007
BEST BOWLING: 6-32 Kent vs Durham, Chester-le-Street, 2008

FAMILY TIES? Cousin Sylvester Joseph played for West Indies
WHY CRICKET? Watching highlights of West Indies on Saturday mornings and being inspired by Viv Richards and his teammates
CAREER HIGHLIGHTS? Being selected for England Lions tour in 2009, taking 5-13 in a Pro40 game, taking nine wickets in a game on two occasions
CRICKETING HEROES? Viv Richards, Andy Roberts, Malcolm Marshall
NON-CRICKETING HEROES? Nelson Mandela, Muhammad Ali, Lance Armstrong
BEST PLAYER IN COUNTY CRICKET? Marcus Trescothick
TIP FOR THE TOP? Daniel Bell-Drummond
IF YOU WEREN'T A CRICKETER? Teaching maybe, or something business related
FAVOURITE TV? The Big Bang Theory, Dexter, Entourage
FAVOURITE FILM? Green Mile, Gladiator, Man On Fire, The Shawshank Redemption
FAVOURITE BOOK? Bounce, Livingston Seagull, The Alchemist
DREAM HOLIDAY? Home to Antigua
ACCOMPLISHMENTS? Getting a degree
GUILTY PLEASURES? KFC

| Batting | Mat | Inns | NO | Runs | HS | Ave | SR | 100 | 50 | Ct | St |
|---|---|---|---|---|---|---|---|---|---|---|---|
| First-class | 53 | 71 | 28 | 456 | 36* | 10.60 | | 0 | 0 | 10 | 0 |
| List A | 33 | 14 | 12 | 43 | 15 | 21.50 | 61.42 | 0 | 0 | 4 | 0 |
| Twenty20 | 9 | 1 | 1 | 1 | 1* | - | 100.00 | 0 | 0 | 3 | 0 |

| Bowling | Mat | Balls | Runs | Wkts | BBI | BBM | Ave | Econ | SR | 5w | 10 |
|---|---|---|---|---|---|---|---|---|---|---|---|
| First-class | 53 | 7853 | 4810 | 150 | 6/32 | | 32.06 | 3.67 | 52.3 | 5 | 0 |
| List A | 33 | 1307 | 1114 | 39 | 5/13 | 5/13 | 28.56 | 5.11 | 33.5 | 1 | 0 |
| Twenty20 | 9 | 168 | 213 | 10 | 2/14 | 2/14 | 21.30 | 7.60 | 16.8 | 0 | 0 |

FULL NAME: Edmund Christopher Joyce
BORN: September 22, 1978, Dublin
SQUAD NO: 24
HEIGHT: 5ft 10in
NICKNAME: Joycey, Spud, Piece
EDUCATION: Presentation College, Bray;
Trinity College, Dublin
TEAMS: England, Ireland, England Lions,
Marylebone Cricket Club, Middlesex, Sussex
CAREER: ODI: 2006; T20I: 2006; First-class:
1997; List A: 1998; T20: 2003

SUSSEX

BEST BATTING: 211 Middlesex vs Warwickshire, Birmingham, 2006
BEST BOWLING: 2-34 Middlesex vs CUCCE, Fenner's, 2004
COUNTY CAP: 2002 (Middlesex)

FAMILY TIES? Two brothers and two sisters have represented Ireland
CRICKETERS PARTICULARLY ADMIRED? Brian Lara, Larry Gomes
OTHER SPORTS FOLLOWED? Rugby (Leinster), football (Manchester United)
OTHER SPORTS PLAYED? Golf, rugby, soccer, snooker
FAVOURITE BAND? The Mars Volta
RELAXATIONS? Cinema, eating out, listening to music
NOTES: Passed 1,000 first-class runs five English summers in a row between 2002-2006.
Has represented both Ireland and England in ODI cricket. Scored his one ODI century for
England against Australia in the 2007 Commonwealth Bank Series

| Batting | Mat | Inns | NO | Runs | HS | Ave | SR | 100 | 50 | Ct | St |
|---|---|---|---|---|---|---|---|---|---|---|---|
| ODIs | 30 | 30 | 0 | 868 | 107 | 28.93 | 66.51 | 1 | 6 | 9 | 0 |
| T20Is | 5 | 3 | 0 | 63 | 38 | 21.00 | 88.73 | 0 | 0 | 1 | 0 |
| First-class | 169 | 282 | 22 | 11693 | 211 | 44.97 | | 26 | 66 | 148 | 0 |
| List A | 217 | 207 | 20 | 6977 | 146 | 37.31 | | 10 | 42 | 74 | 0 |
| Twenty20 | 64 | 59 | 9 | 801 | 47 | 16.02 | 94.34 | 0 | 0 | 16 | 0 |

| Bowling | Mat | Balls | Runs | Wkts | BBI | BBM | Ave | Econ | SR | 5w | 10 |
|---|---|---|---|---|---|---|---|---|---|---|---|
| ODIs | 30 | - | - | - | - | - | - | - | - | - | - |
| T20Is | 5 | - | - | - | - | - | - | - | - | - | - |
| First-class | 169 | 1287 | 1025 | 11 | 2/34 | | 93.18 | 4.77 | 117.0 | 0 | 0 |
| List A | 217 | 264 | 309 | 6 | 2/10 | 2/10 | 51.50 | 7.02 | 44.0 | 0 | 0 |
| Twenty20 | 64 | 6 | 12 | 0 | - | - | - | 12.00 | - | 0 | 0 |

# ANEESH KAPIL

**RHB RFM**

FULL NAME: Aneesh Kapil
BORN: August 3, 1993, Wolverhampton
SQUAD NO: 22
HEIGHT: 5ft 9in
NICKNAME: Poncherello, Ponch
EDUCATION: Denstone College
TEAMS: England Under-19s, Worcestershire, Worcestershire 2nd XI
CAREER: First-class: 2011; List A: 2011; T20: 2011

BEST BATTING: 54 Worcestershire vs Sussex, Horsham, 2011
BEST BOWLING: 2-38 Worcestershire vs Lancashire, Blackpool, 2011

FAMILY TIES? Dad was a club cricketer – a legendary medium-pacer for the Saturday 5th XI
CAREER HIGHLIGHTS? Making my List A and first-class debuts. Playing for England U19
SUPERSTITIONS? I always wear a Power Balance on my left wrist
CRICKETING HEROES? Sachin Tendulkar, Brian Lara, Brett Lee, Basil D'Oliveira
NON-CRICKETING HEROES? Barack Obama, Roger Federer, Manny Pacquiao
BEST PLAYER IN COUNTY CRICKET? Marcus Trescothick
TIPS FOR THE TOP? Nick Harrison, Ben Cox, Neil Pinner, Matt Pardoe, Jack Manuel, Tom Fell
IF YOU WEREN'T A CRICKETER? I'd play baseball
WHEN RAIN STOPS PLAY? Sleeping and playing poker
FAVOURITE TV? Modern Family, Made In Chelsea
FAVOURITE FILM? The Shawshank Redemption
FAVOURITE BOOK? The Power Of Now
ACCOMPLISHMENTS? Winning a talent show with a group of street dancers
SURPRISING SKILL? Beat boxing!
GUILTY PLEASURES? Pizza Hut, cookie dough
AMAZE ME! I can moonwalk to extreme levels of competence
TWITTER FEED: @aneeshkapil22

| Batting | Mat | Inns | NO | Runs | HS | Ave | SR | 100 | 50 | Ct | St |
|---|---|---|---|---|---|---|---|---|---|---|---|
| First-class | 5 | 8 | 0 | 139 | 54 | 17.37 | 48.26 | 0 | 1 | 2 | 0 |
| List A | 6 | 6 | 1 | 105 | 44 | 21.00 | 74.46 | 0 | 0 | 2 | 0 |
| Twenty20 | 6 | 4 | 2 | 26 | 13 | 13.00 | 104.00 | 0 | 0 | 2 | 0 |

| Bowling | Mat | Balls | Runs | Wkts | BBI | BBM | Ave | Econ | SR | 5w | 10 |
|---|---|---|---|---|---|---|---|---|---|---|---|
| First-class | 5 | 182 | 138 | 4 | 2/38 | 3/64 | 34.50 | 4.54 | 45.5 | 0 | 0 |
| List A | 6 | 132 | 159 | 3 | 1/18 | 1/18 | 53.00 | 7.22 | 44.0 | 0 | 0 |
| Twenty20 | 6 | 54 | 53 | 3 | 3/9 | 3/9 | 17.66 | 5.88 | 18.0 | 0 | 0 |

# MURALI KARTIK                              LHB SLA W1 MVP70

FULL NAME: Murali Kartik
BORN: September 11, 1976, Chennai, India
SQUAD NO: 11
HEIGHT: 6ft
NICKNAME: Pirate, Gary, King, Kat, Special K
TEAMS: India, India Green, Kolkata Knight
Riders, Lancashire, Middlesex, Pune
Warriors, Railways, Somerset
CAREER: Test: 2000; ODI: 2002; T20I: 2007;
First-class: 1996; List A: 1996; T20: 2007

BEST BATTING: 96 Railways vs Rest of India, Delhi, 2005
BEST BOWLING: 9-70 Rest of India vs Mumbai, Mumbai, 2000
COUNTY CAP: 2007 (Middlesex)

CAREER HIGHLIGHTS? First and foremost was getting the India cap in 2000, winning the Man
of the Match award against Aussies in an ODI in 2007, taking 6-27 (world record figures in an
ODI for a left-arm spinner) and winning the T20 Cup with Middlesex in 2008
CRICKETING HEROES? Sir Garfield Sobers, Bishan Singh Bedi, Steve Waugh
BEST PLAYER IN COUNTY CRICKET? Without a shadow of doubt it's Marcus Trescothick
TIPS FOR THE TOP? Alex Hales, Jos Buttler, John Simpson
IF YOU WEREN'T A CRICKETER? I would have been a genetic engineer
FAVOURITE TV? Any programme on Discovery or National Geographic
FAVOURITE FILM? Ben-Hur
FAVOURITE BOOK? Coma by Robin Cook
TWITTER FEED: @kartikmurali

| Batting | Mat | Inns | NO | Runs | HS | Ave | SR | 100 | 50 | Ct | St |
|---|---|---|---|---|---|---|---|---|---|---|---|
| Tests | 8 | 10 | 1 | 88 | 43 | 9.77 | 38.09 | 0 | 0 | 2 | 0 |
| ODIs | 37 | 14 | 5 | 126 | 32* | 14.00 | 70.78 | 0 | 0 | 10 | 0 |
| T20Is | 1 | - | - | - | - | - | - | - | - | 0 | 0 |
| First-class | 181 | 230 | 36 | 3866 | 96 | 19.92 | | 0 | 19 | 128 | 0 |
| List A | 185 | 89 | 28 | 750 | 44 | 12.29 | | 0 | 0 | 64 | 0 |
| Twenty20 | 107 | 30 | 14 | 230 | 28 | 14.37 | 103.13 | 0 | 0 | 29 | 0 |

| Bowling | Mat | Balls | Runs | Wkts | BBI | BBM | Ave | Econ | SR | 5w | 10 |
|---|---|---|---|---|---|---|---|---|---|---|---|
| Tests | 8 | 1932 | 820 | 24 | 4/44 | 7/76 | 34.16 | 2.54 | 80.5 | 0 | 0 |
| ODIs | 37 | 1907 | 1612 | 37 | 6/27 | 6/27 | 43.56 | 5.07 | 51.5 | 1 | 0 |
| T20Is | 1 | 24 | 27 | 0 | - | - | - | 6.75 | - | 0 | 0 |
| First-class | 181 | 39192 | 15719 | 599 | 9/70 | | 26.24 | 2.40 | 65.4 | 35 | 5 |
| List A | 185 | 9340 | 6834 | 238 | 6/27 | 6/27 | 28.71 | 4.39 | 39.2 | 2 | 0 |
| Twenty20 | 107 | 2242 | 2490 | 82 | 5/13 | 5/13 | 30.36 | 6.66 | 27.3 | 1 | 0 |

HAMPSHIRE

**FULL NAME:** Simon Mathew Katich
**BORN:** August 21, 1975, Middle Swan, Western Australia, Australia
**SQUAD NO:** 3
**HEIGHT:** 5ft 10in
**NICKNAME:** Kat
**TEAMS:** Australia, Derbyshire, Durham, Hampshire, Kings XI Punjab, New South Wales, Western Australia, Yorkshire
**CAREER:** Test: 2001; ODI: 2001; T20I: 2005; First-class: 1997; List A: 1995; T20: 2003

**BEST BATTING:** 306 New South Wales vs Queensland, SCG, 2007
**BEST BOWLING:** 7-130 New South Wales vs Victoria, MCG, 2003
**COUNTY CAP:** 2007 (Derbyshire)

**NOTES:** Named Hampshire Cricket Society Player of the Year in 2003. Featured for Australia in the 2005 Ashes in England. Captained Derbyshire in 2007 season. As captain of New South Wales, he scored 1,506 runs in the 2007/08 season as his side won the Sheffield Shield and led NSW to victory in the first Champions League trophy in 2009. Dropped from the Australian Test side following the defeat against England in the 2010/11 Ashes and was not offered a new contract with the national side

| Batting | Mat | Inns | NO | Runs | HS | Ave | SR | 100 | 50 | Ct | St |
|---|---|---|---|---|---|---|---|---|---|---|---|
| Tests | 56 | 99 | 6 | 4188 | 157 | 45.03 | 49.36 | 10 | 25 | 39 | 0 |
| ODIs | 45 | 42 | 5 | 1324 | 107* | 35.78 | 68.74 | 1 | 9 | 13 | 0 |
| T20Is | 3 | 2 | 0 | 69 | 39 | 34.50 | 146.80 | 0 | 0 | 2 | 0 |
| First-class | 239 | 409 | 49 | 19091 | 306 | 53.03 | | 53 | 100 | 212 | 0 |
| List A | 226 | 215 | 22 | 7023 | 136* | 36.38 | | 7 | 55 | 102 | 0 |
| Twenty20 | 66 | 57 | 10 | 1354 | 75 | 28.80 | 126.54 | 0 | 5 | 31 | 0 |

| Bowling | Mat | Balls | Runs | Wkts | BBI | BBM | Ave | Econ | SR | 5w | 10 |
|---|---|---|---|---|---|---|---|---|---|---|---|
| Tests | 56 | 1039 | 635 | 21 | 6/65 | 6/90 | 30.23 | 3.66 | 49.4 | 1 | 0 |
| ODIs | 45 | - | - | - | - | - | - | - | - | - | - |
| T20Is | 3 | - | - | - | - | - | - | - | - | - | - |
| First-class | 239 | 6231 | 3685 | 105 | 7/130 | | 35.09 | 3.54 | 59.3 | 3 | 0 |
| List A | 226 | 877 | 817 | 24 | 3/21 | 3/21 | 34.04 | 5.58 | 36.5 | 0 | 0 |
| Twenty20 | 66 | 12 | 14 | 0 | - | - | - | 7.00 | - | 0 | 0 |

# GARY KEEDY

**LHB SLA W4 MVP24**

FULL NAME: Gary Keedy
BORN: November 27, 1974, Sandal, Wakefield, Yorkshire
SQUAD NO: 23
HEIGHT: 5ft 11in
NICKNAME: Keeds
EDUCATION: Garforth Comprehensive; University of Salford
TEAMS: Lancashire, Marylebone Cricket Club, Yorkshire
CAREER: First-class: 1994; List A: 1995; T20: 2004

**LANCASHIRE**

BEST BATTING: 64 Lancashire vs Sussex, Hove, 2001
BEST BOWLING: 7-68 Lancashire vs Durham, Manchester, 2010
COUNTY CAPS: 2000; BENEFIT YEAR: 2009

FAMILY TIES? Twin brother is a Castleford CC legend
WHY CRICKET? Started at school because I was bored of athletics
CAREER HIGHLIGHTS? Receiving my cap in 2000. My one and only outing as an England Lion vs Australia in 2009. All my games for Lancashire
SUPERSTITIONS? No
CRICKETING HEROES? Shane Warne
BEST PLAYER IN COUNTY CRICKET? According to the MVP it's Marcus Trescothick
TIPS FOR THE TOP? Jordan Clark, Luke Procter
IF YOU WEREN'T A CRICKETER? Working!
WHEN RAIN STOPS PLAY? Studying or training mainly
FAVOURITE TV? MasterChef
FAVOURITE FILM? The Untouchables
DREAM HOLIDAY? Naples
ACCOMPLISHMENTS? Almost qualified as a chartered physiotherapist
GUILTY PLEASURES? Chardonnay and chocolate
TWITTER FEED: @keeds23

| Batting | Mat | Inns | NO | Runs | HS | Ave | SR | 100 | 50 | Ct | St |
|---------|-----|------|-----|------|-----|-------|-------|-----|----|----|----|
| First-class | 211 | 245 | 121 | 1415 | 64 | 11.41 | | 0 | 2 | 51 | 0 |
| List A | 79 | 27 | 11 | 143 | 33 | 8.93 | | 0 | 0 | 13 | 0 |
| Twenty20 | 63 | 11 | 6 | 27 | 9* | 5.40 | 79.41 | 0 | 0 | 7 | 0 |

| Bowling | Mat | Balls | Runs | Wkts | BBI | BBM | Ave | Econ | SR | 5w | 10 |
|---------|-----|-------|------|------|------|------|-------|------|------|----|----|
| First-class | 211 | 42938 | 20020 | 648 | 7/68 | | 30.89 | 2.79 | 66.2 | 32 | 7 |
| List A | 79 | 3244 | 2534 | 94 | 5/30 | 5/30 | 26.95 | 4.68 | 34.5 | 1 | 0 |
| Twenty20 | 63 | 1270 | 1355 | 63 | 4/15 | 4/15 | 21.50 | 6.40 | 20.1 | 0 | 0 |

## SAM KELSALL

**RHB RM**

NOTTINGHAMSHIRE

**FULL NAME:** Samuel Kelsall
**BORN:** March 14, 1993, Stoke-on-Trent, Staffordshire
**SQUAD NO:** 18
**NICKNAME:** Kels, Rugrat, Mouse
**EDUCATION:** Priory Primary School; Trentham High School; South Nottingham College.
**TEAMS:** England Under-17s, England Under-19s, Nottinghamshire, Nottinghamshire 2nd XI
**CAREER:** First-class: 2011; List A: 2011

BEST BATTING: 11 Nottinghamshire vs Durham, Chester-le-Street, 2011

WHY CRICKET? My old man – I have had a bat in my hand since I can remember and was always playing in the back garden with my dad
CAREER HIGHLIGHTS? Representing England at U15 and U19. Earning my first professional contract with Notts, having been a member since age 11
CRICKETING HEROES? Ian Bell has always been a role model to me
NON-CRICKETING HEROES? Phil Taylor
BEST PLAYER IN COUNTY CRICKET? Andre Adams and Marcus Trescothick
TIP FOR THE TOP? Thomas Rowe from Nottinghamshire
IF YOU WEREN'T A CRICKETER? Hopefully a PE teacher or coach of some sort
WHEN RAIN STOPS PLAY? Listening to music, resting, playing Doodle Jump
FAVOURITE TV? Eastenders, Emmerdale, MasterChef, TOWIE
FAVOURITE FILM? Billy Elliot
FAVOURITE BOOK? Andre Agassi – Open
DREAM HOLIDAY? Barbados
ACCOMPLISHMENTS? Completing my Level 2 coaching badge, completing my BTEC course
GUILTY PLEASURES? Watching Loose Women or crying at The Lion King
FANTASY SLIP CORDON? Keeper: Shaka Hislop, 1st: Rihanna, 2nd: Chris Kelsall, 3rd: James Corden, Gully: David English
TWITTER FEED: @Kelsall93

| Batting | Mat | Inns | NO | Runs | HS | Ave | SR | 100 | 50 | Ct | St |
|---|---|---|---|---|---|---|---|---|---|---|---|
| First-class | 1 | 2 | 0 | 15 | 11 | 7.50 | 41.66 | 0 | 0 | 1 | 0 |
| List A | 1 | 1 | 0 | 40 | 40 | 40.00 | 64.51 | 0 | 0 | 0 | 0 |

| Bowling | Mat | Balls | Runs | Wkts | BBI | BBM | Ave | Econ | SR | 5w | 10 |
|---|---|---|---|---|---|---|---|---|---|---|---|
| First-class | 1 | - | - | - | - | - | - | - | - | - | - |
| List A | 1 | - | - | - | - | - | - | - | - | - | - |

## BENEDICT KEMP                                    RHB RFM

FULL NAME: Benedict William Kemp
BORN: May 26, 1993, Canterbury, Kent
SQUAD NO: 18
HEIGHT: 6ft 4in
NICKNAME: Kempy, The Technician
EDUCATION: St. Edmund's School,
Canterbury; Oxford Brookes University
TEAMS: Kent 2nd XI, Kent Under-13s, Kent
Under-15s, Kent Under-17s
CAREER: Yet to make first-team debut

KENT

FAMILY TIES? Grandad played competitively, father played for Kent and Young England
CAREER HIGHLIGHTS? Being signed by Kent was probably my proudest moment so far, although taking out the Surrey 2nd XI top-order last season and being named Wisden's best schoolboy bowler during the 2009/2010 season were both good too
CRICKETING HEROES? Glenn McGrath, Shaun Pollock, Andrew Flintoff, WG Grace
NON-CRICKETING HEROES? Muhammad Ali, Steven Gerrard, 50 Cent
BEST PLAYER IN COUNTY CRICKET? Jade Dernbach
TIPS FOR THE TOP? Daniel Bell-Drummond, Ivan Thomas
IF YOU WEREN'T A CRICKETER? Trying to be a businessman (and probably failing), poker player, working in SportsDirect
WHEN RAIN STOPS PLAY? Catching up on my fitness, eating, calorie building
FAVOURITE TV? Luther, Silent Witness, Ford Football Special, Family Guy
FAVOURITE FILM? Inception, The Shawshank Redemption
FAVOURITE BOOK? Bounce – Mathew Syed
DREAM HOLIDAY? An island without British tourists
ACCOMPLISHMENTS? AAB at A-Levels, winning a poker tournament online and being named Mr. Canterbury
GUILTY PLEASURES? Ice cream, creative writing and gambling
AMAZE ME! Prolific poker player on Sky Poker – my alias is bwkemp_93. Secret aspirations to run the country. Own about 10 failed websites
FANTASY SLIP CORDON? Keeper: Sir Winston Churchill, 1st: WG Grace, 2nd: Myself, 3rd: Boris Johnson, 4th: Albert Einstein, Gully: Sir Stephen Hawking
TWITTER FEED: @benkemp18

# ROBERT KEOGH

**RHB OB**

**FULL NAME:** Robert Ian Keogh
**BORN:** October 21, 1991, Dunstable
**SQUAD NO:** TBC
**HEIGHT:** 6ft 1in
**NICKNAME:** Keezy
**EDUCATION:** Queensbury School; Central Beds College
**TEAMS:** Bedfordshire, Northamptonshire, Northamptonshire 2nd XI
**CAREER:** List A: 2010; T20: 2011

**FAMILY TIES?** Dad plays for local cricket club Dunstable Town

**CAREER HIGHLIGHTS?** Making my List A debut on Sky Sports against a strong Yorkshire side and making some T20 appearances last season

**SUPERSTITIONS?** Have to put my kit on in a certain way, same pre-match routine and can't take first ball when opening

**CRICKETING HEROES?** Sachin Tendulkar, Ricky Ponting, Michael Clarke, AB de Villiers, Ian Bell

**NON-CRICKETING HEROES?** Floyd Mayweather Jr, David Beckham, Drake

**TIPS FOR THE TOP?** Ben Duckett and Christian Davis

**IF YOU WEREN'T A CRICKETER?** Coaching or a fireman

**WHEN RAIN STOPS PLAY?** Cards, music, darts and sometimes sleep

**FAVOURITE TV?** Ross Kemp's documentaries, Jersey Shore, The Only Way Is Essex, Soccer AM

**FAVOURITE FILM?** Lock Stock And Two Smoking Barrels, Snatch

**DREAM HOLIDAY?** St. Lucia

**ACCOMPLISHMENTS?** Played for Luton Town FC up until age 15

**AMAZE ME!** Played football with Jack Wilshere for three years before he moved to Arsenal, made my senior club debut at just seven years of age

**FANTASY SLIP CORDON?** Keeper: Jimmy Carr, 1st: Sachin Tendulkar, 2nd: David Beckham, 3rd: Floyd Mayweather Jr, Gully: Drake

| Batting | Mat | Inns | NO | Runs | HS | Ave | SR | 100 | 50 | Ct | St |
|---------|-----|------|-----|------|-----|-------|-------|-----|-----|-----|-----|
| List A | 1 | 1 | 0 | 11 | 11 | 11.00 | 42.30 | 0 | 0 | 1 | 0 |
| Twenty20 | 3 | 1 | 0 | 1 | 1 | 1.00 | 14.28 | 0 | 0 | 2 | 0 |

| Bowling | Mat | Balls | Runs | Wkts | BBI | BBM | Ave | Econ | SR | 5w | 10 |
|---------|-----|-------|------|------|-----|-----|-----|------|-----|-----|-----|
| List A | 1 | - | - | - | - | - | - | - | - | - | - |
| Twenty20 | 3 | 12 | 18 | 0 | - | - | - | 9.00 | - | 0 | 0 |

# SIMON KERRIGAN

## RHB SLA

**FULL NAME:** Simon Christopher Kerrigan
**BORN:** May 10, 1989, Preston, Lancashire
**SQUAD NO:** 10
**HEIGHT:** 5ft 9in
**NICKNAME:** Kegsy, Kegs, Kegger, Bish
**EDUCATION:** Corpus Christi High School;
Preston College; Edge Hill University
**TEAMS:** England Lions, Lancashire,
Lancashire 2nd XI
**CAREER:** First-class: 2010; List A: 2011; T20:
2010

---

**BEST BATTING:** 40 Lancashire vs Somerset, Taunton, 2010
**BEST BOWLING:** 9-51 Lancashire vs Hampshire, Liverpool, 2011

---

**CAREER HIGHLIGHTS?** Winning the Championship
**SUPERSTITIONS?** Not really, they come and go
**CRICKETING HEROES?** Andrew Flintoff, Darren Gough
**NON-CRICKETING HEROES?** Phil Ivey
**BEST PLAYER IN COUNTY CRICKET?** Marcus Trescothick
**TIP FOR THE TOP?** Karl Brown
**IF YOU WEREN'T A CRICKETER?** Jobless
**WHEN RAIN STOPS PLAY?** Sleep and make tea for everyone
**FAVOURITE TV?** Modern Family
**FAVOURITE FILM?** The Other Guys
**DREAM HOLIDAY?** Blackpool
**GUILTY PLEASURES?** All bad foods
**TWITTER FEED:** @Kegs10

| Batting | Mat | Inns | NO | Runs | HS | Ave | SR | 100 | 50 | Ct | St |
|---|---|---|---|---|---|---|---|---|---|---|---|
| First-class | 18 | 22 | 8 | 125 | 40 | 8.92 | 28.08 | 0 | 0 | 4 | 0 |
| List A | 15 | 5 | 2 | 10 | 5 | 3.33 | 43.47 | 0 | 0 | 3 | 0 |
| Twenty20 | 19 | 2 | 2 | 4 | 4* | - | 200.00 | 0 | 0 | 6 | 0 |

| Bowling | Mat | Balls | Runs | Wkts | BBI | BBM | Ave | Econ | SR | 5w | 10 |
|---|---|---|---|---|---|---|---|---|---|---|---|
| First-class | 18 | 3192 | 1461 | 56 | 9/51 | 12/192 | 26.08 | 2.74 | 57.0 | 5 | 1 |
| List A | 15 | 590 | 498 | 12 | 3/21 | 3/21 | 41.50 | 5.06 | 49.1 | 0 | 0 |
| Twenty20 | 19 | 408 | 469 | 15 | 3/17 | 3/17 | 31.26 | 6.89 | 27.2 | 0 | 0 |

## ALEXEI KERVEZEE

**RHB RM R1**

WORCESTERSHIRE

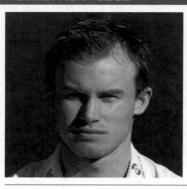

FULL NAME: Alexei Nicolaas Kervezee
BORN: September 11, 1989, Walvis Bay, Namibia
SQUAD NO: 5
HEIGHT: 5ft 7in
NICKNAME: Cub, Rowdy
TEAMS: Netherlands, Netherlands Under-19s, Worcestershire, Worcestershire 2nd XI
CAREER: ODI: 2006; T20I: 2009; First-class: 2005; List A: 2006; T20: 2009

BEST BATTING: 155 Worcestershire vs Derbyshire, Derby, 2010
BEST BOWLING: 1-14 Netherlands vs Namibia, Windhoek, 2008

NOTES: Made first-class debut for Netherlands vs Scotland at Utrecht in the ICC Intercontinental Cup 2005, aged 15. Made ODI debut for Netherlands vs Sri Lanka at Amstelveen in 2006, aged 16, scoring 47. Was still only 17 when playing in the World Cup in 2007. Played in the BPL over the winter for Dhaka Gladiators

| Batting | Mat | Inns | NO | Runs | HS | Ave | SR | 100 | 50 | Ct | St |
|---------|-----|------|----|----- |----|-----|-----|-----|----|----|----|
| ODIs | 37 | 34 | 2 | 794 | 92 | 24.81 | 69.16 | 0 | 3 | 17 | 0 |
| T20Is | 8 | 8 | 1 | 222 | 58* | 31.71 | 109.90 | 0 | 1 | 4 | 0 |
| First-class | 52 | 91 | 6 | 2926 | 155 | 34.42 | | 4 | 17 | 25 | 0 |
| List A | 68 | 65 | 3 | 1804 | 121* | 29.09 | 74.57 | 2 | 7 | 27 | 0 |
| Twenty20 | 46 | 44 | 5 | 724 | 58* | 18.56 | 111.21 | 0 | 2 | 17 | 0 |

| Bowling | Mat | Balls | Runs | Wkts | BBI | BBM | Ave | Econ | SR | 5w | 10 |
|---------|-----|-------|------|------|-----|-----|-----|------|----|----|----|
| ODIs | 37 | 24 | 34 | 0 | - | - | - | 8.50 | - | 0 | 0 |
| T20Is | 8 | - | - | - | - | - | - | - | - | - | - |
| First-class | 52 | 183 | 145 | 2 | 1/14 | 1/14 | 72.50 | 4.75 | 91.5 | 0 | 0 |
| List A | 68 | 48 | 73 | 0 | - | - | - | 9.12 | - | 0 | 0 |
| Twenty20 | 46 | 12 | 13 | 0 | - | - | - | 6.50 | - | 0 | 0 |

# ROBERT KEY
## RHB OB R6

FULL NAME: Robert William Trevor Key
BORN: May 12, 1979, East Dulwich, London
SQUAD NO: 4
HEIGHT: 6ft 2in
NICKNAME: Keysy
EDUCATION: Langley Park Boys' School
TEAMS: England, Kent, Marylebone Cricket Club
CAREER: Test: 2002; ODI: 2003; T20I: 2009; First-class: 1998, List A: 1998; T20: 2004

KENT

BEST BATTING: 270* Kent vs Glamorgan, Cardiff, 2009
BEST BOWLING: 2-31 Kent vs Somerset, Canterbury, 2010
COUNTY CAP: 2001; BENEFIT YEAR: 2011

CAREER HIGHLIGHTS? 221 for England plus 90* vs West Indies. Winning T20 in 2007
NON-CRICKETING HEROES? Eddy Stanford, Darren Scott
BEST PLAYER IN COUNTY CRICKET? Marcus Trescothick
TIPS FOR THE TOP? Anyone coached by Simon Willis
WHEN RAIN STOPS PLAY? iPad
FAVOURITE TV? 24
FAVOURITE FILM? Inception
FAVOURITE BOOK? Steve Jobs' autobiography
DREAM HOLIDAY? Antigua
ACCOMPLISHMENTS? Being a dad
TWITTER FEED: @Robkey612

| Batting | Mat | Inns | NO | Runs | HS | Ave | SR | 100 | 50 | Ct | St |
|---|---|---|---|---|---|---|---|---|---|---|---|
| Tests | 15 | 26 | 1 | 775 | 221 | 31.00 | 47.28 | 1 | 3 | 11 | 0 |
| ODIs | 5 | 5 | 0 | 54 | 19 | 10.80 | 40.00 | 0 | 0 | 0 | 0 |
| T20Is | 1 | 1 | 1 | 10 | 10* | - | 125.00 | 0 | 0 | 1 | 0 |
| First-class | 238 | 414 | 30 | 15934 | 270* | 41.49 | | 45 | 61 | 139 | 0 |
| List A | 199 | 192 | 13 | 5593 | 120* | 31.24 | | 5 | 35 | 41 | 0 |
| Twenty20 | 73 | 73 | 9 | 1659 | 98* | 25.92 | 124.45 | 0 | 9 | 18 | 0 |

| Bowling | Mat | Balls | Runs | Wkts | BBI | BBM | Ave | Econ | SR | 5w | 10 |
|---|---|---|---|---|---|---|---|---|---|---|---|
| Tests | 15 | - | - | - | - | - | - | - | - | - | - |
| ODIs | 5 | - | - | - | - | - | - | - | - | - | - |
| T20Is | 1 | - | - | - | - | - | - | - | - | - | - |
| First-class | 238 | 392 | 206 | 3 | 2/31 | 2/31 | 68.66 | 3.15 | 130.6 | 0 | 0 |
| List A | 199 | - | - | - | - | - | - | - | - | - | - |
| Twenty20 | 73 | - | - | - | - | - | - | - | - | - | - |

## AMJAD KHAN

### RHB RFM W2

FULL NAME: Amjad Khan
BORN: October 14, 1980, Copenhagen, Denmark
SQUAD NO: 2
HEIGHT: 6ft
NICKNAME: Ammy
EDUCATION: Skolen pa Duevej, Denmark; Falkonergardens Gymnasium
TEAMS: Denmark, England, Kent, Sussex
CAREER: Test: 2009; T20I: 2009; First-class: 2001; List A: 1999; T20: 2004

BEST BATTING: 78 Kent vs Middlesex, Lord's, 2003
BEST BOWLING: 6-52 Kent vs Yorkshire, Canterbury, 2002
COUNTY CAP: 2005 (Kent)

CAREER HIGHLIGHTS? Test debut
CRICKETING HEROES? Wasim Akram, Dennis Lillee
NON-CRICKETING HEROES? Muhammad Ali
BEST PLAYER IN COUNTY CRICKET? Marcus Trescothick
TIPS FOR THE TOP? Matt Machan, Callum Jackson
FAVOURITE TV? Dexter
FAVOURITE FILM? The Godfather 1 and 2
FAVOURITE BOOK? The Magus
DREAM HOLIDAY? Hawaii
SURPRISING SKILL? Speak five languages
GUILTY PLEASURES? Danish pastry
AMAZE ME! I will never tan more than Carl Hopkinson. I don't like football. My phone is my best friend

| Batting | Mat | Inns | NO | Runs | HS | Ave | SR | 100 | 50 | Ct | St |
|---|---|---|---|---|---|---|---|---|---|---|---|
| Tests | 1 | - | - | - | - | - | - | - | - | 0 | 0 |
| T20Is | 1 | 1 | 0 | 2 | 2 | 2.00 | 50.00 | 0 | 0 | 0 | 0 |
| First-class | 100 | 120 | 37 | 1324 | 78 | 15.95 | 47.98 | 0 | 5 | 26 | 0 |
| List A | 66 | 33 | 8 | 295 | 65* | 11.80 | | 0 | 1 | 16 | 0 |
| Twenty20 | 29 | 14 | 7 | 47 | 15 | 6.71 | 94.00 | 0 | 0 | 7 | 0 |

| Bowling | Mat | Balls | Runs | Wkts | BBI | BBM | Ave | Econ | SR | 5w | 10 |
|---|---|---|---|---|---|---|---|---|---|---|---|
| Tests | 1 | 174 | 122 | 1 | 1/111 | 1/122 | 122.00 | 4.20 | 174.0 | 0 | 0 |
| T20Is | 1 | 24 | 34 | 2 | 2/34 | 2/34 | 17.00 | 8.50 | 12.0 | 0 | 0 |
| First-class | 100 | 16943 | 10410 | 325 | 6/52 | | 32.03 | 3.68 | 52.1 | 8 | 0 |
| List A | 66 | 2594 | 2266 | 66 | 4/26 | 4/26 | 34.33 | 5.24 | 39.3 | 0 | 0 |
| Twenty20 | 29 | 501 | 761 | 31 | 3/11 | 3/11 | 24.54 | 9.11 | 16.1 | 0 | 0 |

# USMAN KHAWAJA · LHB RM

**FULL NAME:** Usman Tariq Khawaja
**BORN:** December 18, 1986, Islamabad, Pakistan
**SQUAD NO:** 8
**HEIGHT:** 5ft 7in
**NICKNAME:** Usie
**EDUCATION:** Westfield Sports High School; University of New South Wales
**TEAMS:** Australia, Australia A, Australia Under-19s, Derbyshire, New South Wales, Sydney Thunder
**CAREER:** Test: 2011; First-class: 2008; List A: 2008; T20: 2010

BEST BATTING: 214 New South Wales vs South Australia, Adelaide, 2010
BEST BOWLING: 1-21 New South Wales vs South Australia, Adelaide, 2010

TWITTER FEED: @Uz_Khawaja
NOTES: Khawaja is the first Muslim to represent Australia at cricket. He made his Test debut against England at Sydney during the 2010/11 Ashes, scoring 37 and 21. He is returning for his second stint with Derbyshire, having made four Championship appearances for them during the summer of 2011, scoring 319 runs at an average of 39.87. "We were hugely impressed with Usman during his previous spell with the club," Derbyshire head coach Karl Krikken told the BBC when his return was announced back in January. "The 2012 season will give him the opportunity of settling into a longer spell and hopefully scoring plenty of runs"

| Batting | Mat | Inns | NO | Runs | HS | Ave | SR | 100 | 50 | Ct | St |
|---|---|---|---|---|---|---|---|---|---|---|---|
| Tests | 6 | 11 | 2 | 263 | 65 | 29.22 | 39.07 | 0 | 1 | 3 | 0 |
| First-class | 46 | 78 | 6 | 3070 | 214 | 42.63 | 50.29 | 9 | 11 | 27 | 0 |
| List A | 17 | 17 | 1 | 652 | 121 | 40.75 | 77.99 | 3 | 2 | 6 | 0 |
| Twenty20 | 14 | 13 | 1 | 225 | 65 | 18.75 | 105.63 | 0 | 1 | 4 | 0 |

| Bowling | Mat | Balls | Runs | Wkts | BBI | BBM | Ave | Econ | SR | 5w | 10 |
|---|---|---|---|---|---|---|---|---|---|---|---|
| Tests | 6 | - | - | - | - | - | - | - | - | - | - |
| First-class | 46 | 72 | 47 | 1 | 1/21 | 1/21 | 47.00 | 3.91 | 72.0 | 0 | 0 |
| List A | 17 | - | - | - | - | - | - | - | - | - | - |
| Twenty20 | 14 | - | - | - | - | - | - | - | - | - | - |

SOMERSET

FULL NAME: Craig Kieswetter
BORN: November 28, 1987, Johannesburg, South Africa
SQUAD NO: 22
HEIGHT: 6ft
NICKNAME: Hobnob
EDUCATION: Bishops Diocesan College; Millfield School
TEAMS: England, England Lions, Somerset, South Africa Under-19s
CAREER: ODI: 2010; T20I: 2010; First-class: 2007; List A: 2007; T20: 2007

BEST BATTING: 164 Somerset vs Nottinghamshire, Nottingham, 2011
COUNTY CAPS: 2009

WHY CRICKET? As soon as I could walk I carried a bat. I have always loved the game
CAREER HIGHLIGHTS? Man of the Match in World T20 final (Barbados 2010), second youngest ODI century scorer for England
CRICKETING HEROES? Jonty Rhodes, Adam Gilchrist, Justin Langer
NON-CRICKETING HEROES? Ayrton Senna, Jose Mourinho
TIPS FOR THE TOP? Lewis Gregory, Joe Root
IF YOU WEREN'T A CRICKETER? I'd be studying Law
WHEN RAIN STOPS PLAY? iPod, PS3, TV, books
FAVOURITE TV? House, Lost, Made In Chelsea
FAVOURITE FILM? Sherlock Holmes
FAVOURITE BOOK? The Monk Who Sold His Ferrari – Robin Sharma
ACCOMPLISHMENTS? Helping charities with donations of cricket equipment
GUILTY PLEASURES? Chocolate and travelling
TWITTER FEED: @kiesy_22

| Batting | Mat | Inns | NO | Runs | HS | Ave | SR | 100 | 50 | Ct | St |
|---|---|---|---|---|---|---|---|---|---|---|---|
| ODIs | 32 | 30 | 1 | 861 | 107 | 29.68 | 91.59 | 1 | 5 | 31 | 8 |
| T20Is | 17 | 17 | 1 | 408 | 63 | 25.50 | 115.25 | 0 | 2 | 10 | 2 |
| First-class | 76 | 111 | 13 | 3765 | 164 | 38.41 | | 8 | 20 | 219 | 3 |
| List A | 104 | 99 | 10 | 3500 | 143 | 39.32 | 93.28 | 9 | 15 | 101 | 21 |
| Twenty20 | 72 | 70 | 10 | 1710 | 84 | 28.50 | 122.14 | 0 | 11 | 43 | 12 |
| Bowling | Mat | Balls | Runs | Wkts | BBI | BBM | Ave | Econ | SR | 5w | 10 |
| ODIs | 32 | - | - | - | - | - | - | - | - | - | - |
| T20Is | 17 | - | - | - | - | - | - | - | - | - | - |
| First-class | 76 | - | - | - | - | - | - | - | - | - | - |
| List A | 104 | - | - | - | - | - | - | - | - | - | - |
| Twenty20 | 72 | - | - | - | - | - | - | - | - | - | - |

# STEVE KIRBY      RHB RFM W3 MVP30

**FULL NAME:** Steven Paul Kirby
**BORN:** October 4, 1977, Bury, Lancashire
**SQUAD NO:** 9
**HEIGHT:** 6ft 3in
**NICKNAME:** Tango
**EDUCATION:** Elton High School; Bury College
**TEAMS:** England Lions, Gloucestershire, Leicestershire, Marylebone Cricket Club, Somerset, Yorkshire
**CAREER:** First-class: 2001; List A: 2001; T20: 2004

SOMERSET

**BEST BATTING:** 57 Yorkshire vs Hampshire, Leeds, 2002
**BEST BOWLING:** 8-80 Yorkshire vs Somerset, Taunton, 2003
**COUNTY CAPS:** 2003 (Yorkshire); 2005 (Gloucestershire)

**CRICKET MOMENTS TO FORGET?** Being knocked out by Nixon McLean trying to take a return catch
**CRICKETERS PARTICULARLY ADMIRED?** Steve Waugh, Richard Hadlee, Glenn McGrath, Michael Atherton, Curtly Ambrose, Sachin Tendulkar
**OTHER SPORTS PLAYED?** Basketball, table tennis, squash, golf
**NOTES:** Left Leicestershire for Yorkshire before playing a first-class match. Made 7-50 on debut for the White Rose. At his most prolific in 2003, when he claimed 67 first-class wickets. Moved to Gloucestershire in 2005. Moved to Somerset at the end of the 2010 season. Took 53 wickets in his first year at Taunton. Dismissed Mike Atherton in both innings of the former England skipper's last County Championship match

| Batting | Mat | Inns | NO | Runs | HS | Ave | SR | 100 | 50 | Ct | St |
|---|---|---|---|---|---|---|---|---|---|---|---|
| First-class | 147 | 206 | 61 | 1212 | 57 | 8.35 | 28.61 | 0 | 1 | 29 | 0 |
| List A | 86 | 34 | 13 | 88 | 15 | 4.19 | 42.51 | 0 | 0 | 15 | 0 |
| Twenty20 | 60 | 23 | 7 | 66 | 25 | 4.12 | 70.96 | 0 | 0 | 12 | 0 |

| Bowling | Mat | Balls | Runs | Wkts | BBI | BBM | Ave | Econ | SR | 5w | 10 |
|---|---|---|---|---|---|---|---|---|---|---|---|
| First-class | 147 | 26012 | 14709 | 522 | 8/80 | | 28.17 | 3.39 | 49.8 | 17 | 4 |
| List A | 86 | 3485 | 3292 | 117 | 5/36 | 5/36 | 28.13 | 5.66 | 29.7 | 1 | 0 |
| Twenty20 | 60 | 1129 | 1475 | 67 | 3/17 | 3/17 | 22.01 | 7.83 | 16.8 | 0 | 0 |

WORCESTERSHIRE

**FULL NAME:** Michael Klinger
**BORN:** July 4, 1980, Kew, Melbourne, Australia
**SQUAD NO:** TBC
**HEIGHT:** 5ft 9in
**NICKNAME:** Maxy
**TEAMS:** Adelaide Strikers, Australia A, Kochi Tuskers Kerala, South Australia, Victoria
**CAREER:** First-class: 1999; List A: 1999; T20: 2006

**BEST BATTING:** 255 South Australia vs Western Australia, Adelaide, 2008

**NOTES:** Klinger's career took off after his move from Victoria to South Australia in 2008. He was Australia's State Cricketer of the Year in his first two seasons at his new home. His first foray into county cricket comes late in his career – he is 31 – but Worcestershire may well have chosen wisely as his reputation is as high as it has ever been. He scored the third double century of his first-class career against Tasmania early ths year and was also the leading runscorer in the Ryobi Cup one-day competition, with 498 runs at 55.33

| Batting | Mat | Inns | NO | Runs | HS | Ave | SR | 100 | 50 | Ct | St |
|---|---|---|---|---|---|---|---|---|---|---|---|
| First-class | 82 | 146 | 15 | 5006 | 255 | 38.21 | 42.94 | 10 | 23 | 74 | 0 |
| List A | 94 | 94 | 10 | 3471 | 133* | 41.32 | | 9 | 22 | 31 | 0 |
| Twenty20 | 41 | 39 | 4 | 949 | 78 | 27.11 | 124.05 | 0 | 5 | 15 | 0 |

| Bowling | Mat | Balls | Runs | Wkts | BBI | BBM | Ave | Econ | SR | 5w | 10 |
|---|---|---|---|---|---|---|---|---|---|---|---|
| First-class | 82 | 6 | 3 | 0 | - | - | - | 3.00 | - | 0 | 0 |
| List A | 94 | - | - | - | - | - | - | - | - | - | - |
| Twenty20 | 41 | - | - | - | - | - | - | - | - | - | - |

# TOM KNIGHT

## RHB SLA

FULL NAME: Thomas Craig Knight
BORN: June 28, 1993, Sheffield, Yorkshire
SQUAD NO: 27
HEIGHT: 6ft 2in
NICKNAME: Knighty
EDUCATION: Eckington School
TEAMS: Derbyshire, Derbyshire 2nd XI, Derbyshire Under-15s, Derbyshire Under-17s, England Under-19s
CAREER: First-class: 2011; List A: 2011; T20: 2011

---

BEST BATTING: 14 Derbyshire vs Surrey, The Oval, 2011
BEST BOWLING: 2-32 Derbyshire vs Glamorgan, Cardiff, 2011

---

CAREER HIGHLIGHTS? Making T20 debut at Trent Bridge, taking 3-16 for Derbyshire vs Worcestershire, playing for England U19. Also taking 3-27 for England U19 vs South Africa U19
CRICKETING HEROES? Shane Warne and Andy Flintoff
NON-CRICKETING HEROES? Muhammad Ali, Tiger Woods, David Beckham
BEST PLAYER IN COUNTY CRICKET? Marcus Trescothick
TIPS FOR THE TOP? Alex Hughes, Paul Borrington
IF YOU WEREN'T A CRICKETER? I would have gone to university
WHEN RAIN STOPS PLAY? Do a crossword
FAVOURITE TV? Criminal Minds
FAVOURITE FILM? Saving Private Ryan
FAVOURITE BOOK? Holes
DREAM HOLIDAY? Caribbean
GUILTY PLEASURES? Chris Durham's fajitas
TWITTER FEED: @tomknight28

| Batting | Mat | Inns | NO | Runs | HS | Ave | SR | 100 | 50 | Ct | St |
|---|---|---|---|---|---|---|---|---|---|---|---|
| First-class | 2 | 3 | 1 | 15 | 14 | 7.50 | 39.47 | 0 | 0 | 1 | 0 |
| List A | 3 | 1 | 1 | 1 | 1* | - | 100.00 | 0 | 0 | 0 | 0 |
| Twenty20 | 10 | 1 | 1 | 2 | 2* | - | 100.00 | 0 | 0 | 3 | 0 |

| Bowling | Mat | Balls | Runs | Wkts | BBI | BBM | Ave | Econ | SR | 5w | 10 |
|---|---|---|---|---|---|---|---|---|---|---|---|
| First-class | 2 | 288 | 143 | 2 | 2/32 | 2/59 | 71.50 | 2.97 | 144.0 | 0 | 0 |
| List A | 3 | 144 | 113 | 5 | 2/27 | 2/27 | 22.60 | 4.70 | 28.8 | 0 | 0 |
| Twenty20 | 10 | 180 | 201 | 9 | 3/16 | 3/16 | 22.33 | 6.70 | 20.0 | 0 | 0 |

# TOM LANCEFIELD

**LHB LM**

FULL NAME: Thomas John Lancefield
BORN: October 8, 1990, Epsom, Surrey
SQUAD NO: 21
HEIGHT: 5ft 9in
NICKNAME: Creature, Lancey
EDUCATION: Whitgift and Twyford CofE
TEAMS: Surrey, Surrey 2nd XI, Tamil Union Cricket and Athletic Club
CAREER: First-class: 2010; List A: 2009; T20: 2010

BEST BATTING: 74 Surrey vs Worcestershire, Worcester, 2010
BEST BOWLING: 1-12 Tamil Union vs Colts, Colombo, 2011

FAMILY TIES? My uncle played a bit for Surrey 2nd XI and my whole family are cricket mad!
CAREER HIGHLIGHTS? Making my first-class debut for Surrey and playing at Lord's in a first-class game
SUPERSTITIONS? Double tap the crease at the end of every over!
CRICKETING HEROES? Brian Lara
NON-CRICKETING HEROES? Lawrence Dallaglio, Martin Rowlands and Winston Churchill
BEST PLAYER IN COUNTY CRICKET? Marcus Trescothick
TIPS FOR THE TOP? Jason Roy and Matthew Dunn
IF YOU WEREN'T A CRICKETER? Rugby or doing some sort of wheeling and dealing!
FAVOURITE TV? Dexter
FAVOURITE BOOK? Maggie Gee – The Ice People
DREAM HOLIDAY? Mars or any Caribbean island!
ACCOMPLISHMENTS? One A and two Bs at A-Level, England U16 A rugby
SURPRISING SKILL? I can lick my nose with my tongue
FANTASY SLIP CORDON? Keeper: Jon Surtees (Surrey's communication officer), 1st: Prince, 2nd: Gordon Brown, 3rd: Freddie Mercury, Gully: The Queen
TWITTER FEED? @tommylancefield

| Batting | Mat | Inns | NO | Runs | HS | Ave | SR | 100 | 50 | Ct | St |
|---|---|---|---|---|---|---|---|---|---|---|---|
| First-class | 11 | 18 | 1 | 464 | 74 | 27.29 | 47.25 | 0 | 2 | 5 | 0 |
| List A | 1 | 1 | 0 | 20 | 20 | 20.00 | 117.64 | 0 | 0 | 1 | 0 |
| Twenty20 | 5 | 3 | 0 | 65 | 27 | 21.66 | 125.00 | 0 | 0 | 1 | 0 |

| Bowling | Mat | Balls | Runs | Wkts | BBI | BBM | Ave | Econ | SR | 5w | 10 |
|---|---|---|---|---|---|---|---|---|---|---|---|
| First-class | 11 | 30 | 21 | 1 | 1/12 | 1/12 | 21.00 | 4.20 | 30.0 | 0 | 0 |
| List A | 1 | - | - | - | - | - | - | - | - | - | - |
| Twenty20 | 5 | 0 | 0 | 0 | - | - | - | - | - | 0 | 0 |

FULL NAME: Matthew Jack Leach
BORN: June 22, 1991, Taunton, Somerset
SQUAD NO: 17
HEIGHT: 6ft
NICKNAME: Leachy, Donkey, Snoz
EDUCATION: Trinity Primary School; Bishop Fox's Community School
TEAMS: Cardiff MCCU, Dorset, Somerset 2nd XI, Somerset Under-17s
CAREER: Yet to make first-team debut

SOMERSET

WHY CRICKET? The fact that it was a non-contact sport played in the summer suited me!
CAREER HIGHLIGHTS? Represented England U15 (six-wicket haul against Barbados). Regional victory at U17 tournament at Loughborough
SUPERSTITIONS? Not that I know of
CRICKETING HEROES? Jacques Kallis, MS Dhoni, Ricky Ponting
NON-CRICKETING HEROES? Roger Federer
BEST PLAYER IN COUNTY CRICKET? Marcus Trescothick
TIPS FOR THE TOP? Chris Jones, Danny Briggs
IF YOU WEREN'T A CRICKETER? Working a lot harder at my degree
WHEN RAIN STOPS PLAY? I play cards or read a good book
FAVOURITE TV? Friends, An Idiot Abroad
FAVOURITE FILM? The Hangover
FAVOURITE BOOK? The Game
DREAM HOLIDAY? Vegas
SURPRISING FACT? I throw with my right arm and bowl with my left. My dad took me to watch my first Somerset game when I was two weeks old
FANTASY SLIP CORDON? Keeper: Joey Barton (listen to his brilliant sledges), 1st: Karl Pilkington (I'd love to hear his views on the game), 2nd: Myself, 3rd: Jay from The Inbetweeners (I'd like to hear his lies and excuses), Gully: Phil 'The Power' Taylor (direct hitting ability)
TWITTER FEED: @jackleach1991

**WORCESTERSHIRE**

FULL NAME: Joseph Leach
BORN: October 30, 1990, Stafford, Staffordshire
SQUAD NO: 23
HEIGHT: 6ft 1in
NICKNAME: Hugh Jed
EDUCATION: Shrewsbury School; Leeds University
TEAMS: Leeds/Bradford MCCU, Shropshire, Staffordshire, Worcestershire 2nd XI
CAREER: Yet to make first-team debut

WHY CRICKET? Really not sure, I think it might just have been the fact that ever since I can remember I have had a bat and ball in my hand!

CAREER HIGHLIGHTS? Playing at Worcestershire and winning the National Knockout with Shrewsbury CC

SUPERSTITIONS? None, I try not to let things like that affect me

CRICKETING HEROES? Jacques Kallis, Andrew Flintoff

NON-CRICKETING HEROES? None

BEST PLAYER IN COUNTY CRICKET? Being loyal, I'll have to say Alan Richardson

TIPS FOR THE TOP? Ben Slater and Luis Reece

IF YOU WEREN'T A CRICKETER? I'd probably spend more time working on my degree!

WHEN RAIN STOPS PLAY? Taking the mickey out of Chris Russell or traipsing through Twitter

FAVOURITE TV? An Idiot Abroad

FAVOURITE FILM? The Hangover 2

DREAM HOLIDAY? Somewhere in the Caribbean

ACCOMPLISHMENTS? I can speak French (fairly well)

SURPRISING SKILL? I study Philosophy at Leeds University

FANTASY SLIP CORDON? Keeper: Ricky Gervais, 1st: Al Murray, 2nd: Karl Pilkington, 3rd: Me

TWITTER FEED: @joeleach23

FULL NAME: Stephen Geoffrey Leach
BORN: November 19, 1993, Stafford
SQUAD NO: 30
HEIGHT: 6ft 2in
NICKNAME: Screech, Leachy, Scratch
EDUCATION: Shrewsbury School
TEAMS: Shropshire, Worcestershire 2nd XI
CAREER: Yet to make first-team debut

**WORCESTERSHIRE**

FAMILY TIES? My older brother Joe plays for Worcestershire as well as playing for Leeds/Bradford MCCU and I've played a lot with him growing up but beyond that there are no real connections with cricket in the famiy

CAREER HIGHLIGHTS? Playing for Worcestershire 2nd XI. Shrewsbury CC – Birmingham League Champions 2010, National Knockout winners 2011. Shrewsbury School – Silk Trophy winners, National T20 winners 2011

SUPERSTITIONS? Not that I'd like to admit to

CRICKETING HEROES? Brian Lara, Marcus Trescothick, Matthew Hayden

BEST PLAYER IN COUNTY CRICKET? Bowler: Alan Richardson. Leading wicket-taker in the County Championship last year and he's been kind enough to give me a fair few nets this winter so it would be rude not to give him a mention! Batsman: James Taylor – an old Shrewsbury School pupil

FAVOURITE TV? One Tree Hill

FAVOURITE FILM? Mean Girls – a second to none chick flick!

FAVOURITE BOOK? Lance Armstrong – It's Not About The Bike

DREAM HOLIDAY? Cape Town, South Africa

SURPRISING SKILL? I have a party trick where I can eat a Jaffa Cake, leaving the orange bit till last, without using my hands

GUILTY PLEASURES? Power naps – not sure how else I'd get through the day!

FANTASY SLIP CORDON? Keeper: Jack Whitehall (interesting accent and outstanding one liners to keep everyone going through the day), 1st: Brian Blessed (would surely have some classic stories and the best sledges on the circuit), 2nd: Myself, 3rd: Gillian Zinser (actress in 90210 and just an unbelievable piece of eye candy), Gully: Benjamin Francis (my favourite artist at the moment, definitely worth a listen)

TWITTER FEED: @Screech71

YORKSHIRE

FULL NAME: Alexander Zak Lees
BORN: April 14, 1993, Halifax, Yorkshire
SQUAD NO: 14
HEIGHT: 6ft 4in
NICKNAME: Leesy
EDUCATION: Holy Trinity Senior School and Sixth Form
TEAMS: Yorkshire, Yorkshire 2nd XI, Yorkshire Academy, Yorkshire Under-17s
CAREER: First-class: 2010; List A: 2011

BEST BATTING: 38 Yorkshire vs Indians, Leeds, 2010

FAMILY TIES? My late father played the game
CAREER HIGHLIGHTS? Making my CB40 debut at Headingley
SUPERSTITIONS? No, just a certain routine
CRICKETING HEROES? Matthew Hayden, Shane Warne, Brian Lara
NON-CRICKETING HEROES? Lance Armstrong
TIP FOR THE TOP? Joe Root
IF YOU WEREN'T A CRICKETER? I'd be a PE teacher
WHEN RAIN STOPS PLAY? Catching some sleep or relaxing
FAVOURITE TV? The Shawshank Redemption
FAVOURITE BOOK? Dan Brown – Angels And Demons
DREAM HOLIDAY? Maldives
ACCOMPLISHMENTS? Fundraising for Macmillan
GUILTY PLEASURES? Jeremy Kyle
FANTASY SLIP CORDON? Keeper: The Big Show, 1st: Megan Fox, 2nd: Alan Carr, 3rd: Boris Johnson, Gully: The Queen

| Batting | Mat | Inns | NO | Runs | HS | Ave | SR | 100 | 50 | Ct | St |
|---|---|---|---|---|---|---|---|---|---|---|---|
| First-class | 2 | 2 | 0 | 38 | 38 | 19.00 | 35.18 | 0 | 0 | 0 | 0 |
| List A | 1 | 1 | 1 | 12 | 12* | - | 85.71 | 0 | 0 | 0 | 0 |

| Bowling | Mat | Balls | Runs | Wkts | BBI | BBM | Ave | Econ | SR | 5w | 10 |
|---|---|---|---|---|---|---|---|---|---|---|---|
| First-class | 2 | - | - | - | - | - | - | - | - | - | - |
| List A | 1 | - | - | - | - | - | - | - | - | - | - |

**FULL NAME:** Jonathan Lewis
**BORN:** August 26, 1975, Aylesbury, Buckinghamshire
**SQUAD NO:** 7
**HEIGHT:** 6ft 2in
**NICKNAME:** JJ, Lewy
**EDUCATION:** Churchfields School, Swindon
**TEAMS:** England, Gloucestershire, Surrey
**CAREER:** Test: 2006; ODI: 2005; T20I: 2005; First-class: 1995; List A: 1995; T20: 2003

SURREY

---

**BEST BATTING:** 71 Gloucestershire vs Middlesex, Uxbridge, 2011
**BEST BOWLING:** 8-95 Gloucestershire vs Zimbabweans, Gloucester, 2000
**COUNTY CAP:** 1998 (Gloucestershire); **BENEFIT YEAR:** 2007 (Gloucestershire)

---

**CAREER HIGHLIGHTS?** Every time I pulled on an England shirt. Also all my wins for Gloucestershire, especially the Lord's finals
**SUPERSTITIONS?** I usually get a haircut if I go for a gallon
**CRICKETING HEROES?** Courtney Walsh, Richard Hadlee, Jack Russell, Malcolm Marshall
**NON-CRICKETING HEROES?** Tiger Woods
**BEST PLAYER IN COUNTY CRICKET?** Marcus Trescothick
**TIP FOR THE TOP?** Will Carpenter
**IF YOU WEREN'T A CRICKETER?** Golf pro
**FAVOURITE TV?** Take Me Out
**DREAM HOLIDAY?** Mozambique
**GUILTY PLEASURES?** Vino Rosso!

| Batting | Mat | Inns | NO | Runs | HS | Ave | SR | 100 | 50 | Ct | St |
|---|---|---|---|---|---|---|---|---|---|---|---|
| Tests | 1 | 2 | 0 | 27 | 20 | 13.50 | 60.00 | 0 | 0 | 0 | 0 |
| ODIs | 13 | 8 | 2 | 50 | 17 | 8.33 | 79.36 | 0 | 0 | 0 | 0 |
| T20Is | 2 | 2 | 1 | 1 | 1 | 1.00 | 25.00 | 0 | 0 | 1 | 0 |
| First-class | 228 | 327 | 63 | 4191 | 71 | 15.87 | | 0 | 13 | 58 | 0 |
| List A | 213 | 123 | 44 | 879 | 54 | 11.12 | | 0 | 1 | 39 | 0 |
| Twenty20 | 56 | 37 | 9 | 353 | 43 | 12.60 | 125.62 | 0 | 0 | 10 | 0 |

| Bowling | Mat | Balls | Runs | Wkts | BBI | BBM | Ave | Econ | SR | 5w | 10 |
|---|---|---|---|---|---|---|---|---|---|---|---|
| Tests | 1 | 246 | 122 | 3 | 3/68 | 3/122 | 40.66 | 2.97 | 82.0 | 0 | 0 |
| ODIs | 13 | 716 | 500 | 18 | 4/36 | 4/36 | 27.77 | 4.18 | 39.7 | 0 | 0 |
| T20Is | 2 | 42 | 55 | 4 | 4/24 | 4/24 | 13.75 | 7.85 | 10.5 | 0 | 0 |
| First-class | 228 | 41278 | 20623 | 798 | 8/95 | | 25.84 | 2.99 | 51.7 | 34 | 5 |
| List A | 213 | 9790 | 7470 | 285 | 5/19 | 5/19 | 26.21 | 4.57 | 34.3 | 2 | 0 |
| Twenty20 | 56 | 1146 | 1600 | 54 | 4/24 | 4/24 | 29.62 | 8.37 | 21.2 | 0 | 0 |

# CHRIS LIDDLE

## RHB LMF

**FULL NAME:** Christopher John Liddle
**BORN:** February 1, 1984, Middlesbrough, Yorkshire
**SQUAD NO:** 11
**HEIGHT:** 6ft 4in
**NICKNAME:** Lids, Chuck
**EDUCATION:** Nunthorpe Comprehensive, Middlesborough; Teeside Tertiary College
**TEAMS:** Leicestershire, Leicestershire 2nd XI, Sussex
**CAREER:** First-class: 2005; List A: 2006; T20: 2008

**BEST BATTING:** 53 Sussex vs Worcestershire, Hove, 2007
**BEST BOWLING:** 3-42 Leicestershire vs Somerset, Leicester, 2006

**FAMILY TIES?** Brother Andrew plays in the North Yorkshire South Division cricket league
**WHY CRICKET?** The banter with teammates. The competitive side of the game
**CAREER HIGHLIGHTS?** T20 debut. 2011 season having previously missed the 2009 and 2010 seasons with injury
**CRICKETING HEROES?** Darren Gough, AB de Villiers, Marc Rosenberg
**NON-CRICKETING HEROES?** Jamie Redknapp
**BEST PLAYER IN COUNTY CRICKET?** Chris Nash
**TIP FOR THE TOP?** Luke Wells
**IF YOU WEREN'T A CRICKETER?** I'd be an electrician
**WHEN RAIN STOPS PLAY?** On my iPad or messing around with some teammates
**FAVOURITE FILM?** Snatch
**FAVOURITE TV?** An Idiot Abroad, Emmerdale
**DREAM HOLIDAY?** Sea apartment in the Maldives
**SURPRISING SKILL?** Occasional DJ for friends
**FANTASY SLIP CORDON?** Keeper: Karl Pilkington, 1st: Cheryl Cole, 2nd: Jamie Redknapp, 3rd: Mila Kunis, 4th: Me, Gully: Jessica Biel
**TWITTER FEED:** @chrisliddle11

| Batting | Mat | Inns | NO | Runs | HS | Ave | SR | 100 | 50 | Ct | St |
|---------|-----|------|-----|------|-----|-------|-------|-----|-----|-----|-----|
| First-class | 15 | 14 | 5 | 113 | 53 | 12.55 | 62.08 | 0 | 1 | 5 | 0 |
| List A | 29 | 9 | 0 | 36 | 11 | 4.00 | 67.92 | 0 | 0 | 9 | 0 |
| Twenty20 | 25 | 10 | 6 | 45 | 16 | 11.25 | 70.31 | 0 | 0 | 5 | 0 |

| Bowling | Mat | Balls | Runs | Wkts | BBI | BBM | Ave | Econ | SR | 5w | 10 |
|---------|-----|-------|------|------|------|------|-------|------|------|-----|-----|
| First-class | 15 | 1796 | 976 | 18 | 3/42 | 4/82 | 54.22 | 3.26 | 99.7 | 0 | 0 |
| List A | 29 | 1026 | 1038 | 36 | 5/18 | 5/18 | 28.83 | 6.07 | 28.5 | 1 | 0 |
| Twenty20 | 25 | 499 | 596 | 35 | 4/15 | 4/15 | 17.02 | 7.16 | 14.2 | 0 | 0 |

# ALEX LILLEY

## RHB LM

FULL NAME: Alexander Edward Lilley
BORN: April 17, 1992, Halifax, Yorkshire
SQUAD NO: 37
HEIGHT: 5ft 10in
NICKNAME: Lils, Scampi, Frog
EDUCATION: St Aidan's Church of England High School
TEAMS: Yorkshire, Yorkshire 2nd XI, Yorkshire Academy, Yorkshire Under-13s, Yorkshire Under-14s, Yorkshire Under-15s, Yorkshire Under-17s
CAREER: First-class: 2011

**YORKSHIRE**

BEST BATTING: 0 Yorkshire vs DMCCU, Durham University, 2011

WHY CRICKET? My local village team were short of players so I turned up and loved it!
CAREER HIGHLIGHTS? Being selected for the Yorkshire first team
CRICKETING HEROES? Wasim Akram
NON-CRICKETING HEROES? Lance Armstrong
BEST PLAYER IN COUNTY CRICKET? Marcus Trescothick
TIPS FOR THE TOP? Azeem Rafiq, Zafar Ansari
IF YOU WEREN'T A CRICKETER? I'd be a landscape gardener
WHEN RAIN STOPS PLAY? Listen to music
FAVOURITE TV? Modern Family
FAVOURITE FILM? Gladiator
DREAM HOLIDAY? Barbados
FANTASY SLIP CORDON? Keeper: Karl Pilkington, 1st: Russell Brand, 2nd: Myself, 3rd: Keith Lemon, Gully: Peter Kay. Would be a very, very funny afternoon in the field!
TWITTER FEED: @AlexLilley1

| Batting | Mat | Inns | NO | Runs | HS | Ave | SR | 100 | 50 | Ct | St |
|---|---|---|---|---|---|---|---|---|---|---|---|
| First-class | 1 | 1 | 0 | 0 | 0 | 0.00 | 0.00 | 0 | 0 | 0 | 0 |

| Bowling | Mat | Balls | Runs | Wkts | BBI | BBM | Ave | Econ | SR | 5w | 10 |
|---|---|---|---|---|---|---|---|---|---|---|---|
| First-class | 1 | 78 | 34 | 0 | - | - | - | 2.61 | - | 0 | 0 |

# MATT LINEKER

## LHB SLA

**DERBYSHIRE**

FULL NAME: Matthew Steven Lineker
BORN: January 22, 1985, Derby
SQUAD NO: 15
HEIGHT: 6ft 2in
NICKNAME: Lurch, Lurks
EDUCATION: Swanwick Hall School
TEAMS: Derbyshire, Derbyshire 2nd XI,
Nottinghamshire 2nd XI
CAREER: First-class: 2011; List A: 2011

---

BEST BATTING: 71 Derbyshire vs Kent, Derby, 2011

---

CAREER HIGHLIGHTS? First-class debut, 73 vs Kent in my second game
SUPERSTITIONS? Left pad first
CRICKETING HEROES? Graham Thorpe, Brian Lara
NON-CRICKETING HEROES? Michael Jordan, Muhammad Ali
BEST PLAYER IN COUNTY CRICKET? Marcus Trescothick
TIPS FOR THE TOP? Dan Redfern, Ross Whiteley
IF YOU WEREN'T A CRICKETER? An electrician
WHEN RAIN STOPS PLAY? Annoying fellow teammates
FAVOURITE TV? How Stuff Works
FAVOURITE FILM? Step Brothers
FAVOURITE BOOK? Lord Of The Rings
DREAM HOLIDAY? Australia
ACCOMPLISHMENTS? Owning my own company, Leading Edge Cricket
TWITTER FEED: @mattlineker

| Batting | Mat | Inns | NO | Runs | HS | Ave | SR | 100 | 50 | Ct | St | |
|---|---|---|---|---|---|---|---|---|---|---|---|---|
| First-class | 3 | 6 | 0 | 107 | 71 | 17.83 | 44.58 | 0 | 1 | 1 | 0 | |
| List A | 1 | 1 | 0 | 13 | 13 | 13.00 | 56.52 | 0 | 0 | 0 | 0 | |
| Bowling | Mat | Balls | Runs | Wkts | BBI | BBM | Ave | Econ | SR | 5w | 10 | |
| First-class | 3 | - | - | - | - | - | - | - | - | - | - | - |
| List A | 1 | - | - | - | - | - | - | - | - | - | - | - |

**FULL NAME:** Timothy Edward Linley
**BORN:** March 23, 1982, Horsforth, Leeds
**SQUAD NO:** 12
**HEIGHT:** 6ft 2in
**NICKNAME:** Sheephead, Bambi, Viscount, Linners
**EDUCATION:** St Mary's RC Comprehensive; Notre Dame Sixth Form College; Oxford Brookes University
**TEAMS:** Middlesex 2nd XI, Nottinghamshire 2nd XI, Oxford MCCU, Surrey, Sussex
**CAREER:** First-class: 2003; List A: 2009; T20: 2009

**BEST BATTING:** 42 OUCCE vs Derbyshire, The Parks, 2005
**BEST BOWLING:** 6-57 Surrey vs Leicestershire, Leicester, 2011

**FAMILY TIES?** Dad played cricket for his work side and my childhood was dominated by playing cricket with my five brothers. Four out of five still play: Matthew representing Brightlingsea CC, Thomas, Wimbledon CC and Simon and Nick at Garforth CC. Dom has far better things to do with his time
**CAREER HIGHLIGHTS?** Gaining promotion to Division One last year and getting a standing ovation from the members in the Long Room at The Oval for my contribution to the season
**CRICKETING HEROES?** Curtly Ambrose, Shaun Pollock, Glenn McGrath, Mark Ramprakash
**BEST PLAYER IN COUNTY CRICKET?** Marcus Trescothick's record last year spoke for itself
**TIPS FOR THE TOP?** Jason Roy, Tom Maynard, Stuart Meaker, James Taylor
**IF YOU WEREN'T A CRICKETER?** I'd be dreaming about playing cricket professionally
**WHEN RAIN STOPS PLAY?** Playing the card game 500 with Matt Spriegel, Gary Wilson, and Chris Schofield. Plus Arun Harinath if we are really desperate!
**FAVOURITE BOOK?** The Alchemist by Paulo Coelho changed my life
**ACCOMPLISHMENTS?** I somehow managed to get a 2:1 at uni whilst having a part-time job and trying to train like a professional cricketer
**AMAZE ME!** I'm an eighth Indian, I'm dyspraxic (look it up) and I spent two years before I became a cricketer working for J.W. Hinchliffe Ltd, decommissioning petrol tanks

| Batting | Mat | Inns | NO | Runs | HS | Ave | SR | 100 | 50 | Ct | St |
|---|---|---|---|---|---|---|---|---|---|---|---|
| First-class | 34 | 48 | 10 | 350 | 42 | 9.21 | 35.03 | 0 | 0 | 10 | 0 |
| List A | 18 | 6 | 5 | 37 | 20* | 37.00 | 78.72 | 0 | 0 | 2 | 0 |
| Twenty20 | 7 | 2 | 0 | 9 | 8 | 4.50 | 112.50 | 0 | 0 | 2 | 0 |

| Bowling | Mat | Balls | Runs | Wkts | BBI | BBM | Ave | Econ | SR | 5w | 10 |
|---|---|---|---|---|---|---|---|---|---|---|---|
| First-class | 34 | 5571 | 2800 | 111 | 6/57 | | 25.22 | 3.01 | 50.1 | 3 | 1 |
| List A | 18 | 592 | 554 | 12 | 3/50 | 3/50 | 46.16 | 5.61 | 49.3 | 0 | 0 |
| Twenty20 | 7 | 122 | 148 | 6 | 2/28 | 2/28 | 24.66 | 7.27 | 20.3 | 0 | 0 |

MIDDLESEX

**FULL NAME:** Adam Brian London
**BORN:** October 12, 1988, Surrey
**SQUAD NO:** 19
**HEIGHT:** 5ft 8in
**NICKNAME:** Londers, Lon, Simple
**EDUCATION:** Ashford CofE Primary School;
Bishop Wand CofE and Sixth Form College
**TEAMS:** Middlesex, Middlesex 2nd XI
**CAREER:** First-class: 2009; List A: 2009

---

**BEST BATTING:** 77 Middlesex vs Northamptonshire, Northampton, 2010
**BEST BOWLING:** 1-15 Middlesex vs OMCCU, The Parks, 2010

---

**CAREER HIGHLIGHTS?** Making my debut for Middlesex at Lord's and fielding for England
**SUPERSTITIONS?** Right pad first and have to be wearing the right boxer shorts
**CRICKETING HEROES?** Wouldn't say hero but loved watching Graham Thorpe bat
**NON-CRICKETING HEROES?** Alex Ferguson. The commitment, loyalty and the success he has
had with one club is a great achievement
**TIP FOR THE TOP?** Sam Robson
**IF YOU WEREN'T A CRICKETER?** Probably coaching
**FAVOURITE TV?** TOWIE
**FAVOURITE FILM?** Training Day
**ACCOMPLISHMENTS?** Got scouted for Chelsea FC when I was 12
**GUILTY PLEASURES?** FIFA 12
**TWITTER FEED:** @londers19
**NOTES:** Hit a half-century on first-class debut against Gloucestershire at Lord's in 2009

| Batting | Mat | Inns | NO | Runs | HS | Ave | SR | 100 | 50 | Ct | St |
|---------|-----|------|-----|------|-----|-------|-------|-----|-----|-----|-----|
| First-class | 8 | 15 | 2 | 327 | 77 | 25.15 | 38.51 | 0 | 3 | 4 | 0 |
| List A | 2 | - | - | - | - | - | - | - | - | 0 | 0 |

| Bowling | Mat | Balls | Runs | Wkts | BBI | BBM | Ave | Econ | SR | 5w | 10 |
|---------|-----|-------|------|------|------|------|-------|------|------|-----|-----|
| First-class | 8 | 96 | 54 | 1 | 1/15 | 1/15 | 54.00 | 3.37 | 96.0 | 0 | 0 |
| List A | 2 | 6 | 5 | 0 | - | - | - | 5.00 | - | 0 | 0 |

FULL NAME: David Scott Lucas
BORN: August 19, 1978, Nottingham
SQUAD NO: 6
HEIGHT: 6ft 3in
NICKNAME: Muke, Lukey, Luca
EDUCATION: Djanogly City Techology College, Nottingham
TEAMS: Lincolnshire, Northamptonshire, Nottinghamshire, Yorkshire
CAREER: First-class: 1999; List A: 1999; T20: 2007

**WORCESTERSHIRE**

BEST BATTING: 60 Northamptonshire vs Leicestershire, Leicester, 2011
BEST BOWLING: 7-24 Northamptonshire vs Gloucestershire, Cheltenham, 2009
COUNTY CAP: 2009 (Northamptonshire)

WHY CRICKET? Not good enough at football
CRICKETING HEROES? Craig White, Chaminda Vaas
NON-CRICKETING HEROES? Tony Adams, Keith Lemon
BEST PLAYER IN COUNTY CRICKET? Marcus Trescothick
TIP FOR THE TOP? David Willey
IF YOU WEREN'T A CRICKETER? Running my cleaning business and coaching
WHEN RAIN STOPS PLAY? Annoying others, stuff that needs to be done, impersonating James Middlebrook
FAVOURITE TV? Celebrity Juice
FAVOURITE FILM? The Hangover
FAVOURITE BOOK? Andre Agassi's autobiography
DREAM HOLIDAY? Turks and Caicos, St Lucia, Cape Town
ACCOMPLISHMENTS? Setting up a business
SURPRISING SKILL? I can talk exactly like James Middlebrook
GUILTY PLEASURES? PS3, chocolate, whisky

| Batting | Mat | Inns | NO | Runs | HS | Ave | SR | 100 | 50 | Ct | St |
|---|---|---|---|---|---|---|---|---|---|---|---|
| First-class | 85 | 110 | 27 | 1590 | 60 | 19.15 | | 0 | 2 | 15 | 0 |
| List A | 73 | 31 | 10 | 212 | 32* | 10.09 | | 0 | 0 | 17 | 0 |
| Twenty20 | 22 | 7 | 4 | 16 | 5* | 5.33 | 64.00 | 0 | 0 | 3 | 0 |

| Bowling | Mat | Balls | Runs | Wkts | BBI | BBM | Ave | Econ | SR | 5w | 10 |
|---|---|---|---|---|---|---|---|---|---|---|---|
| First-class | 85 | 12815 | 7529 | 239 | 7/24 | | 31.50 | 3.52 | 53.6 | 9 | 1 |
| List A | 73 | 2769 | 2656 | 87 | 5/48 | 5/48 | 30.52 | 5.75 | 31.8 | 1 | 0 |
| Twenty20 | 22 | 315 | 439 | 15 | 3/19 | 3/19 | 29.26 | 8.36 | 21.0 | 0 | 0 |

**NOTTINGHAMSHIRE**

FULL NAME: Michael John Lumb
BORN: February 12, 1980, Johannesburg, South Africa
SQUAD NO: 45
HEIGHT: 6ft
NICKNAME: Joe, Lumby, China, Slumdog
EDUCATION: St Stithians College
TEAMS: Deccan Chargers, England Lions, Hampshire, Queensland, Rajasthan Royals, Sydney Sixers, Yorkshire, Nottinghamshire
CAREER: T20I: 2010; First-class: 2000; List A: 2001; T20: 2003

BEST BATTING: 219 Hampshire vs Nottinghamshire, Nottingham, 2009
BEST BOWLING: 2-10 Yorkshire vs Kent, Canterbury, 2001
COUNTY CAPS: 2003 (Yorkshire); 2008 (Hampshire)

FAMILY TIES? Father Richard played for Yorkshire and uncle Tich played for Natal and South Africa
CAREER HIGHLIGHTS? It would have to be playing for England and winning the World T20, beating the Aussies in the final! Winning the C&G Trophy with Hampshire at Lord's
SUPERSTITIONS? Too many to mention, they call me Rain Man!
CRICKETING HEROES? Graham Thorpe, Darren Lehmann, Stephen Fleming, Craig White, Shane Warne, Jacques Kallis
BEST PLAYER IN COUNTY CRICKET? Marcus Trescothick – no brainer!
TIPS FOR THE TOP? Danny Briggs, James Vince
IF YOU WEREN'T A CRICKETER? Game ranger
WHEN RAIN STOPS PLAY? Probably read the papers with a coffee or play some form of stupid game in the changing room
SURPRISING SKILL? Surfing, badly!
GUILTY PLEASURES? Chocolate and biltong

| Batting | Mat | Inns | NO | Runs | HS | Ave | SR | 100 | 50 | Ct | St |
|---|---|---|---|---|---|---|---|---|---|---|---|
| T20Is | 8 | 8 | 0 | 139 | 33 | 17.37 | 134.95 | 0 | 0 | 3 | 0 |
| First-class | 135 | 226 | 15 | 7283 | 219 | 34.51 | | 12 | 45 | 92 | 0 |
| List A | 164 | 158 | 11 | 4752 | 110 | 32.32 | 84.18 | 3 | 37 | 56 | 0 |
| Twenty20 | 110 | 110 | 6 | 2251 | 124* | 21.64 | 141.39 | 1 | 12 | 36 | 0 |

| Bowling | Mat | Balls | Runs | Wkts | BBI | BBM | Ave | Econ | SR | 5w | 10 |
|---|---|---|---|---|---|---|---|---|---|---|---|
| T20Is | 8 | - | - | - | - | - | - | - | - | - | - |
| First-class | 135 | 318 | 242 | 6 | 2/10 | | 40.33 | 4.56 | 53.0 | 0 | 0 |
| List A | 164 | 12 | 28 | 0 | - | - | - | 14.00 | - | 0 | 0 |
| Twenty20 | 110 | 36 | 65 | 3 | 3/32 | 3/32 | 21.66 | 10.83 | 12.0 | 0 | 0 |

# ADAM LYTH

## LHB OB R1

FULL NAME: Adam Lyth
BORN: September 25, 1987, Whitby, Yorkshire
SQUAD NO: 9
HEIGHT: 5ft 9in
NICKNAME: Peanut, Lythy
EDUCATION: Caedmon School; Whitby Community College
TEAMS: England Under-19s, Yorkshire, Yorkshire 2nd XI
CAREER: First-class: 2007; List A: 2006; T20: 2008

BEST BATTING: 142 Yorkshire vs Somerset, Taunton, 2010
BEST BOWLING: 1-12 Yorkshire vs LUCCE, Leeds, 2007
COUNTY CAP: 2010

FAMILY TIES? My dad and brother played for Scarborough in the Yorkshire League. My brother, Ashley, played for Yorkshire 2nd XI in 2010
WHY CRICKET? I played because my dad and brother did
CAREER HIGHLIGHTS? PCA Young Player of the Year in 2010, scoring a century against Lancashire in 2010, being the first person to score 1,000 runs in 2010
CRICKETING HEROES? Graham Thorpe, Brian Lara
NON-CRICKETING HEROES? David Beckham
BEST PLAYER IN COUNTY CRICKET? Marcus Trescothick
IF YOU WEREN'T A CRICKETER? No idea!
WHEN RAIN STOPS PLAY? Chill out time
FAVOURITE TV? Arsenal TV
FAVOURITE FILM? Man On Fire
FAVOURITE BOOK? Bahamas
AMAZE ME! I played football for Manchester City, Sunderland and Scarborough
FANTASY SLIP CORDON? Keeper: Kim Kardashian, 1st: Me, 2nd: Mila Kunis, 3rd: John Bishop, Gully: David Beckham

| Batting | Mat | Inns | NO | Runs | HS | Ave | SR | 100 | 50 | Ct | St |
|---|---|---|---|---|---|---|---|---|---|---|---|
| First-class | 52 | 88 | 1 | 3176 | 142 | 36.50 | | 4 | 24 | 44 | 0 |
| List A | 53 | 47 | 3 | 1197 | 109* | 27.20 | 85.13 | 1 | 5 | 18 | 0 |
| Twenty20 | 34 | 30 | 1 | 550 | 59 | 18.96 | 126.43 | 0 | 1 | 12 | 0 |

| Bowling | Mat | Balls | Runs | Wkts | BBI | BBM | Ave | Econ | SR | 5w | 10 |
|---|---|---|---|---|---|---|---|---|---|---|---|
| First-class | 52 | 325 | 181 | 3 | 1/12 | 1/12 | 60.33 | 3.34 | 108.3 | 0 | 0 |
| List A | 53 | 18 | 14 | 0 | - | - | - | 4.66 | - | 0 | 0 |
| Twenty20 | 34 | - | - | - | - | - | - | - | - | - | - |

# MATT MACHAN LHB OB

SUSSEX

FULL NAME: Matthew William Machan
BORN: February 15, 1991, Brighton, Sussex
SQUAD NO: 15
HEIGHT: 5ft 9in
NICKNAME: Mach
EDUCATION: Brighton College
TEAMS: Sussex, Sussex 2nd XI
CAREER: First-class: 2010; List A: 2010; T20: 2012

BEST BATTING: 99 Sussex vs OMCCU, The Parks, 2011

CAREER HIGHLIGHTS? Making 1st XI debuts for Sussex
SUPERSTITIONS? Always put right foot on pitch first
CRICKETING HEROES? Andrew Hodd, Will Beer, David Warner
NON-CRICKETING HEROES? Gandhi
BEST PLAYER IN COUNTY CRICKET? Marcus Trescothick
TIPS FOR THE TOP? Ben Brown, Will Beer
WHEN RAIN STOPS PLAY? Monopoly on iPad or dressing room golf
FAVOURITE TV? The Only Way Is Essex
FAVOURITE FILM? The Shawshank Redemption
FAVOURITE BOOK? Of Mice And Men
DREAM HOLIDAY? Cape Town
ACCOMPLISHMENTS? Yellow belt in judo
SURPRISING SKILL? Qualified personal trainer and nutritionist
GUILTY PLEASURES? Skittles, Lola Lo (bar in Brighton)
AMAZE ME! Used to play county rugby. Part-time garage DJ
FANTASY SLIP CORDON? Keeper: John Bishop, 1st: Jessica Wright, 2nd: Joey Essex, 3rd: Mike 'The Situation', Gully: Tinie Tempah
TWITTER FEED: @Mattmachan

| Batting | Mat | Inns | NO | Runs | HS | Ave | SR | 100 | 50 | Ct | St |
|---|---|---|---|---|---|---|---|---|---|---|---|
| First-class | 3 | 4 | 0 | 181 | 99 | 45.25 | 73.27 | 0 | 2 | 0 | 0 |
| List A | 2 | 2 | 0 | 66 | 56 | 33.00 | 77.64 | 0 | 1 | 1 | 0 |
| Twenty20 | 4 | 4 | 0 | 14 | 6 | 3.50 | 41.17 | 0 | 0 | 0 | 0 |

| Bowling | Mat | Balls | Runs | Wkts | BBI | BBM | Ave | Econ | SR | 5w | 10 |
|---|---|---|---|---|---|---|---|---|---|---|---|
| First-class | 3 | 6 | 4 | 0 | - | - | - | 4.00 | - | 0 | 0 |
| List A | 2 | - | - | - | - | - | - | - | - | - | - |
| Twenty20 | 4 | - | - | - | - | - | - | - | - | - | - |

# DARREN MADDY

RHB RM R4

FULL NAME: Darren Lee Maddy
BORN: May 23, 1974, Leicester
SQUAD NO: 43
HEIGHT: 5ft 8in
NICKNAME: Roaster, Dazza, Madds, Mr C
EDUCATION: Roundhill, Thurmaston;
Wreake Valley, Syston
TEAMS: England, Leicestershire,
Warwickshire
CAREER: Test: 1999; ODI: 1998; T20I: 2007;
First-class: 1994; List A: 1993; T20: 2003

BEST BATTING: 229* Leicestershire vs LUCCE, Leicester, 2003
BEST BOWLING: 5-37 Leicestershire vs Hampshire, Southampton, 2002
COUNTY CAPS: 1996 (Leicestershire); 2007 (Warwickshire); BENEFIT YEAR: 2006
(Leicestershire)

CAREER HIGHLIGHTS? Playing cricket for England in Tests, ODIs and T20s, winning
two Championships with Leicestershire in 1996 and 1998, winning two T20 Cups with
Leicestershire in 2004 and 2006, captaining Warwickshire in 2007 and 2008, winning the
CB40 with Warwickshire in 2010
CRICKETING HEROES? Ian Botham, David Gower
BEST PLAYER IN COUNTY CRICKET? Marcus Trescothick and Ian Bell
TIP FOR THE TOP? Chris Woakes
AMAZE ME! I've played several gigs with my band Too Tone Deaf, I'm currently training to
become a strength and conditioning coach and I'm allergic to seafood
TWITTER FEED: @DarrenMaddy

| Batting | Mat | Inns | NO | Runs | HS | Ave | SR | 100 | 50 | Ct | St |
|---|---|---|---|---|---|---|---|---|---|---|---|
| Tests | 3 | 4 | 0 | 46 | 24 | 11.50 | 24.21 | 0 | 0 | 4 | 0 |
| ODIs | 8 | 6 | 0 | 113 | 53 | 18.83 | 54.85 | 0 | 1 | 1 | 0 |
| T20Is | 4 | 4 | 0 | 113 | 50 | 28.25 | 141.25 | 0 | 1 | 1 | 0 |
| First-class | 266 | 433 | 29 | 13161 | 229* | 32.57 | | 26 | 62 | 277 | 0 |
| List A | 343 | 316 | 36 | 8681 | 167* | 31.00 | | 11 | 51 | 134 | 0 |
| Twenty20 | 79 | 78 | 8 | 2113 | 111 | 30.18 | 132.97 | 1 | 13 | 38 | 0 |

| Bowling | Mat | Balls | Runs | Wkts | BBI | BBM | Ave | Econ | SR | 5w | 10 |
|---|---|---|---|---|---|---|---|---|---|---|---|
| Tests | 3 | 84 | 40 | 0 | - | - | - | 2.85 | - | 0 | 0 |
| ODIs | 8 | - | - | - | - | - | - | - | - | - | - |
| T20Is | 4 | 18 | 26 | 3 | 2/6 | 2/6 | 8.66 | 8.66 | 6.0 | 0 | 0 |
| First-class | 266 | 14496 | 7544 | 238 | 5/37 | | 31.69 | 3.12 | 60.9 | 5 | 0 |
| List A | 343 | 7088 | 6106 | 209 | 4/16 | 4/16 | 29.21 | 5.16 | 33.9 | 0 | 0 |
| Twenty20 | 79 | 791 | 1049 | 44 | 3/10 | 3/10 | 23.84 | 7.95 | 17.9 | 0 | 0 |

# WAYNE MADSEN

## RHB OB

FULL NAME: Wayne Lee Madsen
BORN: January 2, 1984, Durban, South Africa
SQUAD NO: 77
HEIGHT: 6ft
NICKNAME: Madders, Mads
EDUCATION: Highbury Prep School; Kearsney College; University of South Africa (UNISA)
TEAMS: Derbyshire, Derbyshire 2nd XI, KwaZulu-Natal
CAREER: First-class: 2004; List A: 2004; T20: 2010

BEST BATTING: 179 Derbyshire vs Northamptonshire, Northampton, 2010
BEST BOWLING: 3-45 KwaZulu-Natal vs Eastern Province, Port Elizabeth, 2008

FAMILY TIES? My uncles [Trevor Madsen and Henry Fotheringham] played cricket for South Africa. Another uncle [Mike Madsen] and my cousin [Greg Fotheringham] both played first-class cricket in South Africa. My father Paddy played Natal Schools cricket
CAREER HIGHLIGHTS? Scoring 170* on debut for Derbyshire against Gloucestershire at Cheltenham in 2009
CRICKETING HEROES? Jonty Rhodes, Hansie Cronje, Shaun Pollock, Dale Benkenstein
NON-CRICKETING HEROES? Nelson Mandela, my grandfather Lionel Madsen, Lance Armstrong
TIPS FOR THE TOP? James Taylor, Ross Whiteley, Tom Knight
IF YOU WEREN'T A CRICKETER? I'd be playing hockey or coaching sport. Might have had a stint as a game ranger
FAVOURITE TV? The X Factor
ACCOMPLISHMENTS? Playing 39 hockey Test matches for South Africa. Playing in the 2006 Commonwealth Games and the 2006 Hockey World Cup
AMAZE ME! I'm one of 10 people in my family to represent South Africa at hockey, my right leg is shorter than my left by 1.5cm, and I've shot a -4 round of 68 on a Championship golf course (when I was a student and playing regular golf!)

| Batting | Mat | Inns | NO | Runs | HS | Ave | SR | 100 | 50 | Ct | St |
|---|---|---|---|---|---|---|---|---|---|---|---|
| First-class | 63 | 113 | 7 | 3784 | 179 | 35.69 | 47.59 | 10 | 18 | 61 | 0 |
| List A | 36 | 35 | 6 | 1105 | 75 | 38.10 | 84.86 | 0 | 9 | 29 | 0 |
| Twenty20 | 19 | 18 | 3 | 375 | 61* | 25.00 | 119.80 | 0 | 3 | 4 | 0 |

| Bowling | Mat | Balls | Runs | Wkts | BBI | BBM | Ave | Econ | SR | 5w | 10 |
|---|---|---|---|---|---|---|---|---|---|---|---|
| First-class | 63 | 686 | 372 | 7 | 3/45 | | 53.14 | 3.25 | 98.0 | 0 | 0 |
| List A | 36 | 102 | 74 | 5 | 2/18 | 2/18 | 14.80 | 4.35 | 20.4 | 0 | 0 |
| Twenty20 | 19 | - | - | - | - | - | - | - | - | - | - |

## AZHAR MAHMOOD
### RHB RFM MVP12

**FULL NAME:** Azhar Mahmood Sagar
**BORN:** February 28, 1975, Rawalpindi, Punjab, Pakistan
**SQUAD NO:** 11
**HEIGHT:** 6ft
**NICKNAME:** Aju
**EDUCATION:** FG No.1 High School, Islamabad
**TEAMS:** Pakistan, Auckland, Dhaka Gladiators, Islamabad Cricket Association, Kent, Lahore Badshahs, Rawalpindi, Surrey, United Bank Limited
**CAREER:** Test: 1997; ODI: 1996; First-class: 1994; List A: 1994; T20: 2003

**BEST BATTING:** 204* Surrey vs Middlesex, The Oval, 2005
**BEST BOWLING:** 8-61 Surrey vs Lancashire, The Oval, 2002
**COUNTY CAPS:** 2004 (Surrey); 2008 (Kent)

**CAREER HIGHLIGHTS?** First Test match against South Africa in 1997 in Pakistan. I scored 128* in first innings, 50* in the second and took two wickets to be named as Man of the Match
**CRICKET MOMENTS TO FORGET?** World Cup 1999 – the final against Australia
**OTHER SPORTS PLAYED?** Snooker, football, kite-flying
**OTHER SPORTS FOLLOWED?** Football (Manchester United)
**RELAXATIONS?** Listening to music, training, spending time with my family

| Batting | Mat | Inns | NO | Runs | HS | Ave | SR | 100 | 50 | Ct | St |
|---|---|---|---|---|---|---|---|---|---|---|---|
| Tests | 21 | 34 | 4 | 900 | 136 | 30.00 | 50.79 | 3 | 1 | 14 | 0 |
| ODIs | 143 | 110 | 26 | 1521 | 67 | 18.10 | 76.50 | 0 | 3 | 37 | 0 |
| First-class | 175 | 272 | 32 | 7654 | 204* | 31.89 | | 9 | 42 | 141 | 0 |
| List A | 301 | 242 | 47 | 4192 | 101* | 21.49 | | 2 | 17 | 89 | 0 |
| Twenty20 | 117 | 105 | 26 | 2357 | 106* | 29.83 | 143.19 | 2 | 10 | 23 | 0 |

| Bowling | Mat | Balls | Runs | Wkts | BBI | BBM | Ave | Econ | SR | 5w | 10 |
|---|---|---|---|---|---|---|---|---|---|---|---|
| Tests | 21 | 3015 | 1402 | 39 | 4/50 | 5/95 | 35.94 | 2.79 | 77.3 | 0 | 0 |
| ODIs | 143 | 6242 | 4813 | 123 | 6/18 | 6/18 | 39.13 | 4.62 | 50.7 | 3 | 0 |
| First-class | 175 | 29672 | 15266 | 609 | 8/61 | | 25.06 | 3.08 | 48.7 | 27 | 3 |
| List A | 301 | 13277 | 10356 | 328 | 6/18 | 6/18 | 31.57 | 4.67 | 40.4 | 5 | 0 |
| Twenty20 | 117 | 2369 | 2991 | 120 | 4/20 | 4/20 | 24.92 | 7.57 | 19.7 | 0 | 0 |

# SAJ MAHMOOD

## RHB RF MVP80

**FULL NAME:** Sajid Iqbal Mahmood
**BORN:** December 21, 1981, Bolton, Lancashire
**SQUAD NO:** 19
**HEIGHT:** 6ft 4in
**NICKNAME:** Saj, King
**EDUCATION:** Smithills School
**TEAMS:** England, England A, England Lions, Lancashire, Lancashire Cricket Board, Marylebone Cricket Club, Western Australia
**CAREER:** Test: 2006; ODI: 2004; T20I: 2006; First-class: 2002; List A: 2002; T20: 2003

**BEST BATTING:** 94 Lancashire vs Sussex, Manchester, 2004
**BEST BOWLING:** 6-30 Lancashire vs Durham, Chester-le-Street, 2009
**COUNTY CAP:** 2007

**CAREER HIGHLIGHTS?** Playing for England and winning the County Championship
**CRICKETING HEROES?** Wasim Akram, Imran Khan
**NON-CRICKETING HEROES?** Muhammad Ali
**BEST PLAYER IN COUNTY CRICKET?** Oliver Newby
**TIP FOR THE TOP?** Karl Brown
**IF YOU WEREN'T A CRICKETER?** I'd have my own astrology business
**WHEN RAIN STOPS PLAY?** Drink cups of tea, play one hand-one bounce
**FAVOURITE TV?** Wildlife documentaries
**ACCOMPLISHMENTS?** Doing level 11 on the bleep test
**SURPRISING SKILL?** I'm a qualified sailor, I play the banjo and I'm a very good listener
**TWITTER FEED:** @sajmahmood19

| Batting | Mat | Inns | NO | Runs | HS | Ave | SR | 100 | 50 | Ct | St |
|---|---|---|---|---|---|---|---|---|---|---|---|
| Tests | 8 | 11 | 1 | 81 | 34 | 8.10 | 50.31 | 0 | 0 | 0 | 0 |
| ODIs | 26 | 15 | 4 | 85 | 22* | 7.72 | 84.15 | 0 | 0 | 1 | 0 |
| T20Is | 4 | 2 | 2 | 1 | 1* | - | 50.00 | 0 | 0 | 1 | 0 |
| First-class | 107 | 139 | 18 | 1985 | 94 | 16.40 | 69.18 | 0 | 9 | 25 | 0 |
| List A | 142 | 75 | 21 | 477 | 29 | 8.83 | | 0 | 0 | 19 | 0 |
| Twenty20 | 68 | 30 | 7 | 180 | 34 | 7.82 | 147.54 | 0 | 0 | 18 | 0 |

| Bowling | Mat | Balls | Runs | Wkts | BBI | BBM | Ave | Econ | SR | 5w | 10 |
|---|---|---|---|---|---|---|---|---|---|---|---|
| Tests | 8 | 1130 | 762 | 20 | 4/22 | 6/130 | 38.10 | 4.04 | 56.5 | 0 | 0 |
| ODIs | 26 | 1197 | 1169 | 30 | 4/50 | 4/50 | 38.96 | 5.85 | 39.9 | 0 | 0 |
| T20Is | 4 | 84 | 155 | 3 | 1/31 | 1/31 | 51.66 | 11.07 | 28.0 | 0 | 0 |
| First-class | 107 | 15855 | 9847 | 303 | 6/30 | | 32.49 | 3.72 | 52.3 | 9 | 2 |
| List A | 142 | 6239 | 5425 | 199 | 5/16 | 5/16 | 27.26 | 5.21 | 31.3 | 1 | 0 |
| Twenty20 | 68 | 1435 | 1878 | 76 | 4/21 | 4/21 | 24.71 | 7.85 | 18.8 | 0 | 0 |

# DAWID MALAN

LHB LB R1

FULL NAME: Dawid Johannes Malan
BORN: September 3, 1987, Roehampton
SQUAD NO: 29
HEIGHT: 6ft
NICKNAME: AC
EDUCATION: Paarl Boys' High School; UNISA
TEAMS: Boland, Marylebone Cricket Club, Middlesex
CAREER: First-class: 2006; List A: 2006; T20: 2006

BEST BATTING: 143 Middlesex vs Derbyshire, Lord's, 2011
BEST BOWLING: 4-20 MCC vs Durham, Abu Dhabi, 2010
COUNTY CAP: 2010

SUPERSTITIONS? The way I pack my cricket bag
CRICKETERS PARTICULARLY ADMIRED? Gary Kirsten
OTHER SPORTS FOLLOWED? Rugby (Blue Bulls)
RELAXATIONS? Fishing
FAVOURITE BAND? The Killers
CRICKET MOMENTS TO FORGET? Getting a first-baller in my school's annual interschool match in my final year at school
FAMILY TIES? Father played for the University of Stellenbosch and for Western Province B. Brother [Charl] was an MCC Young Cricketer
NOTES: Of South African parentage, Malan made his first-class debut for Boland before signing for Middlesex in 2006. Finished as leading runscorer in 2nd XI cricket in 2007 and hit 132* on County Championship debut in 2008 against Northamptonshire before scoring 103 off 51 balls against Lancashire in the T20 Cup quarter-final a week later at The Oval. Has featured in England Performance Programme squads. Signed a contract in November 2010 that ties him to the club until at least the end of the 2014 season

| Batting | Mat | Inns | NO | Runs | HS | Ave | SR | 100 | 50 | Ct | St |
|---|---|---|---|---|---|---|---|---|---|---|---|
| First-class | 64 | 112 | 10 | 3717 | 143 | 36.44 | 51.79 | 7 | 21 | 72 | 0 |
| List A | 54 | 54 | 4 | 1252 | 107 | 25.04 | 76.52 | 1 | 5 | 17 | 0 |
| Twenty20 | 49 | 46 | 14 | 1029 | 103 | 32.15 | 118.00 | 1 | 2 | 10 | 0 |

| Bowling | Mat | Balls | Runs | Wkts | BBI | BBM | Ave | Econ | SR | 5w | 10 |
|---|---|---|---|---|---|---|---|---|---|---|---|
| First-class | 64 | 2055 | 1364 | 31 | 4/20 | 4/80 | 44.00 | 3.98 | 66.2 | 0 | 0 |
| List A | 54 | 503 | 505 | 14 | 2/4 | 2/4 | 36.07 | 6.02 | 35.9 | 0 | 0 |
| Twenty20 | 49 | 240 | 276 | 12 | 2/10 | 2/10 | 23.00 | 6.90 | 20.0 | 0 | 0 |

# NADEEM MALIK

**RHB RMF**

FULL NAME: Muhammad Nadeem Malik
BORN: October 6, 1982, Nottingham
SQUAD NO: 21
HEIGHT: 6ft 5in
NICKNAME: Nads, Nigel, Nodda
EDUCATION: Wilford Meadows Comprehensive; Bilborough College
TEAMS: Leicestershire, Leicestershire 2nd XI, Nottinghamshire, Nottinghamshire Cricket Board, Worcestershire
CAREER: First-class: 2001; List A: 2000; T20: 2004

BEST BATTING: 41 Leicestershire vs Essex, Leicester, 2008
BEST BOWLING: 6-46 Leicestershire vs Essex, Chelmsford, 2008
COUNTY CAP: 2004 (Worcestershire)

CAREER HIGHLIGHTS? Worcestershire Pro40 Division One winners, Leicestershire T20 winners 2011
CRICKETING HEROES? Glenn McGrath, Wasim Akram, Curtly Ambrose
NON-CRICKETING HEROES? Muhammad Ali, Eric Cantona
BEST PLAYER IN COUNTY CRICKET? Mark Ramprakash, Marcus Treschothick
TIPS FOR THE TOP? Ben Collins, Shiv Thakor, James Sykes
WHEN RAIN STOPS PLAY? Sleeping and watching TV
FAVOURITE TV? Grand Designs, Homes Under The Hammer
FAVOURITE FILM? The Shawshank Redemption
FAVOURITE BOOK? The Quran
DREAM HOLIDAY? Maldives
ACCOMPLISHMENTS? My baby
FANTASY SLIP CORDON? Keeper: Gandhi, 1st: Myself, 2nd: Angelina Jolie, 3rd: Genghis Khan (to scare the oppo), Gully: Jamie Oliver (to leave the field early to make a good lunch)

| Batting | Mat | Inns | NO | Runs | HS | Ave | SR | 100 | 50 | Ct | St |
|---|---|---|---|---|---|---|---|---|---|---|---|
| First-class | 85 | 113 | 41 | 717 | 41 | 9.95 | 36.99 | 0 | 0 | 11 | 0 |
| List A | 80 | 32 | 20 | 107 | 11 | 8.91 | | 0 | 0 | 10 | 0 |
| Twenty20 | 38 | 9 | 4 | 12 | 3* | 2.40 | 50.00 | 0 | 0 | 3 | 0 |

| Bowling | Mat | Balls | Runs | Wkts | BBI | BBM | Ave | Econ | SR | 5w | 10 |
|---|---|---|---|---|---|---|---|---|---|---|---|
| First-class | 85 | 13618 | 8072 | 229 | 6/46 | | 35.24 | 3.55 | 59.4 | 7 | 0 |
| List A | 80 | 3160 | 2792 | 83 | 4/40 | 4/40 | 33.63 | 5.30 | 38.0 | 0 | 0 |
| Twenty20 | 38 | 751 | 1021 | 41 | 4/16 | 4/16 | 24.90 | 8.15 | 18.3 | 0 | 0 |

# JACK MANUEL

## LHB OB

**FULL NAME:** Jack Kenneth Manuel
**BORN:** February 13, 1991, Sutton Coldfield, Warwickshire
**SQUAD NO:** 26
**HEIGHT:** 6ft 1in
**NICKNAME:** Manwell, JK, Slug, Jackieman
**EDUCATION:** Wilnecote High School
**TEAMS:** England Under-19s, Worcestershire, Worcestershire 2nd XI
**CAREER:** First-class: 2011; List A: 2010; T20: 2010

**BEST BATTING:** 5 Worcestershire vs Somerset, Worcester, 2011

**FAMILY TIES?** My grandad and father both played cricket with the latter being my coach while I grew up

**CAREER HIGHLIGHTS?** One moment that will stay with me will be scoring 203* in a T20 when I was 13 or 14. But also obviously making my debut for Worcestershire in all forms of the game and playing for England U19 for three years

**CRICKETING HEROES?** Growing up Matthew Hayden was always one of my heroes in the way he attacked the bowlers and scored quickly. Also Brian Lara for the same reason and for his Caribbean flair!

**BEST PLAYER IN COUNTY CRICKET?** I would say Marcus Trescothick. Making my debut against Somerset and watching him score a double hundred with the ease he did was a real eye opener!

**TIPS FOR THE TOP?** A couple of the lads that are already making noise within the county scene who I played with during my time with England U19 are Ben Stokes, Joe Root and Jos Buttler. But also I would say Aneesh Kapil has a very bright future ahead of him

**FAVOURITE TV?** The Inbetweeners, without a doubt!

**DREAM HOLIDAY?** Having already been to Barbados, I would have to say there!

**GUILTY PLEASURES?** Internet shopping! If I'm not playing cricket I will more often than not be surfing the net on my laptop

| Batting | Mat | Inns | NO | Runs | HS | Ave | SR | 100 | 50 | Ct | St |
|---|---|---|---|---|---|---|---|---|---|---|---|
| First-class | 1 | 2 | 0 | 5 | 5 | 2.50 | 45.45 | 0 | 0 | 0 | 0 |
| List A | 7 | 7 | 0 | 142 | 48 | 20.28 | 99.30 | 0 | 0 | 3 | 0 |
| Twenty20 | 13 | 11 | 1 | 111 | 31 | 11.10 | 105.71 | 0 | 0 | 3 | 0 |

| Bowling | Mat | Balls | Runs | Wkts | BBI | BBM | Ave | Econ | SR | 5w | 10 |
|---|---|---|---|---|---|---|---|---|---|---|---|
| First-class | 1 | - | - | - | - | - | - | - | - | - | - |
| List A | 7 | - | - | - | - | - | - | - | - | - | - |
| Twenty20 | 13 | - | - | - | - | - | - | - | - | - | - |

# HAMISH MARSHALL

### RHB RM R1

**FULL NAME:** Hamish John Hamilton Marshall
**BORN:** February 15, 1979, Warkworth, Auckland, New Zealand
**SQUAD NO:** 9
**NICKNAME:** Marshy
**EDUCATION:** Southwell School; Mahurangi College; King's College
**TEAMS:** New Zealand, Buckinghamshire, Gloucestershire, Northern Districts, Royal Bengal Tigers
**CAREER:** Test: 2000; ODI: 2003; T20I: 2005; First-class: 1999; List A: 1998; T20: 2005

**BEST BATTING:** 170 Northern Districts vs Canterbury, Rangiora, 2010
**BEST BOWLING:** 4-24 Gloucestershire vs Leicestershire, Leicester, 2009

**FAMILY TIES?** Twin brother James also played for New Zealand
**CAREER HIGHLIGHTS?** My first Test and maiden Test century
**CRICKETING HEROES?** Mark Waugh when I was growing up
**NON-CRICKETING HEROES?** Andre Agassi
**BEST PLAYER IN COUNTY CRICKET?** Marcus Trescothick
**TIPS FOR THE TOP?** Chris Woakes and Jonathan Bairstow
**FAVOURITE FILM?** The Shawshank Redemption
**DREAM HOLIDAY?** New York
**FANTASY SLIP CORDON?** Keeper: Ayrton Senna (I thought he was a legend after watching his documentary), 1st: Michael McIntyre (for pure comedy), 2nd: Me, 3rd: Rory McIlroy, Gully: Keith Lemon (more laughs from him)

| Batting | Mat | Inns | NO | Runs | HS | Ave | SR | 100 | 50 | Ct | St |
|---|---|---|---|---|---|---|---|---|---|---|---|
| Tests | 13 | 19 | 2 | 652 | 160 | 38.35 | 47.31 | 2 | 2 | 1 | 0 |
| ODIs | 66 | 62 | 9 | 1454 | 101* | 27.43 | 73.06 | 1 | 12 | 18 | 0 |
| T20Is | 3 | 3 | 0 | 12 | 8 | 4.00 | 85.71 | 0 | 0 | 1 | 0 |
| First-class | 175 | 297 | 19 | 9904 | 170 | 35.62 | | 19 | 51 | 97 | 0 |
| List A | 254 | 241 | 24 | 6228 | 122 | 28.70 | | 6 | 43 | 95 | 0 |
| Twenty20 | 74 | 72 | 6 | 1669 | 102 | 25.28 | 136.13 | 2 | 5 | 36 | 0 |

| Bowling | Mat | Balls | Runs | Wkts | BBI | BBM | Ave | Econ | SR | 5w | 10 |
|---|---|---|---|---|---|---|---|---|---|---|---|
| Tests | 13 | 6 | 4 | 0 | - | - | - | 4.00 | - | 0 | 0 |
| ODIs | 66 | - | - | - | - | - | - | - | - | - | - |
| T20Is | 3 | - | - | - | - | - | - | - | - | - | - |
| First-class | 175 | 3499 | 1768 | 37 | 4/24 | | 47.78 | 3.03 | 94.5 | 0 | 0 |
| List A | 254 | 284 | 295 | 4 | 2/21 | 2/21 | 73.75 | 6.23 | 71.0 | 0 | 0 |
| Twenty20 | 74 | 6 | 14 | 0 | - | - | - | 14.00 | - | 0 | 0 |

# DIMITRI MASCARENHAS          RHB RM W1 MVP57

FULL NAME: Adrian Dimitri Mascarenhas
BORN: October 30, 1977, Chiswick, Middlesex
SQUAD NO: 17
HEIGHT: 6ft 1in
NICKNAME: Dimi
EDUCATION: Trinity College, Perth
TEAMS: England, England Lions, Hampshire, Hampshire 2nd XI, Otago, Rajasthan Royals
CAREER: ODI: 2007; T20I: 2007; First-class: 1996; List A: 1996; T20: 2003

HAMPSHIRE

BEST BATTING: 131 Hampshire vs Kent, Canterbury, 2006
BEST BOWLING: 6-25 Hampshire vs Derbyshire, Southampton, 2004
COUNTY CAP: 1998; BENEFIT YEAR: 2007

FAMILY TIES? Father and uncle played in Sri Lanka, both brothers are retired club cricketers
WHY CRICKET? My older brother played and I copied him
CRICKETING HEROES? Viv Richards, Malcolm Marshall
NON-CRICKETING HEROES? Michael Jordan
BEST PLAYER IN COUNTY CRICKET? Marcus Trescothick, Glen Chapple
TIPS FOR THE TOP? James Vince, Liam Dawson, Alex Hales
FAVOURITE TV? The Simpsons
FAVOURITE FILM? Lock Stock And Two Smoking Barrels
FAVOURITE BOOK? Breaking Vegas
DREAM HOLIDAY? Las Vegas
AMAZE ME! I have a surprise piercing, I was a sprinter at school (100m,200m,400m) and I'm a couch potato
TWITTER FEED: @dimimascarenhas

| Batting | Mat | Inns | NO | Runs | HS | Ave | SR | 100 | 50 | Ct | St |
|---|---|---|---|---|---|---|---|---|---|---|---|
| ODIs | 20 | 13 | 2 | 245 | 52 | 22.27 | 95.33 | 0 | 1 | 4 | 0 |
| T20Is | 14 | 13 | 5 | 123 | 31 | 15.37 | 123.00 | 0 | 0 | 7 | 0 |
| First-class | 189 | 285 | 32 | 6375 | 131 | 25.19 | | 8 | 23 | 74 | 0 |
| List A | 251 | 210 | 43 | 4171 | 79 | 24.97 | | 0 | 27 | 63 | 0 |
| Twenty20 | 91 | 79 | 21 | 1169 | 57* | 20.15 | 128.32 | 0 | 3 | 22 | 0 |

| Bowling | Mat | Balls | Runs | Wkts | BBI | BBM | Ave | Econ | SR | 5w | 10 |
|---|---|---|---|---|---|---|---|---|---|---|---|
| ODIs | 20 | 822 | 634 | 13 | 3/23 | 3/23 | 48.76 | 4.62 | 63.2 | 0 | 0 |
| T20Is | 14 | 252 | 309 | 12 | 3/18 | 3/18 | 25.75 | 7.35 | 21.0 | 0 | 0 |
| First-class | 189 | 27557 | 12399 | 439 | 6/25 | | 28.24 | 2.69 | 62.7 | 17 | 0 |
| List A | 251 | 10707 | 7651 | 290 | 5/27 | 5/27 | 26.38 | 4.28 | 36.9 | 1 | 0 |
| Twenty20 | 91 | 1777 | 2078 | 105 | 5/14 | 5/14 | 19.79 | 7.01 | 16.9 | 1 | 0 |

# DAVID MASTERS RHB RMF W2 MVP11

FULL NAME: David Daniel Masters
BORN: April 22, 1978, Chatham, Kent
SQUAD NO: 9
HEIGHT: 6ft 4in
NICKNAME: Hod, Race Horse, Hoddy
EDUCATION: Fort Luton High School, Chatham; Mid-Kent College
TEAMS: Essex, Kent, Leicestershire
CAREER: First-class: 2000; List A: 2000; T20: 2003

BEST BATTING: 119 Leicestershire vs Sussex, Hove, 2003
BEST BOWLING: 8-10 Essex vs Leicestershire, Southend, 2011
COUNTY CAPS: 2007 (Leicestershire); 2008 (Essex)

CRICKETERS PARTICULARLY ADMIRED? Ian Botham
OTHER SPORTS PLAYED? Football, boxing and most other sports
OTHER SPORTS FOLLOWED? Football (Manchester United)
RELAXATIONS? Going out with mates
NOTES: An outstanding 2011 campaign saw Masters claim 93 first-class wickets, the highest tally in the 2011 English domestic season, with eight five-wicket hauls. His 8-10 vs Leicestershire at Southend were the best figures by any bowler and were also the best recorded figures by an Essex bowler since Mark Ilott took 9-19 against Northamptonshire in 1995. Shortlisted for the PCA Player of the Year 2011. He has now taken 233 first-class wickets for Essex at an average of 21.90, since his debut for the county in 2008. His father Kevin played four matches for Kent between 1983-1984; brother Daniel played three first-class matches for Leicestershire between 2009-2010

| Batting | Mat | Inns | NO | Runs | HS | Ave | SR | 100 | 50 | Ct | St |
|---|---|---|---|---|---|---|---|---|---|---|---|
| First-class | 148 | 189 | 29 | 2273 | 119 | 14.20 | | 1 | 5 | 49 | 0 |
| List A | 139 | 68 | 29 | 487 | 39 | 12.48 | | 0 | 0 | 16 | 0 |
| Twenty20 | 83 | 28 | 14 | 80 | 14 | 5.71 | 70.79 | 0 | 0 | 18 | 0 |

| Bowling | Mat | Balls | Runs | Wkts | BBI | BBM | Ave | Econ | SR | 5w | 10 |
|---|---|---|---|---|---|---|---|---|---|---|---|
| First-class | 148 | 27383 | 12579 | 469 | 8/10 | | 26.82 | 2.75 | 58.3 | 20 | 0 |
| List A | 139 | 5781 | 4314 | 134 | 5/17 | 5/17 | 32.19 | 4.47 | 43.1 | 2 | 0 |
| Twenty20 | 83 | 1571 | 1942 | 62 | 3/7 | 3/7 | 31.32 | 7.41 | 25.3 | 0 | 0 |

# TOM MAYNARD

## RHB OB R1

FULL NAME: Thomas Lloyd Maynard
BORN: March 25, 1989, Cardiff
SQUAD NO: 55
HEIGHT: 6ft 3in
NICKNAME: T-bone, T-train
EDUCATION: Millfield School, Whitchurch
TEAMS: England Lions, Glamorgan, Glamorgan 2nd XI, Surrey, Sylhet Royals, Wales Minor Counties
CAREER: First-class: 2007; List A: 2007; T20: 2007

SURREY

---

BEST BATTING: 141 Surrey vs Middlesex, Guildford, 2011

---

FAMILY TIES? Dad [Matthew] played for Glamorgan and England
CAREER HIGHLIGHTS? Winning the CB40 and promotion in the Championship in 2011
CRICKETING HEROES? Brian Lara, Herschelle Gibbs
NON-CRICKETING HEROES? Scott Murphy, Kenny Powers
BEST PLAYER IN COUNTY CRICKET? Marcus Trescothick
TIPS FOR THE TOP? James Vince, Jason Roy
IF YOU WEREN'T A CRICKETER? Poker player, superstar DJ
WHEN RAIN STOPS PLAY? Lurking, pranks, questionable magazines
FAVOURITE TV? Eastbound And Down
FAVOURITE FILM? Old School
FAVOURITE BOOK? FHM?
DREAM HOLIDAY? Las Vegas
SURPRISING SKILL? Pretty good at Guitar Hero
GUILTY PLEASURES? Jagermeister
TWITTER FEED: @TomMaynard55

| Batting | Mat | Inns | NO | Runs | HS | Ave | SR | 100 | 50 | Ct | St |
|---------|-----|------|----|----|----|----|----|----|----|----|----|
| First-class | 40 | 63 | 4 | 1749 | 141 | 29.64 | 65.95 | 3 | 8 | 36 | 0 |
| List A | 58 | 56 | 4 | 1645 | 108 | 31.63 | 97.56 | 2 | 12 | 27 | 0 |
| Twenty20 | 49 | 46 | 9 | 1027 | 78* | 27.75 | 131.49 | 0 | 6 | 18 | 0 |

| Bowling | Mat | Balls | Runs | Wkts | BBI | BBM | Ave | Econ | SR | 5w | 10 |
|---------|-----|-------|------|------|-----|-----|-----|------|----|----|----|
| First-class | 40 | 42 | 45 | 0 | - | - | - | 6.42 | - | 0 | 0 |
| List A | 58 | 12 | 32 | 0 | - | - | - | 16.00 | - | 0 | 0 |
| Twenty20 | 49 | - | - | - | - | - | - | - | - | - | - |

## GRAEME MCCARTER

### RHB RM

**GLOUCESTERSHIRE**

FULL NAME: Graeme John McCarter
BORN: October 10, 1992, Londonderry, Northern Ireland
SQUAD NO: 33
HEIGHT: 6ft 2in
NICKNAME: Macca
EDUCATION: Foyle and Londonderry College
TEAMS: Ireland, Gloucestershire 2nd XI, Ireland Under-13s, Ireland Under-15s, Ireland Under-19s
CAREER: First-class: 2011

BEST BATTING: 10 Ireland vs Namibia, Belfast, 2011
BEST BOWLING: 1-47 Ireland vs Namibia, Belfast, 2011

FAMILY TIES? My whole family love cricket, they are badgers!
CAREER HIGHLIGHTS? Getting a professional contract and playing for Ireland's senior team
CRICKETING HEROES? Glenn McGrath
NON-CRICKETING HEROES? Steven Gerrard
BEST PLAYER IN COUNTY CRICKET? David Payne
TIP FOR THE TOP? David Payne
WHEN RAIN STOPS PLAY? Looking for good jokes on the Internet and using them for my own
FAVOURITE TV? Not Going Out
FAVOURITE FILM? Perfect Storm
DREAM HOLIDAY? Magaluf, Cancun
SURPRISING SKILL? I'm a Grade 2 pianist
AMAZE ME! I played badminton for Ireland

| Batting | Mat | Inns | NO | Runs | HS | Ave | SR | 100 | 50 | Ct | St |
|---|---|---|---|---|---|---|---|---|---|---|---|
| First-class | 1 | 1 | 0 | 10 | 10 | 10.00 | 34.48 | 0 | 0 | 0 | 0 |

| Bowling | Mat | Balls | Runs | Wkts | BBI | BBM | Ave | Econ | SR | 5w | 10 |
|---|---|---|---|---|---|---|---|---|---|---|---|
| First-class | 1 | 114 | 90 | 1 | 1/47 | 1/90 | 90.00 | 4.73 | 114.0 | 0 | 0 |

# ANTHONY MCGRATH

## RHB RM R3

**FULL NAME:** Anthony McGrath
**BORN:** October 6, 1975, Bradford, Yorkshire
**SQUAD NO:** 10
**HEIGHT:** 6ft 1in
**NICKNAME:** Gripper, Mags, Terry, Pidge
**EDUCATION:** Yorkshire Martyrs Collegiate School
**TEAMS:** England, Yorkshire
**CAREER:** Test: 2003; ODI: 2003; First-class: 1995; List A: 1995; T20: 2004

**BEST BATTING:** 211 Yorkshire vs Warwickshire, Birmingham, 2009
**BEST BOWLING:** 5-39 Yorkshire vs Derbyshire, Derby, 2004
**COUNTY CAP:** 1999; **BENEFIT YEAR:** 2009

**CAREER HIGHLIGHTS?** Playing for England, being made Yorkshire captain
**SUPERSTITIONS?** I mark my guard six times when batting
**CRICKETING HEROES?** Robin Smith, Darren Lehmann
**NON-CRICKETING HEROES?** Bryan Robson, Ryan Giggs, Paul Scholes, David Brent
**BEST PLAYER IN COUNTY CRICKET?** Marcus Trescothick, Jacques Rudolph
**ACCOMPLISHMENTS?** Reaching the semi-final of the 1987 World Pac-Man Championship in Luxembourg
**SURPRISING SKILL?** I can count from one to 10 in 25 languages
**AMAZE ME!** I once got to the final 16 in the Take That dance auditions in 1995
**FANTASY SLIP CORDON?** Keeper: Rod Hull (for his enthusiasm), 1st: Susan Boyle (great voice), 2nd: Franz Klammer (good agility), 3rd: Heather Locklear (great looks), Gully: Orville (can fly)

| Batting | Mat | Inns | NO | Runs | HS | Ave | SR | 100 | 50 | Ct | St |
|---|---|---|---|---|---|---|---|---|---|---|---|
| Tests | 4 | 5 | 0 | 201 | 81 | 40.20 | 50.00 | 0 | 2 | 3 | 0 |
| ODIs | 14 | 12 | 2 | 166 | 52 | 16.60 | 47.02 | 0 | 1 | 4 | 0 |
| First-class | 243 | 412 | 27 | 14050 | 211 | 36.49 | | 33 | 67 | 176 | 0 |
| List A | 293 | 271 | 41 | 7548 | 148 | 32.81 | | 7 | 45 | 97 | 0 |
| Twenty20 | 66 | 61 | 12 | 1403 | 73* | 28.63 | 114.43 | 0 | 8 | 26 | 0 |

| Bowling | Mat | Balls | Runs | Wkts | BBI | BBM | Ave | Econ | SR | 5w | 10 |
|---|---|---|---|---|---|---|---|---|---|---|---|
| Tests | 4 | 102 | 56 | 4 | 3/16 | 3/16 | 14.00 | 3.29 | 25.5 | 0 | 0 |
| ODIs | 14 | 228 | 175 | 4 | 1/13 | 1/13 | 43.75 | 4.60 | 57.0 | 0 | 0 |
| First-class | 243 | 8562 | 4290 | 115 | 5/39 | | 37.30 | 3.00 | 74.4 | 1 | 0 |
| List A | 293 | 3137 | 2650 | 80 | 4/41 | 4/41 | 33.12 | 5.06 | 39.2 | 0 | 0 |
| Twenty20 | 66 | 475 | 698 | 23 | 3/17 | 3/17 | 30.34 | 8.81 | 20.6 | 0 | 0 |

# NEIL MCKENZIE

## RHB RM R1 MVP40

**FULL NAME:** Neil Douglas McKenzie
**BORN:** November 24, 1975, Johannesburg, South Africa
**SQUAD NO:** 44
**HEIGHT:** 6ft
**NICKNAME:** Bertie
**EDUCATION:** King Edward VII; RAU, Johannesburg
**TEAMS:** South Africa, Durham, Gauteng, Hampshire, Lions, Northerns, Transvaal
**CAREER:** Test: 2000; ODI: 2000; T20I: 2006; First-class: 1995; List A: 1995; T20: 2004

**BEST BATTING:** 237 Hampshire vs Yorkshire, Southampton, 2011
**BEST BOWLING:** 2-13 Lions vs Eagles, Kimberley, 2007
**COUNTY CAP:** 2010 (Hampshire)

**FAMILY TIES?** Father Kevin played for North Eastern Transvaal and Transvaal
**NOTES:** Captained South African Schools and South Africa U19. South African Cricket Annual Cricketer of the Year in 2001. Part of a world record-breaking opening stand with Graeme Smith in the Test against Bangladesh in Chittagong in 2008

| Batting | Mat | Inns | NO | Runs | HS | Ave | SR | 100 | 50 | Ct | St |
|---|---|---|---|---|---|---|---|---|---|---|---|
| Tests | 58 | 94 | 7 | 3253 | 226 | 37.39 | 42.00 | 5 | 16 | 54 | 0 |
| ODIs | 64 | 55 | 10 | 1688 | 131* | 37.51 | 69.40 | 2 | 10 | 21 | 0 |
| T20Is | 2 | 1 | 1 | 7 | 7* | - | 87.50 | 0 | 0 | 0 | 0 |
| First-class | 242 | 410 | 49 | 16244 | 237 | 44.99 | | 45 | 75 | 216 | 0 |
| List A | 252 | 229 | 35 | 7299 | 131* | 37.62 | | 10 | 51 | 73 | 0 |
| Twenty20 | 85 | 80 | 23 | 1997 | 89* | 35.03 | 119.93 | 0 | 12 | 29 | 0 |

| Bowling | Mat | Balls | Runs | Wkts | BBI | BBM | Ave | Econ | SR | 5w | 10 |
|---|---|---|---|---|---|---|---|---|---|---|---|
| Tests | 58 | 90 | 68 | 0 | - | - | - | 4.53 | - | 0 | 0 |
| ODIs | 64 | 46 | 27 | 0 | - | - | - | 3.52 | - | 0 | 0 |
| T20Is | 2 | - | - | - | - | - | - | - | - | - | - |
| First-class | 242 | 930 | 519 | 10 | 2/13 | | 51.90 | 3.34 | 93.0 | 0 | 0 |
| List A | 252 | 255 | 248 | 4 | 2/19 | 2/19 | 62.00 | 5.83 | 63.7 | 0 | 0 |
| Twenty20 | 85 | 24 | 34 | 1 | 1/4 | 1/4 | 34.00 | 8.50 | 24.0 | 0 | 0 |

# STUART MEAKER                                    RHB RF

FULL NAME: Stuart Christopher Meaker
BORN: January 21, 1989, Pietermaritzburg, South Africa
SQUAD NO: 18
HEIGHT: 6ft
NICKNAME: Ten Bears
EDUCATION: Cranleigh School
TEAMS: England, England Lions, England Under-19s, Surrey, Surrey 2nd XI
CAREER: ODI: 2011; First-class: 2008; List A: 2008; T20: 2010

BEST BATTING: 94 Surrey vs Bangladeshis, The Oval, 2010
BEST BOWLING: 5-37 Surrey vs Northamptonshire, Northampton, 2011

WHY CRICKET? I liked bowling gas
CAREER HIGHLIGHTS? Making ODI debut against India
CRICKETING HEROES? Allan Donald, Dale Steyn
BEST PLAYER IN COUNTY CRICKET? Marcus Trescothick
TIP FOR THE TOP? Jason Roy
IF YOU WEREN'T A CRICKETER? Attempting to play rugby
FAVOURITE TV? Family Guy
ACCOMPLISHMENTS? I was Pumba in the school play
SURPRISING SKILL? I can do a backflip
GUILTY PLEASURES? Chocolate brownies
AMAZE ME! I was a library monitor at school, my favourite song used to be Blue (Da Ba Dee) and I cannot grow a moustache
FANTASY SLIP CORDON? Keeper: Will Ferrell, 1st: Michael McIntyre, 2nd: Robin Williams, 3rd: Peter Griffin, Gully: Me
TWITTER FEED: @SMeaker18

| Batting | Mat | Inns | NO | Runs | HS | Ave | SR | 100 | 50 | Ct | St |
|---|---|---|---|---|---|---|---|---|---|---|---|
| ODIs | 2 | 2 | 0 | 2 | 1 | 1.00 | 12.50 | 0 | 0 | 0 | 0 |
| First-class | 29 | 38 | 3 | 566 | 94 | 16.17 | 39.44 | 0 | 4 | 5 | 0 |
| List A | 27 | 14 | 4 | 38 | 10* | 3.80 | 39.58 | 0 | 0 | 5 | 0 |
| Twenty20 | 14 | 4 | 3 | 27 | 17 | 27.00 | 150.00 | 0 | 0 | 6 | 0 |

| Bowling | Mat | Balls | Runs | Wkts | BBI | BBM | Ave | Econ | SR | 5w | 10 |
|---|---|---|---|---|---|---|---|---|---|---|---|
| ODIs | 2 | 114 | 110 | 2 | 1/45 | 1/45 | 55.00 | 5.78 | 57.0 | 0 | 0 |
| First-class | 29 | 4279 | 2707 | 90 | 5/37 | 8/81 | 30.07 | 3.79 | 47.5 | 5 | 0 |
| List A | 27 | 1017 | 1008 | 28 | 4/47 | 4/47 | 36.00 | 5.94 | 36.3 | 0 | 0 |
| Twenty20 | 14 | 240 | 368 | 10 | 2/16 | 2/16 | 36.80 | 9.20 | 24.0 | 0 | 0 |

# CRAIG MESCHEDE

## RHB RMF

FULL NAME: Craig Anthony Joseph Meschede
BORN: November 21, 1991, Johannesburg, South Africa
SQUAD NO: 26
TEAMS: Somerset, Somerset 2nd XI
CAREER: First-class: 2011; List A: 2011; T20: 2011

---

BEST BATTING: 53 Somerset vs Hampshire, Taunton, 2011
BEST BOWLING: 1-14 Somerset vs Indians, Taunton, 2011

---

NOTES: A brisk seamer and hard-hitting batsman. Has a German passport through his father. Made his full debut in early 2011. Awarded a contract in June 2010 after impressing in the 2nd XI. Hit 28* against Windward Islands, before smashing 26 off 11 balls against Combined Campuses and Colleges in the 2011 Caribbean T20. Dismissed Sachin Tendulkar for his maiden first-class wicket. Hit 53 from just 28 balls to help Somerset beat Glamorgan at Taunton in last year's FL t20

| Batting | Mat | Inns | NO | Runs | HS | Ave | SR | 100 | 50 | Ct | St |
|---|---|---|---|---|---|---|---|---|---|---|---|
| First-class | 5 | 8 | 1 | 149 | 53 | 21.28 | 46.13 | 0 | 1 | 0 | 0 |
| List A | 9 | 5 | 0 | 66 | 19 | 13.20 | 80.48 | 0 | 0 | 4 | 0 |
| Twenty20 | 16 | 13 | 3 | 180 | 53 | 18.00 | 125.00 | 0 | 1 | 4 | 0 |

| Bowling | Mat | Balls | Runs | Wkts | BBI | BBM | Ave | Econ | SR | 5w | 10 |
|---|---|---|---|---|---|---|---|---|---|---|---|
| First-class | 5 | 205 | 141 | 2 | 1/14 | 1/37 | 70.50 | 4.12 | 102.5 | 0 | 0 |
| List A | 9 | 168 | 160 | 5 | 2/16 | 2/16 | 32.00 | 5.71 | 33.6 | 0 | 0 |
| Twenty20 | 16 | 63 | 82 | 6 | 3/9 | 3/9 | 13.66 | 7.80 | 10.5 | 0 | 0 |

# CHRIS METTERS

## RHB SLA

FULL NAME: Christopher Liam Metters
BORN: September 12, 1990, Torquay, Devon
SQUAD NO: 35
HEIGHT: 6ft 1in
NICKNAME: Metts
EDUCATION: Coombeshead College
TEAMS: Devon, Essex 2nd XI, Minor Counties, Warwickshire, Warwickshire 2nd XI
CAREER: First-class: 2011; List A: 2011

BEST BATTING: 30 Warwickshire vs Hampshire, Southampton, 2011
BEST BOWLING: 6-65 Warwickshire vs Worcestershire, Birmingham, 2011

WHY CRICKET? Started playing Kwik Cricket as a youngster at primary school and developed a love for the game from that
CAREER HIGHLIGHTS? Taking 6-65 on my Championship debut vs Worcestershire. Taking a five-fer live on Sky in the last game of the season against Hampshire
SUPERSTITIONS? Always put my left pad on first and if I do well in a certain piece of kit then I try to use it for as long as possible
CRICKETING HEROES? Always enjoyed watching Shane Warne bowl because he made something happen every time he came on
BEST PLAYER IN COUNTY CRICKET? Marcus Trescothick
TIP FOR THE TOP? Chris Woakes
IF YOU WEREN'T A CRICKETER? Probably working for my dad as a painter and decorator
WHEN RAIN STOPS PLAY? Playing games or trying to annoy people to keep myself occupied
FAVOURITE TV? I like most comedy shows and Only Fools And Horses is a classic!
FAVOURITE FILM? The Business
DREAM HOLIDAY? Las Vegas
TWITTER FEED: @metters7

| Batting | Mat | Inns | NO | Runs | HS | Ave | SR | 100 | 50 | Ct | St |
|---|---|---|---|---|---|---|---|---|---|---|---|
| First-class | 10 | 12 | 5 | 167 | 30 | 23.85 | 39.66 | 0 | 0 | 15 | 0 |
| List A | 3 | 2 | 0 | 3 | 2 | 1.50 | 30.00 | 0 | 0 | 1 | 0 |

| Bowling | Mat | Balls | Runs | Wkts | BBI | BBM | Ave | Econ | SR | 5w | 10 |
|---|---|---|---|---|---|---|---|---|---|---|---|
| First-class | 10 | 1330 | 695 | 29 | 6/65 | 8/186 | 23.96 | 3.13 | 45.8 | 2 | 0 |
| List A | 3 | 108 | 94 | 2 | 2/41 | 2/41 | 47.00 | 5.22 | 54.0 | 0 | 0 |

# JAIK MICKLEBURGH

**RHB RM**

ESSEX

**FULL NAME:** Jaik Charles Mickleburgh
**BORN:** March 30, 1990, Norwich, Norfolk
**SQUAD NO:** 32
**HEIGHT:** 5ft 10in
**NICKNAME:** Juddy
**EDUCATION:** Earsham Primary; Bungay Middle; Bungay High School
**TEAMS:** England Under-19s, Essex, Essex 2nd XI, Norfolk
**CAREER:** First-class: 2008; List A: 2010; T20: 2010

**BEST BATTING:** 174 Essex vs Durham, Chester-le-Street, 2010

**CAREER HIGHLIGHTS?** Record partnership with James Foster [339 vs Durham, 2010]
**CRICKETING HEROES?** Darren Gough
**NON-CRICKETING HEROES?** Rafa Nadal, David Beckham
**TIPS FOR THE TOP?** Adam Wheater, Reece Topley, Tymal Mills
**BEST PLAYER IN COUNTY CRICKET?** Marcus Trescothick
**IF YOU WEREN'T A CRICKETER?** Utility warehouse distributor
**WHEN RAIN STOPS PLAY?** Watching the clouds to see where the next batch is coming from
**FAVOURITE TV?** The Only Way Is Essex
**FAVOURITE FILM?** Saving Private Ryan
**FAVOURITE BOOK?** The Slight Edge
**DREAM HOLIDAY?** Mauritius
**FANTASY SLIP CORDON?** Keeper: James Foster, 1st: Wentworth Miller, 2nd: David Beckham, 3rd: Tori Wilson, Gully: Jamie T
**TWITTER FEED:** @jaikmickleburgh

| Batting | Mat | Inns | NO | Runs | HS | Ave | SR | 100 | 50 | Ct | St |
|---|---|---|---|---|---|---|---|---|---|---|---|
| First-class | 41 | 76 | 0 | 2080 | 174 | 27.36 | 44.69 | 2 | 11 | 28 | 0 |
| List A | 7 | 6 | 0 | 141 | 56 | 23.50 | 84.93 | 0 | 1 | 5 | 0 |
| Twenty20 | 10 | 5 | 2 | 76 | 32 | 25.33 | 89.41 | 0 | 0 | 7 | 0 |

| Bowling | Mat | Balls | Runs | Wkts | BBI | BBM | Ave | Econ | SR | 5w | 10 |
|---|---|---|---|---|---|---|---|---|---|---|---|
| First-class | 41 | 78 | 50 | 0 | - | - | - | 3.84 | - | 0 | 0 |
| List A | 7 | - | - | - | - | - | - | - | - | - | - |
| Twenty20 | 10 | - | - | - | - | - | - | - | - | - | - |

# JAMES MIDDLEBROOK  RHB OB W1 MVP72

FULL NAME: James Daniel Middlebrook
BORN: May 13, 1977, Leeds, Yorkshire
SQUAD NO: 7
HEIGHT: 6ft 1in
NICKNAME: Minders, Midhouse, Midi, Dog, Doggy, Brook
EDUCATION: Pudsey Crawshaw School, Pudsey
TEAMS: Essex, Northamptonshire, Yorkshire
CAREER: First-class: 1998; List A: 1998; T20: 2004

BEST BATTING: 127 Essex vs Middlesex, Lord's, 2007
BEST BOWLING: 6-82 Yorkshire vs Hampshire, Southampton, 2000
COUNTY CAPS: 2003 (Essex); 2011 (Northamptonshire)

FAMILY TIES? Father managed the Indoor Cricket School at Headingley
CAREER HIGHLIGHTS? Making debut for Yorkshire at Lord's aged 21, winning the County Championship with Yorkshire in 2001, signing for Essex in 2002 and joining Northamptonshire in 2010
SUPERSTITIONS? Always get dressed for batting in same order
CRICKETING HEROES? John Emburey, Ian Botham, Geoff Boycott
NON-CRICKETING HEROES? Ayrton Senna, Seve Ballesteros
TIPS FOR THE TOP? Alex Wakely, Simon Kerrigan
IF YOU WEREN'T A CRICKETER? Police or fire service
WHEN RAIN STOPS PLAY? iPad
FAVOURITE TV? CSI, Top Gear
FAVOURITE FILM? The Italian Job
FAVOURITE BOOK? Tony Adams' autobiography
DREAM HOLIDAY? Australia
ACCOMPLISHMENTS? Being a great uncle to my nieces
TWITTER FEED: @midders07

| Batting | Mat | Inns | NO | Runs | HS | Ave | SR | 100 | 50 | Ct | St |
|---|---|---|---|---|---|---|---|---|---|---|---|
| First-class | 172 | 245 | 37 | 5528 | 127 | 26.57 | | 7 | 20 | 86 | 0 |
| List A | 168 | 112 | 37 | 1507 | 57* | 20.09 | | 0 | 1 | 48 | 0 |
| Twenty20 | 75 | 53 | 15 | 461 | 43 | 12.13 | 119.74 | 0 | 0 | 18 | 0 |

| Bowling | Mat | Balls | Runs | Wkts | BBI | BBM | Ave | Econ | SR | 5w | 10 |
|---|---|---|---|---|---|---|---|---|---|---|---|
| First-class | 172 | 27878 | 14620 | 384 | 6/82 | | 38.07 | 3.14 | 72.5 | 10 | 1 |
| List A | 168 | 6001 | 4687 | 131 | 4/27 | 4/27 | 35.77 | 4.68 | 45.8 | 0 | 0 |
| Twenty20 | 75 | 1044 | 1317 | 31 | 3/13 | 3/13 | 42.48 | 7.56 | 33.6 | 0 | 0 |

# CRAIG MILES

## RHB RMF

GLOUCESTERSHIRE

FULL NAME: Craig Neil Miles
BORN: July 20, 1994, Swindon, Wiltshire
SQUAD NO: TBC
HEIGHT: 6ft 4in
NICKNAME: Milo
EDUCATION: Bradon Forest Secondary School
TEAMS: Gloucestershire, Gloucestershire 2nd XI
CAREER: First-class: 2011; List A: 2011

BEST BATTING: 19 Gloucestershire vs Northamptonshire, Bristol, 2011
BEST BOWLING: 2-80 Gloucestershire vs Northamptonshire, Bristol, 2009

WHY CRICKET? Enjoyed watching my dad and brother play for our local side. I also liked to watch the likes of Brett Lee and Andrew Flintoff bowl
CAREER HIGHLIGHTS? Being selected for England U15 following the 2009 Bunbury Festival at Charterhouse School. My first-team debut vs Northamptonshire in May 2011, making me the fourth youngest player to play for Gloucestershire
SUPERSTITIONS? None really, but always put the left pad on before right
CRICKETING HEROES? Andrew Flintoff, Stuart Broad
NON-CRICKETING HEROES? My brother
BEST PLAYER IN COUNTY CRICKET? Marcus Trescothick
TIPS FOR THE TOP? David Payne and Chris Dent
IF YOU WEREN'T A CRICKETER? I'd just be finishing off my second year at Filton College, then would have been looking to apply for university. I may have taken a gap year to do some travelling
WHEN RAIN STOPS PLAY? Listening to music or relaxing
FAVOURITE TV? You've got to love a bit of The Simpsons
FAVOURITE FILM? Dumb And Dumber
FANTASY SLIP CORDON? Keeper: Lee Evans, 1st: Jim Carrey, 2nd: Myself, 3rd: Drake (rapper), Gully: Tim Cahill
TWITTER FEED: @CMiles34

| Batting | Mat | Inns | NO | Runs | HS | Ave | SR | 100 | 50 | Ct | St |
|---|---|---|---|---|---|---|---|---|---|---|---|
| First-class | 1 | 2 | 0 | 24 | 19 | 12.00 | 25.80 | 0 | 0 | 0 | 0 |
| List A | 2 | - | - | - | - | - | - | - | - | 0 | 0 |

| Bowling | Mat | Balls | Runs | Wkts | BBI | BBM | Ave | Econ | SR | 5w | 10 |
|---|---|---|---|---|---|---|---|---|---|---|---|
| First-class | 1 | 114 | 80 | 2 | 2/80 | 2/80 | 40.00 | 4.21 | 57.0 | 0 | 0 |
| List A | 2 | 66 | 63 | 2 | 2/32 | 2/32 | 31.50 | 5.72 | 33.0 | 0 | 0 |

# ANDREW MILLER

## RHB RFM

**FULL NAME:** Andrew Stephen Miller
**BORN:** September 27, 1987, Preston, Lancashire
**SQUAD NO:** 11
**HEIGHT:** 6ft 4in
**NICKNAME:** Millsy, Donk
**EDUCATION:** St Cecilia's RC High School; Preston College
**TEAMS:** England Under-19s, Lancashire 2nd XI, Warwickshire, Warwickshire 2nd XI
**CAREER:** First-class: 2008; List A: 2011; T20: 2011

**BEST BATTING:** 35 Warwickshire vs Durham, Birmingham, 2010
**BEST BOWLING:** 5-58 Warwickshire vs Lancashire, Birmingham, 2010

**CAREER HIGHLIGHTS?** Signing a professional deal with Warwickshire at the age of 17 and playing for England at the U19 World Cup in Sri Lanka in 2006
**SUPERSTITIONS?** Before I go on and off the field I make sure I step fully over the rope
**CRICKETING HEROES?** Glenn McGrath, Peter Martin, Tim Munton
**NON-CRICKETING HEROES?** Karl Pilkington
**BEST PLAYER IN COUNTY CRICKET?** Marcus Trescothick
**TIPS FOR THE TOP?** Chris Woakes, Steven Finn and James Taylor
**IF YOU WEREN'T A CRICKETER?** Commercial director
**WHEN RAIN STOPS PLAY?** Have a brew, listen to music or play the stupid dressing room games that we make up
**FAVOURITE TV?** Family Guy
**FAVOURITE FILM?** Anchorman
**FANTASY SLIP CORDON?** Keeper: Bear Grylls (he has the sort of character it takes to be a keeper, i.e. completely crazy!), 1st: Peter Griffin (absolute legend, he would make the day interesting), 2nd: Will Ferrell (he would just make the sessions fly by with his comedy), 3rd: Cheryl Cole (obvious reasons), Gully: Myself
**TWITTER FEED:** @asmiller11

| Batting | Mat | Inns | NO | Runs | HS | Ave | SR | 100 | 50 | Ct | St |
|---|---|---|---|---|---|---|---|---|---|---|---|
| First-class | 17 | 25 | 11 | 85 | 35 | 6.07 | 25.37 | 0 | 0 | 4 | 0 |
| List A | 4 | 2 | 1 | 4 | 2* | 4.00 | 57.14 | 0 | 0 | 1 | 0 |
| Twenty20 | 3 | 1 | 1 | 0 | 0* | - | - | 0 | 0 | 2 | 0 |

| Bowling | Mat | Balls | Runs | Wkts | BBI | BBM | Ave | Econ | SR | 5w | 10 |
|---|---|---|---|---|---|---|---|---|---|---|---|
| First-class | 17 | 2290 | 1216 | 34 | 5/58 | 8/103 | 35.76 | 3.18 | 67.3 | 2 | 0 |
| List A | 4 | 186 | 145 | 6 | 2/31 | 2/31 | 24.16 | 4.67 | 31.0 | 0 | 0 |
| Twenty20 | 3 | 48 | 69 | 3 | 2/16 | 2/16 | 23.00 | 8.62 | 16.0 | 0 | 0 |

## TYMAL MILLS RHB LF

ESSEX

FULL NAME: Tymal Solomon Mills
BORN: August 12, 1992, Dewsbury, Yorkshire
SQUAD NO: 5
HEIGHT: 6ft 1in
NICKNAME: T, Tyrone, T-bone, T-bomb
EDUCATION: Mildenhall College of Technology; University of East London
TEAMS: England Lions, England Under-19s, Essex, Essex 2nd XI, Suffolk
CAREER: First-class: 2011; List A: 2011

BEST BATTING: 8 Essex vs Sri Lankans, Chelmsford, 2010
BEST BOWLING: 3-48 Essex vs Leicestershire, Leicester, 2011

WHY CRICKET? A friend asked me to play for his village side as they were short when I was 14

CAREER HIGHLIGHTS? Being selected to represent England U19, making my first-class debut and taking my first wicket vs Sri Lanka, 3-48 on County Championship debut vs Leicestershire

CRICKETING HEROES? Michael Holding, Malcolm Marshall

NON-CRICKETING HEROES? Don't really have one

BEST PLAYER IN COUNTY CRICKET? Marcus Trescothick

TIPS FOR THE TOP? Daniel Bell-Drummond, Ben Foakes, Reece Topley, Lewis Gregory

IF YOU WEREN'T A CRICKETER? I'd be at university

WHEN RAIN STOPS PLAY? Eating, listening to music, having banter with the lads

FAVOURITE FILM? Cool Runnings, American Gangster

ACCOMPLISHMENTS? Passing my driving test first time and passing my first year at uni

SURPRISING SKILL? I can do an uncanny Louis Armstrong impersonation!

AMAZE ME! I have very oddly shaped toes, I didn't start playing cricket until I was 14 and I'm the first person from Suffolk on the Essex Academy

FANTASY SLIP CORDON? Keeper: Dion Dublin, 1st: Emile Heskey, 2nd: Myself, 3rd: Beyoncé, Gully: Kelly Brook

TWITTER FEED: @tmills15

| Batting | Mat | Inns | NO | Runs | HS | Ave | SR | 100 | 50 | Ct | St |
|---|---|---|---|---|---|---|---|---|---|---|---|
| First-class | 4 | 6 | 2 | 19 | 8 | 4.75 | 46.34 | 0 | 0 | 2 | 0 |
| List A | 3 | 1 | 0 | 0 | 0 | 0.00 | 0.00 | 0 | 0 | 0 | 0 |

| Bowling | Mat | Balls | Runs | Wkts | BBI | BBM | Ave | Econ | SR | 5w | 10 |
|---|---|---|---|---|---|---|---|---|---|---|---|
| First-class | 4 | 390 | 241 | 7 | 3/48 | 3/99 | 34.42 | 3.70 | 55.7 | 0 | 0 |
| List A | 3 | 128 | 114 | 4 | 2/40 | 2/40 | 28.50 | 5.34 | 32.0 | 0 | 0 |

# TOM MILNES

## RHB RFM

FULL NAME: Thomas Patrick Milnes
BORN: October 6, 1992, Stourbridge, Worcestershire
SQUAD NO: 8
TEAMS: England Under-17s, England Under-19s, Warwickshire, Warwickshire 2nd XI, Warwickshire Under-14s, Warwickshire Under-15s, Warwickshire Under-17s
CAREER: First-class: 2011

BEST BATTING: 23 Warwickshire vs DMCCU, Durham University, 2011
BEST BOWLING: 4-15 Warwickshire vs DMCCU, Durham University, 2011

NOTES: Represented England at U17, U18 and U19 level. Took 2-64 in his solitary England U19 match against Sri Lanka U19. Yet to make County Championship debut

| Batting | Mat | Inns | NO | Runs | HS | Ave | SR | 100 | 50 | Ct | St |
|---|---|---|---|---|---|---|---|---|---|---|---|
| First-class | 1 | 1 | 0 | 23 | 23 | 23.00 | 38.33 | 0 | 0 | 0 | 0 |

| Bowling | Mat | Balls | Runs | Wkts | BBI | BBM | Ave | Econ | SR | 5w | 10 |
|---|---|---|---|---|---|---|---|---|---|---|---|
| First-class | 1 | 72 | 39 | 4 | 4/15 | 4/39 | 9.75 | 3.25 | 18.0 | 0 | 0 |

# DARYL MITCHELL

### RHB RM R2 MVP64

**WORCESTERSHIRE**

FULL NAME: Daryl Keith Henry Mitchell
BORN: November 25, 1983, Badsey, nr Evesham
SQUAD NO: 27
HEIGHT: 5ft 10in
NICKNAME: Mitch, Touc
EDUCATION: Prince Henry's, Evesham; University College, Worcester
TEAMS: Mountaineers, Worcestershire, Worcestershire 2nd XI
CAREER: First-class: 2005; List A: 2005; T20: 2005

BEST BATTING: 298 Worcestershire vs Somerset, Taunton, 2009
BEST BOWLING: 4-49 Worcestershire vs Yorkshire, Leeds, 2009

FAMILY TIES? Dad played club cricket and coaches Worcestershire Young Cricketers U13
CAREER HIGHLIGHTS? Winning the Pro40 in 2011, scoring 298 against Somerset at Taunton
CRICKETING HEROES? Ian Botham, Graeme Hick
NON-CRICKETING HEROES? Paul McGrath, John Carew
BEST PLAYER IN COUNTY CRICKET? Marcus Trescothick
TIP FOR THE TOP? Alexei Kervezee
IF YOU WEREN'T A CRICKETER? PE teacher
WHEN RAIN STOPS PLAY? Playing Perudo or Football Manager
FAVOURITE TV? Shameless, Match Of The Day
FAVOURITE FILM? Dumb And Dumber
ACCOMPLISHMENTS? BSc in Sports Studies, won loads of football and darts trophies when I was younger, played for Aston Villa's School of Excellence as a kid
FANTASY SLIP CORDON? Keeper: Tiger Woods (he'd have a few stories and maybe the odd golf tip), 1st: Paul McGrath (favourite Villa player), 2nd: Me (always stand at second slip), 3rd: Ian Botham (cricketing hero), Gully: Rhod Gilbert (bit of comedy for the long days in the dirt!)
TWITTER FEED: @mitchwccc

| Batting | Mat | Inns | NO | Runs | HS | Ave | SR | 100 | 50 | Ct | St |
|---|---|---|---|---|---|---|---|---|---|---|---|
| First-class | 80 | 147 | 19 | 5092 | 298 | 39.78 | 44.93 | 10 | 24 | 113 | 0 |
| List A | 67 | 56 | 12 | 1357 | 92 | 30.84 | 79.87 | 0 | 8 | 25 | 0 |
| Twenty20 | 65 | 44 | 13 | 632 | 45 | 20.38 | 112.45 | 0 | 0 | 24 | 0 |

| Bowling | Mat | Balls | Runs | Wkts | BBI | BBM | Ave | Econ | SR | 5w | 10 |
|---|---|---|---|---|---|---|---|---|---|---|---|
| First-class | 80 | 1347 | 683 | 17 | 4/49 | | 40.17 | 3.04 | 79.2 | 0 | 0 |
| List A | 67 | 1426 | 1375 | 34 | 4/42 | 4/42 | 40.44 | 5.78 | 41.9 | 0 | 0 |
| Twenty20 | 65 | 833 | 1111 | 38 | 4/11 | 4/11 | 29.23 | 8.00 | 21.9 | 0 | 0 |

## STEPHEN MOORE                    RHB RM R4 MVP31

**FULL NAME:** Stephen Colin Moore
**BORN:** November 4, 1980, Johannesburg, South Africa
**SQUAD NO:** 6
**HEIGHT:** 6ft
**NICKNAME:** Rog, Mandy, Circles
**EDUCATION:** St Stithians College, South Africa; Exeter University
**TEAMS:** England Lions, Lancashire, Marylebone Cricket Club, Sussex 2nd XI, Worcestershire
**CAREER:** First-class: 2003; List A: 2003; T20: 2003

BEST BATTING: 246 Worcestershire vs Derbyshire, Worcester, 2005
BEST BOWLING: 1-13 Worcestershire vs Lancashire, Worcester, 2004

CAREER HIGHLIGHTS? Winning the Championship with Lancashire in 2011, scoring a hundred against the Australians for England Lions at Worcester, and playing in a Lord's final in 2004
CRICKETING HEROES? Steve Waugh, Jacques Kallis
NON-CRICKETING HEROES? Roger Federer, Rafa Nadal
BEST PLAYER IN COUNTY CRICKET? Marcus Trescothick
TIP FOR THE TOP? Simon Kerrigan
FAVOURITE TV? Friends
FAVOURITE FILM? The Prestige
FAVOURITE BOOK? Rainbow Six
DREAM HOLIDAY? The African Bush
ACCOMPLISHMENTS? Achieving a Masters degree in Electronic Engineering
SURPRISING SKILL? Play alto saxophone and a little guitar
GUILTY PLEASURES? Coke and Pringles
FANTASY SLIP CORDON? Keeper: Roger Federer, 1st: Kate Beckinsale, 2nd: Michael McIntyre, 3rd: Myself, Gully: Professor Brian Cox
TWITTER FEED? @stephen_moore6

| Batting | Mat | Inns | NO | Runs | HS | Ave | SR | 100 | 50 | Ct | St |
|---|---|---|---|---|---|---|---|---|---|---|---|
| First-class | 129 | 234 | 19 | 8384 | 246 | 38.99 | 57.59 | 17 | 41 | 64 | 0 |
| List A | 115 | 110 | 10 | 2836 | 118 | 28.36 | 71.65 | 4 | 16 | 29 | 0 |
| Twenty20 | 80 | 74 | 10 | 1753 | 83* | 27.39 | 129.56 | 0 | 10 | 24 | 0 |

| Bowling | Mat | Balls | Runs | Wkts | BBI | BBM | Ave | Econ | SR | 5w | 10 |
|---|---|---|---|---|---|---|---|---|---|---|---|
| First-class | 129 | 342 | 321 | 5 | 1/13 | | 64.20 | 5.63 | 68.4 | 0 | 0 |
| List A | 115 | 41 | 53 | 1 | 1/1 | 1/1 | 53.00 | 7.75 | 41.0 | 0 | 0 |
| Twenty20 | 80 | - | - | - | - | - | - | - | - | - | - |

# EOIN MORGAN

**LHB RM R1**

MIDDLESEX

**FULL NAME:** Eoin Joseph Gerard Morgan
**BORN:** September 10, 1986, Dublin, Ireland
**SQUAD NO:** 7
**HEIGHT:** 5ft 10in
**NICKNAME:** Moggie, Morgs
**EDUCATION:** Catholic University School, Dublin
**TEAMS:** England, Ireland, Bangalore Royal Challengers, England A, Ireland A, Ireland Under-19s, Kolkata Knight Riders, Middlesex, Middlesex 2nd XI, Sir Paul Getty's XI
**CAREER:** Test: 2010; ODI: 2006; T20I: 2009; First-class: 2004; List A: 2004; T20: 2006

**BEST BATTING:** 209* Ireland vs UAE, Abu Dhabi, 2007
**BEST BOWLING:** 2-24 Middlesex vs Nottinghamshire, Lord's, 2007
**COUNTY CAPS:** 2008

**FAMILY TIES?** My father, three brothers, two sisters, grandfather and great-grandfather all played
**CRICKETERS PARTICULARLY ADMIRED?** Ricky Ponting, Brian Lara
**OTHER SPORTS PLAYED?** Rugby, Gaelic football
**FAVOURITE BAND?** Aslan
**RELAXATIONS?** Watching sport and listening to music
**NOTES:** Switched his allegiance from Ireland to England in April 2009 after he was named in England's 30-man provisional squad for the 2009 World T20. Made his ODI debut for his adopted nation against West Indies in May 2009 at Bristol and his T20I debut a month later in the defeat to Netherlands at Lord's. Test debut followed against Bangladesh in May 2010 and he struck his maiden century in his third match – 130 vs Pakistan at Trent Bridge in July

| Batting | Mat | Inns | NO | Runs | HS | Ave | SR | 100 | 50 | Ct | St |
|---|---|---|---|---|---|---|---|---|---|---|---|
| Tests | 16 | 24 | 1 | 700 | 130 | 30.43 | 54.77 | 2 | 3 | 11 | 0 |
| ODIs | 75 | 73 | 13 | 2307 | 115 | 38.45 | 83.07 | 4 | 15 | 31 | 0 |
| T20Is | 21 | 21 | 6 | 601 | 85* | 40.06 | 135.36 | 0 | 3 | 13 | 0 |
| First-class | 69 | 113 | 13 | 3592 | 209* | 35.92 | 52.09 | 9 | 16 | 55 | 1 |
| List A | 155 | 146 | 23 | 4558 | 161 | 37.05 | 84.14 | 7 | 28 | 52 | 0 |
| Twenty20 | 83 | 76 | 11 | 1665 | 85* | 25.61 | 129.67 | 0 | 7 | 37 | 0 |

| Bowling | Mat | Balls | Runs | Wkts | BBI | BBM | Ave | Econ | SR | 5w | 10 |
|---|---|---|---|---|---|---|---|---|---|---|---|
| Tests | 16 | - | - | - | - | - | - | - | - | - | - |
| ODIs | 75 | - | - | - | - | - | - | - | - | - | - |
| T20Is | 21 | - | - | - | - | - | - | - | - | - | - |
| First-class | 69 | 97 | 83 | 2 | 2/24 | 2/24 | 41.50 | 5.13 | 48.5 | 0 | 0 |
| List A | 155 | 42 | 49 | 0 | - | - | - | 7.00 | - | 0 | 0 |
| Twenty20 | 83 | - | - | - | - | - | - | - | - | - | - |

# ALBIE MORKEL LHB RMF

**FULL NAME:** Johannes Albertus Morkel
**BORN:** June 10, 1981, Vereeniging, South Africa
**SQUAD NO:** 81
**HEIGHT:** 6ft
**TEAMS:** South Africa, Africa XI, Chennai Super Kings, Durham, Easterns, South Africa Under-19s, Somerset, Titans
**CAREER:** Test: 2009; ODI: 2004; T20I: 2005; First-class: 1999; List A: 1999; T20: 2004

**BEST BATTING:** 204* Titans vs Western Province Boland, Paarl, 2005
**BEST BOWLING:** 6-36 Easterns vs Griqualand West, Kimberley, 1999

**NOTES:** Rose to prominence playing for Easterns against the touring West Indians in the 2003/04 season when he defied food poisoning to score a century and take five wickets at Benoni. Received his first international call-up when he was picked for the 2003/04 tour of New Zealand. His one Test cap to date came against Australia in 2009, at Cape Town. His brother Morne also plays for South Africa. Has scored 422 runs at 32.46 in 19 T20 innings for Durham. Signed by Somerset as a replacement for Roelof van der Merwe due to work permit concerns

| Batting | Mat | Inns | NO | Runs | HS | Ave | SR | 100 | 50 | Ct | St |
|---|---|---|---|---|---|---|---|---|---|---|---|
| Tests | 1 | 1 | 0 | 58 | 58 | 58.00 | 81.69 | 0 | 1 | 0 | 0 |
| ODIs | 58 | 43 | 10 | 782 | 97 | 23.69 | 100.25 | 0 | 2 | 15 | 0 |
| T20Is | 34 | 27 | 7 | 466 | 43 | 23.30 | 140.78 | 0 | 0 | 15 | 0 |
| First-class | 75 | 111 | 21 | 4046 | 204* | 44.95 | | 8 | 23 | 32 | 0 |
| List A | 177 | 137 | 36 | 2728 | 97 | 27.00 | | 0 | 11 | 40 | 0 |
| Twenty20 | 164 | 133 | 50 | 2323 | 71* | 27.98 | 141.73 | 0 | 6 | 35 | 0 |

| Bowling | Mat | Balls | Runs | Wkts | BBI | BBM | Ave | Econ | SR | 5w | 10 |
|---|---|---|---|---|---|---|---|---|---|---|---|
| Tests | 1 | 192 | 132 | 1 | 1/44 | 1/132 | 132.00 | 4.12 | 192.0 | 0 | 0 |
| ODIs | 58 | 2073 | 1899 | 50 | 4/29 | 4/29 | 37.98 | 5.49 | 41.4 | 0 | 0 |
| T20Is | 34 | 478 | 641 | 18 | 2/12 | 2/12 | 35.61 | 8.04 | 26.5 | 0 | 0 |
| First-class | 75 | 11493 | 5977 | 203 | 6/36 | | 29.44 | 3.12 | 56.6 | 5 | 0 |
| List A | 177 | 6719 | 5659 | 184 | 4/23 | 4/23 | 30.75 | 5.05 | 36.5 | 0 | 0 |
| Twenty20 | 164 | 2760 | 3674 | 134 | 4/30 | 4/30 | 27.41 | 7.98 | 20.5 | 0 | 0 |

# GORDON MUCHALL                                    RHB RM

FULL NAME: Gordon James Muchall
BORN: November 2, 1982, Newcastle-upon-Tyne, Northumberland
SQUAD NO: 24
HEIGHT: 6ft 1in
NICKNAME: Muchy
EDUCATION: Durham School
TEAMS: Durham
CAREER: First-class: 2002; List A: 2002; T20: 2003

BEST BATTING: 219 Durham vs Kent, Canterbury, 2006
BEST BOWLING: 3-26 Durham vs Yorkshire, Headingley, 2003
COUNTY CAP: 2005

FAMILY TIES? Grandad played for Northumberlad, brother Paul plays at Gloucestershire, brother Matthew plays for Northumberland and dad Arthur plays for Durham over 50s
CAREER HIGHLIGHTS? Winning the Championship twice with Durham
CRICKETING HEROES? Mike Hussey, Robin Smith, Dale Benkenstein
TIPS FOR THE TOP? Hayden and Rory Mustard, Jack and Luke Benkenstein, Adam Muchall, Mitchell Killeen, Luca Di Venuto, Charlie Harmison
IF YOU WEREN'T A CRICKETER? Coaching or personal trainer
WHEN RAIN STOPS PLAY? 500, card school or some fitness
FAVOURITE TV? None at the minute, but loved 24 and Prison Break
FAVOURITE FILM? Forrest Gump, The Shawshank Redemption, Old School, Wedding Crashers
AMAZE ME! The last game of rugby I ever played was at Twickenham
FANTASY SLIP CORDON? Keeper: Phil Mustard (safe hands, always good for a pearl of wisdom), 1st: James Corden (to make fun out of the rest), 2nd: Andrew Flintoff (able to cover 1st slip), 3rd: Me (I need to fit in somewhere!), Gully: Lee Evans (lots of energy to keep everyone going)

| Batting | Mat | Inns | NO | Runs | HS | Ave | SR | 100 | 50 | Ct | St |
|---|---|---|---|---|---|---|---|---|---|---|---|
| First-class | 130 | 224 | 11 | 6412 | 219 | 30.10 | 54.20 | 11 | 33 | 88 | 0 |
| List A | 106 | 97 | 17 | 2558 | 101* | 31.97 | | 1 | 15 | 38 | 0 |
| Twenty20 | 56 | 47 | 8 | 960 | 64* | 24.61 | 108.84 | | 4 | 21 | 0 |

| Bowling | Mat | Balls | Runs | Wkts | BBI | BBM | Ave | Econ | SR | 5w | 10 |
|---|---|---|---|---|---|---|---|---|---|---|---|
| First-class | 130 | 896 | 617 | 15 | 3/26 | | 41.13 | 4.13 | 59.7 | 0 | 0 |
| List A | 106 | 168 | 144 | 1 | 1/15 | 1/15 | 144.00 | 5.14 | 168.0 | 0 | 0 |
| Twenty20 | 56 | 12 | 8 | 1 | 1/8 | 1/8 | 8.00 | 4.00 | 12.0 | 0 | 0 |

FULL NAME: Paul Bernard Muchall
BORN: March 17, 1987, Newcastle-upon-Tyne
SQUAD NO: TBC
TEAMS: Durham 2nd XI, Durham Under-17s, Gloucestershire, Kent, Kent 2nd XI, Minor Counties Under-25s, Northumberland
CAREER: List A: 2010

GLOUCESTERSHIRE

NOTES: Handed a six-week trial by Gloucestershire in March. Made his List A debut for Kent in 2010 against Durham and took the wicket of his older brother Gordon, who remains on the books at Chester-le-Street. Represented MCC Young Cricketers last season

| Batting | Mat | Inns | NO | Runs | HS | Ave | SR | 100 | 50 | Ct | St |
|---------|-----|------|-----|------|-----|-------|-------|-----|-----|-----|-----|
| List A | 1 | 1 | 0 | 22 | 22 | 22.00 | 57.89 | 0 | 0 | 0 | 0 |

| Bowling | Mat | Balls | Runs | Wkts | BBI | BBM | Ave | Econ | SR | 5w | 10 |
|---------|-----|-------|------|------|------|------|-------|------|------|-----|-----|
| List A | 1 | 24 | 34 | 1 | 1/34 | 1/34 | 34.00 | 8.50 | 24.0 | 0 | 0 |

## STEVEN MULLANEY

RHB RM

NOTTINGHAMSHIRE

FULL NAME: Steven John Mullaney
BORN: November 19, 1986, Warrington, Cheshire
SQUAD NO: 5
HEIGHT: 5ft 10in
NICKNAME: Mull, Cadet Mahoney
EDUCATION: St Mary's RC High School, Astley
TEAMS: England Under-19s, Lancashire, Lancashire 2nd XI, Nottinghamshire
CAREER: First-class: 2006; List A: 2006; T20: 2006

BEST BATTING: 165* Lancashire vs DUCCE, Durham University, 2007
BEST BOWLING: 4-31 Nottinghamshire vs Essex, Nottingham, 2010

FAMILY TIES? Dad was a club professional in the 80s and 90s
IF YOU WEREN'T A CRICKETER? PE teacher
CRICKET MOMENT TO FORGET? A duck on my Championship debut vs Nottinghamshire
FAVOURITE BAND? Westlife
CRICKETERS PARTICULARLY ADMIRED? Andrew Flintoff, VVS Laxman
OTHER SPORTS FOLLOWED? Football (Manchester City), rugby league (St Helens)
OTHER SPORTS PLAYED? Rugby league (toured France with England U15)
NOTES: Played for England in the 2006 U19 World Cup. Left Lancashire after the 2009 season and joined Nottinghamshire

| Batting | Mat | Inns | NO | Runs | HS | Ave | SR | 100 | 50 | Ct | St |
|---|---|---|---|---|---|---|---|---|---|---|---|
| First-class | 33 | 54 | 5 | 1418 | 165* | 28.93 | 63.21 | 2 | 6 | 25 | 0 |
| List A | 31 | 25 | 2 | 438 | 61 | 19.04 | 97.11 | 0 | 2 | 16 | 0 |
| Twenty20 | 37 | 26 | 8 | 312 | 53 | 17.33 | 128.39 | 0 | 1 | 16 | 0 |

| Bowling | Mat | Balls | Runs | Wkts | BBI | BBM | Ave | Econ | SR | 5w | 10 |
|---|---|---|---|---|---|---|---|---|---|---|---|
| First-class | 33 | 1578 | 841 | 16 | 4/31 | 4/48 | 52.56 | 3.19 | 98.6 | 0 | 0 |
| List A | 31 | 866 | 763 | 31 | 3/13 | 3/13 | 24.61 | 5.28 | 27.9 | 0 | 0 |
| Twenty20 | 37 | 624 | 782 | 25 | 3/12 | 3/12 | 31.28 | 7.51 | 24.9 | 0 | 0 |

# MUTTIAH MURALITHARAN　　RHB OB W3

FULL NAME: Muttiah Muralitharan
BORN: April 17, 1972, Kandy, Sri Lanka
SQUAD NO: 800
HEIGHT: 5ft 7in
NICKNAME: Murali
EDUCATION: St Anthony's College, Kandy
TEAMS: Sri Lanka, Asia XI, Chennai Super Kings, Gloucestershire, ICC World XI, Kandurata, Kent, Kochi Tuskers Kerala, Lancashire, Tamil Union Cricket and Athletic Club, Wellington
CAREER: Test: 1992; ODI: 1993; T20I: 2006; First-class: 1990; List A: 1992; T20: 2005

BEST BATTING: 67 Sri Lanka vs India, Kandy, 2001
BEST BOWLING: 9-51 Sri Lanka vs Zimbabwe, Kandy, 2002
COUNTY CAPS: 1999 (Lancashire); 2003 (Kent)

NOTES: The highest wicket-taker in Test history, with 67 five-wicket hauls. A World Cup winner with Sri Lanka in 1996. Has won numerous international series and match awards, including Man of the Match against England at The Oval in 1998, when he took 16 wickets to orchestrate Sri Lanka's first Test victory on English soil. One of Wisden's Five Cricketers of the Year in 1999. The highest Test wicket-taker for the calendar year 2000, with 75 wickets from 10 matches. He took his 500th Test wicket (Michael Kasprowicz) in 2003/04, during the second Test against Australia in his home town of Kandy, becoming the third bowler to reach the milestone. In the first Test vs Bangladesh at Chittagong 2005/06, his 100th Test, he became the first man to take 1,000 international wickets (589 Test / 411 ODI). And in 2010 he became the first man to take 800 Test wickets when he removed Pragyan Ojha in the first Test in Galle, retiring from Test cricket straight after that match

| Batting | Mat | Inns | NO | Runs | HS | Ave | SR | 100 | 50 | Ct | St |
|---|---|---|---|---|---|---|---|---|---|---|---|
| Tests | 133 | 164 | 56 | 1261 | 67 | 11.67 | 70.28 | 0 | 1 | 72 | 0 |
| ODIs | 350 | 162 | 63 | 674 | 33* | 6.80 | 77.56 | 0 | 0 | 130 | 0 |
| T20Is | 12 | 2 | 0 | 1 | 1 | 0.50 | 20.00 | 0 | 0 | 1 | 0 |
| First-class | 232 | 276 | 83 | 2192 | 67 | 11.35 | | 0 | 1 | 123 | 0 |
| List A | 453 | 205 | 76 | 945 | 33* | 7.32 | | 0 | 0 | 159 | 0 |
| Twenty20 | 108 | 28 | 10 | 66 | 11 | 3.66 | 81.48 | 0 | 0 | 23 | 0 |

| Bowling | Mat | Balls | Runs | Wkts | BBI | BBM | Ave | Econ | SR | 5w | 10 |
|---|---|---|---|---|---|---|---|---|---|---|---|
| Tests | 133 | 44039 | 18180 | 800 | 9/51 | 16/220 | 22.72 | 2.47 | 55.0 | 67 | 22 |
| ODIs | 350 | 18811 | 12326 | 534 | 7/30 | 7/30 | 23.08 | 3.93 | 35.2 | 10 | 0 |
| T20Is | 12 | 282 | 297 | 13 | 3/29 | 3/29 | 22.84 | 6.31 | 21.6 | 0 | 0 |
| First-class | 232 | 66933 | 26997 | 1374 | 9/51 | | 19.64 | 2.42 | 48.7 | 119 | 34 |
| List A | 453 | 23734 | 15270 | 682 | 7/30 | 7/30 | 22.39 | 3.85* | 35.1* | 12 | 0 |
| Twenty20 | 108 | 2430 | 2598 | 124 | 4/16 | 4/16 | 20.95 | 6.41 | 19.5 | 0 | 0 |

# DAVID MURPHY RHB WK

FULL NAME: David Murphy
BORN: June 24, 1989, Welwyn Garden City, Hertfordshire
SQUAD NO: 19
HEIGHT: 6ft
NICKNAME: Murph, Smurf
EDUCATION: Richard Hale School; Loughborough University
TEAMS: Loughborough MCCU, Loughborough UCCE, Northamptonshire, Northamptonshire 2nd XI
CAREER: First-class: 2009; List A: 2010; T20: 2010

BEST BATTING: 79 Northamptonshire vs Glamorgan, Northampton, 2011

CAREER HIGHLIGHTS? 69* on first-class debut for Loughborough, 79 vs Glamorgan as a nightwatchman
CRICKETING HEROES? Steve Waugh, Jack Russell
NON-CRICKETING HEROES? Nelson Mandela
BEST PLAYER IN COUNTY CRICKET? Chaminda Vaas
TIPS FOR THE TOP? Alex Wakely, Rob Newton, Maurice Holmes, David Ripley
IF YOU WEREN'T A CRICKETER? Something more fun
WHEN RAIN STOPS PLAY? Reading and chatting
FAVOURITE TV? Family Guy
FAVOURITE FILM? Gone Baby Gone
FAVOURITE BOOK? The Shadow Of The Wind
DREAM HOLIDAY? Barbados
ACCOMPLISHMENTS? Finishing my degree with a 2:1 in Politics
SURPRISING SKILL? I play the saxophone
GUILTY PLEASURES? Magners
AMAZE ME! I am deaf in my left ear
FANTASY SLIP CORDON? Keeper: Myself, 1st: David English, 2nd: James Corden, 3rd: Graham Dilley

| Batting | Mat | Inns | NO | Runs | HS | Ave | SR | 100 | 50 | Ct | St |
|---|---|---|---|---|---|---|---|---|---|---|---|
| First-class | 23 | 34 | 9 | 783 | 79 | 31.32 | 46.00 | 0 | 7 | 65 | 3 |
| List A | 12 | 8 | 6 | 81 | 31* | 40.50 | 83.50 | 0 | 0 | 7 | 3 |
| Twenty20 | 14 | 7 | 2 | 54 | 20 | 10.80 | 112.50 | 0 | 0 | 8 | 2 |

| Bowling | Mat | Balls | Runs | Wkts | BBI | BBM | Ave | Econ | SR | 5w | 10 |
|---|---|---|---|---|---|---|---|---|---|---|---|
| First-class | 23 | 6 | 3 | 0 | - | - | - | 3.00 | - | 0 | 0 |
| List A | 12 | - | - | - | - | - | - | - | - | - | - |
| Twenty20 | 14 | - | - | - | - | - | - | - | - | - | - |

# TIM MURTAGH

## LHB RFM W3 MVP49

FULL NAME: Timothy James Murtagh
BORN: August 2, 1981, Lambeth, London
SQUAD NO: 34
HEIGHT: 6ft 1in
NICKNAME: Dial M, Murts
EDUCATION: John Fisher, Purley; St Mary's University
TEAMS: British Universities, Middlesex, Middlesex 2nd XI, Surrey
CAREER: First-class: 2000; List A: 2000; T20: 2003

BEST BATTING: 74* Surrey vs Middlesex, The Oval, 2004
BEST BOWLING: 7-82 Middlesex vs Derbyshire, Derby, 2009
COUNTY CAPS: 2008 (Middlesex)

FAMILY TIES? Uncle played for Hampshire
WHY CRICKET? Enjoy the contests within the contest
CAREER HIGHLIGHTS? Winning T20 Cup with Middlesex in 2008. Growing up in a fantastic era and squad at Surrey
SUPERSTITIONS? I always have a shave the day before a Championship game starts!
CRICKETING HEROES? Darren Gough, Graham Thorpe, Glenn McGrath
TIPS FOR THE TOP? Jonny Bairstow, Sam Robson
IF YOU WEREN'T A CRICKETER? Editor of the Cricketers' Who's Who
WHEN RAIN STOPS PLAY? Get the physio to rub me to prevent him sleeping, getting stuck into one of the youngsters or taking the mickey out of Finny's physique!
FAVOURITE TV? Friends, Entourage
ACCOMPLISHMENTS? Plucking up the courage to propose to my girlfriend
SURPRISING SKILL? I could say but I'd have to kill you
GUILTY PLEASURES? Chocolate
AMAZE ME! My cousin is a famous jockey
TWITTER FEED: @tjmurtagh

| Batting | Mat | Inns | NO | Runs | HS | Ave | SR | 100 | 50 | Ct | St |
|---|---|---|---|---|---|---|---|---|---|---|---|
| First-class | 114 | 158 | 48 | 2437 | 74* | 22.15 | | 0 | 10 | 33 | 0 |
| List A | 125 | 81 | 30 | 614 | 35* | 12.03 | | 0 | 0 | 34 | 0 |
| Twenty20 | 75 | 31 | 10 | 199 | 40* | 9.47 | 108.15 | 0 | 0 | 16 | 0 |

| Bowling | Mat | Balls | Runs | Wkts | BBI | BBM | Ave | Econ | SR | 5w | 10 |
|---|---|---|---|---|---|---|---|---|---|---|---|
| First-class | 114 | 18150 | 10415 | 365 | 7/82 | | 28.53 | 3.44 | 49.7 | 16 | 2 |
| List A | 125 | 5516 | 4799 | 172 | 4/14 | 4/14 | 27.90 | 5.22 | 32.0 | 0 | 0 |
| Twenty20 | 75 | 1486 | 2124 | 80 | 6/24 | 6/24 | 26.55 | 8.57 | 18.5 | 1 | 0 |

## PHIL MUSTARD — LHB WK MVP28

DURHAM

FULL NAME: Philip Mustard
BORN: October 8, 1982, Sunderland, Co Durham
SQUAD NO: 19
HEIGHT: 5ft 11in
NICKNAME: Colonel
EDUCATION: Usworth Comprehensive
TEAMS: England, Barisal Burners, Durham, Durham Cricket Board, England Under-19s, Mountaineers
CAREER: ODI: 2007; T20I: 2008; First-class: 2002; List A: 2000; T20: 2003

BEST BATTING: 130 Durham vs Kent, Canterbury, 2006

CAREER HIGHLIGHTS? Making my England debut in Sri Lanka and New Zealand in 2007/08 and playing 10 ODIs. Winning our first trophy for Durham, the FP Trophy, in 2007, and then following that up with two Championship victories in 2008 and 2009. Being asked to captain Durham in the middle of 2010

SUPERSTITIONS? A little one when I go out to bat: I always look high to my left. Not sure why, but it happens

TIP FOR THE TOP? Tom Maynard

IF YOU WEREN'T A CRICKETER? Probably selling things, which wouldn't be exciting, but it would be a job

WHEN RAIN STOPS PLAY? Playing cards, reading newspapers, every now and then the gym

FAVOURITE TV? An Idiot Abroad

DREAM HOLIDAY? Brazil

ACCOMPLISHMENTS? Bringing up my two boys

GUILTY PLEASURES? Crisps

TWITTER FEED: @colonel19

| Batting | Mat | Inns | NO | Runs | HS | Ave | SR | 100 | 50 | Ct | St |
|---|---|---|---|---|---|---|---|---|---|---|---|
| ODIs | 10 | 10 | 0 | 233 | 83 | 23.30 | 92.46 | 0 | 1 | 9 | 2 |
| T20Is | 2 | 2 | 0 | 60 | 40 | 30.00 | 162.16 | 0 | 0 | 0 | 0 |
| First-class | 132 | 201 | 24 | 5592 | 130 | 31.59 | 65.21 | 6 | 33 | 438 | 17 |
| List A | 142 | 128 | 8 | 3562 | 139* | 29.68 | | 4 | 23 | 142 | 33 |
| Twenty20 | 98 | 93 | 6 | 2214 | 88* | 25.44 | 129.54 | 0 | 12 | 46 | 23 |

| Bowling | Mat | Balls | Runs | Wkts | BBI | BBM | Ave | Econ | SR | 5w | 10 |
|---|---|---|---|---|---|---|---|---|---|---|---|
| ODIs | 10 | - | - | - | - | - | - | - | - | - | - |
| T20Is | 2 | - | - | - | - | - | - | - | - | - | - |
| First-class | 132 | - | - | - | - | - | - | - | - | - | - |
| List A | 142 | | - | - | - | - | - | - | - | - | - |
| Twenty20 | 98 | - | - | - | - | - | - | - | - | - | - |

# JIGAR NAIK

## RHB OB

FULL NAME: Jigar Kumar Hakumatrai Naik
BORN: August 10, 1984, Leicester
SQUAD NO: 22
HEIGHT: 6ft 2in
NICKNAME: Jigs, Jigsy, Jigglybits
EDUCATION: Rushey Mead School; Gateway Sixth Form College; Nottingham Trent University; Loughborough University
TEAMS: Colombo Cricket Club, Leicestershire, Leicestershire 2nd XI, Loughborough UCCE
CAREER: First-class: 2006; List A: 2003; T20: 2008

LEICESTERSHIRE

BEST BATTING: 109* Leicestershire vs Derbyshire, Leicester, 2009
BEST BOWLING: 7-96 Leicestershire vs Surrey, The Oval, 2010

CAREER HIGHLIGHTS? Getting my maiden first-class century, getting my maiden five-wicket haul (7-96), topping the national bowling averages in 2010, getting selected for the Potential England Performance Programme
CRICKETING HEROES? Claude Henderson, Erapalli Prasanna, Sachin Tendulkar
NON-CRICKETING HEROES? My father, Roger Federer and Gandhi
TIPS FOR THE TOP? Shiv Thakor, James Taylor, Nathan Buck
IF YOU WEREN'T A CRICKETER? Systems engineer
FAVOURITE TV? 24, Smallville
FAVOURITE BOOK? Robin Sharma – The Monk Who Sold His Ferrari
DREAM HOLIDAY? Maldives with my beautiful wife
ACCOMPLISHMENTS? Getting my degree and getting married
SURPRISING SKILL? I play the tabla
FANTASY SLIP CORDON? Keeper: Lee Evans (comedy value), 1st: Will Jefferson (will reach just about anything), 2nd: Superman (will get to everything so I won't have to), 3rd: Myself (can watch the likes of Jefferson and Superman take everything), Gully: Claude Henderson (so I can talk cricket whilst the other two are busy catching balls)
TWITTER FEED: @jigarnaik

| Batting | Mat | Inns | NO | Runs | HS | Ave | SR | 100 | 50 | Ct | St |
|---|---|---|---|---|---|---|---|---|---|---|---|
| First-class | 41 | 64 | 16 | 1165 | 109* | 24.27 | 39.02 | 1 | 3 | 18 | 0 |
| List A | 27 | 19 | 8 | 100 | 18 | 9.09 | | 0 | 0 | 4 | 0 |
| Twenty20 | 18 | 7 | 5 | 16 | 7* | 8.00 | 94.11 | 0 | 0 | 4 | 0 |
| Bowling | Mat | Balls | Runs | Wkts | BBI | BBM | Ave | Econ | SR | 5w | 10 |
| First-class | 41 | 5619 | 3146 | 101 | 7/96 | 8/133 | 31.14 | 3.35 | 55.6 | 3 | 0 |
| List A | 27 | 1037 | 918 | 22 | 3/21 | 3/21 | 41.72 | 5.31 | 47.1 | 0 | 0 |
| Twenty20 | 18 | 276 | 348 | 11 | 3/3 | 3/3 | 31.63 | 7.56 | 25.0 | 0 | 0 |

# DIRK NANNES

## RHB LF

FULL NAME: Dirk Peter Nannes
BORN: May 16, 1976, Mount Waverley, Melbourne, Australia
SQUAD NO: 29
HEIGHT: 6ft 2in
NICKNAME: Diggler
EDUCATION: Wesley College, Melbourne
TEAMS: Australia, Netherlands, Canterbury, Delhi Daredevils, Melbourne Renegades, Middlesex, Mountaineers, Royal Challengers Bangalore, Surrey, Victoria
CAREER: ODI: 2009; T20I: 2009; First-class: 2006; List A: 2006; T20: 2007

BEST BATTING: 31* Victoria vs South Australia, Adelaide, 2007
BEST BOWLING: 7-50 Victoria vs Queensland, Brisbane, 2008
COUNTY CAP: 2008 (Middlesex)

NOTES: A former mogul ski racer who has competed in alpine skiing World Cup competition. Started playing club cricket (for Fitzroy Doncaster, Victoria) in 1999. Made his first-class debut for Victoria in 2006 at the age of 29. Played only once for Victoria in 2006/07, having injured himself playing in England, for Netherfield CC (Northern Premier League), the previous summer. Recovered to play a key role in Victoria's T20 title win in 2007/08, and claimed 22 Pura Cup wickets at an average of 28.54 in the same season. Played for Middlesex in 2008. Returned highly unusual figures of 1-2 off 0.1 overs for Victoria against Western Australia (Sheffield Shield, November 2008) – after dismissing Shaun Marsh with his first ball, he bowled two beamers and was banned from bowling for the rest of the innings. Part of the Dutch side that beat England in the 2009 World T20, but switched allegiance to Australia after just two appearances for the Netherlands. Played for Nottinghamshire in the 2010 FP t20, and Surrey in last year's FL t20

| Batting | Mat | Inns | NO | Runs | HS | Ave | SR | 100 | 50 | Ct | St |
|---|---|---|---|---|---|---|---|---|---|---|---|
| ODIs | 1 | 1 | 0 | 1 | 1 | 1.00 | 50.00 | 0 | 0 | 0 | 0 |
| T20Is | 17 | 5 | 3 | 22 | 12* | 11.00 | 122.22 | 0 | 0 | 1 | 0 |
| First-class | 23 | 24 | 8 | 108 | 31* | 6.75 | 33.12 | 0 | 0 | 7 | 0 |
| List A | 32 | 10 | 5 | 18 | 5* | 3.60 | 40.90 | 0 | 0 | 2 | 0 |
| Twenty20 | 139 | 21 | 15 | 47 | 12* | 7.83 | 88.67 | 0 | 0 | 21 | 0 |

| Bowling | Mat | Balls | Runs | Wkts | BBI | BBM | Ave | Econ | SR | 5w | 10 |
|---|---|---|---|---|---|---|---|---|---|---|---|
| ODIs | 1 | 42 | 20 | 1 | 1/20 | 1/20 | 20.00 | 2.85 | 42.0 | 0 | 0 |
| T20Is | 17 | 366 | 459 | 28 | 4/18 | 4/18 | 16.39 | 7.52 | 13.0 | 0 | 0 |
| First-class | 23 | 4139 | 2327 | 93 | 7/50 | 11/95 | 25.02 | 3.37 | 44.5 | 2 | 1 |
| List A | 32 | 1737 | 1396 | 47 | 4/38 | 4/38 | 29.70 | 4.82 | 36.9 | 0 | 0 |
| Twenty20 | 139 | 3059 | 3664 | 175 | 5/40 | 5/40 | 20.93 | 7.18 | 17.4 | 1 | 0 |

# GRAHAM NAPIER

## RHB RFM MVP99

FULL NAME: Graham Richard Napier
BORN: January 6, 1980, Colchester, Essex
SQUAD NO: 17
HEIGHT: 5ft 10in
NICKNAME: Plank, George, Napes
EDUCATION: Gilberd School, Colchester
TEAMS: England, Central Districts, England Lions, Essex, Essex Cricket Board, Mumbai Indians, Wellington
CAREER: First-class: 1997; List A: 1997; T20: 2003

**ESSEX**

BEST BATTING: 196 Essex vs Surrey, Whitgift School, 2011
BEST BOWLING: 6-53 Essex vs Surrey, Chelmsford, 2011
COUNTY CAP: 2003; BENEFIT YEAR: 2012

CRICKET MOMENT TO FORGET? Being run out in a Lord's final
TIP FOR THE TOP? Adam Wheater
RELAXATIONS? Fly fishing in New Zealand
OTHER SPORTS PLAYED? Golf, fly fishing, tennis
FAVOURITE BAND? Elton John, Stereophonics
CAREER HIGHLIGHTS? Testing myself against the world's best and scoring some runs. Winning the FP Trophy. Scoring 152*, including 16 sixes, in a T20 match. Being included in England's World T20 squad. Playing in the IPL for Mumbai Indians
TWITTER FEED: @Graham_Napier
NOTES: Has hit 16 sixes in an innings twice, a world record. The first occasion was against Sussex in a T20 match in 2008, and he did it again in 2011, hitting 196 from 130 balls in a County Championship match vs Surrey at Whitgift School

| Batting | Mat | Inns | NO | Runs | HS | Ave | SR | 100 | 50 | Ct | St |
|---------|-----|------|----|------|----|----|----|-----|----|----|----|
| First-class | 110 | 154 | 31 | 3733 | 196 | 30.34 | | 4 | 21 | 42 | 0 |
| List A | 208 | 158 | 20 | 2523 | 79 | 18.28 | | 0 | 12 | 47 | 0 |
| Twenty20 | 76 | 57 | 7 | 786 | 152* | 15.72 | 147.19 | 1 | 0 | 21 | 0 |

| Bowling | Mat | Balls | Runs | Wkts | BBI | BBM | Ave | Econ | SR | 5w | 10 |
|---------|-----|-------|------|------|-----|-----|-----|------|----|----|----|
| First-class | 110 | 14413 | 8824 | 238 | 6/53 | | 37.07 | 3.67 | 60.5 | 5 | 0 |
| List A | 208 | 7062 | 6086 | 237 | 6/29 | 6/29 | 25.67 | 5.17 | 29.7 | 1 | 0 |
| Twenty20 | 76 | 1617 | 1984 | 96 | 4/10 | 4/10 | 20.66 | 7.36 | 16.8 | 0 | 0 |

## BRENDAN NASH                                                    LHB LM

**FULL NAME:** Brendan Paul Nash
**BORN:** December 14, 1977, Attadale, Western Australia, Australia
**SQUAD NO:** TBC
**HEIGHT:** 5ft 7in
**NICKNAME:** Bubba
**TEAMS:** West Indies, Jamaica, Queensland, West Indies A, Kent
**CAREER:** Test: 2008; ODI: 2008; First-class: 2001; List A: 2001; T20: 2008

**BEST BATTING:** 207 Jamaica vs Trinidad and Tobago, St Augustine, 2011
**BEST BOWLING:** 2-7 Jamaica vs Combined Campuses and Colleges, Kingston, 2008

**NOTES:** Signed for Kent in March and will be their overseas player for the entire season. Scored his maiden Test century against England, striking 109 in Trinidad in March 2009. Dropped from the West Indies squad last summer, despite being vice-captain. Now reunited with fellow Jamaican, Jimmy Adams, who worked as technical director at the Jamaican Cricket Association prior to taking to taking the role of coach at Kent at the start of the year. "Brendan's ability, coupled with his experience, will be of great value to the club," Adams told the BBC when the signing was announced

| Batting | Mat | Inns | NO | Runs | HS | Ave | SR | 100 | 50 | Ct | St |
|---|---|---|---|---|---|---|---|---|---|---|---|
| Tests | 21 | 33 | 0 | 1103 | 114 | 33.42 | 43.28 | 2 | 8 | 6 | 0 |
| ODIs | 9 | 7 | 3 | 104 | 39* | 26.00 | 73.75 | 0 | 0 | 1 | 0 |
| First-class | 86 | 144 | 19 | 4579 | 207 | 36.63 | | 9 | 18 | 32 | 0 |
| List A | 62 | 45 | 10 | 932 | 71 | 26.62 | | 0 | 4 | 22 | 0 |
| Twenty20 | 1 | - | - | - | - | - | - | - | - | 0 | 0 |

| Bowling | Mat | Balls | Runs | Wkts | BBI | BBM | Ave | Econ | SR | 5w | 10 |
|---|---|---|---|---|---|---|---|---|---|---|---|
| Tests | 21 | 492 | 247 | 2 | 1/21 | 1/21 | 123.50 | 3.01 | 246.0 | 0 | 0 |
| ODIs | 9 | 294 | 224 | 5 | 3/56 | 3/56 | 44.80 | 4.57 | 58.8 | 0 | 0 |
| First-class | 86 | 1268 | 580 | 17 | 2/7 | | 34.11 | 2.74 | 74.5 | 0 | 0 |
| List A | 62 | 672 | 472 | 13 | 4/20 | 4/20 | 36.30 | 4.21 | 51.6 | 0 | 0 |
| Twenty20 | 1 | 6 | 8 | 0 | - | - | - | 8.00 | - | 0 | 0 |

# CHRIS NASH

## RHB OB R2 MVP4

**FULL NAME:** Christopher David Nash
**BORN:** May 19, 1983, Cuckfield, Sussex
**SQUAD NO:** 23
**HEIGHT:** 6ft
**NICKNAME:** Nashy, Nashdog, Bill, Beaut, Knocker, Hummel
**EDUCATION:** Heron Way; Tanbridge House; Collyer's Sixth Form College; Loughborough University
**TEAMS:** England Lions, Loughborough MCCU, Otago, Sussex
**CAREER:** First-class: 2002; List A: 2006; T20: 2006

SUSSEX

**BEST BATTING:** 184 Sussex vs Leicestershire, Leicester, 2010
**BEST BOWLING:** 4-12 Sussex vs Glamorgan, Cardiff, 2010
**COUNTY CAP:** 2008

**FAMILY TIES?** Brother played 2nd XI cricket with Sussex and club cricket for Horsham
**CAREER HIGHLIGHTS?** Winning the T20 Cup in 2009, Championship wins in 2006 and 2007, Pro40 title in 2008 and 2009. England Lions debut in 2011 vs Sri Lanka A. Winning the Cockspur Cup with Horsham in 2005
**SUPERSTITIONS?** I like to be the first on the pitch when I go out to bat
**CRICKETING HEROES?** Edmund Joyce, Dr John Dew, Philip Hudson, Mark Nash, Ryan Leverton, Richard Hawkes, Luke Marshall, Les Lenham
**NON-CRICKETING HEROES?** Gus Poyet
**TIPS FOR THE TOP?** Tom Maynard, Matt Machan, Joe Gatting
**FAVOURITE TV?** Spooks
**FAVOURITE FILM?** Old School, Van Wilder, Top Gun
**FAVOURITE BOOK?** Lee Child books
**DREAM HOLIDAY?** New Zealand
**SURPRISING SKILL?** I used to play drums in a band and I was ranked in the top 10 in in England for U15 squash
**GUILTY PLEASURES?** Cookie dough ice cream, KFC chicken skin!

| Batting | Mat | Inns | NO | Runs | HS | Ave | SR | 100 | 50 | Ct | St |
|---|---|---|---|---|---|---|---|---|---|---|---|
| First-class | 94 | 162 | 11 | 5662 | 184 | 37.49 | 57.24 | 10 | 31 | 41 | 0 |
| List A | 66 | 62 | 2 | 2013 | 124* | 33.55 | 89.70 | 2 | 13 | 15 | 0 |
| Twenty20 | 76 | 70 | 11 | 1265 | 64* | 21.44 | 114.89 | 0 | 4 | 25 | 0 |

| Bowling | Mat | Balls | Runs | Wkts | BBI | BBM | Ave | Econ | SR | 5w | 10 |
|---|---|---|---|---|---|---|---|---|---|---|---|
| First-class | 94 | 2490 | 1458 | 38 | 4/12 | | 38.36 | 3.51 | 65.5 | 0 | 0 |
| List A | 66 | 747 | 684 | 24 | 4/40 | 4/40 | 28.50 | 5.49 | 31.1 | 0 | 0 |
| Twenty20 | 76 | 486 | 549 | 30 | 4/7 | 4/7 | 18.30 | 6.77 | 16.2 | 0 | 0 |

## RANA NAVED-UL-HASAN     RHB RFM W2 MVP74

DERBYSHIRE

FULL NAME: Rana Naved-ul-Hasan
BORN: February 28, 1978, Sheikhupura, Punjab, Pakistan
SQUAD NO: 24
HEIGHT: 5ft 11in
EDUCATION: Government High School, Sheikhupura
TEAMS: Pakistan, Allied Bank, Hobart Hurricanes, Lahore Badshahs, Lahore Division, Sheikhupura Cricket Association, Sialkot Cricket Association, Sussex, Tasmania, Yorkshire
CAREER: Test: 2004; ODI: 2003; T20I: 2006; First-class: 1995; List A: 1999; T20: 2005

BEST BATTING: 139 Sussex vs Middlesex, Lord's, 2005
BEST BOWLING: 7-49 Sheikhupura vs Sialkot, Muridke, 2002
COUNTY CAP: 2005 (Sussex)

CRICKET MOMENT TO FORGET? When we lost the World Cup match to Ireland
CRICKETERS PARTICULARLY ADMIRED? Brian Lara
RELAXATIONS? Music
OTHER SPORTS FOLLOWED? Hockey
NOTES: "He is a world-class bowler with vast experience and immense quality and has tremendous striking ability with the bat," Derbyshire head coach Karl Krikken explained to the BBC when the signing was announced back in February. "We wanted our second overseas player for the Friends Life t20 competition to be a game-changer and a matchwinner. Rana's performances throughout his career and in particular during the recent T20 Big Bash demonstrate that we have ticked those boxes with this signing"

| Batting | Mat | Inns | NO | Runs | HS | Ave | SR | 100 | 50 | Ct | St |
|---|---|---|---|---|---|---|---|---|---|---|---|
| Tests | 9 | 15 | 3 | 239 | 42* | 19.91 | 84.15 | 0 | 0 | 3 | 0 |
| ODIs | 74 | 51 | 18 | 524 | 33 | 15.87 | 84.51 | 0 | 0 | 16 | 0 |
| T20Is | 4 | 2 | 1 | 18 | 17* | 18.00 | 112.50 | 0 | 0 | 2 | 0 |
| First-class | 147 | 209 | 22 | 4258 | 139 | 22.77 | | 5 | 12 | 68 | 0 |
| List A | 180 | 138 | 37 | 2198 | 74 | 21.76 | | 0 | 10 | 47 | 0 |
| Twenty20 | 90 | 62 | 24 | 773 | 95 | 20.34 | 134.90 | 0 | 1 | 38 | 0 |

| Bowling | Mat | Balls | Runs | Wkts | BBI | BBM | Ave | Econ | SR | 5w | 10 |
|---|---|---|---|---|---|---|---|---|---|---|---|
| Tests | 9 | 1565 | 1044 | 18 | 3/30 | 5/93 | 58.00 | 4.00 | 86.9 | 0 | 0 |
| ODIs | 74 | 3466 | 3221 | 110 | 6/27 | 6/27 | 29.28 | 5.57 | 31.5 | 1 | 0 |
| T20Is | 4 | 85 | 101 | 5 | 3/19 | 3/19 | 20.20 | 7.12 | 17.0 | 0 | 0 |
| First-class | 147 | 27146 | 15248 | 626 | 7/49 | | 24.35 | 3.37 | 43.3 | 33 | 7 |
| List A | 180 | 8470 | 7431 | 276 | 6/27 | 6/27 | 26.92 | 5.26 | 30.6 | 3 | 0 |
| Twenty20 | 90 | 1874 | 2196 | 111 | 5/17 | 5/17 | 19.78 | 7.03 | 16.8 | 1 | 0 |

FULL NAME: Jake Needham
BORN: September 30, 1986, Portsmouth
SQUAD NO: 24
HEIGHT: 6ft 2in
NICKNAME: Snake
EDUCATION: Nottingham Bluecoat School
TEAMS: Derbyshire, England Under-19s
CAREER: First-class: 2005; List A: 2005; T20: 2007

**DERBYSHIRE**

BEST BATTING: 48 Derbyshire vs Nottinghamshire, Chesterfield, 2007
BEST BOWLING: 6-49 Derbyshire vs Leicestershire, Leicester, 2008

FAVOURITE BOOK? From Guzzler To Dazzler
CRICKETING HEROES? Mark Waugh
DREAM HOLIDAY? Rome
ACCOMPLISHMENTS? Getting my first 180 in darts
SURPRISING SKILL? I speak three languages
GUILTY PLEASURES? Jon Bon Jovi's Slippery When Wet
AMAZE ME! I play the steel drums and I'm a fully qualified will salesman
CAREER HIGHLIGHTS? Hitting Steffan Jones for six at Taunton
SUPERSTITIONS? Always keep my box in a wool sock
IF YOU WEREN'T A CRICKETER? Selling wills and cheap utilities
FAVOURITE TV? Deal Or No Deal
FAVOURITE FILM? Godfather III

| Batting | Mat | Inns | NO | Runs | HS | Ave | SR | 100 | 50 | Ct | St |
|---|---|---|---|---|---|---|---|---|---|---|---|
| First-class | 19 | 31 | 12 | 384 | 48 | 20.21 | 37.72 | 0 | 0 | 10 | 0 |
| List A | 42 | 29 | 12 | 224 | 42 | 13.17 | 72.49 | 0 | 0 | 13 | 0 |
| Twenty20 | 14 | 5 | 3 | 16 | 7* | 8.00 | 66.66 | 0 | 0 | 4 | 0 |

| Bowling | Mat | Balls | Runs | Wkts | BBI | BBM | Ave | Econ | SR | 5w | 10 |
|---|---|---|---|---|---|---|---|---|---|---|---|
| First-class | 19 | 2263 | 1268 | 35 | 6/49 | | 36.22 | 3.36 | 64.6 | 1 | 0 |
| List A | 42 | 1395 | 1208 | 26 | 3/36 | 3/36 | 46.46 | 5.19 | 53.6 | 0 | 0 |
| Twenty20 | 14 | 159 | 212 | 8 | 4/21 | 4/21 | 26.50 | 8.00 | 19.8 | 0 | 0 |

# OLIVER NEWBY

**RHB RFM**

LANCASHIRE

FULL NAME: Oliver James Newby
BORN: August 26, 1984, Blackburn, Lancashire
SQUAD NO: 8
HEIGHT: 6ft 5in
NICKNAME: Newbz, News
EDUCATION: Ribblesdale High School; Myerscough College
TEAMS: Lancashire, Lancashire Cricket Board, Nottinghamshire
CAREER: First-class: 2003; List A: 2003; T20: 2003

BEST BATTING: 38* Nottinghamshire vs Kent, Nottingham, 2004
BEST BOWLING: 5-69 Gloucestershire vs Northamptonshire, Bristol, 2008

FAMILY TIES? Father played club cricket
WHY CRICKET? Travelling the world playing sport
TIP FOR THE TOP? Jordan Clark
IF YOU WEREN'T A CRICKETER? I'd be looking for a rich widow
WHEN RAIN STOPS PLAY? Winding up Tom Smith for being bald and Glen Chapple for being old, ginger and rubbish at golf
FAVOURITE TV? Pointless
FAVOURITE FILM? Blades Of Glory
DREAM HOLIDAY? Thailand

| Batting | Mat | Inns | NO | Runs | HS | Ave | SR | 100 | 50 | Ct | St |
|---|---|---|---|---|---|---|---|---|---|---|---|
| First-class | 47 | 42 | 11 | 313 | 38* | 10.09 | 41.18 | 0 | 0 | 8 | 0 |
| List A | 24 | 15 | 8 | 73 | 35* | 10.42 | 92.40 | 0 | 0 | 3 | 0 |
| Twenty20 | 10 | 4 | 2 | 14 | 6* | 7.00 | 87.50 | 0 | 0 | 3 | 0 |

| Bowling | Mat | Balls | Runs | Wkts | BBI | BBM | Ave | Econ | SR | 5w | 10 |
|---|---|---|---|---|---|---|---|---|---|---|---|
| First-class | 47 | 5977 | 3828 | 117 | 5/69 | | 32.71 | 3.84 | 51.0 | 1 | 0 |
| List A | 24 | 846 | 905 | 21 | 4/41 | 4/41 | 43.09 | 6.41 | 40.2 | 0 | 0 |
| Twenty20 | 10 | 162 | 216 | 6 | 2/34 | 2/34 | 36.00 | 8.00 | 27.0 | 0 | 0 |

# SCOTT NEWMAN

## LHB RM R4

FULL NAME: Scott Alexander Newman
BORN: November 3, 1979, Epsom, Surrey
SQUAD NO: 23
HEIGHT: 6ft 1in
NICKNAME: Ronaldo, Newms, Dogger
EDUCATION: Trinity School, Croydon
TEAMS: Middlesex, Nottinghamshire, Surrey,
Surrey Cricket Board
CAREER: First-class: 2002; List A: 2001; T20:
2003

BEST BATTING: 219 Surrey vs Glamorgan, The Oval, 2005
COUNTY CAPS: 2005 (Surrey); 2011 (Middlesex)

FAMILY TIES? Dad and brother both played club cricket and mum loves watching
CAREER HIGHLIGHTS? My first contract which made a dream come true
SUPERSTITIONS? The way I pad up
CRICKETING HEROES? Malcolm Marshall, Viv Richards and Brian Lara
NON-CRICKETING HEROES? My family
TIPS FOR THE TOP? John Simpson, Toby Roland-Jones, Jason Roy, Brandon Newman
IF YOU WEREN'T A CRICKETER? Probably some type of trade, plumbing maybe
FAVOURITE TV? True Blood, Supernatural and any sport
FAVOURITE FILM? Most Marvel Comic films
FAVOURITE BOOK? The Bible
DREAM HOLIDAY? Vegas
GUILTY PLEASURES? Ice cream
SURPRISING FACT? I'm Anglo Indian, I have two snakes
FANTASY SLIP CORDON? Keeper: Kevin Hart, 1st: Me, 2nd: Viv Richards, 3rd: Jesus, Gully: Superman
TWITTER FEED: @scottynewms
NOTES: Will start the 2012 county season on loan at Kent

| Batting | Mat | Inns | NO | Runs | HS | Ave | SR | 100 | 50 | Ct | St |
|---|---|---|---|---|---|---|---|---|---|---|---|
| First-class | 129 | 221 | 4 | 8415 | 219 | 38.77 | 63.18 | 16 | 50 | 96 | 0 |
| List A | 106 | 104 | 5 | 2967 | 177 | 29.96 | | 4 | 17 | 25 | 0 |
| Twenty20 | 65 | 61 | 6 | 1237 | 81* | 22.49 | 107.19 | 0 | 5 | 20 | 0 |
| Bowling | Mat | Balls | Runs | Wkts | BBI | BBM | Ave | Econ | SR | 5w | 10 |
| First-class | 129 | 84 | 59 | 0 | - | - | - | 4.21 | - | 0 | 0 |
| List A | 106 | - | - | - | - | - | - | - | - | - | - |
| Twenty20 | 65 | - | - | - | - | - | - | - | - | - | - |

## ROB NEWTON · RHB LB

**FULL NAME:** Robert Irving Newton
**BORN:** January 18, 1990, Taunton, Somerset
**SQUAD NO:** 21
**HEIGHT:** 5ft 8in
**NICKNAME:** E-wok, Bomb, JJ
**EDUCATION:** Framlingham College
**TEAMS:** Northamptonshire, Northamptonshire 2nd XI
**CAREER:** First-class: 2010; List A: 2009; T20: 2010

---

BEST BATTING: 113 Northamptonshire vs Middlesex, Northampton, 2011

---

FAMILY TIES? Very few but dad likes to think he can bat a bit!
CAREER HIGHLIGHTS? Taking the new ball in a four-day game alongside David Sales
CRICKETING HEROES? Always loved watching Viv Richards bat. Ben Howgego for the same reasons as Viv
NON-CRICKETING HEROES? Tucker Max, George Best and Sergio
BEST PLAYER IN COUNTY CRICKET? Marcus Trescothick
TIP FOR THE TOP? Ben Duckett
IF YOU WEREN'T A CRICKETER? Bumming around off Ben Howgego's inheritance
WHEN RAIN STOPS PLAY? Darts, cards or a trip to the driving range. We have also invented a great chipping game around the offices at Wantage Road
FAVOURITE TV? Anything by David Attenborough
FAVOURITE FILM? Shutter Island
FAVOURITE BOOK? No Country For Old Men
DREAM HOLIDAY? Middlesbrough Revs
GUILTY PLEASURES? Mainly ale
FANTASY SLIP CORDON? Keeper: Marilyn Monroe, 1st: Myself, 2nd: Johnny Cash, 3rd: Bobby Robson, Gully: Keith Richards

| Batting | Mat | Inns | NO | Runs | HS | Ave | SR | 100 | 50 | Ct | St |
|---------|-----|------|-----|------|-----|-------|-------|-----|-----|-----|-----|
| First-class | 14 | 25 | 1 | 835 | 113 | 34.79 | 67.17 | 2 | 4 | 4 | 0 |
| List A | 14 | 13 | 0 | 324 | 66 | 24.92 | 94.18 | 0 | 1 | 1 | 0 |
| Twenty20 | 7 | 7 | 1 | 71 | 37 | 11.83 | 88.75 | 0 | 0 | 0 | 0 |

| Bowling | Mat | Balls | Runs | Wkts | BBI | BBM | Ave | Econ | SR | 5w | 10 |
|---------|-----|-------|------|------|-----|-----|-----|------|-----|-----|-----|
| First-class | 14 | 13 | 19 | 0 | - | - | - | 8.76 | - | 0 | 0 |
| List A | 14 | - | - | - | - | - | - | - | - | - | - |
| Twenty20 | 7 | - | - | - | - | - | - | - | - | - | - |

FULL NAME: Aneurin John Norman
BORN: March 22, 1991, Cardiff, Glamorgan
SQUAD NO: 37
HEIGHT: 6ft 1in
NICKNAME: Noddy, Mr Bean
EDUCATION: Millfield School
TEAMS: Glamorgan, Glamorgan 2nd XI,
Wales Minor Counties
CAREER: First-class: 2011; List A: 2011

**GLAMORGAN**

BEST BATTING: 34 Kent vs Glamorgan, Canterbury, 2011

OTHER SPORTS FOLLOWED? Football (Cardiff City)
FAVOURITE BAND? Stereophonics
RELAXATIONS? Football Manager
CRICKET MOMENTS TO FORGET? Being run out by a girl
OPINIONS ON CRICKET? One-day cricket played at weekends will attract more spectators to
support their county
TIP FOR THE TOP? Daniel Bell-Drummond
CRICKETERS PARTICULARLY ADMIRED? Alan Jones

| Batting | Mat | Inns | NO | Runs | HS | Ave | SR | 100 | 50 | Ct | St |
|---------|-----|------|----|------|-----|-------|--------|-----|----|-----|----|
| First-class | 1 | 1 | 0 | 34 | 34 | 34.00 | 41.97 | 0 | 0 | 0 | 0 |
| List A | 1 | 1 | 0 | 15 | 15 | 15.00 | 107.14 | 0 | 0 | 0 | 0 |

| Bowling | Mat | Balls | Runs | Wkts | BBI | BBM | Ave | Econ | SR | 5w | 10 |
|---------|-----|-------|------|------|-----|-----|-----|------|-----|-----|----|
| First-class | 1 | 102 | 49 | 0 | - | - | - | 2.88 | - | 0 | 0 |
| List A | 1 | 42 | 31 | 0 | - | - | - | 4.42 | - | 0 | 0 |

# MARCUS NORTH · LHB OB

GLAMORGAN

FULL NAME: Marcus James North
BORN: July 28, 1979, Pakenham, Melbourne, Australia
SQUAD NO: 12
HEIGHT: 6ft 1in
NICKNAME: Snorks
EDUCATION: Kent Street Senior High School, Perth
TEAMS: Australia, Australia A, Derbyshire, Durham, Durham Cricket Board, Gloucestershire, Hampshire, Lancashire, Western Australia
CAREER: Test: 2009; ODI: 2009; T20I: 2009; First-class: 1999; List A: 1999; T20: 2004

BEST BATTING: 239* Western Australia vs Victoria, Perth, 2006
BEST BOWLING: 6-55 Australia vs Pakistan, Lords, 2010
COUNTY CAP: 2007 (Gloucestershire)

NOTES: Made a century on Test debut for Australia against South Africa at The Wanderers in 2009. Hit two centuries in the 2009 Ashes in England. Scored 900 runs – including one century and eight fifties – in the 2008 season for Gloucestershire. Captain of Western Australia and Perth Scorchers

| Batting | Mat | Inns | NO | Runs | HS | Ave | SR | 100 | 50 | Ct | St |
|---|---|---|---|---|---|---|---|---|---|---|---|
| Tests | 21 | 35 | 2 | 1171 | 128 | 35.48 | 48.14 | 5 | 4 | 17 | 0 |
| ODIs | 2 | 2 | 0 | 6 | 5 | 3.00 | 31.57 | 0 | 0 | 1 | 0 |
| T20Is | 1 | 1 | 0 | 20 | 20 | 20.00 | 95.23 | 0 | 0 | 0 | 0 |
| First-class | 173 | 302 | 28 | 11576 | 239* | 42.24 | | 33 | 57 | 137 | 0 |
| List A | 146 | 138 | 17 | 4386 | 134* | 36.24 | | 8 | 30 | 48 | 0 |
| Twenty20 | 44 | 41 | 6 | 924 | 70 | 26.40 | 113.23 | 0 | 3 | 13 | 0 |

| Bowling | Mat | Balls | Runs | Wkts | BBI | BBM | Ave | Econ | SR | 5w | 10 |
|---|---|---|---|---|---|---|---|---|---|---|---|
| Tests | 21 | 1258 | 591 | 14 | 6/55 | 6/55 | 42.21 | 2.81 | 89.8 | 1 | 0 |
| ODIs | 2 | 18 | 16 | 0 | - | - | - | 5.33 | - | 0 | 0 |
| T20Is | 1 | - | - | - | - | - | - | - | - | - | - |
| First-class | 173 | 10503 | 5281 | 129 | 6/55 | | 40.93 | 3.01 | 81.4 | 2 | 0 |
| List A | 146 | 2528 | 2133 | 69 | 4/26 | 4/26 | 30.91 | 5.06 | 36.6 | 0 | 0 |
| Twenty20 | 44 | 404 | 503 | 8 | 2/19 | 2/19 | 62.87 | 7.47 | 50.5 | 0 | 0 |

# SAM NORTHEAST

## RHB OB

FULL NAME: Sam Alexander Northeast
BORN: October 16, 1989, Ashford, Kent
SQUAD NO: 17
HEIGHT: 5ft 11in
NICKNAME: North, Bam, Nick Knight
EDUCATION: Harrow
TEAMS: England Under-15s, England Under-19s, Harrow School, Kent, Kent 2nd XI
CAREER: First-class: 2007; List A: 2007; T20: 2010

BEST BATTING: 176 Kent vs LMCCU, Canterbury, 2011

CRICKET MOMENTS TO FORGET? Not scoring many runs in my first two appearances at Lord's in the Eton vs Harrow match
SUPERSTITIONS? Right pad on first
CRICKETERS PARTICULARLY ADMIRED? Graham Thorpe, Steve Waugh
TIP FOR THE TOP? Alex Blake
OTHER SPORTS PLAYED? Rackets, squash, cross-country running, football, rugby
OTHER SPORTS FOLLOWED? Football (Spurs), rugby (Bath)
FAVOURITE BAND? Starsailor, Snow Patrol, Florence And The Machine
RELAXATIONS? Fishing, gardening and playing rackets

| Batting | Mat | Inns | NO | Runs | HS | Ave | SR | 100 | 50 | Ct | St |
|---|---|---|---|---|---|---|---|---|---|---|---|
| First-class | 46 | 84 | 2 | 2271 | 176 | 27.69 | 51.51 | 3 | 11 | 25 | 0 |
| List A | 23 | 20 | 2 | 467 | 69 | 25.94 | 75.20 | 0 | 4 | 5 | 0 |
| Twenty20 | 19 | 13 | 6 | 163 | 39* | 23.28 | 114.78 | 0 | 0 | 6 | 0 |

| Bowling | Mat | Balls | Runs | Wkts | BBI | BBM | Ave | Econ | SR | 5w | 10 |
|---|---|---|---|---|---|---|---|---|---|---|---|
| First-class | 46 | 42 | 10 | 0 | - | - | - | 1.42 | - | 0 | 0 |
| List A | 23 | - | - | - | - | - | - | - | - | - | - |
| Twenty20 | 19 | - | - | - | - | - | - | - | - | - | - |

GLOUCESTERSHIRE

**FULL NAME:** Liam Connor Norwell
**BORN:** December 27, 1991, Bournemouth, Dorset
**SQUAD NO:** 24
**HEIGHT:** 6ft 3in
**NICKNAME:** Pasty
**EDUCATION:** Redruth School and Sixth Form
**TEAMS:** Gloucestershire, Gloucestershire 2nd XI
**CAREER:** First-class: 2011

**BEST BATTING:** 26 Gloucestershire vs Middlesex, Bristol, 2011
**BEST BOWLING:** 6-46 Gloucestershire vs Derbyshire, Bristol, 2011

**CRICKETING HEROES?** Andy Caddick, Andy Flintoff
**NON-CRICKETING HEROES?** Martin Johnson, Brett Favre
**TIPS FOR THE TOP?** Joe Root, Chris Dent, Tymal Mills
**IF YOU WEREN'T A CRICKETER?** Probably struggling at university or still working at Card Factory
**FAVOURITE TV?** One Tree Hill, The Mentalist
**FAVOURITE FILM?** Bill And Ted's Excellent Adventure
**FAVOURITE BOOK?** The Great Gatsby
**ACCOMPLISHMENTS?** Four consecutive county titles with Redruth RFC and scoring the winning try in the Redruth vs Camborne derby
**SURPRISING SKILL?** I can make a decent banana bread and various other cakes
**GUILTY PLEASURES?** Glee, and I occasionally watch Power Rangers
**AMAZE ME!** The only 'A' I got in school was on my Food Technology practical/coursework based on fruit-based desserts, I'm obsessed with American football and the NFL, one day I would like to be a history teacher
**FANTASY SLIP CORDON?** Keeper: James Corden (funny, keep spirits high on a long day), 1st: Jeremy Clarkson (keep you entertained with stories and car talk), 2nd: Me, 3rd: Richie McCaw (amazing rugby player and a great leader), Gully: Joe Montana (just a legend and one of the best quarterbacks ever)
**TWITTER FEED:** @LCNorwell24

| Batting | Mat | Inns | NO | Runs | HS | Ave | SR | 100 | 50 | Ct | St |
|---|---|---|---|---|---|---|---|---|---|---|---|
| First-class | 3 | 5 | 2 | 59 | 26 | 19.66 | 30.89 | 0 | 0 | 0 | 0 |

| Bowling | Mat | Balls | Runs | Wkts | BBI | BBM | Ave | Econ | SR | 5w | 10 |
|---|---|---|---|---|---|---|---|---|---|---|---|
| First-class | 3 | 521 | 341 | 12 | 6/46 | 7/112 | 28.41 | 3.92 | 43.4 | 1 | 0 |

# NIALL O'BRIEN

## LHB LB WK

**FULL NAME:** Niall John O'Brien
**BORN:** November 8, 1981, Dublin, Ireland
**SQUAD NO:** 81
**HEIGHT:** 5ft 9in
**NICKNAME:** Paddy, Nobby
**EDUCATION:** Marian College, Dublin
**TEAMS:** Ireland, Ireland Under-19s, Kent, Khulna Royal Bengals, Northamptonshire
**CAREER:** ODI: 2006; T20I: 2008; First-class: 2004; List A: 2003; T20: 2004

**BEST BATTING:** 176 Ireland vs UAE, Windhoek, 2005
**BEST BOWLING:** 1-4 Kent vs CUCCE, Fenner's, 2006
**COUNTY CAP:** 2011 (Northamptonshire)

**FAMILY TIES?** Dad captained Ireland and played for them 52 times and my brother Kevin currently plays with me for Ireland
**CAREER HIGHLIGHTS?** Making my Ireland debut, playing in four World Cups (two 50 overs and two T20) and gaining two Man of the Match awards vs Pakistan in Jamaica in 2007 and vs Bangladesh in T20 in 2009
**WHEN RAIN STOPS PLAY?** Making calls and doing some business for my two companies www.niallobriencricket.net and www.cricketagents.com
**ACCOMPLISHMENTS?** Turning my life around at 16 or so from going down a dark road with some dodgy people to getting my cricket career and life on the straight and narrow
**SURPRISING SKILL?** Used to sing in a band (badly)
**AMAZE ME!** I once had a trial for Rangers, I'm useless at DIY and I'm an ambassador for a charity called SUAS
**TWITTER FEED:** @niallnobiobrien

| Batting | Mat | Inns | NO | Runs | HS | Ave | SR | 100 | 50 | Ct | St |
|---|---|---|---|---|---|---|---|---|---|---|---|
| ODIs | 49 | 49 | 4 | 1198 | 72 | 26.62 | 68.06 | 0 | 8 | 38 | 7 |
| T20Is | 16 | 15 | 1 | 260 | 50 | 18.57 | 97.74 | 0 | 1 | 10 | 8 |
| First-class | 98 | 150 | 18 | 4705 | 176 | 35.64 | 59.02 | 10 | 20 | 290 | 30 |
| List A | 135 | 114 | 14 | 2949 | 121 | 29.49 | 77.30 | 1 | 20 | 117 | 31 |
| Twenty20 | 82 | 69 | 10 | 1344 | 84 | 22.77 | 115.26 | 0 | 5 | 40 | 27 |

| Bowling | Mat | Balls | Runs | Wkts | BBI | BBM | Ave | Econ | SR | 5w | 10 |
|---|---|---|---|---|---|---|---|---|---|---|---|
| ODIs | 49 | - | - | - | - | - | - | - | - | - | - |
| T20Is | 16 | - | - | - | - | - | - | - | - | - | - |
| First-class | 98 | 12 | 16 | 2 | 1/4 | 1/4 | 8.00 | 8.00 | 6.0 | 0 | 0 |
| List A | 135 | - | - | - | - | - | - | - | - | - | - |
| Twenty20 | 82 | - | - | - | - | - | - | - | - | - | - |

## MIKE O'SHEA

### RHB RMF

**FULL NAME:** Michael Paul O'Shea
**BORN:** September 4, 1987, Barry
**SQUAD NO:** 13
**HEIGHT:** 5ft 11in
**NICKNAME:** Rik, Ricky Bobbie, Kiwi
**EDUCATION:** Barry Comprehensive; Millfield School
**TEAMS:** England Under-19s, Glamorgan, Glamorgan 2nd XI, Unicorns, Wales Minor Counties
**CAREER:** First-Class: 2005; List A: 2005; T20: 2009

**BEST BATTING:** 50 Glamorgan vs Kent, Canterbury, 2009

**SUPERSTITIONS?** Left pad first
**CRICKETING HEROES?** Damien Martyn, AB de Villiers
**NON-CRICKETING HEROES?** David Beckham, my family
**TIPS FOR THE TOP?** Tom Maynard, James Harris, Adam Sylvester
**IF YOU WEREN'T A CRICKETER?** Hopefully working in a sporting capacity in some way in either coaching, sports clothing or equipment
**FAVOURITE TV?** Eastenders, TOWIE, Eastbound And Down, Celebrity Juice
**FAVOURITE FILM?** Snatch
**DREAM HOLIDAY?** Maldives
**ACCOMPLISHMENTS?** Passed two thirds of an electrician course, with one part still to complete at Access Training Wales. Worked this winter for Macron Cardiff (technical sports clothing company). Helped my father overcome throat cancer six years ago
**SURPRISING SKILL?** I am the best underwater wood welder around!
**AMAZE ME!** I got Kevin Pietersen with my first delivery in Pro40 cricket. I can't ride a bike
**FANTASY SLIP CORDON?** Keeper: David English (legend of Bunbury and some great stories), 1st: Me, 2nd: Tom Maynard (only if he has brushed his teeth though!), 3rd: Lee Evans (great comedian), Gully: Joe Calzaghe (don't think anyone would be sledging us with Joe around)
**TWITTER FEED:** @mikeoshea13

| Batting | Mat | Inns | NO | Runs | HS | Ave | SR | 100 | 50 | Ct | St |
|---|---|---|---|---|---|---|---|---|---|---|---|
| First-class | 6 | 9 | 0 | 137 | 50 | 15.22 | 45.06 | 0 | 1 | 1 | 0 |
| List A | 26 | 23 | 2 | 557 | 90 | 26.52 | 86.49 | 0 | 3 | 7 | 0 |
| Twenty20 | 4 | 3 | 0 | 23 | 11 | 7.66 | 104.54 | 0 | 0 | 1 | 0 |

| Bowling | Mat | Balls | Runs | Wkts | BBI | BBM | Ave | Econ | SR | 5w | 10 |
|---|---|---|---|---|---|---|---|---|---|---|---|
| First-class | 6 | - | - | - | - | - | - | - | - | - | - |
| List A | 26 | 488 | 491 | 10 | 2/32 | 2/32 | 49.10 | 6.03 | 48.8 | 0 | 0 |
| Twenty20 | 4 | 48 | 50 | 1 | 1/25 | 1/25 | 50.00 | 6.25 | 48.0 | 0 | 0 |

# GRAHAM ONIONS

## RHB RFM W3 MVP73

FULL NAME: Graham Onions
BORN: September 9, 1982, Gateshead
SQUAD NO: 9
HEIGHT: 6ft 2in
NICKNAME: Bunny
EDUCATION: St Thomas More RC School, Blaydon
TEAMS: England, Durham, Durham Cricket Board, Marylebone Cricket Club
CAREER: Test: 2009; ODI: 2009; First-class: 2004; List A: 2003; T20: 2004

DURHAM

---

BEST BATTING: 41 Durham vs Yorkshire, Headingley, 2007
BEST BOWLING: 8-101 Durham vs Warwickshire, Birmingham, 2007

---

CRICKET MOMENT TO FORGET? Getting out to my dad in a charity game
RELAXATIONS? Sleep, music, the pub with mates
OTHER SPORTS FOLLOWED? Football (Newcastle United)
OTHER SPORTS PLAYED? Badminton
IF YOU WEREN'T A CRICKETER? Newcastle United manager
NOTES: Durham's Young Player of the Year in 2006. Represented England Lions in 2007, and was part of England's victorious Ashes team of 2009. He was the saviour in two Tests against South Africa in December 2009, finishing not out at Cape Town and Centurion when England were nine wickets down. He missed all of the 2010 season with a stress fracture of the back, but returned in 2011, and was rewarded with a winter tour berth in 2011/12 to the UAE with the full England side

| Batting | Mat | Inns | NO | Runs | HS | Ave | SR | 100 | 50 | Ct | St |
|---|---|---|---|---|---|---|---|---|---|---|---|
| Tests | 8 | 10 | 7 | 30 | 17* | 10.00 | 30.92 | 0 | 0 | 0 | 0 |
| ODIs | 4 | 1 | 0 | 1 | 1 | 1.00 | 50.00 | 0 | 0 | 1 | 0 |
| First-class | 84 | 110 | 37 | 869 | 41 | 11.90 | 51.32 | 0 | 0 | 21 | 0 |
| List A | 62 | 24 | 7 | 112 | 19 | 6.58 | 71.33 | 0 | 0 | 9 | 0 |
| Twenty20 | 28 | 10 | 5 | 54 | 31 | 10.80 | 112.50 | 0 | 0 | 6 | 0 |

| Bowling | Mat | Balls | Runs | Wkts | BBI | BBM | Ave | Econ | SR | 5w | 10 |
|---|---|---|---|---|---|---|---|---|---|---|---|
| Tests | 8 | 1429 | 869 | 28 | 5/38 | 7/102 | 31.03 | 3.64 | 51.0 | 1 | 0 |
| ODIs | 4 | 204 | 185 | 4 | 2/58 | 2/58 | 46.25 | 5.44 | 51.0 | 0 | 0 |
| First-class | 84 | 14081 | 8492 | 287 | 8/101 | | 29.58 | 3.61 | 49.0 | 11 | 0 |
| List A | 62 | 2575 | 2225 | 68 | 3/39 | 3/39 | 32.72 | 5.18 | 37.8 | 0 | 0 |
| Twenty20 | 28 | 564 | 631 | 21 | 3/25 | 3/25 | 30.04 | 6.71 | 26.8 | 0 | 0 |

## WILL OWEN

**RHB RMF**

**FULL NAME:** William Thomas Owen
**BORN:** September 2, 1988, St Asaph, Flintshire
**SQUAD NO:** 34
**HEIGHT:** 6ft
**NICKNAME:** Swillo
**EDUCATION:** Prestatyn High School
**TEAMS:** Glamorgan, Glamorgan 2nd XI, Wales Minor Counties
**CAREER:** First-class: 2007; List A: 2010; T20: 2010

**BEST BATTING:** 69 Glamorgan vs Derbyshire, Derby, 2011
**BEST BOWLING:** 5-124 Glamorgan vs Middlesex, Cardiff, 2011

**CAREER HIGHLIGHTS?** Five-wicket haul on one-day debut against the Unicorns. Maiden first-class 50 against Derby in 2011
**CRICKETING HEROES?** Simon Jones, being a Welsh lad growing up watching the 2005 Ashes series
**BEST PLAYER IN COUNTY CRICKET?** Marcus Trescothick is a prize scalp
**TIP FOR THE TOP?** Andrew Salter
**IF YOU WEREN'T A CRICKETER?** Policeman
**WHEN RAIN STOPS PLAY?** On the pool table in our dressing room – the time flies by!
**FAVOURITE TV?** Eastbound And Down
**FAVOURITE FILM?** Cool Runnings
**FAVOURITE BOOK?** Anything by Robert G Barrett
**DREAM HOLIDAY?** Barbados on a beach
**SURPRISING SKILL?** Pro at FIFA
**GUILTY PLEASURES?** Chocolate cookies
**FANTASY SLIP CORDON?** Keeper: Will Bragg, 1st: Ricky Gervais, 2nd: Michael McIntyre, Gully: Darren Hughes
**TWITTER FEED:** @swill88

| Batting | Mat | Inns | NO | Runs | HS | Ave | SR | 100 | 50 | Ct | St |
|---|---|---|---|---|---|---|---|---|---|---|---|
| First-class | 13 | 15 | 5 | 205 | 69 | 20.50 | 71.92 | 0 | 1 | 1 | 0 |
| List A | 17 | 8 | 3 | 38 | 12 | 7.60 | 76.00 | 0 | 0 | 2 | 0 |
| Twenty20 | 10 | 1 | 0 | 8 | 8 | 8.00 | 114.28 | 0 | 0 | 0 | 0 |

| Bowling | Mat | Balls | Runs | Wkts | BBI | BBM | Ave | Econ | SR | 5w | 10 |
|---|---|---|---|---|---|---|---|---|---|---|---|
| First-class | 13 | 1748 | 1310 | 33 | 5/124 | 6/61 | 39.69 | 4.49 | 52.9 | 1 | 0 |
| List A | 17 | 534 | 553 | 28 | 5/49 | 5/49 | 19.75 | 6.21 | 19.0 | 1 | 0 |
| Twenty20 | 10 | 153 | 218 | 7 | 3/21 | 3/21 | 31.14 | 8.54 | 21.8 | 0 | 0 |

# TONY PALLADINO

## RHB RMF W1

**FULL NAME:** Antonio Paul Palladino
**BORN:** June 29, 1983, London
**SQUAD NO:** 28
**HEIGHT:** 6ft
**NICKNAME:** Dino, Italian Stallion
**EDUCATION:** Holy Family Primary School; Cardinal Pole Secondary School; Anglia Polytechnic University
**TEAMS:** Namibia, British Universities, Cambridge MCCU, Derbyshire, Essex, Essex 2nd XI, Essex Cricket Board
**CAREER:** First-class: 2003; List A: 2003; T20: 2005

**DERBYSHIRE**

---

**BEST BATTING:** 66 Essex vs Durham, Chelmsford, 2010
**BEST BOWLING:** 6-41 Essex vs Kent, Canterbury, 2003

---

**CAREER HIGHLIGHTS?** Bowler of the tournament in the Stanbic T20 in Zimbabwe 2010, two 2nd XI hundreds, 52 first-class wickets with Derbyshire in 2011, Derbyshire County Championship Player of the Year for 2011
**SUPERSTITIONS?** Wear watch on left wrist, sweatband on right wrist and wear black socks
**CRICKETING HEROES?** Ian Botham and my dad
**NON-CRICKETING HEROES?** Curt Schilling, Dustin Pedroia and Pedro Martinez (baseball)
**BEST PLAYER IN COUNTY CRICKET?** Marcus Trescothick
**TIPS FOR THE TOP?** Ross Whiteley, Adam Wheater
**IF YOU WEREN'T A CRICKETER?** Coaching cricket or something to do with marketing
**WHEN RAIN STOPS PLAY?** Play on the iPhone, go to the gym, drink coffee, crosswords
**FAVOURITE TV?** The Office and Phoenix Nights
**FAVOURITE FILM?** The Shawshank Redemption, Goodfellas or Casino
**FAVOURITE BOOK?** Juiced, Game Of Shadows, Metro 2033
**DREAM HOLIDAY?** Las Vegas
**ACCOMPLISHMENTS?** A few 180s in darts and trapping Chris Wright with aces
**SURPRISING SKILL?** I have a geek-like knowledge of baseball
**TWITTER FEED:** @APalladino28

| Batting | Mat | Inns | NO | Runs | HS | Ave | SR | 100 | 50 | Ct | St |
|---|---|---|---|---|---|---|---|---|---|---|---|
| First-class | 66 | 88 | 23 | 861 | 66 | 13.24 | 43.81 | 0 | 3 | 25 | 0 |
| List A | 40 | 22 | 4 | 153 | 31 | 8.50 | 78.86 | 0 | 0 | 4 | 0 |
| Twenty20 | 16 | 5 | 3 | 21 | 8* | 10.50 | 87.50 | 0 | 0 | 2 | 0 |

| Bowling | Mat | Balls | Runs | Wkts | BBI | BBM | Ave | Econ | SR | 5w | 10 |
|---|---|---|---|---|---|---|---|---|---|---|---|
| First-class | 66 | 9836 | 5373 | 169 | 6/41 | | 31.79 | 3.27 | 58.2 | 5 | 0 |
| List A | 40 | 1488 | 1348 | 39 | 4/32 | 4/32 | 34.56 | 5.43 | 38.1 | 0 | 0 |
| Twenty20 | 16 | 287 | 347 | 22 | 4/21 | 4/21 | 15.77 | 7.25 | 13.0 | 0 | 0 |

SUSSEX

**FULL NAME:** Mudhsuden Singh Panesar
**BORN:** April 25, 1982, Luton, Bedfordshire
**SQUAD NO:** 7
**HEIGHT:** 6ft 1in
**EDUCATION:** Bedford Modern School; Stopsley High School, Luton, Bedfordshire; Loughborough University
**TEAMS:** England, British Universities, England Lions, England Under-19s, Lions, Loughborough MCCU, Marylebone Cricket Club, Northamptonshire, Sussex
**CAREER:** Test: 2006; ODI: 2007; T20I: 2007; First-class: 2001; List A: 2002; T20: 2006

**BEST BATTING:** 46* Sussex vs Middlesex, Hove, 2010
**BEST BOWLING:** 7-181 Northamptonshire vs Essex, Chelmsford, 2005
**COUNTY CAPS:** 2006 (Northamptonshire); 2010 (Sussex)

**FAMILY TIES?** Father used to play cricket
**CAREER HIGHLIGHTS?** Playing for England
**CRICKETERS PARTICULARLY ADMIRED?** Sachin Tendulkar
**OTHER SPORTS FOLLOWED?** Football (Luton Town, Arsenal)
**RELAXATIONS?** Reading
**NOTES:** His first Test wicket was Sachin Tendulkar. Claimed a five-wicket haul (and eight wickets in all) in his first Ashes Test, at Perth in 2006. Helped secure an improbable draw in the first Ashes Test at Cardiff in 2009, batting with James Anderson for 37 minutes to deny Australia. Moved to Sussex after 10 years at Northamptonshire ahead of the 2010 season. Took 14 wickets in two matches against Pakistan in the UAE on his return to England's Test side in January

| Batting | Mat | Inns | NO | Runs | HS | Ave | SR | 100 | 50 | Ct | St |
|---|---|---|---|---|---|---|---|---|---|---|---|
| Tests | 41 | 55 | 19 | 195 | 26 | 5.41 | 29.86 | 0 | 0 | 9 | 0 |
| ODIs | 26 | 8 | 3 | 26 | 13 | 5.20 | 28.57 | 0 | 0 | 3 | 0 |
| T20Is | 1 | 1 | 0 | 1 | 1 | 1.00 | 50.00 | 0 | 0 | 0 | 0 |
| First-class | 152 | 196 | 64 | 1162 | 46* | 8.80 | 32.76 | 0 | 0 | 32 | 0 |
| List A | 79 | 27 | 12 | 136 | 17* | 9.06 | 56.66 | 0 | 0 | 13 | 0 |
| Twenty20 | 31 | 7 | 2 | 7 | 3* | 1.40 | 46.66 | 0 | 0 | 3 | 0 |

| Bowling | Mat | Balls | Runs | Wkts | BBI | BBM | Ave | Econ | SR | 5w | 10 |
|---|---|---|---|---|---|---|---|---|---|---|---|
| Tests | 41 | 9888 | 4633 | 140 | 6/37 | 10/187 | 33.09 | 2.81 | 70.6 | 10 | 1 |
| ODIs | 26 | 1308 | 980 | 24 | 3/25 | 3/25 | 40.83 | 4.49 | 54.5 | 0 | 0 |
| T20Is | 1 | 24 | 40 | 2 | 2/40 | 2/40 | 20.00 | 10.00 | 12.0 | 0 | 0 |
| First-class | 152 | 34881 | 16094 | 516 | 7/181 | | 31.18 | 2.76 | 67.5 | 27 | 3 |
| List A | 79 | 3497 | 2700 | 78 | 5/20 | 5/20 | 34.61 | 4.63 | 44.8 | 1 | 0 |
| Twenty20 | 31 | 618 | 758 | 27 | 3/14 | 3/14 | 28.07 | 7.35 | 22.8 | 0 | 0 |

# MATTHEW PARDOE                                    LHB LM

FULL NAME: Matthew Graham Pardoe
BORN: January 5, 1991, Stourbridge, Worcestershire
SQUAD NO: 19
HEIGHT: 6ft 1in
NICKNAME: Pards
EDUCATION: Haybridge High School and Sixth Form College
TEAMS: Worcestershire, Worcestershire 2nd XI
CAREER: First-class: 2011; List A: 2011

BEST BATTING: 74 Worcestershire vs Nottinghamshire, Nottingham, 2011

FAMILY TIES? My dad and brother both play the game
CAREER HIGHLIGHTS? My first-class and List A debuts, scoring 74 vs Nottinghamshire and being part of the Worcestershire team that maintained Division One status
SUPERSTITIONS? Sometimes, but they change all the time
CRICKETING HEROES? Graeme Hick, Matthew Hayden and Marcus Trescothick
NON-CRICKETING HEROES? Rafael Nadal, Tiger Woods and Michael Jackson to name a few
BEST PLAYER IN COUNTY CRICKET? Marcus Trescothick
TIPS FOR THE TOP? Ben Stokes and James Taylor
IF YOU WEREN'T A CRICKETER? I'd be a Geography teacher or work on the family farm
WHEN RAIN STOPS PLAY? Snoozing, eating and chatting
FAVOURITE TV? Dr Who
FAVOURITE FILM? Gladiator
FAVOURITE BOOK? A Brief History Of Time by Stephen Hawking
DREAM HOLIDAY? The Caribbean
ACCOMPLISHMENTS? County swimming, and dancing at a national competition in Blackpool
SURPRISING SKILL? Ballroom dancing
GUILTY PLEASURES? Michael Buble and sweets
AMAZE ME! I have seen every episode of Dr Who that has ever been shown
FANTASY SLIP CORDON? Keeper: Brian Cox, 1st: Stephen Fry, 2nd: Myself, 3rd: Michael McIntyre, Gully: Michael Jackson

| Batting | Mat | Inns | NO | Runs | HS | Ave | SR | 100 | 50 | Ct | St |
|---|---|---|---|---|---|---|---|---|---|---|---|
| First-class | 13 | 26 | 0 | 507 | 74 | 19.50 | 37.41 | 0 | 4 | 3 | 0 |
| List A | 1 | 1 | 0 | 11 | 11 | 11.00 | 55.00 | 0 | 0 | 1 | 0 |

| Bowling | Mat | Balls | Runs | Wkts | BBI | BBM | Ave | Econ | SR | 5w | 10 |
|---|---|---|---|---|---|---|---|---|---|---|---|
| First-class | 13 | - | - | - | - | - | - | - | - | - | - |
| List A | 1 | - | - | - | - | - | - | - | - | - | - |

## GARRY PARK

**RHB RMF WK R1**

FULL NAME: Garry Terence Park
BORN: April 19, 1983, Empangeni, South Africa
SQUAD NO: 9
HEIGHT: 5ft 6in
EDUCATION: Eshowe High School; Anglia Ruskin University
TEAMS: Cambridge MCCU, Derbyshire, Durham, Durham 2nd XI
CAREER: First-class: 2003; List A: 2005; T20: 2007

BEST BATTING: 178* Derbyshire vs Kent, Derby, 2009
BEST BOWLING: 3-25 Derbyshire vs Surrey, Derby, 2009

FAMILY TIES? My brother Sean Park plays for the Unicorns and Cambridgeshire
WHY CRICKET? Regular trips to watch professional cricket as a kid allowed me to choose my career very early, then a little bit of luck and the rest is history!
CAREER HIGHLIGHTS? My century at Headingley against Yorkshire to keep Durham in Division One, and scoring 1,000 runs in my first season for Derbyshire
SUPERSTITIONS? Always put my left pad on first
CRICKETING HEROES? Ricky Ponting, Jonty Rhodes
NON-CRICKETING HEROES? Tiger Woods, Lance Armstrong
BEST PLAYER IN COUNTY CRICKET? Marcus Trescothick, Darren Stevens
TIPS FOR THE TOP? Scott Borthwick and James Taylor
IF YOU WEREN'T A CRICKETER? Ideally fishing every day, realistically I don't know
WHEN RAIN STOPS PLAY? YouTube, gym
FAVOURITE TV? Two And A Half Men, Takeshi's Castle, Scrubs
FAVOURITE FILM? The Lion King
DREAM HOLIDAY? Los Rogues in Venezuela
FANTASY SLIP CORDON? Keeper: Fearne Cotton, 1st: Keith Lemon, 2nd: Holly Willoughby, 3rd: Rufus Hound

| Batting | Mat | Inns | NO | Runs | HS | Ave | SR | 100 | 50 | Ct | St |
|---|---|---|---|---|---|---|---|---|---|---|---|
| First-class | 47 | 79 | 10 | 2354 | 178* | 34.11 | 46.43 | 4 | 14 | 43 | 0 |
| List A | 47 | 41 | 10 | 730 | 64 | 23.54 | 63.36 | 0 | 1 | 20 | 0 |
| Twenty20 | 47 | 36 | 9 | 707 | 66 | 26.18 | 108.43 | 0 | 4 | 11 | 0 |

| Bowling | Mat | Balls | Runs | Wkts | BBI | BBM | Ave | Econ | SR | 5w | 10 |
|---|---|---|---|---|---|---|---|---|---|---|---|
| First-class | 47 | 1458 | 974 | 18 | 3/25 | 3/25 | 54.11 | 4.00 | 81.0 | 0 | 0 |
| List A | 47 | 646 | 613 | 10 | 2/21 | 2/21 | 61.30 | 5.69 | 64.6 | 0 | 0 |
| Twenty20 | 47 | 336 | 428 | 19 | 3/11 | 3/11 | 22.52 | 7.64 | 17.6 | 0 | 0 |

FULL NAME: Stephen David Parry
BORN: January 12, 1986, Manchester
SQUAD NO: 4
HEIGHT: 6ft
NICKNAME: Pazza
EDUCATION: Audenshaw High School, Greater Manchester
TEAMS: Cumberland, England Lions, Lancashire, Lancashire 2nd XI
CAREER: First-class: 2007; List A: 2009; T20: 2009

**LANCASHIRE**

BEST BATTING: 2 Lancashire vs Durham, Manchester, 2009
BEST BOWLING: 5-23 Lancashire vs Durham MCCU, Durham University, 2007

CAREER HIGHLIGHTS? Playing for Lancashire and England Lions
CRICKETING HEROES? Shane Warne
NON-CRICKETING HEROES? Muhammad Ali
BEST PLAYER IN COUNTY CRICKET? Marcus Trescothick
TIP FOR THE TOP? Jos Buttler
IF YOU WEREN'T A CRICKETER? Fishing or travelling the world
WHEN RAIN STOPS PLAY? Relaxing or working on my game
FAVOURITE TV? Sky Sports News
FAVOURITE FILM? The Hangover, Man On Fire
DREAM HOLIDAY? Barbados
ACCOMPLISHMENTS? Running a marathon
SURPRISING SKILL? Elite table tennis player
GUILTY PLEASURES? San Carlo for a meal and a bottle of Sancerre white wine
TWITTER FEED? @sdparry86

| Batting | Mat | Inns | NO | Runs | HS | Ave | SR | 100 | 50 | Ct | St |
|---|---|---|---|---|---|---|---|---|---|---|---|
| First-class | 3 | 2 | 0 | 3 | 2 | 1.50 | 10.34 | 0 | 0 | 1 | 0 |
| List A | 34 | 15 | 5 | 117 | 31 | 11.70 | 72.67 | 0 | 0 | 7 | 0 |
| Twenty20 | 43 | 13 | 7 | 52 | 11 | 8.66 | 106.12 | 0 | 0 | 7 | 0 |

| Bowling | Mat | Balls | Runs | Wkts | BBI | BBM | Ave | Econ | SR | 5w | 10 |
|---|---|---|---|---|---|---|---|---|---|---|---|
| First-class | 3 | 523 | 256 | 9 | 5/23 | 5/46 | 28.44 | 2.93 | 58.1 | 1 | 0 |
| List A | 34 | 1438 | 1191 | 40 | 3/40 | 3/40 | 29.77 | 4.96 | 35.9 | 0 | 0 |
| Twenty20 | 43 | 960 | 1074 | 53 | 4/23 | 4/23 | 20.26 | 6.71 | 18.1 | 0 | 0 |

WARWICKSHIRE

FULL NAME: Jeetan Shashi Patel
BORN: May 7, 1980, Wellington, New Zealand
SQUAD NO: 5
TEAMS: New Zealand, Warwickshire,
Wellington
CAREER: Test: 2006; ODI: 2005; T20I: 2005;
First-class: 2000; List A: 1999; T20: 2005

BEST BATTING: 120 Warwickshire vs Yorkshire, Birmingham, 2009
BEST BOWLING: 6-32 Wellington vs Otago, Queenstown, 2005

NOTES: Took 5-145 on debut for Wellington against Auckland in 1999/00. Made New Zealand
Test debut in Cape Town against South Africa in April 2006 and took 3-117 in 42 overs,
dismissing Graeme Smith, Boeta Dippenaar and AB de Villiers. Took Test-best figures of
5-110 against West Indies in Napier in 2008. Overseas player with Warwickshire in 2009 and
2011

| Batting | Mat | Inns | NO | Runs | HS | Ave | SR | 100 | 50 | Ct | St |
|---|---|---|---|---|---|---|---|---|---|---|---|
| Tests | 13 | 18 | 3 | 188 | 27* | 12.53 | 44.33 | 0 | 0 | 8 | 0 |
| ODIs | 39 | 13 | 7 | 88 | 34 | 14.66 | 58.66 | 0 | 0 | 12 | 0 |
| T20Is | 11 | 4 | 1 | 9 | 5 | 3.00 | 64.28 | 0 | 0 | 4 | 0 |
| First-class | 111 | 138 | 39 | 2025 | 120 | 20.45 | | 1 | 9 | 43 | 0 |
| List A | 120 | 63 | 22 | 409 | 34 | 9.97 | | 0 | 0 | 38 | 0 |
| Twenty20 | 71 | 24 | 7 | 76 | 12 | 4.47 | 97.43 | 0 | 0 | 21 | 0 |

| Bowling | Mat | Balls | Runs | Wkts | BBI | BBM | Ave | Econ | SR | 5w | 10 |
|---|---|---|---|---|---|---|---|---|---|---|---|
| Tests | 13 | 3552 | 1936 | 40 | 5/110 | 6/151 | 48.40 | 3.27 | 88.8 | 1 | 0 |
| ODIs | 39 | 1804 | 1513 | 42 | 3/11 | 3/11 | 36.02 | 5.03 | 42.9 | 0 | 0 |
| T20Is | 11 | 199 | 269 | 16 | 3/20 | 3/20 | 16.81 | 8.11 | 12.4 | 0 | 0 |
| First-class | 111 | 21788 | 10732 | 260 | 6/32 | | 41.27 | 2.95 | 83.8 | 8 | 1 |
| List A | 120 | 5749 | 4491 | 120 | 4/16 | 4/16 | 37.42 | 4.68 | 47.9 | 0 | 0 |
| Twenty20 | 71 | 1384 | 1710 | 74 | 4/27 | 4/27 | 23.10 | 7.41 | 18.7 | 0 | 0 |

FULL NAME: Ravi Hasmukh Patel
BORN: August 4, 1991, Harrow, Middlesex
SQUAD NO: 36
EDUCATION: Merchant Taylors' School,
Northwood; Loughborough University
TEAMS: Loughborough MCCU, Middlesex,
Middlesex 2nd XI
CAREER: First-class: 2010; List A: 2010

MIDDLESEX

BEST BATTING: 19* Middlesex vs OMCCU, The Parks, 2010
BEST BOWLING: 3-25 LMCCU vs Leicestershire, Leicester, 2011

NOTES: Studying a degree in Economics at Loughborough University. Made his first-class
debut for Middlesex against Oxford MCCU in 2010 and made his List A debut against the
touring Australians in the same season, returning figures of 0-38 in a five-over spell. Played
three first-class matches in 2011 for Loughborough MCCU against Northamptonshire,
Leicestershire and Kent, taking seven wickets in total – including a second innings haul of
3-25 at Grace Road

| Batting | Mat | Inns | NO | Runs | HS | Ave | SR | 100 | 50 | Ct | St |
|---|---|---|---|---|---|---|---|---|---|---|---|
| First-class | 4 | 6 | 3 | 42 | 19* | 14.00 | 34.71 | 0 | 0 | 0 | 0 |
| List A | 1 | - | - | - | - | - | - | - | - | 0 | 0 |

| Bowling | Mat | Balls | Runs | Wkts | BBI | BBM | Ave | Econ | SR | 5w | 10 |
|---|---|---|---|---|---|---|---|---|---|---|---|
| First-class | 4 | 688 | 368 | 12 | 3/25 | 5/134 | 30.66 | 3.20 | 57.3 | 0 | 0 |
| List A | 1 | 30 | 38 | 0 | - | - | - | 7.60 | - | 0 | 0 |

## SAMIT PATEL

### RHB SLA R1 MVP6

NOTTINGHAMSHIRE

FULL NAME: Samit Rohit Patel
BORN: November 30, 1984, Leicester
SQUAD NO: 21
HEIGHT: 5ft 8in
NICKNAME: Pilchy
EDUCATION: Worksop College
TEAMS: England, England Lions, England Under-19s, Nottinghamshire
CAREER: ODI: 2008; T20I: 2011; First-class: 2002; List A: 2002; T20: 2003

BEST BATTING: 176 Nottinghamshire vs Gloucestershire, Bristol, 2007
BEST BOWLING: 7-68 Nottinghamshire vs Hampshire, Southampton, 2011
COUNTY CAP: 2008

CRICKET MOMENT TO FORGET? Playing at Headingley in the T20 Cup against Yorkshire, when I got hit for 28 in an over by Michael Lumb
CRICKETERS PARTICULARLY ADMIRED? Sachin Tendulkar, Brian Lara
OTHER SPORTS FOLLOWED? Football (Nottingham Forest)
NOTES: Represented England at U15, U17 and U19 levels. Test Match Special Young Cricketer of the Year award in 2000 for performances in the U15 World Cup. Made Nottinghamshire 2nd XI debut at the age of 14

| Batting | Mat | Inns | NO | Runs | HS | Ave | SR | 100 | 50 | Ct | St |
|---|---|---|---|---|---|---|---|---|---|---|---|
| ODIs | 25 | 15 | 4 | 340 | 70* | 30.90 | 91.15 | 0 | 1 | 7 | 0 |
| T20Is | 8 | 7 | 1 | 77 | 25* | 12.83 | 101.31 | 0 | 0 | 0 | 0 |
| First-class | 92 | 145 | 10 | 5550 | 176 | 41.11 | 64.41 | 13 | 31 | 50 | 0 |
| List A | 143 | 121 | 20 | 3229 | 114 | 31.97 | 82.26 | 2 | 17 | 38 | 0 |
| Twenty20 | 93 | 87 | 14 | 1826 | 84* | 25.01 | 123.29 | 0 | 11 | 23 | 0 |

| Bowling | Mat | Balls | Runs | Wkts | BBI | BBM | Ave | Econ | SR | 5w | 10 |
|---|---|---|---|---|---|---|---|---|---|---|---|
| ODIs | 25 | 905 | 839 | 23 | 5/41 | 5/41 | 36.47 | 5.56 | 39.3 | 1 | 0 |
| T20Is | 8 | 144 | 168 | 5 | 2/22 | 2/22 | 33.60 | 7.00 | 28.8 | 0 | 0 |
| First-class | 92 | 9742 | 4949 | 131 | 7/68 | | 37.77 | 3.04 | 74.3 | 3 | 1 |
| List A | 143 | 4323 | 3780 | 131 | 6/13 | 6/13 | 28.85 | 5.24 | 33.0 | 2 | 0 |
| Twenty20 | 93 | 1561 | 1866 | 69 | 3/11 | 3/11 | 27.04 | 7.17 | 22.6 | 0 | 0 |

# STEVEN PATTERSON

## RHB RMF

FULL NAME: Steven Andrew Patterson
BORN: October 3, 1983, Beverley Westwood Hospital, Beverley, Humberside
SQUAD NO: 17
HEIGHT: 6ft 4in
NICKNAME: Dead
EDUCATION: Malet Lambert School; St Mary's Sixth Form College; Leeds University
TEAMS: Yorkshire, Yorkshire 2nd XI, Yorkshire Cricket Board
CAREER: First-class: 2005; List A: 2003; T20: 2009

YORKSHIRE

BEST BATTING: 53 Yorkshire vs Sussex, Hove, 2011
BEST BOWLING: 5-50 Yorkshire vs Essex, Scarborough, 2010

CAREER HIGHLIGHTS? First five-fer vs Essex at Scarborough, 2010
TIPS FOR THE TOP? Jonny Bairstow and Joe Root
FAVOURITE FILM? The Shawshank Redemption
DREAM HOLIDAY? Skiing in the Alps
GUILTY PLEASURES? Chocolate
CRICKETING HEROES? Glenn McGrath, Allan Donald
FAVOURITE BAND? Coldplay

| Batting | Mat | Inns | NO | Runs | HS | Ave | SR | 100 | 50 | Ct | St |
|---|---|---|---|---|---|---|---|---|---|---|---|
| First-class | 40 | 49 | 15 | 480 | 53 | 14.11 | 30.74 | 0 | 1 | 10 | 0 |
| List A | 45 | 15 | 13 | 83 | 25* | 41.50 | | | 0 | 0 | 5 | 0 |
| Twenty20 | 20 | 4 | 3 | 3 | 3* | 3.00 | 42.85 | 0 | 0 | 3 | 0 |

| Bowling | Mat | Balls | Runs | Wkts | BBI | BBM | Ave | Econ | SR | 5w | 10 |
|---|---|---|---|---|---|---|---|---|---|---|---|
| First-class | 40 | 5932 | 3157 | 88 | 5/50 | 7/69 | 35.87 | 3.19 | 67.4 | 1 | 0 |
| List A | 45 | 1917 | 1637 | 56 | 6/32 | 6/32 | 29.23 | 5.12 | 34.2 | 1 | 0 |
| Twenty20 | 20 | 429 | 653 | 17 | 4/30 | 4/30 | 38.41 | 9.13 | 25.2 | 0 | 0 |

## DARREN PATTINSON · RHB RFM

**NOTTINGHAMSHIRE**

FULL NAME: Darren John Pattinson
BORN: August 2, 1979, Grimsby, Lincolnshire
SQUAD NO: 14
HEIGHT: 6ft 2in
NICKNAME: Les
TEAMS: England, England Lions, Nottinghamshire, Victoria
CAREER: Test: 2008; First-class: 2007; List A: 2006; T20: 2007

BEST BATTING: 59 Nottinghamshire vs Durham, Chester-le-Street, 2009
BEST BOWLING: 8-35 Victoria vs Western Australia, Perth, 2010
COUNTY CAP: 2008

FAMILY TIES? Brother James plays for Australia
CAREER HIGHLIGHTS? Winning the Championship with Notts
CRICKETING HEROES? Ian Botham
BEST PLAYER IN COUNTY CRICKET? Marcus Trescothick
TIP FOR THE TOP? Michael Robson
IF YOU WEREN'T A CRICKETER? Greyhound trainer
WHEN RAIN STOPS PLAY? Reading the form guide
FAVOURITE TV? True Blood
FAVOURITE FILM? The Waterboy
FAVOURITE BOOK? To Kill A Mockingbird
DREAM HOLIDAY? Greece
ACCOMPLISHMENTS? My two daughters
AMAZE ME! I had my toe shortened

| Batting | Mat | Inns | NO | Runs | HS | Ave | SR | 100 | 50 | Ct | St |
|---|---|---|---|---|---|---|---|---|---|---|---|
| Tests | 1 | 2 | 0 | 21 | 13 | 10.50 | 42.00 | 0 | 0 | 0 | 0 |
| First-class | 62 | 75 | 16 | 763 | 59 | 12.93 | 42.84 | 0 | 1 | 7 | 0 |
| List A | 53 | 19 | 8 | 78 | 13* | 7.09 | 62.90 | 0 | 0 | 15 | 0 |
| Twenty20 | 48 | 11 | 7 | 32 | 12* | 8.00 | 94.11 | 0 | 0 | 13 | 0 |

| Bowling | Mat | Balls | Runs | Wkts | BBI | BBM | Ave | Econ | SR | 5w | 10 |
|---|---|---|---|---|---|---|---|---|---|---|---|
| Tests | 1 | 181 | 96 | 2 | 2/95 | 2/96 | 48.00 | 3.18 | 90.5 | 0 | 0 |
| First-class | 62 | 9840 | 5642 | 171 | 8/35 | 9/97 | 32.99 | 3.44 | 57.5 | 8 | 0 |
| List A | 53 | 2055 | 1825 | 68 | 4/29 | 4/29 | 26.83 | 5.32 | 30.2 | 0 | 0 |
| Twenty20 | 48 | 904 | 1172 | 58 | 5/25 | 5/25 | 20.20 | 7.77 | 15.5 | 1 | 0 |

# DAVID PAYNE

FULL NAME: David Alan Payne
BORN: February 15, 1991, Poole, Dorset
SQUAD NO: 14
HEIGHT: 6ft 2in
NICKNAME: Sid, Payney
EDUCATION: Lytchett Minster Secondary and Sixth Form
TEAMS: Dorset, England Under-19s, Gloucestershire, Gloucestershire 2nd XI
CAREER: First-class: 2011; List A: 2009; T20: 2010

**GLOUCESTERSHIRE**

BEST BATTING: 62 Gloucestershire vs Glamorgan, Bristol, 2011
BEST BOWLING: 6-26 Gloucestershire vs Leicestershire, Bristol, 2011

CAREER HIGHLIGHTS? Record one-day figures for the club of 7-29 against Essex, and first-class debut
BEST PLAYER IN COUNTY CRICKET? Marcus Trescothick
IF YOU WEREN'T A CRICKETER? University
FAVOURITE FILM? Superbad
DREAM HOLIDAY? California
ACCOMPLISHMENTS? Being on AFC Bournemouth's Academy
FANTASY SLIP CORDON? Keeper: Lee Evans, 1st: Mila Kunis, 2nd: Me, 3rd: David Beckham, Gully: Pixie Lott
TWITTER FEED: @sidpayne7

| Batting | Mat | Inns | NO | Runs | HS | Ave | SR | 100 | 50 | Ct | St |
|---|---|---|---|---|---|---|---|---|---|---|---|
| First-class | 14 | 21 | 6 | 255 | 62 | 17.00 | 41.12 | 0 | 1 | 5 | 0 |
| List A | 19 | 9 | 7 | 28 | 13 | 14.00 | 62.22 | 0 | 0 | 4 | 0 |
| Twenty20 | 13 | 6 | 2 | 14 | 10 | 3.50 | 87.50 | 0 | 0 | 0 | 0 |

| Bowling | Mat | Balls | Runs | Wkts | BBI | BBM | Ave | Econ | SR | 5w | 10 |
|---|---|---|---|---|---|---|---|---|---|---|---|
| First-class | 14 | 2072 | 1298 | 42 | 6/26 | 9/96 | 30.90 | 3.75 | 49.3 | 2 | 0 |
| List A | 19 | 732 | 695 | 35 | 7/29 | 7/29 | 19.85 | 5.69 | 20.9 | 1 | 0 |
| Twenty20 | 13 | 222 | 302 | 18 | 3/20 | 3/20 | 16.77 | 8.16 | 12.3 | 0 | 0 |

NORTHAMPTONSHIRE

FULL NAME: Stephen David Peters
BORN: December 10, 1978, Harold Wood, Essex
SQUAD NO: 11
HEIGHT: 5ft 11in
NICKNAME: Pedro, Geezer
EDUCATION: Coopers' Coborn Company School
TEAMS: Essex, Marylebone Cricket Club, Worcestershire
CAREER: First-class: 1996; List A: 1996; T20: 2003

BEST BATTING: 222 Northamptonshire vs Glamorgan, Swansea, 2011
BEST BOWLING: 1-19 Essex vs OUCCE, Chelmsford, 1999
COUNTY CAPS: 2002 (Worcestershire); 2007 (Northamptonshire)

FAMILY TIES? Dad played local club cricket for Upminster
CAREER HIGHLIGHTS? Scoring a double hundred, anytime I make a hundred, anytime the team wins, the 1998 Benson and Hedges Cup final with Essex and winning the U19 World Cup in 1998
SUPERSTITIONS? Loads! More habits really, like how I put my kit on before I bat
NON-CRICKETING HEROES? Paolo Di Canio. Any winner of a golf Major Championship
TIP FOR THE TOP? Rob Newton. If he goes on a diet!
IF YOU WEREN'T A CRICKETER? Would like to be a corporate account manager
WHEN RAIN STOPS PLAY? Papers, gym, fingers in pies!
FAVOURITE TV? Golf followed by Match Of The Day
FAVOURITE FILM? JFK and A Few Good Men
FAVOURITE BOOK? I love Lonely Planet books and magazines
GUILTY PLEASURES? Chocolate and lots of it. McDonald's when I'm hungover
AMAZE ME! I've got five race horses, an Aston Martin and a yacht in Cannes
FANTASY SLIP CORDON? Keeper: Natalie Imbruglia, 1st: Cheryl Cole, 2nd: Kate Beckinsale, 3rd: Stephen Peters, Gully: Lucy Verasamy

| Batting | Mat | Inns | NO | Runs | HS | Ave | SR | 100 | 50 | Ct | St |
|---|---|---|---|---|---|---|---|---|---|---|---|
| First-class | 210 | 357 | 28 | 11610 | 222 | 35.28 | | 27 | 56 | 169 | 0 |
| List A | 169 | 156 | 10 | 3284 | 107 | 22.49 | | 2 | 20 | 45 | 0 |
| Twenty20 | 24 | 20 | 3 | 300 | 61* | 17.64 | 98.36 | 0 | 1 | 7 | 0 |

| Bowling | Mat | Balls | Runs | Wkts | BBI | BBM | Ave | Econ | SR | 5w | 10 |
|---|---|---|---|---|---|---|---|---|---|---|---|
| First-class | 210 | 35 | 31 | 1 | 1/19 | | 31.00 | 5.31 | 35.0 | 0 | 0 |
| List A | 169 | - | - | - | - | - | - | - | - | - | - |
| Twenty20 | 24 | | | | | | | | | | |

**FULL NAME:** Alviro Nathan Petersen
**BORN:** November 25, 1980, Port Elizabeth,
South Africa
**SQUAD NO:** 73
**NICKNAME:** Viro
**TEAMS:** South Africa, Glamorgan, Lions,
North West, Northerns, Titans, Essex
**CAREER:** Test: 2010; ODI: 2006; T20I: 2010;
First-class: 2000; List A: 2000; T20: 2004

ESSEX

**BEST BATTING:** 210 Glamorgan vs Surrey, The Oval, 2011
**BEST BOWLING:** 2-7 Northerns vs Easterns, Benoni, 2002

**NOTES:** South African Test opening batsman who captained Glamorgan last season. Made his debut for Northerns in 2001. Came through the South African system, making his ODI debut in 2006 against Zimbabwe and hitting 80 in his second appearance. Made his Test debut in February 2010 against India at Kolkata and hit a century (100) in his first innings, becoming only the third South African to make a hundred on Test debut. After a spell out of the side, he returned to make a second Test hundred vs Sri Lanka (109) at Cape Town in January 2012. Was installed as Graeme Smith's opening partner in the March 2012 Test series in New Zealand. Will appear for Essex during the first half of the 2012 season up until June 10

| Batting | Mat | Inns | NO | Runs | HS | Ave | SR | 100 | 50 | Ct | St |
|---|---|---|---|---|---|---|---|---|---|---|---|
| Tests | 11 | 21 | 1 | 718 | 109 | 35.90 | 53.78 | 2 | 3 | 6 | 0 |
| ODIs | 17 | 15 | 1 | 437 | 80 | 31.21 | 83.23 | 0 | 4 | 3 | 0 |
| T20Is | 2 | 2 | 0 | 14 | 8 | 7.00 | 73.68 | 0 | 0 | 1 | 0 |
| First-class | 133 | 240 | 13 | 9049 | 210 | 39.86 | | 26 | 39 | 101 | 0 |
| List A | 143 | 138 | 10 | 4408 | 145* | 34.43 | | 7 | 26 | 50 | 0 |
| Twenty20 | 65 | 60 | 9 | 1561 | 84* | 30.60 | 123.01 | 0 | 13 | 35 | 0 |

| Bowling | Mat | Balls | Runs | Wkts | BBI | BBM | Ave | Econ | SR | 5w | 10 |
|---|---|---|---|---|---|---|---|---|---|---|---|
| Tests | 11 | 72 | 36 | 1 | 1/2 | 1/2 | 36.00 | 3.00 | 72.0 | 0 | 0 |
| ODIs | 17 | 6 | 7 | 0 | - | - | - | 7.00 | - | 0 | 0 |
| T20Is | 2 | - | - | - | - | - | - | - | - | - | - |
| First-class | 133 | 1070 | 552 | 11 | 2/7 | | 50.18 | 3.09 | 97.2 | 0 | 0 |
| List A | 143 | 323 | 289 | 6 | 2/48 | 2/48 | 48.16 | 5.36 | 53.8 | 0 | 0 |
| Twenty20 | 65 | 151 | 169 | 7 | 1/5 | 1/5 | 24.14 | 6.71 | 21.5 | 0 | 0 |

## MARK PETTINI

### RHB RM R1

ESSEX

FULL NAME: Mark Lewis Pettini
BORN: August 7, 1983, Brighton, Sussex
SQUAD NO: 24
HEIGHT: 5ft 11in
NICKNAME: Swampy
EDUCATION: Hills Road Sixth Form College;
Cardiff University
TEAMS: England Under-19s, Essex,
Mountaineers
CAREER: First-class: 2001; List A: 2001; T20:
2003

BEST BATTING: 208 Essex vs Derbyshire, Chelmsford, 2006
COUNTY CAP: 2006

CRICKETERS PARTICULARLY ADMIRED? Graham Gooch, Andy Flower, Ronnie Irani
TIPS FOR THE TOP? Adam Wheater, Tom Westley
OTHER SPORTS PLAYED? Darts
OTHER SPORTS FOLLOWED? Football (Liverpool)
FAVOURITE BAND? The White Stripes, Foo Fighters, Editors
RELAXATIONS? Fishing, surfing, travelling, music
CAREER HIGHLIGHTS? Winning two Pro40 titles with Essex, being made Essex captain in
2007, and winning the FP Trophy in 2008
NOTES: Represented England U19 in 2002. Was Essex 2nd XI Player of the Year 2002.
Represented British Universities in 2003 and 2004. Stood as Essex captain from 2007 season
until handing over to James Foster in June 2010. Later that month he signed a contract
extension with Essex until the end of the 2012 season

| Batting | Mat | Inns | NO | Runs | HS | Ave | SR | 100 | 50 | Ct | St |
|---|---|---|---|---|---|---|---|---|---|---|---|
| First-class | 104 | 177 | 23 | 5083 | 208* | 33.00 | 47.27 | 5 | 30 | 73 | 0 |
| List A | 126 | 115 | 9 | 2930 | 144 | 27.64 | 85.37 | 5 | 19 | 49 | 0 |
| Twenty20 | 75 | 71 | 5 | 1715 | 87 | 25.98 | 128.08 | 0 | 11 | 28 | 0 |

| Bowling | Mat | Balls | Runs | Wkts | BBI | BBM | Ave | Econ | SR | 5w | 10 |
|---|---|---|---|---|---|---|---|---|---|---|---|
| First-class | 104 | 113 | 191 | 0 | - | - | - | 10.14 | - | 0 | 0 |
| List A | 126 | - | - | - | - | - | - | - | - | - | - |
| Twenty20 | 75 | - | - | - | - | - | - | - | - | - | - |

# VERNON PHILANDER

## RHB RFM

**FULL NAME:** Vernon Darryl Philander
**BORN:** June 24, 1985, Bellville, South Africa
**SQUAD NO:** TBC
**NICKNAME:** Pro, V-Dawg
**TEAMS:** South Africa, Cape Cobras, Devon, Middlesex, South Africa A, South Africa Under-19s, Western Province, Western Province Boland, Western Province Under-19s
**CAREER:** Test: 2011; ODI: 2007; T20I: 2007; First-class: 2004; List A: 2004; T20: 2005

**BEST BATTING:** 168 Western Province vs Griqualand West, Kimberley, 2004
**BEST BOWLING:** 7-61 Cape Cobras vs Knights, Newlands, 2012

**NOTES:** Played for Devon in 2004, appearing in two C&G Trophy matches, including a famous win over Leicestershire. In the 2006/07 South African season he averaged 72 with the bat and 30 with the ball in one-day cricket for the Cape Cobras. Took 35 wickets at an average of 16.11 in first-class cricket during the 2010/11 South African season. Claimed the Man of the Match award on Test debut, taking 8-78 against Australia, including a second-innings haul of 5-15. Has taken four wickets or more in seven of his 12 innings as a Test bowler

| Batting | Mat | Inns | NO | Runs | HS | Ave | SR | 100 | 50 | Ct | St |
|---|---|---|---|---|---|---|---|---|---|---|---|
| Tests | 5 | 5 | 0 | 53 | 23 | 10.60 | 30.11 | 0 | 0 | 2 | 0 |
| ODIs | 8 | 6 | 3 | 75 | 23 | 25.00 | 85.22 | 0 | 0 | 2 | 0 |
| T20Is | 7 | 4 | 0 | 14 | 6 | 3.50 | 50.00 | 0 | 0 | 1 | 0 |
| First-class | 76 | 103 | 15 | 2339 | 168 | 26.57 | 46.97 | 2 | 6 | 20 | 0 |
| List A | 95 | 69 | 22 | 1182 | 79* | 25.14 | 74.38 | 0 | 4 | 7 | 0 |
| Twenty20 | 63 | 45 | 26 | 576 | 56* | 30.31 | 132.41 | 0 | 1 | 17 | 0 |

| Bowling | Mat | Balls | Runs | Wkts | BBI | BBM | Ave | Econ | SR | 5w | 10 |
|---|---|---|---|---|---|---|---|---|---|---|---|
| Tests | 5 | 937 | 498 | 35 | 5/15 | 10/102 | 14.22 | 3.18 | 26.7 | 4 | 1 |
| ODIs | 8 | 311 | 248 | 7 | 4/12 | 4/12 | 35.42 | 4.78 | 44.4 | 0 | 0 |
| T20Is | 7 | 83 | 114 | 4 | 2/23 | 2/23 | 28.50 | 8.24 | 20.7 | 0 | 0 |
| First-class | 76 | 13178 | 5693 | 297 | 7/61 | | 19.16 | 2.59 | 44.3 | 13 | 1 |
| List A | 95 | 3965 | 3147 | 89 | 4/12 | 4/12 | 35.35 | 4.76 | 44.5 | 0 | 0 |
| Twenty20 | 63 | 979 | 1331 | 44 | 5/17 | 5/17 | 30.25 | 8.15 | 22.2 | 1 | 0 |

## BEN PHILLIPS     RHB RMF

FULL NAME: Ben James Phillips
BORN: September 30, 1974, Lewisham, London
SQUAD NO: 13
HEIGHT: 6ft 6in
NICKNAME: Bennyphil, Bus
EDUCATION: Langley Park School, Beckenham
TEAMS: Kent, Northamptonshire, Somerset
CAREER: First-class: 1996; List A: 1996; T20: 2003

BEST BATTING: 100* Kent vs Lancashire, Manchester, 1997
BEST BOWLING: 6-29 Northamptonshire vs CUCCE, Fenner's, 2006
COUNTY CAP: 2005 (Northamptonshire)

FAMILY TIES? Father and brother are both keen club cricketers for Hayes CC
SUPERSTITIONS? Arrive at the ground early – hate rushing!
RELAXATIONS? Enjoy swimming, watching a good movie, and just generally spending time with family and friends
OTHER SPORTS FOLLOWED? Football (West Ham), rugby (Northampton Saints)
CRICKETERS PARTICULARLY ADMIRED? Glenn McGrath, Jason Gillespie
NOTES: Set the Langley Park School record for the fastest half-century, off 11 balls. Represented England U19 Schools 1993/94

| Batting | Mat | Inns | NO | Runs | HS | Ave | SR | 100 | 50 | Ct | St |
|---|---|---|---|---|---|---|---|---|---|---|---|
| First-class | 109 | 151 | 27 | 2652 | 100* | 21.38 | | 1 | 15 | 32 | 0 |
| List A | 137 | 85 | 29 | 1042 | 51* | 18.60 | | 0 | 1 | 37 | 0 |
| Twenty20 | 63 | 39 | 11 | 438 | 41* | 15.64 | 134.35 | 0 | 0 | 19 | 0 |

| Bowling | Mat | Balls | Runs | Wkts | BBI | BBM | Ave | Econ | SR | 5w | 10 |
|---|---|---|---|---|---|---|---|---|---|---|---|
| First-class | 109 | 15049 | 7260 | 238 | 6/29 | | 30.50 | 2.89 | 63.2 | 5 | 0 |
| List A | 137 | 5556 | 4623 | 153 | 4/25 | 4/25 | 30.21 | 4.99 | 36.3 | 0 | 0 |
| Twenty20 | 63 | 1281 | 1723 | 62 | 4/18 | 4/18 | 27.79 | 8.07 | 20.6 | 0 | 0 |

# TIM PHILLIPS
## LHB SLA

FULL NAME: Timothy James Phillips
BORN: March 13, 1981, Cambridge
SQUAD NO: 23
HEIGHT: 6ft 1in
NICKNAME: Pips
EDUCATION: Felsted School; Durham University
TEAMS: Durham MCCU, England Under-19s, Essex, Essex 2nd XI, Essex Cricket Board
CAREER: First-class: 1999; List A: 1999; T20: 2006

ESSEX

BEST BATTING: 89 Essex vs Worcestershire, Worcester, 2005
BEST BOWLING: 5-41 Essex vs Derbyshire, Chelmsford, 2006
COUNTY CAP: 2006

FAMILY TIES? Father played in the Manchester leagues and then some serious village cricket, brother Nick represented Essex to U16 level
CAREER HIGHLIGHTS? Representing England U19 at the U19 World Cup in 2000, earning my 1st XI cap at Essex in 2006, winning one-day trophies with Essex
CRICKETING HEROES? Brian Lara and Graham Thorpe for batting, Phil Tufnell and Daniel Vettori for bowling
NON-CRICKETING HEROES? Michael Johnson for his unique and amazing technique. And Jack White (The White Stripes) – singer guitar player!
TIPS FOR THE TOP? A couple of young Essex players – Adam Wheater and Reece Topley
WHEN RAIN STOPS PLAY? Normally playing some cards, and consequently making Ryan ten Doeschate coffee all day long
FAVOURITE BOOK? The Catcher In The Rye – JD Salinger
ACCOMPLISHMENTS? Completing a degree at Durham University
FANTASY SLIP CORDON? Keeper: Jack White, 1st: Rory McIlroy, 2nd: Myself, 3rd: Steve Buscemi, Gully: Thierry Henry
TWITTER FEED: @timphillips23

| Batting | Mat | Inns | NO | Runs | HS | Ave | SR | 100 | 50 | Ct | St |
|---|---|---|---|---|---|---|---|---|---|---|---|
| First-class | 71 | 101 | 15 | 1709 | 89 | 19.87 | | 0 | 6 | 47 | 0 |
| List A | 60 | 32 | 13 | 343 | 58* | 18.05 | | 0 | 1 | 19 | 0 |
| Twenty20 | 48 | 25 | 11 | 239 | 57* | 17.07 | 123.19 | 0 | 1 | 22 | 0 |

| Bowling | Mat | Balls | Runs | Wkts | BBI | BBM | Ave | Econ | SR | 5w | 10 |
|---|---|---|---|---|---|---|---|---|---|---|---|
| First-class | 71 | 9482 | 5703 | 121 | 5/41 | | 47.13 | 3.60 | 78.3 | 1 | 0 |
| List A | 60 | 1889 | 1595 | 69 | 5/28 | 5/28 | 23.11 | 5.06 | 27.3 | 3 | 0 |
| Twenty20 | 48 | 717 | 901 | 42 | 4/22 | 4/22 | 21.45 | 7.53 | 17.0 | 0 | 0 |

KENT

FULL NAME: Christopher Damien Piesley
BORN: March 12, 1992, Chatham, Kent
SQUAD NO: 32
HEIGHT: 5ft 11in
NICKNAME: Pies, Pilo, Porky
EDUCATION: Fulston Manor School, Sittingbourne
TEAMS: Kent, Kent 2nd XI, Kent Under-13s, Kent Under-14s, Kent Under-15s, Kent Under-17s
CAREER: First-class: 2010; List A: 2011

---

BEST BATTING: 43 Kent vs Pakistanis, Canterbury, 2010

---

CRICKETING HEROES? Brian Lara and my dad
NON-CRICKETING HEROES? Roger Federer and Ronnie O'Sullivan
BEST PLAYER IN COUNTY CRICKET? Marcus Trescothick
TIP FOR THE TOP? Shaun Piesley
WHEN RAIN STOPS PLAY? iPad or reading the newspaper (The Sun), starting at the back
FAVOURITE BAND? Sunshine Band
FAVOURITE FILM? The Lion King
QUOTE TO LIVE BY? "Hakuna Matata"
TWITTER FEED: @Cpiesley32

| Batting | Mat | Inns | NO | Runs | HS | Ave | SR | 100 | 50 | Ct | St |
|---------|-----|------|----|------|-----|-------|-------|-----|----|----|----|
| First-class | 3 | 5 | 0 | 69 | 43 | 13.80 | 52.27 | 0 | 0 | 0 | 0 |
| List A | 1 | 1 | 0 | 4 | 4 | 4.00 | 40.00 | 0 | 0 | 0 | 0 |

| Bowling | Mat | Balls | Runs | Wkts | BBI | BBM | Ave | Econ | SR | 5w | 10 |
|---------|-----|-------|------|------|-----|-----|-----|------|----|----|----|
| First-class | 3 | - | - | - | - | - | - | - | - | - | - |
| List A | 1 | - | - | - | - | - | - | - | - | - | - |

# KEVIN PIETERSEN RHB OB R3

**FULL NAME:** Kevin Peter Pietersen
**BORN:** June 27, 1980, Pietermaritzburg
**SQUAD NO:** 24
**HEIGHT:** 6ft 4in
**NICKNAME:** KP, Kelves, Kapes, Kev
**EDUCATION:** Maritzburg College; University of SA
**TEAMS:** England, Deccan Chargers, Dolphins, Hampshire, ICC World XI, KwaZulu-Natal, Natal, Nottinghamshire, Royal Challengers Bangalore, Surrey
**CAREER:** Test: 2005; ODI: 2004; T20I: 2005; First-class: 1997; List A: 1999; T20: 2003

BEST BATTING: 254* Nottinghamshire vs Middlesex, Nottingham, 2002
BEST BOWLING: 4-31 Nottinghamshire vs DUCCE, Nottinghham, 2003
COUNTY CAPS: 2002 (Nottinghamshire); 2005 (Hampshire)

SUPERSTITIONS? Left pad first
CRICKETERS PARTICULARLY ADMIRED? Shaun Pollock, Errol Stewart
OTHER SPORTS PLAYED? Golf, swimming, running
OTHER SPORTS FOLLOWED? Formula One, rugby (Natal Sharks)
NOTES: Began his career as a bowling allrounder. Left South Africa for England in 2000. Scored three centuries in only his second ODI series, against South Africa in 2004. Reached 1,000 ODI runs in just 21 innings – equalling Viv Richards' record. Second innings 158 at The Oval helped secure the 2005 Ashes for England. Made more runs in his first 25 Tests than anyone except Don Bradman. Ill-fated stint as England captain (2008-2009) ended in the sacking of then coach Peter Moores. Averages 52.71 in 17 Ashes Tests

| Batting | Mat | Inns | NO | Runs | HS | Ave | SR | 100 | 50 | Ct | St |
|---|---|---|---|---|---|---|---|---|---|---|---|
| Tests | 81 | 139 | 7 | 6428 | 227 | 48.69 | 62.24 | 19 | 25 | 50 | 0 |
| ODIs | 127 | 116 | 16 | 4184 | 130 | 41.84 | 86.76 | 9 | 23 | 39 | 0 |
| T20Is | 36 | 36 | 5 | 1176 | 79 | 37.93 | 141.51 | 0 | 7 | 14 | 0 |
| First-class | 178 | 291 | 19 | 13208 | 254* | 48.55 | | 41 | 56 | 135 | 0 |
| List A | 240 | 220 | 33 | 7783 | 147 | 41.62 | | 15 | 44 | 83 | 0 |
| Twenty20 | 67 | 66 | 8 | 1931 | 79 | 33.29 | 138.22 | 0 | 11 | 25 | 0 |

| Bowling | Mat | Balls | Runs | Wkts | BBI | BBM | Ave | Econ | SR | 5w | 10 |
|---|---|---|---|---|---|---|---|---|---|---|---|
| Tests | 81 | 1089 | 731 | 5 | 1/0 | 1/10 | 146.20 | 4.02 | 217.8 | 0 | 0 |
| ODIs | 127 | 400 | 370 | 7 | 2/22 | 2/22 | 52.85 | 5.55 | 57.1 | 0 | 0 |
| T20Is | 36 | 30 | 53 | 1 | 1/27 | 1/27 | 53.00 | 10.60 | 30.0 | 0 | 0 |
| First-class | 178 | 6055 | 3517 | 65 | 4/31 | | 54.10 | 3.48 | 93.1 | 0 | 0 |
| List A | 240 | 2390 | 2122 | 41 | 3/14 | 3/14 | 51.75 | 5.32 | 58.2 | 0 | 0 |
| Twenty20 | 67 | 324 | 425 | 17 | 3/33 | 3/33 | 25.00 | 7.87 | 19.0 | 0 | 0 |

# NEIL PINNER

## RHB OB

**WORCESTERSHIRE**

FULL NAME: Neil Douglas Pinner
BORN: September 28, 1990, Wordsley, Stourbridge, Worcestershire
SQUAD NO: 20
HEIGHT: 6ft
NICKNAME: Pins, Besty
EDUCATION: RGS Worcester
TEAMS: Worcestershire, Worcestershire 2nd XI
CAREER: First-class: 2011; List A: 2011

BEST BATTING: 0 Worcestershire vs Nottinghamshire, Worcester, 2011

**CAREER HIGHLIGHTS?** Selection for England U15, one-day and first-class debuts for Worcestershire in the 2011 season
**SUPERSTITIONS?** I tap the boundary rope or line with my bat on the way out to the middle
**CRICKETING HEROES?** I used to love watching Michael Vaughan bat when he was in form, but my biggest hero would be Graeme Hick. I spent a lot of time watching him bat at New Road when I was growing up
**TIPS FOR THE TOP?** Ben Stokes, James Taylor, Aneesh Kapil
**WHEN RAIN STOPS PLAY?** I spend a lot of time listening to music or trying very hard to complete The Sun crossword! I also enjoy a game of Stickman Golf against other members of the squad
**FAVOURITE FILM?** Anchorman
**DREAM HOLIDAY?** I'd love to tour America one day
**ACCOMPLISHMENTS?** 100 per cent completion of Call of Duty: MW3 (I had a lot of spare time whilst I was in Adelaide this winter)
**GUILTY PLEASURES?** I enjoy a good sing-along when I'm fairly sure no one can hear me
**AMAZE ME!** 1. I'm not Matt Pardoe (might be a surprise to some of my teammates) 2. I attended the Darren Lehmann Cricket Academy in Adelaide in 2009/10 3. I have currently won more first-class games than I have scored first-class runs (one win, zero runs)
**TWITTER FEED:** @Neil_Pinner

| Batting | Mat | Inns | NO | Runs | HS | Ave | SR | 100 | 50 | Ct | St |
|---|---|---|---|---|---|---|---|---|---|---|---|
| First-class | 1 | 1 | 0 | 0 | 0 | 0.00 | 0.00 | 0 | 0 | 1 | 0 |
| List A | 9 | 9 | 0 | 122 | 37 | 13.55 | 72.61 | 0 | 0 | 2 | 0 |

| Bowling | Mat | Balls | Runs | Wkts | BBI | BBM | Ave | Econ | SR | 5w | 10 |
|---|---|---|---|---|---|---|---|---|---|---|---|
| First-class | 1 | - | - | - | - | - | - | - | - | - | - |
| List A | 9 | 18 | 20 | 0 | - | - | - | 6.66 | - | 0 | 0 |

# STEFFAN PIOLET

**RHB RMF**

**FULL NAME:** Steffan Andreas Piolet
**BORN:** August 8, 1988, Redhill, Surrey
**SQUAD NO:** 14
**HEIGHT:** 6ft 1in
**NICKNAME:** Squiff, Piles
**EDUCATION:** Warden Park School; Central Sussex College
**TEAMS:** Sussex 2nd XI, Warwickshire, Worcestershire 2nd XI
**CAREER:** First-class: 2009; List A: 2009; T20; 2009

---

**BEST BATTING:** 26* Warwickshire vs DUCCE, Durham University, 2009
**BEST BOWLING:** 6-17 Warwickshire vs DUCCE, Durham University, 2009

---

**CAREER HIGHLIGHTS?** Winning one-day trophies with Warwickshire, scoring hundreds in 2nd XI
**SUPERSTITIONS?** They vary
**CRICKETING HEROES?** Jacques Kallis
**NON-CRICKETING HEROES?** Dave Grohl, Glenn Hoddle
**TIP FOR THE TOP?** Ateeq Javid
**IF YOU WEREN'T A CRICKETER?** I'd be selling something!
**FAVOURITE TV?** Entourage
**FAVOURITE FILM?** Gran Torino, Old School
**FAVOURITE BOOK?** Lance Armstrong's autobiography
**SURPRISING SKILL?** I can copy any accent in the world easily!
**GUILTY PLEASURES?** Dancing, even though I'm terrible at it
**AMAZE ME!** I'm half Norwegian, my birthday was 8/8/88, I was born at 8am and weighed eight pounds, I can't stand chewing gum
**FANTASY SLIP CORDON?** Keeper: Dave Grohl, 1st: Rafael van der Vaart, 2nd: Chris Metters, 3rd: Me, Gully: Pixie Lott
**TWITTER FEED:** @spiolet14

| Batting | Mat | Inns | NO | Runs | HS | Ave | SR | 100 | 50 | Ct | St |
|---|---|---|---|---|---|---|---|---|---|---|---|
| First-class | 3 | 5 | 1 | 47 | 26* | 11.75 | 39.49 | 0 | 0 | 3 | 0 |
| List A | 19 | 6 | 2 | 56 | 39 | 14.00 | 86.15 | 0 | 0 | 5 | 0 |
| Twenty20 | 33 | 10 | 3 | 67 | 21 | 9.57 | 88.15 | 0 | 0 | 10 | 0 |

| Bowling | Mat | Balls | Runs | Wkts | BBI | BBM | Ave | Econ | SR | 5w | 10 |
|---|---|---|---|---|---|---|---|---|---|---|---|
| First-class | 3 | 342 | 182 | 13 | 6/17 | 10/43 | 14.00 | 3.19 | 26.3 | 1 | 1 |
| List A | 19 | 569 | 541 | 18 | 3/34 | 3/34 | 30.05 | 5.70 | 31.6 | 0 | 0 |
| Twenty20 | 33 | 666 | 746 | 35 | 3/25 | 3/25 | 21.31 | 6.72 | 19.0 | 0 | 0 |

**DURHAM**

FULL NAME: Liam Edward Plunkett
BORN: April 6, 1985, Middlesbrough
SQUAD NO: 20
HEIGHT: 6ft 3in
NICKNAME: Pudsy
EDUCATION: Nunthorpe Comprehensive
TEAMS: England, Dolphins, Durham, Durham Cricket Board, England Lions, England Under-19s
CAREER: Test: 2005; ODI: 2005; T20I: 2006; First-class: 2003; List A: 2003; T20: 2003

BEST BATTING: 107* Durham vs DMCCU, Durham University, 2011
BEST BOWLING: 6-63 Durham vs Worcestershire, Chester-le-Street, 2009

CAREER HIGHLIGHTS? England debut
CRICKETING HEROES? Glenn McGrath
OTHER SPORTS PLAYED? Swimming, golf
OTHER SPORTS FOLLOWED? Football (Middlesbrough, Arsenal)
NOTES: Became only the second player to record a five-wicket haul on his Championship debut for Durham, 5-53 vs Yorkshire at Headingley, 2003. Represented England U19 that same year, and received the NBC Denis Compton Award for the most promising young Durham player in 2003 and 2005. He made his senior Test debut in November 2005 vs Pakistan at Lahore and his home Test debut in 2006 against Sri Lanka at Lord's

| Batting | Mat | Inns | NO | Runs | HS | Ave | SR | 100 | 50 | Ct | St |
|---|---|---|---|---|---|---|---|---|---|---|---|
| Tests | 9 | 13 | 2 | 126 | 44* | 11.45 | 39.62 | 0 | 0 | 3 | 0 |
| ODIs | 29 | 25 | 10 | 315 | 56 | 21.00 | 83.33 | 0 | 1 | 7 | 0 |
| T20Is | 1 | - | - | - | - | - | - | - | - | 0 | 0 |
| First-class | 106 | 144 | 28 | 2621 | 107* | 22.59 | | 1 | 12 | 64 | 0 |
| List A | 113 | 76 | 27 | 927 | 72 | 18.91 | 90.26 | 0 | 2 | 24 | 0 |
| Twenty20 | 54 | 30 | 13 | 302 | 41 | 17.76 | 125.83 | 0 | 0 | 12 | 0 |

| Bowling | Mat | Balls | Runs | Wkts | BBI | BBM | Ave | Econ | SR | 5w | 10 |
|---|---|---|---|---|---|---|---|---|---|---|---|
| Tests | 9 | 1538 | 916 | 23 | 3/17 | 6/60 | 39.82 | 3.57 | 66.8 | 0 | 0 |
| ODIs | 29 | 1363 | 1321 | 39 | 3/24 | 3/24 | 33.87 | 5.81 | 34.9 | 0 | 0 |
| T20Is | 1 | 24 | 37 | 1 | 1/37 | 1/37 | 37.00 | 9.25 | 24.0 | 0 | 0 |
| First-class | 106 | 16743 | 10123 | 321 | 6/63 | | 31.53 | 3.62 | 52.1 | 8 | 1 |
| List A | 113 | 4716 | 4237 | 132 | 4/15 | 4/15 | 32.09 | 5.39 | 35.7 | 0 | 0 |
| Twenty20 | 54 | 926 | 1212 | 42 | 5/31 | 5/31 | 28.85 | 7.85 | 22.0 | 1 | 0 |

FULL NAME: William Thomas Stuart Porterfield
BORN: September 6, 1984, Londonderry
SQUAD NO: 10
HEIGHT: 5ft 11in
NICKNAME: Purdy, Porty
EDUCATION: Strabane Grammar School; Leeds Metropolitan University
TEAMS: Ireland, Gloucestershire, Marylebone Cricket Club, Warwickshire
CAREER: ODI: 2006; T20I: 2008; First-class: 2006; List A; 2006; T20: 2008

WARWICKSHIRE

BEST BATTING: 175 Gloucestershire vs Worcestershire, Cheltenham, 2010
BEST BOWLING: 1-29 Ireland vs Jamaica, Spanish Town, 2010

CAREER HIGHLIGHTS? Playing in the World Cup, captaining Ireland
SUPERSTITIONS? None
BEST PLAYER IN COUNTY CRICKET? Marcus Trescothick
TIP FOR THE TOP? Paul Stirling
IF YOU WEREN'T A CRICKETER? Maybe a farmer
WHEN RAIN STOPS PLAY? Anything that kills a bit of time
FAVOURITE TV? Two And A Half Men
FAVOURITE FILM? The Guard
DREAM HOLIDAY? Anywhere laid back
GUILTY PLEASURES? A few pints
FANTASY SLIP CORDON? Keeper: Frankie Boyle, 1st: Jimmy Carr, 2nd: John Bishop, 3rd: Kerry Katona
TWITTER FEED: @purdy34

| Batting | Mat | Inns | NO | Runs | HS | Ave | SR | 100 | 50 | Ct | St |
|---|---|---|---|---|---|---|---|---|---|---|---|
| ODIs | 58 | 58 | 3 | 1745 | 112* | 31.72 | 67.58 | 5 | 8 | 29 | 0 |
| T20Is | 21 | 20 | 2 | 346 | 56* | 19.22 | 111.61 | 0 | 1 | 6 | 0 |
| First-class | 62 | 106 | 3 | 3150 | 175 | 30.58 | 45.94 | 4 | 20 | 67 | 0 |
| List A | 127 | 126 | 4 | 4068 | 112* | 33.34 | 71.98 | 5 | 25 | 54 | 0 |
| Twenty20 | 65 | 64 | 3 | 1447 | 83 | 23.72 | 124.41 | 0 | 8 | 28 | 0 |

| Bowling | Mat | Balls | Runs | Wkts | BBI | BBM | Ave | Econ | SR | 5w | 10 |
|---|---|---|---|---|---|---|---|---|---|---|---|
| ODIs | 58 | - | - | - | - | - | - | - | - | - | - |
| T20Is | 21 | - | - | - | - | - | - | - | - | - | - |
| First-class | 62 | 108 | 138 | 2 | 1/29 | 1/29 | 69.00 | 7.66 | 54.0 | 0 | 0 |
| List A | 127 | - | - | - | - | - | - | - | - | - | - |
| Twenty20 | 65 | - | - | - | - | - | - | - | - | - | - |

KENT

FULL NAME: Michael John Powell
BORN: February 3, 1977, Abergavenny,
Monmouthshire
SQUAD NO: 14
HEIGHT: 6ft 1in
NICKNAME: Powelly
EDUCATION: Crickhowell Secondary School;
Pontypool School
TEAMS: Glamorgan, Kent
CAREER: First-class: 1997; List A: 1997; T20:
2003

BEST BATTING: 299 Glamorgan vs Gloucestershire, Cheltenham, 2006
BEST BOWLING: 2-39 Glamorgan vs Oxford UCCE, The Parks, 1999
COUNTY CAP: 2000 (Glamorgan); BENEFIT YEAR: 2011 (Glamorgan)

CAREER OUTSIDE CRICKET? Financial advisor
FAMILY TIES? Dad and uncle Mike both played for Abergavenny
CAREER HIGHLIGHTS? The trophies I've won with Glamorgan over the years
CRICKET MOMENTS TO FORGET? Missing the 2007 season due to illness
SUPERSTITIONS? None
OTHER SPORTS PLAYED? Rugby (Crickhowell RFC)
OTHER SPORTS FOLLOWED? Rugby (Cardiff)
RELAXATIONS? Eating, sleeping
FAVOURITE BAND? Foo Fighters, Stereophonics
CRICKETERS PARTICULARLY ADMIRED? Matthew Elliott, Steve James

| Batting | Mat | Inns | NO | Runs | HS | Ave | SR | 100 | 50 | Ct | St |
|---------|-----|------|-----|------|-----|-------|--------|-----|-----|-----|-----|
| First-class | 212 | 358 | 33 | 12461 | 299 | 38.34 | | 25 | 64 | 130 | 0 |
| List A | 204 | 193 | 20 | 4665 | 114* | 26.96 | | 1 | 25 | 79 | 0 |
| Twenty20 | 44 | 41 | 4 | 844 | 68* | 22.81 | 116.41 | 0 | 5 | 16 | 0 |

| Bowling | Mat | Balls | Runs | Wkts | BBI | BBM | Ave | Econ | SR | 5w | 10 |
|---------|-----|-------|------|------|------|------|-------|------|------|-----|-----|
| First-class | 212 | 164 | 132 | 2 | 2/39 | | 66.00 | 4.82 | 82.0 | 0 | 0 |
| List A | 204 | 24 | 26 | 1 | 1/26 | 1/26 | 26.00 | 6.50 | 24.0 | 0 | 0 |
| Twenty20 | 44 | - | - | - | - | - | - | - | - | - | - |

# TOM POYNTON

## RHB WK

FULL NAME: Thomas Poynton
BORN: November 25, 1989, Burton-on-Trent, Staffordshire
SQUAD NO: 23
HEIGHT: 5ft 10in
NICKNAME: TP, Poynts
EDUCATION: John Taylor High School; Repton School
TEAMS: Derbyshire, Derbyshire 2nd XI, England Under-19s
CAREER: First-class: 2007; List A: 2007; T20: 2007

**DERBYSHIRE**

BEST BATTING: 25 Derbyshire vs Glamorgan, Cardiff, 2010
BEST BOWLING: 2-96 Derbyshire vs Glamorgan, Cardiff, 2010

CAREER HIGHLIGHTS? Making my first-class debut for Derbyshire and touring South Africa with England U19

CRICKETING HEROES? Adam Gilchrist was my hero whilst growing up. Such a destructive batsman and great gloveman. As I have grown older, seen more footage and heard more stories, I would also have to add Bob Taylor and Ian Healy to my heroes

NON-CRICKETING HEROES? Ted 'The Tinman' McMinn, a Derby and Rangers legend. He is our kitman now but has some amazing stories and is a true legend of a man

BEST PLAYER IN COUNTY CRICKET? Marcus Trescothick. Such a consistent performer year in year out for Somerset in all forms of the game

TIPS FOR THE TOP? Dan Redfern, Tom Knight, Peter Burgoyne

FAVOURITE FILM? Scent Of A Woman

FAVOURITE BOOK? Flat Stanley

DREAM HOLIDAY? Sandy Lane, Barbados or Al Qasr, Dubai

GUILTY PLEASURES? Eating out, FIFA 12, Call Of Duty, trash TV

AMAZE ME! I take all the complimentary slippers from all the hotels I stop in, I am a serious FIFA 12 player and I sponsor the meerkats at Twycross Zoo

TWITTER FEED: @tompoynton

| Batting | Mat | Inns | NO | Runs | HS | Ave | SR | 100 | 50 | Ct | St |
|---|---|---|---|---|---|---|---|---|---|---|---|
| First-class | 7 | 11 | 0 | 105 | 25 | 9.54 | 22.92 | 0 | 0 | 12 | 2 |
| List A | 10 | 6 | 2 | 96 | 40 | 24.00 | 105.49 | 0 | 0 | 7 | 2 |
| Twenty20 | 2 | 1 | 0 | 3 | 3 | 3.00 | 37.50 | 0 | 0 | 0 | 2 |

| Bowling | Mat | Balls | Runs | Wkts | BBI | BBM | Ave | Econ | SR | 5w | 10 |
|---|---|---|---|---|---|---|---|---|---|---|---|
| First-class | 7 | 48 | 96 | 2 | 2/96 | 2/96 | 48.00 | 12.00 | 24.0 | 0 | 0 |
| List A | 10 | - | - | - | - | - | - | - | - | - | - |
| Twenty20 | 2 | - | - | - | - | - | - | - | - | - | - |

**LANCASHIRE**

FULL NAME: Ashwell Gavin Prince
BORN: May 28, 1977, Port Elizabeth, South Africa
SQUAD NO: 5
EDUCATION: St Thomas Senior Secondary, UPE
TEAMS: South Africa, Africa XI, Eastern Province, Lancashire, Mumbai Indians, Nottinghamshire, Warriors, Western Province, Western Province Boland
CAREER: Test: 2002; ODI: 2002; T20I: 2005; First-class: 1995; List A: 1996; T20: 2004

BEST BATTING: 254 Warriors vs Titans, Centurion, 2009
BEST BOWLING: 2-11 South Africans vs Middlesex, Uxbridge, 2008
COUNTY CAPS: 2008 (Nottinghamshire), 2010 (Lancashire)

NOTES: Top-scored on Test debut, making 49 against Australia in 2001/02. Became South Africa's first black Test captain when, in the absence of the injured Graeme Smith, he led the side against Sri Lanka in July 2006. Joined Nottinghamshire as their overseas player in August 2008 after the signing of Adam Voges as a replacement for Mike Hussey fell through. Signed by Lancashire as a temporary replacement for VVS Laxman during the early part of the 2009 season, scoring 497 Championship runs at an average of 62.12, including a century and three half-centuries. Returned to Lancashire for the 2010 season, making 450 runs at 40.90, including a century and four half-centuries

| Batting | Mat | Inns | NO | Runs | HS | Ave | SR | 100 | 50 | Ct | St |
|---|---|---|---|---|---|---|---|---|---|---|---|
| Tests | 66 | 104 | 16 | 3665 | 162* | 41.64 | 43.70 | 11 | 11 | 47 | 0 |
| ODIs | 52 | 41 | 12 | 1018 | 89* | 35.10 | 67.77 | 0 | 3 | 26 | 0 |
| T20Is | 1 | 1 | 0 | 5 | 5 | 5.00 | 83.33 | 0 | 0 | 0 | 0 |
| First-class | 208 | 335 | 44 | 12711 | 254 | 43.68 | | 31 | 62 | 144 | 0 |
| List A | 213 | 187 | 35 | 4766 | 128 | 31.35 | | 2 | 24 | 96 | 0 |
| Twenty20 | 48 | 46 | 4 | 1068 | 74 | 25.42 | 110.21 | 0 | 6 | 18 | 0 |

| Bowling | Mat | Balls | Runs | Wkts | BBI | BBM | Ave | Econ | SR | 5w | 10 |
|---|---|---|---|---|---|---|---|---|---|---|---|
| Tests | 66 | 96 | 47 | 1 | 1/2 | 1/2 | 47.00 | 2.93 | 96.0 | 0 | 0 |
| ODIs | 52 | 12 | 3 | 0 | - | - | - | 1.50 | - | 0 | 0 |
| T20Is | 1 | - | - | - | - | - | - | - | - | - | - |
| First-class | 208 | 276 | 166 | 4 | 2/11 | | 41.50 | 3.60 | 69.0 | 0 | 0 |
| List A | 213 | 91 | 86 | 0 | - | - | - | 5.67 | - | 0 | 0 |
| Twenty20 | 48 | 4 | 5 | 0 | - | - | - | 7.50 | - | 0 | 0 |

# MATT PRIOR

## RHB WK R3

**FULL NAME:** Matthew James Prior
**BORN:** February 26, 1982, Johannesburg, South Africa
**SQUAD NO:** 13
**HEIGHT:** 5ft 11in
**NICKNAME:** Matty, Cheese
**EDUCATION:** Brighton College, East Sussex
**TEAMS:** England, England A, England Lions, England Under-19s, Sussex, Sussex Cricket Board, Victoria
**CAREER:** Test: 2007; ODI: 2004; T20I: 2007; First-class: 2001; List A: 2000; T20: 2003

SUSSEX

**BEST BATTING:** 201* Sussex vs LUCCE, Hove, 2004
**COUNTY CAP:** 2003; **BENEFIT YEAR:** 2012

**WHY CRICKET?** I had a net session as an eight-year-old and loved it. After that I wanted to become a professional cricketer
**CAREER HIGHLIGHTS?** Winning the County Championship with Sussex – the first one in 2003 was the best. Making my England debut and scoring 126* at Lord's in 2007. Winning the Ashes back-to-back, but especially in Australia. Being part of the No.1 Test team in the world
**SUPERSTITIONS?** Many, probably too many to disclose!
**CRICKETING HEROES?** Alec Stewart, Steve Waugh, Brian Lara, Adam Gilchrist
**NON-CRICKETING HEROES?** Tiger Woods
**IF YOU WEREN'T A CRICKETER?** I like to think I could have pursued a golf career
**WHEN RAIN STOPS PLAY?** Sleep and talk rubbish with teammates
**GUILTY PLEASURES?** Hot chocolate. Grey Goose!
**TWITTER FEED:** @mattprior13

| Batting | Mat | Inns | NO | Runs | HS | Ave | SR | 100 | 50 | Ct | St |
|---|---|---|---|---|---|---|---|---|---|---|---|
| Tests | 50 | 76 | 15 | 2699 | 131* | 44.24 | 65.57 | 6 | 19 | 149 | 7 |
| ODIs | 68 | 62 | 9 | 1282 | 87 | 24.18 | 76.76 | 0 | 3 | 71 | 8 |
| T20Is | 10 | 8 | 2 | 127 | 32 | 21.16 | 127.00 | 0 | 0 | 6 | 3 |
| First-class | 198 | 306 | 37 | 10935 | 201* | 40.65 | 67.65 | 26 | 61 | 505 | 34 |
| List A | 218 | 200 | 17 | 4946 | 144 | 27.02 | - | 4 | 27 | 185 | 31 |
| Twenty20 | 72 | 67 | 5 | 1586 | 117 | 25.58 | 140.47 | 1 | 9 | 42 | 6 |
| Bowling | Mat | Balls | Runs | Wkts | BBI | BBM | Ave | Econ | SR | 5w | 10 |
| Tests | 50 | - | - | - | - | - | - | - | - | - | - |
| ODIs | 68 | - | - | - | - | - | - | - | - | - | - |
| T20Is | 10 | - | - | - | - | - | - | - | - | - | - |
| First-class | 198 | - | - | - | - | - | - | - | - | - | - |
| List A | 218 | - | - | - | - | - | - | - | - | - | - |
| Twenty20 | 72 | - | - | - | - | - | - | - | - | - | - |

## LUKE PROCTER

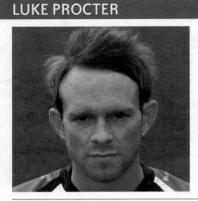

**FULL NAME:** Luke Anthony Procter
**BORN:** June 24, 1988, Oldham, Lancashire
**SQUAD NO:** 2
**HEIGHT:** 5ft 11in
**TEAMS:** Cumberland, Lancashire, Lancashire 2nd XI, Marylebone Cricket Club Young Cricketers
**CAREER:** First-class: 2010; List A: 2009; T20: 2011

**BEST BATTING:** 89 Lancashire vs Sussex, Hove, 2011
**BEST BOWLING:** 3-33 Lancashire vs Warwickshire, Birmingham, 2011

**FAMILY TIES?** My dad played cricket and my mum was an umpire
**CAREER HIGHLIGHTS?** Winning the County Championship
**SUPERSTITIONS?** Putting my right pad on first
**CRICKETING HEROES?** Marcus Trescothick
**TIP FOR THE TOP?** Simon Kerrigan
**IF YOU WEREN'T A CRICKETER?** I'd not be doing a lot
**WHEN RAIN STOPS PLAY?** I listen to music and chat to the lads
**FAVOURITE TV?** Take Me Out
**FAVOURITE FILM?** Happy Gilmore
**FAVOURITE BOOK?** The Twilight series
**DREAM HOLIDAY?** Las Vegas
**GUILTY PLEASURES?** Chocolate
**TWITTER FEED:** @vvsprocter

| Batting | Mat | Inns | NO | Runs | HS | Ave | SR | 100 | 50 | Ct | St |
|---|---|---|---|---|---|---|---|---|---|---|---|
| First-class | 9 | 13 | 1 | 430 | 89 | 35.83 | 42.03 | 0 | 2 | 2 | 0 |
| List A | 16 | 13 | 5 | 244 | 97 | 30.50 | 85.31 | 0 | 2 | 4 | 0 |
| Twenty20 | 15 | 10 | 5 | 85 | 25* | 17.00 | 91.39 | 0 | 0 | 5 | 0 |

| Bowling | Mat | Balls | Runs | Wkts | BBI | BBM | Ave | Econ | SR | 5w | 10 |
|---|---|---|---|---|---|---|---|---|---|---|---|
| First-class | 9 | 543 | 379 | 10 | 3/33 | 4/50 | 37.90 | 4.18 | 54.3 | 0 | 0 |
| List A | 16 | 348 | 346 | 11 | 3/29 | 3/29 | 31.45 | 5.96 | 31.6 | 0 | 0 |
| Twenty20 | 15 | 66 | 94 | 4 | 3/22 | 3/22 | 23.50 | 8.54 | 16.5 | 0 | 0 |

**FULL NAME:** Richard Michael Pyrah
**BORN:** November 1, 1982, Dewsbury, Yorkshire
**SQUAD NO:** 27
**HEIGHT:** 6ft
**NICKNAME:** RP, Pyro, Iceman
**EDUCATION:** Ossett High School
**TEAMS:** Yorkshire, Yorkshire Cricket Board
**CAREER:** First-class: 2004; List A: 2001; T20: 2005

YORKSHIRE

**BEST BATTING:** 134* Yorkshire vs LMCCU, Leeds, 2010
**BEST BOWLING:** 5-58 Yorkshire vs Nottinghamshire, Leeds, 2011
**COUNTY CAP:** 2010

**CAREER HIGHLIGHTS?** Receiving my 1st XI cap, scoring 117 vs Lancashire after we were 45-8
**CRICKETING HEROES?** Jacques Kallis, Sachin Tendulkar
**TIPS FOR THE TOP?** Joe Root, Jonny Bairstow
**IF YOU WEREN'T A CRICKETER?** I'd be some sort of businessman
**WHEN RAIN STOPS PLAY?** Playing Tiger Woods PGA Tour on iPad against Anthony McGrath
**FAVOURITE TV?** EastEnders, One Born Every Minute
**FAVOURITE FILM?** Dumb And Dumber
**FAVOURITE BOOK?** The Beano comics!
**DREAM HOLIDAY?** Barbados
**ACCOMPLISHMENTS?** Having twins with my girlfriend
**SURPRISING SKILL?** I can down a bottle of VK in one second
**GUILTY PLEASURES?** Golf and babysitting my kids
**AMAZE ME!** I played for Sheffield Wednesday as a youngster
**FANTASY SLIP CORDON?** Keeper: Me, 1st: My dog Charlie, 2nd: Tiger Woods, 3rd: Mila Kunis
**TWITTER FEED:** @pyrah27

| Batting | Mat | Inns | NO | Runs | HS | Ave | SR | 100 | 50 | Ct | St |
|---|---|---|---|---|---|---|---|---|---|---|---|
| First-class | 33 | 44 | 5 | 1177 | 134* | 30.17 | 55.28 | 3 | 5 | 15 | 0 |
| List A | 89 | 59 | 15 | 868 | 69 | 19.72 | | 0 | 2 | 30 | 0 |
| Twenty20 | 62 | 41 | 12 | 312 | 33* | 10.75 | 105.76 | 0 | 0 | 24 | 0 |

| Bowling | Mat | Balls | Runs | Wkts | BBI | BBM | Ave | Econ | SR | 5w | 10 |
|---|---|---|---|---|---|---|---|---|---|---|---|
| First-class | 33 | 2972 | 1773 | 45 | 5/58 | | 39.40 | 3.57 | 66.0 | 1 | 0 |
| List A | 89 | 2794 | 2672 | 107 | 5/50 | 5/50 | 24.97 | 5.73 | 26.1 | 1 | 0 |
| Twenty20 | 62 | 1014 | 1261 | 64 | 5/16 | 5/16 | 19.70 | 7.46 | 15.8 | 1 | 0 |

# AZEEM RAFIQ

RHB OB

YORKSHIRE

**FULL NAME:** Azeem Rafiq
**BORN:** February 27, 1991, Karachi, Pakistan
**SQUAD NO:** 30
**HEIGHT:** 5ft 9in
**NICKNAME:** Az, RAF, Raffa
**EDUCATION:** Holgate School, Barnsley
**TEAMS:** England Under-15s, England Under-17s, England Under-19s, Yorkshire, Yorkshire 2nd XI
**CAREER:** First-class: 2009; List A : 2009; T20: 2008

**BEST BATTING:** 100 Yorkshire vs Worcestershire, Worcester, 2009
**BEST BOWLING:** 4-92 Yorkshire vs Lancashire, Manchester, 2010

**WHY CRICKET?** My uncle introduced me to the game and I've always loved watching it
**CAREER HIGHLIGHTS?** Man of the Match in the Roses T20 match and scoring a hundred in my second first-class match
**CRICKETING HEROES?** Saqlain Mushtaq, Sachin Tendulkar
**NON-CRICKETING HEROES?** My dad, Tiger Woods
**BEST PLAYER IN COUNTY CRICKET?** Marcus Trescothick
**TIPS FOR THE TOP?** Jonny Bairstow, Nathan Buck, Jos Buttler, Ben Stokes
**IF YOU WEREN'T A CRICKETER?** No idea!
**FAVOURITE TV?** The Inbetweeners
**FAVOURITE FILM?** The Hangover
**FAVOURITE BOOK?** Harry Potter
**DREAM HOLIDAY?** Mauritius
**GUILTY PLEASURES?** Pick 'n' mix when at the cinema, Ben and Jerry's ice cream
**AMAZE ME!** I love Nando's!
**FANTASY SLIP CORDON?** Keeper: Karl Pilkington, 1st: Megan Fox 2nd: Myself, 3rd: Charlotte Jackson, Gully: Sachin Tendulkar
**TWITTER FEED:** @AzeemRafiq30

| Batting | Mat | Inns | NO | Runs | HS | Ave | SR | 100 | 50 | Ct | St |
|---|---|---|---|---|---|---|---|---|---|---|---|
| First-class | 10 | 12 | 2 | 198 | 100 | 19.80 | 49.62 | 1 | 0 | 1 | 0 |
| List A | 7 | 3 | 2 | 30 | 18 | 30.00 | 85.71 | 0 | 0 | 4 | 0 |
| Twenty20 | 23 | 10 | 6 | 42 | 11* | 10.50 | 80.76 | 0 | 0 | 10 | 0 |

| Bowling | Mat | Balls | Runs | Wkts | BBI | BBM | Ave | Econ | SR | 5w | 10 |
|---|---|---|---|---|---|---|---|---|---|---|---|
| First-class | 10 | 1869 | 1048 | 23 | 4/92 | 6/91 | 45.56 | 3.36 | 81.2 | 0 | 0 |
| List A | 7 | 181 | 151 | 3 | 1/29 | 1/29 | 50.33 | 5.00 | 60.3 | 0 | 0 |
| Twenty20 | 23 | 457 | 615 | 19 | 3/15 | 3/15 | 32.36 | 8.07 | 24.0 | 0 | 0 |

FULL NAME: Benjamin Alexander Raine
BORN: September 14, 1991, Sunderland, Co Durham
SQUAD NO: 88
HEIGHT: 6ft
NICKNAME: Rainedeer, Kung Fu Panda
EDUCATION: St. Aidans RC Secondary School for Boys
TEAMS: Durham, Durham 2nd XI, Northumberland
CAREER: First-class: 2011; List A: 2011

BEST BATTING: 7 Durham vs Sri Lanka A, Chester-le-Street, 2011

WHY CRICKET? It's an excuse to try to hit a ball as far as you can
CAREER HIGHLIGHTS? My first-class debut vs Sri Lanka A, and my List A debut vs Warwickshire
SUPERSTITIONS? If I'm not happy with how I got out I will always clean my pads and gloves
CRICKETING HEROES? Matthew Hayden, Chris Gayle
NON-CRICKETING HEROES? Tiger Woods
BEST PLAYER IN COUNTY CRICKET? Dale Benkenstein
TIP FOR THE TOP? Ben Stokes
IF YOU WEREN'T A CRICKETER? I would be struggling. The army is probably the only option
FAVOURITE TV? QI – the amount of useless facts I know is astounding
FAVOURITE TV? Kevin And Perry Go Large
FAVOURITE BOOK? Count Of Monte Cristo
DREAM HOLIDAY? Ibiza
ACCOMPLISHMENTS? Scoring a hat-trick for Newbottle after playing the first-half in goal
GUILTY PLEASURES? Reasonably partial to a night out in Sunderland/Newcastle
AMAZE ME! I have a ridiculous tattoo, I have experienced and survived a terrorist suicide attack and an earthquake, and I once dropped Andrew Symonds when I was a ball boy at the Emirates
TWITTER FEED: @BenRaine88

| Batting | Mat | Inns | NO | Runs | HS | Ave | SR | 100 | 50 | Ct | St |
|---|---|---|---|---|---|---|---|---|---|---|---|
| First-class | 1 | 2 | 0 | 11 | 7 | 5.50 | 36.66 | 0 | 0 | 1 | 0 |
| List A | 1 | - | - | - | - | - | - | - | - | 1 | 0 |

| Bowling | Mat | Balls | Runs | Wkts | BBI | BBM | Ave | Econ | SR | 5w | 10 |
|---|---|---|---|---|---|---|---|---|---|---|---|
| First-class | 1 | 18 | 7 | 0 | - | - | - | 2.33 | - | 0 | 0 |
| List A | 1 | - | - | - | - | - | - | - | - | - | - |

# MARK RAMPRAKASH

RHB OB R20

FULL NAME: Mark Ravin Ramprakash
BORN: September 5, 1969, Bushey, Hertfordshire
SQUAD NO: 77
HEIGHT: 5ft 10in
NICKNAME: Ramps, Bloodaxe
EDUCATION: Gayton Boys School; Harrow Weald Sixth Form College
TEAMS: England, Middlesex, Surrey
CAREER: Test: 1991; ODI: 1991; First-class: 1987; List A: 1987; T20: 2003

BEST BATTING: 301* Surrey vs Northamptonshire, The Oval, 2006
BEST BOWLING: 3-32 Middlesex vs Glamorgan, Lord's, 1998
COUNTY CAPS: 1990 (Middlesex); 2002 (Surrey); BENEFIT YEAR: 2000 (Middlesex); 2008 (Surrey)

CAREER HIGHLIGHTS? My England, Middlesex and Surrey debuts and winning trophies
SUPERSTITIONS? I have the same piece of chewing gum throughout my innings
CRICKETING HEROES? Tony Greig and Viv Richards
TIPS FOR THE TOP? All the young players at Surrey, Jos Buttler and Alex Hales
IF YOU WEREN'T A CRICKETER? I'd like to be Arsene Wenger's No.2
WHEN RAIN STOPS PLAY? Reading
FAVOURITE TV? The Mentalist
FAVOURITE FILM? Ocean's Eleven
FAVOURITE BOOK? The Pelican Brief by John Grisham
FANTASY SLIP CORDON? Keeper: Arsene Wenger, 1st: Muhammad Ali, 2nd: Karen Hardy, 3rd: Kim Kardashian, Gully: Mark Ramprakash
TWITTER FEED: @MarkRamprakash

| Batting | Mat | Inns | NO | Runs | HS | Ave | SR | 100 | 50 | Ct | St |
|---|---|---|---|---|---|---|---|---|---|---|---|
| Tests | 52 | 92 | 6 | 2350 | 154 | 27.32 | 36.18 | 2 | 12 | 39 | 0 |
| ODIs | 18 | 18 | 4 | 376 | 51 | 26.85 | 69.11 | 0 | 1 | 8 | 0 |
| First-class | 455 | 752 | 93 | 35539 | 301* | 53.92 | | 114 | 147 | 259 | 0 |
| List A | 407 | 394 | 64 | 13273 | 147* | 40.22 | | 17 | 85 | 137 | 0 |
| Twenty20 | 63 | 63 | 10 | 1719 | 85* | 32.43 | 125.01 | 0 | 13 | 21 | 0 |

| Bowling | Mat | Balls | Runs | Wkts | BBI | BBM | Ave | Econ | SR | 5w | 10 |
|---|---|---|---|---|---|---|---|---|---|---|---|
| Tests | 52 | 895 | 477 | 4 | 1/2 | 1/2 | 119.25 | 3.19 | 223.7 | 0 | 0 |
| ODIs | 18 | 132 | 108 | 4 | 3/28 | 3/28 | 27.00 | 4.90 | 33.0 | 0 | 0 |
| First-class | 455 | 4177 | 2202 | 34 | 3/32 | | 64.76 | 3.16 | 122.8 | 0 | 0 |
| List A | 407 | 1734 | 1354 | 46 | 5/38 | 5/38 | 29.43 | 4.68 | 37.6 | 1 | 0 |
| Twenty20 | 63 | - | - | - | - | | - | - | - | - | - |

## HARRY RAMSDEN

**LHB OB**

FULL NAME: Henry Douglas Ramsden
BORN: November 11, 1992
SQUAD NO: 12
HEIGHT: 6ft 4in
NICKNAME: H, Raaaaambo
EDUCATION: Oundle School
TEAMS: Hertfordshire
CAREER: Yet to make first-team debut

CAREER HIGHLIGHTS? Playing for ESCA at Lord's
CRICKETING HEROES? Brian Lara, Stuart Broad, Alastair Cook
NON-CRICKETING HEROES? Jonny Wilkinson, Steve Gerrard
BEST PLAYER IN COUNTY CRICKET? Marcus Trescothick
TIPS FOR THE TOP? Ben Foakes, Tymal Mills
IF YOU WEREN'T A CRICKETER? I'd be studying
WHEN RAIN STOPS PLAY? Sleeping or listening to music
FAVOURITE TV? Top Gear
FAVOURITE FILM? The Other Guys
DREAM HOLIDAY? Beach holiday in Tanzania with fishing involved
SURPRISING FACT? I'm a sleep walker, a sleep talker and my real name is Henry
FANTASY SLIP CORDON?: Keeper: James Corden, 1st: Mila Kunis, 2nd: Me, 3rd: Graeme Swann, Gully: Megan Fox
TWITTER FEED: @HRamsden150

## GURMAN RANDHAWA

**LHB SLA**

FULL NAME: Gurman Singh Randhawa
BORN: January 15, 1992, Huddersfield, Yorkshire
SQUAD NO: 25
HEIGHT: 5ft 10in
NICKNAME: Gurm
EDUCATION: Huddersfield New College
TEAMS: England Under-19s, Yorkshire 2nd XI, Yorkshire Academy, Yorkshire Under-13s, Yorkshire Under-14s, Yorkshire Under-15s, Yorkshire Under-17s
CAREER: First-class: 2011

BEST BATTING: 5 Yorkshire vs DMCCU, Durham University, 2011
BEST BOWLING: 2-54 Yorkshire vs DMCCU, Durham University, 2011

WHY CRICKET? Father playing for a local club side
CAREER HIGHLIGHTS? Playing for England U19, Academy Player of the Year 2009 and 2010
CRICKETING HEROES? Daniel Vettori, Graham Thorpe
NON-CRICKETING HEROES? Mario Balotelli
BEST PLAYER IN COUNTY CRICKET? Marcus Trescothick
TIPS FOR THE TOP? Moin Ashraf
IF YOU WEREN'T A CRICKETER? Tennis player
WHEN RAIN STOPS PLAY? Tiger Woods PGA Tour
FAVOURITE TV? Super Sunday
FAVOURITE FILM? Gladiator
FAVOURITE BOOK? Herschelle Gibbs' autobiography
DREAM HOLIDAY? Barbados
TWITTER FEED: @Gurm1

| Batting | Mat | Inns | NO | Runs | HS | Ave | SR | 100 | 50 | Ct | St |
|---|---|---|---|---|---|---|---|---|---|---|---|
| First-class | 1 | 1 | 0 | 5 | 5 | 5.00 | 23.80 | 0 | 0 | 0 | 0 |

| Bowling | Mat | Balls | Runs | Wkts | BBI | BBM | Ave | Econ | SR | 5w | 10 |
|---|---|---|---|---|---|---|---|---|---|---|---|
| First-class | 1 | 126 | 62 | 2 | 2/54 | 2/62 | 31.00 | 2.95 | 63.0 | 0 | 0 |

# BOYD RANKIN

## LHB RMF W1

FULL NAME: William Boyd Rankin
BORN: July 5, 1984, Derry
SQUAD NO: 30
HEIGHT: 6ft 7in
NICKNAME: Boydo, Pierre
EDUCATION: Strabane Grammar School;
Harper Adams University College
TEAMS: Ireland, Derbyshire, England Lions,
Ireland Under-19s, Warwickshire
CAREER: ODI: 2007; T20I: 2009; First-class:
2007; List A: 2006; T20: 2009

WARWICKSHIRE

BEST BATTING: 43 ICC Combined XI vs England XI, Dubai, 2012
BEST BOWLING: 5-16 Warwickshire vs Essex, Birmingham, 2010

FAMILY TIES? Dad played club cricket, brothers Robert and David have played for Ireland at U19 level. David has played for Ireland A. My sister plays Ireland development cricket
CAREER HIGHLIGHTS? Playing for Ireland in World Cups. Beating Pakistan and England
IF YOU WEREN'T A CRICKETER? Would be back home in Ireland on the family farm
FAVOURITE TV? Two And A Half Men
FAVOURITE FILM? Gladiator
DREAM HOLIDAY? Somewhere in the Caribbean – great beaches, rum and friendly people
ACCOMPLISHMENTS? Higher diploma in Agricultural Mechanisation
SURPRISING SKILL? I can weld, does that count?!
FANTASY SLIP CORDON? Keeper: Michael McIntyre (get a few jokes in between balls), 1st: Brian O'Driscoll (I'm a big Ireland rugby fan and he's a great player), 2nd: Holly Valance (always had a crush on her when I was younger), 3rd: Myself, Gully: Steven Gerard (I'm a massive Liverpool fan and I love how he plays)
TWITTER FEED: @boydrankin

| Batting | Mat | Inns | NO | Runs | HS | Ave | SR | 100 | 50 | Ct | St |
|---|---|---|---|---|---|---|---|---|---|---|---|
| ODIs | 37 | 16 | 11 | 35 | 7* | 7.00 | 33.33 | 0 | 0 | 6 | 0 |
| T20Is | 9 | 3 | 2 | 13 | 7* | 13.00 | 81.25 | 0 | 0 | 3 | 0 |
| First-class | 48 | 60 | 24 | 304 | 43 | 8.44 | 40.69 | 0 | 0 | 16 | 0 |
| List A | 72 | 27 | 16 | 67 | 9 | 6.09 | 39.88 | 0 | 0 | 10 | 0 |
| Twenty20 | 14 | 6 | 4 | 16 | 7* | 8.00 | 84.21 | 0 | 0 | 4 | 0 |

| Bowling | Mat | Balls | Runs | Wkts | BBI | BBM | Ave | Econ | SR | 5w | 10 |
|---|---|---|---|---|---|---|---|---|---|---|---|
| ODIs | 37 | 1700 | 1391 | 43 | 3/32 | 3/32 | 32.34 | 4.90 | 39.5 | 0 | 0 |
| T20Is | 9 | 216 | 232 | 13 | 3/20 | 3/20 | 17.84 | 6.44 | 16.6 | 0 | 0 |
| First-class | 48 | 7044 | 4393 | 159 | 5/16 | 8/115 | 27.62 | 3.74 | 44.3 | 5 | 0 |
| List A | 72 | 2993 | 2488 | 85 | 4/34 | 4/34 | 29.27 | 4.98 | 35.2 | 0 | 0 |
| Twenty20 | 14 | 324 | 329 | 18 | 3/16 | 3/16 | 18.27 | 6.09 | 18.0 | 0 | 0 |

## ADIL RASHID

### RHB LB W2 MVP19

**YORKSHIRE**

FULL NAME: Adil Usman Rashid
BORN: February 17, 1988, Bradford, Yorkshire
SQUAD NO: 3
HEIGHT: 5ft 9in
NICKNAME: Dilly, Dilo, Rash
TEAMS: England, England Lions, England Under-19s, Marylebone Cricket Club, South Australia, Yorkshire, Yorkshire 2nd XI
CAREER: ODI: 2009; T20I: 2009; First-class: 2006; List A: 2006; T20: 2008

BEST BATTING: 157* Yorkshire vs Lancashire, Leeds, 2009
BEST BOWLING: 7-107 Yorkshire vs Hampshire, Southampton, 2008
COUNTY CAP: 2008

CAREER HIGHLIGHTS? Playing for England
CRICKETING HEROES? Sachin Tendulkar, Shane Warne
NON-CRICKETING HEROES? Muhammad Ali
BEST PLAYER IN COUNTY CRICKET? Marcus Trescothick
TIPS FOR THE TOP? Moin Ashraf
IF YOU WEREN'T A CRICKETER? Taxi driver
FAVOURITE TV? Friends
FAVOURITE FILM? Scarface
DREAM HOLIDAY? Barbados
TWITTER FEED: @AdilRashid03

| Batting | Mat | Inns | NO | Runs | HS | Ave | SR | 100 | 50 | Ct | St |
|---|---|---|---|---|---|---|---|---|---|---|---|
| ODIs | 5 | 4 | 1 | 60 | 31* | 20.00 | 111.11 | 0 | 0 | 2 | 0 |
| T20Is | 5 | 2 | 1 | 10 | 9* | 10.00 | 52.63 | 0 | 0 | 0 | 0 |
| First-class | 89 | 129 | 24 | 3580 | 157* | 34.09 | | 4 | 22 | 47 | 0 |
| List A | 66 | 42 | 14 | 467 | 43 | 16.67 | 75.81 | 0 | 0 | 24 | 0 |
| Twenty20 | 59 | 33 | 8 | 260 | 34 | 10.40 | 94.89 | 0 | 0 | 16 | 0 |

| Bowling | Mat | Balls | Runs | Wkts | BBI | BBM | Ave | Econ | SR | 5w | 10 |
|---|---|---|---|---|---|---|---|---|---|---|---|
| ODIs | 5 | 204 | 191 | 3 | 1/16 | 1/16 | 63.66 | 5.61 | 68.0 | 0 | 0 |
| T20Is | 5 | 84 | 120 | 3 | 1/11 | 1/11 | 40.00 | 8.57 | 28.0 | 0 | 0 |
| First-class | 89 | 16337 | 9650 | 280 | 7/107 | 11/114 | 34.46 | 3.54 | 58.3 | 15 | 1 |
| List A | 66 | 2481 | 2111 | 64 | 3/28 | 3/28 | 32.98 | 5.10 | 38.7 | 0 | 0 |
| Twenty20 | 59 | 1200 | 1479 | 74 | 4/20 | 4/20 | 19.98 | 7.39 | 16.2 | 0 | 0 |

# OLLIE RAYNER                    RHB OB

**FULL NAME:** Oliver Philip Rayner
**BORN:** November 1, 1985, Fallingbostel, Germany
**SQUAD NO:** 2
**HEIGHT:** 6ft 5in
**NICKNAME:** Mervin, Rocket, Morag, Kalvin, Donk
**EDUCATION:** St Bede's, Eastbourne
**TEAMS:** Sussex, Sussex 2nd XI, Sussex Cricket Board, Middlesex
**CAREER:** First-class: 2006; List A: 2006; T20: 2006

**MIDDLESEX**

BEST BATTING: 101 Sussex vs Sri Lankans, Hove, 2006
BEST BOWLING: 5-49 Sussex vs Hampshire, Arundel, 2008

WHY CRICKET? Was originally into rugby and tennis, then found cricket fairly late and enjoyed a new challenge. Dad got me some second hand kit to see if I liked it before having to spend a fortune on new gear, and unluckily for him I loved it!
CAREER HIGHLIGHTS? Have been fortunate enough to be with Sussex through a very fruitful period regarding trophies, a ton on debut, and winning Division Two of the County Championship whilst on loan to Middlesex in 2011
CRICKETING HEROES? Freddie Flintoff, Chris Gayle, Adam Blackburn, Richard Smith
NON-CRICKETING HEROES? Kelly Brook, Harry Potter, the Top Gear crew
TIPS FOR THE TOP? Sam Robson, Jonny Bairstow
IF YOU WEREN'T A CRICKETER? Used car salesman, toy boy or a stay at home dad
GUILTY PLEASURES? Harry Potter nut
AMAZE ME! I can actually spin the ball, have lived in army barracks most of my life through my old man and I can only eat small sweets or chocolates in an even number – as an example Maltesers have to go in my mouth in multiples of two. Hence the weight!
FANTASY SLIP CORDON? Keeper: Peter Griffin, 1st: Alan Sugar, 2nd: Me, 3rd: Rihanna, Gully: Simon Cowell

| Batting | Mat | Inns | NO | Runs | HS | Ave | SR | 100 | 50 | Ct | St |
|---|---|---|---|---|---|---|---|---|---|---|---|
| First-class | 52 | 64 | 15 | 1291 | 101 | 26.34 | 56.44 | 1 | 8 | 60 | 0 |
| List A | 26 | 21 | 11 | 293 | 61 | 29.30 | 94.51 | 0 | 1 | 8 | 0 |
| Twenty20 | 29 | 17 | 5 | 152 | 41* | 12.66 | 100.00 | 0 | 0 | 8 | 0 |

| Bowling | Mat | Balls | Runs | Wkts | BBI | BBM | Ave | Econ | SR | 5w | 10 |
|---|---|---|---|---|---|---|---|---|---|---|---|
| First-class | 52 | 7738 | 3893 | 108 | 5/49 | 8/96 | 36.04 | 3.01 | 71.6 | 3 | 0 |
| List A | 26 | 894 | 846 | 20 | 2/20 | 2/20 | 42.30 | 5.67 | 44.7 | 0 | 0 |
| Twenty20 | 29 | 493 | 604 | 21 | 5/18 | 5/18 | 28.76 | 7.35 | 23.4 | 1 | 0 |

# ABDUL RAZZAQ
## RHB RFM

FULL NAME: Abdul Razzaq
BORN: December 2, 1979, Lahore, Punjab, Pakistan
SQUAD NO: 10
HEIGHT: 5ft 11in
NICKNAME: Razi
TEAMS: Pakistan, Asia XI, Hampshire, Hyderabad Heroes, Khan Research Labs, Lahore, Lahore Lions, Leicestershire, Melbourne Renegades, Middlesex, Surrey, Worcestershire
CAREER: Test: 1999; ODI: 1996; T20I: 2006; First-class: 1996; List A: 1996; T20: 2003

---

BEST BATTING: 203* Middlesex vs Glamorgan, Cardiff, 2002
BEST BOWLING: 7-51 Lahore City vs Karachi Whites, Thatta, 1996
COUNTY CAPS: 2002 (Middlesex); 2007 (Worcestershire)

---

WHY CRICKET? I used to see Imran Khan and Wasim Akram play and I developed passion
CAREER HIGHLIGHTS? Against India when I took five wickets and scored 75 runs
CRICKETING HEROES? Imran Khan and Wasim Akram
NON-CRICKETING HEROES? Quaid-e-Azam
TIP FOR THE TOP? There are many good players but I like Josh Cobb the most
WHEN RAIN STOPS PLAY? I play with my iPhone
FAVOURITE FILM? Lord Of The Rings
FAVOURITE BOOK? Nelson Mandela's autobiography
DREAM HOLIDAY? England
ACCOMPLISHMENTS? My ODI matchwinning innings against South Africa when I made 109*
GUILTY PLEASURES? Eating a lot of ice cream

| Batting | Mat | Inns | NO | Runs | HS | Ave | SR | 100 | 50 | Ct | St |
|---|---|---|---|---|---|---|---|---|---|---|---|
| Tests | 46 | 77 | 9 | 1946 | 134 | 28.61 | 41.04 | 3 | 7 | 15 | 0 |
| ODIs | 265 | 228 | 57 | 5080 | 112 | 29.70 | 81.25 | 3 | 23 | 35 | 0 |
| T20Is | 26 | 24 | 9 | 346 | 46* | 23.06 | 126.27 | 0 | 0 | 2 | 0 |
| First-class | 117 | 183 | 27 | 5254 | 203* | 33.67 | | 8 | 28 | 32 | 0 |
| List A | 326 | 280 | 67 | 6375 | 112 | 29.92 | | 3 | 33 | 49 | 0 |
| Twenty20 | 108 | 95 | 23 | 2024 | 109 | 28.11 | 139.68 | 1 | 7 | 15 | 0 |

| Bowling | Mat | Balls | Runs | Wkts | BBI | BBM | Ave | Econ | SR | 5w | 10 |
|---|---|---|---|---|---|---|---|---|---|---|---|
| Tests | 46 | 7008 | 3694 | 100 | 5/35 | 7/155 | 36.94 | 3.16 | 70.0 | 1 | 0 |
| ODIs | 265 | 10941 | 8564 | 269 | 6/35 | 6/35 | 31.83 | 4.69 | 40.6 | 3 | 0 |
| T20Is | 26 | 315 | 360 | 18 | 3/13 | 3/13 | 20.00 | 6.85 | 17.5 | 0 | 0 |
| First-class | 117 | 18564 | 10818 | 340 | 7/51 | | 31.81 | 3.49 | 54.6 | 11 | 2 |
| List A | 326 | 13893 | 11125 | 366 | 6/35 | 6/35 | 30.39 | 4.80 | 37.9 | 3 | 0 |
| Twenty20 | 108 | 1947 | 2470 | 109 | 4/13 | 4/13 | 22.66 | 7.61 | 17.8 | 0 | 0 |

# CHRIS READ RHB WK R2 MVP29

FULL NAME: Christopher Mark Wells Read
BORN: August 10, 1978, Paignton, Devon
SQUAD NO: 7
HEIGHT: 5ft 8in
NICKNAME: Reados, Readie
EDUCATION: Torquay Boys' Grammar School; University of Bath; Loughborough University
TEAMS: England, Devon, Gloucestershire, Nottinghamshire
CAREER: Test: 1999; ODI: 2000; T20I: 2006; First-class: 1998; List A: 1995; T20: 2004

NOTTINGHAMSHIRE

BEST BATTING: 240 Nottinghamshire vs Essex, Chelmsford, 2007
COUNTY CAP: 1999 (Nottinghamshire); BENEFIT YEAR: 2007 (Nottinghamshire)

CAREER HIGHLIGHTS? Winning the County Championship twice
SUPERSTITIONS? Anything to keep the cricketing gods onside!
CRICKETING HEROES? Ian Botham, Ian Healy, Jack Russell
NON-CRICKETING HEROES? Sebastian Loeb
TIP FOR THE TOP? Jos Buttler
IF YOU WEREN'T A CRICKETER? Racing and roadtesting cars or living the dream as a rock star
FAVOURITE TV? Top Gear
FAVOURITE BOOK? Redwall – my son is named after a character in the book
ACCOMPLISHMENTS? Running the NYC marathon
FANTASY SLIP CORDON? Keeper: Me, 1st: Natalie Portman, 2nd: Noel Gallagher, 3rd: Will Ferrell, Gully: Jeremy Clarkson

| Batting | Mat | Inns | NO | Runs | HS | Ave | SR | 100 | 50 | Ct | St |
|---|---|---|---|---|---|---|---|---|---|---|---|
| Tests | 15 | 23 | 4 | 360 | 55 | 18.94 | 39.47 | 0 | 1 | 48 | 6 |
| ODIs | 36 | 24 | 7 | 300 | 30* | 17.64 | 73.17 | 0 | 0 | 41 | 2 |
| T20Is | 1 | 1 | 0 | 13 | 13 | 13.00 | 118.18 | 0 | 0 | 1 | 0 |
| First-class | 257 | 386 | 65 | 11693 | 240 | 36.42 | | 20 | 62 | 759 | 44 |
| List A | 274 | 220 | 54 | 4674 | 135 | 28.15 | | 2 | 18 | 262 | 61 |
| Twenty20 | 75 | 68 | 24 | 1143 | 58* | 25.97 | 121.46 | 0 | 1 | 39 | 16 |

| Bowling | Mat | Balls | Runs | Wkts | BBI | BBM | Ave | Econ | SR | 5w | 10 |
|---|---|---|---|---|---|---|---|---|---|---|---|
| Tests | 15 | - | - | - | - | - | - | - | - | - | - |
| ODIs | 36 | - | - | - | - | - | - | - | - | - | - |
| T20Is | 1 | - | - | - | - | - | - | - | - | - | - |
| First-class | 257 | 96 | 90 | 0 | - | - | - | 5.62 | - | 0 | 0 |
| List A | 274 | - | - | - | - | - | - | - | - | - | - |
| Twenty20 | 75 | - | - | - | - | - | - | - | - | - | - |

# DAN REDFERN

## LHB OB

FULL NAME: Daniel James Redfern
BORN: April 18, 1990, Shrewsbury
SQUAD NO: 19
HEIGHT: 5ft 11in
NICKNAME: Redders, Reddog
EDUCATION: Adams' Grammar School
TEAMS: Derbyshire, Derbyshire 2nd XI,
England Under-19s
CAREER: First-class: 2007; List A: 2006; T20: 2008

BEST BATTING: 99 Derbyshire vs Glamorgan, Derby, 2011
BEST BOWLING: 1-7 Derbyshire vs Warwickshire, Birmingham, 2008

FAMILY TIES? Father, grandfather, brother, uncles and cousins played cricket at Leycett CC
CAREER HIGHLIGHTS? Scoring 63* to win the National T20 Club Final at Chelmsford in 2011
SUPERSTITIONS? Always have to turn over my left shoulder at the end of my run-up
NON-CRICKETING HEROES? Andrew Flintoff, Ian Botham
TIP FOR THE TOP? James Taylor
IF YOU WEREN'T A CRICKETER? Probably playing golf
WHEN RAIN STOPS PLAY? Sleeping mostly, The Sun crossword, inventing stupid games to occupy ourselves
FAVOURITE TV? 24
FAVOURITE FILM? Robin Hood, but the Disney version!
FAVOURITE BOOK? Bad Luck And Trouble by Lee Child
DREAM HOLIDAY? Elbow Quay, Bahamas
ACCOMPLISHMENTS? Building a table at school and actually getting into university
SURPRISING SKILL? Relatively good at technical things, such as fixing and building
GUILTY PLEASURES? Rum, Mr Bean and Mamma Mia
FANTASY SLIP CORDON? Keeper: Lee Evans, 1st: Rowan Atkinson, 2nd: Me, 3rd: Frankie Boyle, 4th: Steven Spielberg, Gully: Alan Davies

| Batting | Mat | Inns | NO | Runs | HS | Ave | SR | 100 | 50 | Ct | St |
|---|---|---|---|---|---|---|---|---|---|---|---|
| First-class | 45 | 76 | 4 | 2113 | 99 | 29.34 | 51.17 | 0 | 15 | 23 | 0 |
| List A | 28 | 25 | 1 | 496 | 57* | 20.66 | 72.83 | 0 | 2 | 6 | 0 |
| Twenty20 | 1 | 1 | 0 | 9 | 9 | 9.00 | 81.81 | 0 | 0 | 0 | 0 |

| Bowling | Mat | Balls | Runs | Wkts | BBI | BBM | Ave | Econ | SR | 5w | 10 |
|---|---|---|---|---|---|---|---|---|---|---|---|
| First-class | 45 | 450 | 269 | 5 | 1/7 | 2/15 | 53.80 | 3.58 | 90.0 | 0 | 0 |
| List A | 28 | 226 | 188 | 5 | 2/10 | 2/10 | 37.60 | 4.99 | 45.2 | 0 | 0 |
| Twenty20 | 1 | - | - | - | - | - | - | - | - | - | - |

**FULL NAME:** Michael Thomas Reed
**BORN:** September 10, 1988, Leicester
**SQUAD NO:** 35
**HEIGHT:** 6ft 7in
**NICKNAME:** Frank, Denis Stracqualursi, Trigger, Long, Marouane Fellaini
**EDUCATION:** De Lisle Catholic Science College; Cardiff University
**TEAMS:** Cardiff MCCU, Glamorgan 2nd XI, Wales Minor Counties
**CAREER:** Yet to make first-team debut

**FAMILY TIES?** Brother [Dominic] was part of 2011 Unicorns squad
**CAREER HIGHLIGHTS?** Signing for Glamorgan, playing against first-class counties for Cardiff MCCU
**CRICKETING HEROES?** Brett Lee, Steve Harmison, Andrew Flintoff
**NON-CRICKETING HEROES?** Martin O'Neill
**BEST PLAYER IN COUNTY CRICKET?** Marcus Trescothick
**TIPS FOR THE TOP?** James Harris, Joe Root
**IF YOU WEREN'T A CRICKETER?** Plugging numbers
**FAVOURITE TV?** Prison Break
**FAVOURITE FILM?** Blood Diamond
**FAVOURITE BOOK?** Any decent autobiography
**DREAM HOLIDAY?** Seychelles
**ACCOMPLISHMENTS?** Getting a Maths degree
**GUILTY PLEASURES?** Chocolate raisins
**SURPRISING FACT?** I have a large scar on my back from my time in Australia and I support Leicester City

# GARETH REES

## LHB LM R2 MVP79

GLAMORGAN

FULL NAME: Gareth Peter Rees
BORN: April 8, 1985, Swansea
SQUAD NO: 28
HEIGHT: 6ft 2in
NICKNAME: Gums
EDUCATION: Coedcae Comprehensive;
Coleg Sir Gar; Bath University
TEAMS: Glamorgan, Glamorgan 2nd XI,
Wales Minor Counties
CAREER: First-class: 2006; List A: 2003; T20:
2009

BEST BATTING: 154 Glamorgan vs Surrey, The Oval, 2009
COUNTY CAP: 2009

CAREER HIGHLIGHTS? Being capped by Glamorgan. Having the pleasure of sitting next to
Dean Cosker in the Glamorgan changing room
CRICKETING HEROES? Brian Lara – best ever player to watch. Tom Maynard – any man who
can get a set of lugs that big into a helmet deserves recognition
NON-CRICKETING HEROES? Alan Turing
TIPS FOR THE TOP? James Harris – best young bowler on the circuit and looking at a big loss
on his really nice car in the near future. James Taylor – best young batter around.
Tom Maynard – prolific, on and off the field
IF YOU WEREN'T A CRICKETER? Working in finance. Possibly a chef or model...
WHEN RAIN STOPS PLAY? Generally harass James Harris, educate Mark Wallace and and
help Robert Croft in and out of his lounge chair in the corner of the dressing room
ACCOMPLISHMENTS? Always felt getting a 1st in my degree was my biggest accomplishment
SURPRISING SKILL? Can rattle off a tax return pretty sharp at the moment
AMAZE ME! 1. Most intelligent man at Glamorgan, comfortably 2. Am a better squash and
chess player than Mark Wallace 3. Not much else, I am an open book
FANTASY SLIP CORDON? Keeper: Russell Howard, 1st: Ricky Gervais, 2nd: Me, 3rd: Einstein
TWITTER FEED: @garethprees28

| Batting | Mat | Inns | NO | Runs | HS | Ave | SR | 100 | 50 | Ct | St |
|---|---|---|---|---|---|---|---|---|---|---|---|
| First-class | 79 | 137 | 8 | 4534 | 154 | 35.14 | 48.62 | 11 | 26 | 63 | 0 |
| List A | 33 | 32 | 4 | 1123 | 123* | 40.10 | | 3 | 8 | 10 | 0 |
| Twenty20 | 27 | 26 | 5 | 350 | 38 | 16.66 | 105.74 | 0 | 0 | 7 | 0 |
| Bowling | Mat | Balls | Runs | Wkts | BBI | BBM | Ave | Econ | SR | 5w | 10 |
| First-class | 79 | 6 | 3 | 0 | - | - | - | 3.00 | - | 0 | 0 |
| List A | 33 | 3 | 2 | 0 | - | - | - | 4.00 | - | 0 | 0 |
| Twenty20 | 27 | 12 | 25 | 0 | - | - | - | 12.50 | - | 0 | 0 |

# HAMZA RIAZUDDIN

**RHB RMF**

FULL NAME: Hamza Riazuddin
BORN: December 19, 1989, Hendon, Middlesex
SQUAD NO: 38
TEAMS: England Under-19s, Hampshire, Hampshire 2nd XI
CAREER: First-class: 2008; List A: 2008; T20: 2008

HAMPSHIRE

BEST BATTING: 4 Hampshire vs Somerset, Taunton, 2008
BEST BOWLING: 1-0 Hampshire vs OMCCU, The Parks, 2010

NOTES: Played for England U19 in 2008-09. Captained England U19 in 2009. Member of Hampshire's 2009 FP Trophy winning squad. Took the wicket of Ian Blackwell on first-class debut against Somerset in 2008

| Batting | Mat | Inns | NO | Runs | HS | Ave | SR | 100 | 50 | Ct | St |
|---|---|---|---|---|---|---|---|---|---|---|---|
| First-class | 3 | 2 | 0 | 7 | 4 | 3.50 | 22.58 | 0 | 0 | 0 | 0 |
| List A | 21 | 7 | 3 | 64 | 23* | 16.00 | 90.14 | 0 | 0 | 7 | 0 |
| Twenty20 | 17 | 6 | 3 | 24 | 13* | 8.00 | 88.88 | 0 | 0 | 2 | 0 |

| Bowling | Mat | Balls | Runs | Wkts | BBI | BBM | Ave | Econ | SR | 5w | 10 |
|---|---|---|---|---|---|---|---|---|---|---|---|
| First-class | 3 | 384 | 200 | 5 | 1/0 | 2/29 | 40.00 | 3.12 | 76.8 | 0 | 0 |
| List A | 21 | 822 | 684 | 16 | 3/37 | 3/37 | 42.75 | 4.99 | 51.3 | 0 | 0 |
| Twenty20 | 17 | 348 | 417 | 21 | 4/15 | 4/15 | 19.85 | 7.18 | 16.5 | 0 | 0 |

# ALAN RICHARDSON

## RHB RMF W3 MVP37

WORCESTERSHIRE

**FULL NAME:** Alan Richardson
**BORN:** May 6, 1975, Newcastle-under-Lyme, Staffordshire
**SQUAD NO:** 9
**HEIGHT:** 6ft 3in
**NICKNAME:** Richo
**EDUCATION:** Alleyne's High School, Stone; Stafford College
**TEAMS:** Derbyshire, Middlesex, Staffordshire, Warwickshire, Worcestershire
**CAREER:** First-class: 1995; List A: 1995; T20: 2004

**BEST BATTING:** 91 Warwickshire vs Hampshire, Birmingham, 2002
**BEST BOWLING:** 8-46 Warwickshire vs Sussex, Birmingham, 2002
**COUNTY CAPS:** 2002 (Warwickshire); 2005 (Middlesex)

**FAMILY TIES?** My grandad patrolled the boundary at both Stone CC and Little Stoke CC. My dad captained Little Stoke 3rd XI and now umpires my nephew's team there
**CAREER HIGHLIGHTS?** My debuts for Warwickshire, Middlesex and Worcestershire. Winning the Minor Counties title with Staffordshire in 1998 and the NSSC League with Little Stoke as the pro in the same year. Getting promoted with Worcestershire in 2010 and being selected on an England Lions tour in 2007/08 to India
**SUPERSTITIONS?** Not really, they're more like habits and I'm not telling you
**BEST PLAYER IN COUNTY CRICKET?** Marcus Trescothick and Glen Chapple have the most influence on their teams at the moment. Both are top quality players
**FAVOURITE TV?** Entourage, Wilfred
**FAVOURITE FILM?** The Other Guys
**FAVOURITE BOOK?** Shantaram
**GUILTY PLEASURES?** Grey's Anatomy
**AMAZE ME!** My voice is occasionally used on Doctors (BBC1 weekdays 1.45-2.15) for background announcements
**TWITTER FEED:** @alricho21

| Batting | Mat | Inns | NO | Runs | HS | Ave | SR | 100 | 50 | Ct | St |
|---|---|---|---|---|---|---|---|---|---|---|---|
| First-class | 138 | 153 | 64 | 983 | 91 | 11.04 | | 0 | 1 | 43 | 0 |
| List A | 64 | 28 | 18 | 105 | 21* | 10.50 | | 0 | 0 | 14 | 0 |
| Twenty20 | 11 | 2 | 1 | 6 | 6* | 6.00 | 60.00 | 0 | 0 | 2 | 0 |

| Bowling | Mat | Balls | Runs | Wkts | BBI | BBM | Ave | Econ | SR | 5w | 10 |
|---|---|---|---|---|---|---|---|---|---|---|---|
| First-class | 138 | 26735 | 12482 | 442 | 8/46 | | 28.23 | 2.80 | 60.4 | 14 | 1 |
| List A | 64 | 2806 | 2199 | 62 | 5/35 | 5/35 | 35.46 | 4.70 | 45.2 | 1 | 0 |
| Twenty20 | 11 | 228 | 268 | 10 | 3/13 | 3/13 | 26.80 | 7.05 | 22.8 | 0 | 0 |

# MICHAEL RICHARDSON RHB WK

**FULL NAME:** Michael John Richardson
**BORN:** October 4, 1986, Port Elizabeth, South Africa
**SQUAD NO:** 18
**HEIGHT:** 5ft 10in
**NICKNAME:** Richie
**EDUCATION:** Stonyhurst College; Nottingham University
**TEAMS:** Durham, Durham 2nd XI, Marylebone Cricket Club Young Cricketers
**CAREER:** First-class: 2010

BEST BATTING: 73* Durham vs Yorkshire, Headingley, 2011

FAMILY TIES? My dad is Dave Richardson [former South Africa wicketkeeper now ICC general manager]
CAREER HIGHLIGHTS? County Championship debut
SUPERSTITIONS? Don't like the score being on 111, never look at the time on the treadmill when it's 1min 11secs or stop reading on page 111
CRICKETING HEROES? Brian Lara, Neil McKenzie
TIPS FOR THE TOP? Ben Stokes, Chris Woakes
IF YOU WEREN'T A CRICKETER? Working in business
WHEN RAIN STOPS PLAY? Sleeping or on the phone
FAVOURITE TV? Geordie Shore
FAVOURITE FILM? John Q, Cool Runnings
FAVOURITE BOOK? The Take
DREAM HOLIDAY? Indonesia
GUILTY PLEASURES? Crisps
TWITTER FEED: @Richo18howu

| Batting | Mat | Inns | NO | Runs | HS | Ave | SR | 100 | 50 | Ct | St |
|---|---|---|---|---|---|---|---|---|---|---|---|
| First-class | 6 | 9 | 1 | 169 | 73* | 21.12 | 52.81 | 0 | 2 | 27 | 1 |

| Bowling | Mat | Balls | Runs | Wkts | BBI | BBM | Ave | Econ | SR | 5w | 10 |
|---|---|---|---|---|---|---|---|---|---|---|---|
| First-class | 6 | - | - | - | - | - | - | - | - | - | - |

## ADAM RILEY                                          RHB OB

**FULL NAME:** Adam Edward Nicholas Riley
**BORN:** March 23, 1992, Sidcup, Kent
**SQUAD NO:** 33
**HEIGHT:** 6ft 3in
**NICKNAME:** Riles, Sherman, Ron Weasley, Saggs
**EDUCATION:** Beths Grammar School; Loughborough University
**TEAMS:** Kent, Kent 2nd XI
**CAREER:** First-class: 2011; List A: 2011; T20: 2011

**BEST BATTING:** 5 Kent vs Derbyshire, Derby, 2011
**BEST BOWLING:** 5-76 Kent vs LMCCU, Canterbury, 2011

**CAREER HIGHLIGHTS?** First-class debut vs Northamptonshire. Playing in the T20 vs India at Canterbury. Playing in the first floodlit/pink ball Championship game. 2-32 vs Sussex in CB40 last year
**SUPERSTITIONS?** Have to rub my fingers in my footmarks at the beginning of every over!
**CRICKETING HEROES?** Shane Warne
**NON-CRICKETING HEROES?** Alan Curbishley, Chris Powell, Johnnie Jackson
**TIPS FOR THE TOP?** James Taylor, Daniel Bell-Drummond, Matt Coles
**ACCOMPLISHMENTS?** Getting the grades to get a place at Loughborough University
**SURPRISING SKILL?** Can hold my own in table tennis using a frying pan
**GUILTY PLEASURES?** Packets of Aero Bubbles at service stations
**AMAZE ME!** I didn't play cricket for a club until I was 13, I have to smell most food before I eat it and I'm an avid Charlton Athletic fan
**FANTASY SLIP CORDON?** Keeper: Michael McIntyre (watching him try to keep and tell jokes would be gold), 1st: Derren Brown (something different to watch between balls), 2nd: Myself (to catch flies), 3rd: Ian Holloway (to talk tactics and half-time rants), Gully: Rowan Atkinson (to act out Mr. Bean scenes between overs)
**TWITTER FEED:** @AdamRiley92

| Batting | Mat | Inns | NO | Runs | HS | Ave | SR | 100 | 50 | Ct | St |
|---|---|---|---|---|---|---|---|---|---|---|---|
| First-class | 6 | 8 | 4 | 17 | 5 | 4.25 | 37.77 | 0 | 0 | 2 | 0 |
| List A | 6 | 1 | 1 | 3 | 3* | - | 42.85 | 0 | 0 | 2 | 0 |
| Twenty20 | 1 | - | - | - | - | - | - | - | - | 0 | 0 |

| Bowling | Mat | Balls | Runs | Wkts | BBI | BBM | Ave | Econ | SR | 5w | 10 |
|---|---|---|---|---|---|---|---|---|---|---|---|
| First-class | 6 | 788 | 547 | 14 | 5/76 | 5/76 | 39.07 | 4.16 | 56.2 | 1 | 0 |
| List A | 6 | 216 | 197 | 5 | 2/32 | 2/32 | 39.40 | 5.47 | 43.2 | 0 | 0 |
| Twenty20 | 1 | 18 | 34 | 1 | 1/34 | 1/34 | 34.00 | 11.33 | 18.0 | 0 | 0 |

# SAM ROBSON

## RHB LB

FULL NAME: Sam David Robson
BORN: July 1, 1989, Paddington, Sydney, Australia
SQUAD NO: 12
HEIGHT: 6ft
NICKNAME: Robbo, Mike
EDUCATION: Marcellin College, Randwick
TEAMS: Australia Under-19s, Eastern Suburbs, Middlesex, Middlesex 2nd XI, New South Wales Under-19s, Sydney South East, University of New South Wales
CAREER: First-class: 2009; List A: 2008; T20: 2011

**MIDDLESEX**

BEST BATTING: 204 Middlesex vs OMCCU, The Parks, 2010

FAMILY TIES? Father played 2nd XI cricket for Worcestershire and captained Australian Universities vs England in 1979
CAREER HIGHLIGHTS? Winning County Championship Division Two with Middlesex in 2011, four first-class hundreds, 231-run opening partnership with Andrew Strauss vs Leicestershire at Lord's 2011, every time I have played at Lord's
CRICKETING HEROES? Shane Warne, Andrew Flintoff, Michael Atherton, Michael Vaughan
TIPS FOR THE TOP? Adam London, Angus Robson, Daniel Rootes
IF YOU WEREN'T A CRICKETER? Journalist
WHEN RAIN STOPS PLAY? Listen to music, throwing around left-field unorthodox dressing room banter
FAVOURITE TV? Seinfeld
FAVOURITE FILM? Gladiator
ACCOMPLISHMENTS? Surviving the Flyfish (a watersport common off the coast of Cyprus involving two people being towed along off the back of a speedboat)
SURPRISING SKILL? Drawing, art
GUILTY PLEASURES? Chocolate milkshakes
FANTASY SLIP CORDON? Keeper: Jessica Biel, 1st: Alan from The Hangover, 2nd: Jennifer Aniston, 3rd: Happy Gilmore, 4th: Lafferty Daniel, Gully: Rod Stewart

| Batting | Mat | Inns | NO | Runs | HS | Ave | SR | 100 | 50 | Ct | St |
|---|---|---|---|---|---|---|---|---|---|---|---|
| First-class | 27 | 48 | 3 | 1857 | 204 | 41.26 | 49.85 | 4 | 8 | 32 | 0 |
| List A | 6 | 4 | 0 | 165 | 65 | 41.25 | 78.57 | 0 | 1 | 3 | 0 |
| Twenty20 | 4 | 4 | 2 | 53 | 28* | 26.50 | 103.92 | 0 | 0 | 2 | 0 |

| Bowling | Mat | Balls | Runs | Wkts | BBI | BBM | Ave | Econ | SR | 5w | 10 |
|---|---|---|---|---|---|---|---|---|---|---|---|
| First-class | 27 | 30 | 30 | 0 | - | - | - | 6.00 | - | 0 | 0 |
| List A | 6 | - | - | - | - | - | - | - | - | - | - |
| Twenty20 | 4 | - | - | - | - | - | - | - | - | - | - |

**MIDDLESEX**

FULL NAME: Christopher John Llewellyn Rogers
BORN: August 31, 1977, Sydney, Australia
SQUAD NO: 1
HEIGHT: 5ft 11in
NICKNAME: Bucky
EDUCATION: Wesley College; Curtin University
TEAMS: Australia, Derbyshire, Leicestershire, Middlesex, Northamptonshire, Victoria, Western Australia
CAREER: Test: 2008; First-class: 1998; List A: 1998; T20: 2005

BEST BATTING: 319 Northamptonshire vs Gloucestershire, Northampton, 2006
BEST BOWLING: 1-16 Northamptonshire vs Leicestershire, Northampton, 2006
COUNTY CAPS: 2008 (Derbyshire); 2011 (Middlesex)

FAMILY TIES? Father John played for New South Wales
CAREER HIGHLIGHTS? Test debut in 2008 for Australia vs India, 209 against Australia for Leicestershire 2005, 319 against Gloucestershire 2006
CRICKETING HEROES? Allan Border, Steve Waugh
NON-CRICKETING HEROES? Michael Jordan, Cadel Evans, Jack Reacher
TIPS FOR THE TOP? Sam Robson, Alex Hales
FAVOURITE BOOK? Power Of One
DREAM HOLIDAY? South America
ACCOMPLISHMENTS? Journalism degree
GUILTY PLEASURES? Motorway service Burger Kings
AMAZE ME! Sudoku and cryptic crossword Middlesex champion (now Jamie Dalrymple has left). Perth first grade rugby player
FANTASY SLIP CORDON? Keeper: Peter Kay, 1st: Michael Jordan, 2nd: Fergie (Black Eyed Peas), 3rd: Me, Gully: Sir Bobby Robson

| Batting | Mat | Inns | NO | Runs | HS | Ave | SR | 100 | 50 | Ct | St |
|---|---|---|---|---|---|---|---|---|---|---|---|
| Tests | 1 | 2 | 0 | 19 | 15 | 9.50 | 70.37 | 0 | 0 | 1 | 0 |
| First-class | 204 | 361 | 25 | 17112 | 319 | 50.92 | | 52 | 79 | 185 | 0 |
| List A | 139 | 135 | 9 | 4443 | 140 | 35.26 | | 4 | 30 | 64 | 0 |
| Twenty20 | 33 | 27 | 1 | 523 | 58 | 20.11 | 122.48 | 0 | 3 | 20 | 0 |

| Bowling | Mat | Balls | Runs | Wkts | BBI | BBM | Ave | Econ | SR | 5w | 10 |
|---|---|---|---|---|---|---|---|---|---|---|---|
| Tests | 1 | - | - | - | - | - | - | - | - | - | - |
| First-class | 204 | 230 | 131 | 1 | 1/16 | 1/16 | 131.00 | 3.41 | 230.0 | 0 | 0 |
| List A | 139 | 24 | 26 | 2 | 2/22 | 2/22 | 13.00 | 6.50 | 12.0 | 0 | 0 |
| Twenty20 | 33 | - | - | - | - | - | - | - | - | - | - |

# TOBY ROLAND-JONES

**RHB RMF**

FULL NAME: Tobias Skelton Roland-Jones
BORN: January 29, 1988, Ashford, Middlesex
SQUAD NO: 21
EDUCATION: Hampton School; Leeds University
TEAMS: Marylebone Cricket Club, Middlesex, Middlesex 2nd XI
CAREER: First-class: 2010; List A: 2010; T20: 2011

**MIDDLESEX**

BEST BATTING: 30* MCC vs Nottinghamshire, Abu Dhabi, 2011
BEST BOWLING: 5-41 Middlesex vs Surrey, Lord's, 2010

NOTES: Middlesex's joint leading County Championship wicket-taker in 2010 with a haul of 36 at 19.60 despite only featuring in eight matches, including five-wicket hauls against Surrey and Worcestershire. Represented MCC against County Championship winners Nottinghamshire in March 2011, taking four wickets in the floodlit match in Abu Dhabi. Older brother Oliver has played for Middlesex 2nd XI and Leeds/Bradford MCCU

| Batting | Mat | Inns | NO | Runs | HS | Ave | SR | 100 | 50 | Ct | St |
|---|---|---|---|---|---|---|---|---|---|---|---|
| First-class | 16 | 22 | 4 | 263 | 30* | 14.61 | 47.55 | 0 | 0 | 6 | 0 |
| List A | 13 | 9 | 3 | 56 | 23* | 9.33 | 84.84 | 0 | 0 | 3 | 0 |
| Twenty20 | 2 | 1 | 0 | 12 | 12 | 12.00 | 200.00 | 0 | 0 | 0 | 0 |

| Bowling | Mat | Balls | Runs | Wkts | BBI | BBM | Ave | Econ | SR | 5w | 10 |
|---|---|---|---|---|---|---|---|---|---|---|---|
| First-class | 16 | 2671 | 1498 | 68 | 5/41 | 9/134 | 22.02 | 3.36 | 39.2 | 3 | 0 |
| List A | 13 | 574 | 556 | 19 | 3/51 | 3/51 | 29.26 | 5.81 | 30.2 | 0 | 0 |
| Twenty20 | 2 | 48 | 70 | 2 | 2/42 | 2/42 | 35.00 | 8.75 | 24.0 | 0 | 0 |

# JOE ROOT

**RHB OB R1**

YORKSHIRE

FULL NAME: Joseph Edward Root
BORN: December 30, 1990, Sheffield, Yorkshire
SQUAD NO: 5
HEIGHT: 6ft
NICKNAME: PT, Ted, Casper, Rooty, The Milkybar Kid
EDUCATION: Worksop College; King Ecgbert School
TEAMS: England Lions, England Under-19s, Yorkshire, Yorkshire 2nd XI
CAREER: First-class: 2010; List A: 2009; T20: 2011

BEST BATTING: 160 Yorkshire vs Sussex, Scarborough, 2011
BEST BOWLING: 3-33 Yorkshire vs Warwickshire, Leeds, 2011

FAMILY TIES? My dad played a few games for Notts 2nd XI and captained their colts side. My brother will be playing for the MCC Young Cricketers this year
CAREER HIGHLIGHTS? Making my first-class debut and scoring a century against Sri Lanka A in a 50-over game for England Lions
CRICKETING HEROES? Michael Vaughan, Shane Warne and Sachin Tendulkar
NON-CRICKETING HEROES? Tiger Woods, Stevie Wonder
TIP FOR THE TOP? Daniel Bell-Drummond
IF YOU WEREN'T A CRICKETER? Playing golf where possible and trying to get into university
WHEN RAIN STOPS PLAY? I'll be found annoying people
FAVOURITE TV? How I Met Your Mother
DREAM HOLIDAY? Camps Bay, South Africa
ACCOMPLISHMENTS? Sheffield table tennis champion aged 12
SURPRISING SKILL? I can play the ukulele
AMAZE ME! I like cooking, I'm very tidy and a poor mover on a night out!
FANTASY SLIP CORDON? Keeper: Tiger Woods, 1st: Me, 2nd: David Beckham, 3rd: Stevie Wonder, 4th: Chris Gayle, Gully: Peter Griffin, Short leg: Peter Crouch
TWITTER FEED: @joeroot05

| Batting | Mat | Inns | NO | Runs | HS | Ave | SR | 100 | 50 | Ct | St |
|---|---|---|---|---|---|---|---|---|---|---|---|
| First-class | 18 | 35 | 5 | 1051 | 160 | 35.03 | 44.57 | 1 | 5 | 6 | 0 |
| List A | 18 | 18 | 2 | 540 | 110* | 33.75 | 71.05 | 1 | 4 | 4 | 0 |
| Twenty20 | 9 | 7 | 2 | 106 | 46* | 21.20 | 100.00 | 0 | 0 | 2 | 0 |

| Bowling | Mat | Balls | Runs | Wkts | BBI | BBM | Ave | Econ | SR | 5w | 10 |
|---|---|---|---|---|---|---|---|---|---|---|---|
| First-class | 18 | 549 | 346 | 7 | 3/33 | 3/33 | 49.42 | 3.78 | 78.4 | 0 | 0 |
| List A | 18 | 317 | 239 | 6 | 2/10 | 2/10 | 39.83 | 4.52 | 52.8 | 0 | 0 |
| Twenty20 | 9 | 18 | 34 | 1 | 1/12 | 1/12 | 34.00 | 11.33 | 18.0 | 0 | 0 |

## ADAM ROSSINGTON                                           RHB WK

FULL NAME: Adam Matthew Rossington
BORN: May 5, 1993, Edgware, Middlesex
SQUAD NO: 17
HEIGHT: 6ft
NICKNAME: Rosso, Big Lad, Mitchell Brother
EDUCATION: Mill Hill School
TEAMS: England Under-19s, Middlesex,
Middlesex 2nd XI
CAREER: First-class: 2010; T20: 2011

**MIDDLESEX**

BEST BATTING: 4 Middlesex vs Sri Lankans, Uxbridge, 2011

CAREER HIGHLIGHTS? Scoring a hundred for England U19 vs Sri Lanka U19
SUPERSTITIONS? Left pad first, always
CRICKETING HEROES? Alec Stewart, Paul Weekes
NON-CRICKETING HEROES? My dad, also Ray Mears
BEST PLAYER IN COUNTY CRICKET? Marcus Trescothick
TIPS FOR THE TOP? Dan Housego, Daniel Bell-Drummond
IF YOU WEREN'T A CRICKETER? Golfer
WHEN RAIN STOPS PLAY? Reading the paper, card games
FAVOURITE TV? Eastenders
FAVOURITE FILM? Gladiator
FAVOURITE BOOK? Of Mice And Men
DREAM HOLIDAY? Las Vegas or Cuba
GUILTY PLEASURES? Nachos
SURPRISING FACT? Support Barnet FC, cannot ride a bicycle
TWITTER FEED: @Rossington17

| Batting | Mat | Inns | NO | Runs | HS | Ave | SR | 100 | 50 | Ct | St |
|---|---|---|---|---|---|---|---|---|---|---|---|
| First-class | 2 | 3 | 0 | 5 | 4 | 1.66 | 16.12 | 0 | 0 | 2 | 0 |
| Twenty20 | 4 | 4 | 0 | 27 | 25 | 6.75 | 112.50 | 0 | 0 | 2 | 0 |

| Bowling | Mat | Balls | Runs | Wkts | BBI | BBM | Ave | Econ | SR | 5w | 10 |
|---|---|---|---|---|---|---|---|---|---|---|---|
| First-class | 2 | - | - | - | - | - | - | - | - | - | - |
| Twenty20 | 4 | - | - | - | - | - | - | - | - | - | - |

## ADAM ROUSE                                    RHB WK

FULL NAME: Adam Paul Rouse
BORN: June 30, 1992, Harare, Zimbabwe
SQUAD NO: 20
HEIGHT: 5ft 7in
NICKNAME: Rousie
EDUCATION: Lilfordia School, Zimbabwe; Perins Community Sports College; Peter Symonds College
TEAMS: England Under-19s, Hampshire, Hampshire 2nd XI, Hampshire Cricket Board, Hampshire Under-15s, Leicestershire 2nd XI
CAREER: Yet to make first-team debut

**FAMILY TIES?** Brother played for Hampshire 2nd XI and was involved in the England U15 set-up

**WHY CRICKET?** Sport was compulsory at school. My older brothers played, so I always went to their games and watched them play. Also, cricket was the main sport in Zimbabwe, so there was a lot of emphasis on it there

**CAREER HIGHLIGHTS?** Represented England U19 a year early in the series vs Sri Lanka U19. Caught out Kumar Sangakkara as sub fielder for England in The Rose Bowl Test match vs Sri Lanka in 2011. Touring India with England U18 Elite Player Development squad

**SUPERSTITIONS?** Left pad on first. Mark a line on off stump every ball when standing up. Mark my guard most balls. Avoid lines

**CRICKETING HEROES?** Sachin Tendulkar, Brian Lara, Andy Flower, AB de Villiers, Kumar Sangakkara

**TIPS FOR THE TOP?** James Taylor, James Vince, Danny Briggs

**IF YOU WEREN'T A CRICKETER?** Strength and conditioning coach or personal trainer

**FAVOURITE TV?** Two And A Half Men

**FAVOURITE FILM?** Gladiator

**FAVOURITE BOOK?** Henry Olonga – Blood, Sweat and Treason

**DREAM HOLIDAY?** Barbados

**ACCOMPLISHMENTS?** Played rugby for London Irish silver academy and London Irish U16. Played county (Hampshire) level rugby for two seasons

**GUILTY PLEASURES?** Chocolate

**FANTASY SLIP CORDON?** Keeper: Myself, 1st: Viv Richards (he is a fascinating person and legend of the game), 2nd: Lee Evans (someone to make me laugh), 3rd: Blake Lively (someone to look at/celebrity crush), Gully: Lionel Messi (legend!)

**TWITTER FEED:** @Rousie20

# JASON ROY

**RHB RM MVP48**

FULL NAME: Jason Jonathan Roy
BORN: July 21, 1990, Durban, South Africa
SQUAD NO: 20
HEIGHT: 6ft
NICKNAME: JRoy
EDUCATION: Whitgift School
TEAMS: England Lions, Surrey, Surrey 2nd XI
CAREER: First-class: 2010; List A: 2008; T20: 2008

**SURREY**

---

BEST BATTING: 106* Surrey vs Glamorgan, The Oval, 2011
BEST BOWLING: 2-29 Surrey vs Glamorgan, The Oval, 2011

---

FAMILY TIES? Nobody in the family has played cricket before me
WHY CRICKET? I liked hitting the ball a long way
CAREER HIGHLIGHTS? Winning the CB40 with Surrey, getting promoted back to Division
One with Surrey, my maiden first-class hundred against Glamorgan and being the first
Surrey player to score a T20 hundred
CRICKETING HEROES? Jacques Kallis and Chris Gayle
BEST PLAYER IN COUNTY CRICKET? Marcus Trescothick
TIPS FOR THE TOP? All the Surrey youngsters
IF YOU WEREN'T A CRICKETER? Professional surfer
WHEN RAIN STOPS PLAY? Chatting in the dressing room
FAVOURITE TV? Two And A Half Men
FAVOURITE FILM? The Hangover
DREAM HOLIDAY? Mauritius or the Caribbean
GUILTY PLEASURES? Watching TV whilst eating a tub of ice cream
FANTASY SLIP CORDON? Keeper: Will Ferrell, 1st: Vince Vaughn, 2nd: Owen Wilson, 3rd:
Jason Roy, Gully: Spiderman
TWITTER FEED: @JasonRoy20

| Batting | Mat | Inns | NO | Runs | HS | Ave | SR | 100 | 50 | Ct | St |
|---|---|---|---|---|---|---|---|---|---|---|---|
| First-class | 15 | 27 | 1 | 793 | 106* | 30.50 | 87.72 | 1 | 3 | 11 | 0 |
| List A | 25 | 24 | 0 | 704 | 131 | 29.33 | 107.31 | 2 | 5 | 11 | 0 |
| Twenty20 | 37 | 34 | 1 | 874 | 101* | 26.48 | 141.19 | 1 | 5 | 19 | 0 |

| Bowling | Mat | Balls | Runs | Wkts | BBI | BBM | Ave | Econ | SR | 5w | 10 |
|---|---|---|---|---|---|---|---|---|---|---|---|
| First-class | 15 | 56 | 61 | 2 | 2/29 | 2/43 | 30.50 | 6.53 | 28.0 | 0 | 0 |
| List A | 25 | 6 | 12 | 0 | - | - | - | 12.00 | - | 0 | 0 |
| Twenty20 | 37 | - | - | - | - | - | - | - | - | - | - |

SURREY

FULL NAME: Jacobus Andries Rudolph
BORN: May 4, 1981, Springs, South Africa
SQUAD NO: TBC
HEIGHT: 5ft 10in
NICKNAME: Jakes
EDUCATION: Afrikaanse Hoer Seunskool
TEAMS: South Africa, Africa XI, Eagles,
Northerns, South Africa A, Titans, Yorkshire
CAREER: Test: 2003; ODI: 2003; T20I: 2006;
First-class: 1997; List A: 2000; T20: 2004

BEST BATTING: 228* Yorkshire vs Durham, Leeds, 2010
BEST BOWLING: 5-80 Eagles vs Cape Cobras, Newlands, 2007
COUNTY CAP: 2007 (Yorkshire)

CRICKETING HEROES? Justin Langer
CAREER HIGHLIGHTS? Making 222* on my Test debut
OTHER SPORTS FOLLOWED? Football (Manchester United)
FAVOURITE BAND? U2, Dire Straits, The Killers
RELAXATIONS? Fly fishing and adventure motorbiking
NOTES: Recalled to South Africa's Test side last October after more than five years out of the
side – he was unavailable for selection for most of this time having signed a Kolpak contract
with Yorkshire. Passed 1,000 runs in four consecutive seasons (2007-2010) while playing
for Yorkshire. Scored his sixth Test century, 105* against New Zealand at Dunedin, this year.
Will be Surrey's overseas player while Murali Kartik is at the IPL. Father Johan is the current
coach of Namibia

| Batting | Mat | Inns | NO | Runs | HS | Ave | SR | 100 | 50 | Ct | St |
|---|---|---|---|---|---|---|---|---|---|---|---|
| Tests | 41 | 73 | 9 | 2395 | 222* | 37.42 | 44.21 | 6 | 10 | 24 | 0 |
| ODIs | 45 | 39 | 6 | 1174 | 81 | 35.57 | 68.05 | 0 | 7 | 11 | 0 |
| T20Is | 1 | 1 | 1 | 6 | 6* | - | 85.71 | 0 | 0 | 0 | 0 |
| First-class | 214 | 366 | 25 | 15664 | 228* | 45.93 | | 46 | 70 | 197 | 0 |
| List A | 218 | 206 | 29 | 8559 | 134* | 48.35 | | 13 | 59 | 80 | 0 |
| Twenty20 | 75 | 69 | 11 | 1830 | 71 | 31.55 | 116.48 | 0 | 12 | 23 | 0 |

| Bowling | Mat | Balls | Runs | Wkts | BBI | BBM | Ave | Econ | SR | 5w | 10 |
|---|---|---|---|---|---|---|---|---|---|---|---|
| Tests | 41 | 664 | 432 | 4 | 1/1 | 1/1 | 108.00 | 3.90 | 166.0 | 0 | 0 |
| ODIs | 45 | 24 | 26 | 0 | - | - | - | 6.50 | - | 0 | 0 |
| T20Is | 1 | - | - | - | - | - | - | - | - | - | - |
| First-class | 214 | 4523 | 2572 | 58 | 5/80 | | 44.34 | 3.41 | 77.9 | 3 | 0 |
| List A | 218 | 418 | 390 | 12 | 4/41 | 4/41 | 32.50 | 5.59 | 34.8 | 0 | 0 |
| Twenty20 | 75 | 163 | 221 | 10 | 3/16 | 3/16 | 22.10 | 8.13 | 16.3 | 0 | 0 |

# CHRIS RUSHWORTH

**RHB RMF**

FULL NAME: Christopher Rushworth
BORN: July 11, 1986, Sunderland
SQUAD NO: 22
HEIGHT: 6ft 2in
NICKNAME: Rushy, Sponge
EDUCATION: Castle View Comprehensive
TEAMS: Durham, Northumberland
CAREER: First-class: 2010; List A: 2004; T20: 2011

BEST BATTING: 28 Durham vs Yorkshire, Chester-le-Street, 2010
BEST BOWLING: 4-90 Durham vs Essex, Chelmsford, 2010

**FAMILY TIES?** My father played local cricket, brother Lee represented England and Durham at junior levels and my cousin Phil Mustard is current captain of Durham

**CAREER HIGHLIGHTS?** My first-class debut against Yorkshire at Headingley is the highlight so far but I'm sure winning trophies with Durham will overshadow that

**CRICKETING HEROES?** Loved watching the two South Africans Shaun Pollock and Allan Donald tear teams apart as a young bowler! Sheer aggression was exciting to watch

**TIPS FOR THE TOP?** Ben Stokes and Scott Borthwick both have brilliant futures and I'm sure they will feature for England and be a great success

**IF YOU WEREN'T A CRICKETER?** No idea. Thankfully I've had the opportunities at Durham

**WHEN RAIN STOPS PLAY?** Usually cards or just general relaxation. Mitch Claydon finds a way to entertain the lads with his magic tricks!

**FAVOURITE TV?** Love watching sports, football takes up a lot of time on the box

**DREAM HOLIDAY?** I've spent a few years in Australia playing cricket and that's probably my ideal holiday destination. The weather is marvellous and the people are friendly

**GUILTY PLEASURES?** Midget gems and wine gums. Takes me back to my school days

**TWITTER FEED:** @rushworth22

| Batting | Mat | Inns | NO | Runs | HS | Ave | SR | 100 | 50 | Ct | St |
|---------|-----|------|-----|------|------|------|------|------|------|------|------|
| First-class | 12 | 17 | 3 | 155 | 28 | 11.07 | 56.98 | 0 | 0 | 2 | 0 |
| List A | 14 | 7 | 4 | 28 | 12* | 9.33 | 80.00 | 0 | 0 | 2 | 0 |
| Twenty20 | 14 | 3 | 2 | 2 | 2 | 2.00 | 66.66 | 0 | 0 | 2 | 0 |

| Bowling | Mat | Balls | Runs | Wkts | BBI | BBM | Ave | Econ | SR | 5w | 10 |
|---------|-----|-------|------|------|------|------|------|------|------|------|------|
| First-class | 12 | 1618 | 990 | 26 | 4/90 | 5/159 | 38.07 | 3.67 | 62.2 | 0 | 0 |
| List A | 14 | 513 | 402 | 22 | 3/6 | 3/6 | 18.27 | 4.70 | 23.3 | 0 | 0 |
| Twenty20 | 14 | 234 | 342 | 11 | 3/20 | 3/20 | 31.09 | 8.76 | 21.2 | 0 | 0 |

# CHRIS RUSSELL

**RHB RMF**

**WORCESTERSHIRE**

FULL NAME: Christopher James Russell
BORN: February 16, 1989, Newport, Isle of Wight
SQUAD NO: 18
HEIGHT: 6ft 1in
NICKNAME: Goobs
EDUCATION: Wroxall Primary School, Ventnor; Medina High School
TEAMS: Worcestershire, Worcestershire 2nd XI
CAREER: List A: 2010

NOTES: Career highlight was playing first game for Worcestershire (2nd XI). Follows football, tennis and rugby. Likes golf, music, surfing and socialising

| Batting | Mat | Inns | NO | Runs | HS | Ave | SR | 100 | 50 | Ct | St |
|---------|-----|------|----|----|------|-----|-----|-----|----|----|----|
| List A | 2 | - | - | - | - | - | - | - | - | 0 | 0 |

| Bowling | Mat | Balls | Runs | Wkts | BBI | BBM | Ave | Econ | SR | 5w | 10 |
|---------|-----|-------|------|------|-----|-----|-----|------|-----|----|----|
| List A | 2 | 54 | 68 | 1 | 1/23 | 1/23 | 68.00 | 7.55 | 54.0 | 0 | 0 |

# DAVID SALES

## RHB RM R6

FULL NAME: David John Grimwood Sales
BORN: December 3, 1977, Carshalton, Surrey
SQUAD NO: 5
HEIGHT: 6ft
NICKNAME: Jumble, Car-boot
EDUCATION: Caterham School
TEAMS: Northamptonshire, Wellington
CAREER: First-class: 1996; List A: 1994; T20: 2003

BEST BATTING: 303* Northamptonshire vs Essex, Northampton, 1999
BEST BOWLING: 4-25 Northamptonshire vs Sri Lanka A, Northampton, 1999
COUNTY CAP: 1999; BENEFIT YEAR: 2007

NON-CRICKETING HEROES? Phil Taylor
BEST PLAYER IN COUNTY CRICKET? Stephen Peters
TIP FOR THE TOP? Alex Wakely
IF YOU WEREN'T A CRICKETER? Cricket coach, brick layer
WHEN RAIN STOPS PLAY? Drink coffee and talk rubbish
FAVOURITE TV? I'm A Celebrity… Get Me Out Of Here!
FAVOURITE FILM? Any Given Sunday
FAVOURITE BOOK? Bravo Two Zero
DREAM HOLIDAY? Spain
ACCOMPLISHMENTS? My three boys
GUILTY PLEASURES? A cheeky Chinese and a few beers

| Batting | Mat | Inns | NO | Runs | HS | Ave | SR | 100 | 50 | Ct | St |
|---------|-----|------|-----|------|------|-------|--------|-----|-----|-----|-----|
| First-class | 216 | 345 | 29 | 12412 | 303* | 39.27 | | 24 | 60 | 202 | 0 |
| List A | 249 | 237 | 34 | 6937 | 161 | 34.17 | | 4 | 49 | 113 | 0 |
| Twenty20 | 56 | 53 | 12 | 1209 | 78* | 29.48 | 129.86 | 0 | 10 | 28 | 0 |

| Bowling | Mat | Balls | Runs | Wkts | BBI | BBM | Ave | Econ | SR | 5w | 10 |
|---------|-----|-------|------|------|------|------|-------|-------|------|-----|-----|
| First-class | 216 | 345 | 184 | 9 | 4/25 | | 20.44 | 3.20 | 38.3 | 0 | 0 |
| List A | 249 | 84 | 67 | 0 | - | - | - | 4.78 | - | 0 | 0 |
| Twenty20 | 56 | 12 | 23 | 1 | 1/10 | 1/10 | 23.00 | 11.50 | 12.0 | 0 | 0 |

# ANDREW SALTER RHB OB

FULL NAME: Andrew Graham Salter
BORN: June 1, 1993, Haverfordwest, Pembrokeshire
SQUAD NO: 21
EDUCATION: Milford Haven Sixth Form College
TEAMS: England Under-17s, England Under-19s, Glamorgan 2nd XI, Wales Minor Counties
CAREER: Yet to make first-team debut

NOTES: Captained England U15. Toured Sri Lanka with England U19 in 2011

# GURJIT SANDHU

## RHB LMF

FULL NAME: Gurjit Singh Sandhu
BORN: March 24, 1992, Isleworth, Middlesex
SQUAD NO: 92
HEIGHT: 6ft 4in
NICKNAME: Gurj
EDUCATION: Isleworth and Syon School
TEAMS: Middlesex, Middlesex 2nd XI
CAREER: First-class: 2011

MIDDLESEX

BEST BATTING: 8 Middlesex vs Sri Lankans, Uxbridge, 2011

**CAREER HIGHLIGHTS?** Making my first-class debut against Sri Lanka at Uxbridge
**SUPERSTITIONS?** My chain, can't play without it. I feel naked when I don't have it around my neck
**CRICKETING HEROES?** Wasim Akram, Brian Lara
**NON-CRICKETING HEROES?** Dimitar Berbatov of Manchester United, Karl Pilkington, Batman
**BEST PLAYER IN COUNTY CRICKET?** Marcus Trescothick
**TIP FOR THE TOP?** James Taylor
**WHEN RAIN STOPS PLAY?** Few of the boys start off a horse racing game with cards and guys making bets
**FAVOURITE TV?** Fresh Prince Of Bel-Air
**FAVOURITE FILM?** Inception, Gladiator
**FAVOURITE BOOK?** Lance Armstrong – It's Not About The Bike
**DREAM HOLIDAY?** Caribbean islands
**ACCOMPLISHMENTS?** Winning a Football Manger season with Brentford
**GUILTY PLEASURES?** Junk food

| Batting | Mat | Inns | NO | Runs | HS | Ave | SR | 100 | 50 | Ct | St |
|---|---|---|---|---|---|---|---|---|---|---|---|
| First-class | 1 | 2 | 1 | 15 | 8 | 15.00 | 51.72 | 0 | 0 | 0 | 0 |

| Bowling | Mat | Balls | Runs | Wkts | BBI | BBM | Ave | Econ | SR | 5w | 10 |
|---|---|---|---|---|---|---|---|---|---|---|---|
| First-class | 1 | 78 | 69 | 0 | - | - | - | 5.30 | - | 0 | 0 |

## RAMNARESH SARWAN                                    RHB LB

FULL NAME: Ramnaresh Ronnie Sarwan
BORN: June 23, 1980, Wakenaam Island,
Essequibo, Guyana
SQUAD NO: 53
TEAMS: West Indies, Gloucestershire,
Guyana, Kings XI Punjab, Stanford
Superstars
CAREER: Test: 2000; ODI: 2000; T20I: 2007;
First-class: 1996; List A: 1996; T20: 2006

BEST BATTING: 291 West Indies vs England, Bridgetown, 2009
BEST BOWLING: 6-62 Guyana vs Leeward Islands, St John's, 2001
COUNTY CAP: 2005 (Gloucestershire)

NOTES: Scored 84* against Pakistan on Test debut in 2000. Played seven first-class matches
for Gloucestershire in 2005 and scored 441 runs, including an innings of 117 against
Sussex at Cheltenham. Succeeded Brian Lara as captain of West Indies after his retirement
following the 2007 World Cup. Topped the batting averages in the 2008/09 Wisden Trophy
against England, scoring 626 runs in six innings at an average of 104.33. Will be with
Leicestershire for the entirety of the 2012 season

| Batting | Mat | Inns | NO | Runs | HS | Ave | SR | 100 | 50 | Ct | St |
|---------|-----|------|-----|------|-----|------|--------|-----|-----|-----|-----|
| Tests | 87 | 154 | 8 | 5842 | 291 | 40.01 | 46.79 | 15 | 31 | 53 | 0 |
| ODIs | 173 | 161 | 31 | 5644 | 115* | 43.41 | 75.76 | 4 | 38 | 45 | 0 |
| T20Is | 18 | 16 | 3 | 298 | 59 | 22.92 | 104.19 | 0 | 2 | 7 | 0 |
| First-class | 192 | 324 | 23 | 11836 | 291 | 39.32 | | 31 | 62 | 137 | 0 |
| List A | 242 | 228 | 39 | 7824 | 118* | 41.39 | | 8 | 48 | 66 | 0 |
| Twenty20 | 48 | 45 | 5 | 872 | 70 | 21.80 | 108.45 | 0 | 5 | 16 | 0 |

| Bowling | Mat | Balls | Runs | Wkts | BBI | BBM | Ave | Econ | SR | 5w | 10 |
|---------|-----|-------|------|------|-----|-----|------|------|------|-----|-----|
| Tests | 87 | 2022 | 1163 | 23 | 4/37 | 7/96 | 50.56 | 3.45 | 87.9 | 0 | 0 |
| ODIs | 173 | 581 | 586 | 16 | 3/31 | 3/31 | 36.62 | 6.05 | 36.3 | 0 | 0 |
| T20Is | 18 | 12 | 10 | 2 | 2/10 | 2/10 | 5.00 | 5.00 | 6.0 | 0 | 0 |
| First-class | 192 | 4193 | 2224 | 54 | 6/62 | | 41.18 | 3.18 | 77.6 | 1 | 0 |
| List A | 242 | 1130 | 1001 | 35 | 5/10 | 5/10 | 28.60 | 5.31 | 32.2 | 1 | 0 |
| Twenty20 | 48 | 18 | 22 | 2 | 2/10 | 2/10 | 11.00 | 7.33 | 9.0 | 0 | 0 |

# IAN SAXELBY

## RHB RMF

FULL NAME: Ian David Saxelby
BORN: May 22, 1989, Nottingham
SQUAD NO: 21
HEIGHT: 6ft 2in
NICKNAME: Sax
EDUCATION: Tuxford Comp; Oakham School
TEAMS: England Under-19s, Gloucestershire, Gloucestershire 2nd XI, Nottinghamshire 2nd XI
CAREER: First-class: 2008; List A: 2009; T20: 2009

---

BEST BATTING: 60* Gloucestershire vs Northamptonshire, Northampton, 2009
BEST BOWLING: 6-69 Gloucestershire vs Surrey, The Oval, 2011

---

FAMILY TIES? Dad played county 2nd XI and my uncles Kevin and Mark were both county cricketers
CAREER HIGHLIGHTS? Playing for England U19
SUPERSTITIONS? I never change my seat when there's a partnership developing!
CRICKETING HEROES? Brian Lara
TIPS FOR THE TOP? Alex Hales, Jos Buttler
IF YOU WEREN'T A CRICKETER? Working on the family farm
WHEN RAIN STOPS PLAY? Playing cards/games, watching TV, and drinking coffee
FAVOURITE TV? Hustle, Top Gear
FAVOURITE FILM? Gladiator
FAVOURITE BOOK? Not a reader!
DREAM HOLIDAY? Barbados
ACCOMPLISHMENTS? Leicester Tigers Academy
GUILTY PLEASURES? McDonald's, Twix, Chocolate Digestives
FANTASY SLIP CORDON? Keeper: Jeremy Clarkson, 1st: Me, 2nd: Megan Fox, 3rd: Chris Martin, Gully: Richard Attenborough
TWITTER FEED: @saxelby21

| Batting | Mat | Inns | NO | Runs | HS | Ave | SR | 100 | 50 | Ct | St |
|---|---|---|---|---|---|---|---|---|---|---|---|
| First-class | 27 | 39 | 10 | 426 | 60* | 14.68 | 42.01 | 0 | 1 | 8 | 0 |
| List A | 10 | 7 | 2 | 27 | 7* | 5.40 | 56.25 | 0 | 0 | 0 | 0 |
| Twenty20 | 14 | 8 | 2 | 15 | 5 | 2.50 | 44.11 | 0 | 0 | 2 | 0 |

| Bowling | Mat | Balls | Runs | Wkts | BBI | BBM | Ave | Econ | SR | 5w | 10 |
|---|---|---|---|---|---|---|---|---|---|---|---|
| First-class | 27 | 3754 | 2367 | 71 | 6/69 | 10/142 | 33.33 | 3.78 | 52.8 | 2 | 1 |
| List A | 10 | 367 | 417 | 15 | 4/31 | 4/31 | 27.80 | 6.81 | 24.4 | 0 | 0 |
| Twenty20 | 14 | 279 | 385 | 12 | 2/23 | 2/23 | 32.08 | 8.27 | 23.2 | 0 | 0 |

YORKSHIRE

**FULL NAME:** Joseph John Sayers
**BORN:** November 5, 1983, Leeds, Yorkshire
**SQUAD NO:** 22
**HEIGHT:** 6ft
**NICKNAME:** JJ, Squirrel
**EDUCATION:** St Mary's RC Comprehensive School, Menston; Oxford University
**TEAMS:** England Under-19s, Oxford MCCU, Oxford University, Yorkshire
**CAREER:** First-class: 2002; List A: 2003; T20: 2005

**BEST BATTING:** 187 Yorkshire vs Kent, Tunbridge Wells, 2007
**BEST BOWLING:** 3-15 Yorkshire vs DMCCU, Durham University, 2011
**COUNTY CAP:** 2007

**CAREER HIGHLIGHTS?** Captaining Yorkshire in 2011, playing for England Lions in 2011
**CRICKETING HEROES?** Mike Atherton
**TIP FOR THE TOP?** Jonny Bairstow
**IF YOU WEREN'T A CRICKETER?** Working in the City
**WHEN RAIN STOPS PLAY?** Making and drinking tea
**FAVOURITE TV?** Mock The Week
**FAVOURITE FILM?** Legends Of The Fall
**FAVOURITE BOOK?** Mitch Albom – Tuesdays With Morrie
**ACCOMPLISHMENTS?** Physics degree from Oxford, marrying my wife, my son Sebastian
**SURPRISING SKILL?** Playing guitar, oil painting
**GUILTY PLEASURES?** Twitter and Jedward – although preferably not simultaneously!
**AMAZE ME!** I own a racehorse called Simply The Best and my nickname is Squirrel, but I don't know why!
**FANTASY SLIP CORDON?** Keeper: Stephen Fry, 1st: Anthony Hopkins, 2nd: Peter Kay, 3rd: Abraham Lincoln, Gully: Brian Blessed
**TWITTER FEED:** @Joe_Sayers

| Batting | Mat | Inns | NO | Runs | HS | Ave | SR | 100 | 50 | Ct | St |
|---|---|---|---|---|---|---|---|---|---|---|---|
| First-class | 96 | 161 | 12 | 5133 | 187 | 34.44 | 38.30 | 11 | 28 | 56 | 0 |
| List A | 27 | 27 | 2 | 515 | 62 | 20.60 | 59.81 | 0 | 4 | 2 | 0 |
| Twenty20 | 12 | 9 | 0 | 172 | 44 | 19.11 | 120.27 | 0 | 0 | 2 | 0 |

| Bowling | Mat | Balls | Runs | Wkts | BBI | BBM | Ave | Econ | SR | 5w | 10 |
|---|---|---|---|---|---|---|---|---|---|---|---|
| First-class | 96 | 361 | 178 | 6 | 3/15 | 3/15 | 29.66 | 2.95 | 60.1 | 0 | 0 |
| List A | 27 | 60 | 79 | 1 | 1/31 | 1/31 | 79.00 | 7.90 | 60.0 | 0 | 0 |
| Twenty20 | 12 | - | - | - | - | - | - | - | - | - | - |

# TOM SCOLLAY

## RHB OB

FULL NAME: Thomas Edward Scollay
BORN: November 28, 1987, Alice Springs, Australia
SQUAD NO: 5
HEIGHT: 5ft 8in
NICKNAME: Scolls
EDUCATION: St Philip's College, Alice Springs, Australia
TEAMS: Hampshire 2nd XI, Middlesex, Middlesex 2nd XI, Nightcliff, Northern Territory, Northern Territory Under-19s
CAREER: List A: 2010; T20: 2011

**MIDDLESEX**

WHY CRICKET? My best friend played on a Saturday morning when I was nine years old and I would sleep at his house every Friday night and wear my white clothes to the ground hoping I would get a game because it looked like heaps of fun!

CAREER HIGHLIGHTS? Debuting for Middlesex in Pro40 at Lord's. Still early in my career so hopefully many more to come and lots of success with Middlesex

CRICKETING HEROES? I grew up idolising Mark Waugh and modelled my batting as a young player on him

TIP FOR THE TOP? Paul Stirling is a very special player for us at Middlesex. Currently playing for Ireland and could one day be one of the best ODI/T20 batsmen in the world. Also Sam Robson is still young and doing very well. I like the look of James Vince at Hampshire, he looks like a future England player

IF YOU WEREN'T A CRICKETER? I would probably be living back in Australia and have gone to uni. Maybe studied Sports Science, Psychology or Economics. Otherwise I would have been an international DJ, travelling the world mixing music!

FAVOURITE TV? Entourage is the best show ever made! Closely followed by The Inbetweeners, Two And A Half Men, Flight Of The Conchords and Californication

SURPRISING FACT? I have a twin brother. His name is Clancy and I'm two minutes older. I was in a Bollywood movie about cricket called Patiala House. It was shot all around England at Test grounds and was a big hit in India

TWITTER FEED: @scolls5

| Batting | Mat | Inns | NO | Runs | HS | Ave | SR | 100 | 50 | Ct | St |
|---|---|---|---|---|---|---|---|---|---|---|---|
| List A | 9 | 9 | 0 | 115 | 32 | 12.77 | 83.94 | 0 | 0 | 3 | 0 |
| Twenty20 | 5 | 4 | 0 | 36 | 15 | 9.00 | 90.00 | 0 | 0 | 1 | 0 |
| Bowling | Mat | Balls | Runs | Wkts | BBI | BBM | Ave | Econ | SR | 5w | 10 |
| List A | 9 | 24 | 21 | 1 | 1/21 | 1/21 | 21.00 | 5.25 | 24.0 | 0 | 0 |
| Twenty20 | 5 | - | - | - | - | - | - | - | - | - | - |

## BEN SCOTT        RHB WK

FULL NAME: Ben James Matthew Scott
BORN: August 4, 1981, Isleworth, Middlesex
SQUAD NO: 7
HEIGHT: 5ft 8in
NICKNAME: Scotty, Singh
EDUCATION: Whitton School; Richmond College
TEAMS: England Lions, Middlesex, Middlesex Cricket Board, Surrey, Worcestershire
CAREER: First-class: 2003; List A: 1999; T20: 2004

BEST BATTING: 164* Middlesex vs Northamptonshire, Uxbridge, 2008
COUNTY CAP: 2007 (Middlesex)

FAMILY TIES? Dad played local cricket and was a legendary legspinner in his day. Brother was, according to dad, a classy bat. My nephew Joel Pope played for Leicestershire
CAREER HIGHLIGHTS? My first hundred at Lord's, winning the T20 competition in 2008 and Lions tour to New Zealand
SUPERSTITIONS? I have to touch something white on my way to the crease
CRICKETING HEROES? Alec Stewart, Alan Knott, Jack Russell
TIPS FOR THE TOP? Paul Stirling, Aneesh Kapil, Moeen Ali
IF YOU WEREN'T A CRICKETER? I'd be a personal trainer
WHEN RAIN STOPS PLAY? You'll find me annoying Vikram Solanki
FAVOURITE FILM? Lemonade Mouth
FAVOURITE BOOK? The Curious Incident Of The Dog In The Night-time
SURPRISING SKILL? Play guitar, piano and I'm almost a professional body popper
GUILTY PLEASURES? Burgers, pancakes, bubble tea
AMAZE ME! I speak Hindi, Urdu and Afrikaans so I understand all the sledges I've been getting over the years! It was me that put glue on Miss Chohan's chair in primary school that landed the whole class in detention! I'm actually taller that I look, I've just had my knees bent the whole time

| Batting | Mat | Inns | NO | Runs | HS | Ave | SR | 100 | 50 | Ct | St |
|---|---|---|---|---|---|---|---|---|---|---|---|
| First-class | 89 | 139 | 27 | 3173 | 164* | 28.33 | 50.28 | 3 | 18 | 242 | 26 |
| List A | 111 | 72 | 23 | 926 | 73* | 18.89 | | 0 | 4 | 84 | 32 |
| Twenty20 | 85 | 61 | 26 | 545 | 43* | 15.57 | 103.41 | 0 | 0 | 30 | 34 |

| Bowling | Mat | Balls | Runs | Wkts | BBI | BBM | Ave | Econ | SR | 5w | 10 |
|---|---|---|---|---|---|---|---|---|---|---|---|
| First-class | 89 | 3 | 1 | 0 | - | - | - | 2.00 | - | 0 | 0 |
| List A | 111 | - | - | - | - | - | - | - | - | - | - |
| Twenty20 | 85 | - | - | - | - | - | - | - | - | - | - |

# OWAIS SHAH

## RHB OB R8

**FULL NAME:** Owais Alam Shah
**BORN:** October 22, 1978, Karachi, Pakistan
**SQUAD NO:** 3
**HEIGHT:** 6ft 1in
**NICKNAME:** Ace, The Mauler
**EDUCATION:** Isleworth and Syon School; Westminster University
**TEAMS:** England, Cape Cobras, Delhi Daredevils, England Lions, Essex, Hobart Hurricanes, Kochi Tuskers Kerala, Kolkata Knight Riders, Middlesex, Wellington
**CAREER:** Test: 2006; ODI: 2001; T20I: 2007; First-class: 1996; List A: 1995; T20: 2003

**BEST BATTING:** 203 Middlesex vs Derbyshire, Southgate, 2001
**BEST BOWLING:** 3-33 Middlesex vs Gloucestershire, Bristol, 1999
**COUNTY CAP:** 2000 (Middlesex); **BENEFIT YEAR:** 2008 (Middlesex)

**CAREER HIGHLIGHTS?** My Test debut against India in Mumbai
**OTHER SPORTS FOLLOWED?** Football (I like to watch Manchester United play)
**CRICKETERS PARTICULARLY ADMIRED?** Viv Richards, Sachin Tendulkar, Mark Waugh
**NOTES:** Captained England U19 to victory in the 1997/98 U19 World Cup in South Africa. Cricket Writers' Young Player of the Year for 2001. Made his Test debut in the third Test vs India at Mumbai in March 2006, scoring 88. His first and only ODI century came six years later against India at The Oval (107* from 95 balls). Made 98 from 89 balls in an ODI vs South Africa at Centurion in September 2007. Bought by Delhi Daredevils for IPL 2009, and by Kolkata Knight Riders a year later. Signed for Rajasthan Royals for IPL 2012 following a run to the semi-finals of the Big Bash League with Hobart Hurricanes, averaging 70.50 from eight games. Signed a two-year deal with Essex in November 2010

| Batting | Mat | Inns | NO | Runs | HS | Ave | SR | 100 | 50 | Ct | St |
|---|---|---|---|---|---|---|---|---|---|---|---|
| Tests | 6 | 10 | 0 | 269 | 88 | 26.90 | 41.90 | 0 | 2 | 2 | 0 |
| ODIs | 71 | 66 | 6 | 1834 | 107* | 30.56 | 78.67 | 1 | 12 | 21 | 0 |
| T20Is | 17 | 15 | 1 | 347 | 55* | 24.78 | 122.18 | 0 | 1 | 5 | 0 |
| First-class | 237 | 404 | 36 | 15461 | 203 | 42.01 | | 42 | 76 | 187 | 0 |
| List A | 348 | 328 | 41 | 10165 | 134 | 35.41 | | 14 | 66 | 116 | 0 |
| Twenty20 | 136 | 129 | 29 | 3520 | 80 | 35.20 | 130.46 | 0 | 20 | 50 | 0 |

| Bowling | Mat | Balls | Runs | Wkts | BBI | BBM | Ave | Econ | SR | 5w | 10 |
|---|---|---|---|---|---|---|---|---|---|---|---|
| Tests | 6 | 30 | 31 | 0 | - | - | - | 6.20 | - | 0 | 0 |
| ODIs | 71 | 193 | 184 | 7 | 3/15 | 3/15 | 26.28 | 5.72 | 27.5 | 0 | 0 |
| T20Is | 17 | - | - | - | - | - | - | - | - | - | - |
| First-class | 237 | 2254 | 1493 | 26 | 3/33 | | 57.42 | 3.97 | 86.6 | 0 | 0 |
| List A | 348 | 924 | 910 | 27 | 4/11 | 4/11 | 33.70 | 5.90 | 34.2 | 0 | 0 |
| Twenty20 | 136 | 57 | 78 | 5 | 2/26 | 2/26 | 15.60 | 8.21 | 11.4 | 0 | 0 |

# AJMAL SHAHZAD

**RHB RFM**

FULL NAME: Ajmal Shahzad
BORN: July 27, 1985, Huddersfield, Yorkshire
SQUAD NO: 4
HEIGHT: 6ft
NICKNAME: Ajy, AJ
EDUCATION: Bradford Grammar School; Woodhouse Grove School; Bradford University; Leeds Metropolitan University
TEAMS: England, England Lions, Yorkshire
CAREER: Test: 2010; ODI: 2010; T20I: 2010; First-class: 2006; List A: 2004; T20: 2006

BEST BATTING: 88 Yorkshire vs Sussex, Hove, 2009
BEST BOWLING: 5-51 Yorkshire vs Durham, Chester-le-Street, 2010
COUNTY CAP: 2010

CAREER HIGHLIGHTS? County cap, England caps, Ashes tour, T20 and ODI World Cups
SUPERSTITIONS? Right pad first
CRICKETING HEROES? Imran Khan, Wasim Akram, Waqar Younis, Shoaib Akhtar
BEST PLAYER IN COUNTY CRICKET? Marcus Trescothick
TIP FOR THE TOP? Joe Root
IF YOU WEREN'T A CRICKETER? Doctor, pharmacist or professional badminton player
WHEN RAIN STOPS PLAY? Watching TV programmes on the iPad
FAVOURITE TV? PhoneShop
DREAM HOLIDAY? Adelaide
GUILTY PLEASURES? Frozen yoghurt

| Batting | Mat | Inns | NO | Runs | HS | Ave | SR | 100 | 50 | Ct | St |
|---|---|---|---|---|---|---|---|---|---|---|---|
| Tests | 1 | 1 | 0 | 5 | 5 | 5.00 | 41.66 | 0 | 0 | 2 | 0 |
| ODIs | 11 | 8 | 2 | 39 | 9 | 6.50 | 65.00 | 0 | 0 | 4 | 0 |
| T20Is | 3 | 1 | 1 | 0 | 0* | - | 0.00 | 0 | 0 | 1 | 0 |
| First-class | 46 | 59 | 16 | 1155 | 88 | 26.86 | 42.60 | 0 | 3 | 8 | 0 |
| List A | 46 | 31 | 10 | 288 | 59* | 13.71 | 95.36 | 0 | 1 | 12 | 0 |
| Twenty20 | 25 | 17 | 5 | 129 | 20 | 10.75 | 135.78 | 0 | 0 | 6 | 0 |

| Bowling | Mat | Balls | Runs | Wkts | BBI | BBM | Ave | Econ | SR | 5w | 10 |
|---|---|---|---|---|---|---|---|---|---|---|---|
| Tests | 1 | 102 | 63 | 4 | 3/45 | 4/63 | 15.75 | 3.70 | 25.5 | 0 | 0 |
| ODIs | 11 | 588 | 490 | 17 | 3/41 | 3/41 | 28.82 | 5.00 | 34.5 | 0 | 0 |
| T20Is | 3 | 66 | 97 | 3 | 2/38 | 2/38 | 32.33 | 8.81 | 22.0 | 0 | 0 |
| First-class | 46 | 7514 | 4354 | 127 | 5/51 | 8/121 | 34.28 | 3.47 | 59.1 | 3 | 0 |
| List A | 46 | 2188 | 1865 | 58 | 5/51 | 5/51 | 32.15 | 5.11 | 37.7 | 1 | 0 |
| Twenty20 | 25 | 510 | 673 | 20 | 3/30 | 3/30 | 33.65 | 7.91 | 25.5 | 0 | 0 |

FULL NAME: Jack David Shantry
BORN: January 29, 1988, Shrewsbury, Shropshire
SQUAD NO: 11
HEIGHT: 6ft 4in
NICKNAME: Shants, Mincer, Length
EDUCATION: Priory School; Shrewsbury Sixth Form College; Manchester University
TEAMS: Minor Counties Under-25s, Shropshire, Worcestershire, Worcestershire 2nd XI
CAREER: First-class: 2009; List A: 2009; T20: 2010

**WORCESTERSHIRE**

BEST BATTING: 47* Worcestershire vs Yorkshire, Scarborough, 2011
BEST BOWLING: 5-49 Worcestershire vs Leicestershire, Leicester, 2010

FAMILY TIES? My brother [Adam] played for Northamptonshire, Warwickshire and Glamorgan before retiring due to injury in 2011. Dad played for Gloucestershire in the late 70s. Mum won 'most whites washed in a calendar year' in 1997

SUPERSTITIONS? Never wear underpants on day four. Always seek new, innovative ways to put the batsman off his game. Always try to beat Matt Pardoe to the lunch queue. NB – not always possible

BEST PLAYER IN COUNTY CRICKET? You can't say yourself can you, it sounds arrogant! I'll say Marcus Trescothick. Or me

ACCOMPLISHMENTS? My castles and moats report in Year 6. Thorough, in-depth and accurate. Not my words, the words of Mrs Pashley

AMAZE ME! 1. I was once half-an-hour away from playing in the FA Cup (qualifying round) for Hyde United but the first-choice goalkeeper passed a late fitness test 2. I played in the same local football and cricket teams as Joe Hart before he moved on to bigger and better things. He recently told me there's not a day goes by when he regrets not choosing a career in cricket 3. In minor counties cricket I opened the batting as an 18-year-old. Worcestershire fans may find that very surprising

TWITTER FEED: @JackShantry

| Batting | Mat | Inns | NO | Runs | HS | Ave | SR | 100 | 50 | Ct | St |
|---|---|---|---|---|---|---|---|---|---|---|---|
| First-class | 22 | 31 | 10 | 215 | 47* | 10.23 | 45.07 | 0 | 0 | 6 | 0 |
| List A | 28 | 12 | 7 | 62 | 18 | 12.40 | 80.51 | 0 | 0 | 5 | 0 |
| Twenty20 | 28 | 8 | 5 | 11 | 6* | 3.66 | 64.70 | 0 | 0 | 7 | 0 |

| Bowling | Mat | Balls | Runs | Wkts | BBI | BBM | Ave | Econ | SR | 5w | 10 |
|---|---|---|---|---|---|---|---|---|---|---|---|
| First-class | 22 | 3836 | 1961 | 49 | 5/49 | 6/111 | 40.02 | 3.06 | 78.2 | 1 | 0 |
| List A | 28 | 1158 | 1141 | 37 | 3/33 | 3/33 | 30.83 | 5.91 | 31.2 | 0 | 0 |
| Twenty20 | 28 | 574 | 684 | 34 | 3/23 | 3/23 | 20.11 | 7.14 | 16.8 | 0 | 0 |

## ASHLEY SHAW RHB LFM

FULL NAME: Stuart Ashley Shaw
BORN: April 15, 1991, Crewe, Cheshire
SQUAD NO: 22
HEIGHT: 5ft 10in
NICKNAME: Ash, Reem
EDUCATION: Shavington High School, Crewe
TEAMS: Kent, Kent 2nd XI
CAREER: First-class: 2011; List A: 2011; T20: 2010

BEST BATTING: 22* Kent vs Derbyshire, Canterbury, 2011
BEST BOWLING: 5-118 Kent vs Derbyshire, Canterbury, 2011

CAREER HIGHLIGHTS? Taking five-fer on debut in the County Championship
CRICKETING HEROES? Charl Langeveldt, David Balcombe
NON-CRICKETING HEROES? Floyd Mayweather Jr, Justin Bieber and Jack Wilshere
BEST PLAYER IN COUNTY CRICKET? Darren Stevens
IF YOU WEREN'T A CRICKETER? Laying bricks
WHEN RAIN STOPS PLAY? Doing quizzes with Rob Key and Joe Denly to find out which of us is most clever
FAVOURITE TV? The Only Way Is Essex
FAVOURITE FILM? Adulthood
GUILTY PLEASURES? Big Brother
SURPRISING FACT? I have a budgie named Dappy. There is a video of me singing on YouTube!
FANTASY SLIP CORDON? Keeper: David Seaman, 1st: Floyd Mayweather Jr, 2nd: Kelly Rowland, 3rd: Russell Brand, Gully: Me
TWITTER FEED: @stuashshaw

| Batting | Mat | Inns | NO | Runs | HS | Ave | SR | 100 | 50 | Ct | St |
|---|---|---|---|---|---|---|---|---|---|---|---|
| First-class | 4 | 5 | 3 | 50 | 22* | 25.00 | 71.42 | 0 | 0 | 3 | 0 |
| List A | 6 | 5 | 3 | 8 | 4* | 4.00 | 88.88 | 0 | 0 | 0 | 0 |
| Twenty20 | 4 | 2 | 2 | 4 | 3* | - | 133.33 | 0 | 0 | 2 | 0 |
| Bowling | Mat | Balls | Runs | Wkts | BBI | BBM | Ave | Econ | SR | 5w | 10 |
| First-class | 4 | 487 | 400 | 11 | 5/118 | 6/175 | 36.36 | 4.92 | 44.2 | 1 | 0 |
| List A | 6 | 162 | 184 | 5 | 3/26 | 3/26 | 36.80 | 6.81 | 32.4 | 0 | 0 |
| Twenty20 | 4 | 60 | 84 | 2 | 1/10 | 1/10 | 42.00 | 8.40 | 30.0 | 0 | 0 |

# CHARLIE SHRECK

**RHB RFM W2**

FULL NAME: Charles Edward Shreck
BORN: January 6, 1978, Truro, Cornwall
SQUAD NO: 19
HEIGHT: 6ft 7in
NICKNAME: Shrecker, Ogre, Stoat, Chough
EDUCATION: Truro School
TEAMS: Cornwall, Kent, Marylebone Cricket
Club, Nottinghamshire, Wellington
CAREER: First-class: 2003; List A: 1999; T20:
2003

**KENT**

BEST BATTING: 19 Nottinghamshire vs Essex, Chelmsford, 2003
BEST BOWLING: 8-31 Nottinghamshire vs Middlesex, Nottingham, 2006
COUNTY CAP: 2006 (Nottinghamshire)

CRICKETERS PARTICULARLY ADMIRED? Viv Richards, Michael Holding, Ian Botham
CRICKET MOMENTS TO FORGET? Being run out off the last ball of the game against
Shropshire when walking off – we lost!
FAVOURITE FILM? The Lives Of Others
FAVOURITE BAND? Katchafire
QUOTE TO LIVE BY? "When I get sad, I stop being sad and be awesome instead. True story"
RELAXATIONS? Swimming, music

| Batting | Mat | Inns | NO | Runs | HS | Ave | SR | 100 | 50 | Ct | St |
|---|---|---|---|---|---|---|---|---|---|---|---|
| First-class | 96 | 112 | 65 | 183 | 19 | 3.89 | 17.68 | 0 | 0 | 33 | 0 |
| List A | 52 | 19 | 12 | 45 | 9* | 6.42 | | 0 | 0 | 13 | 0 |
| Twenty20 | 22 | 6 | 5 | 10 | 6* | 10.00 | 62.50 | 0 | 0 | 4 | 0 |

| Bowling | Mat | Balls | Runs | Wkts | BBI | BBM | Ave | Econ | SR | 5w | 10 |
|---|---|---|---|---|---|---|---|---|---|---|---|
| First-class | 96 | 19206 | 10404 | 341 | 8/31 | | 30.51 | 3.25 | 56.3 | 19 | 2 |
| List A | 52 | 2309 | 2010 | 63 | 5/19 | 5/19 | 31.90 | 5.22 | 36.6 | 2 | 0 |
| Twenty20 | 22 | 457 | 597 | 23 | 4/22 | 4/22 | 25.95 | 7.83 | 19.8 | 0 | 0 |

**DERBYSHIRE**

FULL NAME: Hamza Ghani Siddique
BORN: January 19, 1991, Stoke-on-Trent, Staffordshire
SQUAD NO: 14
HEIGHT: 5ft 11in
NICKNAME: Hamz, H, Waj
EDUCATION: Denstone College; Repton School; Cardiff University
TEAMS: Derbyshire 2nd XI, Derbyshire Under-13s, Derbyshire Under-15s, Derbyshire Under-17s
CAREER: Yet to make first-team debut

FAMILY TIES? Brother played for Derbyshire age groups
WHY CRICKET? I was just brought up playing it (Asian roots!)
CAREER HIGHLIGHTS? Midlands Player of the Festival at Loughborough, first 2nd XI hundred for Derbyshire, three hundreds for the Cardiff MCCU last year (one against the Somerset 1st XI)
CRICKETING HEROES? Mark Waugh, Sachin Tendulkar
NON-CRICKETING HEROES? My father. I hope to become half the man that he is
BEST PLAYER IN COUNTY CRICKET? Still Marcus Trescothick
TIPS FOR THE TOP? Jos Buttler, Zafar Ansari, Ben Stokes
IF YOU WEREN'T A CRICKETER? I'd still be at university pondering what my future holds
WHEN RAIN STOPS PLAY? On my iPod. I'm a music fanatic!
FAVOURITE TV? The Vampire Diaries
FAVOURITE FILM? The Lion King, Gladiator, Snatch
FAVOURITE BOOK? Birdsong – Sebastian Faulks, A Million Little Pieces – James Frey
TWITTER FEED: @hamzasiddique

# PETER SIDDLE

**RHB RFM**

FULL NAME: Peter Matthew Siddle
BORN: November 25, 1984, Traralgon, Victoria, Australia
SQUAD NO: 10
HEIGHT: 6ft 1in
NICKNAME: Vicious, Dermie
TEAMS: Australia, Australia A, Victoria, Essex
CAREER: Test: 2008; ODI: 2009; T20I: 2009; First-class: 2005; List A: 2005; T20: 2006

ESSEX

BEST BATTING: 45* Victoria vs New South Wales, Melbourne, 2011
BEST BOWLING: 6-43 Victoria vs South Australia, Melbourne, 2012

NOTES: Made his Victoria debut in 2005 against the touring West Indians. Three years later, in October 2008, he debuted for Australia's Test team against India at Mohali. Took eight wickets (5-59 and 3-53) against South Africa at Sydney in January 2009 to claim his first Man of the Match award at Test level. A month later he made his ODI debut against New Zealand at Brisbane. Took 20 wickets during the 2009 Ashes. In the return series in Australia, took a hat-trick and a Test-best 6-54 on day one of the series from Brisbane to become the ninth man to perform the feat in Ashes cricket. It was also his 26th birthday. Will appear for Essex in the FL t20 competition in 2012

| Batting | Mat | Inns | NO | Runs | HS | Ave | SR | 100 | 50 | Ct | St |
|---|---|---|---|---|---|---|---|---|---|---|---|
| Tests | 31 | 44 | 8 | 587 | 43 | 16.30 | 50.95 | 0 | 0 | 13 | 0 |
| ODIs | 17 | 4 | 2 | 21 | 9* | 10.50 | 116.66 | 0 | 0 | 1 | 0 |
| T20Is | 2 | 1 | 1 | 1 | 1* | - | 100.00 | 0 | 0 | 0 | 0 |
| First-class | 61 | 83 | 16 | 1097 | 45* | 16.37 | 48.21 | 0 | 0 | 28 | 0 |
| List A | 38 | 17 | 8 | 94 | 25* | 10.44 | 87.03 | 0 | 0 | 6 | 0 |
| Twenty20 | 16 | 5 | 4 | 14 | 9* | 14.00 | 100.00 | 0 | 0 | 2 | 0 |

| Bowling | Mat | Balls | Runs | Wkts | BBI | BBM | Ave | Econ | SR | 5w | 10 |
|---|---|---|---|---|---|---|---|---|---|---|---|
| Tests | 31 | 6418 | 3310 | 114 | 6/54 | 8/113 | 29.03 | 3.09 | 56.2 | 5 | 0 |
| ODIs | 17 | 751 | 581 | 15 | 3/55 | 3/55 | 38.73 | 4.64 | 50.0 | 0 | 0 |
| T20Is | 2 | 48 | 58 | 3 | 2/24 | 2/24 | 19.33 | 7.25 | 16.0 | 0 | 0 |
| First-class | 61 | 11830 | 6050 | 231 | 6/43 | 9/77 | 26.19 | 3.06 | 51.2 | 12 | 0 |
| List A | 38 | 1816 | 1410 | 41 | 4/27 | 4/27 | 34.39 | 4.65 | 44.2 | 0 | 0 |
| Twenty20 | 16 | 359 | 446 | 15 | 4/29 | 4/29 | 29.73 | 7.45 | 23.9 | 0 | 0 |

## RYAN SIDEBOTTOM — LHB LFM W3 MVP20

FULL NAME: Ryan Jay Sidebottom
BORN: January 15, 1978, Huddersfield, Yorkshire
SQUAD NO: 11
HEIGHT: 6ft 4in
NICKNAME: Siddy
EDUCATION: King James Grammar School, Almondbury
TEAMS: England, Nottinghamshire, Yorkshire
CAREER: Test: 2001; ODI: 2001; T20I: 2007; First-class: 1997; List A: 1997; T20: 2003

BEST BATTING: 61 Yorkshire vs Worcestershire, Worcester, 2011
BEST BOWLING: 7-37 Yorkshire vs Somerset, Leeds, 2011
COUNTY CAPS: 2000 (Yorkshire); 2004 (Nottinghamshire); BENEFIT YEAR: 2010 (Nottinghamshire)

FAMILY TIES? My father [Arnie] played for Yorkshire and England
CAREER HIGHLIGHTS? Test hat-trick against New Zealand, World T20 winner in 2010
SUPERSTITIONS? I always put my front foot first over the boundary rope
CRICKETING HEROES? Mark Ealham, Sir Ian Botham, my dad
TIPS FOR THE TOP? Jonny Bairstow, Joe Root
FAVOURITE TV? Game Of Thrones
FAVOURITE BOOK? Harry Potter
SURPRISING SKILL? Canvas drawing
AMAZE ME! I love bird watching and collecting Steiff bears
TWITTER FEED: @RyanSidebottom

| Batting | Mat | Inns | NO | Runs | HS | Ave | SR | 100 | 50 | Ct | St |
|---|---|---|---|---|---|---|---|---|---|---|---|
| Tests | 22 | 31 | 11 | 313 | 31 | 15.65 | 34.66 | 0 | 0 | 5 | 0 |
| ODIs | 25 | 18 | 8 | 133 | 24 | 13.30 | 68.55 | 0 | 0 | 6 | 0 |
| T20Is | 18 | 1 | 1 | 5 | 5* | - | 125.00 | 0 | 0 | 5 | 0 |
| First-class | 163 | 209 | 65 | 1981 | 61 | 13.75 | | 0 | 3 | 51 | 0 |
| List A | 180 | 86 | 39 | 540 | 32 | 11.48 | | 0 | 0 | 39 | 0 |
| Twenty20 | 58 | 18 | 12 | 116 | 17* | 19.33 | 110.47 | 0 | 0 | 22 | 0 |

| Bowling | Mat | Balls | Runs | Wkts | BBI | BBM | Ave | Econ | SR | 5w | 10 |
|---|---|---|---|---|---|---|---|---|---|---|---|
| Tests | 22 | 4812 | 2231 | 79 | 7/47 | 10/139 | 28.24 | 2.78 | 60.9 | 5 | 1 |
| ODIs | 25 | 1277 | 1039 | 29 | 3/19 | 3/19 | 35.82 | 4.88 | 44.0 | 0 | 0 |
| T20Is | 18 | 367 | 437 | 23 | 3/16 | 3/16 | 19.00 | 7.14 | 15.9 | 0 | 0 |
| First-class | 163 | 28710 | 13470 | 537 | 7/37 | | 25.08 | 2.81 | 53.4 | 23 | 3 |
| List A | 180 | 7962 | 5846 | 189 | 6/40 | 6/40 | 30.93 | 4.40 | 42.1 | 2 | 0 |
| Twenty20 | 58 | 1229 | 1434 | 63 | 3/16 | 3/16 | 22.76 | 7.00 | 19.5 | 0 | 0 |

# JOHN SIMPSON LHB WK

FULL NAME: John Andrew Simpson
BORN: July 13, 1988, Bury, Lancashire
SQUAD NO: 20
HEIGHT: 5ft 10in
NICKNAME: Simmo
EDUCATION: St Gabriels R.C High School
TEAMS: England Under-19s, Lancashire, Lancashire 2nd XI, Marylebone Cricket Club, Marylebone Cricket Club Young Cricketers, Middlesex, Middlesex 2nd XI
CAREER: First-class: 2009; List A: 2009; T20: 2009

**MIDDLESEX**

BEST BATTING: 143 Middlesex vs Surrey, Lord's, 2011
COUNTY CAP: 2011

FAMILY TIES? Dad played Lancashire 2nd XI and England amateurs. Currently holds batting and wicketkeeping records in the Lancashire League and Central Lancashire League
CAREER HIGHLIGHTS? Winning Division Two of the Championship with Middlesex. Being capped by Middlesex. First hundred at Lord's. Representing England U19 in the World Cup
CRICKETING HEROES? Adam Gilchrist, Ian Healy, Brian Lara, Jack Russell, Gary Kirsten
NON-CRICKETING HEROES? Roger Federer, Tiger Woods, Michael Jordan
TIP FOR THE TOP? Mitchell Starc
FAVOURITE TV? The Inbetweeners, Two And A Half Men, The Simpsons, Family Guy
DREAM HOLIDAY? Cape Verde and travel around America
ACCOMPLISHMENTS? Holding a school record in javelin, winning golf tournaments as a junior at my local club
GUILTY PLEASURES? Watching WWE wrestling
AMAZE ME! Dad played lacrosse for England. Grandad and great grandad played rugby league for Great Britain. Played my first game of 1st XI cricket when I was 10
FANTASY SLIP CORDON? Keeper: Karl Pilkington, 1st: Charlie Sheen, 2nd: Natalie Portman, 3rd: Roger Federer, Gully: David Guetta
TWITTER FEED: @johnsimpson_88

| Batting | Mat | Inns | NO | Runs | HS | Ave | SR | 100 | 50 | Ct | St |
|---|---|---|---|---|---|---|---|---|---|---|---|
| First-class | 37 | 59 | 8 | 1696 | 143 | 33.25 | 47.74 | 2 | 10 | 114 | 3 |
| List A | 27 | 18 | 1 | 363 | 82 | 21.35 | 76.58 | 0 | 1 | 19 | 4 |
| Twenty20 | 17 | 14 | 1 | 227 | 60* | 17.46 | 128.97 | 0 | 1 | 9 | 5 |

| Bowling | Mat | Balls | Runs | Wkts | BBI | BBM | Ave | Econ | SR | 5w | 10 |
|---|---|---|---|---|---|---|---|---|---|---|---|
| First-class | 37 | - | - | - | - | - | - | - | - | - | - |
| List A | 27 | - | - | - | - | - | - | - | - | - | - |
| Twenty20 | 17 | - | - | - | - | - | - | - | - | - | - |

# RAMMY SINGH

**RHB OB**

DURHAM

FULL NAME: Ramanpreet Singh
BORN: February 19, 1993, Newcastle-upon-Tyne, Northumberland
SQUAD NO: 11
HEIGHT: 5ft 7in
NICKNAME: Loose Man
EDUCATION: Gosforth High School
TEAMS: Durham 2nd XI, England Under-19s, Northumberland
CAREER: Yet to make first-team debut

WHY CRICKET? My dad's passion for the game
CAREER HIGHLIGHTS? Representing England U19, scoring back-to-back hundreds for the academy last season
CRICKETING HEROES? Sachin Tendulkar, Viv Richards, MS Dhoni
NON-CRICKETING HEROES? Bhagat Singh, Mahatma Gandhi, Manny Pacquiao
BEST PLAYER IN COUNTY CRICKET? Marcus Trescothick
TIPS FOR THE TOP? Ben Stokes, Jonny Bairstow
IF YOU WEREN'T A CRICKETER? Lawyer
FAVOURITE FILM? The Shawshank Redemption
FAVOURITE BOOK? Wolf Brother
DREAM HOLIDAY? Marbella
ACCOMPLISHMENTS? Charity work in India
GUILTY PLEASURES? The casino
SURPRISING FACT? I have a deep hatred for tomatoes

# BEN SLATER

## LHB OB

FULL NAME: Benjamin Thomas Slater
BORN: August 26, 1991, Chesterfield, Derbyshire
SQUAD NO: 26
HEIGHT: 5ft 8in
NICKNAME: Slats, Slatsy
EDUCATION: Netherthorpe School and Sixth Form; Leeds Metropolitan University
TEAMS: Bradford/Leeds UCCE, Derbyshire, Derbyshire 2nd XI, Derbyshire Under-13s, Derbyshire Under-15s, Derbyshire Under-17s
CAREER: Yet to make first-team debut

FAMILY TIES? Most of my family have played the game. Dad played local league cricket for Chesterfield CC and grandad was a league legend for about 40 years until he retired, aged 63
CAREER HIGHLIGHTS? Earning a summer contract for Derbyshire, scoring 100* vs Warwickshire 1st XI in my first year at university for Leeds/Bradford MCCU, winning the Derbyshire Premier League with Chesterfield CC in 2008
CRICKETING HEROES? Past: Brian Lara; present: Wes Durston and Paul Borrington
NON-CRICKETING HEROES? Stone Cold Steve Austin, Eminem, David Beckham
BEST PLAYER IN COUNTY CRICKET? Marcus Trescothick
TIPS FOR THE TOP? Dan Hodgson, Joe Leach, Peter Burgoyne
WHEN RAIN STOPS PLAY? Stealing Jake Needham's newspapers and playing Tiny Wings on the iPhone
FAVOURITE TV? The Only Way Is Essex, Made In Chelsea, PhoneShop, Soccer AM
FAVOURITE FILM? Coach Carter
FAVOURITE BOOK? The Harry Potter series
DREAM HOLIDAY? Maldives
ACCOMPLISHMENTS? Passing my GCSEs and A-Levels and going to university
GUILTY PLEASURES? Flapjacks and Football Manager
FANTASY SLIP CORDON? Keeper: Peter Kay, 1st: David Beckham, 2nd: Joey Essex, 3rd: Rickie Fowler, Gully: Paul Borrington
TWITTER FEED: @BennySlats

# GREG SMITH

## RHB RMF/OB MVP60

ESSEX

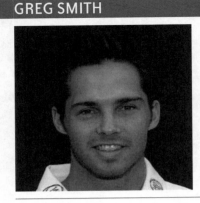

**FULL NAME:** Gregory Marc Smith
**BORN:** April 20, 1983, Johannesburg, South Africa
**SQUAD NO:** 83
**HEIGHT:** 5ft 9in
**NICKNAME:** Smithy
**EDUCATION:** St Stithians College; UNISA
**TEAMS:** Derbyshire, Derbyshire 2nd XI, Griqualand West, Mountaineers, South Africa Academy, South Africa Under-19s, Essex
**CAREER:** First-class: 2003; List A: 2003; T20: 2007

**BEST BATTING:** 165* Derbyshire vs Glamorgan, Derby, 2010
**BEST BOWLING:** 5-54 Derbyshire vs Northamptonshire, Chesterfield, 2010
**COUNTY CAP:** 2009 (Derbyshire)

**FAMILY TIES?** My dad used to be the financial advisor at the South African Cricket Board
**CAREER HIGHLIGHTS?** Playing in the U19 World Cup final in New Zealand and scoring my maiden Championship ton
**CRICKETING HEROES?** I have always admired Jacques Kallis as he is a genuine allrounder and Sachin Tendulkar is also a true great of the game
**NON-CRICKETING HEROES?** Roger Federer and Rafael Nadal
**TIPS FOR THE TOP?** Reece Topley and Tymal Mills
**WHEN RAIN STOPS PLAY?** We normally get the laptops out, watch a movie or some of the boys enjoy their poker
**FAVOURITE FILM?** I am a film geek so I have millions but one that sticks out is probably Blood Diamond
**DREAM HOLIDAY?** I would like to go to Thailand

| Batting | Mat | Inns | NO | Runs | HS | Ave | SR | 100 | 50 | Ct | St |
|---|---|---|---|---|---|---|---|---|---|---|---|
| First-class | 88 | 152 | 13 | 4299 | 165* | 30.92 | 57.14 | 5 | 29 | 27 | 0 |
| List A | 78 | 78 | 5 | 1694 | 88 | 23.20 | 83.57 | 0 | 7 | 28 | 0 |
| Twenty20 | 54 | 52 | 2 | 1020 | 100* | 20.40 | 113.20 | 1 | 4 | 20 | 0 |

| Bowling | Mat | Balls | Runs | Wkts | BBI | BBM | Ave | Econ | SR | 5w | 10 |
|---|---|---|---|---|---|---|---|---|---|---|---|
| First-class | 88 | 9722 | 5229 | 146 | 5/54 | | 35.81 | 3.22 | 66.5 | 2 | 0 |
| List A | 78 | 2179 | 2047 | 62 | 4/53 | 4/53 | 33.01 | 5.63 | 35.1 | 0 | 0 |
| Twenty20 | 54 | 610 | 782 | 31 | 5/27 | 5/27 | 25.22 | 7.69 | 19.6 | 1 | 0 |

FULL NAME: Greg Phillip Smith
BORN: November 16, 1988, Leicester
SQUAD NO: 14
HEIGHT: 5ft 11in
EDUCATION: Oundle School; Durham University
TEAMS: Durham MCCU, Durham UCCE, England Under-19s, Kibworth, Leicestershire, Leicestershire 2nd XI
CAREER: First-class: 2008; List A: 2008

**LEICESTERSHIRE**

BEST BATTING: 158* Leicestershire vs Gloucestershire, Leicester, 2010
BEST BOWLING: 1-64 Leicestershire vs Gloucestershire, Leicester, 2008

FAMILY TIES? Step grandad [Peter Kelland] played for Sussex
CAREER HIGHLIGHTS? Topping the first-class averages in 2010
SUPERSTITIONS? Always listen to music before I bat
CRICKETING HEROES? Claude Henderson is my cricketing hero
NON-CRICKETING HEROES? General Richard Dannatt
BEST PLAYER IN COUNTY CRICKET? Chris Woakes
TIP FOR THE TOP? James Taylor
FAVOURITE TV? Geordie Shore
FAVOURITE FILM? Gladiator
FAVOURITE BOOK? The Kite Runner
DREAM HOLIDAY? Southend
ACCOMPLISHMENTS? I have created my own breed of apple
SURPRISING SKILL? I play the cello
GUILTY PLEASURES? Making boy band videos and posting them on the Internet
AMAZE ME! My best sport is in fact Laser Quest, I have been a member of two boy bands and I used to have a pet sheep called Lambert
FANTASY SLIP CORDON? Keeper: Paul Nixon, 1st: Steve Irwin, 2nd: Myself, 3rd: Mila Kunis, Gully: Chris Martin
TWITTER FEED: @Greg_smith14

| Batting | Mat | Inns | NO | Runs | HS | Ave | SR | 100 | 50 | Ct | St |
|---|---|---|---|---|---|---|---|---|---|---|---|
| First-class | 34 | 64 | 6 | 1871 | 158* | 32.25 | 47.99 | 4 | 9 | 20 | 0 |
| List A | 12 | 12 | 2 | 141 | 58 | 14.10 | 61.30 | 0 | 1 | 4 | 0 |

| Bowling | Mat | Balls | Runs | Wkts | BBI | BBM | Ave | Econ | SR | 5w | 10 |
|---|---|---|---|---|---|---|---|---|---|---|---|
| First-class | 34 | 30 | 64 | 1 | 1/64 | 1/64 | 64.00 | 12.80 | 30.0 | 0 | 0 |
| List A | 12 | - | - | - | - | - | - | - | - | - | - |

# TOM SMITH

## LHB RM MVP27

FULL NAME: Thomas Christopher Smith
BORN: December 26, 1985, Liverpool
SQUAD NO: 24
HEIGHT: 6ft 3in
NICKNAME: Smudger
EDUCATION: Parklands High School;
Runshaw College
TEAMS: England Under-19s, Lancashire,
Lancashire 2nd XI, Matabeleland Tuskers
CAREER: First-class: 2005; List A: 2005; T20:
2006

BEST BATTING: 128 Lancashire vs Hampshire, Southampton, 2010
BEST BOWLING: 6-46 Lancashire vs Yorkshire, Manchester, 2009
COUNTY CAP: 2010

CAREER HIGHLIGHTS? Winning the County Championship
CRICKETING HEROES? Brian Lara, Andrew Flintoff
BEST PLAYER IN COUNTY CRICKET? Marcus Trescothick
TIP FOR THE TOP? Jordan Clark
WHEN RAIN STOPS PLAY? Listen to music
FAVOURITE TV? Entourage
FAVOURITE FILM? Wedding Crashers
DREAM HOLIDAY? Thailand
GUILTY PLEASURES? Curry
TWITTER FEED: @Tcp24

| Batting | Mat | Inns | NO | Runs | HS | Ave | SR | 100 | 50 | Ct | St |
|---|---|---|---|---|---|---|---|---|---|---|---|
| First-class | 68 | 97 | 17 | 2085 | 128 | 26.06 | 44.44 | 3 | 9 | 72 | 0 |
| List A | 52 | 42 | 7 | 1024 | 117 | 29.25 | 83.72 | 1 | 7 | 14 | 0 |
| Twenty20 | 61 | 55 | 12 | 1323 | 92* | 30.76 | 115.74 | 0 | 7 | 25 | 0 |

| Bowling | Mat | Balls | Runs | Wkts | BBI | BBM | Ave | Econ | SR | 5w | 10 |
|---|---|---|---|---|---|---|---|---|---|---|---|
| First-class | 68 | 8947 | 4539 | 141 | 6/46 | | 32.19 | 3.04 | 63.4 | 2 | 0 |
| List A | 52 | 1976 | 1706 | 64 | 4/48 | 4/48 | 26.65 | 5.18 | 30.8 | 0 | 0 |
| Twenty20 | 61 | 858 | 1119 | 37 | 3/12 | 3/12 | 30.24 | 7.82 | 23.1 | 0 | 0 |

# TOM SMITH

## RHB SLA

**FULL NAME:** Thomas Michael John Smith
**BORN:** August 22, 1987, Eastbourne, Sussex
**SQUAD NO:** 11
**HEIGHT:** 5ft 8in
**NICKNAME:** Smudge, The Egg
**EDUCATION:** Seaford Head Community College
**TEAMS:** Middlesex, Middlesex 2nd XI, Surrey, Sussex, Sussex 2nd XI
**CAREER:** First-class: 2007; List A: 2006; T20: 2007

**BEST BATTING:** 33 Middlesex vs Derbyshire, Derby, 2010
**BEST BOWLING:** 3-38 Middlesex vs Derbyshire, Lord's, 2011

**CAREER HIGHLIGHTS?** 5-24 at Lord's in a T20 match against Kent
**CRICKETING HEROES?** Dan Vettori, Adam Gilchrist
**NON-CRICKETING HEROES?** James "Sawyer" Ford from Lost
**BEST PLAYER IN COUNTY CRICKET?** Marcus Trescothick
**TIP FOR THE TOP?** Paul Stirling
**IF YOU WEREN'T A CRICKETER?** Either a plumber or a cricket coach
**WHEN RAIN STOPS PLAY?** Crossword
**FAVOURITE TV?** Modern Family, Lost, Spooks
**FAVOURITE FILM?** Inception
**FAVOURITE BOOK?** Moneyball by Michael Lewis
**DREAM HOLIDAY?** Cape Town
**ACCOMPLISHMENTS?** NVQ Level 2 in Plumbing and Level 3 cricket coach
**GUILTY PLEASURES?** Cinnamon doughnuts and chocolate marzipan
**SURPRISING SKILL?** Qualified plumber
**FANTASY SLIP CORDON?** Keeper: Ross Kemp, 1st: Me, 2nd: Jason Manford, 3rd: Shane Warne, Gully: Sofia Vergara

| Batting | Mat | Inns | NO | Runs | HS | Ave | SR | 100 | 50 | Ct | St |
|---|---|---|---|---|---|---|---|---|---|---|---|
| First-class | 10 | 16 | 1 | 165 | 33 | 11.00 | 29.83 | 0 | 0 | 3 | 0 |
| List A | 25 | 10 | 0 | 153 | 65 | 15.30 | 79.27 | 0 | 1 | 10 | 0 |
| Twenty20 | 32 | 18 | 12 | 135 | 36* | 22.50 | 109.75 | 0 | 0 | 14 | 0 |

| Bowling | Mat | Balls | Runs | Wkts | BBI | BBM | Ave | Econ | SR | 5w | 10 |
|---|---|---|---|---|---|---|---|---|---|---|---|
| First-class | 10 | 1204 | 780 | 11 | 3/38 | 4/107 | 70.90 | 3.88 | 109.4 | 0 | 0 |
| List A | 25 | 924 | 846 | 20 | 3/26 | 3/26 | 42.30 | 5.49 | 46.2 | 0 | 0 |
| Twenty20 | 32 | 563 | 725 | 30 | 5/24 | 5/24 | 24.16 | 7.72 | 18.7 | 1 | 0 |

**DURHAM**

FULL NAME: William Rew Smith
BORN: September 28, 1982, Luton, Bedfordshire
SQUAD NO: 2
HEIGHT: 5ft 9in
NICKNAME: Smudger, Jiggy
EDUCATION: Bedford School; Durham University
TEAMS: Bedfordshire, British Universities, Durham, Nottinghamshire
CAREER: First-class: 2002; List A: 2002; T20: 2003

BEST BATTING: 201* Durham vs Surrey, Guildford, 2008
BEST BOWLING: 3-34 DUCCE vs Leicestershire, Leicester, 2005

CAREER HIGHLIGHTS? Winning the County Championship with Durham in 2008 and 2009, being Player of the Year in 2008 and captaining the club in 2009
CRICKETING HEROES? Mike Atherton, Graeme Fowler, Dale Benkenstein
TIPS FOR THE TOP? Scott Borthwick, Ben Stokes, Jos Buttler, Jonny Bairstow
IF YOU WEREN'T A CRICKETER? Professional gambler, pundit or journalist
FAVOURITE TV? QI
FAVOURITE FILM? Top Gun
SURPRISING SKILL? Racing tipster, dog whisperer...
GUILTY PLEASURES? Starbucks coffee
AMAZE ME! I have a tattoo, I was a Latin scholar at school, I'm the best surfer yet to take up the sport...
FANTASY SLIP CORDON? Keeper: Myself (hugely underrated as a keeper), 1st: AP McCoy (the personification of dedication and bravery), 2nd: Stephen Fry (the wittiest, most intelligent man alive), 3rd: Bobby Robson (would have loved to meet him, don't know of one person who doesn't hold him in the highest regard), Gully: Inspector Gadget (he can use his go-go gadget arms to catch everything while the rest of us pay no attention)
TWITTER FEED: @Will_Smith2

| Batting | Mat | Inns | NO | Runs | HS | Ave | SR | 100 | 50 | Ct | St |
|---|---|---|---|---|---|---|---|---|---|---|---|
| First-class | 91 | 147 | 8 | 4606 | 201* | 33.13 | 43.83 | 11 | 16 | 47 | 0 |
| List A | 74 | 67 | 5 | 1538 | 103 | 24.80 | 69.78 | 1 | 11 | 28 | 0 |
| Twenty20 | 59 | 47 | 11 | 653 | 55 | 18.13 | 117.02 | 0 | 3 | 35 | 0 |

| Bowling | Mat | Balls | Runs | Wkts | BBI | BBM | Ave | Econ | SR | 5w | 10 |
|---|---|---|---|---|---|---|---|---|---|---|---|
| First-class | 91 | 759 | 557 | 8 | 3/34 | | 69.62 | 4.40 | 94.8 | 0 | 0 |
| List A | 74 | 71 | 74 | 2 | 1/6 | 1/6 | 37.00 | 6.25 | 35.5 | 0 | 0 |
| Twenty20 | 59 | 95 | 132 | 1 | 1/31 | 1/31 | 132.00 | 8.33 | 95.0 | 0 | 0 |

FULL NAME: Vikram Singh Solanki
BORN: April 1, 1976, Udaipur, Rajasthan, India
SQUAD NO: 3
HEIGHT: 6ft
NICKNAME: Vik
EDUCATION: Merridale Primary School; Regis School; Open University
TEAMS: England, Rajasthan, Worcestershire
CAREER: ODI: 2000; T20I: 2005; First-class: 1995; List A: 1993; T20: 2004

**WORCESTERSHIRE**

BEST BATTING: 270 Worcestershire vs Gloucestershire, Cheltenham, 2008
BEST BOWLING: 5-40 Worcestershire vs Middlesex, Lord's, 2004
COUNTY CAP: 1998; BENEFIT YEAR: 2007

FAMILY TIES? My father played in India and my brother is a keen club cricketer
CAREER HIGHLIGHTS? Playing for England and captaining Worcestershire
SUPERSTITIONS? Many habits, but no superstitions
CRICKETING HEROES? Sachin Tendulkar, Graeme Hick, Wasim Akram
NON-CRICKETING HEROES? My father
BEST PLAYER IN COUNTY CRICKET? Marcus Trescothick
TIPS FOR THE TOP? Moeen Ali, Alexei Kervezee, Richard Jones
IF YOU WEREN'T A CRICKETER? I have no idea!
WHEN RAIN STOPS PLAY? You'll find me reading
FAVOURITE TV? House, Human Planet
FAVOURITE FILM? Gladiator
FAVOURITE BOOK? The Alchemist by Paulo Coelho
DREAM HOLIDAY? India, completing my Open University degree

| Batting | Mat | Inns | NO | Runs | HS | Ave | SR | 100 | 50 | Ct | St |
|---|---|---|---|---|---|---|---|---|---|---|---|
| ODIs | 51 | 46 | 5 | 1097 | 106 | 26.75 | 72.93 | 2 | 5 | 16 | 0 |
| T20Is | 3 | 3 | 0 | 76 | 43 | 25.33 | 124.59 | 0 | 0 | 3 | 0 |
| First-class | 283 | 476 | 29 | 16187 | 270 | 36.21 | | 30 | 85 | 299 | 0 |
| List A | 370 | 342 | 28 | 10064 | 164* | 32.05 | | 14 | 59 | 143 | 0 |
| Twenty20 | 59 | 57 | 1 | 1425 | 100 | 25.44 | 125.77 | 1 | 9 | 32 | 0 |

| Bowling | Mat | Balls | Runs | Wkts | BBI | BBM | Ave | Econ | SR | 5w | 10 |
|---|---|---|---|---|---|---|---|---|---|---|---|
| ODIs | 51 | 111 | 105 | 1 | 1/17 | 1/17 | 105.00 | 5.67 | 111.0 | 0 | 0 |
| T20Is | 3 | - | - | - | - | - | - | - | - | - | - |
| First-class | 283 | 7105 | 4120 | 86 | 5/40 | | 47.90 | 3.47 | 82.6 | 4 | 1 |
| List A | 370 | 1122 | 987 | 28 | 4/14 | 4/14 | 35.25 | 5.27 | 40.0 | 0 | 0 |
| Twenty20 | 59 | 96 | 145 | 5 | 1/6 | 1/6 | 29.00 | 9.06 | 19.2 | 0 | 0 |

# MATTHEW SPRIEGEL                    LHB OB

FULL NAME: Matthew Neil William Spriegel
BORN: March 4, 1987, Epsom, Surrey
SQUAD NO: 28
HEIGHT: 6ft 3in
NICKNAME: Spriegs
EDUCATION: Whitgift School; Loughborough University
TEAMS: Loughborough MCCU, Surrey, Surrey 2nd XI
CAREER: First-class: 2007; List A: 2008; T20: 2008

BEST BATTING: 108* Surrey vs Bangladeshis, The Oval, 2010
BEST BOWLING: 2-28 Surrey vs Hampshire, The Oval, 2008

CAREER HIGHLIGHTS? Scoring the winning runs in the CB40 final against Somerset at Lord's last season
CRICKETING HEROES? Alec Stewart, Graham Thorpe, Brian Lara
NON-CRICKETING HEROES? David Beckham, Jonny Wilkinson
TIPS FOR THE TOP? The majority of the Surrey squad
IF YOU WEREN'T A CRICKETER? Not a clue. Maybe coaching or personal training
WHEN RAIN STOPS PLAY? Playing cards, causing mischief, getting a bit of shut eye
FAVOURITE TV? The Office
FAVOURITE FILM? Gladiator
ACCOMPLISHMENTS? 2:1 in Sports Science at Loughborough
SURPRISING SKILL? Handy golfer, but I doubt that's too unexpected for a cricketer
GUILTY PLEASURES? Sweets. The pick 'n' mix takes a hammering at the cinema
FANTASY SLIP CORDON? Keeper: Gary Wilson (best mate, massive head, infectious laugh), 1st: Me (I can hide between keeper and 2nd), 2nd: Andrew Flintoff (bucket hands, apparently enjoys a beer), 3rd: Jack Bauer (if anything kicks off he'll have our back), Gully: Stephen Merchant (great wingspan and very funny man)
TWITTER FEED: @spriegs

| Batting | Mat | Inns | NO | Runs | HS | Ave | SR | 100 | 50 | Ct | St |
|---|---|---|---|---|---|---|---|---|---|---|---|
| First-class | 32 | 52 | 3 | 1237 | 108* | 25.24 | 42.21 | 3 | 3 | 24 | 0 |
| List A | 49 | 45 | 16 | 1218 | 86 | 42.00 | 91.30 | 0 | 9 | 26 | 0 |
| Twenty20 | 35 | 26 | 11 | 235 | 25* | 15.66 | 94.00 | 0 | 0 | 12 | 0 |

| Bowling | Mat | Balls | Runs | Wkts | BBI | BBM | Ave | Econ | SR | 5w | 10 |
|---|---|---|---|---|---|---|---|---|---|---|---|
| First-class | 32 | 1357 | 823 | 19 | 2/28 | 2/28 | 43.31 | 3.63 | 71.4 | 0 | 0 |
| List A | 49 | 1362 | 1241 | 31 | 3/39 | 3/39 | 40.03 | 5.46 | 43.9 | 0 | 0 |
| Twenty20 | 35 | 558 | 701 | 24 | 4/33 | 4/33 | 29.20 | 7.53 | 23.2 | 0 | 0 |

# DARREN STEVENS

## RHB RM R2 MVP3

**FULL NAME:** Darren Ian Stevens
**BORN:** April 30, 1976, Leicester
**SQUAD NO:** 3
**HEIGHT:** 5ft 11in
**NICKNAME:** Stevo, Hoover
**EDUCATION:** Mount Grace High School; John College
**TEAMS:** Dhaka Gladiators, England Lions, Kent, Leicestershire, Otago
**CAREER:** First-class: 1997; List A: 1997; T20: 2003

KENT

**BEST BATTING:** 208 Kent vs Middlesex, Canterbury, 2009
**BEST BOWLING:** 7-21 Kent vs Surrey, Canterbury, 2011
**COUNTY CAPS:** 2002 (Leicestershire); 2005 (Kent)

**WHY CRICKET?** I played softball as a kid and the schools I went to were rugby and soccer dominated. It was my father that persuaded me to go along to a training session and I've never looked back
**CAREER HIGHLIGHTS?** Winning three T20 finals
**SUPERSTITIONS?** Left pad first
**CRICKETING HEROES?** Sir Vivian Richards, Sir Ian Botham
**NON-CRICKETING HEROES?** Tiger Woods for what he has achieved in the game
**TIPS FOR THE TOP?** Alex Hales, Jos Buttler
**IF YOU WEREN'T A CRICKETER?** Golfer
**WHEN RAIN STOPS PLAY?** Sleep, cards
**FAVOURITE TV?** Hawaii Five-O
**FAVOURITE FILM?** The Warrior
**FAVOURITE BOOK?** Anything by Lee Child
**DREAM HOLIDAY?** Maldives
**GUILTY PLEASURES?** Chocolate
**TWITTER FEED?** @stevo208

| Batting | Mat | Inns | NO | Runs | HS | Ave | SR | 100 | 50 | Ct | St |
|---|---|---|---|---|---|---|---|---|---|---|---|
| First-class | 186 | 307 | 20 | 9655 | 208 | 33.64 | | 22 | 46 | 141 | 0 |
| List A | 236 | 222 | 25 | 6026 | 133 | 30.58 | | 4 | 40 | 89 | 0 |
| Twenty20 | 117 | 110 | 30 | 2393 | 77 | 29.91 | 131.99 | 0 | 10 | 35 | 0 |

| Bowling | Mat | Balls | Runs | Wkts | BBI | BBM | Ave | Econ | SR | 5w | 10 |
|---|---|---|---|---|---|---|---|---|---|---|---|
| First-class | 186 | 8516 | 4269 | 135 | 7/21 | | 31.62 | 3.00 | 63.0 | 2 | 1 |
| List A | 236 | 2765 | 2331 | 64 | 5/32 | 5/32 | 36.42 | 5.05 | 43.2 | 1 | 0 |
| Twenty20 | 117 | 936 | 1189 | 51 | 4/14 | 4/14 | 23.31 | 7.62 | 18.3 | 0 | 0 |

# PAUL STIRLING                                     RHB OB

MIDDLESEX

FULL NAME: Paul Robert Stirling
BORN: September 3, 1990, Belfast
SQUAD NO: 39
EDUCATION: Belfast High School
TEAMS: Ireland, Ireland Under-13s, Ireland
Under-15s, Ireland Under-17s, Ireland
Under-19s, Ireland Under-23s
CAREER: ODI: 2008; T20I: 2009; First-class:
2008; List A: 2008; T20: 2008

BEST BATTING: 107 Ireland vs Canada, Dublin, 2011
BEST BOWLING: 2-45 Ireland vs Jamaica, Spanish Town, 2010

NOTES: Signed for Middlesex in 2009. Older brother Richard represented Ireland U19. Holds
the record for the highest ODI score by an Ireland batsman for the 177 he made against
Canada in September 2010. Nominated in the Emerging Player of the Year and Associate and
Affiliate Player of the Year categories for the 2010 ICC Awards. Represented Ireland at the
2011 World Cup, scoring 101 off 70 deliveries in the victory over Netherlands. Shortlisted for
Associate and Affiliate Player of the Year at the 2011 ICC Awards. Scored 109 off 99 balls for
Middlesex against Derbyshire at Chesterfield last year's CB40. Represented Ireland in the
World T20 qualifiers in March

| Batting | Mat | Inns | NO | Runs | HS | Ave | SR | 100 | 50 | Ct | St |
|---|---|---|---|---|---|---|---|---|---|---|---|
| ODIs | 36 | 36 | 1 | 1418 | 177 | 40.51 | 96.26 | 4 | 6 | 20 | 0 |
| T20Is | 10 | 10 | 2 | 169 | 65* | 21.12 | 94.41 | 0 | 1 | 1 | 0 |
| First-class | 13 | 21 | 0 | 547 | 107 | 26.04 | 62.51 | 2 | 2 | 9 | 0 |
| List A | 67 | 67 | 3 | 2303 | 177 | 35.98 | 95.52 | 5 | 11 | 32 | 0 |
| Twenty20 | 32 | 32 | 3 | 544 | 65* | 18.75 | 116.73 | 0 | 2 | 7 | 0 |

| Bowling | Mat | Balls | Runs | Wkts | BBI | BBM | Ave | Econ | SR | 5w | 10 |
|---|---|---|---|---|---|---|---|---|---|---|---|
| ODIs | 36 | 918 | 686 | 18 | 4/11 | 4/11 | 38.11 | 4.48 | 51.0 | 0 | 0 |
| T20Is | 10 | 90 | 89 | 3 | 2/21 | 2/21 | 29.66 | 5.93 | 30.0 | 0 | 0 |
| First-class | 13 | 363 | 195 | 4 | 2/45 | 3/92 | 48.75 | 3.22 | 90.7 | 0 | 0 |
| List A | 67 | 1122 | 880 | 20 | 4/11 | 4/11 | 44.00 | 4.70 | 56.1 | 0 | 0 |
| Twenty20 | 32 | 258 | 275 | 11 | 3/20 | 3/20 | 25.00 | 6.39 | 23.4 | 0 | 0 |

# BEN STOKES

## LHB RM

FULL NAME: Benjamin Andrew Stokes
BORN: June 4, 1991, Christchurch, Canterbury, New Zealand
SQUAD NO: 38
HEIGHT: 6ft 1in
NICKNAME: Stokesy, Beast
EDUCATION: Cockermouth School
TEAMS: England, Durham, Durham 2nd XI, England Lions, England Under-19s
CAREER: ODI: 2011; T20I: 2011; First-class: 2010; List A: 2009; T20: 2010

BEST BATTING: 185 Durham vs Lancashire, Chester-le-Street, 2011
BEST BOWLING: 6-68 Durham vs Hampshire, Southampton, 2011

CAREER HIGHLIGHTS? Making my debut for England
SUPERSTITIONS? Left pad on first
CRICKETING HEROES? Herschelle Gibbs
BEST PLAYER IN COUNTY CRICKET? Marcus Trescothick, Dale Benkenstein, Michael Di Venuto
TIPS FOR THE TOP? Scott Borthwick, Jos Buttler, James Vince
WHEN RAIN STOPS PLAY? Sleeping, playing cards, Angry Birds
FAVOURITE TV? Friends, Scrubs
FAVOURITE FILM? Chopper
DREAM HOLIDAY? Ibiza
GUILTY PLEASURES? Don't think I can go there
SURPRISING FACTS? Born in New Zealand and lived there for 12 years, my father played one Test match for New Zealand at rugby league and I was a right-hander when I was younger
TWITTER FEED: @benstokes38

| Batting | Mat | Inns | NO | Runs | HS | Ave | SR | 100 | 50 | Ct | St |
|---|---|---|---|---|---|---|---|---|---|---|---|
| ODIs | 5 | 3 | 0 | 30 | 20 | 10.00 | 57.69 | 0 | 0 | 3 | 0 |
| T20Is | 2 | 1 | 0 | 31 | 31 | 31.00 | 134.78 | 0 | 0 | 0 | 0 |
| First-class | 28 | 42 | 5 | 1615 | 185 | 43.64 | | 5 | 6 | 17 | 0 |
| List A | 29 | 27 | 3 | 694 | 150* | 28.91 | 93.02 | 1 | 3 | 10 | 0 |
| Twenty20 | 18 | 14 | 1 | 239 | 44 | 18.38 | 112.73 | 0 | 0 | 4 | 0 |

| Bowling | Mat | Balls | Runs | Wkts | BBI | BBM | Ave | Econ | SR | 5w | 10 |
|---|---|---|---|---|---|---|---|---|---|---|---|
| ODIs | 5 | - | - | - | - | - | - | - | - | - | - |
| T20Is | 2 | - | - | - | - | - | - | - | - | - | - |
| First-class | 28 | 1398 | 1046 | 28 | 6/68 | 7/145 | 37.35 | 4.48 | 49.9 | 1 | 0 |
| List A | 29 | 236 | 207 | 14 | 4/29 | 4/29 | 14.78 | 5.26 | 16.8 | 0 | 0 |
| Twenty20 | 18 | 30 | 37 | 1 | 1/23 | 1/23 | 37.00 | 7.40 | 30.0 | 0 | 0 |

# MARK STONEMAN                                        LHB

**DURHAM**

FULL NAME: Mark Daniel Stoneman
BORN: June 26, 1987, Newcastle-upon-Tyne, Northumberland
SQUAD NO: 26
HEIGHT: 5ft 10in
NICKNAME: Rocky
EDUCATION: Whickham Comprehensive
TEAMS: Durham, Durham 2nd XI, England Under-19s
CAREER: First-class: 2007; List A: 2008; T20: 2010

---

BEST BATTING: 128 Durham vs Sussex, Hove, 2011

---

FAMILY TIES? Grandfather played and umpired, and father played
CAREER HIGHLIGHTS? Being part of two Championship winning squads
SUPERSTITIONS? Right pad goes on first
CRICKETING HEROES? My dad, Brian Lara, Michael Di Venuto
NON-CRICKETING HEROES? Billy Slater, Vincent Chase
BEST PLAYER IN COUNTY CRICKET? Marcus Trescothick
TIPS FOR THE TOP? Jonny Bairstow, Ben Stokes, Scott Borthwick
IF YOU WEREN'T A CRICKETER? I'd be a PE teacher
WHEN RAIN STOPS PLAY? Playing cards, reading magazines or annoying people
FAVOURITE TV? Entourage
FAVOURITE FILM? The Patriot
DREAM HOLIDAY? Las Vegas
GUILTY PLEASURES? Guinness, Southern Comfort and lemonade, pizza

| Batting | Mat | Inns | NO | Runs | HS | Ave | SR | 100 | 50 | Ct | St |
|---|---|---|---|---|---|---|---|---|---|---|---|
| First-class | 52 | 86 | 3 | 2345 | 128 | 28.25 | 47.56 | 3 | 14 | 34 | 0 |
| List A | 9 | 9 | 0 | 224 | 73 | 24.88 | 86.82 | 0 | 1 | 4 | 0 |
| Twenty20 | 3 | 3 | 0 | 85 | 46 | 28.33 | 100.00 | 0 | 0 | 1 | 0 |
| Bowling | Mat | Balls | Runs | Wkts | BBI | BBM | Ave | Econ | SR | 5w | 10 |
| First-class | 52 | - | - | - | - | - | - | - | - | - | - |
| List A | 9 | - | - | - | - | - | - | - | - | - | - |
| Twenty20 | 3 | - | - | - | - | - | - | - | - | - | - |

# ANDREW STRAUSS                                        LHB LM R5

FULL NAME: Andrew John Strauss
BORN: March 2, 1977, Johannesburg, South Africa
SQUAD NO: 6
HEIGHT: 5ft 11in
NICKNAME: Straussy, Levi, Mareman, Muppet, Johann
EDUCATION: Radley College; Durham University
TEAMS: England, Middlesex, Northern Districts
CAREER: Test: 2004; ODI: 2003; T20I: 2005; First-class: 1998; List A: 1997; T20: 2003

BEST BATTING: 241* Middlesex vs Leicestershire, Lord's, 2011
BEST BOWLING: 1-16 Middlesex vs Nottinghamshire, Lord's, 2007
COUNTY CAP: 2001; BENEFIT YEAR: 2009

CRICKETERS PARTICULARLY ADMIRED? Allan Donald, Brian Lara, Saqlain Mushtaq
OTHER SPORTS PLAYED? Golf (Durham University 1998), rugby (Durham University 1996-97)
NOTES: Middlesex Player of the Year in 2001. Scored century (112) plus 83 in second innings on Test debut in the first Test vs New Zealand at Lord's in 2004, winning the Man of the Match award. Captain of Middlesex 2002-04. Scored 126 in the first Test vs South Africa at Port Elizabeth 2004/05, achieving feat of scoring a Test century on home and away debuts and becoming first player to score a Test century in his first innings against each of his first three opponents. Man of the Series vs New Zealand, summer 2008. Captained England's 2009 Ashes-winning side and became the first England captain to win the Ashes in Australia for 24 years in 2010/11. Captained England to 4-0 whitewash over India in summer 2011 to become the world's No.1 ranked Test side

| Batting | Mat | Inns | NO | Runs | HS | Ave | SR | 100 | 50 | Ct | St |
|---|---|---|---|---|---|---|---|---|---|---|---|
| Tests | 92 | 163 | 6 | 6490 | 177 | 41.33 | 49.17 | 19 | 26 | 109 | 0 |
| ODIs | 127 | 126 | 8 | 4205 | 158 | 35.63 | 80.94 | 6 | 27 | 57 | 0 |
| T20Is | 4 | 4 | 0 | 73 | 33 | 18.25 | 114.06 | 0 | 0 | 1 | 0 |
| First-class | 227 | 400 | 23 | 16082 | 241* | 42.65 | | 42 | 72 | 208 | 0 |
| List A | 254 | 247 | 14 | 7631 | 163 | 32.75 | | 10 | 49 | 90 | 0 |
| Twenty20 | 28 | 28 | 0 | 519 | 60 | 18.53 | 117.42 | 0 | 2 | 12 | 0 |

| Bowling | Mat | Balls | Runs | Wkts | BBI | BBM | Ave | Econ | SR | 5w | 10 |
|---|---|---|---|---|---|---|---|---|---|---|---|
| Tests | 92 | - | - | - | - | - | - | - | - | - | - |
| ODIs | 127 | 6 | 3 | 0 | - | - | - | 3.00 | - | 0 | 0 |
| T20Is | 4 | - | - | - | - | - | - | - | - | - | - |
| First-class | 227 | 132 | 142 | 3 | 1/16 | | 47.33 | 6.45 | 44.0 | 0 | 0 |
| List A | 254 | 6 | 3 | 0 | - | - | - | 3.00 | - | 0 | 0 |
| Twenty20 | 28 | - | - | - | - | - | - | - | - | - | - |

# SCOTT STYRIS                                                                RHB RM

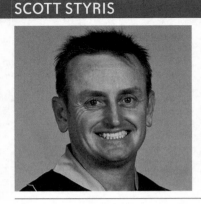

**FULL NAME:** Scott Bernard Styris
**BORN:** July 10, 1975, Brisbane, Australia
**SQUAD NO:** 56
**HEIGHT:** 5ft 10in
**NICKNAME:** Miley, The Rus
**EDUCATION:** Hamilton Boys High School
**TEAMS:** New Zealand, Auckland, Chennai
Super Kings, Deccan Chargers, Durham,
Essex, Middlesex, New Zealand Emerging
Players, New Zealand Under-19s, Northern
Districts, PCA Masters XI, Sylhet Royals
**CAREER:** Test: 2002; ODI: 1999; T20I: 2005;
First-class: 1994; List A: 1994; T20: 2005

**BEST BATTING:** 212* Northern Districts vs Otago, Hamilton, 2002
**BEST BOWLING:** 6-32 Northern Districts vs Otago, Gisborne, 2000
**COUNTY CAP:** 2006 (Middlesex)

**NOTES:** Distinguished limited-overs career with more than 5,000 runs and 150 wickets for
the Black Caps. Five Test match centuries. He was awarded his Test cap on the eve of the
Karachi Test in May 2002, but it was taken back when the match was cancelled because of a
bomb blast. He had 10 years of domestic experience before he was awarded his Test cap.
Having given up Test cricket in 2008, he announced his retirement from all international
cricket in June 2011

| Batting | Mat | Inns | NO | Runs | HS | Ave | SR | 100 | 50 | Ct | St |
|---|---|---|---|---|---|---|---|---|---|---|---|
| Tests | 29 | 48 | 4 | 1586 | 170 | 36.04 | 51.34 | 5 | 6 | 23 | 0 |
| ODIs | 188 | 161 | 23 | 4483 | 141 | 32.48 | 79.41 | 4 | 28 | 73 | 0 |
| T20Is | 31 | 29 | 2 | 578 | 66 | 21.40 | 119.66 | 0 | 1 | 8 | 0 |
| First-class | 128 | 213 | 20 | 6048 | 212* | 31.33 | | 10 | 30 | 102 | 0 |
| List A | 339 | 297 | 48 | 8325 | 141 | 33.43 | | 6 | 57 | 130 | 0 |
| Twenty20 | 137 | 127 | 18 | 2800 | 106* | 25.68 | 134.03 | 1 | 9 | 36 | 0 |
| Bowling | Mat | Balls | Runs | Wkts | BBI | BBM | Ave | Econ | SR | 5w | 10 |
| Tests | 29 | 1960 | 1015 | 20 | 3/28 | 3/44 | 50.75 | 3.10 | 98.0 | 0 | 0 |
| ODIs | 188 | 6114 | 4839 | 137 | 6/25 | 6/25 | 35.32 | 4.74 | 44.6 | 1 | 0 |
| T20Is | 31 | 309 | 349 | 18 | 3/5 | 3/5 | 19.38 | 6.77 | 17.1 | 0 | 0 |
| First-class | 128 | 12826 | 6446 | 204 | 6/32 | | 31.59 | 3.01 | 62.8 | 9 | 1 |
| List A | 339 | 12036 | 9227 | 298 | 6/25 | 6/25 | 30.96 | 4.59 | 40.3 | 1 | 0 |
| Twenty20 | 137 | 2044 | 2566 | 93 | 3/5 | 3/5 | 27.59 | 7.53 | 21.9 | 0 | 0 |

# ARUL SUPPIAH
## RHB SLA R1 MVP51

**FULL NAME:** Arul Vivasvan Suppiah
**BORN:** August 30, 1983, Kuala Lumpur, Malaysia
**SQUAD NO:** 23
**HEIGHT:** 6ft
**NICKNAME:** Ruley, Ja , Shilpa, Ruler
**EDUCATION:** Millfield School; Exeter University
**TEAMS:** Somerset
**CAREER:** First-class: 2002; List A: 2002; T20: 2005

BEST BATTING: 156 Somerset vs Indians, Taunton, 2011
BEST BOWLING: 3-46 Somerset vs West Indies A, Taunton, 2002
COUNTY CAP: 2009

**CAREER HIGHLIGHTS?** Holding the world record bowling figures in T20 cricket. 156 against India in July 2011
**NON-CRICKETING HEROES?** Nelson Mandela, Nicol David (world No.1 squash player)
**TIPS FOR THE TOP?** Jos Buttler, Chris Jones, Danny Briggs
**IF YOU WEREN'T A CRICKETER?** Cooking somewhere as a chef
**WHEN RAIN STOPS PLAY?** Listen to music, go to the gym, annoy James Hildreth
**FAVOURITE TV?** Grey's Anatomy, Fawlty Towers
**FAVOURITE FILM?** 3 Idiots, Bad Boys, The King's Speech
**FAVOURITE BOOK?** Lord Of The Flies, Andre Agassi's autobiography
**DREAM HOLIDAY?** New York
**GUILTY PLEASURES?** Comfort food, especially chocolates
**AMAZE ME!** I'm a black tip belt holder in taekwando, I can speak three languages, and I played badminton for Somerset
**FANTASY SLIP CORDON?** Keeper: Po (Kung Fu Panda), 1st: James Hildreth (best hands in the game), 2nd: Eva Mendes (stunning to look at), 3rd: Michael McIntyre (to keep us entertained for a long day in the field), Gully: Mila Kunis (for the benefits)

| Batting | Mat | Inns | NO | Runs | HS | Ave | SR | 100 | 50 | Ct | St |
|---|---|---|---|---|---|---|---|---|---|---|---|
| First-class | 77 | 130 | 8 | 4257 | 156 | 34.89 | 48.62 | 6 | 24 | 45 | 0 |
| List A | 82 | 66 | 13 | 1478 | 80 | 27.88 | | 0 | 8 | 31 | 0 |
| Twenty20 | 75 | 48 | 15 | 417 | 32* | 12.63 | 104.51 | 0 | 0 | 32 | 0 |

| Bowling | Mat | Balls | Runs | Wkts | BBI | BBM | Ave | Econ | SR | 5w | 10 |
|---|---|---|---|---|---|---|---|---|---|---|---|
| First-class | 77 | 4173 | 2379 | 42 | 3/46 | | 56.64 | 3.42 | 99.3 | 0 | 0 |
| List A | 82 | 1508 | 1397 | 44 | 4/39 | 4/39 | 31.75 | 5.55 | 34.2 | 0 | 0 |
| Twenty20 | 75 | 575 | 697 | 37 | 6/5 | 6/5 | 18.83 | 7.27 | 15.5 | 1 | 0 |

## GRAEME SWANN

### RHB OB W1

FULL NAME: Graeme Peter Swann
BORN: March 24, 1979, Northampton
SQUAD NO: 6
HEIGHT: 6ft 1in
NICKNAME: Chin, Swanny, G, Jimmy Hill
EDUCATION: Sponne School, Towcester
TEAMS: England, Northamptonshire, Nottinghamshire
CAREER: Test: 2008; ODI: 2000; T20I: 2008; First-class: 1998; List A: 1997; T20: 2003

BEST BATTING: 183 Northamptonshire vs Gloucestershire, Bristol, 2002
BEST BOWLING: 7-33 Northamptonshire vs Derbyshire, Northampton, 2003
COUNTY CAP: 1999 (Northamptonshire)

CAREER HIGHLIGHTS? Winning the Northamptonshire U13 pairs cricket competition with Horton House juniors in the early 90s for the first time
GUILTY PLEASURES? I like listening to the back catalogue of Kylie Minogue in my car. I reduce the volume when driving through town centres or neighbourhoods where the queen of Australia isn't considered to be 'street' enough
AMAZE ME! 1. My doorbell plays the Blaydon Races, the famous anthem of the magnificent Newcastle United FC 2. My favourite motorbike is the Triumph Thunderbird 3. My favourite meal would be sausages in batter, chips and mushy peas followed by a Krispy Kreme Doughnut. Kevin Paxton, the Notts strength and conditioning guy, does not think this is fuel for a modern athlete. I think he was bullied at school
TWITTER FEED: @swannyg66

| Batting | Mat | Inns | NO | Runs | HS | Ave | SR | 100 | 50 | Ct | St |
|---|---|---|---|---|---|---|---|---|---|---|---|
| Tests | 39 | 46 | 6 | 905 | 85 | 22.62 | 79.45 | 0 | 4 | 33 | 0 |
| ODIs | 67 | 44 | 12 | 468 | 34 | 14.62 | 89.82 | 0 | 0 | 25 | 0 |
| T20Is | 30 | 13 | 10 | 52 | 15* | 17.33 | 98.11 | 0 | 0 | 3 | 0 |
| First-class | 221 | 300 | 26 | 7135 | 183 | 26.04 | | 4 | 35 | 167 | 0 |
| List A | 254 | 192 | 28 | 3118 | 83 | 19.01 | | 0 | 14 | 84 | 0 |
| Twenty20 | 71 | 51 | 14 | 739 | 90* | 19.97 | 135.34 | 0 | 3 | 18 | 0 |

| Bowling | Mat | Balls | Runs | Wkts | BBI | BBM | Ave | Econ | SR | 5w | 10 |
|---|---|---|---|---|---|---|---|---|---|---|---|
| Tests | 39 | 9592 | 4736 | 166 | 6/65 | 10/217 | 28.53 | 2.96 | 57.7 | 11 | 1 |
| ODIs | 67 | 3204 | 2385 | 92 | 5/28 | 5/28 | 25.92 | 4.46 | 34.8 | 1 | 0 |
| T20Is | 30 | 618 | 659 | 40 | 3/13 | 3/13 | 16.47 | 6.39 | 15.4 | 0 | 0 |
| First-class | 221 | 39910 | 19921 | 623 | 7/33 | | 31.97 | 2.99 | 64.0 | 26 | 4 |
| List A | 254 | 10434 | 7669 | 292 | 5/17 | 5/17 | 26.26 | 4.41 | 35.7 | 3 | 0 |
| Twenty20 | 71 | 1500 | 1651 | 87 | 3/13 | 3/13 | 18.97 | 6.60 | 17.2 | 0 | 0 |

**FULL NAME:** Samuel Alan Sweeney
**BORN:** March 15, 1990, Preston, Lancashire
**SQUAD NO:** 17
**HEIGHT:** 5ft 11in
**NICKNAME:** The Sweeney, Sweens, Sweendog
**EDUCATION:** Parklands High School, Chorley; Myerscough College, Manchester
**TEAMS:** Northamptonshire, Northamptonshire 2nd XI
**CAREER:** List A: 2011

**FAMILY TIES?** Dad was the local league sledger
**CAREER HIGHLIGHTS?** Getting a contract at Northamptonshire
**SUPERSTITIONS?** Last one out of the changing room
**CRICKETING HEROES?** Brett Lee, Rob Newton, Andrew Flintoff
**NON-CRICKETING HEROES?** Charlie Sheen, Robert De Niro
**BEST PLAYER IN COUNTY CRICKET?** Marcus Trescothick
**TIP FOR THE TOP?** James Taylor
**WHEN RAIN STOPS PLAY?** One hand-one bounce and sleeping
**FAVOURITE TV?** Geordie Shore
**FAVOURITE FILM?** Superbad
**FAVOURITE BOOK?** BFG
**DREAM HOLIDAY?** Benidorm
**ACCOMPLISHMENTS?** Signing for Bolton Wanderers U12
**SURPRISING SKILL?** I can play the trombone
**GUILTY PLEASURES?** Terry's Chocolate Orange
**FANTASY SLIP CORDON?** Keeper: Sheldon from The Big Bang Theory, 1st: James Corden, 2nd: Peter Kay, 3rd: Alan from The Hangover

| Batting | Mat | Inns | NO | Runs | HS | Ave | SR | 100 | 50 | Ct | St |
|---------|-----|------|-----|------|-----|------|------|------|-----|-----|-----|
| List A | 1 | - | - | - | - | - | - | - | - | 1 | 0 |

| Bowling | Mat | Balls | Runs | Wkts | BBI | BBM | Ave | Econ | SR | 5w | 10 |
|---------|-----|-------|------|------|-----|-----|------|-------|-----|-----|-----|
| List A | 1 | 18 | 31 | 0 | - | - | - | 10.33 | - | 0 | 0 |

## JAMES SYKES LHB SLA

FULL NAME: James Stuart Sykes
BORN: April 26, 1992, Huntingdon
SQUAD NO: 20
HEIGHT: 6ft 2in
NICKNAME: Sykesy
EDUCATION: St Ivo School
TEAMS: Cambridgeshire, Leicestershire 2nd XI
CAREER: Yet to make first-team debut

WHY CRICKET? Enjoyed watching Shane Warne bowling in the Ashes
CAREER HIGHLIGHTS? Being offered a professional contract at Leicestershire
SUPERSTITIONS? Always put my right pad and right glove on first
CRICKETING HEROES? Shane Warne, Claude Henderson
NON-CRICKETING HEROES? Tom Hardy, Samuel L Jackson, Channing Tatum
BEST PLAYER IN COUNTY CRICKET? Chris Rogers
TIPS FOR THE TOP? Nathan Buck, Josh Cobb, Ned Eckersley, Alex Wyatt
IF YOU WEREN'T A CRICKETER? Ski season working as a chalet boy
WHEN RAIN STOPS PLAY? Listen to music, lots of talking, lots of sleeping
FAVOURITE TV? Hollyoaks, Geordie Shore, TOWIE
FAVOURITE FILM? Coach Carter, Any Given Sunday
FAVOURITE BOOK? The Beano
DREAM HOLIDAY? Switzerland
ACCOMPLISHMENTS? Passing A-Levels
SURPRISING FACT? Can dance ballet (seriously). Season ticket holder at Norwich City
GUILTY PLEASURES? Reality TV, McFlurrys, One Direction
FANTASY SLIP CORDON? Keeper: Michael Jordan, 1st: Tom Hardy, 2nd: Eminem, 3rd: Myself, Gully: Drake
TWITTER FEED: @jsykes321

# NAQAASH TAHIR

**RHB RFM**

FULL NAME: Naqaash Sarosh Tahir
BORN: November 14, 1983, Birmingham, Warwickshire
SQUAD NO: 17
HEIGHT: 5ft 10in
NICKNAME: Naq
EDUCATION: Moseley School; Spring Hill College
TEAMS: Warwickshire, Warwickshire 2nd XI
CAREER: First-class: 2004; List A: 2005

**LANCASHIRE**

BEST BATTING: 53 Warwickshire vs Durham, Birmingham, 2011
BEST BOWLING: 7-107 Warwickshire vs Lancashire, Blackpool, 2006

FAMILY TIES? Dad played club cricket and brother played for Worcestershire and Warwickshire
SUPERSTITIONS? Putting my pads on in a certain way
CRICKETERS PARTICULARLY ADMIRED? Waqar Younis, Wasim Akram, Brett Lee, Darren Gough
OTHER SPORTS FOLLOWED? Football (Manchester United)
RELAXATIONS? Watching TV, PlayStation
NOTES: Made his first-class debut while playing for Warwickshire against Cambridge MCCU in 2004. Released by Warwickshire at the end of last season but signed by Lancashire for the start of this summer. "We are delighted to secure Naqaash for the coming season," said Lancashire head coach Peter Moores. "He is a very talented swing bowler who will provide the necessary depth to an already strong seam attack, which is essential for the demands of a first-class county season"

| Batting | Mat | Inns | NO | Runs | HS | Ave | SR | 100 | 50 | Ct | St |
|---|---|---|---|---|---|---|---|---|---|---|---|
| First-class | 56 | 65 | 16 | 751 | 53 | 15.32 | 36.35 | 0 | 1 | 7 | 0 |
| List A | 15 | 5 | 3 | 19 | 13* | 9.50 | 73.07 | 0 | 0 | 1 | 0 |

| Bowling | Mat | Balls | Runs | Wkts | BBI | BBM | Ave | Econ | SR | 5w | 10 |
|---|---|---|---|---|---|---|---|---|---|---|---|
| First-class | 56 | 7677 | 4163 | 139 | 7/107 | – | 29.94 | 3.25 | 55.2 | 2 | – |
| List A | 15 | 523 | 439 | 5 | 2/47 | 2/47 | 87.80 | 5.03 | 104.6 | 0 | 0 |

**GLOUCESTERSHIRE**

FULL NAME: Jack Martin Robert Taylor
BORN: November 12, 1991, Banbury, Oxfordshire
SQUAD NO: 10
HEIGHT: 5ft 9in
NICKNAME: Schlidd
EDUCATION: Chipping Norton School
TEAMS: Gloucestershire, Gloucestershire 2nd XI, Oxfordshire
CAREER: First-class: 2010; List A: 2011; T20: 2011

---

BEST BATTING: 39 Gloucestershire vs Surrey, Cheltenham, 2011
BEST BOWLING: 2-81 Gloucestershire vs Middlesex, Uxbridge, 2011
COUNTY CAP: 2010

---

FAMILY TIES? Father and grandfather both played minor counties cricket, brother [Matthew] also made list A debut in 2011 for Gloucestershire
CAREER HIGHLIGHTS? First-class debut vs Derbyshire in 2010 and beating Somerset in T20 at Bristol having taken 4-16 off four overs and hit 38 off 28 balls
CRICKETING HEROES? Ricky Ponting, Muttiah Muralitharan, Dan Vettori
NON-CRICKETING HEROES? Liam Neeson, Stifler!
BEST PLAYER IN COUNTY CRICKET? Marcus Trescothick with the bat, Simon Jones with the ball, Chris Taylor in the field
TIPS FOR THE TOP? Chris Dent, David Payne, James Fuller
FAVOURITE TV? Jersey Shore, Criminal Minds
FAVOURITE FILM? Taken, The Girl Next Door
FAVOURITE BOOK? The Game by Neil Strauss
ACCOMPLISHMENTS? Passing my driving test
GUILTY PLEASURES? Glamour Sunday, Big Macs, TOWIE
AMAZE ME! I have a tattoo and I love cooking
TWITTER FEED: @ jacktaylor141

| Batting | Mat | Inns | NO | Runs | HS | Ave | SR | 100 | 50 | Ct | St |
|---|---|---|---|---|---|---|---|---|---|---|---|
| First-class | 5 | 9 | 0 | 122 | 39 | 13.55 | 50.00 | 0 | 0 | 3 | 0 |
| List A | 5 | 3 | 1 | 18 | 9* | 9.00 | 180.00 | 0 | 0 | 1 | 0 |
| Twenty20 | 7 | 7 | 1 | 51 | 38 | 8.50 | 89.47 | 0 | 0 | 1 | 0 |

| Bowling | Mat | Balls | Runs | Wkts | BBI | BBM | Ave | Econ | SR | 5w | 10 |
|---|---|---|---|---|---|---|---|---|---|---|---|
| First-class | 5 | 498 | 368 | 7 | 2/81 | 2/81 | 52.57 | 4.43 | 71.1 | 0 | 0 |
| List A | 5 | 154 | 151 | 7 | 3/37 | 3/37 | 21.57 | 5.88 | 22.0 | 0 | 0 |
| Twenty20 | 7 | 97 | 118 | 8 | 4/16 | 4/16 | 14.75 | 7.29 | 12.1 | 0 | 0 |

# JAMES TAYLOR

## RHB LB R3 MVP93

FULL NAME: James William Arthur Taylor
BORN: January 6, 1990, Nottingham
SQUAD NO: 4
HEIGHT: 5ft 7in
NICKNAME: Jimmy, Titch
EDUCATION: Shrewsbury School
TEAMS: England, England Lions, England Under-19s, Leicestershire, Shropshire, Worcestershire 2nd XI
CAREER: ODI: 2011; First-class: 2008; List A: 2008; T20: 2008

**NOTTINGHAMSHIRE**

BEST BATTING: 237 Leicestershire vs LMCCU, Leicester, 2011
COUNTY CAP: 2009 (Leicestershire)

CRICKETERS PARTICULARLY ADMIRED? Sachin Tendulkar
TIP FOR THE TOP? Shiv Thakor
RELAXATIONS? Fishing, shooting, hunting
FAVOURITE BAND? Pussycat Dolls
NOTES: Represented England in the 2008 U19 World Cup. Cricket Writers' Young Player of the Year 2009. Captain of England Lions in 2011/12. Made ODI debut against Ireland in August 2011. Joined Nottinghamshire after four successful seasons with Leicestershire, having graduated from minor counties cricket with Shropshire and the academy at Worcestershire

| Batting | Mat | Inns | NO | Runs | HS | Ave | SR | 100 | 50 | Ct | St |
|---|---|---|---|---|---|---|---|---|---|---|---|
| ODIs | 1 | 1 | 0 | 1 | 1 | 1.00 | 12.50 | 0 | 0 | 0 | 0 |
| First-class | 63 | 106 | 15 | 4534 | 237 | 49.82 | | 10 | 23 | 48 | 0 |
| List A | 59 | 55 | 10 | 1987 | 111 | 44.15 | 79.83 | 5 | 11 | 10 | 0 |
| Twenty20 | 49 | 45 | 13 | 1124 | 62* | 35.12 | 115.40 | 0 | 6 | 15 | 0 |

| Bowling | Mat | Balls | Runs | Wkts | BBI | BBM | Ave | Econ | SR | 5w | 10 |
|---|---|---|---|---|---|---|---|---|---|---|---|
| ODIs | 1 | - | - | - | - | - | - | - | - | - | - |
| First-class | 63 | 216 | 160 | 0 | - | - | - | 4.44 | - | 0 | 0 |
| List A | 59 | 138 | 170 | 5 | 4/61 | 4/61 | 34.00 | 7.39 | 27.6 | 0 | 0 |
| Twenty20 | 49 | 74 | 100 | 2 | 1/10 | 1/10 | 50.00 | 8.10 | 37.0 | 0 | 0 |

# ROBERT TAYLOR

## LHB LM

**FULL NAME:** Robert Meadows Liam Taylor
**BORN:** December 21, 1989, Northampton
**SQUAD NO:** 42
**HEIGHT:** 6ft 3in
**NICKNAME:** Tayls
**EDUCATION:** Harrow School; Loughborough University
**TEAMS:** Harrow School, Leicestershire, Leicestershire 2nd XI, Loughborough MCCU, Northamptonshire 2nd XI
**CAREER:** First-class: 2010

**BEST BATTING:** 101* LMCCU vs Leicestershire, Leicester, 2011
**BEST BOWLING:** 3-53 Leicestershire vs Surrey, Leicester, 2011

**FAMILY TIES?** Father played In the Northants Leagues, brother played 1st XI cricket at Stowe School
**CAREER HIGHLIGHTS?** Scoring 101* against Leicestershire for Loughborough MCCU, scoring 70 and taking 3-53 against Surrey on debut
**CRICKETING HEROES?** Mike Hussey, Mitchell Johnson
**NON-CRICKETING HEROES?** My brother
**BEST PLAYER IN COUNTY CRICKET?** James Taylor
**TIPS FOR THE TOP?** James Taylor, Josh Cobb, Sam Billings
**IF YOU WEREN'T A CRICKETER?** Trying to find a job somewhere that didn't involve sitting in an office all day
**WHEN RAIN STOPS PLAY?** Go on Twitter and see what everyone on there is up to
**FAVOURITE TV?** Top Gear
**FAVOURITE FILM?** The Shawshank Redemption
**FAVOURITE BOOK?** The Cat In The Hat
**GUILTY PLEASURES?** Ben and Jerry's
**AMAZE ME!** I used to play the drums, four players who were in my school team are now signed at counties, I bowl with my left arm and throw with my right arm
**FANTASY SLIP CORDON?** Keeper: Karl Pilkington, 1st: Lee Evans, 2nd: Myself, 3rd: Michael McIntyre, Gully: Ricky Gervais
**TWITTER FEED:** @robtaylor1989

| Batting | Mat | Inns | NO | Runs | HS | Ave | SR | 100 | 50 | Ct | St |
|---|---|---|---|---|---|---|---|---|---|---|---|
| First-class | 9 | 16 | 1 | 397 | 101* | 26.46 | 56.47 | 1 | 1 | 4 | 0 |

| Bowling | Mat | Balls | Runs | Wkts | BBI | BBM | Ave | Econ | SR | 5w | 10 |
|---|---|---|---|---|---|---|---|---|---|---|---|
| First-class | 9 | 970 | 734 | 16 | 3/53 | 4/165 | 45.87 | 4.54 | 60.6 | 0 | 0 |

# RYAN TEN DOESCHATE

## RHB RMF

FULL NAME: Ryan Neil ten Doeschate
BORN: June 30, 1980, Port Elizabeth, South Africa
SQUAD NO: 27
HEIGHT: 5ft 11in
NICKNAME: Tendo
EDUCATION: Fairbairn College; University of Cape Town
TEAMS: Netherlands, Canterbury, Essex, Impi, Kolkata Knight Riders, Mashonaland Eagles, Tasmania, Western Province
CAREER: ODI: 2006; T20I: 2008; First-class: 2003; List A: 2003; T20: 2003

BEST BATTING: 259* Netherlands vs Canada, Pretoria, 2006
BEST BOWLING: 6-20 Netherlands vs Canada, Pretoria, 2006
COUNTY CAP: 2006

CRICKETERS PARTICULARLY ADMIRED? Jacques Kallis, Kepler Wessels
OTHER SPORTS PLAYED? Rugby
OTHER SPORTS FOLLOWED? Football (Arsenal), rugby (Stormers)
FAVOURITE MUSICIAN? Phil Collins
RELAXATIONS? Golf, tennis, reading
NOTES: Netherlands international who won the inaugural ICC Associate ODI Player of the Year in 2007 and the ICC Associate and Affiliate Player of the Year Award in 2010. Scored 686 runs at an average of 228.66 in the ICC Intercontinental Cup in 2006, recording four consecutive hundreds, including a competition record 259* vs Canada in Pretoria. Made a century (119) against England at Nagpur in the World Cup 2011, becoming the first batsman from the Netherlands to make a hundred in the World Cup finals, and a second century against Ireland at Kolkata. Leading first-class wicket-taker for Essex in 2008

| Batting | Mat | Inns | NO | Runs | HS | Ave | SR | 100 | 50 | Ct | St |
|---|---|---|---|---|---|---|---|---|---|---|---|
| ODIs | 33 | 32 | 9 | 1541 | 119 | 67.00 | 87.70 | 5 | 9 | 13 | 0 |
| T20Is | 9 | 9 | 4 | 214 | 56 | 42.80 | 128.91 | 0 | 1 | 3 | 0 |
| First-class | 90 | 132 | 16 | 5451 | 259* | 46.99 | | 18 | 19 | 54 | 0 |
| List A | 139 | 113 | 33 | 3667 | 134* | 45.83 | | 7 | 20 | 43 | 0 |
| Twenty20 | 129 | 111 | 24 | 2267 | 121* | 26.05 | 131.34 | 2 | 6 | 42 | 0 |

| Bowling | Mat | Balls | Runs | Wkts | BBI | BBM | Ave | Econ | SR | 5w | 10 |
|---|---|---|---|---|---|---|---|---|---|---|---|
| ODIs | 33 | 1580 | 1327 | 55 | 4/31 | 4/31 | 24.12 | 5.03 | 28.7 | 0 | 0 |
| T20Is | 9 | 204 | 241 | 12 | 3/23 | 3/23 | 20.08 | 7.08 | 17.0 | 0 | 0 |
| First-class | 90 | 8333 | 5528 | 167 | 6/20 | | 33.10 | 3.98 | 49.8 | 7 | 0 |
| List A | 139 | 4051 | 3765 | 133 | 5/50 | 5/50 | 28.30 | 5.57 | 30.4 | 1 | 0 |
| Twenty20 | 129 | 1087 | 1447 | 61 | 4/24 | 4/24 | 23.72 | 7.98 | 17.8 | 0 | 0 |

## SEAN TERRY

### RHB OB

**HAMPSHIRE**

FULL NAME: Sean Paul Terry
BORN: August 1, 1991, Southampton, Hampshire
SQUAD NO: 10
HEIGHT: 5ft 11in
NICKNAME: Seaney, Tez
EDUCATION: Aquinas College, Perth, Western Australia
TEAMS: Derbyshire 2nd XI, Hampshire 2nd XI, Marylebone Cricket Club Young Cricketers
CAREER: Yet to make first-team debut

FAMILY TIES? My dad [Paul] played for Hampshire and England
WHY CRICKET? Watching my dad play
CAREER HIGHLIGHTS? Being an MCC Young Cricketer was something special, being at Lord's every day was awesome
SUPERSTITIONS? Left pad on first
CRICKETING HEROES? Michael Clarke, Sachin Tendulkar, AB de Villiers
NON-CRICKETING HEROES? Mum, Michael Jordan
TIPS FOR THE TOP? Jamie Porter, Christian Marsh, Omar Ali and all the MCC YCs
IF YOU WEREN'T A CRICKETER? Hopefully be involved in sport somewhere
WHEN RAIN STOPS PLAY? Sleeping or playing poker
FAVOURITE TV? The Simpsons
FAVOURITE FILM? Wedding Crashers, Cool Runnings
FAVOURITE BOOK? Not a big reader!
DREAM HOLIDAY? Bali or somewhere in Spain
ACCOMPLISHMENTS? Year 12 English award!
SURPRISING SKILL? Unfortunately not, fancy myself as a bit of a singer though
GUILTY PLEASURES? McDonalds
AMAZE ME! 1. Born in England 2. Grew up in Australia 3. Can play for Ireland
FANTASY SLIP CORDON? Keeper: Katy Perry (something to look at), 1st: Myself, 2nd: Ricky Ponting, 3rd: Chris Rock (bit of banter), Gully: Mark Waugh
TWITTER FEED: @sterry91

FULL NAME: Shivsinh Jaysinh Thakor
BORN: October 22, 1993, Leicester
SQUAD NO: 57
HEIGHT: 5ft 11in
NICKNAME: King Kong, Jarhead, Bear, Shiva
EDUCATION: Uppingham School
TEAMS: England Under-17s, England Under-19s, Leicestershire, Leicestershire 2nd XI
CAREER: First-class: 2011; List A: 2011

BEST BATTING: 134 Leicestershire vs LMCCU, Leicester, 2011
BEST BOWLING: 3-57 Leicestershire vs Surrey, Leicester, 2011

FAMILY TIES? My father played cricket both in Leicestershire and back in India, representing youth age groups followed by club cricket
CAREER HIGHLIGHTS? Making 134 on first-class debut, playing for England U19, winning the U13 Schools National Cup and getting 237* in the semi-final. Being part of the Leicestershire squad for the T20 win in 2011
CRICKETING HEROES? Sachin Tendulkar, Ricky Ponting
TIPS FOR THE TOP? Aryian Patel, Ben Collins, Salman Mir
IF YOU WEREN'T A CRICKETER? Something that fits in with the degree I plan to do, PPE
WHEN RAIN STOPS PLAY? Talking, listening to music or in the nets
FAVOURITE TV? 90210, Made In Chelsea, Desperate Housewives
FAVOURITE FILM? Secretariat
FAVOURITE BOOK? Richard Dawkins – The God Delusion
ACCOMPLISHMENTS? Uppingham School prefect, CCF sergeant, meeting the prime minister at 10 Downing Street
AMAZE ME! I have a teddy bear, I was lead vocal in a house singing competition and I cannot swim
FANTASY SLIP CORDON? Keeper: Trevor Ward, 1st: Me, 2nd: Oliver William Packer, 3rd: David Beggs, Gully: Paul Martin
TWITTER FEED: @Thakor57

| Batting | Mat | Inns | NO | Runs | HS | Ave | SR | 100 | 50 | Ct | St |
|---|---|---|---|---|---|---|---|---|---|---|---|
| First-class | 3 | 5 | 0 | 190 | 134 | 38.00 | 54.13 | 1 | 0 | 0 | 0 |
| List A | 2 | 2 | 0 | 26 | 13 | 13.00 | 65.00 | 0 | 0 | 0 | 0 |

| Bowling | Mat | Balls | Runs | Wkts | BBI | BBM | Ave | Econ | SR | 5w | 10 |
|---|---|---|---|---|---|---|---|---|---|---|---|
| First-class | 3 | 102 | 74 | 3 | 3/57 | 3/57 | 24.66 | 4.35 | 34.0 | 0 | 0 |
| List A | 2 | - | - | - | - | - | - | - | - | - | - |

# ALFONSO THOMAS

RHB RFM

SOMERSET

FULL NAME: Alfonso Clive Thomas
BORN: February 9, 1977, Cape Town, South Africa
SQUAD NO: 8
TEAMS: South Africa, Adelaide Strikers, Dolphins, North West, Northerns, Pune Warriors, Somerset, Staffordshire, Titans, Warwickshire, Western Province
CAREER: T20I: 2007; First-class: 1998; List A: 2000; T20: 2004

BEST BATTING: 119* North West vs Northerns, Centurion, 2002
BEST BOWLING: 7-54 Titans vs Cape Cobras, Newlands, 2005
COUNTY CAP: 2008 (Somerset)

NOTES: Came to prominence in 2003/04, after 36 wickets in eight SuperSport Series matches for Northern Titans. Replaced the injured Andre Nel in South Africa's Test squad to India in late 2004. Made his international debut aged 30 in 2007, but signed with Somerset as a Kolpak player the following year. Leading wicket-taker in the 2010 FP t20, with 33 wickets. Took 109 wickets across all competitions in 2010

| Batting | Mat | Inns | NO | Runs | HS | Ave | SR | 100 | 50 | Ct | St |
|---|---|---|---|---|---|---|---|---|---|---|---|
| T20Is | 1 | - | - | - | - | - | - | - | - | 0 | 0 |
| First-class | 120 | 168 | 33 | 3491 | 119* | 25.85 | | 2 | 12 | 32 | 0 |
| List A | 143 | 70 | 33 | 550 | 28* | 14.86 | | 0 | 0 | 30 | 0 |
| Twenty20 | 130 | 43 | 24 | 229 | 30* | 12.05 | 103.61 | 0 | 0 | 38 | 0 |

| Bowling | Mat | Balls | Runs | Wkts | BBI | BBM | Ave | Econ | SR | 5w | 10 |
|---|---|---|---|---|---|---|---|---|---|---|---|
| T20Is | 1 | 24 | 25 | 3 | 3/25 | 3/25 | 8.33 | 6.25 | 8.0 | 0 | 0 |
| First-class | 120 | 21609 | 10495 | 386 | 7/54 | | 27.18 | 2.91 | 55.9 | 18 | 2 |
| List A | 143 | 6088 | 5169 | 185 | 4/18 | 4/18 | 27.94 | 5.09 | 32.9 | 0 | 0 |
| Twenty20 | 130 | 2601 | 3125 | 151 | 4/27 | 4/27 | 20.69 | 7.20 | 17.2 | 0 | 0 |

# IVAN THOMAS RHB RM

FULL NAME: Ivan Thomas
BORN: September 25, 1991
SQUAD NO: 5
HEIGHT: 6ft 4in
NICKNAME: Drago
EDUCATION: The John Roan Secondary School; University of Leeds
TEAMS: Kent 2nd XI, Kent Under-17s
CAREER: Yet to make first-team debut

KENT

WHY CRICKET? I enjoyed a tournament I played in at primary school and realised playing it got me out of lessons!

CAREER HIGHLIGHTS? Taking my first hat-trick against Surrey 2nd XI at Cheam

SUPERSTITIONS? Have to turn the same way at the top of my run-up

CRICKETING HEROES? Andrew Flintoff

NON-CRICKETING HEROES? Che Guevara

TIPS FOR THE TOP? Adam Ball, Daniel Bell-Drummond

IF YOU WEREN'T A CRICKETER? Studying Physics at uni

WHEN RAIN STOPS PLAY? Normally eating

FAVOURITE TV? The Wire

FAVOURITE FILM? The Usual Suspects

FAVOURITE BOOK? The Hitchhiker's Guide To The Galaxy or The Lord Of The Rings

DREAM HOLIDAY? Jamaica

ACCOMPLISHMENTS? Getting in to the University of Leeds

GUILTY PLEASURES? Custard slices

SURPRISING SKILL? Can complete a Rubik's Cube in just over a minute

AMAZE ME! I can tear an apple in half, I'm a quarter Jamaican and I'm a trained silver-service waiter and barman

FANTASY SLIP CORDON? Keeper: Me, 1st: Idris Elba, 2nd: Biggie Smalls, 3rd: Eminem, Gully: Peter Griffin

## CALLUM THORP

### RHB RMF W1 MVP76

**DURHAM**

FULL NAME: Callum David Thorp
BORN: January 11, 1975, Mount Lawley,
Perth, Australia
SQUAD NO: 36
HEIGHT: 6ft 3in
EDUCATION: Servite College
TEAMS: Durham, Western Australia
CAREER: First-class: 2003; List A: 2003; T20:
2005

BEST BATTING: 79* Durham vs MCC, Abu Dhabi, 2009
BEST BOWLING: 7-88 Durham vs Kent, Canterbury, 2008

CAREER HIGHLIGHTS? One-day final win for Wanneroo DCC, County Championship wins in 2008 and 2009 for Durham, and my first-class debut for Western Australia
SUPERSTITIONS? All clothing and kit must be put on left side first
CRICKETING HEROES? Dennis Lillee, Viv Richards and Steve Waugh
NON-CRICKETING HEROES? Michael Jordan, Pele, Stefan Edberg and Carl Lewis
BEST PLAYER IN COUNTY CRICKET? Marcus Trescothick
TIPS FOR THE TOP? Ben Stokes and Scott Borthwick
WHEN RAIN STOPS PLAY? Sleep or harass the physio
FAVOURITE TV? Suits
FAVOURITE FILM? Gladiator
DREAM HOLIDAY? Maldives
GUILTY PLEASURES? Eating a slice of cake almost every day
FANTASY SLIP CORDON? Keeper: Billy Connolly, 1st: Me, 2nd: Michael Jordan, 3rd: Tiger Woods, Gully: Usain Bolt

| Batting | Mat | Inns | NO | Runs | HS | Ave | SR | 100 | 50 | Ct | St |
|---------|-----|------|-----|------|-----|-------|--------|-----|-----|-----|-----|
| First-class | 72 | 94 | 12 | 1286 | 79* | 15.68 | 57.92 | 0 | 3 | 42 | 0 |
| List A | 42 | 28 | 9 | 323 | 52 | 17.00 | 99.69 | 0 | 1 | 8 | 0 |
| Twenty20 | 9 | 6 | 0 | 63 | 13 | 10.50 | 114.54 | 0 | 0 | 1 | 0 |

| Bowling | Mat | Balls | Runs | Wkts | BBI | BBM | Ave | Econ | SR | 5w | 10 |
|---------|-----|-------|------|------|-----|-----|-------|------|------|-----|-----|
| First-class | 72 | 11277 | 5580 | 205 | 7/88 | | 27.21 | 2.96 | 55.0 | 8 | 1 |
| List A | 42 | 1897 | 1438 | 53 | 6/17 | 6/17 | 27.13 | 4.54 | 35.7 | 1 | 0 |
| Twenty20 | 9 | 162 | 266 | 3 | 2/32 | 2/32 | 88.66 | 9.85 | 54.0 | 0 | 0 |

## JAMES TOMLINSON     LHB LMF W1

FULL NAME: James Andrew Tomlinson
BORN: June 12, 1982, Winchester, Hampshire
SQUAD NO: 21
HEIGHT: 6ft 2in
NICKNAME: Tommo
EDUCATION: Cricklade College, Andover;
Cardiff University
TEAMS: British Universities, Cardiff MCCU,
Hampshire, Hampshire 2nd XI, Hampshire
Cricket Board, Wiltshire
CAREER: First-class: 2002; List A: 2000; T20:
2006

BEST BATTING: 42 Hampshire vs Somerset, Southampton, 2010
BEST BOWLING: 8-46 Hampshire vs Somerset, Taunton, 2008
COUNTY CAP: 2008

FAMILY TIES? Both brothers play and both grandfathers played to a high standard
CAREER HIGHLIGHTS? Leading wicket-taker in Championship (67 wickets in 2008 season)
and 8-46 vs Somerset in 2008
CRICKETING HEROES? Wasim Akram, Darren Gough, Ryan Sidebottom, Mark Ilott
NON-CRICKETING HEROES? Chris Packham, Chris d'Albuquerque
BEST PLAYER IN COUNTY CRICKET? Marcus Trescothick, Glen Chapple, Alfonso Thomas,
Andre Adams
TIPS FOR THE TOP? Chris Wood, Tim Ravenscroft
FAVOURITE TV? Springwatch
FAVOURITE FILM? Gladiator
FAVOURITE BOOK? All Harry Potter books
DREAM HOLIDAY? A remote Scottish island
ACCOMPLISHMENTS? Getting married to Lucy and digging a pond!
GUILTY PLEASURES? Terry's Chocolate Orange
AMAZE ME! I really enjoy birdwatching and can recite my top 50 birds… 1. Osprey 2.
Nightjar 3. Bittern, etc

| Batting | Mat | Inns | NO | Runs | HS | Ave | SR | 100 | 50 | Ct | St |
|---|---|---|---|---|---|---|---|---|---|---|---|
| First-class | 71 | 95 | 41 | 566 | 42 | 10.48 | 29.54 | 0 | 0 | 17 | 0 |
| List A | 27 | 14 | 5 | 34 | 14 | 3.77 | | 0 | 0 | 3 | 0 |
| Twenty20 | 2 | 1 | 0 | 5 | 5 | 5.00 | 125.00 | 0 | 0 | 0 | 0 |

| Bowling | Mat | Balls | Runs | Wkts | BBI | BBM | Ave | Econ | SR | 5w | 10 |
|---|---|---|---|---|---|---|---|---|---|---|---|
| First-class | 71 | 12413 | 7308 | 205 | 8/46 | | 35.64 | 3.53 | 60.5 | 8 | 1 |
| List A | 27 | 1089 | 910 | 29 | 4/47 | 4/47 | 31.37 | 5.01 | 37.5 | 0 | 0 |
| Twenty20 | 2 | 42 | 48 | 1 | 1/20 | 1/20 | 48.00 | 6.85 | 42.0 | 0 | 0 |

# REECE TOPLEY

## RHB LFM

**ESSEX**

FULL NAME: Reece James William Topley
BORN: February 21, 1994, Ipswich, Suffolk
SQUAD NO: 6
HEIGHT: 6ft 7in
EDUCATION: Royal Hospital School, Ipswich
TEAMS: England Under-19s, Essex, Essex
2nd XI
CAREER: First-class: 2011; List A: 2011

BEST BATTING: 9 Essex vs Derbyshire, Chelmsford, 2011
BEST BOWLING: 5-46 Essex vs Kent, Chelmsford, 2011

NOTES: Burst on the scene in 2011 aged 17 with 14 Championship wickets in his first three Championship matches including five-wicket hauls in each of his first two games against Kent and Middlesex. His season was truncated due to having to sit his summer exams, at the school where his father is a teacher. Made his England U19 debut against South Africa U19 in July 2011. Father Don was a first-class cricketer for Essex and Surrey. Uncle Peter was also a first-class cricketer

| Batting | Mat | Inns | NO | Runs | HS | Ave | SR | 100 | 50 | Ct | St |
|---|---|---|---|---|---|---|---|---|---|---|---|
| First-class | 9 | 11 | 5 | 21 | 9 | 3.50 | 29.16 | 0 | 0 | 1 | 0 |
| List A | 3 | 1 | 0 | 19 | 19 | 19.00 | 95.00 | 0 | 0 | 0 | 0 |

| Bowling | Mat | Balls | Runs | Wkts | BBI | BBM | Ave | Econ | SR | 5w | 10 |
|---|---|---|---|---|---|---|---|---|---|---|---|
| First-class | 9 | 1337 | 801 | 34 | 5/46 | 7/114 | 23.55 | 3.59 | 39.3 | 2 | 0 |
| List A | 3 | 120 | 109 | 3 | 2/45 | 2/45 | 36.33 | 5.45 | 40.0 | 0 | 0 |

# JAMES TREDWELL LHB OB W1 MVP59

**FULL NAME:** James Cullum Tredwell
**BORN:** February 27, 1982, Ashford, Kent
**SQUAD NO:** 15
**HEIGHT:** 5ft 11in
**NICKNAME:** Tredders, Pingu, Tredman, Chad
**EDUCATION:** Southlands Community Comprehensive
**TEAMS:** England, England A, England Lions, England Under-19s, Kent, Kent Cricket Board
**CAREER:** Test: 2010; ODI: 2010; First-class: 2001; List A: 2000; T20: 2003

BEST BATTING: 123* Kent vs New Zealanders, Canterbury, 2008
BEST BOWLING: 8-66 Kent vs Glamorgan, Canterbury, 2009
COUNTY CAP: 2007

**FAMILY TIES?** Father played club cricket for Folkestone in the Kent League
**CAREER HIGHLIGHTS?** The pride of firstly representing my county then getting noticed and eventually picked by England. Getting told I was playing and then picking up my Test cap from Michael Atherton was a moment I won't forget
**CRICKETING HEROES?** Shane Warne
**NON-CRICKETING HEROES?** My dad was a pretty big inspiration
**TIPS FOR THE TOP?** Joe Root, Daniel Bell-Drummond
**IF YOU WEREN'T A CRICKETER?** I dabble a bit in growing my own fruit and veg (as sad as it may sound!)
**FAVOURITE TV?** Dexter, Grand Designs, all the old school comedy sitcoms
**FAVOURITE FILM?** The Da Vinci Code
**DREAM HOLIDAY?** Masai Mara safari in Kenya

| Batting | Mat | Inns | NO | Runs | HS | Ave | SR | 100 | 50 | Ct | St |
|---|---|---|---|---|---|---|---|---|---|---|---|
| Tests | 1 | 1 | 0 | 37 | 37 | 37.00 | 58.73 | 0 | 0 | 1 | 0 |
| ODIs | 5 | 3 | 1 | 27 | 16 | 13.50 | 52.94 | 0 | 0 | 0 | 0 |
| First-class | 113 | 167 | 21 | 3367 | 123* | 23.06 | 43.31 | 3 | 13 | 120 | 0 |
| List A | 167 | 117 | 38 | 1399 | 88 | 17.70 | | 0 | 4 | 69 | 0 |
| Twenty20 | 91 | 40 | 12 | 360 | 34* | 12.85 | 107.14 | 0 | 0 | 30 | 0 |

| Bowling | Mat | Balls | Runs | Wkts | BBI | BBM | Ave | Econ | SR | 5w | 10 |
|---|---|---|---|---|---|---|---|---|---|---|---|
| Tests | 1 | 390 | 181 | 6 | 4/82 | 6/181 | 30.16 | 2.78 | 65.0 | 0 | 0 |
| ODIs | 5 | 222 | 200 | 4 | 4/48 | 4/48 | 50.00 | 5.40 | 55.5 | 0 | 0 |
| First-class | 113 | 20402 | 10709 | 309 | 8/66 | | 34.65 | 3.14 | 66.0 | 11 | 3 |
| List A | 167 | 6786 | 5322 | 159 | 6/27 | 6/27 | 33.47 | 4.70 | 42.6 | 1 | 0 |
| Twenty20 | 91 | 1698 | 2012 | 79 | 4/21 | 4/21 | 25.46 | 7.10 | 21.4 | 0 | 0 |

# PETER TREGO

## RHB RM MVP17

FULL NAME: Peter David Trego
BORN: June 12, 1981, Weston-super-Mare, Somerset
SQUAD NO: 7
HEIGHT: 6ft
NICKNAME: Tregs, Darcy, Pedro Tregos, Pirate
EDUCATION: Wyvern Comprehensive
TEAMS: England, England Lions, Herefordshire, Kent, Mashonaland Eagles, Middlesex, Minor Counties, Somerset, Sylhet Royals
CAREER: First-class: 2000; List A: 1999; T20: 2003

BEST BATTING: 140 Somerset vs West Indies A, Taunton, 2002
BEST BOWLING: 6-59 Middlesex vs Nottinghamshire, Nottingham, 2005
COUNTY CAP: 2007 (Somerset)

CAREER HIGHLIGHTS? County cap, England Lions tours, Champions League twice with Somerset, fighting early on to keep my career alive
SUPERSTITIONS? Many, but mostly silly things like keeping the same sweat band for each different competition, same batting socks, pants – but washed on a regular basis of course!
CRICKETING HEROES? Graham Rose, Ian Botham, Justin Langer
NON-CRICKETING HEROES? George Best, Brian Robson, Gerard Bromley
IF YOU WEREN'T A CRICKETER? Buying, selling and making a loss! Maybe in the candle industry with Darren Veness
DREAM HOLIDAY? Perth, Australia or Weston-super-Mare – it's home but we're away so much it's like being on holiday
ACCOMPLISHMENTS? Making my three beautiful children Amelia, Davis and Dexter; playing conference standard football for five years or so; playing in three FA Cup first round ties
SURPRISING SKILL? I do awesome animal noises! Not always consciously
GUILTY PLEASURES? The Golden Arches, cars, clothes and sunglasses
AMAZE ME! What you see is what you get, but many of Somerset's supporters don't know my name is pronounced 'tree-go' not 'tray-go'

| Batting | Mat | Inns | NO | Runs | HS | Ave | SR | 100 | 50 | Ct | St |
|---|---|---|---|---|---|---|---|---|---|---|---|
| First-class | 116 | 169 | 25 | 5028 | 140 | 34.91 | | 9 | 31 | 47 | 0 |
| List A | 122 | 102 | 19 | 2025 | 147 | 24.39 | | 2 | 8 | 36 | 0 |
| Twenty20 | 103 | 94 | 12 | 2018 | 79 | 24.60 | 122.45 | 0 | 10 | 26 | 0 |
| Bowling | Mat | Balls | Runs | Wkts | BBI | BBM | Ave | Econ | SR | 5w | 10 |
| First-class | 116 | 11583 | 7334 | 194 | 6/59 | | 37.80 | 3.79 | 59.7 | 1 | 0 |
| List A | 122 | 4160 | 3886 | 121 | 5/40 | 5/40 | 32.11 | 5.60 | 34.3 | 2 | 0 |
| Twenty20 | 103 | 1207 | 1737 | 58 | 4/27 | 4/27 | 29.94 | 8.63 | 20.8 | 0 | 0 |

# CHRIS TREMLETT

## RHB RFM

FULL NAME: Christopher Timothy Tremlett
BORN: September 2, 1981, Southampton, Hampshire
SQUAD NO: 33
HEIGHT: 6ft 7in
NICKNAME: Twiggy, Goober
EDUCATION: Taunton's College, Southampton
TEAMS: England, ECB National Academy, England Lions, Hampshire, Hampshire Cricket Board, Surrey
CAREER: Test: 2007; ODI: 2005; T20I: 2007; First-class: 2000; List A: 2000; T20: 2004

BEST BATTING: 64 Hampshire vs Gloucestershire, Southampton, 2005
BEST BOWLING: 6-44 Hampshire vs Sussex, Hove, 2005
COUNTY CAP: 2004 (Hampshire)

CRICKETING HEROES? Glenn McGrath, Mark Waugh, Shane Warne
OTHER SPORTS PLAYED? Basketball, volleyball
OTHER SPORTS FOLLOWED? Football (Arsenal)
RELAXATIONS? Socialising with friends, cinema
NOTES: Son of Tim Tremlett, the former Hampshire seamer, and the grandson of Maurice, who played for Somerset and England in the 1940s and 50s. Denied a hat-trick against Bangladesh in 2005 when the ball bounced off middle stump without dislodging the bails. Persistent injury has dogged his international career. Joined Surrey in 2010. Dismissed Michael Beer in Sydney to seal England's 2010/11 Ashes series victory, and claimed a total of 17 wickets at 23.35 in three Tests

| Batting | Mat | Inns | NO | Runs | HS | Ave | SR | 100 | 50 | Ct | St |
|---|---|---|---|---|---|---|---|---|---|---|---|
| Tests | 11 | 13 | 4 | 98 | 25* | 10.88 | 42.42 | 0 | 0 | 4 | 0 |
| ODIs | 15 | 11 | 4 | 50 | 19* | 7.14 | 56.17 | 0 | 0 | 4 | 0 |
| T20Is | 1 | - | - | - | - | - | - | - | - | 0 | 0 |
| First-class | 118 | 152 | 41 | 1979 | 64 | 17.82 | | 0 | 7 | 32 | 0 |
| List A | 125 | 76 | 24 | 521 | 38* | 10.01 | | 0 | 0 | 26 | 0 |
| Twenty20 | 44 | 15 | 6 | 72 | 13 | 8.00 | 105.88 | 0 | 0 | 5 | 0 |

| Bowling | Mat | Balls | Runs | Wkts | BBI | BBM | Ave | Econ | SR | 5w | 10 |
|---|---|---|---|---|---|---|---|---|---|---|---|
| Tests | 11 | 2686 | 1311 | 49 | 6/48 | 8/150 | 26.75 | 2.92 | 54.8 | 2 | 0 |
| ODIs | 15 | 784 | 705 | 15 | 4/32 | 4/32 | 47.00 | 5.39 | 52.2 | 0 | 0 |
| T20Is | 1 | 24 | 45 | 2 | 2/45 | 2/45 | 22.50 | 11.25 | 12.0 | 0 | 0 |
| First-class | 118 | 20490 | 10723 | 390 | 6/44 | | 27.49 | 3.13 | 52.5 | 9 | 0 |
| List A | 125 | 5787 | 4718 | 170 | 4/25 | 4/25 | 27.75 | 4.89 | 34.0 | 0 | 0 |
| Twenty20 | 44 | 963 | 1159 | 62 | 4/16 | 4/16 | 18.69 | 7.22 | 15.5 | 0 | 0 |

**SOMERSET**

FULL NAME: Marcus Edward Trescothick
BORN: December 25, 1975, Keynsham, Somerset
SQUAD NO: 2
HEIGHT: 6ft 3in
NICKNAME: Banger, Tresco
EDUCATION: Sir Bernard Lovell School
TEAMS: England, Somerset
CAREER: Test: 2000; ODI: 2000; T20I: 2005; First-class: 1993; List A: 1993; T20: 2004

BEST BATTING: 284 Somerset vs Northamptonshire, Northampton, 2007
BEST BOWLING: 4-36 Somerset vs Young Australia, Taunton, 1995
COUNTY CAP: 1999; BENEFIT YEAR: 2008

FAMILY TIES? Father played Somerset 2nd XI, uncle played club cricket
CRICKETERS PARTICULARLY ADMIRED? Adam Gilchrist, Andy Caddick
OTHER SPORTS FOLLOWED? Golf, football (Bristol City)
RELAXATIONS? Spending time at home, playing golf
NOTES: Made his Test debut against West Indies at Old Trafford in 2000. Played his last Test against Pakistan at The Oval in 2006. Retired from international cricket in 2008. Wisden Cricketer of the Year in 2005. PCA Player of the Year in 2000, 2009 and 2011. Has scored more ODI centuries than any other Englishman. Has topped 1,000 first-class runs in the last five seasons, scoring almost 7,500 runs. Made almost 3,000 runs in all competitions in 2009

| Batting | Mat | Inns | NO | Runs | HS | Ave | SR | 100 | 50 | Ct | St |
|---|---|---|---|---|---|---|---|---|---|---|---|
| Tests | 76 | 143 | 10 | 5825 | 219 | 43.79 | 54.51 | 14 | 29 | 95 | 0 |
| ODIs | 123 | 122 | 6 | 4335 | 137 | 37.37 | 85.21 | 12 | 21 | 49 | 0 |
| T20Is | 3 | 3 | 0 | 166 | 72 | 55.33 | 126.71 | 0 | 2 | 2 | 0 |
| First-class | 284 | 489 | 29 | 19715 | 284 | 42.85 | | 49 | 97 | 369 | 0 |
| List A | 346 | 332 | 27 | 11474 | 184 | 37.61 | | 28 | 57 | 136 | 0 |
| Twenty20 | 67 | 66 | 5 | 2120 | 108* | 34.75 | 157.27 | 2 | 17 | 22 | 0 |

| Bowling | Mat | Balls | Runs | Wkts | BBI | BBM | Ave | Econ | SR | 5w | 10 |
|---|---|---|---|---|---|---|---|---|---|---|---|
| Tests | 76 | 300 | 155 | 1 | 1/34 | 1/34 | 155.00 | 3.10 | 300.0 | 0 | 0 |
| ODIs | 123 | 232 | 219 | 4 | 2/7 | 2/7 | 54.75 | 5.66 | 58.0 | 0 | 0 |
| T20Is | 3 | - | - | - | - | - | - | - | - | - | - |
| First-class | 284 | 2704 | 1551 | 36 | 4/36 | | 43.08 | 3.44 | 75.1 | 0 | 0 |
| List A | 346 | 2010 | 1644 | 57 | 4/50 | 4/50 | 28.84 | 4.90 | 35.2 | 0 | 0 |
| Twenty20 | 67 | - | - | - | - | - | - | - | - | - | - |

# JONATHAN TROTT

## RHB RM R6

FULL NAME: Ian Jonathan Leonard Trott
BORN: April 22, 1981, Cape Town, South Africa
SQUAD NO: 9
HEIGHT: 6ft
NICKNAME: Booger, Trotters
EDUCATION: Rondebosch Boys' High School; Stellenbosch University
TEAMS: England, Boland, England Lions, Otago, South Africa Under-15s, South Africa Under-19s, Warwickshire, Western Province
CAREER: Test: 2009; ODI: 2009; T20I: 2007; First-class: 2000; List A: 2000; T20: 2003

BEST BATTING: 226 England vs Bangladesh, Lord's, 2010
BEST BOWLING: 7-39 Warwickshire vs Kent, Canterbury, 2003
COUNTY CAP: 2005

CRICKETERS PARTICULARLY ADMIRED? Sachin Tendulkar, Adam Hollioake, Steve Waugh
OTHER SPORTS FOLLOWED? Football (Tottenham Hotspur), American football
FAVOURITE BAND? Roxette, Robbie Williams
RELAXATIONS? Music, watching sport
NOTES: Represented South Africa A. Scored 245 on debut for Warwickshire 2nd XI. Hit 134 on Championship debut for Warwickshire vs Sussex at Edgbaston in 2003. Made 119 on Test debut for England in the deciding match of the 2009 Ashes at The Oval

| Batting | Mat | Inns | NO | Runs | HS | Ave | SR | 100 | 50 | Ct | St |
|---|---|---|---|---|---|---|---|---|---|---|---|
| Tests | 26 | 44 | 4 | 2126 | 226 | 53.15 | 47.95 | 6 | 8 | 11 | 0 |
| ODIs | 44 | 42 | 4 | 1836 | 137 | 48.31 | 77.76 | 3 | 15 | 11 | 0 |
| T20Is | 7 | 7 | 1 | 138 | 51 | 23.00 | 95.83 | 0 | 1 | 0 | 0 |
| First-class | 174 | 292 | 34 | 11496 | 226 | 44.55 | | 26 | 56 | 159 | 0 |
| List A | 207 | 193 | 34 | 7309 | 137 | 45.96 | | 14 | 50 | 65 | 0 |
| Twenty20 | 77 | 72 | 16 | 2082 | 86* | 37.17 | 114.90 | 0 | 13 | 18 | 0 |

| Bowling | Mat | Balls | Runs | Wkts | BBI | BBM | Ave | Econ | SR | 5w | 10 |
|---|---|---|---|---|---|---|---|---|---|---|---|
| Tests | 26 | 336 | 227 | 3 | 1/5 | 1/5 | 75.66 | 4.05 | 112.0 | 0 | 0 |
| ODIs | 44 | 183 | 166 | 2 | 2/31 | 2/31 | 83.00 | 5.44 | 91.5 | 0 | 0 |
| T20Is | 7 | - | - | - | - | - | - | - | - | - | - |
| First-class | 174 | 4628 | 2636 | 58 | 7/39 | | 45.44 | 3.41 | 79.7 | 1 | 0 |
| List A | 207 | 1552 | 1459 | 54 | 4/55 | 4/55 | 27.01 | 5.64 | 28.7 | 0 | 0 |
| Twenty20 | 77 | 144 | 234 | 8 | 2/19 | 2/19 | 29.25 | 9.75 | 18.0 | 0 | 0 |

# JIM TROUGHTON

## LHB SLA R1

WARWICKSHIRE

FULL NAME: Jamie Oliver Troughton
BORN: March 2, 1979, Camden, London
SQUAD NO: 24
HEIGHT: 5ft 11in
NICKNAME: Troughts
EDUCATION: Trinity School, Leamington Spa; Birmingham University
TEAMS: England, Warwickshire, Warwickshire Cricket Board
CAREER: ODI: 2003; First-class: 2001; List A: 1999; T20: 2003

BEST BATTING: 223 Warwickshire vs Hampshire, Birmingham, 2009
BEST BOWLING: 3-1 Warwickshire vs CUCCE, Fenner's, 2004
COUNTY CAP: 2002

FAMILY TIES? Great grandfather [Henry Crighton] played for Warwickshire. Younger brother [Wigsy Troughton] played for Warwickshire youth and is a Stratford Panther
CAREER HIGHLIGHTS? Warwickshire debut, Benson and Hedges Cup final 2002, playing for England, Championship winners in 2004, CB40 finalists in 2010, captaining Warwickshire
SUPERSTITIONS? Don't leave straight ones
CRICKETING HEROES? Graham Thorpe, Brian Lara
IF YOU WEREN'T A CRICKETER? Actor, teacher or graphic designer
FAVOURITE BOOK? 1984
SURPRISING SKILL? Guitar, drawing caricatures and movie-making
GUILTY PLEASURES? The X Factor, banoffee pie, Angelina Jolie
AMAZE ME! I suffered from a form of epilepsy as a child. I come from a family of actors. I played youth football for Stoke City
FANTASY SLIP CORDON? Keeper: Eric Cantona, 1st: Me, 2nd: Angelina Jolie, 3rd: Eddie Izzard, 4th: Shakespeare, Gully: Bear Grylls

| Batting | Mat | Inns | NO | Runs | HS | Ave | SR | 100 | 50 | Ct | St |
|---|---|---|---|---|---|---|---|---|---|---|---|
| ODIs | 6 | 5 | 1 | 36 | 20 | 9.00 | 47.36 | 0 | 0 | 1 | 0 |
| First-class | 140 | 217 | 17 | 7132 | 223 | 35.66 | 49.33 | 17 | 34 | 71 | 0 |
| List A | 148 | 132 | 16 | 3365 | 115* | 29.00 | | 2 | 20 | 52 | 0 |
| Twenty20 | 83 | 77 | 8 | 1617 | 66 | 23.43 | 122.77 | | 9 | 35 | 0 |

| Bowling | Mat | Balls | Runs | Wkts | BBI | BBM | Ave | Econ | SR | 5w | 10 |
|---|---|---|---|---|---|---|---|---|---|---|---|
| ODIs | 6 | - | - | - | - | - | - | - | - | - | - |
| First-class | 140 | 2357 | 1416 | 22 | 3/1 | | 64.36 | 3.60 | 107.1 | 0 | 0 |
| List A | 148 | 736 | 644 | 25 | 4/23 | 4/23 | 25.76 | 5.25 | 29.4 | 0 | 0 |
| Twenty20 | 83 | 96 | 127 | 6 | 2/10 | 2/10 | 21.16 | 7.93 | 16.0 | 0 | 0 |

# KARL TURNER

## LHB RMF

FULL NAME: Karl Turner
BORN: November 29, 1987, Dryburn, Durham
SQUAD NO: 3
HEIGHT: 5ft 9in
NICKNAME: Freddie, Tina, Karlos
EDUCATION: Deerness Valley Comprehensive School
TEAMS: Durham 2nd XI, Hampshire, Hampshire 2nd XI, Nottinghamshire, Nottinghamshire 2nd XI
CAREER: First-class: 2011; List A: 2011

BEST BATTING: 64 Nottinghamshire vs Sussex, Nottingham, 2011

CAREER HIGHLIGHTS? Being a part of a very successful Durham squad. Making my first-class debut for Nottinghamshire against my old club in my home town. Taking the winning catch of the final Test against the West Indies as 12th man in 2009
SUPERSTITIONS? Right pad on first
CRICKETING HEROES? Mike Hussey, Brian Lara, Justin Langer, Shiv Chanderpaul
NON-CRICKETING HEROES? Alan Shearer, Gazza, Sir Bobby Robson, Floyd Mayweather Jr, Oscar de la Hoya, Ricky Hatton. I love Newcastle and boxing, as you can see!
BEST PLAYER IN COUNTY CRICKET? Marcus Trescothick
TIPS FOR THE TOP? Ben Stokes, Alex Hales, Scott Borthwick
IF YOU WEREN'T A CRICKETER? All my friends are in groundworks so that or I'd like to get into personal training
WHEN RAIN STOPS PLAY? I can't sit still so card tricks, telling jokes and trying to make people laugh
FAVOURITE TV? Heartbeat, The Bill, UK Gold, I like old stuff
FAVOURITE FILM? Law Abiding Citizen, all the Rockys
DREAM HOLIDAY? Las Vegas is unreal
ACCOMPLISHMENTS? Played district football and Middlesbrough U13, also played ice hockey for North of England

| Batting | Mat | Inns | NO | Runs | HS | Ave | SR | 100 | 50 | Ct | St |
|---|---|---|---|---|---|---|---|---|---|---|---|
| First-class | 5 | 9 | 0 | 227 | 64 | 25.22 | 49.45 | 0 | 1 | 1 | 0 |
| List A | 2 | 2 | 0 | 22 | 18 | 11.00 | 100.00 | 0 | 0 | 0 | 0 |

| Bowling | Mat | Balls | Runs | Wkts | BBI | BBM | Ave | Econ | SR | 5w | 10 |
|---|---|---|---|---|---|---|---|---|---|---|---|
| First-class | 5 | - | - | - | - | - | - | - | - | - | - |
| List A | 2 | - | - | - | - | - | - | - | - | - | - |

# MARK TURNER                                        RHB RMF

**FULL NAME:** Mark Leif Turner
**BORN:** October 23, 1984, Sunderland
**SQUAD NO:** 6
**HEIGHT:** 5ft 11in
**NICKNAME:** Tina, Beak
**EDUCATION:** Thornhill Comprehensive School, Sunderland
**TEAMS:** Derbyshire, Durham, England Under-19s, Somerset, Somerset 2nd XI
**CAREER:** First-class: 2005; List A: 2007; T20: 2005

**BEST BATTING:** 57 Somerset vs Derbyshire, Taunton, 2007
**BEST BOWLING:** 5-32 Derbyshire vs Northamptonshire, Northampton, 2011

**CAREER HIGHLIGHTS?** Playing in a Lord's final, even though we lost and I had a night to forget. Five-wicket haul for England U19
**SUPERSTITIONS?** Look up at the sky for help before every spell (never works!)
**CRICKETING HEROES?** Allan Donald, Andrew Caddick, Dale Benkenstein, Marcus Trescothick, Sachin Tendulkar
**NON-CRICKETING HEROES?** Steve Jobs, David Beckham, Maxwell (singer)
**BEST PLAYER IN COUNTY CRICKET?** Marcus Trescothick
**TIPS FOR THE TOP?** Jos Buttler, Adam Dibble (Somerset); Dan Redfern, Pete Burgoyne (Derbyshire)
**IF YOU WEREN'T A CRICKETER?** Maybe policeman or firefighter
**FAVOURITE FILM?** Blade, Superbad, Old School, The Kingdom
**TWITTER FEED:** @Tina2310

| Batting | Mat | Inns | NO | Runs | HS | Ave | SR | 100 | 50 | Ct | St |
|---|---|---|---|---|---|---|---|---|---|---|---|
| First-class | 16 | 19 | 10 | 202 | 57 | 22.44 | 65.58 | 0 | 1 | 3 | 0 |
| List A | 24 | 11 | 6 | 51 | 15* | 10.20 | 64.55 | 0 | 0 | 6 | 0 |
| Twenty20 | 36 | 11 | 5 | 26 | 11* | 4.33 | 68.42 | 0 | 0 | 6 | 0 |

| Bowling | Mat | Balls | Runs | Wkts | BBI | BBM | Ave | Econ | SR | 5w | 10 |
|---|---|---|---|---|---|---|---|---|---|---|---|
| First-class | 16 | 2235 | 1500 | 38 | 5/32 | | 39.47 | 4.02 | 58.8 | 1 | 0 |
| List A | 24 | 868 | 892 | 33 | 4/36 | 4/36 | 27.03 | 6.16 | 26.3 | 0 | 0 |
| Twenty20 | 36 | 613 | 915 | 33 | 3/22 | 3/22 | 27.72 | 8.95 | 18.5 | 0 | 0 |

FULL NAME: Warnakulasuriya Patabendige Ushantha Joseph Chaminda Vaas
BORN: January 27, 1974, Mattumagala, Sri Lanka
SQUAD NO: 4
HEIGHT: 5ft 10in
EDUCATION: St. Joseph's College, Maradana
TEAMS: Sri Lanka, Basnahira North, Colts Cricket Club, Deccan Chargers, Hampshire, Middlesex, Northamptonshire, Worcestershire
CAREER: Test: 1994; ODI: 1994; T20I: 2006; First-class: 1990; List A: 1993; T20: 2005

BEST BATTING: 134 Colts Cricket Club vs Burgher Recreation Club, Sinhalese Sports Club Ground, 2004
BEST BOWLING: 7-28 Colts Cricket Club vs Colombo Cricket Club, Colombo Cricket Club Ground, 2011
COUNTY CAPS: 2007 (Middlesex); 2011 (Northamptonshire)

NOTES: Took the first ever ODI eight-fer, against Zimbabwe in 2001/02, returning figures of 8-19 including a hat-trick. Claimed a hat-trick with the first three balls of the match against Bangladesh in the 2003 World Cup. Selected for the World XI at the inaugural ICC Awards in 2004. Reached the 300-wicket milestone in Tests against India in 2005/06. Scored his first Test ton in his 97th match – hitting 100* against Bangladesh in 2007 – before becoming the third Sri Lankan to play 100 Tests or more. Announced his Test retirement in July 2009. Northamptonshire became his fourth county when he represented the Steelbacks in the FP t20 in 2010 and he was their overseas player across all competitions last season – taking 76 first-class wickets at 21.86

| Batting | Mat | Inns | NO | Runs | HS | Ave | SR | 100 | 50 | Ct | St |
|---|---|---|---|---|---|---|---|---|---|---|---|
| Tests | 111 | 162 | 35 | 3089 | 100* | 24.32 | 43.92 | 1 | 13 | 31 | 0 |
| ODIs | 322 | 220 | 72 | 2025 | 50* | 13.68 | 72.52 | 0 | 1 | 60 | 0 |
| T20Is | 6 | 2 | 1 | 33 | 21 | 33.00 | 80.48 | 0 | 0 | 0 | 0 |
| First-class | 221 | 296 | 58 | 6204 | 134 | 26.06 | | 4 | 29 | 57 | 0 |
| List A | 409 | 284 | 90 | 3220 | 76* | 16.59 | | 0 | 8 | 83 | 0 |
| Twenty20 | 49 | 43 | 8 | 643 | 73 | 18.37 | 110.48 | 0 | 4 | 8 | 0 |

| Bowling | Mat | Balls | Runs | Wkts | BBI | BBM | Ave | Econ | SR | 5w | 10 |
|---|---|---|---|---|---|---|---|---|---|---|---|
| Tests | 111 | 23438 | 10501 | 355 | 7/71 | 14/191 | 29.58 | 2.68 | 66.0 | 12 | 2 |
| ODIs | 322 | 15775 | 11014 | 400 | 8/19 | 8/19 | 27.53 | 4.18 | 39.4 | 4 | 0 |
| T20Is | 6 | 132 | 128 | 6 | 2/14 | 2/14 | 21.33 | 5.81 | 22.0 | 0 | 0 |
| First-class | 221 | 40624 | 18747 | 766 | 7/28 | | 24.47 | 2.76* | 53.4* | 34 | 4 |
| List A | 409 | 19345 | 13425 | 504 | 8/19 | 8/19 | 26.63 | 4.16 | 38.3 | 4 | 0 |
| Twenty20 | 49 | 1005 | 1147 | 57 | 3/16 | 3/16 | 20.12 | 6.84 | 17.6 | 0 | 0 |

## FREDDIE VAN DEN BERGH RHB SLA

SURREY

FULL NAME: Freddie Oliver Edward van den Bergh
BORN: June 14, 1992, Bickley, Kent
SQUAD NO: 15
HEIGHT: 6ft 2in
NICKNAME: Vanders
EDUCATION: Whitgift School; Durham University
TEAMS: Surrey, Surrey 2nd XI
CAREER: First-class: 2011

BEST BATTING: 0 Surrey vs CMCCU, Fenner's, 2011
BEST BOWLING: 3-79 Surrey vs CMCCU, Fenner's, 2011

CAREER HIGHLIGHTS? Making my first-class debut for Surrey with Kevin Pietersen playing and taking 3-79 off 24 overs
CRICKETING HEROES? Andrew Flintoff, Daniel Vettori and AB de Villiers
NON-CRICKETING HEROES? Nelson Mandela, Lance Armstrong and Jonny Wilkinson
BEST PLAYER IN COUNTY CRICKET? Marcus Trescothick
TIPS FOR THE TOP? Jason Roy and Tom Maynard
IF YOU WEREN'T A CRICKETER? I'd be studying at Durham University
WHEN RAIN STOPS PLAY? Game of cards or read a paper
FAVOURITE TV? Spooks
FAVOURITE FILM? Gladiator
FAVOURITE BOOK? To Kill A Mockingbird
DREAM HOLIDAY? Maldives
ACCOMPLISHMENTS? Getting a place at Durham University
GUILTY PLEASURES? Chocolate
FANTASY SLIP CORDON? Keeper: James Corden (he would keep me amused throughout the day), 1st: Jonny Wilkinson (he is a hero of mine), 2nd: Andrew Flintoff (he would be good fun in the slips), 3rd: Myself, Gully: Viv Richards (a legend of the game)

| Batting | Mat | Inns | NO | Runs | HS | Ave | SR | 100 | 50 | Ct | St |
|---|---|---|---|---|---|---|---|---|---|---|---|
| First-class | 1 | 1 | 0 | 0 | 0 | 0.00 | 0.00 | 0 | 0 | 0 | 0 |

| Bowling | Mat | Balls | Runs | Wkts | BBI | BBM | Ave | Econ | SR | 5w | 10 |
|---|---|---|---|---|---|---|---|---|---|---|---|
| First-class | 1 | 144 | 79 | 3 | 3/79 | 3/79 | 26.33 | 3.29 | 48.0 | 0 | 0 |

FULL NAME: Kishen Shailesh Velani
BORN: September 2, 1994, Newham, London
SQUAD NO: 8
EDUCATION: Brentwood School
TEAMS: England Under-19s, Essex 2nd XI, Essex Under-13s, Essex Under-15s, Essex Under-17s
CAREER: Yet to make first-team debut

ESSEX

CRICKETING HEROES? Sachin Tendulkar
FAVOURITE FOOD? Chicken
NOTES: Essex academy graduate who plays club cricket for Wanstead CC. First represented England U19 in July 2011. Has played nine matches at that level with a highest score of 54 against South Africa U19 at Canterbury

**HAMPSHIRE**

FULL NAME: James Michael Vince
BORN: March 14, 1991, Cuckfield, Sussex
SQUAD NO: 14
HEIGHT: 6ft 2in
NICKNAME: Vincey
EDUCATION: Warminster School
TEAMS: England Lions, England Under-19s, Hampshire, Hampshire 2nd XI, Wiltshire
CAREER: First-class: 2009; List A: 2009; T20: 2010

BEST BATTING: 180 Hampshire vs Yorkshire, Scarborough, 2010

FAMILY TIES? My old man couldn't have been any worse
CAREER HIGHLIGHTS? Winning the T20 and my first hundred for Hampshire
SUPERSTITIONS? Put my kit on in the same order
CRICKETING HEROES? Stephen Parry, Jimmy Adams, Neil McKenzie
BEST PLAYER IN COUNTY CRICKET? Marcus Trescothick
TIP FOR THE TOP? Jos Buttler
IF YOU WEREN'T A CRICKETER? Not a lot
WHEN RAIN STOPS PLAY? Chill out and abuse Batesy [Michael Bates]
FAVOURITE TV? TOWIE
FAVOURITE FILM? Taken
DREAM HOLIDAY? Maldives
TWITTER FEED: @vincey14

| Batting | Mat | Inns | NO | Runs | HS | Ave | SR | 100 | 50 | Ct | St |
|---|---|---|---|---|---|---|---|---|---|---|---|
| First-class | 41 | 67 | 7 | 1915 | 180 | 31.91 | 57.80 | 3 | 7 | 23 | 0 |
| List A | 33 | 33 | 1 | 1067 | 131 | 33.34 | 93.18 | 1 | 5 | 13 | 0 |
| Twenty20 | 38 | 36 | 4 | 905 | 85* | 28.28 | 126.39 | 0 | 6 | 32 | 0 |

| Bowling | Mat | Balls | Runs | Wkts | BBI | BBM | Ave | Econ | SR | 5w | 10 |
|---|---|---|---|---|---|---|---|---|---|---|---|
| First-class | 41 | 92 | 61 | 0 | - | - | - | 3.97 | - | 0 | 0 |
| List A | 33 | - | - | - | - | - | - | - | - | - | - |
| Twenty20 | 38 | - | - | - | - | - | - | - | - | - | - |

# ADAM VOGES

## RHB SLA MVP58

FULL NAME: Adam Charles Voges
BORN: October 4, 1979, Subiaco, Perth, Australia
SQUAD NO: 32
HEIGHT: 6ft 1in
NICKNAME: Kenny, Hank
TEAMS: Australia, Australia A, Hampshire, Melbourne Stars, Nottinghamshire, Rajasthan Royals, Western Australia
CAREER: ODI: 2007; T20I: 2007; First-class: 2002; List A: 2004; T20: 2006

BEST BATTING: 180 Western Australia vs Tasmania, Hobart, 2007
BEST BOWLING: 4-92 Western Australia vs South Australia, Adelaide, 2007
COUNTY CAP: 2008 (Nottinghamshire)

NOTES: Hit 62-ball 100 not out against New South Wales at Sydney in 2004/05 – his maiden one-day century and at the time the fastest one-day hundred in Australian domestic history. Captained Australia A. Temporary overseas player for Hampshire in 2007 as replacement for Stuart Clark. Played with Nottinghamshire since 2008. Hit top ODI score of 80 not out from 72 balls in the seventh ODI against England at Perth in 2011

| Batting | Mat | Inns | NO | Runs | HS | Ave | SR | 100 | 50 | Ct | St |
|---|---|---|---|---|---|---|---|---|---|---|---|
| ODIs | 15 | 14 | 5 | 392 | 80* | 43.55 | 91.16 | 0 | 2 | 2 | 0 |
| T20Is | 4 | 3 | 1 | 63 | 26 | 31.50 | 121.15 | 0 | 0 | 2 | 0 |
| First-class | 114 | 195 | 25 | 7120 | 180 | 41.88 | 50.82 | 14 | 40 | 149 | 0 |
| List A | 128 | 123 | 28 | 4143 | 104* | 43.61 | 79.01 | 3 | 33 | 45 | 0 |
| Twenty20 | 87 | 82 | 11 | 2160 | 82* | 30.42 | 131.70 | 0 | 9 | 32 | 0 |

| Bowling | Mat | Balls | Runs | Wkts | BBI | BBM | Ave | Econ | SR | 5w | 10 |
|---|---|---|---|---|---|---|---|---|---|---|---|
| ODIs | 15 | 150 | 159 | 1 | 1/22 | 1/22 | 159.00 | 6.36 | 150.0 | 0 | 0 |
| T20Is | 4 | 12 | 5 | 2 | 2/5 | 2/5 | 2.50 | 2.50 | 6.0 | 0 | 0 |
| First-class | 114 | 2650 | 1433 | 41 | 4/92 | | 34.95 | 3.24 | 64.6 | 0 | 0 |
| List A | 128 | 1340 | 1197 | 23 | 3/25 | 3/25 | 52.04 | 5.35 | 58.2 | 0 | 0 |
| Twenty20 | 87 | 311 | 444 | 12 | 2/4 | 2/4 | 37.00 | 8.56 | 25.9 | 0 | 0 |

## DAVID WADE

**GLOUCESTERSHIRE**

FULL NAME: David Neil Wade
BORN: September 27, 1983, Chichester, Sussex
SQUAD NO: 27
HEIGHT: 6ft 5in
NICKNAME: Wadey, Wadeozz
EDUCATION: Bishop Luffa Church of England School, Chichester, Sussex; Havant College, Hampshire
TEAMS: Gloucestershire 2nd XI
CAREER: Yet to make first-team debut

FAMILY TIES? Father and brother played high level Premier League club cricket
WHY CRICKET? Father's influence
CAREER HIGHLIGHTS? Getting signed by Gloucestershire CCC
CRICKETING HEROES? Ian Botham, Viv Richards, Courtney Walsh, Curtly Ambrose
NON-CRICKETING HEROES? The armed forces
BEST PLAYER IN COUNTY CRICKET? Marcus Trescothick
TIP FOR THE TOP? James Fuller
IF YOU WEREN'T A CRICKETER? Probably back in Afghanistan with the army
WHEN RAIN STOPS PLAY? Reading
FAVOURITE TV? Match Of The Day
FAVOURITE FILM? Scarface
DREAM HOLIDAY? Maldives or Rio de Janeiro
ACCOMPLISHMENTS? Served as a soldier in the British Army for eight years and completed seven months in Helmand Province in 2007
SURPRISING SKILL? Can disassemble and reassemble an AK47 blindfolded
AMAZE ME! I played semi-pro football, I can abseil from helicopters, I'm a carp fisherman/angler
FANTASY SLIP CORDON? Keeper: Margaret Thatcher, 1st: Micky Flanagan, 2nd: Hugh Hefner, 3rd: Andy McNab, Gully: Me
TWITTER FEED: @Wadey461

## GRAHAM WAGG RHB LMF W2 MVP71

FULL NAME: Graham Grant Wagg
BORN: April 28, 1983, Rugby, Warwickshire
SQUAD NO: 8
HEIGHT: 6ft
NICKNAME: Waggy
EDUCATION: Ashlawn High School;
Warwickshire College
TEAMS: Glamorgan, Derbyshire, England
A, England Under-19s, Warwickshire,
Warwickshire Cricket Board
CAREER: First-class: 2002; List A: 2000; T20:
2003

**GLAMORGAN**

BEST BATTING: 108 Derbyshire vs Northampton, Northampton, 2008
BEST BOWLING: 6-35 Derbyshire vs Surrey, Derby, 2009
COUNTY CAP: 2007 (Derbyshire)

FAMILY TIES? My dad played 2nd XI cricket, minor counties, and a good standard of Premier League – he could bowl a heavy ball and hit a long ball – and my little man Brayden Wagg is just learning, so watch his name

WHY CRICKET? My dad was coaching a local side in Rugby and I was wanting to give it a try and he coached me along with a guy called Alan Morgan, who put a lot of time in with me as well. But my dad has to take the credit for where I am now

CAREER HIGHLIGHTS? Getting my first contract at Warwickshire and playing for England Schools in all the age groups

CRICKETING HEROES? Ian Botham, Allan Donald, Viv Richards

TIPS FOR THE TOP? James Taylor, James Harris, Brayden Wagg

IF YOU WEREN'T A CRICKETER? Full-time dad I suppose

WHEN RAIN STOPS PLAY? Feet up, maybe a bit of poker

FAVOURITE TV? Banged Up Abroad

FAVOURITE FILM? Green Mile

SURPRISING SKILL? Dark horse on the snooker table

GUILTY PLEASURES? Eating too much in the winter

| Batting | Mat | Inns | NO | Runs | HS | Ave | SR | 100 | 50 | Ct | St |
|---|---|---|---|---|---|---|---|---|---|---|---|
| First-class | 82 | 117 | 12 | 2470 | 108 | 23.52 | 66.99 | 1 | 13 | 28 | 0 |
| List A | 87 | 72 | 10 | 1096 | 48* | 17.67 | | 0 | 0 | 24 | 0 |
| Twenty20 | 56 | 47 | 10 | 606 | 62 | 16.37 | 126.25 | 0 | 1 | 16 | 0 |

| Bowling | Mat | Balls | Runs | Wkts | BBI | BBM | Ave | Econ | SR | 5w | 10 |
|---|---|---|---|---|---|---|---|---|---|---|---|
| First-class | 82 | 14017 | 8406 | 249 | 6/35 | | 33.75 | 3.59 | 56.2 | 8 | 1 |
| List A | 87 | 3247 | 3048 | 93 | 4/35 | 4/35 | 32.77 | 5.63 | 34.9 | 0 | 0 |
| Twenty20 | 56 | 907 | 1190 | 44 | 3/23 | 3/23 | 27.04 | 7.87 | 20.6 | 0 | 0 |

## JAMES WAINMAN                                           RHB LM

YORKSHIRE

FULL NAME: James Charles Wainman
BORN: January 25, 1993, Harrogate, Yorkshire
SQUAD NO: 15
HEIGHT: 6ft 4in
NICKNAME: Wainers
EDUCATION: Leeds Grammar School
TEAMS: Yorkshire 2nd XI, Yorkshire Academy, Yorkshire Under-14s, Yorkshire Under-15s, Yorkshire Under-17s
CAREER: Yet to make first-team debut

WHY CRICKET? I started playing for my local team after watching cricket on TV

CAREER HIGHLIGHTS? Winning the Yorkshire Knockout Cup with the academy and gaining a professional contract

SUPERSTITIONS? I always wear two pairs of socks

CRICKETING HEROES? Andrew Flintoff

BEST PLAYER IN COUNTY CRICKET? Marcus Trescothick

TIP FOR THE TOP? Alex Lees

IF YOU WEREN'T A CRICKETER? I'd be at Northumbria University studying Design Technology and Business

WHEN RAIN STOPS PLAY? I'll be chilling, reading magazines, or listening to music

FAVOURITE TV? Prison Break, Made in Chelsea

FAVOURITE FILM? Taken

DREAM HOLIDAY? Barbados

ACCOMPLISHMENTS? Getting three A-Levels

GUILTY PLEASURES? Sweet popcorn

AMAZE ME! I took three attempts to pass my driving test; I have walked the Three Peaks

FANTASY SLIP CORDON? Keeper: Karl Pilkington, 1st: Megan Fox, 2nd: Me, 3rd: Zinedine Zidane, Gully: Lee Evans

TWITTER FEED: @JCWainman

# DAVID WAINWRIGHT
## LHB SLA

FULL NAME: David John Wainwright
BORN: March 21, 1985, Pontefract, Yorkshire
SQUAD NO: 21
HEIGHT: 5ft 9in
NICKNAME: Wainers
EDUCATION: Hemsworth High School;
Loughborough University
TEAMS: Derbyshire, Loughborough MCCU,
Police Sports Club, Yorkshire
CAREER: First-class: 2004; List A: 2005; T20:
2007

**DERBYSHIRE**

BEST BATTING: 104* Yorkshire vs Sussex, Hove, 2008
BEST BOWLING: 6-40 Yorkshire vs DMCCU, Durham University, 2011
COUNTY CAP: 2010 (Yorkshire)

FAMILY TIES? Grandfather (Harry Heritage, also a slow left-armer) represented Yorkshire Schoolboys in 1950 and 1951
CAREER HIGHLIGHTS? Winning at Lord's in the BUSA final for Loughborough, scoring a century at Scarborough in front of my family
CRICKETING HEROES? Brian Lara, Daniel Vettori
NON-CRICKETING HEROES? Will Smith, Steven Gerrard
TIPS FOR THE TOP? Alex Lees, Barney Gibson
FAVOURITE TV? Family Guy
FAVOURITE FILM? Bad Boys
FAVOURITE BOOK? Facebook
DREAM HOLIDAY? Orlando, Florida
ACCOMPLISHMENTS? My 20 and 0 undefeated streak against Oliver Hannon-Dalby at golf
FANTASY SLIP CORDON? Keeper: Will Smith (the Fresh Prince himself), 1st: Myself (mixing it with Big Will and the Smooth Criminal), 2nd: Michael Jackson (keeping us going with a few 'hee hees' and 'shamones'), 3rd: Steven Gerrard (talking the guys through Istanbul 2005), Gully: James Corden (because no cordon is complete without James Corden)

| Batting | Mat | Inns | NO | Runs | HS | Ave | SR | 100 | 50 | Ct | St |
|---|---|---|---|---|---|---|---|---|---|---|---|
| First-class | 37 | 47 | 12 | 1115 | 104* | 31.85 | 53.55 | 2 | 3 | 13 | 0 |
| List A | 51 | 24 | 14 | 153 | 26 | 15.30 | 70.50 | 0 | 0 | 16 | 0 |
| Twenty20 | 26 | 9 | 6 | 23 | 6* | 7.66 | 62.16 | 0 | 0 | 9 | 0 |

| Bowling | Mat | Balls | Runs | Wkts | BBI | BBM | Ave | Econ | SR | 5w | 10 |
|---|---|---|---|---|---|---|---|---|---|---|---|
| First-class | 37 | 5595 | 3106 | 84 | 6/40 | | 36.97 | 3.33 | 66.6 | 2 | 0 |
| List A | 51 | 1887 | 1534 | 43 | 3/26 | 3/26 | 35.67 | 4.87 | 43.8 | 0 | 0 |
| Twenty20 | 26 | 455 | 551 | 21 | 3/6 | 3/6 | 26.23 | 7.26 | 21.6 | 0 | 0 |

## ALEX WAKELY RHB RMF MVP90

NORTHAMPTONSHIRE

FULL NAME: Alex George Wakely
BORN: November 3, 1988, London
SQUAD NO: 8
HEIGHT: 6ft 1in
NICKNAME: Wakers, Allan, Baby Seal
EDUCATION: Bedford School
TEAMS: Bedfordshire, England Under-19s, Northamptonshire, Northamptonshire 2nd XI
CAREER: First-class: 2007; List A: 2005; T20: 2009

BEST BATTING: 113* Northamptonshire vs Glamorgan, Cardiff, 2009
BEST BOWLING: 2-62 Northamptonshire vs Somerset, Taunton, 2007

FAMILY TIES? Father played minor counties
WHY CRICKET? As a small child my grandfather made me a bat
CAREER HIGHLIGHTS? England U19 captain, T20 Finals Day in 2009
CRICKETING HEROES? Ricky Ponting, David Ripley
NON-CRICKETING HEROES? Muhammad Ali, my grandfather
BEST PLAYER IN COUNTY CRICKET? Mark Ramprakash
TIPS FOR THE TOP? Rob Newton, Dan Housego
IF YOU WEREN'T A CRICKETER? Journalist or sports scientist
WHEN RAIN STOPS PLAY? Darts, cards, hide Dave Murphy's kit
FAVOURITE TV? Hung, Californication
FAVOURITE FILM? The Lion King
FAVOURITE BOOK? The Girl With The Dragon Tattoo
DREAM HOLIDAY? Bora Bora
SURPRISING SKILL? Play piano to grade five
GUILTY PLEASURES? Diet Coke
FANTASY SLIP CORDON? Keeper: Mario Balotelli, 1st: Michael McIntyre, 2nd: John McEnroe, 3rd: David Beckham

| Batting | Mat | Inns | NO | Runs | HS | Ave | SR | 100 | 50 | Ct | St |
|---|---|---|---|---|---|---|---|---|---|---|---|
| First-class | 50 | 80 | 2 | 2240 | 113* | 28.71 | 45.17 | 2 | 14 | 29 | 0 |
| List A | 31 | 30 | 4 | 632 | 94 | 24.30 | 82.29 | 0 | 3 | 12 | 0 |
| Twenty20 | 37 | 36 | 4 | 833 | 62 | 26.03 | 117.32 | 0 | 4 | 13 | 0 |

| Bowling | Mat | Balls | Runs | Wkts | BBI | BBM | Ave | Econ | SR | 5w | 10 |
|---|---|---|---|---|---|---|---|---|---|---|---|
| First-class | 50 | 351 | 284 | 6 | 2/62 | 2/62 | 47.33 | 4.85 | 58.5 | 0 | 0 |
| List A | 31 | 120 | 90 | 4 | 2/14 | 2/14 | 22.50 | 4.50 | 30.0 | 0 | 0 |
| Twenty20 | 37 | 12 | 29 | 0 | - | - | - | 14.50 | - | 0 | 0 |

# MATT WALKER

**LHB RM R4**

FULL NAME: Matthew Jonathan Walker
BORN: January 2, 1974, Gravesend, Kent
SQUAD NO: 22
HEIGHT: 5ft 6in
NICKNAME: Walks
EDUCATION: King's School, Rochester
TEAMS: Essex, Kent
CAREER: First-class: 1993; List A: 1994; T20: 2003

ESSEX

BEST BATTING: 275* Kent vs Somerset, Canterbury, 1996
BEST BOWLING: 3-35 Essex vs Kent, Canterbury, 2010
COUNTY CAPS: 2000 (Kent), 2010 (Essex); BENEFIT YEAR: 2008 (Kent)

FAMILY TIES? Dad played Kent and Middlesex 2nd XI and was on Lord's groundstaff.
Grandfather kept wicket for Kent. Mum was women's cricket coach
CRICKETERS PARTICULARLY ADMIRED? Darren Lehmann, Nick Knight, Mark Ramprakash
OTHER SPORTS PLAYED? Hockey (England U14-21), rugby (Kent U18)
CRICKET MOMENT TO FORGET? Losing the Benson and Hedges final vs Surrey in 1997
OTHER SPORTS FOLLOWED? Football (Charlton Athletic), hockey (Gore Court HC)
FAVOURITE BAND? Razorlight, Arctic Monkeys, Jeff Buckley
RELAXATIONS? Music and films
NOTES: Was installed as Essex assistant coach to Paul Grayson in December 2011

| Batting | Mat | Inns | NO | Runs | HS | Ave | SR | 100 | 50 | Ct | St |
|---|---|---|---|---|---|---|---|---|---|---|---|
| First-class | 223 | 377 | 39 | 12197 | 275* | 36.08 | | 28 | 51 | 155 | 0 |
| List A | 285 | 255 | 40 | 6269 | 117 | 29.15 | | 3 | 37 | 75 | 0 |
| Twenty20 | 82 | 75 | 11 | 1397 | 74* | 21.82 | 116.12 | 0 | 4 | 10 | 0 |

| Bowling | Mat | Balls | Runs | Wkts | BBI | BBM | Ave | Econ | SR | 5w | 10 |
|---|---|---|---|---|---|---|---|---|---|---|---|
| First-class | 223 | 2154 | 1274 | 28 | 3/35 | | 45.50 | 3.54 | 76.9 | 0 | 0 |
| List A | 285 | 904 | 759 | 30 | 4/24 | 4/24 | 25.30 | 5.03 | 30.1 | 0 | 0 |
| Twenty20 | 82 | - | - | - | - | - | - | - | - | - | - |

GLAMORGAN

**FULL NAME:** Mark Alexander Wallace
**BORN:** November 19, 1981, Abergavenny, Monmouthshire
**SQUAD NO:** 18
**HEIGHT:** 5ft 9in
**NICKNAME:** Wally, Grommit, Wash, Screech, Kyle, Chesney
**EDUCATION:** Crickhowell High School; Staffordshire University; University of Wales
**TEAMS:** Glamorgan, Wales Minor Counties
**CAREER:** First-class: 1999; List A: 1999; T20: 2003

**BEST BATTING:** 139 Glamorgan vs Surrey, The Oval, 2009
**COUNTY CAP:** 2003

**FAMILY TIES?** Father still plays club cricket for Abergavenny and turns out for Wales Over 50s and 60s
**CAREER HIGHLIGHTS?** Winning one-day trophies and captaining Glamorgan
**CRICKETING HEROES?** Ian Healy, Alec Stewart, Steve James, Brendon McCullum, Justin Langer
**NON-CRICKETING HEROES?** Lance Armstrong, Rory McIlroy, Harry Potter
**BEST PLAYER IN COUNTY CRICKET?** Steve Davies
**TIPS FOR THE TOP?** James Taylor, James Harris, Andrew Salter
**IF YOU WEREN'T A CRICKETER?** Journalist, student
**WHEN RAIN STOPS PLAY?** Reading, playing pool, talking rubbish
**FAVOURITE TV?** Spooks, Eastenders
**DREAM HOLIDAY?** New York
**GUILTY PLEASURES?** Lego
**SURPRISING FACT?** Work as a rugby writer in the winter. Single handicap golfer
**FANTASY SLIP CORDON?** Keeper: Me, 1st: Michael McIntyre, 2nd: Rory McIlroy, 3rd: Lance Armstrong, 4th: Del Trotter, Gully: David Harrison, 2nd gully: Ian Thomas
**TWITTER FEED:** @markwallace18

| Batting | Mat | Inns | NO | Runs | HS | Ave | SR | 100 | 50 | Ct | St |
|---|---|---|---|---|---|---|---|---|---|---|---|
| First-class | 183 | 294 | 21 | 7868 | 139 | 28.82 | | 11 | 39 | 457 | 42 |
| List A | 165 | 131 | 27 | 1940 | 85 | 18.65 | | 0 | 3 | 150 | 41 |
| Twenty20 | 83 | 66 | 21 | 826 | 42* | 18.35 | 127.66 | 0 | 0 | 32 | 20 |

| Bowling | Mat | Balls | Runs | Wkts | BBI | BBM | Ave | Econ | SR | 5w | 10 |
|---|---|---|---|---|---|---|---|---|---|---|---|
| First-class | 183 | 6 | 3 | 0 | - | - | - | 3.00 | - | 0 | 0 |
| List A | 165 | - | - | - | - | - | - | - | - | - | - |
| Twenty20 | 83 | - | - | - | - | - | - | - | - | - | - |

# MAX WALLER

## RHB LB

FULL NAME: Max Thomas Charles Waller
BORN: March 3, 1988, Salisbury, Wiltshire
SQUAD NO: 10
HEIGHT: 6ft
NICKNAME: Steam Kat
EDUCATION: Millfield School; Bournemouth University
TEAMS: Dorset, Gloucestershire 2nd XI, Somerset, Somerset 2nd XI
CAREER: First-class: 2009; List A: 2009; T20: 2009

BEST BATTING: 28 Somerset vs Hampshire, Southampton, 2009
BEST BOWLING: 2-27 Somerset vs Sussex, Hove, 2009

FAMILY TIES? Dad is an MCC playing member
CAREER HIGHLIGHTS? Playing in the Champions League T20. Man of the Match in a Caribbean T20 match. Playing in Finals Day. First-class debut
SUPERSTITIONS? Like to have the ball in my hand before handing my stuff to the umpire!
CRICKETING HEROES? Shane Warne, Jonty Rhodes
NON-CRICKETING HEROES? Ayrton Senna
TIPS FOR THE TOP? Jamie Overton and Lewis Gregory
IF YOU WEREN'T A CRICKETER? Something business related or a failed artist!
WHEN RAIN STOPS PLAY? On the laptop, beating everyone at FIFA 12 as Chelsea, and cards
FAVOURITE TV? MOTD, Take Me Out, The OC, Prison Break, Hawaii Five-O
FAVOURITE FILM? Top Gun, Spread, Senna, Wedding Crashers, Cool Runnings
FAVOURITE BOOK? The Secret
ACCOMPLISHMENTS? Having my paintings in an art shop (acrylics on canvas)
FANTASY SLIP CORDON? Keeper: Muhammad Ali (great hands!), 1st: Tiger Woods (get a few tips for my swing), 2nd: Shane Warne (has some great stories and obviously brilliant to talk to about bowling), 3rd: Me, Gully: Jimmy Carr (funniest man ever)
TWITTER FEED: @maxtcwaller

| Batting | Mat | Inns | NO | Runs | HS | Ave | SR | 100 | 50 | Ct | St |
|---|---|---|---|---|---|---|---|---|---|---|---|
| First-class | 5 | 6 | 1 | 67 | 28 | 13.40 | 44.96 | 0 | 0 | 1 | 0 |
| List A | 22 | 7 | 6 | 13 | 5 | 13.00 | 48.14 | 0 | 0 | 4 | 0 |
| Twenty20 | 28 | 8 | 3 | 7 | 3 | 1.40 | 33.33 | 0 | 0 | 10 | 0 |

| Bowling | Mat | Balls | Runs | Wkts | BBI | BBM | Ave | Econ | SR | 5w | 10 |
|---|---|---|---|---|---|---|---|---|---|---|---|
| First-class | 5 | 528 | 348 | 6 | 2/27 | 3/57 | 58.00 | 3.95 | 88.0 | 0 | 0 |
| List A | 22 | 676 | 621 | 16 | 2/24 | 2/24 | 38.81 | 5.51 | 42.2 | 0 | 0 |
| Twenty20 | 28 | 456 | 528 | 30 | 3/16 | 3/16 | 17.60 | 6.94 | 15.2 | 0 | 0 |

# STEWART WALTERS

**RHB LB**

**FULL NAME:** Stewart Jonathan Walters
**BORN:** June 25, 1983, Mornington, Australia
**SQUAD NO:** 26
**HEIGHT:** 6ft 1in
**NICKNAME:** Forrest, Walts
**EDUCATION:** Guildford Grammar School, Perth
**TEAMS:** Glamorgan, Glamorgan 2nd XI, Surrey, Surrey 2nd XI
**CAREER:** First-class: 2006; List A: 2005; T20: 2006

**BEST BATTING:** 188 Surrey vs Leicestershire, The Oval, 2009
**BEST BOWLING:** 1-4 Surrey vs Durham, Chester-le-Street, 2007

**FAMILY TIES?** Father and grandfather played for Carlton in Victoria
**WHY CRICKET?** Inspired watching Dean Jones bat for Australia
**CAREER HIGHLIGHTS?** Signing a contract at Glamorgan and being given the opportunity to express myself
**SUPERSTITIONS?** Put right pad on first, always talk to myself whilst batting
**CRICKETING HEROES?** Steve Waugh
**NON-CRICKETING HEROES?** My daughter Maddison
**TIPS FOR THE TOP?** James Harris, Tom Maynard, Will Owen
**IF YOU WEREN'T A CRICKETER?** Professional sports coach/trainer
**WHEN RAIN STOPS PLAY?** Sadly in the indoor school or playing cards
**FAVOURITE TV?** The X Factor, BGT
**FAVOURITE FILM?** Gladiator
**DREAM HOLIDAY?** The theme parks at Orlando to watch my daughter have so much fun
**FANTASY SLIP CORDON?** Keeper: Ali Brown (the man could do anything, handy No.7 too), 1st: Jon Albert (you need a fiery ginger in the cordon), 2nd: Daughter Maddison (just so I knew where she was), 3rd: Gareth Rees (keeps him away from short leg)
**TWITTER FEED:** @stewiewalters

| Batting | Mat | Inns | NO | Runs | HS | Ave | SR | 100 | 50 | Ct | St |
|---|---|---|---|---|---|---|---|---|---|---|---|
| First-class | 41 | 68 | 5 | 1844 | 188 | 29.26 | 50.58 | 4 | 5 | 43 | 0 |
| List A | 56 | 53 | 9 | 1302 | 91 | 29.59 | 85.15 | 0 | 9 | 18 | 0 |
| Twenty20 | 37 | 28 | 9 | 450 | 53* | 23.68 | 109.48 | 0 | 1 | 24 | 0 |

| Bowling | Mat | Balls | Runs | Wkts | BBI | BBM | Ave | Econ | SR | 5w | 10 |
|---|---|---|---|---|---|---|---|---|---|---|---|
| First-class | 41 | 426 | 239 | 3 | 1/4 | 1/9 | 79.66 | 3.36 | 142.0 | 0 | 0 |
| List A | 56 | 165 | 179 | 3 | 1/12 | 1/12 | 59.66 | 6.50 | 55.0 | 0 | 0 |
| Twenty20 | 37 | 18 | 26 | 1 | 1/9 | 1/9 | 26.00 | 8.66 | 18.0 | 0 | 0 |

# IAIN WARDLAW

**RHB RFM**

FULL NAME: Iain Wardlaw
BORN: June 29, 1985, Dewsbury, Yorkshire
SQUAD NO: 7
HEIGHT: 6ft 3in
NICKNAME: Wardy
EDUCATION: Whitcliffe Mount School;
Huddersfield University
TEAMS: Yorkshire, Yorkshire 2nd XI
CAREER: First-class: 2011; List A: 2011; T20:
2011

**YORKSHIRE**

BEST BOWLING: 1-68 Yorkshire vs Lancashire, Leeds, 2011

FAMILY TIES? Sister played for Yorkshire and England Women
WHY CRICKET? Enjoyed watching it as a youngster
CAREER HIGHLIGHTS? First-team debut vs Notts in T20
CRICKETING HEROES? Andrew Flintoff
BEST PLAYER IN COUNTY CRICKET? Marcus Trescothick
TIP FOR THE TOP? Jonny Bairstow
IF YOU WEREN'T A CRICKETER? Sales director
WHEN RAIN STOPS PLAY? Playing on iPad

| Batting | Mat | Inns | NO | Runs | HS | Ave | SR | 100 | 50 | Ct | St |
|---|---|---|---|---|---|---|---|---|---|---|---|
| First-class | 1 | - | - | - | - | - | - | - | - | 0 | 0 |
| List A | 1 | 1 | 0 | 1 | 1 | 1.00 | 25.00 | 0 | 0 | 0 | 0 |
| Twenty20 | 4 | - | - | - | - | - | - | - | - | 0 | 0 |

| Bowling | Mat | Balls | Runs | Wkts | BBI | BBM | Ave | Econ | SR | 5w | 10 |
|---|---|---|---|---|---|---|---|---|---|---|---|
| First-class | 1 | 78 | 68 | 1 | 1/68 | 1/68 | 68.00 | 5.23 | 78.0 | 0 | 0 |
| List A | 1 | 24 | 15 | 0 | - | - | - | 3.75 | - | 0 | 0 |
| Twenty20 | 4 | 67 | 65 | 2 | 2/17 | 2/17 | 32.50 | 5.82 | 33.5 | 0 | 0 |

**GLAMORGAN**

FULL NAME: Huw Thomas Waters
BORN: September 26, 1986, Cardiff
SQUAD NO: 17
HEIGHT: 6ft 2in
NICKNAME: Muds, Muddy, Mudification of the Nation
EDUCATION: Llantarnam Comprehensive; Monmouth School; The Open University
TEAMS: Glamorgan, Wales Minor Counties
CAREER: First-class 2005; List A 2005; T20: 2010

BEST BATTING: 54 Glamorgan vs Surrey, Cardiff, 2011
BEST BOWLING: 5-86 Glamorgan vs Somerset, 2006

FAMILY TIES? Big Don played for Usk Cricket Club during their time in the Three Counties League. My uncle, grandfather and great uncle also played for Usk
CAREER HIGHLIGHTS? Making my debut for Glamorgan. Going on tour with England U19. First first-class five-fer
CRICKETING HEROES? Father, Glenn McGrath
NON-CRICKETING HEROES? Sir Alex Ferguson
BEST PLAYER IN COUNTY CRICKET? Too many to mention just one
TIPS FOR THE TOP? Our academy players
IF YOU WEREN'T A CRICKETER? Coaching/PE teacher, something involved in sport
WHEN RAIN STOPS PLAY? Listen to music, play a few games on a phone and putting the world to rights whilst getting mocked by various members of our dressing room!
FAVOURITE TV? Top Gear
FAVOURITE FILM? The Shawshank Redemption, Die Hard
DREAM HOLIDAY? St Lucia or Barbados
GUILTY PLEASURES? Desserts
FANTASY SLIP CORDON? Keeper: Peter Kay, 1st: Brandon Flowers, 2nd: Alex Ferguson, 3rd: Me, 4th: Glenn McGrath, Gully: Morgan Freeman

| Batting | Mat | Inns | NO | Runs | HS | Ave | SR | 100 | 50 | Ct | St |
|---|---|---|---|---|---|---|---|---|---|---|---|
| First-class | 37 | 55 | 24 | 305 | 54 | 9.83 | 17.97 | 0 | 1 | 7 | 0 |
| List A | 21 | 8 | 3 | 24 | 8 | 4.80 | 42.10 | 0 | 0 | 3 | 0 |
| Twenty20 | 4 | 2 | 2 | 11 | 11* | - | 84.61 | 0 | 0 | 0 | 0 |

| Bowling | Mat | Balls | Runs | Wkts | BBI | BBM | Ave | Econ | SR | 5w | 10 |
|---|---|---|---|---|---|---|---|---|---|---|---|
| First-class | 37 | 4672 | 2538 | 68 | 5/86 | | 37.32 | 3.25 | 68.7 | 1 | 0 |
| List A | 21 | 798 | 836 | 14 | 3/47 | 3/47 | 59.71 | 6.28 | 57.0 | 0 | 0 |
| Twenty20 | 4 | 85 | 118 | 3 | 3/30 | 3/30 | 39.33 | 8.32 | 28.3 | 0 | 0 |

# LUKE WELLS

## LHB OB

FULL NAME: Luke William Peter Wells
BORN: December 29, 1990, Eastbourne, Sussex
SQUAD NO: 31
HEIGHT: 6ft 4in
NICKNAME: Wellsy, Rinser
EDUCATION: St Bede's School; Loughborough University
TEAMS: Colombo Cricket Club, England Under-19s, Sussex, Sussex 2nd XI
CAREER: First-class: 2010; List A: 2010; T20: 2011

BEST BATTING: 174 Sussex vs Yorkshire, Hove, 2011
BEST BOWLING: 2-28 Sussex vs Worcestershire, Horsham, 2011

FAMILY TIES? Father [Alan] played for Sussex, Kent and England. Uncle [Colin] played for Sussex, Derbyshire and England

CAREER HIGHLIGHTS? In my short career so far my highlights are undoubtedly scoring three hundreds in last year's County Championship. Also, to get my first hundred in a run-chase with heaps of pressure was great and to get it so early in my career was a great relief. Hopefully it has opened the flood gates for many more!

CRICKETING HEROES? I'd say Matthew Hayden is a great inspiration for me being a tall left-handed opening/top-order batsman. And of course Sachin Tendulkar

IF YOU WEREN'T A CRICKETER? I'd be in my final year of university at Loughborough and possibly looking into a career in teaching/coaching

WHEN RAIN STOPS PLAY? Either laughing and joking with the lads or inventing some sort of ball game in the changing room

ACCOMPLISHMENTS? Coming through extreme family/personal adversity and coming out the other side as a stronger and successful person

GUILTY PLEASURES? Definitely chocolate ice cream and probably a few too many drinks with my mates! But I reckon worst of all is that I actually quite like Justin Bieber songs!

TWITTER FEED: @luke_wells07

| Batting | Mat | Inns | NO | Runs | HS | Ave | SR | 100 | 50 | Ct | St |
|---|---|---|---|---|---|---|---|---|---|---|---|
| First-class | 18 | 35 | 4 | 951 | 174 | 30.67 | 43.56 | 3 | 1 | 8 | 0 |
| List A | 6 | 3 | 0 | 28 | 17 | 9.33 | 73.68 | 0 | 0 | 1 | 0 |
| Twenty20 | 1 | 1 | 0 | 3 | 3 | 3.00 | 50.00 | 0 | 0 | 0 | 0 |

| Bowling | Mat | Balls | Runs | Wkts | BBI | BBM | Ave | Econ | SR | 5w | 10 |
|---|---|---|---|---|---|---|---|---|---|---|---|
| First-class | 18 | 414 | 260 | 4 | 2/28 | 2/33 | 65.00 | 3.76 | 103.5 | 0 | 0 |
| List A | 6 | 77 | 61 | 3 | 3/19 | 3/19 | 20.33 | 4.75 | 25.6 | 0 | 0 |
| Twenty20 | 1 | - | - | - | - | - | - | - | - | - | - |

# KIRK WERNARS

**LHB RFM**

**FULL NAME:** Kirk Ogilvy Wernars
**BORN:** June 14, 1991, Cape Town, South Africa
**SQUAD NO:** 4
**HEIGHT:** 6ft 2in
**NICKNAME:** Baloo, Leupels
**EDUCATION:** SACS High School
**TEAMS:** South Africa Under-19s, Sussex, Sussex 2nd XI, Western Province, Western Province Under-19s
**CAREER:** First-class: 2010; List A: 2010; T20: 2011

BEST BATTING: 53 Sussex vs Worcestershire, Horsham, 2011
BEST BOWLING: 2-11 Western Province vs Boland, Newlands, 2010

CAREER HIGHLIGHTS? Being selected for SA U19. Making debut for Sussex 1st XI
SUPERSTITIONS? I always walk with my left foot first over the boundary rope on to a cricket field when going into bat
CRICKETING HEROES? Brian Lara, Steve Waugh
NON-CRICKETING HEROES? Douglas Bader, Gerry Wernars
BEST PLAYER IN COUNTY CRICKET? Marcus Trescothick or Murray Goodwin
IF YOU WEREN'T A CRICKETER? A firefighter or an entrepreneur
WHEN RAIN STOPS PLAY? Usually sit talking with teammates or sometimes spend some time in the gym
FAVOURITE FILM? Gladiator
FAVOURITE TV? CSI Miami
FAVOURITE BOOK? The Power Of One
DREAM HOLIDAY? Europe
SURPRISING FACT? I am Dutch from my father's side of the family, and Scottish from my mother's side. I played rugby, water polo, squash, golf and cricket to a good standard when growing up at school. I am a volunteer fire fighter in Cape Town
TWITTER FEED: @KirkWernars

| Batting | Mat | Inns | NO | Runs | HS | Ave | SR | 100 | 50 | Ct | St |
|---|---|---|---|---|---|---|---|---|---|---|---|
| First-class | 5 | 8 | 3 | 181 | 53 | 36.20 | 45.13 | 0 | 1 | 4 | 0 |
| List A | 12 | 9 | 4 | 115 | 37* | 23.00 | 90.55 | 0 | 0 | 5 | 0 |
| Twenty20 | 6 | 5 | 0 | 22 | 9 | 4.40 | 70.96 | 0 | 0 | 4 | 0 |

| Bowling | Mat | Balls | Runs | Wkts | BBI | BBM | Ave | Econ | SR | 5w | 10 |
|---|---|---|---|---|---|---|---|---|---|---|---|
| First-class | 5 | 249 | 153 | 7 | 2/11 | 3/30 | 21.85 | 3.68 | 35.5 | 0 | 0 |
| List A | 12 | 249 | 239 | 7 | 6/27 | 6/27 | 34.14 | 5.75 | 35.5 | 1 | 0 |
| Twenty20 | 6 | 18 | 41 | 1 | 1/21 | 1/21 | 41.00 | 13.66 | 18.0 | 0 | 0 |

# RIKI WESSELS

## RHB WK

**FULL NAME:** Mattheus Hendrik Wessels
**BORN:** November 12, 1985, Marougudoore, Queensland, Australia
**SQUAD NO:** 9
**HEIGHT:** 5ft 11in
**NICKNAME:** Blood, Weasel, Riki Bobby
**EDUCATION:** Woodridge College, Port Elizabeth; University of Northampton
**TEAMS:** Marylebone Cricket Club, Mid West Rhinos, Nondescripts Cricket Club, Northamptonshire, Nottinghamshire
**CAREER:** First-class: 2004; List A: 2005; T20: 2005

**BEST BATTING:** 197 Mid West Rhinos vs Matabeleland Tuskers, Bulawayo, 2011
**BEST BOWLING:** 1-10 Mid West Rhinos vs Matabeleland Tuskers, Bulawayo, 2009

**CAREER HIGHLIGHTS?** Has to be my first first-class hundred and the finals I've taken part in
**CRICKETING HEROES?** Michael Slater, Justin Langer
**NON-CRICKETING HEROES?** All the soldiers fighting currently, having lost a few friends to the war myself
**BEST PLAYER IN COUNTY CRICKET?** Mark Ramprakash, Marcus Trescothick
**TIPS FOR THE TOP?** Chris Woakes, Alex Hales, Sam Wood
**IF YOU WEREN'T A CRICKETER?** Probably in the army on the front line
**WHEN RAIN STOPS PLAY?** iPad or avoiding Paul Franks and his bad banter
**FAVOURITE TV?** Dr Who
**FAVOURITE FILM?** Any Given Sunday
**FAVOURITE BOOK?** Anything by Chris Ryan
**DREAM HOLIDAY?** Zanzibar. Heat, beaches and beer
**ACCOMPLISHMENTS?** Helping Macmillan Cancer UK raise money and helping people who need it more than myself
**SURPRISING FACTS?** I've bungee jumped at Vic Falls, I lived in Colombo for six months and I love hunting
**TWITTER FEED:** @rikiwessels

| Batting | Mat | Inns | NO | Runs | HS | Ave | SR | 100 | 50 | Ct | St |
|---|---|---|---|---|---|---|---|---|---|---|---|
| First-class | 99 | 165 | 15 | 5100 | 197 | 34.00 | 64.37 | 11 | 28 | 188 | 12 |
| List A | 98 | 91 | 9 | 2266 | 100 | 27.63 | 96.75 | 1 | 13 | 67 | 0 |
| Twenty20 | 79 | 69 | 12 | 1532 | 86* | 26.87 | 137.89 | 0 | 6 | 25 | 13 |

| Bowling | Mat | Balls | Runs | Wkts | BBI | BBM | Ave | Econ | SR | 5w | 10 |
|---|---|---|---|---|---|---|---|---|---|---|---|
| First-class | 99 | 78 | 42 | 2 | 1/10 | 1/10 | 21.00 | 3.23 | 39.0 | 0 | 0 |
| List A | 98 | 49 | 48 | 1 | 1/0 | 1/0 | 48.00 | 5.87 | 49.0 | 0 | 0 |
| Twenty20 | 79 | - | - | - | - | - | - | - | - | - | - |

## TOM WESTLEY — RHB OB

**FULL NAME:** Thomas Westley
**BORN:** March 13, 1989, Cambridge
**SQUAD NO:** 21
**HEIGHT:** 6ft 2in
**NICKNAME:** Spongebob, Pup
**EDUCATION:** Linton Village College; Hills Road Sixth Form College (both Cambridge)
**TEAMS:** Cambridgeshire, England Under-19s, Essex, Essex 2nd XI, Marylebone Cricket Club
**CAREER:** First-class: 2007; List A: 2006; T20: 2010

**BEST BATTING:** 132 Essex vs Derbyshire, Derby, 2009
**BEST BOWLING:** 4-55 DMCCU vs Durham, Durham University, 2010

**SUPERSTITIONS?** I mark my crease three times before every over and after every boundary
**CRICKETERS PARTICULARLY ADMIRED?** Steve Waugh, Sachin Tendulkar, Andy Flower, Alastair Cook
**OTHER SPORTS FOLLOWED?** Football (Newcastle United)
**NOTES:** Played for MCC in 2007, and for England U19 in 2008, appearing in the U19 World Cup, and again in 2009 as captain. Won the NBC Denis Compton Award for Essex's most promising young player in 2008 and 2009. Represented Essex and Durham MCCU in 2011, playing 10 Championship matches and making a highest score of 67

| Batting | Mat | Inns | NO | Runs | HS | Ave | SR | 100 | 50 | Ct | St |
|---|---|---|---|---|---|---|---|---|---|---|---|
| First-class | 48 | 85 | 9 | 2217 | 132 | 29.17 | 48.98 | 3 | 12 | 27 | 0 |
| List A | 11 | 8 | 0 | 106 | 50 | 13.25 | 71.62 | 0 | 1 | 1 | 0 |
| Twenty20 | 4 | 1 | 1 | 2 | 2* | - | 100.00 | 0 | 0 | 1 | 0 |

| Bowling | Mat | Balls | Runs | Wkts | BBI | BBM | Ave | Econ | SR | 5w | 10 |
|---|---|---|---|---|---|---|---|---|---|---|---|
| First-class | 48 | 1490 | 760 | 20 | 4/55 | 4/55 | 38.00 | 3.06 | 74.5 | 0 | 0 |
| List A | 11 | 102 | 77 | 2 | 1/18 | 1/18 | 38.50 | 4.52 | 51.0 | 0 | 0 |
| Twenty20 | 4 | 12 | 13 | 1 | 1/7 | 1/7 | 13.00 | 6.50 | 12.0 | 0 | 0 |

# IAN WESTWOOD

## LHB OB

**FULL NAME:** Ian James Westwood
**BORN:** July 13, 1982, Birmingham, Warwickshire
**SQUAD NO:** 22
**HEIGHT:** 5ft 7in
**NICKNAME:** Westy, Wezzo, Tot
**EDUCATION:** Wheelers Lane Boys' School; Solihull Sixth Form College
**TEAMS:** Warwickshire, Warwickshire Cricket Board
**CAREER:** First-class: 2003; List A: 2001; T20: 2005

**BEST BATTING:** 178 Warwickshire vs West Indies A, Birmingham, 2006
**BEST BOWLING:** 2-39 Warwickshire vs Hampshire, Southampton, 2009
**COUNTY CAP:** 2008

**FAMILY TIES?** Grandad was a member at Warwickshire. Brother played Warwickshire junior cricket
**CAREER HIGHLIGHTS?** Getting my county cap and being named club captain
**SUPERSTITIONS?** None
**CRICKETING HEROES?** Stuart Eustace, Phil Stephenson, Vanraaj Padhaal
**BEST PLAYER IN COUNTY CRICKET?** Marcus Trescothick
**TIPS FOR THE TOP?** George and Isaac Maddy
**IF YOU WEREN'T A CRICKETER?** No idea!
**WHEN RAIN STOPS PLAY?** Playing iPhone games, eating, annoying the balding physio
**FAVOURITE TV?** House
**FAVOURITE FILM?** Old School
**FAVOURITE BOOK?** The Cricketers' Who's Who
**DREAM HOLIDAY?** Skegness
**GUILTY PLEASURES?** Sweets, Birmingham City FC

| Batting | Mat | Inns | NO | Runs | HS | Ave | SR | 100 | 50 | Ct | St |
|---|---|---|---|---|---|---|---|---|---|---|---|
| First-class | 95 | 163 | 17 | 4842 | 178 | 33.16 | 45.33 | 10 | 25 | 55 | 0 |
| List A | 59 | 49 | 9 | 928 | 65 | 23.20 | | 0 | 3 | 6 | 0 |
| Twenty20 | 38 | 27 | 12 | 342 | 49* | 22.80 | 114.00 | 0 | 0 | 5 | 0 |

| Bowling | Mat | Balls | Runs | Wkts | BBI | BBM | Ave | Econ | SR | 5w | 10 |
|---|---|---|---|---|---|---|---|---|---|---|---|
| First-class | 95 | 389 | 238 | 6 | 2/39 | | 39.66 | 3.67 | 64.8 | 0 | 0 |
| List A | 59 | 252 | 215 | 3 | 1/28 | 1/28 | 71.66 | 5.11 | 84.0 | 0 | 0 |
| Twenty20 | 38 | 54 | 91 | 5 | 3/29 | 3/29 | 18.20 | 10.11 | 10.8 | 0 | 0 |

# ADAM WHEATER

## RHB WK

ESSEX

FULL NAME: Adam Jack Wheater
BORN: February 13, 1990, Whipps Cross, Essex
SQUAD NO: 31
HEIGHT: 5ft 6in
NICKNAME: Wheates
TEAMS: Badureliya Sports Club, Cambridge MCCU, England Under-19s, Essex, Essex 2nd XI, Essex Under-17s, Matabeleland Tuskers
CAREER: First-class: 2008; List A: 2010; T20: 2009

BEST BATTING: 164 Essex vs Northamptonshire, Chelmsford, 2011

IF YOU WEREN'T A CRICKETER? An entrepreneur
CRICKETERS PARTICULARLY ADMIRED? James Foster and Adam Gilchrist
OTHER SPORTS FOLLOWED? Hockey (Old Loughtonians)
FAVOURITE BAND? Kings Of Leon
NOTES: After touring South Africa with England U19 in 2008/09 and featuring on the England Performance Programme in 2009/10, he made his first-class mark with Essex in June 2011, hitting 164 from 143 balls against Northants and sharing an Essex-record sixth-wicket partnership of 253 with James Foster. The innings followed a run of three half-centuries in consecutive Championship matches. Also represents Matabeleland Tuskers and Badureliya Sports Club in Zimbabwe domestic cricket

| Batting | Mat | Inns | NO | Runs | HS | Ave | SR | 100 | 50 | Ct | St |
|---|---|---|---|---|---|---|---|---|---|---|---|
| First-class | 32 | 47 | 6 | 1857 | 164 | 45.29 | 70.90 | 3 | 12 | 50 | 0 |
| List A | 28 | 18 | 2 | 372 | 69 | 23.25 | 97.63 | 0 | 2 | 9 | 0 |
| Twenty20 | 25 | 19 | 3 | 185 | 29 | 11.56 | 98.93 | 0 | 0 | 8 | 6 |

| Bowling | Mat | Balls | Runs | Wkts | BBI | BBM | Ave | Econ | SR | 5w | 10 |
|---|---|---|---|---|---|---|---|---|---|---|---|
| First-class | 32 | - | - | - | - | - | - | - | - | - | - |
| List A | 28 | - | - | - | - | - | - | - | - | - | - |
| Twenty20 | 25 | - | - | - | - | - | - | - | - | - | - |

# GRAEME WHITE

## RHB SLA

FULL NAME: Graeme Geoffrey White
BORN: April 18, 1987, Milton Keynes, Buckinghamshire
SQUAD NO: 87
HEIGHT: 5ft 11in
NICKNAME: Chalky, Whitey, Pony
EDUCATION: Stowe School, Buckingham
TEAMS: England Under-19s, Northamptonshire, Northamptonshire 2nd XI, Nottinghamshire
CAREER: First-class: 2006; List A: 2007; T20: 2007

BEST BATTING: 65 Northamptonshire vs Glamorgan, Colwyn Bay, 2007
BEST BOWLING: 4-72 Nottinghamshire vs Durham, Nottingham, 2011

FAMILY TIES? Sister Rachel played England Women U17
CAREER HIGHLIGHTS? Representing my country at the U19 World Cup in Sri Lanka in 2006 and reaching the semi-finals
CRICKET MOMENTS TO FORGET? Getting hit for five sixes in one over playing for Stowe School
SUPERSTITIONS? Putting pads on from the top down
CRICKETERS PARTICULARLY ADMIRED? Phil Tufnell, Bishan Bedi, Daniel Vettori
OTHER SPORTS PLAYED? Badminton, hockey, football
OTHER SPORTS FOLLOWED? Football (Manchester United)
FAVOURITE BAND? Kings Of Leon, Bloc Party
NOTES: Represented England at U15, U17 and U19 level. Moved from Northamptonshire to Nottinghamshire in October 2009

| Batting | Mat | Inns | NO | Runs | HS | Ave | SR | 100 | 50 | Ct | St |
|---|---|---|---|---|---|---|---|---|---|---|---|
| First-class | 15 | 21 | 3 | 309 | 65 | 17.16 | 47.32 | 0 | 2 | 6 | 0 |
| List A | 27 | 15 | 5 | 104 | 25 | 10.40 | 80.62 | 0 | 0 | 9 | 0 |
| Twenty20 | 28 | 8 | 3 | 64 | 26* | 12.80 | 114.28 | 0 | 0 | 10 | 0 |

| Bowling | Mat | Balls | Runs | Wkts | BBI | BBM | Ave | Econ | SR | 5w | 10 |
|---|---|---|---|---|---|---|---|---|---|---|---|
| First-class | 15 | 1662 | 961 | 19 | 4/72 | 7/89 | 50.57 | 3.46 | 87.4 | 0 | 0 |
| List A | 27 | 792 | 720 | 24 | 5/35 | 5/35 | 30.00 | 5.45 | 33.0 | 1 | 0 |
| Twenty20 | 28 | 349 | 464 | 18 | 3/22 | 3/22 | 25.77 | 7.97 | 19.3 | 0 | 0 |

# ROB WHITE

### RHB LB R1

**FULL NAME:** Robert Allan White
**BORN:** October 15, 1979, Chelmsford, Essex
**SQUAD NO:** 18
**HEIGHT:** 5ft 11in
**NICKNAME:** Chalky, Toff
**EDUCATION:** Stowe School; Durham University; Loughborough University
**TEAMS:** Loughborough MCCU, Northamptonshire
**CAREER:** First-class: 2000; List A: 2002; T20: 2003

**BEST BATTING:** 277 Northamptonshire vs Gloucestershire, Northampton, 2002
**BEST BOWLING:** 2-30 Northamptonshire vs Gloucestershire, Northampton, 2002
**COUNTY CAP:** 2008

**FAMILY TIES?** Grandfather was on the Essex committee for many years
**CAREER HIGHLIGHTS?** Scoring 277 for my maiden first-class century
**CRICKETING HEROES?** Viv Richards and Robin Smith when I was growing up
**TIPS FOR THE TOP?** I would tip Alex Wakely and Rob Newton to have great careers
**FAVOURITE TV?** Boardwalk Empire
**FAVOURITE FILM?** The Shawshank Redemption
**FAVOURITE BOOK?** Beyond A Boundary is the best cricket book I've read
**ACCOMPLISHMENTS?** Gaining a degree in Politics. Fathering my first son
**SURPRISING SKILL?** This winter I entered Northamptonshire's version of Strictly Come Dancing to raise money for a new cancer unit at Northampton General Hospital. We raised over £30k and I somehow managed to win the competition
**GUILTY PLEASURES?** Pastries
**AMAZE ME!** I'm into ballroom dancing. My family are all Essex supporters. My wife once clean bowled me in a benefit game
**FANTASY SLIP CORDON?** Keeper: Myself, 1st: Viv Richards, 2nd: Stephen Fry, 3rd: Che Guevara, Gully: Barack Obama

| Batting | Mat | Inns | NO | Runs | HS | Ave | SR | 100 | 50 | Ct | St |
|---|---|---|---|---|---|---|---|---|---|---|---|
| First-class | 110 | 187 | 16 | 5644 | 277 | 33.00 | | 8 | 28 | 67 | 0 |
| List A | 92 | 87 | 3 | 1992 | 111 | 23.71 | 79.11 | 2 | 10 | 19 | 0 |
| Twenty20 | 67 | 64 | 5 | 1326 | 94* | 22.47 | 113.81 | 0 | 7 | 12 | 0 |

| Bowling | Mat | Balls | Runs | Wkts | BBI | BBM | Ave | Econ | SR | 5w | 10 |
|---|---|---|---|---|---|---|---|---|---|---|---|
| First-class | 110 | 1516 | 1071 | 18 | 2/30 | | 59.50 | 4.23 | 84.2 | 0 | 0 |
| List A | 92 | 62 | 79 | 2 | 2/18 | 2/18 | 39.50 | 7.64 | 31.0 | 0 | 0 |
| Twenty20 | 67 | - | - | - | - | - | - | - | - | - | - |

# WAYNE WHITE

## RHB RMF

FULL NAME: Wayne Andrew White
BORN: September 22, 1985, Derby
SQUAD NO: 35
HEIGHT: 6ft 3in
NICKNAME: Chalky, Sticks, Waz
EDUCATION: John Port School; Nottingham Trent University
TEAMS: Derbyshire, Derbyshire 2nd XI, Leicestershire
CAREER: First-class: 2005; List A: 2006; T20: 2009

BEST BATTING: 101* Leicestershire vs Derbyshire, Derby, 2010
BEST BOWLING: 5-87 Derbyshire vs Northamptonshire, Northampton, 2007

FAMILY TIES? Brother [Harry] is on the Derbyshire academy
CAREER HIGHLIGHTS? Winning the FL t20 and first hundred
CRICKETING HEROES? Mike Hendrick, Dominic Cork
BEST PLAYER IN COUNTY CRICKET? Marcus Trescothick
TIPS FOR THE TOP? Shiv Thakor, Liam Kinch
IF YOU WEREN'T A CRICKETER? Trying to be a footballer
WHEN RAIN STOPS PLAY? iPod, Football Manager, annoying everyone
FAVOURITE TV? 90210
FAVOURITE FILM? Saving Private Ryan, Gladiator
FAVOURITE BOOK? Cricketers' Who's Who
DREAM HOLIDAY? Grenada, Ibiza
ACCOMPLISHMENTS? Playing in the FA Cup, four years no claims on my car insurance
SURPRISING SKILL? DJ
GUILTY PLEASURES? Dunking biscuits
AMAZE ME! I'm a Derby County fan, I'm unbeaten on FIFA 12 on PS3, I took Burton Albion to the Premier League on Football Manager
TWITTER FEED: @wayneAwhite

| Batting | Mat | Inns | NO | Runs | HS | Ave | SR | 100 | 50 | Ct | St |
|---|---|---|---|---|---|---|---|---|---|---|---|
| First-class | 46 | 74 | 8 | 1669 | 101* | 25.28 | 51.49 | 1 | 8 | 19 | 0 |
| List A | 47 | 38 | 13 | 468 | 46* | 18.72 | 89.82 | 0 | 0 | 11 | 0 |
| Twenty20 | 39 | 27 | 12 | 231 | 26 | 15.40 | 114.92 | 0 | 0 | 21 | 0 |

| Bowling | Mat | Balls | Runs | Wkts | BBI | BBM | Ave | Econ | SR | 5w | 10 |
|---|---|---|---|---|---|---|---|---|---|---|---|
| First-class | 46 | 5506 | 3717 | 96 | 5/87 | | 38.71 | 4.05 | 57.3 | 1 | 0 |
| List A | 47 | 1522 | 1615 | 40 | 6/29 | 6/29 | 40.37 | 6.36 | 38.0 | 1 | 0 |
| Twenty20 | 39 | 495 | 765 | 16 | 3/27 | 3/27 | 47.81 | 9.27 | 30.9 | 0 | 0 |

# ROSS WHITELEY

**LHB LM**

DERBYSHIRE

**FULL NAME:** Ross Andrew Whiteley
**BORN:** September 13, 1988, Sheffield, Yorkshire
**SQUAD NO:** 44
**HEIGHT:** 6ft 2in
**NICKNAME:** Rossco, Pico, Brick
**EDUCATION:** Westfield School; Repton School; Leeds Metropolitan University
**TEAMS:** Derbyshire, Derbyshire 2nd XI
**CAREER:** First-class: 2008; List A: 2008; T20: 2011

**BEST BATTING:** 130* Derbyshire vs Kent, Derby, 2011
**BEST BOWLING:** 1-21 Derbyshire vs Glamorgan, Derby, 2011

**FAMILY TIES?** Brother Adam played Derbyshire age groups and 2nd XI cricket
**CAREER HIGHLIGHTS?** Maiden century at Northampton, signing my first professional contract
**SUPERSTITIONS?** Every time I am on strike I scrape my mark three times
**CRICKETING HEROES?** Martin Guptill, Shane Warne, Ben Hilfenhaus
**NON-CRICKETING HEROES?** Buddy Franklin – Hawthorn Hawks
**TIPS FOR THE TOP?** Will Beer, Tom Poynton, Greg Smith
**IF YOU WEREN'T A CRICKETER?** Playing some other form of sport
**FAVOURITE BOOK?** Sniper One
**TWITTER FEED:** @RossWhiteley44

| Batting | Mat | Inns | NO | Runs | HS | Ave | SR | 100 | 50 | Ct | St |
|---|---|---|---|---|---|---|---|---|---|---|---|
| First-class | 12 | 22 | 4 | 689 | 130* | 38.27 | 49.71 | 2 | 2 | 9 | 0 |
| List A | 11 | 10 | 1 | 147 | 40 | 16.33 | 88.55 | 0 | 0 | 4 | 0 |
| Twenty20 | 12 | 11 | 7 | 215 | 40* | 53.75 | 141.44 | 0 | 0 | 2 | 0 |

| Bowling | Mat | Balls | Runs | Wkts | BBI | BBM | Ave | Econ | SR | 5w | 10 |
|---|---|---|---|---|---|---|---|---|---|---|---|
| First-class | 12 | 618 | 423 | 6 | 1/21 | 2/82 | 70.50 | 4.10 | 103.0 | 0 | 0 |
| List A | 11 | 72 | 70 | 1 | 1/26 | 1/26 | 70.00 | 5.83 | 72.0 | 0 | 0 |
| Twenty20 | 12 | 36 | 46 | 2 | 1/12 | 1/12 | 23.00 | 7.66 | 18.0 | 0 | 0 |

# DAVID WILLEY

## LHB LFM

**FULL NAME:** David Jonathan Willey
**BORN:** February 28, 1990, Northampton
**SQUAD NO:** 15
**HEIGHT:** 6ft 1in
**NICKNAME:** Willow, Will
**EDUCATION:** Northampton School for Boys
**TEAMS:** England Under-19s, Northamptonshire, Northamptonshire 2nd XI
**CAREER:** First-class: 2009; List A: 2009; T20: 2009

---

**BEST BATTING:** 64 Northamptonshire vs Gloucestershire, Northampton, 2011
**BEST BOWLING:** 5-29 Northamptonshire vs Gloucestershire, Northampton, 2011

---

**FAMILY TIES?** Father played for Leicester, Northants and England
**SUPERSTITIONS?** Left pad on first, turn right before starting run-up when bowling
**TIP FOR THE TOP?** Ben Duckett
**IF YOU WEREN'T A CRICKETER?** On the beach somewhere hot!
**FAVOURITE TV?** 24
**FAVOURITE FILM?** The Inbetweeners
**FAVOURITE BOOK?** Muhammad Ali – The Soul of a Butterfly
**DREAM HOLIDAY?** Cook Islands
**GUILTY PLEASURES?** Gardening
**FANTASY SLIP CORDON?** Keeper: Celine Dion, 1st: Princess Diana, 2nd: Myself, 3rd: Jamie Oliver, Gully: Kevin Richardson (the Lion Whisperer)
**TWITTER FEED:** @david_willey

| Batting | Mat | Inns | NO | Runs | HS | Ave | SR | 100 | 50 | Ct | St |
|---|---|---|---|---|---|---|---|---|---|---|---|
| First-class | 15 | 23 | 4 | 490 | 64 | 25.78 | 40.16 | 0 | 3 | 4 | 0 |
| List A | 30 | 22 | 4 | 348 | 74 | 19.33 | 83.85 | 0 | 2 | 11 | 0 |
| Twenty20 | 39 | 22 | 9 | 163 | 22* | 12.53 | 104.48 | 0 | 0 | 14 | 0 |

| Bowling | Mat | Balls | Runs | Wkts | BBI | BBM | Ave | Econ | SR | 5w | 10 |
|---|---|---|---|---|---|---|---|---|---|---|---|
| First-class | 15 | 1109 | 681 | 25 | 5/29 | 10/75 | 27.24 | 3.68 | 44.3 | 2 | 1 |
| List A | 30 | 755 | 735 | 20 | 3/49 | 3/49 | 36.75 | 5.84 | 37.7 | 0 | 0 |
| Twenty20 | 39 | 372 | 442 | 27 | 3/9 | 3/9 | 16.37 | 7.12 | 13.7 | 0 | 0 |

# ROBBIE WILLIAMS

### RHB RFM

FULL NAME: Robert Edward Morgan Williams
BORN: January 19, 1987, Pembury, Kent
SQUAD NO: 16
HEIGHT: 6ft
EDUCATION: Marlborough School; Durham University
TEAMS: Durham MCCU, Marylebone Cricket Club, Middlesex, Middlesex 2nd XI
CAREER: First-class: 2007; List A: 2007; T20: 2010

BEST BATTING: 31 DUCCE vs Lancashire, Durham University, 2009
BEST BOWLING: 5-70 DUCCE vs Lancashire, Durham University, 2007

CAREER HIGHLIGHTS? Taking five wickets on Championship debut and playing against the Australians with Adam Gilchrist
CRICKETING HEROES? Malcolm Marshall, Dale Steyn, Adam Gilchrist
NON-CRICKETING HEROES? Roger Federer, David Attenborough, Jamie Oliver
BEST PLAYER IN COUNTY CRICKET? Marcus Trescothick
TIP FOR THE TOP? Adam Rossington
IF YOU WEREN'T A CRICKETER? Playing table tennis
WHEN RAIN STOPS PLAY? I attempt to do crosswords
FAVOURITE TV? Family Guy
FAVOURITE FILM? Willy Wonka And The Chocolate Factory or Inception
FAVOURITE BOOK? Man's Search For Meaning by Victor Frankl
DREAM HOLIDAY? A villa in France or Italy
ACCOMPLISHMENTS? Getting a degree from university
GUILTY PLEASURES? Fast food, Dr Pepper, a couple of Katy Perry songs
AMAZE ME! I do Bikram Yoga and I can move my eyebrows independently of each other
FANTASY SLIP CORDON? Keeper: Michael McIntyre, 1st: Doctor Who, 2nd: Sherlock Holmes, 3rd: Myself, Gully: Jamie Oliver

| Batting | Mat | Inns | NO | Runs | HS | Ave | SR | 100 | 50 | Ct | St |
|---|---|---|---|---|---|---|---|---|---|---|---|
| First-class | 9 | 15 | 5 | 119 | 31 | 11.90 | 35.95 | 0 | 0 | 4 | 0 |
| List A | 7 | 1 | 1 | 2 | 2* | - | 28.57 | 0 | 0 | 1 | 0 |
| Twenty20 | 2 | - | - | - | - | - | - | - | - | 0 | 0 |

| Bowling | Mat | Balls | Runs | Wkts | BBI | BBM | Ave | Econ | SR | 5w | 10 |
|---|---|---|---|---|---|---|---|---|---|---|---|
| First-class | 9 | 1241 | 755 | 23 | 5/70 | 5/115 | 32.82 | 3.65 | 53.9 | 2 | 0 |
| List A | 7 | 227 | 305 | 2 | 2/60 | 2/60 | 152.50 | 8.06 | 113.5 | 0 | 0 |
| Twenty20 | 2 | 24 | 55 | 0 | - | - | - | 13.75 | - | 0 | 0 |

# CHARL WILLOUGHBY

## LHB LFM W6

**FULL NAME:** Charl Myles Willoughby
**BORN:** December 3, 1974, Cape Town, South Africa
**SQUAD NO:** 1
**HEIGHT:** 6ft 3in
**NICKNAME:** Puppy, Harry
**EDUCATION:** Wynberg Boys' High School; Stellenbosch University
**TEAMS:** South Africa, Boland, Cape Cobras, Essex, Leicestershire, Somerset, Western Province, Western Province Boland
**CAREER:** Test: 2003; ODI: 2000; First-class 1994; List A 1994; T20: 2004

**ESSEX**

---

**BEST BATTING:** 47 Somerset vs Worcestershire, Taunton, 2006
**BEST BOWLING:** 7-44 Somerset vs Gloucestershire, Taunton, 2006
**COUNTY CAPS:** 2005 (Leicestershire); 2007 (Somerset)

---

**CAREER HIGHLIGHTS?** Test and ODI debuts, taking four wickets in four balls in first-class match vs Dolphins
**CRICKET MOMENT TO FORGET?** Dislocating my shoulder diving on the boundary
**CRICKETERS PARTICULARLY ADMIRED?** Graeme Smith, Andrew Flintoff, Wasim Akram
**OTHER SPORTS FOLLOWED?** Rugby (Stormers)
**FAVOURITE BAND?** Coldplay
**NOTES:** Signed a two-year contract with Essex in November 2011 after six years at Somerset. Took 54 first-class wickets for Somerset in 15 matches in 2011, to go with 347 first-class wickets in all for the club

| Batting | Mat | Inns | NO | Runs | HS | Ave | SR | 100 | 50 | Ct | St |
|---|---|---|---|---|---|---|---|---|---|---|---|
| Tests | 2 | - | - | - | - | - | - | - | - | 0 | 0 |
| ODIs | 3 | 2 | 0 | 0 | 0 | 0.00 | 0.00 | 0 | 0 | 0 | 0 |
| First-class | 225 | 253 | 111 | 871 | 47 | 6.13 | | 0 | 0 | 44 | 0 |
| List A | 209 | 61 | 32 | 147 | 15 | 5.06 | | 0 | 0 | 26 | 0 |
| Twenty20 | 67 | 16 | 11 | 28 | 11 | 5.60 | 112.00 | 0 | 0 | 11 | 0 |

| Bowling | Mat | Balls | Runs | Wkts | BBI | BBM | Ave | Econ | SR | 5w | 10 |
|---|---|---|---|---|---|---|---|---|---|---|---|
| Tests | 2 | 300 | 125 | 1 | 1/47 | 1/79 | 125.00 | 2.50 | 300.0 | 0 | 0 |
| ODIs | 3 | 168 | 148 | 2 | 2/39 | 2/39 | 74.00 | 5.28 | 84.0 | 0 | 0 |
| First-class | 225 | 45104 | 21418 | 829 | 7/44 | | 25.83 | 2.84 | 54.4 | 32 | 3 |
| List A | 209 | 10164 | 7094 | 255 | 6/16 | 6/16 | 27.81 | 4.18 | 39.8 | 5 | 0 |
| Twenty20 | 67 | 1463 | 1729 | 71 | 4/9 | 4/9 | 24.35 | 7.09 | 20.6 | 0 | 0 |

# GARY WILSON

## RHB WK

**FULL NAME:** Gary Craig Wilson
**BORN:** February 5, 1986, Dundonald, Northern Ireland
**SQUAD NO:** 14
**HEIGHT:** 5ft 9in
**NICKNAME:** Gaz, Wils, Suede
**EDUCATION:** Methodist College, Belfast
**TEAMS:** Ireland, Ireland Under-19s, Surrey, Surrey 2nd XI
**CAREER:** ODI: 2007; T20I: 2008; First-class: 2005; List A: 2006; T20: 2008

**BEST BATTING:** 125 Surrey vs Leicestershire, Leicester, 2010

**CAREER HIGHLIGHTS?** Playing in the World Cup and beating England, plus my maiden Championship and ODI hundreds
**CRICKETING HEROES?** Alec Stewart
**NON-CRICKETING HEROES?** David Beckham, Sir Alex Ferguson
**TIPS FOR THE TOP?** Jason Roy, Tom Maynard, Paul Stirling
**IF YOU WEREN'T A CRICKETER?** Probably a fireman or policeman
**WHEN RAIN STOPS PLAY?** On the Internet, thinking about where I can play golf next
**FAVOURITE TV?** Spooks, The Apprentice, TOWIE
**DREAM HOLIDAY?** Zanzibar
**GUILTY PLEASURES?** Haribo sweets, Sensations crisps
**AMAZE ME!** I have the biggest head in the changing room in terms of volume, I played Ulster Schools rugby
**FANTASY SLIP CORDON?** Keeper: David Beckham, 1st: Myself, 2nd: Sir Alex Ferguson, 3rd: Michael McIntyre, Gully: Tiger Woods
**TWITTER FEED:** @Gwilson14

| Batting | Mat | Inns | NO | Runs | HS | Ave | SR | 100 | 50 | Ct | St |
|---|---|---|---|---|---|---|---|---|---|---|---|
| ODIs | 37 | 36 | 3 | 952 | 113 | 28.84 | 75.85 | 1 | 6 | 23 | 7 |
| T20Is | 17 | 15 | 2 | 247 | 32 | 19.00 | 82.60 | 0 | 0 | 8 | 0 |
| First-class | 24 | 37 | 3 | 888 | 125 | 26.11 | | 1 | 3 | 41 | 1 |
| List A | 89 | 79 | 6 | 1735 | 113 | 23.76 | 69.98 | 1 | 12 | 60 | 18 |
| Twenty20 | 45 | 36 | 8 | 486 | 49 | 17.35 | 99.38 | 0 | 0 | 25 | 5 |

| Bowling | Mat | Balls | Runs | Wkts | BBI | BBM | Ave | Econ | SR | 5w | 10 |
|---|---|---|---|---|---|---|---|---|---|---|---|
| ODIs | 37 | - | - | - | - | - | - | - | - | - | - |
| T20Is | 17 | - | - | - | - | - | - | - | - | - | - |
| First-class | 24 | 66 | 46 | 0 | - | - | - | 4.18 | - | 0 | 0 |
| List A | 89 | - | - | - | - | - | - | - | - | - | - |
| Twenty20 | 45 | - | - | - | - | - | - | - | - | - | - |

# MITCH WILSON

## RHB RFM

**FULL NAME:** Mitchell James Wilson
**BORN:** June 10, 1992, Poole, Dorset
**SQUAD NO:** 25
**HEIGHT:** 5ft 11in
**EDUCATION:** Poole Grammar School;
Bryanston School, Blandford; Cardiff
Metropolitan University
**TEAMS:** Cardiff MCCU, Dorset, Dorset Under-
17s, Gloucestershire, Gloucestershire 2nd XI
**CAREER:** Yet to make first-team debut

**TWITTER FEED:** @Mitch_Wilson25
**NOTES:** Claimed 10 wickets at 28.20 in the 2010 Minor Counties Championship, which led former Derbyshire head coach John Morris to offer him a contract at the start of the 2011 season. Plays for Swarkestone CC in the Derbyshire County Cricket League Divison One, alongside Derbyshire teammates Tom Poynton and Ross Whiteley. Claimed 29 wickets at 23.38 for the club in 2011. His Twitter account description of himself reads: "Derbyshire CCC cricketer, student at UWIC. From Poole. Bryanston alumni. Appreciates good food, good music, good coffee, and good company. Boar"

## CHRIS WOAKES      RHB RMF W2 MVP7

**WARWICKSHIRE**

FULL NAME: Christopher Roger Woakes
BORN: March 2, 1989, Birmingham, Warwickshire
SQUAD NO: 19
HEIGHT: 6ft 1in
NICKNAME: Woaksy, Woako, Wiz, GB
EDUCATION: Barr Beacon School
TEAMS: England, England Lions, England Under-19s, Herefordshire, Marylebone Cricket Club, Warwickshire
CAREER: ODI: 2011; T20I: 2011; First-class: 2006; List A: 2007; T20: 2008

BEST BATTING: 136* Warwickshire vs Hampshire, Birmingham, 2010
BEST BOWLING: 7-20 Warwickshire vs Hampshire, Birmingham, 2011
COUNTY CAP: 2009

CAREER HIGHLIGHTS? Winning the CB40 in 2010 with Warwickshire. Making debut for England in Australia in January 2011
CRICKETING HEROES? Jacques Kallis
NON-CRICKETING HEROES? Paul 'God' McGrath
TIP FOR THE TOP? Tom Milnes
WHEN RAIN STOPS PLAY? Eat, relax, or play a silly game called Tit!
FAVOURITE TV? An Idiot Abroad or A League Of Their Own
FAVOURITE FILM? Gladiator, The Hangover, Old School
FAVOURITE BOOK? Paul McGrath's autobiography
FANTASY SLIP CORDON? Keeper: Shay Given, 1st: Myself, 2nd: Angelina Jolie, 3rd: Karl Pilkington, Gully: David Beckham
TWITTER FEED: @crwoakes19

| Batting | Mat | Inns | NO | Runs | HS | Ave | SR | 100 | 50 | Ct | St |
|---|---|---|---|---|---|---|---|---|---|---|---|
| ODIs | 4 | 4 | 2 | 39 | 19* | 19.50 | 73.58 | 0 | 0 | 1 | 0 |
| T20Is | 3 | 3 | 2 | 37 | 19* | 37.00 | 123.33 | 0 | 0 | 1 | 0 |
| First-class | 61 | 81 | 21 | 2002 | 136* | 33.36 | | 4 | 8 | 32 | 0 |
| List A | 59 | 36 | 12 | 444 | 49* | 18.50 | 90.06 | 0 | 0 | 13 | 0 |
| Twenty20 | 45 | 24 | 14 | 252 | 44* | 25.20 | 134.75 | 0 | 0 | 22 | 0 |

| Bowling | Mat | Balls | Runs | Wkts | BBI | BBM | Ave | Econ | SR | 5w | 10 |
|---|---|---|---|---|---|---|---|---|---|---|---|
| ODIs | 4 | 194 | 169 | 7 | 6/45 | 6/45 | 24.14 | 5.22 | 27.7 | 1 | 0 |
| T20Is | 3 | 60 | 94 | 2 | 1/29 | 1/29 | 47.00 | 9.40 | 30.0 | 0 | 0 |
| First-class | 61 | 10695 | 5487 | 223 | 7/20 | 11/97 | 24.60 | 3.07 | 47.9 | 12 | 3 |
| List A | 59 | 2218 | 2015 | 58 | 6/45 | 6/45 | 34.74 | 5.45 | 38.2 | 1 | 0 |
| Twenty20 | 45 | 796 | 1088 | 38 | 4/21 | 4/21 | 28.63 | 8.20 | 20.9 | 0 | 0 |

## CHRIS WOOD
### RHB LMF

**FULL NAME:** Christopher Philip Wood
**BORN:** June 27, 1990, Basingstoke, Hampshire
**SQUAD NO:** 25
**HEIGHT:** 6ft 3in
**NICKNAME:** Woody
**EDUCATION:** Amery Hill Secondary School; Alton College
**TEAMS:** England Under-19s, Hampshire, Hampshire 2nd XI
**CAREER:** First-class: 2010; List A: 2010; T20: 2010

BEST BATTING: 56* Hampshire vs Worcestershire, Southampton, 2011
BEST BOWLING: 5-54 Hampshire vs OMCCU, The Parks, 2010

FAMILY TIES? Dad played for Witley CC
CAREER HIGHLIGHTS? Winning the 2010 T20 competition
SUPERSTITIONS? Always put my right shoe on before the left
CRICKETING HEROES? Freddie Flintoff
NON-CRICKETING HEROES? David Beckham
TIPS FOR THE TOP? James Vince, James Taylor, Ben Stokes
IF YOU WEREN'T A CRICKETER? Dustbin man
WHEN RAIN STOPS PLAY? Listening to music, playing on my phone, or playing poker
FAVOURITE TV? League Of Their Own
FAVOURITE FILM? Snatch
DREAM HOLIDAY? Las Vegas
ACCOMPLISHMENTS? Played in the FA Cup
AMAZE ME! I'm the best in the Hampshire dressing room at FIFA, trialled for Chelsea, addicted to McDonald's
FANTASY SLIP CORDON? Keeper: Kelly Brook, 1st: Katy Perry, 2nd: Cheryl Cole, 3rd: Kim Kardashian, Gully: Delta White – why do you think?
TWITTER FEED: @CWoody27

| Batting | Mat | Inns | NO | Runs | HS | Ave | SR | 100 | 50 | Ct | St |
|---|---|---|---|---|---|---|---|---|---|---|---|
| First-class | 11 | 15 | 1 | 327 | 56* | 23.35 | 70.47 | 0 | 1 | 4 | 0 |
| List A | 20 | 11 | 3 | 49 | 14* | 6.12 | 70.00 | 0 | 0 | 7 | 0 |
| Twenty20 | 32 | 10 | 3 | 50 | 18 | 7.14 | 94.33 | 0 | 0 | 12 | 0 |

| Bowling | Mat | Balls | Runs | Wkts | BBI | BBM | Ave | Econ | SR | 5w | 10 |
|---|---|---|---|---|---|---|---|---|---|---|---|
| First-class | 11 | 1583 | 911 | 37 | 5/54 | 7/84 | 24.62 | 3.45 | 42.7 | 1 | 0 |
| List A | 20 | 784 | 727 | 36 | 4/33 | 4/33 | 20.19 | 5.56 | 21.7 | 0 | 0 |
| Twenty20 | 32 | 594 | 831 | 31 | 3/27 | 3/27 | 26.80 | 8.39 | 19.1 | 0 | 0 |

## MARK WOOD — RHB RMF

**DURHAM**

FULL NAME: Mark Andrew Wood
BORN: January 11, 1990, Ashington, Northumberland
SQUAD NO: 33
HEIGHT: 6ft
NICKNAME: Woody
EDUCATION: Ashington High School
TEAMS: Durham, Durham 2nd XI, Durham Academy, Northumberland, Northumberland Under-13s, Northumberland Under-15s, Northumberland Under-17s
CAREER: First-class 2011; List A 2011

BEST BATTING: 48 Durham vs Sri Lanka A, Chester-le-Street, 2011
BEST BOWLING: 3-72 Durham vs Nottinghamshire, Trent Bridge, 2011

FAMILY TIES? Neil Wood (uncle) and Derek Wood (dad) played minor counties cricket for Northumberland
CAREER HIGHLIGHTS? Championship debut at Trent Bridge
CRICKETING HEROES? Stephen Harmison, Graham Onions and Michael Holding
NON-CRICKETING HEROES? Lennox Lewis, Vinnie Jones
BEST PLAYER IN COUNTY CRICKET? Marcus Trescothick
TIPS FOR THE TOP? Ben Stokes, Jonny Bairstow and Scott Borthwick
IF YOU WEREN'T A CRICKETER? I'd be a PE teacher
WHEN RAIN STOPS PLAY? Kicking the football around with Chris Rushworth or watching Mitchell Claydon's card tricks
FAVOURITE TV? Misfits, Scrubs, and Two And A Half Men
FAVOURITE FILM? The Other Guys
DREAM HOLIDAY? Barbados
SURPRISING FACTS? I share the same birthday as my dad, I played football for Newcastle United as a kid and I support AFC Wimbledon

| Batting | Mat | Inns | NO | Runs | HS | Ave | SR | 100 | 50 | Ct | St |
|---|---|---|---|---|---|---|---|---|---|---|---|
| First-class | 3 | 5 | 1 | 118 | 48 | 29.50 | 73.75 | 0 | 0 | 2 | 0 |
| List A | 3 | 2 | 0 | 6 | 5 | 3.00 | 50.00 | 0 | 0 | 1 | 0 |

| Bowling | Mat | Balls | Runs | Wkts | BBI | BBM | Ave | Econ | SR | 5w | 10 |
|---|---|---|---|---|---|---|---|---|---|---|---|
| First-class | 3 | 342 | 264 | 10 | 3/72 | 5/129 | 26.40 | 4.63 | 34.2 | 0 | 0 |
| List A | 3 | 84 | 62 | 1 | 1/28 | 1/28 | 62.00 | 4.42 | 84.0 | 0 | 0 |

# SAM WOOD

**LHB OB**

**FULL NAME:** Samuel Kenneth William Wood
**BORN:** April 3, 1993, Nottingham
**SQUAD NO:** 23
**HEIGHT:** 6ft
**NICKNAME:** Woody, Swood, Gorm
**EDUCATION:** Colonel Frank Seely School; West Nottinghamshire College; South Nottinghamshire College
**TEAMS:** England Under-19s, Nottinghamshire, Nottinghamshire 2nd XI, Nottinghamshire Under-15s, Nottinghamshire Under-17s
**CAREER:** First-class: 2011; List A: 2011

**CAREER HIGHLIGHTS?** Representing England U19, making my debut for Notts in one-day and four-day cricket, signing my first professional contract
**CRICKETING HEROES?** Marcus Trescothick, Mike Hussey, Brian Lara
**NON-CRICKETING HEROES?** Muhammad Ali
**BEST PLAYER IN COUNTY CRICKET?** Andre Adams
**TIPS FOR THE TOP?** Tom Rowe, Simon Webster
**IF YOU WEREN'T A CRICKETER?** I'd be going to university
**WHEN RAIN STOPS PLAY?** Listen to music, put the feet up
**FAVOURITE TV?** Coronation Street, The Inbetweeners
**FAVOURITE FILM?** Man On Fire
**FAVOURITE BOOK?** Muhammad Ali's autobiography
**DREAM HOLIDAY?** Abu Dhabi
**AMAZE ME!** I made my Notts Premier League debut when I was 10 for Blidworth
**FANTASY SLIP CORDON?** Keeper: Peter Kay, 1st: Michael Hall, 2nd: Megan Fox, 3rd: Luke Fletcher, Gully: Myself

| Batting | Mat | Inns | NO | Runs | HS | Ave | SR | 100 | 50 | Ct | St |
|---|---|---|---|---|---|---|---|---|---|---|---|
| First-class | 1 | - | - | - | - | - | - | - | - | 0 | 0 |
| List A | 4 | 3 | 0 | 8 | 8 | 2.66 | 47.05 | 0 | 0 | 2 | 0 |

| Bowling | Mat | Balls | Runs | Wkts | BBI | BBM | Ave | Econ | SR | 5w | 10 |
|---|---|---|---|---|---|---|---|---|---|---|---|
| First-class | 1 | 24 | 8 | 0 | - | - | - | 2.00 | - | 0 | 0 |
| List A | 4 | 66 | 72 | 3 | 2/24 | 2/24 | 24.00 | 6.54 | 22.0 | 0 | 0 |

## BEN WRIGHT

**RHB RM**

GLAMORGAN

FULL NAME: Ben James Wright
BORN: December 5, 1987, Preston, Lancashire
SQUAD NO: 29
HEIGHT: 5ft 11in
NICKNAME: Bej, Killer
EDUCATION: Cowbridge Comprehensive
TEAMS: England Under-19s, Glamorgan, Wales Minor Counties
CAREER: First-class: 2006; List A: 2006; T20: 2007

BEST BATTING: 172 Glamorgan vs Gloucestershire, Cardiff, 2007
BEST BOWLING: 1-14 Glamorgan vs Essex, Chelmsford, 2007
COUNTY CAP: 2011

CAREER HIGHLIGHTS? Scoring a hundred vs Middlesex at Lord's
CRICKETING HEROES? Andrew Flintoff, Matthew Maynard
NON-CRICKETING HEROES? Jonny Wilkinson
BEST PLAYER IN COUNTY CRICKET? Marcus Trescothick
TIP FOR THE TOP? Andrew Salter
IF YOU WEREN'T A CRICKETER? Fitness trainer
WHEN RAIN STOPS PLAY? Annoying people
FAVOURITE TV? Eastbound And Down
FAVOURITE FILM? Wedding Crashers
FAVOURITE BOOK? Jonny Wilkinson's autobiography
DREAM HOLIDAY? Hawaii
ACCOMPLISHMENTS? Playing rugby at U16 for Wales
GUILTY PLEASURES? Pizza
TWITTER FEED: @bej29w

| Batting | Mat | Inns | NO | Runs | HS | Ave | SR | 100 | 50 | Ct | St |
|---|---|---|---|---|---|---|---|---|---|---|---|
| First-class | 47 | 76 | 4 | 1987 | 172 | 27.59 | 52.00 | 4 | 10 | 28 | 0 |
| List A | 54 | 51 | 7 | 1037 | 79 | 23.56 | 70.30 | 0 | 5 | 12 | 0 |
| Twenty20 | 33 | 29 | 10 | 433 | 55* | 22.78 | 105.86 | 0 | 1 | 11 | 0 |

| Bowling | Mat | Balls | Runs | Wkts | BBI | BBM | Ave | Econ | SR | 5w | 10 |
|---|---|---|---|---|---|---|---|---|---|---|---|
| First-class | 47 | 192 | 137 | 2 | 1/14 | 1/14 | 68.50 | 4.28 | 96.0 | 0 | 0 |
| List A | 54 | 132 | 126 | 1 | 1/19 | 1/19 | 126.00 | 5.72 | 132.0 | 0 | 0 |
| Twenty20 | 33 | 24 | 22 | 1 | 1/16 | 1/16 | 22.00 | 5.50 | 24.0 | 0 | 0 |

# CHRIS WRIGHT

### RHB RFM

**FULL NAME:** Christopher Julian Clement Wright
**BORN:** July 14, 1985, Chipping Norton, Oxfordshire
**SQUAD NO:** 31
**HEIGHT:** 6ft 3in
**NICKNAME:** Wrighty, Baron, Almunia,
**EDUCATION:** Eggars Grammar School, Alton
**TEAMS:** British Universities, Cambridge MCCU, Essex, Hampshire 2nd XI, Middlesex, Tamil Union Cricket and Athletic Club, Warwickshire
**CAREER:** First-class: 2004; List A: 2004; T20: 2004

**BEST BATTING:** 77 Essex vs CMCCU, Fenner's, 2011
**BEST BOWLING:** 6-22 Essex vs Leicestershire, Leicester, 2008

**CAREER HIGHLIGHTS?** FP Trophy win at Lord's for Essex and getting promoted to Division One the following season
**SUPERSTITIONS?** If I give my cap or jumper to the umpire in a certain way and I bowl well then I repeat it. If not, I get someone else to do it until I bowl well
**TIP FOR THE TOP?** Tymal Mills
**IF YOU WEREN'T A CRICKETER?** I'd try to be a master chef or poker player. Or maybe coaching or working for my dad's business
**FAVOURITE TV?** Prison Break, Modern Family, Dexter and Biggest Loser
**ACCOMPLISHMENTS?** Having an awesome little boy who is very clever and well-behaved, with his mum being key to this!
**GUILTY PLEASURES?** Gambling, Krispy Kreme Doughnuts and watching too much sport
**AMAZE ME!** When I was very young and naive I missed a pre-season cricket match to play in the Irish Open Poker Tournament, with a buy-in of 10,000 Euros. I got knocked out on day one, got drunk and missed my flight home!
**FANTASY SLIP CORDON?** Keeper: Jimmy Carr, 1st: Tony Palladino, 2nd: Phil Edwards, 3rd: Matt Hooper, Gully: Me
**TWITTER FEED:** @chriswright1985

| Batting | Mat | Inns | NO | Runs | HS | Ave | SR | 100 | 50 | Ct | St |
|---|---|---|---|---|---|---|---|---|---|---|---|
| First-class | 63 | 82 | 20 | 1152 | 77 | 18.58 | 52.60 | 0 | 4 | 13 | 0 |
| List A | 67 | 28 | 11 | 183 | 42 | 10.76 | 78.87 | 0 | 0 | 14 | 0 |
| Twenty20 | 38 | 9 | 6 | 16 | 6* | 5.33 | 106.66 | 0 | 0 | 5 | 0 |

| Bowling | Mat | Balls | Runs | Wkts | BBI | BBM | Ave | Econ | SR | 5w | 10 |
|---|---|---|---|---|---|---|---|---|---|---|---|
| First-class | 63 | 9982 | 6166 | 157 | 6/22 | | 39.27 | 3.70 | 63.5 | 4 | 0 |
| List A | 67 | 2531 | 2350 | 60 | 4/20 | 4/20 | 39.16 | 5.57 | 42.1 | 0 | 0 |
| Twenty20 | 38 | 752 | 1114 | 35 | 4/24 | 4/24 | 31.82 | 8.88 | 21.4 | 0 | 0 |

## LUKE WRIGHT                                    RHB RMF

**SUSSEX**

FULL NAME: Luke James Wright
BORN: March 7, 1985, Grantham, Lincolnshire
SQUAD NO: 10
HEIGHT: 6ft
NICKNAME: Wrighty
EDUCATION: Belvoir High School; Ratcliffe College; Loughborough University
TEAMS: England, England Lions, England Under-19s, Impi, Leicestershire, Melbourne Stars, Sussex, Wellington
CAREER: ODI: 2007; T20I: 2007; First-class: 2003; List A 2002; T20: 2004

BEST BATTING: 155* Sussex vs MCC, Lord's, 2008
BEST BOWLING: 5-65 Sussex vs Derbyshire, Derby, 2010
COUNTY CAP: 2007 (Sussex)

FAMILY TIES? Father very keen cricketer (Level 2 coach). Brother Ashley played for Leicestershire
SUPERSTITIONS? Too many to name
CRICKETERS PARTICULARLY ADMIRED? Jacques Kallis, Andrew Flintoff
OTHER SPORTS FOLLOWED? Football (Newcastle United)
OTHER SPORTS PLAYED? Football, hockey, squash, tennis
RELAXATIONS? Music, cinema, going out
NOTES: Has won the Denis Compton Medal three times. Scored exactly 100 on his first-class debut for Sussex, against Loughborough UCCE – both the bowler (Chris Nash) and the catcher (Monty Panesar) involved in his dismissal are now teammates at Sussex. Scored a half-century on ODI debut against India at The Oval

| Batting | Mat | Inns | NO | Runs | HS | Ave | SR | 100 | 50 | Ct | St |
|---|---|---|---|---|---|---|---|---|---|---|---|
| ODIs | 46 | 35 | 4 | 701 | 52 | 22.61 | 89.29 | 0 | 2 | 17 | 0 |
| T20Is | 30 | 25 | 2 | 355 | 71 | 15.43 | 125.44 | 0 | 1 | 10 | 0 |
| First-class | 70 | 100 | 15 | 3104 | 155* | 36.51 | 65.84 | 9 | 15 | 29 | 0 |
| List A | 147 | 114 | 19 | 2305 | 125 | 24.26 | | | 1 | 6 | 45 | 0 |
| Twenty20 | 113 | 97 | 10 | 2110 | 117 | 24.25 | 144.71 | 2 | 7 | 37 | 0 |

| Bowling | Mat | Balls | Runs | Wkts | BBI | BBM | Ave | Econ | SR | 5w | 10 |
|---|---|---|---|---|---|---|---|---|---|---|---|
| ODIs | 46 | 1020 | 863 | 15 | 2/34 | 2/34 | 57.53 | 5.07 | 68.0 | 0 | 0 |
| T20Is | 30 | 156 | 219 | 6 | 1/5 | 1/5 | 36.50 | 8.42 | 26.0 | 0 | 0 |
| First-class | 70 | 6965 | 4070 | 106 | 5/65 | | 38.39 | 3.50 | 65.7 | 3 | 0 |
| List A | 147 | 4527 | 3973 | 102 | 4/12 | 4/12 | 38.95 | 5.26 | 44.3 | 0 | 0 |
| Twenty20 | 113 | 1278 | 1764 | 56 | 3/17 | 3/17 | 31.50 | 8.28 | 22.8 | 0 | 0 |

# ALEX WYATT

FULL NAME: Alexander Wyatt
BORN: July 23, 1990, Roehampton
SQUAD NO: 16
HEIGHT: 6ft 7in
NICKNAME: Waz, Goobs
EDUCATION: Oakham School
TEAMS: Leicestershire, Leicestershire 2nd XI
CAREER: First-class: 2009; List A: 2009; T20: 2009

BEST BATTING: 4* Leicestershire vs Middlesex, Leicester, 2011
BEST BOWLING: 3-42 Leicestershire vs West Indians, Leicester, 2009

WHY CRICKET? When I was six I started playing Kwik Cricket with school friends and then got hooked
CAREER HIGHLIGHTS? Making my first-class, List A and T20 debuts in 2009. Being able to travel the world through links with the game
CRICKETING HEROES? Glenn McGrath, Darren Gough, Andrew Caddick, Wayne White
NON-CRICKETING HEROES? My parents
BEST PLAYER IN COUNTY CRICKET? David Masters is an amazing bowler and the epitome of a hard-working county seamer
TIPS FOR THE TOP? Josh Cobb, Nathan Buck, Greg Smith
IF YOU WEREN'T A CRICKETER? I'd still be at university trying to obtain a degree
WHEN RAIN STOPS PLAY? Listening to music, engaging in an intellectual debate with either Will Jefferson, Matt Boyce or James Sykes, or playing changing room cricket
FAVOURITE TV? Nothing quite beats Friends
FAVOURITE FILM? Airplane!
FAVOURITE BOOK? Anything written by Wilbur Smith
DREAM HOLIDAY? The Caribbean

| Batting | Mat | Inns | NO | Runs | HS | Ave | SR | 100 | 50 | Ct | St |
|---|---|---|---|---|---|---|---|---|---|---|---|
| First-class | 7 | 7 | 3 | 14 | 4* | 3.50 | 46.66 | 0 | 0 | 1 | 0 |
| List A | 9 | 3 | 2 | 4 | 2* | 4.00 | 50.00 | 0 | 0 | 2 | 0 |
| Twenty20 | 2 | - | - | - | - | - | - | - | - | 1 | 0 |

| Bowling | Mat | Balls | Runs | Wkts | BBI | BBM | Ave | Econ | SR | 5w | 10 |
|---|---|---|---|---|---|---|---|---|---|---|---|
| First-class | 7 | 1032 | 554 | 20 | 3/42 | 4/65 | 27.70 | 3.22 | 51.6 | 0 | 0 |
| List A | 9 | 272 | 284 | 7 | 2/36 | 2/36 | 40.57 | 6.26 | 38.8 | 0 | 0 |
| Twenty20 | 2 | 42 | 36 | 3 | 3/14 | 3/14 | 12.00 | 5.14 | 14.0 | 0 | 0 |

FULL NAME: Michael Howard Yardy
BORN: November 27, 1980, Pembury, Kent
SQUAD NO: 20
HEIGHT: 6ft
NICKNAME: Yards, Paolo, Moo Moo
EDUCATION: William Parker School, Hastings
TEAMS: England, Central Districts, Sussex, Sussex Cricket Board
CAREER: ODI: 2006; T20I: 2006; First-class: 2000; List A: 1999; T20: 2004

---

BEST BATTING: 257 Sussex vs Bangladeshis, Hove, 2005
BEST BOWLING: 5-83 Sussex vs Bangladeshis, Hove, 2005
COUNTY CAP: 2005

---

CAREER HIGHLIGHTS? The successes with Sussex. Winning World T20 in 2010
CRICKETING HEROES? Graham Gooch, Michael Atherton, Alec Stewart, Graham Thorpe
NON-CRICKETING HEROES? Paolo Di Canio, Paul Gascoigne
BEST PLAYER IN COUNTY CRICKET? Marcus Trescothick
TIP FOR THE TOP? Too many good young cricketers to pick!
IF YOU WEREN'T A CRICKETER? Doing a proper job
WHEN RAIN STOPS PLAY? Reading, irritating people
FAVOURITE TV? Outnumbered
FAVOURITE FILM? Snatch
FAVOURITE BOOK? Tony Cascarino's autobiography
DREAM HOLIDAY? Maldives
SURPRISING SKILL? Very sweet left foot
GUILTY PLEASURES? West Ham United

| Batting | Mat | Inns | NO | Runs | HS | Ave | SR | 100 | 50 | Ct | St |
|---|---|---|---|---|---|---|---|---|---|---|---|
| ODIs | 28 | 24 | 8 | 326 | 60* | 20.37 | 69.06 | 0 | 2 | 10 | 0 |
| T20Is | 14 | 8 | 5 | 96 | 35* | 32.00 | 133.33 | 0 | 0 | 8 | 0 |
| First-class | 139 | 233 | 23 | 8223 | 257 | 39.15 | | 17 | 41 | 116 | 0 |
| List A | 186 | 161 | 28 | 3233 | 98* | 24.30 | | 0 | 21 | 74 | 0 |
| Twenty20 | 89 | 71 | 26 | 1061 | 76* | 23.57 | 105.36 | 0 | 2 | 34 | 0 |

| Bowling | Mat | Balls | Runs | Wkts | BBI | BBM | Ave | Econ | SR | 5w | 10 |
|---|---|---|---|---|---|---|---|---|---|---|---|
| ODIs | 28 | 1332 | 1075 | 21 | 3/24 | 3/24 | 51.19 | 4.84 | 63.4 | 0 | 0 |
| T20Is | 14 | 276 | 299 | 11 | 2/19 | 2/19 | 27.18 | 6.50 | 25.0 | 0 | 0 |
| First-class | 139 | 3459 | 2010 | 26 | 5/83 | | 77.30 | 3.48 | 133.0 | 1 | 0 |
| List A | 186 | 5677 | 4823 | 127 | 6/27 | 6/27 | 37.97 | 5.09 | 44.7 | 1 | 0 |
| Twenty20 | 89 | 1681 | 1805 | 71 | 3/21 | 3/21 | 25.42 | 6.44 | 23.6 | 0 | 0 |

# ED YOUNG

## RHB SLA

FULL NAME: Edward George Christopher Young
BORN: May 21, 1989, Chertsey, Surrey
SQUAD NO: 30
HEIGHT: 6ft 1in
NICKNAME: EY
EDUCATION: Wellington College; Oxford Brookes University
TEAMS: Gloucestershire, Gloucestershire 2nd XI, Oxford MCCU, Unicorns, Valley End
CAREER: First-class: 2009; List A: 2010; T20: 2011

BEST BATTING: 133 OMCCU vs Lancashire, The Parks, 2011
BEST BOWLING: 2-74 OUCCE vs Nottinghamshire, The Parks, 2009
COUNTY CAP: 2010

CAREER HIGHLIGHTS? Scoring my maiden first-class hundred vs Lancashire for Oxford MCCU in April 2011. Bowling in tandem in the T20s with Muttiah Muralitharan was a fantastic privilege
CRICKETING HEROES? Marcus Trescothick, Daniel Vettori, Shane Warne, Chris Gayle
NON-CRICKETING HEROES? Michael Jordan, Jason Bourne, Barney Stinson (suit up!)
TIPS FOR THE TOP? Ross Whiteley, Greg Smith
WHEN RAIN STOPS PLAY? Doing crosswords
FAVOURITE TV? How I Met Your Mother
ACCOMPLISHMENTS? Getting a degree in Anthropology/Sociology
SURPRISING SKILL? I can moonwalk
GUILTY PLEASURES? A bit of blackjack
AMAZE ME! I won a national schoolboy rackets competition. I watched every episode of Lost and still didn't know what was going on
FANTASY SLIP CORDON? Keeper: Lee Evans (he's a very funny man and has a great work rate), 1st: Morgan Freeman (great actor, great voice), 2nd: Me (just so I am in the middle), 3rd: Mr Motivator (obvious reasons), Gully: Michael McIntyre (just because he is a hero!)

| Batting | Mat | Inns | NO | Runs | HS | Ave | SR | 100 | 50 | Ct | St |
|---|---|---|---|---|---|---|---|---|---|---|---|
| First-class | 12 | 18 | 3 | 658 | 133 | 43.86 | 55.15 | 1 | 4 | 8 | 0 |
| List A | 19 | 14 | 3 | 155 | 50 | 14.09 | 79.48 | 0 | 1 | 7 | 0 |
| Twenty20 | 15 | 12 | 2 | 78 | 28 | 7.80 | 100.00 | 0 | 0 | 0 | 0 |

| Bowling | Mat | Balls | Runs | Wkts | BBI | BBM | Ave | Econ | SR | 5w | 10 |
|---|---|---|---|---|---|---|---|---|---|---|---|
| First-class | 12 | 893 | 619 | 5 | 2/74 | 2/129 | 123.80 | 4.15 | 178.6 | 0 | 0 |
| List A | 19 | 736 | 603 | 12 | 2/32 | 2/32 | 50.25 | 4.91 | 61.3 | 0 | 0 |
| Twenty20 | 15 | 300 | 325 | 11 | 2/14 | 2/14 | 29.54 | 6.50 | 27.2 | 0 | 0 |

# Wormsley

## "Quintessentially English"
Arguably the most beautiful cricket ground in the world.

Visit The Wormsley Cricket Website for more details of a select number of public events in 2012.

# www.wormsleycricket.co.uk

**CB40 Cricket at Wormsley • May 6th, July 29th and August 19th**

**British Universities One Day Final • Wednesday 20th June**

**"The Wormsley July Festival" • 11th to 24th July which includes:**
England Women v India Wednesday 11th July
Wormsley Armed Forces Cricket Day Sunday 15th July

Veuve Clicquot

SUMARIDGE
ESTATE WINES

mantis

JAMIE OLIVER'S
FABULOUS
FEASTS

Additional *Clydesdale Bank 40* Teams

**SCOTLAND**
FORMED: 1980
HOME GROUND: Citylets Grange, Edinburgh
ONE-DAY NAME: Scottish Saltires
CAPTAIN: Gordon Drummond
HEAD COACH: Peter Steindl
2011 RESULTS: CB40 7/7 in Group B

**THE NETHERLANDS**
FORMED: 1883
BOARD: Koninklijke Nederlandse Cricket Bond (Royal Dutch Cricket Board)
HOMEGROUND: Various
CAPTAIN: Peter Borren
HEAD COACH: Peter Drinnen
ICC MEMBER STATUS: 1966
2011 RESULTS: CB40 5/7 in Group A

**UNICORNS**
FORMED: 2010
HOME GROUND: Various, several fixtures at Wormsley
CAPTAIN: Keith Parsons
HEAD COACH: Phil Oliver
2011 RESULTS: CB40 7/7 in Group C

| | Mat | Inns | NO | Runs | HS | Ave | SR | 100 | 50 | 4s | 6s |
|---|---|---|---|---|---|---|---|---|---|---|---|
| PL Mommsen | 11 | 11 | 4 | 408 | 81* | 58.28 | 108.51 | 0 | 2 | 37 | 8 |
| KJ Coetzer | 3 | 3 | 0 | 172 | 122 | 57.33 | 103.61 | 1 | 1 | 16 | 4 |
| CG Burnett | 3 | 3 | 2 | 52 | 31* | 52.00 | 104.00 | 0 | 0 | 6 | 0 |
| JH Davey | 11 | 10 | 0 | 257 | 91 | 25.70 | 76.03 | 0 | 2 | 21 | 0 |
| DF Watts | 6 | 6 | 0 | 146 | 62 | 24.33 | 74.11 | 0 | 1 | 13 | 0 |
| GH Worker | 3 | 3 | 0 | 73 | 46 | 24.33 | 90.12 | 0 | 0 | 8 | 0 |
| LR Butterworth | 4 | 4 | 1 | 72 | 24 | 24.00 | 87.80 | 0 | 0 | 4 | 0 |
| RM Haq | 11 | 7 | 3 | 95 | 30 | 23.75 | 79.83 | 0 | 0 | 5 | 0 |
| OJ Hairs | 1 | 1 | 0 | 20 | 20 | 20.00 | 86.95 | 0 | 0 | 2 | 0 |
| EF Chalmers | 4 | 4 | 0 | 74 | 50 | 18.50 | 67.27 | 0 | 1 | 7 | 0 |
| RD Berrington | 7 | 7 | 0 | 126 | 31 | 18.00 | 55.50 | 0 | 0 | 9 | 0 |
| R Flannigan | 6 | 6 | 0 | 92 | 39 | 15.33 | 63.44 | 0 | 0 | 9 | 0 |
| CS MacLeod | 6 | 6 | 0 | 92 | 33 | 15.33 | 87.61 | 0 | 0 | 8 | 0 |
| NFI McCallum | 4 | 4 | 0 | 58 | 53 | 14.50 | 92.06 | 0 | 1 | 3 | 2 |
| G Goudie | 9 | 7 | 2 | 61 | 13 | 12.20 | 132.60 | 0 | 0 | 7 | 1 |
| GI Maiden | 10 | 9 | 2 | 78 | 32* | 11.14 | 68.42 | 0 | 0 | 4 | 0 |
| CD Wallace | 1 | 1 | 0 | 11 | 11 | 11.00 | 50.00 | 0 | 0 | 0 | 0 |
| GD Drummond | 11 | 7 | 1 | 50 | 25 | 8.33 | 111.11 | 0 | 0 | 4 | 1 |
| S Sharif | 4 | 3 | 1 | 16 | 13* | 8.00 | 76.19 | 0 | 0 | 1 | 0 |
| MA Parker | 6 | 4 | 4 | 10 | 8* | - | 71.42 | 0 | 0 | 1 | 0 |

Batting & Fielding

| | Overs | Mdns | Runs | Wkts | BBI | Ave | Econ | SR | 4w | 5w |
|---|---|---|---|---|---|---|---|---|---|---|
| RM Haq | 77.0 | 1 | 376 | 6 | 2/32 | 62.66 | 4.88 | 77.0 | 0 | 0 |
| PL Mommsen | 30.0 | 0 | 163 | 6 | 2/11 | 27.16 | 5.43 | 30.0 | 0 | 0 |
| S Sharif | 15.0 | 0 | 88 | 2 | 1/15 | 44.00 | 5.86 | 45.0 | 0 | 0 |
| JH Davey | 45.2 | 3 | 276 | 11 | 3/30 | 25.09 | 6.08 | 24.7 | 0 | 0 |
| GD Drummond | 64.2 | 1 | 403 | 7 | 2/51 | 57.57 | 6.26 | 55.1 | 0 | 0 |
| RD Berrington | 5.0 | 1 | 32 | 0 | - | | 6.40 | - | 0 | 0 |
| G Goudie | 53.0 | 0 | 344 | 11 | 4/36 | 31.27 | 6.49 | 28.9 | 1 | 0 |
| GH Worker | 17.4 | 0 | 115 | 1 | 1/23 | 115.00 | 6.50 | 106.0 | 0 | 0 |
| MA Parker | 36.0 | 0 | 235 | 10 | 5/47 | 23.50 | 6.52 | 21.6 | 0 | 1 |
| LR Butterworth | 21.1 | 0 | 145 | 1 | 1/44 | 145.00 | 6.85 | 127.0 | 0 | 0 |
| CG Burnett | 18.0 | 0 | 125 | 0 | - | | 6.94 | - | 0 | 0 |

Bowling

**Catches/Stumpings:**
9 Mommsen, 5 Berrington, 4 Davey, Maiden (+3st), 3 McCallum, 2 Butterworth, Drummond, Goudie, MacLeod, Parker, 1 Haq, Wallace (+0st)

| | Mat | Inns | NO | Runs | HS | Ave | SR | 100 | 50 | 4s | 6s |
|---|---|---|---|---|---|---|---|---|---|---|---|
| SJ Myburgh | 1 | 1 | 0 | 55 | 55 | 55.00 | 114.58 | 0 | 1 | 11 | 0 |
| TLW Cooper | 7 | 7 | 1 | 255 | 126* | 42.50 | 91.72 | 1 | 0 | 31 | 2 |
| Mudassar Bukhari | 11 | 11 | 4 | 249 | 78* | 35.57 | 111.16 | 0 | 1 | 27 | 6 |
| PW Borren | 11 | 11 | 2 | 268 | 71* | 29.77 | 97.45 | 0 | 2 | 24 | 7 |
| W Barresi | 11 | 11 | 1 | 288 | 97* | 28.80 | 76.39 | 0 | 2 | 30 | 5 |
| TN de Grooth | 11 | 11 | 2 | 238 | 58 | 26.44 | 78.54 | 0 | 1 | 22 | 1 |
| SM Mott | 9 | 6 | 3 | 65 | 50* | 21.66 | 95.58 | 0 | 1 | 5 | 1 |
| ES Szwarczynski | 11 | 11 | 0 | 197 | 111 | 17.90 | 71.89 | 1 | 0 | 23 | 1 |
| PM Seelaar | 10 | 3 | 2 | 17 | 15* | 17.00 | 54.83 | 0 | 0 | 0 | 0 |
| WP Diepeveen | 6 | 6 | 0 | 85 | 27 | 14.16 | 56.29 | 0 | 0 | 9 | 0 |
| TGJ Gruijters | 4 | 4 | 2 | 26 | 23 | 13.00 | 38.23 | 0 | 0 | 1 | 0 |
| MF Cleary | 2 | 2 | 0 | 23 | 16 | 11.50 | 74.19 | 0 | 0 | 1 | 1 |
| MR Swart | 10 | 10 | 0 | 108 | 57 | 10.80 | 51.67 | 0 | 1 | 9 | 1 |
| BP Kruger | 4 | 3 | 0 | 24 | 11 | 8.00 | 44.44 | 0 | 0 | 0 | 0 |
| TJ Heggelman | 9 | 5 | 2 | 22 | 8 | 7.33 | 33.33 | 0 | 0 | 0 | 0 |
| N Kruger | 1 | 1 | 0 | 3 | 3 | 3.00 | 17.64 | 0 | 0 | 0 | 0 |
| BA Westdijk | 3 | 1 | 1 | 0 | 0* | - | - | 0 | 0 | 0 | 0 |

*Batting & Fielding*

| | Overs | Mdns | Runs | Wkts | BBI | Ave | Econ | SR | 4w | 5w |
|---|---|---|---|---|---|---|---|---|---|---|
| Mudassar Bukhari | 83.0 | 5 | 392 | 19 | 4/41 | 20.63 | 4.72 | 26.2 | 1 | 0 |
| SM Mott | 69.4 | 8 | 335 | 21 | 4/29 | 15.95 | 4.80 | 19.9 | 1 | 0 |
| TGJ Gruijters | 10.0 | 0 | 49 | 2 | 1/12 | 24.50 | 4.90 | 30.0 | 0 | 0 |
| PW Borren | 68.0 | 2 | 336 | 12 | 3/29 | 28.00 | 4.94 | 34.0 | 0 | 0 |
| MR Swart | 44.0 | 0 | 224 | 4 | 2/14 | 56.00 | 5.09 | 66.0 | 0 | 0 |
| BP Kruger | 15.0 | 1 | 79 | 1 | 1/24 | 79.00 | 5.26 | 90.0 | 0 | 0 |
| TJ Heggelman | 25.0 | 1 | 136 | 2 | 1/19 | 68.00 | 5.44 | 75.0 | 0 | 0 |
| PM Seelaar | 64.0 | 0 | 350 | 7 | 2/36 | 50.00 | 5.46 | 54.8 | 0 | 0 |
| BA Westdijk | 15.0 | 0 | 96 | 1 | 1/44 | 96.00 | 6.40 | 90.0 | 0 | 0 |
| MF Cleary | 16.0 | 0 | 114 | 3 | 2/57 | 38.00 | 7.12 | 32.0 | 0 | 0 |

*Bowling*

**Catches/Stumpings:**
11 Barresi (+0st), 7 Cooper, Swart, 5 Seelaar, 4 Borren, Gruijters, 3 Diepeveen, BP Kruger, 2 de Grooth, Heggelman, Mott, Szwarczynski, 1 Bukhari, Westdijk

www.kncb.nl / tel: 0031 30 751 3780

unicorns

| | Mat | Inns | NO | Runs | HS | Ave | SR | 100 | 50 | 4s | 6s |
|---|---|---|---|---|---|---|---|---|---|---|---|
| MA Thornely | 12 | 11 | 1 | 425 | 105* | 42.50 | 82.84 | 1 | 1 | 51 | 3 |
| JE Ord | 3 | 3 | 0 | 116 | 55 | 38.66 | 74.83 | 0 | 2 | 7 | 2 |
| CC Benham | 8 | 6 | 1 | 167 | 58 | 33.40 | 69.29 | 0 | 2 | 14 | 0 |
| JRA Campbell | 10 | 9 | 0 | 226 | 58 | 25.11 | 65.88 | 0 | 1 | 24 | 0 |
| JG Thompson | 3 | 3 | 0 | 70 | 44 | 23.33 | 95.89 | 0 | 0 | 10 | 2 |
| LM Reece | 9 | 7 | 2 | 115 | 26 | 23.00 | 91.26 | 0 | 0 | 12 | 0 |
| KA Parsons | 12 | 11 | 2 | 204 | 62* | 22.66 | 74.72 | 0 | 1 | 15 | 1 |
| JR Levitt | 3 | 3 | 0 | 65 | 33 | 21.66 | 84.41 | 0 | 0 | 6 | 1 |
| CM Park | 3 | 2 | 0 | 40 | 38 | 20.00 | 65.57 | 0 | 0 | 3 | 0 |
| CT Peploe | 4 | 3 | 2 | 20 | 11* | 20.00 | 80.00 | 0 | 0 | 1 | 0 |
| JPT Knappett | 12 | 11 | 0 | 207 | 43 | 18.81 | 63.10 | 0 | 0 | 13 | 1 |
| NC Saker | 7 | 5 | 1 | 58 | 18 | 14.50 | 61.70 | 0 | 0 | 6 | 0 |
| A Rashid | 9 | 6 | 1 | 61 | 24* | 12.20 | 87.14 | 0 | 0 | 6 | 1 |
| RG Querl | 12 | 8 | 2 | 64 | 23 | 10.66 | 62.74 | 0 | 0 | 4 | 0 |
| T Friend | 3 | 3 | 1 | 19 | 14 | 9.50 | 70.37 | 0 | 0 | 2 | 0 |
| DM Wheeldon | 5 | 4 | 0 | 26 | 14 | 6.50 | 100.00 | 0 | 0 | 2 | 1 |
| RJH Lett | 3 | 3 | 0 | 14 | 10 | 4.66 | 41.17 | 0 | 0 | 1 | 0 |
| BL Wadlan | 2 | 1 | 0 | 3 | 3 | 3.00 | 33.33 | 0 | 0 | 0 | 0 |
| AC McGarry | 3 | 1 | 0 | 0 | 0 | 0.00 | 0.00 | 0 | 0 | 0 | 0 |
| LE Beaven | 5 | 2 | 2 | 11 | 9* | - | 64.70 | 0 | 0 | 1 | 0 |
| TR Craddock | 2 | 2 | 2 | 4 | 3* | - | 23.52 | 0 | 0 | 0 | 0 |
| JS Miles | 2 | 1 | 1 | 3 | 3* | - | 42.85 | 0 | 0 | 0 | 0 |

*Batting & Fielding*

| | Overs | Mdns | Runs | Wkts | BBI | Ave | Econ | SR | 4w | 5w |
|---|---|---|---|---|---|---|---|---|---|---|
| JR Levitt | 3.0 | 0 | 9 | 0 | - | - | 3.00 | - | 0 | 0 |
| CT Peploe | 30.0 | 0 | 116 | 1 | 1/32 | 116.00 | 3.86 | 180.0 | 0 | 0 |
| TR Craddock | 16.0 | 1 | 65 | 1 | 1/33 | 65.00 | 4.06 | 96.0 | 0 | 0 |
| NC Saker | 44.0 | 5 | 196 | 8 | 3/33 | 24.50 | 4.45 | 33.0 | 0 | 0 |
| LE Beaven | 29.1 | 2 | 142 | 4 | 3/35 | 35.50 | 4.86 | 43.7 | 0 | 0 |
| DM Wheeldon | 35.5 | 4 | 181 | 4 | 3/31 | 45.25 | 5.05 | 53.7 | 0 | 0 |
| BL Wadlan | 11.0 | 0 | 57 | 2 | 2/39 | 28.50 | 5.18 | 33.0 | 0 | 0 |
| MA Thornely | 13.2 | 0 | 71 | 1 | 1/28 | 71.00 | 5.32 | 80.0 | 0 | 0 |
| RG Querl | 83.3 | 3 | 456 | 13 | 3/33 | 35.07 | 5.46 | 38.5 | 0 | 0 |
| JS Miles | 15.5 | 0 | 87 | 0 | - | - | 5.49 | - | 0 | 0 |
| LM Reece | 30.1 | 0 | 172 | 5 | 4/35 | 34.40 | 5.70 | 36.2 | 1 | 0 |
| A Rashid | 50.4 | 0 | 290 | 4 | 1/30 | 72.50 | 5.72 | 76.0 | 0 | 0 |
| T Friend | 19.0 | 3 | 122 | 1 | 1/49 | 122.00 | 6.42 | 114.0 | 0 | 0 |
| AC McGarry | 17.0 | 1 | 126 | 1 | 1/47 | 126.00 | 7.41 | 102.0 | 0 | 0 |
| JRA Campbell | 1.0 | 0 | 8 | 0 | - | - | 8.00 | - | 0 | 0 |
| CC Benham | 0.1 | 0 | 4 | 0 | - | - | 24.00 | - | 0 | 0 |

*Bowling*

**Catches/Stumpings:**
10 Knappett (+2st), 4 Thornely, 2 Parsons, Reece, 1 Benham, Lett, Peploe, Querl, Rashid, Thompson

 ICC **WORLD TWENTY20** SRI LANKA 2012

# TICKETS ON SALE NOW
**TO BUY TICKETS VISIT WWW.ICC-CRICKET.COM**

COMMERCIAL PARTNERS

 RELIANCE   LG   PEPSI   Hero   Emirates   Reebok   Castrol   MoneyGram  HYUNDAI

BROADCAST PARTNER   INTERNET PARTNER

 ESPN stars  YAHOO! icc.yahoo

Scotland

# RICHIE BERRINGTON

## RHB RMF

**FULL NAME:** Richard Douglas Berrington
**BORN:** April 3, 1987, Pretoria, South Africa
**SQUAD NO:** 44
**HEIGHT:** 6ft
**NICKNAME:** Richie, Berro
**EDUCATION:** Greenock Academy
**TEAMS:** Scotland, Scotland Under-19s
**CAREER:** ODI: 2008; T20I: 2008; First-class: 2007; List A: 2007; T20: 2008

**BEST BATTING:** 110 Scotland vs UAE, Sharjah, 2012
**BEST BOWLING:** 3-13 Scotland vs Kenya, Nairobi, 2010

**WHY CRICKET?** I watched South Africa playing from a very young age and played backyard cricket with my dad before playing for my school team in South Africa

**CAREER HIGHLIGHTS?** Receiving my first and 50th caps for Scotland. Beating India A at Titwood and scoring my first hundred for Scotland is a day I will always remember. Our win against Ireland last summer was also pretty special

**CRICKETING HEROES?** Shaun Pollock and Jonty Rhodes. Both great players who always gave everything and Jonty was inspirational in the field

**BEST PLAYER IN COUNTY CRICKET?** Kyle Coetzer

**IF YOU WEREN'T A CRICKETER?** I would love to have been a professional footballer but most likely a personal trainer/fitness instructor

**FAVOURITE TV?** MasterChef

**FAVOURITE FILM?** Gladiator

**AMAZE ME!** I've been lucky enough to visit over 15 countries as well as nine islands, not bad for a bad flyer. I was born in a military hospital in South Africa

| Batting | Mat | Inns | NO | Runs | HS | Ave | SR | 100 | 50 | Ct | St |
|---|---|---|---|---|---|---|---|---|---|---|---|
| ODIs | 20 | 18 | 1 | 387 | 84 | 22.76 | 81.30 | 0 | 3 | 11 | 0 |
| T20Is | 9 | 7 | 1 | 72 | 28 | 12.00 | 105.88 | 0 | 0 | 0 | 0 |
| First-class | 11 | 19 | 2 | 509 | 110 | 29.94 | 41.89 | 1 | 2 | 13 | 0 |
| List A | 49 | 45 | 2 | 1110 | 106 | 25.81 | 76.76 | 1 | 7 | 22 | 0 |
| Twenty20 | 19 | 17 | 2 | 248 | 63 | 16.53 | 116.43 | 0 | 1 | 4 | 0 |

| Bowling | Mat | Balls | Runs | Wkts | BBI | BBM | Ave | Econ | SR | 5w | 10 |
|---|---|---|---|---|---|---|---|---|---|---|---|
| ODIs | 20 | 590 | 472 | 11 | 2/14 | 2/14 | 42.90 | 4.80 | 53.6 | 0 | 0 |
| T20Is | 9 | 118 | 126 | 5 | 2/21 | 2/21 | 25.20 | 6.40 | 23.6 | 0 | 0 |
| First-class | 11 | 892 | 500 | 18 | 3/13 | 3/39 | 27.77 | 3.36 | 49.5 | 0 | 0 |
| List A | 49 | 1184 | 1068 | 30 | 4/47 | 4/47 | 35.60 | 5.41 | 39.4 | 0 | 0 |
| Twenty20 | 19 | 280 | 335 | 12 | 2/12 | 2/12 | 27.91 | 7.17 | 23.3 | 0 | 0 |

# TYLER BUCHAN

## RHB RMF

FULL NAME: Tyler John Buchan
BORN: September 12, 1985, Aberdeen
SQUAD NO: TBC
HEIGHT: 6ft 2in
NICKNAME: Bucco
EDUCATION: Aberdeen Grammar School; Aberdeen University
TEAMS: Scotland, Scotland A, Scotland Under-19s
CAREER: T20: 2011

**SCOTLAND**

CAREER HIGHLIGHTS? Playing in the U19 World Cup in Sri Lanka. It was a fantastic experience, but making my debut for Scotland in Namibia would have to be the highlight

SUPERSTITIONS? Usually like to sit in the same seat to watch the game when we're batting, but I think you make a lot of your own luck in cricket

CRICKETING HEROES? Glenn McGrath – great bowler and a fierce competitor

NON-CRICKETING HEROES? Lance Armstrong is an inspirational athlete who succeeded despite facing incredible adversity. On a personal note my cousin Steven is a hero of mine, protecting our country on the frontline in Afghanistan

BEST PLAYER IN COUNTY CRICKET? Kyle Coetzer, hundreds for and against Scotland in the CB40 last year

TIP FOR THE TOP? Watching England U19 on Sky last year, Daniel Bell-Drummond looked a real talent

IF YOU WEREN'T A CRICKETER? Well, I'm a chartered accountant full-time and a cricketer part-time, so if I wasn't an accountant I'd be a cricketer!

FAVOURITE TV? The Wire, or more recently I've really got into Breaking Bad – the story of a high school chemistry teacher who begins to sell drugs to pay for his chemotherapy

ACCOMPLISHMENTS? Becoming a chartered accountant. Seven years of study through uni and some tough professional exams, but a real accomplishment to get there

GUILTY PLEASURES? TOWIE

AMAZE ME! 1. I can juggle, 2. I got engaged last summer in New York, 3. I turned down an interview to appear on The Apprentice because I was playing cricket

TWITTER FEED: @tjbuchan

| Batting | Mat | Inns | NO | Runs | HS | Ave | SR | 100 | 50 | Ct | St |
|---------|-----|------|----|------|----|-----|----|-----|----|----|----|
| Twenty20 | 5 | 2 | 0 | 5 | 3 | 2.50 | 38.46 | 0 | 0 | 1 | 0 |

| Bowling | Mat | Balls | Runs | Wkts | BBI | BBM | Ave | Econ | SR | 5w | 10 |
|---------|-----|-------|------|------|-----|-----|-----|------|----|----|----|
| Twenty20 | 5 | 60 | 99 | 2 | 1/17 | 1/17 | 49.50 | 9.90 | 30.0 | 0 | 0 |

## CALVIN BURNETT

### LHB RMF

SCOTLAND

FULL NAME: Calvin Gary Burnett
BORN: October 23, 1990, Dundee
SQUAD NO: 33
HEIGHT: 6ft 1in
NICKNAME: Calv, Burno, Clive
EDUCATION: Arbroath High School;
Edinburgh Telford College
TEAMS: Scotland, Scotland Under-13s,
Scotland Under-15s, Scotland Under-17s,
Scotland Under-19s
CAREER: List A: 2011

FAMILY TIES? My father was our club captain and was heavily involved. However, my uncle Neil Burnett was the more successful cricketer, earning caps for Scotland

CAREER HIGHLIGHTS? Earning my first caps this year has been my biggest achievement, and travelling around the world, including Australia, India and all over Europe

SUPERSTITIONS? I used to be very bad for it! Needing to put each right sided bit of my kit on before the left and always getting the ball from the off side when bowling! Also I can't touch the lines on the crease when walking past

CRICKETING HEROES? Alastair Cook, Andrew Strauss and Marcus Trescothick are my current heroes. Even though I'm an allrounder, I respect these guys. And for my role in the team, Kieron Pollard is up there too

NON-CRICKETING HEROES? Outside of cricket I look up to my father and take a lot from him as a person

BEST PLAYER IN COUNTY CRICKET? Best county cricketer just now I think is Jason Roy as he hits an unbelievable ball!

TIPS FOR THE TOP? James Vince and Jos Buttler are going to be big stars. And also a friend of mine from an academy in Australia, Joe Root

WHEN RAIN STOPS PLAY? Riddles and card games are very popular, with the odd quiz kicking about

FAVOURITE TV? Entourage and Grey's Anatomy

ACCOMPLISHMENTS? I did win the college go-karting competition, so that's got to be up there!

TWITTER FEED: @calvgburnett

| Batting | Mat | Inns | NO | Runs | HS | Ave | SR | 100 | 50 | Ct | St |
|---------|-----|------|-----|------|-----|-------|--------|-----|-----|-----|-----|
| List A | 3 | 3 | 2 | 52 | 31* | 52.00 | 104.00 | 0 | 0 | 0 | 0 |

| Bowling | Mat | Balls | Runs | Wkts | BBI | BBM | Ave | Econ | SR | 5w | 10 |
|---------|-----|-------|------|------|-----|-----|-----|------|-----|-----|-----|
| List A | 3 | 108 | 125 | 0 | - | - | - | 6.94 | - | 0 | 0 |

# EWAN CHALMERS

## RHB RM

FULL NAME: Ewan Fraser Chalmers
BORN: October 19, 1989, Edinburgh
SQUAD NO: 7
HEIGHT: 6ft
NICKNAME: Chubby
EDUCATION: George Watson's College;
University of St Andrews
TEAMS: Scotland, Scotland Under-13s,
Scotland Under-15s
CAREER: First-class: 2009; List A: 2010

BEST BATTING: 67 Scotland vs Afghanistan, Ayr, 2010

CAREER HIGHLIGHTS? Gaining my first cap for Scotland in 2009 and scoring my first century for my country at Lord's last year
CRICKETING HEROES? Jacques Kallis, Sachin Tendulkar
NON-CRICKETING HEROES? Chris Hoy, Jonny Wilkinson
BEST PLAYER IN COUNTY CRICKET? Kyle Coetzer
TIP FOR THE TOP? Craig Wallace
IF YOU WEREN'T A CRICKETER? Club rep in Malia
WHEN RAIN STOPS PLAY? Napping
FAVOURITE TV? The Apprentice
FAVOURITE FILM? Braveheart
FAVOURITE BOOK? Touching The Void
DREAM HOLIDAY? New York
ACCOMPLISHMENTS? Getting a Maths degree
SURPRISING SKILL? I can play the bagpipes
GUILTY PLEASURES? Bourbon biscuits, One Direction
AMAZE ME! I have won the World Pipe Band Championships, the first single I bought was Words by Boyzone, I have had a hit with Andy Murray
FANTASY SLIP CORDON? Keeper: Sonny Bill Williams, 1st: Me, 2nd: Will Ferrell, 3rd: Michael McIntyre, 4th: Michael Buble, Gully: Barack Obama
TWITTER FEED: @EFChubby

| Batting | Mat | Inns | NO | Runs | HS | Ave | SR | 100 | 50 | Ct | St |
|---|---|---|---|---|---|---|---|---|---|---|---|
| First-class | 5 | 10 | 1 | 170 | 67 | 18.88 | 38.28 | 0 | 1 | 6 | 0 |
| List A | 5 | 5 | 0 | 82 | 50 | 16.40 | 67.76 | 0 | 1 | 0 | 0 |

| Bowling | Mat | Balls | Runs | Wkts | BBI | BBM | Ave | Econ | SR | 5w | 10 |
|---|---|---|---|---|---|---|---|---|---|---|---|
| First-class | 5 | - | - | - | - | - | - | - | - | - | - |
| List A | 5 | - | - | - | - | - | - | - | - | - | - |

## GORDON DRUMMOND  RHB RMF

SCOTLAND

FULL NAME: Gordon David Drummond
BORN: April 21, 1980, Meigle, Perthshire
SQUAD NO: 24
HEIGHT: 6ft
NICKNAME: Big Toby
EDUCATION: Blairgowrie High School;
Telford College; Edinburgh Napier
University
TEAMS: Scotland, Scotland A
CAREER: ODI: 2007; T20I: 2008; First-class:
2007; List A: 2007; T20: 2008

BEST BATTING: 52 Scotland vs Canada, Aberdeen, 2009
BEST BOWLING: 3-18 Scotland vs Kenya, Nairobi, 2010

CAREER HIGHLIGHTS? Playing in the T20 World Cup in England and being part of Kyle Coetzer's amazing catch in the game against SA
CRICKETING HEROES? I loved Ian Botham as a kid and used to watch Botham's Ashes over and over again. I was amazed with how one man could have such an effect on a series
BEST PLAYER IN COUNTY CRICKET? Marcus Trescothick
TIPS FOR THE TOP? Ben Stokes and James Vince
IF YOU WEREN'T A CRICKETER? Probably a plumber and playing football
FAVOURITE FILM? Bloodsport – Jean-Claude Van Damme is a legend
FAVOURITE BOOK? Don't read much, but Fraser Watts gave me a book called Sacred Hoops which is a good read
ACCOMPLISHMENTS? Scored a three-minute hat-trick in amateur football – honest!
AMAZE ME! I don't think the county fans will know me anyway, so any fact I write would be surprising!
TWITTER FEED: @drummo639

| Batting | Mat | Inns | NO | Runs | HS | Ave | SR | 100 | 50 | Ct | St |
|---|---|---|---|---|---|---|---|---|---|---|---|
| ODIs | 25 | 16 | 7 | 207 | 35* | 23.00 | 93.24 | 0 | 0 | 4 | 0 |
| T20Is | 10 | 7 | 0 | 54 | 35 | 7.71 | 83.07 | 0 | 0 | 0 | 0 |
| First-class | 11 | 14 | 0 | 187 | 52 | 13.35 | 46.05 | 0 | 1 | 5 | 0 |
| List A | 61 | 45 | 12 | 391 | 35* | 11.84 | 78.35 | 0 | 0 | 11 | 0 |
| Twenty20 | 18 | 13 | 2 | 102 | 35 | 9.27 | 100.99 | 0 | 0 | 1 | 0 |

| Bowling | Mat | Balls | Runs | Wkts | BBI | BBM | Ave | Econ | SR | 5w | 10 |
|---|---|---|---|---|---|---|---|---|---|---|---|
| ODIs | 25 | 1107 | 794 | 23 | 4/41 | 4/41 | 34.52 | 4.30 | 48.1 | 0 | 0 |
| T20Is | 10 | 203 | 241 | 10 | 3/20 | 3/20 | 24.10 | 7.12 | 20.3 | 0 | 0 |
| First-class | 11 | 1494 | 562 | 16 | 3/18 | 3/44 | 35.12 | 2.25 | 93.3 | 0 | 0 |
| List A | 61 | 2489 | 1992 | 47 | 4/41 | 4/41 | 42.38 | 4.80 | 52.9 | 0 | 0 |
| Twenty20 | 18 | 341 | 401 | 20 | 3/20 | 3/20 | 20.05 | 7.05 | 17.0 | 0 | 0 |

## ALASDAIR EVANS                                    RHB RMF

**FULL NAME:** Alasdair Campbell Evans
**BORN:** January 12, 1989, Tunbridge Wells, Kent
**SQUAD NO:** 45
**HEIGHT:** 6ft 5in
**NICKNAME:** Evo, Pipe, Mellers, Whittle
**EDUCATION:** George Watson's College, Edinburgh; Loughborough University
**TEAMS:** Scotland, Loughborough MCCU, Scotland Under-13s, Scotland Under-15s, Scotland Under-17s, Scotland Under-19s
**CAREER:** ODI: 2009; First-class: 2009; List A: 2009

BEST BATTING: 2 Scotland vs Ireland, Aberdeen, 2009
BEST BOWLING: 2-41 LUCCE vs Leicestershire, Leicester, 2009

CAREER HIGHLIGHTS? Gaining first full cap for Scotland in 2009
CRICKETING HEROES? Lance Klusener, Shaun Pollock
NON-CRICKETING HEROES? Thierry Henry, Jason White
BEST PLAYER IN COUNTY CRICKET? Marcus Trescothick
TIP FOR THE TOP? Preston Mommsen
IF YOU WEREN'T A CRICKETER? Using my degree in Psychology
WHEN RAIN STOPS PLAY? Sporting trivia questions
FAVOURITE TV? Prison Break, 24, Scrubs
FAVOURITE FILM? Madagascar, Madagascar 2
FAVOURITE BOOK? Where's Wally?
ACCOMPLISHMENTS? Playing for Scotland at hockey at age group level
SURPRISING SKILL? Can play Three Blind Mice on the recorder!
GUILTY PLEASURES? Westlife, musicals and crisps
AMAZE ME! I used to sing in a Gaelic choir, I played hockey for Scotland at U16 and U18 level, I have played Malvolio in Twelfth Night and Lysander in A Midsummer Night's Dream
FANTASY SLIP CORDON? Keeper: Michael McIntrye (to make us laugh), 1st: Frank Sinatra (to sing to us), 2nd: Katy Perry (to look at), 3rd: Myself, Gully: Jack Bauer (to save the world)

| Batting | Mat | Inns | NO | Runs | HS | Ave | SR | 100 | 50 | Ct | St |
|---|---|---|---|---|---|---|---|---|---|---|---|
| ODIs | 2 | - | - | - | - | - | - | - | - | 0 | 0 |
| First-class | 4 | 2 | 0 | 3 | 2 | 1.50 | 18.75 | 0 | 0 | 1 | 0 |
| List A | 3 | 1 | 1 | 1 | 1* | - | 33.33 | 0 | 0 | 0 | 0 |

| Bowling | Mat | Balls | Runs | Wkts | BBI | BBM | Ave | Econ | SR | 5w | 10 |
|---|---|---|---|---|---|---|---|---|---|---|---|
| ODIs | 2 | 102 | 99 | 1 | 1/55 | 1/55 | 99.00 | 5.82 | 102.0 | 0 | 0 |
| First-class | 4 | 318 | 247 | 4 | 2/41 | 2/41 | 61.75 | 4.66 | 79.5 | 0 | 0 |
| List A | 3 | 138 | 137 | 2 | 1/38 | 1/38 | 68.50 | 5.95 | 69.0 | 0 | 0 |

**SCOTLAND**

FULL NAME: Ryan Flannigan
BORN: June 30, 1988, Kelso
SQUAD NO: 88
HEIGHT: 6ft
NICKNAME: Pieman
EDUCATION: Edenside Primary School; Kelso High School; Edinburgh Napier University
TEAMS: Scotland, Scotland Under-19s
CAREER: ODI: 2010; T20I: 2012; First-class: 2010; List A: 2010; T20: 2011

BEST BATTING: 102 Scotland vs Namibia, Windhoek, 2011

**FAMILY TIES?** Uncle Jack Kerr played 55 times for Scotland. Father Ian captained and played for Kelso CC for many years. All uncles played cricket as well
**CAREER HIGHLIGHTS?** Maiden first-class century in Namibia for Scotland. Playing for my country at Test venues in England. Travelling the world
**NON-CRICKETING HEROES?** Russell Latapy (Hibernian legend)
**BEST PLAYER IN COUNTY CRICKET?** Kyle Coetzer
**TIPS FOR THE TOP?** Jos Buttler, Ben Stokes
**IF YOU WEREN'T A CRICKETER?** Looking for a job
**WHEN RAIN STOPS PLAY?** iPod or annoying the boys
**FAVOURITE TV?** The Inbetweeners, Gavin And Stacey, Entourage
**FAVOURITE FILM?** Saving Private Ryan
**DREAM HOLIDAY?** Barbados, Australia
**ACCOMPLISHMENTS?** Honours degree in Sport Science. Nine golf trophies in one season at Kelso Golf Club
**TWITTER FEED:** @flanners_man88

| Batting | Mat | Inns | NO | Runs | HS | Ave | SR | 100 | 50 | Ct | St |
|---|---|---|---|---|---|---|---|---|---|---|---|
| ODIs | 1 | 1 | 0 | 0 | 0 | 0.00 | 0.00 | 0 | 0 | 0 | 0 |
| T20Is | 1 | 1 | 0 | 5 | 5 | 5.00 | 125.00 | 0 | 0 | 0 | 0 |
| First-class | 4 | 7 | 0 | 238 | 102 | 34.00 | 42.12 | 1 | 1 | 3 | 0 |
| List A | 11 | 11 | 0 | 134 | 39 | 12.18 | 57.26 | 0 | 0 | 3 | 0 |
| Twenty20 | 3 | 2 | 0 | 15 | 10 | 7.50 | 100.00 | 0 | 0 | 0 | 0 |

| Bowling | Mat | Balls | Runs | Wkts | BBI | BBM | Ave | Econ | SR | 5w | 10 |
|---|---|---|---|---|---|---|---|---|---|---|---|
| ODIs | 1 | - | - | - | - | - | - | - | - | - | - |
| T20Is | 1 | - | - | - | - | - | - | - | - | - | - |
| First-class | 4 | - | - | - | - | - | - | - | - | - | - |
| List A | 11 | - | - | - | - | - | - | - | - | - | - |
| Twenty20 | 3 | - | - | - | - | - | - | - | - | - | - |

**FULL NAME:** Gordon Goudie
**BORN:** August 12, 1987, Aberdeen
**SQUAD NO:** 16
**HEIGHT:** 6ft
**NICKNAME:** Goudz
**EDUCATION:** Bankhead Academy
**TEAMS:** Scotland, Scotland Under-19s
**CAREER:** ODI: 2008; T20I: 2010; First-class: 2005; List A: 2004; T20: 2010

SCOTLAND

---

**BEST BATTING:** 44* Scotland vs Netherlands, Deventer, 2010
**BEST BOWLING:** 4-58 Scotland vs Ireland, Aberdeen, 2009

---

**CAREER HIGHLIGHTS?** Representing Scotland U19 at two World Cups. Taking five wickets in an ODI against Australia in Edinburgh
**SUPERSTITIONS?** I always put on my left pad before the right one
**CRICKETING HEROES?** Darren Gough, Andrew Flintoff, Dale Steyn
**NON-CRICKETING HEROES?** Tiger Woods, Lance Armstrong
**BEST PLAYER IN COUNTY CRICKET?** Kyle Coetzer
**WHEN RAIN STOPS PLAY?** Just messing around in the dressing room and listening to music
**GUILTY PLEASURES?** Shania Twain
**AMAZE ME!** Played age group football for Dundee United
**FANTASY SLIP CORDON?** Keeper: Lee Evans (he brings me to tears laughing), 1st: Me, 2nd: Herschelle Gibbs (he would have some good stories), 3rd: Cheryl Cole (something nice to look at)
**TWITTER FEED:** @Goudz16

| Batting | Mat | Inns | NO | Runs | HS | Ave | SR | 100 | 50 | Ct | St |
|---|---|---|---|---|---|---|---|---|---|---|---|
| ODIs | 14 | 9 | 3 | 40 | 17* | 6.66 | 63.49 | 0 | 0 | 5 | 0 |
| T20Is | 2 | 2 | 0 | 8 | 4 | 4.00 | 80.00 | 0 | 0 | 0 | 0 |
| First-class | 10 | 11 | 2 | 129 | 44* | 14.33 | 61.42 | 0 | 0 | 4 | 0 |
| List A | 50 | 35 | 12 | 246 | 45 | 10.69 | 96.85 | 0 | 0 | 16 | 0 |
| Twenty20 | 8 | 7 | 0 | 68 | 26 | 9.71 | 170.00 | 0 | 0 | 0 | 0 |

| Bowling | Mat | Balls | Runs | Wkts | BBI | BBM | Ave | Econ | SR | 5w | 10 |
|---|---|---|---|---|---|---|---|---|---|---|---|
| ODIs | 14 | 615 | 503 | 21 | 5/73 | 5/73 | 23.95 | 4.90 | 29.2 | 1 | 0 |
| T20Is | 2 | 24 | 52 | 0 | - | - | - | 13.00 | - | 0 | 0 |
| First-class | 10 | 1190 | 560 | 21 | 4/58 | 8/119 | 26.66 | 2.82 | 56.6 | 0 | 0 |
| List A | 50 | 2068 | 1943 | 71 | 5/73 | 5/73 | 27.36 | 5.63 | 29.1 | 1 | 0 |
| Twenty20 | 8 | 144 | 219 | 4 | 1/17 | 1/17 | 54.75 | 9.12 | 36.0 | 0 | 0 |

SCOTLAND

## MAJID HAQ

**LHB OB**

FULL NAME: Rana Majid Haq Khan
BORN: February 11, 1983, Paisley, Renfrewshire
SQUAD NO: 77
HEIGHT: 5ft 11in
NICKNAME: Maj, Panther, Haqy
EDUCATION: Todholm Primary School; South Primary School; Castlehead High School; Reid Kerr College; University of the West of Scotland
TEAMS: Scotland
CAREER: ODI: 2006; T20I: 2007; First-class: 2004; List A: 2003; T20: 2007

BEST BATTING: 120* Scotland vs Netherlands, Aberdeen, 2011
BEST BOWLING: 6-32 Scotland vs Namibia, Windhoek, 2011

FAMILY TIES? My uncles used to play club cricket. My cousin Omer Hussain has played for the Scotland national side in recent times
CAREER HIGHLIGHTS? Representing my country at three World Cups
CRICKETING HEROES? Brian Lara, Saeed Anwar, Saqlain Mushtaq, Saeed Ajmal
NON-CRICKETING HEROES? Muhammad Ali, Lionel Messi, Paolo Maldini
BEST PLAYER IN COUNTY CRICKET? Batting: Kevin Pietersen; bowling: James Anderson
TIPS FOR THE TOP? Batting: Paul Stirling; bowling: Steven Finn
IF YOU WEREN'T A CRICKETER? An accountant
WHEN RAIN STOPS PLAY? Praying it doesn't stop!
FAVOURITE TV? Crimewatch, Eastenders and documentaries about lions
FAVOURITE FILM? Cool Runnings
ACCOMPLISHMENTS? Being a good Muslim, getting my BAcc (Hons) in Accountancy, playing football and badminton at district level
GUILTY PLEASURES? Eating tubs of Nutella with a spoon!

| Batting | Mat | Inns | NO | Runs | HS | Ave | SR | 100 | 50 | Ct | St |
|---|---|---|---|---|---|---|---|---|---|---|---|
| ODIs | 31 | 24 | 0 | 445 | 71 | 18.54 | 64.68 | 0 | 3 | 6 | 0 |
| T20Is | 9 | 7 | 3 | 54 | 21* | 13.50 | 64.28 | 0 | 0 | 3 | 0 |
| First-class | 16 | 24 | 5 | 587 | 120* | 30.89 | 51.90 | 1 | 1 | 7 | 0 |
| List A | 100 | 72 | 14 | 1102 | 71 | 19.00 | 66.10 | 0 | 4 | 10 | 0 |
| Twenty20 | 19 | 11 | 6 | 100 | 27* | 20.00 | 81.30 | 0 | 0 | 7 | 0 |
| Bowling | Mat | Balls | Runs | Wkts | BBI | BBM | Ave | Econ | SR | 5w | 10 |
| ODIs | 31 | 1541 | 1196 | 38 | 4/28 | 4/28 | 31.47 | 4.65 | 40.5 | 0 | 0 |
| T20Is | 9 | 174 | 212 | 8 | 2/16 | 2/16 | 26.50 | 7.31 | 21.7 | 0 | 0 |
| First-class | 16 | 3102 | 1166 | 49 | 6/32 | 9/118 | 23.79 | 2.25 | 63.3 | 2 | 0 |
| List A | 100 | 4309 | 3549 | 89 | 4/28 | 4/28 | 39.87 | 4.94 | 48.4 | 0 | 0 |
| Twenty20 | 19 | 396 | 473 | 19 | 3/18 | 3/18 | 24.89 | 7.16 | 20.8 | 0 | 0 |

# CALUM MACLEOD

**RHB RMF**

FULL NAME: Calum Scott MacLeod
BORN: November 15, 1988, Glasgow, Lanarkshire
SQUAD NO: 10
HEIGHT: 6ft 2in
NICKNAME: Cloudy, Highlander, Scot
EDUCATION: Hillpark Secondary School
TEAMS: Scotland, Scotland Under-19s, Warwickshire, Warwickshire 2nd XI
CAREER: ODI: 2008; T20I: 2009; First-class: 2007; List A: 2008; T20: 2009

SCOTLAND

BEST BATTING: 26 Warwickshire vs DUCCE, Durham University, 2009
BEST BOWLING: 4-66 Scotland vs Canada, Aberdeen, 2009

FAMILY TIES? Both brothers play club cricket at Uddingston CC
WHY CRICKET? Dad took me to the local club when I was about six years old and played the game ever since
CAREER HIGHLIGHTS? Opening bowling in T20 World Cup, also opening batting for Scotland and my first Scotland cap
CRICKETING HEROES? Glenn McGrath – loved watching him bowl when I was growing up
NON-CRICKETING HEROES? Mark Knopfler, Tiger Woods
BEST PLAYER IN COUNTY CRICKET? Jonathan Trott
TIP FOR THE TOP? Gavin Main
IF YOU WEREN'T A CRICKETER? A sports psychologist
SURPRISING SKILL? Chef, guitarist, artist and poet. In truth, none of the above!
AMAZE ME! I have a pet rabbit called Alfie and a family pet giraffe called Seoras. I speak the fine Scottish language that is Gaelic
TWITTER FEED: @calummacleod640

| Batting | Mat | Inns | NO | Runs | HS | Ave | SR | 100 | 50 | Ct | St |
|---|---|---|---|---|---|---|---|---|---|---|---|
| ODIs | 8 | 7 | 1 | 80 | 35 | 13.33 | 68.37 | 0 | 0 | 4 | 0 |
| T20Is | 3 | 2 | 0 | 55 | 55 | 27.50 | 144.73 | 0 | 1 | 1 | 0 |
| First-class | 7 | 7 | 2 | 93 | 26 | 18.60 | 48.18 | 0 | 0 | 5 | 0 |
| List A | 25 | 21 | 2 | 248 | 46 | 13.05 | 77.74 | 0 | 0 | 11 | 0 |
| Twenty20 | 10 | 9 | 0 | 248 | 62 | 27.55 | 145.88 | 0 | 2 | 2 | 0 |

| Bowling | Mat | Balls | Runs | Wkts | BBI | BBM | Ave | Econ | SR | 5w | 10 |
|---|---|---|---|---|---|---|---|---|---|---|---|
| ODIs | 8 | 138 | 139 | 3 | 2/46 | 2/46 | 46.33 | 6.04 | 46.0 | 0 | 0 |
| T20Is | 3 | 30 | 56 | 0 | - | - | - | 11.20 | - | 0 | 0 |
| First-class | 7 | 413 | 214 | 11 | 4/66 | 6/102 | 19.45 | 3.10 | 37.5 | 0 | 0 |
| List A | 25 | 360 | 338 | 8 | 2/38 | 2/38 | 42.25 | 5.63 | 45.0 | 0 | 0 |
| Twenty20 | 10 | 30 | 56 | 0 | - | - | - | 11.20 | - | 0 | 0 |

# PRESTON MOMMSEN  RHB OB

SCOTLAND

**FULL NAME:** Preston Luke Mommsen
**BORN:** October 14, 1987, Durban, South Africa
**SQUAD NO:** 1
**HEIGHT:** 5ft 8in
**NICKNAME:** Gok
**EDUCATION:** Hilton College; Gordonstoun School; Glasgow Caledonian University
**TEAMS:** Scotland, Kent 2nd XI, Northamptonshire 2nd XI, Scotland A
**CAREER:** ODI: 2010; T20I: 2012; First-class: 2010; List A: 2010; T20: 2011

---

**BEST BATTING:** 102 Scotland vs Namibia, Windhoek, 2011
**BEST BOWLING:** 3-67 Scotland vs Netherlands, Aberdeen, 2011

---

**FAMILY TIES?** Heath Streak – second cousin. Norman Featherstone [Middlesex] – uncle
**CAREER HIGHLIGHTS?** The 2011 CB40 and chasing 320 to beat Ireland in an ODI
**SUPERSTITIONS?** Yes, but don't enjoy discussing them!
**CRICKETING HEROES?** Jonty Rhodes, Hansie Cronje, Brian Lara
**BEST PLAYER IN COUNTY CRICKET?** Jos Buttler
**TIP FOR THE TOP?** James Vince
**IF YOU WEREN'T A CRICKETER?** Quantity surveyor
**ACCOMPLISHMENTS?** Surviving a Scottish winter!
**GUILTY PLEASURES?** Haagen-Dazs
**AMAZE ME!** 1. Played in the same SA Schools team as Craig Kieswetter 2. Represented the Natal Sharks up to U19 level 3. Quickest schoolboy to 1,000 runs in the UK in 2006
**FANTASY SLIP CORDON?** Keeper: David Attenborough, 1st: Chris Gayle, 2nd: Jonny Wilkinson, 3rd: Barack Obama, Gully: Myself
**TWITTER FEED:** @prestonmommsen

| Batting | Mat | Inns | NO | Runs | HS | Ave | SR | 100 | 50 | Ct | St |
|---|---|---|---|---|---|---|---|---|---|---|---|
| ODIs | 10 | 10 | 0 | 204 | 80 | 20.40 | 53.12 | 0 | 1 | 3 | 0 |
| T20Is | 1 | 1 | 1 | 22 | 22* | - | 146.66 | 0 | 0 | 0 | 0 |
| First-class | 5 | 9 | 0 | 177 | 102 | 19.66 | 42.75 | 1 | 0 | 8 | 0 |
| List A | 30 | 29 | 5 | 719 | 81* | 29.95 | 76.24 | 0 | 3 | 20 | 0 |
| Twenty20 | 8 | 8 | 3 | 159 | 39 | 31.80 | 124.21 | 0 | 0 | 5 | 0 |

| Bowling | Mat | Balls | Runs | Wkts | BBI | BBM | Ave | Econ | SR | 5w | 10 |
|---|---|---|---|---|---|---|---|---|---|---|---|
| ODIs | 10 | 90 | 88 | 6 | 3/26 | 3/26 | 14.66 | 5.86 | 15.0 | 0 | 0 |
| T20Is | 1 | 24 | 32 | 1 | 1/32 | 1/32 | 32.00 | 8.00 | 24.0 | 0 | 0 |
| First-class | 5 | 192 | 127 | 4 | 3/67 | 3/67 | 31.75 | 3.96 | 48.0 | 0 | 0 |
| List A | 30 | 378 | 345 | 14 | 3/26 | 3/26 | 24.64 | 5.47 | 27.0 | 0 | 0 |
| Twenty20 | 8 | 118 | 166 | 8 | 3/12 | 3/12 | 20.75 | 8.44 | 14.7 | 0 | 0 |

# DEWALD NEL

## RHB RMF

**FULL NAME:** Johann Dewald Nel
**BORN:** June 6, 1980, Klerksdorp, South Africa
**SQUAD NO:** 17
**HEIGHT:** 6ft
**NICKNAME:** Nella
**EDUCATION:** George Watson's College; UWS
**TEAMS:** Scotland, Kent, Worcestershire
**CAREER:** ODI: 2006; T20I: 2007; First-class: 2004; List A: 2004; T20: 2007

**BEST BATTING:** 36 Scotland vs Afghanistan, Ayr, 2010
**BEST BOWLING:** 6-62 Kent vs Yorkshire, Leeds, 2010
**COUNTY CAP:** 2007 (Worcestershire)

**WHY CRICKET?** I started playing aged six and never looked back since
**CAREER HIGHLIGHTS?** 2007 World Cup, 2007 World T20
**CRICKETING HEROES?** Shaun Pollock
**WHEN RAIN STOPS PLAY?** Drinking coffee, eating and being bored
**FAVOURITE TV?** CSI Miami
**FAVOURITE FILM?** The Shawshank Redemption
**ACCOMPLISHMENTS?** Catching my first salmon!
**GUILTY PLEASURES?** Chocolate covered chocolate, double dipped in chocolate!
**AMAZE ME!** In 2008 I became the first ever player to bowl two maiden overs in a single international T20 match
**FANTASY SLIP CORDON?** Keeper: Tiger Woods, 1st: Michael Jackson, 2nd: Me, 3rd: Muhammad Ali, Gully: The Invisible Man
**TWITTER FEED:** @dewaldnel619

| Batting | Mat | Inns | NO | Runs | HS | Ave | SR | 100 | 50 | Ct | St |
|---|---|---|---|---|---|---|---|---|---|---|---|
| ODIs | 19 | 10 | 8 | 31 | 11* | 15.50 | 57.40 | 0 | 0 | 3 | 0 |
| T20Is | 10 | 5 | 2 | 34 | 13* | 11.33 | 136.00 | 0 | 0 | 1 | 0 |
| First-class | 19 | 25 | 11 | 156 | 36 | 11.14 | 32.77 | 0 | 0 | 6 | 0 |
| List A | 84 | 49 | 28 | 202 | 36* | 9.61 | 52.74 | 0 | 0 | 15 | 0 |
| Twenty20 | 15 | 5 | 2 | 34 | 13* | 11.33 | 136.00 | 0 | 0 | 1 | 0 |

| Bowling | Mat | Balls | Runs | Wkts | BBI | BBM | Ave | Econ | SR | 5w | 10 |
|---|---|---|---|---|---|---|---|---|---|---|---|
| ODIs | 19 | 730 | 649 | 14 | 4/25 | 4/25 | 46.35 | 5.33 | 52.1 | 0 | 0 |
| T20Is | 10 | 186 | 169 | 12 | 3/10 | 3/10 | 14.08 | 5.45 | 15.5 | 0 | 0 |
| First-class | 19 | 2514 | 1434 | 52 | 6/62 | | 27.57 | 3.42 | 48.3 | 2 | 0 |
| List A | 84 | 3398 | 2969 | 83 | 4/25 | 4/25 | 35.77 | 5.24 | 40.9 | 0 | 0 |
| Twenty20 | 15 | 289 | 278 | 17 | 3/10 | 3/10 | 16.35 | 5.77 | 17.0 | 0 | 0 |

# MATTHEW PARKER

**LHB RMF**

SCOTLAND

**FULL NAME:** Matthew Archibald Parker
**BORN:** March 2, 1990, Dundee
**SQUAD NO:** 23
**HEIGHT:** 6ft
**NICKNAME:** Hoggy, Warren, Roof
**EDUCATION:** Timergreens Primary School; Arbroath High School
**TEAMS:** Scotland, Scotland A, Scotland Under-13s, Scotland Under-15s, Scotland Under-17s
**CAREER:** ODI: 2010; T20I: 2012; First-class: 2010; List A: 2009; T20: 2012

**BEST BATTING:** 65 Scotland vs Netherlands, Deventer, 2010
**BEST BOWLING:** 4-63 Scotland vs Netherlands, Deventer, 2010

**FAMILY TIES?** Grandfather Chris Plomer MBE was the coach at my school and club
**CAREER HIGHLIGHTS?** Getting my first cap for Scotland
**TIPS FOR THE TOP?** Freddie Coleman and Ross McLean from Scotland
**FAVOURITE TV?** Modern Family
**FAVOURITE FILM?** Remember The Titans
**FAVOURITE BOOK?** Kane And Abel, The Da Vinci Code
**ACCOMPLISHMENTS?** In P7 my project about the Amazon rainforest was published in a book. I was offered the chance to play basketball at high school in America but decided to go to Australia and play cricket instead
**GUILTY PLEASURES?** Irn Bru and Percy Pigs
**AMAZE ME!** I was given 'bad boy' fitness/fielding practice on the morning of my debut, I forget the reason why There is video evidence that I am the world's worst at downing a pint of lager – wet feet! Justin Bieber is in my Top 25 Most Played playlist on my iTunes library
**TWITTER FEED:** @Matthew23P

| Batting | Mat | Inns | NO | Runs | HS | Ave | SR | 100 | 50 | Ct | St |
|---|---|---|---|---|---|---|---|---|---|---|---|
| ODIs | 10 | 8 | 2 | 59 | 22 | 9.83 | 56.73 | 0 | 0 | 3 | 0 |
| First-class | 3 | 6 | 0 | 122 | 65 | 20.33 | 41.21 | 0 | 1 | 2 | 0 |
| List A | 28 | 24 | 9 | 171 | 23 | 11.40 | 55.70 | 0 | 0 | 7 | 0 |
| Twenty20 | 1 | - | - | - | - | - | - | - | - | 1 | 0 |

| Bowling | Mat | Balls | Runs | Wkts | BBI | BBM | Ave | Econ | SR | 5w | 10 |
|---|---|---|---|---|---|---|---|---|---|---|---|
| ODIs | 10 | 414 | 327 | 12 | 4/33 | 4/33 | 27.25 | 4.73 | 34.5 | 0 | 0 |
| First-class | 3 | 630 | 333 | 14 | 4/63 | 7/119 | 23.78 | 3.17 | 45.0 | 0 | 0 |
| List A | 28 | 1096 | 1022 | 36 | 5/47 | 5/47 | 28.38 | 5.59 | 30.4 | 1 | 0 |
| Twenty20 | 1 | 6 | 7 | 0 | - | - | - | 7.00 | - | 0 | 0 |

**FULL NAME:** Marc John Petrie
**BORN:** March 2, 1990, Dundee
**SQUAD NO:** 3
**HEIGHT:** 5ft 8in
**NICKNAME:** Sparkie
**EDUCATION:** Arbroath High School; Edinburgh's Telford College
**TEAMS:** Scotland, Scotland Under-15s, Scotland Under-17s, Scotland Under-19s
**CAREER:** ODI: 2009; List A: 2009; T20: 2011

SCOTLAND

**FAMILY TIES?** My dad played club cricket for Arbroath United CC as a wicketkeeper/batsman
**WHY CRICKET?** Was taken to Kwik Cricket at an early age, met new friends and enjoyed the sport instantly. I enjoyed the big hitting involved and the fact that everybody got a shot to do everything
**CAREER HIGHLIGHTS?** Making my full Scotland debut in 2009 vs Canada at the age of 19 and also playing against Australia in an ODI in the same season
**SUPERSTITIONS?** No, just routines
**CRICKETING HEROES?** Adam Gilchrist
**NON-CRICKETING HEROES?** David Beckham
**BEST PLAYER IN COUNTY CRICKET?** Jos Buttler
**TIPS FOR THE TOP?** Jos Buttler, Jonny Bairstow, James Taylor, David Warner, Trent Copeland
**FAVOURITE TV?** One Tree Hill, The Big Bang Theory
**FAVOURITE FILM?** Star Wars
**FAVOURITE BOOK?** Adam Gilchrist's autobiography
**DREAM HOLIDAY?** Orlando, Florida
**SURPRISING SKILL?** I play a little guitar
**GUILTY PLEASURES?** The X Factor
**TWITTER FEED:** @marcpetrie3

| Batting | Mat | Inns | NO | Runs | HS | Ave | SR | 100 | 50 | Ct | St |
|---------|-----|------|-----|------|-----|------|-------|-----|-----|-----|-----|
| ODIs | 4 | 2 | 0 | 3 | 3 | 1.50 | 16.66 | 0 | 0 | 3 | 1 |
| List A | 7 | 5 | 1 | 16 | 7* | 4.00 | 39.02 | 0 | 0 | 3 | 1 |
| Twenty20 | 2 | 2 | 1 | 0 | 0* | 0.00 | 0.00 | 0 | 0 | 0 | 0 |

| Bowling | Mat | Balls | Runs | Wkts | BBI | BBM | Ave | Econ | SR | 5w | 10 |
|---------|-----|-------|------|------|-----|-----|-----|------|-----|-----|-----|
| ODIs | 4 | - | - | - | - | - | - | - | - | - | - |
| List A | 7 | - | - | - | - | - | - | - | - | - | - |
| Twenty20 | 2 | - | - | - | - | - | - | - | - | - | - |

# SAFYAAN SHARIF

## RHB RMF

SCOTLAND

FULL NAME: Safyaan Mohammed Sharif
BORN: May 24, 1991, Huddersfield
SQUAD NO: 50
HEIGHT: 6ft 2in
NICKNAME: Saf
EDUCATION: Buckhaven High School
TEAMS: Scotland, Scotland Under-15s,
Scotland Under-17s, Scotland Under-19s
CAREER: ODI: 2011; T20I: 2012; First-class:
2011; List A: 2011; T20: 2011

BEST BATTING: 11 Scotland vs Namibia, Windhoek, 2011
BEST BOWLING: 3-27 Scotland vs UAE, Sharjah, 2012

CAREER HIGHLIGHTS? My debut match against Holland
CRICKETING HEROES? Wasim Akram
NON-CRICKETING HEROES? My dad
BEST PLAYER IN COUNTY CRICKET? Owais Shah
IF YOU WEREN'T A CRICKETER? Studying
WHEN RAIN STOPS PLAY? I just chill and chat with mates
FAVOURITE TV? Soccer AM
FAVOURITE FILM? Bad Boys
FAVOURITE BOOK? The holy book of Quran
DREAM HOLIDAY? Saudi Arabia
SURPRISING SKILL? Good dancer

| Batting | Mat | Inns | NO | Runs | HS | Ave | SR | 100 | 50 | Ct | St |
|---|---|---|---|---|---|---|---|---|---|---|---|
| ODIs | 3 | 2 | 2 | 10 | 9* | - | 43.47 | 0 | 0 | 1 | 0 |
| T20Is | 1 | - | - | - | - | - | - | - | - | 0 | 0 |
| First-class | 2 | 2 | 1 | 11 | 11 | 11.00 | 47.82 | 0 | 0 | 2 | 0 |
| List A | 11 | 7 | 4 | 35 | 13* | 11.66 | 60.34 | 0 | 0 | 1 | 0 |
| Twenty20 | 7 | 2 | 1 | 20 | 13* | 20.00 | 133.33 | 0 | 0 | 1 | 0 |

| Bowling | Mat | Balls | Runs | Wkts | BBI | BBM | Ave | Econ | SR | 5w | 10 |
|---|---|---|---|---|---|---|---|---|---|---|---|
| ODIs | 3 | 120 | 119 | 5 | 4/27 | 4/27 | 23.80 | 5.95 | 24.0 | 0 | 0 |
| T20Is | 1 | 24 | 20 | 1 | 1/20 | 1/20 | 20.00 | 5.00 | 24.0 | 0 | 0 |
| First-class | 2 | 348 | 194 | 5 | 3/27 | 5/88 | 38.80 | 3.34 | 69.6 | 0 | 0 |
| List A | 11 | 424 | 376 | 12 | 4/27 | 4/27 | 31.33 | 5.32 | 35.3 | 0 | 0 |
| Twenty20 | 7 | 132 | 145 | 10 | 3/29 | 3/29 | 14.50 | 6.59 | 13.2 | 0 | 0 |

FULL NAME: Simon James Stevenson Smith
BORN: December 8, 1979, Ashington, Northumberland
SQUAD NO: 32
HEIGHT: 5ft 8in
NICKNAME: Smudger
EDUCATION: Loretto School, Musselburgh; Loughborough University
TEAMS: Scotland
CAREER: T20I: 2010; First-class: 2004; List A: 2004; T20: 2010

**SCOTLAND**

---

BEST BATTING: 54 Scotland vs UAE, Sharjah, 2012

---

FAMILY TIES? Father played for his local team Belford CC for over 40 years, mother coached at various levels, brother played for Loughborough University and Scotland U19 and sister played a bit too

WHY CRICKET? Mad about competitive sports from the very beginning, and with the whole family being into their cricket that was the one I became most keen on

CAREER HIGHLIGHTS? Playing in the 2010 Intercontinental Cup final and the 2010 World T20 qualifiers. Neither of them ended with the desired result, but playing in global tournaments is the pinnacle. Hopefully more opportunities will come

BEST PLAYER IN COUNTY CRICKET? Kyle Coetzer

TIP FOR THE TOP? Josh Davey

IF YOU WEREN'T A CRICKETER? Finding a way of being involved in cricket in some way

WHEN RAIN STOPS PLAY? Newspapers, crosswords and trying to retain a modicum of sanity. Not easy in our dressing room

GUILTY PLEASURES? My fiancée's homemade orange and poppyseed cake and the music of Bruce Springsteen

AMAZE ME! In my final year at Loughborough I compered the annual comedy cabaret

| Batting | Mat | Inns | NO | Runs | HS | Ave | SR | 100 | 50 | Ct | St |
|---|---|---|---|---|---|---|---|---|---|---|---|
| T20Is | 4 | 4 | 1 | 21 | 9 | 7.00 | 52.50 | 0 | 0 | 0 | 1 |
| First-class | 12 | 13 | 4 | 286 | 54 | 31.77 | 37.09 | 0 | 1 | 31 | 1 |
| List A | 12 | 8 | 2 | 103 | 41* | 17.16 | 72.02 | 0 | 0 | 7 | 5 |
| Twenty20 | 6 | 5 | 2 | 24 | 9 | 8.00 | 55.81 | 0 | 0 | 2 | 2 |

| Bowling | Mat | Balls | Runs | Wkts | BBI | BBM | Ave | Econ | SR | 5w | 10 |
|---|---|---|---|---|---|---|---|---|---|---|---|
| T20Is | 4 | - | - | - | - | - | - | - | - | - | - |
| First-class | 12 | - | - | - | - | - | - | - | - | - | - |
| List A | 12 | - | - | - | - | - | - | - | - | - | - |
| Twenty20 | 6 | - | - | - | - | - | - | - | - | - | - |

FULL NAME: Jan Hendrik Stander
BORN: January 4, 1982, Port Elizabeth, South Africa
SQUAD NO: 31
HEIGHT: 5ft 8in
EDUCATION: Daniel Pienaar Technical High School, Port Elizabeth; NNMU University
TEAMS: Scotland, Eastern Province Academy XI, Scotland Lions
CAREER: ODI: 2009; T20I: 2009; First-class: 2009; List A: 2009; T20: 2009

BEST BATTING: 64 Scotland vs Canada, Aberdeen, 2009
BEST BOWLING: 3-43 Scotland vs Canada, Aberdeen, 2009

CAREER HIGHLIGHTS? Playing in the World T20
CRICKETING HEROES? Jacques Kallis
NON-CRICKETING HEROES? Nelson Mandela
IF YOU WEREN'T A CRICKETER? Working for the family business
WHEN RAIN STOPS PLAY? Listen to music or watch cricket on Sky
FAVOURITE TV? The Apprentice
FAVOURITE FILM? Men Of Honour
FAVOURITE BOOK? Don't read
DREAM HOLIDAY? New York
NOTES: Completed his four-year residency qualification in 2008 to become eligible to represent Scotland

| Batting | Mat | Inns | NO | Runs | HS | Ave | SR | 100 | 50 | Ct | St |
|---|---|---|---|---|---|---|---|---|---|---|---|
| ODIs | 4 | 4 | 1 | 36 | 22* | 12.00 | 69.23 | 0 | 0 | 1 | 0 |
| T20Is | 7 | 7 | 1 | 56 | 45 | 9.33 | 96.55 | 0 | 0 | 2 | 0 |
| First-class | 1 | 2 | 0 | 64 | 64 | 32.00 | 49.61 | 0 | 1 | 0 | 0 |
| List A | 20 | 19 | 3 | 288 | 80* | 18.00 | 73.09 | 0 | 1 | 5 | 0 |
| Twenty20 | 16 | 16 | 3 | 309 | 116* | 23.76 | 147.14 | 1 | 0 | 5 | 0 |

| Bowling | Mat | Balls | Runs | Wkts | BBI | BBM | Ave | Econ | SR | 5w | 10 |
|---|---|---|---|---|---|---|---|---|---|---|---|
| ODIs | 4 | 150 | 166 | 6 | 2/25 | 2/25 | 27.66 | 6.64 | 25.0 | 0 | 0 |
| T20Is | 7 | 57 | 114 | 1 | 1/28 | 1/28 | 114.00 | 12.00 | 57.0 | 0 | 0 |
| First-class | 1 | 180 | 91 | 5 | 3/43 | 5/91 | 18.20 | 3.03 | 36.0 | 0 | 0 |
| List A | 20 | 865 | 821 | 24 | 4/41 | 4/41 | 34.20 | 5.69 | 36.0 | 0 | 0 |
| Twenty20 | 16 | 135 | 220 | 2 | 1/16 | 1/16 | 110.00 | 9.77 | 67.5 | 0 | 0 |

# JEAN SYMES

## LHB SLA

FULL NAME: Jean Symes
BORN: November 13, 1986, Johannesburg, South Africa
SQUAD NO: TBC
TEAMS: Gauteng, Lions, South Africa Under-19s
CAREER: First-class: 2005; List A: 2006; T20: 2008

SCOTLAND

BEST BATTING: 193 Gauteng vs Free State, Bloemfontein, 2006
BEST BOWLING: 6-61 Gauteng vs KwaZulu-Natal Inland, 2010

NOTES: Signed by Scotland in March as a replacement overseas player for George Worker, who was unavailable due to his selection for the New Zealand Emerging Player programme. Symes represented South Africa at the U19 World Cup in Sri Lanka in 2006, when he was named Man of the Match in a win over Scotland. He has had two stints playing for Norden CC in the Lancashire League where he scored almost 2,500 runs, including an unbeaten 268 against Royton in 2009. He will turn out for club side Watsonian CC when not on Saltires duties

| Batting | Mat | Inns | NO | Runs | HS | Ave | SR | 100 | 50 | Ct | St |
|---------|-----|------|-----|------|-----|--------|--------|-----|----|-----|-----|
| First-class | 54 | 90 | 6 | 2865 | 193 | 34.10 | 65.24 | 6 | 12 | 41 | 0 |
| List A | 56 | 54 | 1 | 1714 | 170 | 32.33 | 86.13 | 2 | 10 | 25 | 0 |
| Twenty20 | 23 | 17 | 6 | 297 | 40 | 27.00 | 121.72 | 0 | 0 | 12 | 0 |

| Bowling | Mat | Balls | Runs | Wkts | BBI | BBM | Ave | Econ | SR | 5w | 10 |
|---------|-----|-------|------|------|-----|-----|-------|------|------|-----|-----|
| First-class | 54 | 4117 | 2403 | 65 | 6/61 | 8/100 | 36.96 | 3.50 | 63.3 | 1 | 0 |
| List A | 56 | 1529 | 1220 | 47 | 4/8 | 4/8 | 25.95 | 4.78 | 32.5 | 0 | 0 |
| Twenty20 | 23 | 218 | 297 | 15 | 3/5 | 3/5 | 19.80 | 8.17 | 14.5 | 0 | 0 |

## CRAIG WALLACE

## RHB WK

**FULL NAME:** Craig Donald Wallace
**BORN:** June 27, 1990, Dundee, Angus
**SQUAD NO:** 18
**HEIGHT:** 5ft 9in
**NICKNAME:** Smiler
**EDUCATION:** Dundee High School; Edinburgh University
**TEAMS:** Scotland, Scotland Under-15s, Scotland Under-17s, Scotland Under-19s
**CAREER:** T20I: 2012; List A: 2011; T20: 2011

**FAMILY TIES?** Dad and mum both used to play for their local clubs
**WHY CRICKET?** Parents just sent me to training at Forfarshire CC when I was five and have played ever since
**CAREER HIGHLIGHTS?** Making my debut for Scotland against Hampshire last season
**SUPERSTITIONS?** Walking right for runs and left for wickets
**CRICKETING HEROES?** Brendon McCullum, Andrew Flintoff
**NON-CRICKETING HEROES?** Jonny Wilkinson
**BEST PLAYER IN COUNTY CRICKET?** Marcus Trescothick
**TIP FOR THE TOP?** Alex Hales
**IF YOU WEREN'T A CRICKETER?** PE teacher
**WHEN RAIN STOPS PLAY?** Cards, poker, golf if it brightens up but the game has been called off
**FAVOURITE TV?** The Inbetweeners
**FAVOURITE FILM?** Coach Carter
**FAVOURITE BOOK?** Steig Larsson – The Girl Who Played With Fire
**DREAM HOLIDAY?** Barbados
**ACCOMPLISHMENTS?** Playing junior football for Dundee United
**AMAZE ME!** My grandad Russell Crossley played goalkeeper for Liverpool FC

| Batting | Mat | Inns | NO | Runs | HS | Ave | SR | 100 | 50 | Ct | St |
|---------|-----|------|----|----|----|-----|----|-----|----|----|----|
| T20Is | 1 | 1 | 1 | 7 | 7* | - | 233.33 | 0 | 0 | 2 | 0 |
| List A | 5 | 4 | 0 | 58 | 40 | 14.50 | 52.25 | 0 | 0 | 3 | 0 |
| Twenty20 | 7 | 6 | 4 | 52 | 24* | 26.00 | 136.84 | 0 | 0 | 2 | 2 |

| Bowling | Mat | Balls | Runs | Wkts | BBI | BBM | Ave | Econ | SR | 5w | 10 |
|---------|-----|-------|------|------|-----|-----|-----|------|----|----|----|
| T20Is | 1 | - | - | - | - | - | - | - | - | - | - |
| List A | 5 | - | - | - | - | - | - | - | - | - | - |
| Twenty20 | 7 | - | - | - | - | - | - | - | - | - | - |

# FRASER WATTS

## RHB RM

**FULL NAME:** David Fraser Watts
**BORN:** June 5, 1979, King's Lynn, Norfolk
**SQUAD NO:** 12
**HEIGHT:** 6ft
**NICKNAME:** Fraggle
**EDUCATION:** Boroughmuir High School; Durham School; Loughborough University
**TEAMS:** Scotland, Carlton (Scotland), Loughborough MCCU
**CAREER:** ODI: 2006; T20I: 2007; First-class: 1999; List A: 2002; T20: 2007

---

BEST BATTING: 146 Scotland vs Kenya, Abu Dhabi, 2004

---

**WHY CRICKET?** My dad is a huge cricket fan and took me down to our local cricket club Carlton CC at an early age

**CRICKETING HEROES?** Growing up it was Robin Smith, he scored a hundred in the first game I ever saw. More recently Justin Langer – the way he went about training and playing is pretty inspirational

**BEST PLAYER IN COUNTY CRICKET?** The best player not to have played for England yet is probably James Vince

**TIPS FOR THE TOP?** Young Scottish players for the future are Gavin Main, Freddie Coleman and Kyle MacPherson

**IF YOU WEREN'T A CRICKETER?** I work for Lloyds Banking Group, so probably doing that

**WHEN RAIN STOPS PLAY?** Generally trying to avoid [Richie] Berrington and [Gordon] Goudie who are usually up to no good. Otherwise reading the papers, crosswords and cards

**FAVOURITE FILM?** A Beautiful Mind, Gladiator, Big Daddy

**FAVOURITE BOOK?** Birdsong, Rubicon, Sacred Hoops, A Good Walk Spoiled

**TWITTER FEED:** @Fragglewatts

| Batting | Mat | Inns | NO | Runs | HS | Ave | SR | 100 | 50 | Ct | St |
|---|---|---|---|---|---|---|---|---|---|---|---|
| ODIs | 36 | 35 | 1 | 974 | 101 | 28.64 | 62.47 | 1 | 9 | 7 | 0 |
| T20Is | 8 | 6 | 0 | 81 | 46 | 13.50 | 103.84 | 0 | 0 | 5 | 0 |
| First-class | 21 | 34 | 1 | 942 | 146 | 28.54 | | 2 | 4 | 13 | 0 |
| List A | 135 | 132 | 11 | 2707 | 101 | 22.37 | | 1 | 15 | 26 | 0 |
| Twenty20 | 18 | 16 | 1 | 305 | 73 | 20.33 | 127.08 | 0 | 2 | 12 | 0 |
| Bowling | Mat | Balls | Runs | Wkts | BBI | BBM | Ave | Econ | SR | 5w | 10 |
| ODIs | 36 | - | - | - | - | - | - | - | - | - | - |
| T20Is | 8 | - | - | - | - | - | - | - | - | - | - |
| First-class | 21 | - | - | - | - | - | - | - | - | - | - |
| List A | 135 | - | - | - | - | - | - | - | - | - | - |
| Twenty20 | 18 | - | - | - | - | - | - | - | - | - | - |

# ALL**OUT**CRICKET

### The *magazine* the *players* read

Check out the AOC website, Facebook and
Twitter pages for all your cricketing needs

*The*
Netherlands

## WESLEY BARRESI

### RHB OB WK

FULL NAME: Wesley Barresi
BORN: May 3, 1984, Johannesburg, South Africa
SQUAD NO: 2
HEIGHT: 6ft
NICKNAME: Pepe
EDUCATION: SBHS, Ekurhuleni East College Campus
TEAMS: Netherlands, Easterns, Easterns Under-15s, Easterns Under-19s, Easterns Under-23s
CAREER: ODI: 2010; T20I: 2012; First-class: 2004; List A: 2004; T20: 2012

BEST BATTING: 81 Netherlands vs Zimbabwe XI, Amstelveen, 2010

WHY CRICKET? When South Africa resumed official international cricket in 1991, I really enjoyed watching the likes of Peter Kirsten, Adrian Kuiper and Jonty Rhodes

CAREER HIGHLIGHTS? I'd have to say helping Netherlands secure their first-ever ODI victory against a full member nation in Glasgow last year, scoring 65* off 43 balls

SUPERSTITIONS? I have a couple but won't mention them. You just never know what the opposition will get up to with that kind of information!

FAVOURITE FILM? A Beautiful Mind

DREAM HOLIDAY? The Maldives

SURPRISING SKILL? I produce my own electronic music and DJ

GUILTY PLEASURES? Oh gee, you wouldn't want to know. No seriously, you wouldn't want to know!

AMAZE ME! I am Italian but have never been to Italy, I occasionally stutter, I can't sleep at night after watching a horror movie

FANTASY SLIP CORDON? Keeper: Adam Gilchrist, 1st: Me, 2nd: Adriana Lima, 3rd: Eric Cartman, Gully: Adam Sandler

| Batting | Mat | Inns | NO | Runs | HS | Ave | SR | 100 | 50 | Ct | St |
|---|---|---|---|---|---|---|---|---|---|---|---|
| ODIs | 19 | 19 | 2 | 457 | 67 | 26.88 | 71.51 | 0 | 3 | 6 | 4 |
| T20Is | 2 | 2 | 0 | 17 | 14 | 8.50 | 85.00 | 0 | 0 | 0 | 0 |
| First-class | 10 | 19 | 0 | 325 | 81 | 17.10 | 46.03 | 0 | 2 | 13 | 1 |
| List A | 40 | 40 | 4 | 916 | 97* | 25.44 | 71.73 | 0 | 5 | 25 | 4 |
| Twenty20 | 8 | 7 | 1 | 88 | 45* | 14.66 | 101.14 | 0 | 0 | 2 | 0 |

| Bowling | Mat | Balls | Runs | Wkts | BBI | BBM | Ave | Econ | SR | 5w | 10 |
|---|---|---|---|---|---|---|---|---|---|---|---|
| ODIs | 19 | 18 | 20 | 0 | - | - | - | 6.66 | - | 0 | 0 |
| T20Is | 2 | - | - | - | - | - | - | - | - | - | - |
| First-class | 10 | 12 | 3 | 0 | - | - | - | 1.50 | - | 0 | 0 |
| List A | 40 | 18 | 20 | 0 | - | - | - | 6.66 | - | 0 | 0 |
| Twenty20 | 8 | - | - | - | - | - | - | - | - | - | - |

# PETER BORREN

RHB RM

FULL NAME: Peter William Borren
BORN: August 21, 1983, Christchurch, Canterbury, New Zealand
SQUAD NO: 83
HEIGHT: 5ft 8in
NICKNAME: Baldrick
EDUCATION: St Andrew's College, Christchurch
TEAMS: Netherlands, Canterbury Under-19s, Netherlands A, New Zealand Under-19s
CAREER: ODI: 2006; T20I: 2008; First-class: 2006; List A: 2006; T20: 2008

BEST BATTING: 109 Netherlands vs Scotland, Deventer, 2010
BEST BOWLING: 3-21 Netherlands vs Afghanistan, Amstelveen, 2009

WHY CRICKET? My mates were playing, I wanted to join, so I switched from tennis
CAREER HIGHLIGHTS? Beating England at Lord's in the opening match of the World T20. Captaining Netherlands to their first ODI win over a full member vs Bangladesh
CRICKETING HEROES? Viv Richards, Martin Crowe, Darron Reekers
NON-CRICKETING HEROES? My auntie Sylvia
WHEN RAIN STOPS PLAY? Coffee, boredom and generally annoying people
FAVOURITE TV? Luther
FAVOURITE FILM? Michael Clayton
FAVOURITE BOOK? Bryce Courtenay – Power Of One and Tandia
DREAM HOLIDAY? Santorini
ACCOMPLISHMENTS? Helping less fortunate people
SURPRISING SKILL? Fat man, skinny man party trick
GUILTY PLEASURES? No comment!
TWITTER FEED: @dutchiepdb

| Batting | Mat | Inns | NO | Runs | HS | Ave | SR | 100 | 50 | Ct | St |
|---|---|---|---|---|---|---|---|---|---|---|---|
| ODIs | 49 | 43 | 3 | 791 | 96 | 19.77 | 78.86 | 0 | 4 | 23 | 0 |
| T20Is | 12 | 10 | 2 | 123 | 37* | 15.37 | 96.85 | 0 | 0 | 6 | 0 |
| First-class | 16 | 28 | 0 | 870 | 109 | 31.07 | 56.64 | 2 | 3 | 18 | 0 |
| List A | 84 | 72 | 7 | 1359 | 96 | 20.90 | 79.80 | 0 | 6 | 34 | 0 |
| Twenty20 | 19 | 16 | 3 | 234 | 45 | 18.00 | 100.00 | 0 | 0 | 9 | 0 |

| Bowling | Mat | Balls | Runs | Wkts | BBI | BBM | Ave | Econ | SR | 5w | 10 |
|---|---|---|---|---|---|---|---|---|---|---|---|
| ODIs | 49 | 1667 | 1403 | 40 | 3/30 | 3/30 | 35.07 | 5.04 | 41.6 | 0 | 0 |
| T20Is | 12 | 240 | 269 | 9 | 2/19 | 2/19 | 29.88 | 6.72 | 26.6 | 0 | 0 |
| First-class | 16 | 2277 | 1179 | 29 | 3/21 | 4/54 | 40.65 | 3.10 | 78.5 | 0 | 0 |
| List A | 84 | 3065 | 2557 | 73 | 3/29 | 3/29 | 35.02 | 5.00 | 41.9 | 0 | 0 |
| Twenty20 | 19 | 342 | 387 | 12 | 3/14 | 3/14 | 32.25 | 6.78 | 28.5 | 0 | 0 |

## MUDASSAR BUKHARI                                    RHB RMF

THE NETHERLANDS

**FULL NAME:** Mudassar Bukhari
**BORN:** December 26, 1983, Gujrat, Punjab, Pakistan
**SQUAD NO:** 7
**HEIGHT:** 6ft
**TEAMS:** Netherlands, Netherlands A
**CAREER:** ODI: 2007; T20I: 2008; First-class: 2007; List A: 2006; T20: 2008

**BEST BATTING:** 66* Netherlands vs Canada, King City, 2007
**BEST BOWLING:** 5-79 Netherlands vs Scotland, Aberdeen, 2011

**NOTES:** Moved from Pakistan at the age of 14 along with his family. Plays club cricket in Amsterdam. First came to the Netherlands selectors' attention when he apeared for a KNCB Invitation XI against a Denmark XI at Sportpark Maarschalkerweerd, Utrecht in 2007. Made his ODI debut against Canada in Toronto on July 3, 2007, bowling first change and claiming figures of 3-24 from eight overs. His top List A score of 84 came against Canada during the 2009 World Cup Qualifiers, while his highest ODI score of 71 came off 114 deliveries against Ireland at Belfast in 2007. Impressed many observers with his performances with the ball during the 2011 World Cup, where he claimed five wickets from six matches with an economy rate of 5.25

| Batting | Mat | Inns | NO | Runs | HS | Ave | SR | 100 | 50 | Ct | St |
|---|---|---|---|---|---|---|---|---|---|---|---|
| ODIs | 37 | 28 | 4 | 457 | 71 | 19.04 | 76.67 | 0 | 2 | 5 | 0 |
| T20Is | 10 | 7 | 3 | 52 | 28* | 13.00 | 133.33 | 0 | 0 | 1 | 0 |
| First-class | 9 | 16 | 2 | 359 | 66* | 25.64 | 71.08 | 0 | 3 | 1 | 0 |
| List A | 71 | 57 | 10 | 1033 | 84 | 21.97 | 87.32 | 0 | 5 | 11 | 0 |
| Twenty20 | 17 | 13 | 4 | 80 | 28* | 8.88 | 111.11 | 0 | 0 | 2 | 0 |

| Bowling | Mat | Balls | Runs | Wkts | BBI | BBM | Ave | Econ | SR | 5w | 10 |
|---|---|---|---|---|---|---|---|---|---|---|---|
| ODIs | 37 | 1680 | 1216 | 46 | 3/17 | 3/17 | 26.43 | 4.34 | 36.5 | 0 | 0 |
| T20Is | 10 | 184 | 214 | 10 | 4/33 | 4/33 | 21.40 | 6.97 | 18.4 | 0 | 0 |
| First-class | 9 | 1372 | 674 | 23 | 5/79 | 5/79 | 29.30 | 2.94 | 59.6 | 1 | 0 |
| List A | 71 | 3091 | 2417 | 85 | 4/41 | 4/41 | 28.43 | 4.69 | 36.3 | 0 | 0 |
| Twenty20 | 17 | 303 | 359 | 15 | 4/33 | 4/33 | 23.93 | 7.10 | 20.2 | 0 | 0 |

**FULL NAME:** Atse Folkert Buurman
**BORN:** March 21, 1982, Dordrecht, Netherlands
**SQUAD NO:** 82
**HEIGHT:** 5ft 9in
**NICKNAME:** Ace
**TEAMS:** Netherlands, Voorburg CC, VRA Cricket
**CAREER:** ODI: 2007; T20I: 2010; First-class: 2007; List A: 2003; T20: 2010

BEST BATTING: 41 Netherlands vs Kenya, Amstelveen, 2008

FAMILY TIES? My grandfather used to play and umpire, and my parents took me to watch cricket in the Netherlands and England
CAREER HIGHLIGHTS? The 2011 World Cup
NON-CRICKETING HEROES? Ricky Gervais, Mike Myers, The Rock, Alistair Overeem
TIP FOR THE TOP? Alexei Kervezee
WHEN RAIN STOPS PLAY? I listen to music, talk cricket, make jokes and organise my kit
FAVOURITE TV? Fight Night, Ultimate Survivor
FAVOURITE FILM? The Hangover, Step Brothers, Ong Bak
DREAM HOLIDAY? French Polynesia, Fiji, Miami
ACCOMPLISHMENTS? My family, wife and daughter
SURPRISING SKILL? I play the saxophone and can also balance large objects on my chin, like chairs and bats
GUILTY PLEASURES? Biltong. Fortunately I can't buy it that often in the Netherlands
TWITTER FEED: @Aceman0082

| Batting | Mat | Inns | NO | Runs | HS | Ave | SR | 100 | 50 | Ct | St |
|---|---|---|---|---|---|---|---|---|---|---|---|
| ODIs | 17 | 11 | 2 | 140 | 34 | 15.55 | 78.21 | 0 | 0 | 17 | 3 |
| T20Is | 4 | 2 | 0 | 0 | 0 | 0.00 | 0.00 | 0 | 0 | 1 | 1 |
| First-class | 5 | 10 | 1 | 176 | 41 | 19.55 | 55.00 | 0 | 0 | 16 | 1 |
| List A | 29 | 20 | 2 | 262 | 53 | 14.55 | | 0 | 1 | 25 | 5 |
| Twenty20 | 8 | 4 | 0 | 8 | 5 | 2.00 | 57.14 | 0 | 0 | 3 | 2 |

| Bowling | Mat | Balls | Runs | Wkts | BBI | BBM | Ave | Econ | SR | 5w | 10 |
|---|---|---|---|---|---|---|---|---|---|---|---|
| ODIs | 17 | - | - | - | - | - | - | - | - | - | - |
| T20Is | 4 | - | - | - | - | - | - | - | - | - | - |
| First-class | 5 | - | - | - | - | - | - | - | - | - | - |
| List A | 29 | - | - | - | - | - | - | - | - | - | - |
| Twenty20 | 8 | - | - | - | - | - | - | - | - | - | - |

# TOM COOPER

**RHB OB**

**FULL NAME:** Tom Lexley William Cooper
**BORN:** November 26, 1986, Wollongong, New South Wales, Australia
**SQUAD NO:** 26
**HEIGHT:** 6ft 1in
**NICKNAME:** Coops
**EDUCATION:** University of NSW
**TEAMS:** Netherlands, Australia Under-19s, New South Wales Institute of Sport, New South Wales Second XI, South Australia, South Australia Second XI
**CAREER:** ODI: 2010; T20I: 2012; First-class: 2008; List A: 2008; T20: 2008

**BEST BATTING:** 203* South Australia vs New South Wales, Sydney, 2011
**BEST BOWLING:** 1-11 South Australia vs New South Wales, SCG, 2010

**NOTES:** Qualifies for the Netherlands through his Dutch mother. Represented Australia at the 2006 U19 World Cup, making 104 against South Africa. Made his first-class debut for Western Australia against South Australia at Adelaide in November, 2008. Made his List A debut against the same opponents at the same venue three days later, scoring 53 off 67 deliveries from the top of the order. Impressed many judges with a brutal 160* for the Prime Minister's XI against the touring West Indians at Canberra in February 2010, a knock that contained six sixes and 14 fours. Made his ODI debut against Scotland at Rotterdam on June 15, 2010 and notched a half-century, a feat he then repeated in his next two ODIs. Notched his maiden first-class double-hundred – 203* off 291 deliveries – against New South Wales at Sydney in November 2011

| Batting | Mat | Inns | NO | Runs | HS | Ave | SR | 100 | 50 | Ct | St |
|---|---|---|---|---|---|---|---|---|---|---|---|
| ODIs | 18 | 18 | 2 | 864 | 101 | 54.00 | 70.58 | 1 | 7 | 10 | 0 |
| T20Is | 2 | 2 | 0 | 36 | 29 | 18.00 | 100.00 | 0 | 0 | 2 | 0 |
| First-class | 20 | 34 | 2 | 1213 | 203* | 37.90 | 53.34 | 1 | 8 | 17 | 0 |
| List A | 65 | 64 | 8 | 2393 | 126* | 42.73 | 77.89 | 4 | 17 | 33 | 0 |
| Twenty20 | 34 | 29 | 4 | 391 | 50 | 15.64 | 121.42 | 0 | 1 | 13 | 0 |

| Bowling | Mat | Balls | Runs | Wkts | BBI | BBM | Ave | Econ | SR | 5w | 10 |
|---|---|---|---|---|---|---|---|---|---|---|---|
| ODIs | 18 | 353 | 299 | 9 | 2/19 | 2/19 | 33.22 | 5.08 | 39.2 | 0 | 0 |
| T20Is | 2 | 18 | 15 | 0 | - | - | - | 5.00 | - | 0 | 0 |
| First-class | 20 | 421 | 287 | 4 | 1/11 | 2/97 | 71.75 | 4.09 | 105.2 | 0 | 0 |
| List A | 65 | 359 | 301 | 9 | 2/19 | 2/19 | 33.44 | 5.03 | 39.8 | 0 | 0 |
| Twenty20 | 34 | 42 | 35 | 1 | 1/11 | 1/11 | 35.00 | 5.00 | 42.0 | 0 | 0 |

# TOM DE GROOTH

## RHB OB

FULL NAME: Tom Nico de Grooth
BORN: May 14, 1979, The Hague, Netherlands
SQUAD NO: 99
HEIGHT: 5ft 10in
TEAMS: Netherlands, HCC
CAREER: ODI: 2006; T20I: 2008; First-class: 2004; List A: 2005; T20: 2008

BEST BATTING: 196 Netherlands vs Bermuda, Amstelveen, 2007
BEST BOWLING: 1-2 Netherlands vs Canada, Rotterdam, 2009

NOTES: One of Holland's most experienced cricketers, de Grooth first played for his country in an ICC Intercontinental Cup match against Scotland at Aberdeen in August 2004, scoring 59 from the top of the order in the second innings. Scored a crucial 49 during the Netherlands' historic victory over England in the opening match of the 2009 World T20 at Lord's. Struggled during the 2011 World Cup, only mustering 50 runs from five innings with a top-score of 28 coming against England at Nagpur

| Batting | Mat | Inns | NO | Runs | HS | Ave | SR | 100 | 50 | Ct | St |
|---|---|---|---|---|---|---|---|---|---|---|---|
| ODIs | 31 | 30 | 4 | 467 | 97 | 17.96 | 62.18 | 0 | 1 | 6 | 0 |
| T20Is | 9 | 7 | 3 | 107 | 49 | 26.75 | 110.30 | 0 | 0 | 4 | 0 |
| First-class | 19 | 34 | 1 | 887 | 196 | 26.87 | | 1 | 5 | 6 | 0 |
| List A | 62 | 58 | 7 | 919 | 97 | 18.01 | 64.13 | 0 | 3 | 10 | 0 |
| Twenty20 | 14 | 11 | 3 | 123 | 49 | 15.37 | 92.48 | 0 | 0 | 5 | 0 |

| Bowling | Mat | Balls | Runs | Wkts | BBI | BBM | Ave | Econ | SR | 5w | 10 |
|---|---|---|---|---|---|---|---|---|---|---|---|
| ODIs | 31 | 6 | 2 | 1 | 1/2 | 1/2 | 2.00 | 2.00 | 6.0 | 0 | 0 |
| T20Is | 9 | - | - | - | - | - | - | - | - | - | - |
| First-class | 19 | 45 | 36 | 1 | 1/2 | 1/2 | 36.00 | 4.80 | 45.0 | 0 | 0 |
| List A | 62 | 42 | 34 | 3 | 2/32 | 2/32 | 11.33 | 4.85 | 14.0 | 0 | 0 |
| Twenty20 | 14 | - | - | - | - | - | - | - | - | - | - |

# WILFRED DIEPEVEEN                                    RHB LB

**THE NETHERLANDS**

FULL NAME: Wilfred Peter Diepeveen
BORN: June 18, 1985, Utrecht, Netherlands
SQUAD NO: TBC
HEIGHT: 5ft 8in
NICKNAME: Willy, DVT
EDUCATION: Hogeschool, Utrecht
TEAMS: Netherlands, Netherlands A
CAREER: ODI: 2011; First-class: 2010; List A: 2010

BEST BATTING: 72* Netherlands vs Scotland, Deventer, 2010

FAMILY TIES? I am the first one in my family to start playing cricket but my sister now also plays and has represented the Netherlands
CAREER HIGHLIGHTS? Scoring 72* on my debut for the Netherlands and playing at Lord's
SUPERSTITIONS? Always put my left pad on first before batting
CRICKETING HEROES? Shane Warne, Shane Watson, Sachin Tendulkar, Peter Cantrell
NON-CRICKETING HEROES? Eddie Vedder, Dirk Kuyt, Lance Armstrong
BEST PLAYER IN COUNTY CRICKET? Ryan ten Doeschate
FAVOURITE BOOK? Good To Great by Jim Collins
DREAM HOLIDAY? Maldives, Fiji or Seychelles
ACCOMPLISHMENTS? Getting a degree and a great job at a great company which has taken me to almost all parts of the world already
GUILTY PLEASURES? Toasted cheese sandwiches
SURPRISING FACT? Have played cricket in Cyprus, have worked as a waiter during my studies, support the Pittsburgh Steelers in American football
FANTASY SLIP CORDON? Keeper: Ian Healy, 1st: Shane Warne, 2nd: Johnny Depp, 3rd: Myself, Gully: Sachin Tendulkar
TWITTER FEED: @incrediwil

| Batting | Mat | Inns | NO | Runs | HS | Ave | SR | 100 | 50 | Ct | St |
|---|---|---|---|---|---|---|---|---|---|---|---|
| ODIs | 1 | 1 | 0 | 6 | 6 | 6.00 | 85.71 | 0 | 0 | 0 | 0 |
| First-class | 3 | 6 | 1 | 171 | 72* | 34.20 | 54.98 | 0 | 1 | 2 | 0 |
| List A | 9 | 9 | 1 | 128 | 27 | 16.00 | 54.23 | 0 | 0 | 3 | 0 |

| Bowling | Mat | Balls | Runs | Wkts | BBI | BBM | Ave | Econ | SR | 5w | 10 |
|---|---|---|---|---|---|---|---|---|---|---|---|
| ODIs | 1 | - | - | - | - | - | - | - | - | - | - |
| First-class | 3 | - | - | - | - | - | - | - | - | - | - |
| List A | 9 | - | - | - | - | - | - | - | - | - | - |

# TIM GRUIJTERS

## RHB OB

FULL NAME: Timothy George Johannus Gruijters
BORN: August 28, 1991, The Hague, Netherlands
SQUAD NO: 51
HEIGHT: 6ft 1in
TEAMS: Netherlands, Netherlands Under-13s, Netherlands Under-15s, Netherlands Under-17s, Netherlands Under-19s
CAREER: ODI: 2010; List A: 2010; T20: 2012

NOTES: One of four cricket-mad brothers. Selected for the Dutch U12 side at the age of nine. Captained Holland at U19 level. Originally an allrounder who bowled seamers, his career seemed to be in doubt two years ago, when a severe back condition threatened to force him out of the game – he has since converted to bowling offspin. Played for Walmley in the Birmingham and District League for the past three seasons, scoring 895 runs in 28 league and other one-day appearances, 732 of them in 2011 at an average of 40.67 – in total he passed 50 five times, with his highest score 142 against Smethwick in the ECB National Club Championship. Also played nine times for Warwickshire U19 and was included in the Warwickshire 2nd XI for one match in 2010. Will play club cricket for Dutch side Quick Haag in 2012, alongside his younger brother James

| Batting | Mat | Inns | NO | Runs | HS | Ave | SR | 100 | 50 | Ct | St |
|---|---|---|---|---|---|---|---|---|---|---|---|
| ODIs | 4 | 4 | 1 | 68 | 32 | 22.66 | 58.62 | 0 | 0 | 2 | 0 |
| List A | 8 | 8 | 3 | 94 | 32 | 18.80 | 51.08 | 0 | 0 | 6 | 0 |
| Twenty20 | 3 | 2 | 0 | 11 | 6 | 5.50 | 55.00 | 0 | 0 | 0 | 0 |
| Bowling | Mat | Balls | Runs | Wkts | BBI | BBM | Ave | Econ | SR | 5w | 10 |
| ODIs | 4 | 120 | 79 | 2 | 2/37 | 2/37 | 39.50 | 3.95 | 60.0 | 0 | 0 |
| List A | 8 | 180 | 128 | 4 | 2/37 | 2/37 | 32.00 | 4.26 | 45.0 | 0 | 0 |
| Twenty20 | 3 | 12 | 11 | 0 | - | - | - | 5.50 | - | 0 | 0 |

## TOM HEGGELMAN

RHB RM

THE NETHERLANDS

FULL NAME: Thomas Josephus Heggelman
BORN: January 16, 1987, Schiedam, Netherlands
SQUAD NO: 87
HEIGHT: 6ft
NICKNAME: Hagelslag
EDUCATION: Johan Cruyff University, Amsterdam
TEAMS: Netherlands, Excelsior, Netherlands A, Netherlands Under-17s, Netherlands Under-19s, Netherlands Under-23s
CAREER: ODI: 2010; First-class: 2010; List A: 2010; T20: 2012

---

BEST BATTING: 30 Netherlands vs Ireland, Dublin, 2010

---

FAMILY TIES? My father arranges a lot of things at my club Excelsior'20 and is involved with the KNCB youth teams. In 2007 he was voted World Volunteer of the Year in the ICC Development Programme. My sister is a scorer for the 1st XI of my club and also does a lot of scoring at international level for KNCB youth. My mum also makes the best lunches in Holland for all our home games!

CAREER HIGHLIGHTS? Becoming champions with my club team in 2009. Making my first century – 128 vs Denmark. Every game I play for the Netherlands!

SUPERSTITIONS? Not that I am aware of

BEST PLAYER IN COUNTY CRICKET? Murray Goodwin, still going strong!

TIPS FOR THE TOP? Joost Kroesen, a young player who plays for my club and also plays in the KNCB youth teams

IF YOU WEREN'T A CRICKETER? I'd be playing soccer

WHEN RAIN STOPS PLAY? Playing cards with teammates, listening to music or eating!

DREAM HOLIDAY? Maldives

ACCOMPLISHMENTS? Finishing my studies in Sport and Movement

GUILTY PLEASURES? I love eating, a lot!

| Batting | Mat | Inns | NO | Runs | HS | Ave | SR | 100 | 50 | Ct | St |
|---|---|---|---|---|---|---|---|---|---|---|---|
| ODIs | 5 | 5 | 0 | 27 | 22 | 5.40 | 31.76 | 0 | 0 | 1 | 0 |
| First-class | 1 | 2 | 0 | 46 | 30 | 23.00 | 52.27 | 0 | 0 | 0 | 0 |
| List A | 16 | 11 | 2 | 52 | 22 | 5.77 | 33.12 | 0 | 0 | 3 | 0 |
| Twenty20 | 1 | - | - | - | - | - | - | - | - | 0 | 0 |

| Bowling | Mat | Balls | Runs | Wkts | BBI | BBM | Ave | Econ | SR | 5w | 10 |
|---|---|---|---|---|---|---|---|---|---|---|---|
| ODIs | 5 | 102 | 86 | 5 | 3/29 | 3/29 | 17.20 | 5.05 | 20.4 | 0 | 0 |
| First-class | 1 | 72 | 54 | 0 | - | - | - | 4.50 | - | 0 | 0 |
| List A | 16 | 252 | 222 | 7 | 3/29 | 3/29 | 31.71 | 5.28 | 36.0 | 0 | 0 |
| Twenty20 | 1 | - | - | - | - | - | - | - | - | - | - |

# MARK JONKMAN
## RHB RFM

FULL NAME: Mark Benjamin Sebastiaan Jonkman
BORN: March 20, 1986, The Hague, Netherlands
SQUAD NO: TBC
TEAMS: Netherlands, Netherlands A
CAREER: ODI: 2006; T20I: 2010; First-class: 2006; List A: 2006; T20: 2010

THE NETHERLANDS

BEST BATTING: 43* Netherlands vs Canada, King City, 2007
BEST BOWLING: 5-21 Netherlands vs Scotland, Deventer, 2010

NOTES: Made his international debut in an ODI against Canada at Potchefstroom on November 26, 2006 and recorded match figures of 0-37 off seven overs as Netherlands coasted to a 17-run win. Reportedly modelled his action on Brett Lee and was described by former Netherlands bowling coach Ian Pont as having the potential to become the fastest bowler outside the Test nations. His identical twin Maurits has also played for the Netherlands. In August 2010, the ICC suspended him from bowling in international cricket after an independent test found that his deliveries exceeded the tolerance threshold level of 15 degrees for bending of the elbow. He is currently undergoing remedial work on his action and it is hoped he will return to action soon, although he has not featured for the Netherlands since July 2010

| Batting | Mat | Inns | NO | Runs | HS | Ave | SR | 100 | 50 | Ct | St |
|---|---|---|---|---|---|---|---|---|---|---|---|
| ODIs | 16 | 9 | 4 | 59 | 16 | 11.80 | 74.68 | 0 | 0 | 1 | 0 |
| T20Is | 3 | 1 | 0 | 1 | 1 | 1.00 | 12.50 | 0 | 0 | 2 | 0 |
| First-class | 6 | 10 | 3 | 144 | 43* | 20.57 | 38.91 | 0 | 0 | 3 | 0 |
| List A | 24 | 14 | 6 | 95 | 16 | 11.87 | 74.21 | 0 | 0 | 3 | 0 |
| Twenty20 | 3 | 1 | 0 | 1 | 1 | 1.00 | 12.50 | 0 | 0 | 2 | 0 |

| Bowling | Mat | Balls | Runs | Wkts | BBI | BBM | Ave | Econ | SR | 5w | 10 |
|---|---|---|---|---|---|---|---|---|---|---|---|
| ODIs | 16 | 719 | 565 | 24 | 3/24 | 3/24 | 23.54 | 4.71 | 29.9 | 0 | 0 |
| T20Is | 3 | 48 | 47 | 4 | 2/21 | 2/21 | 11.75 | 5.87 | 12.0 | 0 | 0 |
| First-class | 6 | 858 | 419 | 15 | 5/21 | 7/83 | 27.93 | 2.93 | 57.2 | 1 | 0 |
| List A | 24 | 1091 | 898 | 37 | 3/24 | 3/24 | 24.27 | 4.93 | 29.4 | 0 | 0 |
| Twenty20 | 3 | 48 | 47 | 4 | 2/21 | 2/21 | 11.75 | 5.87 | 12.0 | 0 | 0 |

# MAURITS JONKMAN

**RHB RM**

FULL NAME: Maurits Maarten Alexander Jonkman
BORN: March 20, 1986, The Hague, Netherlands
SQUAD NO: TBC
HEIGHT: 5ft 10in
TEAMS: Netherlands, Netherlands Under-15s, Netherlands Under-17s, Netherlands Under-19s, Netherlands Under-23s
CAREER: ODI: 2007; First-class: 2007; List A: 2007

BEST BATTING: 18* Netherlands vs Bermuda, Amstelveen, 2007
BEST BOWLING: 2-63 Netherlands vs Zimbabwe XI, Amstelveen, 2010

NOTES: Identical twin of fellow Netherlands international Mark. Made his ODI debut against Bermuda on August 20, 2007, at Hazelaarweg, Rotterdam; bowling first change, he claimed the wickets of Lionel Cann, captain Irving Romaine and Chris Lonsdale on his way to match-figures of 3-22 off 5.4 overs as Netherlands registered an eight-wicket victory. Currently undergoing a training programme designed to change his bowling action, although the ICC has not suspended him from bowling as they did his brother. Hasn't played for Netherlands since August 2010, it remains to be seen if he will take part in Holland's CB40 campaign

| Batting | Mat | Inns | NO | Runs | HS | Ave | SR | 100 | 50 | Ct | St |
|---|---|---|---|---|---|---|---|---|---|---|---|
| ODIs | 4 | 2 | 0 | 20 | 13 | 10.00 | 39.21 | 0 | 0 | 1 | 0 |
| First-class | 4 | 7 | 1 | 62 | 18* | 10.33 | 32.12 | 0 | 0 | 1 | 0 |
| List A | 8 | 6 | 1 | 55 | 25* | 11.00 | 59.13 | 0 | 0 | 2 | 0 |

| Bowling | Mat | Balls | Runs | Wkts | BBI | BBM | Ave | Econ | SR | 5w | 10 |
|---|---|---|---|---|---|---|---|---|---|---|---|
| ODIs | 4 | 136 | 113 | 6 | 3/22 | 3/22 | 18.83 | 4.98 | 22.6 | 0 | 0 |
| First-class | 4 | 420 | 297 | 8 | 2/63 | 3/101 | 37.12 | 4.24 | 52.5 | 0 | 0 |
| List A | 8 | 260 | 198 | 10 | 3/18 | 3/18 | 19.80 | 4.56 | 26.0 | 0 | 0 |

# MOHAMMAD KASHIF

**RHB OB**

FULL NAME: Mohammad Kashif
BORN: December 3, 1984, Khanewal, Punjab, Pakistan
SQUAD NO: TBC
HEIGHT: 5ft 9in
TEAMS: Netherlands
CAREER: ODI: 2006; T20I: 2010; First-class: 2006; List A: 2006; T20: 2010

BEST BATTING: 24* Netherlands vs Kenya, Amstelveen, 2008
BEST BOWLING: 5-53 Netherlands vs Ireland, Dublin, 2010

NOTES: Made his international debut in an ODI against Sri Lanka at Amstelveen in 2006, returning match-figures of 2-79 from his 10 overs, dismissing both Sanath Jayasuriya and Kumar Sangakkara in the process. Described by coach Peter Drinnen as "a big turner of the ball with several useful variations," and someone who would "have probably played more international cricket were it not for the consistency of Pieter Seelaar and the fact that Tom Cooper, one of our best batsmen, bowls handy offbreaks." Hasn't represented the Netherlands since a rain-affected CB40 fixture against Essex at Chelmsford in 2010

| Batting | Mat | Inns | NO | Runs | HS | Ave | SR | 100 | 50 | Ct | St |
|---|---|---|---|---|---|---|---|---|---|---|---|
| ODIs | 11 | 3 | 0 | 1 | 1 | 0.33 | 5.88 | 0 | 0 | 2 | 0 |
| T20Is | 3 | 1 | 1 | 0 | 0* | - | - | 0 | 0 | 1 | 0 |
| First-class | 6 | 9 | 4 | 59 | 24* | 11.80 | 56.73 | 0 | 0 | 3 | 0 |
| List A | 19 | 7 | 0 | 16 | 9 | 2.28 | 42.10 | 0 | 0 | 5 | 0 |
| Twenty20 | 4 | 1 | 1 | 0 | 0* | - | - | 0 | 0 | 1 | 0 |

| Bowling | Mat | Balls | Runs | Wkts | BBI | BBM | Ave | Econ | SR | 5w | 10 |
|---|---|---|---|---|---|---|---|---|---|---|---|
| ODIs | 11 | 450 | 410 | 9 | 3/42 | 3/42 | 45.55 | 5.46 | 50.0 | 0 | 0 |
| T20Is | 3 | 42 | 55 | 4 | 2/28 | 2/28 | 13.75 | 7.85 | 10.5 | 0 | 0 |
| First-class | 6 | 919 | 502 | 16 | 5/53 | 5/53 | 31.37 | 3.27 | 57.4 | 1 | 0 |
| List A | 19 | 774 | 747 | 16 | 3/42 | 3/42 | 46.68 | 5.79 | 48.3 | 0 | 0 |
| Twenty20 | 4 | 66 | 81 | 4 | 2/28 | 2/28 | 20.25 | 7.36 | 16.5 | 0 | 0 |

# AHSAN MALIK

### RHB RMF

**FULL NAME:** Malik Ahsan Ahmad Jamil
**BORN:** August 29, 1989, Rotterdam, Netherlands
**SQUAD NO:** 17
**HEIGHT:** 6ft 1in
**TEAMS:** Netherlands
**CAREER:** ODI: 2011; T20I: 2012; First-class: 2011; List A: 2011; T20: 2012

**BEST BATTING:** 1* Netherlands vs Scotland, Aberdeen, 2011

**NOTES:** Only took up cricket at the age of 16. Plays club cricket for Rotterdam CC. Made his ODI debut on June 29, 2011, against Scotland at Mannofield Park, Aberdeen during the ICC World Cricket League Championship 2011/12, producing match-figures of 0-45 off eight overs with the new ball. Made his international debut on March 13, 2012 in a T20 against Canada in Dubai during the World T20 Qualifiers 2011/12, claiming match-figures of 2-18 off 2.4 overs

| Batting | Mat | Inns | NO | Runs | HS | Ave | SR | 100 | 50 | Ct | St |
|---|---|---|---|---|---|---|---|---|---|---|---|
| ODIs | 3 | - | - | - | - | - | - | - | - | 0 | 0 |
| T20Is | 2 | - | - | - | - | - | - | - | - | 0 | 0 |
| First-class | 1 | 1 | 1 | 1 | 1* | - | 100.00 | 0 | 0 | 0 | 0 |
| List A | 3 | - | - | - | - | - | - | - | - | 0 | 0 |
| Twenty20 | 6 | 4 | 3 | 6 | 3* | 6.00 | 75.00 | 0 | 0 | 0 | 0 |

| Bowling | Mat | Balls | Runs | Wkts | BBI | BBM | Ave | Econ | SR | 5w | 10 |
|---|---|---|---|---|---|---|---|---|---|---|---|
| ODIs | 3 | 168 | 115 | 4 | 3/38 | 3/38 | 28.75 | 4.10 | 42.0 | 0 | 0 |
| T20Is | 2 | 38 | 50 | 4 | 2/18 | 2/18 | 12.50 | 7.89 | 9.5 | 0 | 0 |
| First-class | 1 | 102 | 51 | 0 | - | - | - | 3.00 | - | 0 | 0 |
| List A | 3 | 168 | 115 | 4 | 3/38 | 3/38 | 28.75 | 4.10 | 42.0 | 0 | 0 |
| Twenty20 | 6 | 98 | 117 | 8 | 2/18 | 2/18 | 14.62 | 7.16 | 12.2 | 0 | 0 |

# GEERT-MAARTEN MOL

**RHB RM**

**FULL NAME:** Geert-Maarten Christopher Mol
**BORN:** October 12, 1983, The Hague, Netherlands
**SQUAD NO:** TBC
**HEIGHT:** 6ft 1in
**TEAMS:** Netherlands, Netherlands A, Netherlands Under-15, Netherlands Under-17s, Netherlands Under-19s, Quick Haag
**CAREER:** ODI: 2007; T20I: 2008; First-class: 2007; List A: 2007; T20: 2008

**BEST BATTING:** 21 Netherlands vs Scotland, Amstelveen, 2007
**BEST BOWLING:** 2-78 Netherlands vs Scotland, Aberdeen, 2007

**NOTES:** An allrounder who has played youth cricket at all levels for the Netherlands. His older brother Henk-Jan Mol played 11 ODIs and four T20Is for the country. Geert-Maarten made his first-class debut against Scotland in the ICC Intercontinental Cup 2007/08 – batting at No.6, he made 15 off 44 balls in the first innings before being dismissed by Gordon Drummond and 21 runs in the second innings as the Netherlands slumped to an innings and 59-run defeat. His last ODI appearance came in a rain-affected match against Kenya at Rotterdam in August 2008 – returning match-figures of 0-14 off two overs and scoring 5* as Netherlands claimed a six-wicket victory with six balls remaining

| Batting | Mat | Inns | NO | Runs | HS | Ave | SR | 100 | 50 | Ct | St |
|---|---|---|---|---|---|---|---|---|---|---|---|
| ODIs | 6 | 4 | 2 | 25 | 14 | 12.50 | 46.29 | 0 | 0 | 2 | 0 |
| T20Is | 1 | - | - | - | - | - | - | - | - | - | - |
| First-class | 3 | 5 | 0 | 53 | 21 | 10.60 | 25.85 | 0 | 0 | 5 | 0 |
| List A | 6 | 4 | 2 | 25 | 14 | 12.50 | 46.29 | 0 | 0 | 2 | 0 |
| Twenty20 | 1 | - | - | - | - | - | - | - | - | - | - |

| Bowling | Mat | Balls | Runs | Wkts | BBI | BBM | Ave | Econ | SR | 5w | 10 |
|---|---|---|---|---|---|---|---|---|---|---|---|
| ODIs | 6 | 162 | 111 | 3 | 2/23 | 2/23 | 37.00 | 4.11 | 54.0 | 0 | 0 |
| T20Is | 1 | - | - | - | - | - | - | - | - | - | - |
| First-class | 3 | 162 | 118 | 2 | 2/78 | 2/78 | 59.00 | 4.37 | 81.0 | 0 | 0 |
| List A | 6 | 162 | 111 | 3 | 2/23 | 2/23 | 37.00 | 4.11 | 54.0 | 0 | 0 |
| Twenty20 | 1 | - | - | - | - | - | - | - | - | - | - |

# STEPHAN MYBURGH

### LHB OB

THE NETHERLANDS

**FULL NAME:** Stephanus Johannes Myburgh
**BORN:** February 28, 1984, Pretoria, South Africa
**SQUAD NO:** 97
**HEIGHT:** 5ft 8in
**NICKNAME:** Uzzi, Mybs, Stef
**EDUCATION:** PBHS, SATS
**TEAMS:** Netherlands, KwaZulu-Natal Inland, Northerns
**CAREER:** ODI: 2011; T20I: 2012; First-class: 2006; List A: 2006; T20: 2011

---

BEST BATTING: 59 KwaZulu-Natal Inland vs Gauteng, Johannesburg, 2012

---

**FAMILY TIES?** My brother Johann and my brother-in-law both play professionally
**WHY CRICKET?** My dad spent hours and hours coaching my brother and I started to love the game at a young age
**CAREER HIGHLIGHTS?** Making my international debut
**SUPERSTITIONS?** None
**CRICKETING HEROES?** Andrew Hudson, Michael Slater, Matthew Hayden, Johann Myburgh
**NON-CRICKETING HEROES?** Tiger Woods
**TIP FOR THE TOP?** Marchant de Lange – a quickie from South Africa
**IF YOU WEREN'T A CRICKETER?** Golf player
**WHEN RAIN STOPS PLAY?** Sudoku
**FAVOURITE TV?** How I Met Your Mother, Friends
**FAVOURITE FILM?** Facing The Giants
**FAVOURITE BOOK?** The Bible
**DREAM HOLIDAY?** Mauritius
**ACCOMPLISHMENTS?** Degree in Engineering and Theology

| Batting | Mat | Inns | NO | Runs | HS | Ave | SR | 100 | 50 | Ct | St |
|---|---|---|---|---|---|---|---|---|---|---|---|
| ODIs | 2 | 2 | 0 | 61 | 56 | 30.50 | 77.21 | 0 | 1 | 1 | 0 |
| T20Is | 2 | 2 | 0 | 35 | 19 | 17.50 | 94.59 | 0 | 0 | 1 | 0 |
| First-class | 14 | 19 | 2 | 323 | 59 | 19.00 | 80.95 | 0 | 1 | 10 | 0 |
| List A | 26 | 26 | 2 | 732 | 105 | 30.50 | 85.11 | 1 | 6 | 6 | 0 |
| Twenty20 | 10 | 10 | 1 | 195 | 55* | 21.66 | 98.98 | 0 | 1 | 3 | 0 |

| Bowling | Mat | Balls | Runs | Wkts | BBI | BBM | Ave | Econ | SR | 5w | 10 |
|---|---|---|---|---|---|---|---|---|---|---|---|
| ODIs | 2 | - | - | - | - | - | - | - | - | - | - |
| T20Is | 2 | - | - | - | - | - | - | - | - | - | - |
| First-class | 14 | 60 | 42 | 0 | - | - | - | 4.20 | - | 0 | 0 |
| List A | 26 | 55 | 34 | 2 | 2/30 | 2/30 | 17.00 | 3.70 | 27.5 | 0 | 0 |
| Twenty20 | 10 | - | - | - | - | - | - | - | - | - | - |

# JELTE SCHOONHEIM  RHB RM

FULL NAME: Jelte D Schoonheim
BORN: November 16, 1981, Rotterdam, Netherlands
SQUAD NO: TBC
HEIGHT: 6ft 3in
NICKNAME: Scooner
EDUCATION: The Hague School of Higher Education
TEAMS: Netherlands, Netherlands Under-19s, Netherlands Under-23s
CAREER: T20I: 2008; First-class: 2007; T20: 2008

THE NETHERLANDS

BEST BATTING: 15 Netherlands vs Scotland, Aberdeen, 2007

FAMILY TIES? My father Rene has played cricket his whole life and played for the Dutch team several times
WHY CRICKET? It was a part of my life from the moment I could understand it
CAREER HIGHLIGHTS? There are many, but with the Dutch team it was winning the World T20 qualification tournament in Ireland in 2008
SUPERSTITIONS? To have superstitions is a sign of insecurity so I try to have none
CRICKETING HEROES? Jacques Kallis
NON-CRICKETING HEROES? Everyone who does good to other people out of charity
TIP FOR THE TOP? Alexei Kervezee, maybe even for England
IF YOU WEREN'T A CRICKETER? I would be playing baseball
WHEN RAIN STOPS PLAY? Playing cards, Risk or Settlers Of Catan
FAVOURITE TV? I don't really watch TV
FAVOURITE FILM? Saving Private Ryan
FAVOURITE BOOK? Komt Een Vrouw Bij De Dokter
DREAM HOLIDAY? The Maldives
ACCOMPLISHMENTS? I've managed to teach myself a few DIY skills, does that count?
FANTASY SLIP CORDON? It should be made up of anyone that has fishing as a hobby because it takes patience to wait for a long time for that one big catch when I'm batting!

| Batting | Mat | Inns | NO | Runs | HS | Ave | SR | 100 | 50 | Ct | St |
|---|---|---|---|---|---|---|---|---|---|---|---|
| T20Is | 1 | - | - | - | - | - | - | - | - | - | - |
| First-class | 1 | 2 | 0 | 17 | 15 | 8.50 | 56.66 | 0 | 0 | 0 | 0 |
| Twenty20 | 1 | - | - | - | - | - | - | - | - | - | - |

| Bowling | Mat | Balls | Runs | Wkts | BBI | BBM | Ave | Econ | SR | 5w | 10 |
|---|---|---|---|---|---|---|---|---|---|---|---|
| T20Is | 1 | - | - | - | - | - | - | - | - | - | - |
| First-class | 1 | 48 | 34 | 0 | - | - | - | 4.25 | - | 0 | 0 |
| Twenty20 | 1 | - | - | - | - | - | - | - | - | - | - |

**THE NETHERLANDS**

FULL NAME: Pieter Marinus Seelaar
BORN: July 2, 1987, Schiedam, Netherlands
SQUAD NO: 8
HEIGHT: 6ft 1in
NICKNAME: Vuvu, Pinguin
TEAMS: Netherlands, Netherlands Under-15s, Netherlands Under-17s, Hermes DVS
CAREER: ODI: 2006; T20I: 2008; First-class: 2006; List A: 2005; T20: 2008

BEST BATTING: 81* Netherlands vs Zimbabwe XI, Amstelveen, 2010
BEST BOWLING: 5-57 Netherlands vs Kenya, Amstelveen, 2008

WHY CRICKET? The passion the coaches had for the game got me hooked. It was a real treat to go out on Saturdays to play cricket because you knew it was a lot of fun. I also liked making people look funny when I was bowling!

CAREER HIGHLIGHTS? The victory vs England during the World T20 in 2009 at Lord's. The game we played vs India in Delhi during the ICC World Cup 2011 when I took the wickets of Sehwag, Pathan and Tendulkar

CRICKETING HEROES? First are Adam Gilchrist and Andy Flower. As I became older, I always wanted to learn from Daniel Vettori

TIPS FOR THE TOP? Ben Stokes, Paul Stirling

WHEN RAIN STOPS PLAY? When allowed, on my phone. Play a bit of cards and making jokes about my teammates

FAVOURITE TV? Californication

FAVOURITE FILM? Mega Shark Vs Giant Octopus – a must watch!

FAVOURITE BOOK? Millennium Trilogy

| Batting | Mat | Inns | NO | Runs | HS | Ave | SR | 100 | 50 | Ct | St |
|---|---|---|---|---|---|---|---|---|---|---|---|
| ODIs | 31 | 19 | 10 | 92 | 34* | 10.22 | 53.17 | 0 | 0 | 8 | 0 |
| T20Is | 11 | 3 | 0 | 2 | 1 | 0.66 | 28.57 | 0 | 0 | 7 | 0 |
| First-class | 13 | 22 | 5 | 265 | 81* | 15.58 | 40.09 | 0 | 1 | 3 | 0 |
| List A | 65 | 36 | 17 | 179 | 34* | 9.42 | 48.11 | 0 | 0 | 19 | 0 |
| Twenty20 | 18 | 8 | 3 | 29 | 12 | 5.80 | 67.44 | 0 | 0 | 8 | 0 |

| Bowling | Mat | Balls | Runs | Wkts | BBI | BBM | Ave | Econ | SR | 5w | 10 |
|---|---|---|---|---|---|---|---|---|---|---|---|
| ODIs | 31 | 1429 | 1129 | 34 | 3/22 | 3/22 | 33.20 | 4.74 | 42.0 | 0 | 0 |
| T20Is | 11 | 252 | 252 | 16 | 4/19 | 4/19 | 15.75 | 6.00 | 15.7 | 0 | 0 |
| First-class | 13 | 1863 | 1093 | 26 | 5/57 | 5/57 | 42.03 | 3.52 | 71.6 | 1 | 0 |
| List A | 65 | 2926 | 2356 | 63 | 3/22 | 3/22 | 37.39 | 4.83 | 46.4 | 0 | 0 |
| Twenty20 | 18 | 390 | 407 | 21 | 4/19 | 4/19 | 19.38 | 6.26 | 18.5 | 0 | 0 |

# MICHAEL SWART

### RHB OB

FULL NAME: Michael Richard Swart
BORN: October 1, 1982, Subiaco, Perth, Australia
SQUAD NO: 25
TEAMS: Netherlands, Lombard XI, Western Australia, Western Australia Under-17s, Western Australia Under-19s
CAREER: ODI: 2011; T20I: 2012; First-class: 2010; List A: 2010; T20: 2010

BEST BATTING: 104 Western Australia vs Victoria, Perth, 2010
BEST BOWLING: 1-0 Western Australia vs Victoria, Perth, 2010

NOTES: Relative latecomer to Australian state cricket, having previously scored heavily in Perth's first-grade competition. Made his first-class debut for Western Australia against Tasmania at Perth on February 19, 2010 and made scores of 25 and 83, although they weren't enough to stave off a 70-run defeat. Spent two years on Western Australia's books but was cut from their squad by coach Mickey Arthur in March 2011, shortly before Arthur himself moved on to take charge of the Australian national side. Swart qualifies to represent the Netherlands in international cricket through his father

| Batting | Mat | Inns | NO | Runs | HS | Ave | SR | 100 | 50 | Ct | St |
|---|---|---|---|---|---|---|---|---|---|---|---|
| ODIs | 4 | 4 | 0 | 46 | 30 | 11.50 | 56.09 | 0 | 0 | 2 | 0 |
| T20Is | 2 | 2 | 0 | 25 | 22 | 12.50 | 125.00 | 0 | 0 | 0 | 0 |
| First-class | 10 | 18 | 0 | 556 | 104 | 30.88 | 47.39 | 1 | 4 | 3 | 0 |
| List A | 19 | 19 | 0 | 236 | 57 | 12.42 | 58.12 | 0 | 2 | 10 | 0 |
| Twenty20 | 10 | 10 | 0 | 184 | 57 | 18.40 | 102.22 | 0 | 2 | 2 | 0 |

| Bowling | Mat | Balls | Runs | Wkts | BBI | BBM | Ave | Econ | SR | 5w | 10 |
|---|---|---|---|---|---|---|---|---|---|---|---|
| ODIs | 4 | 90 | 73 | 0 | - | - | - | 4.86 | - | 0 | 0 |
| T20Is | 2 | 36 | 37 | 1 | 1/26 | 1/26 | 37.00 | 6.16 | 36.0 | 0 | 0 |
| First-class | 10 | 72 | 73 | 2 | 1/0 | 1/0 | 36.50 | 6.08 | 36.0 | 0 | 0 |
| List A | 19 | 360 | 306 | 4 | 2/14 | 2/14 | 76.50 | 5.10 | 90.0 | 0 | 0 |
| Twenty20 | 10 | 177 | 189 | 7 | 3/31 | 3/31 | 27.00 | 6.40 | 25.2 | 0 | 0 |

**THE NETHERLANDS**

FULL NAME: Eric Stefan Szwarczynski
BORN: February 13, 1983, Vanderbijlpark, South Africa
SQUAD NO: 13
HEIGHT: 6ft
NICKNAME: Turtle
EDUCATION: Anna van Rijn College; Erasmus Universiy of Rotterdam; Open University
TEAMS: Netherlands, Netherlands Under-23s
CAREER: ODI: 2006; T20I: 2008; First-class: 2005; List A: 2006; T20: 2008

BEST BATTING: 93 Netherlands vs Kenya, Nairobi, 2010
BEST BOWLING: 2-24 Netherlands vs Canada, King City, 2007

WHY CRICKET? I liked taking diving catches
CAREER HIGHLIGHTS? Playing in two World Cups and making my maiden century at Hove last year
SUPERSTITIONS? Always put my gear on in the same order
CRICKETING HEROES? Jonty Rhodes and Andrew Hudson
NON-CRICKETING HEROES? Gary Player
BEST PLAYER IN COUNTY CRICKET? Murray Goodwin
IF YOU WEREN'T A CRICKETER? Hopefully making money playing golf
WHEN RAIN STOPS PLAY? Reading
FAVOURITE TV? The Big Bang Theory
FAVOURITE FILM? The Road To Redemption
FAVOURITE BOOK? The Sword Of Truth
DREAM HOLIDAY? Any tropical island
GUILTY PLEASURES? I have a bit of a sweet tooth

| Batting | Mat | Inns | NO | Runs | HS | Ave | SR | 100 | 50 | Ct | St |
|---|---|---|---|---|---|---|---|---|---|---|---|
| ODIs | 35 | 34 | 2 | 825 | 84* | 25.78 | 68.63 | 0 | 7 | 6 | 0 |
| T20Is | 8 | 7 | 0 | 185 | 45 | 26.42 | 100.00 | 0 | 0 | 2 | 0 |
| First-class | 14 | 23 | 1 | 453 | 93 | 20.59 |  | 0 | 3 | 5 | 0 |
| List A | 68 | 66 | 2 | 1371 | 111 | 21.42 | 67.67 | 1 | 10 | 17 | 0 |
| Twenty20 | 10 | 9 | 0 | 235 | 45 | 26.11 | 98.73 | 0 | 0 | 3 | 0 |
| Bowling | Mat | Balls | Runs | Wkts | BBI | BBM | Ave | Econ | SR | 5w | 10 |
| ODIs | 35 | - | - | - | - | - | - | - | - | - | - |
| T20Is | 8 | - | - | - | - | - | - | - | - | - | - |
| First-class | 14 | 136 | 98 | 3 | 2/24 | 2/25 | 32.66 | 4.32 | 45.3 | 0 | 0 |
| List A | 68 | 36 | 32 | 0 | - | - | - | 5.33 | - | 0 | 0 |
| Twenty20 | 10 | - | - | - | - | - | - | - | - | - | - |

# TIMM VAN DER GUGTEN

**RHB RFM**

FULL NAME: Timm van der Gugten
BORN: February 25, 1991, Hornsby, New South Wales, Australia
SQUAD NO: 10
HEIGHT: 6ft 2in
NICKNAME: Lady Gaga, Vander
EDUCATION: Hornsby Heights Public School; University of New South Wales
TEAMS: Netherlands, New South Wales, New South Wales Under-17s, New South Wales Under-19s, University of New South Wales
CAREER: T20I: 2012; First-class: 2011; List A: 2011; T20: 2012

BEST BATTING: 12* New South Wales vs Western Australia, Perth, 2012
BEST BOWLING: 1-19 New South Wales vs Western Australia, Sydney, 2011

NOTES: Timm's father is from The Hague while his mother is from Australia. Born and raised in the Sydney area, he has progressed through the New South Wales youth teams into the senior squad. Made his first-class debut against Western Australia at Sydney in November 2011 and took his maiden first-class wicket – that of Tom Beaton – in Western Australia's first innings. Got in contact with the Dutch team management last year through former New South Wales and current Glamorgan coach Matthew Mott just before the 2011 World Cup and made his Netherlands debut during the Caribbean T20

| Batting | Mat | Inns | NO | Runs | HS | Ave | SR | 100 | 50 | Ct | St |
|---|---|---|---|---|---|---|---|---|---|---|---|
| T20Is | 2 | - | - | - | - | - | - | - | - | 0 | 0 |
| First-class | 2 | 2 | 2 | 12 | 12* | - | 42.85 | 0 | 0 | 1 | 0 |
| List A | 1 | - | - | - | - | - | - | - | - | 0 | 0 |
| Twenty20 | 8 | 4 | 0 | 6 | 3 | 1.50 | 42.85 | 0 | 0 | 1 | 0 |

| Bowling | Mat | Balls | Runs | Wkts | BBI | BBM | Ave | Econ | SR | 5w | 10 |
|---|---|---|---|---|---|---|---|---|---|---|---|
| T20Is | 2 | 24 | 29 | 1 | 1/8 | 1/8 | 29.00 | 7.25 | 24.0 | 0 | 0 |
| First-class | 2 | 288 | 209 | 1 | 1/19 | 1/98 | 209.00 | 4.35 | 288.0 | 0 | 0 |
| List A | 1 | 60 | 42 | 1 | 1/42 | 1/42 | 42.00 | 4.20 | 60.0 | 0 | 0 |
| Twenty20 | 8 | 140 | 165 | 11 | 5/21 | 5/21 | 15.00 | 7.07 | 12.7 | 1 | 0 |

# BEREND WESTDIJK

## RHB RM

FULL NAME: Berend Arnold Westdijk
BORN: March 5, 1985, The Hague, Netherlands
SQUAD NO: 53
TEAMS: Netherlands, HBS, Netherlands Under-19s, Netherlands Under-23s
CAREER: ODI: 2011; First-class: 2009; List A: 2010

BEST BATTING: 17 Netherlands vs Scotland, Deventer, 2010
BEST BOWLING: 4-46 Netherlands vs Zimbabwe XI, Amstelveen, 2010

NOTES: Claimed match-figures of 4-127 on first-class debut against Canada during the ICC Intercontinental Cup 2009/10. Made his ODI debut against England at Nagpur on February 22 during the 2011 World Cup, returning figures of 0-41 off seven overs. To date, his only wicket in ODI cricket is former West Indies captain Ramnaresh Sarwan, while his one catch dismissed Scottish allrounder Preston Mommsen. Narrowly missed the cut for the Netherlands squad for the World T20 Qualifiers, but is described by Dutch coach Peter Drinnen as "a player for the future"

| Batting | Mat | Inns | NO | Runs | HS | Ave | SR | 100 | 50 | Ct | St |
|---|---|---|---|---|---|---|---|---|---|---|---|
| ODIs | 4 | 3 | 1 | 1 | 1* | 0.50 | 16.66 | 0 | 0 | 1 | 0 |
| First-class | 4 | 5 | 0 | 22 | 17 | 4.40 | 16.05 | 0 | 0 | 3 | 0 |
| List A | 10 | 5 | 3 | 4 | 3* | 2.00 | 50.00 | 0 | 0 | 2 | 0 |

| Bowling | Mat | Balls | Runs | Wkts | BBI | BBM | Ave | Econ | SR | 5w | 10 |
|---|---|---|---|---|---|---|---|---|---|---|---|
| ODIs | 4 | 156 | 195 | 1 | 1/56 | 1/56 | 195.00 | 7.50 | 156.0 | 0 | 0 |
| First-class | 4 | 576 | 336 | 12 | 4/46 | 4/91 | 28.00 | 3.50 | 48.0 | 0 | 0 |
| List A | 10 | 294 | 365 | 3 | 1/31 | 1/31 | 121.66 | 7.44 | 98.0 | 0 | 0 |

Unicorns

## GAVIN BAKER

### RHB RMF

UNICORNS

FULL NAME: Gavin Charles Baker
BORN: October 3, 1988, Edgware, Middlesex
SQUAD NO: 1
HEIGHT: 6ft 3in
NICKNAME: Bakes, Gavlar, Ghost, Sap
EDUCATION: Haberdashers' Aske's Boys;
Loughborough University
TEAMS: Loughborough MCCU,
Middlesex 2nd XI, Northamptonshire,
Northamptonshire 2nd XI
CAREER: First-class: 2009; List A: 2010

BEST BATTING: 66 LUCCE vs Hampshire, Southampton, 2009
BEST BOWLING: 2-35 LMCCU vs Kent, Canterbury, 2010

FAMILY TIES? My great, great grandfather was cricket master at Charterhouse
WHY CRICKET? As a youngster I played a lot of sport and cricket was the one which I enjoyed the most
CAREER HIGHLIGHTS? First-class debut for Loughborough, five-fer at Lord's in university final. Championship and List A debuts for Northamptonshire
SUPERSTITIONS? Right pad on first
CRICKETING HEROES? James Anderson, Brett Lee
NON-CRICKETING HEROES? All Arsenal legends, David Beckham, Jonny Wilkinson
BEST PLAYER IN COUNTY CRICKET? Jack Brooks
TIPS FOR THE TOP? Alex Hales, Alex Wakely, Ben Howgego
IF YOU WEREN'T A CRICKETER? I would still be at university
WHEN RAIN STOPS PLAY? I listen to music, eat a lot and annoy my teammates
FAVOURITE TV? Modern Family
FAVOURITE FILM? American Pie
FAVOURITE BOOK? Wisden
DREAM HOLIDAY? Cape Town
ACCOMPLISHMENTS? Getting a 2:1 in Psychology
SURPRISING SKILL? I play the clarinet
GUILTY PLEASURES? Playing PS3, McDonald's, Glee

| Batting | Mat | Inns | NO | Runs | HS | Ave | SR | 100 | 50 | Ct | St |
|---|---|---|---|---|---|---|---|---|---|---|---|
| First-class | 5 | 7 | 1 | 196 | 66 | 32.66 | 48.87 | 0 | 2 | 1 | 0 |
| List A | 1 | 1 | 0 | 0 | 0 | 0.00 | 0.00 | 0 | 0 | 0 | 0 |

| Bowling | Mat | Balls | Runs | Wkts | BBI | BBM | Ave | Econ | SR | 5w | 10 |
|---|---|---|---|---|---|---|---|---|---|---|---|
| First-class | 5 | 543 | 390 | 5 | 2/35 | 2/112 | 78.00 | 4.30 | 108.6 | 0 | 0 |
| List A | 1 | 42 | 63 | 1 | 1/63 | 1/63 | 63.00 | 9.00 | 42.0 | 0 | 0 |

UNICORNS

FULL NAME: Luke Edward Beaven
BORN: August 31, 1989, Reading, Berkshire
SQUAD NO: 2
HEIGHT: 6ft 3in
NICKNAME: Bevo
EDUCATION: Highdown School
TEAMS: Berkshire, Minor Counties, Unicorns, Unicorns A
CAREER: List A: 2011

FAMILY TIES? My father, uncle and brother all played/play club cricket
CAREER HIGHLIGHTS? Beating Glamorgan and taking three wickets in one over against them
SUPERSTITIONS? None
CRICKETING HEROES? Brian Lara, Jonty Rhodes, Courtney Walsh
NON-CRICKETING HEROES? My nan, Gianfranco Zola
BEST PLAYER IN COUNTY CRICKET? Marcus Trescothick
TIP FOR THE TOP? Jonny Bairstow
IF YOU WEREN'T A CRICKETER? I'd be working and travelling abroad
WHEN RAIN STOPS PLAY? Any sort of reading material
FAVOURITE FILM? Blood Diamond, Lock Stock And Two Smoking Barrels, Snatch, Man On Fire
DREAM HOLIDAY? The Caribbean
FANTASY SLIP CORDON? Keeper: James Corden, 1st: Denzel Washington, 2nd: Harry Redknapp, 3rd: Mark Knopfler, Gully: Myself

| Batting | Mat | Inns | NO | Runs | HS | Ave | SR | 100 | 50 | Ct | St |
|---------|-----|------|-----|------|-----|-----|-------|-----|-----|-----|-----|
| List A | 5 | 2 | 2 | 11 | 9* | - | 64.70 | 0 | 0 | 0 | 0 |

| Bowling | Mat | Balls | Runs | Wkts | BBI | BBM | Ave | Econ | SR | 5w | 10 |
|---------|-----|-------|------|------|------|------|-------|------|------|-----|-----|
| List A | 5 | 175 | 142 | 4 | 3/35 | 3/35 | 35.50 | 4.86 | 43.7 | 0 | 0 |

**UNICORNS**

FULL NAME: James Robert Alexander Campbell
BORN: November 25, 1988, Dorchester, Dorset
SQUAD NO: 3
HEIGHT: 6ft
NICKNAME: JC, Cambo
EDUCATION: Prior Park College; Leeds Metropolitan University
TEAMS: Gloucestershire 2nd XI, Leeds/Bradford UCCE, Somerset 2nd XI, Staffordshire, Unicorns
CAREER: List A: 2011

**WHY CRICKET?** The headmaster of my primary school loved the game, which happened to be the only ball game we were allowed to play in the playground

**CAREER HIGHLIGHTS?** Scoring my first hundred as a youngster will always stand out but representing the Unicorns against some of the best players in the game is up there

**SUPERSTITIONS?** Left pad always goes on before the right

**CRICKETING HEROES?** Most of the guys in both the English and Australian teams that battled for the 2005 Ashes. If I were to choose one player it would be Brian Lara. I loved watching him entertain

**NON-CRICKETING HEROES?** Muhammad Ali, no explanation needed. Jonny Wilkinson, ultimate professional

**BEST PLAYER IN COUNTY CRICKET?** Marcus Trescothick – would still be dominating international cricket

**TIP FOR THE TOP?** Jos Buttler. Pleasure to watch and gives youngsters someone to look up to with the way he carries himself

**IF YOU WEREN'T A CRICKETER?** Playing another sport, either rugby or hockey

**WHEN RAIN STOPS PLAY?** If there's the luxury of a dartboard then that's me. If not I'll probably be looking for food or annoying the nearest person

**FAVOURITE TV?** Saturday Kitchen

**FAVOURITE FILM?** Step Brothers

**DREAM HOLIDAY?** Tahiti

**GUILTY PLEASURES?** Ice cream. Couldn't live without it!

| Batting | Mat | Inns | NO | Runs | HS | Ave | SR | 100 | 50 | Ct | St |
|---------|-----|------|-----|------|-----|-------|-------|-----|-----|-----|-----|
| List A | 10 | 9 | 0 | 226 | 58 | 25.11 | 65.88 | 0 | 1 | 0 | 0 |

| Bowling | Mat | Balls | Runs | Wkts | BBI | BBM | Ave | Econ | SR | 5w | 10 |
|---------|-----|-------|------|------|-----|-----|-----|------|-----|-----|-----|
| List A | 10 | 6 | 8 | 0 | - | - | - | 8.00 | - | 0 | 0 |

**FULL NAME:** Nicky Thomas Caunce
**BORN:** June 7, 1989, Southport, Lancashire
**SQUAD NO:** 4
**HEIGHT:** 6ft 2in
**NICKNAME:** Cauncey, Weaponhead
**EDUCATION:** Rufford Primary; Hutton Grammar School; Runshaw College
**TEAMS:** Lancashire 2nd XI, Lancashire Under-17s, Lancashire Under-19s
**CAREER:** Yet to make first-team debut

UNICORNS

**FAMILY TIES?** Father played local club cricket
**WHY CRICKET?** Started playing with my mates at the age of 11 and loved it
**CAREER HIGHLIGHTS?** Playing for Lancashire 2nd XI in various finals and being part of a few first team squads. Winning titles at club level
**SUPERSTITIONS?** Always put my left pad on first
**CRICKETING HEROES?** Andrew Flintoff, Brett Lee, Shane Warne
**NON-CRICKETING HEROES?** Steven Gerrard, LeBron James
**BEST PLAYER IN COUNTY CRICKET?** Marcus Trescothick
**TIP FOR THE TOP?** Simon Kerrigan
**IF YOU WEREN'T A CRICKETER?** I'd be a groundsman/curator
**WHEN RAIN STOPS PLAY?** Play card games, play on my iPhone or read the paper
**FAVOURITE TV?** Entourage, Geordie Shore
**FAVOURITE FILM?** The Shawshank Redemption, Taken
**FAVOURITE BOOK?** Of Mice And Men
**DREAM HOLIDAY?** Fiji
**ACCOMPLISHMENTS?** Travelling around Australia
**GUILTY PLEASURES?** Nando's, ice cream
**AMAZE ME!** I've spent four of the last five winters in Australia and I'm only 22. I was a correspondent reporting for the local newspaper. Before I played cricket I owned a gardening business
**FANTASY SLIP CORDON?** Keeper: John Bishop (to make us laugh), 1st: Andrew Flintoff (for the antics), 2nd: Shane Warne (to get us some wickets), 3rd: Mario Balotelli (for the stories), Gully: Rihanna (for the voice and the looks)
**TWITTER FEED:** @nickytcaunce

## STEVEN CHEETHAM — RHB RFM

**FULL NAME:** Steven Philip Cheetham
**BORN:** September 5, 1987, Oldham, Lancashire
**SQUAD NO:** 5
**HEIGHT:** 6ft 5in
**NICKNAME:** Cheets
**EDUCATION:** Bury Grammar School; Holy Cross College
**TEAMS:** Lancashire, Lancashire 2nd XI, Surrey
**CAREER:** First-class: 2007; List A: 2008

---

**BEST BATTING:** 0* Surrey vs Leicestershire, Leicester, 2010
**BEST BOWLING:** 2-71 Surrey vs Leicestershire, Leicester, 2010

---

**CAREER HIGHLIGHTS?** First-team debut Lancashire vs Durham UCCE, representing England U17, taking a hat-trick in the VCTA Cup semi-final vs Mentonians in Melbourne, March 2008, 7-30 for Lancashire 2nd XI vs Leicester and 5-11 in Dubai

**CRICKET MOMENTS TO FORGET?** Two seasons of injuries – stress fracture of back and double hernia. Having my hat-trick ball and five-wicket haul dropped at Derby, first game of the 2008 season. Breaking my finger in the pre-match warm-up before the first game of the 2009 season

**SUPERSTITIONS?** Too many to mention

**CRICKETERS PARTICULARLY ADMIRED?** Marcus Trescothick, Andrew Flintoff, Chris Gayle, Brett Lee

**OTHER SPORTS FOLLOWED?** Football (Oldham Athletic), AFL (Collingwood)

**FAVOURITE BAND?** Arctic Monkeys, The Courteeners, Pendulum

**OTHER SPORTS PLAYED?** Football (Bury GS Old Boys, Oldham Athletic Academy)

| Batting | Mat | Inns | NO | Runs | HS | Ave | SR | 100 | 50 | Ct | St |
|---|---|---|---|---|---|---|---|---|---|---|---|
| First-class | 2 | 1 | 1 | 0 | 0* | - | 0.00 | 0 | 0 | 1 | 0 |
| List A | 10 | 5 | 3 | 20 | 13* | 10.00 | 43.47 | 0 | 0 | 1 | 0 |

| Bowling | Mat | Balls | Runs | Wkts | BBI | BBM | Ave | Econ | SR | 5w | 10 |
|---|---|---|---|---|---|---|---|---|---|---|---|
| First-class | 2 | 240 | 198 | 3 | 2/71 | 2/71 | 66.00 | 4.95 | 80.0 | 0 | 0 |
| List A | 10 | 378 | 399 | 14 | 4/32 | 4/32 | 28.50 | 6.33 | 27.0 | 0 | 0 |

# SAM DAVIES

RHB

**FULL NAME:** Samuel Llyr Davies
**BORN:** January 30, 1992, Neath, Glamorgan
**SQUAD NO:** 6
**HEIGHT:** 5ft 10in
**NICKNAME:** Sambo, Roider
**EDUCATION:** Ysgol Gyfun Ystalyfera; Neath College; University of UWIC
**TEAMS:** Glamorgan 2nd XI, Wales Minor Counties
**CAREER:** Yet to make first-team debut

---

**FAMILY TIES?** My dad played for Glamorgan
**WHY CRICKET?** Enjoyed smashing the ball around the park with my mates
**CAREER HIGHLIGHTS?** Scoring 177* for Wales U16, being selected for the Glamorgan academy and 2nd XI
**SUPERSTITIONS?** None
**CRICKETING HEROES?** Michael Clarke and Viv Richards
**NON-CRICKETING HEROES?** Brendan Rodgers, Craig Clemson
**BEST PLAYER IN COUNTY CRICKET?** Tom Maynard
**TIPS FOR THE TOP?** Will Owen, Tom Maynard
**IF YOU WEREN'T A CRICKETER?** Studying at UWIC and playing rugby
**WHEN RAIN STOPS PLAY?** Listen to music and read newspapers
**FAVOURITE TV?** Geordie Shore
**FAVOURITE FILM?** The Blind Side
**DREAM HOLIDAY?** Las Vegas
**SURPRISING SKILL?** Used to play the piano as a youngster
**GUILTY PLEASURES?** Watching Desperate Housewives
**AMAZE ME!** I used to sing at the Eisteddfod! Welsh is my first language
**FANTASY SLIP CORDON?** Keeper: Matt LeBlanc, 1st: Lucy Pinder, 2nd: Adam Sandler, 3rd: Me, Gully: Pixie Lott – interesting stories, great shapes and guaranteed laughter!
**TWITTER FEED:** @SLDavies4

UNICORNS

FULL NAME: Rhodri Francis Evans
BORN: December 6, 1989, Swansea, Glamorgan
SQUAD NO: 7
HEIGHT: 5ft 9in
NICKNAME: Rodders, Evs
EDUCATION: Bishopston Comprehensive; Gorseinon College; Loughborough University
TEAMS: Glamorgan 2nd XI, Loughborough MCCU, Loughborough UCCE, Wales Minor Counties
CAREER: First-class: 2009

BEST BATTING: 44 LMCCU vs Kent, Canterbury, 2010
BEST BOWLING: 1-57 LMCCU vs Kent, Canterbury, 2010

FAMILY TIES? Father played, great uncle is Don Shepherd
WHY CRICKET? Watching my dad play and the excitement of the game
CAREER HIGHLIGHTS? Touring to South Africa, Abu Dhabi and playing a season in Australia
SUPERSTITIONS? They come and go, must put front pad on first!
CRICKETING HEROES? Michael Hussey, Justin Langer, Allan Donald
NON-CRICKETING HEROES? Shane Williams, Benji Marshall
BEST PLAYER IN COUNTY CRICKET? Mark Ramprakash
TIP FOR THE TOP? Pat Cummins
IF YOU WEREN'T A CRICKETER? Playing rugby
WHEN RAIN STOPS PLAY? Playing changing room cricket or any kind of games that keep me occupied
FAVOURITE TV? Ninja Warrior
FAVOURITE FILM? Old School
FAVOURITE BOOK? Atlas
DREAM HOLIDAY? Snowboarding in the Alps
ACCOMPLISHMENTS? Geography degree (hopefully!)
GUILTY PLEASURES? Doodling, Marmite
SURPRISING FACT? Like to bodyboard, interested in rocks and pebbles
TWITTER FEED: @RodEvs

| Batting | Mat | Inns | NO | Runs | HS | Ave | SR | 100 | 50 | Ct | St |
|---------|-----|------|-----|------|-----|-----|------|-----|-----|-----|-----|
| First-class | 4 | 4 | 0 | 67 | 44 | 16.75 | 32.36 | 0 | 0 | 2 | 0 |

| Bowling | Mat | Balls | Runs | Wkts | BBI | BBM | Ave | Econ | SR | 5w | 10 |
|---------|-----|-------|------|------|------|------|--------|------|-------|-----|-----|
| First-class | 4 | 264 | 217 | 2 | 1/57 | 1/73 | 108.50 | 4.93 | 132.0 | 0 | 0 |

# PHIL HARRIS
## RHB RMF

FULL NAME: Philip Graham Harris
BORN: May 12, 1990, Worcester
SQUAD NO: 9
HEIGHT: 5ft 10in
NICKNAME: PH
EDUCATION: Chase High School and Sixth Form, Malvern; UWIC University
TEAMS: Cardiff MCCU
CAREER: Yet to make first-team debut

UNICORNS

FAMILY TIES? My dad played cricket for Barnards Green CC
WHY CRICKET? It was my summer sport
CAREER HIGHLIGHTS? Gaining promotion with Barnards Green CC in consecutive seasons
SUPERSTITIONS? None
CRICKETING HEROES? Ricky Ponting, Shane Watson
NON-CRICKETING HEROES? David Beckham
BEST PLAYER IN COUNTY CRICKET? Jonny Bairstow
TIP FOR THE TOP? Ben Stokes
IF YOU WEREN'T A CRICKETER? I'd be living the student dream
WHEN RAIN STOPS PLAY? Listening to my iPod
FAVOURITE TV? Geordie Shore
FAVOURITE FILM? Iron Man, Rocky IV
DREAM HOLIDAY? Perth, Australia
ACCOMPLISHMENTS? Playing football in America on a two-month scholarship
GUILTY PLEASURES? Takeaways
AMAZE ME! I played semi-professional football, I'm a fully qualified sports masseur and I have a metal plate in my jaw from where I broke it playing rugby
FANTASY SLIP CORDON? Keeper: David Beckham (absolute hero), 1st: Peter Kay (for the entertainment), 2nd: Pixie Lott (something to look at), 3rd: Me, Gully: Liam Paddock (best mate)
TWITTER FEED: @Phily_H1

## LEWIS HILL — RHB RM

UNICORNS

FULL NAME: Lewis John Hill
BORN: October 5, 1990, Leicester
SQUAD NO: 10
HEIGHT: 5ft 8in
NICKNAME: Hilly, Lew, Show Pony
EDUCATION: John Cleveland College;
Hastings High School
TEAMS: Leicestershire 2nd XI
CAREER: Yet to make first-team debut

FAMILY TIES? My dad is a junior coach
CAREER HIGHLIGHTS? Scoring my first century at the age of 13, scoring 173 for Leicestershire
Academy and 143 for Leicestershire 2nd XI
SUPERSTITIONS? Always put left pad on first
CRICKETING HEROES? Craig Wilson (Lutterworth CC), Marcus Trescothick
NON-CRICKETING HEROES? Mum and dad
BEST PLAYER IN COUNTY CRICKET? Marcus Trescothick
TIPS FOR THE TOP? Shiv Thakor, Joe Root
IF YOU WEREN'T A CRICKETER? I'd be working for the family business
WHEN RAIN STOPS PLAY? On the phone
FAVOURITE TV? Two And A Half Men, Wild at Heart, Mrs Brown's Boys
FAVOURITE FILM? Cool Runnings
FAVOURITE BOOK? Journey's End
DREAM HOLIDAY? Australia
ACCOMPLISHMENTS? GCSEs and A-Levels
SURPRISING SKILL? I must be the only 5ft 8in football goalkeeper
GUILTY PLEASURES? Chocolate, ice cream
AMAZE ME! I have been held up in an armed robbery!
FANTASY SLIP CORDON? Keeper: Happy Gilmore, 1st: Mr Bean, 2nd: Me, 3rd: Sanka from
Cool Runnings, Gully: Jay from The Inbetweeners

## ANDY KERR

**RHB RM**

FULL NAME: Andrew Philip Kerr
BORN: January 6, 1986, Bolton, Lancashire
SQUAD NO: 11
HEIGHT: 6ft 3in
NICKNAME: Gooba, Kerr-dog, Plon
EDUCATION: Tonge Moor CP School Smithills
High School; University of Salford
TEAMS: Derbyshire 2nd XI
CAREER: Yet to make first-team debut

UNICORNS

FAMILY TIES? My brother Jason played for Somerset and Derbyshire and is currently academy director and assistant coach at Somerset

WHY CRICKET? I spent all my spare time at my local club as a youngster

CAREER HIGHLIGHTS? Playing for various Lancashire age group sides, winning the treble in 2011 with Greenmount CC

SUPERSTITIONS? When padding up my kit goes on in a certain order

CRICKETING HEROES? Marcus Trescothick, Brian Lara, Mark Stewart (Greenmount legend)

NON-CRICKETING HEROES? Tiger Woods

BEST PLAYER IN COUNTY CRICKET? Marcus Trescothick

TIPS FOR THE TOP? Karl Brown, Jos Buttler

IF YOU WEREN'T A CRICKETER? I'd be playing golf

WHEN RAIN STOPS PLAY? Listen to Mark Stewart tell stories about how easy batting is

FAVOURITE TV? Grand Designs

FAVOURITE FILM? Beverly Hills Cop

FAVOURITE BOOK? Russell Brand – My Booky Wook

DREAM HOLIDAY? Fiji

SURPRISING SKILL? Darts, average of 114

FANTASY SLIP CORDON? Keeper: Tiger Woods, 1st: Russell Brand, 2nd: Barack Obama, 3rd: Andy Kerr, Gully: Mila Kunis

TWITTER FEED: @ak85err

UNICORNS

FULL NAME: Joshua Philip Thomas Knappett
BORN: April 15, 1985, Middlesex Hospital, London
SQUAD NO: 12
HEIGHT: 6ft
NICKNAME: Badger, Edwin
EDUCATION: East Barnet School; Oxford Brookes University
TEAMS: British Universities, Middlesex Cricket Board, Oxford MCCU, Unicorns, Worcestershire
CAREER: First-class: 2004; List A: 2010

BEST BATTING: 100* OUCCE vs Durham, The Parks, 2006
COUNTY CAP: 2007 (Worcestershire)

CAREER OUTSIDE CRICKET? Coaching and coach education
CAREER HIGHLIGHTS? My Championship debut vs Sussex in 2007
CRICKET MOMENTS TO FORGET? Being hit on the head by Jimmy Ormond on first-class debut for Oxford. Getting out to Mushtaq twice in a day for 7 and 4
CRICKETERS PARTICULARLY ADMIRED? Jack Russell, Adam Gilchrist
OTHER SPORTS PLAYED? Squash, trampolining
OTHER SPORTS FOLLOWED? Football (Tottenham Hotspur)
RELAXATIONS? Listening to music, films, eating

| Batting | Mat | Inns | NO | Runs | HS | Ave | SR | 100 | 50 | Ct | St |
|---------|-----|------|-----|------|-----|-------|-------|-----|-----|-----|-----|
| First-class | 13 | 20 | 3 | 523 | 100* | 30.76 | 50.67 | 1 | 3 | 26 | 3 |
| List A | 23 | 21 | 0 | 571 | 91 | 27.19 | 75.03 | 0 | 4 | 16 | 4 |

| Bowling | Mat | Balls | Runs | Wkts | BBI | BBM | Ave | Econ | SR | 5w | 10 |
|---------|-----|-------|------|------|-----|-----|-----|------|-----|-----|-----|
| First-class | 13 | - | - | - | - | - | - | - | - | - | - |
| List A | 23 | - | - | - | - | - | - | - | - | - | - |

FULL NAME: Warren Wain Lee
BORN: July 28, 1987, New Delhi, India
SQUAD NO: 14
HEIGHT: 6ft 4in
NICKNAME: Wozza, Waz
EDUCATION: Eaglesfield Secondary School;
Greenwich Community College
TEAMS: Kent, Kent 2nd XI
CAREER: List A: 2009

UNICORNS

WHY CRICKET? I was brought up in India where everyone loves cricket
CAREER HIGHLIGHTS? Playing my two List A games against Somerset and Middlesex
SUPERSTITIONS? None
CRICKETING HEROES? Sachin Tendulkar, Glenn McGrath, Brett Lee
NON-CRICKETING HEROES? Muhammad Ali
BEST PLAYER IN COUNTY CRICKET? Alastair Cook
TIPS FOR THE TOP? Reece Topley, Daniel Bell-Drummond, Ivan Thomas
IF YOU WEREN'T A CRICKETER? Electrician or a teacher
WHEN RAIN STOPS PLAY? Listen to music or play changing room cricket
FAVOURITE TV? Match Of The Day
FAVOURITE FILM? 300
DREAM HOLIDAY? Somewhere in the Himalayas
ACCOMPLISHMENTS? Helping other children with similar backgrounds and facing the same challenges I had growing up to develop their own cricketing skills. Also, working for the Tower Hamlets Youth Sport Foundation has been a moving experience
SURPRISING SKILL? Good at drawing
GUILTY PLEASURES? Got To Dance, Road Wars
AMAZE ME! I speak Hindi
FANTASY SLIP CORDON? Keeper: Peter Schmeichel, 1st: Eric Cantona, 2nd: Usain Bolt, 3rd: Me, Gully: James Corden

| Batting | Mat | Inns | NO | Runs | HS | Ave | SR | 100 | 50 | Ct | St |
|---------|-----|------|-----|------|-----|------|------|-----|-----|-----|-----|
| List A | 2 | 1 | 0 | 0 | 0 | 0.00 | 0.00 | 0 | 0 | 2 | 0 |

| Bowling | Mat | Balls | Runs | Wkts | BBI | BBM | Ave | Econ | SR | 5w | 10 |
|---------|-----|-------|------|------|------|------|-------|------|------|-----|-----|
| List A | 2 | 81 | 110 | 4 | 3/39 | 3/39 | 27.50 | 8.14 | 20.2 | 0 | 0 |

# JAYDEN LEVITT

**RHB OB**

FULL NAME: Jayden Ross Levitt
BORN: June 23, 1986, Johannesburg, South Africa
SQUAD NO: 15
HEIGHT: 5ft 10in
NICKNAME: Jaydos, Saffa, Bokie
EDUCATION: Brislinton Sixth Form
TEAMS: Gloucestershire 2nd XI, Unicorns, Unicorns A, Wiltshire
CAREER: List A: 2011

**WHY CRICKET?** Living two minutes away from my local cricket ground always helped. From an early age I showed potential as a decent window-smasher. Mum was impressed!

**CAREER HIGHLIGHTS?** Making my List A debut in the CB40 against Gloucestershire

**SUPERSTITIONS?** Never chirp a fast bowler

**CRICKETING HEROES?** Mike Hussey is without doubt my favourite cricketer. Really appreciate his passion for the game and his never give up attitude

**NON-CRICKETING HEROES?** Nick Husbands. Has had a profound effect on me outside of the game. I use him as my benchmark when it comes to any challenge

**BEST PLAYER IN COUNTY CRICKET?** Marcus Trescothick

**TIP FOR THE TOP?** Brett D'Oliveira

**WHEN RAIN STOPS PLAY?** Try and set aside some reading material or just sit and watch Tom Friend try and read. Fairly entertaining

**FAVOURITE TV?** An Idiot Abroad has to be the most entertaining thing on TV

**FAVOURITE FILM?** Gladiator

**DREAM HOLIDAY?** Have a massive soft spot for Cape Town. Kalk Bay is a fairly decent night out

**ACCOMPLISHMENTS?** Being nominated for Bromsgrove Sports Personality. And then coming third

**GUILTY PLEASURES?** Eating a ridiculous amount of banoffee pie. Having an eclectic array of skinny jeans. Singing along to Hanson. Watching Love Actually on DVD at least once a month

**AMAZE ME!** 1. It took me five attempts to pass my driving test, 2. I eventually passed in Australia whilst wintering abroad, 3. I still can't drive

**TWITTER FEED:** @Jaydenlevitt

| Batting | Mat | Inns | NO | Runs | HS | Ave | SR | 100 | 50 | Ct | St |
|---------|-----|------|-----|------|-----|-------|-------|-----|-----|-----|-----|
| List A | 3 | 3 | 0 | 65 | 33 | 21.66 | 84.41 | 0 | 0 | 0 | 0 |

| Bowling | Mat | Balls | Runs | Wkts | BBI | BBM | Ave | Econ | SR | 5w | 10 |
|---------|-----|-------|------|------|-----|-----|-----|------|-----|-----|-----|
| List A | 3 | 18 | 9 | 0 | - | - | - | 3.00 | - | 0 | 0 |

# TOM NEW

## LHB WK

FULL NAME: Thomas James New
BORN: January 18, 1985, Sutton-In-Ashfield, Nottinghamshire
SQUAD NO: 16
HEIGHT: 5ft 10in
NICKNAME: Newy, P
EDUCATION: Quarrydale Comprehensive
TEAMS: Derbyshire, England Under-15s, England Under-19s, Leicestershire, Leicestershire 2nd XI, Leicestershire Cricket Board
CAREER: First-class: 2004; List A: 2001; T20: 2008

BEST BATTING: 125 Leicestershire vs OUCCE, The Parks, 2007
BEST BOWLING: 2-18 Leicestershire vs Gloucestershire, Leicester, 2007
COUNTY CAP: 2009 (Leicestershire)

CRICKET MOMENT TO FORGET? Losing the semi-final of Costcutter World Challenge 2000 in Pakistan
SUPERSTITIONS? None
CRICKETERS PARTICULARLY ADMIRED? Ian Healy, Jack Russell
OTHER SPORTS PLAYED? Golf, football
OTHER SPORTS FOLLOWED? Football (Mansfield Town)
RELAXATIONS? Golf, music

| Batting | Mat | Inns | NO | Runs | HS | Ave | SR | 100 | 50 | Ct | St |
|---|---|---|---|---|---|---|---|---|---|---|---|
| First-class | 95 | 160 | 18 | 4338 | 125 | 30.54 | 49.85 | 2 | 33 | 160 | 8 |
| List A | 58 | 49 | 6 | 1134 | 68 | 26.37 | | 0 | 4 | 30 | 8 |
| Twenty20 | 1 | 1 | 0 | 18 | 18 | 18.00 | 94.73 | 0 | 0 | 1 | 1 |

| Bowling | Mat | Balls | Runs | Wkts | BBI | BBM | Ave | Econ | SR | 5w | 10 |
|---|---|---|---|---|---|---|---|---|---|---|---|
| First-class | 95 | 229 | 211 | 5 | 2/18 | 2/18 | 42.20 | 5.52 | 45.8 | 0 | 0 |
| List A | 58 | - | - | - | - | - | - | - | - | - | - |
| Twenty20 | 1 | - | - | - | - | - | - | - | - | - | - |

UNICORNS

FULL NAME: James Edward Ord
BORN: November 9, 1987, Birmingham, Warwickshire
SQUAD NO: 17
HEIGHT: 5ft 10in
NICKNAME: Ordy
EDUCATION: Solihull School; Loughborough University
TEAMS: Leicestershire 2nd XI, Loughborough MCCU, Unicorns, Unicorns A, Warwickshire, Warwickshire 2nd XI
CAREER: First-class: 2009; List A: 2009

BEST BATTING: 9 LUCCE vs Hampshire, Southampton, 2009

FAMILY TIES? My grandad [Jimmy] played for Warwickshire
WHY CRICKET? Just had a passion for any ball sports as a young boy whether it was cricket, tennis or football
CAREER HIGHLIGHTS? Making my County Championship and List A debut for Warwickshire, winning CB40 game with Unicorns, winning Birmingham Premier League with Barnt Green CC
SUPERSTITIONS? None
CRICKETING HEROES? Brian Lara
NON-CRICKETING HEROES? Don't think I have any heroes but really look up to Novak Djokovic, and my dad of course!
BEST PLAYER IN COUNTY CRICKET? Glen Chapple
TIPS FOR THE TOP? Jos Buttler, Chris Woakes, Ateeq Javid
IF YOU WEREN'T A CRICKETER? I'd be travelling around
WHEN RAIN STOPS PLAY? Annoying people or laid out horizontally
FAVOURITE TV? Entourage
FAVOURITE FILM? Back To The Future
DREAM HOLIDAY? Hawaii
GUILTY PLEASURES? Beer
TWITTER FEED: @jamesord1

| Batting | Mat | Inns | NO | Runs | HS | Ave | SR | 100 | 50 | Ct | St |
|---|---|---|---|---|---|---|---|---|---|---|---|
| First-class | 2 | 4 | 0 | 17 | 9 | 4.25 | 21.51 | 0 | 0 | 1 | 0 |
| List A | 5 | 4 | 0 | 143 | 55 | 35.75 | 69.41 | 0 | 2 | 0 | 0 |
| Bowling | Mat | Balls | Runs | Wkts | BBI | BBM | Ave | Econ | SR | 5w | 10 |
| First-class | 2 | - | - | - | - | - | - | - | - | - | - |
| List A | 5 | - | - | - | - | - | - | - | - | - | - |

# MAX OSBORNE

**RHB RMF**

FULL NAME: Max Osborne
BORN: November 21, 1990, Orsett, Essex
SQUAD NO: 18
HEIGHT: 6ft 3in
NICKNAME: Ozzie
EDUCATION: Sawyers Hall College
TEAMS: Essex, Essex 2nd XI, Essex Under-15s, Essex Under-19s
CAREER: First-class: 2010

BEST BATTING: 5 Essex vs Durham, Chelmsford, 2010
BEST BOWLING: 3-35 Essex vs Bangladeshis, Chelmsford, 2010

WHY CRICKET? Enjoyed watching my dad and brother play when I was younger
CAREER HIGHLIGHTS? First-class debut against Bangladesh, County Championship debut against Durham, taking four wickets in four balls for local side Horndon when I was 16
SUPERSTITIONS? None
CRICKETING HEROES? Freddie Flintoff
NON-CRICKETING HEROES? Tiger Woods
BEST PLAYER IN COUNTY CRICKET? David Masters
IF YOU WEREN'T A CRICKETER? No idea!
WHEN RAIN STOPS PLAY? Take my boots off and chill out
FAVOURITE TV? Two And A Half Men, Friends, Prison Break
FAVOURITE FILM? The Hangover
FAVOURITE BOOK? Harry Potter
DREAM HOLIDAY? Somewhere I could ski and be around the pool in the sun on the same day
ACCOMPLISHMENTS? Getting to the national swimming finals
GUILTY PLEASURES? Desserts
FANTASY SLIP CORDON? Keeper: Zach Galifianakis (a very funny man), 1st: Me, 2nd: Rosie Huntington-Whitely (pretty self-explanatory), 3rd: Freddie Flintoff (England legend), Gully: Superman (to take the catches)

| Batting | Mat | Inns | NO | Runs | HS | Ave | SR | 100 | 50 | Ct | St |
|---|---|---|---|---|---|---|---|---|---|---|---|
| First-class | 2 | 3 | 2 | 5 | 5 | 5.00 | 19.23 | 0 | 0 | 0 | 0 |

| Bowling | Mat | Balls | Runs | Wkts | BBI | BBM | Ave | Econ | SR | 5w | 10 |
|---|---|---|---|---|---|---|---|---|---|---|---|
| First-class | 2 | 216 | 151 | 6 | 3/35 | 5/95 | 25.16 | 4.19 | 36.0 | 0 | 0 |

UNICORNS

**FULL NAME:** Craig Mitchell Park
**BORN:** March 1, 1986, Empangeni, Natal, South Africa
**SQUAD NO:** 19
**HEIGHT:** 5ft 8in
**NICKNAME:** Parky
**EDUCATION:** Grantleigh College, Kwa-Zulu Natal, South Africa; Anglia Ruskin University, Cambridge
**TEAMS:** Cambridge MCCU, Cambridgeshire
**CAREER:** First-class: 2010; List A: 2011

**BEST BATTING:** 81 CMCCU vs Surrey, Fenner's, 2011
**BEST BOWLING:** 1-34 CMCCU vs Sussex, Fenner's, 2010

**FAMILY TIES?** Brother [Garry] plays for Derbyshire and another brother [Sean] played for Unicorns and Cambridgeshire
**CAREER HIGHLIGHTS?** Playing for the Unicorns last season, making career best 191 against Loughborough in MCCU Championship last year, beating Surrey in our MCCU first-class match
**CRICKETING HEROES?** Jonty Rhodes, Lance Klusener, Shaun Pollock
**BEST PLAYER IN COUNTY CRICKET?** Marcus Trescothick
**TIPS FOR THE TOP?** Rob Woolley, Tom Craddock, Adam Wheater, Tymal Mills
**IF YOU WEREN'T A CRICKETER?** Working in marketing
**WHEN RAIN STOPS PLAY?** Play card games or Articulate
**FAVOURITE TV?** Any nature documentaries
**FAVOURITE FILM?** Lucky Number Slevin, Maching Gun Preacher, Superbad
**SURPRISING SKILL?** I can stick my tongue up my nose!
**GUILTY PLEASURES?** Cheesy music
**AMAZE ME!** I have killed a monkey with a catapult, I've been on the world's highest gorge swing, my Zulu nickname translates as Cabbage Ears – wonder why?!
**FANTASY SLIP CORDON?** Keeper: Lee Mack, 1st: Tiger Woods, 2nd: Sacha Baron Cohen, 3rd: Me, Gully: John Rzeznik from the Goo Goo Dolls
**TWITTER FEED:** @cpark49

| Batting | Mat | Inns | NO | Runs | HS | Ave | SR | 100 | 50 | Ct | St |
|---|---|---|---|---|---|---|---|---|---|---|---|
| First-class | 6 | 8 | 0 | 279 | 81 | 34.87 | 54.17 | 0 | 3 | 4 | 0 |
| List A | 3 | 2 | 0 | 40 | 38 | 20.00 | 65.57 | 0 | 0 | 0 | 0 |

| Bowling | Mat | Balls | Runs | Wkts | BBI | BBM | Ave | Econ | SR | 5w | 10 |
|---|---|---|---|---|---|---|---|---|---|---|---|
| First-class | 6 | 384 | 295 | 2 | 1/34 | 2/93 | 147.50 | 4.60 | 192.0 | 0 | 0 |
| List A | 3 | - | - | - | - | - | - | - | - | - | - |

FULL NAME: Keith Alan Parsons
BORN: May 2, 1973, Taunton, Somerset
SQUAD NO: 20
HEIGHT: 6ft 1in
NICKNAME: Pilot, Pars, Orv
EDUCATION: The Castle School, Taunton; Richard Huish Sixth Form College, Taunton
TEAMS: Cornwall, Somerset, Unicorns
CAREER: First-class: 1992; List A: 1993; T20: 2003

UNICORNS

BEST BATTING: 193* Somerset vs West Indians, Taunton, 2000
BEST BOWLING: 5-13 Somerset vs Lancashire, Taunton, 2000
COUNTY CAP: 1999; BENEFIT YEAR: 2004

WHY CRICKET? Father was playing each weekend so used to go along and soon was putting my kit in the back in case there was a late cry-off
CAREER HIGHLIGHTS? Man of the Match in the C&G final at Lord's in 2001
SUPERSTITIONS? None
CRICKETING HEROES? Ian Botham
NON-CRICKETING HEROES? Anyone who consistently excels at their sport – Tiger Woods, AP McCoy etc
BEST PLAYER IN COUNTY CRICKET? Marcus Trescothick
TIP FOR THE TOP? Jos Buttler
IF YOU WEREN'T A CRICKETER? Ideally performing on the US PGA Tour!
WHEN RAIN STOPS PLAY? Playing cards or The Racing Post
FAVOURITE TV? Hustle or anything on sports channels
FAVOURITE BOOK? Don't read anything bigger than a newspaper
DREAM HOLIDAY? Family time in Florida
ACCOMPLISHMENTS? My two boys, Joseph and Alex
GUILTY PLEASURES? Anything with chocolate in!

| Batting | Mat | Inns | NO | Runs | HS | Ave | SR | 100 | 50 | Ct | St |
|---|---|---|---|---|---|---|---|---|---|---|---|
| First-class | 130 | 209 | 23 | 5324 | 193* | 28.62 | | 6 | 28 | 115 | 0 |
| List A | 270 | 237 | 44 | 5817 | 121 | 30.13 | | 2 | 32 | 102 | 0 |
| Twenty20 | 31 | 30 | 7 | 464 | 57* | 20.17 | 117.76 | | 1 | 9 | 0 |

| Bowling | Mat | Balls | Runs | Wkts | BBI | BBM | Ave | Econ | SR | 5w | 10 |
|---|---|---|---|---|---|---|---|---|---|---|---|
| First-class | 130 | 8005 | 4646 | 106 | 5/13 | | 43.83 | 3.48 | 75.5 | 2 | 0 |
| List A | 270 | 6345 | 5319 | 146 | 5/39 | 5/39 | 36.43 | 5.02 | 43.4 | 1 | 0 |
| Twenty20 | 31 | 338 | 467 | 18 | 3/12 | 3/12 | 25.94 | 8.28 | 18.7 | 0 | 0 |

# JOEL POPE

## RHB WK

**FULL NAME:** Joel Ian Pope
**BORN:** October 23, 1988, Ashford, Middlesex
**SQUAD NO:** 21
**HEIGHT:** 5ft 7in
**NICKNAME:** Popey
**EDUCATION:** Whitton School
**TEAMS:** Leicestershire, Leicestershire 2nd XI, Marylebone Cricket Club Young Cricketers, Middlesex 2nd XI
**CAREER:** List A: 2008

**FAMILY TIES?** Uncle Ben Scott plays for Worcester, dad and grandad played club cricket
**CAREER HIGHLIGHTS?** Signing my first professional contract with Leicestershire, playing my first 40-over game against Derbyshire
**SUPERSTITIONS?** Left pad on first, mark my guard every ball
**CRICKETING HEROES?** Jack Russell
**NON-CRICKETING HEROES?** Derrick Rose (Chicago Bulls), David Beckham, my dad
**BEST PLAYER IN COUNTY CRICKET?** Marcus Trescothick
**TIP FOR THE TOP?** Shiv Thakor
**IF YOU WEREN'T A CRICKETER?** Something in design
**WHEN RAIN STOPS PLAY?** Usually a card game
**FAVOURITE TV?** The Inbetweeners, An Idiot Abroad
**FAVOURITE FILM?** The Shawshank Redemption, City Of God
**FAVOURITE BOOK?** The Sun
**DREAM HOLIDAY?** Fiji
**SURPRISING SKILL?** I can play the banjo, I am a certified scuba diver, I can leapfrog a 6ft person
**FANTASY SLIP CORDON?** Keeper: Peter Kay, 1st: Karl Pilkington, 2nd: Me; 3rd: Denzel Washington, Gully: Will Smith
**TWITTER FEED:** @popey1010

| Batting | Mat | Inns | NO | Runs | HS | Ave | SR | 100 | 50 | Ct | St |
|---------|-----|------|----|----|----|----|----|----|----|----|----|
| List A | 3 | 3 | 0 | 22 | 9 | 7.33 | 146.66 | 0 | 0 | 3 | 1 |

| Bowling | Mat | Balls | Runs | Wkts | BBI | BBM | Ave | Econ | SR | 5w | 10 |
|---------|-----|-------|------|------|-----|-----|-----|------|----|----|----|
| List A | 3 | - | - | - | - | - | - | - | - | - | - |

# GLENN QUERL

## RHB RFM

**FULL NAME:** Reginald Glenn Querl
**BORN:** April 4, 1988, Harare, Zimbabwe
**SQUAD NO:** 22
**HEIGHT:** 5ft 8in
**NICKNAME:** Querlie
**EDUCATION:** Harrow School
**TEAMS:** Essex 2nd XI, Hampshire 2nd XI, Marylebone Cricket Club, Marylebone Cricket Club Young Cricketers, Matabeleland Tuskers, Unicorns, Zimbabwe Under-19s
**CAREER:** First-class: 2011; List A: 2010; T20: 2011

**BEST BATTING:** 26* Matabeleland Tuskers vs Mashonaland Eagles, Harare, 2011
**BEST BOWLING:** 6-20 Matabeleland Tuskers vs Mashonaland Eagles, Harare, 2011

**TWITTER FEED:** @glenn911
**NOTES:** Querl played for Zimbabwe in the U19 World Cup in 2006 and for Essex 2nd XI in 2007. This will be his third year in the Unicorns' set-up. He admires Jacques Kallis and Michael Clarke and his interests outside cricket are coaching, hockey and fishing

| Batting | Mat | Inns | NO | Runs | HS | Ave | SR | 100 | 50 | Ct | St |
|---|---|---|---|---|---|---|---|---|---|---|---|
| First-class | 7 | 8 | 3 | 77 | 26* | 15.40 | 61.11 | 0 | 0 | 1 | 0 |
| List A | 27 | 20 | 6 | 191 | 34 | 13.64 | 81.62 | 0 | 0 | 4 | 0 |
| Twenty20 | 7 | - | - | - | - | - | - | - | - | 2 | 0 |

| Bowling | Mat | Balls | Runs | Wkts | BBI | BBM | Ave | Econ | SR | 5w | 10 |
|---|---|---|---|---|---|---|---|---|---|---|---|
| First-class | 7 | 1664 | 579 | 45 | 6/20 | 9/38 | 12.86 | 2.08 | 36.9 | 5 | 0 |
| List A | 27 | 1180 | 1049 | 34 | 4/41 | 4/41 | 30.85 | 5.33 | 34.7 | 0 | 0 |
| Twenty20 | 7 | 140 | 170 | 10 | 3/13 | 3/13 | 17.00 | 7.28 | 14.0 | 0 | 0 |

UNICORNS

FULL NAME: Amar Rashid
BORN: May 16, 1986, Bradford, Yorkshire
SQUAD NO: 23
TEAMS: Leeds/Bradford MCCU,
Leicestershire 2nd XI, Unicorns
CAREER: List A: 2011

NOTES: Rashid will be turning out for the Unicorns again this year, looking to join his brother Adil in the ranks of first-class cricketers. He was a steady performer for the full Unicorns side and their 2nd XI last year but will be looking to make more eye-catching contributions this season

| Batting | Mat | Inns | NO | Runs | HS | Ave | SR | 100 | 50 | Ct | St |
|---------|-----|------|-----|------|-----|------|------|-----|----|----|-----|
| List A | 9 | 6 | 1 | 61 | 24* | 12.20 | 87.14 | 0 | 0 | 1 | 0 |

| Bowling | Mat | Balls | Runs | Wkts | BBI | BBM | Ave | Econ | SR | 5w | 10 |
|---------|-----|-------|------|------|------|------|-------|------|------|----|----|
| List A | 9 | 304 | 290 | 4 | 1/30 | 1/30 | 72.50 | 5.72 | 76.0 | 0 | 0 |

# LUIS REECE

## LHB LM

FULL NAME: Luis Michael Reece
BORN: August 4, 1990, Taunton, Somerset
SQUAD NO: 24
TEAMS: Lancashire 2nd XI, Leeds/Bradford MCCU, Unicorns
CAREER: List A: 2011

UNICORNS

NOTES: Reece played for Lancashire 2nd XI, the Unicorns and MCCU last season. He says his biggest influence is his dad and admires Brett Lee and AB de Villiers. He follows football, snooker and squash

| Batting | Mat | Inns | NO | Runs | HS | Ave | SR | 100 | 50 | Ct | St |
|---|---|---|---|---|---|---|---|---|---|---|---|
| List A | 9 | 7 | 2 | 115 | 26 | 23.00 | 91.26 | 0 | 0 | 2 | 0 |

| Bowling | Mat | Balls | Runs | Wkts | BBI | BBM | Ave | Econ | SR | 5w | 10 |
|---|---|---|---|---|---|---|---|---|---|---|---|
| List A | 9 | 181 | 172 | 5 | 4/35 | 4/35 | 34.40 | 5.70 | 36.2 | 0 | 0 |

## MIKE THORNELY

**RHB RM**

UNICORNS

**FULL NAME:** Michael Alistair Thornely
**BORN:** October 19, 1987, Camden, London
**SQUAD NO:** 25
**HEIGHT:** 6ft 1in
**NICKNAME:** Thorners, T-Bone
**EDUCATION:** Brighton College
**TEAMS:** Kent 2nd XI, Mashonaland Eagles, Nottinghamshire 2nd XI, Somerset 2nd XI, Sussex, Sussex 2nd XI, Sussex Under-15s, Sussex Under-17s, Unicorns, Unicorns A
**CAREER:** First-class: 2007; List A: 2007

**BEST BATTING:** 89 Sussex vs Northamptonshire, Hove, 2010
**BEST BOWLING:** 2-14 Sussex vs Worcestershire, Hove, 2010

**FAMILY TIES?** Uncle played minor counties for Cambridgeshire
**WHY CRICKET?** Played it since a young age and love the team environment
**CAREER HIGHLIGHTS?** Playing for Sussex
**SUPERSTITIONS?** Try to avoid them
**CRICKETING HEROES?** Mark Waugh
**NON-CRICKETING HEROES?** Maverick from Top Gun
**BEST PLAYER IN COUNTY CRICKET?** Marcus Trescothick
**TIP FOR THE TOP?** Jos Buttler
**IF YOU WEREN'T A CRICKETER?** Would have gone to university
**FAVOURITE TV?** Top Gear, Mock The Week
**FAVOURITE FILM?** Top Gun
**FAVOURITE BOOK?** Michael McIntyre's Life And Laughing
**ACCOMPLISHMENTS?** Skiing a double-black diamond slope in Banff, Canada
**SURPRISING SKILL?** I play the saxophone and the drums
**GUILTY PLEASURES?** Banoffee pie
**AMAZE ME!** I was a national junior triple jump champion, Princess Diana held me when I was a baby, I enjoy a fancy dress night out
**FANTASY SLIP CORDON?** Keeper: Tom Hanks, 1st: Me, 2nd: Charlie Sheen, 3rd: Jonty Rhodes
**TWITTER FEED:** @Thorners87

| Batting | Mat | Inns | NO | Runs | HS | Ave | SR | 100 | 50 | Ct | St |
|---|---|---|---|---|---|---|---|---|---|---|---|
| First-class | 19 | 34 | 2 | 638 | 89 | 19.93 | 37.66 | 0 | 4 | 16 | 0 |
| List A | 21 | 19 | 1 | 645 | 105* | 35.83 | 77.43 | 1 | 3 | 8 | 0 |

| Bowling | Mat | Balls | Runs | Wkts | BBI | BBM | Ave | Econ | SR | 5w | 10 |
|---|---|---|---|---|---|---|---|---|---|---|---|
| First-class | 19 | 150 | 100 | 4 | 2/14 | 2/14 | 25.00 | 4.00 | 37.5 | 0 | 0 |
| List A | 21 | 80 | 71 | 1 | 1/28 | 1/28 | 71.00 | 5.32 | 80.0 | 0 | 0 |

## VISHAL TRIPATHI

**RHB LB**

FULL NAME: Vishal Tripathi
BORN: March 3, 1988, Burnley, Lancashire
SQUAD NO: 26
HEIGHT: 5ft 7in
NICKNAME: Vish, Vee, Trip, Triple, Triplar
EDUCATION: Rosehill Primary; Habergham High School; University of Sunderland
TEAMS: Lancashire 2nd XI, Northamptonshire
CAREER: First-class: 2010; List A: 2010; T20: 2010

BEST BATTING: 71 Northamptonshire vs Derbyshire, Northampton, 2010

FAMILY TIES? Brother Bharat and father Pankaj Tripathi
CAREER HIGHLIGHTS? Scoring 55* on my first-class debut vs Oxford University for Northants in 2010
CRICKETING HEROES? Sachin Tendulkar, Rahul Dravid, VVS Laxman, MS Dhoni
NON-CRICKETING HEROES? Nelson Mandela, Joe Frazier, Muhammad Ali, Will Smith, Denzel Washington
BEST PLAYER IN COUNTY CRICKET? Marcus Trescothick
TIPS FOR THE TOP? Simon Kerrigan, Aneesh Kapil
IF YOU WEREN'T A CRICKETER? I'd be a broadcast journalist or presenter
WHEN RAIN STOPS PLAY? Listening to music or watching a film on my iPod
FAVOURITE BOOK? Bounce by Matthew Syed
DREAM HOLIDAY? Orlando, Florida
ACCOMPLISHMENTS? Getting a degree in Broadcast Journalism
SURPRISING SKILL? Cooking
GUILTY PLEASURES? Eating at KFC, Nando's and Krispy Kremes
FANTASY SLIP CORDON? Keeper: Muhammad Ali, 1st: Keith Lemon, 2nd: Myself, 3rd: Sachin Tendulkar, 4th: Denzel Washington, Gully: Dave Chappelle
TWITTER FEED: @Vishal_Tripathi

| Batting | Mat | Inns | NO | Runs | HS | Ave | SR | 100 | 50 | Ct | St |
|---|---|---|---|---|---|---|---|---|---|---|---|
| First-class | 4 | 7 | 1 | 196 | 71 | 32.66 | 54.29 | 0 | 2 | 3 | 0 |
| List A | 1 | 1 | 0 | 0 | 0 | 0.00 | 0.00 | 0 | 0 | 1 | 0 |
| Twenty20 | 3 | 1 | 0 | 6 | 6 | 6.00 | 120.00 | 0 | 0 | 2 | 0 |

| Bowling | Mat | Balls | Runs | Wkts | BBI | BBM | Ave | Econ | SR | 5w | 10 |
|---|---|---|---|---|---|---|---|---|---|---|---|
| First-class | 4 | 36 | 28 | 0 | - | - | - | 4.66 | - | 0 | 0 |
| List A | 1 | - | - | - | - | - | - | - | - | - | - |
| Twenty20 | 3 | - | - | - | - | - | - | - | - | - | - |

## BRADLEY WADLAN — LHB SLA

FULL NAME: Bradley Lewis Wadlan
BORN: December 14, 1988, Bridgend, Glamorgan
SQUAD NO: 27
HEIGHT: 6ft 2in
NICKNAME: Wadderz, Waddington, Scheemo
EDUCATION: Brynteg School; Cardiff University
TEAMS: Cardiff MCCU, Glamorgan 2nd XI, Herefordshire, Unicorns, Wales Minor Counties
CAREER: List A: 2011

WHY CRICKET? I love fielding for 80-plus overs every day

CAREER HIGHLIGHTS? Winning the UCCE final at Lord's 2009, making 88* at Lord's, playing in the Combined Universities team, being top of the batting and bowling averages in the one-day competition for UCCE cricket, making 205 off 125 balls in a league match. Making 187 in A-grade cricket in Australia

SUPERSTITIONS? Put on my batting gloves when I'm on the pitch and never before

CRICKETING HEROES? Marcus Trescothick, Andrew Symonds, David Warner, Dan Vettori

NON-CRICKETING HEROES? Tito Ortiz, Hunter Mahan, Chuck Liddell, Keith 'The Lean' Jardine

BEST PLAYER IN COUNTY CRICKET? Batsman: Marcus Trescothick; allrounder: Ryan ten Doeschate; bowler: Alfonso Thomas

TIP FOR THE TOP? James Taylor (Notts), Tom Maynard (Surrey), James Harris (Glamorgan), Glenn Querl (Unicorns)

IF YOU WEREN'T A CRICKETER? I'd be playing another sport or involved in property development or management

WHEN RAIN STOPS PLAY? Playing poker, on my iPod or badgering Facebook

FAVOURITE TV? The Inbetweeners

FAVOURITE FILM? The Hangover, Rush Hour

DREAM HOLIDAY? Cape Town, South Africa

SURPRISING SKILL? Dancefloor specialist

GUILTY PLEASURES? Kim Weller

AMAZE ME! Qualified sports masseur, Jagerbomb disposal expert

| Batting | Mat | Inns | NO | Runs | HS | Ave | SR | 100 | 50 | Ct | St |
|---------|-----|------|-----|------|-----|------|-------|-----|-----|-----|-----|
| List A | 2 | 1 | 0 | 3 | 3 | 3.00 | 33.33 | 0 | 0 | 0 | 0 |

| Bowling | Mat | Balls | Runs | Wkts | BBI | BBM | Ave | Econ | SR | 5w | 10 |
|---------|-----|-------|------|------|------|------|-------|------|------|-----|-----|
| List A | 2 | 66 | 57 | 2 | 2/39 | 2/39 | 28.50 | 5.18 | 33.0 | 0 | 0 |

# DAN WHEELDON

## RHB RFM

**FULL NAME:** Daniel Maurice Wheeldon
**BORN:** March 14, 1989, Nottingham
**SQUAD NO:** 28
**HEIGHT:** 6ft 4in
**NICKNAME:** Donk, Wheelo
**EDUCATION:** Wilsthorpe Community School
**TEAMS:** Derbyshire Under-15s, Derbyshire Under-17s, Unicorns, Yorkshire 2nd XI
**CAREER:** List A: 2011

UNICORNS

---

**CAREER HIGHLIGHTS?** Taking 3-31 on List A debut against Gloucestershire. Youngest player to score a hundred and take five wickets in the Derbyshire Premier League
**SUPERSTITIONS?** No
**CRICKETING HEROES?** Chris Gayle, Dale Steyn
**NON-CRICKETING HEROES?** Anderson Silva, Tiger Woods
**BEST PLAYER IN COUNTY CRICKET?** Samit Patel
**WHEN RAIN STOPS PLAY?** I catch up on sleep!
**FAVOURITE TV?** Spooks, Question Of Sport
**FAVOURITE FILM?** Gladiator
**FAVOURITE BOOK?** Guinness Book Of Records
**DREAM HOLIDAY?** Miami
**ACCOMPLISHMENTS?** Starting my business at the age of 20. Hitting a hole in one on the golf course
**GUILTY PLEASURES?** Elton John, Simply Red

| Batting | Mat | Inns | NO | Runs | HS | Ave | SR | 100 | 50 | Ct | St |
|---|---|---|---|---|---|---|---|---|---|---|---|
| List A | 5 | 4 | 0 | 26 | 14 | 6.50 | 100.00 | 0 | 0 | 0 | 0 |

| Bowling | Mat | Balls | Runs | Wkts | BBI | BBM | Ave | Econ | SR | 5w | 10 |
|---|---|---|---|---|---|---|---|---|---|---|---|
| List A | 5 | 215 | 181 | 4 | 3/31 | 3/31 | 45.25 | 5.05 | 53.7 | 0 | 0 |

## ROBERT WOOLLEY

### RHB RMF

UNICORNS

FULL NAME: Robert James Joseph Woolley
BORN: August 6, 1990, Tameside, Greater Manchester
SQUAD NO: 29
HEIGHT: 5ft 9in
NICKNAME: Woollers, Wools
EDUCATION: St.Bedes College, Manchester
TEAMS: Cambridge MCCU
CAREER: First-class: 2009

BEST BATTING: 89* CMCCU vs Middlesex, Fenner's, 2011
BEST BOWLING: 3-54 CMCCU vs Surrey, Fenner's, 2011

CAREER HIGHLIGHTS? Captaining Cambridge MCCU to a 10-wicket first-class victory over Surrey and also getting Kevin Pietersen out bowled in the second innings. Captaining the Combined Universities team on an unbeaten tour of Abu Dhabi
CRICKETING HEROES? Jaques Kallis is in my opinion the greatest allrounder that I have witnessed play, bowling-wise I have always admired James Anderson
NON-CRICKETING HEROES? Roger Federer because he has stayed at the top of his game for such a long period of time and Lance Armstrong due to reading his book
BEST PLAYER IN COUNTY CRICKET? Kyle Hogg
TIPS FOR THE TOP? Tom Craddock, Craig Park
IF YOU WEREN'T A CRICKETER? Accountant
WHEN RAIN STOPS PLAY? Any card games are hugely appreciated, and you can't forget a good old fashioned game of one hand-one bounce!
FAVOURITE TV? Don't Tell The Bride, Sun, Sea, Sex and Suspicious Parents (any terrible BBC Three reality programme, really)
FAVOURITE FILM? 500 Days Of Summer
ACCOMPLISHMENTS? Represented the full England Independent Schools Football Association team on tour in Italy and played an international at Tynecastle against Scotland
FANTASY SLIP CORDON? Keeper: Alfie Boe, 1st: Reginald D Hunter, 2nd: Charles Dickens, 3rd: Myself, Gully: Sacha Baron Cohen
TWITTER FEED: @Robwoolley2

| Batting | Mat | Inns | NO | Runs | HS | Ave | SR | 100 | 50 | Ct | St |
|---|---|---|---|---|---|---|---|---|---|---|---|
| First-class | 9 | 10 | 3 | 283 | 89* | 40.42 | 73.50 | 0 | 2 | 8 | 0 |

| Bowling | Mat | Balls | Runs | Wkts | BBI | BBM | Ave | Econ | SR | 5w | 10 |
|---|---|---|---|---|---|---|---|---|---|---|---|
| First-class | 9 | 1469 | 970 | 19 | 3/54 | 4/100 | 51.05 | 3.96 | 77.3 | 0 | 0 |

# THE LEADING ONLINE CRICKET MANAGEMENT GAME

- Free to play
- T20, 50 Over, First Class and International matches
- Buy, sell and train players
- Develop your own winning formula
- Welcoming global community
- Be the next Andy Flower

Sign Up Now

# FREE
# www.battrick.org

JELLYFISH
PRINT SOLUTIONS

# JELLYFISH SOLUTIONS
## First Class Delivery

www.jellyfishsolutions.co.uk

JELLYFISH SOLUTIONS LTD
SUITE B, HOLLYTHORN HOUSE, THE HOLLYTHORNS, NEW ROAD,
SWANMORE, HAMPSHIRE SO32 2NW
TELEPHONE 01489 89 73 73

*The*
Umpires

**ROB BAILEY**

NAME: Robert John Bailey
BORN: October 28, 1963, Biddulph
HEIGHT: 6ft 3in
NICKNAME: Bailers
APPOINTED TO FIRST-CLASS LIST: 2006
INTERNATIONAL PANEL: 2011-
ODIS UMPIRED: 1
T20IS UMPIRED: 2
COUNTIES AS PLAYER: Northamptonshire, Derbyshire
ROLE: Right-hand bat, offspin bowler
COUNTY DEBUT: 1982 (Northamptonshire), 2000 (Derbyshire)
TEST DEBUT: 1988
ODI DEBUT: 1985

NOTES: Officiated at T20 Cup Finals Day 2008, 2009, 2010 and 2011, including the final in the last two years

| Batting | Mat | Inns | NO | Runs | HS | Ave | SR | 100 | 50 | Ct | St |
|---|---|---|---|---|---|---|---|---|---|---|---|
| Tests | 4 | 8 | 0 | 119 | 43 | 14.87 | 36.50 | 0 | 0 | 0 | 0 |
| ODIs | 4 | 4 | 2 | 137 | 43* | 68.50 | 69.89 | 0 | 0 | 1 | 0 |
| First-class | 374 | 628 | 89 | 21844 | 224* | 40.52 | - | 47 | 111 | 272 | 0 |
| List A | 396 | 376 | 65 | 12076 | 153* | 38.82 | - | 10 | 79 | 111 | 0 |

| Bowling | Mat | Balls | Runs | Wkts | BBI | BBM | Ave | Econ | SR | 5w | 10 |
|---|---|---|---|---|---|---|---|---|---|---|---|
| Tests | 4 | - | - | - | - | - | - | - | - | - | - |
| ODIs | 4 | 36 | 25 | 0 | - | - | - | 4.16 | - | 0 | 0 |
| First-class | 374 | 9713 | 5144 | 121 | 5/54 | - | 42.51 | 3.17 | 80.2 | 2 | 0 |
| List A | 396 | 3092 | 2564 | 72 | 5/45 | 5/45 | 35.61 | 4.97 | 42.9 | 1 | 0 |

UMPIRES

B

# NEIL BAINTON

**NAME:** Neil Laurence Bainton
**BORN:** October 2, 1970, Romford, Essex
**HEIGHT:** 5ft 8in
**APPOINTED TO FIRST-CLASS LIST:** 2006
**FAVOURITE GROUND?** Colwyn Bay and Arundel. Most outgrounds are nice to go to
**FIRST COUNTY PLAYER YOU GAVE OUT?** I can't remember, but it was probably wrong!
**CAREER HIGHLIGHT AS AN UMPIRE?** Being appointed to the first-class list and my two Tests as fourth umpire

NOTES: Has been reserve umpire in two Tests, two ODIs and two T20Is, as well as umpiring in four women's ODIs

## 2012 RESERVE UMPIRE LIST

Paul Baldwin

Mike Burns

Ismail Dawood

Ben Debenham

Mark Eggleston

Russell Evans

Graham Lloyd

Paul Pollard

Billy Taylor

Alex Wharf

## MARK BENSON

NAME: Mark Richard Benson
BORN: July 6, 1958, Shoreham, Sussex
HEIGHT: 5ft 10in
NICKNAME: Benny
APPOINTED TO FIRST-CLASS LIST: 2000
INTERNATIONAL PANEL: 2004-2006
ELITE PANEL: 2006-2010
TESTS UMPIRED: 27 (plus 9 as TV umpire)
ODIS UMPIRED: 72 (plus 25 as TV umpire)
T20IS UMPIRED: 19 (plus 6 as TV umpire)
COUNTY AS PLAYER: Kent
ROLE: Left-hand bat
COUNTY DEBUT: 1980
TEST DEBUT: 1986
ODI DEBUT: 1986

NOTES: Stood in the C&G Trophy final in 2003. Umpired in the 2007 World Cup and the 2007 World T20, including the final

| Batting | Mat | Inns | NO | Runs | HS | Ave | SR | 100 | 50 | Ct | St |
|---|---|---|---|---|---|---|---|---|---|---|---|
| Tests | 1 | 2 | 0 | 51 | 30 | 25.50 | 31.48 | 0 | 0 | 0 | 0 |
| ODIs | 1 | 1 | 0 | 24 | 24 | 24.00 | 41.37 | 0 | 0 | 0 | 0 |
| First-class | 292 | 491 | 34 | 18387 | 257 | 40.23 | - | 48 | 99 | 140 | 0 |
| List A | 269 | 257 | 11 | 7838 | 119 | 31.86 | - | 5 | 53 | 68 | 0 |

| Bowling | Mat | Balls | Runs | Wkts | BBI | BBM | Ave | Econ | SR | 5w | 10 |
|---|---|---|---|---|---|---|---|---|---|---|---|
| Tests | 1 | - | - | - | - | - | - | - | - | - | - |
| ODIs | 1 | - | - | - | - | - | - | - | - | - | - |
| First-class | 292 | 467 | 493 | 5 | 2/55 | - | 98.60 | 6.33 | 93.4 | 0 | 0 |
| List A | 269 | - | - | - | - | - | - | - | - | - | - |

# MARTIN BODENHAM

NAME: Martin John Dale Bodenham
BORN: 23 April, 1950, Brighton
HEIGHT: 6ft 1in
APPOINTED TO FIRST-CLASS LIST: 2009
COUNTY AS PLAYER: 'Played for Sussex in a number of 2nd XI Championship matches'
ROLE: Batsman, wicketkeeper

NOTES: He is the first man to referee in football's Premier League and umpire first-class cricket. As a ref, he was in charge of three FA Cup semis and the League Cup final in 1997, as well as being reserve referee for the European Cup final between AC Milan and Barcelona in 1994. In his career he sent off Vinnie Jones for threatening to break an opponent's legs and gave Roy Keane a yellow card while he was going off on a stretcher. Umpired in three women's ODIs and five women's T20Is

# NICK COOK

**NAME:** Nicholas Grant Billson Cook
**BORN:** June 17, 1956, Leicester
**HEIGHT:** 6ft
**NICKNAME:** Beast
**APPOINTED TO FIRST-CLASS LIST:** 2009
**COUNTIES AS PLAYER:** Leicestershire, Northamptonshire
**ROLE:** Right-hand bat, slow left-arm bowler
**COUNTY DEBUT:** 1978 (Leicestershire), 1986 (Northamptonshire)
**TEST DEBUT:** 1983
**ODI DEBUT:** 1984
**RITUALS OR QUIRKS?** I like to walk out to the left of my colleague
**SOMETHING WE DON'T KNOW ABOUT YOU?** I have two Siamese cats

NOTES: Officiated as TV umpire in the Clydesdale Bank 40 final at Lord's in 2011

| Batting | Mat | Inns | NO | Runs | HS | Ave | SR | 100 | 50 | Ct | St |
|---|---|---|---|---|---|---|---|---|---|---|---|
| Tests | 15 | 25 | 4 | 179 | 31 | 8.52 | 23.58 | 0 | 0 | 5 | 0 |
| ODIs | 3 | - | - | - | - | - | - | - | - | 2 | 0 |
| First-class | 356 | 365 | 96 | 3137 | 75 | 11.66 | - | 0 | 4 | 197 | 0 |
| List A | 223 | 89 | 36 | 491 | 23 | 9.26 | - | 0 | 0 | 74 | 0 |

| Bowling | Mat | Balls | Runs | Wkts | BBI | BBM | Ave | Econ | SR | 5w | 10 |
|---|---|---|---|---|---|---|---|---|---|---|---|
| Tests | 15 | 4174 | 1689 | 52 | 6/65 | 11/83 | 32.48 | 2.42 | 80.2 | 4 | 1 |
| ODIs | 3 | 144 | 95 | 5 | 2/18 | 2/18 | 19.00 | 3.95 | 28.8 | 0 | 0 |
| First-class | 356 | 64460 | 25507 | 879 | 7/34 | - | 29.01 | 2.37 | 73.3 | 31 | 4 |
| List A | 223 | 10077 | 6812 | 200 | 4/22 | 4/22 | 34.06 | 4.05 | 50.3 | 0 | 0 |

**NAME:** Nigel Geoffrey Charles Cowley
**BORN:** March 1, 1953, Shaftesbury
**HEIGHT:** 5ft 6in
**APPOINTED TO FIRST-CLASS LIST:** 2000
**COUNTIES AS PLAYER:** Hampshire, Glamorgan
**ROLE:** Right-hand bat, offspin bowler
**COUNTY DEBUT:** 1974 (Hampshire), 1990 (Glamorgan)

UMPIRES

NOTES: Has stood as reserve umpire in four Tests and three ODIs

| Batting | Mat | Inns | NO | Runs | HS | Ave | SR | 100 | 50 | Ct | St |
|---|---|---|---|---|---|---|---|---|---|---|---|
| First-class | 271 | 375 | 62 | 7309 | 109* | 23.35 | - | 2 | 36 | 105 | 0 |
| List A | 305 | 226 | 45 | 3022 | 74 | 16.69 | - | 0 | 5 | 69 | 0 |

| Bowling | Mat | Balls | Runs | Wkts | BBI | BBM | Ave | Econ | SR | 5w | 10 |
|---|---|---|---|---|---|---|---|---|---|---|---|
| First-class | 271 | 32662 | 14879 | 437 | 6/48 | | 34.04 | 2.73 | 74.7 | 5 | 0 |
| List A | 305 | 11704 | 8038 | 248 | 5/24 | 5/24 | 32.41 | 4.12 | 47.1 | 1 | 0 |

UMPIRES

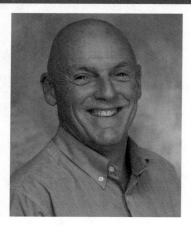

NAME: Jeffrey Howard Evans
BORN: August 7, 1954, Llanelli
HEIGHT: 5ft 8in
APPOINTED TO FIRST-CLASS LIST: 2001

NOTES: Played league cricket in South Wales as a right-hand bat. Has stood as reserve umpire in four Tests, three ODIs and two T20Is

# STEVE GALE

NAME: Stephen Clifford Gale
BORN: 3 June 1952, Shrewsbury
APPOINTED TO FIRST-CLASS LIST: 2011
WHAT'S YOUR FAVOURITE COUNTY
GROUND? Durham
FIRST COUNTY PLAYER YOU GAVE OUT?
Jim Troughton
RITUALS OR QUIRKS? I always count with
six pound coins
CAREER HIGHLIGHT AS AN UMPIRE? My
first televised game, a full house between
Lancashire and Yorkshire at Old Trafford

NOTES: Gale spent three seasons on the reserve list following a playing career representing Shropshire in minor counties cricket between 1975 and 1987 before joining the full list in 2011. He umpired the Second XI Knockout final at Horsham and the Cockspur T20 Cup Final at The Rose Bowl in 2010

| Batting | Mat | Inns | NO | Runs | HS | Ave | SR | 100 | 50 | Ct | St |
|---------|-----|------|-----|------|-----|-------|-----|-----|-----|-----|-----|
| List A | 5 | 5 | 0 | 156 | 68 | 31.20 | 0 | 1 | 0 | 0 | 0 |

| Bowling | Mat | Balls | Runs | Wkts | BBI | BBM | Ave | Econ | SR | 5w | 10 |
|---------|-----|-------|------|------|-----|-----|-----|------|-----|-----|-----|
| List A | 5 | - | - | - | - | - | - | - | - | - | - |

# STEVE GARRATT

NAME: Steven Arthur Garratt
BORN: July 5, 1953, Nottingham
HEIGHT: 6ft 2in
NICKNAME: Trigger
APPOINTED TO FIRST-CLASS LIST: 2008
FAVOURITE GROUND? My favourite ground has to be Lord's, although the more traditional grounds such as Canterbury, Taunton and Worcester certainly have a special charm
SOMETHING WE DON'T KNOW ABOUT YOU? My nickname Trigger is a reference to the speed of my decision-making early in my career and NOT the character in Only Fools And Horses, although some may beg to differ...

NOTES: Garratt is a retired police officer

# MICHAEL GOUGH

NAME: Michael Andrew Gough
BORN: December 18, 1979, Hartlepool
HEIGHT: 6ft 5in
NICKNAME: Goughy
APPOINTED TO FIRST-CLASS LIST: 2009
COUNTIES AS PLAYER: Durham
ROLE: Right-hand bat; offspin bowler
COUNTY DEBUT: 1998
SOMETHING WE DON'T KNOW ABOUT YOU? I'm a qualified football referee and a season ticket holder at Hartlepool United
FAVOURITE GROUND? Worcester
RITUALS AND QUIRKS? I step onto the pitch with my left foot first and my left foot is the first off the pitch

NOTES: Gough started umpiring in 2005 after retiring from the first-class game; he was appointed to the ECB reserve list in 2006. He is believed to be the youngest first-class umpire in the history of the game. In 2011 he officiated at T20 Finals Day at Edgbaston and was named PCA Umpire of the Year

| Batting | Mat | Inns | NO | Runs | HS | Ave | SR | 100 | 50 | Ct | St |
|---|---|---|---|---|---|---|---|---|---|---|---|
| First-class | 67 | 119 | 3 | 2952 | 123 | 25.44 | - | 2 | 15 | 57 | 0 |
| List A | 49 | 45 | 4 | 974 | 132 | 23.75 | - | 1 | 3 | 14 | 0 |

| Bowling | Mat | Balls | Runs | Wkts | BBI | BBM | Ave | Econ | SR | 5w | 10 |
|---|---|---|---|---|---|---|---|---|---|---|---|
| First-class | 67 | 2486 | 1350 | 30 | 5/66 | - | 45.00 | 3.25 | 82.8 | 1 | 0 |
| List A | 49 | 1136 | 947 | 21 | 3/26 | 3/26 | 45.09 | 5.00 | 54.0 | 0 | 0 |

# IAN GOULD

NAME: Ian James Gould
BORN: August 19, 1957, Taplow
HEIGHT: 5ft 7in
NICKNAME: Gunner
APPOINTED TO FIRST-CLASS LIST: 2002
INTERNATIONAL PANEL: 2006-
ELITE PANEL: 2010-
TESTS UMPIRED: 25
ODIS UMPIRED: 70
T20IS UMPIRED: 15
COUNTIES AS PLAYER: Middlesex, Sussex
ROLE: Left-hand bat, wicketkeeper
COUNTY DEBUT: 1975 (Middlesex), 1981
(Sussex)
ODI DEBUT: 1983

NOTES: Officiated at the T20 Finals Day at Edgbaston in 2004 and at The Oval in 2005 –
including standing in both finals – and again at Edgbaston in 2009. PCA Umpire of the Year
2005, 2007. Umpired in the 2007 World Cup. Stood in the FP Trophy final at Lord's in 2007

| Batting | Mat | Inns | NO | Runs | HS | Ave | SR | 100 | 50 | Ct | St |
|---------|-----|------|-----|------|-----|-------|-------|-----|-----|-----|-----|
| ODIs | 18 | 14 | 2 | 155 | 42 | 12.91 | 63.78 | 0 | 0 | 15 | 3 |
| First-class | 298 | 399 | 63 | 8756 | 128 | 26.05 | - | - | 4 | 47 | 536 | 67 |
| List A | 315 | 270 | 41 | 4377 | 88 | 19.11 | - | - | 0 | 20 | 242 | 37 |

| Bowling | Mat | Balls | Runs | Wkts | BBI | BBM | Ave | Econ | SR | 5w | 10 |
|---------|-----|-------|------|------|-----|-----|------|------|-----|-----|-----|
| ODIs | 18 | - | - | - | - | - | - | - | - | - | - |
| First-class | 298 | 478 | 365 | 7 | 3/10 | - | 52.14 | 4.58 | 68.2 | 0 | 0 |
| List A | 315 | 20 | 16 | 1 | 1/0 | 1/0 | 16.00 | 4.80 | 20.0 | 0 | 0 |

# PETER HARTLEY

NAME: Peter John Hartley
BORN: April 18, 1960, Keighley
HEIGHT: 6ft
NICKNAME: Jack
APPOINTED TO FIRST-CLASS LIST: 2003
INTERNATIONAL PANEL: 2006-
TESTS UMPIRED: 9 as TV umpire and 5 as
reserve umpire
ODIS UMPIRED: 6
T20IS UMPIRED: 3
COUNTIES AS PLAYER: Warwickshire,
Yorkshire, Hampshire
ROLE: Right-hand bat, right-arm fast-
medium bowler
COUNTY DEBUT: 1982 (Warwickshire),
1985 (Yorkshire), 1998 (Hampshire)

NOTES: Officiated at T20 Finals Day in 2006 at Trent Bridge, including standing in the final.
Umpired the FP Trophy final in 2007, the 2008 U19 World Cup final in Malaysia and the
2010 CB40 final

| Batting | Mat | Inns | NO | Runs | HS | Ave | SR | 100 | 50 | Ct | St |
|---|---|---|---|---|---|---|---|---|---|---|---|
| First-class | 232 | 283 | 66 | 4321 | 127* | 19.91 | - | 2 | 14 | 68 | 0 |
| List A | 269 | 170 | 62 | 1765 | 83 | 16.34 | - | 0 | 4 | 46 | 0 |

| Bowling | Mat | Balls | Runs | Wkts | BBI | BBM | Ave | Econ | SR | 5w | 10 |
|---|---|---|---|---|---|---|---|---|---|---|---|
| First-class | 232 | 37108 | 20635 | 683 | 9/41 | - | 30.21 | 3.33 | 54.3 | 23 | 3 |
| List A | 269 | 12636 | - | - | - | - | - | - | - | - | - |

# RICHARD ILLINGWORTH

NAME: Richard Keith Illingworth
BORN: August 23, 1963, Greengates
HEIGHT: 5ft 11in
NICKNAME: Harry, Lucy
APPOINTED TO FIRST-CLASS LIST: 2006
INTERNATIONAL PANEL: 2009-
TESTS UMPIRED: 1 as TV umpire
ODIS UMPIRED: 10
T20IS UMPIRED: 3
COUNTIES AS PLAYER: Worcestershire, Derbyshire
ROLE: Right-hand bat, slow left-arm bowler
COUNTY DEBUT: 1982 (Worcestershire), 2001 (Derbyshire)
TEST DEBUT: 1991
ODI DEBUT: 1991

NOTES: Officiated at T20 Finals Day at Edgbaston in 2011

| Batting | Mat | Inns | NO | Runs | HS | Ave | SR | 100 | 50 | Ct | St |
|---|---|---|---|---|---|---|---|---|---|---|---|
| Tests | 9 | 14 | 7 | 128 | 28 | 18.28 | 32.08 | 0 | 0 | 5 | 0 |
| ODIs | 25 | 11 | 5 | 68 | 14 | 11.33 | 57.14 | 0 | 0 | 8 | 0 |
| First-class | 376 | 435 | 122 | 7027 | 120* | 22.45 | - | 4 | 21 | 161 | 0 |
| List A | 381 | 185 | 87 | 1458 | 53* | 14.87 | - | 0 | 1 | 93 | 0 |

| Bowling | Mat | Balls | Runs | Wkts | BBI | BBM | Ave | Econ | SR | 5w | 10 |
|---|---|---|---|---|---|---|---|---|---|---|---|
| Tests | 9 | 1485 | 615 | 19 | 4/96 | 6/150 | 32.36 | 2.48 | 78.1 | 0 | 0 |
| ODIs | 25 | 1501 | 1059 | 30 | 3/33 | 3/33 | 35.30 | 4.23 | 50.0 | 0 | 0 |
| First-class | 376 | 65868 | 26213 | 831 | 7/50 | - | 31.54 | 2.38 | 79.2 | 27 | 6 |
| List A | 381 | 16918 | 11157 | 412 | 5/24 | 5/24 | 27.08 | 3.95 | 41.0 | 2 | 0 |

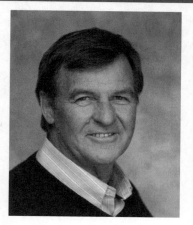

NAME: Trevor Edward Jesty
BORN: June 2, 1948, Gosport
HEIGHT: 5ft 9in
NICKNAME: Jets
APPOINTED TO FIRST-CLASS LIST: 1994
TESTS UMPIRED: 4 as reserve umpire
ODIS UMPIRED: 3 as TV umpire and 1 as reserve umpire
T20IS UMPIRED: 1 as reserve umpire
COUNTIES AS PLAYER: Hampshire, Surrey, Lancashire
ROLE: Right-hand bat, right-arm medium bowler
COUNTY DEBUT: 1966 (Hampshire), 1985 (Surrey), 1988 (Lancashire)
ODI DEBUT: 1983

NOTES: Stood in the CB40 final at Lord's in 2011

| Batting | Mat | Inns | NO | Runs | HS | Ave | SR | 100 | 50 | Ct | St |
|---|---|---|---|---|---|---|---|---|---|---|---|
| ODIs | 10 | 10 | 4 | 127 | 52* | 21.16 | 69.78 | 0 | 1 | 5 | 0 |
| First-class | 490 | 777 | 107 | 21916 | 248 | 32.71 | - | 35 | 110 | 265 | 1 |
| List A | 428 | 394 | 54 | 9216 | 166* | 27.10 | - | 7 | 46 | 106 | 0 |

| Bowling | Mat | Balls | Runs | Wkts | BBI | BBM | Ave | Econ | SR | 5w | 10 |
|---|---|---|---|---|---|---|---|---|---|---|---|
| ODIs | 10 | 108 | 93 | 1 | 1/23 | 1/23 | 93.00 | 5.16 | 108.0 | 0 | 0 |
| First-class | 490 | 36864 | 16075 | 585 | 7/75 | - | 27.47 | 2.61 | 63.0 | 19 | 0 |
| List A | 428 | 13309 | 9283 | 372 | 6/20 | 6/20 | 24.95 | 4.18 | 35.7 | 5 | 0 |

# RICHARD KETTLEBOROUGH

NAME: Richard Allan Kettleborough
BORN: March 15, 1973, Sheffield
HEIGHT: 5ft 10in
NICKNAME: Ketts
APPOINTED TO FIRST-CLASS LIST: 2006
INTERNATIONAL PANEL: 2008-2011
ELITE PANEL: 2011-
TESTS UMPIRED: 7
ODIS UMPIRED: 18
T20IS UMPIRED: 3
COUNTIES AS PLAYER: Yorkshire, Middlesex
ROLE: Left-hand bat
COUNTY DEBUT: 1994 (Yorkshire), 1998
(Middlesex)

NOTES: Rates Trent Bridge and Scarborough as his favourite county grounds and always takes a picture of his children out to the middle with him. He describes his career highlight as an umpire as his first Test match between Sri Lanka and West Indies in Galle in 2010 and being appointed to the ICC Elite Panel

| Batting | Mat | Inns | NO | Runs | HS | Ave | SR | 100 | 50 | Ct | St |
|---|---|---|---|---|---|---|---|---|---|---|---|
| First-class | 33 | 56 | 6 | 1258 | 108 | 25.16 | - | 1 | 7 | 20 | 0 |
| List A | 21 | 16 | 4 | 290 | 58 | 24.16 | - | 0 | 1 | 6 | 0 |

| Bowling | Mat | Balls | Runs | Wkts | BBI | BBM | Ave | Econ | SR | 5w | 10 |
|---|---|---|---|---|---|---|---|---|---|---|---|
| First-class | 33 | 378 | 243 | 3 | 2/26 | - | 81.00 | 3.85 | 126.0 | 0 | 0 |
| List A | 21 | 270 | - | - | - | - | - | - | - | - | - |

# NIGEL LLONG

NAME: Nigel James Llong
BORN: February 11, 1969, Ashford, Kent
HEIGHT: 6ft
NICKNAME: Nidge
APPOINTED TO FIRST-CLASS LIST: 2002
INTERNATIONAL PANEL: 2004-2006 as TV umpire; 2006-present as full member
TESTS UMPIRED: 12
ODIS UMPIRED: 55
T20IS UMPIRED: 16
COUNTY AS PLAYER: Kent
ROLE: Left-hand bat, right-arm offspin bowler
COUNTY DEBUT: 1990

NOTES: Officiated at T20 Finals Day at Edgbaston in 2004, including standing in the final, and again in 2007, 2009 and 2010. Umpired at 2007 World T20 in South Africa

| Batting | Mat | Inns | NO | Runs | HS | Ave | SR | 100 | 50 | Ct | St |
|---|---|---|---|---|---|---|---|---|---|---|---|
| First-class | 68 | 108 | 11 | 3024 | 130 | 31.17 | - | 6 | 16 | 59 | 0 |
| List A | 136 | 115 | 24 | 2302 | 123 | 25.29 | - | 2 | 8 | 41 | 0 |

| Bowling | Mat | Balls | Runs | Wkts | BBI | BBM | Ave | Econ | SR | 5w | 10 |
|---|---|---|---|---|---|---|---|---|---|---|---|
| First-class | 68 | 2273 | 1259 | 35 | 5/21 | - | 35.97 | 3.32 | 64.9 | 2 | 0 |
| List A | 136 | 1317 | 1210 | 40 | 4/24 | 4/24 | 30.25 | 5.51 | 32.9 | 0 | 0 |

# JEREMY LLOYDS

NAME: Jeremy William Lloyds
BORN: November 17, 1954, Penang, Malaysia
HEIGHT: 5ft 11in
NICKNAME: Jerry
APPOINTED TO FIRST-CLASS LIST: 1998
INTERNATIONAL PANEL: 2002-2004 as TV umpire; 2004-2006
TESTS UMPIRED: 5
ODIS UMPIRED: 18
T20IS UMPIRED: 1
COUNTIES AS PLAYER: Somerset, Gloucestershire
ROLE: Left-hand bat, offspin bowler
COUNTY DEBUT: 1979 (Somerset), 1985 (Gloucestershire)

NOTES: Stood in the C&G final in 2006. Officiated at T20 Finals Day in 2007 and 2008

| Batting | Mat | Inns | NO | Runs | HS | Ave | SR | 100 | 50 | Ct | St |
|---|---|---|---|---|---|---|---|---|---|---|---|
| First-class | 267 | 408 | 64 | 10679 | 132* | 31.04 | - | 10 | 62 | 229 | 0 |
| List A | 177 | 150 | 26 | 1982 | 73* | 15.98 | - | 0 | 5 | 58 | 0 |

| Bowling | Mat | Balls | Runs | Wkts | BBI | BBM | Ave | Econ | SR | 5w | 10 |
|---|---|---|---|---|---|---|---|---|---|---|---|
| First-class | 267 | 24175 | 12943 | 333 | 7/88 | - | 38.86 | 3.21 | 72.5 | 13 | 1 |
| List A | 177 | 1522 | 1129 | 26 | 3/14 | 3/14 | 43.42 | 4.45 | 58.5 | 0 | 0 |

# NEIL MALLENDER

**NAME:** Neil Alan Mallender
**BORN:** August 13, 1961, Kirk Sandall
**HEIGHT:** 6ft
**NICKNAME:** Ghostie
**APPOINTED TO FIRST-CLASS LIST:** 1999
**INTERNATIONAL PANEL:** 2002-2004
**TESTS UMPIRED:** 3
**ODIS UMPIRED:** 22
**COUNTIES AS PLAYER:** Northamptonshire, Somerset
**ROLE:** Right-hand bat, right-arm fast-medium bowler
**COUNTY DEBUT:** 1980 (Northamptonshire), 1987 (Somerset)
**TEST DEBUT:** 1992

NOTES: PCA Umpire of the Year 2001, 2002, 2003, 2004, 2006, 2008. Stood in the 2003 World Cup. Describes his two favourite grounds, discounting Lord's, as Taunton and Chester-le-Street and loves to listen to rock/metal music before going out to umpire. Officiated at T20 Finals Day at Edgbaston in 2011, including the final

| Batting | Mat | Inns | NO | Runs | HS | Ave | SR | 100 | 50 | Ct | St |
|---|---|---|---|---|---|---|---|---|---|---|---|
| Tests | 2 | 3 | 0 | 8 | 4 | 2.66 | 36.36 | 0 | 0 | 0 | 0 |
| First-class | 345 | 396 | 122 | 4709 | 100* | 17.18 | - | 1 | 10 | 111 | 0 |
| List A | 325 | 163 | 75 | 1146 | 38* | 13.02 | - | 0 | 0 | 60 | 0 |

| Bowling | Mat | Balls | Runs | Wkts | BBI | BBM | Ave | Econ | SR | 5w | 10 |
|---|---|---|---|---|---|---|---|---|---|---|---|
| Tests | 2 | 449 | 215 | 10 | 5/50 | 8/122 | 21.50 | 2.87 | 44.9 | 1 | 0 |
| First-class | 345 | 53215 | 24654 | 937 | 7/27 | - | 26.31 | 2.77 | 56.7 | 36 | 5 |
| List A | 325 | 15488 | 9849 | 387 | 7/37 | 7/37 | 25.44 | 3.81 | 40.0 | 3 | 0 |

## DAVID MILLNS

NAME: David James Millns
BORN: February 27, 1965, Clipstone
HEIGHT: 6ft 3in
NICKNAME: Rocket Man
APPOINTED TO FIRST-CLASS LIST: 2009
COUNTIES AS PLAYER: Nottinghamshire, Leicestershire
ROLE: Left-hand bat, right-arm fast bowler
COUNTY DEBUT: 1988 (Nottinghamshire), 1990 (Leicestershire)
SOMETHING WE DON'T KNOW ABOUT YOU? I spend my winters scuba diving, skiing and sailing

NOTES: Has stood as reserve umpire in one Test and one T20I

| Batting | Mat | Inns | NO | Runs | HS | Ave | SR | 100 | 50 | Ct | St |
|---|---|---|---|---|---|---|---|---|---|---|---|
| First-class | 171 | 203 | 63 | 3082 | 121 | 22.01 | - | - | 3 | 8 | 76 | 0 |
| List A | 91 | 49 | 26 | 338 | 39* | 14.69 | - | 0 | 0 | 18 | 0 |

| Bowling | Mat | Balls | Runs | Wkts | BBI | BBM | Ave | Econ | SR | 5w | 10 |
|---|---|---|---|---|---|---|---|---|---|---|---|
| First-class | 171 | 26571 | 15129 | 553 | 9/37 | - | 27.35 | 3.41 | 48.0 | 23 | 4 |
| List A | 91 | 3931 | 3144 | 83 | 4/26 | 4/26 | 37.87 | 4.79 | 47.3 | 0 | 0 |

# STEVE O'SHAUGHNESSY

NAME: Steven Joseph O'Shaughnessy
BORN: September 9, 1961, Bury
APPOINTED TO FIRST-CLASS LIST: 2011
COUNTIES AS PLAYER: Lancashire, Worcestershire
ROLE: Right-hand bat, right-arm medium bowler
COUNTY DEBUT: 1980 (Lancashire), 1988 (Worcestershire)

NOTES: O'Shaughnessy started umpiring in 2007 and was appointed to the full list for the 2011 season

| Batting | Mat | Inns | NO | Runs | HS | Ave | SR | 100 | 50 | Ct | St |
|---|---|---|---|---|---|---|---|---|---|---|---|
| First-class | 112 | 181 | 28 | 3720 | 159* | 24.31 | - | 5 | 16 | 57 | 0 |
| List A | 176 | 151 | 23 | 2999 | 101* | 23.42 | - | 1 | 15 | 44 | 0 |

| Bowling | Mat | Balls | Runs | Wkts | BBI | BBM | Ave | Econ | SR | 5w | 10 |
|---|---|---|---|---|---|---|---|---|---|---|---|
| First-class | 112 | 7179 | 4108 | 114 | 4/66 | - | 36.03 | 3.43 | 62.9 | 0 | 0 |
| List A | 176 | 5389 | 4184 | 115 | 4/17 | 4/17 | 36.38 | 4.65 | 46.8 | 0 | 0 |

## TIM ROBINSON

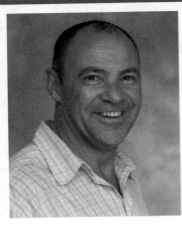

NAME: Robert Timothy Robinson
BORN: November 21, 1958,
Sutton-in-Ashfield
HEIGHT: 6ft
NICKNAME: Robbo, Chop
APPOINTED TO FIRST-CLASS LIST: 2007
TESTS UMPIRED: 4 as reserve umpire
ODIS UMPIRED: 1 as reserve umpire
T20IS UMPIRED: 3 as reserve umpire
COUNTY AS PLAYER: Nottinghamshire
ROLE: Right-hand opening bat
COUNTY DEBUT: 1978
TEST DEBUT: 1984
ODI DEBUT: 1984

NOTES: TV umpire in the CB40 final in 2010 and stood in the CB40 final at Lord's in 2011

| Batting | Mat | Inns | NO | Runs | HS | Ave | SR | 100 | 50 | Ct | St |
|---|---|---|---|---|---|---|---|---|---|---|---|
| Tests | 29 | 49 | 5 | 1601 | 175 | 36.38 | 41.62 | 4 | 6 | 8 | 0 |
| ODIs | 26 | 26 | 0 | 597 | 83 | 22.96 | 58.18 | 0 | 3 | 6 | 0 |
| First-class | 425 | 739 | 85 | 27571 | 220* | 42.15 | - | - | 63 | 141 | 257 | 0 |
| List A | 397 | 386 | 40 | 11879 | 139 | 34.33 | - | - | 9 | 75 | 120 | 0 |

| Bowling | Mat | Balls | Runs | Wkts | BBI | BBM | Ave | Econ | SR | 5w | 10 |
|---|---|---|---|---|---|---|---|---|---|---|---|
| Tests | 29 | 6 | 0 | 0 | - | - | - | 0.00 | - | 0 | 0 |
| ODIs | 26 | - | - | - | - | - | - | - | - | - | - |
| First-class | 425 | 259 | 289 | 4 | 1/22 | - | 72.25 | 6.69 | 64.7 | 0 | 0 |
| List A | 397 | - | - | - | - | - | - | - | - | - | - |

# MARTIN SAGGERS

NAME: Martin John Saggers
BORN: May 23, 1972, King's Lynn
HEIGHT: 6ft 2in
NICKNAME: Saggs
APPOINTED TO FIRST-CLASS LIST: 2012
COUNTIES AS PLAYER: Durham, Kent
ROLE: Right-hand bat, right-arm fast-medium bowler
COUNTY DEBUT: 1996 (Durham), 1999 (Kent)
TEST DEBUT: 2003

NOTES: Retired from first-class cricket in 2009 and added to the reserve list of umpires in 2010

| Batting | Mat | Inns | NO | Runs | HS | Ave | SR | 100 | 50 | Ct | St |
|---|---|---|---|---|---|---|---|---|---|---|---|
| Tests | 3 | 3 | 0 | 1 | 1 | 0.33 | 3.33 | 0 | 0 | 1 | 0 |
| First-class | 119 | 147 | 43 | 1165 | 64 | 11.20 | - | 0 | 2 | 27 | 0 |
| List A | 124 | 68 | 34 | 313 | 34* | 9.20 | - | 0 | 0 | 23 | 0 |
| Twenty20 | 10 | 1 | 0 | 5 | 5 | 5.00 | 62.50 | 0 | 0 | 2 | 0 |

| Bowling | Mat | Balls | Runs | Wkts | BBI | BBM | Ave | Econ | SR | 5w | 10 |
|---|---|---|---|---|---|---|---|---|---|---|---|
| Tests | 3 | 493 | 247 | 7 | 2/29 | 3/62 | 35.28 | 3.00 | 70.4 | 0 | 0 |
| First-class | 119 | 20676 | 10513 | 415 | 7/79 | - | 25.33 | 3.05 | 49.8 | 18 | 0 |
| List A | 124 | 5622 | 4229 | 166 | 5/22 | 5/22 | 25.47 | 4.51 | 33.8 | 2 | 0 |
| Twenty20 | 10 | 186 | 256 | 6 | 2/14 | 2/14 | 42.66 | 8.25 | 31.0 | 0 | 0 |

# GEORGE SHARP

NAME: George Sharp
BORN: March 12, 1950, West Hartlepool
HEIGHT: 5ft 11in
NICKNAME: Sharpie, Blunt, Razor
APPOINTED TO FIRST-CLASS LIST: 1992
INTERNATIONAL PANEL: 1996-2002
TESTS UMPIRED: 15 (plus 1 as TV umpire)
ODIS UMPIRED: 31 (plus 13 as TV umpire)
COUNTY AS PLAYER: Northamptonshire
ROLE: Right-hand bat, wicketkeeper
COUNTY DEBUT: 1968

NOTES: Stood in the 1997 and 2001 Ashes

| Batting | Mat | Inns | NO | Runs | HS | Ave | SR | 100 | 50 | Ct | St |
|---|---|---|---|---|---|---|---|---|---|---|---|
| First-class | 306 | 396 | 81 | 6254 | 98 | 19.85 | - | 0 | 21 | 565 | 90 |
| List A | 285 | 203 | 52 | 2377 | 51* | 15.74 | - | 0 | 1 | 242 | 50 |

| Bowling | Mat | Balls | Runs | Wkts | BBI | BBM | Ave | Econ | SR | 5w | 10 |
|---|---|---|---|---|---|---|---|---|---|---|---|
| First-class | 306 | 114 | 70 | 1 | 1/47 | - | 70.00 | 3.68 | 114.0 | 0 | 0 |
| List A | 285 | - | - | - | - | - | - | - | - | - | - |

# PETER WILLEY

NAME: Peter Willey
BORN: December 6, 1949, Sedgefield
HEIGHT: 6ft 1in
NICKNAME: Will
APPOINTED TO FIRST-CLASS LIST: 1993
INTERNATIONAL PANEL: 1996-2003
TESTS UMPIRED: 25
ODIS UMPIRED: 34
COUNTIES AS PLAYER: Northamptonshire, Leicestershire
ROLE: Right-hand bat, offspin bowler
COUNTY DEBUT: 1966 (Northamptonshire), 1984 (Leicestershire)
TEST DEBUT: 1976
ODI DEBUT: 1977

NOTES: Stood in the 1999 and 2003 World Cups, in the 1999 Benson and Hedges Super Cup final and in the 2004 C&G Trophy final. Officiated at T20 Finals Day at The Oval in 2005 and Edgbaston in 2007, including standing in both finals. Willey is chairman of the First-Class Umpires' Association

| Batting | Mat | Inns | NO | Runs | HS | Ave | SR | 100 | 50 | Ct | St |
|---|---|---|---|---|---|---|---|---|---|---|---|
| Tests | 26 | 50 | 6 | 1184 | 102* | 26.90 | 42.37 | 2 | 5 | 3 | 0 |
| ODIs | 26 | 24 | 1 | 538 | 64 | 23.39 | 62.92 | 0 | 5 | 4 | 0 |
| First-class | 559 | 918 | 121 | 24361 | 227 | 30.56 | - | 44 | 101 | 235 | 0 |
| List A | 458 | 436 | 43 | 11105 | 154 | 28.25 | - | 10 | 67 | 124 | 0 |

| Bowling | Mat | Balls | Runs | Wkts | BBI | BBM | Ave | Econ | SR | 5w | 10 |
|---|---|---|---|---|---|---|---|---|---|---|---|
| Tests | 26 | 1091 | 456 | 7 | 2/73 | 2/73 | 65.14 | 2.50 | 155.8 | 0 | 0 |
| ODIs | 26 | 1031 | 659 | 13 | 3/33 | 3/33 | 50.69 | 3.83 | 79.3 | 0 | 0 |
| First-class | 559 | 58635 | 23400 | 756 | 7/37 | - | 30.95 | 2.39 | 77.5 | 26 | 3 |
| List A | 458 | 18520 | 11143 | 347 | 4/17 | 4/17 | 32.11 | 3.61 | 53.3 | 0 | 0 |

# opta

---

## the world of cricket covered

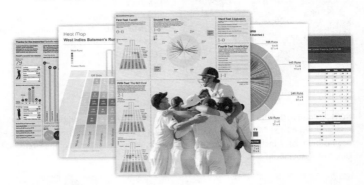

- Ball-by-ball live data feeds
- Detailed performance analysis
- Editorial features and social media content
- Graphics, widgets and hosted online services

---

## coverage

- English domestic cricket
- All Test, ODI and
  international T-20 games
- Indian Premier League

## contact us

info@optasports.com

optasports.com

twitter.com/optajim

Roll *of* **Honour**

# ROLL OF HONOUR, 2011 AVERAGES AND MVPS
## LV=COUNTY CHAMPIONSHIP TABLES

### Division One

| Team | Mat | Won | Lost | Tied | Draw | Aban | Pts |
|------|-----|-----|------|------|------|------|-----|
| Lancashire | 16 | 10 | 4 | 0 | 2 | 0 | 246 |
| Warwickshire | 16 | 9 | 4 | 0 | 3 | 0 | 235 |
| Durham | 16 | 8 | 4 | 0 | 4 | 0 | 232 |
| Somerset | 16 | 6 | 7 | 0 | 3 | 0 | 189 |
| Sussex | 16 | 6 | 6 | 0 | 4 | 0 | 182 |
| Nottinghamshire | 16 | 5 | 6 | 0 | 5 | 0 | 173 |
| Worcestershire | 16 | 4 | 11 | 0 | 1 | 0 | 142 |
| Yorkshire | 16 | 3 | 6 | 0 | 7 | 0 | 138 |
| Hampshire | 16 | 3 | 6 | 0 | 7 | 0 | 127 |

### Division Two

| Team | Mat | Won | Lost | Tied | Draw | Aban | Pts |
|------|-----|-----|------|------|------|------|-----|
| Middlesex | 16 | 8 | 2 | 0 | 6 | 0 | 240 |
| Surrey | 16 | 8 | 4 | 0 | 4 | 0 | 227 |
| Northamptonshire | 16 | 7 | 2 | 0 | 7 | 0 | 226 |
| Gloucestershire | 16 | 6 | 5 | 0 | 5 | 0 | 198 |
| Derbyshire | 16 | 5 | 6 | 0 | 5 | 0 | 181 |
| Glamorgan | 16 | 5 | 6 | 0 | 5 | 0 | 178 |
| Essex | 16 | 4 | 4 | 0 | 8 | 0 | 159 |
| Kent | 16 | 5 | 9 | 0 | 2 | 0 | 149 |
| Leicestershire | 16 | 1 | 11 | 0 | 4 | 0 | 88 |

### Group A

| Team | Mat | Won | Lost | Tied | N/R | Pts | Net RR |
|---|---|---|---|---|---|---|---|
| Sussex | 12 | 8 | 4 | 0 | 0 | 16 | +1.070 |
| Middlesex | 12 | 8 | 4 | 0 | 0 | 16 | +0.213 |
| Derbyshire | 12 | 6 | 5 | 1 | 0 | 13 | -0.079 |
| Kent | 12 | 6 | 6 | 0 | 0 | 12 | -0.017 |
| Netherlands | 12 | 5 | 5 | 1 | 1 | 12 | -0.361 |
| Yorkshire | 12 | 5 | 7 | 0 | 0 | 10 | -0.147 |
| Worcestershire | 12 | 2 | 9 | 0 | 1 | 5 | -0.710 |

### Group B

| Team | Mat | Won | Lost | Tied | N/R | Pts | Net RR |
|---|---|---|---|---|---|---|---|
| Surrey | 12 | 10 | 1 | 0 | 1 | 21 | +1.047 |
| Durham | 12 | 9 | 2 | 0 | 1 | 19 | +0.901 |
| Northamptonshire | 12 | 6 | 6 | 0 | 0 | 12 | -0.304 |
| Hampshire | 12 | 5 | 6 | 0 | 1 | 11 | +0.224 |
| Warwickshire | 12 | 5 | 7 | 0 | 0 | 10 | -0.274 |
| Leicestershire | 12 | 2 | 8 | 0 | 2 | 6 | -0.833 |
| Scotland | 12 | 2 | 9 | 0 | 1 | 5 | -0.857 |

### Group C

| Team | Mat | Won | Lost | Tied | N/R | Pts | Net RR |
|---|---|---|---|---|---|---|---|
| Somerset | 12 | 9 | 2 | 0 | 1 | 19 | +1.008 |
| Nottinghamshire | 12 | 7 | 4 | 0 | 1 | 15 | +0.260 |
| Essex | 12 | 6 | 3 | 0 | 3 | 15 | +0.255 |
| Lancashire | 12 | 6 | 5 | 0 | 1 | 13 | -0.172 |
| Glamorgan | 12 | 4 | 5 | 0 | 3 | 11 | +0.161 |
| Gloucestershire | 12 | 4 | 8 | 0 | 0 | 8 | -0.488 |
| Unicorns | 12 | 1 | 10 | 0 | 1 | 3 | -0.640 |

| | |
|---|---|
| SEMI-FINALS | Somerset vs Durham at Taunton – Sep 4, 2011 *Somerset won by 39 runs (D/L)* |
| | Durham 219 (38.5/40 ov); Somerset 165/3 (27/27 ov) |
| | Surrey vs Sussex at The Oval – Sep 4, 2011 *Surrey won by 71 runs* |
| | Surrey 228/7 (24/24 ov); Sussex 157 (22/24 ov) |
| FINAL | Somerset vs Surrey at Lord's – Sep 17, 2011 |
| | *Surrey won by 5 wickets (with 15 balls remaining) (D/L)* |
| | Somerset 214 (39.2/40 ov); Surrey 189/5 (27.3/30 ov) |

| North Group | | | | | | | |
| Team | Mat | Won | Lost | Tied | N/R | Pts | Net RR |
|---|---|---|---|---|---|---|---|
| Nottinghamshire | 16 | 11 | 2 | 0 | 3 | 25 | +1.087 |
| Leicestershire | 16 | 10 | 2 | 0 | 4 | 24 | +0.541 |
| Lancashire | 16 | 9 | 5 | 1 | 1 | 20 | +0.459 |
| Durham | 16 | 6 | 6 | 0 | 4 | 16 | +0.678 |
| Worcestershire | 16 | 6 | 7 | 0 | 3 | 15 | -0.089 |
| Yorkshire | 16 | 6 | 7 | 0 | 3 | 15 | -0.548 |
| Derbyshire | 16 | 4 | 8 | 1 | 3 | 12 | -0.489 |
| Warwickshire | 16 | 4 | 10 | 0 | 2 | 10 | -0.598 |
| Northamptonshire | 16 | 2 | 11 | 0 | 3 | 7 | -0.912 |

| South Group | | | | | | | |
| Team | Mat | Won | Lost | Tied | N/R | Pts | Net RR |
|---|---|---|---|---|---|---|---|
| Hampshire* | 16 | 11 | 2 | 0 | 3 | 23 | +1.093 |
| Sussex | 16 | 9 | 5 | 0 | 2 | 20 | +0.061 |
| Kent | 16 | 9 | 5 | 0 | 2 | 20 | -0.205 |
| Somerset | 16 | 7 | 4 | 1 | 4 | 19 | +0.978 |
| Surrey | 16 | 7 | 6 | 0 | 3 | 17 | +0.131 |
| Essex | 16 | 7 | 7 | 0 | 2 | 16 | -0.086 |
| Glamorgan | 16 | 5 | 9 | 0 | 2 | 12 | +0.045 |
| Gloucestershire | 16 | 4 | 11 | 0 | 1 | 9 | -0.473 |
| Middlesex | 16 | 2 | 12 | 1 | 1 | 6 | -1.247 |

*Hampshire were docked two points for producing a poor pitch last season

QUARTER-FINALS  Leicestershire vs Kent at Leicester – Aug 6, 2011
*Leicestershire won by 3 wickets (with 4 balls remaining)*
Kent 203/3 (20/20 ov); Leicestershire 206/7 (19.2/20 ov)
Nottinghamshire vs Somerset at Nottingham – Aug 7, 2011
*Somerset won by 6 wickets (with 5 balls remaining)*
Nottinghamshire 169/5 (20/20 ov); Somerset 172/4 (19.1/20 ov)
Hampshire vs Durham at Southampton – Aug 7, 2011 *Hampshire won by 55 runs*
Hampshire 154/6 (20/20 ov); Durham 99 (18.3/20 ov)
Sussex vs Lancashire at Hove – Aug 8, 2011 *Lancashire won by 20 runs*
Lancashire 152/8 (20/20 ov); Sussex 132/8 (20/20 ov)

SEMI-FINALS  Lancashire vs Leicestershire at Birmingham – Aug 27, 2011
*Match tied (D/L method) (Leicestershire won the one-over eliminator)*
Leicestershire 132/6 (18/18 ov); Lancashire 79/6 (11/11 ov)
Hampshire vs Somerset at Birmingham – Aug 27, 2011
*Match tied (D/L method) (Somerset won the one-over eliminator)*
Hampshire 138/4 (15.5/15.5 ov); Somerset 94/6 (10/10 ov)

FINAL  Leicestershire vs Somerset at Birmingham – Aug 27, 2011 *Leicestershire won by 18 runs*
Leicestershire 145/6 (20/20 ov); Somerset 127/9 (20/20 ov)

FIRST-CLASS AVERAGES

| Name | Mat | Mat | NO | Runs | HS | Ave | BF | SR | 100 | 50 | 0 | 4s | 6s |
|---|---|---|---|---|---|---|---|---|---|---|---|---|---|
| ME Trescothick | 13 | 23 | 2 | 1673 | 227 | 79.66 | 2392 | 69.94 | 6 | 6 | 0 | 242 | 18 |
| DM Benkenstein | 17 | 27 | 4 | 1366 | 150 | 59.39 | 2457 | 55.59 | 4 | 9 | 3 | 162 | 5 |
| NRD Compton | 14 | 23 | 4 | 1098 | 254* | 57.78 | 2311 | 47.51 | 2 | 6 | 2 | 124 | 1 |
| AN Cook | 14 | 24 | 0 | 1372 | 294 | 57.16 | 2527 | 54.29 | 5 | 5 | 0 | 171 | 1 |
| AJ Strauss | 14 | 22 | 3 | 1057 | 241* | 55.63 | 1806 | 58.52 | 4 | 2 | 1 | 150 | 3 |
| Z de Bruyn | 16 | 27 | 2 | 1383 | 179 | 55.32 | 2314 | 59.76 | 4 | 9 | 2 | 194 | 9 |
| JWA Taylor | 17 | 32 | 3 | 1602 | 237 | 55.24 | 3047 | 52.57 | 3 | 10 | 3 | 155 | 16 |
| CJL Rogers | 16 | 27 | 3 | 1303 | 148 | 54.29 | 2135 | 61.03 | 4 | 6 | 0 | 183 | 6 |
| SD Robson | 12 | 20 | 3 | 903 | 146 | 53.11 | 1672 | 54.00 | 2 | 4 | 1 | 131 | 2 |
| MW Goodwin | 16 | 29 | 3 | 1372 | 274* | 52.76 | 2685 | 51.09 | 4 | 4 | 1 | 166 | 1 |
| AJ Hall | 16 | 23 | 4 | 960 | 146 | 50.52 | 2005 | 47.88 | 2 | 5 | 1 | 116 | 9 |
| JM Bairstow | 15 | 28 | 3 | 1213 | 205 | 48.52 | 1741 | 69.67 | 3 | 7 | 1 | 187 | 10 |
| GS Ballance | 12 | 23 | 5 | 862 | 111 | 47.88 | 1679 | 51.34 | 1 | 10 | 4 | 108 | 5 |
| SR Patel | 14 | 25 | 2 | 1094 | 124 | 47.56 | 1724 | 63.45 | 3 | 7 | 2 | 164 | 4 |
| AD Hales | 14 | 26 | 2 | 1127 | 184 | 46.95 | 1714 | 65.75 | 3 | 8 | 2 | 164 | 8 |
| JS Foster | 16 | 28 | 7 | 964 | 117* | 45.90 | 1926 | 50.05 | 2 | 4 | 2 | 111 | 3 |
| WRS Gidman | 16 | 28 | 6 | 1006 | 116* | 45.72 | 1963 | 51.24 | 1 | 8 | 1 | 134 | 3 |
| EC Joyce | 16 | 29 | 1 | 1269 | 140 | 45.32 | 2359 | 53.79 | 2 | 9 | 1 | 181 | 3 |
| V Chopra | 17 | 28 | 1 | 1203 | 228 | 44.55 | 2087 | 57.64 | 3 | 4 | 1 | 158 | 8 |
| AC Voges | 12 | 20 | 1 | 845 | 165 | 44.47 | 1562 | 54.09 | 1 | 7 | 2 | 121 | 0 |
| ID Blackwell | 17 | 26 | 2 | 1063 | 158 | 44.29 | 1339 | 79.38 | 3 | 6 | 2 | 121 | 18 |
| JA Simpson | 18 | 26 | 6 | 869 | 143 | 43.45 | 1723 | 50.43 | 1 | 7 | 1 | 111 | 5 |
| SD Peters | 15 | 21 | 1 | 864 | 222 | 43.20 | 1596 | 54.13 | 3 | 2 | 2 | 120 | 0 |
| ND McKenzie | 16 | 28 | 2 | 1120 | 237 | 43.07 | 2422 | 46.24 | 3 | 3 | 4 | 145 | 2 |
| JD Middlebrook | 16 | 20 | 5 | 644 | 109 | 42.93 | 1178 | 54.66 | 3 | 1 | 2 | 75 | 8 |
| AN Petersen | 15 | 27 | 2 | 1069 | 210 | 42.76 | 1784 | 59.92 | 2 | 5 | 3 | 141 | 4 |
| VS Solanki | 16 | 30 | 3 | 1148 | 173 | 42.51 | 1953 | 58.78 | 3 | 6 | 3 | 162 | 10 |
| AJ Wheater | 11 | 20 | 1 | 804 | 164 | 42.31 | 971 | 82.80 | 2 | 4 | 2 | 109 | 17 |
| TL Maynard | 16 | 28 | 3 | 1022 | 141 | 40.88 | 1485 | 68.82 | 3 | 3 | 3 | 123 | 13 |
| MA Wallace | 16 | 29 | 4 | 1020 | 107 | 40.80 | 1646 | 61.96 | 2 | 7 | 2 | 122 | 9 |
| RWT Key | 12 | 24 | 2 | 895 | 162 | 40.68 | 1675 | 53.43 | 2 | 5 | 3 | 104 | 3 |
| CG Taylor | 16 | 29 | 1 | 1139 | 196 | 40.67 | 1825 | 62.41 | 3 | 6 | 2 | 160 | 2 |
| WJ Durston | 16 | 31 | 3 | 1138 | 151 | 40.64 | 1731 | 65.74 | 3 | 6 | 2 | 171 | 7 |
| SC Moore | 16 | 28 | 3 | 1013 | 169* | 40.52 | 1795 | 56.43 | 2 | 5 | 2 | 135 | 5 |
| AW Gale | 12 | 22 | 3 | 769 | 145* | 40.47 | 1464 | 52.52 | 2 | 4 | 2 | 92 | 3 |
| RA Whiteley | 11 | 20 | 4 | 644 | 130* | 40.25 | 1273 | 50.58 | 2 | 2 | 1 | 82 | 14 |
| SM Davies | 16 | 27 | 1 | 1035 | 156 | 39.80 | 1759 | 58.84 | 2 | 5 | 3 | 143 | 3 |
| AG Wakely | 16 | 22 | 0 | 869 | 98 | 39.50 | 1608 | 54.04 | 0 | 5 | 0 | 109 | 8 |
| TR Ambrose | 16 | 22 | 3 | 744 | 95* | 39.15 | 1416 | 52.54 | 0 | 8 | 3 | 93 | 0 |
| WR Smith | 15 | 25 | 0 | 978 | 166 | 39.12 | 2328 | 42.01 | 3 | 4 | 2 | 139 | 4 |
| MJ Di Venuto | 16 | 25 | 1 | 935 | 132 | 38.95 | 1525 | 61.31 | 3 | 4 | 0 | 130 | 0 |
| JJ Sayers | 11 | 22 | 2 | 773 | 139 | 38.65 | 1895 | 40.79 | 1 | 6 | 1 | 75 | 4 |
| JC Hildreth | 17 | 27 | 1 | 996 | 186 | 38.30 | 1563 | 63.72 | 2 | 4 | 5 | 139 | 6 |
| RS Bopara | 15 | 26 | 2 | 917 | 178 | 38.20 | 1791 | 51.20 | 3 | 3 | 3 | 104 | 2 |
| JL Denly | 14 | 28 | 1 | 1024 | 199 | 37.92 | 1655 | 61.87 | 2 | 5 | 1 | 148 | 5 |
| PJ Horton | 17 | 30 | 1 | 1099 | 99 | 37.89 | 2196 | 50.04 | 0 | 9 | 1 | 145 | 2 |
| APR Gidman | 15 | 27 | 3 | 903 | 168 | 37.62 | 1450 | 62.27 | 1 | 6 | 2 | 117 | 7 |
| NJ O'Brien | 14 | 22 | 4 | 676 | 166 | 37.55 | 1126 | 60.03 | 1 | 4 | 5 | 86 | 2 |
| RJ Hamilton-Brown | 16 | 30 | 2 | 1039 | 159 | 37.10 | 1327 | 78.29 | 1 | 5 | 2 | 163 | 9 |
| DJ Malan | 17 | 28 | 2 | 947 | 143 | 36.42 | 1637 | 57.84 | 3 | 2 | 4 | 126 | 0 |

| Name | Mat | Overs | Mdns | Runs | Wkts | BBI | BBM | Ave | Econ | SR | 5 | 10 |
|------|-----|-------|------|------|------|-----|-----|-----|------|-----|---|----|
| DD Masters | 16 | 637.1 | 169 | 1687 | 93 | 8/10 | 9/55 | 18.13 | 2.64 | 41.1 | 8 | 0 |
| TE Linley | 14 | 482.3 | 102 | 1339 | 73 | 6/57 | 10/107 | 18.34 | 2.77 | 39.6 | 2 | 1 |
| G Chapple | 13 | 434.3 | 104 | 1126 | 57 | 6/70 | 9/117 | 19.75 | 2.59 | 45.7 | 3 | 0 |
| TJ Murtagh | 16 | 514.5 | 103 | 1774 | 85 | 5/27 | 10/128 | 20.87 | 3.44 | 36.3 | 4 | 1 |
| WRS Gidman | 16 | 375.2 | 84 | 1088 | 51 | 6/92 | 6/114 | 21.33 | 2.89 | 44.1 | 3 | 0 |
| WPUJC Vaas | 14 | 499.0 | 119 | 1501 | 70 | 6/46 | 10/82 | 21.44 | 3.00 | 42.7 | 6 | 1 |
| CR Woakes | 11 | 406.4 | 90 | 1220 | 56 | 7/20 | 10/123 | 21.78 | 3.00 | 43.5 | 3 | 1 |
| RJ Sidebottom | 16 | 467.4 | 107 | 1364 | 62 | 7/37 | 11/98 | 22.00 | 2.91 | 45.2 | 3 | 1 |
| AR Adams | 16 | 479.3 | 93 | 1515 | 67 | 6/31 | 11/85 | 22.61 | 3.15 | 42.9 | 7 | 2 |
| J Lewis | 16 | 513.3 | 109 | 1521 | 65 | 5/65 | 8/100 | 23.40 | 2.96 | 47.4 | 1 | 0 |
| G Keedy | 16 | 562.4 | 110 | 1442 | 61 | 6/133 | 10/177 | 23.63 | 2.56 | 55.3 | 3 | 1 |
| A Richardson | 16 | 663.1 | 179 | 1783 | 73 | 6/22 | 9/114 | 24.42 | 2.68 | 54.5 | 3 | 0 |
| SCJ Broad | 10 | 381.5 | 87 | 1120 | 44 | 6/46 | 8/76 | 25.45 | 2.93 | 52.0 | 2 | 0 |
| WB Rankin | 13 | 387.5 | 42 | 1419 | 55 | 5/57 | 8/115 | 25.80 | 3.65 | 42.3 | 2 | 0 |
| CD Collymore | 16 | 456.2 | 100 | 1289 | 49 | 4/28 | 6/100 | 26.30 | 2.82 | 55.8 | 0 | 0 |
| AP Palladino | 14 | 435.1 | 94 | 1379 | 52 | 5/39 | 9/124 | 26.51 | 3.16 | 50.2 | 3 | 0 |
| R Clarke | 15 | 410.5 | 70 | 1225 | 46 | 5/10 | 7/32 | 26.63 | 2.98 | 53.5 | 1 | 0 |
| MS Panesar | 16 | 750.0 | 223 | 1880 | 69 | 5/58 | 7/134 | 27.24 | 2.50 | 65.2 | 3 | 0 |
| JAR Harris | 11 | 371.2 | 68 | 1289 | 47 | 5/39 | 8/101 | 27.42 | 3.47 | 47.4 | 3 | 0 |
| G Onions | 12 | 397.3 | 73 | 1479 | 53 | 6/95 | 8/153 | 27.90 | 3.72 | 45.0 | 2 | 0 |
| JC Tredwell | 12 | 394.5 | 78 | 1175 | 42 | 5/35 | 6/141 | 27.97 | 2.97 | 56.4 | 2 | 0 |
| TD Groenewald | 14 | 469.0 | 107 | 1422 | 48 | 5/59 | 8/97 | 29.62 | 3.03 | 58.6 | 1 | 0 |
| GM Andrew | 16 | 384.1 | 63 | 1545 | 52 | 5/59 | 8/106 | 29.71 | 4.02 | 44.3 | 1 | 0 |
| JD Middlebrook | 16 | 426.4 | 86 | 1307 | 43 | 5/123 | 9/190 | 30.39 | 3.06 | 59.5 | 2 | 0 |
| CD Thorp | 16 | 476.4 | 124 | 1412 | 46 | 6/20 | 8/73 | 30.69 | 2.96 | 62.1 | 1 | 0 |
| SR Patel | 14 | 333.4 | 57 | 1017 | 33 | 7/68 | 11/111 | 30.81 | 3.04 | 60.6 | 1 | 1 |
| ID Blackwell | 17 | 482.5 | 167 | 1172 | 38 | 5/102 | 7/91 | 30.84 | 2.42 | 76.2 | 1 | 0 |
| DA Payne | 14 | 345.2 | 61 | 1298 | 42 | 6/26 | 9/96 | 30.90 | 3.75 | 49.3 | 2 | 0 |
| LJ Fletcher | 13 | 409.0 | 89 | 1247 | 40 | 5/82 | 7/124 | 31.17 | 3.04 | 61.3 | 1 | 0 |
| JKH Naik | 17 | 462.4 | 73 | 1528 | 49 | 5/34 | 7/109 | 31.18 | 3.30 | 56.6 | 2 | 0 |
| ID Saxelby | 15 | 393.2 | 53 | 1529 | 49 | 6/69 | 10/142 | 31.20 | 3.88 | 48.1 | 2 | 1 |
| SP Kirby | 16 | 490.5 | 89 | 1672 | 53 | 6/115 | 6/115 | 31.54 | 3.40 | 55.5 | 1 | 0 |
| CW Henderson | 13 | 495.1 | 127 | 1269 | 40 | 4/43 | 7/128 | 31.72 | 2.56 | 74.2 | 0 | 0 |
| A Khan | 13 | 381.5 | 72 | 1259 | 39 | 4/70 | 6/85 | 32.28 | 3.29 | 58.7 | 0 | 0 |
| JE Anyon | 13 | 450.1 | 50 | 1785 | 55 | 5/136 | 8/156 | 32.45 | 3.96 | 49.1 | 1 | 0 |
| CM Willoughby | 15 | 507.3 | 106 | 1721 | 53 | 6/76 | 6/92 | 32.47 | 3.39 | 57.4 | 1 | 0 |
| JW Dernbach | 11 | 375.3 | 82 | 1125 | 34 | 5/41 | 9/138 | 33.08 | 2.99 | 66.2 | 2 | 0 |
| GJ Batty | 16 | 390.5 | 69 | 1200 | 36 | 5/76 | 6/124 | 33.33 | 3.07 | 65.1 | 1 | 0 |
| DA Cosker | 16 | 613.1 | 162 | 1650 | 49 | 5/48 | 8/91 | 33.67 | 2.69 | 75.0 | 1 | 0 |
| LM Daggett | 15 | 451.5 | 91 | 1551 | 46 | 4/35 | 6/132 | 33.71 | 3.43 | 58.9 | 0 | 0 |
| DR Briggs | 11 | 449.5 | 89 | 1393 | 38 | 6/65 | 7/156 | 36.65 | 3.09 | 71.0 | 3 | 0 |
| GG Wagg | 14 | 401.2 | 64 | 1380 | 33 | 3/52 | 6/138 | 41.81 | 3.43 | 72.9 | 0 | 0 |
| AU Rashid | 16 | 448.3 | 56 | 1692 | 39 | 6/77 | 11/114 | 43.38 | 3.77 | 69.0 | 2 | 1 |
| AJ Hall | 16 | 351.1 | 66 | 1267 | 28 | 3/8 | 4/81 | 45.25 | 3.60 | 75.2 | 0 | 0 |
| NL Buck | 13 | 345.4 | 83 | 1197 | 25 | 5/99 | 5/124 | 47.88 | 3.46 | 82.9 | 1 | 0 |

**FIRST-CLASS AVERAGES**

| Name | Mat | Mat | Dis | Ct | St | Max Dis Mat | Dis/Inn |
|---|---|---|---|---|---|---|---|
| JA Simpson | 18 | 35 | 68 | 67 | 1 | 5 (5ct 0st) | 1.942 |
| GO Jones | 16 | 29 | 61 | 57 | 4 | 5 (5ct 0st) | 2.103 |
| LD Sutton | 16 | 29 | 61 | 59 | 2 | 4 (4ct 0st) | 2.103 |
| GD Cross | 17 | 33 | 58 | 48 | 10 | 6 (4ct 2st) | 1.757 |
| SM Davies | 16 | 31 | 55 | 53 | 2 | 4 (4ct 0st) | 1.774 |
| NJ O'Brien | 14 | 26 | 53 | 49 | 4 | 4 (4ct 0st) | 2.038 |
| JS Foster | 16 | 31 | 52 | 48 | 4 | 4 (4ct 0st) | 1.677 |
| CMW Read | 17 | 31 | 52 | 48 | 4 | 4 (3ct 1st) | 1.677 |
| P Mustard | 13 | 24 | 50 | 48 | 2 | 4 (4ct 0st) | 2.083 |
| JM Bairstow | 15 | 26 | 46 | 46 | 0 | 5 (5ct 0st) | 1.769 |
| MA Wallace | 16 | 29 | 44 | 39 | 5 | 4 (4ct 0st) | 1.517 |
| TR Ambrose | 16 | 31 | 41 | 39 | 2 | 5 (5ct 0st) | 1.322 |
| MJ Prior | 12 | 18 | 37 | 33 | 4 | 4 (4ct 0st) | 2.055 |
| RG Coughtrie | 18 | 22 | 36 | 35 | 1 | 6 (6ct 0st) | 1.636 |
| BJM Scott | 12 | 22 | 35 | 31 | 4 | 5 (5ct 0st) | 1.590 |
| C Kieswetter | 10 | 17 | 32 | 31 | 1 | 5 (5ct 0st) | 1.882 |
| JC Buttler | 13 | 14 | 29 | 28 | 1 | 6 (6ct 0st) | 2.071 |
| MJ Richardson | 5 | 10 | 28 | 27 | 1 | 5 (5ct 0st) | 2.800 |
| JN Batty | 6 | 11 | 28 | 28 | 0 | 6 (6ct 0st) | 2.545 |
| D Murphy | 7 | 11 | 26 | 24 | 2 | 4 (4ct 0st) | 2.363 |
| MD Bates | 8 | 14 | 22 | 18 | 4 | 4 (3ct 1st) | 1.571 |
| TJ New | 10 | 16 | 21 | 20 | 1 | 4 (4ct 0st) | 1.312 |
| N Pothas | 8 | 15 | 20 | 20 | 0 | 3 (3ct 0st) | 1.333 |

| Name | Mat | Mat | Ct | Max | Ct/Inn |
|------|-----|-----|-----|-----|--------|
| R Clarke | 15 | 29 | 39 | 7 | 1.344 |
| DKH Mitchell | 13 | 25 | 33 | 4 | 1.320 |
| PJ Horton | 17 | 33 | 32 | 3 | 0.969 |
| AJ Hall | 16 | 31 | 31 | 4 | 1.000 |
| ME Trescothick | 13 | 23 | 29 | 5 | 1.260 |
| MJ Di Venuto | 16 | 30 | 27 | 3 | 0.900 |
| JC Hildreth | 17 | 30 | 26 | 3 | 0.866 |
| DJ Malan | 17 | 33 | 25 | 2 | 0.757 |
| M van Jaarsveld | 14 | 25 | 24 | 3 | 0.960 |
| WI Jefferson | 15 | 26 | 24 | 3 | 0.923 |
| VS Solanki | 16 | 30 | 23 | 4 | 0.766 |
| TC Smith | 12 | 23 | 22 | 4 | 0.956 |
| EC Joyce | 16 | 28 | 22 | 3 | 0.785 |
| SJ Croft | 17 | 33 | 21 | 3 | 0.636 |
| A Lyth | 11 | 21 | 20 | 4 | 0.952 |
| AC Voges | 12 | 24 | 20 | 3 | 0.833 |
| GJ Batty | 16 | 31 | 20 | 3 | 0.645 |
| AJ Strauss | 14 | 28 | 19 | 3 | 0.678 |
| OP Rayner | 14 | 26 | 18 | 3 | 0.692 |
| WTS Porterfield | 16 | 31 | 18 | 3 | 0.580 |
| MH Yardy | 10 | 19 | 17 | 3 | 0.894 |
| CDJ Dent | 12 | 22 | 17 | 3 | 0.772 |
| LA Dawson | 15 | 27 | 17 | 3 | 0.629 |
| JHK Adams | 16 | 30 | 16 | 2 | 0.533 |
| V Chopra | 17 | 33 | 16 | 3 | 0.484 |

| # | Name | County | Batting | Bowling | Field | Capt. | Wins | Pld | Pts | Average |
|---|------|--------|---------|---------|-------|-------|------|-----|-----|---------|
| 1 | Trescothick, Marcus | Somerset | 504.67 | 0.00 | 45 | 23 | 25.0 | 41 | 597 | 14.55 |
| 2 | Andrew, Gareth | Worcs | 206.77 | 317.19 | 18 | 0 | 11.0 | 39 | 553 | 14.18 |
| 3 | Stevens, Darren | Kent | 276.69 | 223.32 | 22 | 0 | 20.0 | 43 | 541 | 12.59 |
| 4 | Nash, Chris | Sussex | 366.61 | 121.09 | 22 | 0 | 22.0 | 43 | 532 | 12.37 |
| 5 | Blackwell, Ian | Durham | 262.58 | 227.69 | 9 | 0 | 21.0 | 41 | 520 | 12.69 |
| 6 | Patel, Samit | Notts | 252.76 | 217.01 | 13 | 0 | 20.0 | 34 | 503 | 14.79 |
| 7 | Woakes, Chris | Warks | 127.30 | 338.57 | 17 | 0 | 11.0 | 28 | 494 | 17.64 |
| 8 | Panesar, Monty | Sussex | 16.34 | 445.34 | 7 | 0 | 20.0 | 41 | 489 | 11.92 |
| 9 | Clarke, Rikki | Warks | 171.22 | 230.49 | 59 | 0 | 18.0 | 42 | 479 | 11.40 |
| 10 | Adams, Andre | Notts | 105.66 | 346.53 | 10 | 0 | 11.0 | 24 | 473 | 19.72 |
| 11 | Masters, David | Essex | 33.65 | 413.09 | 6 | 0 | 13.0 | 36 | 465 | 12.92 |
| 12 | Mahmood, Azhar | Kent | 238.98 | 194.62 | 15 | 0 | 15.0 | 32 | 464 | 14.49 |
| 13 | Ali, Moeen | Worcs | 312.94 | 114.89 | 22 | 1 | 12.0 | 40 | 463 | 11.57 |
| 14 | Croft, Steven | Lancs | 353.83 | 24.85 | 40 | 14 | 28.0 | 45 | 460 | 10.22 |
| 15 | Hall, Andrew | Northants | 178.90 | 221.74 | 31 | 15 | 15.0 | 38 | 460 | 12.10 |
| 16 | Benkenstein, Dale | Durham | 341.99 | 54.28 | 19 | 16 | 22.0 | 43 | 453 | 10.54 |
| 17 | Trego, Peter | Somerset | 251.08 | 152.72 | 21 | 0 | 26.0 | 46 | 450 | 9.78 |
| 18 | Davies, Steven | Surrey | 305.23 | 0.00 | 112 | 0 | 27.0 | 43 | 443 | 10.30 |
| 19 | Rashid, Adil | Yorks | 109.01 | 302.94 | 19 | 0 | 12.0 | 41 | 443 | 10.80 |
| 20 | Sidebottom, Ryan | Yorks | 69.99 | 348.03 | 11 | 0 | 9.0 | 31 | 438 | 14.13 |
| 21 | Petersen, Alviro | Glamorgan | 367.00 | 24.47 | 17 | 14 | 14.0 | 43 | 435 | 10.12 |
| 22 | Durston, Wesley | Derbyshire | 315.58 | 89.08 | 14 | 0 | 17.0 | 42 | 434 | 10.34 |
| 23 | Hales, Alex | Notts | 392.44 | 0.00 | 20 | 0 | 19.0 | 34 | 431 | 12.69 |
| 24 | Keedy, Gary | Lancs | 17.59 | 373.32 | 11 | 0 | 23.0 | 35 | 424 | 12.13 |
| 25 | de Bruyn, Zander | Surrey | 284.45 | 99.03 | 13 | 0 | 27.0 | 43 | 422 | 9.82 |
| 26 | Goodwin, Murray | Sussex | 371.48 | 0.00 | 15 | 5 | 22.0 | 44 | 413 | 9.40 |
| 27 | Smith, Tom | Lancs | 212.58 | 141.42 | 29 | 0 | 24.0 | 35 | 406 | 11.60 |
| 28 | Mustard, Philip | Durham | 267.57 | 0.00 | 104 | 6 | 21.0 | 41 | 399 | 9.72 |
| 29 | Read, Chris | Notts | 253.59 | 0.00 | 108 | 12 | 23.0 | 43 | 397 | 9.22 |
| 30 | Kirby, Steven | Somerset | 21.83 | 341.44 | 11 | 0 | 21.0 | 39 | 395 | 10.12 |
| 31 | Moore, Stephen | Lancs | 351.39 | 0.00 | 14 | 0 | 28.0 | 45 | 392 | 8.72 |
| 32 | Vince, James | Hants | 339.11 | 0.00 | 29 | 0 | 21.0 | 45 | 389 | 8.64 |
| 33 | Vaas, Chaminda | Northants | 68.36 | 308.40 | 2 | 0 | 10.0 | 24 | 388 | 16.16 |
| 34 | Bopara, Ravinder | Essex | 201.21 | 157.87 | 11 | 1 | 12.0 | 30 | 383 | 12.77 |
| 35 | Bairstow, Jonathan | Yorks | 299.92 | 0.00 | 69 | 0 | 13.0 | 38 | 382 | 10.05 |
| 36 | Joyce, Ed | Sussex | 338.66 | 0.00 | 28 | 0 | 15.0 | 31 | 382 | 12.31 |
| 37 | Richardson, Alan | Worcs | 26.85 | 341.69 | 7 | 0 | 4.0 | 16 | 380 | 23.72 |
| 38 | Chopra, Varun | Warks | 333.56 | 0.00 | 21 | 0 | 19.0 | 41 | 374 | 9.11 |
| 39 | Hamilton-Brown, Rory | Surrey | 285.88 | 14.75 | 20 | 27 | 27.0 | 43 | 372 | 8.65 |
| 40 | McKenzie, Neil | Hants | 335.97 | -2.30 | 20 | 0 | 18.0 | 39 | 371 | 9.52 |
| 41 | Henderson, Claude | Leics | 75.37 | 268.58 | 13 | 0 | 14.0 | 39 | 370 | 9.49 |
| 42 | Maynard, Tom | Surrey | 315.23 | -0.28 | 29 | 0 | 27.0 | 43 | 370 | 8.61 |
| 43 | Gidman, William | Gloucs | 152.45 | 199.11 | 9 | 0 | 10.0 | 32 | 370 | 11.56 |
| 44 | Pyrah, Richard | Yorks | 98.70 | 248.62 | 10 | 0 | 11.0 | 33 | 368 | 11.16 |
| 45 | Buttler, Jos | Somerset | 254.91 | 0.00 | 90 | 0 | 23.0 | 41 | 367 | 8.95 |
| 46 | Lewis, Jon | Gloucs | 76.90 | 270.29 | 6 | 0 | 10.0 | 28 | 363 | 12.96 |
| 47 | Cross, Gareth | Lancs | 150.75 | 0.00 | 185 | 0 | 28.0 | 44 | 363 | 8.24 |
| 48 | Roy, Jason | Surrey | 301.49 | 6.13 | 27 | 0 | 27.0 | 39 | 361 | 9.25 |
| 49 | Murtagh, Tim | Middx | 31.37 | 304.61 | 8 | 0 | 16.0 | 34 | 358 | 10.54 |
| 50 | Solanki, Vikram | Worcs | 308.73 | 1.40 | 34 | 0 | 11.0 | 35 | 355 | 10.15 |

| # | Name | County | Batting | Bowling | Field | Capt. | Wins | Pld | Pts | Average |
|---|------|--------|---------|---------|-------|-------|------|-----|-----|---------|
| 51 | Suppiah, Arul | Somerset | 151.81 | 155.68 | 21 | 0 | 26.0 | 46 | 353 | 7.68 |
| 52 | Chapple, Glen | Lancs | 60.07 | 268.80 | 2 | 9 | 11.0 | 17 | 350 | 20.58 |
| 53 | Adams, James | Hants | 301.34 | 0.00 | 21 | 7 | 21.0 | 42 | 350 | 8.33 |
| 54 | Hogg, Kyle | Lancs | 69.17 | 265.09 | 4 | 0 | 12.0 | 20 | 350 | 17.49 |
| 55 | Briggs, Danny | Hants | 23.40 | 303.74 | 8 | 0 | 15.0 | 35 | 350 | 9.99 |
| 56 | Hughes, Chesney | Derbyshire | 190.94 | 132.32 | 12 | 0 | 15.0 | 39 | 349 | 8.95 |
| 57 | Mascarenhas, Dimitri | Hants | 62.76 | 258.81 | 5 | 0 | 19.0 | 32 | 345 | 10.78 |
| 58 | Voges, Adam | Notts | 288.48 | 1.67 | 28 | 4 | 19.0 | 35 | 341 | 9.75 |
| 59 | Tredwell, James | Kent | 76.99 | 221.40 | 21 | 0 | 20.0 | 38 | 339 | 8.91 |
| 60 | Smith, Greg | Derbyshire | 148.16 | 164.06 | 11 | 0 | 12.0 | 31 | 334 | 10.78 |
| 61 | Cosker, Dean | Glamorgan | 53.32 | 257.99 | 11 | 0 | 12.0 | 39 | 334 | 8.57 |
| 62 | Linley, Timothy | Surrey | 13.45 | 300.72 | 4 | 0 | 14.0 | 22 | 331 | 15.04 |
| 63 | Gale, Andrew | Yorks | 299.09 | 0.00 | 9 | 11 | 11.0 | 36 | 330 | 9.17 |
| 64 | Mitchell, Daryl | Worcs | 215.96 | 40.29 | 49 | 11 | 11.0 | 35 | 327 | 9.35 |
| 65 | Claydon, Mitchell | Durham | 27.65 | 272.64 | 8 | 0 | 18.0 | 36 | 326 | 9.06 |
| 66 | Ervine, Sean | Hants | 205.02 | 89.28 | 16 | 0 | 16.0 | 37 | 326 | 8.81 |
| 67 | Cobb, Joshua | Leics | 229.21 | 63.09 | 19 | 0 | 14.0 | 36 | 325 | 9.03 |
| 68 | Hildreth, James | Somerset | 261.82 | 0.00 | 37 | 0 | 26.0 | 45 | 324 | 7.20 |
| 69 | Clare, Jonathan | Derbyshire | 109.91 | 185.12 | 14 | 0 | 16.0 | 36 | 324 | 8.99 |
| 70 | Kartik, Murali | Somerset | 64.32 | 231.23 | 12 | 0 | 16.0 | 29 | 323 | 11.12 |
| 71 | Wagg, Graham | Glamorgan | 130.16 | 169.68 | 12 | 0 | 11.0 | 36 | 322 | 8.96 |
| 72 | Middlebrook, James | Northants | 113.28 | 185.86 | 11 | 0 | 13.0 | 37 | 322 | 8.71 |
| 73 | Onions, Graham | Durham | 14.13 | 283.38 | 6 | 0 | 17.0 | 29 | 321 | 11.05 |
| 74 | Naved-ul-Hasan, Rana | Sussex | 64.58 | 227.72 | 10 | 0 | 17.0 | 28 | 319 | 11.40 |
| 75 | Horton, Paul | Lancs | 259.48 | 0.00 | 38 | 0 | 22.0 | 36 | 318 | 8.85 |
| 76 | Thorp, Callum | Durham | 55.18 | 242.20 | 11 | 0 | 10.0 | 20 | 318 | 15.92 |
| 77 | Taylor, Chris | Gloucs | 286.44 | 1.97 | 16 | 0 | 14.0 | 42 | 318 | 7.57 |
| 78 | Foster, James | Essex | 203.97 | 0.00 | 84 | 15 | 15.0 | 36 | 318 | 8.82 |
| 79 | Rees, Gareth | Glamorgan | 290.35 | -3.11 | 18 | 0 | 12.0 | 37 | 316 | 8.55 |
| 80 | Mahmood, Sajid | Lancs | 64.48 | 226.81 | 7 | 0 | 17.0 | 26 | 315 | 12.11 |
| 81 | Fletcher, Luke | Notts | 28.34 | 259.27 | 9 | 0 | 18.0 | 31 | 315 | 10.15 |
| 82 | McDonald, Andrew | Leics | 189.29 | 87.38 | 18 | 5 | 13.0 | 26 | 313 | 12.03 |
| 83 | Williamson, Kane | Gloucs | 199.95 | 79.87 | 18 | 3 | 11.0 | 39 | 312 | 7.99 |
| 84 | van Jaarsveld, Martin | Kent | 250.51 | 17.13 | 28 | 2 | 14.0 | 34 | 311 | 9.14 |
| 85 | Yardy, Michael | Sussex | 159.53 | 92.06 | 22 | 18 | 18.0 | 31 | 310 | 9.99 |
| 86 | Barker, Keith | Warks | 111.05 | 165.39 | 18 | 0 | 14.0 | 35 | 308 | 8.81 |
| 87 | Batty, Gareth | Surrey | 66.85 | 195.90 | 23 | 0 | 23.0 | 39 | 307 | 7.88 |
| 88 | Phillips, Tim | Essex | 49.26 | 227.27 | 16 | 0 | 15.0 | 34 | 307 | 9.03 |
| 89 | Groenewald, Timothy | Derbyshire | 41.16 | 240.24 | 9 | 0 | 15.0 | 34 | 304 | 8.94 |
| 90 | Wakely, Alex | Northants | 257.79 | 8.38 | 20 | 0 | 15.0 | 38 | 300 | 7.90 |
| 91 | Porterfield, William | Warks | 252.03 | 0.00 | 30 | 0 | 17.0 | 41 | 299 | 7.29 |
| 92 | Stokes, Ben | Durham | 193.53 | 84.44 | 9 | 0 | 11.0 | 18 | 298 | 16.55 |
| 93 | Taylor, James | Leics | 269.43 | 0.00 | 15 | 0 | 13.0 | 39 | 298 | 7.63 |
| 94 | Kieswetter, Craig | Somerset | 215.16 | 0.00 | 65 | 0 | 15.0 | 26 | 294 | 11.31 |
| 95 | Rogers, Chris | Middx | 266.67 | 0.00 | 10 | 4 | 14.0 | 33 | 294 | 8.90 |
| 96 | Gidman, Alex | Gloucs | 234.57 | 20.94 | 14 | 10 | 11.0 | 33 | 289 | 8.75 |
| 97 | Guptill, Martin | Derbyshire | 260.07 | 0.00 | 19 | 0 | 10.0 | 27 | 288 | 10.67 |
| 98 | Payne, David | Gloucs | 37.78 | 234.77 | 6 | 0 | 10.0 | 33 | 287 | 8.71 |
| 99 | Napier, Graham | Essex | 100.59 | 168.31 | 9 | 0 | 9.0 | 27 | 287 | 10.64 |
| 100 | Arafat, Yasir | Surrey | 60.75 | 199.45 | 7 | 0 | 19.0 | 30 | 286 | 9.53 |

# ALLOUTCRICKET

## The *magazine* the *players* read

## SAVE 25% WHEN YOU SUBSCRIBE TO ALL OUT CRICKET AND WE'LL DONATE £10 TO YOUR FAVOURITE COUNTY'S YOUTH CRICKET

**Subscriber Benefits**

- *Save £13.50 and pay just £37.50 for 12 issues*
- *Free delivery to your door every month*
- *Access to AOC Extra, the online subscribers club offering exclusive prizes, discounts and free gifts all year round*

**Call the number opposite to start your subscription. Remember to quote the offer code (3_AOCCLUB07) and be sure to state the name of the county you wish to support**

**SAVE 25%**
**OFF THE COVER PRICE**

DIRK NANNES 'THE DIGGLER' JOINS AOC!

# ALLOUTCRICKET

*magazine the players read* | www.alloutcricket.com

THE **MOST INFLUENTIAL** 2**5**

WIN BIG!

**Brit** Insurance

635

EARN MONEY FOR YOUR COUNTY'S YOUTH CRICKET!

PRIOR · KEVIN KEEGAN

WIN An antique bat PAGE 64

# MATT + PRIOR

IT'S BEEN EMOTIONA...

ISSUE 90
APRIL 2012
£4.25

9 771743 315

"AOC - THE ONLY MAG YOU NEED TO PAC...

**ALLOUTCRICKET**

**ALLOUTCRIC**

Reinventing the wheels

Tracing the lineage of the fast men from Spofforth to Finn

THE **FAST**

James Anderson
He's Not The Mess...

## CALL THE ORDER HOTLINE NOW
**0844 322 1229** and quote offer code: **3_AOCCLUB07**

The county payment of £10 per subscriber will be made upon confirmed receipt of each subscription payment. This can take up to four weeks for collections made by Direct Debit.